Postrevolutionary Iran

Postrevolutionary Iran

A POLITICAL HANDBOOK

Mehrzad Boroujerdi
and Kourosh Rahimkhani

Syracuse University Press

∞ The paper used in this publication meets the minimum requirements
of the American National Standard for Information Sciences—Permanence
of Paper for Printed Library Materials, ANSI Z39.48-1992.

For a listing of books published and distributed by Syracuse University Press,
visit www.SyracuseUniversityPress.syr.edu.

ISBN: 978-0-8156-3574-1 (hardcover)
978-0-8156-5432-2 (e-book)

Library of Congress Cataloging-in-Publication Data

Names: Boroujerdi, Mehrzad, author. | Rahimkhani, Kourosh, author.
Title: Postrevolutionary Iran : a political handbook / Mehrzad Boroujerdi and Kourosh Rahimkhani.
Description: First edition. | Syracuse, New York : Syracuse University Press, 2018. |
Includes bibliographical references and index.
Identifiers: LCCN 2018007516 (print) | LCCN 2018012110 (ebook) | ISBN 9780815654322 (e-book) |
ISBN 9780815635741 | ISBN 9780815635741¬(hardcover :¬alk. paper)
Subjects: LCSH: Iran—Politics and government—1979–1997. | Iran—Politics and government—1997– |
Elite (Social sciences)—Political activity—Iran. | Politicians—Iran.
Classification: LCC JQ1785 (ebook) | LCC JQ1785 .B67 2018 (print) | DDC 955.05/4—dc23
LC record available at https://lccn.loc.gov/2018007516

Manufactured in the United States of America

Dedicated to our children,

Mateen, Avva, Saanya, and Neela,

for all the time their daddies had to work (yet again!) on the computer.

I keep six honest serving-men
(They taught me all I knew);
Their names are What and Why and When
And How and Where and Who.
             —Rudyard Kipling (1865–1936)

Contents

Illustrations

Tables

Preface

The flaw in the pluralist heaven is that the heavenly chorus sings with a strong upper-class accent.
—ELMER E. SCHATTSNEIDER (1960)

In early 2000, a reformist member of the Iranian parliament, Akbar Alami, claimed that a cabal-like group of 200 individuals had controlled Iranian politics since the revolution. Some years later, John Limbert (2008), a former American hostage in Iran who became a deputy assistant secretary of state for Iran, opined: "Controlling this system is a group of about twenty-five individuals, members of an elite inner circle who, with varying titles, have held the reins of power in the Islamic Republic since its beginning in 1979." As political scientists and as political observers of Iran from abroad, we realized that there was no empirical evidence to either confirm or reject Alami's and Limbert's propositions. Meanwhile, we appreciated the fact that Iranians, like political subjects everywhere, were curious to know the identities of the heavyweights that pull the strings of power and oversee the grave matters of the state. We recalled that before the 1979 revolution, a widely used expression referred to the "thousand families" who ruled Iran. After the revolution, the effort to identify the elites who were "truly in charge" did not lose any appeal. Paraphrasing Schattsneider, we recognized that not only the "size" but also the "accent" of the heavenly chorus in theocratic Iran, this novel form of political regime, remained unknown. This desire to understand the practical functioning of Iranian politics is what inspired the book before you.

The 1979 revolution fundamentally altered Iran's political landscape as a generation of inexperienced new men, who did not hail from the ranks of the upper class and were not tainted by association with the old regime, came to power. The political inclinations of the new truculent clerics and their lay allies fundamentally altered the nature of state–clergy relations in Iran and caused major international concern about their actions and intentions. Imposition of theocratic rule and religious ethos on the disconcerted modern landscape of Iran with its inorganic body politic has been an uphill battle. The author of a major work on the Iranian constitution concludes his book by maintaining that within the confines of Iran's authoritarian theocracy, "the state has conquered the clergy and along with them religion" (Schirazi 1997, 303). Roy (1999) refers to the politicization, "Iranization," and secularization of Shiite clergy. Finally, Alamdari (2005, 408) notes, "political rivals now use the religious umbrella to justify their economic and political interests."

For much of the last two decades, Iran's domestic and foreign policy and its nuclear program have loomed large in daily news coverage. Yet, despite all the consternation over their rule, the knowledge about Iran's political elite remains skeletal. Elite theorists maintain that elites have agency and can act to maximize their interests, profits, and power. Following Best and Higley (2010, 6), we defined "political elites" as those "persons who are able, by virtue of their strategic positions in powerful organizations and movements, to affect political outcomes and the workings of political institutions regularly and seriously." To be more precise, we wanted to study those whom Perthes (2004, 5) defines as the "politically relevant elite," meaning those "who wield political influence and power in that they make strategic decisions or participate in decision-making on a national level, contribute to defining political norms and values, and directly influence political discourse on strategic issues." However, it should be noted that we did not aim to study the social impact of elites or present a discursive analysis of them. Furthermore, we excluded the economic, literary or intellectual elite from this study.

Beyond the attention paid to a few leading political figures (e.g., the supreme leader, the president, or the chief nuclear negotiator), scholars and policy analysts know very little about the characteristics of other high-ranking individuals and almost nothing about the middle and lower echelons of government.[1] We know embarrassingly little about the class origin, ethnic background, age composition, educational pedigree, prerevolutionary prison experience, familial ties, party affiliations, or patterns of political mobility of the revolutionaries who came to power in 1979.

Once we consider that postrevolutionary politics in Iran are defined by an opaque structure, a top-heavy state, contentious politics, parallel institutions, an ideologically divided elite, weak political parties, and lack of transparency (see Boroujerdi 2004), the deficiency of our prima facie knowledge becomes more glaring. The problem is further compounded by the observation that Iranian politics do not run along strict party lines and are rather influenced by filial dependence, paternal authority, and local connections. Graham Fuller (1991, 26) writes: "Because the Iranian political and social systems decree that one deal with personalities and not with institutions, the personal relationship to this day transcends any formal or institutionalized relationship." Hence, a shortage of biographical information can seriously handicap all analytical work of political analysis. Scholars and analysts implicitly acknowledge their lack of understanding. It is not surprising that the adjectives commonly used to describe postrevolutionary Iranian politics include "arcane," "anachronistic," "bewildering," "enigmatic," "incongruent," "intricate," "ironic,"

"multi-dimensional," "paradoxical," "permutable," "recondite," and "unpredictable."[2]

Nearly four decades after the clergy became the state elite par excellence, there has not been a large-scale empirical study that could shed light on the recruitment, composition, and circulation of the Iranian ruling political elite after 1979. Consequently, we are left with two competing theoretical approaches, with accompanying narratives of Iranian politics. In the first approach and narrative, commentators employ an agent-focused conceptual framework and analyze the complexity of the polity and politics in the postrevolutionary state through the prism of clashes of personalities and factions (e.g., Akhavi 1987, Baktiari 1996, and Moslem 2002). Alternatively, the competing narrative emphasizes the role of institutions and collective action at the expense of everything else (Parsa 1989, Buchta 2001, and Hen-Tov and Gonzalez 2011). A focus on factions requires the creation of more and more labels and typologies to cover ever-narrower shades on the political spectrum. At the same time, interpretations that stress institutions fail to explain the crucial and inevitable evolution of key individuals and groups over time. Nor are they able to explain why despite their extensive socioeconomic web and evident resourcefulness, the bazaaris have so far failed to produce leadership cadres on par with those of the clergy or the secularly minded middle class. One scholar laments this epistemological deficit when he writes that Iran is generally analyzed "in a framework of a revolution that occurred more than a generation ago, as if all that has transpired [in and outside of Iran] since is inconsequential" (Ansari 2006, 239).

Our dissatisfaction with the quality of analysis on a theocracy born through popular revolution was the impetus for undertaking the current work. We were convinced that the generally available sources—dramatized journalistic accounts, government propaganda, partisan policy briefs by Western think tanks,

1. Previous attempts to gather information on Iranian elites include the reports of the American Central Intelligence Agency (1976, 1985, 1987).

2. See for example Kurzman (2004), Takeyh (2006), and Katouzian (2010, 45).

and slanted commentary by exiled activists—all fell short in capturing the nuances and vicissitudes of Iranian politics. Conventional analysis suffers from the dearth of in-depth knowledge of political players and the almost total lack of quantitative analysis, not to speak of the ubiquitous subjective bias.

The gestation for this book began in earnest in 2004. Convinced that gathering empirical data about political elites and institutions might allow us to move beyond the two frail narratives described, we decided to assemble a mountain of hard empirical data that might eventually facilitate new insights based in evidence. We started methodically to collect large amounts of data regarding political elites, elections, demographic indicators, women, and political parties. This data-gathering was accomplished through doggedly scouring archives, books, yearbooks, obituary notices, newspapers, and online sources, as well as correspondence and interviews with former politicians, opposition activists, political analysts, scholars, and journalists. We also drew upon a rich array of English and original Persian-language sources, including the proceedings of institutions such as the Iranian Parliament (Majlis), the Assembly of Experts, and the Guardian Council, memoirs written by numerous postrevolutionary clerics and political figures, and websites of various political personalities, government organs, and political parties. We think it is fair to say that the present book contains the most comprehensive collection of data on political life in postrevolutionary Iran. Hitherto, there has simply been no work in any Western language that covers Iranian politics as

empirically and comprehensively. Indeed, we can even safely say that there is no empirical study of political elites in any Middle Eastern country that can match the depth, range, volume, and originality of information assembled here. Free from the limitations of strict censorship and the restraints of state-imposed "historiography," we were able to provide more detailed, objective information about Iranian political institutions and elites in this volume than one might find in a Persian-language book on elites published in Iran. For example, the biographies contained in the Who Is Who section of this book provide accounts of political defeats, fraudulent university degrees, corruption charges, and other unflattering details about individuals that are often whitewashed in official biographies.

Scope

Much of our research was inserted into a database, which ultimately contained sociobiographical data on over 2,300 political personalities. The biographical dataset covers ministers in fifteen different cabinets, members of ten parliaments, members of the Assembly for the Final Examination of the Constitution (AFEC), members of seven Guardian Councils, members of eight Expediency Discernment Assemblies, and members of five Assemblies of Experts. Also included are supreme leaders, presidents, vice presidents, prime ministers, leading commanders of the military and Revolutionary Guards Corps,[3] high-level judiciary officials,[4] and other assorted prominent personalities.[5] In addition to the over 2,300 individual biographical

---

3. Including the chief of the joint staff of the Islamic Republic of Iran Army, general commander of the army, deputy general commander of the army, chief of the Armed Forces General Staff, first deputy chief of the Armed Forces General Staff, commander of the Islamic Republic of Iran Ground Forces, commander of the Islamic Republic of Iran Air Force, commander of the Islamic Republic of Iran Navy, supreme commander of Revolutionary Guards, commander of the IRGC Navy, deputy commander in chief of the IRGC, commander of the IRGC's Basij Force, commander of the IRGC's Quds Force, deputy commander of the IRGC's Basij Force, commander of the Khatam al-Anbia Air Defense Base, and chief of Law Enforcement Forces.

4. Including members of the High Council of the Judiciary, chief justice, first deputy to the chief justice, head of the Supreme Court, prosecutor-general, prosecutor-general of Tehran, chief prosecutor of revolutionary courts, chief judge of the Special Court for Clergy, head prosecutor of the Special Court for Clergy, and head of the State General Inspectorate Organization.

5. Including permanent representatives to the United Nations, secretary of the Supreme National Security Council, governors of the Central Bank, director-general of the Islamic Republic of Iran Broadcasting, rector of Islamic Azad University, and the mayor of Tehran.

listings, we have collected data on the thirty-six national elections held so far, 166 outlawed political organizations, 248 legal political parties (with lists of their original founders), various ministerial impeachments, and women's political participation. The book also contains an extensive political chronology spanning thirty-nine years (1978–2017), as well as a comprehensive list of family ties among the revolutionary elite.

Much of the information contained in this volume is not available in English. For example, you could not find the complete list of Iranian deputies (or MPs) in the First through Tenth Majlis in any publicly available English-language source. This book not only provides the reader or researcher with such lists of political figures, but also enables her or him to understand the individuals better through the construction and collation of personal biographies. In addition, it is not just Iran's Byzantine political structure with multiple nodes of power (i.e., supreme leader, Guardian Council, Expediency Discernment Assembly, and Assembly of Experts), concentric circles of influence, informal networks of patronage, and opaque system of checks and balances that makes Iranian politics impenetrable to outsider audiences. Also perplexing is the formation, merger, or withering away of political institutions, cabinet posts, clerical bodies, and judicial organs, by the constantly fluctuating voting rules such as age requirements, and by the establishment of new provinces and voting districts. We have attempted to explain such complicated issues by providing detailed and easy-to-understand notes.

In summary, this volume provides a cartography of the complex structure of power in postrevolutionary Iran through a longitudinal study of political elites. It provides a window into not only the immediate years before and after the Iranian revolution, but also what has happened over the course of the last four turbulent decades, a complex story that remains to be told. A longitudinal approach has many benefits. The approach enables us to assess changes in the voting behavior of Iranian citizens over four decades, and it helps to demonstrate how former Revolutionary Guards and war veterans managed to make significant inroads into the highest political offices, while clergy have been increasingly unsuccessful in winning parliamentary seats.

On Data

Any researcher who has ever tried to gather accurate empirical data on politics and politicians in an authoritarian state knows that it is a vexing exercise. The state often regards information through a security lens, and the lack of transparency brings many frustrations and difficulties. In the case of postrevolutionary Iran, we faced a multitude of additional problems. Poor recordkeeping in non-digital formats and partial or contradictory information and statistics from official sources were the first hurdles we faced. For example, it has become commonplace for the Ministry of Interior and the Statistical Center of Iran to offer different statistics on the number of eligible voters in any given election. The researcher has to decide which source to use. In addition, Iranian government agencies often put information about current legislation or election results on official websites for a short period of time, and later make it unavailable to the general public. This phenomenon required us to monitor official websites vigilantly to save needed information before it disappeared.[6] When it comes to election data, the government may discontinue providing an indicator that they had provided in previous elections, thereby making comparisons difficult. For example, while the Islamic Parliament Research Center (the research arm of the Majlis) provided data on the father's occupation of MPs elected to the First Majlis in 1980, they refused to provide the same information for any other round. Furthermore, ascertaining the religious rank of individuals also proved to be a challenge. While an individual may

---

6. We have placed some of this hard-to-find data on the Iran Data Portal (http://irandataportal.syr.edu/). As further information becomes available and as users inform us of inaccuracies and missing data, we will do our best to update this information.

be referred to as a hojjat al-Islam (HI, a clerical rank immediately below ayatollah) in some government or media pronouncements, others may use the inflated title of ayatollah for that same individual. The data surrounding the contested 2009 presidential election is riddled with inaccuracies and dubious claims. The statistics put out by the government regarding the number of actual voters, votes received by President Ahmadinejad, and his margin of victory in that election should be taken with a great degree of skepticism.[7]

Considering the sensitive nature of our research, conducting personal interviews or distributing surveys in Iran was not possible for us as emigrants living in the United States.[8] Therefore, we had to conduct semistructured interviews with a number of interlocutors in person in such countries as Canada, England, France, Norway, and the United States, or through email correspondence, phone calls, or Skype with correspondents inside and outside of Iran. These limitations meant that there was often no way of independently verifying the information individuals would provide about themselves (for example, their educational degrees). Again, confronted with the choice of using this weakly verifiable data or nothing at all, we opted for the former with the caveats mentioned above. We faced significant challenges in obtaining certain types of information about individuals. Father's occupation, spouses' names, names of universities individuals attended, and year of graduation from universities or religious seminaries proved to be particularly hard forms of data to obtain.[9] While we had some luck with the others, names of spouses proved to be such an arduous problem that we had to more or less abandon it as a data field. A final challenge was the fact that more than 85 percent of the 2,300 people included in our

database are still alive. This means that data on these figures will change over time. To make the publication of this book possible, however, we decided to draw the line at the end of 2017.

The reader should be aware of discrepancies between our statistics and those of governmental bodies. For example, the Majlis often publishes statistics on the backgrounds of MPs based on the first session in which they are elected. However, we have included in our calculations all those MPs who were elected in midterm Majlis elections. Since our data was therefore more inclusive, we have relied on our own data rather than those published by the Majlis in making descriptive statistics and various calculations.

Considering our narrower focus on politically relevant elite, we decided not to include such categories of people as ambassadors, deputy ministers, Friday prayer leaders, provincial governor-generals, mayors (except for Tehran), heads of parastatal foundations, members of municipal councils, and leading clerics who did not hold official governmental posts.[10] However, it should be kept in mind that while our study focuses on the upper echelons of the Iranian political elite, it also provides a treasure trove of derivative information about the second-tier positions that helped so many of these elites jump-start their careers. By analyzing the types of occupations individuals held before entering the upper echelons, the scholarly community can better grasp how the grooming and circulation of elites takes place in a revolutionary theocracy.

With a database containing well over 100,000 data fields, it is also inevitable that despite our best efforts, some data entry mistakes (improper transliteration of names, years of birth or tenure, or typographical errors) may have occurred, or that we did not incorporate

---

7. In the absence of any other source of comprehensive authoritative data, we have had to rely on government data. We acknowledge that this data may not always be accurate and objective.

8. We have relied entirely on open sources in assembling our data.

9. We were more successful in verifying the educational pedigree of those Iranian elite who had studied abroad. This was done partly through consulting dissertation databases in England, France, and the United States, or contacting the registrar's office at some universities.

10. The formidable challenges of gathering data on so many people were not lost on us. For a list of some 334 provincial governors after the revolution, see http://irandataportal.syr.edu/provincial-governments.

all pertinent information about an individual in the Who Is Who section (chapter 15).[11] By running database queries, consulting multiple sources, and hiring fact checkers, and by using other methods, we have tried to minimize the frequency of mistakes.

Future Research

Our fundamental purpose in compiling this compendium was to address what we perceived to be an enormous gap in the otherwise large corpus of scholarship on contemporary Iranian politics. We decided to share our empirical "sandbox" to provide the scholarly community with the kind of raw data that can enrich numerous books, student research projects, dissertations, policy papers, editorials, and social media posts about Iranian politics.[12] We consider our venture a success if the data presented here will swing the pendulum of research on Iranian politics a bit more toward fact-based, empirical analysis and thereby open up new vistas of understanding.

Here are a few examples of how the raw data assembled in this volume can support future research. One researcher could investigate the effects of voter turnout on such elected offices as the presidency, parliament, and Assembly of Experts. A second researcher with an interest in political economy could explore the correlation between candidate incumbency and the level of economic development in any given region.[13] A third scholar could examine whether there is any correlation between the educational background of ministers and the ministerial posts they occupied. A fourth academic could identify what districts have voted for clerical or female candidates and posit explanations. A fifth investigator could explore the commonalities in the backgrounds of individuals who have served as party leaders. Yet a sixth scholar can examine the Islamicity of names of the postrevolutionary political elite.

By providing information on kinship and patronage ties, who sits on what council, and who serves as the representative of the supreme leader, we might enable various scholars of network analysis to draw sophisticated mappings of the Iranian political elite.[14]

We believe the present study can help the scholarly community address the following types of questions:

Elite Studies: What is the socioeconomic background of the political elite? What institutions are the incubators for the emerging elites? What is the degree of elite circulation in Iran? What discernable trends can we see in the evolving careers of Iranian politicians? What percentage of the elite comes from Tehran as compared to other provinces?

Electoral Behavior: What are the dynamics and patterns of voter turnout in Iranian elections? Do candidate disqualifications affect voter turnout? Do "native sons" win elections? Do reformist politicians get more votes in urban centers and restive provinces?

Gender and Politics: How and why are women underrepresented in elected offices? Is it due to conservative attitudes, not being placed on party lists, or facing insurmountable challenges in winning single-member districts?

Party Politics: Are Iranian political parties primarily collections of individuals gathered around a prominent political activist? Are Iranian elections unpredictable because of weak political parties?

Institutional Design: How sclerotic is the Iranian political system? How have changes in electoral rules, gerrymandering, or candidate disqualifications impacted election results? Does the asymmetry of power guarantee that upper-chamber institutions (e.g., the Guardian Council or the Expediency Discernment Assembly) can control lower chambers (e.g., the Majlis)?

Comparing Pre- and Postrevolutionary Elite: Another advantage of compiling such a resource is that it

---

11. Indeed, we have encountered these same types of mistakes in publications put out by governmental agencies and online news agencies. Since government data was not error free, we relied on data generated from our own database whenever possible.

12. We took one step toward this goal in a publication about the supreme leader. See Boroujerdi and Rahimkhani (2016).

13. For an example of this type of research, see Mahdavi (2015).

14. For a discussion of network analysis of elites, see Knoke (1993).

enables the scholarly community to compare the politically relevant elite before and after the revolution. For example, one can compare our data on the elite with the seminal works of Zahra Shaji'i (1996; 2004) or Marvin Zonis (1971).[15] While the political biographies we have provided in the Who Is Who section of the present book may invite comparisons to such works as Khajehnuri (1952), Bamdad (1978), and Alamuti (1995; 1998), it should be mentioned that we do not share their inclination toward the "Great Man" theory of history, their recourse to political psychology explanations, and their often apologetic or sympathetic accounts of their subjects' lives.

Structure of the Book

The Islamic Republic of Iran supplements nominally democratic institutions such as local councils, the Office of the President, the Assembly of Experts, and the parliament with a plethora of unique "narrow institutions" that include the Office of the Supreme Leader, the Guardian Council, and the Expediency Discernment Assembly. In this book, after providing a comprehensive chronology and a bird's eye view of the overall structure of power in Iran, we present hundreds of charts, graphs, tables, and data points about each of these key institutions of power in theocratic Iran. This is supplemented with electoral data as well as information about political parties.

The second part of the book consists of short biographical sketches of over 2,300 political personalities presented in alphabetical order. The last section presents a detailed account of family ties among ten prominent clerical families[16] as well as other members of the political elites.

---

15. Unfortunately, after the revolution no analogous high-quality works on the political elite have been undertaken. A couple of "Who Is Who" volumes were published by minor outlets in Iran and in the West (e.g., Behrooz 1999, Iran Publishing House 2003) but these were woefully inadequate in their coverage and seriously out of date. An almanac (http://www.iranalmanac.com/), which was active until a couple of years ago, can still be found online, but it offers a potpourri of information on everything from the history of pre-Islamic Persia to present-day economic conditions. Its biographies of elites are riddled with inaccuracies.

16. Afshar (1985, 221) aptly describes the ulema as "an affluent semi-closed elite with tightly knit matrimonial patterns linking families together."

Acknowledgments

For their support toward the research and authorship of this volume, we wish to express our thanks to the United States Institute of Peace (USIP), the Violet Jabara Charitable Trust, and Syracuse University. A 2008 grant from USIP enabled us to hire research assistants and computer programmers to improve the quality of the database on which much of this project is based. A 2016 grant from the Violet Jabara Charitable Trust and its generous benefactor, Dr. Linda Jacobs, enabled us to hire fact checkers, a copy editor, an indexer, and a webmaster. We also thank Mrs. Mary Selden Evans for her financial support and boundless encouragement. Syracuse University's Maxwell School of Citizenship and Public Affairs also provided valuable research, travel, and technology support.

We thank the following research assistants for their marvelous help during the crafting of this book over the last decade: Artin Afkhami, Kambiz Aminshakib, Parsa Ghahramani, Azadeh Haratian, Pedram Magsoud-Nia, Nicholas Stephen Patriciu, Arash Pourebrahimi, Carmel Rabin, Cassandra Lynn Schneider, and Sheida Soleimani. Thanks are also due to Patrick McGraw and Todd Fine for their editing help, and Amit Gupta and Saranya Balakrishnan Jothi for their superb programming skills. We also wish to express our thanks to Ervand Abrahamian, Touraj Atabaki, Maziar Behrooz, Mohammad-Reza Jalaeipour, Nasser Pakdaman, Nouradin Pirmoazen, Eskandar Sadeghi-Boroujerdi, Alireza Shomali, Ebrahim Soltani, Peyman Vahabzadeh, and Morad Vaisi for providing information and feedback on certain parts of this book. We are grateful to Suzanne E. Guiod, the editor-in-chief of Syracuse University Press, for taking this project under her wing, and to Kaitlin Carruthers-Busser for her careful copyediting. We would be remiss if we did not also thank those individuals who shared their intimate knowledge of Iranian politics with us but wish to remain anonymous.

Fragments of the research contained in this book have been presented at talks at Yale (2005, 2017), Princeton (2007, 2015), UCLA (2007), Brandeis (2008), Georgetown (2009), Stanford (2010), NYU (2011), Harvard (2016), and University of Michigan (2017), and at conferences organized by the Middle East Studies Association (2006, 2010), the International Society for Iranian Studies (now renamed Association for Iranian Studies; 2006, 2012, 2014, 2016), Brookings Institution (2008, 2010), the Norwegian Institute of International Affairs (2010), and the United States Institute of Peace (2010). We thank our interlocutors at all of these events whose comments and questions helped us greatly. Lastly, we should mention that particle elements from the current manuscript have been published in Iran Data Portal (http://irandataportal.syr.edu/) and the Iran Primer (http://iranprimer.usip.org/).

Acronyms

ACC	Assembly of Combatant Clergy	IISP	Islamic Iran's Solidarity Party
ADVIR	Alliance for the Defense of Values of the Islamic Revolution	IKRF	Imam Khomeini Relief Foundation
		INF	Iran's National Front
AE	Assembly of Experts	IRGC	Islamic Revolutionary Guards Corps
AEOI	Atomic Energy Organization of Iran	IRIB	Islamic Republic of Iran Broadcasting
AFEC	Assembly for the Final Examination of the Constitution	IRP	Islamic Republic Party
		ISFPD	Islamic Society of Former Parliament Deputies
AFGS	Armed Forces General Staff	JAMA	Revolutionary Movement of the People of Iran (Persian acronym)
AILF	Assembly of Imam's Line Forces		
ASLQS	Assembly of Scholars and Lecturers of Qom Seminary	JSIRIA	Joint Staff of the Islamic Republic of Iran Army
		KDPI	Kurdistan Democratic Party of Iran
AVIR	Alliance of Veterans of the Islamic Revolution	LMI	Liberation Movement of Iran
CAJ	Court of Administrative Justice	MDAFL	Ministry of Defense and Armed Forces Logistics
CIC/PCIC	(Party of) Confederated Islamic Congregations		
CIRD	Center for Islamic Revolution Documentation	MI	Ministry of Interior
DAFOOS	Iranian Army's Command and General Staff College (Persian acronym)	MIIRI	Ministry of Intelligence of the Islamic Republic of Iran
		MNP	Muslim Nations' Party
DCII	Developers' Coalition of Islamic Iran	MP	Member of Parliament
EDA	Expediency Discernment Assembly (of the State)	NIOC	National Iranian Oil Company
		NTP	National Trust Party
FDWI	Foundation for Dispossessed and War-Invalids	OCU	Office for Consolidation of Unity
FMVA	Foundation of Martyrs and Veterans Affairs	OIPFG	Organization of Iranian People's Feda'i Guerrillas
FPAVSD	Foundation for Preservation of Artifacts and Values of Sacred Defense	OMIRI	Organization of Mojahedin of the Islamic Revolution of Iran
GC	Guardian Council		
HCCR	High Council of Cultural Revolution	OSPWCE	Organization for Struggle on the Path of Working Class Emancipation
HCJ	High Council of the Judiciary		
HCRSQ	High Council of Religious Seminaries of Qom	PBO	Plan and Budget Organization
HI	Hojjat al-Islam (honorific)	PECI	Party of Executives of Construction of Iran
IAEA	International Atomic Energy Agency	PIIPU	Party of Islamic Iran's People's Unity
IIPF	Islamic Iran's Participation Front		

PM   Prime Minister

PMD   Party of Moderation and Development

PMOI   People's Mojahedin Organization of Iran

SAVAK   Persian acronym for the shah's secret police

SCC   Society of Combatant Clergy

SCFC   Special Court for Clergy

SCNS   Supreme Council for National Security

SFIR   Steadfastness Front of the Islamic Revolution

SFPD   Society of Former Parliament Deputies

SG   Secretary-General

SQSS   Society of Qom Seminary Scholars

VP   Vice President

WFPIST   World Forum for Proximity of Islamic Schools
            of Thought

Translated List of Iranian Offices, Organizations, and Groups

Abode of the Supreme Leader: *Beyt-e Rahbari*

Absolute Mandate of the Jurist: *Velayat-e motlaqeh-ye faqih*

Academy of Medical Sciences of the Islamic Republic of Iran: *Farhangestan-e Olum-e Pezeshki-ye Jomhuri-ye Islami-ye Iran*

Academy of Persian Language and Literature: *Farhangestan-e Zaban va Adab-e Farsi*

Academy of Sciences of the Islamic Republic of Iran: *Farhangestan-e Olum-e Jomhuri-ye Islami-ye Iran*

Administrative and Recruitment Organization: *Sazman-e Edari va Estekhdami-ye Keshvar*

Aerospace Industries Organization: *Sazman-e Sanaye Hava Faza*

Agricultural Jihad: *Jahad-e keshavarzi*

Ahlulbeyt World Assembly: *Majma'-e Jahani-ye Ahl-ul-Beyt*

Air Defense Base: *Padafand-e Hava'i*

Alliance for the Defense of Values of the Islamic Revolution: *Jam'iyyat-e Defa' az Arzeshha-ye Enqelab-e Islami*

Alliance of Steadfast Supporters of the Islamic Revolution: *Jam'iyyat-e Vafadaran-e Enqelab-e Islami*

Alliance of Veterans of the Islamic Revolution: *Jam'iyyat-e Issargaran-e Enqelab-e Islami*

Alliance of Wayfarers of the Islamic Revolution: *Jam'iyyat-e Rahpuyan-e Enqelab-e Islami*

Armed Forces General Staff: *Setad-e Kol-e Niruha-ye Mosalah*

Assembly for the Final Examination of the Constitution: *Majlis-e Barrasi-ye Naha'i-ye Qanun-e Asasi-ye Jomhuri-ye Islami-ye Iran* (commonly referred to as *Majlis-e Khebregan Qanun-e Asasi* or the Constitutional Assembly of Experts)

Assembly of Combatant Clergy: *Majma'-e Ruhaniyun-e Mobarez*

Assembly of Former MPs: *Majma'-e Namayandegan-e Advar-e Mokhtalef-e Majlis-e Showra-ye Islami*

Assembly of Imam's Line Forces: *Majma'-e Niruha-ye Khat-e Imam*

Assembly of Experts for the Leadership: *Majlis-e Khebregan-e Rahbari* (commonly known as the Assembly of Experts)

Assembly of Scholars and Lecturers of Qom Seminary: *Majma'-e Modarresin va Mohaqqeqin-e Howzeh-ye Elmiyyeh-ye Qom*

Association for Defense of the Freedom of the Press: *Anjoman-e Defa' Az Azadi-ye Matbu'at*

Association for Safeguarding of National Production: *Jam'iyyat-e Defa' Az Towlid-e Melli*

Association of Industrial and Economic Managers and Professionals of Iran: *Anjoman-e Modiran va Motekhassesin-e San'ati va Eqtesadi-ye Iran*

Association of Modern Muslim Women Thinkers of Iran: *Jam'iyyat-e Zanan-e Mosalman-e Nowandish-e Iran*

Association of Muslim Journalists: *Anjoman-e Ruznamehnegaran-e Mosalman*

Association of Petrochemical Industry Corporations: *Anjoman-e Senfi-ye Karfarma'i-ye San'at-e Petroshimi*

Association of Women of the Islamic Republic: *Jam'iyyat-e Zanan-e Jomhuri-ye Islami-ye Iran*

Atomic Energy Organization of Iran: *Sazman-e Energi-ye Atomi-ye Iran*

Basij Resistance Force: *Neyrou-ye Moqavemat-e Basij*

Be'sat Foundation: *Bonyad-e Be'sat*

Bureau for Cooperation between Religious Seminaries and Universities: *Daftar-e Hamkari-ye Howzeh va Daneshgah*

Bureau of Islamic Sciences Academy: *Daftar-e Farhangestan-e Olum-e Islami*

Center for Islamic Revolution Documentation: *Markaz-e Asnad-e Enqelab-e Islami*

Center for Media Studies and Research: *Markaz-e Motale'eat va Tahqiqat-e Resanehha*

Center for Representing the Supreme Leader in Universities: *Nahad-e Namayandegi-ye Maqqam-e Mo'azzem-e Rahbari dar Daneshgahha*

Center for Strategic Research: *Markaz-e Tahqiqat-e Estrategik*

Center for Supervision of Mosque Affairs: *Markaz-e Residegi be Omur-e Masajed*

Central Khatam al-Anbia Headquarters: *Qarargah-e Markazi-ye Khatam al Anbia*

Chamber of Commerce: *Otaq-e Bazargani*

Chief Justice: *Ra'is-e Qoveh-ye Qaza'i-ye*

Chief of the Armed Forces General Staff: *Farmandehe Setad-e Kolle Niroohaye Mosallah*

Confederated Islamic Congregations: *Hey'atha-ye Mo'talefeh-ye Islami* (later renamed Party of Confederated Islamic Congregations: *Hezb-e Mo'talefeh-ye Islami*)

Construction Jihad: *Jahad-e Sazandegi*

Council for Coordination of Islamic Propaganda: *Showra-ye Hamahangi-ye Tabliqat-e Islami*

Council for Revision of the Constitution: *Showra-ye Baznegari-ye Qanun-e Asasi*

Council for Selection of Judges: *Showra-ye Gozinesh-e Qozat*

Court of Administrative Justice: *Divan-e Edalat-e Edari*

Defense Industries Organization: *Sazman-e Sanaye Defa'*

Developers' Coalition of Islamic Iran: *E'telaf Abadgaran-e Iran-e Islami*

Devotees of Islam: *Feda'iyan-e Islam*

Disciplinary Court for Judges and Public Prosecutors: *Dadsara va Dadgah-e Ali-ye Entezami-ye Qozat*

Dispute Settlement Council of Branches: *Showra-ye Hal-e Ekhtelaf Meyan-e Se Qoveh*

Encyclopedia of Islam Foundation: *Bonyad-e Da'eratolm'aref Islami*

Environmental Protection Organization: *Sazman-e Hefz-e Mohit-e Zist*

Expediency Discernment Assembly (of the State): *Majma'-e Tashkhis-e Maslahat-e Nezam*

Fifteenth of Khordad Foundation: *Bonyad-e Panzdahe Khordad*

Foundation for Affairs of People Displaced by the Imposed War: *Bonyad-e Omur-e Mohajerin-e Jang-e Tahmili*

Foundation for Dispossessed and War-Invalids: *Bonyad-e Mostaz'afan va Janbazan*

Foundation for History of the Islamic Revolution in Iran: *Bonyad-e Tarikh-e Enqelab-e Islami-ye Iran*

Foundation for Islamic Thought: *Bonyad-e Andisheh-ye Islami*

Foundation of Martyrs and Veterans Affairs: *Bonyad-e Shahid va Omur-e Issargaran*

Foundation for Preservation of Artifacts and Values of Sacred Defense: *Bonyad-e Hefz-e Asar va Arzeshhay-e Defa' Moqadas*

Freedom-Seeking Movement of People of Iran: *Jonbesh-e Azadikhahi-ye Mardom-e Iran*

Friday Prayer Policymaking Council: *Showra-ye Siyasatgozari-ye A'emmeh-ye Jom'eh*

Front for Followers of the Line of Imam and the Leader: *Jebheh-ye Peyrowan-e Khat-e Imam va Rahbari*

Good Scent of Service: *Rayeh-ye Khosh-e Khedmat*

Green Party of Iran: *Hezb-e Sabz*

Ground Forces Officers' Academy: *Daneshkadeh-ye Afsari*

Guardian Council: *Showra-ye Negahban*

Headquarters for Cultural Revolution: *Setad-e Enqelab-e Farhangi*

Headquarters for Implementation of Imam's (Khomeini) Order: *Setad-e Ejra'i-ye Farman-e Imam*

Headquarters for Islamic Revolution: *Setad-e Enqelab-e Islami*

Headquarters for Prayer Adduction: *Setad-e Eqameh-ye Namaz*

Headquarters for Propagation of Virtue and Prohibition of Vice: *Setad-e Amr-e be Ma'ruf va Nahy-e Az Monkar*

Headquarters for War Propagation: *Setad-e Tabliqat-e Jang*

High Council of Cultural Revolution: *Showra-ye Ali-ye Enqelab-e Farhangi*

High Council of Defense: *Showra-ye Ali-ye Defa'*

High Council of Judiciary: *Showra-ye Ali-ye Qaza'i*

High Council of Reconstruction: *Showra-ye Ali-ye Bazsazi*

High Council of Religious Seminaries of Qom: *Showra-ye Ali-ye Howzeh-ye Elmiyyeh-ye Qom*

House of (Political) Parties: *Khaneh-ye Ahzab*

House of the Farmer: *Khaneh-ye Keshavarz*

House of the Worker: *Khaneh-ye Kargar*

Housing Foundation of the Islamic Revolution: *Bonyad-e Maskan-e Enqelab-e Islami*

Imam Hoseyn University: *Daneshgah-e Imam Hoseyn*

Imam Khomeini and Islamic Revolution Research Institute: *Pazouheshkadeh-e Imam Khomeini va Enqelab-e Islami*

Imam Khomeini Relief Foundation: *Komiteh-e Emdad-e Imam Khomeini*

Imam Sadeq University: *Daneshgah-e Imam Sadeq*

Industrial Development and Renovation Organization of Iran: *Sazman-e Gostaresh va Nowsazi-ye Sanaye Iran*

Institute for Compilation and Publication of Imam Khomeini's Work: *Mo'asseseh-ye Tanzim va Nashr-e Asar-e Imam Khomeini*

Institute for Management and Planning Studies: *Mo'assesseh Ali-ye Amouzesh-e Modiriyat va Barnamehrizi*

Institute for Planning and Development Research: *Mo'assesseh Ali-ye Pazouhesh dar Barnamehrizi va Towse'eh*

Intelligence Organization of the IRGC: *Sazman-e Ettela'at Sepah-e Pasdaran-e Enqelab-e Islami*

In the Righteous Path Institute: *Mo'asseseh-ye Dar Rah-e Haq*

Iran Academy of Arts: *Farhangestan-e Honar-e Jomhuri-ye Islami-ye Iran*

Iran Army Aviation: *Havaniruz*

Iranian Army's Command and General Staff College: *Daneshkadeh-ye Farmandehi va Setad*

Iranian Central Oil Fields Company: *Sherkat-e Naft-e Manateq-e Markazi*

Iranian Fuel Conservation Company: *Sherkat-e Behinehsazi-ye Masraf-e Sokht*

Iranian National Standards Organization: *Sazman-e Estandard-e Melli Iran*

Iranian Offshore Engineering and Construction Company: *Sherkat-e Mohandesi va sakht-e Tasisat-e Darya'i-ye Iran*

Iranian Offshore Oil Company: *Sherkat-e Naft-e Falat Qareh-ye Iran*

Iranian Privatization Organization: *Sazman-e Khososizasi-ye Iran*

Iranian Tobacco Company: *Sherkat-e Dokhaniyat-e Iran*

Iran's National Front: *Jebheh-ye Melli-ye Iran*

IRGC Cooperative Foundation: *Bonyad-e Ta'avon-e Sepah*

Islamic Assembly of Ladies: *Majma'-e Islami-ye Banovan*

Islamic Association of Iranian Medical Society: *Anjoman-e Islami-ye Jame'eh-ye Pezeshki-ye Iran*

Islamic Association of Iranian Teachers: *Anjoman-e Islami-ye Mo'alleman-e Iran*

Islamic Association of University Instructors: *Anjoman-e Islami-ye Modarresin-e Daneshgahha*

Islamic Azad University: *Daneshgah-e Azad-e Islami*

Islamic Civilization Party: *Hezb-e Tamaddon-e Islami*

Islamic Consultative Assembly: *Majlis-e Showra-ye Islami* (commonly known as Majlis)

Islamic Culture and Communication Organization: *Sazman-e Farhang va Ertebatat-e Islami*

Islamic Iran's Participation Front: *Hezb-e Jebheh-ye Mosharekat-e Iran-e Islami*

Islamic Iran's Solidarity Party: *Hezb-e Hambastegi-ye Iran-e Islami*

Islamic Labor Party: *Hezb-e Islami-ye Kar*

Islamic Majlis Research Center: *Markaz-e Pazhuheshha-ye Majlis-e Showra-ye Islami*

Islamic People's Republican Party of Iran: *Hezb-e Jomhuri-ye Khalq-e Mosalman-e Iran*

Islamic Propaganda Organization: *Sazman-e Tabliqat-e Islami*

Islamic Republic of Iran Broadcasting: *Seda va Sima-ye Jomhuri-ye Islami-ye Iran* (literal translation is The Voice and Vision of The Islamic Republic of Iran, but its English website refers to it as IRIB)

Islamic Republic of Iran Medical Council: *Sazman-e Nezam Pezehski-ye Jomhuri-ye Islami-ye Iran*

Islamic Republic Party: *Hezb-e Jomhuri-ye Islami*

Islamic Revolutionary Committees: *Komitehha-ye Enqelab-e Islami*

Islamic Revolutionary Guards Corps: *Sepah-e Pasdaran-e Enqelab-e Islami*

Islamic Revolutionary Tribunals: *Dadgahay-e Enqelab-e Islami*

Islamic Revolution Documentation Center: *Markaz-e Asnad-e Enqelab-e Islami*

Islamic Revolution Guard Corps Cooperative Organization: *Bonyad-e Ta'avon-e Sepah-e Pasdaran-e Enqelab-e Islami*

Islamic Schools of Thought Educational and Research Institute: *Mo'asseseh-ye Amouzeshi Pazhuheshi-ye Mazaheb-e Islami*

Islamic Sciences Academy of Qom: *Farhangestan-e Olum-e Islami-ye Qom*

Islamic Seminaries Management Center for Ladies: *Markaz-e Modiriyat-e Howzeha-ye Elmiyyeh-ye Khaharan*

Islamic Society of Academics of Iran: *Jame'eh-ye Islami-ye Daneshgahiyan-e Iran*

Islamic Society of Alumni of Shiraz University: *Anjoman-e Islami-ye Daneshamukhtegan-e Daneshgah-e Shiraz*

Islamic Society of Alumni of Tehran University's College of Engineering: *Anjoman-e Islami-ye Fareghottahsilan-e Daneshkadeh-ye Fanni-ye Daneshgah-e Tehran*

Islamic Society of Athletes: *Jame'eh-ye Islami-ye Varzeshkaran*

Islamic Society of Bakhtiaris: *Jame'eh-ye Islami-ye Bakhtiariha*

Islamic Society of Educators: *Jame'eh-ye Islami-ye Farhangiyan*

Islamic Society of Engineers: *Jame'eh-ye Islami-ye Mohandesin*

Islamic Society of Former Parliament Deputies: *Jame'eh-ye Islami-ye Namayandegan-e Advar-e Mokhtalef-e Majlis*

Islamic Society of Iranian Physicians: *Anjoman-e Islami-ye Pezeshkan-e Iran*

Joint Staff of the Islamic Republic of Iran Army: *Setad-e Moshtark-e Artesh Jomhuri-ye Islami-ye Iran*

Judicial Organization of the Armed Forces: *Sazman-e Qaza'i-e Neyrouha-ye Mosalah*

Judicial Police: *Polis-e Qaza'i*

Justice Administration of the Islamic Revolution: *Dadsaraye Enqelab-e Islami*

Law Enforcement Forces: *Niruy-e Entezami*

Liberation Movement of Iran: *Nehzat-e Azadi-ye Iran*

Management and Planning Organization: *Sazman-e Modiriyat va Barnamehrizi*

Mandate of the Jurist: *Velayat-e faqih*

Ministry of Intelligence: *Vezarat-e Ettela'at*

Ministry of Interior: Vezarat-e Keshvar

Ministry of Revolutionary Guards: *Vezarat-e Sepah-e Pasdaran-e Enqelab-e Islami*

Ministry of Roads and Urban Development: *Vezarat-e Rah va Shahrsazi*

Ministry of Sports and Youth: *Vezarat-e Varzesh va Javanan*

Mofid University: *Daneshgah-e Mofid*

Movement of Combatant Muslims: *Jonbesh-e Mosalmanan-e Mobarez*

Muslim Nations' Party: *Hezb-e Mellal-e Islami*

National Elites Foundation: *Bonyad-e Melli-ye Nokhbegan*

National Iranian Oil Company Pension Fund: *Sherkat-e Sarmayehgozari-ye Sandoq-e Bazneshastegi-ye Karkonan-e San'at-e Naft*

National Iranian Oil Refining and Distribution Company: *Sherkat-e Melli-ye Palayesh va Pakhsh-e Faravardeha-ye Nafti-ye Iran*

National Trust Party: *Hezb-e E'temad-e Melli*

Office of the President: *Ra'is-e Jomhur*

Organization for Battling Price Gouging: *Sazman-e Mobarez-eh ba Geranforushi*

Organization for Investment, and Economic, and Technical Assistance of Iran: *Sazman-e Sarmayehgozari va Komakha-ye Eqtesadi va Fani-ye Iran*

Organization for Struggle on the Path of Working Class Emancipation: *Sazman-e Peykar dar Rah-e Azadi-ye Tabaqeh-ye Kargar*

Organization of Erudite of Islamic Iran: *Sazman-e Daneshamukhtegan-e Iran-e Islami* (commonly known as *Advar-e Tahkim-e Vahdat*)

Organization of Iranian People's Feda'i Guerrillas: *Sazman-e Cherikha-ye Feda'i-ye Khalq-e Iran*

Organization of Mobilization of the Dispossessed: *Sazman-e Basij-e Mostaz'afin*

Organization of Mobilization of University Students: *Sazman-e Basij-e Daneshjuie*

Organization of Mojahedin of the Islamic Revolution of Iran: *Sazman-e Mojahedin-e Enqelab-e Islami-ye Iran*

Organization of National Industries of Iran: *Sazman-e Sanaye Melli-ye Iran*

Organization of Targeted Subsidies: *Sazman-e Hadafmand-Sazi-ye Yaranehha*

Pars Oil and Gas Company: *Sherkat-e Naft va Gaz-e Pars*

Party of Democracy: *Hezb-e Mardomsalari*

Party of Executives of Construction of Iran: *Hezb-e Kargozaran-e Sazandegi-e Iran*

Party of Iranian Independence: *Hezb-e Esteqlal-e Iran*

Party of Iranian People's Will: *Hezb-e Eradeh-ye Mellat-e Iran*

Party of Islamic Iran's People's Unity: *Hezb-e Ettehad-e Mellat-e Iran-e Islami*

Party of Moderation and Development: *Hezb-e E'tedal va Towse'eh*

Party of the Iranian Nation: *Hezb-e Mellat-e Iran*

Party of Women of the Islamic Republic of Iran: *Hezb-e Zanan-e Jomhuri-ye Islami-ye Iran*

Penitentiary Organization: *Sazman-e Ta'zirat*

People's Mojahedin Organization of Iran: *Sazman-e Mojahedin-e Khalq-e Iran*

Perseverance Front of the Islamic Revolution: *Jebheh-ye Istadegi-ye Enqelab-e Islami*

Petroleum Ministry's Management Development Center: *Markaz-e Towse'eh-ye Modiriyat-e Vezarat-e Naft*

Petropars Company: *Sherkat-e Petropars*

Physical Training Organization: *Sazman-e Tarbiat Badani*

Pious Endowments and Charity Affairs Organization: *Sazman-e Owqaf va Omour-e Kheyriyeh*

Plan and Budget Organization: *Sazman-e Barnameh va Budjeh* (after the revolution renamed as Management and Planning Organization of Iran [*Sazman-e Modiriyat va Barnamehrizi-ye Keshvar*])

Popular Front of Islamic Revolution Forces: *Jebh-ye Mardomi-ye Niruha-ye Enqelab-e Islami*

Ports and Maritime Organization: *Sazman-e Banader va Daryanavardi*

Prime Minister's Intelligence Bureau: *Daftar-e Ettela'at Nokhost Vaziri*

Prosecutor-general: *Dadsetan-e Kol-e Keshvar*

Public Health Organization: *Sazman-e Behzisti*

Qods Aviation Industries: *Sherkat-e Sanaye Hava'i-ye Qods*

Qom Higher Education Complex: *Mojtamah-e Amuzesh-e Ali-ye Qom*

Qom Islamic Society of Admonishers: *Jame'eh-ye Islami-ye Nasehin-e Qom*

Qom Seminary Islamic Propaganda Office: *Daftar-e Tabliqat-e Islami-ye Howzeh-ye Elmiyyeh-ye Qom*

Radical Movement of Iran: *Nehzat-e Radikal-e Iran*

Research Institute of Seminaries and University: *Pazouheshkah-e Howzeh va Daneshgah*

Revolutionary Council: *Showra-ye Enqelab*

Revolutionary Movement of People of Iran: *Jonbesh-e Enqelabi-ye Mardom-e Iran*

Seven-Member Committees for Land Distribution: *Hey'atha-ye Haft Nafareh-ye Taqsim-e Zamin*

Shahed University: *Daneshgah-e Shahed*

Social Security Organization: *Sazman-e Ta'min-e Ejtema'i*

Society for Islamic Education: *Kanun-e Tarbiyat-e Islami*

Society of Alumni of the Indian Subcontinent: *Kanun-e Fareghottahsilan-e Shebhehqarreh-ye Hend*

Society of Combatant Clergy: *Jame'eh-ye Ruhaniyyat-e Mobarez*

Society of Former Members of the Union of Islamic Student Associations in Europe: *Kanun-e Islami-ye Daneshamukhtegan-e Ozv-e Sabeq-e Ettehadiyyeh-ye Anjomanha-ye Islami-ye Daneshjuyan-e Orupa*

Society of Former Parliament Deputies: *Kanun-e Namayandegan-e Advar-e Majlis-e Showra-ye Islami*

Society of Prerevolution Muslim Political Prisoners: *Kanun-e Zendaniyan-e Siyasi-ye Mosalman-e Dowran-e Qabl Az Piruzi-ye Enqelab-e Islami*

Society of Qom Seminary Scholars: *Jame'eh-ye Modarresin-e Howzeh-ye Elmiyyeh-ye Qom*

Society of Women of the Islamic Revolution: *Jame'eh-ye Zanan-e Enqelab-e Islami*

Source of emulation: *Marja'-e taqlid*

South Zagros Oil and Gas Production Company: *Sherkat-e Bahrebardari-ye Naft va Gaz-e Zagros-e Jonubi*

Special Court for Clergy: *Dadgah-e Vizheh-ye Ruhaniyyat*

State Audit Court: *Divan-e Mohasebat-e Keshvar*

State Educational Assessment Organization: *Sazman-e Sanjesh-e Amouzesh-e Keshvar*

State General Inspectorate Organization: *Sazman-e Bazrasi-ye Kol-e Keshvar*

State Management Training Center: *Markaz-e Amouzesh-e Modiriyat-e Dowlati*

State Organization for Registration of Deeds and Properties: *Sazman-e Sabt-e Asnad va Amlak-e Keshvar*

State Prisons and Security and Corrective Measures Organization: *Sazman-e Zendanha va Eqdamat-e Ta'mini va Tarbiyati-ye Keshvar*

State Security Council: *Showra-ye Amniyyat-e Keshvar*

State Supreme Court: *Divan-e Ali-ye Keshvar*

State Welfare Organization of Iran: *Sazman-e Behzisti-ye Keshvar*

Statistical Center of Iran: *Sazman-e Amar-e Iran*

Steadfastness Front of the Islamic Revolution: *Jebheh-ye Payedari-ye Enqelab-e Islami*

Strategic Council on Foreign Relations: *Showra-ye Rahbordi-ye Ravabet-e Khareji*

Supreme Council for National Security: *Showra-ye Ali-ye Amniyyat-e Melli*

Supreme Council for Reconstruction: *Showra-ye Ali-ye Bazsazi va Nowsazi-ye Manateq-e Janqzadeh*

Supreme Council of Cyberspace: *Showra-ye Ali-ye Fazay-e Majazi*

Supreme Defense Council: *Showra-ye Ali-ye Defa'*

Tehran Chamber of Commerce: *Otaq-e Bazargani-ye Tehran*

Tehran's Higher Teachers' Training College: Daneshsara-ye Ali-ye Tehran

Telecommunications Company of Iran: *Sherkat-e Mokhaberat-e Iran*

Theological Seminaries Center for Services: *Markaz-e Khadamat-e Howzeha-ye Elmiyyeh*

Toilers Party: *Hezb-e Zahmatkeshan-e Mellat-e Iran*

Tribal Affairs Organization of Iran: *Sazman-e Omur-e Ashayer-e Iran*

Union of Students' Islamic Associations: *Ettehadiyyeh-ye Anjomanha-ye Islami-ye Daneshamouzan*

United Front of Principalist and Skilled Women: *Jebheh-ye Mottahed-e Zanan-e Usulgara va Karamad*

Unity Consolidation Bureau (among Union of Islamic Student Associations in Universities throughout Iran): *Daftar-e Tahkim-e Vahdat (Ettehadiyyeh-ye Anjomanha-ye Islami-ye Daneshjuyan-e Daneshgahha-ye Sarasar-e Keshvar)*

University Jihad: *Jahad-e Daneshgahi*

University of Judicial Sciences and Administrative Services: *Daneshkadeh-e Olum-e Qaza'i va Khadamat-e Edari*

University of Social Welfare and Rehabilitation Sciences: *Daneshkadeh-e Olum-e Behzisti va Tavanbakhshi*

Vice President for Implementation of the Constitution: *Moaven-e Ra'is-e Jomhur dar Ejra-ye Qanun-e Asasi*

Vice President for Management and Human Capital Development: *Moavenat-e Towse'eh-ye Modiriyat va Sarmayeh Ensani-ye Ra'is-e Jomhuri*

Vice President for Planning and Strategic Supervision: *Moavenat-e Barnamehrizi va Nezarat-e Rahbordi-ye Reyasat-e Jomhuri*

Women's Organization of the Islamic Revolution: *Sazman-e Zanan-e Enqelab-e Islami*

World Center for Islamic Sciences: *Markaz-e Jahani-ye Olum-e Islami*

World Forum for Proximity of Islamic Schools of Thought: *Majma'-e Jahani-ye Taqrib-e Mazaheb-e Islami*

Youth Alliance of the Islamic Revolution of Iran: *Jam'iyyat-e Javanan-e Enqelab-e Islami-ye Iran*

Zeynab Society: *Jame'eh-ye Zeynab*

A Note on Translation and Transliteration

All translations from Persian are ours unless indicated otherwise. We have tried to use a simple and consistent transliteration system.

All the diacritical marks for Persian and Arabic terms were dispensed with except for *ayn* and *hamza* (represented respectively by an opening quotation mark and an apostrophe), which are dropped only at the initial position.

Anglicized forms for foreign words (Islam, shari'a, Shaikh, ulama) and place names (Isfahan, Kurdistan) found in the 5th edition of the *American Heritage Dictionary* or the *Oxford English Dictionary Online* have been used. However, where appropriate, deference has been accorded to colloquial Persian pronunciations (e.g., ayatollah, hejab, Hezbollah, shaikholislam).

Names of key political figures known in the West have been written based on their Western spelling in newspapers such as the *New York Times* (Mahmoud Ahmadinejad, Akbar Hashemi-Rafsanjani, Seyyed Ali Khamenei, and Hassan Rouhani).

A hyphen has been used in the case of both compound first names (Ali-Akbar, Gholam-Reza) and compound last names (Abbaspur-Tehranifard, Roghani-Zanjani).

In the Who Is Who section of the volume, more rarely used elements of a compound personal name appear in brackets, as in Mir Hoseyn Musavi [-Khameneh], to fully identify the person. However, in the rest of the book such brackets are dropped unless they were deemed essential to avoid any confusion.

Except in the case of first and last names, -e and -ye are used respectively after each consonant and vowel to capture *ezafeh*. For example, Jam'iyyat-e Zanan or Jame'eh-ye Zeynab, but not Hashemi-ye-Rafsanjani.

Titles and forms of address for dignitaries or descendants of the family of Prophet Muhammad such as Aqa, Haj(i), Khan, Mir, Mirza, Molla, and Seyyed have been separated from both the first names and the last names.

All dates are given as Western-calendar dates and were calculated using the Khayam Persian Calendar program (http://www.payvand.com/calendar/) as a conversion tool. The equivalent Persian solar dates have been dropped except in the References section where sources are cited.

PART ONE

Political Institutions

1

Chronology of Major Political Events
(1978–2017)

1978

January 7 — An article is published under a pseudonym in *Ettela'at* insulting Ayatollah Seyyed Ruhollah Khomeini by calling him a "British agent," questioning his Iranian parentage, and accusing him of living an immoral life.

January 9 — In protests that follow in Qom, at least six protesters are killed.

February 18 — Demonstrations take place in a dozen Iranian cities to commemorate forty days since the deaths in Qom.

July 10 — The US–Iranian Nuclear Energy Agreement is signed in Tehran.

August 11 — Isfahan's military commander, Lieutenant General Reza Naji, declares the first imposition of martial law.

August 19 — Arson at Rex Cinema in Abadan during a movie screening kills 377 people.

August 26 — Prime Minister Jamshid Amouzegar resigns his post.

August 27 — The shah appoints Ja'far Sharif-Emami as prime minister. The new premier announces that the calendar will change from an imperial calendar (based on the coronation of Cyrus the Great) to the hijri calendar. He also orders the closure of all casinos and cabarets in the country.

August 29 — Fourteen political parties announce their formation.

September 4 — Millions take part in anti-shah demonstrations throughout the country.

September 7 — After massive demonstrations in Tehran, the cabinet imposes martial law in twelve Iranian cities for up to six months.

September 8 — In an event that later became known as Black Friday, hundreds of demonstrators are killed in Tehran's Jaleh Square.

September 16 — Over 10,000 people die in an earthquake in the city of Tabas.

September 23 — Oil workers in Ahvaz go on strike.

September 24 — Iran's only official party, the Resurrection (Rastakhiz) Party, announces its dissolution.

October 2	The secretary-general of the Resurrection Party, Javad Sa'id, resigns.
October 5	Khomeini leaves his exile in Najaf but is denied entry into Kuwait.
October 6	Khomeini arrives in France and settles in the Paris suburb of Neauphle-le-Château.
October 7	Field Marshal Ne'matollah Nasiri, head of the SAVAK, is dismissed.
October 14	Employees of Iran's largest oil refinery in Abadan go on strike.
October 15	The Iranian government announces the end of media censorship after a four-day strike by the major media outlets.
October 17	Employees of the main office of the National Iranian Oil Company (NIOC) go on strike.
October 21	Mehdi Bazargan, the leader of the Liberation Movement of Iran (LMI), travels to Paris to meet with Ayatollah Khomeini the next day. Employees of the Tehran oil refinery begin a strike.
October 25	1,126 political prisoners are released.
October 30	Ayatollah Hoseyn-Ali Montazeri and Ayatollah Seyyed Mahmud Taleqani are released from prison. Nationwide strike of workers in the Iranian oil industry begins.
October 31	Exports of Iranian oil and gas are stopped.
November 4	The American government warns its citizens to leave Iran. Karim Sanjabi, secretary-general of Iran's National Front, meets with Ayatollah Khomeini in Paris. Students clash with members of the imperial guard in front of Tehran University.
November 5	Ja'far Sharif-Emami resigns as prime minister.
November 6	The shah appoints General Gholam-Reza Azhari (1912–2001), chief of staff of Iran's armed forces, as premier in a cabinet made up of military officers. In a televised speech, the shah announces, "I too have heard the message of the people's revolution."
November 8	Former premier Amir-Abbas Hoveyda is arrested.
November 9	William Sullivan, US ambassador to Iran, sends a cable to Washington titled "Thinking the Unthinkable," stating that the shah's regime is doomed.
December 1	People start chanting "God is great" from rooftops.
December 10	The largest public demonstration against the regime (known as the Tasu'a demonstration) takes place in Tehran.
December 18	Ayatollah Montazeri goes to Paris to meet Ayatollah Khomeini.
December 23	Two oil executives (an American, Paul E. Grimm, and an Iranian, Malek-Mohammad Boroujerdi)

are assassinated in street ambushes carried out by Mansurron group in Ahvaz. Grimm, the acting managing director of the Oil Service Company of Iran, is the first foreigner killed in the unrest.

December 28–29 A five-member delegation—Mehdi Bazargan, Akbar Hashemi-Rafsanjani, Mostafa Katira'i, Kazem Hasibi, and Hashem Sabbaghiyan—dispatched by Khomeini, convinces striking oil workers to produce enough oil for domestic consumption.

December 31 General Azhari resigns as prime minister.

1979

January 4–7 At a conference in Guadeloupe, the leaders of France, the United Kingdom, the United States, and West Germany conclude that the events in Iran are unfolding in such a way that the crisis cannot be resolved with the shah remaining in power.

January 4 The shah signs a decree appointing Shapur Bakhtiar as prime minister, and Bakhtiar later presents his cabinet to the shah. Ayatollah Khomeini urges civil servants not to obey the new government. General Robert E. Huyser (1924–97), deputy commander of the US European Command, visits Iran to assess the situation on behalf of the American government.

January 6 Premier Bakhtiar declares new measures including the cessation of

press censorship and the easing of martial law. However, thousands of protesters oppose him in Qom. Khomeini announces in Paris that there should be no collaboration with the new administration.

January 7 Despite the appointment of a new government, demonstrations against the shah's regime continue in various Iranian cities.

January 9 In a secret memo (since declassified) to Zbigniew Brzezinski, David L. Aaron, US deputy national security adviser, writes, "the Bakhtiar government is not working politically, and the way in which the Shah is leaving will not help Bakhtiar make the government work . . . The best that can result in my view is a military coup against Bakhtiar and then a deal struck between the military and Khomeini that finally pushes the Shah out of power . . . it seems clear that the Shah is through and that his protracted and indecisive presence is counterproductive."

January 10 Bakhtiar is left with no tribal political support, as Bakhtiari tribesmen support Khomeini.

January 12 Khomeini announces the formation of a Revolutionary Council as a shadow government to Bakhtiar's government.

January 13 Millions demonstrate in Iran demanding the return of Khomeini and the abdication of power by the shah.

January 14   A regency council headed by Seyyed Jalaleddin Tehrani holds its first meeting, and the shah prepares to leave for his "temporary vacation" abroad.

January 16   The shah and Queen Farah Diba leave Tehran for Aswan in Egypt on their way to the United States. Khomeini congratulates his followers in Iran for their success in forcing the shah out. Bakhtiar's cabinet is approved by the Majlis.

January 18   Khomeini demands that the shah be brought back to Iran to face trial for causing bloodshed and for plundering Iran's economy.

January 20   Khomeini announces his intention to return to Iran in response to his followers' demands.

January 21   A committee is formed to coordinate the logistics of Ayatollah Khomeini's return to Iran. Some of its prominent members are Asadollah Badamchiyan, Ali Danesh-Monfared, Mohammad Mofatteh, Morteza Motahhari, Hashem Sabbaghiyan, and Kazem Sami.

January 22   The shah leaves Egypt for Morocco. Tehrani resigns as head of the regency council. Hasan-Ebrahim Habibi presents Khomeini the preliminary draft of the new constitution.

January 24   Bakhtiar announces a plebiscite to decide whether Iranians desire a monarchy or a republic. He also announces the closure of Iran's airports to prevent the return of

Khomeini but the latter insists that he will soon return to Tehran.

January 26–29   Khomeini's supporters continue to demonstrate in Tehran. In an attempt at reconciliation, Bakhtiar expresses a desire to meet Khomeini in Paris but the Ayatollah refuses to see him unless he first resigns from office.

January 30   Mehdi Bazargan holds talks with General Abbas Gharabaghi (1918–2000), the last chief of staff of the Iranian Armed Forces under the shah, on such issues as Khomeini's return to Iran and the military's position on political change. Meanwhile, American citizens prepare to leave Iran due to rising anti-American sentiment.

February 1   After spending 135 days in France, Khomeini triumphantly returns to Tehran and is welcomed by millions of supporters. In a brief speech, he criticizes foreign intervention in Iran, and urges the army to join the revolution. Bakhtiar promises strong action against the ayatollah if he declares Iran an Islamic state. The prime minister offers to form a "national unity" government, but Khomeini rejects the offer.

February 4   Khomeini announces the appointment of Mehdi Bazargan as the prime minister of the provisional government.

February 6   Bakhtiar goes to the Majlis and asks for the dissolution of SAVAK. He refuses to resign from his post, even though fifty-seven members of the Majlis already resigned in response to the call by Khomeini. The US government continues to express its support for the Bakhtiar government.

February 7 — Supporters of the opposition parties take over the police, judicial institutions, and administrative buildings in Qom, Shiraz, Isfahan, and other cities. Bazargan meets Bakhtiar and General Gharabaghi.

February 8 — Bakhtiar refuses to hand over power to the revolutionaries, and describes Khomeini's vision of the future state as "archaic and medieval."

February 9 — In a mutiny, air force cadets and technicians at the Dowshan Tappeh air base declare their support for Khomeini. Bazargan delivers a speech at Tehran University, outlining a number of proposals for his government, including the resignation of Bakhtiar's government, a referendum to form an Islamic Republic, and appointment of a committee to draft a new constitution.

February 10–11 — Revolutionaries acquire arms from Dowshan Tappeh air base and other bases, and gain control of the police stations and army garrisons in Tehran. Several high-ranking military officials are arrested or killed, prompting the chiefs of staff to declare their neutrality. The revolutionaries capture the shah's Niavaran Palace, and Bakhtiar's government collapses.

February 11 — The shah's government collapses as the revolutionaries proclaim victory.

The official tenure of Bazargan's government begins.

February 12–13 — The armed forces accept Bazargan's de facto government. National Front leaders, supporters of Khomeini, and technocrats form the new cabinet. Bazargan appoints Major General Valiyollah Qarani as chief of the joint staff of the Islamic Republic of Iran Army, while Karim Sanjabi is appointed minister of foreign affairs. Clashes between pro-shah and anti-shah groups continue throughout the country. Khomeini establishes the new Islamic revolution committees.

February 14 — People's Mojahedin Organization of Iran (PMOI) submits a list of demands to the government, including "equal rights for men and women, nationalization of all industries and the expulsion of all foreign military advisers from Iran." Meanwhile, on Valentine's Day, some individuals attack the American embassy in Tehran and hold embassy personnel hostage for a few hours, before government forces free the hostages.

February 15 — The government announces a national referendum on the replacement of the Pahlavi monarchy by an Islamic Republic to take place on March 30. On the same day, the former head of the SAVAK (Ne'matollah Nasiri), Tehran's military governor (Lieutenant General Mehdi Rahimi), the commander of the air force (Major General Manuchehr Khosrowdad), and Isfahan's military governor (Lieutenant General Reza Naji) are executed.

February 17	Oil industry workers return to work and the 30,000-strong Imperial Guard is dissolved. The Islamic Republic Party (IRP) is formed.
February 19	Iran breaks diplomatic relations with Israel.
February 24	Bazargan announces the dissolution of the SAVAK.
February 26	The interior minister tells the press that on the order of Khomeini, the Family Protection Law has been annulled.
February 27	Supporters of Grand Ayatollah Seyyed Mohammad-Kazem Shari'atmadari establish the Islamic People's Republican Party of Iran.
March 1	Khomeini leaves Tehran, takes up residence in Qom, and urges the people to vote for the Islamic Republic in the upcoming referendum.
March 7	Khomeini announces that Bazargan's government has been weak in dealing with Western pressure; he also orders female government employees to wear hijab.
March 8	Thousands of women pour into the streets of Tehran to protest against the enforcement of hijab.
March 12	Shari'atmadari criticizes the upcoming national referendum.
March 14	Bazargan denounces the summary executions of former officials in February as a "sacrilegious, inhuman, and disgraceful" violation of human rights. He also criticizes Khomeini for interfering with the work of his government.
March 16	Khomeini bans all trials and summary executions of former government officials, and asks the judiciary to draw up proper trial procedures. Supporters of the Kurdistan Democratic Party of Iran (KDPI) stage protests in Saqqez and Baneh, and the party opens its official headquarters in these cities.
March 18	The two leading guerrilla organizations, PMOI and the Organization of Iranian People's Feda'i Guerrillas (OIPFG), oppose the referendum.
March 18–21	Iranian Kurds in the city of Sanandaj rebel against the government, demanding autonomy. Scores of people are killed in clashes between Kurdish and security forces.
March 21	Ayatollah Taleqani heads a delegation to Sanandaj that includes Ayatollah Mohammad Beheshti, HI Akbar Hashemi-Rafsanjani, Abolhasan Banisadr, and Seyyed Ahmad Sadr Haj Seyyed Javadi.
March 24	Taleqani tells a crowd in Sanandaj that the city will be the first in Iran to have its own municipal election.
March 26	The government announces its intention to grant autonomy to the Kurds and appoints a Kurd, Ebrahim Yunesi, as governor-general of Kurdistan province. Violence breaks out in the Gonbad-e Kavus area between autonomy-seeking Turkomen tribesmen and security forces. The

chief of the joint staff, Valiyollah Qarani, leaves his post.

March 28 A delegation from KDPI presents an autonomy proposal to Khomeini in Qom.

March 30 The shah leaves Morocco for the Bahamas.

March 30–31 A national referendum approves the formation of the Islamic Republic; many Kurds and Turkomen do not take part in the referendum.

April 1 Khomeini proclaims the foundation of the Islamic Republic of Iran and the end of Iranian monarchy.

April 5 Seven underground Islamic guerrilla organizations join to form the Organization of Mojahedin of the Islamic Revolution of Iran (OMIRI).

April 7 Former prime minister Hoveyda is killed in Qasr Prison, but not by firing squad as ordered by the judge.

April 11 Eleven more high-level officials of the prerevolutionary era are executed. They include a former head of the SAVAK (Hasan Pakravan), a former mayor of Tehran, a former foreign minister (Abbas-Ali Khalatbari), and former members of the Senate and the Majlis, as well as military officials.

April 13 Taleqani leaves Tehran to protest the arrest and beating of two of his sons affiliated with OSPWCE.

April 15 Foreign minister Sanjabi resigns.

April 20 Street fights erupt between Kurdish supporters of KDPI and Azeri supporters of the revolution in the ethnically divided small northwest town of Naqadeh. According to reports up to seventy people are killed in twenty-four hours.

April 22 The Islamic Revolutionary Guards Corps (IRGC) is formed.

April 23 Major General Valiyollah Qarani is assassinated by members of the Forqan group—a militant Islamic group that was opposed to clerical political rule—in Tehran in their first terrorist operation. Ayatollah Mohammad-Taher Al-e Shobayr-Khaqani, spiritual leader of Arabs in the Khuzestan province, threatens to leave Iran in protest of the revolutionary committees' (*komitehs*) excessive powers.

April 25 Ayatollah Mohammad-Reza Mahdavi-Kani, supervisor of the revolutionary committees, announces his intention to reform the organization.

April 26 Tens of thousands of Arabs in Khuzestan Province demand autonomy for Iranian Arabs and express their support for Ayatollah Shobayr-Khaqani.

April 30 Iran breaks diplomatic relations with Egypt after Egypt signs a peace accord with Israel.

May 1 Ayatollah Morteza Motahhari, the leading member of the Revolutionary Council, is assassinated.

May 8 — Thousands of women protest against the new headscarf law.

May 9 — Habib Elghanian, an industrialist and former head of Tehran's Jewish society, is subjected to a summary trial and execution on the charge of contact with Israel.

May 12 — *Ayandegan*, a liberal mass-circulation newspaper, publishes three blank pages to show its protest after a remark by Khomeini that he will no longer be reading the newspaper. Ayatollah Mohammad-Sadeq Khalkhali, head judge of the revolutionary tribunals, issues a death sentence in absentia for the deposed shah, Queen Farah, Princess Ashraf (the shah's twin sister), former prime minister Bakhtiar, and a number of other high-level officials.

May 13 — PMOI leaders Mas'ud Rajavi and Musa Khiyabani meet with Khomeini in Qom. One of the top leaders of PMOI, Mohammad-Reza Sa'adati, is arrested by the security forces on charges of spying on behalf of the Soviet Union. Khomeini issues an order limiting executions.

May 25 — Hashemi-Rafsanjani, a close confidant of Khomeini, survives an assassination attempt.

May 30 — The daily newspaper *Jomhuri-ye Islami* begins its publication as the organ of the IRP. Bloody clashes take place between government forces and the Arabs of Khorramshahr who demand autonomy.

June 5 — Khomeini warns writers, lawyers, and secular critics who oppose Islam of a similar fate to that of the shah.

June 7 — The Islamic Republic nationalizes thirty-seven banks.

June 10 — The shah leaves the Bahamas for Mexico.

June 12 — Khomeini accuses the USSR of interfering in the internal affairs of Iran and Afghanistan.

June 14 — The Revolutionary Council publishes the official preliminary draft of the constitution.

June 16 — Bruce Laingen arrives in Iran as the new American interim chargé d'affaires. The Construction Jihad is officially established.

June 25 — The Islamic government announces the nationalization of all insurance companies.

July 5 — The Revolutionary Council passes the bill for the election of the Assembly for the Final Examination of the Constitution (AFEC).

July 9 — Khomeini grants general amnesty, releasing some 3,000 political prisoners.

July 21 — Khomeini bans the broadcast of music on television and radio.

July 22 — A former press attaché at the Iranian embassy in Washington, DC, Ali-Akbar Tabataba'i, is murdered on his doorstep in Bethesda, Maryland.

July 27   The first massive Friday prayer ceremony after the revolution, led by Ayatollah Taleqani, is held at Tehran University.

August 3   Elections are held for the AFEC.

August 7–11   *Ayandegan* and over twenty other newspapers and periodicals are banned on the orders of Ayatollah Ahmad Azari-Qomi, the revolutionary prosecutor-general of Tehran. This represented the revolutionary regime's first imposition of a restrictive press law.

August 12   The National Democratic Front of Iran and many other organizations hold a large demonstration in Tehran to protest the banning of *Ayandegan* and other newspapers.

August 18   Ayatollah Khomeini orders the armed forces to advance toward Paveh, a Kurdish city next to the Iraqi border.

August 19   The AFEC begins deliberations on drafting a new constitution.

August 24   Ayatollah Khomeini orders the establishment of Islamic revolutionary tribunals.

September 2   At least forty-five civilian Kurds, including women and children, are killed in Qarna (a village south of Naqadeh) by forces under the control of HI Gholam-Reza Hasani,

according to Ayatollah Montazeri's special envoy.

September 4–6   The city of Mahabad, a Kurdish stronghold, falls to government troops.

September 6   The city of Sardasht falls to government troops. The government nationalizes the two leading national dailies, *Keyhan* and *Ettela'at*.

September 10   Ayatollah Taleqani dies at the age of 68.

October 5   The US resumes shipment of military spare parts to Iran.

October 22   The shah arrives in New York City to undergo cancer treatment at the New York Hospital-Cornell Medical Center.

October 30   Islamic Republic introduced its new one-, two-, five-, and twenty-rial coins.

November 1   Premier Bazargan shakes hands with Zbigniew Brzezinski, the US national security adviser, on the sidelines of a meeting in Algiers. Conservatives attack him vehemently for this gesture. HI Seyyed Mohammad Qazi-Tabatabai, Khomeini's representative and Friday prayer leader of Tabriz, is assassinated.

November 4   A group of students calling themselves the Muslim Student Followers of the Imam's Line seizes the American embassy in Tehran. Sixty-six American embassy personnel are held hostage, spurring a political and diplomatic drama labeled by the media as the Iran hostage crisis, which ultimately lasts 444 days.

November 5   PM Bazargan and his cabinet resign over the hostage crisis.

November 6   Based on Khomeini's order, the Revolutionary Council cabinet starts acting in place of the Bazargan cabinet.

November 14   With Executive Order 12170, President Jimmy Carter freezes $6 billion of Iranian assets in the US in retaliation for the embassy takeover.

November 15   The AFEC holds its final meeting.

November 19   Khomeini declares that the American hostages will be tried as foreign spies.

November 23   PMOI's paramilitary volunteer militia is established.

November 26   Grand Ayatollah Shari'atmadari denounces the taking of the American hostages.

December 2–3 The newly drafted constitution is overwhelmingly ratified in a nationwide referendum.

December 4   The UN Security Council passes a resolution demanding the release of the American hostages.

December 5   Shari'atmadari's home is attacked by a pro-Khomeini mob for his criticism of the constitution.

December 13   Hundreds of thousands gather in Tabriz in support of Shari'atmadari and denounce the constitution.

December 15   The shah leaves the United States for Panama. The Muslim People's Republican Party of Iran, which supports Shari'atmadari, is ordered to close.

December 18   The Forqan group assassinates Ayatollah Mohammad Mofatteh, a member of the Revolutionary Council and close aide to Khomeini, in front of Tehran University's faculty of theology.

December 20–22 Sectarian fighting breaks out between the Shiite Sistanis and the Sunni Baluchis in Sistan and Baluchestan.

December 24   The Soviet Union invades Afghanistan.

1980

January 1–3   Kurt Waldheim, secretary-general of the UN, arrives in Tehran and meets members of the Revolutionary Council regarding the possible release of the American hostages.

January 5   PMOI's leader, Mas'ud Rajavi, announces his candidacy for the presidential election.

January 14   Khomeini appoints HI Seyyed Ali Khamenei as the Friday prayer leader in Tehran.

January 18   Abbas Omani, a man working for Rajavi's presidential campaign, is fatally beaten in the streets of Tehran.

January 19   Khomeini issues a ruling stating those who did not vote for the establishment of the Islamic Republic cannot run for its presidency. This ruling disqualifies Rajavi from running in the first presidential election.

January 23 Khomeini is hospitalized due to heart disease.

January 25 Seyyed Abolhasan Banisadr is elected president of the Islamic Republic of Iran, winning 75 percent of the vote in the first presidential election in Iranian history.

January 30 In a speech at Tehran University, PMOI leader Rajavi warns that his group will answer fists with fists and bullets with bullets.

February 4 Banisadr is sworn in as president in a ceremony attended by Khomeini.

February 7 Banisadr is appointed head of the Revolutionary Council.

February 19 Khomeini also appoints Banisadr as commander in chief of the Iranian Armed Forces.

February 23 Khomeini suggests that the Iranian Majlis should decide the fate of the American hostages.

February 24 HI Seyyed Ali Khamenei resigns from the post of deputy defense minister.

March 3 Seven members of Forqan group are executed.

March 12 The Foundation of Martyrs is established.

March 14 Iran's first Majlis election since the revolution is held.

March 23 The shah leaves Panama for Egypt, where he undergoes an operation on his spleen.

April 7 The United States breaks diplomatic relations with Iran.

April 15 The Revolutionary Council approves a decree to distribute agrarian land among landless farmers. It calls for the creation of seven-member committees across Iran to oversee the implementation of the law. This legislation proves to be controversial as it mandates limiting land ownership to only three times what was deemed sufficient for making a living. After protests from many quarters, including conservative clergy, the law is shelved.

April 18 A campaign begins to purge opposition political forces from university campuses by attacking their supporters. It is labeled the Cultural Revolution.

April 24 US commandos launch an abortive rescue mission to secure the release of the fifty-two American hostages.

April 30 A bill approved by the Revolutionary Council forms the Basij Resistance Force.

May 8 Iran's first female minister, Mrs. Farrokhroo Parsa—appointed as education minister in 1968—is executed. The chief prosecutor of the revolutionary courts bans the publication of forty independent newspapers and magazines.

May 28	The tenure of the Revolutionary Council cabinet comes to an end and the first postrevolutionary Majlis begins its work.	July 24	Prominent Marxist activist Taqi Shahram is executed.
		July 27	The deposed shah dies of cancer in Cairo at the age of sixty-one and is buried there.
June 4	OIPFG splits into two factions—Majority (aksariyat) and Minority (aqalliyat). The majority faction is close to the Tudeh Party and supports the regime, while the minority faction retains a militant policy against the Islamic Republic.	August 10	President Banisadr introduces Mohammad-Ali Raja'i to the Majlis as the designated prime minister.
		August 11	Raja'i is elected prime minister by the MPs.
June 5	The end of the academic year enables the state to properly start its cultural revolution by fully closing the universities. The closure lasts for some two years.	August 20	President Banisadr signs the official order appointing Mohammad-Ali Raja'i as the prime minister.
June 13	The Headquarters for Cultural Revolution (later renamed the High Council of Cultural Revolution) is established with seven members appointed by Khomeini. They are tasked with the Islamization of university campuses and the revision of educational curricula.	August 31	PM Raja'i presents his cabinet to the Majlis.
		September 6	President Banisadr endorses a slate of fourteen ministers proposed by Raja'i and sends that list to the Majlis for a vote.
		September 10	Raja'i's government officially begins after the Majlis approves the slate of fourteen ministers.
July 5	The entry of women into government offices without proper hijab is forbidden.	September 22	The Iran–Iraq War begins as Iraqi forces invade Iran.
July 9	A plan by military officers for a coup (known as the Nojeh coup) is discovered, and the officers are arrested.	September 27	The Headquarters for Economic Basij is formed and the government starts rationing essential goods.
July 17	The original Revolutionary Council holds its last meeting.	October 26	Iraqi forces occupy the port city of Khorramshahr.
July 21	Hashemi-Rafsanjani is elected as the first Majlis Speaker in the Islamic Republic.	November 7	Foreign minister Sadeq Qotbzadeh is dismissed.

November 22 | The government tasks the defense and interior ministers and the head of the Plan and Budget Organization to deal with the unrest in Kurdistan.

1981

January 18 | The Basij Resistance Force is dissolved into the IRGC.

January 19 | Iran and the US sign the Algiers Accord to resolve the hostage crisis.

January 20 | Within hours of the inauguration of President Ronald Reagan, the Iranian government releases all of the remaining American hostages.

March 5 | Club wielders attack a meeting at Tehran University where Banisadr is speaking. The marshals, ordered by the president to arrest the club wielders, find IRP identification cards in their pockets.

May 25 | Khomeini accuses Banisadr of promoting a personality cult not approved by Islam.

May 30 | National television broadcasts the first of a number of debates between the main ideologues of the state—Ayatollah Beheshti, Ayatollah Mohammad-Taqi Mesbah-Yazdi, and Abdolkarim Sorush—and representatives of opposition forces—Ehsan Tabari and Nureddin Kiyanuri representing the Tudeh Party, Farrokh Negahdar and Mehdi Fatahpur representing OIPFG, and Habibollah Peyman representing the Movement of Combatant Muslims.

June 1 | Banisadr demands a referendum so that the citizenry can render judgment on his differences with the Majlis.

June 7 | Tehran's prosecutor-general orders the closing of the following newspapers: *Arman-e Mellat, Edalat, Enqelab-e Islami, Jebheh-ye Melli, Mizan,* and *Nameh-e Mardom.*

June 10 | Khomeini dismisses Banisadr as commander in chief.

June 12 | Banisadr goes into hiding along with the leader of PMOI.

June 15 | The National Front organizes a demonstration against the imposition of the law of retaliation (*qisas*), which is one form of punishment in Islamic penal law. Khomeini calls the National Front a heretical organization.

June 16 | More than 136 MPs file a motion to impeach Banisadr.

June 20 | Bloody street confrontations take place between PMOI supporters and regime forces. This marks the beginning of PMOI's military campaign against the regime.

June 21 | The Majlis votes to impeach Banisadr, citing political incompetence. In total, 177 MPs vote for the impeachment, one votes against it, and twelve abstain. Sa'id Soltanpur, a leftist poet close to OIPFG, is executed.

June 22 | Banisadr is dismissed from his post by Khomeini, who appoints a three-member Presidential Council made up of Ayatollah Beheshti, HI Hashemi-Rafsanjani, and Moham-mad-Ali Raja'i.

June 27   HI Seyyed Ali Khamenei survives an assassination attempt, but his right hand is permanently paralyzed.

June 28   A bomb explosion in the head-quarters of the IRP kills over seventy high-level political figures, including the powerful Ayatollah Beheshti, head of the State Su-preme Court.

June 29   Mohammad Kochu'i, warden of Evin Prison, is assassinated by PMOI.

July 2   The Majlis approves the formation of the Court of Administrative Justice.

July 21   Rajavi, leader of PMOI, announces the formation of the National Council of Resistance of Iran.

July 24   Former prime minister Moham-mad-Ali Raja'i wins the second presidential election with 90 per-cent of the vote.

July 29   Fearful for his life, former president Banisadr flees to Paris in the com-pany of Rajavi. The French govern-ment grants them political asylum upon arrival the next day.

August 2   Raja'i begins his term as president.

August 5   Mohammad-Javad Bahonar was confirmed PM by the Majlis with 130 votes in favor, fourteen

opposed, and twenty-four in abstention.

August 30   President Raja'i and PM Ba-honar are killed in another bomb explosion.

September 2   Ayatollah Mahdavi-Kani is ap-proved by the Majlis as the interim prime minister with 178 votes in favor, ten opposed, and eight in abstention. Mahdavi-Kani, Akbar Hashemi-Rafsanjani, and Seyyed Abdolkarim Musavi-Ardabili constitute an interim presidential commission.

September 3   Mahdavi-Kani's entire cabinet is approved by the Majlis on a single slate with 170 in favor, four op-posed, and thirteen in abstention.

September 30   Plane crash kills minister of defense Seyyed Musa Namju, former minis-ter of defense Javad Fakuri, chief of the joint staff of the Islamic Repub-lic of Iran army Valiyollah Fallahi, deputy commander in chief of the IRGC Yusef Kolahduz, and another high-level IRGC commander.

October 2   HI Seyyed Ali Khamenei is elected president, receiving 95 percent of the votes cast.

October 13   Khamenei begins serving his term as president. Khomeini appoints Hashemi-Rafsanjani as his repre-sentative in the Supreme Defense Council, replacing Khamenei.

October 18   Mahdavi-Kani and his cabinet turn in their resignations after serving for forty-five days so that Khamenei can appoint a new prime minister and cabinet.

October 22
Khamenei's first choice for prime minister, Ali-Akbar Velayati, is rejected by the Majlis.

October 29
Mir Hoseyn Musavi is approved by the Majlis as the next prime minister, receiving 115 out of 202 votes.

November 15
Learned Shiite philosopher and theologian Ayatollah Allameh Seyyed Mohammad-Hoseyn Tabataba'i dies at the age of eighty.

December 11
Ayatollah Seyyed Abdolhoseyn Dastgheyb, Friday prayer leader of Shiraz, is assassinated by PMOI.

1982

January 26
A leftist organization called Sarbedaran attacks the city of Amol. Over sixty guerrillas and government forces are killed before the guerrillas retreat into the jungle. They are completely eliminated by March 3, 1983.

February 8
PMOI's second-in-command Musa Khiyabani, his wife, Ashraf Rabi'i (the wife of PMOI leader Rajavi), and eight other guerrillas are killed in Tehran in a clash with IRGC.

February/March
Security forces kill leaders of the Marxist organizations OIPFG—Minority and OSPWCE.

May 24
Iranian forces free the city of Khorramshahr from Iraqi forces. This serves as a major boost to the morale of the Iranian forces.

June 10
The Iraqi government proposes a ceasefire and acceptance of internationally recognized borders to end the war, but the Iranian government insists that the aggressor (i.e., Iraq) must be punished.

June 11
Iran sends hundreds of IRGC militiamen to Lebanon after Israel's June 6 invasion of Lebanon.

July 23
Majlis Speaker Hashemi-Rafsanjani puts forward the conditions for a ceasefire, which include the trial of Saddam Hussein as a war criminal. Khomeini suggests that the condition for a ceasefire should be an Iraqi admission that it initiated the war.

July 28
US Secretary of Defense Caspar Weinberger comments that Iran is led by "a bunch of madmen" who would endanger the security of the region if Iran wins the war.

August 12
Iraq declares a total maritime exclusion zone around Kharg Island, an Iranian oil export terminal.

September 15
Sadeq Qotbzadeh, former minister of foreign affairs and confidant to Ayatollah Khomeini, is executed for plotting to overthrow the regime.

October 1
Iran launches a fresh attack on the central front to the northeast of Iraq's capital Baghdad in an operation with the code name Moslem Ibn Eqil.

December 10
Iran holds elections for the eighty-three-member Assembly of Experts

(AE), which will deliberate on the appointment of a successor to Khomeini.

December 18   Universities reopen after thirty months of closure due to the cultural revolution.

1983

February 6   Over fifty leaders of the Marxist Tudeh Party are arrested and forced to participate in televised confessions.

February 15   Khomeini writes his political will and deposits one copy in the safe of the Majlis and another copy in the safe of the Imam Reza Shrine in Mashhad.

May 5   The prosecutor-general officially bans the Tudeh Party.

May 6   Tudeh Party theoretician Ehsan Tabari, under arrest, appears on national television declaring the bankruptcy of socialism.

May 10   More than 1,000 members of the Tudeh Party are arrested.

August 15   The first AE begins its work.

August 18   The Majlis passes a law establishing the Ministry of Intelligence, which is approved by the Guardian Council (GC) on August 25, 1983.

1984

January 19   The US State Department adds Iran to its list of nations that support international terrorism.

February 7   The "war of the cities" between Iraq and Iran begins as each side starts firing missiles into the other's urban centers.

February 10   Khamenei warns that Iran will close down shipping lanes in the Persian Gulf if the US intervenes in the war.

Feb. 26–March 20   The Iranians accuse the Iraqis of using chemical weapons against them in response to Operation Kheybar.

March 24   Banisadr leaves the National Council of Resistance.

April 15   Elections for the Second Majlis take place.

May 27   The First Majlis holds its last meeting.

May 28   The Second Majlis begins.

August 5   During a Majlis speech, Ayatollah Azari-Qomi argues that the supreme leader, Ayatollah Khomeini, has no right to tell the Majlis what to do.

1985

January 27   PMOI leader Rajavi announces the appointment of Maryam Azodanlu as the organization's co-equal leader. The two later marry and Mrs. Maryam Rajavi is proclaimed as the organization's choice for president after the collapse of the current regime.

March 6–20   The "war of the cities" escalates as Iran accuses Iraq of using poison gas and chemical weapons against its soldiers on battlefields near Basra. Iraqi airplanes bomb Tehran on March 11, and on March 14, Iran fires rockets on Baghdad.

August 15   Iraqi aircraft attack Kharg Island, causing considerable damage but failing to end export shipments.

August 16   Khamenei is reelected to his second term as president, receiving 85 percent of the vote.

September 4   Khamenei's second term as president begins.

October 28   Mir Hoseyn Musavi's second cabinet is approved by the Majlis.

November 16–19   The first AE officially appoints Ayatollah Montazeri as designated successor to Ayatollah Khomeini and bestows upon him the title of deputy supreme leader.

1986

January 9   *Resalat*, a mouthpiece for conservative forces, publishes its first issue.

February 24   The UN Security Council passes Resolution 582, urging Iran and Iraq to observe an immediate ceasefire.

March 14   The UN secretary-general announces that Iraqi forces used chemical weapons in the war.

April 3   Grand Ayatollah Seyyed Mohammad-Kazem Shari'atmadari passes away (1905–86).

May 28–31   Robert C. McFarlane, a former national security adviser to President

Ronald Reagan, makes a secret trip to Iran to deliver planeloads of weapons in return for the release of all American hostages held in Lebanon.

June 2   IRP disbands due to serious ideological differences.

October 6   OMIRI disbands due to serious ideological differences.

November 3   The Lebanese newspaper *Ash-Shiraa* first reveals the Iran-Contra scandal, which involves the sales of weapons to Iran in return for the release of American hostages. The revenue generated from the sales is allocated to fund the Contras in Nicaragua.

1987

January 7   Khomeini issues a fatwa, stating in no uncertain terms that the supreme leader is the ultimate arbiter within the Iranian political system, and that, based on the interests of the state, he can suspend religious rules such as praying, fasting, or pilgrimage. By this ruling, Khomeini articulates what becomes known as the principle of the absolute mandate of the jurist (*velayat-e motlaqeh-ye faqih*).

January 9   Iran launches its most expensive and deadliest military campaign, code named Karbala 5, against Iraqi forces.

April 28   Khomeini promotes ten military men to such ranks as major general, brigadier general, and commodore.

June 1	In response to a request by President Khamenei and Majlis Speaker Hashemi-Rafsanjani, Khomeini issues a decree to disband the IRP.
July 20	UN Security Council Resolution 598 urges Iran and Iraq to observe an immediate ceasefire. This resolution became the basis for ending the war a year later.
July 31	During the annual Hajj pilgrimage, 320 Iranian pilgrims are killed in clashes with Saudi security forces. The two countries cut diplomatic ties.
September 21	American helicopters destroy an Iranian landing craft (Iran Ajr), which allegedly was laying mines in the shipping lanes of the Persian Gulf.
September 28	Seyyed Mehdi Hashemi (brother of Ayatollah Montazeri's son-in-law), who was responsible for revealing the secret negotiations which became known as the Iran-Contra affair, is executed after being condemned to death by the Special Court for Clergy.
October 8	Battle takes place between American helicopters and Iranian gunboats in the Persian Gulf.
December 10	Khomeini amends his political will and orders two new copies to be deposited in the Majlis and the Imam Reza Shrine in Mashhad for safekeeping.
December 21	In response to a letter from Khamenei asking about the

appropriateness of the Islamic Republic of Iran Broadcasting (IRIB) showing the faces of women in films and the bodies of athletes, Khomeini puts the burden on viewers and says that if these images cause lust in them they should not view them.

1988

January 6	Khomeini admonishes Khamenei for not understanding clearly the idea of an absolute mandate of the jurist. In a departure from prevailing religious views, Khomeini states that if a measure is in the interest of the state, it can overrule such Islamic ordinances as fasting, pilgrimage to Mecca, and prayer.
February 6	Ayatollah Khomeini orders the establishment of the Expediency Discernment Assembly (EDA).
March 15	Two days after the Iraqi Kurdish city of Halabja falls to Iranian forces, the Iraqi army attacks the city with chemical weapons and kills between 3,000 and 5,000 people.
April 8	Elections are held for the third Majlis.
April 14	Ayatollah Khomeini approves the split of Assembly of Combatant Clergy (ACC) from the Society of Combatant Clergy (SCC). The missile frigate USS Samuel B. Roberts is struck by an Iranian mine, injuring some American sailors. Four days later, the American Navy retaliates by attacking two Iranian oil terminals, sinking one ship (Sahand)

and one patrol boat (Joshan) and damaging a second ship (Sabalan).

April 17   Iraqi forces regain the Faw Peninsula to the south of the mainland in a major offensive that lasts thirty-six hours.

April 27   Saudi Arabia breaks diplomatic relations with Iran. They remain suspended for three years.

May 26   The last meeting of the Second Majlis is held.

May 28   The Third Majlis begins.

June 2   Ayatollah Khomeini designates Majlis Speaker Hashemi-Rafsanjani as deputy chief of the armed forces.

July 3   The USS Vincennes, a guided missile cruiser, fires at and brings down a civilian Iran Air plane, killing all 290 passengers and crewmembers onboard.

July 18   Iran informs the UN of its willingness to accept Resolution 598, ending the Iran–Iraq War.

July 19   The regime starts a mass execution of political prisoners.

July 20   Khomeini issues a decree accepting a ceasefire with Iraq. He calls his decision to end the Gulf War "worse than drinking hemlock." In his letter to UN Secretary-General Javier Perez de Cueller, President Ali Khamenei writes, "The Islamic Republic of Iran, because of the importance it attaches to the lives of human beings and the

establishment of justice and regional and international peace and security, accepts Security Council Resolution 598," implementing a ceasefire. Lloyd's of London announces that 546 ships were hit during the eight-year Gulf War (1980–88).

July 25   Thousands of PMOI militiamen enter Iran from Iraq in Operation Forouq-e-Javidan but are defeated in three days, after suffering heavy casualties (1,300–2,500). Iran's counterattack is called Operation Mersad.

July 28   Khomeini issues a fatwa calling for execution of imprisoned members and supporters of PMOI.

July 29   Mass execution of imprisoned PMOI and other dissident groups begins; over 4,000 are executed.

August 15   In a private meeting, Ayatollah Montazeri asks four high-level judiciary officials to stop the mass execution of political prisoners.

August 20   The Iran–Iraq War officially ends.

September 7   Mir Hoseyn Musavi tenders his resignation to Ayatollah Khamenei.

1989

January 3   Khomeini sends an envoy with a letter to Soviet leader Mikhail Gorbachev, suggesting that communism is moribund and that Moscow's leaders should study Islam.

February 14   Khomeini issues a fatwa calling for the death of Salman Rushdie for his blasphemous novel, *The Satanic Verses*.

February 17   Khamenei suggests that Salman Rushdie could be granted a pardon if he repents.

February 28   The Majlis approves a resolution to break off diplomatic relations with Britain over the Rushdie affair.

March 25   BBC Persian radio service broadcasts a letter written from Montazeri to Khomeini some eight months ago, in which Montazeri sharply criticized the mass execution of political prisoners.

March 26   Khomeini dismisses Montazeri as his successor and bans him from engaging in any political activity.

April 24   Khomeini writes a letter to President Khamenei informing him that he has appointed a twenty-member Council for the Revision of the Constitution, which will also include five deputies to be chosen by the Majlis.

April 29   In a public letter to Ali-Akber Meshkini, the chair of the AE, Khomeini states: "From the beginning I believed and I had insisted that the condition marja'iyyat is not necessary [as a requirement for the office of supreme leader]."

May 18   Khomeini's doctors secretly inform the heads of the three branches that he is suffering from advanced cancer.

June 3   Khomeini dies of a heart attack.

June 4   The AE meets in a special session to decide who should replace Khomeini. They first vote forty-five to twenty-three in favor of electing a sole supreme leader rather than a leadership council. When mentioned as a leading candidate, Seyyed Ali Khamenei argues that he does not feel qualified for the role and considers his selection to be a violation of both the letter of the constitution and clerical protocol. Despite his reservations, the AE votes sixty to fourteen to choose Khamenei over ninety-two-year-old Ayatollah Mohammad-Reza Golpayegani as the temporary supreme leader until a new referendum is held. However, no such referendum was ever held and, until a leaked videotape of the meeting was posted by an exiled Iranian journalist in January 2018, the public did not know that the appointment was supposed to be temporary.

July 13   Abdorrahman Qasemlu (b. 1930), secretary-general of the Kurdistan Democratic Party of Iran, is assassinated in Vienna by agents of the Islamic Republic of Iran.

July 28   Majlis Speaker Akbar Hashemi-Rafsanjani is elected as the new president of Iran. In an election held concurrently with the presidential election, an amended constitution is approved.

August 3   Hashemi-Rafsanjani begins his term as president. Mir Hoseyn Musavi completes his term as prime minister, and the position is abolished.

August 15 — Hashemi-Rafsanjani resigns from the Majlis in order to serve solely as president.

August 16 — Khamenei resigns from the presidency to serve solely as supreme leader.

August 17 — Hashemi-Rafsanjani begins serving his term as president.

August 22 — The Ministry of Revolutionary Guards is abolished.

December 25 — Nicolae Ceaușescu, president and secretary-general of the Romanian Communist Party, is executed a week after returning from a trip to Tehran.

1990

January 31 — The Majlis approves the first five-year development plan after the revolution.

April 24 — Kazem Rajavi, older brother of PMOI leader Mas'ud Rajavi, is assassinated outside Geneva, Switzerland.

June 21 — A strong earthquake in the city of Rudbar (Gilan Province) kills over 35,000 people.

July 3 — The foreign ministers of Iran and Iraq, Ali-Akbar Velayati and Tariq Aziz, meet in Geneva under UN auspices to discuss the release of prisoners of war and evacuation of their armies from each other's territories. These are the first direct talks between ministers of the two countries since the implementation of the ceasefire in August 1988.

July 8 — The first meeting of the governing council of the newly established Center for Strategic Studies (overseen by the president) is held. This center later becomes affiliated with the EDA.

August 2 — Iraq invades Kuwait, a move that is later condemned by the Iranian government.

August 17 — A large number of Iranian POWs imprisoned in Iraq are returned to Iran.

September 27 — Iran and Britain announce that they will restore diplomatic relations, which were broken off in February 1989 after the controversy over Rushdie.

October 8 — Elections are held for the second AE.

1991

April 18 — Abdorrahman Borumand, an ally of former prime minister Bakhtiar active in the opposition group the National Movement of the Iranian Resistance, is stabbed to death in Paris.

August 6 — Former prime minister Bakhtiar and his secretary are assassinated in Paris.

1992

April 10 — Elections are held for the Fourth Majlis.

May 24 — Seyyed Mohammad Khatami resigns his post as minister of culture and Islamic guidance. President

Hashemi-Rafsanjani accepts the resignation on July 18.

May 27 The Third Majlis meets for the last time.

May 28 The Fourth Majlis begins.

August 8 Grand Ayatollah Seyyed Abolqasem Kho'i, a leading Shiite mojtahed in Iraq, dies.

September 17 Agents of the Iranian regime assassinate the secretary-general of the Kurdistan Democratic Party of Iran, Dr. Sadeq Sharafkandi, and three of his colleagues at the Mykonos restaurant in Berlin.

November 2 The Fifteenth of Khordad Foundation increases its bounty on Salman Rushdie to more than $2 million, shortly after his visit to Germany.

November 12 The Iranian authorities decree that men and women should be segregated on buses.

1993

June 11 In the presidential election, President Hashemi-Rafsanjani is re-elected with 63 percent of the vote.

August 3 Hashemi-Rafsanjani begins his second term as president.

December 9 Grand Ayatollah Golpayegani dies in Tehran at the age of ninety-six.

December 15 Grand Ayatollah Mohammad-Ali Araki is declared a source of emulation after the death of Ayatollah Golpayegani.

1994

July 18 The Jewish Community Center (Asociación Mutual Israelita Argentina) in Buenos Aires is bombed, killing eighty-five and wounding hundreds. Iran and Hezbollah are later blamed for the bombing.

November 27 Ali-Akbar Sa'idi-Sirjani (b. 1931), a literary writer, historical researcher, and critic of the theocratic rulers of Iran, dies under suspicious circumstances after being imprisoned by the security forces for eight months.

November 29 Grand Ayatollah Araki dies at the age of 100.

December 1 The SCC announces that it considers the following three ayatollahs suitable candidates for becoming the marja': Ali Khamenei (b. 1939), Mohammad Fazel-Lankarani (1931–2007), and Mirza Javad Tabrizi (1926–2006).

December 2 The Society of Qom Seminary Scholars (SQSS) announces that it considers the following seven ayatollahs suitable candidates for becoming the marja': Mohammad-Taqi Behjat (1915–2009), Mohammad Fazel-Lankarani, Ali Khamenei, Naser Makarem-Shirazi (b. 1926), Seyyed Musa Shobeiri-Zanjani (b. 1927), Mirza Javad Tabrizi, and Hoseyn Vahid-Khorasani (b. 1921).

December 14 Ayatollah Khamenei announces that he considers himself a marja' for the Shii community outside Iran and not within the country.

1995

January 20   Mehdi Bazargan, the first prime minister of the Islamic Republic of Iran, dies in Zurich, Switzerland, at the age of eighty-eight.

February 6   Members of the LMI elect Ebrahim Yazdi (b. 1931) as their new leader, replacing Bazargan.

February 12   The Majlis passes a bill, presented by the minister of culture and Islamic guidance, banning the import and private use of satellite dishes. The Iranian state bans *Jahan-e Islam* (World of Islam) for castigating political leaders.

March 14   US President Bill Clinton vetoes a billion-dollar contract offered to US oil company Conoco by Iran and bans all direct American trade with Iran.

March 16   Ayatollah Khomeini's son Seyyed Ahmad Khomeini, who served as a member of the AE and EDA, dies at the age of forty-nine. Some consider the death suspicious.

1996

January 17   The Party of Executives of Construction of Iran, made up of close confidants of President Hashemi-Rafsanjani, announces its formation.

March 8   Two hundred seventy new members are elected to the Fifth Majlis.

May 26   The Fourth Majlis holds its last meeting.

June 1   The Fifth Majlis begins.

June 25   A truck bomb explodes outside the Khobar Towers in Dhahran, Saudi Arabia, killing nineteen American service members and injuring 500 others. Iran is suspected of masterminding the attack.

August 5   President Clinton, imposing economic sanctions on any firms doing business with Iran and Libya, signs the Iran and Libya Sanctions Act of 1996 into law.

1997

April 10   A German court convicts an Iranian and three Lebanese of involvement in the Mykonos restaurant assassination. The court accuses Supreme Leader Khamenei, President Hashemi-Rafsanjani, foreign minister Ali-Akbar Velayati, and intelligence minister Ali Fallahiyan of having ordered the assassination. The next day, a number of European countries, as well as Australia, Canada, and New Zealand, withdraw their ambassadors from Iran.

May 23   Seyyed Mohammad Khatami wins the presidential election in a landslide, receiving 20 million votes, while his opponent receives 7.2 million votes. The Reformist movement begins.

May 25   The Majlis creates the new province of Qazvin by adding territory from Tehran to the city of Qazvin.

August 3   Seyyed Mohammad Khatami begins his term as president.

October 8　The US State Department designates PMOI as a foreign terrorist organization.

October 25　The EDA revises its internal bylaws.

November 14　Ayatollah Montazeri publically states that Ayatollah Khamenei does not have the qualifications to be a source of emulation.

November 19–21　Demonstrators protest at Montazeri's office in Qom for questioning the legitimacy of the clergy's right to rule.

November 26　Khamenei threatens to prosecute those who question his authority.

1998

January 7　President Khatami says in a CNN interview that he wants to see an improvement in Iran's relations with the American people.

January 29　Responding to President Khatami's public statement to seek improved relations with the United States, President Bill Clinton expresses optimism regarding the prospect of cultural exchange programs.

February 5　*Jame'eh* (Society), a reformist daily newspaper, publishes its first issue and becomes hugely popular.

April 4　The mayor of Tehran, Gholam-Hoseyn Karbaschi, a reformist ally of President Khatami, is arrested on corruption charges.

June 21　The Majlis votes in favor of dismissing the interior minister, Abdollah Nuri, for causing social tension.

July 21　The editor of *Jame'eh* is convicted of libel, and his newspaper is closed down.

July 23　Mayor Karbaschi is sentenced to five years in prison for mismanagement of state funds but is acquitted of a bribery charge.

August 8　Iran deploys troops to the Afghan border after the Taliban kills eight Iranian diplomats in Afghanistan.

August 23　Asadollah Ladjvardi (1935–98), the former Evin Prison warden and chief of the State Prisons Organization (1989–98), is assassinated by PMOI.

October 23　Elections are held for the third AE.

November 14　Ayatollah Montazeri delivers a speech in Qom on the necessity of protecting the Shia principle of marja'iyyat from state interference. A week later, the Supreme Council for National Security sentences him to house arrest, which stays in effect for the next five years.

November 22　Daryush Foruhar, leader of the banned People's Party, and his wife are stabbed to death in their home. In the following weeks, three notable Iranian writers, Mohammad Mokhtari, Mohammad-Ja'far Puyandeh, and Majid Sharif, are kidnapped and killed.

December 5　The Islamic Iran Participation Front (IIPF), a new political party that supports President Khatami's reform agenda, is officially inaugurated.

December 10   The body of Mohammad Mokhtari (1942–98), a poet and writer, is found. This is part of a wave of killings of dissident intellectuals.

December 24   The Court of Appeals reduces former Mayor Karbaschi's sentence from five years to two.

1999

January 5   The intelligence ministry announces that rogue officials were behind the serial killings of dissident intellectuals.

February 26   In the first municipal council elections, some 200,000 councilors are elected for local administration. Reformers win the municipal elections.

April 10   The first deputy chief of staff of the Iranian Armed Forces, Brigadier General Ali Sayyad-Shirazi, is assassinated by PMOI.

April 29   The municipal councils start their work.

May 1   Seyyed Ataollah Mohajerani, minister of culture and Islamic guidance, survives an interpellation vote in the Majlis.

May 5   President Khatami goes on a five-day visit to Saudi Arabia to improve bilateral relations.

June 19   The death of Sa'id Emami, a conservative deputy minister of intelligence in detention, sparks a major political controversy.

July 7–13   The closure of the journal *Salam* provokes riots by students in Tehran. Three people are killed, 200 are injured, and hundreds of students are arrested.

July 9   Twenty-four high-level IRGC commanders publish a threatening letter of ultimatum to President Khatami about dealing with the student protests.

September 28   Iran's largest oil discovery in thirty years is made at Azadegan oil field, which covers 520 square miles and lies twenty-five miles from Iraq's Majnon oil field. It is estimated to contain oil reserves of 26 billion barrels.

October 31   The trial of Abdollah Nuri, former interior minister under President Khatami, begins.

December 29   Ebrahim Yazdi announces that members of the LMI have been barred from taking part in the February 2000 Majlis elections.

2000

February 18   Elections are held for the Sixth Majlis. Reformers take control of Majlis.

March 12   Sa'id Hajjarian, a former intelligence official and leading strategist for the reform movement, survives an assassination attempt in front of the Tehran City Council building but is paralyzed.

March 17   US Secretary of State Madeleine Albright acknowledges America's role in the 1953 coup toppling PM Mohammad Mossadeq.

April 7–9 A conference on Iran organized by the Heinrich Böll Foundation in Berlin becomes controversial when regime opponents strongly criticize the Iranian state. A week later, the main Iranian TV station broadcasts a program about the conference; subsequently, two of the speakers, former MP HI Hasan Yusefi-Eshkevari and investigative journalist Akbar Ganji, are respectively condemned to seven- and six-year prison terms.

April A new press law comes into effect, banning over a dozen newspapers.

May 18 The World Bank approves two loans to Iran for a total of $232 million (the first in seven years). The loans are for a primary health project and the Tehran sewer project.

May 24 The last meeting of the Fifth Majlis is held.

May 27 The Sixth Majlis begins.

2001

June 8 President Khatami wins reelection to a second term.

August 2 President Khatami begins serving his second term.

September 27 Iranian leaders condemn the September 11 attacks by Al-Qaeda on US soil.

October 7 The American invasion of Afghanistan begins.

2002

January 29 In his State of the Union address, President George W. Bush calls Iran, Iraq, and North Korea an "Axis of Evil."

August 14 Exiled opposition group PMOI reveals the operation of a uranium enrichment plant in Natanz and a heavy water reactor in Arak.

2003

February 28 The second nationwide municipal council elections take place.

March 20 The American invasion of Iraq begins.

July 6 Voice of America (VOA) begins its Persian-language television program broadcasting to Iran.

October 10 Mrs. Shirin Ebadi, a human rights lawyer, wins Iran's first ever Nobel Peace Prize.

October 21 Iran reaches an agreement with Britain, France, and Germany to stop producing enriched uranium and formally decides to sign the Additional Protocol with the International Atomic Energy Association (IAEA).

December 18 Iran and IAEA sign an agreement for enhanced, unannounced, and on-the-spot inspections of Iran's nuclear facilities.

December 26 A strong earthquake in the city of Bam kills over 50,000 people.

2004

Jan. 11–Feb. 5   One hundred thirty-nine deputies of the Sixth Majlis hold a sit-in to protest the massive disqualifications of candidates for the Seventh Majlis, including eighty-five sitting MPs. On February 1, 129 of the deputies resign their posts in protest.

February 20   Elections are held for the Seventh Majlis and conservatives gain control of it.

May 26   The last meeting of the Sixth Majlis is held.

May 27   The Seventh Majlis begins.

June 14   IAEA condemns Iran for its lack of cooperation in the investigation of its nuclear program.

November 14   In talks with Britain, France, and Germany (known as the Paris Accord), Iran voluntarily agrees to temporarily suspend uranium enrichment activities and allow the IAEA to monitor the suspension.

2005

June 17   In an eight-man presidential race, Hashemi-Rafsanjani receives 21 percent and Mahmoud Ahmadinejad 19.4 percent of the vote, requiring a runoff election.

June 24   Ahmadinejad wins the runoff election, receiving 61.7 percent of the vote.

August 3   Ahmadinejad begins serving his term as president.

August 8   Iran announces that it has resumed uranium conversion at the Isfahan facility under the surveillance of the IAEA.

August 9   Khamenei issues a fatwa forbidding the "production, stockpiling and use of nuclear weapons."

October 26   Ahmadinejad delivers a controversial speech and, quoting Ayatollah Khomeini, calls for Israel to be wiped from the map.

2006

January 10   Iran breaks IAEA seals at its Natanz nuclear research facility and abandons its voluntary suspension of enrichment-related activities, as well as the interim application of the Additional Protocol.

February 4   After a vote, the IAEA announces that it will report Iran to the UN Security Council for noncompliance with its NPT Safeguards Agreement obligations.

July 31   The UN adopts Resolution 1696 against Iran as the Security Council demands that Iran suspend "all enrichment-related and reprocessing activities, including research and development."

December 11–12   At a conference held in Iran titled "The International Conference on Review of the Holocaust: Global Visions," attendees deny the Holocaust.

December 15   Concurrent elections are held for the fourth AE and the third municipal councils.

December 30 Saddam Hussein is executed.

2007

March 23 Diplomatic ties with Britain are strained after Iran seizes fifteen British sailors and marines on the Shatt al-Arab waterway.

June 26 Petrol rationing results in protests.

October 25 The US imposes new sanctions against Iran, the most severe in nearly thirty years.

2008

March 14 Elections are held for the Eighth Majlis.

May 3 Abbas Palizar, a member of the judicial inquiry and review commission of the Majlis, discloses cases of financial corruption by various clerics and claims that the plane crash death of former minister of roads and transportation Rahman Dadman involved foul play.

May 25 The last meeting of the Seventh Majlis is held.

May 27 The Eighth Majlis begins.

November 4 The Majlis dismisses interior minister Ali Kordan for fabricating his educational degree.

2009

January 14 BBC Persian Television starts broadcasting its programs to Iran and Afghanistan.

June 3 Mir Hoseyn Musavi and Mahmoud Ahmadinejad face each other in a televised presidential debate, marking the first time a sitting president has debated an opponent on live television.

June 12 Ahmadinejad is reelected to a second term as president. Opponents charge that the vote was rigged. Massive protests follow and last for eight months.

June 13 Mass arrest of opposition political activists begins.

June 15 Students in the dormitories of Tehran University are attacked in a violent nighttime raid.

June 19 In his first Friday prayer sermon after the presidential election, Ayatollah Khamenei endorses the results and defends the fairness of the election.

July 3 Under pressure from the supreme leader, Ahmadinejad's first vice president, Esfandiyar Rahimma-sha'i, resigns. In a defiant move, the president appoints him as his chief of staff.

August 3 President Ahmadinejad begins serving his second term.

December 19 Ayatollah Montazeri passes away while under house arrest.

2010

February 23 Abdolmalek Rigi, the leader of Jundollah (the army of God), an

Islamist Sunni militant organization active in Sistan and Baluchestan, is arrested and later executed.

September 23   Reports emerge that Stuxnet, a powerful computer virus, had compromised a number of nuclear facilities in Iran.

December 19   The government implements a subsidy reform plan that replaces energy handouts with a universal cash transfer program for households.

2011

March 8   Mahdavi-Kani replaces Hashemi-Rafsanjani as secretariat of the AE.

July 25   Khamenei forms a five-member committee titled Supreme Board to Resolve Disputes and Regulate Relations among the Three Branches of Government.

November 29   A group of protesters attack the British embassy in Tehran to protest the imposition of new sanctions on Iran.

2012

January 12   An Iranian nuclear scientist is killed in an explosion. Three other people affiliated with the Iranian nuclear program are assassinated during the next two years.

January 23   European Union foreign ministers adopt an unprecedented oil embargo against Iran over its nuclear program. At the time, Europe was buying 20 percent of Iran's oil exports.

March 2   Elections are held for the Ninth Majlis.

May 23   The Eighth Majlis meets for the last time.

May 27   The Ninth Majlis begins.

September 7   Canada severs diplomatic relations with Iran.

September 28   The US State Department removes PMOI from its list of foreign terrorist organizations.

October 3   Iranian riot police clash with protesters in the Tehran bazaar who are blaming President Ahmadinejad for the plummeting value of the currency—an 80 percent drop in the value of the Iranian rial.

2013

June 14   Hassan Rouhani is elected president. Concurrently, the fourth nationwide municipal council elections take place, with 259,664 candidates participating.

July 6   Iran's Central Bank devalues the national currency's official rate to $1=24,777 rials, a 102 percent depreciation over the January 2012 rate of $1=12,260 rials.

August 3   Rouhani begins serving his first term as president.

September 27   President Obama calls President Rouhani, marking the highest-level contact between the two countries since 1979.

November 24 | An interim agreement known as the Joint Plan of Action is signed in Geneva, Switzerland, between Iran, the European Union, and P5+1—a group of world powers comprising the five permanent members of the UN Security Council, plus Germany. It represents the first formal agreement between the US and Iran in thirty-four years.

2014

January 20 | The interim nuclear accord between Iran, P5+1, and the European Union (EU) goes into effect.

May 24 | Businessman Mahafarid Amir-Khosravi is executed on charges of embezzling, money laundering, and bribery of 3 trillion tomans. The Iranian media labels this as the largest case of fraud since the 1979 revolution.

August 20 | The Majlis impeaches Reza Faraji-Dana, the minister of science, research, and technology, for sympathizing with prodemocracy demonstrators.

August 23 | Britain reopens its embassy in Tehran, restoring diplomatic ties.

2015

April 2 | Iran and P5+1 agree to the Iran nuclear deal framework in Lausanne, Switzerland.

July 14 | P5+1, the European Union, and Iran reach a Joint Comprehensive Plan of Action (JCPOA).

September 17 | Opponents of the "Iran deal" in the US Congress fail to stop its implementation.

September 24 | Close to 500 Iranian pilgrims die during a stampede near Mecca in Saudi Arabia during the annual Hajj pilgrimage.

October 13 | The Majlis approves the nuclear deal with P5+1 by a vote of 161 in favor, fifty-nine opposed, and thirteen in abstention.

October 14 | The GC approves the nuclear agreement.

2016

January 3 | Saudi Arabia cuts diplomatic ties with Iran.

January 16 | The JCPOA is implemented.

February 26 | The elections for the Tenth Majlis and the fifth AE are held simultaneously.

May 24 | The Ninth Majlis meets for the last time. Ayatollah Ahmad Jannati is elected as the chairperson of the AE.

May 28 | The Tenth Majlis begins.

2017

January 8 | Akbar Hashemi-Rafsanjani, one of the most important political personalities of postrevolutionary Iran, dies.

May 19 | President Rouhani is elected to a second term in the twelfth presidential election held in Iran.

June 7	ISIS forces attack the Iranian Parliament and the mausoleum of Ayatollah Khomeini, killing seventeen people.
August 3	Rouhani begins serving his second term as president.
August 14	Khamenei appointed the members of the Eighth Expediency Discernment Assembly to serve for a five-year term.
August 20	The Majlis approves all but one of President Rouhani's proposed ministers.
December 28	Antiregime protests erupt in Mashhad and engulf many other Iranian cities over the next two weeks, resulting in at least twenty-five deaths and thousands arrested.

2

Revolutionaries and Political Institutions

Selected List of New Institutions
Formed after the Revolution

1979

Assembly of Experts (for the Leadership)
Basij Resistance Force[1]
Be'sat Foundation
Construction Jihad
Foundation for Dispossessed and War-Invalids
Guardian Council
High Council of Defense[2]
Housing Foundation of the Islamic Revolution
Imam Khomeini Relief Foundation
Islamic Revolutionary Committees[3]
Islamic Revolutionary Guards Corps (IRGC)
Islamic Revolutionary Tribunals
Justice Administration of the Islamic Revolution
Office of the President
Qom Seminary Islamic Propaganda Office
Revolutionary Council

1980

Disciplinary Court for Judges and Public Prosecutors
Foundation of Martyrs and Veterans Affairs

High Council of Cultural Revolution[4]
High Council of Judiciary[5]
Judicial Police[6]
State Welfare Organization
University Jihad

1981

Center for Islamic Revolution Documentation
Fifteenth of Khordad Foundation
Foundation for Affairs of People Displaced by the
    Imposed War
Islamic Propaganda Organization
Prime Minister's Intelligence Bureau
Shahed University
State General Inspectorate Organization
Tarbiyat-e Modarres University

1982

Bureau for Cooperation between Religious Seminaries
    and Universities (later renamed Research Institute
    of Seminaries and University)
Court of Administrative Justice
Islamic Azad University
Ministry of Revolutionary Guards[7]

---

1. Basij was absorbed into the IRGC in January 1981 and later became the Organization of Mobilization of the Dispossessed.
2. Dissolved in 1989.
3. Absorbed into Law Enforcement Forces in 1991.
4. Name changed on February 10, 1984.
5. Dissolved in 1989.
6. Absorbed into Low Enforcement Forces in 1991.
7. Abolished in 1989.

1983

Encyclopedia of Islam Foundation
Imam Sadeq University
State Security Council

1984

Ministry of Intelligence and Security
State Prisons and Security and Corrective Measures
    Organization[8]

1985

Imam Hoseyn University
Qods Aviation Industries

1987

Organization for Battling Price Gouging[9]
Penitentiary Organization
Special Court for Clergy[10]

1988

Academy of Sciences of the Islamic Republic
    of Iran
Expediency Discernment Assembly of the
    System
Islamic Revolution Guard Corps Cooperative
    Organization
Mofid University
Supreme Council for Reconstruction

1989

Armed Forces General Staff
Center for Strategic Research
Center for Supervision of Mosque Affairs
Head of Judiciary
Headquarters for Implementation of Imam's Order
Central Khatam al-Anbia Headquarters
Supreme Council for National Security[11]
World Assembly for Proximity of Islamic Schools
    of Thought

1990

Academy of Persian Language and Literature
Ahlulbeyt World Assembly
Headquarters for Prayer Adduction

1991

Academy of Medical Sciences
Law Enforcement Forces[12]
Theological Seminaries Center for Services
High Council of Quran

1992

Foundation for Preservation of Artifacts and Values
    of Sacred Defense

1993

Friday Prayer Policymaking Council

8. Emerged out of the Supervisory Council for Prisons.

9. Absorbed into Ministry of Justice.

10. Origins in courts set up in 1979.

11. SCNS emerged out of the High Council of Defense (*Showra-ye Ali-ye Defa'*) that was formed in 1983. The new council became responsible for Iran's intelligence, military, security, and strategic policies. The thirteen-member council is made up of heads of the three branches of government, the chief of staff of the Iranian Armed Forces, the vice president for planning and strategic supervision, two representatives assigned by the supreme leader, ministers of foreign affairs, interior and intelligence, and two senior military officials. In addition, other ministers or relevant experts attend meetings depending on the subject matter at hand.

12. Established because of the merger of police force, gendarmerie, and Islamic Revolutionary Committees.

Headquarters for Rejuvenating Commanding Good
and Prohibiting Vice

1994

Center for Representing the Supreme Leader in
Universities

1995

High Council of Religious Seminaries of Qom
Islamic Majlis Research Center

1996

Imam Khomeini and Islamic Revolution Research
Institute
Supreme Council for Intelligence Affairs

1997

Islamic Seminaries Management Center for
Ladies

1998

Aerospace Industries Organization

1999

Iran Academy of Arts

2000

Management and Planning Organization

2002

Institute for Management and Planning Studies[13]

2005

Administrative and Recruitment Organization

2006

Strategic Council on Foreign Relations

2007

Vice President for Management and Human Capital
Development
Vice President for Planning and Strategic Supervision

2009

Intelligence Organization of IRGC

2011

Ministry of Roads and Urban Development
Ministry of Sports and Youth

2012

Vice President for Implementation of the Constitution
Supreme Council of Cyberspace

2016

Administrative and Recruitment Organization

13. The institute was formed on June 24, 2002, from the merger of the State Management Training Center and the Institute for Planning and Development Research. It is affiliated with the Office of the President.

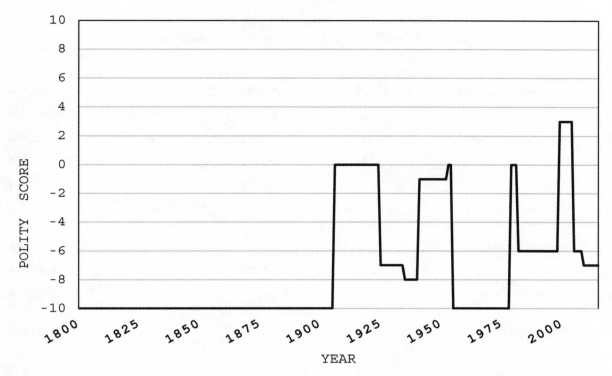

1. Authority Trends in Iran (1800–2015). Source: Marshall, Gurr, and Jaggers (2016).

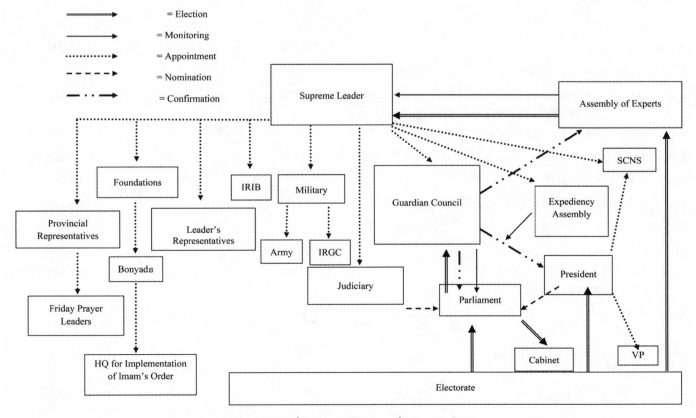

2. Structure of Power in Postrevolutionary Iran.

Table 1
Budget of Select New State Institutions (in millions of rials)

Name of institution	2008	2012	2014	2016
High Council of Cultural Revolution	128,615	607,162	429,311	507,986
University Jihad	447,724	117,127	1,386,065	1,819,430
Assembly of Experts for the Leadership	28,000	33,272	29,615	32,491
Supreme Council for National Security	49,898	282,812	150,190	175,218
Office of the President	4,315,291	3,752,798	2,920,907	5,073,791
Expediency Discernment Assembly (of the State)	192,670	344,132	469,750	678,750
Islamic Majlis Research Center	99,962	106,087	230,300	286,763
Guardian Council	238,126	479,518	650,000	1,000,383
Ministry of Intelligence of the Islamic Republic of Iran	4,165,813	10,999,677	17,031,570	32,463,498
Center for Strategic Research	35,000	62,524	66,200	111,800
State Management and Planning Organization	492,341	0	0	8,143,264
State Management Training Center	0	78,710	76,908	130,770
Institute for Management and Planning Studies	57,352	0	0	270,870
Law Enforcement Forces	15,567,834	32,860,268	46,134,484	63,974,611
Special Court for Clergy	58,589	226,292	135,354	231,000
Court of Administrative Justice	87,803	261,457	218,890	402,001
State Prisons and Security and Corrective Measures Organization	526,730	4,829,649	4,915,402	6,177,225
State General Inspectorate Organization	209,364	519,087	540,065	1,055,000
Islamic Revolutionary Guards Corp	40,788,460	132,526,546	115,689,445	146,287,290
Imam Hoseyn University	31,000	55,998	47,598	78,219
Intelligence Organization of IRGC	45,200	95,056	72,830	253,586
Basij Resistance Force	3,115,000	7,152,359	8,522,500	10,701,638
Construction Jihad	0	0	0	200,000
Foundation for Preservation of Artifacts and Values of Sacred Defense	0	433,079	234,461	620,585
Qom Seminary Islamic Propaganda Office	473,858	662,695	758,883	960,740
Council for Coordination of Islamic Propaganda	0	260,242	271,865	361,641
High Council of Religious Seminaries of Qom	1,150,000	2,963,575	2,791,021	3,289,000

Table 1 (Cont.)
Budget of Select New State Institutions (in millions of rials)

Name of institution	2008	2012	2014	2016
Ministry of Sports and Youth	0	4,760,292	3,134,340	8,717,487
Imam Khomeini Relief Foundation	14,972,530	24,327,201	31,164,000	38,091,901
Foundation of Martyrs and Veterans Affairs	22,138,456	49,268,191	68,740,100	92,685,548
Housing Foundation of the Islamic Revolution	644,995	2,844,916	1,850,000	3,665,000
Ministry of Roads and Urban Development	20,506,996	56,411,452	46,503,983	75,101,721
Shahed University	310,662	791,467	1,386,617	1,885,310
Tarbiyat-e Modarres University	454,971	1,685,672	1,858,372	2,234,975
Research Institute of Seminaries and University	0	93,168	79,665	126,350
Foundation for Affairs of People Displaced by the Imposed War	0	100,000	147,410	147,000
Cultural and Islamic Communications Organization	597,580	3,082,759	4,537,985	5,825,000
World Forum for Proximity of Islamic Schools of Thought	33,474	100,150	132,250	210,000
Ahlulbeyt World Assembly	584,261	1,698,827	1,791,534	2,301,326
Institute for Compilation and Publication of Imam Khomeini's Work	57,113	221,000	240,000	255,000
Imam Khomeini and Islamic Revolution Research Institute	78,254	330,000	335,000	365,000
Theological Seminaries Center for Services	91,539	158,583	154,230	512,978
Imam Khomeini Educational Research Institute	0	24,180	33,200	82,394
Islamic Propaganda Organization	1,062,995	1,331,740	2,446,569	3,140,522
Encyclopedia of Islam Foundation	0	0	74,025	79240
Friday Prayer Policymaking Council	0	0	312,400	277159
Center for Supervision of Mosque Affairs	0	0	320,350	332,439
Headquarters for Prayer Adduction	0	0	161,000	200,000
Total budget of the government	512,383,662	1,644,177,061	2,350,084,641	3,073,805,947

Note: Budget laws are published by the Management and Planning Organization of Iran (http://irandataportal.syr.edu/annual-budgets).

Table 2
Members of the Revolutionary Council

First name	Last name
Mohammad-Javad	Bahonar
Seyyed Abolhasan	Banisadr
Mehdi	Bazargan
Seyyed Mohammad	Beheshti
Hasan-Ebrahim	Habibi
Akbar	Hashemi-Rafsanjani
Ahmad	Jalali
Mostafa	Katira'i
Seyyed Ali	Khamenei
Mohammad-Reza	Mahdavi-Kani
Ali-Asghar	Mas'udi
Mohammad	Mofatteh
Ali-Akbar	Mo'infar
Morteza	Motahhari
Mir Hoseyn	Musavi
Seyyed Abdolkarim	Musavi-Ardabili
Habibollah	Peyman
Valiyollah	Qarani
Sadeq	Qotbzadeh
Mohammad-Ali	Raja'i
Seyyed Ahmad	Sadr Haj Seyyed Javadi
Ezzatollah	Sahabi
Yadollah	Sahabi
Karim	Sanjabi
Abbas	Sheybani
Seyyed Mahmud	Taleqani
Ebrahim	Yazdi

Note: The individuals listed took part in meetings of the Revolutionary Council at various points during the eighteen months it was in existence (January 12, 1979–July 17, 1980).

Number and Percentage of Political Elite in Key
Institutions Imprisoned or Exiled before 1979

Table 3
Number of Guardian Council Members Imprisoned before 1979

Session (years)	Number of members	Number imprisoned	Percentage
First (1980–86)	20	8	40.0
Second (1986–92)	16	5	31.3
Third (1992–98)	15	5	33.3
Fourth (1998–2004)	20	7	35.0
Fifth (2004–10)	15	4	26.7
Sixth (2010–16)	15	4	26.7
Seventh (2016–22)	12	4	33.3

Source for Tables 3–7: Authors' database.

Note: Prison and exile experience before the 1979 revolution can be an indicator of the revolutionary pedigree of the new elite who came to power. The data in each of these tables covers all members who were originally elected or appointed (depending on the institution) to their posts, as well as all those who were added midterm. All percentages have been rounded to the nearest decimal.

Table 4
Number of Assembly of Experts Members Imprisoned before 1979

Session (years)	Number of deputies	Number imprisoned	Percentage
First (1983–90)	86	37	43.0
Second (1991–98)	85	31	36.5
Third (1999–2006)	90	30	33.3
Fourth (2007–16)	96	33	34.4
Fifth (2016–22)[a]	88	20	22.7

[a] The data for the fifth session of the Assembly of Experts only includes those elected originally in 2016 since as of January 1, 2018, no midterm elections had been held.

Table 5
Number of Expediency Discernment Assembly Members Imprisoned before 1979

Session (years)	Number of members	Number imprisoned	Percentage
First (1988–89)	7	4	57.1
Second (1989–92)	11	5	45.5
Third (1992–97)	10	4	40.0
Fourth (1997–2002)	27	14	51.9
Fifth (2002–7)	31	16	51.6
Sixth (2007–12)	36	16	44.4
Seventh (2012–17)	38	13	34.2
Eighth (2017–22)[a]	38	10	26.3

[a] The data for the eighth session of the Expediency Assembly only includes those appointed originally on August 14, 2017.

Table 6
Number of Majlis Deputies Imprisoned before 1979

Session (years)	Number of MPs	Number imprisoned	Percentage
First (1980–84)	327	87	26.6
Second (1984–88)	277	44	15.9
Third (1988–92)	278	43	15.5
Fourth (1992–96)	274	33	12.0
Fifth (1996–2000)	274	29	10.6
Sixth (2000–2004)	297	19	6.4
Seventh (2004–8)	294	18	6.1
Eighth (2008–12)	291	22	7.6
Ninth (2012–16)	290	12	4.1
Tenth (2016–20)	290	6	2.1

Table 7
Number of Cabinet Ministers and VPs Imprisoned before 1979

PM/President, years	Number of ministers and VPs combined[a]	Number imprisoned	Percentage
Bazargan, Feb. 2–Nov. 5, 1979	29	13	44.8
Revolutionary Council, Nov. 6, 1979–May 28, 1980	21	10	47.6
Banisadr, Feb. 4, 1980–June 21, 1981	23	7	30.4
Raja'i, Aug. 20, 1980–Aug. 1, 1981	21	10	47.6
Mahdavi-Kani, Sept. 2–Oct. 18, 1981	22	9	40.9
Khamenei, 1981–85	39	16	41.0
Khamenei, 1985–89	28	8	28.6
Hashemi-Rafsanjani, 1989–93	32	4	12.5
Hashemi-Rafsanjani, 1993–97	32	6	18.8
Khatami, 1997–2001	34	6	17.7
Khatami, 2001–5	34	6	17.7
Ahmadinejad, 2005–9	45	1	2.2
Ahmadinejad, 2009–13	42	1	2.4
Rouhani, 2013–17	35	1	2.9
Rouhani, 2017–21	29	0	0

Note: Of the seven individuals who have so far held the post of president in postrevolutionary Iran, five (Banisadr, Raja'i, Khamenei, Hashemi-Rafsanjani, and Rouhani) had spent time in prison before the revolution. Similarly, four of the prime ministers (Bazargan, Raja'i, Mahdavi-Kani, and Mohammad-Javad Bahonar) were imprisoned before 1979. The information included for Rouhani's second cabinet is accurate as of January 1, 2018. The numbers may change because of possible turnovers that may take place before his term ends in 2021.

[a] The count includes both those who had the title of ministerial adviser (1979–89) and those, starting in President Hashemi-Rafsanjani's first term, who had the title of vice president (1989–2017).

Age Profile of Political Elite in Key Institutions

Table 8
Age Profile of Members of the Guardian Council

Session (years)	Minimum age	Maximum age	Median age
First (1980–86)	37	61	50
Second (1986–92)	35	67	53
Third (1992–98)	41	70	58
Fourth (1998–2004)	35	73	57
Fifth (2004–10)	38	77	53
Sixth (2010–16)	43	83	60
Seventh (2016–22)	50	89	66

Source: Authors' database.
Note: The data in each of these tables covers all members who were originally elected or appointed (depending on the institution) to their posts as well as all those who were added midterm. All percentages have been rounded to the nearest decimal. The minimum, maximum, and median ages were calculated based on the year that body (e.g., the Guardian Council) started its first session.

Table 9
Age Profile of Members of the Assembly of Experts

Session (years)	Minimum age	Maximum age	Median age
First (1983–90)[a]	33	83	55
Second (1991–98)	36	88	61
Third (1999–2006)	37	96	64
Fourth (2007–16)	31	88	65
Fifth (2016–22)	33	93	68

[a] The age of one member, Hasan Hemmati-Moqaddam, was not found.

Table 10
Age Profile of Members of the Expediency Discernment Assembly

Session (years)	Minimum age	Maximum age	Median age
First (1988–89)	42	62	51
Second (1989–92)	39	59	50
Third (1992–97)	42	62	53
Fourth (1997–2002)	40	72	56
Fifth (2002–7)	45	77	59
Sixth (2007–12)	47	82	62
Seventh (2012–17)[a]	48	87	64
Eighth (2017–22)	52	92	68

[a] The age of one member, Hoseyn Mohammadi, was not found.

Table 11
Age Profile of Majlis Deputies

Session (years)	Minimum age	Maximum age	Median age
First (1980–84)	26	74	41
Second (1984–88)	26	69	40
Third (1988–92)	26	68	40
Fourth (1992–96)	28	62	42
Fifth (1996–2000)	31	69	44
Sixth (2000–2004)	30	71	45
Seventh (2004–8)	31	75	47
Eighth (2008–12)	32	73	48
Ninth (2012–16)	31	73	49
Tenth (2016–20)	31	75	51

Table 12
Age Profile of Cabinet Members

Cabinet, years	Minimum age	Maximum age	Median age
Bazargan, Feb. 5–Nov. 5, 1979	36	75	52
Revolutionary Council, Nov. 6, 1979–May 28, 1980	34	52	45
Raja'i, Feb. 4, 1980–June 21, 1981	29	49	38
Bahonar, Aug. 20, 1980–Aug. 1, 1981	29	50	38
Mahdavi-Kani, Sept. 2–Oct. 18, 1981	29	49	38
Musavi's first term, 1981–85	29	49	38
Musavi's second term, 1985–89	32	48	39
Hashemi-Rafsanjani's first term, 1989–93	34	52	41
Hashemi-Rafsanjani's second term, 1993–97	33	56	45
Khatami's first term, 1997–2001	37	60	46
Khatami's second term, 2001–5	41	57	48
Ahmadinejad's first term, 2005–9	38	67	49
Ahmadinejad's second term, 2009–13	29	68	50
Rouhani's first term, 2013–17	41	68	57
Rouhani's second term, 2017–21	33	68	57

Note: The count of cabinet members does not include the vice presidents. The title of VP did not exist before President Hashemi-Rafsanjani began his term in 1989. Also, the information included for Rouhani's second cabinet is accurate as of January 1, 2018. The numbers may change because of possible turnovers that may take place before his term ends in 2021.

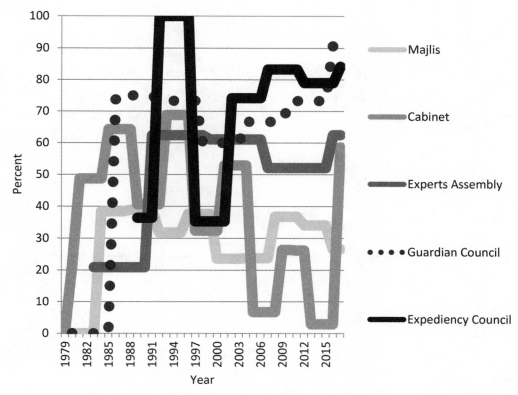

3. Incumbency Rates Compared for Key Political Institutions. Incumbency was determined by looking at whether any individual had served back-to-back terms in an institution (e.g., serving in the second and third session of the Majlis). Source: Authors' database.

3
Supreme Leader

Table 13
Supreme Leaders

Name	Province of birth	Lifespan	Age when inaugurated	Tenure
Supreme leaders				
Seyyed Ruhollah Khomeini	Markazi	1902–89	77	Dec. 3, 1979[a]–June 3, 1989
Seyyed Ali Khamenei	Razavi Khorasan	1939–	50	June 4, 1989–present[b]
Deputy supreme leader				
Hoseyn-Ali Montazeri	Isfahan	1922–2009	63	Nov. 23, 1985–March 26, 1989[c]

[a] Date of the approval of the first postrevolutionary constitution.

[b] Upon becoming the leader, Khamenei could not be recognized as a *marja'* because of his junior status. As explained in Boroujerdi and Rahimkhani (2016), it took some years before he could present himself as a *marja'*. Please note that Khamenei served concurrently as the supreme leader and president from June 4 to August 16, 1989, when he resigned from the presidency to serve solely as the supreme leader.

[c] Date appointed by the Assembly of Experts and date dismissed by Ayatollah Khomeini. There has been no deputy supreme leader since Montazeri.

Table 14
Partial List of Officials Appointed by the Supreme Leader

Guardian Council
- Six experts of Islamic law, all clergymen

Expediency Discernment Assembly
- Forty-four members, including the chairman

Islamic Republic of Iran Broadcasting (IRIB)
- Director-general of IRIB
- Members of the Policymaking Council of IRIB

Judicial system of Iran
- Chief justice
- Chief judge of the Special Court for Clergy

Supreme Council for National Security (SCNS)
- Supreme leader's representative to the SCNS
- Supreme leader's representative to the SCNS

Table 14 (Cont.)
Partial List of Officials Appointed by the Supreme Leader

Military

Islamic Revolutionary Guard Corps (IRGC)

- Commander in chief of the IRGC
- Deputy commander in chief of the IRGC
- Commanders of the IRGC ground forces, aerospace force, and the navy
- Commander of the IRGC's Basij Force
- Commander of the IRGC's Qods Force
- Supreme leader's representative to the IRGC
- Supreme leader's deputy representative to the IRGC
- Deputy coordinator of the IRGC
- Director of the IRGC's Intelligence Organization
- Head of the IRGC's Center for Strategic Research
- Supreme leader's representative to provincial units of the IRGC (e.g., West Azerbaijan, Mahabad, Bandar-e Abbas, Gilan, and Markazi)

Ministry of Defense and Armed Forces Logistics

- Head of the ideological-political bureau of the Ministry of Defense

Law Enforcement Forces (LEF)

- Commander of the LEF
- Chief of the LEF's ideological–political bureau
- Chief of the LEF's Intelligence Protection Organization

Iranian Army

- General commander of the army
- Deputy general commander of the army
- Commanders of the ground forces, air force, and the navy
- Commander of the Khatam al-Anbia Air Defense Base
- Chief of the army's ideological–political bureau
- Chief of the navy's ideological–political bureau
- Chief of the army's intelligence protection bureau
- Deputy inspectorate of the chief of staff of the Iranian Armed Forces
- Deputy chief of the General Headquarters of Armed Forces in Basij Affairs

Charity foundations

- Head of the FMVA
- Supervisor of the Fifteenth of Khordad Foundation
- Head of the FDWI
- Representative at the Housing Foundation of the Islamic Revolution
- Head and members of the board of trustees of IKRF
- Head of the Headquarters for Implementation of Imam's Order

Culture and media

- Members of the HCCR
- Supervisor of the Ettela'at Institute
- Supervisor of the Keyhan Institute

Table 14 (Cont.)
Partial List of Officials Appointed by the Supreme Leader

- Head of the Islamic Propaganda Organization
- Secretary of the Council for Coordination of Islamic Propaganda
- Members of the board of trustees of the FPAVSD
- Members of the Supreme Council of Cyberspace

Representatives and Friday prayer leaders

- Supreme leader's representatives in all provinces
- Friday prayer leaders in provincial capitals and other big cities
- Head and members of the Friday Prayer Policymaking Council
- Head of the Headquarters for Prayer Adduction
- Supreme leader's representatives in overseas offices

Religious institutions

- Grand custodians of holy shrines, including Qods-e Razavi, Shahcheragh, Jamkaran, Fatemeh Ma'sumeh, and Shah-Abdolazim
- Superintendent of *Astan-e Qods-e Razavi*
- Haj affairs representative and supervisor of Iranian pilgrims
- Head of the High Council of Quran
- Representative in Nahj al-Balagha Foundation
- Secretary-general and members of the Supreme Council of WAPIST
- All members of the central council of the Theological Seminaries Center for Services
- Secretary-general of the Ahlulbeyt World Assembly
- Head of the Center for Supervision of Mosque Affairs
- Representative in Najaf Seminary
- Representative and Friday prayer leader of the Islamic Center of London
- Representative and Friday prayer leader of Dubai
- Representative and head of the office of Sunni Brethren of Baluchestan
- Representative for the affairs of Sunni Brethren of Bushehr Province
- Representative in religious affairs of the people of Pakistan
- Head of the policy council of the Headquarters for Rejuvenating Commanding Good and Prohibiting Vice
- Head of the Pious Endowments and Charity Affairs Organization
- Head of the Foundation for Islamic Thought

Education institutions

- Center for Representing the Supreme Leader in Universities
- All members of the board of trustees of Imam Sadeq Society, the Center for the Great Islamic Encyclopedia, and Al-Zahra Women's Seminary (in Qom)
- Executive board and chief executive officer of the Qom Seminary Islamic Propaganda Office
- Secretary, head and supreme members of religious seminaries in Khorasan
- Representative in the Union of Students' Islamic Associations
- Representative for liaison with Iranian Islamic student associations in Europe
- Representative for liaison with Iranian university students and the student association in Asia and Oceania

Table 14 (Cont.)
Partial List of Officials Appointed by the Supreme Leader

- Head of the founding committee of the Islamic Azad University
- Managing director of CIRD
- Managing director of the Encyclopedia of Islam Foundation
- One of the nine members of the board of trustees of University Jihad

Other miscellaneous organizations

- Representative to the Construction Jihad
- Representative in Iraq and Syria
- President of the Red Crescent Society of the Islamic Republic of Iran
- Supreme board to resolve disputes and regulate relations among the three branches of government
- Representative to the Iran Veterinary Organization
- Representative to the Plant Protection Organization
- Representative to the Central Organization of Rural Cooperatives of Iran

Abode of the Supreme Leader and advisers

- Members of the Abode of the Supreme Leader
- Supreme leader's special advisor
- Supreme leader's international affairs adviser
- Chair and members of the Strategic Council on Foreign Relations
- Head of the supreme leader's inspectorate office

Note: This list was compiled based on information available in the constitution, the websites of Ayatollah Khomeini (http://farsi.rouhollah.ir/) and Ayatollah Khamenei (www.Khamenei.ir), newspaper accounts, and the BBC (http://www.bbc.com).

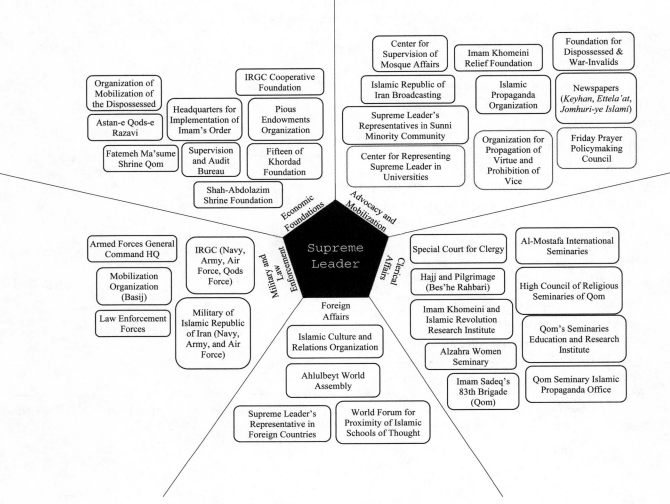

Economic Foundations: Organization of Mobilization of the Dispossessed; Astan-e Qods-e Razavi; Fatemeh Ma'sume Shrine Qom; Headquarters for Implementation of Imam's Order; Supervision and Audit Bureau; Shah-Abdolazim Shrine Foundation; IRGC Cooperative Foundation; Pious Endowments Organization; Fifteen of Khordad Foundation

Advocacy and Mobilization: Center for Supervision of Mosque Affairs; Islamic Republic of Iran Broadcasting; Supreme Leader's Representatives in Sunni Minority Community; Center for Representing Supreme Leader in Universities; Imam Khomeini Relief Foundation; Islamic Propaganda Organization; Organization for Propagation of Virtue and Prohibition of Vice; Foundation for Dispossessed & War-Invalids; Newspapers (Keyhan, Ettela'at, Jomhuri-ye Islami); Friday Prayer Policymaking Council

Supreme Leader

Military and Law Enforcement: Armed Forces General Command HQ; Mobilization Organization (Basij); Law Enforcement Forces; IRGC (Navy, Army, Air Force, Qods Force); Military of Islamic Republic of Iran (Navy, Army, and Air Force)

Clerical Affairs: Special Court for Clergy; Hajj and Pilgrimage (Bes'he Rahbari); Imam Khomeini and Islamic Revolution Research Institute; Alzahra Women Seminary; Imam Sadeq's 83th Brigade (Qom); Al-Mostafa International Seminaries; High Council of Religious Seminaries of Qom; Qom's Seminaries Education and Research Institute; Qom Seminary Islamic Propaganda Office

Foreign Affairs: Islamic Culture and Relations Organization; Ahlulbeyt World Assembly; Supreme Leader's Representative in Foreign Countries; World Forum for Proximity of Islamic Schools of Thought

4. Partial List of Institutions under the Supreme Leader.

4

Guardian Council

All Members of the Guardian Council (1980–2022)

Table 15
Members of the First Guardian Council

Last name	First name	Start	End
Arad	Ali	1980	1986
Bizhani	Khosrow	1983	1986
Eftekhar-Jahromi	Gudarz	1980	1983
Emami-Kashani	Mohammad	1983	1986
Fakheri	Hasan	1983	1986
Hadavi	Mehdi	1980	1983
Hadavi	Mohsen	1980	1983
Jannati	Ahmad	1980	1986
Khaz'ali	Seyyed Abolqasem	1981	1986
Madani-Kermani	Seyyed Jalaleddin	1983	1986
Mahdavi-Kani	Mohammad-Reza	1980	1980
		1982	1983
Mehrpur-Mohammadabadi	Hoseyn	1980	1986
Mohammadi-Gilani	Mohammad	1983	1986
Mo'men	Mohammad	1983	1986
Rabbani-Amlashi	Mohammad-Mehdi	1983	1983
Rabbani-Shirazi	Abdorrahim	1980	1982
Rezvani	Gholam-Reza	1980	1983
Safi-Golpayegani	Lotfollah	1980	1986
Salehi	Mohammad	1980	1986
Sane'i	Yusef	1980	1983

Note: Much of the data was taken from the Guardian Council website (http://www.majlesekhobregan.ir).

Table 16
Members of the Second Guardian Council

Last name	First name	Start	End
Alizadeh	Ahmad	1989	1992
Alizadeh	Mohammad-Reza	1986	1992
Bizhani	Khosrow	1986	1989
Eftekhar-Jahromi	Gudarz	1986	1992
Emami-Kashani	Mohammad	1986	1992
Fakheri	Hasan	1986	1992
Habibi	Hasan-Ebrahim	1989	1992
Jannati	Ahmad	1986	1992
Khaz'ali	Seyyed Abolqasem	1986	1992
Madani-Kermani	Seyyed Jalaleddin	1986	1989
Mehrpur-Mohammadabadi	Hoseyn	1986	1992
Mohammadi-Gilani	Mohammad	1986	1992
Mo'men	Mohammad	1986	1992
Rezvani	Gholam-Reza	1989	1992
Safi-Golpayegani	Lotfollah	1986	1988
Yazdi	Mohammad	1988	1989

Table 17
Members of the Third Guardian Council

Last Name	First Name	Start	End
Abbasifard	Mohammad-Reza	1992	1998
Alizadeh	Ahmad	1992	1998
Alizadeh	Mohammad-Reza	1992	1998
Arad	Ali	1997	1998
Bizhani	Khosrow	1992	1998
Emami-Kashani	Mohammad	1992	1998
Fakheri	Hasan	1992	1995
Habibi	Hasan-Ebrahim	1992	1998
Hashemi-Shahrudi	Seyyed Mahmud	1995	1998
Jannati	Ahmad	1992	1998
Khaz'ali	Seyyed Abolqasem	1992	1998
Mohammadi-Gilani	Mohammad	1992	1995
Mo'men	Mohammad	1992	1998
Rezvani	Gholam-Reza	1992	1998
Zavareh'i	Seyyed Reza	1995	1996

Table 18
Members of the Fourth Guardian Council

Last name	First name	Start	End
Abbasifard	Mohammad-Reza	1998	2003
Alizadeh	Ahmad	1998	2001
Alizadeh	Mohammad-Reza	1998	2004
Arad	Ali	1998	2001
Azizi	Ebrahim	2001	2004
Emami-Kashani	Mohammad	1998	1999
Esma'ili	Mohsen	2001	2004
Habibi	Hasan-Ebrahim	1998	2001
Hashemi-Shahrudi	Seyyed Mahmud	1998	1999
Jannati	Ahmad	1998	2004
Kadkhoda'i	Abbas-Ali	2001	2004
Khaz'ali	Seyyed Abolqasem	1998	1999
Larijani-Amoli	Sadeq	2001	2004
Mo'men	Mohammad	1998	2004
Ostadi-Moqaddam	Reza	1999	2001
Qadiri	Mohammad-Hasan	2001	2004
Rezvani	Gholam-Reza	1998	2004
Taheri-Khorramabadi	Seyyed Hasan	1999	2001
Yazdi	Mohammad	1999	2004
Zavareh'i	Seyyed Reza	1998	2004

Table 19
Members of the Fifth Guardian Council

Last name	First name	Start	End
Alizadeh	Mohammad-Reza	2004	2010
Amiri	Hoseyn-Ali	2007	2010
Azizi	Ebrahim	2004	2009
Elham	Gholam-Hoseyn	2004	2010
Esma'ili	Mohsen	2004	2010
Hashemi-Shahrudi	Seyyed Mahmud	2009	2010
Jannati	Ahmad	2004	2010
Ka'bi	Abbas	2004	2010
Kadkhoda'i	Abbas-Ali	2004	2010
Larijani-Amoli	Sadeq	2004	2009
Modarresi-Yazdi	Seyyed Mohammad-Reza	2004	2010
Mo'men	Mohammad	2004	2010
Rezvani	Gholam-Reza	2004	2010
Salimi [Hamadan]	Mohammad	2004	2010
Yazdi	Mohammad	2004	2010

Table 20
Members of the Sixth Guardian Council

Last name	First name	Start	End
Alizadeh	Mohammad-Reza	2010	2016
Amiri	Hoseyn-Ali	2010	2013
Ebrahimiyan	Nejatollah	2013	2016
Esma'ili	Mohsen	2010	2016
Hashemi-Shahrudi	Seyyed Mahmud	2010	2016
Jannati	Ahmad	2010	2016
Kadkhoda'i	Abbas-Ali	2010	2013
Modarresi-Yazdi	Seyyed Mohammad-Reza	2010	2016
Mo'men	Mohammad	2010	2016
Rahpeyk	Siyamak	2010	2016
Rezvani	Gholam-Reza	2010	2013
Salimi [Hamadan]	Mohammad	2010	2016
Savadkuhifar	Sam	2013	2016
Shabzendehdar	Mohammad-Mehdi	2013	2016
Yazdi	Mohammad	2010	2016

Table 21
Members of the Seventh Guardian Council

Last name	First name	Start	End
Alizadeh	Mohammad-Reza	2016	2019
Ebrahimiyan	Nejatollah	2016	2019
Esma'ili	Mohsen	2016	2019
Hashemi-Shahrudi	Seyyed Mahmud	2016	2019
Jannati	Ahmad	2016	2019
Kadkhoda'i	Abbas-Ali	2016	2019
Modarresi-Yazdi	Seyyed Mohammad-Reza	2016	2019
Mo'men	Mohammad	2016	2019
Musavi	Seyyed Fazlollah	2016	2019
Savadkuhifar	Sam	2016	2019
Shabzendehdar	Mohammad-Mehdi	2016	2019
Yazdi	Mohammad	2016	2019

Note: The members of the Guardian Council are supposed to serve six-year terms. However, halfway through their term three clerical members and three lay legal jurists will change based on a lottery system to create staggered terms. Considering that the Seventh Guardian Council will reach its half point mark in 2019 we have used that year here and in Part Two of the book as the closing date, not knowing who will continue to serve until 2022. It is also quite possible that due to advanced age, resignations, or accidents, some of the members may not be able to complete their full term.

Table 22
Clerical Jurist Members of the Guardian Council (1980–2022)

	SESSION (YEARS)[a]						
	First (1980–86)	Second (1986–92)	Third (1992–98)	Fourth (1998–2004)	Fifth (2004–10)	Sixth (2010–16)	Seventh (2016–22)
Emami-Kashani, Mohammad	* (1983–86)	*	*	* (1998–99)			
Hashemi-Shahrudi, Seyyed Mahmud			* (1995–98)	* (1998–99)	* (2009–10)	*	*
Jannati, Ahmad	*	*	*	*	*	*	*
Khaz'ali, Seyyed Abolqasem	* (1981–86)	*	*	* (1998–99)			
Larijani-Amoli, Sadeq				* (2001–4)	* (2004–9)		
Mahdavi-Kani, Mohammad-Reza	* (July–Dec. 1980; 1982–83)						
Modarresi-Yazdi, Seyyed Mohammad-Reza					*	*	*
Mo'men, Mohammad	* (1983–86)	*	*	*	*	*	*
Mohammadi-Gilani, Mohammad	* (1983–86)	*	* (1992–95)				
Ostadi-Moqaddam, Reza				* (1999–2001)			
Qadiri, Mohammad-Hasan				* (2001–4)			
Rabbani-Amlashi, Mohammad-Mehdi	* (Jan.–July 1983)						
Rabbani-Shirazi, Abdorrahim	* (1980–82)						
Rezvani, Gholam-Reza	* (1980–83)	* (1989–92)	*	*	*	* (2010–13)	
Safi-Golpayegani, Lotfollah	*	* (1986–88)					
Sane'i, Yusef	* (1980–83)						
Shabzendehdar, Mohammad-Mehdi						* (2013–16)	*
Taheri-Khorramabadi, Seyyed Hasan				* (1999–2001)			
Yazdi, Mohammad		* (1988–89)		* (1999–2004)	*	*	*

Source: Guardian Council website (http://www.shora-gc.ir).

[a] The years in parentheses represent the actual years of a term served, if less than a full term. Some members of the Seventh Guardian Council may not finish their full term due to old age or other reasons.

Table 23
Legal Jurist Members of the Guardian Council (1980–2019)

	SESSION (YEARS)[a]				
	1 (1980–83)	1 (1983–86)	2 (1986–89)	2 (1989–92)	3 (1992–95)
Abbasifard, Mohammad-Reza[b]					*
Alizadeh, Ahmad				*	*
Alizadeh, Mohammad-Reza			*	*	*
Amiri, Hoseyn-Ali					
Arad, Ali	*	*			
Azizi, Ebrahim					
Bizhani, Khosrow		*	*		*
Ebrahimiyan, Nejatollah					
Eftekhar-Jahromi, Gudarz	*		*	*	
Elham, Gholam-Hoseyn					
Esma'ili, Mohsen					
Fakheri, Hasan		*	*	*	*
Habibi, Hasan-Ebrahim				*	*
Hadavi, Mehdi	*				
Hadavi, Mohsen	*				
Ka'bi, Abbas[c]					
Kadkhoda'i, Abbas-Ali					
Madani-Kermani, Seyyed Jalaleddin		*	*		
Mehrpur-Mohammadabadi, Hoseyn	*	*	*	*	
Musavi, Seyyed Fazlollah					
Rahpeyk, Siyamak					
Salehi, Mohammad	*	*			
Salimi [Hamadan], Mohammad[d]					
Savadkuhifar, Sam					
Zavareh'i, Seyyed Reza					

Source: Guardian Council website (http://www.shora-gc.ir).
[a] The years in parentheses represent the actual years of a term served, if less than a full term. Some members of the Seventh Guardian Council may not finish their full terms due to old age or other reasons.
[b] Some clerics can be appointed to the Guardian Council as lay legal jurists. Abbasifard is one such cleric.
[c] Ka'bi is another cleric appointed as a lay legal jurist.
[d] Salimi [Hamadan] is another cleric appointed as a lay legal jurist.

Table 23 (Cont.)
Legal Jurist Members of the Guardian Council (1980–2019)

			SESSION (YEARS)[A]				
3 (1995–98)	4 (1998–2001)	4 (2001–4)	5 (2004–7)	5 (2007–10)	6 (2010–13)	6 (2013–16)	7 (2016–19)
*	*	*					
		(2001–3)					
*	*						
*	*	*	*	*	*	*	*
				*	*		
*	*						
(1997–98)							
		*	*	*			
				(2007–9)			
*							
						*	*
			*	*			
		*	*	*	*	*	*
*	*						
			*	*			
		*	*	*	*		*
							*
					*	*	
			*	*	*	*	
						*	*
*	*	*					
(1995–96)							

Table 24
Percentage of Legislation from Each Majlis Approved by the Guardian Council

Majlis session	Date of first GC opinion on legislations	Date of last GC opinion on legislations	Number of legislations ratified by the Majlis	Final number of legislations approved by GC	Percentage of legislations approved
First	July 22, 1980	May 26, 1984	410	357	87.0%
Second	July 5, 1984	June 8, 1988	336	284	84.5%
Third	June 23, 1988	June 15, 1992	265	226	85.2%
Fourth	July 17, 1992	June 12, 1996	357	321	89.9%
Fifth	July 29, 1996	May 24, 2000	371	326	87.9%
Sixth	June 29, 2000	May 26, 2004	444	337	75.9%
Seventh	July 19, 2004	June 11, 2008	364	300	82.4%
Eighth	July 2, 2008	June 27, 2012	355	301	84.8%
Ninth	July 7, 2012	July 4, 2015	132	107	81.0%

Source: Peyqambari (2015, 6–7).

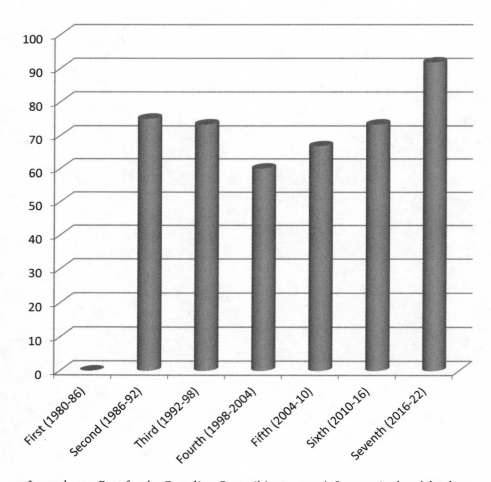

5. Incumbency Rate for the Guardian Council (1980–2022). Source: Authors' database.

Table 25
Place of Birth of All Guardian Council Members (1980–2017)

Province	Number and percentage of members from each province	Percentage of members born in each provincial capital
Tehran	9 (20.5%)	Tehran (78%)
Isfahan	8 (18.2%)	Isfahan (62%)
Mazandaran	4 (9.1%)	Sari (0%)
Fars	3 (6.8%)	Shiraz (33%)
Qom	3 (6.8%)	Qom (100%)
Lorestan	3 (6.8%)	Khorramabad (33%)
Iraq[a]	2 (4.5%)	0%
Khuzestan	2 (4.5%)	Ahvaz (50%)
Kermanshah	2 (4.5%)	Kermanshah (50%)
Yazd	2 (4.5%)	Yazd (50%)
East Azerbaijan	1 (2.3%)	Tabriz (0%)
Kerman	1 (2.3%)	Kerman (100%)
Gilan	1 (2.3%)	Rasht (0%)
Markazi	1 (2.3%)	Arak (0%)
Hamadan	1 (2.3%)	Hamadan (100%)
Unknown	1 (2.3%)	NA
Alborz	0	NA
Ardabil	0	NA
Bushehr	0	NA
Chahar Mahal and Bakhtiari	0	NA
Golestan	0	NA
Hormozgan	0	NA
Ilam	0	NA
Kohgiluyeh and Buyer Ahmad	0	NA
Kurdistan	0	NA
North Khorasan	0	NA
Qazvin	0	NA
Razavi Khorasan	0	NA
Semnan	0	NA
Sistan and Baluchestan	0	NA
South Khorasan	0	NA
West Azerbaijan	0	NA
Zanjan	0	NA
Total	44 (100%)	(51%)

Source: Authors' database.
Note: The table includes data on forty-four individuals who have served in the Guardian Council in sessions one through seven from 1980 to 2017. The birth province of one individual, Mehdi Hadavi, could not be found and we have not counted him. Numbers have been rounded to the nearest integer.
[a] Seyyed Mahmud Hashemi-Shahrudi and Sadeq Larijani-Amoli were born in neighboring Iraq.

5

Expediency Discernment Assembly

Explanatory Note on the Expediency Discernment Assembly

Ayatollah Khomeini ordered the establishment of the EDA on February 6, 1988, as the final arbiter between the GC and the Majlis. In 1989, with the amendment of the constitution, changes were made to the makeup of the EDA. The members were divided into two categories. Juristic members (*afrad-e Hoquqi*) included the clerical jurists of the GC, heads of the three branches of government, and cabinet ministers and parliament committee chairs authorized to attend the meetings of the EDA based on the issue at hand. Natural members (*afrad-e Haqiqi*) were individuals specifically named by the supreme leader in the official appointment letter. Between February 1988 and December 2017, fifty-nine natural members were officially appointed, first by Ayatollah Khomeini and then by Ayatollah

Khamenei (many with multiple appointments). Table 26 only includes natural members. The breakdown of the natural members who served in the first through eighth sessions of the EDA is seven, eleven, ten, twenty-seven, thirty-one, thirty-six, thirty-eight, and thirty-eight, respectively.[1] Of these fifty-nine individuals, twenty-seven (46 percent) have been clerics, and they have been identified in the table in italics. It should be noted that some individuals, like Ali Larijani, were sometimes designated as natural members while serving simultaneously in a juristic capacity as head of the legislative branch. On the other hand, someone like Mohammad Khatami could only attend assembly meetings in his juristic capacity since he was never named as a natural member. In addition, starting in 1997, the terms of appointment of members of the assembly officially changed from three years to five years.

---

1. The official website of the Expediency Assembly (http://81.91.157.27/) mentions seven sessions but seems to have omitted those who were appointed in 2002 (session five). The list of those members is available at http://www.iran-resist.org/IMG/pdf/_Discernement _membres.pdf.

Table 26
Natural Members of the Expediency Discernment Assembly (1988–2022)

	First (1988–89)	Second (1989–92)	Third (1992–97)	Fourth (1997–2002)	Fifth (2002–7)	Sixth (2007–12)	Seventh (2012–17)	Eighth (2017–22)[a]
Ahmadinejad, Mahmoud							* (2013–17)	*
Amini, Ebrahim				*	*	*	*	*
Ansari, Majid					*	*	*	*
Aqa Mohammadi, Ali						*	*	*
Aqa Zadeh, Gholam-Reza				*	*	*	*	*
Aref, Mohammad-Reza					*	*	*	*
Asgarowladi, Habibollah				*	*	*	* (2012–13)	
Bahonar, Mohammad-Reza					*	*	*	*
Danesh-Ja'fari, Davud						*	*	*
Davudi, Parviz						*	*	*
Dorri-Najafabadi, Qorbanali				*	*	*	*	
Emami-Kashani, Mohammad				*	*	*		
Firuzabadi, Seyyed Hasan				*	*	*	*	*
Foruzandeh, Mohammad						*	*	*
Habibi, Hasan-Ebrahim		* (May 8, 1991–92)	*	*	*	*	* (2012–13)	
Haddad-Adel, Gholam-Ali					*	*	*	*
Hashemi-Bahremani, Mohammad				*	*	*		
Hashemi-Rafsanjani, Akbar	*			*	*	*	* (2012–17)	
Hashemi-Shahrudi, Seyyed Mahmud						* (2009–12)	*	*
Iravani, Mohammad-Javad					*	*	*	*
Jalili, Sa'id							* (2013–17)	*
Jannati, Ahmad				*	*	*	*	*
Karrubi, Mehdi					* (2004–7)			
Khamenei, Seyyed Ali	*							
Khomeini, Seyyed Ahmad	*	*	* (1992–95)					
Larijani, Ali				*	*	*	*	
Mahdavi-Kani, Mohammad-Reza		*	*	*				
Mesbahi-Moqaddam, Gholam-Reza							*	*
Mir Mohammadi, Seyyed Mohammad								*

[a] The members listed for the eighth session were appointed on August 14, 2017, and some of them may not finish their full term due to resignations or death.

Table 26 (Cont.)
Natural Members of the Expediency Discernment Assembly (1988–2022)

	SESSION (YEARS)							
	First (1988–89)	Second (1989–92)	Third (1992–97)	Fourth (1997–2002)	Fifth (2002–7)	Sixth (2007–12)	Seventh (2012–17)	Eighth (2017–22)[a]
Mir Salim, Seyyed Mostafa				*	*	*	*	*
Mohammadi, Hoseyn							*	*
Mohammadi-Araqi, Mahmud							*	*
Mohseni-Ezheh'i, Gholam-Hoseyn						*	*	*
Mojtahed-Shabestari, Mohsen								*
Movahhedi-Kermani, Mohammad-Ali			*	*	*	*	*	*
Mozaffar, Hoseyn					*	*	*	*
Musavi, Mir Hoseyn	*	*	*	*	*	* (2007–9)[b]		
Musavi-Ardabili, Seyyed Abdolkarim	*							
Musavi-Kho'iniha, Seyyed Mohammad	*	*	*	*				
Nabavi, Seyyed Morteza				*	*	*	*	*
Namdar-Zangeneh, Bizhan				*	*	*		
Nateq-Nuri, Ali-Akbar					*	*	*	*
Nurbakhsh, Mohsen				*				
Nuri, Abdollah		*	*	*				
Qalibaf, Mohammad-Baqer								*
Ra'isi, Seyyed Ebrahim								*
Reyshahri, Mohammad				*	*	*		
Reza'i, Mohsen				*	*	*	*	*
Rouhani, Hassan		* (1991–92)	*	*	*	*	*	
Sadr, Seyyed Mohammad								*
Saffar-Harandi, Mohammad-Hoseyn							*	*
Sane'i, Hasan		*	*	*	*	*	*	*
Sane'i, Yusef		*						
Tavakkoli, Ahmad								*
Tavassoli-Mahallati, Mohammad-Reza	*	*	*		*	* (2007–8)		
Va'ez-Tabasi, Abbas				*	*	*	* (2012–16)	
Va'ezzadeh-Khorasani, Sadeq							*	*
Vahidi, Ahmad							*	*
Velayati, Ali-Akbar				*	*	*	*	*

Sources: http://farsi.khamenei.ir; http://www.iran-resist.org/IMG/pdf/_Discernement_membres.pdf.

Note: Clerical members of the Expediency Discernment Assembly have been identified by italics.

[b] While Musavi was not officially expelled from the EDA, he was placed under house arrest after protesting the 2009 election irregularities.

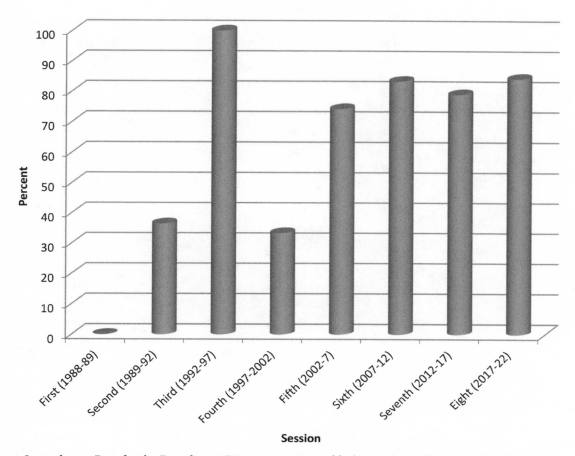

6. Incumbency Rate for the Expediency Discernment Assembly (1988–2022). Source: Authors' database.

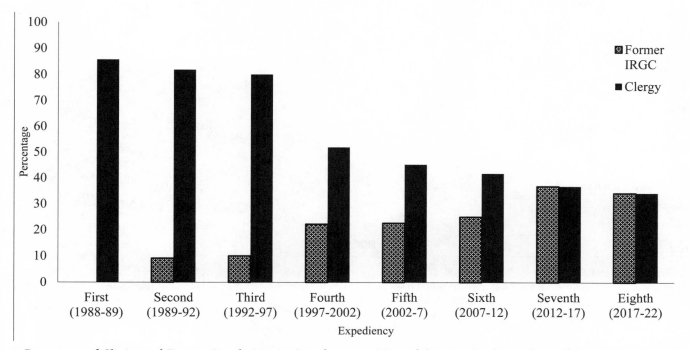

7. Percentage of Clerics and Former Revolutionary Guards among Natural (Non-Juristic) Members of the Expediency Discernment Assembly. Source: Authors' database.

Table 27
Place of Birth of All Natural Members of the Expediency Discernment Assembly (1988–2022)

Province	Number and percentage of deputies from each province	Percentage of deputies born in provincial capitals
Tehran	11 (19%)	Tehran (82%)
Isfahan	9 (16%)	Isfahan (33%)
Razavi Khorasan	8 (14%)	Mashhad (75%)
Kerman	5 (9%)	Kerman (40%)
Iraq[a]	3 (5%)	0%
Qom	3 (5%)	Qom (100%)
East Azerbaijan	2 (4%)	Tabriz (0%)
Hamadan	2 (4%)	Hamadan (50%)
Kermanshah	2 (4%)	Kermanshah (50%)
Mazandaran	2 (4%)	Sari (0%)
Qazvin	2 (4%)	Qazvin (100%)
Semnan	2 (4%)	Semnan (0%)
Ardabil	1 (2%)	Ardabil (100%)
Fars	1 (2%)	Shiraz (100%)
Khuzestan	1 (2%)	Ahvaz (0%)
Lorestan	1 (2%)	Khorramabad (0%)
Markazi	1 (2%)	Arak (0%)
West Azerbaijan	1 (2%)	Urmia (0%)
Yazd	1 (2%)	Yazd (100%)
Alborz	0	NA
Bushehr	0	NA
Chahar Mahal and Bakhtiari	0	NA
Gilan	0	NA
Golestan	0	NA
Hormozgan	0	NA
Ilam	0	NA
Kohgiluyeh and Buyer Ahmad	0	NA
Kurdistan	0	NA
North Khorasan	0	NA
Sistan and Baluchestan	0	NA
South Khorasan	0	NA
Zanjan	0	NA
Total	58 (100%)	(55%)

Source: Authors' database.

Note: Of the fifty-nine individuals who have served in the EDA (from 1988 to 2017), the birth province of one individual (Hoseyn Mohammadi) could not be found and we have not counted him in the above table. Numbers have been rounded to the nearest integer. It is possible that new individuals may be added to the eighth session of the EDA before the current term is over in 2022.

[a] The following individuals were born in neighboring Iraq: Seyyed Mahmoud Hashemi-Shahrudi, Mohamad-Javad Iravani, and Ali Larijani.

6

Judiciary and Military Officials

Explanatory Note on the Judiciary

According to Article 157 of the 1979 constitution, the High Council of the Judiciary (HCJ) was formed as the highest authority of judiciary power. Article 158 stated that this council would consist of five members: the head of the State Supreme Court, the prosecutor-general, and three just and learned judges who are scholars of jurisprudence, as selected by the judges of the country. HCJ members were selected for five-year terms. Between 1979 and 1982, the two highest judicial positions were head of the State Supreme Court and the prosecutor-general. In his capacity as supreme leader, Ayatollah Khomeini appointed Ayatollah Seyyed Mohammad Beheshti and Ayatollah Seyyed Abdolkarim Musavi-Ardabili to the above two respective posts. However, after Beheshti's assassination in 1981, Ayatollah Khomeini promoted Musavi-Ardabili to the post of head of the State Supreme Court and a new prosecutor-general had to be appointed. The HCJ became very active in 1982 but suffered from major disagreements among members. In 1989, as part of the constitutional amendments that were introduced, the HCJ was abolished in favor of a chief justice. The revised amendment stipulated that: "In order to fulfil the responsibilities of the judiciary power in all the matters concerning judiciary, administrative and executive areas, the Leader shall appoint a just, honorable man well versed in judiciary affairs and possessing prudence and administrative abilities as the head of the judiciary power for a period of five years who shall be the highest judicial authority."[1]

1. http://irandataportal.syr.edu.

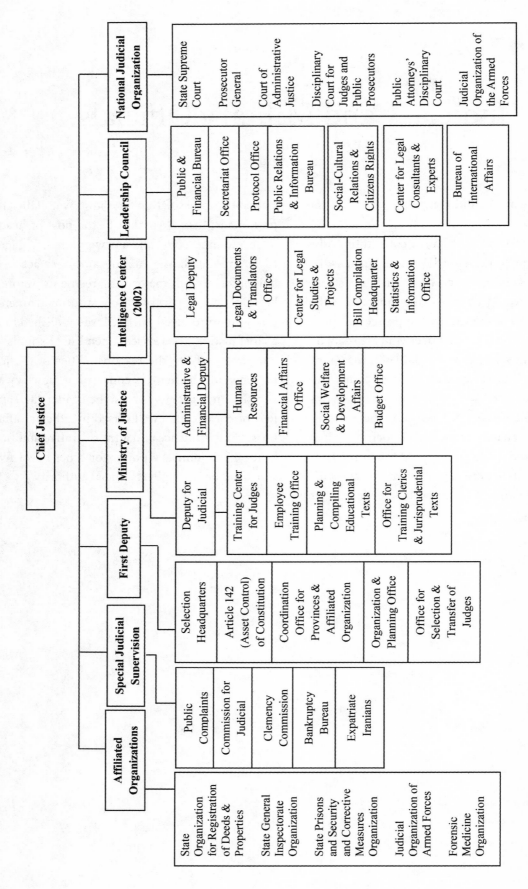

8. Organizational Chart of the Judiciary. For the Persian, see http://noperator.persiangig.com/image/%DA%86%D8%A7%D8%B1%D8%AA%20%D8%AF%D8%A7%D8%AF%DA%AF%D8%B3%D8%AA%D8%B1%DB%8C.gif.

Partial List of High-Level Judiciary Officials[2]

MEMBERS OF THE HIGH COUNCIL OF THE JUDICIARY[3]

Name	Tenure
Qoddusi, Ali	July 13, 1980–Sept. 5, 1981
Rabbani-Amlashi, Mohammad-Mehdi	July 13, 1980–Jan. 6, 1983
Javadi-Amoli, Abdollah	July 13, 1980–Jan. 6, 1983
Mo'men, Mohammad[4]	Oct. 4, 1981–Jan. 6, 1983
Moqtada'i, Morteza	Oct. 4, 1981–July 1989
Mir Mohammadi, Seyyed Abolfazl	May 1983–June 1985
Musavi-Bojnurdi, Seyyed Mohammad	May 1983–July 1989
Mar'ashi-Shushtari, Mohammad-Hasan	June 1985–Jan. 1989

HEAD OF THE STATE SUPREME COURT

Name	Tenure
Beheshti, Seyyed Mohammad	Feb. 23, 1980–June 28, 1981
Musavi-Ardabili, Seyyed Abdolkarim	June 29, 1981–June 30, 1989
Moqtada'i, Morteza	1989–94
Mohammadi-Gilani, Mohammad	Aug. 28, 1994–Aug. 15, 2004
Mofid, Hoseyn	Aug. 15, 2004–Aug. 25, 2009
Mohseni-Garakani, Ahmad	Aug. 25, 2009–Aug. 20, 2014
Karimi, Hoseyn	Aug. 23, 2014–present

PROSECUTOR-GENERAL OF THE REVOLUTIONARY COURTS[5]

Name	Tenure
Hadavi, Mehdi	Feb. 28–Aug. 6, 1979
Qoddusi, Ali	Aug. 6, 1979–Sept. 5, 1981
Musavi-Tabrizi, Seyyed Hoseyn	Sept. 7, 1981–Jan. 28, 1984

2. This list has been put together based on the authors' database and various other sources including http://hamshahrionline.ir.

3. From 1982 to 1989, the two heads of the State Supreme Court, Ayatollah Beheshti and Ayatollah Seyyed Abdolkarim Musavi-Ardabili, served as the chairs of the HCJ. Apparently, the two chief state prosecutors during this period, Yusef Sane'i (1980–85) and Seyyed Mohammad Musavi-Kho'iniha (1985–89), also attended the meetings of HCJ.

4. http://nbo.ir.

5. In 1984, this position merged with that of the prosecutor-general.

CHIEF JUSTICE

Name	Tenure
Yazdi, Mohammad	Aug. 15, 1989–Aug. 14, 1999
Hashemi-Shahrudi, Seyyed Mahmud	Aug. 14, 1999–Aug. 14, 2009
Larijani-Amoli, Sadeq	Aug. 14, 2009–present

FIRST DEPUTY TO THE CHIEF JUSTICE

Name	Tenure
Marvi, Mohammad-Hadi	1999–2004
Ra'isi, Seyyed Ebrahim	2004–Aug. 23, 2014
Mohseni-Ezheh'i, Gholam-Hoseyn	Aug. 23, 2014–present

PROSECUTOR-GENERAL

Name	Tenure
Banisadr, Seyyed Fathollah	1979–80
Musavi-Ardabili, Seyyed Abdolkarim	Feb. 23, 1980–June 29, 1981
Rabbani-Amlashi, Mohammad-Mehdi	June 29, 1981–Jan. 6, 1983
Sane'i, Yusef	Jan. 9, 1983–July 10, 1985
Musavi-Kho'iniha, Seyyed Mohammad	July 10, 1985–Aug. 1989
Reyshahri, Mohammad	Aug. 21, 1989–91
Musavi-Tabrizi, Seyyed Abolfazl	1991–94
Moqtada'i, Morteza	Aug. 28, 1994–98
Namazi, Abdolnnabi	1998–Aug. 14, 2004
Dorri-Najafabadi, Qorbanali	Aug. 15, 2004–Aug. 25, 2009
Mohseni-Ezheh'i, Gholam-Hoseyn	Aug. 25, 2009–Aug. 23, 2014
Ra'isi, Seyyed Ebrahim	Aug. 23, 2014–Mar. 6, 2016
Montazeri, Mohammad-Ja'far	Apr. 3, 2016–present

PUBLIC PROSECUTOR-GENERAL OF TEHRAN

Name	Tenure
Mir Shams-Shahshahani, Abolfazl	1979–Oct. 31, 1979
Dadgar, Hoseyn	1980–84
Mir Emadi, Seyyed Ziya'eddin	1984–88
Yunesi, Ali	1988–90
Qandi, [unknown first name]	1990–date unknown
Naseri-Salehabadi, Mohammad	date unknown–1994

REVOLUTIONARY PROSECUTOR-GENERAL OF TEHRAN

Name	Tenure
Zavareh'i, Seyyed Reza	1979
Azari-Qomi, Ahmad	July 2[6]–Sept. 16, 1979
Ladjvardi, Asadollah	Sept. 11, 1980–Dec. 1984
Razini, Ali	1985–86
Eshraqi, Morteza	1986–89
Ra'isi, Seyyed Ebrahim	1989–94

PUBLIC AND REVOLUTIONARY PROSECUTOR-GENERAL OF TEHRAN

Name	Tenure
Mortazavi, Sa'id	2003–Aug. 29, 2009
Ja'fari-Dowlatabadi, Abbas	Aug. 30, 2009–present

PROSECUTOR-GENERAL OF THE SPECIAL COURT FOR CLERGY[7]

Name	Tenure
Fallahiyan, Ali	June 12, 1987–Jan. 3, 1990
Reyshahri, Mohammad	Jan. 3, 1990–Dec. 16, 1998
Mohseni-Ezheh'i, Gholam-Hoseyn	Dec. 16, 1998–Sept. 24, 2005
Salimi, Mohammad	Sept. 24, 2005–May 1, 2012
Ra'isi, Seyyed Ebrahim	June 16, 2012–present

CHIEF JUDGE OF THE SPECIAL COURT FOR CLERGY

Name	Tenure
Azari-Qomi, Ahmad	1986–87
Razini, Ali	June 15, 1987–June 2012
Montazeri, Mohammad-Ja'far	May 2, 2012–present

HEAD OF THE COURT OF ADMINISTRATIVE JUSTICE

Name	Tenure
Emami-Kashani, Mohammad	June 10, 1982–July 1983
Rezvani, Gholam-Reza	July 1983–85

6. http://www.imam-khomeini.ir.

7. The SCC was established in 1987. See Künkler (2012).

Feyz-Gilani, Mohammad-Ali	1986–89
Musavi-Tabrizi, Seyyed Abolfazl	1989–91
Abbasifard, Mohammad-Reza	1991–93
Ferdowsipur, Esma'il	Dec. 5, 1993–July 16, 1997
Musavi-Tabrizi, Seyyed Abolfazl	1997–99
Dorri-Najafabadi, Qorbanali	1999–Aug. 17, 2004
Razini, Ali	Aug. 17, 2004–Aug. 19, 2009
Montazeri, Mohammad-Ja'far	Aug. 26, 2009–Apr. 10, 2016
Bahrami, Mohammad-Kazem	Apr. 10, 2016–present

HEAD OF THE STATE GENERAL INSPECTORATE ORGANIZATION

Name	Tenure
Mohaqqeq-Damad, Seyyed Mostafa	Oct. 10, 1981–94
Ra'isi, Seyyed Ebrahim	1994–2004
Niyazi, Mohammad	2004–June 28, 2008
Purmohammadi, Mostafa	July 2, 2008–Aug. 2013
Seraj, Naser	Aug. 21, 2013–present

Partial List of High-Level Military-Security Officials[8]

Military

THE SUPREME COMMANDER OF ARMED FORCES

Supreme Leader

CHIEF OF THE JOINT STAFF OF THE ISLAMIC REPUBLIC OF IRAN ARMY

Name	Tenure
Qarani, Valiyollah	Feb. 11–Mar. 26, 1979
Farbod, Naser	Mar. 26–July 19, 1979
Shaker, Mohammad-Hoseyn	July 21–Dec. 22, 1979
Shadmehr, Mohammad-Hadi	Dec. 22, 1979–June 19, 1980
Fallahi, Valiyollah	June 19, 1980–Sept. 30, 1981
Zahirnezhad, Qasemali	Oct. 1, 1981–Oct. 25, 1984
Sohrabi, Esma'il	Oct. 25, 1984–May 3, 1988
Shahbazi, Ali	May 3, 1988–Sept. 29, 1998
Torabipur, Mostafa	Oct. 14, 1998–date unknown

8. Much of this data was taken from the websites of Ayatollah Khomeini (http://farsi.rouhollah.ir/) and Ayatollah Khamenei (www.Khamenei.ir).

Rostami, Shahram   date unknown–Feb. 5, 2001

Purshasb, Abdolali   Feb. 5, 2001–Sept. 25, 2005

Musavi, Seyyed Abdorrahim   Sept. 26, 2005–Aug. 25, 2008

Dadras, Mohammad-Hoseyn   Aug. 26, 2008–Nov. 5, 2017[9]

Sayyari, Habibollah   Nov. 5, 2017–present

GENERAL COMMANDER OF THE ARMY[10]

Name	Tenure
Shahbazi, Ali	Sept. 30, 1998–May 21, 2000
Salimi, Mohammad	May 21, 2000–Sept. 11, 2005
Salehi, Seyyed Ataollah	Sept. 11, 2005–Aug. 21, 2017
Musavi, Seyyed Abdorrahim	Aug. 21, 2017–present

CHIEF OF THE ARMED FORCES GENERAL STAFF[11]

Name	Tenure
Firuzabadi, Seyyed Hasan	Sept. 26, 1989–June 28, 2016
Baqeri, Mohammad-Hoseyn	June 28, 2016–present

FIRST DEPUTY CHIEF OF THE ARMED FORCES GENERAL STAFF

Name	Tenure
Foruzandeh, Mohammad	Oct. 1, 1989–93
Sayyad-Shirazi, Ali	Sept. 11, 1993–Apr. 10, 1999
Rashid, Gholam-Ali	Aug. 15, 1999–July 5, 2016
Musavi, Seyyed Abdorrahim	July 5, 2016–Aug. 21, 2017
Salehi, Seyyed Ataollah	Aug. 21, 2017–present

DEPUTY GENERAL COMMANDER OF THE ARMY

Name	Tenure
Arasteh, Naser	Oct. 14, 1998–date unknown
Baqa'i, Habib	May 26, 2004–Sept. 26, 2005
Qarayi-Ashtiyani, Mohammad-Reza	Sept. 26, 2005–Aug. 25, 2008

9. Beginning with Dadras in 2008, the official title changed to coordinating deputy and chief of the joint staff of the Islamic Republic of Iran.

10. This position was established in September 1998 as the highest position in the army, which reduced the significance of the chief of the joint staff of the Islamic Republic of Iran Army.

11. Created in 1989, this is the most senior military position in Iran after the supreme leader. The chief of staff of the Iranian Armed Forces coordinates the common activities of the army, IRGC, and the LEF.

Musavi, Seyyed Abdorrahim	Aug. 26, 2008–July 5, 2016
Purdastan, Ahmad-Reza	Nov. 19, 2016–Nov. 5, 2017
Dadras, Mohammad-Hoseyn	Nov. 5, 2017–present

COMMANDER OF THE ISLAMIC REPUBLIC OF IRAN GROUND FORCES

Name	Tenure
Fallahi, Valiyollah	ca. Mar. 1979–June 19, 1980
Zahirnezhad, Qasemali	June 19, 1980–Oct. 1, 1981
Sayyad-Shirazi, Ali	Oct. 1, 1981–Aug. 2, 1986
Hasani-Sa'di, Hoseyn	Aug. 2, 1986–May 8, 1991
Najafi, Abdollah	May 8, 1991–Oct. 25, 1994
Dadbin, Ahmad	Oct. 25, 1994–Oct. 1, 1997
Purshasb, Abdolali	Oct. 1, 1997–Feb. 7, 2001
Mohammadifar, Naser	Feb. 7, 2001–Sept. 25, 2005
Dadras, Mohammad-Hoseyn	Sept. 26, 2005–Aug. 25, 2008
Purdastan, Ahmad-Reza	Aug. 25, 2008–Nov. 15, 2016
Heydari, Kiyumars	Nov. 15, 2016–present

COMMANDER OF THE ISLAMIC REPUBLIC OF IRAN AIR FORCE

Name	Tenure
Imaniyan, Asghar	Feb. 25–Aug. 15, 1979
Baqeri, Amir-Bahman	Aug. 15, 1979–June 3, 1980
Fakuri, Javad	June 19, 1980–Sept. 29, 1981
Mo'inipur, Mohammad-Hasan	Oct. 1, 1981–Nov. 25, 1983
Sadiq, Hushang	Nov. 25, 1983–Jan. 30, 1987
Sattari, Mansur	Jan. 30, 1987–Jan. 5, 1995
Baqa'i, Habib	Jan. 26, 1995–May 27, 2001
Pardis, Seyyed Reza	May 27, 2001–Oct. 5, 2004
Qavami, Karim	Oct. 5, 2004–Oct. 29, 2006
Meyqani, Ahmad	Oct. 29, 2006–Aug. 31, 2008
Shahsafi, Hasan	Aug. 31, 2008–present

COMMANDER OF THE KHATAM AL-ANBIA AIR DEFENSE BASE[12]

Name	Tenure
Meyqani, Ahmad	Aug. 31, 2008–Jan. 25, 2011
Esma'ili, Farzad	Jan. 25, 2011–present

12. This position was established in 2008 and Meyqani was its founder and first commander.

COMMANDER OF THE ISLAMIC REPUBLIC OF IRAN NAVY

Name	Tenure
Madani, Seyyed Ahmad	Feb.–Mar. 2, 1979
Afzali, Bahram	May/June 1980–Apr. 24, 1983
Hoseyni, Esfandiyar	Apr. 30, 1983–June 27, 1985
Malekzadehgan, Mohammad-Hoseyn	June 27, 1985–Oct. 30, 1989
Shamkhani, Ali	Oct. 31, 1989–Aug. 26, 1997
Mohtaj, Abbas	Aug. 27, 1997–Sept. 25, 2005
Kuchaki-Badelani, Sajjad	Sept. 26, 2005–Aug. 20, 2007
Sayyari, Habibollah	Aug. 20, 2007–Nov. 5, 2017
Khanzadi, Hoseyn	Nov. 5, 2017–present

IRGC and Basij

COMMANDER IN CHIEF OF THE IRGC

Name	Tenure
Mansuri, Javad	1979
Aqa Zamani, Abbas	1979–Feb. 1980
Duzduzani, Abbas	Feb.–July 1980
Reza'i, Morteza	July 19, 1980–81
Reza'i, Mohsen	1981–Sept. 9, 1997
Safavi, Seyyed Yahya	Sept. 10, 1997–Sept. 1, 2007
Ja'fari, Mohammad-Ali	Sept. 1, 2007–present

DEPUTY COMMANDER IN CHIEF OF THE IRGC

Name	Tenure
Kolahduz, Yusef	date unknown–Sept. 29, 1981
Shamkhani, Ali	1985–88
Safavi, Seyyed Yahya	Sept. 24, 1989–Sept. 1997
Zolqadr, Mohammad-Baqer	Sept. 13, 1997–Nov. 23, 2005
Reza'i, Morteza	Apr. 30, 2006–May 22, 2008
Hejazi, Seyyed Mohammad	May 22, 2008–Oct. 4, 2009
Salami, Hoseyn	Oct. 4, 2009–present

COMMANDER OF THE IRGC NAVY

Name	Tenure
Fadavi, Ali	May 3, 2010–present

COMMANDER OF THE IRGC'S QODS FORCE

Name	Tenure
Soleymani, Qasem	1997–present

COMMANDER OF THE IRGC'S BASIJ FORCE[13]

Name	Tenure
Majd, Amir (HI)	1980 (three months)
Salek, Ahmad (HI)	1980–81
Rahmani, Mohammad-Ali (HI)	Mar. 11, 1983–Mar. 1, 1990
Afshar, Ali-Reza	Mar. 1, 1990–98
Hejazi, Seyyed Mohammad	Mar. 11, 1998–2007
Ja'fari, Mohammad-Ali	2008
Ta'eb, Hoseyn (HI)	July 12, 2008–Oct. 4, 2009
Naqdi, Mohammad-Reza	Oct. 4, 2009–Dec. 7, 2016
Gheybparvar, Gholam-Hoseyn	Dec. 7, 2016–present

DEPUTY COMMANDER OF THE IRGC'S BASIJ FORCE

Name	Tenure
Fazli, Ali[14]	Dec. 10, 2009–present

DEPUTY CHIEF OF THE GENERAL STAFF OF ARMED FORCES IN BASIJ AFFAIRS

Name	Tenure
Zolqadr, Mohammad-Baqer	Dec. 11, 2007–May 23, 2010
Ebrahimzadeh, Akbar	May 23, 2010–present

Other

SECRETARY OF THE SUPREME COUNCIL FOR NATIONAL SECURITY

Name	Tenure
Rouhani, Hassan	Nov. 13, 1989–2005
Larijani, Ali	May 25, 2004–June 27, 2008
Jalili, Sa'id	June 28, 2008–Oct. 9, 2013
Shamkhani, Ali	Oct. 9, 2013–present

13. The official title is head of the Organization for the Mobilization of the Dispossessed. Basij was absorbed into IRGC in January 1981.

14. To date, Fazli has been the only person to hold this position.

CHIEF OF LAW ENFORCEMENT FORCES

Name	Tenure
Sohrabi, Mohammad	Apr. 1, 1991–Sept. 24, 1992
Seyfollahi, Reza	Sept. 24, 1992–Feb. 15, 1997
Latifiyan, Hedayat	Feb. 15, 1997–June 27, 2000
Qalibaf, Mohammad-Baqer	June 27, 2000–Apr. 4, 2005
Ahmadi-Moqaddam, Esma'il	July 9, 2005–Mar. 9, 2015
Ashtari, Hoseyn	Mar. 9, 2015–present

DEPUTY CHIEF OF LAW ENFORCEMENT FORCES

Name	Tenure
Radan, Ahmad-Reza	Oct. 11, 2008–May 26, 2014
Ashtari, Hoseyn	May 26, 2014–Mar. 9, 2015
Mo'meni, Eskandar	Apr. 4, 2015–present

7
Provinces and Elections

**Explanatory Note on Iranian Provinces
after the Revolution**[1]

In 1937, Iran was divided into six provinces; a few months later, in February 1938 it was further divided into ten provinces. At the time of the February 1979 revolution, Iran had twenty-four provinces. After the revolution the following seven provinces were formed:

Jul. 1, 1992   The name of Bakhtaran Province was changed back to Kermanshah Province after 149 MPs requested the name change. The Majlis approved this change on April 7, 1993.

Apr. 11, 1993   The Majlis approved the formation of Ardabil as an independent province by incorporating the eastern part of East Azerbaijan Province and the northern part of Gilan Province. Ardabil became its capital city.

Apr. 23, 1996   Final permission was granted for the formation of Qom as an independent province with Qom as its capital city. This new province was carved out of Markazi Province.

May 25, 1997   Qazvin was separated from Zanjan Province and became an independent province. Such cities as Qazvin and Takestan became parts of Qazvin Province.

Dec. 7, 1997   The Majlis approved the formation of Golestan Province with Gorgan as its capital city. It was split off from Mazandaran Province.

May 29, 2004   The GC approved a Majlis resolution to divide the huge province of Khorasan into three smaller independent provinces: Razavi Khorasan (with Mashhad as capital city), North Khorasan (with Bojnurd as capital city), and South Khorasan (with Birjand as capital city).[2]

Aug. 12, 2010   The government officially announced the formation of Alborz Province as an independent province with Karaj as its capital city.[3]

As such, as of the beginning of 2017, Iran has thirty-one provinces.

---

1. Data collected from Ahmadipur (1999), Hashemi-Rafsanjani (2015, 210), and the Statistical Center of Iran (2013–14, 2014–15, 2015–16).

2. http://rc.majlis.ir/fa.

3. http://www.farsnews.com.

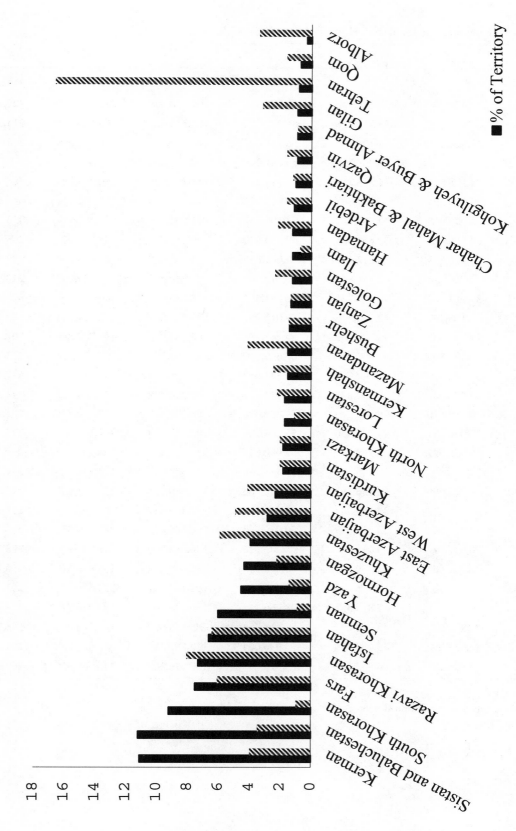

9. Provinces by Territorial Size and Population Percentage in 2016. Source: Statistical Yearbook of Iran 2015–16.

Province

Percentage

■ % of Territory

▨ % of Population

Table 28
Gross Income for Urban Households in Various Provinces (in rials)

Province	2001	2003	2005	2009	2013	2014
Alborz	*	*		*	277,796,495	327,996,692
Ardabil	24,656,633	37,411,502	58,931,245	94,478,188	244,096,097	229,395,839
Bushehr	30,442,102	53,513,286	81,283,534	133,324,628	263,645,585	314,846,640
Chahar Mahal and Bakhtiari	27,994,814	44,103,993	68,817,602	126,722,955	286,158,200	320,876,597
East Azerbaijan	24,730,531	30,955,563	49,841,201	110,556,202	331,675,025	272,592,089
Fars	34,176,838	44,378,338	71,714,216	114,820,568	266,394,398	306,428,531
Gilan	30,588,291	51,620,088	67,042,177	113,466,056	250,081,914	304,500,396
Golestan	31,031,418	44,488,361	53,497,287	111,754,919	223,696,017	235,244,152
Hamadan	18,546,815	38,653,433	49,454,500	95,157,722	208,837,002	266,570,567
Hormozgan	31,252,599	34,812,940	52,041,030	89,961,890	185,819,004	239,006,333
Ilam	Missing	47,848,842	62,014,641	94,249,299	213,529,393	240,969,913
Isfahan	30,927,172	48,390,743	62,801,584	128,896,062	300,387,505	325,264,921
Kerman	28,178,067	42,393,772	59,019,087	113,572,081	248,153,911	302,188,091
Kermanshah	22,802,558	35,808,280	49,165,738	88,784,963	195,747,890	207,394,228
Khuzestan	40,597,803	47,257,516	66,699,219	113,805,711	252,751,715	272,716,389
Kohgiluyeh and Buyer Ahmad	35,533,793	41,449,795	65,332,653	122,006,302	283,151,713	317,059,040
Kurdistan	19,676,625	29,092,225	55,032,251	102,224,279	231,109,462	241,006,294
Lorestan	26,114,616	36,433,213	54,888,808	88,750,623	172,736,814	185,917,789
Markazi	32,055,191	44,480,556	53,158,127	103,147,359	235,181,361	278,510,492
Mazandaran	29,640,077	42,237,450	71,990,653	121,229,733	258,106,897	293,208,099
North Khorasan	*	*	44,481,297	77,334,376	186,649,713	234,449,457
Qazvin	34,711,900	53,956,397	71,260,664	102,619,294	272,448,835	317,200,744
Qom	*	33,290,248	51,011,164	92,330,087	204,568,094	239,309,650
Razavi Khorasan	25,017,881	32,731,959	50,039,995	96,298,826	217,899,854	244,301,449
Semnan	30,627,927	40,131,636	78,283,726	100,367,040	226,055,536	298,799,404
Sistan and Baluchestan	22,096,881	25,889,594	46,439,434	82,047,029	155,483,628	175,264,038
South Khorasan	*	*	58,661,995	100,164,421	234,523,354	287,431,756
Tehran	42,698,659	65,815,377	88,966,143	179,239,263	403,056,795	475,860,830
West Azerbaijan	22,771,479	33,718,537	58,418,384	95,453,629	206,013,985	254,177,372
Yazd	23,539,992	36,053,265	56,996,004	112,892,389	236,506,976	291,841,649
Zanjan	Missing	40,541,658	60,926,707	107,796,489	225,909,026	269,939,856

Source: Central Bank of Iran: http://www.cbi.ir/simplelist/1600.aspx.
Note: An asterisk (*) means that the province was not yet formed at that time.

Table 29
Data on Thirty-Six Elections (1979–2017)

Elections	Year	Eligible voters	Actual voters	Voter turnout (%)	No. of candidates registered	No. of final candidates who competed	No. of seats contested	Candidates who competed (%)
Referendum on the Islamic Republic	1979	20,857,391	20,440,108	98%	–	–	–	–
Assembly for Final Examination of Constitution	1979	20,857,391	10,784,932	51.7%	428	428	73	100%
Referendum approving the constitution	1979	20,857,391	15,690,142	75.2%	–	–	–	–
First presidential election	1980	20,993,643	14,152,907	67.4%	124	106	1	85.4%
First Majlis election	1980	20,857,391	10,875,969	52.1%	3,694	1,910	270	51.70%
Second presidential election	1981	22,687,017	14,572,493	64.2%	71	4	1	5.63%
Third presidential election	1981	22,687,017	16,847,715	74.3%	46	5	1	10.9%
First Assembly of Experts election	1982	23,277,871	18,013,061	77.4%	168	146	83	86.9%
Second Majlis election	1984	24,143,498	15,607,306	64.6%	1,592	1,231	270	77.32%
Fourth presidential election	1985	25,993,802	14,238,587	54.8%	50	3	1	6.0%
Third Majlis election	1988	27,986,736	16,714,281	59.7%	1,999	1,417	270	70.88%
Fifth presidential election	1989	30,139,598	16,452,562	54.6%	79	2	1	2.53%
Referendum amending the constitution	1989	30,139,598	16,428,976	54.5%	–	–	–	–
Second Assembly of Experts election	1990	31,280,084	11,602,613	37.1%	180	106	83	58.9%
Fourth Majlis election	1992	32,465,558	18,767,042	57.8%	3,233	2,741	270	84.78%
Sixth presidential election	1993	33,156,055	16,796,755	50.7%	128	4	1	3.12%
Fifth Majlis election	1996	34,716,000	24,682,386	71.1%	8,365	6,954	270	83.13%
Seventh presidential election	1997	36,466,487	29,145,745	79.9%	238	4	1	1.68%
Third Assembly of Experts election	1998	38,570,597	17,857,869	46.3%	396	146	86	36.9%
First municipal council elections	1999	36,739,982	23,668,739	64.4%	336,138	–	–	–
Sixth Majlis election	2000	38,726,431	26,082,157	67.3%	6,853	5,742	290	83.78%
Eighth presidential election	2001	42,170,230	28,155,969	66.8%	814	10	1	1.23%
Second municipal council elections	2003	40,501,783	20,235,898	49.9%	218,957	–	109,588	–
Seventh Majlis election	2004	46,351,032	23,734,677	51.21%	8,172	5,450	290	66.69%

Table 29 (Cont.)
Data on Thirty-Six Elections (1979–2017)

Elections	Year	Eligible voters	Actual voters	Voter turnout (%)	No. of candidates registered	No. of final candidates who competed	No. of seats contested	Candidates who competed (%)
Ninth presidential election (first round)	2005	46,786,418	29,400,857	62.8%	1,014	8	1	0.79%
Ninth presidential election (second round)	2005	46,786,418	27,958,931	59.8%	2	2	1	100%
Fourth Assembly of Experts election	2006	46,549,042	28,321,270	60.8%	493	167	86	33.9%
Third municipal council elections	2006	43,500,000	28,199,903	64.8%	247,759	–	109,536	–
Eighth Majlis election	2008	43,824,254	24,279,717	55.4%	7,600	4,476	290	58.89%
Tenth presidential election	2009	46,199,997	39,371,214	85.2%	475	4	1	0.84%
Ninth Majlis election	2012	48,288,799	30,844,462	63.8%	5,283	3,323	290	69.04%
Eleventh presidential election	2013	50,483,192	36,821,538	72.9%	686	8	1	1.1%
Fourth municipal council elections	2013	50,483,192	31,627,704	62.6%	259,664		126,153	
Tenth Majlis election	2016	54,915,024	33,847,117	61.6%	12,072	4,844	290	40.1%
Fifth Assembly of Experts election	2016	54,915,024	33,480,548	61.0%	801	161	88	20.1%
Twelfth presidential election	2017	56,410,234	41,366,085	73.3%	1,636	6	1	0.36%

Source: Ministry of Interior (http://www.moi.ir).
Note: More information has been provided for each of these elections separately in chapters 8, 10, 11, and 12.

Table 30
Official Voting Age in Postrevolutionary Elections

Election	Election date	Voting age
Referendum approving the Islamic Republic	Mar. 30–31, 1979	16[a]
Assembly for the Final Examination of the Constitution	Aug. 3, 1979	16[b]
Approving the constitution	Dec. 2–3, 1979	16[c]
First presidential	Jan. 25, 1980	16[d]
First Majlis	Mar. 14, 1980	16
Second presidential	July 24, 1981	15[e]
Third presidential	Oct. 2, 1981	15
First Assembly of Experts	Dec. 10, 1982	15
Second Majlis	Apr. 15, 1984	15
Fourth presidential	Aug. 16, 1985	15
Third Majlis	Apr. 8, 1988	15
Fifth presidential and referendum on amending the constitution	July 28, 1989	15
Second Assembly of Experts	Oct. 8, 1990	15
Fourth Majlis	Apr. 10, 1992	15
Sixth presidential	June 11, 1993	15
Fifth Majlis	Mar. 8, 1996	15
Seventh presidential	May 23, 1997	15
Third Assembly of Experts	Oct. 23, 1998	15
First municipal	Feb. 26, 1999	15
Sixth Majlis	Feb. 18, 2000	16[f]
Eighth presidential	June 8, 2001	15[g]
Second municipal	Feb. 28, 2003	15
Seventh Majlis	Feb. 20, 2004	15
Ninth presidential	June 17, 2005	15
Fourth Assembly of Experts and third municipal	Dec. 15, 2006	15
Eighth Majlis	Mar. 14, 2008	18[h]
Tenth presidential	June 12, 2009	18[i]
Ninth Majlis	Mar. 2, 2012	18
Eleventh presidential and fourth municipal	June 14, 2013	18
Tenth Majlis and Fifth Assembly of Experts	Feb. 26, 2016	18

Note: With thanks to Anoosheh Modarresi for sharing some of her research in her forthcoming doctoral dissertation at the University of Oxford, entitled "Childhood and Politics in Post-Revolution Iran (A Case Study of High School Students)."

[a] On March 18, 1979, the Revolutionary Council set the voting age at sixteen years old. See http://rc.majlis.ir.

[b] http://rc.majlis.ir.

[c] http://rc.majlis.ir.

[d] On December 19, 1979, the Revolutionary Council again confirmed sixteen full years as the voting age. See http://rc.majlis.ir.

[e] On July 6, 1981, the Majlis approved lowering the voting age from sixteen full years to fifteen full years. See http://rc.majlis.ir.

[f] On December 15, 1999, the Majlis raised the voting age from fifteen full years to sixteen full years. See http://ical.ir.

[g] On November 15, 2000, the Majlis once again approved lowering the voting age from sixteen full years to fifteen full years. Ibid.

[h] On January 2, 2007, the Majlis raised the voting age from fifteen full years to eighteen full years. See http://www.shora-gc.ir. In 2008, President Ahmadinejad submitted a bill to the Majlis to lower the voting age for Majlis elections from eighteen full years to fifteen full years but it was not approved by the MPs. See http://rc.majlis.ir.

[i] President Ahmadinejad submitted another bill to the Majlis on April 22, 2009, to lower the voting age from eighteen full years to fifteen full years but it was not approved.

Table 31
Election Data for the Assembly for the Final Examination of the Constitution (AFEC)

Date of election	Aug. 3, 1979
Number of eligible voters	20,857,391
Number of actual voters	10,784,932
Voter turnout rate	51.71%
Number of precincts	24
Number of candidates needed	73
Number of registered entrants	428
Number of entrants positively vetted	428
Percentage of candidates positively vetted	No one was disqualified from running, but Abdolrahman Qasemlou, leader of the Democratic Party of Iranian Kurdistan, was prevented from occupying his seat.

Source: http://www.moi.ir.

Referendums

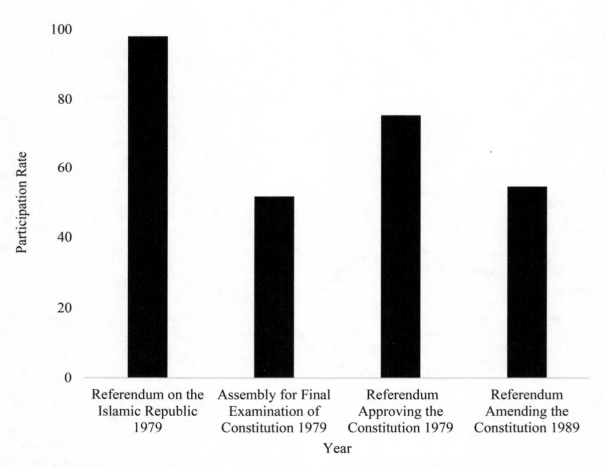

10. Average Voter Participation Rate in Three Referendums and AFEC Election. Source: Ministry of Interior (http://www.moi.ir/portal/File/ShowFile.aspx?ID=30759931-94c9-487d-9368-6426279490c8).

Table 32
Voter Turnout Rate in Presidential, Majlis, and Assembly of Experts Elections

Election	Majlis	Presidential	AE
First	52.1%	67.4%	77.4%
Second	64.6%	64.2%	37.1%
Third	59.7%	74.3%	46.3%
Fourth	57.8%	54.8%	60.8%
Fifth	71.1%	54.6%	61.0%
Sixth	67.3%	50.7%	
Seventh	51.2%	79.9%	
Eighth	55.4%	66.8%	
Ninth	63.8%	62.8%	
Tenth	61.6%	85.2%	
Eleventh		72.9%	
Twelfth		73.3%	

Source: Data from the Ministry of Interior including at http://www.moi.ir.

8

Presidency

Table 33
Presidents

Name	Province of birth	Lifespan	Age when first occupying office	Tenure
Seyyed Abolhasan Banisadr	Hamadan	1933–	47	Feb. 4, 1980–June 21, 1981[a]
Mohammad-Ali Raja'i	Qazvin	1933–81	48	Aug. 2–30, 1981
Seyyed Ali Khamenei	Razavi Khorasan	1939–	42	Oct. 13, 1981–Aug. 16, 1989
Akbar Hashemi-Rafsanjani	Kerman	1934–2017	55	Aug. 17, 1989–Aug. 2, 1997
Seyyed Mohammad Khatami	Yazd	1943–	54	Aug. 3, 1997–Aug. 2, 2005
Mahmoud Ahmadinejad	Semnan	1956–	49	Aug. 3, 2005–Aug. 2, 2013
Hassan Rouhani	Semnan	1948–	65	Aug. 3, 2013–2021

[a] Between the time President Banisadr was dismissed and President Raja'i took over, a three-member Presidential Council made up of Ayatollah Beheshti, HI Hashemi-Rafsanjani, and Mohammad-Ali Raja'i was in charge.

Table 34
Data on the 1980 Presidential Election

Date of election	Jan. 25, 1980[a]	
Number of eligible voters	20,993,643	
Number of actual voters	14,152,907	
Voter turnout rate	67.4%	
Number of registered entrants	124	
Number of entrants positively vetted	106	
Percentage of entrants positively vetted	85.4%	
Final number of entrants who stood for election	96[b]	
Number of female candidates	0	
Election winner	Seyyed Abolhasan Banisadr	
Winner's number and percentage of vote received	10,709,330	75.6%
First runner-up	Seyyed Ahmad Madani	
First runner-up number and percentage of vote received	2,224,554	15.71%

Table 34 (Cont.)
Data on the 1980 Presidential Election

Margin of victory by the winner	59.9%		
Names and votes of other top candidates	Hasan-Ebrahim Habibi	474,859	3.35%
	Daryush Foruhar	133,478	0.94%
	Seyyed Sadeq Tabataba'i	114,776	0.81%
	Kazem Sami	89,270	0.63%
	Sadeq Qotbzadeh	48,547	0.34%

[a] All data on election date, number of eligible and actual voters, voter turnout rate, and number of registered candidates for the first through eleventh presidential elections have been taken from the Ministry of Interior (http://www.moi.ir). Data on each candidate's share of votes is based on statistics published by the Ministry of Interior (http://www.moi.ir) as well as such media outlets as http://www.farsnews.com and http://www.bbc.co.uk/persian.

[b] Of the 124 entrants who registered to compete, eighteen were disqualified and ten dropped out of the race. Therefore, ninety-six candidates stood for election on the day of voting. Two important candidates, Mas'ud Rajavi and Jalaleddin Farsi, did not end up competing. Rajavi was disqualified for not having voted in the referendum for the constitution, while Farsi dropped out after it was revealed that he was not born in Iran.

Table 35
Breakdown of Votes Based on Province in the 1980 Presidential Election

Province	Total votes cast	NUMBER AND PERCENTAGE OF TOTAL VOTES[a]		
		Banisadr	Madani	Habibi
Bushehr	157,538	144,637 (91.81%)	7,951 (5.05%)	2,353 (1.49%)
Chahar Mahal and Bakhtiari	135,709	100,210 (73.84%)	28,762 (21.19%)	4,381 (3.23%)
East Azerbaijan	985,315	734,589 (74.55%)	148,844 (15.11%)	73,893 (7.5%)
Fars	931,244	779,229 (83.68%)	114,596 (12.31%)	20,352 (2.19%)
Gilan	580,436	492,746 (84.89%)	41,756 (7.19%)	13,340 (2.3%)
Hamadan	496,252	452,525 (91.19%)	29,359 (5.92%)	5,081 (1.02%)
Hormozgan	179,763	87,293 (48.56%)	69,711 (38.78%)	19,259 (10.71%)
Ilam	97,202	85,218 (87.67%)	9,127 (9.39%)	1,196 (1.23%)
Kerman	452,511	129,424 (28.60%)	301,862 (66.71%)	18,338 (4.05%)
Isfahan	1,110,801	900,909 (81.10%)	137,999 (12.42%)	39,687 (3.57%)
Kermanshah	337,591	256,067 (75.85%)	34,427 (10.20%)	17,552 (5.2%)

[a] The numbers of votes for the top three candidates are listed.

Table 35 (Cont.)
Breakdown of Votes Based on Province in the 1980 Presidential Election

Province	Total votes cast	NUMBER AND PERCENTAGE OF TOTAL VOTES[a]		
		Banisadr	Madani	Habibi
Khorasan	1,369,640	995,088 (72.65%)	170,694 (12.46%)	158,143 (11.55%)
Khuzestan	920,768	760,572 (82.60%)	120,688 (13.11%)	18,058 (1.96%)
Kohgiluyeh and Buyer Ahmad	96,516	88,029 (91.21%)	6,301 (6.53%)	1,240 (1.28%)
Kurdistan	59,100	46,522 (78.72%)	10,027 (16.97%)	1,210 (2.05%)
Lorestan	388,461	304,908 (78.49%)	19,545 (5.03%)	51,316 (13.21%)
Markazi	537,732	449,090 (83.52%)	45,877 (8.53%)	26,227 (4.88%)
Mazandaran	938,280	814,724 (86.83%)	46,530 (4.96%)	47,051 (5.01%)
Semnan	151,213	127,286 (84.18%)	12,991 (8.59%)	8,052 (5.32%)
Sistan and Baluchestan	143,249	43,075 (30.07%)	94,397 (65.90%)	4,438 (3.1%)
Tehran	3,003,539	2,154,986 (71.75%)	597,120 (19.88%)	97,754 (3.25%)
West Azerbaijan	335,569	206,823 (61.63%)	98,020 (29.21%)	15,876 (4.73%)
Yazd	188,092	135,910 (72.26%)	32,755 (17.41%)	15,915 (8.46%)
Zanjan	488,722	419,470 (85.83%)	45,215 (9.25%)	14,147 (2.89%)
Total votes	14,146,622[b]	10,709,330 (75.70%)	2,224,554 (15.72%)	674,859 (4.77%)

Source: *Ettela'at*, 1358/1980. "Banisadr Ba 10 Million va 709 Hezar Ray Ra'is-e Jomhur Shod [Banisadr Became President with 10,709,000 Votes]," 9 Bahman 1358/January 29, 1980. The total number of votes in each province is provided by the Statistical Center of Iran (2015–16), 911.
[b] The total number of votes includes votes cast outside Iran. Invalid votes are not included.

Table 36
Data on the First 1981 Presidential Election

Date of election	July 24, 1981		
Number of eligible voters	22,687,017		
Number of actual voters	14,572,493		
Voter turnout rate	64.2%		
Number of registered entrants	71		
Number of entrants positively vetted	4[a]		
Percentage of entrants positively vetted	5.6%		
Election winner	Mohammad-Ali Raja'i		
Winner's number and percentage of votes received	12,770,050	87.6%	
First runner-up	Abbas Sheybani		
First runner-up's number and percentage of votes received	658,498	4.5%	
Margin of victory by the winner	83.1%		
Names and votes of other candidates	Seyyed Ali-Akbar Parvaresh	339,646	2.3%
	Habibollah Asgarowladi	249,457	1.7%

[a] Beginning with this election, the Guardian Council started to disqualify candidates.

Table 37
Data on the Second 1981 Presidential Election

Date of election	Oct. 2, 1981[a]		
Number of eligible voters	22,687,017		
Number of actual voters	16,847,715		
Voter turnout rate	74.3%		
Number of registered entrants	46		
Number of entrants positively vetted	5[b]		
Percentage of entrants positively vetted	10.9%		
Election winner	Seyyed Ali Khamenei		
Winner's number and percentage of votes received	16,008,579	95.05%	
First runner-up	Seyyed Ali-Akbar Parvaresh		
First runner-up's number and percentage of vote received	341,874	2.03%	
Margin of victory by the winner	93.02%		
Names and votes of other candidates	Seyyed Reza Zavareh'i	59,058	0.36%
	Hasan Ghafurifard	80,545	0.27%
Nullified Votes	356,411		

[a] A second presidential election was held in 1981 after the sitting president (Raja'i) was assassinated.

[b] Despite being approved to stand for elections, Mohammad-Reza Mahdavi-Kani quit the race in favor of Seyyed Ali Khamenei three days before Election Day.

Table 38
Data on the 1985 Presidential Election

Date of election	Aug. 16, 1985		
Number of eligible voters	25,993,802		
Number of actual voters	14,238,587		
Voter turnout rate	54.8%		
Number of registered entrants	50		
Number of entrants positively vetted	3		
Percentage of entrants positively vetted	6.0%		
Void ballots	355,047[a]		
Election winner	Seyyed Ali Khamenei		
Winner's number and percentage of votes received	12,205,012	85%	
First runner-up	Seyyed Mahmud Kashani[b]		
First runner-up's number and percentage of votes received	1,402,953	9.85%	
Margin of victory by the winner	75.2%		
Names and votes of other candidates	Habibollah Asgarowladi	278,113	1.95%

[a]*Ettela'at*. 1364/1985. "Natayej-e Qat'i-ye Shomaresh-e Aray-e Entekhabat-e Riyasat-e Jomhuri [Final Vote Count of the Presidential Election]," 29 Mordad 1364/August 20, 1985.
[b] BBC Persian Service puts Kashani's votes at 1,397,548, Asgarowladi's at 276,502, and Khamenei's at over 12 million. See http://www.bbc.co.uk/persian.

Table 39
Breakdown of Votes Based on Province in the 1985 Presidential Election

		NUMBER AND PERCENTAGE OF TOTAL VOTES		
Province	Total votes cast	Khamenei	Kashani	Asgarowladi
Bushehr	184,522	168,841 (91.5%)	8,262 (4.48%)	3,359 (1.82%)
Chahar Mahal and Bakhtiari	183,946	164,983 (89.69%)	12,681 (6.89%)	3,188 (1.73%)
East Azerbaijan	1,053,443	937,188 (88.96%)	69,376 (6.59%)	39,158 (3.72%)
Fars	903,592	805,723 (89.17%)	60,724 (6.72%)	17,058 (1.89%)
Gilan	515,050	448,022 (86.99%)	42,884 (8.33%)	12,284 (2.39%)
Hamadan	468,958	429,863 (91.66%)	20,834 (4.44%)	7,404 (1.58%)
Hormozgan	171,913	143,243 (83.32%)	21,666 (12.6%)	4,230 (2.46%)
Ilam	131,376	118,957 (90.55%)	9,601 (7.31%)	3,379 (2.57%)

Table 39 (Cont.)
Breakdown of Votes Based on Province in the 1985 Presidential Election

Province	Total votes cast	NUMBER AND PERCENTAGE OF TOTAL VOTES		
		Khamenei	Kashani	Asgarowladi
Kerman	449,630	375,257 (83.46%)	63,081 (14.03%)	4,635 (1.03%)
Isfahan	993,193	821,393 (82.7%)	130,817 (13.17%)	10,778 (1.09%)
Kermanshah	350,187	298,734 (85.31%)	28,539 (8.15%)	11,154 (3.19%)
Khorasan	1,489,301	1,331,912 (89.43%)	112,757 (7.57%)	18,105 (1.22%)
Khuzestan	770,976	664,611 (86.2%)	71,179 (9.23%)	13,303 (1.73%)
Kohgiluyeh and Buyer Ahmad	126,656	118,050 (93.21%)	6,153 (4.86%)	2,453 (1.9%)
Kurdistan	280,451	204,117 (72.78%)	40,841 (14.56%)	20,963 (7.47%)
Lorestan	458,737	429,101 (93.54%)	20,359 (4.44%)	4,846 (1.06%)
Markazi	553,314	494,892 (89.44%)	39,577 (7.15%)	6,999 (1.26%)
Mazandaran	990,825	880,706 (88.89%)	75,976 (7.67%)	16,918 (1.71%)
Semnan	162,058	144,025 (88.87%)	11,036 (6.81%)	2,640 (1.63%)
Sistan and Baluchestan	175,967	133,442 (75.83%)	34,142 (19.4%)	5,098 (2.9%)
Tehran	2,425,229	1,900,484 (78.36%)	383,855 (15.83%)	48,582 (2%)
West Azerbaijan	552,424	437,783 (79.25%)	68,731 (12.44%)	26,421 (4.78%)
Yazd	201,205	167,378 (83.19%)	29,708 (14.77%)	1,072 (0.53%)
Zanjan	499,908	448,760 (89.77%)	34,187 (6.84%)	7,952 (1.59%)
Total votes	14,244,630[a]	12,203,870 (85.67%)	1,402,416 (9.84%)	283,297 (1.99%)

Source: *Ettela'at*. 1364/1985. "Natayej-e Qat'i-ye Shomaresh-e Aray-e Entekhabat-e Riyasat-e Jomhuri [Final Vote Count of the Presidential Election]," 29 Mordad 1364/August 20, 1985.

[a] The total number of votes includes votes cast outside Iran. When the total votes cast from all provinces for each candidate (e.g., Asgarowladi) varied from officially announced total votes for that candidate, we went with the latter.

Table 40
Data on the 1989 Presidential Election

Date of election	July 28, 1989	
Number of eligible voters	30,139,598	
Number of actual voters	16,452,562	
Voter turnout rate	54.6%	
Number of registered entrants	79	
Number of entrants positively vetted	2	
Percentage of entrants positively vetted	2.5%	
Election winner	Akbar Hashemi-Rafsanjani	
Winner's number and percentage of votes received	15,550,528	94%
First runner-up	Abbas Sheybani	
First runner-up's number and percentage of votes received	635,165	3.86%
Margin of victory by the winner	90.1%	
Names and votes of other candidates	NA	

Table 41
Data on the 1993 Presidential Election

Date of election	June 11, 1993		
Number of eligible voters	33,156,055		
Number of actual voters	16,796,755		
Voter turnout rate	50.7%		
Number of registered entrants	128		
Number of entrants positively vetted	4		
Percentage of entrants positively vetted	3.1%		
Election winner	Akbar Hashemi-Rafsanjani		
Winner's number and percentage of votes received	10,566,499	63%	
First runner-up	Ahmad Tavakkoli		
First runner-up's number and percentage of votes received	4,026,879	23.97%	
Margin of victory by the winner	39.0%		
Names and votes of other candidates	Rajab-Ali Taheri	387,655[a]	2.31%
	Abdollah Jasbi	1,498,084	8.92%

[a] BBC Persian Service puts Taheri's votes at 114,776 and Jasbi's at 89,280. See http://www.bbc.co.uk/persian.

Table 42
Data on the 1997 Presidential Election

Date of election	May 23, 1997
Number of eligible voters	36,466,487
Number of actual voters	29,145,745
Void ballots	240,966[a]
Voter turnout rate	79.9%
Number of registered entrants	238
Number of entrants positively vetted	4
Percentage of entrants positively vetted	1.68%
Election winner	Seyyed Mohammad Khatami[b]
Winner's number and percentage of votes received	20,138,784[c] 69.1%
First runner-up	Ali-Akbar Nateq-Nuri
First runner-up number and percentage of votes received	7,248,317 24.87%
Margin of victory by the winner	44.2%
Names and votes of other candidates	Seyyed Reza Zavareh'i 772,707 2.65%
	Mohammad Reyshahri 744,205 2.55%

[a] *Ettela'at*. 1376/1997. "Doktor Seyyed Mohammad Khatami Ba Beysh Az 20 Million Ray Ra'is-e Jomhur Iran Shod [Dr. Seyyed Mohammad Khatami Became Iran's President with Over 20 Million Votes]," 4 Khordad 1376/May 25, 1997.

[b] For an analysis of Khatami's win, see Boroujerdi (1997).

[c] Other sources put Khatami's and Nateq-Nuri's votes at 20,088,338 and 7,233,568, respectively. See http://www.bbc.co.uk/persian.

Table 43
Breakdown of Votes Based on Province in the 1997 Presidential Election

Province	Total votes cast	NUMBER AND PERCENTAGE OF TOTAL VOTES			
		Khatami	Zavareh'i	Reyshahri	Nateq-Nuri
Ardabil	484,199	350,491 (72.39%)	16,830 (3.48%)	12,242 (2.53%)	101,997 (21.07%)
Bushehr	356,449	298,427 (83.72%)	3,892 (1.09%)	6,333 (1.78%)	45,826 (12.86%)
Chahar Mahal and Bakhtiari	373,286	223,099 (59.77%)	9,026 (2.42%)	12,462 (3.34%)	125,450 (33.61%)
East Azerbaijan	1,448,334	939,138 (64.84%)	107,105 (7.40%)	52,423 (3.62%)	335,223 (23.15%)
Fars	1,830,828	1,472,031 (80.40%)	21,392 (1.17%)	27,740 (1.52%)	300,886 (16.43%)
Gilan	1,037,251	779,859 (75.19%)	32,516 (3.13%)	19,049 (1.84%)	196,309 (18.93%)
Hamadan	770,472	545,462 (70.80%)	25,423 (3.30%)	39,934 (5.18%)	153,024 (19.86%)
Hormozgan	503,096	402,427 (79.99%)	4,709 (0.94%)	2,325 (0.46%)	90,485 (17.99%)

Table 43 (Cont.)
Breakdown of Votes Based on Province in the 1997 Presidential Election

Province	Total votes cast	NUMBER AND PERCENTAGE OF TOTAL VOTES			
		Khatami	Zavareh'i	Reyshahri	Nateq-Nuri
Ilam	236,851	190,552 (80.45%)	3,409 (1.44%)	7,420 (3.13%)	34,471 (14.55%)
Kerman	992,457	621,809 (62.65%)	10,720 (1.08%)	8,262 (0.83%)	345,705 (34.83%)
Isfahan	1,929,227	1,350,679 (70.01%)	42,653 (2.21%)	29,708 (1.54%)	485,389 (25.16%)
Kermanshah	802,129	644,657 (80.37%)	27,148 (3.38%)	18,377 (2.29%)	103,557 (12.91%)
Khorasan	2,936,367	1,737,041 (59.16%)	93,373 (3.18%)	56,360 (1.92%)	1,032,486 (35.16%)
Khuzestan	1,559,354	1,290,248 (82.74%)	23,219 (1.49%)	33,196 (2.13%)	199,788 (12.81)
Kohgiluyeh and Buyer Ahmad	257,838	148,663 (57.66%)	1,929 (0.75%)	14,399 (5.58%)	91,495 (35.49%)
Kurdistan	617,351	432,569 (70.07%)	11,349 (1.84%)	5,615 (0.91%)	161,222 (26.12%)
Lorestan	974,529	433,136 (44.45%)	8,688 (0.89%)	15,012 (1.54%)	512,037 (52.54%)
Markazi	607,253	410,276 (67.56%)	22,270 (3.67%)	32,057 (5.28%)	136,809 (22.53%)
Mazandaran	2,019,890	882,903 (43.71%)	48,727 (2.41%)	31,544 (1.56%)	1,042,694 (51.62%)
Qom	424,231	249,363 (58.78%)	15,691 (3.70%)	15,033 (3.54%)	139,567 (32.90%)
Semnan	286,047	183,689 (64.22%)	8,200 (2.87%)	12,240 (4.28%)	79,629 (27.84%)
Sistan and Baluchestan	548,057	424,669 (77.49%)	6,910 (1.26%)	3,796 (0.69%)	109,225 (19.93%)
Tehran	6,044,962	4,575,139 (75.69%)	179,399 (2.97%)	245,763 (4.07%)	982,922 (16.26%)
West Azerbaijan	1,108,691	826,186 (74.52%)	32,764 (2.96%)	20,620 (1.84%)	217,335 (19.60%)
Yazd	423,374	359,812 (84.99%)	2,387 (0.56%)	6,125 (1.45%)	53,436 (12.62%)
Zanjan	504,416	316,017 (62.65%)	11,734 (2.33%)	14,564 (2.89%)	156,602 (31.05%)
Total votes	29,076,962[a]	20,088,338 (69.1%)	771,463 (2.7%)	742,599 (2.6%)	7,233,568 (24.9%)

Source: *Ettela'at*. 1376/1997. "Natayej-e Ara-ye Makhuzeh-e Entekhabat-e Riyasat-e Jomhuri Be Tafkik-e Ostanha [Breakdown of Votes Cast by Province in the Presidential Election]," 6 Khordad 1376/May 27, 1997.

[a] The total number of votes reported here is 68,783 fewer than the official figure of 29,145,745 that the Ministry of Interior subsequently reported. This difference is mainly due to the number of votes cast outside of Iran, which was 67,831 votes, according to *Ettela'at* (1376/1997).

Table 44
Data on the 2001 Presidential Election

Date of Election	June 8, 2001	
Number of eligible voters	42,170,230	
Number of actual voters	28,155,969	
Voter turnout rate	66.8%	
Number of registered entrants	814	
Number of entrants positively vetted	10	
Percentage of entrants positively vetted	1.23%	
Election winner	Seyyed Mohammad Khatami	
Winner's number and percentage of votes received	21,659,053[a]	77%
First runner-up	Ahmad Tavakkoli	
First runner-up's number and percentage of votes received	4,393,544	15.6%
Margin of victory by the winner	61.4%	
Names and votes of other candidates	Ali Shamkhani	737,962	2.62%
	Abdollah Jasbi	260,082	0.92%
	Seyyed Mahmud Mostafavi-Kashani	235,363	0.84%
	Hasan Ghafurifard	129,222	0.46%
	Mansur Razavi	114,327	0.41%
	Ali Fallahiyan	55,176	0.20%
	Seyyed Mostafa Hashemi-Taba	28,090	0.10%

[a] BBC Persian Service puts the total number of Khatami's votes at 21,651,521. See http://www.bbc.co.uk/persian.

Table 45
Breakdown of Votes Based on Province in the 2001 Presidential Election

Province	Total votes cast	NUMBER AND PERCENTAGE OF TOTAL VOTES[a] Khatami	Tavakkoli
Ardabil	467,859	382,660 (81.79%)	37,588 (8.03%)
Bushehr	365,099	310,721 (85.11%)	30,920 (8.47%)
Chahar Mahal and Bakhtiari	340,543	235,244 (69.08%)	81,894 (24.05%)
East Azerbaijan	1,294,682	1,020,178 (78.80%)	143,647 (11.10%)
Fars	1,837,556	1,562,362 (85.02%)	161,548 (8.79%)

[a]http://www.parsine.com.

Table 45 (Cont.)
Breakdown of Votes Based on Province in the 2001 Presidential Election

| | | NUMBER AND PERCENTAGE OF TOTAL VOTES[a] | |
Province	Total votes cast	Khatami	Tavakkoli
Gilan	1,097,403	911,499 (83.06%)	106,616 (9.72%)
Golestan	725,934	603,989 (83.20%)	92,095 (12.69%)
Hamadan	743,550	556,359 (74.83%)	129,456 (17.41%)
Hormozgan	530,336	465,544 (87.78%)	46,886 (8.84%)
Ilam	250,795	205,337 (81.87%)	32,052 (12.78%)
Kerman	998,371	717,125 (71.83%)	159,198 (15.95%)
Isfahan	1,735,814	1,197,596 (68.99%)	406,961 (23.45%)
Kermanshah	790,685	666,401 (84.28%)	77,655 (9.82%)
Khorasan	3,124,814	2,239,245 (71.66%)	725,846 (23.23%)
Khuzestan	1,474,820	1,154,652 (78.29%)	108,038 (7.23%)
Kohgiluyeh and Buyer Ahmad	270,417	177,292 (65.56%)	66,248 (24.50%)
Kurdistan	486,596	423,166 (86.97%)	280,72 (5.77%)
Lorestan	702,936	545,983 (77.67%)	121,881 (17.34%)
Markazi	565,018	432,263 (76.50%)	86,362 (15.29%)
Mazandaran	1,302,654	773,516 (59.38%)	448,436 (34.43%)
Qazvin	500,918	398,617 (79.58%)	71,315 (14.24%)
Qom	428,005	255,855 (59.78%)	142,620 (33.32%)
Semnan	285,964	200,242 (70.02%)	68,160 (23.84%)
Sistan and Baluchestan	702,444	638,981 (90.97%)	34,387 (4.90%)
Tehran	5,190,742	3,951,044 (76.12%)	801,721 (15.45%)

Table 45 (Cont.)
Breakdown of Votes Based on Province in the 2001 Presidential Election

		NUMBER AND PERCENTAGE OF TOTAL VOTES[a]	
Province	Total votes cast	Khatami	Tavakkoli
West Azerbaijan	974,181	816,568 (83.82%)	88,219 (9.06%)
Yazd	468,982	415,023 (88.50%)	39,878 (8.50%)
Zanjan	429,389	336,670 (78.41%)	52,491 (12.23%)
Total votes	28,086,507	21,594,132 (76.89%)	4,390,190 (15.63%)

Note: This table gives votes for the top two candidates only. It does not include votes cast by Iranians outside the country.

Table 46
Data on the 2005 Presidential Election (First Round)

Date of election	June 17, 2005	
Number of eligible voters	46,786,418	
Number of actual voters	29,400,857	
Voter turnout rate	62.84%	
Number of registered entrants	1014	
Number of entrants positively vetted	8[a]	
Percentage of entrants positively vetted	0.79%	
Election winner	Akbar Hashemi-Rafsanjani[b]	
Winner's number and percentage of votes received	6,179,653[c]	21.0%
First runner-up	Mahmoud Ahmadinejad	
First runner-up's number and percentage of votes received	5,710,354	19.4%
Margin of victory by the winner	1.6%	
Names and votes of other candidates	Mehdi Karrubi	5,056,686	17.2%
	Mohammad-Baqer Qalibaf	4,075,189	13.9%
	Mostafa Mo'in	4,069,699	13.8%
	Ali Larijani	1,716,081	5.8%
	Mohsen Mehr-Alizadeh	1,287,440	4.4%
Invalid votes	1,200,000	4.2%

[a] Mohsen Reza'i, who was approved by the Guardian Council, dropped out of the race a few days before Election Day.
[b] Because no candidate garnered the needed majority, there was a runoff election between the top two candidates.
[c] BBC Persian Service (http://www.bbc.co.uk/persian) puts Hashemi-Rafsanjani, Ahmadinejad, and Karrubi's votes respectively at 6,190,122, 5,718,129, and 5,073,800.

Table 47
Breakdown of Votes Based on Province in the 2005 Presidential Election (First Round)

Province	Rafsanjani	Ahmadinejad	Karrubi	Qalibaf	Mo'in	Larijani	Mehr-Alizadeh
Ardabil	95,490	34,090	53,906	106,272	67,134	7,766	111,465
Bushehr	97,412	82,376	98,148	46,962	68,547	8,207	4,942
Chahar Mahal and Bakhtiari	59,521	90,960	75,044	64,068	48,357	23,127	5,051
East Azerbaijan	268,954	198,417	121,969	122,160	190,211	28,075	378,604
Fars	403,074	242,535	546,633	273,542	217,122	61,383	22,440
Gilan	215,478	149,026	203,941	171,562	182,321	50,070	33,996
Golestan	155,498	56,776	193,570	87,522	156,862	42,334	8,283
Hamadan	175,997	195,030	218,018	72,986	84,424	24,002	20,496
Hormozgan	75,601	80,154	177,413	25,326	153,648	78,161	9,679
Ilam	40,580	32,383	108,627	41,082	56,526	6,783	3,026
Kerman	480,271	129,284	152,764	112,056	52,896	221,219	9,697
Isfahan	260,858	801,635	196,512	198,409	196,261	73,452	30,325
Kermanshah	137,010	70,117	254,780	115,439	106,804	22,033	12,516
Khuzestan	319,921	232,874	538,735	148,234	148,529	58,564	20,164
Kohgiluyeh and Buyer Ahmad	56,154	34,396	96,459	52,259	50,954	20,306	1,572
Kurdistan	54,004	22,353	111,249	48,913	92,884	7,785	10,261
Lorestan	121,130	69,710	440,247	70,225	53,747	31,169	6,865
Markazi	143,118	161,669	104,522	71,828	65,592	17,258	14,058
Mazandaran	311,949	159,291	103,229	116,763	148,408	464,891	18,467
North Khorasan	70,407	22,954	89,551	100,091	37,330	16,900	8,209
Qazvin	108,928	118,414	81,569	77,399	68,366	18,078	24,649
Qom	104,004	256,110	25,282	25,792	27,824	10,894	14,451
Razavi Khorasan	527,707	377,732	297,967	877,665	325,281	78,976	33,488
Semnan	69,773	98,024	25,899	37,059	26,572	20,190	3,873
Sistan and Baluchestan	155,147	47,743	77,017	68,605	479,125	24,954	7,312
South Khorasan	57,244	101,638	27,705	49,043	39,276	5,716	4,958
Tehran	1,274,276	1,500,829	415,187	614,381	648,598	246,167	281,748
West Azerbaijan	151,525	75,319	99,766	141,289	146,941	15,435	163,091
Yazd	77,924	175,206	58,132	66,892	60,510	9,317	5,186
Zanjan	110,698	93,309	62,845	71,365	68,649	22,869	18,568
Total votes	6,179,653	5,710,354	5,056,686	4,075,189	4,069,699	1,716,081	1,287,440

Note: The votes in each province are based on an Excel database that was published by the Ministry of Interior. The file is no longer on the ministry's website (www.moi.ir).

Table 48
Data on the 2005 Presidential Election (Runoff)

Date of election	June 24, 2005	
Number of eligible voters	46,786,418	
Number of actual voters	27,958,931	
Voter turnout rate	59.8%	
Number of registered entrants	2	
Number of entrants positively vetted	2	
Percentage of entrants positively vetted	100%	
Election winner	Mahmud Ahmadinejad	
Winner's number and percentage of votes received	17,248,782	61.7%
First runner-up	Akbar Hashemi-Rafsanjani	
First runner-up's number and percentage of votes received	9,210,853	38.3%
Margin of victory by the winner	23.4%	

Table 49
Breakdown of Votes Based on Province in the 2005 Presidential Election (Runoff)

Province	Hashemi-Rafsanjani	Ahmadinejad
Ardabil	154,591	280,266
Bushehr	161,654	215,750
Chahar Mahal and Bakhtiari	99,346	269,374
East Azerbaijan	364,110	837,660
Fars	706,898	998,693
Gilan	351,039	684,794
Golestan	294,626	356,619
Hamadan	209,295	533,476
Hormozgan	200,921	317,374
Ilam	113,838	127,258
Isfahan	300,693	300,693
Kerman	570,538	603,117
Kermanshah	332,692	343,319
Khuzestan	518,621	882,682
Kohgiluyeh and Buyer Ahmad	114,874	188,461
Kurdistan	109,170	127,808
Lorestan	350,650	364,790
Markazi	166,887	410,726
Mazandaran	461,207	888,878
North Khorasan[a]	85,976	176,396
Qazvin	128,610	367,874
Qom	120,586	352,019

Table 49 (Cont.)

Breakdown of Votes Based on Province in the 2005 Presidential Election (Runoff)

Province	Hashemi-Rafsanjani	Ahmadinejad
Razavi Khorasan	804,328	1,490,064
Semnan	78,167	214,059
Sistan and Baluchestan	407,063	332,316
South Khorasan	85,976	176,396
Tehran	1,390,839	2,174,734
West Azerbaijan	250,186	428,558
Yazd	144,906	311,654
Zanjan	132,566	294,155
Total Votes	9,210,853	15,457,573

Note: Most sources maintain that Ahmadinejad received 17,248,782 or 61.7 percent of the vote in the second round. The following table on the breakdown of votes by province puts his total at 15,457,573 (55.3 percent) and that of Hashemi-Rafsanjani at 9,210,853. This puts the total number of votes at 24,668,426, which is much lower than the number of total voters released by the Ministry of Interior.

[a] The identical votes for North Khorasan and South Khorasan show that this table has its problems. Alas, it is the only official breakdown of votes available to us.

Table 50

Data on the 2009 Presidential Election

Date of election	June 12, 2009		
Number of eligible voters	46,199,997		
Number of actual voters	39,371,214		
Voter turnout rate	85.2%		
Number of registered entrants	475		
Number of entrants positively vetted	4		
Percentage of entrants positively vetted	0.84%		
Election winner	Mahmud Ahmadinejad		
Winner's number and percentage of votes received	24,592,793	63.1%	
First runner-up	Mir Hoseyn Musavi		
First runner-up's number and percentage of votes received	13,338,121	34.2%	
Margin of victory by the winner	28.9%		
Names and votes of other candidates	Mohsen Reza'i	681,851	1.75%
	Mehdi Karrubi	338,278	0.87%
Invalid ballots	420,171		

Note: The announced election results led to serious complaints and urban unrest as Musavi and Karrubi accused the government of voter fraud. For a critical look at the election results, see Ansari (2009).

Table 51
Breakdown of Votes Based on Province in the 2009 Presidential Election

Province	Ahmadinejad	Reza'i	Karrubi	Musavi
Ardabil	325,911	6,578	2,319	302,825
Bushehr	299,357	7,608	3,563	177,268
Chahar Mahal and Bakhtiari	359,578	22,689	4,127	106,099
East Azerbaijan	1,131,111	16,920	7,246	837,858
Fars	1,758,026	23,871	16,277	706,764
Gilan	998,573	12,022	7,183	453,806
Golestan	525,311	5,987	10,097	325,806
Hamadan	765,723	13,117	12,033	218,481
Hormozgan	482,990	7,237	5,126	241,988
Ilam	199,654	5,221	7,471	96,826
Isfahan	1,799,255	51,788	14,579	746,697
Kerman	1,160,446	12,016	4,977	318,250
Kermanshah	573,568	11,258	10,798	374,188
Khuzestan	1,303,129	139,124	15,934	552,636
Kohgiluyeh and Buyer Ahmad	253,962	8,542	4,274	98,937
Kurdistan	315,689	7,140	13,862	261,772
Lorestan	677,829	14,920	44,036	219,156
Markazi	572,988	10,057	4,675	190,349
Mazandaran	1,289,257	19,587	10,050	585,373
North Khorasan	341,104	4,129	2,478	113,218
Qazvin	498,061	7,978	2,690	177,542
Qom	422,457	16,297	2,314	148,467
Razavi Khorasan	2,214,801	44,809	13,561	884,570
Semnan	295,177	4,440	2,147	77,754
Sistan and Baluchestan	450,269	6,616	12,504	507,946
South Khorasan	285,984	3,962	928	90,363
Tehran	3,819,495	147,487	67,334	3,371,523
West Azerbaijan	623,946	12,199	21,609	656,508
Yazd	337,178	8,406	2,565	255,799
Zanjan	444,480	7,276	2,223	126,561
Total votes	24,525,309	659,281	328,980	13,225,330

Note: The votes in each province are based on an Excel database that was published by the Ministry of Interior and accessed on June 16, 2009. The file is no longer on the ministry's website (www.moi.ir) but we have posted it at http://irandataportal.syr.edu. For number of eligible voters in each province on the eve of the vote, see http://www.tabnak.ir. The total does not include votes cast outside Iran by expatriates (approximately 632,314).

Table 52
Data on the 2013 Presidential Election

Date of election	June 14, 2013[a]	
Number of eligible voters	50,483,192[b]	
Number of actual voters	36,821,538	
Invalid ballots	1,247,327	
Number of accurate votes	35,574,211[c]	
Voter turnout rate	72.9%	
Number of registered entrants	686 (656 males, 30 females)[d]	
Number of entrants positively vetted	8	
Percentage of entrants positively vetted	1.1%	
Election winner	Hassan Rouhani	
Winner's number and percentage of votes received	18,692,500	50.60%
First runner-up	Mohammad-Baqer Qalibaf	
First runner-up's number and percentage of votes received	6,077,292 (16.5%)	
Margin of victory by the winner	34.1%	
Names and votes of other candidates	Sa'id Jalili	4,168,946 (11.28%)
	Mohsen Reza'i	3,884,412 (10.51%)
	Ali-Akbar Velayati	2,268,753 (6.14%)
	Seyyed Mohammad Gharazi	446,015 (1.20%)

[a] The total number of eligible first-time voters in this election was 1,631,206. 125,000 ballot boxes in 60,000 branches were collected inside the country and 290 branches outside Iran.
[b] For the number of eligible voters in each province, see *Mehrnameh* (1392/2013), 109.
[c] https://www.moi.ir.
[d] http://www.mehrnews.com.

Table 53
Breakdown of Votes Based on Province in the 2013 Presidential Election

Province	Rouhani	Qalibaf	Reza'i	Jalili	Velayati	Gharazi
Alborz	519,412	213,904	84,633	105,372	77,288	12,226
Ardabil	384,751	98,298	59,524	44,441	40,531	8,367
Bushehr	278,763	64,881	74,220	54,960	38,499	6,711
Chahar Mahal and Bakhtiari	155,884	43,201	211,101	38,600	21,693	4,034
East Azerbaijan	1,052,345	187,444	202,175	187,227	164,179	25,082
Fars	1,292,943	247,642	211,801	309,929	135,425	23,343
Gilan	784,789	213,424	86,923	149,876	85,156	18,516
Golestan	548,069	158,947	46,100	78,192	74,633	10,401
Hamadan	451,810	139,865	80,340	138,414	69,770	11,378
Hormozgan	414,444	99,277	64,270	122,954	48,743	11,356
Ilam	175,608	35,586	58,182	22,976	15,104	3,889
Isfahan	1,017,516	259,601	270,799	411,098	203,679	59,106
Kerman	855,463	222,800	69,316	215,872	64,247	14,237
Kermanshah	567,784	162,062	108,186	64,597	41,348	9,017
Khuzestan	675,495	117,977	921,570	169,446	78,488	15,251
Kohgiluyeh and Buyer Ahmad	126,395	17,489	142,040	24,138	11,510	1,487
Kurdistan	438,290	75,548	49,695	30,195	17,843	7,048
Lorestan	402,655	99,022	236,451	63,316	40,908	6,596
Markazi	323,631	137,195	65,495	93,343	75,318	9,409
Mazandaran	1,107,494	286,464	94,178	180,772	161,873	20,742
North Khorasan	226,144	157,800	18,870	52,802	17,924	5,684
Qazvin	324,739	111,604	45,884	90,573	47,174	8,108
Qom	201,677	89,987	30,540	121,237	68,356	9,346
Razavi Khorasan	1,300,617	967,432	108,075	406,124	140,142	34,433
Semnan	157,133	87,598	14,541	55,987	26,500	5,051
Sistan and Baluchestan	770,394	109,390	61,986	64,339	36,122	8,785
South Khorasan	192,446	101,713	14,582	103,382	15,185	5,052
Tehran	2,385,890	1,266,568	336,557	550,348	316,592	61,893
West Azerbaijan	885,693	151,508	105,658	93,787	67,874	15,548
Yazd	351,527	52,911	19,793	62,232	27,468	5,137
Zanjan	281,867	106,415	49,654	70,797	42,550	9,170
Total	18,651,668	6,083,553	3,943,139	4,177,326	2,272,122	446,403

Note: Does not include votes cast outside Iran by expatriates.

Table 54
Data on the 2017 Presidential Election

Date of election	May 19, 2017	
Number of eligible voters	56,410,234[a]	
Number of actual voters	41,366,085	
Voter turnout rate	73.3%	
Number of registered entrants[b]	1,636[c]	
Number of entrants positively vetted	6	
Percentage of entrants positively vetted	0.4%	
Election winner	Hassan Rouhani	
Winner's number and percentage of votes received	23,636,652	57.14%
First runner-up	Seyyed Ebrahim Ra'isi	
First runner-up's number and percentage of votes received	15,835,794 (38.28%)	
Names and votes of other candidates	Seyyed Mostafa Mir Salim	478,267 (1.15%)
	Seyyed Mostafa Hashemi-Taba	214,441 (0.51%)

[a] The Ministry of Interior put the total number of eligible voters at 56,410,234, of which 1,350,294 were eligible to vote for the first time. See http://www.moi.ir.

[b] The government has talked occasionally about adopting a more rigorous system for limiting the number of entrants to presidential races, but so far nothing has been done other than massive disqualifications by the Guardian Council after entrants have registered.

[c] http://www.shahrara.com.

Table 55
Breakdown of Votes Based on Province in the 2017 Presidential Election

Province	Rouhani	Ra'isi	Mir Salim	Hashemi-Taba
Alborz	832,045	390,488	16,533	5,906
Ardabil	412,735	261,056	8,543	3,617
Bushehr	328,806	223,278	3,808	1,981
Chahar Mahal and Bakhtiari	272,917	222,313	6,120	2,310
East Azerbaijan	1,281,020	662,263	27,624	14,245
Fars	1,525,792	904,001	18,078	9,115
Gilan	1,043,780	443,309	16,925	7,751
Golestan	616,999	361,472	8,686	4,631
Hamadan	418,636	483,301	14,746	5,630
Hormozgan	480,655	370,388	8,577	4,449
Ilam	188,925	133,023	2,781	1,143
Isfahan	1,401,482	1,045,932	37,775	18,027
Kerman	804,805	717,580	12,310	6,502
Kermanshah	699,666	313,896	8,788	4,173
Khuzestan	1,194,423	920,970	23,507	15,132
Kohgiluyeh and Buyer Ahmad	187,166	179,028	1,717	614

Table 55 (Cont.)
Breakdown of Votes Based on Province in the 2017 Presidential Election

Province	Rouhani	Ra'isi	Mir Salim	Hashemi-Taba
Kurdistan	467,700	155,036	10,241	8,677
Lorestan	459,190	367,955	8,544	3,314
Markazi	376,904	377,145	11,449	4,437
Mazandaran	1,266,889	732,475	25,730	10,408
North Khorasan	231,313	272,690	6,027	2,116
Qazvin	395,911	303,469	11,907	3,958
Qom	219,443	350,269	13,327	5,518
Razavi Khorasan	1,437,382	1,903,067	42,512	14,076
Semnan	182,279	200,658	5,758	2,100
Sistan and Baluchestan	875,694	314,502	5,401	3,071
South Khorasan	159,432	301,976	2,917	1,060
Tehran	4,045,357	1,918,390	82,625	29,860
West Azerbaijan	1,030,286	473,857	18,386	13,971
Yazd	402,995	206,514	6,145	2,900
Zanjan	260,049	294,603	9,760	3,213
Total	23,636,652	15,835,794	478,267	214,441

Source: Based on data released by the Ministry of Interior. See https://www.moi.ir.
Note: This data does not include votes cast outside Iran by expatriates.

Table 56
Percentage of Presidential Candidates Approved versus Voter Turnout Rates

Presidential election date	Percentage of approved candidates	Percentage of voter turnout
Jan. 25, 1980	85.4%	67.4%
July 24, 1981	5.6%	64.2%
Oct. 2, 1981	10.9%	74.3%
Aug. 16, 1985	6.0%	54.8%
July 28, 1989	2.5%	54.6%
June 11, 1993	3.1%	50.7%
May 23, 1997	1.7%	79.9%
June 8, 2001	1.2%	66.8%
June 17, 2005 (First round)	0.8%	62.8%
June 24, 2005 (Runoff)	NA (between top two candidates from first round)	59.8%
June 12, 2009	0.8%	85.2%
June 14, 2013	1.1%	72.9%
May 19, 2017	0.4%	73.3%

Note: Numbers have been rounded to the nearest integer. For sources, see preceding tables regarding presidential election data.

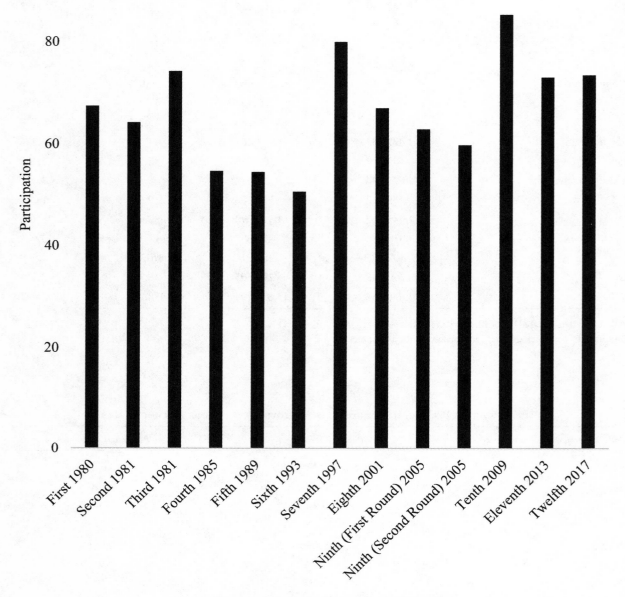

Year and Round of Presidential Elections

11. Average Voter Participation Rate in Presidential Elections (1980–2017). Source: Ministry of Interior (http://www.moi.ir/portal/File/ShowFile.aspx?ID=30759931-94c9-487d-9368-6426279490c8).

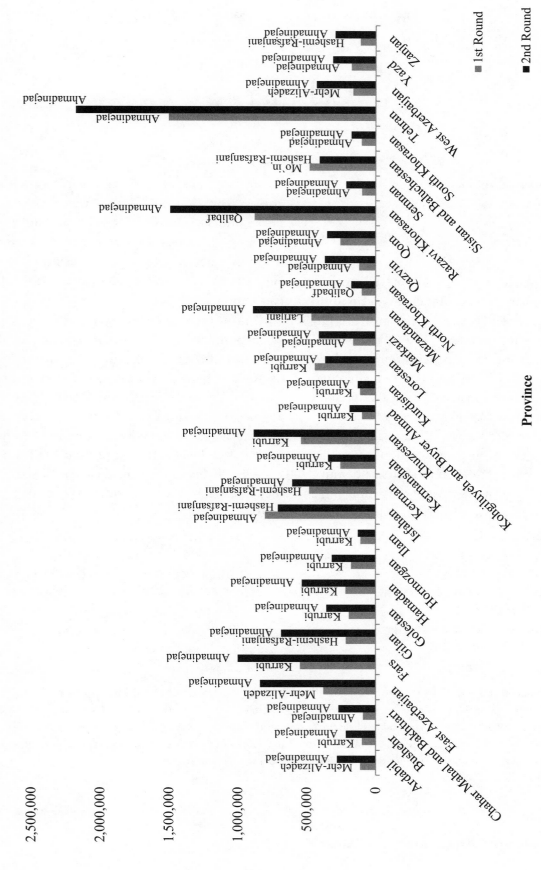

12. Top Presidential Vote Recipients in First- and Second-Round Elections in 2005. Source: http://irandataportal.syr.edu/wp-content/uploads/2005-Presidential-Election-Results-1st-2nd-rounds.pdf.

9
Cabinet

Explanatory Note on Cabinets and History of Ministries

Cabinets

The executive branch in postrevolutionary Iran has undergone a number of important changes. Up until February 4, 1980, when Seyyed Abolhasan Banisadr was sworn in as president, the head of the executive branch was the prime minister. From February 4, 1980, until August 3, 1989, the country had both a president and a prime minister. During this period, the prime minister's office would put together the cabinet and present it to the Majlis for a vote of confidence, but the prime minister also had to secure the consent of the sitting president on the choice of ministers. On August 3, 1989, the post of the prime minister was abolished in favor of a stronger presidency.

Meanwhile, there were times when the country was governed by a Revolutionary Council and an interim prime minister. Moreover, one prime minister (Mohammad-Ali Raja'i) also later served as president. All of this created challenges for decisions of how to label the cabinets. We decided to use the following convention:

During the time (February 5, 1979–August 3, 1989) when Iran had a parliamentary system whereby the prime minister would present the cabinet to the Majlis, we have named the cabinets after the prime minister (e.g., Musavi's first cabinet). Starting on August 29, 1989, when Iran adopted a presidential system, we have labeled the cabinets by the president's name since there was no longer an office of the prime minister.

As such, the tenure of each cabinet, based on when they received a vote of confidence from the Majlis, is as follows:

Bazargan's cabinet	February 11–November 5, 1979[1]
Revolutionary Council cabinet	November 6, 1979–May 28, 1980[2]
PM Raja'i's cabinet	September 10, 1980–June 21, 1981[3]
PM Bahonar's cabinet	August 17–30, 1981[4]
Interim Prime Minister Mahdavi-Kani's cabinet	September 3–October 18, 1981[5]

1. Ayatollah Khomeini announced the appointment of Mehdi Bazargan as the prime minister of the provisional government on February 4, 1979, but his term officially began on February 11, 1979. Bazargan's cabinet did not obtain a confidence vote because the Majlis was not formed until May 28, 1980. Twenty-nine individuals held thirty-seven cabinet posts in Bazargan's cabinet.

2. The Revolutionary Council cabinet also did not obtain a confidence vote from the Majlis for the same reason. Its tenure ended on May 28, 1980, when the First Majlis began. Twenty-one individuals held posts in this cabinet.

3. The confidence vote for PM Raja'i's cabinet occurred during Banisadr's term as president. Twenty-three individuals served in PM Raja'i's cabinet.

4. The confidence vote for PM Bahonar's cabinet occurred during Raja'i's term as president. Twenty-one individuals held posts in this short-lived cabinet.

5. Twenty-two individuals held posts in this interim cabinet.

PM Musavi's first cabinet	November 2, 1981–August 14, 1985[6]
PM Musavi's second cabinet	October 28, 1985–August 3, 1989[7]
President Hashemi-Rafsanjani's first cabinet	August 29, 1989–August 2, 1993[8]
President Hashemi-Rafsanjani's second cabinet	August 16, 1993–August 2, 1997[9]
President Khatami's first cabinet	August 20, 1997–August 1, 2001[10]
President Khatami's second cabinet	August 22, 2001–August 2, 2005[11]
President Ahmadinejad's first cabinet	August 24, 2005–August 2, 2009[12]
President Ahmadinejad's second cabinet	September 3, 2009–August 3, 2013[13]
President Rouhani's first cabinet	August 15, 2013–August 13, 2017[14]
President Rouhani's second cabinet	August 20, 2017–2021[15]

In the first decade of the revolution, when there was a prime minister, there were no such positions as vice presidents. Instead, there were individuals designated as ministerial advisers or ministers of state in charge of such important organizations as the Plan and Budget Organization, Iran National Steel Company, the Public Health Organization, and the Atomic Energy Organization (as of 1989). The ministerial advisers in charge of these organizations were presented to the Majlis (after it was formed) for a confidence vote and were considered members of the cabinet. There were also other portfolios (executive, parliamentary affairs, and revolutionary projects) at the rank of ministerial adviser reserved for those individuals helping the prime minister. After the abolishment of the post of prime minister, the president had the authority to appoint various vice presidents, who did not need to be confirmed by the Majlis. Unless otherwise indicated, the ministerial advisers and the vice presidents have been included in the tables describing the cabinets.

On occasions when a minister left the post, was dismissed, was impeached, or died in office, the position was left vacant or assigned to a caretaker. Since caretakers did not have to receive a vote from the Majlis, we have not included them in the database. For example, between 1987, when Mohammad-Taqi Banki left the post of minister of energy, and 1988, when Bizhan Namdar-Zanganeh took it over, the ministry was run by a caretaker.

Between February 11, 1979, and August 8, 2017, 251 individuals served one or more times in cabinets.

History of Ministries

Below is a list of changes in the status of various ministries after the revolution:

---

6. In the 1980s, the law required that when the Majlis changed, the sitting cabinet needed to obtain another vote of confidence from the Majlis. This rule was later changed, but it required PM Musavi to present his cabinet to the Majlis initially on November 2, 1981, and a second time on August 14, 1984, to receive a vote of confidence. Both of these votes took place during the first term of President Khamenei. Thirty-nine individuals held forty positions in PM Musavi's first cabinet.

7. PM Musavi presented his cabinet to the Majlis on two separate occasions (October 28, 1985, and September 13, 1988) during President Khamenei's second term as well. Twenty-eight individuals held twenty-nine positions in PM Musavi's second cabinet.

8. Thirty-two individuals held posts in President Hashemi-Rafsanjani's first cabinet.

9. Thirty-two individuals held thirty-three posts in President Hashemi-Rafsanjani's second cabinet.

10. Thirty-four individuals held thirty-eight posts in President Khatami's first cabinet.

11. Thirty-four individuals held thirty-five posts in President Khatami's second cabinet.

12. Forty-five individuals held forty-six posts in President Ahmadinejad's first cabinet.

13. Forty-two individuals held fifty posts in President Ahmadinejad's second cabinet.

14. Thirty-five individuals held thirty-seven posts in President Rouhani's first cabinet.

15. In August 2017, a total of twenty-seven individuals were appointed to various posts in President Rouhani's second cabinet. Two more ministers were added on October 29, 2017. It is reasonable to expect changes due to impeachments, resignations, or deaths before President Rouhani's term ends in 2021.

AGRICULTURAL JIHAD

Dec. 26, 2000: The Majlis approved the merger of the two ministries of Agriculture and Construction Jihad into one new ministry called the Ministry of Agricultural Jihad. The GC approved this merger on December 30, 2000.[16]

CONSTRUCTION JIHAD

Nov. 29, 1983: The Majlis approved the establishment of a Ministry of Construction Jihad. Nine days later the GC approved it as well.[17] Up until this point the Construction Jihad, which was formed on June 16, 1979, was operating as a revolutionary organization.

COOPERATIVES, LABOR, AND SOCIAL WELFARE

Sept. 4, 1991: The Majlis approved the creation of a Ministry of Cooperatives.[18] The government did not introduce a ministerial candidate until December 31, 1991.

July 15, 2004: The Ministry of Welfare and Social Security was established.[19]

June 29, 2011: The Majlis voted to merge the Ministry of Cooperatives, Ministry of Labor, and Ministry of Welfare and Social Security into one single ministry called the Ministry of Cooperatives, Labor, and Social Welfare.[20] The GC approved this on July 2, 2011.[21]

CULTURE

May 27, 1979: The prerevolutionary Ministry of Information and Tourism was renamed the Ministry of National Guidance.[22] Four months later the sitting minister changed its name to the Ministry of Islamic Guidance.[23]

Nov. 18, 1981: A good number of museums and cultural centers under the auspices of the Ministry of Higher Education were transferred to the Ministry of Islamic Guidance.[24]

Mar. 3, 1987: The Majlis approved the establishment of a Ministry of Culture and Islamic Guidance.[25]

Sept. 13, 1988: Seyyed Mohammad Khatami received a vote of confidence from the Majlis with the title of minister of culture and Islamic guidance, signifying the official transfer of the culture and arts portfolio to this ministry.[26]

DEFENSE

Feb. 22, 1979: The prerevolutionary Ministry of War was renamed the Ministry of National Defense.

May 23, 1984: The Ministry of National Defense was renamed the Ministry of Defense.[27]

Aug. 19, 1989: The Majlis approved the merger of the two ministries of Defense and Revolutionary

16. http://rc.majlis.ir.
17. http://rc.majlis.ir.
18. http://tarikhirani.ir.
19. http://www.mcls.gov.ir.
20. http://www.bbc.com/persian.
21. http://www.mimt.gov.ir.
22. http://rc.majlis.ir.
23. http://www.farhang.gov.ir.
24. http://rc.majlis.ir.
25. http://rc.majlis.ir.
26. http://ical.ir.
27. http://rc.majlis.ir.

Guards into a unified Ministry of Defense and Armed Forces Logistics. On August 22, 1989, the GC approved this merger.[28]

HEALTH

June 14, 1980: The Public Health Organization was created as a separate entity from the Ministry of Health and Public Health and the position of ministerial adviser and head of the Public Health Organization was created.[29]

Mar. 1, 1981: The Ministry of Health and Public Health was renamed the Ministry of Health.[30]

Jan. 6, 1985: The Public Health Organization (*Sazman-e Behzisti*) was absorbed back into the Ministry of Health and the position of ministerial adviser and head of the Public Health Organization was discontinued.[31] The name of the ministry reverted to its original name of Ministry of Health and Public Health.[32] Later on, a new organization (State Welfare Organization of Iran) began operating with the Persian title of *Sazman-e Behzisti-ye Keshvar* and became a part of the Ministry of Cooperatives, Labor, and Social Welfare.

Oct. 1, 1985: The Majlis approved modifying the name of the Ministry of Health and Public Health to the Ministry of Health and Medical Education. The GC approved the change on October 16, 1985.[33]

HEAVY INDUSTRIES

Apr. 11, 1982: The Majlis approved the establishment of the Ministry of Heavy Industries.[34] On May 31, 1982, Behzad Nabavi became the first minister of heavy industries.

HIGHER EDUCATION

Mar. 8, 1979: The prerevolutionary ministries of Culture and Arts and Science and Higher Education were merged to create a Ministry of Culture and Higher Education.[35] However, in 1981, the cultural portfolio was transferred to the Ministry of Culture and Islamic Guidance.[36]

Apr. 5, 2000: As part of the Third Development Plan, the Majlis approved replacing the Ministry of Higher Education with the Ministry of Science, Research, and Technology. The GC approved the change on April 20, 2000.[37]

INDUSTRIES

July 26, 1981: The Ministry of Mining and Metals was established.[38]

Sept. 13, 1994: The Ministry of Heavy Industries was merged with Ministry of Industries and the new ministry continued with the name Ministry of Industries. On September 21, 1994, the GC formally abolished the Ministry of Heavy Industries.[39] On October 5, 1994, President

28. http://rc.majlis.ir.
29. http://www.behdasht.gov.ir.
30. http://rc.majlis.ir.
31. http://talar.dadparvar.ir.
32. http://www.behdasht.gov.ir.
33. http://rc.majlis.ir.
34. http://rc.majlis.ir.
35. http://rc.majlis.ir.
36. http://www.khabaronline.ir.
37. http://rc.majlis.ir.
38. http://rc.majlis.ir.
39. http://rc.majlis.ir.

Hashemi-Rafsanjani asked the Majlis to approve Mohammad-Reza Ne'matzadeh as the minister of industries, which it did. This action ended Mohammad-Hadi Nezhad-Hoseyniyan's term as minister of heavy industries.[40]

Dec. 26, 2000: The Majlis voted to merge the Ministry of Industries and the Ministry of Mining and Metals into a single Ministry of Industries and Mining. The GC approved this decision five days later.[41]

June 29, 2011: The Majlis voted to merge the Ministry of Industries and Mining and the Ministry of Commerce into a single Ministry of Industry, Mining, and Trade.[42] The GC approved this on July 2, 2011.[43]

INTELLIGENCE

Aug. 18, 1984: The Majlis passed a law establishing the Ministry of Intelligence. The GC approved it on August 25, 1984.

PETROLEUM

Sept. 30, 1979: The Ministry of Petroleum was established.[44]

PLANNING AND BUDGET

Jan. 6, 1985: The Plan and Budget Organization (PBO) became the Ministry of Planning and Budget, and the post of ministerial adviser for plan and budget was changed to the minister of planning and budget. The GC approved this

change on January 17, 1985.[45] However, in February 1989, it was decided to once again make it into an organization rather than a ministry. Thus, the first VP for planning and budget was appointed on August 2, 1989.[46]

Mar. 1, 2000: The PBO merged with the Organization for Administrative and Employment Affairs to create the Management and Planning Organization. In the summer of 2000, Mohammad-Reza Aref became VP and head of the Management and Planning Organization.

July 9, 2007: President Ahmadinejad abolished the Management and Planning Organization. As a result, the post of VP and head of the Management and Planning Organization was also eliminated.

Nov. 10, 2014: President Rouhani restored the Management and Planning Organization.

July 25, 2016: The Management and Planning Organization was split into PBO and the Administrative and Recruitment Organization.

POST, TELEGRAPH, AND TELEPHONES

Dec. 10, 2003: The Ministry of Post, Telegraph, and Telephones was renamed the Ministry of Information and Communications Technology.[47] The GC approved it on the same day.

ROADS AND URBAN DEVELOPMENT

June 21, 2011: The Ministry of Housing and the Ministry of Urban Development and Roads and

40. http://archive.ical.ir.
41. http://rc.majlis.ir.
42. http://www.bbc.com/persian; http://www.mcls.gov.ir; http://rc.majlis.ir.
43. http://www.mimt.gov.ir; http://rc.majlis.ir.
44. http://rc.majlis.ir.
45. http://rc.majlis.ir.
46. http://www.aftabir.com.
47. http://rc.majlis.ir.

Transportation were merged into a single Ministry of Roads and Urban Development.[48]

SPORTS AND YOUTH

Jan. 2, 2011: The Majlis voted to create the Ministry of Sports and Youth. The GC approved the decision on January 19, 2011.[49] However, President Ahmadinejad waited until June 14, 2011, to introduce a ministerial candidate for this post to the Majlis; that person was approved on July 3, 2011. The National Youth Organization, which was dissolved on December 29, 2010, was absorbed into the Ministry of Sports and Youth.

Table 57
Prime Ministers (1979–89)

Name	Province of birth	Lifespan	Age when first occupying office	Tenure
Mehdi Bazargan	Tehran	1907–95	72	Feb. 11–Nov. 5, 1979
Mohammad-Ali Raja'i	Qazvin	1933–81	47	Aug. 11, 1980–Aug. 1, 1981
Mohammad-Javad Bahonar	Kerman	1933–81	48	Aug. 5–30, 1981
Mohammad-Reza Mahdavi-Kani[a]	Tehran	1931–2014	50	Sept. 2–Oct. 18, 1981
Mir Hoseyn Musavi[b]	East Azerbaijan	1942–	39	Oct. 29, 1981–Aug. 3, 1989

[a] Mahdavi-Kani was approved by the Majlis as the interim PM after the assassination of President Raja'i and PM Bahonar.
[b] At the end of Musavi's term, the office of the prime minister was abolished.

Table 58
Ministers in Each Cabinet (1979–2021)

MEMBERS OF PM BAZARGAN'S CABINET (FEB. 11–NOV. 5, 1979)[a]

Minister	Ministry/Portfolio
Mahmud Ahmadzadeh-Heravi	Industries
Ali Ardalan	Economic affairs and finance
Mohammad-Hoseyn Baniasadi	Ministerial adviser for revolutionary affairs; ministerial adviser for executive affairs
Mostafa Chamran	Ministerial adviser for revolutionary affairs; national defense
Abdolali Espahbodi	Labor and social affairs
Daryush Foruhar	Labor and social affairs; ministerial adviser
Hasan-Ebrahim Habibi	Islamic guidance
Mohammad-Hasan Islami	Post, telegraph, and telephones
Ali-Mohammad Izadi	Agriculture

[a] When a cabinet member has held more than one position in any cabinet, a semicolon has been used to separate the positions. Vice presidents have been identified as VP.

48. http://rc.majlis.ir.
49. http://rc.majlis.ir.

Table 58 (Cont.)
Ministers in Each Cabinet (1979–2021)

MEMBERS OF PM BAZARGAN'S CABINET (FEB. 11–NOV. 5, 1979)[a]

Minister	Ministry/Portfolio
Mostafa Katira'i	Housing and urban development
Seyyed Ahmad Madani	National defense
Naser Minachi	Islamic guidance
Ali-Akbar Mo'infar	Ministerial adviser and head of the PBO; petroleum[b]
Asadollah Mobasheri	Justice
Mohammad-Taqi Riyahi	National defense
Hashem Sabbaghiyan	Ministerial adviser for revolutionary affairs; interior
Reza Sadr	Commerce
Seyyed Ahmad Sadr Haj Seyyed Javadi	Interior; justice
Ezzatollah Sahabi	Ministerial adviser and head of the PBO
Yadollah Sahabi	Ministerial adviser for education and research; ministerial adviser for revolutionary affairs
Kazem Sami	Health
Karim Sanjabi	Foreign affairs
Hoseyn Shahhoseyni	Ministerial adviser and head of the Physical Training Organization
Ali Shari'atmadari	Culture and Higher Education
Gholam-Hoseyn Shokuhi	Education
Seyyed Sadeq Tabataba'i	Ministerial adviser for executive affairs
Yusef Taheri	Roads and transportation
Abbas Taj	Energy
Ebrahim Yazdi	Foreign affairs; ministerial adviser for revolutionary affairs

MEMBERS OF THE REVOLUTIONARY COUNCIL CABINET (NOV. 6, 1979–MAY 28, 1980)

Minister	Ministry/Portfolio
Hasan Abbaspur-Tehranifard	Energy
Mahmud Ahmadzadeh-Heravi	Industries
Seyyed Abolhasan Banisadr	Economic affairs and finance
Seyyed Mohammad Beheshti	Head of cabinet
Mostafa Chamran	National defense
Hasan-Ebrahim Habibi	Culture and higher education
Akbar Hashemi-Rafsanjani	Interior
Mostafa Katira'i	Housing and urban development
Mohammad-Reza Mahdavi-Kani	Interior
Naser Minachi	Islamic guidance
Ali-Akbar Mo'infar	Petroleum

Source for all Table 58 subheadings: Authors' database.
[b] Hasan Nazih, Chairman of NIOC, was not included in this list because his status was not one of an official minister. The Petroleum Ministry was established in late September 1979 with Mo'infar as its inaugural minister.

Table 58 (Cont.)
Ministers in Each Cabinet (1979–2021)

MEMBERS OF THE REVOLUTIONARY COUNCIL CABINET (NOV. 6, 1979–MAY 28, 1980)

Minister	Ministry/Portfolio
Mohammad-Reza Ne'matzadeh	Labor and social affairs
Mahmud Qandi	Post, telegraph, and telephones
Sadeq Qotbzadeh	Foreign affairs
Mohammad-Ali Raja'i	Education
Reza Sadr	Commerce
Ezzatollah Sahabi	Ministerial adviser and head of the PBO
Abbas Sheybani	Agriculture
Yusef Taheri	Roads and transportation
Seyyed Mohsen Yahyavi	Housing and urban development
Musa Zargar	Health

MEMBERS OF PM MOHAMMAD-ALI RAJA'I'S CABINET (SEPT. 10, 1980–JUNE 21, 1981)

Minister	Ministry/Portfolio
Hasan Abbaspur-Tehranifard	Energy
Ebrahim Ahadi	Justice
Mahmud Ahmadzadeh-Heravi	Ministerial adviser and head of the Iran National Steel Company
Seyyed Hasan Arefi	Culture and higher education
Seyyed Mohammad Asghari-Bahari	Justice
Mohammad-Javad Bahonar	Education
Abbas Duzduzani	Islamic guidance
Javad Fakuri	Defense
Mahammad-Ali Fayyazbakhsh	Ministerial adviser and head of Public Health Organization
Mohammad-Shahab Gonabadi	Housing and urban development
Musa Kalantari	Roads and transportation
Hoseyn Kazempur-Ardabili	Commerce
Musa Khayyer	Ministerial adviser and head of PBO
Mohammad-Reza Mahdavi-Kani	Interior
Hadi Manafi	Health
Mohammad Mir Mohammad-Sadeqi	Labor and social affairs
Mir Hoseyn Musavi	Foreign affairs
Behzad Nabavi	Ministerial adviser for executive affairs
Hoseyn Namazi	Economic affairs and finance
Mohammad-Reza Ne'matzadeh	Industries
Mahmud Qandi	Post, telegraph, and telephones
Mohammad Salamati	Agriculture
Mohammad-Javad Tondguyan	Petroleum

Table 58 (Cont.)
Ministers in Each Cabinet (1979–2021)

MEMBERS OF PM BAHONAR'S CABINET (AUG. 17–30, 1981)

Minister	Ministry/Portfolio
Habibollah Asgarowladi	Commerce
Seyyed Mohammad Asghari-Bahari	Justice
Mohammad-Taqi Banki	Ministerial adviser and head of PBO
Hasan Ghafurifard	Energy
Seyyed Mohammad Gharazi	Petroleum
Mohammad-Shahab Gonabadi	Housing and urban development
Seyyed Mostafa Hashemi-Taba	Industries
Mohammad-Reza Mahdavi-Kani	Interior
Hadi Manafi	Health
Mohammad Mir Mohammad-Sadeqi	Labor and social affairs
Abdolmajid Mo'adikhah	Islamic guidance
Mir Hoseyn Musavi	Foreign affairs
Seyyed Hoseyn Musaviyani	Mining and Metals
Behzad Nabavi	Ministerial adviser for executive affairs
Seyyed Morteza Nabavi	Post, telegraph and telephones
Mohammad-Ali Najafi	Culture and higher education
Hoseyn Namazi	Economic affairs and finance
Seyyed Musa Namju	National defense
Seyyed Ali-Akbar Parvaresh	Education
Mahmud Ruhani	Ministerial adviser and head of the Public Health Organization
Mohammad Salamati	Agriculture

MEMBERS OF INTERIM PM MOHAMMAD-REZA MAHDAVI-KANI'S CABINET (SEPT. 3–OCT. 18, 1981)

Minister	Ministry/Portfolio
Habibollah Asgarowladi	Commerce
Seyyed Mohammad Asghari-Bahari	Justice
Mohammad-Taqi Banki	Ministerial adviser and head of the PBO
Hasan Ghafurifard	Energy
Seyyed Mohammad Gharazi	Petroleum
Mohammad-Shahab Gonabadi	Housing and urban development
Seyyed Mostafa Hashemi-Taba	Industries
Hadi Manafi	Health
Mohammad Mir Mohammad-Sadeqi	Labor and social affairs
Abdolmajid Mo'adikhah	Islamic guidance
Mir Hoseyn Musavi	Foreign affairs
Seyyed Hoseyn Musaviyani	Mining and metals

Table 58 (Cont.)
Ministers in Each Cabinet (1979–2021)

MEMBERS OF INTERIM PM MOHAMMAD-REZA MAHDAVI-KANI'S CABINET (SEPT. 3–OCT. 18, 1981)

Minister	Ministry/Portfolio
Behzad Nabavi	Ministerial adviser for executive affairs
Seyyed Morteza Nabavi	Post, telegraph, and telephones
Mohammad-Ali Najafi	Culture and higher education
Hoseyn Namazi	Economic affairs and finance
Seyyed Musa Namju	National defense
Mohammad-Hadi Nezhad-Hoseyniyan	Roads and transportation
Seyyed Kamaleddin Nikravesh	Interior
Seyyed Ali-Akbar Parvaresh	Education
Mahmud Ruhani	Ministerial adviser and head of Public Health Organization
Mohammad Salamati	Agriculture

MEMBERS OF PM MIR HOSEYN MUSAVI'S FIRST CABINET (NOV. 2, 1981–AUG. 14, 1985)

Minister	Ministry/Portfolio
Hasan Abedi-Ja'fari	Commerce
Seyyed Kazem Akrami	Education
Gholam-Reza Aqa Zadeh	Ministerial adviser for executive affairs
Habibollah Asgarowladi	Commerce
Seyyed Mohammad Asghari-Bahari	Justice
Mohammad-Taqi Banki	Ministerial adviser and head of the PBO
Mohammad-Javad Ezheh'i	Ministerial adviser and head of Public Health Organization
Iraj Fazel	Culture and higher education
Hasan Ghafurifard	Energy
Seyyed Mohammad Gharazi	Petroleum
Mohammad-Shahab Gonabadi	Housing and urban development
Hasan-Ebrahim Habibi	Justice
Seyyed Mostafa Hashemi-Taba	Industries
Serajeddin Kazeruni	Housing and urban development
Seyyed Mohammad Khatami	Islamic guidance
Hadi Manafi	Health
Seyyed Ali-Reza Marandi	Health
Abdolmajid Mo'adikhah	Islamic guidance
Seyyed Hoseyn Musaviyani	Mining and metals
Behzad Nabavi	Ministerial adviser for executive affairs; heavy industries
Seyyed Morteza Nabavi	Post, telegraph, and telephones
Mohammad-Ali Najafi	Culture and higher education
Hoseyn Namazi	Economic affairs and finance

Table 58 (Cont.)
Ministers in Each Cabinet (1979–2021)

MEMBERS OF PM MIR HOSEYN MUSAVI'S FIRST CABINET (NOV. 2, 1981–AUG. 14, 1985)

Minister	Ministry/Portfolio
Bizhan Namdar-Zangeneh	Construction Jihad
Ali-Akbar Nateq-Nuri	Interior
Mohammad-Hadi Nezhad-Hoseyniyan	Roads and transportation
Seyyed Kamaleddin Nikravesh	Interior
Hoseyn Nili-Ahmadabadi	Mining and metals
Seyyed Ali-Akbar Parvaresh	Education
Mohsen Rafiqdust	Revolutionary guards
Mohammad Reyshahri	Intelligence
Mahmud Ruhani	Ministerial adviser and head of Public Health Organization
Mohammad Salamati	Agriculture
Mohammad Salimi	National defense
Abolqasem Sarhaddizadeh	Labor and social affairs
Gholam-Reza Shafei	Industries
Ahmad Tavakkoli	Labor and social affairs
Ali-Akbar Velayati	Foreign affairs
Abbas-Ali Zali	Agriculture

MEMBERS OF PM MIR HOSEYN MUSAVI'S SECOND CABINET (OCT. 28, 1985–AUG. 3, 1989)

Minister	Ministry/Portfolio
Hasan Abedi-Ja'fari	Commerce
Seyyed Kazem Akrami	Education
Gholam-Reza Aqa Zadeh	Petroleum
Seyyed Mohammad-Reza Ayatollahi	Mining and metals
Mohammad-Taqi Banki	Energy
Mohammad Farhadi	Higher education
Gholam-Reza Foruzesh	Construction Jihad
Seyyed Mohammad Gharazi	Post, telegraph, and telephones
Hasan-Ebrahim Habibi	Justice
Mohammad-Javad Iravani	Economic affairs and finance
Mohammad-Hoseyn Jalali	Defense
Isa Kalantari	Agriculture
Serajeddin Kazeruni	Housing and urban development
Seyyed Mohammad Khatami	Culture and Islamic guidance
Seyyed Ali-Reza Marandi	Health and medical education
Seyyed Ali-Akbar Mohtashamipur	Interior
Behzad Nabavi	Heavy industries

Table 58 (Cont.)
Ministers in Each Cabinet (1979–2021)

MEMBERS OF PM MIR HOSEYN MUSAVI'S SECOND CABINET (OCT. 28, 1985–AUG. 3, 1989)

Minister	Ministry/Portfolio
Mohammad-Ali Najafi	Education
Bizhan Namdar-Zangeneh	Energy; Construction Jihad
Mohsen Rafiqdust	Revolutionary guards
Mohammad Reyshahri	Intelligence
Mas'ud Roghani-Zanjani	Planning and budget
Mohammad Sa'idi-Kiya	Roads and transportation
Abolqasem Sarhaddizadeh	Labor and social affairs
Gholam-Reza Shafei	Industries
Ali Shamkhani	Revolutionary guards
Ali-Akbar Velayati	Foreign affairs
Abbas-Ali Zali	Agriculture

MEMBERS OF PRESIDENT AKBAR HASHEMI-RAFSANJANI'S FIRST CABINET (AUG. 29, 1989–AUG. 2, 1993)

Minister	Ministry/Portfolio
Reza Amrollahi	VP and head of the Atomic Energy Organization
Gholam-Reza Aqa Zadeh	Petroleum
Ali Fallahiyan	Intelligence
Iraj Fazel	Health and medical education
Gholam-Reza Foruzesh	Construction Jihad
Hasan Ghafurifard	VP and head of Physical Training Organization
Seyyed Mohammad Gharazi	Post, telegraph, and telephones
Hasan-Ebrahim Habibi	First vice president
Isa Kalantari	Agriculture
Hoseyn Kamali	Labor and social affairs
Serajeddin Kazeruni	Housing and urban development
Seyyed Mohammad Khatami	Culture and Islamic guidance
Ali Larijani	Culture and Islamic guidance
Hoseyn Mahlujchi	Mining and metals
Reza Malekzadeh	Health and medical education
Hadi Manafi	VP and head of the Environmental Protection Organization
Hamid Mirzadeh	VP for executive affairs
Mostafa Mo'in	Higher education
Seyyed Ataollah Mohajerani	VP for parliamentary affairs
Mohammad-Ali Najafi	Education
Bizhan Namdar-Zangeneh	Energy
Mohammad-Reza Ne'matzadeh	Industries

Table 58 (Cont.)
Ministers in Each Cabinet (1979–2021)

MEMBERS OF PRESIDENT AKBAR HASHEMI-RAFSANJANI'S FIRST CABINET (AUG. 29, 1989–AUG. 2, 1993)

Minister	*Ministry/Portfolio*
Mohammad-Hadi Nezhad-Hoseyniyan	Heavy Industries
Mohsen Nurbakhsh	Economic affairs and finance
Abdollah Nuri	Interior
Mas'ud Roghani-Zanjani	VP and head of the Management and Planning Organization
Mohammad Sa'idi-Kiya	Roads and transportation
Gholam-Reza Shafei	Cooperatives
Mohammad-Esma'il Shushtari	Justice
Akbar Torkan	Defense and armed forces logistics
Abdolhoseyn Vahaji	Commerce
Ali-Akbar Velayati	Foreign affairs

MEMBERS OF PRESIDENT AKBAR HASHEMI-RAFSANJANI'S SECOND CABINET (AUG. 16, 1993–AUG. 2, 1997)

Minister	*Ministry/Portfolio*
Abbas-Ahmad Akhundi	Housing and urban development
Yahya Ale-'Eshaq	Commerce
Reza Amrollahi	VP and head of the Atomic Energy Organization
Gholam-Reza Aqa Zadeh	Petroleum
Ali-Mohammad Besharati	Interior
Ali Fallahiyan	Intelligence
Mohammad Foruzandeh	Defense and armed forces logistics
Gholam-Reza Foruzesh	Construction Jihad
Seyyed Mohammad Gharazi	Post, telegraph, and telephones
Hasan-Ebrahim Habibi	First vice president
Mohammad Hashemi-Bahremani	VP for executive affairs
Seyyed Mohammad-Reza Hashemi-Golpayegani	Higher education
Seyyed Mostafa Hashemi-Taba	VP and head of Physical Training Organization
Isa Kalantari	Agriculture
Hoseyn Kamali	Labor and social affairs
Ali Larijani	Culture and Islamic guidance
Hoseyn Mahlujchi	Mining and metals
Hadi Manafi	VP and head of the Environmental Protection Organization
Seyyed Ali-Reza Marandi	Health and medical education
Seyyed Mostafa Mir Salim	Culture and Islamic guidance
Hamid Mirzadeh	VP for executive affairs; VP and head of the Management and Planning Organization
Seyyed Ataollah Mohajerani	VP for parliamentary affairs

Table 58 (Cont.)
Ministers in Each Cabinet (1979–2021)

MEMBERS OF PRESIDENT AKBAR HASHEMI-RAFSANJANI'S SECOND CABINET (AUG. 16, 1993–AUG. 2, 1997)

Minister	Ministry/Portfolio
Morteza Mohammad Khan	Economic affairs and finance
Mohammad-Ali Najafi	Education
Bizhan Namdar-Zangeneh	Energy
Mohammad-Reza Ne'matzadeh	Industries
Mohammad-Hadi Nezhad-Hoseyniyan	Heavy industries
Mas'ud Roghani-Zanjani	VP and head of the Management and Planning Organization
Gholam-Reza Shafei	Cooperatives
Mohammad-Esma'il Shushtari	Justice
Akbar Torkan	Roads and transportation
Ali-Akbar Velayati	Foreign affairs

MEMBERS OF PRESIDENT MOHAMMAD KHATAMI'S FIRST CABINET (AUG. 20, 1997–AUG. 1, 2001)

Minister	Ministry/Portfolio
Ali Abdolali'zadeh	Housing and urban development
Gholam-Reza Aqa Zadeh	VP and head of the Atomic Energy Organization
Mohammad-Reza Aref	Post, telegraph, and telephones; VP and head of the Management and Planning Organization
Habibollah Bitaraf	Energy
Rahman Dadman	Roads and transportation
Qorbanali Dorri-Najafabadi	Intelligence
Ma'sume Ebtekar	VP and head of Environmental Protection Organization
Mohammad Farhadi	Health and medical education
Hasan-Ebrahim Habibi	First vice president
Morteza Haji	Cooperatives
Seyyed Mostafa Hashemi-Taba	VP and head of the Physical Training Organization
Mohammad Hashemi-Bahremani	VP for executive affairs
Mahmud Hojjati	Roads and transportation; Agricultural Jihad
Eshaq Jahangiri	Mining and metals; industries and mining
Isa Kalantari	Agriculture
Hoseyn Kamali	Labor and social affairs
Seyyed Kamal Kharrazi	Foreign affairs
Ahmad Masjed-Jame'i	Culture and Islamic guidance
Mostafa Mo'in	Higher education
Seyyed Ataollah Mohajerani	Culture and Islamic guidance
Seyyed Ahmad Mo'tamedi	Post, telegraph, and telephones
Hoseyn Mozaffar	Education

Table 58 (Cont.)
Ministers in Each Cabinet (1979–2021)

MEMBERS OF PRESIDENT MOHAMMAD KHATAMI'S FIRST CABINET (AUG. 20, 1997–AUG. 1, 2001)

Minister	Ministry/Portfolio
Seyyed Abdolvahed Musavi-Lari	VP for parliamentary affairs; interior
Mohammad-Ali Najafi	VP and head of the Management and Planning Organization
Hoseyn Namazi	Economic affairs and finance
Bizhan Namdar-Zangeneh	Petroleum
Abdollah Nuri	Interior
Mohammad-Ali Saduqi	VP for parliamentary affairs
Mohammad Sa'idi-Kiya	Construction Jihad
Gholam-Reza Shafei	Industries
Ali Shamkhani	Defense and armed forces logistics
Mohammad Shari'atmadari	Commerce
Mohammad-Esma'il Shushtari	Justice
Ali Yunesi	Intelligence

MEMBERS OF PRESIDENT MOHAMMAD KHATAMI'S SECOND CABINET (AUG. 22, 2001–AUG. 2, 2005)

Minister	Ministry/Portfolio
Ali Abdolali'zadeh	Housing and urban development
Seyyed Mohammad-Ali Abtahi	VP for parliamentary affairs
Majid Ansari	VP for parliamentary affairs
Gholam-Reza Aqa Zadeh	VP and head of the Atomic Energy Organization
Mohammad-Reza Aref	First vice president
Hamid-Reza Baradaran-Shoraka	VP and head of the Management and Planning Organization
Habibollah Bitaraf	Energy
Hoseyn Dehqan	VP and head of Foundation of Martyrs and Veterans Affairs
Ma'sume Ebtekar	VP and head of the Environmental Protection Organization
Morteza Haji	Education
Mahmud Hojjati	Agriculture
Seyyed Safdar Hoseyni	Labor and social affairs; economic affairs and finance
Eshaq Jahangiri	Industries and mining
Naser Khaleqi	Labor and social affairs
Seyyed Kamal Kharrazi	Foreign affairs
Ahmad Khorram	Roads and transportation
Seyyed Hoseyn Mar'ashi	VP and head of the Cultural Heritage Organization
Ahmad Masjed-Jame'i	Culture and Islamic guidance
Tahmaseb Mazaheri	Economic affairs and finance
Mohsen Mehr-Alizadeh	VP and head of the Physical Training Organization
Mostafa Mo'in	Science, research, and technology

Table 58 (Cont.)
Ministers in Each Cabinet (1979–2021)

MEMBERS OF PRESIDENT MOHAMMAD KHATAMI'S SECOND CABINET (AUG. 22, 2001–AUG. 2, 2005)

Minister	Ministry/Portfolio
Seyyed Ahmad Mo'tamedi	Post, telegraph, and telephones
Seyyed Abdolvahed Musavi-Lari	Interior
Bizhan Namdar-Zangeneh	Petroleum
Mas'ud Pezeshkiyan	Health and medical education
Mohammad Rahmati	Roads and transportation
Mohammad Sattarifar	VP and head of the Management and Planning Organization
Ali Shamkhani	Defense and armed forces logistics
Mohammad Shari'atmadari	Commerce
Mohammad-Hoseyn Sharifzadegan	Social welfare
Mohammad-Esma'il Shushtari	Justice
Ali Sufi	Cooperatives
Ja'far Tofiqi	Science, research, and technology
Ali Yunesi	Intelligence

MEMBERS OF PRESIDENT MAHMOUD AHMADINEJAD'S FIRST CABINET (AUG. 24, 2005–AUG. 2, 2009)

Minister	Ministry/Portfolio
Mohammad Abbasi	Cooperatives
Mohammad Aliabadi	VP and head of the Physical Training Organization
Ali-Reza Aliahmadi	Education
Gholam-Reza Aqa Zadeh	VP and head of the Atomic Energy Organization
Ebrahim Azizi	VP for management and human capital development
Kamran Baqeri-Lankarani	Health and medical education
Hamid Behbahani	Roads and transportation
Seyyed Amir-Mansur Borqe'i	VP and head of the Management and Planning Organization
Davud Danesh-Ja'fari	Economic affairs and finance
Parviz Davudi	First vice president
Hoseyn Dehqan	VP and head of Foundation of Martyrs and Veterans Affairs
Gholam-Hoseyn Elham	Justice
Mohammad-Reza Eskandari	Agricultural Jihad
Mahmud Farshidi	Education
Seyyed Parviz Fattah	Energy
Mohammad-Javad Haj Aliakbari	VP and head of the National Youth Organization
Seyyed Shamseddin Hoseyni	Economic affairs and finance
Seyyed Mohammad Jahromi	Labor and social affairs
Jamal Karimirad	Justice
Parviz Kazemi	Welfare and social security

Table 58 (Cont.)
Ministers in Each Cabinet (1979–2021)

MEMBERS OF PRESIDENT MAHMOUD AHMADINEJAD'S FIRST CABINET (AUG. 24, 2005–AUG. 2, 2009)

Minister	Ministry/Portfolio
Ali Kordan	Interior
Sadeq Mahsuli	Interior
Ali-Akbar Mehrabiyan	Industries and mining
Abdorreza Mesri	Welfare and social security
Seyyed Mas'ud Mir Kazemi	Commerce
Mostafa Mohammad-Najjar	Defense and armed forces logistics
Gholam-Hoseyn Mohseni-Ezheh'i	Intelligence
Manouchehr Mottaki	Foreign affairs
Seyyed Ahmad Musavi	VP for parliamentary affairs
Mohammad Nazemi-Ardakani	Cooperatives
Gholam-Hoseyn Nowzari	Petroleum
Mostafa Purmohammadi	Interior
Farhad Rahbar	VP and head of the Management and Planning Organization
Mohammad-Reza Rahimi	VP for parliamentary affairs
Esfandiyar Rahimmasha'i	VP and head of the Cultural Heritage, Handicrafts, and Tourism Organization; first vice president
Mohammad Rahmati	Roads and transportation
Mohammad-Hoseyn Saffar-Harandi	Culture and Islamic guidance
Mohammad Sa'idi-Kiya	Housing and urban development
Ali Sa'idlu	VP for executive affairs
Mohammad Soleymani	Information and communications technology
Ali-Reza Tahmasebi	Industries and mining
Fatemeh Va'ez-Javadi	VP and head of the Environmental Protection Organization
Sadeq Va'ezzadeh	VP for scientific and technological affairs
Seyyed Kazem Vaziri-Hamaneh	Petroleum
Mohammad-Mehdi Zahedi	Science, research, and technology

MEMBERS OF PRESIDENT MAHMOUD AHMADINEJAD'S SECOND CABINET (SEPT. 3, 2009–AUG. 3, 2013)

Minister	Ministry/Portfolio
Mohammad Abbasi	Cooperatives; sports and youth
Fereydun Abbasi-Davani	VP and head of the Atomic Energy Organization
Ruhollah Ahmadzadeh-Kermani	VP and head of the Cultural Heritage, Handicrafts, and Tourism Organization
Ebrahim Azizi	VP for planning and strategic supervision; VP for management and human capital development
Seyyed Morteza Bakhtiari	Justice
Hamid Baqa'i	VP and head of the Cultural Heritage, Handicrafts, and Tourism Organization; VP for executive affairs

Table 58 (Cont.)
Ministers in Each Cabinet (1979–2021)

MEMBERS OF PRESIDENT MAHMOUD AHMADINEJAD'S SECOND CABINET (SEPT. 3, 2009–AUG. 3, 2013)

Minister	Ministry/Portfolio
Mehrdad Bazrpash	VP and head of the National Youth Organization
Hamid Behbahani	Roads and transportation
Fatemeh Bodaghi	VP for legal affairs
Kamran Daneshju	Science, research, and technology
Lotfollah Foruzandeh-Dehkordi	VP for management and human capital development; VP for parliamentary affairs
Mehdi Ghazanfari	Commerce; Industry, Mining and Trade
Hamid-Reza Hajibaba'i	Education
Seyyed Mohammad Hoseyni	Culture and Islamic guidance
Seyyed Shamseddin Hoseyni	Economic affairs and finance
Sadeq Khaliliyan	Agricultural Jihad
Sadeq Mahsuli	Welfare and social security
Mohammad-Sharif Malekzadeh	VP for cultural heritage and tourism
Ali-Akbar Mehrabiyan	Industry, mining, and trade
Seyyed Mas'ud Mir Kazemi	Petroleum
Seyyed Mohammad-Reza Mir Tajeddini	VP for parliamentary affairs; VP for implementation of the constitution
Mostafa Mohammad-Najjar	Interior
Mohammad-Javad Mohammadizadeh	VP and head of the Environmental Protection Organization
Maryam Mojtahedzadeh	VP for women's and family affairs
Behruz Moradi	VP for planning and strategic supervision
Heydar Moslehi	Intelligence
Manouchehr Mottaki	Foreign affairs
Mir Hasan Musavi	VP and head of the Cultural Heritage, Handicrafts, and Tourism Organization
Mohammad-Hasan Nami	Information and communications technology
Majid Namju	Energy
Ali Nikzad	Housing and urban development; roads and urban development
Rostam Qasemi	Petroleum
Mohammad-Reza Rahimi	First vice president
Ali Sa'idlu	VP and head of Physical Training Organization
Ali-Akbar Salehi	VP and head of the Atomic Energy Organization; foreign affairs
Abdorreza Shaikholislami	Cooperatives, Labor, and social welfare
Nasrin Soltankhah	VP for scientific and technological affairs
Reza Taqipur	Information and communications technology
Mohammad-Hasan Tariqat-Monfared	Health and medical education
Marziyeh Vahid-Dastjerdi	Health and medical education
Ahmad Vahidi	Defense and armed forces logistics
Mas'ud Zaribafan	VP and head of Foundation of Martyrs and Veterans Affairs

Table 58 (Cont.)
Ministers in Each Cabinet (1979–2021)

MEMBERS OF PRESIDENT HASSAN ROUHANI'S FIRST CABINET (AUG. 15, 2013–AUG. 13, 2017)

Minister	Ministry/Portfolio
Fakhreddin Ahmadi-Danesh-Ashtiyani	Education
Zahra Ahmadipur	VP and head of the Cultural Heritage, Handicrafts, and Tourism Organization
Abbas-Ahmad Akhundi	Road and urban development
Seyyed Mahmud Alavi	Intelligence
Elham Aminzadeh	VP for legal affairs
Hoseyn-Ali Amiri	VP for parliamentary affairs
Majid Ansari	VP for parliamentary affairs; VP for legal affairs
Hamid Chitchiyan	Energy
Hoseyn Dehqan	Defense and armed forces logistics
Ma'sume Ebtekar	VP and head of the Environmental Protection Organization
Ali-Asghar Fani	Education
Reza Faraji-Dana	Science, research, and technology
Mohammad Farhadi	Science, research, and technology
Mahmud Gudarzi	Sports and youth
Mahmud Hojjati	Agriculture
Eshaq Jahangiri	First vice president
Ali Jannati	Culture and Islamic guidance
Shahindokht Moulaverdi	VP for women's and family affairs
Mohammad-Ali Najafi	VP and head of the Cultural Heritage, Handicrafts, and Tourism Organization
Bizhan Namdar-Zangeneh	Petroleum
Mohammad-Reza Ne'matzadeh	Industry, mining, and trade
Mohammad-Baqer Nowbakht-Haqiqi	VP for planning and strategic supervision
Mostafa Purmohammadi	Justice
Seyyed Hasan Qazizadeh-Hashemi	Health and medical education
Ali Rabi'i	Cooperatives, labor, and social welfare
Abdorreza Rahmani-Fazli	Interior
Ali-Akbar Salehi	VP and head of the Atomic Energy Organization
Seyyed Reza Salehi-Amiri	Culture and Islamic guidance
Sourena Sattari	VP for scientific and technological affairs
Seyyed Mohammad-Ali Shahidi-Mahallati	VP and head of Foundation of Martyrs and Veterans Affairs
Mohammad Shari'atmadari	VP for executive affairs
Mas'ud Soltanifar	VP and head of the Cultural Heritage, Handicrafts, and Tourism Organization; sports and youth
Ali Tayyebniya	Economic affairs and finance
Mahmud Va'ezi	Information and communications technology
Mohammad-Javad Zarif	Foreign affairs

Table 58 (Cont.)
Ministers in Each Cabinet (1979–2021)

MEMBERS OF PRESIDENT HASSAN ROUHANI'S SECOND CABINET (AUG. 20, 2017–2021)

Minister	Ministry/Portfolio
Abbas-Ahmad Akhundi	Road and urban development
Seyyed Mahmud Alavi	Intelligence
Hoseyn-Ali Amiri	VP for parliamentary affairs
Jamshid Ansari	VP and head of the Administrative and Recruitment Organization
Reza Ardakanian	Energy
Seyyed Ali-Reza Ava'i	Justice
Mohammad-Javad Azari-Jahromi	Information and communications technology
Seyyed Mohammad Bathaie	Education
Ma'sume Ebtekar	VP for women's and family affairs
Mansur Gholami	Science, research, and technology
Amir Hatami	Defense and armed forces logistics
Mahmud Hojjati	Agriculture
Eshaq Jahangiri	First vice president
La'ya Joneydi	VP for legal affairs
Isa Kalantari	VP and head of the Environmental Protection Organization
Mas'ud Karbasiyan	Economic affairs and finance
Ali-Asghar Monesan	VP and head of the Cultural Heritage, Handicrafts, and Tourism Organization
Bizhan Namdar-Zangeneh	Petroleum
Mohammad-Baqer Nowbakht-Haqiqi	VP and head of the Plan and Budget Organization
Seyyed Hasan Qazizadeh-Hashemi	Health and medical education
Ali Rabi'i	Cooperatives, labor, and social welfare
Abdorreza Rahmani-Fazli	Interior
Abbas Salehi	Culture and Islamic guidance
Ali-Akbar Salehi	VP and head of the Atomic Energy Organization
Sourena Sattari	VP for scientific and technological affairs
Seyyed Mohammad-Ali Shahidi-Mahallati	VP and head of Foundation of Martyrs and Veterans Affairs
Mohammad Shari'atmadari	Industry, mining, and trade
Mas'ud Soltanifar	Sports and youth
Mohammad-Javad Zarif	Foreign affairs

Table 59
Ministers Based on Portfolio (1979–2021)

MINISTRY OF AGRICULTURAL JIHAD

Mahmud Hojjati	Jan. 14–Aug. 21, 2001	Khatami's first
Mahmud Hojjati	2001–5	Khatami's second
Mohammad-Reza Eskandari	2005–9	Ahmadinejad's first
Sadeq Khaliliyan	2009–13	Ahmadinejad's second
Mahmud Hojjati	2013–17	Rouhani's first
Mahmud Hojjati	2017–21	Rouhani's second

MINISTRY OF AGRICULTURE

Name of minister	Tenure	PM or president's cabinet
Ali-Mohammad Izadi	1979–79	Bazargan
Abbas Sheybani	1980–80	Revolution Council
Mohammad Salamati	1980–81	Raja'i
Mohammad Salamati	1981–81	Bahonar
Mohammad Salamati	1981–81	Mahdavi-Kani
Mohammad Salamati	1981–83	Musavi's first
Abbas-Ali Zali	1983–85	Musavi's first
Abbas-Ali Zali	1985–88	Musavi's second
Isa Kalantari	1988–89	Musavi's second
Isa Kalantari	1989–93	Hashemi-Rafsanjani's first
Isa Kalantari	1993–97	Hashemi-Rafsanjani's second
Isa Kalantari	1997–2000	Khatami's first

MINISTRY OF COMMERCE

Name of minister	Tenure	PM or president's cabinet
Reza Sadr	1979–79	Bazargan
Reza Sadr	1979–80	Revolutionary Council
Hoseyn Kazempur-Ardabili	1981–81	Raja'i
Habibollah Asgarowladi	1981–81	Bahonar
Habibollah Asgarowladi	1981–81	Mahdavi-Kani
Habibollah Asgarowladi	1981–83	Musavi's first
Hasan Abedi-Ja'fari	1983–85	Musavi's first
Hasan Abedi-Ja'fari	1985–89	Musavi's second
Abdolhoseyn Vahaji	1989–93	Hashemi-Rafsanjani's first
Yahya Ale-'Eshaq	1993–97	Hashemi-Rafsanjani's second
Mohammad Shari'atmadari	1997–2001	Khatami's first
Mohammad Shari'atmadari	2001–5	Khatami's second
Seyyed Mas'ud Mir Kazemi	2005–9	Ahmadinejad's first
Mehdi Ghazanfari	2009–11	Ahmadinejad's second

Table 59 (Cont.)
Ministers Based on Portfolio (1979–2021)

MINISTRY OF THE CONSTRUCTION JIHAD

Name of minister	Tenure	PM or president's cabinet
Bizhan Namdar-Zangeneh	1984–85	Musavi's first
Bizhan Namdar-Zangeneh	1985–88	Musavi's second
Gholam-Reza Foruzesh	1988–89	Musavi's second
Gholam-Reza Foruzesh	1989–93	Hashemi-Rafsanjani's first
Gholam-Reza Foruzesh	1993–97	Hashemi-Rafsanjani's second
Mohammad Sa'idi-Kiya	1997–2000	Khatami's first
Mahmud Hojjati	Jan. 14–Aug. 21, 2001	Khatami's first

MINISTRY OF COOPERATIVES

Name of minister	Tenure	PM or president's cabinet
Gholam-Reza Shafei	1991–93	Hashemi-Rafsanjani's first
Gholam-Reza Shafei	1993–97	Hashemi-Rafsanjani's second
Morteza Haji	1997–2001	Khatami's first
Ali Sufi	2001–5	Khatami's second
Mohammad Nazemi-Ardakani	2005–6	Ahmadinejad's first
Mohammad Abbasi	2006–9	Ahmadinejad's first
Mohammad Abbasi	2009–11	Ahmadinejad's second

MINISTRY OF COOPERATIVES, LABOR, AND SOCIAL AFFAIRS

Abdorreza Shaikholislami	Aug. 3, 2011–2013	Ahmadinejad's second
Ali Rabi'i	2013–17	Rouhani's first
Ali Rabi'i	2017–21	Rouhani's second

MINISTRY OF (CULTURE AND) ISLAMIC GUIDANCE[a]

Name of minister	Tenure	PM or president's cabinet
Hasan-Ebrahim Habibi	1979–79	Bazargan
Naser Minachi	1979–79	Bazargan
Naser Minachi	1979–80	Revolutionary Council
Abbas Duzduzani	1980–81	Raja'i
Abdolmajid Mo'adikhah	1981–81	Bahonar
Abdolmajid Mo'adikhah	1981–81	Mahdavi-Kani
Abdolmajid Mo'adikhah	1981–82	Musavi's first
Seyyed Mohammad Khatami	1982–85	Musavi's first
Seyyed Mohammad Khatami	1985–89	Musavi's second
Seyyed Mohammad Khatami	1989–92	Hashemi-Rafsanjani's first

[a] Beginning in 1987, the name of this ministry changed from Ministry of Islamic Guidance to Ministry of Culture and Islamic Guidance.

Table 59 (Cont.)
Ministers Based on Portfolio (1979–2021)

MINISTRY OF (CULTURE AND) ISLAMIC GUIDANCE[a]

Name of minister	Tenure	PM or president's cabinet
Ali Larijani	1992–93	Hashemi-Rafsanjani's first
Ali Larijani	1993–94	Hashemi-Rafsanjani's second
Seyyed Mostafa Mir Salim	1994–97	Hashemi-Rafsanjani's second
Seyyed Ataollah Mohajerani	1997–2000	Khatami's first
Ahmad Masjed-Jame'i	2001–1	Khatami's first
Ahmad Masjed-Jame'i	2001–5	Khatami's second
Mohammad-Hoseyn Saffar-Harandi	2005–9	Ahmadinejad's first
Seyyed Mohammad Hoseyni	2009–13	Ahmadinejad's second
Ali Jannati	2013–16	Rouhani's first
Reza Salehi-Amiri	2016–17	Rouhani's first
Abbas Salehi	2017–21	Rouhani's second

MINISTRY OF (NATIONAL) DEFENSE (AND ARMED FORCES LOGISTICS)

Name of minister	Tenure	PM or president's cabinet
Seyyed Ahmad Madani	1979–79	Bazargan
Mohammad-Taqi Riyahi	1979–79	Bazargan
Mostafa Chamran	1979–79	Bazargan
Mostafa Chamran	1979–80	Revolutionary Council
Javad Fakuri	1980–81	Raja'i
Seyyed Musa Namju	1981–81	Bahonar
Seyyed Musa Namju	1981–81	Mahdavi-Kani
Mohammad Salimi	1981–85	Musavi's first
Mohammad-Hoseyn Jalali	1985–89	Musavi's second
Akbar Torkan	1989–93	Hashemi-Rafsanjani's first
Mohammad Foruzandeh	1993–97	Hashemi-Rafsanjani's second
Ali Shamkhani	1997–2001	Khatami's first
Ali Shamkhani	2001–5	Khatami's second
Mostafa Mohammad-Najjar	2005–9	Ahmadinejad's first
Ahmad Vahidi	2009–13	Ahmadinejad's second
Hoseyn Dehqan	2013–17	Rouhani's first
Amir Hatami	2017–21	Rouhani's second

MINISTRY OF ECONOMIC AFFAIRS AND FINANCE[b]

Name of minister	Tenure	PM or president's cabinet
Ali Ardalan	1979–79	Bazargan
Seyyed Abolhasan Banisadr	1979–80	Revolutionary Council
Hoseyn Namazi	1981–81	Raja'i

[b] This ministry was also referred to as the Ministry of Economics and Finance.

Table 59 (Cont.)
Ministers Based on Portfolio (1979–2021)

MINISTRY OF ECONOMIC AFFAIRS AND FINANCE[b]

Name of minister	Tenure	PM or president's cabinet
Hoseyn Namazi	1981–81	Bahonar
Hoseyn Namazi	1981–81	Mahdavi-Kani
Hoseyn Namazi	1981–85	Musavi's first
Mohammad-Javad Iravani	1986–89	Musavi's second
Mohsen Nurbakhsh	1989–93	Hashemi-Rafsanjani's first
Morteza Mohammad Khan	1993–97	Hashemi-Rafsanjani's second
Hoseyn Namazi	1997–2001	Khatami's first
Tahmaseb Mazaheri	2001–4	Khatami's second
Seyyed Safdar Hoseyni	2004–5	Khatami's second
Davud Danesh-Ja'fari	2005–8	Ahmadinejad's first
Seyyed Shamseddin Hoseyni	2008–9	Ahmadinejad's first
Seyyed Shamseddin Hoseyni	2009–13	Ahmadinejad's second
Ali Tayyebniya	2013–17	Rouhani's first
Mas'ud Karbasiyan	2017–21	Rouhani's second

MINISTRY OF EDUCATION

Name of minister	Tenure	PM or president's cabinet
Gholam-Hoseyn Shokuhi	1979–79	Bazargan
Mohammad-Ali Raja'i	1979–80	Revolutionary Council
Mohammad-Javad Bahonar	1980–81	Raja'i
Seyyed Ali-Akbar Parvaresh	1981–81	Bahonar
Seyyed Ali-Akbar Parvaresh	1981–81	Mahdavi-Kani
Seyyed Ali-Akbar Parvaresh	1981–84	Musavi's first
Seyyed Kazem Akrami	1984–85	Musavi's first
Seyyed Kazem Akrami	1985–88	Musavi's second
Mohammad-Ali Najafi	1988–89	Musavi's second
Mohammad-Ali Najafi	1989–93	Hashemi-Rafsanjani's first
Mohammad-Ali Najafi	1993–97	Hashemi-Rafsanjani's second
Hoseyn Mozaffar	1997–2001	Khatami's first
Morteza Haji	2001–5	Khatami's second
Mahmud Farshidi	2005–7	Ahmadinejad's first
Ali-Reza Aliahmadi	2008–9	Ahmadinejad's first
Hamid-Reza Haji Baba'i	2009–13	Ahmadinejad's second
Ali-Asghar Fani	2013–16	Rouhani's first
Fakhreddin Ahmadi-Danesh-Ashtiyani	2016–17	Rouhani's first
Seyyed Mohammad Bathaie	2017–21	Rouhani's second

Table 59 (Cont.)
Ministers Based on Portfolio (1979–2021)

MINISTRY OF ENERGY

Name of minister	Tenure	PM or president's cabinet
Abbas Taj	1979–79	Bazargan
Hasan Abbaspur-Tehranifard	1979–80	Revolutionary Council
Hasan Abbaspur	1980–81	Raja'i
Hasan Ghafurifard	1981–81	Bahonar
Hasan Ghafurifard	1981–81	Mahdavi-Kani
Hasan Ghafurifard	1981–85	Musavi's first
Mohammad-Taqi Banki	1985–87	Musavi's second
Bizhan Namdar-Zangeneh	1988–89	Musavi's second
Bizhan Namdar-Zangeneh	1989–93	Hashemi-Rafsanjani's first
Bizhan Namdar-Zangeneh	1993–97	Hashemi-Rafsanjani's second
Habibollah Bitaraf	1997–2001	Khatami's first
Habibollah Bitaraf	2001–5	Khatami's second
Seyyed Parviz Fattah	2005–9	Ahmadinejad's first
Majid Namju	2009–13	Ahmadinejad's second
Hamid Chitchiyan	2013–17	Rouhani's first
Reza Ardakanian	2017–21	Rouhani's second

MINISTRY OF FOREIGN AFFAIRS

Name of minister	Tenure	PM or president's cabinet
Karim Sanjabi	1979–79	Bazargan
Ebrahim Yazdi	1979–79	Bazargan
Sadeq Qotbzadeh	1979–80	Revolutionary Council
Mir Hoseyn Musavi	1981–81	Raja'i
Mir Hoseyn Musavi	1981–81	Bahonar
Mir Hoseyn Musavi	1981–81	Mahdavi-Kani
Ali-Akbar Velayati	1981–85	Musavi's first
Ali-Akbar Velayati	1985–89	Musavi's second
Ali-Akbar Velayati	1989–93	Hashemi-Rafsanjani's first
Ali-Akbar Velayati	1993–97	Hashemi-Rafsanjani's second
Seyyed Kamal Kharrazi	1997–2001	Khatami's first
Seyyed Kamal Kharrazi	2001–5	Khatami's second
Manouchehr Mottaki	2005–9	Ahmadinejad's first
Manouchehr Mottaki	2009–10	Ahmadinejad's second
Ali-Akbar Salehi	2011–13	Ahmadinejad's second
Mohammad-Javad Zarif	2013–17	Rouhani's first
Mohammad-Javad Zarif	2017–21	Rouhani's second

Table 59 (Cont.)
Ministers Based on Portfolio (1979–2021)

MINISTRY OF HEALTH (AND MEDICAL EDUCATION)

Name of minister	Tenure	PM or president's cabinet
Kazem Sami	1979–79	Bazargan
Musa Zargar	1979–80	Revolutionary Council
Hadi Manafi	1980–81	Raja'i
Hadi Manafi	1981–81	Bahonar
Hadi Manafi	1981–81	Mahdavi-Kani
Hadi Manafi	1981–84	Musavi's first
Seyyed Ali-Reza Marandi	1984–85	Musavi's first
Seyyed Ali-Reza Marandi	1985–89	Musavi's second
Iraj Fazel	1989–91	Hashemi-Rafsanjani's first
Reza Malekzadeh	1991–93	Hashemi-Rafsanjani's first
Seyyed Ali-Reza Marandi	1993–97	Hashemi-Rafsanjani's second
Mohammad Farhadi	1997–2001	Khatami's first
Mas'ud Pezeshkiyan	2001–5	Khatami's second
Kamran Baqeri-Lankarani	2005–9	Ahmadinejad's first
Marziyeh Vahid-Dastjerdi	2009–12	Ahmadinejad's second
Mohammad-Hasan Tariqat-Monfared	2013–13	Ahmadinejad's second
Seyyed Hasan Qazizadeh-Hashemi	2013–17	Rouhani's first
Seyyed Hasan Qazizadeh-Hashemi	2017–21	Rouhani's second

MINISTRY OF HEAVY INDUSTRIES

Name of minister	Tenure	PM or president's cabinet
Behzad Nabavi	1982–85	Musavi's first
Behzad Nabavi	1985–89	Musavi's second
Mohammad-Hadi Nezhad-Hoseyniyan	1989–93	Hashemi-Rafsanjani's first
Mohammad-Hadi Nezhad-Hoseyniyan	1993–94	Hashemi-Rafsanjani's second

MINISTRY OF HIGHER EDUCATION (SCIENCE, RESEARCH AND TECHNOLOGY)

Name of minister	Tenure	PM or president's cabinet
Ali Shari'atmadari	1979–79	Bazargan
Hasan-Ebrahim Habibi	1979–80	Revolutionary Council
Seyyed Hasan Arefi	1980–81	Raja'i
Mohammad-Ali Najafi	1981–81	Bahonar
Mohammad-Ali Najafi	1981–81	Mahdavi-Kani
Mohammad-Ali Najafi	1981–84	Musavi's first
Iraj Fazel	1984–85	Musavi's first
Mohammad Farhadi	1985–89	Musavi's second
Mostafa Mo'in	1989–93	Hashemi-Rafsanjani's first

Table 59 (Cont.)
Ministers Based on Portfolio (1979–2021)

MINISTRY OF HIGHER EDUCATION (SCIENCE, RESEARCH AND TECHNOLOGY)

Name of minister	Tenure	PM or president's cabinet
Seyyed Mohammad-Reza Hashemi-Golpayegani	1993–97	Hashemi-Rafsanjani's second
Mostafa Mo'in	1997–2001	Khatami's first
Mostafa Mo'in	2001–3	Khatami's second
Ja'far Tofiqi	2003–5	Khatami's second
Mohammad-Mehdi Zahedi	2005–9	Ahmadinejad's first
Kamran Daneshju	2009–13	Ahmadinejad's second
Reza Faraji-Dana	2013–14	Rouhani's first
Mohammad Farhadi	2014–17	Rouhani's first
Mansur Gholami	2017–21	Rouhani's second

MINISTRY OF HOUSING AND URBAN DEVELOPMENT

Name of minister	Tenure	PM or president's cabinet
Mostafa Katira'i	1979–79	Bazargan
Mostafa Katira'i	1979–79	Revolutionary Council
Seyyed Mohsen Yahyavi	1979–80	Revolutionary Council
Mohammad-Shahab Gonabadi	1980–81	Raja'i
Mohammad-Shahab Gonabadi	1981–81	Bahonar
Mohammad-Shahab Gonabadi	1981–81	Mahdavi-Kani
Mohammad-Shahab Gonabadi	1981–83	Musavi's first
Serajeddin Kazeruni	1984–85	Musavi's first
Serajeddin Kazeruni	1985–89	Musavi's second
Serajeddin Kazeruni	1989–93	Hashemi-Rafsanjani's first
Abbas-Ahmad Akhundi	1993–97	Hashemi-Rafsanjani's second
Ali Abdolali'zadeh	1997–2001	Khatami's first
Ali Abdolali'zadeh	2001–5	Khatami's second
Mohammad Sa'idi-Kiya	2005–9	Ahmadinejad's first
Ali Nikzad	2009–11	Ahmadinejad's second

MINISTRY OF INDUSTRIES (INDUSTRY, MINING, AND TRADE)[c]

Name of minister	Tenure	PM or president's cabinet
Mahmud Ahmadzadeh-Heravi	1979–79	Bazargan
Mahmud Ahmadzadeh-Heravi	1979–80	Revolutionary Council
Mohammad-Reza Ne'matzadeh	1980–81	Raja'i
Seyyed Mostafa Hashemi-Taba	1981–81	Bahonar
Seyyed Mostafa Hashemi-Taba	1981–81	Mahdavi-Kani

[c] As mentioned in the explanatory notes at the beginning of this chapter, this ministry went through several name changes: Ministry of Industries, then Ministry of Industries and Mining, then Ministry of Industry, Mining, and Trade. Here we have listed ministers under the broad category of "ministry of industries."

Table 59 (Cont.)
Ministers Based on Portfolio (1979–2021)

MINISTRY OF INDUSTRIES (INDUSTRY, MINING, AND TRADE)[c]

Name of minister	Tenure	PM or president's cabinet
Seyyed Mostafa Hashemi-Taba	1981–84	Musavi's first
Gholam-Reza Shafei	1984–85	Musavi's first
Gholam-Reza Shafei	1985–89	Musavi's second
Mohammad-Reza Ne'matzadeh	1989–93	Hashemi-Rafsanjani's first
Mohammad-Reza Ne'matzadeh	1993–97	Hashemi-Rafsanjani's second
Gholam-Reza Shafei	1997–2001	Khatami's first
Eshaq Jahangiri	2001–1	Khatami's first
Eshaq Jahangiri	2001–5	Khatami's second
Ali-Reza Tahmasebi	2005–7	Ahmadinejad's first
Ali-Akbar Mehrabiyan	2007–9	Ahmadinejad's first
Ali-Akbar Mehrabiyan	2009–11	Ahmadinejad's second
Mehdi Ghazanfari	2011–13	Ahmadinejad's second
Mohammad-Reza Ne'matzadeh	2013–17	Rouhani's first
Mohammad Shari'atmadari	2017–21	Rouhani's second

MINISTRY OF INTELLIGENCE[d]

Name of minister	Tenure	PM or president's cabinet
Mohammad Reyshahri	1984–85	Musavi's first
Mohammad Reyshahri	1985–89	Musavi's second
Ali Fallahiyan	1989–93	Hashemi-Rafsanjani's first
Ali Fallahiyan	1993–97	Hashemi-Rafsanjani's second
Qorbanali Dorri-Najafabadi	1997–99	Khatami's first
Ali Yunesi	1999–2001	Khatami's first
Ali Yunesi	2001–5	Khatami's second
Gholam-Hoseyn Mohseni-Ezheh'i	2005–9	Ahmadinejad's first
Heydar Moslehi	2009–13	Ahmadinejad's second
Seyyed Mahmud Alavi	2013–17	Rouhani's first
Seyyed Mahmud Alavi	2017–21	Rouhani's second

MINISTRY OF INTERIOR

Name of minister	Tenure	PM or president's cabinet
Seyyed Ahmad Sadr Haj Seyyed Javadi	1979–79	Bazargan
Hashem Sabbaghiyan	1979–79	Bazargan
Akbar Hashemi-Rafsanjani	1979–80	Revolutionary Council
Mohammad-Reza Mahdavi-Kani	1980–80	Revolutionary Council
Mohammad-Reza Mahdavi-Kani	1980–81	Raja'i

[d] By law, all ministers of intelligence must be clerics.

Table 59 (Cont.)
Ministers Based on Portfolio (1979–2021)

MINISTRY OF INTERIOR

Name of minister	Tenure	PM or president's cabinet
Mohammad-Reza Mahdavi-Kani	1981–81	Bahonar
Seyyed Kamaleddin Nikravesh	1981–81	Mahdavi-Kani
Seyyed Kamaleddin Nikravesh	1981–81	Musavi's first
Ali-Akbar Nateq-Nuri	1981–85	Musavi's first
Seyyed Ali-Akbar Mohtashamipur	1985–89	Musavi's second
Abdollah Nuri	1989–93	Hashemi-Rafsanjani's first
Ali-Mohammad Besharati	1993–97	Hashemi-Rafsanjani's second
Abdollah Nuri	1997–98	Khatami's first
Seyyed Abdolvahed Musavi-Lari	1998–2001	Khatami's first
Seyyed Abdolvahed Musavi-Lari	2001–5	Khatami's second
Mostafa Purmohammadi	2005–8	Ahmadinejad's first
Ali Kordan	2008–8	Ahmadinejad's first
Sadeq Mahsuli	2008–9	Ahmadinejad's first
Mostafa Mohammad-Najjar	2009–13	Ahmadinejad's second
Abdorreza Rahmani-Fazli	2013–17	Rouhani's first
Abdorreza Rahmani-Fazli	2017–21	Rouhani's second

MINISTRY OF JUSTICE

Name of minister	Tenure	PM or president's cabinet
Asadollah Mobasheri	1979–79	Bazargan
Seyyed Ahmad Sadr Haj Seyyed Javadi	1979–79	Bazargan
Ebrahim Ahadi	1980–81	Raja'i
Seyyed Mohammad Asghari-Bahari	1981–81	Raja'i
Seyyed Mohammad Asghari-Bahari	1981–81	Bahonar
Seyyed Mohammad Asghari-Bahari	1981–81	Mahdavi-Kani
Seyyed Mohammad Asghari-Bahari	1981–84	Musavi's first
Hasan-Ebrahim Habibi	1984–85	Musavi's first
Hasan-Ebrahim Habibi	1985–89	Musavi's second
Mohammad-Esma'il Shushtari	1989–93	Hashemi-Rafsanjani's first
Mohammad-Esma'il Shushtari	1993–97	Hashemi-Rafsanjani's second
Mohammad-Esma'il Shushtari	1997–2001	Khatami's first
Mohammad-Esma'il Shushtari	2001–5	Khatami's second
Jamal Karimirad	2005–6	Ahmadinejad's first
Gholam-Hoseyn Elham	2007–9	Ahmadinejad's second
Seyyed Morteza Bakhtiari	2009–13	Ahmadinejad's second
Mostafa Purmohammadi	2013–17	Rouhani's first
Seyyed Ali-Reza Ava'i	2017–21	Rouhani's second

Table 59 (Cont.)
Ministers Based on Portfolio (1979–2021)

MINISTRY OF LABOR AND SOCIAL AFFAIRS

Name of minister	Tenure	PM or president's cabinet
Daryush Foruhar	1979–79	Bazargan
Abdolali Espahbodi	1979–79	Bazargan
Mohammad-Reza Ne'matzadeh	1979–80	Revolutionary Council
Mohammad Mir Mohammad-Sadeqi	1980–81	Raja'i
Mohammad Mir Mohammad-Sadeqi	1981–81	Bahonar
Mohammad Mir Mohammad-Sadeqi	1981–81	Mahdavi-Kani
Ahmad Tavakkoli	1981–83	Musavi's first
Abolqasem Sarhaddizadeh	1983–85	Musavi's first
Abolqasem Sarhaddizadeh	1985–89	Musavi's second
Hoseyn Kamali	1989–93	Hashemi-Rafsanjani's first
Hoseyn Kamali	1993–97	Hashemi-Rafsanjani's second
Hoseyn Kamali	1997–2001	Khatami's first
Seyyed Safdar Hoseyni	2001–4	Khatami's second
Naser Khaleqi	2004–5	Khatami's second
Seyyed Mohammad Jahromi	2005–9	Ahmadinejad's first
Abdorreza Shaikholislami	2009–Aug. 3, 2011	Ahmadinejad's second

MINISTRY OF MINING (AND METALS)

Name of minister	Tenure	PM or president's cabinet
Seyyed Hoseyn Musaviyani	1981–81	Bahonar
Seyyed Hoseyn Musaviyani	1981–81	Mahdavi-Kani
Seyyed Hoseyn Musaviyani	1981–83	Musavi's first
Hoseyn Nili-Ahmadabadi	1983–85	Musavi's first
Seyyed Mohammad-Reza Ayatollahi	1986–89	Musavi's second
Hoseyn Mahlujchi	1989–93	Hashemi-Rafsanjani's first
Hoseyn Mahlujchi	1993–97	Hashemi-Rafsanjani's second
Eshaq Jahangiri	1997–Jan. 14, 2001	Khatami's first

MINISTRY OF PETROLEUM

Name of minister	Tenure	PM or president's cabinet
Ali-Akbar Mo'infar	1979–79	Bazargan
Ali-Akbar Mo'infar	1979–80	Revolutionary Council
Mohammad-Javad Tondguyan	1980–81	Raja'i
Seyyed Mohammad Gharazi	1981–81	Bahonar
Seyyed Mohammad Gharazi	1981–81	Mahdavi-Kani
Seyyed Mohammad Gharazi	1981–85	Musavi's first
Gholam-Reza Aqa Zadeh	1985–89	Musavi's second

Table 59 (Cont.)
Ministers Based on Portfolio (1979–2021)

MINISTRY OF PETROLEUM

Name of minister	Tenure	PM or president's cabinet
Gholam-Reza Aqa Zadeh	1989–93	Hashemi-Rafsanjani's first
Gholam-Reza Aqa Zadeh	1993–97	Hashemi-Rafsanjani's second
Bizhan Namdar-Zangeneh	1997–2001	Khatami's first
Bizhan Namdar-Zangeneh	2001–5	Khatami's second
Seyyed Kazem Vaziri-Hamaneh	2005–7	Ahmadinejad's first
Gholam-Hoseyn Nowzari	2007–9	Ahmadinejad's first
Seyyed Mas'ud Mir Kazemi	2009–11	Ahmadinejad's second
Rostam Qasemi	2011–13	Ahmadinejad's second
Bizhan Namdar-Zangeneh	2013–17	Rouhani's first
Bizhan Namdar-Zangeneh	2017–21	Rouhani's second

MINISTRY OF PLANNING AND BUDGET

Name of minister	Tenure	PM or president's cabinet
Mas'ud Roghani-Zanjani	1985–89	Musavi's second

MINISTRY OF POST, TELEGRAPH, AND TELEPHONES (INFORMATION AND COMMUNICATIONS TECHNOLOGY)

Name of minister	Tenure	PM or president's cabinet
Mohammad-Hasan Islami	1979–79	Bazargan
Mahmud Qandi	1979–80	Revolutionary Council
Mahmud Qandi	1980–81	Raja'i
Seyyed Morteza Nabavi	1981–81	Bahonar
Seyyed Morteza Nabavi	1981–81	Mahdavi-Kani
Seyyed Morteza Nabavi	1981–85	Musavi's first
Seyyed Mohammad Gharazi	1985–89	Musavi's second
Seyyed Mohammad Gharazi	1989–93	Hashemi-Rafsanjani's first
Seyyed Mohammad Gharazi	1993–97	Hashemi-Rafsanjani's second
Mohammad-Reza Aref	1997–2000	Khatami's first
Seyyed Ahmad Mo'tamedi	2001–1	Khatami's first
Seyyed Ahmad Mo'tamedi	2001–5	Khatami's second
Mohammad Soleymani	2005–9	Ahmadinejad's first
Reza Taqipur	2009–12	Ahmadinejad's second
Mohammad-Hasan Nami	2013–13	Ahmadinejad's second
Mahmud Va'ezi	2013–17	Rouhani's first
Mohammad-Javad Azari-Jahromi	2017–21	Rouhani's second

Table 59 (Cont.)
Ministers Based on Portfolio (1979–2021)

MINISTRY OF REVOLUTIONARY GUARDS

Name of minister	Tenure	PM or president's cabinet
Mohsen Rafiqdust	1982–85	Musavi's first
Mohsen Rafiqdust	1985–88	Musavi's second
Ali Shamkhani	1988–89	Musavi's second

MINISTRY OF ROADS AND TRANSPORTATION[e]

Name of minister	Tenure	PM or president's cabinet
Yusef Taheri	1979–79	Bazargan
Yusef Taheri	1979–79	Revolutionary Council
Musa Kalantari	1980–81	Raja'i
Mohammad-Hadi Nezhad-Hoseyniyan	1981–81	Mahdavi-Kani
Mohammad-Hadi Nezhad-Hoseyniyan	1981–85	Musavi's first
Mohammad Sa'idi-Kiya	1985–89	Musavi's second
Mohammad Sa'idi-Kiya	1989–93	Hashemi-Rafsanjani's first
Akbar Torkan	1993–97	Hashemi-Rafsanjani's second
Mahmud Hojjati	1997–2000	Khatami's first
Rahman Dadman	2001–1	Khatami's first
Ahmad Khorram	2001–4	Khatami's second
Mohammad Rahmati	2005–5	Khatami's second
Mohammad Rahmati	2005–8	Ahmadinejad's first
Hamid Behbahani	2008–9	Ahmadinejad's first
Hamid Behbahani	2009–11	Ahmadinejad's second
Ali Nikzad	2011–13	Ahmadinejad's second
Abbas-Ahmad Akhundi	2013–17	Rouhani's first
Abbas-Ahmad Akhundi	2017–21	Rouhani's second

MINISTRY OF WELFARE AND SOCIAL SECURITY

Name of minister	Tenure	President's cabinet
Mohammad-Hoseyn Sharifzadegan	2004–5	Khatami's second
Parviz Kazemi	2005–6	Ahmadinejad's first
Abdorreza Mesri	2006–8	Ahmadinejad's first
Sadeq Mahsuli	2009–11	Ahmadinejad's second

[e] As mentioned in the explanatory notes at the beginning of this chapter, the name of this ministry changed to the Ministry of Roads and Urban Development in 2011. Here we have kept the original name.

Table 59 (Cont.)
Ministers Based on Portfolio (1979–2021)

MINISTRY OF SPORTS AND YOUTH

Name of minister	Tenure	President's cabinet
Mohammad Abbasi	2011–13	Ahmadinejad's second
Mahmud Gudarzi	2013–16	Rouhani's first
Mas'ud Soltanifar	2016–17	Rouhani's first
Mas'ud Soltanifar	2017–21	Rouhani's second

MINISTERIAL ADVISER (WITHOUT PORTFOLIO)

Name of minister	Tenure	PM's cabinet
Daryush Foruhar	1979–79	Bazargan

MINISTERIAL ADVISER FOR EDUCATION AND RESEARCH

Name of minister	Tenure	PM's cabinet
Yadollah Sahabi	1979–79	Bazargan

MINISTERIAL ADVISER FOR EXECUTIVE AFFAIRS

Name of minister	Tenure	PM or president's cabinet
Seyyed Sadeq Tabataba'i	1979–79	Bazargan
Mohammad-Hoseyn Baniasadi	1979–79	Bazargan
Behzad Nabavi	1980–81	Raja'i
Behzad Nabavi	1981–81	Bahonar
Behzad Nabavi	1981–81	Mahdavi-Kani
Behzad Nabavi	1981–82	Musavi's first
Gholam-Reza Aqa Zadeh	1982–85	Musavi's first

MINISTERIAL ADVISER AND HEAD OF PBO

Name of minister	Tenure	PM or president's cabinet
Ali-Akbar Mo'infar	1979–79	Bazargan
Ezzatollah Sahabi	1979–79	Bazargan
Ezzatollah Sahabi	1979–80	Revolutionary Council
Musa Khayyer	1980–81	Raja'i
Mohammad-Taqi Banki	1981–81	Bahonar
Mohammad-Taqi Banki	1981–81	Mahdavi-Kani
Mohammad-Taqi Banki	1981–85	Musavi's first

Table 59 (Cont.)
Ministers Based on Portfolio (1979–2021)

MINISTERIAL ADVISER FOR REVOLUTIONARY AFFAIRS

Name of minister	Tenure	PM's cabinet
Ebrahim Yazdi	1979–79	Bazargan
Yadollah Sahabi	1979–79	Bazargan
Mohammad-Hoseyn Baniasadi	1979–79	Bazargan

MINISTERIAL ADVISER AND HEAD OF THE IRAN NATIONAL STEEL COMPANY

Name of minister	Tenure	President's cabinet
Mahmud Ahmadzadeh-Heravi	1980–81	Raja'i

MINISTERIAL ADVISER AND HEAD OF THE PUBLIC HEALTH ORGANIZATION

Name of minister	Tenure	PM or president's cabinet
Mohammad-Ali Fayyazbakhsh	1980–81	Raja'i
Mahmud Ruhani	1981–81	Bahonar
Mahmud Ruhani	1981–81	Mahdavi-Kani
Mahmud Ruhani	1981–82	Musavi's first
Mohammad-Javad Ezheh'i	1982–85	Musavi's first

FIRST VICE PRESIDENT

Name of vice president	Tenure	President's cabinet
Hasan-Ebrahim Habibi	1989–93	Hashemi-Rafsanjani's first
Hasan-Ebrahim Habibi	1993–97	Hashemi-Rafsanjani's second
Hasan-Ebrahim Habibi	1997–2001	Khatami's first
Mohammad-Reza Aref	2001–5	Khatami's second
Parviz Davudi	2005–9	Ahmadinejad's first
Esfandiyar Rahimmasha'i	2009–9	Ahmadinejad's first
Mohammad-Reza Rahimi	2009–13	Ahmadinejad's second
Eshaq Jahangiri	2013–17	Rouhani's first
Eshaq Jahangiri	2017–21	Rouhani's second

VICE PRESIDENT AND HEAD OF THE PLAN AND BUDGET ORGANIZATION[f]

Name of vice president	Tenure	President's cabinet
Mas'ud Roghani-Zanjani	1989–93	Hashemi-Rafsanjani's first
Mas'ud Roghani-Zanjani	1993–95	Hashemi-Rafsanjani's second

[f] As mentioned in the explanatory notes at the beginning of this chapter, the title of this organization changed to Management and Planning Organization for a while.

Table 59 (Cont.)
Ministers Based on Portfolio (1979–2021)

VICE PRESIDENT AND HEAD OF THE PLAN AND BUDGET ORGANIZATION[f]

Name of minister	Tenure	PM's cabinet
Hamid Mirzadeh	1995–97	Hashemi-Rafsanjani's second
Mohammad-Ali Najafi	1997–2000	Khatami's first
Mohammad-Reza Aref	2000–2001	Khatami's second
Mohammad Sattarifar	2001–4	Khatami's second
Hamid-Reza Baradaran-Shoraka	2004–5	Khatami's second
Farhad Rahbar	2005–6	Ahmadinejad's first
Seyyed Amir-Mansur Borqe'i	2006–7	Ahmadinejad's first
Mohammad-Baqer Nowbakht-Haqiqi	2017–21	Rouhani's second

VICE PRESIDENT AND HEAD OF THE ADMINISTRATIVE AND RECRUITMENT ORGANIZATION

Name of vice president	Tenure	President's cabinet
Jamshid Ansari	2017–21	Rouhani's second

VICE PRESIDENT AND HEAD OF THE PHYSICAL TRAINING ORGANIZATION[g]

Name of vice president	Tenure	President's cabinet
Hasan Ghafurifard	1990–93	Hashemi-Rafsanjani's first
Seyyed Mostafa Hashemi-Taba	1993–97	Hashemi-Rafsanjani's second
Seyyed Mostafa Hashemi-Taba	1997–2001	Khatami's first
Mohsen Mehr-Alizadeh	2001–5	Khatami's second
Mohammad Aliabadi	2005–9	Ahmadinejad's first
Ali Sa'idlu	2009–11	Ahmadinejad's second

VICE PRESIDENT AND HEAD OF THE NATIONAL YOUTH ORGANIZATION

Name of vice president	Tenure	President's cabinet
Mohammad-Javad Haj Aliakbari	2005–9	Ahmadinejad's first
Mehrdad Bazrpash	2009–10	Ahmadinejad's second

VICE PRESIDENT AND HEAD OF THE ATOMIC ENERGY ORGANIZATION

Name of vice president	Tenure	President's cabinet
Reza Amrollahi	1989–93	Hashemi-Rafsanjani's first
Reza Amrollahi	1993–97	Hashemi-Rafsanjani's second
Gholam-Reza Aqa Zadeh	1997–2001	Khatami's first
Gholam-Reza Aqa Zadeh	2001–5	Khatami's second
Gholam-Reza Aqa Zadeh	2005–9	Ahmadinejad's first
Ali-Akbar Salehi	2009–11	Ahmadinejad's second

[g] Hoseyn Shahhoseyni was ministerial adviser and head of the Physical Training Organization in 1979.

Table 59 (Cont.)
Ministers Based on Portfolio (1979–2021)

VICE PRESIDENT AND HEAD OF THE ATOMIC ENERGY ORGANIZATION

Name of minister	Tenure	PM's cabinet
Fereydun Abbasi-Davani	2011–13	Ahmadinejad's second
Ali-Akbar Salehi	2013–17	Rouhani's first
Ali-Akbar Salehi	2017–21	Rouhani's second

VICE PRESIDENT AND HEAD OF THE CULTURAL HERITAGE, HANDICRAFTS, AND TOURISM ORGANIZATION

Name of vice president	Tenure	PM or president's cabinet
Seyyed Hoseyn Mar'ashi	2004–5	Khatami's second
Esfandiyar Rahimmasha'i	2005–9	Ahmadinejad's first
Hamid Baqa'i	2009–11	Ahmadinejad's second
Ruhollah Ahmadzadeh-Kermani	2011–12	Ahmadinejad's second
Mir Hasan Musavi	2012–12	Ahmadinejad's second
Mohammad-Ali Najafi	2013–14	Rouhani's first
Mas'ud Soltanifar	2014–16	Rouhani's first
Zahra Ahmadipur	2016–17	Rouhani's first
Ali-Asghar Monesan	2017–21	Rouhani's second

VICE PRESIDENT AND HEAD OF THE ENVIRONMENTAL PROTECTION ORGANIZATION[h]

Name of vice president	Tenure	President's cabinet
Hadi Manafi	1989–93	Hashemi-Rafsanjani's first
Hadi Manafi	1993–97	Hashemi-Rafsanjani's second
Ma'sume Ebtekar	1997–2001	Khatami's first
Ma'sume Ebtekar	2001–5	Khatami's second
Fatemeh Va'ez-Javadi	2005–9	Ahmadinejad's first
Mohammad-Javad Mohammadizadeh	2009–13	Ahmadinejad's second
Ma'sume Ebtekar	2013–17	Rouhani's first
Isa Kalantari	2017–21	Rouhani's second

VICE PRESIDENT FOR EXECUTIVE AFFAIRS

Name of vice president	Tenure	President's cabinet
Hamid Mirzadeh	1989–93	Hashemi-Rafsanjani's first
Hamid Mirzadeh	1993–95	Hashemi-Rafsanjani's second
Mohammad Hashemi-Bahremani	1995–97	Hashemi-Rafsanjani's second
Mohammad Hashemi-Bahremani	1997–2001	Khatami's first
Ali Sa'idlu	2005–9	Ahmadinejad's first
Hamid Baqa'i	2011–13	Ahmadinejad's second
Mohammad Shari'atmadari	2013–17	Rouhani's first

[h] Between 1979 and 1989, Abbas Sami'i, Taqi Ebtekar, Reza-Hoseyn Mirza-Taheri, and Hadi Manafi served as heads of the Environmental Protection Organization but they were not designated as vice presidents and were not introduced to the Majlis to secure a vote of confidence like the ministerial advisors had to do. As such, they have not been included.

Table 59 (Cont.)
Ministers Based on Portfolio (1979–2021)

VICE PRESIDENT FOR IMPLEMENTATION OF CONSTITUTION

Name of vice president	Tenure	President's cabinet
Seyyed Mohammad-Reza Mir Tajeddini	2012–13	Ahmadinejad's second

VICE PRESIDENT FOR LEGAL AFFAIRS

Name of vice president	Tenure	President's cabinet
Fatemeh Bodaghi	2009–13	Ahmadinejad's second
Elham Aminzadeh	2013–16	Rouhani's first
Majid Ansari	2016–17	Rouhani's first
La'ya Joneydi	2017–21	Rouhani's second

VICE PRESIDENT FOR MANAGEMENT AND HUMAN CAPITAL DEVELOPMENT

Name of vice president	Tenure	President's cabinet
Ebrahim Azizi	2007–9	Ahmadinejad's first
Lotfollah Foruzandeh-Dehkordi	2009–12	Ahmadinejad's second
Ebrahim Azizi	2012–13	Ahmadinejad's second

VICE PRESIDENT AND HEAD OF FOUNDATION OF MARTYRS AND VETERANS AFFAIRS

Name of vice president	Tenure	President's cabinet
Hoseyn Dehqan	2004–5	Khatami's second
Hoseyn Dehqan	2005–9	Ahmadinejad's first
Mas'ud Zaribafan	2009–13	Ahmadinejad's second
Seyyed Mohammad-Ali Shahidi-Mahallati	2013–17	Rouhani's first
Seyyed Mohammad-Ali Shahidi-Mahallati	2017–21	Rouhani's second

VICE PRESIDENT FOR PARLIAMENTARY AFFAIRS

Name of vice president	Tenure	President's cabinet
Seyyed Ataollah Mohajerani	1989–93	Rafsanjani's first
Seyyed Ataollah Mohajerani	1993–97	Rafsanjani's second
Seyyed Abdolvahed Musavi-Lari	1997–98	Khatami's first
Mohammad-Ali Saduqi	1998–2001	Khatami's first
Seyyed Mohammad-Ali Abtahi	2001–4	Khatami's second
Majid Ansari	2004–5	Khatami's second
Seyyed Ahmad Musavi	2005–7	Ahmadinejad's first
Mohammad-Reza Rahimi	2008–9	Ahmadinejad's first
Seyyed Mohammad-Reza Mir Tajeddini	2009–12	Ahmadinejad's second
Lotfollah Foruzandeh-Dehkordi	2012–13	Ahmadinejad's second
Majid Ansari	2013–16	Rouhani's first

Table 59 (Cont.)
Ministers Based on Portfolio (1979–2021)

VICE PRESIDENT FOR PARLIAMENTARY AFFAIRS

Name of vice president	Tenure	President's cabinet
Hoseyn-Ali Amiri	2016–17	Rouhani's first
Hoseyn-Ali Amiri	2017–21	Rouhani's second

VICE PRESIDENT FOR PLANNING AND STRATEGIC SUPERVISION

Name of vice president	Tenure	President's cabinet
Ebrahim Azizi	2009–12	Ahmadinejad's second
Behruz Moradi	2012–13	Ahmadinejad's second
Mohammad-Baqer Nowbakht-Haqiqi	2013–17	Rouhani's first

VICE PRESIDENT FOR SCIENTIFIC AND TECHNOLOGICAL AFFAIRS

Name of vice president	Tenure	President's cabinet
Sadeq Va'ezzadeh-Khorasani	2005–9	Ahmadinejad's first
Nasrin Soltankhah	2009–13	Ahmadinejad's second
Sourena Sattari	2013–17	Rouhani's first
Sourena Sattari	2017–21	Rouhani's second

VICE PRESIDENT FOR WOMEN'S AND FAMILY AFFAIRS

Name of vice president	Tenure	PM or president's cabinet
Maryam Mojtahedzadeh	2013–13	Ahmadinejad's second
Shahindokht Moulaverdi	2013–17	Rouhani's first
Ma'sume Ebtekar	2017–21	Rouhani's second

Confidence Vote for Each Cabinet (1980–2017)

Table 60
Confidence Vote for Premier Raja'i's Cabinet (Sept. 10, 1980)

Ministry	Ministerial candidate	Approvals	Denials	Abstentions	Total
Agriculture	Mohammad Salamati	169	14	10	193
Culture and higher education	Seyyed Hasan Arefi	169	14	10	193
National defense	Javad Fakuri	169	14	10	193
Energy	Hasan Abbaspur-Tehranifard	169	14	10	193
Health	Hadi Manafi	169	14	10	193
Housing and urban development	Mohammad-Shahab Gonabadi	169	14	10	193
Industries	Mohammad-Reza Ne'matzadeh	169	14	10	193
Interior	Mohammad-Reza Mahdavi-Kani	169	14	10	193
Islamic guidance	Abbas Duzduzani	169	14	10	193
Ministerial adviser for executive affairs	Behzad Nabavi	169	14	10	193
Ministerial adviser and head of the Iran National Steel Company	Mahmud Ahmadzadeh-Heravi	169	14	10	193
Ministerial adviser and head of the Public Health Organization	Mohammad-Ali Fayyazbakhsh	169	14	10	193
Post, telegraph, and telephones	Mahmud Qandi	169	14	10	193
Roads and transportation	Musa Kalantari	169	14	10	193
VOTED ON LATER					
Petroleum	Mohammad-Javad Tondguyan (Sept. 25, 1980)	155	3	18	176
Ministerial adviser and head of PBO	Musa Khayyer (Sept. 25, 1980)	162	2	12	176
Justice	Ebrahim Ahadi (Nov. 5, 1980)	129	19	26[a]	170
Labor and social affairs	Mohammad Mir Mohammad-Sadeqi (Jan. 5, 1981)	156[b]	9	11	174
Commerce	Hoseyn Kazempur-Ardabili (Mar. 11, 1981)	114	13	45	176
Economic affairs and finance	Hoseyn Namazi (Mar. 11, 1981)	150	4	21	172
Justice	Mohammad Asghari-Bahari (June 15, 1981)	134	7	41	175
Foreign affairs	Mir Hoseyn Musavi (July 5, 1981)	126	8	33	182

Source: Islamic Consultative Assembly, Sept. 10, 1980 (19 Shahrivar 1359), p. 38; Sept. 25, 1980 (3 Mehr 1359), p. 25; Nov. 5, 1980 (14 Aban 1359), pp. 28–29; Nov. 25, 1980 (4 Azar 1359), p. 28; Mar. 11, 1981 (20 Bahman 1359); Jun. 15, 1981 (25 Khordad 1360), p. 17; Jul. 5, 1981 (14 Tir 1360).

Note: Bazargan's cabinet and the Revolutionary Council cabinets did not need to get a vote of confidence since the First Majlis had not yet been established. PM Raja'i's slate of ministers was not voted on individually but approved in a general vote. Dates in parentheses refer to when the Majlis voted on the minister.

[a] *Ettela'at* (1359/1980) puts Ahadi's abstained vote at twenty-nine and the total at 177.

[b] *Ettela'at* (1359/1980) puts Mohammad-Sadeqi's positive vote at 160 and the total at 180.

Table 61
Confidence Vote for Premier Bahonar's Cabinet (Aug. 17, 1981)

Ministry	Ministerial candidate	Approvals	Denials	Abstentions	Total
Agriculture	Mohammad Salamati	124	14	24	162
Commerce	Habibollah Asgarowladi	134	0	12	166
Culture and higher education	Mohammad-Ali Najafi	130	11	27	168
National defense	Seyyed Musa Namju	163	1	3	167
Economic affairs and finance	Hoseyn Namazi	143	5	10	158
Education	Seyyed Ali-Akbar Parvaresh	138	14	11	163
Energy	Hasan Ghafurifard	142	8	11	161
Foreign affairs	Mir Hoseyn Musavi	153	5	12	170
Health	Hadi Manafi	133	9	25	167
Housing and urban development	Mohammad-Shahab Gonabadi	156	5	9	170
Industries	Seyyed Mostafa Hashemi-Taba	147	2	15	164
Interior	Mohammad-Reza Mahdavi-Kani	134	17	16	167
Islamic guidance	Abdolmajid Mo'adikhah	116	20	19	155
Justice	Seyyed Mohammad Asghari-Bahari	137	13	12	162
Labor and social affairs	Mohammad Mir Mohammad-Sadeqi	118	18	29	165
Mining and metals	Seyyed Hoseyn Musaviyani	122	3	29	154
Ministerial adviser for executive affairs	Behzad Nabavi	144	6	10	160
Ministerial adviser and head of PBO	Mohammad-Taqi Banki	154	1	10	165
Ministerial adviser and head of the Public Health Organization	Mahmud Ruhani	155	1	10	166
Petroleum	Seyyed Mohammad Gharazi	154	2	11	167
Post, telegraph, and telephones	Seyyed Morteza Nabavi	154	2	6	162
Roads and transportation	Seyyed Hoseyn Tajgardun (rejected)	79	33	51	163

Source: Islamic Consultative Assembly, Aug. 17, 1981 (26 Mordad 1360), pp. 38–39.

Table 62
Confidence Vote for Premier Mahdavi-Kani's Cabinet (Sept. 3, 1981)

Ministry	Ministerial candidate	Approvals	Denials	Abstentions	Total
Agriculture	Mohammad Salamati	170	4	13	187
Commerce	Habibollah Asgarowladi	170	4	13	187
Culture and higher education	Mohammad-Ali Najafi	170	4	13	187
National defense	Seyyed Musa Namju	170	4	13	187
Economic affairs and finance	Hoseyn Namazi	170	4	13	187
Education	Seyyed Ali-Akbar Parvaresh	170	4	13	187
Energy	Hasan Ghafurifard	170	4	13	187
Foreign affairs	Mir Hoseyn Musavi	170	4	13	187
Health	Hadi Manafi	170	4	13	187
Housing and urban development	Mohammad-Shahab Gonabadi	170	4	13	187
Industries	Seyyed Mostafa Hashemi-Taba	170	4	13	187
Interior	Seyyed Kamaleddin Nikravesh	170	4	13	187
Islamic guidance	Abdolmajid Mo'adikhah	170	4	13	187
Justice	Seyyed Mohammad Asghari-Bahari	170	4	13	187
Labor and social affairs	Mohammad Mir Mohammad-Sadeqi	170	4	13	187
Mining and metals	Seyyed Hoseyn Musaviyani	170	4	13	187
Petroleum	Seyyed Mohammad Gharazi	170	4	13	187
Post, telegraph, and telephones	Seyyed Morteza Nabavi	170	4	13	187
Roads and transportation	Mohammad-Hadi Nezhad-Hoseyniyan	170	4	13	187

Source: Islamic Consultative Assembly (1360/1981).
Note: No individual vote was cast and the Majlis approved the cabinet as a whole on September 3, 1981.

Table 63
Confidence Vote for Premier Musavi's First Cabinet (Nov. 2, 1981)

Ministry	Ministerial candidate	Approvals	Denials	Abstentions	Total
Agriculture	Mohammad Salamati	120	16	25	161
Commerce	Habibollah Asgarowladi	131	11	12	154
Culture and higher education	Mohammad-Ali Najafi	135	9	15	159
National defense	Mohammad Salimi	102	27	27	156
Economic affairs and finance	Hoseyn Namazi	148	1	11	160
Education	Seyyed Ali-Akbar Parvaresh	146	12	2	160
Energy	Hasan Ghafurifard	108	24	23	155
Health	Hadi Manafi	124	18	17	159
Housing and urban development	Mohammad-Shahab Gonabadi	132	15	12	159
Industries	Seyyed Mostafa Hashemi-Taba	115	20	22	157
Interior	Seyyed Kamaleddin Nikravesh	102	30	29	161

Table 63 (Cont.)
Confidence Vote for Premier Musavi's First Cabinet (Nov. 2, 1981)

Ministry	Ministerial candidate	Approvals	Denials	Abstentions	Total
Islamic guidance	Abdolmajid Mo'adikhah	137	9	4	150
Justice	Seyyed Mohammad Asghari-Bahari	145	7	7	159
Labor and social affairs	Ahmad Tavakkoli	105	28	23	156
Mining and metals	Seyyed Hoseyn Musaviyani	113	15	22	150
Ministerial adviser for executive affairs	Behzad Nabavi	134	12	11	157
Ministerial adviser and head of PBO	Mohammad-Taqi Banki	158	0	6	164
Ministerial adviser and head of the Public Health Organization	Mahmud Ruhani	154	0	3	157
Petroleum	Seyyed Mohammad Gharazi	141	10	9	160
Post, telegraph, and telephones	Seyyed Morteza Nabavi	153	2	3	158
Roads and transportation	Mohammad-Hadi Nezhad-Hoseyniyan	146	1	12	159

VOTED ON LATER

Ministry	Ministerial candidate	Approvals	Denials	Abstentions	Total
Foreign affairs	Ali-Akbar Velayati (Dec. 15, 1981)	155	19	12	186
Interior	Ali-Akbar Nateq-Nuri (Dec. 15, 1981)	176	6	6	188
Heavy industries	Behzad Nabavi (May 31, 1982)	125	27	15	167
Ministerial adviser for executive affairs	Gholam-Reza Aqa Zadeh (May 31, 1982)	117	7	37	161
Islamic guidance	Seyyed Mohammad Khatami (Nov. 9, 1982)	121	27	22	170
Revolutionary guards	Mohsen Rafiqdust (Nov. 9, 1982)	139	11	23	173
Ministerial adviser and head of the Public Health Organization	Mohammad-Javad Ezheh'i (Nov. 9, 1982)	126	7	38	171
Agriculture	Isa Kalantari (rejected) (Aug. 28, 1983)	74	57	58	189
Commerce	Hasan Abedi-Ja'fari (Aug. 28, 1983)	134	23	32	189
Housing and urban development	Serajeddin Kazeruni (rejected) (Aug. 28, 1983)	66	68	48	182
Labor and social affairs	Abolqasem Sarhaddizadeh (Aug. 28, 1983)	121	17	47	185
Mining and metals	Hoseyn Naji (rejected) (Aug. 28, 1983)	51	40	88	179
Housing and urban development	Mohammad Morovvat (rejected) (Dec. 7, 1983)	66	62	32	160
Agriculture	Abbas-Ali Zali (Dec. 7, 1983)	102	42	21	165
Mining and metals	Hoseyn Nili-Ahmadabadi (Dec. 7, 1983)	102	35	23	160
Construction Jihad	Bizhan Namdar-Zangeneh (Feb. 21, 1984)	110	NA	NA	NA
Intelligence	Esma'il Ferdowsipur (rejected) (Feb. 21, 1984)	74	NA	NA	NA
Housing and urban development	Mohammad-Hasan Tehraninezhad (rejected) (Feb. 21, 1984)	78	NA	NA	NA

Source: Islamic Consultative Assembly, Nov. 2, 1981 (11 Aban 1360), pp. 39–40; Dec. 15, 1981 (24 Azar 1360), p. 29; May 31, 1982 (10 Khordad 1361), p. 37; Nov. 9, 1982 (18 Aban 1361), p. 29; Aug. 28, 1983 (6 Shahrivar 1362), pp. 34–35; Dec. 7, 1983 (16 Azar 1362), p. 40.

Table 64
Confidence Vote for Premier Musavi's First Cabinet: Midterm Confirmation (Aug. 14, 1984)

Ministry	Ministerial candidate	Approvals	Denials	Abstentions	Total
Agriculture	Abbas-Ali Zali	141	26	35	202
Commerce	Hasan Abedi-Ja'fari	156	29	23	208
Construction Jihad	Bizhan Namdar-Zangeneh	161	19	27	207
Culture and higher education	Mohammad-Ali Najafi (rejected)	51	89	64	204
National defense	Mohammad Salimi (rejected)	97	57	51	205
Economic affairs and finance	Hoseyn Namazi	106	38	56	200
Education	Seyyed Ali-Akbar Parvaresh (rejected)	99	81	25	205
Energy	Hasan Ghafurifard	179	11	18	208
Foreign affairs	Ali-Akbar Velayati	166	23	17	206
Health	Hadi Manafi (rejected)	102	53	46	201
Heavy industries	Behzad Nabavi	106	65	32	203
Industries	Seyyed Mostafa Hashemi-Taba (rejected)	62	90	53	205
Interior	Ali-Akbar Nateq-Nuri	107	69	29	205
Islamic guidance	Seyyed Mohammad Khatami	158	28	19	205
Labor and social affairs	Abolqasem Sarhaddizadeh	162	18	23	203
Mining and metals	Hoseyn Nili-Ahmadabadi	106	38	60	204
Ministerial adviser for executive affairs	Gholam-Reza Aqa Zadeh				No vote[a]
Ministerial adviser and head of the PBO	Mohammad-Taqi Banki				No vote
Ministerial adviser and head of the Public Health Organization	Mohammad-Javad Ezheh'i				No vote
Petroleum	Seyyed Mohammad Gharazi	154	29	23	206
Post, telegraph, and telephones	Seyyed Morteza Nabavi	140	43	24	207
Revolutionary guards	Mohsen Rafiqdust	154	28	23	205
Roads and transportation	Mohammad-Hadi Nezhad-Hoseyniyan	190	6	12	208
VOTED ON LATER					
Housing and urban development	Serajeddin Kazeruni (Aug. 15, 1984)	174	12	14	200
Intelligence	Mohammad Reyshahri (Aug. 15, 1984)	176	11	13	200
Justice	Hasan-Ebrahim Habibi (Aug. 15, 1984)	176	14	10	200
Health	Seyyed Ali-Reza Marandi (Aug. 20, 1984)	174	16	19	209
Culture and higher education	Iraj Fazel (Aug. 20, 1984)	178	17	14	209
Industries	Gholam-Reza Shafei (Aug. 20, 1984)	187	15	7	209
Education	Seyyed Kazem Akrami (Oct. 18, 1984)	122	39	26	187
Defense	Farrokh Azimi-Etemadi (rejected) (Oct. 18, 1984)	76	66	40	182

Source: Islamic Consultative Assembly, Aug. 14, 1984 (23 Mordad 1363), pp. 55–56; Aug. 15, 1984 (24 Mordad 1363), pp. 42–43; Oct. 18, 1984 (26 Mehr 1363), p. 37; Hashemi-Rafsanjani (2007), 251.
[a] Ministerial advisers did not need to be approved by the Majlis.

Table 65
Confidence Vote for Premier Musavi's Second Cabinet (Oct. 28, 1985)

Ministry	Ministerial candidate	Approvals	Denials	Abstentions	Total
Agriculture	Abbas-Ali Zali	163	57	38	258
Commerce	Hasan Abedi-Ja'fari	167	46	45	258
Construction Jihad	Bizhan Namdar-Zangeneh	218	14	26	258
Islamic guidance	Seyyed Mohammad Khatami	221	18	19	258
Defense	Mohammad-Hoseyn Jalali	195	17	46	258
Economic affairs and finance	Hoseyn Namazi (rejected)	115	73	70	258
Education	Seyyed Kazem Akrami	192	32	34	258
Energy	Mohammad-Taqi Banki	165	44	49	258
Foreign affairs	Ali-Akbar Velayati	210	17	31	258
Health	Seyyed Ali-Reza Marandi	144	75	39	258
Heavy industries	Behzad Nabavi	159	65	34	258
Higher education	Mohammad Farhadi	217	13	28	258
Housing and urban development	Serajeddin Kazeruni	202	20	36	258
Industries	Gholam-Reza Shafei	161	34	63	258
Intelligence	Mohammad Reyshahri	233	4	21	258
Interior	Seyyed Ali-Akbar Mohtashamipur	163	32	63	258
Justice	Hasan-Ebrahim Habibi	241	3	14	258
Labor and social affairs	Abolqasem Sarhaddizadeh	176	45	37	258
Mining and metals	Hoseyn Nili-Ahmadabadi (rejected)	126	83	49	258
Planning and budget	Mas'ud Roghani-Zanjani	144	55	59	258
Petroleum	Gholam-Reza Aqa Zadeh	146	65	47	258
Post, telegraph, and telephones	Seyyed Mohammad Gharazi	214	14	30	258
Revolutionary guards	Mohsen Rafiqdust	183	32	43	258
Roads and transportation	Mohammad Sa'idi-Kiya	170	25	63	258
VOTED ON LATER					
Economic affairs and finance	Mohammad-Javad Iravani (Jan. 5, 1986)	138	6	32	176
Mining and metals	Seyyed Mohammad-Reza Ayatollahi (Jan. 5, 1986)	143	4	29	176
Education	Mohammad-Ali Najafi (Sept. 20, 1988)[a]	128	49	30	207
Revolutionary guards	Ali Shamkhani (Sept. 20, 1988)	202	10	6	218
Construction Jihad	Gholam-Reza Foruzesh (Sept. 20, 1988)	180	15	13	208
Energy	Bizhan Namdar-Zangeneh (Sept. 20, 1988)	177	14	5	196
Agriculture	Isa Kalantari (Sept. 20, 1988)	171	25	19	215
Commerce	Seyyed Majid Hedayatzadeh (rejected) (Sept. 20, 1988)	NA	NA	NA	NA

[a] Najafi became education minister after Seyyed Kazem Akrami failed to secure enough votes to continue serving in the cabinet.

Table 66
Confidence Vote for President Hashemi-Rafsanjani's First Cabinet (Aug. 29, 1989)

Ministry	Ministerial candidate	Approvals	Denials	Abstentions	Total
Agriculture	Isa Kalantari	186	53	20	259
Commerce	Abdolhoseyn Vahaji	147	93	18	258
Construction Jihad	Gholam-Reza Foruzesh	221	30	10	261
Culture and Islamic guidance	Seyyed Mohammad Khatami	246	10	4	260
Defense and armed forces logistics	Akbar Torkan	242	10	9	261
Economic affairs and finance	Mohsen Nurbakhsh	195	43	19	257
Education	Mohammad-Ali Najafi	160	86	12	258
Energy	Bizhan Namdar-Zangeneh	245	5	7	257
Foreign affairs	Ali-Akbar Velayati	213	35	10	258
Health and medical education	Iraj Fazel	165	86	9	260
Heavy industries	Mohammad-Hadi Nezhad-Hoseyniyan	219	26	11	256
Higher education	Mostafa Mo'in	237	14	6	257
Housing and urban development	Serajeddin Kazeruni	145	97	14	256
Industries	Mohammad-Reza Ne'matzadeh	217	28	12	257
Intelligence	Ali Fallahiyan	158	79	18	255
Interior	Abdollah Nuri	224	20	15	259
Justice	Mohammad-Esma'il Shushtari	209	30	18	257
Labor and social affairs	Hoseyn Kamali	224	18	16	258
Mining and metals	Hoseyn Mahlujchi	150	85	22	257
Petroleum	Gholam-Reza Aqa Zadeh	231	18	10	259
Post, telegraph, and telephones	Seyyed Mohammad Gharazi	230	16	11	257
Roads and transportation	Mohammad Sa'idi-Kiya	222	21	9	252
	VOTED ON LATER				
Health and medical education	Reza Malekzadeh (Mar. 5, 1991)	149	31	24	204
Cooperatives	Gholam-Reza Shafei (Dec. 31, 1991)	147	30	10	187
Culture and Islamic guidance	Ali Larijani (Aug. 11, 1992)	207	8	9	224

Table 67
Confidence Vote for President Hashemi-Rafsanjani's Second Cabinet (Aug. 16, 1993)

Ministry	Ministerial candidate	Approvals	Denials	Abstentions	Total
Agriculture	Isa Kalantari	215	23	23	261
Commerce	Yahya Ale-'Eshaq	222	12	26	260
Construction Jihad	Gholam-Reza Foruzesh	152	70	27	249
Cooperatives	Gholam-Reza Shafei	229	9	18	256
Culture and Islamic guidance	Ali Larijani	219	12	29	260
Defense and armed forces logistics	Mohammad Foruzandeh	233	5	20	258
Economic affairs and finance	Mohsen Nurbakhsh (rejected)	127	75	49	251
Education	Mohammad-Ali Najafi	147	73	36	256
Energy	Bizhan Namdar-Zangeneh	202	37	18	257
Foreign affairs	Ali-Akbar Velayati	207	17	33	257
Health	Seyyed Ali-Reza Marandi	246	4	11	261
Heavy industries	Mohammad-Hadi Nezhad-Hoseyniyan	231	12	16	259
Higher education	Seyyed Mohammad-Reza Hashemi-Golpayegani	220	12	29	261
Housing and urban development	Abbas-Ahmad Akhundi	193	37	22	252
Industries	Mohammad-Reza Ne'matzadeh	194	29	29	252
Intelligence	Ali Fallahiyan	204	24	27	255
Interior	Ali-Mohammad Besharati	225	14	21	260
Justice	Mohammad-Esma'il Shushtari	233	7	18	258
Labor and social affairs	Hoseyn Kamali	223	18	17	258
Mining and metals	Hoseyn Mahlujchi	166	54	38	258
Petroleum	Gholam-Reza Aqa Zadeh	134	88	25	247
Post, telegraph, and telephones	Seyyed Mohammad Gharazi	192	38	21	251
Roads and transportation	Akbar Torkan	176	34	48	258
	VOTED ON LATER				
Economic affairs and finance	Morteza Mohammad Khan (Oct. 6, 1993)	151	46	26	223
Culture and Islamic guidance	Seyyed Mostafa Mir Salim (Feb. 22, 1994)	178	27	19	224
Industries	Mohammad-Reza Ne'matzadeh (Oct. 5, 1994)[a]	127	76	10	213

[a] Ne'matzadeh had to be reconfirmed as minister of industries after the merger of the ministries of industries and heavy industries.

Table 68
Confidence Vote for President Khatami's First Cabinet (Aug. 20, 1997)

Ministry	Ministerial candidate	Approvals	Denials	Abstentions	Total
Agriculture	Isa Kalantari	178	54	26	258
Commerce	Mohammad Shari'atmadari	215	25	20	260
Construction Jihad	Mohammad Sa'idi-Kiya	256	4	4	264
Cooperatives	Morteza Haji	182	54	24	260
Culture and Islamic guidance	Seyyed Ataollah Mohajerani	144	96	20	260
Defense and armed forces logistics	Ali Shamkhani	251	6	7	264
Economic affairs and finance	Hoseyn Namazi	249	6	11	266
Education	Hoseyn Mozaffar	145	84	32	261
Energy	Habibollah Bitaraf	202	35	21	258
Foreign affairs	Seyyed Kamal Kharrazi	241	13	12	266
Health and medical education	Mohammad Farhadi	216	34	16	266
Higher education	Mostafa Mo'in	211	35	20	266
Housing and urban development	Ali Abdolali'zadeh	172	70	21	263
Industries	Gholam-Reza Shafei	244	11	10	265
Intelligence	Qorbanali Dorri-Najafabadi	238	17	9	264
Interior	Abdollah Nuri	153	89	21	263
Justice	Mohammad-Esma'il Shushtari	255	3	6	264
Labor and social affairs	Hoseyn Kamali	222	25	18	265
Mining and metals	Eshaq Jahangiri	182	56	22	260
Petroleum	Bizhan Namdar-Zangeneh	213	34	19	266
Post, telegraph, and telephones	Mohammad-Reza Aref	246	9	8	263
Roads and transportation	Mahmud Hojjati	156	81	24	261
	VOTED ON LATER				
Interior	Seyyed Abdolvahed Musavi-Lari (July 22, 1998)	177	67	22	266
Intelligence	Ali Yunesi (Feb. 24, 1999)	197	9	18	224
Post, telegraph, and telephones	Nasrollah Jahangard (rejected) (Oct. 3, 2000)	117	99	25	241
Culture and Islamic guidance	Ahmad Masjed-Jame'i (Jan. 14, 2001)	214	27	12	253
Post, telegraph, and telephones	Seyyed Ahmad Mo'tamedi (Jan. 14, 2001)	202	38	15	255
Agriculture	Mahmud Hojjati (Jan. 14, 2001)[a]	189	55	11	255
Roads and transportation	Rahman Dadman (Jan. 14, 2001)	223	25	7	255
Industries	Eshaq Jahangiri (Jan. 14, 2001)	210	35	10	255

[a] Hojjati had to be reconfirmed after he switched from being minister of roads and transportation to minister of agriculture.

Table 69
Confidence Vote for President Khatami's Second Cabinet (Aug. 22, 2001)

Ministry	Ministerial candidate	Approvals	Denials	Abstentions	Total
Agriculture	Mahmud Hojjati	173	80	8	261
Commerce	Mohammad Shari'atmadari	205	47	15	267
Cooperatives	Ali Sufi	148	93	21	262
Culture and Islamic guidance	Ahmad Masjed-Jame'i	184	62	18	264
Defense and armed forces logistics	Ali Shamkhani	195	62	11	268
Economic affairs and finance	Tahmaseb Mazaheri	193	16	59	268
Education	Morteza Haji	155	90	16	261
Energy	Habibollah Bitaraf	190	63	10	263
Foreign affairs	Seyyed Kamal Kharrazi	201	11	55	267
Health and medical education	Mas'ud Pezeshkiyan	168	75	15	258
Housing and urban development	Ali Abdolali'zadeh	153	86	14	253
Industries and mining	Eshaq Jahangiri	191	58	11	260
Intelligence	Ali Yunesi	219	39	10	268
Interior	Seyyed Adolvahed Musavi-Lari	203	51	10	264
Justice	Mohammad-Esma'il Shushtari	195	55	13	263
Labor and social affairs	Seyyed Safdar Hoseyni	221	37	5	263
Petroleum	Bizhan Namdar-Zangeneh	166	74	14	254
Post, telegraph, and telephones	Seyyed Ahmad Mo'tamedi	175	71	12	258
Roads and transportation	Ahmad Khorram	186	58	14	258
Science, research, and technology	Mostafa Mo'in	169	86	11	266
	VOTED ON LATER				
Science, research, and technology	Ja'far Tofiqi (Oct. 8, 2003)	163	27	8	198
Economic affairs and finance	Seyyed Safdar Hoseyni (Apr. 25, 2004)[a]	169	25	7	201
Labor and social affairs	Naser Khaleqi (Apr. 25, 2004)	189	16	5	210
Social welfare	Mohammad-Hoseyn Sharifzadegan (July 3, 2004)	132	113	14	259
Roads and transportation	Mohammad Rahmati (Feb. 2, 2005)	117	29	18	164

[a] Hoseyni had to be reconfirmed after he switched from being minister of labor and social affairs to minister of economic affairs and finance.

Table 70
Confidence Vote for President Ahmadinejad's First Cabinet (Aug. 24, 2005)

Ministry	Ministerial candidate	Approvals	Denials	Abstentions	Total
Agriculture	Mohammad-Reza Eskandari	214	45	24	283
Commerce	Seyyed Mas'ud Mir Kazemi	169	85	25	279
Cooperatives	Ali-Reza Aliahmadi (rejected)	105	134	34	273
Culture and Islamic guidance	Mohammad-Hoseyn Saffar-Harandi	181	78	20	279
Defense and armed forces logistics	Mostafa Mohammad-Najjar	205	55	17	277
Economic affairs and finance	Davud Danesh-Ja'fari	216	47	19	282
Education	Ali-Akbar Ash'ari (rejected)	73	175	31	279
Energy	Seyyed Parviz Fattah	194	56	23	273
Foreign affairs	Manouchehr Mottaki	220	47	16	283
Health and medical education	Kamran Baqeri-Lankarani	169	86	27	282
Housing and urban development	Mohammad Sa'idi-Kiya	222	31	25	278
Industries and mining	Ali-Reza Tahmasebi	182	58	30	270
Information and communications technology	Mohammad Soleymani	220	43	16	279
Intelligence	Gholam-Hoseyn Mohseni-Ezheh'i	217	51	13	281
Interior	Mostafa Purmohammadi	153	90	31	274
Justice	Jamal Karimirad	191	59	24	274
Labor and social affairs	Seyyed Mohammad Jahromi	197	59	20	276
Petroleum	Ali Sa'idlu (rejected)	101	133	38	272
Roads and transportation	Mohammad Rahmati	214	43	21	278
Science, research, and technology	Mohammad-Mehdi Zahedi	144	101	35	280
Welfare and social security	Seyyed Mehdi Hashemi (rejected)	131	108	36	275
VOTED ON LATER					
Cooperatives	Mohammad Nazemi-Ardakani (Nov. 9, 2005)	174	51	11	236
Education	Mahmud Farshidi (Nov. 9, 2005)	136	91	21	248
Welfare and social security	Parviz Kazemi (Nov. 9, 2005)	178	61	15	254
Petroleum	Sadeq Mahsuli (rejected) (Nov. 9, 2005)	NA	NA	NA	Withdrew
Petroleum	Mohsen Tasalloti (rejected) (Nov. 23, 2005)	77	139	38	254
Petroleum	Seyyed Kazem Vaziri-Hamaneh (Dec. 11, 2005)	172	53	34	259
Welfare and social security	Abdorreza Mesri (Oct. 29, 2006)	191	42	11	244
Cooperatives	Mohammad Abbasi (Nov. 5, 2006)	155	70	20	245
Justice	Gholam-Hoseyn Elham (2007)	130	101	23	254
Industries and mining	Ali-Akbar Mehrabiyan (Nov. 14, 2007)	174	49	18	241
Petroleum	Gholam-Hoseyn Nowzari (Nov. 14, 2007)	217	20	9	246
Education	Ali-Reza Aliahmadi (Feb. 9, 2008)	133	92	29	254
Roads and transportation	Hamid Behbahani (Aug. 12, 2008)	181	51	37	269
Economic affairs and finance	Seyyed Shamseddin Hoseyni (Aug. 12, 2008)	217	29	23	269
Interior	Ali Kordan (Aug. 12, 2008)	169	64	36	269
Interior	Sadeq Mahsuli (Nov. 18, 2008)	138	112	20	270

Table 71
Confidence Vote for President Ahmadinejad's Second Cabinet (Sept. 3, 2009)

Ministry	Ministerial candidate	Approvals	Denials	Abstentions	Total
Agricultural Jihad	Sadeq Khaliliyan	200	54	32	286
Commerce	Mehdi Ghazanfari	158	91	37	286
Cooperatives	Mohammad Abbasi	163	83	37	283
Culture and Islamic guidance	Seyyed Mohammad Hoseyni	194	61	31	286
Defense and armed forces logistics	Ahmad Vahidi	227	54	5	286
Economic affairs and finance	Seyyed Shamseddin Hoseyni	224	41	21	286
Education	Susan Keshavarz (rejected)	49	209[a]	28	286
Energy	Mohammad Aliabadi (rejected)	137	117	32	286
Foreign affairs	Manouchehr Mottaki	173	79	34	286
Health and medical education	Marziyeh Vahid-Dastjerdi	175	82	29	286
Housing and urban development	Ali Nikzad	219	40	27	286
Industries and mining	Ali-Akbar Mehrabiyan	153	103	27	283
Information and communications technology	Reza Taqipur	197	62	27	286
Intelligence	Heydar Moslehi	194	67	25	286
Interior	Mostafa Mohammad-Najjar	182	75	25	282
Justice	Seyyed Morteza Bakhtiari	225	36	23	284
Cooperatives, labor, and social welfare	Abdorreza Shaikholislami	193	63	30	286
Petroleum	Seyyed Mas'ud Mir Kazemi	147	117	19	283
Roads and transportation	Hamid Behbahani	167	83	33	283
Science, research, and technology	Kamran Daneshju	186	75	25	286
Welfare and social security	Fatemeh Ajorlu (rejected)	76	181	29	286
	VOTED ON LATER				
Education	Hamid-Reza Haji Baba'i (Nov. 15, 2009)	217	33	13	263
Energy	Majid Namju (Nov. 15, 2009)	210	36	19	265
Welfare and social security	Sadeq Mahsuli (Nov. 15, 2009)	149	95	21	265
Foreign affairs	Ali-Akbar Salehi (Jan. 30, 2011)	146	60	35	241
Sports and youth	Hamid Sajjadi (rejected) (June 21, 2011)	87	137	23	247
Roads and urban development	Ali Nikzad (June 26, 2011)	205	16	16	237
Sports and youth	Mohammad Abbasi (Aug. 3, 2011)	165	61	19	245
Industry, mining, and trade	Mehdi Ghazanfari (Aug. 3, 2011)[b]	218	20	7	245
Petroleum	Rostam Qasemi (Aug. 13, 2011)	216	22	7	245
Information and communications technology	Mohammad-Hasan Nami (Feb. 26, 2013)	177	?[c]	?	243
Health and medical education	Mohammad-Hasan Tariqat-Monfared (Mar. 17, 2013)	113	99	12	224

[a] This has been the highest recorded negative vote for any ministerial candidate in postrevolutionary Iran.
[b] Ghazanfari had to be reconfirmed as minister of industry, mining, and trade after the merger of the ministries of industries and mining and commerce.
[c] The exact number of negative and abstaining votes for Nami could not be found.

Table 72
Confidence Vote for President Rouhani's First Cabinet (Aug. 15, 2013)

Ministry	Ministerial candidate	Approvals	Denials	Abstentions	Total
Agriculture	Mahmud Hojjati	177	81	26	284
Cooperatives, labor, and social welfare	Ali Rabi'i	163	100	21	284
Culture and Islamic guidance	Ali Jannati	234	36	12	282
Defense and armed forces logistics	Hoseyn Dehqan	269	10	5	284
Economic affairs and finance	Ali Tayyebniya	274	7	3	284
Education	Mohammad-Ali Najafi (rejected)	142	133	9	284
Energy	Hamid Chitchiyan	272	7	5	284
Foreign affairs	Mohammad-Javad Zarif	232	36	13	281
Health and medical education	Seyyed Hasan Qazizadeh-Hashemi	260	18	6	284
Industry, mining, and trade	Mohammad-Reza Ne'matzadeh	199	60	24	283
Information and communications technology	Mahmud Va'ezi	218	45	20	283
Intelligence	Seyyed Mahmud Alavi	227	38	18	283
Interior	Abdorreza Rahmani-Fazli	256	19	9	284
Justice	Mostafa Purmohammadi	201	64	19	284
Petroleum	Bizhan Namdar-Zangeneh	166	104	13	283
Road and urban development	Abbas-Ahmad Akhundi	159	107	18	284
Science, research, and technology	Ja'far Mili-Monfared (rejected)	105	162	15	282
Sports and youth	Mas'ud Soltanifar (rejected)	117	148	18	283
VOTED ON LATER					
Education	Ali-Asghar Fani (Oct. 27, 2013)	185	53	24	262
Science, research, and technology	Reza Faraji-Dana (Oct. 27, 2013)	159	70	32	261
Sports and youth	Seyyed Reza Salehi-Amiri (rejected) (Oct. 27, 2013)	107	141	13	261
Sports and youth	Nasrollah Sajjadi (rejected) (Nov. 10, 2013)	124	107	22	253
Sports and youth	Mahmud Gudarzi (Nov. 16, 2013)	199	44	24	267
Science, research, and technology	Mahmud Nili-Ahmadabadi (rejected) (Oct. 29, 2014)	79	160	7	246
Science, research, and technology	Fakhreddin Ahmadi-Danesh-Ashtiyani (rejected) (Nov. 18, 2014)	70	171	16	257
Science, research, and technology	Mohammad Farhadi (Nov. 26, 2014)	197	28	10	235
Sports and youth	Mas'ud Soltanifar (Nov. 1, 2016)	193	72	9	274
Education	Fakhreddin Ahmadi-Danesh-Ashtiyani (Nov. 1, 2016)	157	111	6	274
Culture and Islamic guidance	Seyyed Reza Salehi-Amiri (Nov. 1, 2016)	180	89	6	275

Table 73
Confidence Vote for President Rouhani's Second Cabinet (Aug. 20, 2017)

Ministry	Ministerial candidate	Approvals	Denials	Abstentions	Void Ballots	Total
Agriculture	Mahmud Hojjati	164	94	23	7	288
Cooperatives, labor, and social welfare	Ali Rabi'i	191	79	15	3	288
Culture and Islamic guidance	Abbas Salehi	242	25	21	0	288
Defense and armed forces logistics	Amir Hatami	261	10	13	4	288
Economic affairs and finance	Mas'ud Karbasiyan	240	31	15	2	288
Education	Seyyed Mohammad Bathaie	238	35	13	0	286
Energy	Habibollah Bitaraf (rejected)	133	132	17	6	288
Foreign affairs	Mohammad-Javad Zarif	236	26	26	0	288
Health and medical education	Seyyed Hasan Qazizadeh-Hashemi	253	18	14	3	288
Industry, mining, and trade	Mohammad Shari'atmadari	241	25	20	2	288
Information and communications technology	Mohammad-Javad Azari-Jahromi	152	120	7	9	288
Intelligence	Seyyed Mahmud Alavi	252	22	13	1	288
Interior	Abdorreza Rahmani-Fazli	250	25	13	0	288
Justice	Seyyed Ali-Reza Ava'i	244	18	23	3	288
Petroleum	Bizhan Namdar-Zangeneh	230	35	23	0	288
Road and urban development	Abbas-Ahmad Akhundi	198	75	14	1	288
Sports and youth	Mas'ud Soltanifar	225	39	20	4	288
VOTED ON LATER						
Energy	Reza Ardakanian (Oct. 29, 2017)	225	38	13	0	276
Science, research, and technology	Mansur Gholami (Oct. 29, 2017)	180	82	14	0	276

Note: On Aug. 20, 2017, President Rouhani did not introduce anyone as minister of science, research, and technology.

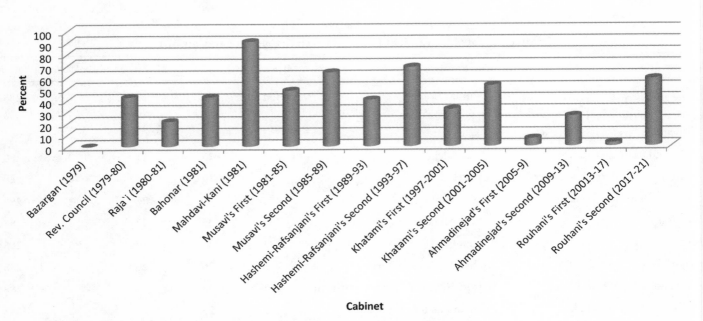

13. Incumbency Rate for Each Cabinet (1979–2021). Source: Authors' database.

Table 74
Ministers Impeached by the Majlis (1982–2017)

Date	Minister	Ministry	First or second term of prime minister or president	In favor of impeachment, against, abstention[a]
Nov. 4, 1982	Mohammad-Shahab Gonabadi	Housing and urban development	Musavi's first	75, 101, 12
Nov. 6, 1983	Ali-Akbar Nateq-Nuri	Interior	Musavi's first	72, 146, 13
Aug. 20, 1989	Behzad Nabavi	Heavy industries	Musavi's second	73, 132, 21
Jan. 13, 1991	Iraj Fazel	Health and medical education	Hashemi-Rafsanjani's first	115, 114, 17 (impeached)
Apr. 24, 1991	Mohammad-Ali Najafi	Education	Hashemi-Rafsanjani's first	77, 137, 11
Mar. 2, 1993	Mohammad Sa'idi-Kiya	Roads and transportation	Hashemi-Rafsanjani's first	121, 121 (against, abstained)[b]
Dec. 14, 1994	Hoseyn Mahlujchi	Mining	Hashemi-Rafsanjani's first	98, 106 (against, abstained)[c]
June 21, 1998	Abdollah Nuri	Interior	Khatami's first	137, 117, 11 (impeached)
May 1, 1999	Seyyed Ataollah Mohajerani	Culture and Islamic guidance	Khatami's first	121, 135, 7
June 2, 2002	Ali Abdolali'zadeh	Housing and urban development	Khatami's second	114, 119, 12
June 17, 2003	Mas'ud Pezeshkiyan	Health and medical education	Khatami's second	60, 170, 5
Aug. 31, 2003	Morteza Haji	Education	Khatami's second	67, 159, 10
Nov. 5, 2003	Seyyed Ahmad Mo'tamedi	Post, telegraph, and telephones	Khatami's second	61, 142, 11

Table 74 (Cont.)
Ministers Impeached by the Majlis (1982–2017)

Date	Minister	Ministry	First or second term of prime minister or president	In favor of impeachment, against, abstention[a]
Oct. 3, 2004	Ahmad Khorram	Roads and transportation	Khatami's second	188, 58, 9 (*impeached*)
Oct. 22, 2006	Mohammad-Reza Eskandari	Agricultural Jihad	Ahmadinejad's first	98, 142, 24
May 16, 2007	Mahmud Farshidi	Education	Ahmadinejad's first	89, 132, 17
Nov. 4, 2008	Ali Kordan	Interior	Ahmadinejad's first	188, 45, 14 (*impeached*)
Feb. 1, 2011	Hamid Behbahani	Road and transportation	Ahmadinejad's second	147, 78, 9 (*impeached*)
Mar. 6, 2011	Majid Namju	Energy	Ahmadinejad's second	101, 102, 6
Nov. 1, 2011	Seyyed Shamseddin Hoseyni	Economic affairs and finance	Ahmadinejad's second	93, 141, 10
Feb. 3, 2013	Abdorreza Shaikholislami	Cooperatives, labor, and social welfare	Ahmadinejad's second	192, 56, 24 (*impeached*)
Aug. 20, 2014	Reza Faraji-Dana	Science, research, and technology	Rouhani's first	145, 110, 15 (*impeached*)[d]
Aug. 20, 2014	Ali-Asghar Fani	Education	Rouhani's first	76, 167, 13[e]
Oct. 5, 2015	Abbas-Ahmad Akhundi	Road and transportation	Rouhani's first	72, 175, 5[f]
Feb. 19, 2017	Abbas-Ahmad Akhundi	Road and transportation	Rouhani's first	74, 176, 5
Mar. 3, 2018	Abbas-Ahmad Akhundi	Road and transportation	Rouhani's second	92, 152, 2
Mar. 3, 2018	Ali Rabi'i	Labor, cooperatives, and social welfare	Rouhani's second	124, 126, 2
Mar. 14, 2018	Mahmud Hojjati	Agricultural Jihad	Rouhani's second	105, 117, 7

Note: This table is based on the actual impeachments that were voted on in the Majlis. There were a number of other impeachment cases that were submitted but never voted upon by the Majlis. For example, in April 2008 a request for interpellation of Seyyed Mas'ud Mir Kazemi, minister of commerce in Ahmadinejad's first cabinet, was received by the Majlis but was never voted on.

[a] Much of the data gathered from Teiri-qazi (2001), http://www.asriran.com, http://www.khabaronline.ir, and other media accounts.

[b] Of the 242 MPs present at the session, 121 voted to impeach Sa'idi-Kiya. This meant that he survived the impeachment because the bylaws of the Majlis state that a vote of no confidence should be half plus one. The Majlis Speaker did not specify how many MPs abstained and how many voted against the impeachment. See Teiri-qazi (2001).

[c] Of the 204 MPs present at the session, ninety-eight voted to impeach Mahlujchi, which was not sufficient. The Majlis Speaker did not specify how many MPs abstained and how many voted against the impeachment. See Teiri-qazi (2001), 812.

[d] http://www.bbc.co.uk.

[e] http://www.khabaronline.ir.

[f] http://www.bbc.com/persian.

Table 75
Ministers Who Resigned, Were Dismissed, Left to Take Other Positions, or Died in Office

MINISTERS WHO RESIGNED

Minister	Position	Prime minister or president's cabinet
Karim Sanjabi	Foreign affairs	Bazargan
Asadollah Mobasheri[a]	Justice	Bazargan
Mohammad-Taqi Riyahi	National defense	Bazargan
Kazem Sami[b]	Health	Bazargan
Ebrahim Ahadi[c]	Justice	Raja'i
Habibollah Asgarowladi	Commerce	Musavi's first
Abdolmajid Mo'adikhah	Islamic guidance	Musavi's first
Ahmad Tavakkoli	Labor and social affairs	Musavi's first
Seyyed Morteza Nabavi	Post, telegraph, and telephones	Musavi's first
Seyyed Mohammad Khatami	Culture and Islamic guidance	Hashemi-Rafsanjani's first
Qorbanali Dorri-Najafabadi	Intelligence	Khatami's first
Seyyed Ataollah Mohajerani	Culture and Islamic guidance	Khatami's first
Mohammad-Reza Aref	Post, telegraph, and telephones	Khatami's first
Mostafa Mo'in	Science, research, and technology	Khatami's second
Davud Danesh-Ja'fari[d]	Economic affairs and finance	Ahmadinejad's first
Ali-Reza Tahmasebi	Industries and mining	Ahmadinejad's first
Mahmud Farshidi	Education	Ahmadinejad's first
Mahmud Gudarzi	Sports and youth	Rouhani's first
Ali Jannati	Culture and Islamic guidance	Rouhani's first
Ali-Asghar Fani	Education	Rouhani's first

MINISTERS WHO WERE DISMISSED

Minister	Position	Prime minister or president's cabinet
Mohammad Sa'idi-Kiya	Construction Jihad	Khatami's first
Tahmaseb Mazaheri	Economic affairs and finance	Khatami's first
Mohammad Nazemi-Ardakani	Cooperatives	Ahmadinejad's first
Mostafa Purmohammadi	Interior	Ahmadinejad's first
Seyyed Kazem Vaziri-Hamaneh	Petroleum	Ahmadinejad's first
Mohammad Rahmati	Roads and transportation	Ahmadinejad's first
Parviz Kazemi	Welfare and social security	Ahmadinejad's first
Manouchehr Mottaki	Foreign affairs	Ahmadinejad's second
Seyyed Mas'ud Mir Kazemi	Petroleum	Ahmadinejad's second

[a] Resigned June 20, 1979.
[b] Resigned Oct. 27, 1979.
[c] Resigned Jan. 30, 1981.
[d] Resigned Aug. 6, 2008.

Table 75 (Cont.)
Ministers Who Resigned, Were Dismissed, Left to Take Other Positions, or Died in Office

MINISTERS WHO LEFT TO TAKE ON OTHER POSITIONS

Minister	Position	Prime minister or president's cabinet
Seyyed Ahmad Madani	National defense	Bazargan
Ali-Akbar Mo'infar	Plan and budget	Bazargan
Ali-Akbar Mehrabiyan[e]	Industries and mining	Ahmadinejad's second

MINISTERS WHO DIED WHILE SERVING IN OFFICE

Minister	Position	Prime minister or president's cabinet
Rahman Dadman[f]	Roads and transportation	Khatami's first
Jamal Karimirad[g]	Justice	Ahmadinejad's first

Note: Information is based on announcements in various Iranian newspapers and government websites.
[e] In May 2011, Ahmadinejad ended Mehrabiyan's tenure when the Ministry of Industries was combined with the Ministry of Commerce.
[f] Died in a plane crash on May 17, 2001.
[g] Died in a car accident on Dec. 28, 2006.

Table 76
Fields of Study of Cabinet Members (1979–2017)

Cabinet	Experimental and medical sciences	Human sciences	Mathematics and engineering	Military sciences	Theology	Unknown	Total number of cabinet members
Bazargan	20.7	41.4	34.5	0	0	3.5	29
Revolutionary Council	19.1	19.1	42.9	0	14.3	4.8	21
Raja'i	17.4	30.4	34.8	4.4	13	0	23
Bahonar	9.5	23.8	47.6	4.8	14.3	0	21
Mahdavi-Kani	9.1	22.7	54.6	4.6	9.1	0	22
Musavi's first	12.8	25.6	43.6	2.6	10.3	5.1	39
Musavi's second	10.7	21.4	46.4	7.1	7.1	7.1	28
Hashemi-Rafsanjani's first	15.6	28.1	46.9	0	9.4	0	32
Hashemi-Rafsanjani's second	9.4	31.3	50	0	6.3	3.1	32
Khatami's first	8.8	35.3	38.2	2.9	14.7	0	34
Khatami's second	11.8	47.1	29.4	2.9	8.8	0	34
Ahmadinejad's first	8.9	48.9	33.3	2.2	6.7	0	45
Ahmadinejad's second	11.9	40.9	31	0	11.9	4.8	42
Rouhani's first	8.6	54.3	25.7	0	8.6	2.9	35

Source: Authors' database.
Note: The academic divisions in this table correspond to categories used in the Iranian educational system. The fields of study of the cabinet members were determined based on their highest educational degree. Percentages have been rounded to the nearest integer. Since President Rouhani's second cabinet had not completed its full term at the time of publication, information about this cabinet has not been included in the table.

Table 77
Pre-Elite Occupations of Cabinet Ministers (1979–2017)

PERCENTAGE

Cabinet	Academia	Bazaar	Clergy	Military/ security	Public sector bureaucracy	Professionals (doctors, lawyers, engineers)	Other (retired, etc.)	Unknown
Bazargan	27.6	0	0	0	24.1	27.6	3.5	13.8
Revolutionary Council	30	0	10	0	30	25		5
Raja'i	21.8	0	8.7	4.4	47.6	8.7	0	8.7
Bahonar	28.6	4.8	9.5	4.8	47.6	4.8	0	0
Mahdavi-Kani	31.8	4.6	4.6	4.6	50	4.6	0	0
Musavi's first	20.5	2.6	10.3	7.7	48.7	10.3	0	0
Musavi's second	18.1	0	10.7	14.3	46.4	7.1	0	3.6
Hashemi-Rafsanjani's first	12.5	0	9.4	3.1	53.1	18.8	0	3.1
Hashemi-Rafsanjani's second	12.5	0	6.3	3.1	59.4	12.5	0	6.3
Khatami's first	20.6	0	11.8	5.9	52.9	8.8	0	0
Khatami's second	8.8	0	8.8	5.9	64.7	11.8	0	0
Ahmadinejad's first	17.8	0	2.2	20	55.6	2.2	0	2.2
Ahmadinejad's second	21.4	0	2.4	14.3	57.1	0	0	4.8
Rouhani's first	42.9	0	8.6	11.4	31.4	5.7	0	0
Average	22.5	0.9	7.4	7.1	47.8	10.6	0.1	3.4

Source: Authors' database.

Note: This table presents information on what type of profession cabinet members held immediately before they entered the ranks of the political elite. For example, a former governor who first becomes a member of the Majlis and then proceeds to become a cabinet minister has been coded as a "public sector bureaucrat" because of his governorship. Clerics have been coded as clerics, even if they were employed in other capacities as well. This was done in light of the special status that they enjoy as clergyman within a theocratic state. Since President Rouhani's second cabinet had not completed its full term at the time we finished writing this book, information about this cabinet has not been included in the table. All percentages have been rounded to the nearest integer.

Table 78
Percentage of All Cabinet Ministers Based on Place of Birth

Province or country (if born outside Iran)	Number and percentage of ministers
Tehran	67 (26.7%)[a]
Isfahan	35 (13.9%)
Fars	16 (6.4%)
East Azerbaijan	13 (5.2%)
Razavi Khorasan	13 (5.2%)
Hamadan	11 (4.4%)
Kerman	10 (4%)
Mazandaran	9 (3.6%)
Khuzestan	8 (3.2%)
Qom	8 (3.2%)
Yazd	7 (2.8%)
West Azerbaijan	6 (2.4%)
Iraq[b]	6 (2.4%)
Kermanshah	6 (2.4%)
Qazvin	5 (2.0%)
Markazi	5 (2.0%)
Gilan	4 (1.6%)
Lorestan	4 (1.6%)
Semnan	3 (1.2%)
Ardabil	3 (1.2%)
Golestan	2 (0.8%)
Afghanistan	1 (0.4%)
Chahar Mahal and Bakhtiari	1 (0.4%)
Hormozgan	1 (0.4%)
Kurdistan	1 (0.4%)
North Khorasan	1 (0.4%)
Zanjan	1 (0.4%)
Sistan and Baluchestan	1 (0.4%)
South Khorasan	1 (0.4%)
Alborz	0 (0%)
Bushehr	0 (0%)
Ilam	0 (0%)
Kohgiluyeh and Buyer Ahmad	0 (0%)
Unknown[c]	2 (0.8%)
Total	251 (100%)

Source: Authors' database.

Note: From Feb. 11, 1979, to Aug. 8, 2017, 251 individuals served in fourteen cabinets in ministerial posts. Since President Rouhani's second cabinet had not completed its full term at the time we finished writing this book, information about this cabinet has not been included in the table. The list also does not include vice presidents who have served in various cabinets.
[a] Percentages have been rounded off to the nearest integer.
[b] Six ministers were born in Iraq and one in Afghanistan.
[c] We could not find the province of birth for Mohammad-Hoseyn Jalali or Abdolhoseyn Vahaji.

Table 79
Top Two Provinces of Birth for All Cabinet Members

Prime minister or president's cabinet	Top province	Second highest province	Total number of cabinet members
Bazargan	Tehran (37.9%)[a]	Isfahan (17.2%)	29
Revolutionary Council	Tehran (47.6%)	Isfahan (14.3%)	21
Raja'i	Tehran (39.1%)	East Azerbaijan (26.1%)	23
Bahonar	Tehran (38.1%)	Isfahan (23.8%)	21
Mahdavi-Kani	Tehran (31.8%)	Isfahan (22.7%)	22
Musavi's first	Tehran (33.3%)	Isfahan (23.1%)	39
Musavi's second	Tehran (35.7%)	Isfahan (17.9%)	28
Hashemi-Rafsanjani's first	Isfahan (25%)	Tehran (15.6%)	32
Hashemi-Rafsanjani's second	Tehran (21.9%)	Isfahan (15.6%)	32
Khatami's first	Tehran (23.5%)	Isfahan (17.6%)	34
Khatami's second	Tehran (23.5%)	Isfahan (17.7%)	34
Ahmadinejad's first	Tehran (22.2%)	Isfahan (11.1%)	45
Ahmadinejad's second	Tehran (19.1%)	Fars and Mazandaran (9.5%)	42
Rouhani's first	Tehran (25.7%)	Isfahan (11.4%)	35

Source: Authors' database.
Note: This table is based on province of birth information for all but two of the ministers and vice presidents who have served in each of the above cabinets. Persons who have been both a minister and a vice president have been counted each time they have served. Since President Rouhani's second cabinet had not completed its full term at the time we finished writing this book, information about this cabinet has not been included in the table.
[a] Percentages have been rounded to the nearest integer.

Table 80
Percentage of Cabinet Members Born in Provincial Capitals

Prime minister or president's cabinet	Percentage born in provincial capitals	Total number of cabinet members
Bazargan	83	29
Revolutionary Council	66.6	21
Raja'i	70	23
Bahonar	71	21
Mahdavi-Kani	68	22
Musavi's first	69	39
Musavi's second	64	28
Hashemi-Rafsanjani's first	53.1	32
Hashemi-Rafsanjani's second	53.1	32
Khatami's first	55.9	34
Khatami's second	52.9	34

Table 80 (Cont.)
Percentage of Cabinet Members Born in Provincial Capitals

Prime minister or president's cabinet	Percentage born in provincial capitals	Total number of cabinet members
Ahmadinejad's first	66.7	45
Ahmadinejad's second	57.1	42
Rouhani's first	51.4	35

Source: Authors' database.
Note: Provincial capitals used to refer to the following cities: Ahvaz, Arak, Bandar-e Abbas, Bandar-e Bushehr, Hamadan, Ilam, Isfahan, Kerman, Kermanshah, Khorramabad, Mashhad, Rasht, Sanandaj, Sari, Semnan, Shahrekord, Shiraz, Tabriz, Tehran, Urmia, Yasouj, Yazd, Zahedan, and Zanjan. After the revolution, the following cities also were added to the ranks of provincial capitals as new provinces were formed: Ardabil (since 1993), Birjand (since 2004), Bojnurd (since 2004), Gorgan (since 1997), Karaj (since 2010), Qazvin (since 1997), and Qom (since 1996). However, as explained in the book's introduction, for our analysis we have treated the new provincial capitals as if they have been long-standing provincial capitals no different from the others. Since President Rouhani's second cabinet had not completed its full term at the time we finished writing this book, information about this cabinet has not been included in the table.

Table 81
Number of Clerics and Former Revolutionary Guards in Each Cabinet

Prime minister or president's cabinet	Number of former IRGC	Number of clerics	Total number of cabinet members
Bazargan	0	0	29
Revolutionary Council	0	3	21
Raja'i	1	2	23
Bahonar	2	2	21
Mahdavi-Kani	2	1	22
Musavi's first	6	5	39
Musavi's second	6	3	28
Hashemi-Rafsanjani's first	3	4	32
Hashemi-Rafsanjani's second	4	2	32
Khatami's first	6	7	34
Khatami's second	8	5	34
Ahmadinejad's first	18	4	45
Ahmadinejad's second	19	2	42
Rouhani's first	12	4	35

Source: Authors' database.
Note: Since President Rouhani's second cabinet had not completed its full term at the time we finished writing this book, information about this cabinet has not been included in the table.

Table 82
Number of Iran-Based versus Foreign-Educated Members of Each Cabinet (1979–2017)

Cabinet	Iran	Asia and Australia	Europe	MENA[a] and Turkey	North America	Unknown	Total number of cabinet members
Bazargan	13	1	9	0	5	1	29
Revolutionary Council	12	1	2	0	5	1	21
Raja'i	13	0	3	1	5	1	23
Bahonar	15	0	2	1	3	0	21
Mahdavi-Kani	14	0	2	1	5	0	22
Musavi's first	25	0	4	1	9	0	39
Musavi's second	19	0	0	1	7	1	28
Hashemi-Rafsanjani's first	18	1	2	1	8	2	32
Hashemi-Rafsanjani's second	17	2	3	1	7	2	32
Khatami's first	25	0	3	0	5	1	34
Khatami's second	25	0	3	0	5	1	34
Ahmadinejad's first	38	1	1	0	5	0	45
Ahmadinejad's second	31	2	3	0	3	3	42
Rouhani's first	22	0	5	0	5	3	35

Source: Authors' database.

Note: Those educated outside Iran must have received at least one higher education degree overseas. Since President Rouhani's second cabinet had not completed its full term at the time we finished writing this book, information about this cabinet has not been included in the table.

[a] MENA refers to Middle East and North Africa.

10

Majlis

Table 83
Number of Seats Allocated to Each Province in the Majlis (1980–2020)

Province	First (1980–84)	Second (1984–88)	Third (1988–92)	Fourth (1992–96)	Fifth (1996–2000)	Sixth (2000–2004)	Seventh (2004–8)	Eighth (2008–12)	Ninth (2012–16)	Tenth (2016–20)
Alborz	*	*	*	*	*	*	*	*	3	3
Ardabil	*	*	*	*	6	7	7	7	7	7
Bushehr	3	3	3	3	3	4	4	4	4	4
Chahar Mahal and Bakhtiari	3	3	3	3	3	4	4	4	4	4
East Azerbaijan	24	24	24	24	18	19	19	19	19	19
Fars	17	17	17	17	17	18	18	18	18	18
Gilan	13	13	13	13	13	13	13	13	13	13
Golestan	*	*	*	*	*	7	7	7	7	7
Hamadan	9	9	9	9	9	9	9	9	9	9
Hormozgan	3	4	4	4	4	5	5	5	5	5
Ilam	2	2	2	2	2	3	3	3	3	3
Isfahan	18	18	18	18	18	19	19	19	19	19
Kerman	10	10	10	10	10	10	10	10	10	10
Kermanshah	8	8	8	8	8	8	8	8	8	8
Khuzestan	17	17	17	17	17	18	18	18	18	18
Kohgiluyeh and Buyer Ahmad	2	2	2	2	2	3	3	3	3	3
Kurdistan	6	6	6	6	6	6	6	6	6	6
Lorestan	9	8	8	8	8	9	9	9	9	9
Markazi	9	7	7	7	7	7	7	7	7	7
Mazandaran	17	17	17	17	17	12	12	12	12	12
North Khorasan	*	*	*	*	*	4	4	4	4	4
Qazvin	*	*	*	*	*	4	4	4	4	4
Qom	*	*	*	*	*	3	3	3	3	3
Razavi Khorasan	25	25	25	25	25	18	18	18	18	18

Table 83 (Cont.)
Number of Seats Allocated to Each Province in the Majlis (1980–2020)

Province	SESSION AND YEARS									
	First (1980–84)	Second (1984–88)	Third (1988–92)	Fourth (1992–96)	Fifth (1996–2000)	Sixth (2000–2004)	Seventh (2004–8)	Eighth (2008–12)	Ninth (2012–16)	Tenth (2016–20)
Semnan	4	4	4	4	4	4	4	4	4	4
Sistan and Baluchestan	7	7	7	7	7	8	8	8	8	8
South Khorasan	*	*	*	*	*	4	4	4	4	4
Tehran	35	37	37	37	37	38	38	38	35	35
West Azerbaijan	12	12	12	12	12	12	12	12	12	12
Yazd	3	3	3	3	3	4	4	4	4	4
Zanjan	9	9	9	9	9	5	5	5	5	5
Religious minorities	5	5	5	5	5	5	5	5	5	5
Total seats	270	270	270	270	270	290	290	290	290	290

Source: Iranian Majlis (http://www.parliran.ir).

Note: From the First to the Fifth Majlis the total number of seats was 270. From the Sixth to the Tenth Majlis the number of seats was increased to 290. In 1989, it was decided that every ten years a total of twenty more seats can be added to the Majlis based on such factors as demographic growth or political and geographical reasons. There are 207 electoral districts in 384 cities that compete for these 290 seats. In this table, an asterisk (*) means that the province was not yet established.

Table 84
Electoral Districts

Electoral district	Province	Number of MPs
Karaj, Eshtehard, Fardis	Alborz	2
Savojblagh, Nazarabad, Taleqan	Alborz	1
Ardabil, Namin, Nir, Sareyn	Ardabil	3
Germi (also known as Moghan)	Ardabil	1
Khalkhal, Kowsar	Ardabil	1
Meshginshahr	Ardabil	1
Parsabad, Bilehsavar	Ardabil	1
Bushehr, Genaveh, Deylam	Bushehr	1
Dashtestan	Bushehr	1
Dashti, Tangestan	Bushehr	1
Kangan, Deyr, Jam, Asaluyeh	Bushehr	1
Ardal, Farsan, Kuhrang, Kiyar, Dastgerd	Chahar Mahal and Bakhtiari	1
Borujen	Chahar Mahal and Bakhtiari	1
Lordegan	Chahar Mahal and Bakhtiari	1
Shahrekord, Ben, Saman	Chahar Mahal and Bakhtiar	1
Ahar, Heris	East Azerbaijan	1
Bonab	East Azerbaijan	1
Bostanabad	East Azerbaijan	1

Table 84 (Cont.)
Electoral Districts

Electoral district	Province	Number of MPs
Hashtrud, Charuymaq	East Azerbaijan	1
Kaleybar, Hurand, Khoda Afarin	East Azerbaijan	1
Malekan	East Azerbaijan	1
Maragheh, Ajab-Shir	East Azerbaijan	1
Marand, Jolfa	East Azerbaijan	1
Miyaneh	East Azerbaijan	2
Sarab	East Azerbaijan	1
Shabestar	East Azerbaijan	1
Tabriz, Azarshahr, Osku	East Azerbaijan	6
Varzaqan	East Azerbaijan	1
Abadeh, Bavanat, Khorrambid	Fars	1
Darab, Zarrindasht	Fars	1
Eqlid	Fars	1
Fasa	Fars	1
Firuzabad, Farashband, Qir, Karzin	Fars	1
Jahrom	Fars	1
Kazerun	Fars	1
Lamerd, Mohr	Fars	1
Larestan, Khonj, Gerash	Fars	1
Mamasani, Rostam	Fars	1
Marvdasht, Pasargad, Arsanjan	Fars	1
Neyriz, Estahban	Fars	1
Sarvestan, Kherameh, Kavar	Fars	1
Sepidan	Fars	1
Shiraz	Fars	4
Astaneh-ye Ashrafiyyeh	Gilan	1
Astara	Gilan	1
Bandar-e Anzali	Gilan	1
Fuman, Shaft	Gilan	1
Lahijan, Siyahkal	Gilan	1
Langarud	Gilan	1
Rasht	Gilan	3
Rudbar	Gilan	1
Rudsar, Amlash	Gilan	1
Sowme'eh Sara	Gilan	1
Talesh, Rezvanshahr, Masal	Gilan	1
Aliabad Katul	Golestan	1
Gonbad-e Kavus	Golestan	1
Gorgan, Aq-Qala	Golestan	2
Kordkuy, Torkaman, Bandar-e Gaz, Gomishan	Golestan	1

Table 84 (Cont.)
Electoral Districts

Electoral district	*Province*	*Number of MPs*
Minudasht, Kalaleh, Maraveh Tappeh, Galikash	Golestan	1
Ramiyan, Azadshahr	Golestan	1
Asadabad	Hamadan	1
Bahar, Kabudarahang	Hamadan	1
Hamadan, Famenin	Hamadan	2
Malayer	Hamadan	2
Nahavand	Hamadan	1
Razan	Hamadan	1
Tuyserkan	Hamadan	1
Bandar-e Abbas, Qeshm, Abumusa, Hajiabad, Khamir	Hormozgan	3
Bandar-e Lengeh, Bastak, Parsian	Hormozgan	1
Minab, Rudan, Jask, Sirik, Bashagard	Hormozgan	1
Dehloran, Darrehshahr, Badreh	Ilam	1
Ilam, Eyvan, Mehran, Malekshahi, Shirvan	Ilam	2
Ardestan	Isfahan	1
Falavarjan	Isfahan	1
Faridan, Chadegan, Fereydunshahr, Buin, Miandasht	Isfahan	1
Golpayegan, Khansar	Isfahan	1
Isfahan	Isfahan	5
Kashan, Aran, Bidgol	Isfahan	1
Khomeinishahr	Isfahan	1
Lenjan	Isfahan	1
Mobarakeh	Isfahan	1
Na'in, Khur, Biabanak	Isfahan	1
Najafabad, Tiran, Karvan	Isfahan	1
Natanz, Qamsar	Isfahan	1
Semirom	Isfahan	1
Shahinshahr, Meymeh, Borkhar	Isfahan	1
Shahreza, Dehaqan, Dare Shoor	Isfahan	1
Baft, Rabor, Arzuiyeh	Kerman	1
Bam, Rigan, Fahraj, Narmashir	Kerman	1
Jiroft, Anbarabad	Kerman	1
Kahnuj, Manujan, South Rudbar, Qaleh Ganj, Faryab	Kerman	1
Kerman, Ravar	Kerman	2
Rafsanjan, Anar	Kerman	1
Shahr-e Babak	Kerman	1
Sirjan, Bardsir	Kerman	1
Zarand, Kuhbanan	Kerman	1
Islamabad-e Gharb, Dalahu	Kermanshah	1
Kangavar, Sahneh, Harsin	Kermanshah	1

Table 84 (Cont.)
Electoral Districts

Electoral district	Province	Number of MPs
Kermanshah	Kermanshah	3
Paveh, Javanrud, Salase Babajani, Ravansar, Sar Qaleh, Jeygaran	Kermanshah	1
Qasr-e Shirin, Sarpol-e Zahab, Gilan-e Gharb	Kermanshah	1
Sonqor	Kermanshah	1
Abadan	Khuzestan	3
Ahvaz, Bavi, Hamidieh, Karun	Khuzestan	3
Andimeshk	Khuzestan	1
Bandar-e Mahshahr, Omidiyeh, Hendijan, Joulaki	Khuzestan	1
Behbahan, Aqajari	Khuzestan	1
Dasht-e Azadegan, Hoveyzeh	Khuzestan	1
Dezful	Khuzestan	1
I'zeh, Baghmalek	Khuzestan	1
Khorramshahr	Khuzestan	1
Masjed Soleyman, Lali, Haftkel, Andika	Khuzestan	1
Ramhormoz, Ramshir	Khuzestan	1
Shadegan	Khuzestan	1
Shush	Khuzestan	1
Shushtar, Gotvand	Khuzestan	1
Buyer Ahmad, Dena	Kohgiluyeh and Buyer Ahmad	1
Gachsaran, Basht	Kohgiluyeh and Buyer Ahmad	1
Kohgiluyeh, Bahmai, Choram, Landeh	Kohgiluyeh and Buyer Ahmad	1
Bijar	Kurdistan	1
Marivan, Sarvabad	Kurdistan	1
Qorveh, Dehgolan	Kurdistan	1
Sanandaj, Divandarreh, Kamyaran	Kurdistan	2
Saqqez, Baneh	Kurdistan	1
Aligudarz	Lorestan	1
Borujerd	Lorestan	2
Delfan, Selseleh	Lorestan	1
Dorud, Azna	Lorestan	1
Khorramabad, Dowreh	Lorestan	2
Kuhdasht, Rumeshkhan	Lorestan	1
Pol-e Dokhtar	Lorestan	1
Arak, Komijan, Khondab	Markazi	2
Khomeyn	Markazi	1
Mahallat, Delijan	Markazi	1
Saveh, Zarandieh	Markazi	1
Shazand	Markazi	1
Tafresh, Ashtiyan, Farahan	Markazi	1
Amol	Mazandaran	1

Table 84 (Cont.)
Electoral Districts

Electoral district	Province	Number of MPs
Babol	Mazandaran	2
Babolsar, Fereydunkenar	Mazandaran	1
Behshahr, Neka, Galugah	Mazandaran	1
Nowshahr, Chalus, Kelardasht	Mazandaran	1
Nur, Mahmudabad	Mazandaran	1
Qaemshahr, Savadkuh, Juybar, Simorgh, North Savadkuh	Mazandaran	2
Sari, Miandorud	Mazandaran	2
Tonekabon, Ramsar, Abbasabad	Mazandaran	1
Bojnurd, Maneh, Samalqan, Jajarm, Garmeh, Raz, and Jargalan	North Khorasan	2
Esfarayen	North Khorasan	1
Shirvan	North Khorasan	1
Bu'inzahra, Avaj	Qazvin	1
Qazvin, Abyek, Alborz	Qazvin	2
Takestan	Qazvin	1
Qom	Qom	3
Chenaran, Binaloud	Razavi Khorasan	1
Dargaz	Razavi Khorasan	1
Fariman, Sarakhs, Ahmadabad, Razaviyeh	Razavi Khorasan	1
Gonabad, Bejestan	Razavi Khorasan	1
Kashmar, Khalilabad, Bardaskan	Razavi Khorasan	1
Khaf, Roshtkhar	Razavi Khorasan	1
Mashhad, Kalat	Razavi Khorasan	5
Neyshabur, Firuzeh	Razavi Khorasan	2
Quchan, Faruj	Razavi Khorasan	1
Torbat-e Heydariyyeh, Mahvelat, Zaveh	Razavi Khorasan	1
Torbat-e Jam, Taybad, Bakharz	Razavi Khorasan	1
Damghan	Semnan	1
Garmsar, Aradan	Semnan	1
Semnan, Mehdishahr, Sorkheh, Shahmirzad	Semnan	1
Shahrud, Meyami, Bastam	Semnan	1
Chabahar, Nikshahr, Konarak, Qasr-e Qand	Sistan and Baluchestan	1
Iranshahr, Sarbaz, Delgan, Fanuj, Bent, Lashar, Ashar, Ahoran	Sistan and Baluchestan	1
Khash, Mirjaveh, Nosratabad, Kurin	Sistan and Baluchestan	1
Saravan, Sib, Suran, Mehrestan	Sistan and Baluchestan	1
Zabol, Zahak, Hirmand, Nimrouz, Hamun	Sistan and Baluchestan	2
Zahedan	Sistan and Baluchestan	2
Birjand, Darmiyan, Khoosf	South Khorasan	1
Ferdows, Sarayan, Tabas, Boshruyeh	South Khorasan	1
Nehbandan, Sarbisheh	South Khorasan	1
Qaenat, Zirkuh	South Khorasan	1

Table 84 (Cont.)
Electoral Districts

Electoral district	Province	Number of MPs
Damavand, Firuzkuh	Tehran	1
Pakdasht	Tehran	1
Robat Karim, Baharestan	Tehran	1
Shahriyar, Qods, Malard	Tehran	1
Tehran, Rey, Shemiranat, Islamshahr, Pardis	Tehran	30
Varamin, Pishva, Qarchak	Tehran	1
Bukan	West Azerbaijan	1
Khoy, Chaypareh	West Azerbaijan	1
Mahabad	West Azerbaijan	1
Maku, Chaldoran, Poldasht, Showt	West Azerbaijan	1
Miyandoab, Shahindezh, Takab	West Azerbaijan	2
Naqadeh, Oshnaviyyeh	West Azerbaijan	1
Piranshahr, Sardasht	West Azerbaijan	1
Salmas	West Azerbaijan	1
Urmia	West Azerbaijan	3
Ardakan	Yazd	1
Mehriz, Bafq, Abarkuh, Khatam, Bahabad	Yazd	1
Taft, Meybod	Yazd	1
Yazd, Ashkezar, Nadushan, Sourck	Yazd	1
Abhar, Khorramdarreh, Soltaniyeh	Zanjan	1
Khodabandeh	Zanjan	1
Mahneshan, Ijrood, Boqdakandi, Qoltugh	Zanjan	1
Zanjan, Tarom	Zanjan	2
Armenians of southern Iran	Minorities	1
Armenians of northern Iran	Minorities	1
Assyrians and Chaldean Christians	Minorities	1
Jews	Minorities	1
Zoroastrians	Minorities	1

Source: Ministry of Interior.
Note: In Iran, MPs represent either territorial districts or religious minorities. In 1975, when elections were held for the last (twenty-fourth) prerevolutionary Majlis, there were 170 territorial districts plus five seats allocated for religious minorities (Shaji'i 2004, 463–559). As of Jan. 1, 2017, there are 202 territorial districts plus five seats allocated for religious minorities. In other words, redistricting has led to the creation of thirty-two new electoral districts.

Table 85
Data on the 1980 Majlis Election

Date of election	Mar. 14, 1980[a]
Number of eligible voters	20,857,391
Number of actual voters	10,875,969
Voter turnout rate	52.14%
Number of precincts	193
Number of candidates needed	270
Number of registered entrants	3,694
Number of entrants positively vetted	1,910
Percentage of entrants positively vetted	51.70%
Number of female registered entrants	90[b]
In session	May 28, 1980–May 27, 1984
Total number of MPs who served during the session	327

[a] For tables 85 to 94, all data on election date, number of eligible and actual voters, voter turnout rate, and number of registered candidates was taken from http://www.moi.ir. Number of eligible and actual voters also consistent with the Statistical Center of Iran (2013, 897–900).
[b] Purardeshir (2008).

Table 86
Data on the 1984 Majlis Election

Date of election	Apr. 15, 1984
Number of eligible voters	24,143,498
Number of actual voters	15,607,306
Voter turnout rate	64.64%
Number of precincts	193
Number of candidates needed	270
Number of registered entrants	1,592
Number of entrants positively vetted	1,231
Percentage of entrants positively vetted	77.32%
Number of female registered entrants	32[a]
In session	May 28, 1984–May 26, 1988
Total number of MPs who served during the session	277

[a] http://iran-newspaper.com.

Table 87
Data on the 1988 Majlis Election

Date of election	Apr. 8, 1988
Number of eligible voters	27,986,736
Number of actual voters	16,714,281
Voter turnout rate	59.72%
Number of precincts	193
Number of candidates needed	270
Number of registered entrants	1,999
Number of entrants positively vetted	1,417
Percentage of entrants positively vetted	70.88%
Number of female registered entrants	47[a]
In session	May 28, 1988–May 27, 1992
Total number of MPs who served during the session	278

[a] http://iran-newspaper.com.

Table 88
Data on the 1992 Majlis Election

Date of election	Apr. 10, 1992
Number of eligible voters	32,465,558
Number of actual voters	18,767,042
Voter turnout rate	57.81%
Number of precincts	196
Number of candidates needed	270
Number of registered entrants	3,233
Number of entrants positively vetted	2,741[a]
Percentage of entrants positively vetted	84.78%
Number of female registered entrants	84[b]
In session	May 28, 1992–May 26, 1996
Total number of MPs who served during the session	274

[a] Quoting Abdollah Nuri, the interior minister at the time, Vaziri (2015, 155) states that 3,110 registered to compete and 2,310 were approved.
[b] http://iran-newspaper.com.

Table 89
Data on the 1996 Majlis Election

Date of election	Mar. 8, 1996
Number of eligible voters	34,716,000
Number of actual voters	24,682,386
Voter turnout rate	71.10%
Number of precincts	196
Number of candidates needed	270
Number of registered entrants	8,365[a]
Number of entrants positively vetted	6,954
Percentage of entrants positively vetted	83.13%
Number of female registered entrants	351[b]
In session	June 1, 1996–May 24, 2000
Total number of MPs who served during the session	274

[a] Vaziri (2015, 191) has used the figure 5,365, which seems to be a typographical mistake on the original Ministry of Interior site (http://www.moi.ir). The correct number must be 8,365.
[b] http://iran-newspaper.com. *Iran* gives the number as 320 female candidates (Feb. 7, 2000).

Table 90
Data on the 2000 Majlis Election

Date of election	Feb. 18, 2000
Number of eligible voters	38,726,431
Number of actual voters	26,082,157
Voter turnout rate	67.35%
Number of precincts	207
Number of candidates needed	290
Number of registered entrants	6,853
Number of entrants positively vetted	5,742
Percentage of entrants positively vetted	83.78%
Number of female registered entrants	504[a]
In session	May 27, 2000–Aug. 24, 2004
Total number of MPs who served during the session	297

[a] http://iran-newspaper.com. Vaziri (2015, 235) gives the figure as 514.

Table 91
Data on the 2004 Majlis Election

Date of election	Feb. 20, 2004
Number of eligible voters	46,351,032
Number of actual voters	23,734,677
Voter turnout rate	51.21%
Number of precincts	207
Number of candidates needed	290
Number of registered entrants	8,172
Number of entrants positively vetted	5,450[a]
Percentage of entrants positively vetted	66.69%
Number of female registered entrants	857[b]
In session	May 27, 2004–May 25, 2008
Total number of MPs who served during the session	294

[a] Vaziri (2015, 279) states that approximately 5,600 candidates were finally approved, but 1,179 of them decided not to actually run in the election.
[b] http://iran-newspaper.com.

Table 92
Data on the 2008 Majlis Election

Date of election	Mar. 14, 2008
Number of eligible voters	43,824,254[a]
Number of actual voters	24,279,717[b]
Voter turnout rate	55.40%
Number of precincts	207
Number of candidates needed	290
Number of registered entrants	7,600
Number of entrants positively vetted	4,476[c]
Percentage of entrants positively vetted	58.89[d]
Number of female registered entrants	585[e]
In session	May 27, 2008–May 23, 2012
Total number of MPs who served during the session	291

[a] The reason the number of eligible voters in 2008 is less than those in 2004 is because on Jan. 2, 2007, the Majlis raised the voting age from fifteen full years to eighteen full years.
[b] http://khabaronline.ir cites the total number of actual voters as 22,350,254, which means the turnout rate was 51 percent.
[c] "Tablighat-e 4476 Namzad-e Vorood be Majlis-e Hashtom Aghaz Shod" [4,476 Candidates for the Parliament Begin Their Campaigns], Fars News Agency, Mar. 6, 2008.
[d] Sanandaji (2009, 629).
[e] http://iran-newspaper.com.

Table 93
Data on the 2012 Majlis Election

Date of election	Mar. 2, 2012
Number of eligible voters	48,288,799
Number of actual voters	30,844,462
Voter turnout rate	63.87%
Number of precincts	207[a]
Number of candidates needed	290[b]
Number of registered entrants	5,283 (5,405)[c]
Number of entrants who withdrew before the election	470
Final number of entrants who actually competed in elections	3,323
Percentage of entrants who actually competed in elections	69.04%[d]
Number of female registered entrants/number positively vetted	390[e]/249[f]
In session	May 27, 2012–May 24, 2016
Total number of MPs who served during the session	290

[a] Since the election results in Damavand, Ilam (one out of two candidates), Ramsar, and Tuyserkan were declared invalid by the Guardian Council, only 286 lawmakers started serving their terms, and the above districts elected the remaining four representatives in midterm elections held in June 2013. See http://www.khabaronline.ir and http://www.moi.ir4.

[b] Ninety-two MPs from the Eighth Majlis were elected to the Ninth Majlis. One hundred ninety-six new MPs were elected to the Ninth Majlis in the first and second sessions combined.

[c] However, the interior minister at the time reported 5,405 candidates (http://www.moi.ir).

[d] This percentage was calculated after deducting the candidates who voluntarily withdrew from the total of registered candidates.

[e] http://iran-newspaper.com. The interior minister, however, reported that 428 female candidates registered. See http://www.moi.ir.

[f] http://www.irna.ir.

Table 94
Data on the 2016 Majlis Election

Date of election	Feb. 26, 2016
Number of eligible voters	54,915,024
Number of actual voters	33,847,117
Voter turnout rate	61.64%
Number of candidates needed	290[a]
Number of registered entrants	12,072[b]
Number of entrants who voluntarily withdrew before the election	1,480[c]
Number of entrants disqualified	5,743
Final number of entrants positively vetted in elections	4,844[d]
Percentage of entrants who actually competed in the election	40.1%
Number of female registered entrants/number positively vetted	1,234[e]/584[f]
Number of precincts	207[g]
In session	May 27, 2016–May 26, 2020
Total number of MPs who served during the session	290[h]

Note: The winners of sixty-eight seats which were not decided in the first round (Feb. 26, 2016) were chosen two months later in the second round, which was held on Apr. 29, 2016. One hundred thirty-six candidates competed in the second round and 5,901,297 votes were cast (33.48% participation rate). One hundred seventy-eight of the 290 MPs were elected for the first time. The Tenth Majlis started its work with 287 instead of 290 deputies. Mohammad-Ali Hoseynzadeh (1977–2016), elected MP from Maragheh, died in a car accident on May 6, 2016, before the Tenth Majlis had convened. The GC prevented an elected MP from Isfahan, Ms. Minoo Khaleqi, from taking her seat after pictures of her not wearing a veil were made public. The GC also nullified the results of the election in Bandar-e Lengeh, Hormozgan Province, and Ahar, East Azerbaijan, thereby preventing elected MPs Khaled Ząmzamnejad and Beytollah Abdollahi from taking their seats.

[a] http://www.majlesekhobregan.ir.

[b] http://www.farsnews.com lists the total number of candidates at 12,067.

[c] https://www.tasnimnews.com.

[d] https://www.tasnimnews.com.

[e] http://www.ilna.ir.

[f] http://www.irna.ir.

[g] http://www.majlesekhobregan.ir.

[h] The total count of MPs who served is only until the end of 2017.

Table 95
Eligible Voters and Valid Votes in the 2016 Majlis Election

Province	Eligible voters[a]	Number of valid votes[b]	Turnout (IRIB)	Turnout (valid votes/ MI eligible voters)
Alborz	1,480,131	713,699	54%	48.2%
Ardabil	998,499	594,458	61.5%	59.5%
Bushehr	691,406	443,070	68%	64.1%
Chahar Mahal and Bakhtiari	702,623	495,050	75%	70.5%
East Azerbaijan	2,909,208	1,714,890	70%	58.9%
Fars	3,374,243	2,109,633	63.6%	62.5%
Gilan	1,861,370	1,123,791	65%	60.4%
Golestan	1,288,536	887,978	81%	68.9%
Hamadan	1,505,279	804,367	58.1%	53.4%
Hormozgan	1,119,093	733,445	67%	65.5%
Ilam	434,636	318,587	75.1%	73.3%
Isfahan	3,445,298	1,837,592	61%	53.3%
Kerman	2,083,887	1,250,835	61%	60%
Kermanshah	1,507,595	858,655	60%	57%
Khuzestan	3,447,959	1,912,676	NA%	55.5%
Kohgiluyeh and Buyer Ahmad	518,811	407,707	80%	78.6%
Kurdistan	1,161,537	555,705	53.3%	47.8%
Lorestan	1,409,036	879,405	70.59%	62.4%
Markazi	1,047,670	597,305	60.4%	57%
Mazandaran	2,235,636	1,551,126	72.3%	69.4%
North Khorasan	624,300	412,097	71%	66%
Qazvin	887,164	502,662	61%	56.7%
Qom	768,730	443,797	60%	57.7%
Razavi Khorasan	4,420,718	2,677,450	68%	60.6%
Semnan	494,712	311,001	66%	62.9%
Sistan and Baluchestan	1,685,760	1,089,802	66	64.6%
South Khorasan	598,205	416,836	72.11%	69.7%
Tehran	8,475,077	4,204,554	50%	49.6%
West Azerbaijan	2,296,591	1,469,164	65.5%	64%
Yazd	665,504	438,591	74%	65.9%
Zanjan	775,820	496,505	67%	64%
Average			65.92%	61.55%

[a] For number of eligible voters of each province, two sources were used: 1) A report on an interview with the head of Iran's election headquarters published by the portal of the Ministry of Interior (MI), and 2) a report published on the portal of the Islamic Republic of Iran Broadcasting (IRIB) (see both reports at http://irandataportal.syr.edu). Number of eligible voters was not the same for four provinces in these two sources. To figure out which number was accurate, all possible scenarios were considered. In only one case, out of all sixteen possible cases, the total number of eligible voters was equal to the total number officially announced by MI. To get this number, we extracted the figures for the provinces of North Khorasan, Sistan and Baluchestan, and Kermanshah from the IRIB source and extracted the number for Hamadan Province from MI's report.

[b] For the following four electoral districts, the total number of votes is included in the number of valid votes of the province: Shahrud, Meyami, and Bastam (Semnan), Marvdasht, Pasargad, and Arsanjan (Fars), Bu'in Zahra, and Avaj (Qazvin), and Mehriz, Bafq, Abarkuh, Khatam, and Bahabad (Yazd).

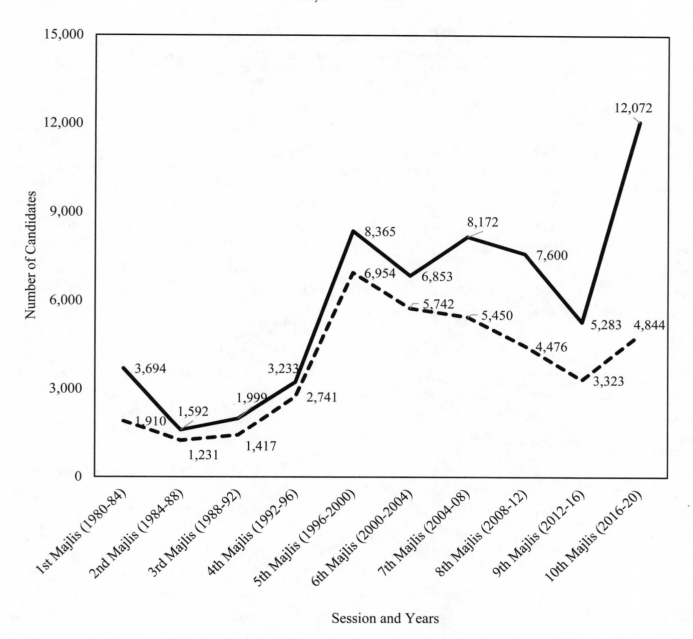

14. Number of Registered Entrants versus Number of Final Candidates Who Competed for Majlis Elections. For sources of data, see chapter 10.

Table 96
Percentage of Voter Turnout Based on Province in Majlis Elections (1980–2016)

Province	1980–84	1984–88	1988–92	1992–96	1996–2000	2000–2004	2004–8	2008–12	2012–16	2016–20
Alborz	*[a]	*	*	*	*	*	*	*	51	54
Ardabil	*	*	*	68.2	70.3	70.2	55.4	59.7	67.5	61.5
Bushehr	52.5	65.8	62.2	56.5	83.4	76.2	61	66.4	72.6	68
Chahar Mahal and Bakhtiari	55	74	74.8	82.3	77	86	75.3	74.4	82.4	75
East Azerbaijan	42.6	57.2	57.9	57.3	69.9	67.2	45.2	55.1	61.7	70
Fars	50.7	66.3	61.2	59.7	75.6	73.1	57.6	63.9	70.2	63.6
Gilan	39.7	60.9	65.3	62.8	82.1	77.8	50.5	65.5	71.3	65
Golestan	*	*	*	*	*	78.6	65.9	71.7	80.2	81
Hamadan	44.3	69.4	63.5	60.7	73.2	68.7	51	54.6	61.6	58.1
Hormozgan	42.2	60.2	62.2	60.3	66.6	71.3	61.7	60.4	71.1	67
Ilam	54.1	72.4	83.8	78.1	90.6	87	73	78.3	86.5	75.1
Isfahan	61	69	59.8	49.4	67.5	60	41.6	46.5	60.9	61
Kerman	36.9	67.5	70.1	63.7	80.4	76.4	64.2	65.3	69.6	61
Kermanshah (Bakhtaran)	37.8	52.3	52.1	63.2	75.9	71.8	50.2	55.9	66	60
Khuzestan	51.8	67.9	70.2	71.4	73	67.5	55.6	54.4	63	NA
Kohgiluyeh and Buyer Ahmad	43.9	78.8	84.9	86.6	96.1	96.5	89.8	87.5	89.9	80
Kurdistan	22.4	47.9	61.4	71.3	77	70.1	32.2	46.5	57.8	53.3
Lorestan	56.5	67.2	63.4	68.6	80.6	78	62.3	65.5	70.6	70.6
Markazi	90.1	72.1	76.7	64.9	72.7	68.3	42.7	54.9	64.9	60.4
Mazandaran	53.4	72	71.9	69.5	83.6	72.2	55.9	64.7	76.3	72.3
North Khorasan	*	*	*	*	*	*	*	66	68.5	71
Qazvin	*	*	*	*	*	70.3	54.8	54.4	68.2	61
Qom	*	*	*	*	*	66.0	52.2	54.2	66.4	60
Razavi Khorasan	55	66.8	55.6	57.2	71.6	73.1	57.5	60.3	66	68
Semnan	62.3	81.1	77.5	71.9	88.5	76.1	56.4	58.1	71.3	66
Sistan and Baluchestan	29.7	38.5	49.9	53.2	62.7	68.7	75.3	67	72.4	66
South Khorasan	*	*	*	*	*	*	*	77	83.8	72.1
Tehran[b]	61.1	60.3	43.2	39.3	55.7	46.8	36.7	35.7	43.1	50
West Azerbaijan	45.2	64.8	60.9	58.3	75.4	71.9	42.3	54.4	69.6	65.5
Yazd	64.9	75.2	74	63.5	70.4	70.8	49.1	56	67.8	74
Zanjan	56	75.5	72.5	67.2	88.5	73.5	59.8	67	72.4	67
Average[c]	50.4	66.0	65.6	64.2	76.3	72.6	56.3	61.4	69.2	65.9

Source: Statistical Center of Iran (1392/2013), 897–900.

Note: The numbers in the table were calculated based on dividing the actual votes cast by the number of eligible voters.

[a] The asterisk means the province was not yet established.

[b] Since 1984, the voter turnout rate for Majlis elections has been substantially lower in Tehran than in the rest of the country.

[c] The "average" voter turnout should not be mistaken for the total turnout.

Table 97
Ratio of Final Candidates to Available Seats in Majlis Elections (1980–2020)

Session (years)	Number of final entrants who competed[a]	Number of available Majlis seats	Ratio[b]
First (1980–84)	1,910	270	7:1
Second (1984–88)	1,231	270	5:1
Third (1988–92)	1,417	270	5:1
Fourth (1992–96)	2,741	270	10:1
Fifth (1996–2000)	6,954	270	26:1
Sixth (2000–2004)	5,742	290	20:1
Seventh (2004–8)	5,450	290	19:1
Eighth (2008–12)	4,476	290	15:1
Ninth (2012–16)	3,323	290	11:1
Tenth (2016–20)	4,844	290	16:7

[a] For an explanation of how the number of candidates was determined, see tables 85 to 94.
[b] Numbers have been rounded off to the nearest full number.

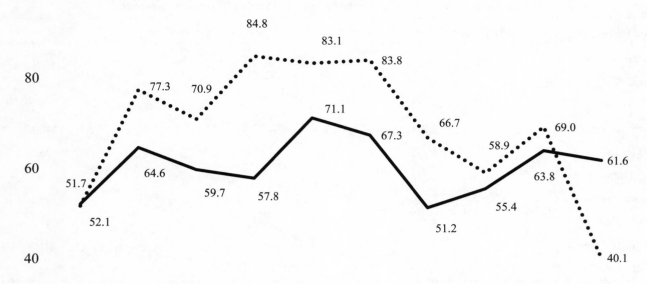

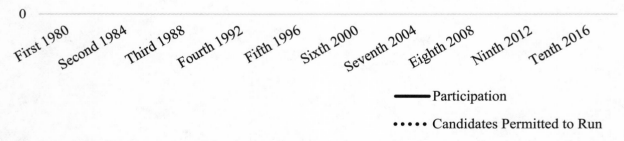

15. Percentage of Majlis Candidates Who Competed Compared to Voter Turnout Rates. For sources of data, see tables 85 to 96.

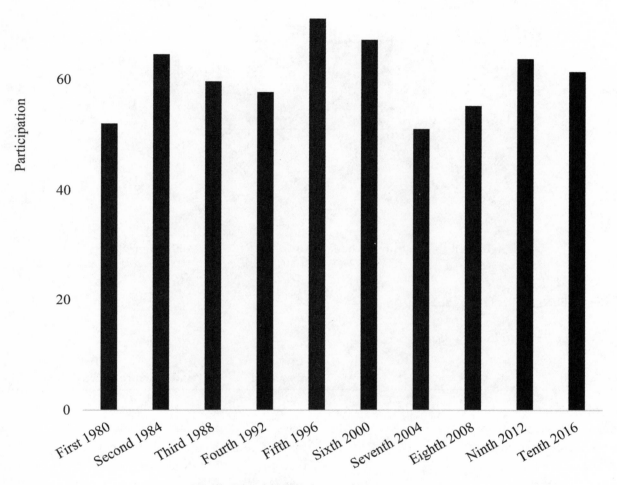

16. Average Voter Participation Rate in Majlis Elections (1980–2016). Source: Ministry of Interior (http://www .moi.ir/portal/File/ShowFile.aspx?ID=30759931-94c9-487d-9368-6426279490c8).

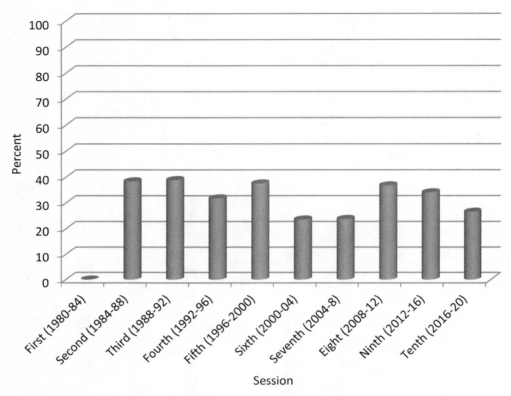

17. Incumbency Rate for Each Majlis (1980–2016). Source: Authors' database.

Deputies in Each Majlis (1980–2020)

Deputies in the First Majlis (1980–84)

Name	Years served	City and province of constituency
Abbasi, Abbas	1980–84	Minab, Hormozgan
Abbasifard, Mohammad-Reza	1980–84	Kuhdasht, Lorestan
Abdekhoda'i, Mohammad-Hadi	1980–84	Mashhad, Razavi Khorasan
Abdolkarimi, Seyfollah	1980–81	Langarud, Gilan
Abedinzadeh, Kamel	1980–84	Khoy and Chaypareh, West Azerbaijan
Abusa'idi-Manuchehri, Abbas	1980–84	Jiroft, Kerman
Abutorabifard, Seyyed Abbas	1980–84	Qazvin, Qazvin
Ahmadi-Danesh-Ashtiyani, Mohammad-Hoseyn	1981–84	Tafresh, Markazi
Ahmadi-Forushani, Seyyed Mohammad	1980–84	Khomeinishahr, Isfahan
Ajam, Ali	1981–84	Mashhad, Razavi Khorasan
Akhlaqinia, Mohammad	1981–84	Sirjan, Kerman
Akhtari, Abbas-Ali	1981–84	Mashhad, Razavi Khorasan
Akrami, Seyyed Kazem	1981–84	Bahar and Kabudarahang, Hamadan
Alamolhoda'i, Bahaeddin	1980–84	Ardabil, Ardabil
Alavi, Seyyed Mahmud	1981–84	Lamerd, Fars
Ale-Kazemi, Ali	1980–84	Delfan and Selseleh, Lorestan

Name	Years served	City and province of constituency
Ale-Seyyed Ghafur, Seyyed Mohammad-Taqi	1981–84	Shushtar, Khuzestan
Alinezhad-Sarkhani, Mohammad	1980–81	Tabriz, East Azerbaijan
Alipur, Ahmad	1983–84	Piranshahr and Sardasht, West Azerbaijan
Alipur, Asadollah	1980–84	Ilam, Ilam
Alizadeh, Ahmad	1980–84	Qaemshahr, Mazandaran
Allahbedashti, Abolhasan	1981–84	Nowshahr, Mazandaran
Alviri, Morteza	1980–84	Damavand, Tehran
Amani, Sa'id	1981–84	Tehran, Tehran
Amin-Naseri, Mohammad-Reza	1980–84	Astaneh-ye Ashrafiyyeh, Gilan
Ansari, Majid	1980–84	Zarand, Kerman
Ansarirad, Hoseyn	1980–84	Neyshabur, Razavi Khorasan
Aqa Hoseyni-Tabataba'i, Seyyed Hasan	1981–84	Zabol, Sistan and Baluchestan
Aqa Mohammadi, Ali	1980–84	Hamadan, Hamadan
Aqa Rahimi, Abdolhamid	1980–84	Shahr-e Babak, Kerman
Arbabi, Abdolkarim	1981–84	Chabahar, Sistan and Baluchestan
Asadiniya, Abdorreza	1980–84	Ahvaz, Khuzestan
Asgarowladi, Habibollah	1980–81	Tehran, Tehran
Asghari, Ali-Akbar	1980–81	Bonab and Malekan, East Azerbaijan
Attari, Ahmad	1980–84	Arak, Markazi
Ayat, Seyyed Hasan	1980–81	Tehran, Tehran
A'zami, Morteza	1980–84	Khorramabad, Lorestan
Baba'i, Alibaba	1982–84	Esfarayen, North Khorasan
Babasafari-Zamani, Mohammad-Reza	1980–84	Borkhar, Isfahan
Baghani, Ali-Asghar	1980–84	Sabzevar, Razavi Khorasan
Bahari-Ardeshiri, Abbas-Ali	1981–84	Sari, Mazandaran
Bahonar, Mohammad-Javad	1980–81	Kerman, Kerman
Bahrami, Ahmad	1981–84	Paveh, Kermanshah
Bakhshi, Hoseyn	1981–84	Ramhormoz, Khuzestan
Bat-Oshonagugtappeh, Sergon	1980–84	Assyrians and Chaldeans (minority)
Bayani, Salaheddin	1980–84	Khaf, Razavi Khorasan
Bayat-Zanjani, Asadollah	1980-84	Mahneshan and Ijrood, Zanjan
Bazargan, Mehdi	1980-84	Tehran, Tehran
Bazqandi, Hoseyn	1981–84	Dorud, Lorestan
Behbahani, Mohammad-Zeyd	1980–80	Bandar-e Mahshahr, Khuzestan
Beheshti, Ahmad	1980–84	Fasa, Fars
Beheshtinezhad, Seyyed Hoseyn	1981–84	Isfahan, Isfahan
Behruzi, Maryam	1981–84	Tehran, Tehran
Besharat, Mohammad-Taqi	1980–81	Semirom, Isfahan
Besharati, Ali-Mohammad	1980–84	Jahrom, Fars
Bimeqdar, Shahabeddin	1981–84	Varzaqan, East Azerbaijan
Borumand, Mohammad-Hadi	1980–84	Borujerd, Lorestan
Chamran, Mostafa	1980–81	Tehran, Tehran
Chehregani-Anzabi, Mohammad-Hoseyn	1980–84	Tabriz, East Azerbaijan
Cheraghzadeh-Dezfuli, Ali-Reza	1980–81	Ramhormoz, Khuzestan

Name	Years served	City and province of constituency
Damani, Hamed	1981–84	Khash, Sistan and Baluchestan
Danesh, Seyyed Mohammad-Kazem	1980–81	Andimeshk and Shush, Khuzestan
Danesh-Ashtiyani, Gholam-Reza	1980–81	Tafresh and Ashtiyan, Markazi
Dastgheyb, Gowharoshshari'eh	1980–84	Tehran, Tehran
Dehqan, Ali-Akbar	1980–81	Torbat-e Jam, Razavi Khorasan
Dehqan, Ezzatollah	1981–84	Torbat-e Jam and Taybad, Razavi Khorasan
Dehqani, Yadollah	1980–84	Ahar, East Azerbaijan
Dialameh, Seyyed Abdolhamid	1980–81	Mashhad, Razavi Khorasan
Didgah, Nazar-Mohammad	1980–84	Iranshahr, Sistan and Baluchestan
Doa'i, Seyyed Mahmud	1981–84	Tehran, Tehran
Dorri-Najafabadi, Qorbanali	1980–84	Ardal, Chahar Mahal and Bakhtiari
Duzduzani, Abbas	1981–84	Tabriz, East Azerbaijan
Emami, Abdollah	1980–83	Torbat-e Heydariyyeh, Razavi Khorasan
Emami-Kashani, Mohammad	1980–82	Kashan, Isfahan
Erfani, Seyyed Mojtaba	1981–84	Talesh, Gilan
Erfani, Seyyed Yunes	1980–82	Talesh, Gilan
Eshaq-Madani, Mohammad	1981–84	Saravan, Sistan and Baluchestan
Estaki, Fereydun	1982–84	Shahrekord, Chahar Mahal and Bakhtiari
Estaki, Mojtaba	1981–81	Shahrekord, Chahar Mahal and Bakhtiari
Estaki, Rahman	1980–81	Shahrekord, Chahar Mahal and Bakhtiari
Ezheh'i, Mehdi	1982–84	Isfahan, Isfahan
Fahim-Kermani, Morteza	1981–84	Kerman, Kerman
Fallahhojjat-Ansari, Arsalan	1980–84	Lahijan, Gilan
Farzpor-Machiyani, Mohammad	1980–84	Astara, Gilan
Fazel-Astarabadi, Mohammad	1980–84	Babol, Mazandaran
Fazel-Harandi, Mohyeddin	1981–84	Eqlid, Fars
Fazlali, Morteza	1980–84	Garmsar, Semnan
Feda'i, Esma'il	1980–84	Shazand (Sarband), Markazi
Ferdowsipur, Esma'il	1980–84	Mashhad, Razavi Khorasan
Foroughi, Mohammad	1981–84	Masjed Soleyman, Khuzestan
Fumani-Ha'eri, Mostafa	1980–84	Fuman, Gilan
Garshasebi, Ghafur	1981–84	Bandar-e Lengeh, Hormozgan
Ghaffari, Hadi	1980–84	Tehran, Tehran
Ghaffari, Mohammad	1980–84	Salmas, West Azerbaijan
Ghaffari-Qarebagh, Seyyed Akbar	1980–84	Urmia, West Azerbaijan
Ghafurifard, Hasan	1981–81	Mashhad, Razavi Khorasan
Gharazi, Seyyed Mohammad	1981–81	Isfahan, Isfahan
Ghazanfarpur, Ahmad	1980–82	Lenjan, Isfahan
Golzadeh-Ghafuri, Ali	1980–82	Tehran, Tehran
Habibi, Hasan-Ebrahim	1980–84	Tehran, Tehran
Hadi-Najafabadi, Mohammad-Ali	1980–84	Tehran, Tehran
Ha'eri-Shirazi, Mohammad-Sadeq	1980–82	Shiraz, Fars
Ha'erizadeh, Seyyed Abolhasan	1980–84	Birjand, South Khorasan
Hamidi, Seyyed Hashem	1980–84	Hamadan, Hamadan

Name	Years served	City and province of constituency
Hamidzadeh-Givi, Ali-Akbar	1982–84	Bu'inzahra, Zanjan
Hamzeh'i, Ali	1981–84	Asadabad, Hamadan
Haqiqat-Afshar, Ali	1980–84	Urmia, West Azerbaijan
Haqqani, Gholam-Hoseyn	1980–81	Bandar-e Abbas, Hormozgan
Haqshenas-Kuddehi, Mazaher	1980–84	Aliabad Katul, Golestan
Harati, Hoseyn	1980–84	Sabzevar, Razavi Khorasan
Hasani, Seyyed Mohammad-Amin	1981–84	Sanandaj, Kurdistan
Hasani, Gholam-Reza	1980–82	Urmia, West Azerbaijan
Hasanzadeh-Mirabadi, Hasan	1981–84	Kashmar, Razavi Khorasan
Hashemi, Seyyed Baqer	1981–84	Falavarjan, Isfahan
Hashemi-Rafsanjani, Akbar	1980–84	Tehran, Tehran
Hashemi-Sanjani, Ali	1980–81	Arak, Markazi
Hashemiyan, Hoseyn	1980–84	Rafsanjan, Kerman
Hatefi, Nosratollah	1981–84	Qorveh, Kurdistan
Hejazi, Fakhreddin	1980–84	Tehran, Tehran
Hejazifar, Hashem	1981–84	Maku, West Azerbaijan
Hemmati, Ahmad	1980–84	Meshginshahr, Ardabil
Heydari, Abbas	1980–81	Bandar-e Bushehr, Bushehr
Heydari, Mohammad-Ali	1980–81	Nahavand, Hamadan
Hojaji, Seyyed Sajjad	1980–84	Miyaneh, East Azerbaijan
Hojjati-Kermani, Mohammad-Javad	1980–84	Tehran, Tehran
Hojjat-Kashfi, Seyyed Ja'far	1980–84	Neyriz and Estahban, Fars
Hoseyni, Seyyed Abolhasan	1980–84	Minudasht, Golestan
Hoseyni, Seyyed Ahmad	1980–84	Marvdasht, Fars
Hoseyni, Seyyed Ali	1981–84	Sanandaj, Kurdistan
Hoseyni-Brameh'i, Seyyed Fazlollah	1981–84	Dargaz, Razavi Khorasan
Hoseyni-Lavasani, Seyyed Mohammad-Baqer	1980–81	Tehran, Tehran
Hoseyni-Na'ini, Seyyed Shamseddin	1980–81	Na'in, Isfahan
Hoseyni-Niya-Kajidi, Mohammad	1981–84	Rudsar, Gilan
Hoseyni-Tabataba'i, Seyyed Mohammad-Taqi	1980–81	Zabol, Sistan and Baluchestan
Hoseyni-Vae'z-Ramiyani, Seyyed Hoseyn	1980–84	Ramiyan, Golestan
Isfahani, Reza	1980–84	Varamin, Tehran
Jaberi-Bonab, Mir Yusef	1983–84	Bonab and Malekan, East Azerbaijan
Ja'fari, Hoseyn	1981–84	Kermanshah, Kermanshah
Ja'fari-Chenijani, Mohammad	1981–84	Langarud, Gilan
Ja'fari, Seyyed Mohammad-Mehdi	1980–84	Dashtestan, Bushehr
Jalali, Abdolhoseyn	1980–84	Neyshabur, Razavi Khorasan
Kamali, Hoseyn	1981–84	Tehran, Tehran
Kamaliniya, Mohammad-Taqi	1980–81	Quchan, Razavi Khorasan
Karami, Mohammad-Mehdi	1980–82	Dasht-e Azadegan, Khuzestan
Karimi, Foad	1980–84	Ahvaz, Khuzestan
Karimi-Bijaninezhad, Emadeddin	1980–81	Nowshahr, Mazandaran
Karrubi, Mehdi	1980–84	Aligudarz, Lorestan
Katira'i, Morteza	1980–84	Malayer, Hamadan

Name	Years served	City and province of constituency
Kermani, Hoseyn	1980–81	Abadeh, Fars
Khachaturian, Herach	1980–84	Armenians of southern Iran (minority)
Khalatian, Hara'i	1980–84	Armenians of northern Iran (minority)
Khalili, Mohammad	1980–84	Baft, Kerman
Khalkhali, Mohammad-Sadeq	1980–84	Qom, Qom
Khamenei, Seyyed Ali	1980–81	Tehran, Tehran
Khamenei, Seyyed Hadi	1981–84	Fariman, Razavi Khorasan
Khamenei, Seyyed Mohammad	1980–84	Mashhad, Razavi Khorasan
Khatami, Seyyed Mohammad	1980–82	Ardakan, Yazd
Khaza'i, Mohammad	1980–84	Rasht, Gilan
Khoshnevis, Esma'il	1980–84	Ardabil, Ardabil
Khosravi, Mohammad-Ali	1981–84	Miyandoab, West Azerbaijan
Kiya'i, Seyyed Mostafa	1981–84	Tuyserkan, Hamadan
Kiyan-Ersi, Asadollah	1980–84	Faridan and Fereydunshahr, Isfahan
Kiyavash, Seyyed Mohammad	1980–84	Ahvaz, Khuzestan
Lahuti-Eshkevari, Hasan	1980–81	Rasht, Gilan
Mahallati, Fazlollah	1980–84	Mahallat, Markazi
Mahlujchi, Hoseyn	1982–84	Kashan, Isfahan
Mahmudi, Morteza	1980–84	Qasr-e Shirin, Kermanshah
Mahmudi-Golpayegani, Seyyed Abutaleb	1980–84	Golpayegan and Khansar, Isfahan
Mahmudi-Sartangi, Seyyed Shahab	1980–84	Borujen, Chahar Mahal and Bakhtiari
Malakuti, Ali	1980–84	Sarab, East Azerbaijan
Malekpur, Parviz	1980–84	Zoroastrian community (minority)
Marvi-Samavarchi, Mahmud	1980–84	Torqabeh and Chenaran, Razavi Khorasan
Ma'sumi, Ali-Akbar	1980–84	Shahrud, Semnan
Matin, Abbas	1981–84	Bandar-e Abbas, Hormozgan
Milani-Hoseyni, Seyyed Mohammad	1980–84	Tabriz, East Azerbaijan
Mir Ja'fari, Seyyed Mojtaba	1981–84	Arak, Markazi
Mir Yunesi, Seyyed Abbas	1980–84	Kangavar, Kermanshah
Mirzapur-Kleshtari, Moslem	1980–84	Rudbar, Gilan
Mo'in, Mostafa	1982–84	Shiraz, Fars
Mo'infar, Ali-Akbar	1980–84	Tehran, Tehran
Mo'adikhah, Abdolmajid	1980–81	Tehran, Tehran
Moarrefi'zadeh, Ali	1980–84	Khorramshahr and Shadegan, Khuzestan
Moezzi, Esma'il	1980–84	Malayer, Hamadan
Mohajerani, Seyyed Ataollah	1980–84	Shiraz, Fars
Mohammadi, Mohammad	1980–84	Gorgan, Golestan
Mohammadi, Seyyed Mohammad-Hoseyn	1981–84	Dashti and Tangestan, Bushehr
Mohammadi, Yunes	1980–84	Khorramshahr, Khuzestan
Mohyeddin-Anvari, Mohammad-Baqer	1980–84	Razan, Hamadan
Mojtahed-Shabestari, Mohammad	1980–84	Shabestar, East Azerbaijan
Mojtahed-Shabestari, Mohsen	1980–84	Tehran, Tehran
Mollazadeh, Ahmad	1980–84	Gonabad, Razavi Khorasan

Name	Years served	City and province of constituency
Montajabniya, Rasul	1981–84	Andimeshk and Shush, Khuzestan
Montazeri, Mohammad-Ali	1980–81	Najafabad, Isfahan
Mostafavi-Kashani, Seyyed Ahmad	1980–84	Qamsar and Natanz, Isfahan
Mostafavi-Siyahmazgi, Seyyed Davud	1982–84	Rasht, Gilan
Motahhari, Mohammad-Taqi	1980–80	Fariman, Razavi Khorasan
Mottaki, Manouchehr	1980–84	Kordkuy, Golestan
Movahhedi-Kermani, Mohammad-Ali	1980–84	Kerman, Kerman
Movahhedi-Savoji, Ali	1980–84	Saveh, Markazi
Mowla'i, Ahmad	1982–84	Tehran, Tehran
Mozaffar, Abbas	1980–84	Bojnurd, North Khorasan
Musavi-Bojnurdi, Seyyed Mohammad-Kazem	1980–84	Tehran, Tehran
Musavi-Jahanabad, Seyyed Hoseyn	1980–84	Mashhad, Razavi Khorasan
Musavi-Kho'iniha, Seyyed Mohammad	1980–84	Tehran, Tehran
Musavi-Lari, Seyyed Abdolvahed	1981–84	Larestan, Fars
Musavi-Nanehkaran, Mir Fakhreddin	1980–84	Ardabil, Ardabil
Musavi-Tabrizi, Seyyed Abolfazl	1980–84	Tabriz, East Azerbaijan
Musavi-Tabrizi, Seyyed Hasan	1981–84	Hashtrud, East Azerbaijan
Musavi-Tabrizi, Seyyed Hoseyn	1980–81	Tabriz, East Azerbaijan
Musavi-Tabrizi, Seyyed Mohsen	1981–84	Tabriz, East Azerbaijan
Musavi-Tareh, Seyyed Mohammad	1982–84	Dasht-e Azadegan, Khuzestan
Nabavi, Seyyed Mohammad-Hasan	1981–84	Bandar-e Bushehr, Bushehr
Nadi, Gholam-Hoseyn	1981–84	Najafabad, Isfahan
Najafi, Qodratollah	1980–84	Shahreza, Isfahan
Naqavi, Seyyed Ali-Naqi	1980–84	Qaenat, South Khorasan
Naqi, Khosrow	1981–84	Jewish community (minority)
Nari'zadeh, Ali	1981–84	Marivan, Kurdistan
Naseri, Mostafa	1981–84	Zanjan, Zanjan
Nasiri-Lari, Mehdi	1980–81	Larestan, Fars
Nasrollahi, Mohammad	1980–84	Abadan, Khuzestan
Nateq-Nuri, Abbas-Ali	1980–81	Nur and Mahmudabad, Mazandaran
Nateq-Nuri, Ahmad	1981–84	Nur and Mahmudabad, Mazandaran
Nateq-Nuri, Ali-Akbar	1980–81	Tehran, Tehran
Nazari-Monfared, Ali	1982–84	Abadeh, Fars
Nowruzi, Kazem	1980–84	Amol, Mazandaran
Nowruzi, Mohammad	1980–84	Gonbad-e Kavus, Golestan
Okhovvatiyan, Abolqasem	1980–84	Sari, Mazandaran
Omid-Najafabadi, Fathollah	1980–84	Isfahan, Isfahan
Orumiyan, Ali	1980–84	Maragheh, East Azerbaijan
Paknezhad, Seyyed Reza	1980–81	Yazd, Yazd
Parvaresh, Seyyed Ali-Akbar	1980–81	Isfahan, Isfahan
Purgol, Mohammad-Mehdi	1981–84	Bandar-e Anzali, Gilan
Purostad, Ali-Akbar	1981–84	Tehran, Tehran
Pursalari, Hoseyn	1982–84	Kahnuj, Kerman

Name	Years served	City and province of constituency
Qaemi-Amiri, Ali	1980–84	Babolsar and Bandpay, Mazandaran
Qaemifar, Mehdi	1981–84	Buyer Ahmad, Dena, Kohgiluyeh and Buyer Ahmad
Qasemi, Abdolvahhab	1980–81	Sari, Mazandaran
Rafi'iyan, Esma'il	1980–84	Marand, East Azerbaijan
Rahbari, Mohammad-Hashem	1982–84	Tehran, Tehran
Rahimi, Seyyed Fakhreddin	1980–81	Malavi, Lorestan
Rahimi, Seyyed Nureddin	1981–84	Pol-e Dokhtar and Malavi, Lorestan
Rahimi-Haji Abadi, Gholam-Reza	1981–84	Bandar-e Mahshahr, Khuzestan
Rahmani, Hoseyn-Ali	1980–84	Bijar, Kurdistan
Rahmani, Qahreman	1980–84	Takestan, Zanjan
Rahmani-Khalili, Ali-Asghar	1981–84	Behshahr, Mazandaran
Raja'i, Mohammad-Ali	1980–80	Tehran, Tehran
Raja'iyan, Mohammad	1980–84	Zanjan, Zanjan
Ramezani-Khorshiddust, Reza	1980–84	Rasht, Gilan
Ranjbar-Chubeh, Mohammad-Taqi	1980–84	Sowme'eh Sara, Gilan
Rashed, Mohammad-Reza	1981–84	Germi (Moghan), Ardabil
Rashidian, Mohammad	1980–84	Abadan, Khuzestan
Rasi, Mohsen	1981–84	Miyandoab and Takab, West Azerbaijan
Razavi-Ardakani, Seyyed Abufazel	1980–84	Sepidan, Fars
Reza'i-Henji, Mahmud	1980–84	Karaj, Tehran
Rezvani, Ali-Akbar	1981–84	Firuzabad, Fars
Rohami, Mohsen	1980–84	Khodabandeh, Zanjan
Rostami-Qarahquz, Asghar	1981–84	Naqadeh, West Azerbaijan
Rouhani, Hassan	1980–84	Semnan, Semnan
Sabbaghiyan, Hashem	1980–84	Tehran, Tehran
Saburi, Mohammad-Kazem	1981–84	Shiravan, North Khorasan
Sadeqi, Mohammad-Hoseyn	1980–81	Dorud and Azna, Lorestan
Sadeqi, Qasem	1980–81	Mashhad, Razavi Khorasan
Sadeqi-Givi, Ghafur	1980–84	Khalkhal, Ardabil
Sadiqi, Ateqeh	1980–84	Tehran, Tehran
Sadr Haj Seyyed Javadi, Seyyed Ahmad	1980–84	Qazvin, Qazvin
Saduqi, Mohammad-Ali	1981–84	Yazd, Yazd
Safa'ipur-Zamani, Arsalan	1983–84	Kermanshah, Kermanshah
Safari, Latif	1980–84	Islamabad-e Gharb, Kermanshah
Sahabi, Ezzatollah	1980–84	Tehran, Tehran
Sahabi, Yadollah	1980–84	Tehran, Tehran
Sahebozzamani, Fathali	1980–81	Asadabad, Hamadan
Sajjadnezhad, Seyyed Mir Ghaffar	1981–84	Bostanabad, East Azerbaijan
Salamatiyan, Seyyed Ahmad	1980–82	Isfahan, Isfahan
Salavati, Fazlollah	1980–84	Isfahan, Isfahan
Salek, Ahmad	1981–84	Isfahan, Isfahan
Salimi-Gamini, Musa	1981–84	Miyaneh, East Azerbaijan
Salmani-Zarji, Mohammad-Hoseyn	1980–84	Sonqor and Koliyayi, Kermanshah

Name	Years served	City and province of constituency
Sami, Kazem	1980–84	Tehran, Tehran
Sazegarnezhad, Mohammad-Amin	1980–84	Sarvestan, Fars
Sefati-Dezfuli, Iraj	1980–84	Abadan, Khuzestan
Seyyed Khamushi, Seyyed Taqi	1981–84	Tehran, Tehran
Seyyed Zadeh, Seyyed Jalil	1981–84	Kermanshah, Kermanshah
Seyyedin, Mohsen	1980–84	Khomeyn, Markazi
Shahabadi, Mehdi	1980–84	Tehran, Tehran
Shahcheraqi, Seyyed Hasan	1980–84	Damghan, Semnan
Shahraki, Gholam-Ali	1980–84	Zabol, Sistan and Baluchestan
Shahriyari, Mir Behzad	1980–81	Dashti, Tangestan, Bushehr
Shahrokhi, Seyyed Mohammad-Taqi	1980–84	Khorramabad, Lorestan
Shar'i, Abdolkarim	1980–84	Darab, Fars
Shari'ati-Dehaqani, Mohammad	1981–84	Semirom, Isfahan
Shaverani, Mohammad	1981–84	Bukan, West Azerbaijan
Sherafat, Seyyed Mohammad-Javad	1980–81	Shushtar, Khuzestan
Sheybani, Abbas	1981–84	Tehran, Tehran
Shiraziyan, Javad	1980–84	Qaemshahr, Mazandaran
Shoja'i, Mohammad	1980–82	Zanjan, Zanjan
Shoja'iyan, Samad	1980–84	Mamasani, Fars
Shojuni, Ja'far	1980–84	Karaj, Tehran
Shushtari, Mohammad-Esma'il	1981–84	Quchan, Razavi Khorasan
Sobhanollahi, Mohammad-Ali	1980–84	Tabriz, East Azerbaijan
Sori, Abdollah	1983–84	Saqqez, Baneh, Kurdistan
Tabataba'inezhad, Seyyed Abbas	1981–84	Ardestan, Isfahan
Tabataba'inezhad, Seyyed Nurollah	1980–81	Ardestan, Isfahan
Tabrizi, Mostafa	1980–84	Bojnurd, North Khorasan
Taheri, Ali	1981–84	I'zeh, Khuzestan
Taheri, Rajab-Ali	1980–84	Kazerun, Fars
Tajgardun, Bahram	1980–84	Gachsaran, Kohgiluyeh and Buyer Ahmad
Taleqani, A'zam	1980–84	Tehran, Tehran
Tatari, Mohammad-Ali	1980–84	Zahedan, Sistan and Baluchestan
Tavakkoli, Ahmad	1980–81	Behshahr, Mazandaran
Tayyeb, Mehdi	1981–84	Na'in, Isfahan
Tayyebi, Mohammad-Hasan	1980–81	Esfarayen, North Khorasan
Va'ezi, Farajollah	1980–84	Abhar, Zanjan
Va'ez-Musavi-Anzabi, Seyyed Hasan	1982–84	Urmia, West Azerbaijan
Vafi-Yazdi, Abolqasem	1980–84	Taft, Yazd
Vahid, Motlleb	1981–84	Kaleybar, East Azerbaijan
Velayati, Ali-Akbar	1980–81	Tehran, Tehran
Yar-Mohammadi, Ali-Reza	1980–84	Bam, Kerman
Yazdi, Ebrahim	1980–84	Tehran, Tehran
Yazdi, Mohammad	1980–84	Qom, Qom
Yusefi-Eshkevari, Hasan	1980–84	Tonekabon, Mazandaran
Za'eri, Gholam-Abbas	1980–84	Bandar-e Abbas, Hormozgan

Name	Years served	City and province of constituency
Zamaniyan, Ahmad	1981–84	Nahavand, Hamadan
Zangeneh, Seyyed Sabah	1980–84	Shiraz, Fars
Zargar, Musa	1980–84	Shahriyar, Tehran
Zarhani, Seyyed Ahmad	1980–84	Dezful, Khuzestan
Zavareh'i, Seyyed Reza	1981–84	Tehran, Tehran
Zeynali, Seyyed Shokrollah	1980–84	Behbahan, Khuzestan

Deputies in the Second Majlis (1984–88)

Name	Tenure	City and province of constituency
Abbasifard, Mohammad-Reza	1984–88	Khorramabad, Lorestan
Abbaspur, Ebrahim	1984–88	Kaleybar, East Azerbaijan
Abdekhoda'i, Mohammad-Hadi	1984–88	Mashhad, Razavi Khorasan
Abdolali'zadeh, Ali	1984–88	Urmia, West Azerbaijan
Abdollahpur, Ali	1984–88	Hashtrud, East Azerbaijan
Abedi, Nurollah	1984–88	Behbahan, Khuzestan
Afrazideh, Seyyed Farajollah	1984–88	Nowshahr and Chalus, Mazandaran
Ahani, Esma'il	1984–88	Astara, Gilan
Ahmadi, Moradali	1984–88	Sonqor, Kermanshah
Ahmadvand, Mohammad-Saleh	1984–88	Malayer, Hamadan
Akhundi, Mohammad-Baqer	1984–88	Shabestar, East Azerbaijan
Akrami, Seyyed Reza	1984–88	Semnan, Semnan
Alavi, Seyyed Mahmud	1984–88	Lamerd, Fars
Alavi-Hoseyni, Seyyed Mohammad-Hasan	1984–88	Gorgan, Golestan
Alizadeh-Barogh, Rahim	1984–88	Ardabil, Ardabil
Amani, Sa'id	1984–88	Tehran, Tehran
Amirzadeh-Irani, Mirza Ahmad	1984–88	Ardabil, Ardabil
Angaji, Seyyed Javad	1984–88	Tabriz, East Azerbaijan
Anjiri-Motlaq, Ahad	1984–88	Mahabad, West Azerbaijan
Aqa Hoseyni-Tabataba'i, Seyyed Hasan	1984–88	Zabol, Sistan and Baluchestan
Aqa Mohammadi, Ali	1984–88	Hamadan, Hamadan
Arabameri, Yar-Mohammad	1984–88	Garmsar, Semnan
A'rabi, Mohammad-Ali	1984–88	Kashmar, Razavi Khorasan
Arbabi, Abdolkarim	1984–88	Chabahar, Sistan and Baluchestan
Asadiniya, Abdorreza	1984–88	Ahvaz, Khuzestan
Asghari-Bahari, Seyyed Mohammad	1984–88	Tehran, Tehran
Ashrafi-Isfahani, Mohammad	1984–88	Kermanshah, Kermanshah
Ata'i, Abdollah	1984–86	Sanandaj, Kurdistan
Ayyubi, Mohammad	1986–88	Bojnurd, North Khorasan
Azari-Qomi, Ahmad	1984–88	Qom, Qom
Azizi, Ahmad	1984–88	Qazvin, Qazvin
Baba'i, Alibaba	1984–88	Esfarayen, North Khorasan

Name	Tenure	City and province of constituency
Badamchiyan, Asadollah	1984–88	Tehran, Tehran
Baghumian, Artavaz	1984–88	Armenians of southern Iran (minority)
Bahari-Ardeshiri, Abbas-Ali	1984–88	Sari, Mazandaran
Bahonar, Mohammad-Reza	1984–88	Baft, Kerman
Bahrami, Mohammad-Baqer	1984–88	Asadabad, Hamadan
Bayat, Gholam-Reza	1984–88	Mahneshan and Ijrood, Zanjan
Bayat-Zanjani, Asadollah	1984–88	Zanjan and Tarom, Zanjan
Beheshti, Ahmad	1984–88	Fasa, Fars
Behruzi, Maryam	1984–88	Tehran, Tehran
Bimeqdar, Shahabeddin	1984–88	Varzaqan, East Azerbaijan
Chehregani-Anzabi, Mohammad-Hoseyn	1984–88	Tabriz, East Azerbaijan
Damani, Hamed	1984–88	Khash, Sistan and Baluchestan
Dashti-Tolier, Motalleb	1984–88	Germi (Moghan), Ardabil
Dastgheyb, Gowharoshshari'eh	1984–88	Tehran, Tehran
Davudi, Mohammad-Baqer	1984–88	Kordkuy, Golestan
Davudolmusavi-Damghani, Seyyed Abolqasem	1984–86	Ramhormoz and Ramshir, Khuzestan
Dehqan, Ezzatollah	1984–88	Torbat-e Jam and Taybad, Razavi Khorasan
Doa'i, Seyyed Mahmud	1984–88	Tehran, Tehran
Dorri-Najafabadi, Qorbanali	1984–88	Tehran, Tehran
Duzduzani, Abbas	1984–88	Tehran, Tehran
Ebrahimi, Hoseyn	1984–88	Varamin, Tehran
Efri, Mohammad-Amin	1984–88	Abadan, Khuzestan
Emammusavi, Seyyed Mohammad-Kazem	1984–88	Shushtar, Khuzestan
Emamzadeh-Vaqfi, Seyyed Mohammad-Reza	1984–88	Isfahan, Isfahan
Erfani, Seyyed Mojtaba	1984–88	Talesh, Gilan
Esfandiyarpur, Ali-Asghar	1984–88	Kuhdasht, Lorestan
Eshaq-Madani, Mohammad	1984–88	Saravan, Sistan and Baluchestan
Esrafiliyan, Ebrahim	1984–88	Tehran, Tehran
Estaki, Fereydun	1984–88	Shahrekord, Chahar Mahal and Bakhtiari
Fahim-Kermani, Morteza	1984–88	Kerman, Kerman
Falasiri, Seyyed Fakhreddin	1984–88	Neyriz and Estahban, Fars
Farsi, Jalaleddin	1984–88	Tehran, Tehran
Farugh, Seyyed Mostafa	1984–88	Dezful, Khuzestan
Faza'eli, Ataollah	1984–88	Semirom, Isfahan
Fazel-Harandi, Mohyeddin	1984–88	Isfahan, Isfahan
Feda'i, Esma'il	1984–88	Shazand (Sarband), Markazi
Feda'i-Araqi, Gholam-Reza	1984–88	Arak, Markazi
Ferdowsipur, Esma'il	1984–88	Mashhad, Razavi Khorasan
Ghaffari, Hadi	1984–88	Tehran, Tehran
Habibi, Abutaleb	1984–88	Qaemshahr, Mazandaran
Hadidchi-Dabbagh, Marziyeh	1984–88	Tehran, Tehran
Hadi-Najafabadi, Mohammad-Ali	1984–88	Tehran, Tehran
Ha'erizadeh, Seyyed Abolhasan	1984–88	Birjand, South Khorasan

Name	Tenure	City and province of constituency
Hamidi, Seyyed Hashem	1984–88	Hamadan, Hamadan
Hamidzadeh-Givi, Ali-Akbar	1984–86	Bu'inzahra, Zanjan
Harati, Hoseyn	1984–88	Sabzevar, Razavi Khorasan
Hashemi, Seyyed Fakhreddin	1984–88	Jahrom, Fars
Hashemi, Seyyed Mohammad-Reza	1984–88	Aligudarz, Lorestan
Hashemi-Rafsanjani, Akbar	1984–88	Tehran, Tehran
Hashemiyan, Hoseyn	1984–88	Rafsanjan, Kerman
Hashemza'i-Nehbandan, Abdorreza	1984–88	Ferdows and Tabas, South Khorasan
Hejazi, Fakhreddin	1984–88	Tehran, Tehran
Hejazifar, Hashem	1984–88	Khoy and Chaypareh, West Azerbaijan
Hejazi-Kamsari, Seyyed Abutaleb	1984–88	Rasht, Gilan
Hejrati-Qazvini, Seyyed Abdollah	1984–88	Qazvin, Qazvin
Hemmati, Ahmad	1984–88	Meshginshahr, Ardabil
Hesari, Mohammad	1984–88	Kangavar, Kermanshah
Heydari, Gholam-Reza	1984–88	Tafresh, Markazi
Hojjati, Aziz	1984–88	Maku, West Azerbaijan
Hoseyni, Seyyed Abolhasan	1984–88	Minudasht, Golestan
Hoseyni, Seyyed Ali	1984–88	Sanandaj, Kurdistan
Hoseyni, Seyyed Hoseyn	1984–88	Qaenat, South Khorasan
Hoseyni-Brameh'i, Seyyed Fazlollah	1984–88	Dargaz, Razavi Khorasan
Hoseyninezhad, Seyyed Mehdi	1984–88	Nur and Mahmudabad, Mazandaran
Hoseyninezhad, Seyyed Mohammad	1984–88	Ardakan, Yazd
Hoseyni-Shahrudi, Seyyed Hoseyn	1984–88	Shahrud, Semnan
Hoseyni, Seyyed Javad	1984-88	Aliabad Katul, Golestan
Hoseynizadeh, Seyyed Ali	1984–88	Borujen and Lordegan, Chahar Mahal and Bakhtiari
Hoseyni-Zeydabadi, Seyyed Ahmad	1984–88	Sirjan, Kerman
Islami-Kheramehi, Ebrahim	1984–88	Eqlid, Fars
Ja'fari, Hasan	1984–88	Shahr-e Babak, Kerman
Ja'fari-Hesarlu, Seyyed Mir Heydar	1984–88	Bonab and Malekan, East Azerbaijan
Jahangiri, Eshaq	1984–88	Jiroft, Kerman
Jalali, Khodakaram	1984–88	Firuzabad, Fars
Jamal-Yusefi, Ebrahim	1984–88	Dashti, Tangestan, Bushehr
Kabiri, Qanbar	1984–88	Marvdasht, Fars
Kalateh'i, Mohammad	1984–86	Bojnurd, North Khorasan
Kalimi-Nikruz, Manuchehr	1984–88	Jewish community (minority)
Kamali, Hoseyn	1984–88	Tehran, Tehran
Kamyar, Ali	1984–88	Urmia, West Azerbaijan
Karimi, Foad	1984–88	Ahvaz, Khuzestan
Karimi, Mohammad-Ali	1984–88	Bojnurd, North Khorasan
Karimi, Reza	1984–88	Marand, East Azerbaijan
Karrubi, Mehdi	1984–88	Tehran, Tehran
Kazemi, Seyyed Motahhar	1984–88	Khalkhal, Ardabil
Khalkhali, Mohammad-Sadeq	1984–88	Qom, Qom

Name	Tenure	City and province of constituency
Khamenei, Seyyed Hadi	1984–88	Mashhad, Razavi Khorasan
Khamenei, Seyyed Mohammad	1984–88	Mashhad, Razavi Khorasan
Khanansu, Ator	1984–88	Assyrians and Chaldeans (minority)
Kharmataei, Ali	1984–88	Saqqez, Baneh, Kurdistan
Khayyati, Taleb	1984–88	Dasht-e Azadegan, Khuzestan
Khaza'i, Mohammad	1984–88	Rasht, Gilan
Kheyrkhah, Kamel	1984–88	Lahijan, Gilan
Kiyan-Ersi, Asadollah	1984–88	Faridan and Fereydunshahr, Isfahan
Kiyavash, Seyyed Mohammad	1984–88	Abadan, Khuzestan
Kosehgharavi, Anehmohammad	1984–88	Gonbad-e Kavus, Golestan
Lotfi, Mohammad-Taqi	1984–88	Ilam, Ilam
Mahbudi, Borzu	1984–88	Kazerun, Fars
Mahdavi Haji, Mehdi	1984–88	Babolsar and Bandpay, Mazandaran
Mahlujchi, Hoseyn	1984–88	Kashan, Isfahan
Mahmudi-Golpayegani, Seyyed Abutaleb	1984–88	Golpayegan and Khansar, Isfahan
Mahmudiyan, Seyyed Nurmohammad	1984–88	Buyer Ahmad, Kohgiluyeh and Buyer Ahmad
Makhzan-Musavi, Seyyed Abolhasan	1984–88	Rudbar, Gilan
Malakuti, Ali	1984–88	Sarab, East Azerbaijan
Malekasa, Karim	1986–88	Pol-e Dokhtar, Lorestan
Malekpur, Parviz	1984–88	Zoroastrian community (minority)
Marvi-Samavarchi, Mahmud	1984–88	Torqabeh and Chenaran, Razavi Khorasan
Matin, Abbas	1984–88	Bandar-e Abbas, Hormozgan
Mazare'i, Jamshid	1986–88	Bandar-e Mahshahr, Khuzestan
Mehdizadeh, Mehdi	1984–88	Gonabad, Razavi Khorasan
Mehrzad-Sedqiyani, Qasem	1984–88	Salmas, West Azerbaijan
Me'mari, Qasem	1984–88	Ahar, East Azerbaijan
Mir, Amir	1984–88	Zahedan, Sistan and Baluchestan
Mir Heydari, Abbas	1984–88	Shahriyar, Tehran
Mir Ja'fari, Seyyed Mojtaba	1984–88	Arak, Markazi
Mirza'i-Ataabadi, Eydimohammad	1984–87?	Falavarjan, Isfahan
Moarrefi'zadeh, Ali	1984–86	Khorramshahr and Shadegan, Khuzestan
Mo'ezi, Mohammad	1984–88	Isfahan, Isfahan
Mohammad-Gharibani, Ali	1984–88	Ardabil, Ardabil
Mohammadi, Mohammad	1984–88	Selseleh and Delfan Lorestan
Mohammadi, Yunes	1984–88	Khorramshahr and Shadegan, Khuzestan
Mohammadiazar, Seyyed Hoseyn	1984–88	Takestan, Zanjan
Mohammadkhani-Shahrudi, Hoseyn	1984–88	Darab, Fars
Mohaqqeq-Banki, Hoseyn	1984–88	Karaj, Tehran
Mohyeddin-Anvari, Mohammad-Baqer	1984–88	Tehran, Tehran
Mojtahed-Shabestari, Mohsen	1984–88	Tehran, Tehran
Molla Zehi, Hamidaddin	1984–88	Iranshahr, Sistan and Baluchestan
Montajabniya, Rasul	1984–88	Shiraz, Fars
Mortazavifar, Ali-Asghar	1984–88	Lenjan, Isfahan

Name	Tenure	City and province of constituency
Mosbet, Ali	1984–88	Bahar and Kabudarahang, Hamadan
Mostafavi-Kashani, Seyyed Ahmad	1984–86	Natanz, Isfahan
Mostafavi-Siyahmazgi, Seyyed Davud	1984–88	Rasht, Gilan
Motahhari, Ali	1984–88	Zarand, Kerman
Movahhedi-Kermani, Mohammad-Ali	1984–88	Tehran, Tehran
Movahhedi-Savoji, Ali	1984–88	Saveh, Markazi
Musavi, Seyyed Abbas	1984–88	Dorud, Lorestan
Musavi, Seyyed Rasul	1984–88	Ahvaz, Khuzestan
Musavi-Abrbekuh, Mir Morteza	1984–88	Andimeshk and Shush, Khuzestan
Musavinasab, Seyyed Ali	1984–88	Shiravan, North Khorasan
Musavipur, Seyyed Hasan	1984–88	Abhar, Zanjan
Musavi-Tabrizi, Seyyed Abolfazl	1984–88	Tabriz, East Azerbaijan
Musaviyani, Seyyed Hoseyn	1984–88	Tehran, Tehran
Nabavi, Seyyed Mohammad-Hasan	1984–88	Bandar-e Bushehr, Bushehr
Nadi, Gholam-Hoseyn	1984–88	Najafabad, Isfahan
Najafi-Rahnani, Hasan-Ali	1984–88	Gachsaran, Kohgiluyeh and Buyer Ahmad
Naru'i, Hatam	1984–88	Bam, Kerman
Naseri, Mostafa	1984–88	Zanjan, Zanjan
Nateq-Nuri, Ali-Akbar	1986–88	Tehran, Tehran
Nazari-Monfared, Ali	1984–88	Abadeh, Fars
Nazri, Ali-Reza	1984–88	Mahallat and Delijan, Markazi
Nikravesh, Seyyed Kamaleddin	1984–88	Tehran, Tehran
Nuri, Abdollah	1984–88	Isfahan, Isfahan
Orumiyan, Ali	1984–88	Maragheh, East Azerbaijan
Panahandeh, Ali	1984–88	Borkhar, Isfahan
Parhizkar, Akbar	1984–87	Tabriz, East Azerbaijan
Pari'zad, Ali	1984–88	Naqadeh, West Azerbaijan
Pezeshki, Hokmollalh	1984–88	Miyaneh, East Azerbaijan
Purgol, Mohammad-Mehdi	1984–88	Bandar-e Anzali, Gilan
Pursalari, Hoseyn	1984–88	Kahnuj, Kerman
Qaderi, Mostafa	1984–88	Piranshahr and Sardasht, West Azerbaijan
Qaemifar, Mehdi	1984–88	Sarvestan, Fars
Qanbari-Qazikolahi, Abdolali	1984–88	Qaemshahr, Mazandaran
Qatmiri, Seyyed Hoseyn	1984–88	Shiraz, Fars
Qazizadeh-Hashemi, Seyyed Hoseyn	1984–88	Fariman, Razavi Khorasan
Qorbani-Panjah, Zeynol'abedin	1984–88	Astaneh-ye Ashrafiyyeh, Gilan
Qoreyshi, Seyyed Mohammad-Ali	1984–88	Khomeyn, Markazi
Rabbani-Amlashi, Mohammad-Mehdi	1984–85	Tehran, Tehran
Rahbari, Mohammad-Hashem	1984–88	Tehran, Tehran
Rahbari-Amlashi, Mohammad-Mehdi	1984–88	Rudsar, Gilan
Rahbarpur, Gholam-Hoseyn	1984–88	Tuyserkan, Hamadan
Rahchamani, Mohammad-Reza	1984–88	Sabzevar, Razavi Khorasan
Rahimi, Abdorrahman	1984–88	Paveh, Kermanshah
Rahimi, Mohammad-Reza	1984–88	Qorveh, Kurdistan

Name	Tenure	City and province of constituency
Rahimi, Seyyed Nureddin	1984–86	Pol-e Dokhtar and Malavi, Lorestan
Rahimi-Haji Abadi, Abbas	1984–88	Dashtestan, Bushehr
Rahimi-Haji Abadi, Gholam-Reza	1984–86	Bandar-e Mahshahr, Khuzestan
Rahmani, Hoseyn-Ali	1984–88	Bijar, Kurdistan
Rahmaniasl, Abolfazl	1984–88	Razan, Hamadan
Rahmani-Khalili, Ali-Asghar	1984–88	Behshahr, Mazandaran
Rahmati, Rahmatollah	1984–88	Qomsheh, Isfahan
Raji, Nabiyollah	1984–88	Na'in, Isfahan
Ranjbar-Chubeh, Mohammad-Taqi	1984–88	Sowme'eh Sara, Gilan
Rashidian, Mohammad	1984–88	Abadan, Khuzestan
Rasti-Lari, Mohammad-Javad	1984–88	Larestan, Fars
Rasi, Mohsen	1984–88	Miyandoab and Takab, West Azerbaijan
Razavi, Morteza	1984–88	Tabriz, East Azerbaijan
Razzaqi, Abolqasem	1984–86	Tonekabon and Ramsar, Mazandaran
Rohami, Mohsen	1984–88	Khodabandeh, Zanjan
Rouhani, Hassan	1984–88	Tehran, Tehran
Ruhanifard, Ali-Akbar	1984–88	Dehloran, Ilam
Ruhaniniya, Ramezan	1984–88	Sepidan, Fars
Sadeqlu, Hasan	1984–88	Ramiyan, Golestan
Sadiqi, Ateqeh	1984–88	Tehran, Tehran
Sadr-Tabataba'i, Seyyed Jalil	1984–88	Yazd, Yazd
Safa'ipur-Zamani, Arsalan	1984–88	Kermanshah, Kermanshah
Safari, Latif	1984–88	Islamabad-e Gharb, Kermanshah
Safari, Mahmud	1984–88	Damavand, Tehran
Safavi-Kuhesareh, Mir Abbas	1984–88	Fuman, Gilan
Sahebozzamani, Mohammad-Ali	1984–88	Urmia, West Azerbaijan
Sahmihesari, Esma'il	1986–88	Torbat-e Heydariyyeh, Razavi Khorasan
Sa'idiyanfar, Mohammad-Ja'far	1984–88	Khomeinishahr, Isfahan
Sajjadnezhad, Seyyed Mir Ghaffar	1984–88	Bostanabad, East Azerbaijan
Salehi-Haji Abadi, Nasrollah	1984–88	Isfahan, Isfahan
Salimi-Gamini, Musa	1984–88	Miyaneh, East Azerbaijan
Salimi-Mahmudjayq, Fereydun	1984–88	Miyandoab and Takab, West Azerbaijan
Saveh, Abdolhoseyn	1984–88	Kerman, Kerman
Seyyed Khavari-Langarudi, Seyyed Mir Ali-Naqi	1984–88	Langarud, Gilan
Seyyed Zadeh, Seyyed Jalil	1984–88	Kermanshah, Kermanshah
Shahcheraqi, Seyyed Hasan	1984–86	Damghan, Semnan
Shahraki, Gholam-Ali	1984–88	Zabol, Sistan and Baluchestan
Shaikhi, Qoli	1984–88	I'zeh, Khuzestan
Shamlu-Mahmudi, Mehdi	1984–88	Malayer, Hamadan
Shaqaqiyan, Javad	1984–88	Shiraz, Fars
Shar'pasand, Abdolmajid	1986–88	Karaj, Tehran
Shaverani, Mohammad	1984–88	Bukan, West Azerbaijan
Shehnimostafa, Mohammad	1984–88	Masjed Soleyman, Khuzestan
Sheybani, Abbas	1984–88	Tehran, Tehran

Name	Tenure	City and province of constituency
Shirzadi, Morteza	1984–88	Qasr-e Shirin, Kermanshah
Shoja'ei-Kiyasari, Seyyed Hasan	1984–88	Sari, Mazandaran
Shoja'iyan, Samad	1984–88	Mamasani, Fars
Shushtari, Ali	1984–88	Neyshabur, Razavi Khorasan
Shushtari, Mohammad-Esma'il	1984–88	Quchan, Razavi Khorasan
Sobhaninia, Hoseyn	1984–88	Neyshabur, Razavi Khorasan
Sobhanollahi, Mohammad-Ali	1984–88	Tabriz, East Azerbaijan
Soltani, Gholam-Reza	1984–86	Karaj, Tehran
Soltani, Hoseyn	1984–88	Ardestan, Isfahan
Tabataba'i-Shirazi, Seyyed Mohammad-Mehdi	1984–88	Mashhad, Razavi Khorasan
Taheri-Khorramabadi, Seyyed Mohammad-Saleh	1984–88	Khorramabad, Lorestan
Taheri-Musavi, Seyyed Abdossaheb	1986–88	Khorramshahr and Shadegan, Khuzestan
Taqavi, Seyyed Reza	1986–88	Damghan, Semnan
Tatali, Abdollah	1984–88	Marivan, Kurdistan
Tavassolizadeh, Mohammad-Naser	1984–88	Khaf, Razavi Khorasan
Vafi-Yazdi, Abolqasem	1984–88	Taft, Yazd
Vartanian, Vartan	1984–88	Armenians of northern Iran (minority)
Vela'i, Isa	1984–88	Amol, Mazandaran
Ya'qubi, Mehdi	1984–86	Torbat-e Heydariyyeh, Razavi Khorasan
Yazdi, Mohammad	1984–88	Tehran, Tehran
Yusefpur, Ali	1984–88	Ardal, Chahar Mahal and Bakhtiari
Za'eri, Gholam-Abbas	1984–88	Bandar-e Abbas, Hormozgan
Zamani, Hojjatollah	1984–88	Borujerd, Lorestan
Zamani, Valiyollah	1984–88	Babol, Mazandaran
Zamaniyan, Ahmad	1984–88	Nahavand, Hamadan
Zargar, Musa	1984–88	Tehran, Tehran
Zavareh'i, Seyyed Reza	1984–88	Tehran, Tehran
Zolqadr, Seyyed Mostafa	1984–88	Minab, Hormozgan

Deputies in the Third Majlis (1988–92)

Name	Tenure	City and province of constituency
Abbasi, Abbas	1988–92	Bandar-e Abbas, Hormozgan
Abdolali'zadeh, Ali	1988–92	Urmia, West Azerbaijan
Abdolkarimi-Natanzi, Ali	1988–92	Qamsar and Natanz, Isfahan
Abdollahi, Reza	1988–92	Mahneshan and Ijrood, Zanjan
Abdollahpuri-Hoseyni, Mir Ali-Ashraf	1988–92	Tabriz, East Azerbaijan
Abedi, Nurollah	1988–92	Behbahan, Khuzestan
Abedi-Shahrekhafri, Asadollah	1988–92	Shiraz, Fars
Afrazideh, Seyyed Farajollah	1988–92	Nowshahr and Chalus, Mazandaran
Ahmadi, Ali-Mohammad	1988–92	Aligudarz, Lorestan
Ahmadi, Vahid	1988–92	Kangavar, Sahneh, and Harsin, Kermanshah

Name	Tenure	City and province of constituency
Ahmadnezhad, Abdolkarim	1988–92	Sanandaj, Kurdistan
Akbarzadeh, Mohammad	1988–92	Neyshabur, Razavi Khorasan
Akrami, Seyyed Reza	1988–92	Semnan, Semnan
Ala', Eynollah	1988–92	Aliabad Katul, Golestan
Alavi-Hoseyni, Seyyed Mohammad-Hasan	1988–92	Gorgan, Golestan
Alhoseyni, Seyyed Hasan	1988–92	Arak, Markazi
Alviri, Morteza	1988–92	Tehran, Tehran
Amid-Zanjani, Abbas-Ali	1988–92	Tehran, Tehran
Aminlu, Hasan	1988–92	Shabestar, East Azerbaijan
Ansari, Majid	1988–92	Zarand, Kerman
Ansari, Mohammad-Sa'id	1988–92	Abadan, Khuzestan
Aqa Mohammadi, Ali	1988–92	Hamadan, Hamadan
Aqa'i, Gholam-Hasan	1988–92	Hamadan, Hamadan
Aqa'i-Ghiyasabadi, Hedayatollah	1988–92	Fasa, Fars
Arabameri, Yar-Mohammad	1988–92	Garmsar, Semnan
Arbabifard, Hoseyn	1988–92	Ramiyan, Golestan
Asadi, Ne'matollah	1988–92	Islamabad-e Gharb, Kermanshah
Asghari-Bahari, Seyyed Mohammad	1988–92	Tehran, Tehran
Asgharzadeh, Mohammad-Ebrahim	1988–92	Tehran, Tehran
Ashrafi-Isfahani, Mohammad	1988–92	Kermanshah, Kermanshah
Astaneh, Mahmud	1988–92	Shazand (Sarband), Markazi
Azimi-Taraqdari, Mohammad	1988–92	Torqabeh and Chenaran, Razavi Khorasan
Azizi, Ahmad	1988–92	Qazvin, Qazvin
Babakhas, Ali-Mohammad	1988–92	Paveh and Uramanat, Kermanshah
Baghumian, Artavaz	1988–92	Armenians of southern Iran (minority)
Bahme'i, Mohammad-Reza	1988–92	Ramhormoz, Khuzestan
Bahonar, Mohammad-Reza	1988–92	Tehran, Tehran
Banihashemi-Chaharom, Seyyed Hashem	1988–92	Mashhad, Razavi Khorasan
Baqeri-Nezhadiyanfard, Mohammad-Baqer	1988–92	Kazerun, Fars
Bayanak, Amin	1988–92	Ahvaz, Khuzestan
Bayat-Zanjani, Asadollah	1988–92	Zanjan and Tarom, Zanjan
Behruzi, Maryam	1989–92	Tehran, Tehran
Behzadiyan, Mohammad-Reza	1988–92	Qaenat, South Khorasan
Besanjideh, Yusef	1990–92	Kordkuy, Golestan
Bolukiyan, Ahmad	1988–92	Kashmar, Razavi Khorasan
Borumand-Dashqapu, Habib	1988–92	Germi (Moghan), Ardabil
Chehregani-Anzabi, Mohammad-Hoseyn	1988–92	Tabriz, East Azerbaijan
Chitchiyan, Hamid	1988–92	Tabriz, East Azerbaijan
Dabestani, Majid	1988–92	Bam, Kerman
Dadgar, Abdolaziz	1988–92	Chabahar, Sistan and Baluchestan
Damadi-Kohnehdeh, Ezzatollah	1988–92	Sari, Mazandaran
Danesh, Jahanshah	1988–92	Masjed Soleyman, Khuzestan
Dastgheyb, Gowharoshshari'eh	1988–92	Tehran, Tehran

Name	Tenure	City and province of constituency
Davudi-Shamsi, Seyyed Esma'il	1988–92	Ardakan, Yazd
Delbari, Mohammad-Esma'il	1988–92	Bostanabad, East Azerbaijan
Doa'i, Seyyed Mahmud	1988–92	Tehran, Tehran
Duzduzani, Abbas	1988–92	Tehran, Tehran
Eftekhari, Mohammad-Hoseyn	1988–90	Fuman, Gilan
Emammusavi, Seyyed Mohammad-Kazem	1988–92	Shushtar, Khuzestan
Emamzadeh-Vaqfi, Seyyed Mohammad-Reza	1988–90	Isfahan, Isfahan
Enayat, Ali	1988–92	Khorramabad, Lorestan
Esma'ili, Ghaffar	1988–92	Hashtrud, East Azerbaijan
Farugh, Seyyed Mostafa	1988–92	Dezful, Khuzestan
Farzad, Ali-Reza	1988–92	Taft, Yazd
Farzpor-Machiyani, Mohammad	1988–92	Astara, Gilan
Faza'eli, Ataollah	1988–92	Semirom, Isfahan
Fazel-Harandi, Mohyeddin	1988–92	Isfahan, Isfahan
Feda'i-Araqi, Gholam-Reza	1988–92	Arak, Markazi
Ferdowsipur, Esma'il	1988–92	Mashhad, Razavi Khorasan
Forutan-Pishbijari, Hoseyn	1988–92	Tehran, Tehran
Ghaffari, Hadi	1988–92	Tehran, Tehran
Habibi, Abutaleb	1988–92	Qaemshahr, Mazandaran
Habibi, Najafqoli	1988–92	Tehran, Tehran
Hadidchi-Dabbagh, Marziyeh	1988–92	Tehran, Tehran
Ha'eri, Seyyed Mohammad	1988–92	Dehloran, Darrehshahr, and Badreh, Ilam
Ha'erizadeh, Seyyed Abolhasan	1988–92	Birjand, South Khorasan
Haji Naseri, Davud	1988–92	Zanjan and Tarom, Zanjan
Hamtaei, Ali-Akbar	1988–92	Neyriz and Estahban, Fars
Haqi-Sarabi, Mohammad-Ali	1988–92	Sarab, East Azerbaijan
Harati, Hoseyn	1988–92	Sabzevar, Razavi Khorasan
Hasanbeygi, Abolfazl	1988–92	Damghan, Semnan
Hasan-Sa'di, Abbas	1988–89	Kerman, Kerman
Hashemi, Seyyed Fakhreddin	1988–92	Jahrom, Fars
Hashemi-Rafsanjani, Akbar	1988–89	Tehran, Tehran
Hashemiyan, Hoseyn	1988–92	Rafsanjan, Kerman
Hashemzadeh-Herisi, Hashem	1988–92	Tabriz, East Azerbaijan
Hashemzehi, Mas'ud	1988–92	Khash, Sistan and Baluchestan
Hazrati, Elyas	1988–92	Rasht, Gilan
Hedayati-Sichani, Seyyed Abbas	1988–92	Faridan and Fereydunshahr, Isfahan
Hejazi, Fakhreddin	1988–92	Tehran, Tehran
Hejazifar, Hashem	1988–92	Khoy and Chaypareh, West Azerbaijan
Hejrati-Qazvini, Seyyed Abdollah	1988–92	Qazvin, Qazvin
Hemmati, Ahmad	1988–92	Meshginshahr, Ardabil
Heydari, Gholam-Reza	1988–92	Tafresh, Markazi
Heydari-Moqaddam, Masha'allah	1988–92	Delfan and Selseleh, Lorestan
Hojaji, Seyyed Sajjad	1988–92	Miyaneh, East Azerbaijan
Hoseyni, Seyyed Abdollah	1988–92	Bandar-e Lengeh, Hormozgan

Name	Tenure	City and province of constituency
Hoseyni, Seyyed Abolqasem	1988–92	Bojnurd, North Khorasan
Hoseyni, Seyyed Mohammad	1988–92	Mahabad, West Azerbaijan
Hoseyni-Almadini, Seyyed Razi	1988–92	Lamerd, Fars
Hoseyni-Barzanji, Abdorrahman	1988–92	Naqadeh, West Azerbaijan
Hoseyni-Kuhestani, Seyyed Rasul	1988–92	Behshahr, Mazandaran
Hoseyni-Shahrudi, Seyyed Hoseyn	1988–92	Shahrud, Semnan
Hoseyni-Zeydabadi, Seyyed Ahmad	1988–92	Sirjan, Kerman
Hoseynzadeh, Javad	1988–92	Dargaz, Razavi Khorasan
Islami, Yadollah	1988–92	Baft, Kerman
Jadri, Jasem	1988–92	Dasht-e Azadegan, Khuzestan
Ja'fari, Beytollah	1988–92	Urmia, West Azerbaijan
Ja'fari, Hasan	1988–92	Shahr-e Babak, Kerman
Jahangiri, Eshaq	1988–92	Jiroft, Kerman
Jahangiri, Mohammad-Hoseyn	1988–92	Qasr-e Shirin, Kermanshah
Jalali, Khodakaram	1988–92	Firuzabad, Fars
Jamali, Mahmud	1989–92	Kashan, Isfahan
Jami, Asadollah	1988–92	Torbat-e Jam and Taybad, Razavi Khorasan
Kabiri, Qanbar	1988–92	Marvdasht, Fars
Kalimi-Nikruz, Manuchehr	1988–92	Jewish community (minority)
Kamali, Hoseyn	1988–89	Tehran, Tehran
Kamyar, Ali	1988–92	Urmia, West Azerbaijan
Karrubi, Mehdi	1988–92	Tehran, Tehran
Katira'i, Morteza	1988–92	Tehran, Tehran
Kavusi, Nader	1988–92	Tuyserkan, Hamadan
Kazem-Dinan, Seyyed Mahmud	1988–92	Amol, Mazandaran
Kazemi, Seyyed Motahhar	1988–92	Khalkhal, Ardabil
Khak-Aji-Bozeh, Ali-Reza	1988–92	Rasht, Gilan
Khalkhali, Mohammad-Sadeq	1988–92	Qom, Qom
Khamenei, Seyyed Hadi	1988–92	Mashhad, Razavi Khorasan
Kharestani, Ahmad	1988–92	Sarvestan, Fars
Khaza'i, Abdolazim	1988–92	Bandar-e Mahshahr, Khuzestan
Khanansu, Ator	1988–92	Assyrians and Chaldeans (minority)
Kheyrkhah, Kamel	1988–92	Lahijan, Gilan
Khosravi, Rahmatollah	1988–92	Abadeh, Fars
Kiya'inezhad, Mofid	1988–92	Savojblagh, Nazarabad, and Taleqan, Tehran
Mahlujchi, Hoseyn	1988–89	Kashan, Isfahan
Mahmudi-Golpayegan, Seyyed Abutaleb	1988–92	Golpayegan and Khansar, Isfahan
Mahmudiyan, Seyyed Nurmohammad	1988–92	Yasouj, Kohgiluyeh and Buyer Ahmad
Mahmud-Robati, Ahmad	1988–92	Shahriyar and Robat Karim, Tehran
Majdara, Mohammad	1988–92	Babolsar and Bandpay, Mazandaran
Malekasa, Karim	1988–92	Pol-e Dokhtar, Lorestan
Mehdizadeh, Mehdi	1988–92	Gonabad, Razavi Khorasan
Mehrzad-Sedqiyani, Qasem	1988–92	Salmas, West Azerbaijan
Me'mari, Qasem	1988–92	Ahar, East Azerbaijan

Name	Tenure	City and province of constituency
Mir, Amir	1988–92	Zahedan, Sistan and Baluchestan
Mir Ghaffari-Marya'i, Seyyed Ebrahim	1988–92	Talesh, Gilan
Mir Valad, Seyyed Kazem	1988–92	Malayer, Hamadan
Mirza Abutalebi, Abbas	1988–92	Bu'inzahra and Avaj, Zanjan
Mirzapur-Kleshtari, Moslem	1988–92	Rudbar, Gilan
Mo'in, Mostafa	1988–89	Tehran, Tehran
Mo'azzenzadeh, Seyyed Mostafa	1988–92	Kerman, Kerman
Mo'ezi, Mohammad	1988–92	Isfahan, Isfahan
Mohammad-Gharibani, Ali	1988–92	Ardabil, Ardabil
Mohammadi, Yunes	1988–92	Khorramshahr and Shadegan, Khuzestan
Mohammadiyan, Ali-Karam	1988–92	Ilam, Shirvan, and Chardavol, Ilam
Mohaqqar, Ali	1988–92	Bojnurd, North Khorasan
Mohtashamipur, Seyyed Ali-Akbar	1989–92	Tehran, Tehran
Mokhtari, Hasan	1988–92	Najafabad, Isfahan
Molla Zehi, Hamidaddin	1988–92	Iranshahr, Sistan and Baluchestan
Montajabniya, Rasul	1988–92	Shiraz, Fars
Moqtada'i, Abdolhasan	1988–92	Abadan, Khuzestan
Moravveji, Mohammad-Karim	1989–92	Borujerd, Lorestan
Morseli, Mostafa	1988–92	Abhar, Zanjan
Mortazavifar, Ali-Asghar	1988–92	Lenjan, Isfahan
Mosbet, Ali	1988–92	Bahar and Kabudarahang, Hamadan
Mo'tamediniya, Gholam-Reza	1988–92	Kahnuj, Kerman
Movahhedi-Kermani, Mohammad-Ali	1989–92	Tehran, Tehran
Movahhedi-Savoji, Ali	1988–92	Saveh, Markazi
Movashah, Seyyed Khalil	1988–92	Bandar-e Anzali, Gilan
Mozaffarinezhad, Hoseyn	1988–92	Tehran, Tehran
Musavi, Seyyed Abbas	1988–92	I'zeh, Khuzestan
Musavi, Seyyed Abdorrasul	1988–92	Mamasani, Fars
Musavi, Seyyed Ahmad	1988–92	Ahvaz, Khuzestan
Musavi, Seyyed Rasul	1988–92	Ahvaz, Khuzestan
Musavi-Lari, Seyyed Abdolvahed	1988–92	Tehran, Tehran
Musavi-Nanehkaran, Mir Fakhreddin	1988–92	Ardabil, Ardabil
Musavinasab, Seyyed Ali	1988–92	Shiravan, North Khorasan
Musavi-Tabrizi, Seyyed Hoseyn	1988–92	Tabriz, East Azerbaijan
Nabavi, Seyyed Mohammad-Hasan	1988–92	Bandar-e Bushehr, Bushehr
Najafi-Sani-Rashtkhari, Hoseyn	1988–92	Khaf and Rashtkhar, Razavi Khorasan
Nariman, Mohsen	1988–92	Babol, Mazandaran
Nateq-Nuri, Ahmad	1988–92	Nur and Mahmudabad, Mazandaran
Nateq-Nuri, Ali-Akbar	1988–92	Tehran, Tehran
Nazripur, Ahmad-Ali	1988–92	Darab, Fars
Nikfar, Ahmad	1988–92	Eqlid, Fars
Niyazi, Mahmud	1988–92	Bijar, Kurdistan
Nowbakht-Haqiqi, Mohammad-Baqer	1988–92	Rasht, Gilan
Nowruzi, Asghar	1988–92	Damavand, Tehran

Name	Tenure	City and province of constituency
Nowruzi-Mishani, Abdollah	1988–92	Malayer, Hamadan
Nowruzzadeh, Seyyed Reza	1988–92	Esfarayen, North Khorasan
Nurbakhsh, Mohsen	1988–89	Tehran, Tehran
Panahandeh, Ali	1988–92	Borkhar, Isfahan
Partovi, Mohammad-Ali	1988–92	Saqqez and Baneh, Kurdistan
Partow, Morovvatollah	1988–92	Khodabandeh, Zanjan
Parvaresh, Seyyed Ali-Akbar	1988–92	Isfahan, Isfahan
Pudineh, Mohammad-Hoseyn	1988–92	Zabol, Sistan and Baluchestan
Purmohammadi-Fallah, Ali	1988–92	Astaneh-ye Ashrafiyyeh, Gilan
Qasemi, Fereydun	1988–92	Varzaqan, East Azerbaijan
Qasemi, Khodanazar	1988–92	Dashtestan, Bushehr
Qazipur, Mir Naqi	1988–92	Ardabil, Ardabil
Qazizadeh-Hashemi, Seyyed Hoseyn	1988–92	Fariman, Razavi Khorasan
Qolizadeh, Yaghmor	1988–92	Minudasht, Golestan
Qomi, Mohammad	1988–92	Varamin, Tehran
Qoreyshi, Seyyed Mohammad-Ali	1988–92	Khomeyn, Markazi
Rahbari, Ahmad	1988–92	Razan and Famenin, Hamadan
Rahbari-Amlashi, Mohammad-Mehdi	1988–92	Rudsar, Gilan
Rahchamani, Mohammad-Reza	1988–92	Sabzevar, Razavi Khorasan
Rahimi, Mohammad-Reza	1988–92	Qorveh, Kurdistan
Rahimnezhad-Baqcheh-Joqi, Bakhshali	1988–92	Maku, West Azerbaijan
Rahmani, Qahreman	1988–92	Takestan, Zanjan
Rahmati, Rahmatollah	1988–92	Shahreza, Isfahan
Ra'isi-Naf'chi, Mohammad	1988–92	Shahrekord, Chahar Mahal and Bakhtiari
Raja'i-Khorasani, Sa'id	1988–92	Tehran, Tehran
Raji, Nabiyollah	1988–92	Na'in, Isfahan
Ranjbar-Chubeh, Mohammad-Taqi	1988–92	Sowme'eh Sara, Gilan
Rashidian, Mohammad	1988–92	Abadan, Khuzestan
Rasti-Lari, Mohammad-Javad	1988–92	Larestan, Fars
Razavi, Seyyed Mohammad	1988–92	Yazd, Yazd
Razavi-Rashtipur, Asadalloh	1989–92	Kerman, Kerman
Reza'i-Dobandari, Hasan	1988–92	Andimeshk and Shush, Khuzestan
Rezazehi, Fakhreddin	1988–92	Saravan, Sistan and Baluchestan
Rostami, Ali-Reza	1988–92	Sonqor and Koliyayi, Kermanshah
Rouhani, Hassan	1988–92	Tehran, Tehran
Ruhaniniya, Ramezan	1988–92	Sepidan, Fars
Ruhanizadeh-Qadikolahi, Saleh	1988–92	Qaemshahr and Savadkuh, Mazandaran
Sadeqi-Azad, Mas'ud	1988–92	Kaleybar, East Azerbaijan
Sadiqi, Ateqeh	1988–92	Tehran, Tehran
Sadiqi-Bonabi, Rasul	1988–92	Bonab and Malekan, East Azerbaijan
Saduqi, Mohammad-Ali	1988–92	Tehran, Tehran
Safa'i, Zabihollah	1988–92	Asadabad, Hamadan
Safa'ipur-Zamani, Arsalan	1988–92	Kermanshah, Kermanshah
Sahmihesari, Esma'il	1988–92	Torbat-e Heydariyyeh, Razavi Khorasan

Name	Tenure	City and province of constituency
Sa'idiyanfar, Mohammad-Ja'far	1988–92	Khomeinishahr, Isfahan
Salamati, Mohammad	1988–92	Tehran, Tehran
Salehabadi, Qorbanali	1988–92	Mashhad, Razavi Khorasan
Salek, Ahmad	1992–92	Isfahan, Isfahan
Salimi-Gamini, Musa	1988–92	Miyaneh, East Azerbaijan
Sarhaddizadeh, Abolqasem	1990–92	Tehran, Tehran
Seyqali-Kumeleh, Parviz	1988–92	Langarud, Gilan
Seyyed Zadeh, Seyyed Jalil	1988–92	Kermanshah, Kermanshah
Shafei, Karim	1988–92	Marand, East Azerbaijan
Shafi'i, Seyyed Mohsen	1988–92	Dorud and Japlaq, Lorestan
Shafi'i-Kas-Ahmadani, Mohammad-Reza	1990–92	Fuman, Gilan
Shahidi-Mahallati, Seyyed Mohammad-Ali	1988–92	Mahallat and Delijan, Markazi
Shahraki, Gholam-Ali	1988–92	Zabol, Sistan and Baluchestan
Shahriyari, Seyyed Kamaleddin	1988–92	Tangestan, Dashti, Kangan, and Deyr, Bushehr
Shahrzad, Mohammad-Karim	1988–92	Isfahan, Isfahan
Shar'i, Mohammad-Ali	1988–92	Qom, Qom
Sharifzadeh, Qader	1988–92	Sardasht and Piranshahr, West Azerbaijan
Shar'pasand, Abdolmajid	1988–89	Karaj, Tehran
Sheybani, Abbas	1988–92	Tehran, Tehran
Shoja'ei-Kiyasari, Seyyed Hasan	1988–92	Sari, Mazandaran
Sho'lehsa'di, Qasem	1988–92	Shiraz, Fars
Sobhaninia, Hoseyn	1988–92	Neyshabur, Razavi Khorasan
Sobhanollahi, Mohammad-Ali	1988–92	Tabriz, East Azerbaijan
Suri-Laki, Ali-Mohammad	1988–92	Khorramabad, Lorestan
Tabataba'inezhad, Seyyed Yusef	1988–92	Ardestan, Isfahan
Tabataba'i-Shirazi, Seyyed Mohammad-Mehdi	1988–92	Mashhad, Razavi Khorasan
Tabe'-Miyandoab, Asadollah	1988–92	Miyandoab and Takab, West Azerbaijan
Taha, Ahmad	1988–92	Bukan, West Azerbaijan
Taha'i, Seyyed Ali-Akbar	1988–92	Tonekabon and Ramsar, Mazandaran
Taheri, Nader	1988–92	Maragheh, East Azerbaijan
Taheri-Musavi, Seyyed Abdossaheb	1988–92	Shadegan and Khorramshahr, Khuzestan
Taherizadeh, Mostafa	1988–92	Falavarjan, Isfahan
Tajgardun, Bahram	1988–92	Gachsaran, Kohgiluyeh and Buyer Ahmad
Taslimi, Mohammad-Sa'id	1988–92	Tehran, Tehran
Tatali, Abdollah	1988–92	Marivan, Kurdistan
Tavassoli, Mohammad-Reza	1988–92	Ferdows and Tabas, South Khorasan
Tohidi, Davud	1988–92	Borujen and Lordegan, Chahar Mahal and Bakhtiari
Vartanian, Vartan	1988–92	Armenians of northern Iran (minority)
Vela'i, Isa	1988–92	Tehran, Tehran
Yusefpur, Ali	1988–92	Ardal, Chahar Mahal and Bakhtiari
Za'eri, Gholam-Abbas	1988–92	Bandar-e Abbas, Hormozgan

Name	Tenure	City and province of constituency
Zakeri, Mohammad-Baqer	1988–92	Quchan, Razavi Khorasan
Zali, Abbas-Ali	1989–92	Karaj and Eshtehard, Tehran
Zamaniyan, Ahmad	1988–92	Nahavand, Hamadan
Zarringol, Morteza	1988–92	Sanandaj, Kurdistan
Ziyafat, Aflatun	1988–92	Zoroastrian community (minority)
Ziya'i, Hoseyn-Ali	1988–92	Miyandoab and Takab, West Azerbaijan
Ziyapur-Razliqqi, Khosrow	1988–92	Gonbad-e Kavus, Golestan
Zolqadr, Seyyed Mostafa	1988–92	Minab, Hormozgan

Deputies in the Fourth Majlis (1992–96)

Name	Tenure	City and province of constituency
Abbasi, Abbas	1992–96	Bandar-e Abbas, Hormozgan
Abbaspur, Mohammad	1992–96	Maku, West Azerbaijan
Abbaspur-Tehranifard, Ali	1992–96	Tehran, Tehran
Abdekhoda'i, Mohammad-Hadi	1992–96	Mashhad, Razavi Khorasan
Abdollahi, Reza	1992–96	Mahneshan and Ijrood, Zanjan
Abedinzadeh, Kamel	1992–96	Khoy, West Azerbaijan
Abutorabifard, Seyyed Ali-Akbar	1992–96	Tehran, Tehran
Afrazideh, Seyyed Farajollah	1992–96	Nowshahr, Mazandaran
Ahmadi, Firuz	1993–96	Germi (Moghan), Ardabil
Ahmadi-Forushani, Seyyed Mohammad	1992–96	Khomeinishahr, Isfahan
Ahmadi-Zadsara'i, Valiyollah	1992–96	Ahar and Heris, East Azerbaijan
Ahmadnezhad, Abdolkarim	1994–96	Sanandaj, Kurdistan
Akrami, Seyyed Reza	1992–96	Semnan, Semnan
Alavi, Seyyed Mahmud	1992–96	Lamerd, Fars
Alavi-Faradanbeh, Abolqasem	1992–96	Borujen and Lordegan, Chahar Mahal and Bakhtiari
Alavi-Hoseyni, Seyyed Mohammad-Hasan	1992–96	Gorgan, Golestan
Alinezhad-Sarkhani, Mohammad	1992–96	Tabriz, East Azerbaijan
Allahyari, Reza-Qoli	1992–96	Mamasani, Fars
Amid-Zanjani, Abbas-Ali	1992–96	Tehran, Tehran
Amini, Hoseyn	1992–96	Qaenat, South Khorasan
Aminlu, Hasan	1992–96	Shabestar, East Azerbaijan
Amirjahani, Seyyed Fazel	1992–96	Abhar, Zanjan
Amirshaqaqi, Fakhrtaj	1992–96	Tabriz, East Azerbaijan
Angaji, Seyyed Javad	1992–96	Tabriz, East Azerbaijan
Ansari, Gholam-Reza	1992–96	Mashhad, Razavi Khorasan
Ansari, Mohammad-Sa'id	1992–96	Abadan, Khuzestan
Aqa Hoseyni-Tabataba'i, Seyyed Hasan	1992–96	Zabol, Sistan and Baluchestan
Asgarowladi, Habibollah	1992–96	Tehran, Tehran
Astaneh, Mahmud	1992–96	Shazand (Sarband), Markazi

Name	Tenure	City and province of constituency
Atazadeh, Mahmud	1992–96	Semirom, Isfahan
Azarkish, Madad	1992–96	Zahedan, Sistan and Baluchestan
Baghani, Ali-Asghar	1992–96	Sabzevar, Razavi Khorasan
Baghumian, Artavaz	1992–96	Armenians of southern Iran (minority)
Bahme'i, Mohammad-Reza	1992–96	Ramhormoz and Ramshir, Khuzestan
Bahonar, Mohammad-Reza	1992–96	Tehran, Tehran
Bahrami, Mohammad-Baqer	1992–96	Asadabad, Hamadan
Banihashemi-Chaharom, Seyyed Hashem	1992–96	Mashhad, Razavi Khorasan
Behruzi, Maryam	1992–96	Tehran, Tehran
Bolfath, Ali	1992–96	Pol-e Dokhtar and Malavi, Lorestan
Dabestani, Majid	1992–96	Bam, Kerman
Dadvar, Khalil	1992–96	Neyriz and Estahban, Fars
Damadi-Kohnehdeh, Ezzatollah	1992–96	Sari, Mazandaran
Dana, Seyyed Mohammad-Hoseyn	1992–96	Abadeh, Fars
Danesh-Monfared, Ali	1992–96	Ashtiyan and Tafresh, Markazi
Daneshyar, Kamal	1992–96	Bandar-e Mahshahr, Khuzestan
Davudi-Shamsi, Seyyed Esma'il	1992–96	Ardakan, Yazd
Delbari, Mohammad-Esma'il	1992–96	Bostanabad, East Azerbaijan
Derakhshandeh, Akhtar	1992–96	Kermanshah, Kermanshah
Doa'i, Seyyed Mahmud	1992–96	Tehran, Tehran
Dorri-Najafabadi, Qorbanali	1992–96	Tehran, Tehran
Ebrahimnezhad, Ja'far	1992–96	Quchan, Razavi Khorasan
Elyasi, Golmohammad	1992–96	Varzaqan, East Azerbaijan
Emami-Rad, Ali	1992–96	Kuhdasht and Chegini, Lorestan
Erfani, Seyyed Mojtaba	1992–96	Talesh, Gilan
Esma'ili, Ghaffar	1992–96	Hashtrud, East Azerbaijan
Ezheh'i, Mehdi	1992–96	Isfahan, Isfahan
Faqih-Aliabadi, Asgari	1993–96	Qaemshahr and Savadkuh, Mazandaran
Farid, Akbar	1992–96	Khorramabad, Lorestan
Fattahi-Ma'sum, Seyyed Hoseyn	1992–96	Mashhad, Razavi Khorasan
Fayyazbakhsh, Nafiseh	1992–96	Tehran, Tehran
Ghayuri-Najafabadi, Seyyed Ali	1992–96	Tehran, Tehran
Golshani, Faramarz	1992–96	Rudbar, Gilan
Habibi, Habibollah	1992–96	Khaf, Razavi Khorasan
Habibiyan, Ahmad	1992–96	Hamadan, Hamadan
Hakimipur, Ahmad	1992–96	Zanjan and Tarom, Zanjan
Hasanbeygi, Abolfazl	1992–96	Damghan, Semnan
Hasani, Mohammad	1992–96	Dehloran, Ilam
Hashemi, Seyyed Hoseyn	1992–96	Miyaneh, East Azerbaijan
Hashemi, Seyyed Mojtaba	1992–96	Shahreza, Isfahan
Hashemiyan, Hoseyn	1992–96	Rafsanjan, Kerman
Hazrati, Elyas	1992–96	Rasht, Gilan
Hemmati, Ahmad	1992–96	Meshginshahr, Ardabil
Holaku, Mo'ami	1993–96	Ramiyan, Golestan

Name	Tenure	City and province of constituency
Homayun-Moqaddam, Fatemeh	1992–96	Tabriz, East Azerbaijan
Hoseyni, Seyyed Abdollah	1992–96	Bandar-e Lengeh, Hormozgan
Hoseyni, Seyyed Abolqasem	1992–96	Bojnurd, North Khorasan
Hoseyni, Seyyed Fathollah	1992–96	Paveh and Uramanat, Kermanshah
Hoseyni, Seyyed Javad	1992-96	Aliabad Katul, Golestan
Hoseyni, Seyyed Mas'ud	1992–96	Qorveh, Kurdistan
Hoseyni [Buyer Ahmad], Seyyed Mas'ud	1992–96	Buyer Ahmad, Kohgiluyeh and Buyer Ahmad
Hoseyni [Torbat-e Jam], Seyyed Mohammad	1992–96	Torbat-e Jam and Taybad, Razavi Khorasan
Hoseyni-Shahrudi, Seyyed Hoseyn	1992–94	Shahrud, Semnan
Hoseyni-Zeydabadi, Seyyed Ahmad	1992–96	Sirjan, Kerman
Irani, Hoseyn	1992–96	Qom, Qom
Irannezhad, Abdolghafur	1992–96	Chabahar, Sistan and Baluchestan
Jabbarzadeh, Esma'il	1992–96	Tabriz, East Azerbaijan
Jadri, Jasem	1992–96	Dasht-e Azadegan, Khuzestan
Ja'fari, Beytollah	1992–96	Urmia, West Azerbaijan
Jalali, Khodakaram	1992–96	Firuzabad, Fars
Jamali, Mahmud	1992–96	Kashan, Isfahan
Jamshidi-Ardeshiri, Mohammad-Hasan	1992–96	Behshahr, Mazandaran
Kahraze'i, Akhtar-Mohammad	1992–96	Khash, Sistan and Baluchestan
Kamran-Dastjerdi, Hasan	1992–96	Isfahan, Isfahan
Kamyar, Ali	1992–96	Urmia, West Azerbaijan
Karami, Ali Mir	1992–96	Qasr-e Shirin, Kermanshah
Karimi, Mohammad-Ali	1992–96	Marivan, Kurdistan
Karimi, Zabihollah	1992–96	Shushtar, Khuzestan
Karimiyan, Mohammad	1993–96	Sardasht and Piranshahr, West Azerbaijan
Karimpur-Natanzi, Mas'ud	1994–96	Qamsar and Natanz, Isfahan
Kazem-Dinan, Seyyed Mahmud	1992–96	Amol, Mazandaran
Kazemi, Seyyed Motahhar	1992–96	Khalkhal, Ardabil
Keyvani, Kuros	1992–96	Jewish community (minority)
Khabbaz, Mohammad-Reza	1992–96	Kashmar, Razavi Khorasan
Khajehpur, Mohammad	1992–96	Bushehr and Genaveh, Bushehr
Khatami, Hadi	1992–96	Borujerd, Lorestan
Khaza'i, Mohammad-Mehdi	1992–96	Fariman, Sarakhs, Ahmadabad, Marzdaran, and Razavieh, Razavi Khorasan
Kia, Mohammad-Qasem	1992–96	Kordkuy and Torkaman, Golestan
Kiya'inezhad, Mofid	1992–96	Savojblagh, Nazarabad, and Taleqan, Tehran
Kiyan-Ersi, Asadollah	1992–96	Faridan and Fereydunshahr, Isfahan
Kiyani-Falavarjani, Hoseyn	1992–96	Falavarjan, Isfahan
Kuhkan-Rizi, Mohsen	1992–96	Lenjan and Mobarakeh, Isfahan
Larijani, Mohammad-Javad	1992–96	Tehran, Tehran
Mahdavi-Khanaki, Seyyed Mohammad-Baqer	1992–96	Kerman, Kerman
Majdara, Mohammad	1992–96	Babolsar and Bandpay, Mazandaran
Majidi, Mohammad-Reza	1993–96	Fasa, Fars
Maqniyan, Mohammad-Ali	1992–96	Bijar, Kurdistan

Name	Tenure	City and province of constituency
Maqsudpursir, Shamshoun	1992–96	Assyrians and Chaldeans (minority)
Marhaba, Shapur	1992–96	Astara, Gilan
Marvi, Ali	1992–96	Neyshabur, Razavi Khorasan
Matori, Ali	1992–96	Ahvaz, Khuzestan
Mehdizadeh, Mehdi	1992–96	Gonabad, Razavi Khorasan
Mir Hoseyni, Abbas	1992–96	Zabol, Sistan and Baluchestan
Mir Khalili, Seyyed Ali	1992–96	Minab, Hormozgan
Mir Valad, Seyyed Kazem	1992–96	Malayer, Hamadan
Mobini-Dehkordi, Ali	1992–96	Shahrekord, Chahar Mahal and Bakhtiari
Mofatteh, Mohammad-Mehdi	1993–96	Razan, Hamadan
Mohammad-Gharibani, Ali	1992–96	Ardabil, Ardabil
Mohammadi, Mohammad	1992–96	Selseleh and Delfan, Lorestan
Mohammadi, Yunes	1993–96	Khorramshahr and Shadegan, Khuzestan
Mohammadifar, Baratali	1992–96	Sonqor, Kermanshah
Mohassel-Hamadani, Seyyed Mohammad-Taqi	1992–96	Taft, Yazd
Mojtahed-Shabestari, Mohsen	1992–96	Tehran, Tehran
Mokhtari, Hasan	1992–96	Najafabad, Isfahan
Moqaddam-Firuz, Mohammad-Reza	1992–96	Arak, Markazi
Moqaddamizad, Isa	1992–96	Shadegan, Khuzestan
Moqtada'i, Abdolhasan	1992–96	Abadan, Khuzestan
Moradi, Ahmad	1993–96	Torqabeh and Chenaran, Razavi Khorasan
Mortazavi, Seyyed Fatah	1992–96	Qazvin, Qazvin
Motahhari, Ali	1992–96	Zarand, Kerman
Mo'tamediniya, Gholam-Reza	1992–96	Kahnuj, Kerman
Movahhed, Seyyed Haji Mohammad	1992–96	Gachsaran, Kohgiluyeh and Buyer Ahmad
Movahhedi-Kermani, Mohammad-Ali	1992–96	Tehran, Tehran
Movahhedi-Savoji, Ali	1992–96	Tehran, Tehran
Movallizadeh, Seyyed Mohammad-Reza	1992–96	Ahvaz, Khuzestan
Musavi, Seyyed Ahmad	1992–96	Ahvaz, Khuzestan
Musavi, Seyyed Heshmat	1992–96	Ilam, Ilam
Musavi, Seyyed Mohammad-Ali	1992–96	Khodabandeh, Zanjan
Musavi, Seyyed Yunes	1992–96	Abadan, Khuzestan
Musavi-Hoseyni, Seyyed Ali-Akbar	1992–96	Tehran, Tehran
Musavi-Ojaq, Seyyed Ayatollah	1992–94	Kermanshah, Kermanshah
Musavi-Shahrudi, Seyyed Mohammad	1995–96	Shahrud, Semnan
Nabavi, Seyyed Morteza	1992–96	Tehran, Tehran
Nabovvati, Mohammad	1992–96	Saveh, Markazi
Naderi, Majid	1992–96	Bu'inzahra and Avaj, Zanjan
Nariman, Mohsen	1992–96	Babol, Mazandaran
Narimani, Aman	1992–96	Islamabad-e Gharb, Kermanshah
Naseri, Mostafa	1992–96	Zanjan, Zanjan
Naseri-Dowlatabadi, Mohammad-Reza	1992–96	Borkhar and Meymeh, Isfahan
Nasri, Seyyed Ahmad	1992–96	Qazvin, Qazvin
Nateq-Nuri, Ahmad	1992–96	Nur and Mahmudabad, Mazandaran

Name	Tenure	City and province of constituency
Nateq-Nuri, Ali-Akbar	1992–96	Tehran, Tehran
Nejabat, Ahmad	1992–96	Shiraz, Fars
Nikfar, Ahmad	1992–96	Eqlid, Fars
Niknam, Abolfath	1992–96	Tonekabon and Ramsar, Mazandaran
Nokhbeh-Alfuqha'i, Mohammad-Hoseyn	1992–96	Larestan, Fars
No'i-Aqdam, Nureddin	1992–96	Ardabil, Ardabil
Noqaba'i, Seyyed Mohammad	1992–96	Tuyserkan, Hamadan
Nosratirad, Ahmad	1992–96	Rasht, Gilan
Nowbakht, Monireh	1992–96	Tehran, Tehran
Nowbakht-Haqiqi, Mohammad-Baqer	1992–96	Rasht, Gilan
Nowruzi, Esma'il	1992–96	Sarvestan and Karbal, Fars
Nowruzi-Mishani, Abdollah	1992–96	Malayer, Hamadan
Nowruzzadeh, Seyyed Reza	1992–96	Esfarayen, North Khorasan
Nowzari, Gholam-Hoseyn	1992–96	Kazerun, Fars
Nurbakhsh, Abdorrahim	1992–96	Mahabad, West Azerbaijan
Paknezhad, Seyyed Abbas	1992–96	Yazd, Yazd
Partovi, Mohammad-Ali	1992–96	Saqqez and Baneh, Kurdistan
Parvaresh, Seyyed Ali-Akbar	1992–96	Isfahan, Isfahan
Pirzadeh, Seyyed Ahmad	1992–96	Dargaz, Razavi Khorasan
Pishbin, Ahmad	1992–96	Baft, Kerman
Purqorban, Khan Ali	1992–96	Kaleybar, East Azerbaijan
Purzaman, Rasul	1992–96	Naqadeh, West Azerbaijan
Qanbari-Maman, Jamshid	1992–96	Miyaneh, East Azerbaijan
Qashqavi, Hasan	1992–96	Shahriyar and Robat Karim, Tehran
Qazipur, Mir Naqi	1992–96	Ardabil, Ardabil
Qoli, Mohammad-Hasan	1994–96	Aligudarz, Lorestan
Qomi, Mohammad	1992–96	Varamin, Tehran
Rabi'i, Abolfazl	1992–96	Garmsar, Semnan
Rahbari, Mohammad-Hashem	1992–96	Tehran, Tehran
Rahbari-Amlashi, Mohammad-Mehdi	1992–96	Rudsar, Gilan
Rahchamani, Mohammad-Reza	1992–96	Sabzevar, Razavi Khorasan
Rahimi, Mohammad-Reza	1992–93	Sanandaj, Kurdistan
Rahmani, Rajab	1992–96	Takestan, Zanjan
Rahmani-Fazli, Abdorreza	1992–96	Shiravan, North Khorasan
Raja'i-Khorasani, Sa'id	1992–96	Tehran, Tehran
Ramezanpur-Nargesi, Qasem	1992–96	Sowme'eh Sara, Gilan
Rashidi, Hoseyn	1992–96	Darab, Fars
Rashidi-Kuchi, Habibollah	1995–96	Marvdasht, Fars
Rashidi-Kuchi, Jalil	1992–94	Marvdasht, Fars
Rasi, Mohsen	1992–96	Miyandoab and Takab, West Azerbaijan
Rasuli, Jalal	1992–96	Miyandoab and Takab, West Azerbaijan
Rasulinezhad, Seyyed Ahmad	1992–96	Damavand and Firuzkuh, Tehran
Ravani, Parviz	1994–96	Zoroastrian community (minority)
Razavi, Seyyed Abolfazl	1992–96	Na'in, Isfahan

Name	Tenure	City and province of constituency
Razavi-Ardakani, Seyyed Abufazel	1992–96	Sepidan, Fars
Razavi-Rashtipur, Asadalloh	1992–96	Kerman, Kerman
Razeqi, Gholam-Reza	1992–96	Dashtestan, Bushehr
Rebosheh, Mohammad	1992–96	Iranshahr, Sistan and Baluchestan
Reza'i, Seyyed Abolqasem	1992–96	Bojnurd, North Khorasan
Reza'i-Darshaki, Fathollah	1992–96	Salmas, West Azerbaijan
Reza'i-Sardareh, Mohammad	1996–96	Bandar-e Abbas, Hormozgan
Rezazehi, Fakhreddin	1992–96	Saravan, Sistan and Baluchestan
Rouhani, Hassan	1992–96	Tehran, Tehran
Ruhani, Seyyed Mostafa	1992–96	Mahallat and Delijan, Markazi
Ruhanizadeh-Qadikolahi, Saleh	1992–96	Qaemshahr and Savadkuh, Mazandaran
Ruhbakhsh-Mehraban, Mahmud	1992–96	Sarab, East Azerbaijan
Sa'adatiyan, Seyyed Jalal	1992–96	Hamadan, Hamadan
Saber-Hamishegi, Mahmud	1992–96	Tehran, Tehran
Sadiq, Jahanshah	1992–96	Dorud and Azna, Lorestan
Sadiqi-Bonabi, Rasul	1992–96	Bonab and Malekan, East Azerbaijan
Sadr, Seyyed Shahabeddin	1992–96	Tehran, Tehran
Sadra, Ali-Reza	1992–96	Dezful, Khuzestan
Sa'edi, Seyyed Jasem	1992–96	Andimeshk and Shush, Khuzestan
Sa'idi, Abdollah-e Sani	1992–96	Minudasht, Golestan
Salehi, Yavar	1992–96	I'zeh, Khuzestan
Salek, Ahmad	1992–96	Isfahan, Isfahan
Salihi-Labafinejad, Parvin	1992–96	Tehran, Tehran
Samadi, Seyyed Ma'ruf	1992–94	Sanandaj, Kurdistan
Samadzadeh, Nosrat	1992–96	Urmia, West Azerbaijan
Sarraf, Ebrahim	1992–96	Marand, East Azerbaijan
Seyfiyan, Mohammad-Kazem	1992–96	Tehran, Tehran
Seyqali-Kumeleh, Parviz	1992–96	Langarud, Gilan
Seyyed Hashemi, Seyyed Mostafa	1992–96	Maragheh, East Azerbaijan
Seyyed Khamushi, Seyyed Ali-Naqi	1992–96	Tehran, Tehran
Seyyedi Alavi, Bibi Qodsiyyeh	1992–96	Mashhad, Razavi Khorasan
Shafi'i-Kas-Ahmadani, Mohammad-Reza	1992–96	Fuman, Gilan
Shahriyari, Seyyed Kamaleddin	1992–96	Tangestan, Dashti, Kangan, and Deyr, Bushehr
Shahrzad, Mohammad-Karim	1992–96	Isfahan, Isfahan
Shakhesi, Hasan	1992–96	Astaneh-ye Ashrafiyyeh, Gilan
Shar'i, Mohammad-Ali	1992–96	Qom, Qom
Sharifi, Seyyed Hoseyn	1992–96	Arak, Markazi
Shayesteh, Morteza	1992–96	Golpayegan and Khansar, Isfahan
Sheybani, Abbas	1992–96	Tehran, Tehran
Shoja', Abdolghaffar	1992–96	Bandar-e Anzali, Gilan
Shoja'eifard, Mohammad-Mehdi	1992–96	Jahrom, Fars
Shoja'ei-Kiyasari, Seyyed Hasan	1992–96	Sari, Mazandaran

Name	Tenure	City and province of constituency
Sho'lehsa'di, Qasem	1992–96	Shiraz, Fars
Sobhaninia, Hoseyn	1992–96	Neyshabur, Razavi Khorasan
Sobhanollahi, Mohammad-Ali	1992–96	Tabriz, East Azerbaijan
Sohrabi, Naser	1992–96	Masjed Soleyman, Khuzestan
Soleymani, Hasan	1992–96	Kangavar, Kermanshah
Soleymani-Meymandi, Mansur	1992–96	Shahr-e Babak, Kerman
Tabataba'inezhad, Seyyed Yusef	1992–96	Ardestan, Isfahan
Taha, Ahmad	1992–96	Bukan, West Azerbaijan
Taheri-Khorramabadi, Seyyed Mohammad-Saleh	1992–96	Khorramabad, Lorestan
Taqavi, Seyyed Reza	1992–96	Tehran, Tehran
Tatari, Esma'il	1992–96	Kermanshah, Kermanshah
Tavakkoli, Mohammad-Baqer	1992–96	Khomeyn, Markazi
Tavassoli, Mohammad-Reza	1992–96	Ferdows and Tabas, South Khorasan
Tavassolizadeh, Mohammad-Naser	1992–96	Torbat-e Heydariyyeh, Razavi Khorasan
Tayyar, Atrak	1993–96	Gonbad-e Kavus, Golestan
Vahid-Dastjerdi, Marziyeh	1992–96	Tehran, Tehran
Vartanian, Vartan	1992–96	Armenians of northern Iran (minority)
Yahyavi, Seyyed Mohsen	1992–96	Tehran, Tehran
Ya'qubi, Ali	1992–96	Bahar and Kabudarahang, Hamadan
Ya'qubi-Bijarbaneh, Bahram	1992–96	Lahijan, Gilan
Yusefpur, Ali	1992–96	Ardal, Chahar Mahal and Bakhtiari
Zadsar-Jirofti, Ali	1992–96	Jiroft, Kerman
Za'eri, Gholam-Abbas	1992–94	Bandar-e Abbas, Hormozgan
Zali, Abbas-Ali	1992–96	Karaj and Eshtehard, Tehran
Zamaniyan, Ahmad	1992–96	Nahavand, Hamadan
Zare', Karim	1992–96	Shiraz, Fars
Zare'i-Qanavati, Lotfollah	1992–96	Behbahan, Khuzestan
Zeynali, Seyyed Mohammad-Hoseyn	1992–96	Birjand, South Khorasan

Deputies in the Fifth Majlis (1996–2000)

Name	Tenure	City and province of constituency
Abbasi, Abbas	1996–2000	Bandar-e Abbas, Hormozgan
Abbaspur-Tehranifard, Ali	1998–2000	Tehran, Tehran
Abdollahi, Reza	1996–2000	Mahneshan, Zanjan
Abdolvand, Gholam-Reza	1996–2000	Dorud and Azna, Lorestan
Abedinzadeh, Kamel	1996–2000	Khoy, West Azerbaijan
Abtahi, Seyyed Mahmud	1996–2000	Khomeinishahr, Isfahan
Abutorabifard, Seyyed Ali-Akbar	1996–2000	Tehran, Tehran
Adab, Bahaeddin	1996–2000	Sanandaj, Kurdistan
Afqahi, Seyyed Ali-Reza	1996–2000	Sabzevar, Razavi Khorasan
Ahmadi, Ali	1996–2000	Maku, West Azerbaijan

Name	Tenure	City and province of constituency
Ahmadi, Ali-Asghar	1996–2000	Shahrud, Semnan
Ahmadiyyeh, Mostafa	1996–2000	Karaj and Eshtehard, Tehran
Ahmadi-Zadsara'i, Valiyollah	1996–2000	Ahar and Heris, East Azerbaijan
Akbari, Saleh	1996–2000	Naqadeh, West Azerbaijan
Akbari-Talarposhti, Ezzatollah	1996–2000	Qaemshahr and Savadkuh, Mazandaran
Akbarzadeh, Ali	1998–2000	Varzaqan and Kharvanagh, East Azerbaijan
Akhavan, Bahman	1996–2000	Tafresh and Ashtiyan, Markazi
Akhavan-Bitaraf, Nayyereh	1996–2000	Isfahan, Isfahan
Akrami, Seyyed Reza	1996–2000	Tehran, Tehran
Ala', Eynollah	1996–2000	Aliabad Katul, Golestan
Alavi, Seyyed Mahmud	1996–2000	Lamerd, Fars
Ale-Kazemi, Ali	1996–2000	Delfan and Selseleh, Lorestan
Alihoseyni-Abbasi, Mohammad-Reza	1996–2000	Nahavand, Hamadan
Allahqolizadeh, Qoli	1996–2000	Kaleybar and Hurand, East Azerbaijan
Almasi, Hasan	1996–2000	Germi (Moghan), Ardabil
Amani-Anganeh, Shahrbanu	1996–2000	Urmia, West Azerbaijan
Ansari, Fariborz	1996–2000	Mamasani and Doshman Ziari, Fars
Ansari, Majid	1996–2000	Tehran, Tehran
Ansarirad, Hoseyn	1996–2000	Neyshabur, Razavi Khorasan
Anvari, Hoseyn	1996–2000	Sarab, East Azerbaijan
Aqa Alikhani, Gholam-Abbas	1996–2000	Bu'inzahra and Avaj, Zanjan
Asgari, Hoseyn	1996–2000	Shahriyar and Robat Karim, Tehran
Ashrafi, Gholam-Reza	1996–2000	Zabol, Sistan and Baluchestan
Ashuri-Qal'erudkhani, Naser	1997–2000	Fuman and Shaft, Gilan
Astaneh, Mahmud	1996–2000	Shazand (Sarband), Markazi
Azimi-Taraqdari, Mohammad	1996–2000	Torqabeh and Chenaran, Razavi Khorasan
Azizi, Ebrahim	1996–2000	Kermanshah, Kermanshah
Baghbaniyan, Ali	1997–2000	Qamsar, Natanz, and Niyasar, Isfahan
Baghumian, Artavaz	1996–2000	Armenians of southern Iran (minority)
Bahme'i, Mohammad-Reza	1997–2000	Ramhormoz, Khuzestan
Bahonar, Mohammad-Reza	1996–2000	Tehran, Tehran
Baqeri-Bonabi, Abdolhamid	1996–2000	Tabriz, East Azerbaijan
Baqerzadeh, Seyyed Javad	1997–2000	Zanjan and Tarom, Zanjan
Barzegar-Tekmehdash, Taher Aqa	1996–2000	Bostanabad, East Azerbaijan
Bayanak, Amin	1996–2000	Ahvaz, Khuzestan
Behnia, Manuchehr	1996–2000	Kermanshah, Kermanshah
Beygmoradi, Hemmat	1996–2000	Qasr-e Shirin, Sarpol-e Zahab, and Gilan-e Gharb, Kermanshah
Bohluli-Qashqa'i, Sohrab	1996–2000	Firuzabad, Fars
Dabestani, Majid	1996–2000	Bam, Kerman
Dahgan, Hasan	1996–2000	Langarud, Gilan
Dana, Seyyed Mohammad-Hoseyn	1996–2000	Abadeh, Fars
Danesh-Ja'fari, Davud	1996–2000	Tehran, Tehran
Daneshyar, Kamal	1996–2000	Bandar-e Mahshahr, Khuzestan

Name	Tenure	City and province of constituency
Darvishzadeh, Mehdi-Reza	1996–2000	Dezful, Khuzestan
Davudi, Yusef	1997–2000	Najafabad, Isfahan
Doa'i, Seyyed Mahmud	1996–2000	Tehran, Tehran
Dorri-Najafabadi, Qorbanali	1996–97	Tehran, Tehran
Dowlati-Bakhshan, Abdolaziz	1996–2000	Saravan, Sistan and Baluchestan
Dusti, Esma'il	1996–2000	Kuhdasht, Lorestan
Ebadi, Seyyed Ali-Reza	1996–2000	Birjand and Nehbandan, South Khorasan
Ebrahim-Baysalami, Gholam-Heydar	1996–2000	Khaf and Roshtkhar, Razavi Khorasan
Elyasi, Manuchehr	1996–2000	Jewish community (minority)
Esma'ilzadeh, Habibollah	1996–2000	Falavarjan, Isfahan
Eydi-Goltapeh'i, Gazanfar	1996–2000	Arak, Markazi
Faker, Mohammad-Reza	1996–2000	Mashhad, Razavi Khorasan
Fayyazbakhsh, Nafiseh	1996–2000	Tehran, Tehran
Fazlali, Morteza	1996–2000	Tuyserkan, Hamadan
Fotuhi, Mohammad-Sharif	1996–2000	Chabahar, Sistan and Baluchestan
Fuladi, Kurosh	1996–2000	Khorramabad, Lorestan
Ghafurifard, Hasan	1996–2000	Tehran, Tehran
Ghanizadeh, Ali-Reza	1996–2000	Urmia, West Azerbaijan
Golbaz, Ja'far	1996–2000	Savojblagh, Nazarabad, and Taleqan, Tehran
Golshani, Faramarz	1996–2000	Rudbar, Gilan
Habibzadeh-Bukani, Anvar	1996–2000	Bukan, West Azerbaijan
Hadidchi-Dabbagh, Marziyeh	1996–2000	Hamadan, Hamadan
Hadizadeh, Ali-Asghar	1996–2000	Mahallat and Delijan, Markazi
Haji Baba'i, Hamid-Reza	1996–2000	Hamadan, Hamadan
Hajiyani, Abdollah	1996–2000	Tangestan, Deyr, Kangan, and Dashti, Bushehr
Harizavi, Abdozzahra	1996–2000	Abadan, Khuzestan
Hashemi, Seyyed Hoseyn	1996–2000	Miyaneh, East Azerbaijan
Hashemi, Seyyed Mohammad	1996–2000	Sirjan and Bardsir, Kerman
Hashemi-Bahremani, Fa'ezeh	1996–2000	Tehran, Tehran
Hashemi-R'iseh, Seyyed Mostafa	1996–2000	Shahr-e Babak, Harat, Marvdast, and Raviz, Kerman
Hashemi-Toghroljerdi, Seyyed Taha	1996–2000	Qom, Qom
Hashemizadeh, Faramand	1996–2000	Ahvaz, Khuzestan
Hashemzadeh-Herisi, Hashem	1996–2000	Tabriz, East Azerbaijan
Hazrati, Elyas	1996–2000	Rasht, Gilan
Heshmatiyan, Qodrat-Ali	1996–2000	Sonqor and Koliyayi, Kermanshah
Heydari-Darani, Gholam-Reza	1996–2000	Faridan and Fereydunshahr, Isfahan
Holaku, Mo'ami	1996–2000	Gonbad-e Kavus, Golestan
Hoseyni, Seyyed Abdollah	1996–2000	Bandar-e Lengeh, Hormozgan
Hoseyni, Seyyed Mohammad	1996–2000	Rafsanjan, Kerman
Hoseyni [Torbat-e Jam], Seyyed Mohammad	1996–2000	Torbat-e Jam and Taybad, Razavi Khorasan
Hoseyninezhad, Seyyed Akbar	1996–2000	Ardakan and Meybod, Yazd
Hoseyni-Vae'z, Seyyed Mahmud	1996–2000	Ramiyan, Golestan

Name	Tenure	City and province of constituency
Irani, Hoseyn	1996–2000	Qom, Qom
Jabbarzadeh, Esma'il	1996–2000	Tabriz, East Azerbaijan
Jadri, Jasem	1996–2000	Dasht-e Azadegan, Khuzestan
Ja'fari-Nasab-Jori, Seyyed Mohammad-Reza	1996–2000	Zarand, Kerman
Jalilkhani, Gholam-Hoseyn	1997–2000	Zanjan and Tarom, Zanjan
Jamali, Mahmud	1996–2000	Kashan, Isfahan
Jamshidi-Ardeshiri, Mohammad-Hasan	1996–2000	Behshahr, Mazandaran
Jamshidinezhad, Iraj	1996–2000	Islamabad-e Gharb, Kermanshah
Jandaqi, Abbas	1996–2000	Garmsar, Semnan
Jelowdarzadeh, Sohayla	1996–2000	Tehran, Tehran
Ka'bi, Abdollah	1996–2000	Abadan, Khuzestan
Kamran-Dastjerdi, Hasan	1999–2000	Isfahan, Isfahan
Karamatlu, Abbas-Ali	1996–2000	Minudasht, Golestan
Karimi, Hamid	1996–2000	Ilam, Eyvan and Chardavol, Ilam
Karimi-Munjermo'i, Ebrahim	1996–2000	Borujen and Lordegan, Chahar Mahal and Bakhtiari
Karimiyan, Mohammad	1996–2000	Sardasht and Piranshahr, West Azerbaijan
Karrubi, Fatemeh	1999–2000	Tehran, Tehran
Kazemi, Seyyed Motahhar	1996–2000	Khalkhal, Ardabil
Khabbaz, Mohammad-Reza	1996–2000	Kashmar, Razavi Khorasan
Khadem-Arabbaghi, Mohsen	1996–2000	Urmia, West Azerbaijan
Khajehpur, Mohammad	1996–2000	Bushehr and Genaveh, Bushehr
Khaleqi, Naser	1997–2000	Isfahan, Isfahan
Khatami, Hadi	1996–99	Borujerd, Lorestan
Khaza'i, Mohammad-Mehdi	1996–2000	Fariman, Sarakhs, Ahmadabad, Marzdaran, and Razavieh, Razavi Khorasan
Kheyrkhah, Kamel	1996–2000	Lahijan, Gilan
Khodadadi, Salman	1996–2000	Bonab and Malekan, East Azerbaijan
Kurdmandani, Khodabakhsh	1996–2000	Khash, Nosratabad, and Mirjaveh, Sistan and Baluchestan
Larijani, Mohammad-Javad	1996–2000	Tehran, Tehran
Maddahi, Mohammad-Ebrahim	1996–2000	Aligudarz, Lorestan
Mahdavi-Abhari, Ahmad	1996–2000	Abhar, Zanjan
Mahjub, Ali-Reza	1996–2000	Tehran, Tehran
Majdara, Mohammad	1996–96	Babolsar and Bandpay, Mazandaran
Majidi, Mohammad-Reza	1996–2000	Fasa, Fars
Maqsudpursir, Shamshoun	1996–2000	Assyrians and Chaldeans (minority)
Mar'ashi, Seyyed Hoseyn	1996–2000	Kerman, Kerman
Marhaba, Shapur	1997–2000	Astara, Gilan
Marvi, Ali	1996–2000	Neyshabur, Razavi Khorasan
Maturzadeh, Mostafa	1996–2000	Khorramshahr, Khuzestan
Mehdizadeh, Mehdi	1996–2000	Gonabad, Razavi Khorasan
Mehrzad-Sedqiyani, Qasem	1999–2000	Salmas, West Azerbaijan
Milani-Hoseyni, Seyyed Mohammad-Reza	1996–2000	Tabriz, East Azerbaijan

Name	Tenure	City and province of constituency
Mir Hoseyni, Abbas	1996–2000	Zabol, Sistan and Baluchestan
Mir Khalili, Seyyed Ali	1996–2000	Minab, Hormozgan
Mo'in, Mostafa	1997–97	Isfahan, Isfahan
Mo'allemi-Juybari, Ali	1996–2000	Qaemshahr and Savadkuh, Mazandaran
Mofatteh, Mohammad-Mehdi	1996–2000	Razan, Hamadan
Mohammadi-Kaftarkari, Abbas	1996–2000	Kordkuy and Torkaman, Mazandaran
Mohammadyari, Bahman	1996–2000	Talesh, Gilan
Mohassel-Hamadani, Seyyed Mohammad-Taqi	1996–2000	Taft, Yazd
Mohebbinia, Jahanbakhsh	1997–2000	Miyandoab, Takab, and Shahindezh, West Azerbaijan
Mojtahed-Shabestari, Mohsen	1996–2000	Tehran, Tehran
Moqaddamizad, Isa	1996–2000	Shadegan, Khuzestan
Mortazavi, Seyyed Fatah	1996–2000	Qazvin, Qazvin
Mo'tamediniya, Gholam-Reza	1996–2000	Kahnuj, Kerman
Movahhed, Seyyed Haji Mohammad	1996–2000	Gachsaran and Kohgiluyeh, Kohgiluyeh and Buyer Ahmad
Movahhedi-Kermani, Mohammad-Ali	1996–2000	Tehran, Tehran
Movahhedi-Savoji, Ali	1996–2000	Tehran, Tehran
Movallizadeh, Seyyed Mohammad-Reza	1996–2000	Ahvaz, Khuzestan
Musavi, Seyyed Abbas	1996–2000	I'zeh, Khuzestan
Musavi, Seyyed Mohammad-Ali	1996–2000	Khodabandeh, Zanjan
Musavi-Hoseyni, Seyyed Ali-Akbar	1996–2000	Tehran, Tehran
Musavi-Jahanabadi, Seyyed Baqer	1996–2000	Yasouj, Kohgiluyeh and Buyer Ahmad
Musavi-Kuzehkonani, Seyyed Ali	1996–2000	Shabestar, East Azerbaijan
Musavi-Nanehkaran, Mir Fakhreddin	1996–2000	Ardabil, Ardabil
Musavinasab, Seyyed Ali	1996–2000	Shiravan, North Khorasan
Musavi-Ojaq, Seyyed Mojtaba	1996–2000	Kermanshah, Kermanshah
Nabavi, Seyyed Morteza	1996–2000	Tehran, Tehran
Nabovvati, Mohammad	1996–2000	Saveh, Markazi
Najafi, Qodratollah	1996–2000	Shahreza, Isfahan
Najafnezhad, Meqdad	1997–2000	Babolsar and Bandpay, Mazandaran
Naserigahar, Ahmad	1996–2000	Dehloran and Mehran, Ilam
Nateq-Nuri, Ahmad	1996–2000	Nur and Mahmudabad, Mazandaran
Nateq-Nuri, Ali-Akbar	1996–2000	Tehran, Tehran
Nazariniya, Qodratollah	1996–2000	Kangavar, Kermanshah
Nejabat, Ahmad	1996–2000	Shiraz, Fars
Ne'matzadeh, Ali	1996–2000	Saqqez and Baneh, Kurdistan
Nokhbeh-Alfuqha'i, Mohammad-Hoseyn	1996–2000	Larestan, Fars
Nowbakht, Monireh	1996–2000	Tehran, Tehran
Nowbakht-Haqiqi, Mohammad-Baqer	1996–2000	Rasht, Gilan
Nowruzzadeh, Seyyed Reza	1996–2000	Esfarayen, North Khorasan
Nowzari, Gholam-Hoseyn	1996–2000	Kazerun, Fars
Nura, Abbas-Ali	1996–2000	Zahedan, Sistan and Baluchestan
Nurbakhsh, Abdorrahim	1996–2000	Mahabad, West Azerbaijan

Name	Tenure	City and province of constituency
Nuri, Abdollah	1996–97	Tehran, Tehran
Nuri, Ezzatollah	1996–2000	Qorveh, Kurdistan
Nurizadeh, Seyyed Mahmud	1996–2000	Meshginshahr, Ardabil
Paknezhad, Seyyed Abbas	1996-2000	Yazd, Yazd
Pirne'mati, Ebrahim	1996–2000	Ardabil, Ardabil
Pishbin, Ahmad	1996–2000	Baft, Kerman
Pishgahifard, Zahra	1997–2000	Isfahan, Isfahan
Qaderi, Mohammad-Rauf	1996–2000	Paveh and Javanrud, Kermanshah
Qahremani, Mohammad-Mehdi	1996–2000	Shiraz, Fars
Qanbari-Adivi, Ali	1996–2000	Ardal, Farsan, and Kiyar, Chahar Mahal and Bakhtiari
Qanbari-Maman, Jamshid	1996–2000	Miyaneh, East Azerbaijan
Qandehari, Qorbanali	1996–2000	Gorgan, Golestan
Qasemi, Abdollah	1996–2000	Marivan, Kurdistan
Qasemi, Khodanazar	1996–2000	Dashtestan, Bushehr
Qasempur, Samad	1996–2000	Tabriz, East Azerbaijan
Qasemzadeh, Hoseyn-Ali	1996–2000	Babol, Mazandaran
Qaza'i-Niyyari, Ahad	1996–2000	Ardabil, Ardabil
Qermezi, Shahriyar	1996–2000	Semirom, Isfahan
Qobadi, Khodadad	1996–2000	Eqlid, Fars
Qolizadeh, Rahman-Qoli	1996–2000	Bojnurd, North Khorasan
Qomi, Mohammad	1996–2000	Varamin, Tehran
Qorbani, Musa	1996–2000	Qaenat, South Khorasan
Qoreyshi, Seyyed Mohammad-Ali	1998–2000	Khomeyn, Markazi
Rahbari-Amlashi, Mohammad-Mehdi	1996–2000	Rudsar, Gilan
Rahchamani, Mohammad-Reza	1996–2000	Sabzevar, Razavi Khorasan
Raheb, Ja'farqoli	1996–2000	Tonekabon and Ramsar, Mazandaran
Rahmani, Rajab	1996–2000	Takestan, Qazvin
Ra'isi, Khodabakhsh	1996–2000	Iranshahr, Bent, Lashar, and Fanuj, Sistan and Baluchestan
Ra'isi-Dehkordi, Asghar	1996–2000	Shahrekord, Chahar Mahal and Bakhtiari
Ramezanpur-Nargesi, Ahmad	1996–2000	Rasht, Gilan
Ramezanpur-Nargesi, Qasem	1996–2000	Sowme'eh Sara, Gilan
Ramezanzadeh, Fatemeh	1996–2000	Tehran, Tehran
Rashidi-Kuchi, Habibollah	1996–2000	Marvdasht, Fars
Rastad, Abdolmohammad	1996–2000	Darab, Fars
Rastgu, Elaheh	1997–2000	Malayer, Hamadan
Rasulinezhad, Seyyed Ahmad	1996–2000	Damavand and Firuzkuh, Tehran
Ravani, Parviz	1996–2000	Zoroastrian community (minority)
Razavi, Seyyed Abolfazl	1996–2000	Na'in, Isfahan
Razavi-Ardakani, Seyyed Abufazel	1996–2000	Sepidan, Fars
Razavi-Rashtipur, Asadalloh	1996–2000	Kerman, Kerman
Razmiyan-Moqaddam, Hasan	1996–2000	Dargaz, Razavi Khorasan

Name	Tenure	City and province of constituency
Reza'i, Seyyed Abolqasem	1996–2000	Bojnurd, North Khorasan
Reza'i, Omidvar	1996–2000	Masjed Soleyman, Khuzestan
Reza'i-Sardareh, Mohammad	1996–2000	Bandar-e Abbas, Hormozgan
Roshancheragh, Hoseyn	1996–2000	Borkhar and Meymeh, Isfahan
Rouhani, Hassan	1996–2000	Tehran, Tehran
Ruhi-Sarokhkala'i, Abolqasem	1996–2000	Sari, Mazandaran
Sadiqi, Marziyeh	1996–2000	Mashhad, Razavi Khorasan
Sadr, Seyyed Shahabeddin	1996–2000	Tehran, Tehran
Sa'edi, Seyyed Jasem	1996–2000	Andimeshk and Shush, Khuzestan
Safa'i, Zabihollah	1996–2000	Asadabad, Hamadan
Salehi-Khansari, Seyyed Morteza	1996–2000	Golpayegan and Khansar, Isfahan
Salimi-Mahmudjayq, Fereydun	1997–2000	Miyandoab and Takab, West Azerbaijan
Samadi, Seyyed Ma'ruf	1996–2000	Sanandaj, Kurdistan
Samarghandi, Balal	1996–2000	Tabriz, East Azerbaijan
Saqqa'i, Mohammad	1996–2000	Neyriz and Estahban, Fars
Sarhaddizadeh, Abolqasem	1996–2000	Tehran, Tehran
Sefati-Dezfuli, Iraj	1996–2000	Abadan, Khuzestan
Sepahvand, Abdorreza	1996–2000	Khorramabad, Lorestan
Seyyed Hashemi, Seyyed Mostafa	1996–2000	Maragheh, East Azerbaijan
Seyyedi Alavi, Bibi Qodsiyyeh	1996–2000	Mashhad, Razavi Khorasan
Seyyedzadeh-Galehban, Seyyed Hoseyn	1996–2000	Marand, East Azerbaijan
Shahi-Arablu, Mohammad	1996–2000	Hashtrud, East Azerbaijan
Shahrokhi, Seyyed Mohammad-Mehdi	1996–2000	Pol-e Dokhtar and Malavi, Lorestan
Shaikh, Mohammad-Ali	1996–2000	Shushtar, Khuzestan
Shakhesi, Hasan	1996–2000	Astaneh-ye Ashrafiyyeh, Gilan
Shakibi, Seyyed Masha'allah	1996–2000	Ferdows and Tabas, South Khorasan
Sharifi, Seyyed Hoseyn	1996–2000	Arak, Markazi
Sheybani, Abbas	1996–2000	Tehran, Tehran
Shiraziyan, Seyyed Gholam-Reza	1996–2000	Mashhad, Razavi Khorasan
Shoja', Abdolghaffar	1996–2000	Bandar-e Anzali, Gilan
Shoja'eifard, Mohammad-Mehdi	1996–2000	Jahrom, Fars
Sobhani, Hasan	1996–2000	Damghan, Semnan
Sohrabi, Ali	1996–2000	Shiraz, Fars
Taheri, Seyyed Taher	1996–2000	Semnan, Semnan
Tahernezhad, Yadollah	1996–2000	Nowshahr, Mazandaran
Tajeddin-Khuzani, Abdorrahman	1997–2000	Isfahan, Isfahan
Taqavi, Seyyed Reza	1996–2000	Tehran, Tehran
Taraqqi, Hamid-Reza	1996–2000	Mashhad, Razavi Khorasan
Tavakkoli-Tabazavareh, Seyyed Valiyollah	1996–2000	Ardestan, Isfahan
Tavassolizadeh, Mohammad-Naser	1996–2000	Torbat-e Heydariyyeh, Razavi Khorasan
Torabizadeh, Heshmatollah	1996–2000	Lenjan and Mobarakeh, Isfahan
Torang, Enayatollah	1996–2000	Amol, Mazandaran
Vahid-Dastjerdi, Marziyeh	1996–2000	Tehran, Tehran

Name	Tenure	City and province of constituency
Vartanian, Vartan	1996–2000	Armenians of northern Iran (minority)
Yahyavi, Seyyed Mohsen	1996–2000	Tehran, Tehran
Ya'qubi, Ali	1996–2000	Bahar and Kabudarahang, Hamadan
Yusefnezhad, Ali-Asghar	1996–2000	Sari, Mazandaran
Zadsar-Jirofti, Ali	1996–2000	Jiroft, Kerman
Zajkaniha, Hoseyn	1996–2000	Qazvin, Qazvin
Zakeri, Mohammad-Baqer	1996–2000	Quchan, Razavi Khorasan
Zamanifar, Hasan-Reza	1997–2000	Malayer, Hamadan
Zare'i, Mostafa	1996–2000	Sarvestan, Kavar, and Karbal, Fars
Zare'i-Qanavati, Lotfollah	1996–2000	Behbahan, Khuzestan
Zargar, Musa	1996–2000	Tehran, Tehran
Zarringol, Morteza	1996–2000	Bijar, Kurdistan

Deputies in the Sixth Majlis (2000–2004)

Name	Tenure	City and province of constituency
Aba'i-Khorasani, Mohammad	2000–2004	Mashhad, Razavi Khorasan
Abbaspur, Mohammad	2000–2004	Maku, West Azerbaijan
Abdollahi, Reza	2000–2004	Mahneshan and Ijrood, Zanjan
Abdollahpuri-Hoseyni, Mir Ali-Ashraf	2000–2004	Tabriz, East Azerbaijan
Abdolvand, Gholam-Reza	2000–2004	Dorud and Azna, Lorestan
Abedi, Gholam-Ali	2000–2004	Nehbandan and Sarbisheh, South Khorasan
Abedinpur, Abolqasem	2000–2004	Torbat-e Heydariyyeh, Razavi Khorasan
Abramiyan, Zhorzhik	2000–2004	Armenians of southern Iran (minority)
Abutorabifard, Seyyed Mohammad-Hasan	2000–2004	Qazvin, Qazvin
Adab, Bahaeddin	2000–2004	Sanandaj, Kurdistan
Afarideh, Hoseyn	2000–2004	Shirvan, North Khorasan
Afghahi-Farimani, Ja'far	2000–2004	Fariman, Sarakhs, Ahmadabad, and Razavieh, Razavi Khorasan
Afkhami, Behruz	2000–2004	Tehran, Tehran
Ahmadi, Ali-Mohammad	2000–2004	Aligudarz, Lorestan
Ahmadiniya, Isaqoli	2000–2004	I'zeh and Baghmalek, Khuzestan
Akbarzadeh, Ali	2000–2004	Varzaqan and Kharvanagh, East Azerbaijan
Akhavan, Bahman	2000–2004	Tafresh and Ashtiyan, Markazi
Akhavan-Bazardeh, Mahmud	2000–2004	Langarud, Gilan
Alami, Akbar	2000–2004	Azarshahr, Osku, and Tabriz, East Azerbaijan
Alemi-Nayesi, Abdozzahra	2000–2004	Dasht-e Azadegan, Khuzestan
Alihoseyni-Abbasi, Mohammad-Reza	2000–2004	Nahavand, Hamadan
Alikhani, Qodratollah	2000–2004	Bu'inzahra and Avaj, Qazvin
Alireza'i, Ne'matollah	2000–2004	Khomeinishahr, Isfahan
Allahqolizadeh, Qoli	2000–2004	Kaleybar and Hurand, East Azerbaijan
Allahyari, Abbas-Ali	2000–2004	Kermanshah, Kermanshah
Almasi, Hasan	2000–2004	Parsabad and Bilehsavar, Ardabil

Name	Tenure	City and province of constituency
Amani-Anganeh, Shahrbanu	2000–2004	Urmia, West Azerbaijan
Amini-Najafabadi, Seyyed Ebrahim	2000–2004	Mamasani, Fars
Amiri-Khamkani, Hoseyn	2000–2004	Zarand, Kerman
Amirjahani, Seyyed Fazel	2000–2004	Abhar, Zanjan
Ansari, Majid	2000–2004	Tehran, Tehran
Ansarirad, Hoseyn	2000–2004	Neyshabur, Razavi Khorasan
Anvari, Hoseyn	2000–2004	Sarab, East Azerbaijan
Aqa'i, Gholam-Hasan	2000–2004	Zabol, Sistan and Baluchestan
Aqa'i-Kahlikbolaghi, Khalil	2000–2004	Meshginshahr, Ardabil
Aqa'i-Moghanjuqi, Ali-Akbar	2000–2004	Salmas, West Azerbaijan
Armin, Mohsen	2000–2004	Tehran, Tehran
Ashuri-Bandari, Peyman	2000–2004	Bandar-e Mahshahr, Khuzestan
Ayati, Mehdi	2000–2004	Birjand, South Khorasan
Azadmanesh, Azadi	2000–2004	Gonabad, Razavi Khorasan
A'zami, Maqsud	2001–4	Naqadeh and Oshnaviyyeh, West Azerbaijan
Azarvash, Vali	2000–2004	Ardabil, Namin, and Nir, Ardabil
Azimi, Seyyed Ahmad	2000–2004	Shiraz, Fars
Azizi, Qasem	2000–2004	Shazand, Markazi
Baghbaniyan, Ali	2000–2004	Qamsar, Natanz, and Niyasar, Isfahan
Baharvand, Abdorrahim	2000–2004	Khorramabad, Lorestan
Bahrami-Hasanabadi, Qahreman	2000–2004	Mobarakeh, Isfahan
Baqeri-Nezhadiyanfard, Mohammad-Baqer	2000–2004	Kazerun, Fars
Barzegar, Gholam-Hoseyn	2000–2004	Sepidan, Fars
Barzegar-Tekmehdash, Taher Aqa	2000–2004	Bostanabad, East Azerbaijan
Behmanesh, Rahman	2000–2004	Mahabad, West Azerbaijan
Betkiliya, Yonaten	2000–2004	Assyrians and Chaldeans (minority)
Bohluli-Qashqa'i, Sohrab	2000–2004	Firuzabad, Fars
Borujerdi, Alaeddin	2000–2004	Borujerd, Lorestan
Burqani-Farahani, Ahmad	2000–2004	Tehran, Tehran
Dabestani, Khosrow	2000–2004	Zoroastrian community (minority)
Dadfar, Mohammad	2000–2004	Bushehr, Genaveh, and Deylam, Bushehr
Daseh, Hasel	2000–2004	Piranshahr and Sardasht, West Azerbaijan
Davidian, Levon	2000–2004	Armenians of northern Iran (minority)
Dirbaz, Ali	2001–4	Bandar-e Abbas, Hormozgan
Doa'i, Seyyed Mahmud	2000–2004	Tehran, Tehran
Dowlatabadi, Mohammad-Reza	2000–2004	Neyshabur, Razavi Khorasan
Ebrahim-Baysalami, Gholam-Heydar	2000–2004	Khaf and Roshtkhar, Razavi Khorasan
Ebrahimi, Ali-Asghar	2001–4	Aliabad Katul, Golestan
Edalat, Hamideh	2000–2004	Dashtestan, Bushehr
Ela'i, Salaheddin	2001–4	Saqqez and Baneh, Kurdistan
Emadi, Seyyed Keramatollah	2000–2004	Semirom, Isfahan
Emami, Baqer	2000–2004	Marand and Jolfa, East Azerbaijan
Emami-Rad, Ali	2000–2004	Kuhdasht and Chegini, Lorestan
Esma'ili-Moqaddam, Mohammad-Reza	2000–2004	Qom, Qom

Name	Tenure	City and province of constituency
Esma'ilzadeh, Habibollah	2000–2004	Falavarjan, Isfahan
Etaa't, Javad	2001–4	Darab and Zarrindasht, Fars
Farrokhi, Mohammad	2001–4	Jiroft, Kerman
Fattahpur-Mavaneh, Karim	2000–2004	Urmia, West Azerbaijan
Gheyasi-Moradi, Karim	2000–2004	Shabestar, East Azerbaijan
Gol, Azim	2000–2001	Bandar-e Torkaman, Kordkuy, and Bandar-e Gaz, Golestan
Golbaz, Ja'far	2000–2004	Savojblagh, Nazarabad, and Taleqan, Tehran
Golcheshmeh, Naqdi	2001–4	Gonbad-e Kavus, Golestan
Gorzin, Gholam-Reza	2000–2004	Qaemshahr, Savadkuh, and Juybar, Mazandaran
Habibi, Ahmad	2001–4	Bandar-e Abbas, Qeshm, Abumusa, and Hajiabad, Hormozgan
Haddad-Adel, Gholam-Ali	2000–2004	Tehran, Tehran
Hadizadeh, Ali-Asghar	2000–2004	Mahallat and Delijan, Markazi
Haji Baba'i, Hamid-Reza	2000–2004	Hamadan, Hamadan
Hajiyani, Abdollah	2000–2004	Deyr and Kangan, Bushehr
Haqiqatju, Fatemeh	2000–2004	Tehran, Tehran
Hasani, Ali	2001–4	Arak, Markazi
Hasanvand, Fereydun	2000–2004	Andimeshk and Shush, Khuzestan
Hasanzadegan-Rudsari, Davud	2000–2004	Rudsar and Amlash, Gilan
Hashemi, Seyyed Hoseyn	2000–2004	Miyaneh, East Azerbaijan
Hashemi, Seyyed Mohammad	2000–2004	Sirjan and Bardsir, Kerman
Hashemi-Bahremani, Ali	2000–2004	Rafsanjan, Kerman
Hashemzehi, Mas'ud	2000–2002	Khash, Sistan and Baluchestan
Hazrati, Elyas	2000–2004	Tehran, Tehran
Heydarizadi, Abdorreza	2000–2004	Chardavol, Eyvan, Ilam, Mehran, and Shirvan, Ilam
Hezarjaribi, Gholam-Ali	2000–2001	Gorgan, Golestan
Hoseyni, Seyyed Abdollah	2000–2004	Bandar-e Lengeh, Hormozgan
Hoseyni, Seyyed Abolqasem	2000–2004	Bojnurd, North Khorasan
Hoseyni, Seyyed Mansur	2000–2001	Minudasht, Golestan
Hoseyni, Seyyed Mas'ud	2000–2004	Qorveh, Kurdistan
Hoseyni, Seyyed Najib	2001–4	Minudasht, Golestan
Hoseyni-Heydarabadi, Seyyed Sobhan	2001–4	Aq-Qala and Gorgan, Golestan
Hoseyninasab, Seyyed Rajab	2000–2004	Abdanan, Darrehshahr, and Dehloran, Ilam
Hoseynzadeh-Taqiabadi, Shahbaz	2000–2004	Miyandoab, Shahindezh, and Takab, West Azerbaijan
Irannezhad, Abdolghafur	2000–2004	Chabahar, Sistan and Baluchestan
Islamdust-Karbandi, Askar	2000–2004	Talesh, Gilan
Jabbarzadeh, Esma'il	2000–2004	Tabriz, East Azerbaijan
Ja'fari, Ali-Akbar	2000–2004	Saveh, Markazi
Jahandideh, Gholam-Mohammad	2000–2004	Saravan, Sistan and Baluchestan
Jalali, Kazem	2000–2004	Shahrud, Semnan

Name	Tenure	City and province of constituency
Jalalizadeh, Jalal	2000–2004	Divandarreh, Kamyaran, and Sanandaj, Kurdistan
Jama'ati-Malvani, Rasul	2000–2004	Fuman, Gilan
Jelowdarzadeh, Sohayla	2000–2004	Tehran, Tehran
Ka'bi, Abdollah	2000–2004	Abadan, Khuzestan
Kadivar, Jamileh	2000–2004	Tehran, Tehran
Kambuzia, Ja'far	2000–2004	Zahedan, Sistan and Baluchestan
Karrubi, Mehdi	2000–2004	Tehran, Tehran
Kashfi, Seyyed Mansur	2000–2004	Larestan, Fars
Kazem-Dinan, Seyyed Mahmud	2000–2004	Amol, Mazandaran
Kazemi, Mohammad	2000–2004	Malayer, Hamadan
Khabbaz, Mohammad-Reza	2000–2004	Kashmar, Razavi Khorasan
Khaleqi, Naser	2000–2004	Isfahan, Isfahan
Khalili-Ardakani, Mohammad-Hoseyn	2000–2004	Karaj, Tehran
Khamenei, Seyyed Hadi	2000–2004	Tehran, Tehran
Khanzadeh, Mostafa	2001–4	Damavand and Firuzkuh, Tehran
Khasahmadi, Ahmad	2000–2004	Taybad and Torbat-e Jam, Razavi Khorasan
Khastehband, Hasan	2000–2004	Bandar-e Anzali, Gilan
Khatami, Seyyed Mohammad-Reza	2000–2004	Tehran, Tehran
Khatami, Seyyedeh Fatemeh	2000–2004	Mashhad, Razavi Khorasan
Kheyrabadi, Morteza	2000–2004	Sabzevar, Razavi Khorasan
Khodadadi, Salman	2000–2004	Malekan, East Azerbaijan
Khoshro, Seyyed Hasan	2000–2004	Kerman, Kerman
Kiyafar, Mohammad	2000–2004	Miyaneh, East Azerbaijan
Kiyan-Ersi, Asadollah	2000–2004	Faridan and Fereydunshahr, Isfahan
Kiyanush-Rad, Mohammad	2000–2004	Ahvaz, Khuzestan
Kohram, Hamid	2000–2004	Ahvaz, Khuzestan
Kuchaki-Borujeni, Mansur-Mirza	2000–2004	Borujen, Chahar Mahal and Bakhtiari
Kuhsari, Ali	2000–2001	Ramiyan and Azadshahr, Golestan
Kuhsari, Gholam-Ali	2001–2004	Azadshahr and Ramiyan, Golestan
Kula'i, Elaheh	2000–2004	Tehran, Tehran
Kurd, Baqer	2000–2004	Zahedan, Sistan and Baluchestan
Kuzehgar, Mohammad-Ali	2000–2004	Shahriyar and Qods, Tehran
Loqmaniyan, Hoseyn	2000–2004	Hamadan, Hamadan
Mahjub, Ali-Reza	2001–4	Tehran, Tehran
Mar'ashi, Salim	2000–2004	Rudbar, Gilan
Mar'ashi, Seyyed Hoseyn	2000–2004	Kerman, Kerman
Mazru'i, Rajab-Ali	2000–2004	Isfahan, Isfahan
Mehrparvar, Rasul	2000–2004	Dargaz, Razavi Khorasan
Me'mari, Qasem	2000–2004	Ahar, East Azerbaijan
Meydari, Ahmad	2000–2004	Abadan, Khuzestan
Mir Damadi, Mohsen	2000–2004	Tehran, Tehran
Mir Khalili, Seyyed Ali	2001–4	Minab, Hormozgan
Mir Mohammadi, Seyyed Mohammad	2000–2004	Qom, Qom

Name	Tenure	City and province of constituency
Mo'addabpur, Seyyed Mohammad	2000–2002	Rasht, Gilan
Mohammad-Gharibani, Ali	2000–2004	Ardabil, Ardabil
Mohammadi, Mohammad	2000–2004	Selseleh and Delfan, Lorestan
Mohammadi, Mostafa	2000–2004	Paveh and Javanrud, Kermanshah
Mohammadi-Jezzi, Amrollah	2000–2004	Borkhar and Meymeh, Isfahan
Mohammad-Reza'i, Mohammad	2000–2004	Bijar, Kurdistan
Mohebbinia, Jahanbakhsh	2000–2004	Miyandoab, Shahindezh, and Takab, West Azerbaijan
Mohseni-Bandpey, Anushiravan	2000–2004	Nowshahr and Chalus, Mazandaran
Mohtashamipur, Seyyed Ali-Akbar	2000–2004	Tehran, Tehran
Mokhtari, Abolqasem	2000–2004	Zabol, Sistan and Baluchestan
Moqaddamizad, Isa	2000–2004	Shadegan, Khuzestan
Moradi, Ahmad	2000–2004	Torqabeh and Chenaran, Razavi Khorasan
Morovvati, Mehrangiz	2002–4	Khalkhal and Kowsar, Ardabil
Mortazavi, Seyyed Mohammad-Kazem	2000–2004	Mehriz, Bafq, Abarkuh, and Khatam , Yazd
Mosavvari-Manesh, Akram	2000–2004	Isfahan, Isfahan
Mo'tamed, Morris	2000–2004	Jewish community (minority)
Movahhed, Seyyed Haji Mohammad	2000–2004	Kohgiluyeh, Kohgiluyeh and Buyer Ahmad
Musavi, Seyyed Afzal	2000–2004	Zanjan and Tarom, Zanjan
Musavi, Seyyed Amrollah	2000–2004	Khomeyn, Markazi
Musavi, Seyyed Jalal	2000–2004	Lamerd, Fars
Musavi, Seyyed Mir Taher	2000–2004	Karaj and Eshtehard, Tehran
Musavi, Seyyed Naser	2000–2004	Ramhormoz and Ramshir, Khuzestan
Musavi [Tabriz], Seyyed Mir Taher	2000–2004	Tabriz, Azarshahr, and Osku, East Azerbaijan
Musaviasl, Mir Gesmat	2000–2004	Germi (Moghan), Ardabil
Musavi-Jahanabad, Seyyed Baqer	2000–2004	Buyer Ahmad, Kohgiluyeh and Buyer Ahmad
Musavi-Kho'ini, Seyyed Ali-Akbar	2000–2004	Tehran, Tehran
Musavinezhad, Seyyed Isa	2000–2004	Khorramabad, Lorestan
Musavi-Ojaq, Seyyed Mojtaba	2000–2004	Kermanshah, Kermanshah
Nabavi, Behzad	2000–2004	Tehran, Tehran
Nabizadeh, Mohammad-Ali	2001–4	Gachsaran, Kohgiluyeh and Buyer Ahmad
Nadimi, Iraj	2000–2004	Lahijan, Gilan
Na'imipur, Mohammad	2000–2004	Tehran, Tehran
Najafnezhad, Meqdad	2000–2004	Babolsar and Bandpay, Mazandaran
Namazi, Ali-Mohammad	2000–2004	Lenjan, Isfahan
Namju, Rahman	2000–2004	Bukan, West Azerbaijan
Nariman, Mohsen	2000–2004	Babol, Mazandaran
Naru'i, Hatam	2000–2004	Bam, Kerman
Naseri, Abdolhoseyn	2001–4	Aq-Qala and Gorgan, Golestan
Naseripur, A'zam	2001–4	Islamabad-e Gharb, Kermanshah
Nateq-Nuri, Ahmad	2000–2004	Nur and Mahmudabad, Mazandaran
Nazari, Ali	2000–2004	Arak, Markazi
Nazariniya, Qodratollah	2000–2000	Kangavar, Kermanshah
Nezamolesalmi, Abdolmohammad	2000–2004	Borujerd, Lorestan

Name	Tenure	City and province of constituency
Noushabadi, Hoseyn	2000–2004	Varamin, Tehran
Nowbakht-Haqiqi, Mohammad-Baqer	2000–2004	Rasht, Gilan
Nowruzzadeh, Seyyed Reza	2000–2004	Esfarayen, North Khorasan
Nuri, Ali-Reza	2000–2002	Tehran, Tehran
Partow, Morovvatollah	2000–2004	Khodabandeh, Zanjan
Piran, Mohammad	2000–2004	Razan, Hamadan
Pirmo'azzen, Nureddin	2000–2004	Ardabil, Nir, and Namin, Ardabil
Pishbin, Ahmad	2000–2004	Baft, Kerman
Purfatemi, Seyyed Mohammad-Mehdi	2000–2004	Dashti and Tangestan, Bushehr
Purjazayeri, Samir	2000–2004	Khorramshahr, Khuzestan
Purnejati, Ahmad	2000–2004	Tehran, Tehran
Qanbari-Adivi, Ali	2000–2004	Ardal, Farsan, and Kiyar, Chahar Mahal and Bakhtiari
Qandehari, Qorbanali	2000–2001	Gorgan, Golestan
Qasemzadeh, Hoseyn-Ali	2000–2004	Babol, Mazandaran
Qashqavi, Hasan	2000–2004	Robat Karim, Tehran
Qavami, Seyyed Naser	2000–2004	Qazvin, Qazvin
Qobadi, Khodadad	2000–2004	Eqlid, Fars
Qomi, Mohammad	2000–2004	Pakdasht, Tehran
Qorbani, Musa	2000–2004	Qaenat, South Khorasan
Rahbari, Ahmad	2000–2004	Garmsar, Semnan
Rahmani, Rajab	2000–2004	Takestan, Qazvin
Rahmani-Khalili, Ali-Asghar	2000–2004	Behshahr, Mazandaran
Ra'isi-Naf'chi, Mohammad	2000–2004	Shahrekord, Chahar Mahal and Bakhtiari
Rake'i, Fatemeh	2000–2004	Tehran, Tehran
Ramezanianpur, Hasan	2000–2004	Shahreza, Isfahan
Ramezanpur-Nargesi, Ahmad	2000–2004	Rasht, Gilan
Ranjbar-Chubeh, Mohammad-Taqi	2000–2004	Sowme'eh Sara, Gilan
Rashidian, Mohammad	2000–2004	Abadan, Khuzestan
Rayat, Vali	2000–2004	Qaemshahr, Savadkuh, and Juybar, Mazandaran
Razavi, Seyyed Abolfazl	2000–2004	Na'in, Isfahan
Razavi, Seyyed Mohammad	2000–2004	Yazd, Yazd
Rebosheh, Mohammad	2000–2004	Iranshahr, Sistan and Baluchestan
Reza'i, Omidvar	2000–2004	Masjed Soleyman, Khuzestan
Rezazadeh-Shiraz, Tahereh	2000–2004	Shiraz, Fars
Rustatasuji, Sa'dollah	2000–2004	Sarvestan, Kherameh, and Karbal, Fars
Ruzbehi, Hoseyn	2000–2004	Sari, Mazandaran
Saberi, Fakhreddin	2000–2004	Tonekabon and Ramsar, Mazandaran
Sa'da'i-Jahromi, Mohammad-Ali	2000–2004	Jahrom, Fars
Sadeqi, Mohammad-Sadeq	2000–2001	Aliabad Katul, Golestan
Sadiqi-Bonabi, Rasul	2000–2004	Bonab, East Azerbaijan
Sa'edi, Mohammad-Reza	2000–2004	Tehran, Tehran
Sa'edi, Seyyed Jasem	2000–2004	Shush, Khuzestan

Name	Tenure	City and province of constituency
Safa'i, Zabihollah	2000–2004	Asadabad, Hamadan
Safa'i-Farahani, Mohsen	2000–2004	Tehran, Tehran
Saleh-Jalali, Reza	2000–2004	Astaneh-ye Ashrafiyyeh, Gilan
Salehi-Salhchini, Golmohammad	2000–2004	Lordegan, Chahar Mahal and Bakhtiari
Salim-Bahrami, Seyyed Masih	2000–2004	Sari, Mazandaran
Saqqa'i, Mohammad	2000–2004	Neyriz and Estahban, Fars
Sarhaddizadeh, Abolqasem	2000–2004	Tehran, Tehran
Sazegarnezhad, Jalil	2000–2004	Shiraz, Fars
Seyyed Abadi, Hasan	2000–2004	Sabzevar, Razavi Khorasan
Seyyed Aqa Miri, Seyyed Ali	2000–2004	Dezful, Khuzestan
Seyyed Hashemi, Seyyed Mostafa	2000–2004	Maragheh, East Azerbaijan
Seyyed Mahdavi-Aqdam, Seyyed Hamid	2000–2004	Tabriz, East Azerbaijan
Sha'banpur, Hasan	2000–2004	Marvdasht and Arsanjan, Fars
Shadidzadeh, Jasem	2000–2004	Ahvaz, Khuzestan
Shahbazkhani, Bizhan	2000–2004	Malayer, Hamadan
Shahi-Arablu, Mohammad	2000–2004	Hashtrud, East Azerbaijan
Shahrokhi, Seyyed Mohammad-Mehdi	2000–2004	Pol-e Dokhtar and Malavi, Lorestan
Shaikh, Mohammad-Ali	2000–2004	Shushtar, Khuzestan
Shakibi, Seyyed Masha'allah	2000–2004	Tabas and Ferdows, South Khorasan
Shakuri, Abolfazl	2000–2004	Zanjan, Zanjan
Shakurirad, Ali	2000–2004	Tehran, Tehran
Shayesteh, Morteza	2000–2004	Golpayegan and Khansar, Isfahan
Sherdust, Ali-Asghar	2000–2004	Tabriz, East Azerbaijan
Shirzad, Ahmad	2000–2004	Isfahan, Isfahan
Shirzadi, Morteza	2000–2004	Qasr-e Shirin, Sarpol-e Zahab, and Gilan-e Gharb, Kermanshah
Shoja'purian, Valiyollah	2000–2004	Behbahan, Khuzestan
Sobhani, Hasan	2000–2004	Damghan, Semnan
Sohrabi, Abdollah	2000–2004	Marivan, Kurdistan
Soleymani, Behyar	2000–2004	Fasa, Fars
Soleymani, Davud	2000–2004	Tehran, Tehran
Soleymani, Hasan	2001–4	Kangavar, Sahneh, and Harsin, Kermanshah
Soleymani-Meymandi, Mansur	2000–2004	Shahr-e Babak, Kerman
Tabataba'i, Seyyed Mehdi	2000–2004	Abadeh, Bavanat, and Khorrambid, Fars
Tabesh, Mohammad-Reza	2000–2004	Ardakan, Yazd
Taheri, Seyyed Taher	2000–2004	Semnan, Semnan
Taheri-Najafabadi, Mostafa	2000–2004	Najafabad, Tiran, and Karvan, Isfahan
Tajeddin-Khuzani, Abdorrahman	2000–2004	Isfahan, Isfahan
Tajerniya, Ali	2000–2004	Mashhad, Razavi Khorasan
Takaffoli, Gholam-Hoseyn	2000–2004	Mashhad, Razavi Khorasan
Tala'inik, Reza	2000–2004	Bahar and Kabudarahang, Hamadan
Taleqani, Vahideh	2000–2004	Tehran, Tehran
Taqi'zadeh, Ali	2001–4	Khoy and Chaypareh, West Azerbaijan

Name	Tenure	City and province of constituency
Tatari, Esma'il	2000–2004	Kermanshah, Kermanshah
Tavakkoli-Tabazavareh, Seyyed Valiyollah	2000–2004	Ardestan, Isfahan
Tayyar, Atrak	2000–2001	Gonbad-e Kavus, Golestan
Tofiqi, Hasan	2000–2004	Kashan, Aran, and Bidgol, Isfahan
Torkashvand, Mohsen	2000–2004	Tuyserkan, Hamadan
Vahhabi, Seyyed Shamseddin	2000–2004	Tehran, Tehran
Vahid-Mehrjerdi, Sarajeddin	2000–2004	Taft, Yazd
Vahidi, Ramezan	2000–2004	Bojnurd and Jajarm, Northern Khorasan
Valipur, Naz-Mohammad	2001–4	Bandar-e Torkaman, Bandar-e Gaz, and Kord-kuy, Golestan
Vaziri, Mokhtar	2000–2004	Kahnuj, Kerman
Yari, Ali	2000–2004	Ilam, Eyvan, Mehran, Malekshahi, Shirvan, and Chardavol, Ilam
Yasrebi, Seyyed Ali-Mohammad	2000–2004	Qom, Qom
Yeganli, Mir Mahmud	2000–2004	Urmia, West Azerbaijan
Yusefiyan, Reza	2000–2004	Shiraz, Fars
Zafarzadeh, Ali	2000–2004	Mashhad, Razavi Khorasan
Zahmatkesh, Hasan	2000–2004	Astara, Gilan
Zakeri, Mohammad-Baqer	2000–2004	Quchan, Razavi Khorasan
Zolqadr, Seyyed Mostafa	2001–4	Bandar-e Abbas, Hormozgan

Deputies in the Seventh Majlis (2004–8)

Name	Tenure	City and province of constituency
Abbasi, Asadollah	2004–8	Rudsar and Amlash, Gilan
Abbasi, Mohammad	2004–6	Aq-Qala and Gorgan, Golestan
Abbasi, Seyyed Hasan	2004–8	Delijan and Mahallat, Markazi
Abbaspur, Mohammad	2004–8	Urmia, West Azerbaijan
Abbaspur-Tehranifard, Ali	2004–8	Tehran, Tehran
Abdollahi, Reza	2004–8	Mahneshan and Ijrood, Zanjan
Abtahi, Seyyed Mahmud	2004–8	Khomeinishahr, Isfahan
Abutaleb, Sa'id	2004–8	Tehran, Tehran
Abutorabifard, Seyyed Mohammad-Hasan	2004–8	Qazvin, Qazvin
Afarideh, Hoseyn	2004–5	Shiravan, North Khorasan
Afrugh, Emad	2004–8	Tehran, Tehran
Afshari, Ali	2004–8	Semirom, Isfahan
Ahmadi, Ahmad	2004–8	Tehran, Tehran
Ahmadi, Ali	2004–8	Mamasani, Fars
A'inparast, Ja'far	2004–8	Mahabad, West Azerbaijan
Ajorlu, Fatemeh	2004–8	Karaj, Tehran
Akhavan-Bitaraf, Nayyereh	2004–8	Isfahan, Isfahan
Akhtari, Abbas-Ali	2004–8	Tehran, Tehran

Name	Tenure	City and province of constituency
Alami, Akbar	2004–8	Azarshahr, Osku, and Tabriz, East Azerbaijan
Alikhani, Mohammad	2004–8	Abyek and Qazvin, Qazvin
Alikhani, Qodratollah	2004–8	Avaj and Bu'inzahra, Qazvin
Allahyari, Abbas-Ali	2004–8	Kermanshah, Kermanshah
Alya, Fatemeh	2004–8	Tehran, Tehran
Amini, Jahanbakhsh	2004–8	Kermanshah, Kermanshah
Amini, Mas'ud	2004–8	Estahban and Neyriz, Fars
Aminzadeh, Elham	2004–8	Tehran, Tehran
Amir-Hasankhani, Mohammad-Reza	2004–8	Ferdows and Tabas, South Khorasan
Amiri-Khamkani, Hoseyn	2004–8	Zarand, Kerman
Ansari, Mohammad-Sa'id	2004–8	Abadan, Khuzestan
Aqa Hoseyni-Tabataba'i, Seyyed Hasan	2004–8	Zabol, Sistan and Baluchestan
Aqa'i-Moghanjuqi, Ali-Akbar	2004–8	Salmas, West Azerbaijan
Ariyanmanesh, Javad	2004–8	Mashhad and Kalat, Razavi Khorasan
Arjomand, Seyyed Jamaleddin	2004–8	Jahrom, Fars
Asgari, Teymurali	2004–8	Mashhad and Kalat, Razavi Khorasan
Ashtiyani-Araqi, Reza	2004–8	Qom, Qom
Ashuri-Qal'erudkhani, Naser	2004–8	Fuman and Shaft, Gilan
Ashuri-Tazyani, Mohammad	2004–8	Abumusa, Bandar-e Abbas, Hajiabad, and Qeshm, Hormozgan
Attarzadeh, Shokrollah	2004–8	Bushehr, Deylam, and Genaveh, Bushehr
Ava'i, Seyyed Ahmad	2004–5	Dezful, Khuzestan
Azar, Adel	2004–8	Abdanan, Darrehshahr, and Dehloran, Ilam
Azarvash, Vali	2004–8	Ardabil, Namin, and Nir, Ardabil
Azizi, Qasem	2004–8	Shazand, Markazi
Baghbaniyan, Ali	2004–8	Natanz, Niyasar, and Qamsar, Isfahan
Bahonar, Mohammad-Reza	2004–8	Kerman, Kerman
Bahrami, Mohammad-Baqer	2004–8	Asadabad, Hamadan
Bahrami-Ahmadi, Hamid	2004–8	Rafsanjan, Kerman
Bameri, Golmohammad	2005–8	Iranshahr and Sarbaz, Sistan and Baluchestan
Bana'i-Qomi, Ali	2004–8	Qom, Qom
Barmak, Bayromgaldi	2004–8	Galikash, Kalaleh, Maraveh Tappeh, and Minudasht, Golestan
Barzegar-Tekmehdash, Taher Aqa	2004–8	Bostanabad, East Azerbaijan
Bayat, Raf'at	2004–8	Zanjan, Zanjan
Beglarian, Robert	2004–8	Armenians of southern Iran (minority)
Betkiliya, Yonaten	2004–8	Assyrians and Chaldeans (minority)
Bolukiyan, Ahmad	2004–8	Kashmar, Razavi Khorasan
Borujerdi, Alaeddin	2004–8	Borujerd, Lorestan
Bozorgiyan, Ahmad	2004–8	Sabzevar, Razavi Khorasan
Danesh-Ja'fari, Davud	2004–5	Tehran, Tehran
Danesh-Monfared, Ali	2004–8	Tafresh, Markazi
Daneshyar, Kamal	2004–8	Bandar-e Mahshahr, Khuzestan

Name	Tenure	City and province of constituency
Dehqani-Nughandar, Mohammad	2004–8	Torqabeh and Chenaran, Razavi Khorasan
Delkhosh-Abatary, Seyyed Kazem	2004–8	Sowme'eh Sara, Gilan
Dini, Valiyollah	2004–8	Ahar, East Azerbaijan
Dirbaz, Ali	2004–8	Bandar-e Abbas, Hormozgan
Dogani-Aghchelu, Mohammad-Hasan	2004–8	Fasa, Fars
Dustmohammadi, Hadi	2004–8	Semnan, Semnan
Ebadi, Seyyed Ali-Reza	2004–8	Birjand, South Khorasan
Eftekhari, Laleh	2004–8	Tehran, Tehran
Elyasi, Bahman	2004–8	Koliyayi and Sonqor, Kermanshah
Elyasi, Golmohammad	2004–8	Varzaqan, East Azerbaijan
Emami-Rad, Ali	2004–8	Kuhdasht, Lorestan
Esma'ili, Ghaffar	2004–8	Hashtrud, East Azerbaijan
Esma'ilzadeh, Habibollah	2004–8	Falavarjan, Isfahan
Estaki, Mohammad-Hoseyn	2004–8	Isfahan, Isfahan
Eyri, Mohammad-Qoli Haji	2004–8	Bandar-e Gaz, Bandar-e Toraman, and Kord-kuy, Golestan
Fahimi-Giglu, Soleyman	2004–8	Bilehsavar and Parsabad, Ardabil
Faker, Mohammad-Reza	2004–8	Mashhad, Razavi Khorasan
Falahatpisheh, Heshmatollah	2004–8	Islamabad-e Gharb, Kermanshah
Farhangi, Mohammad-Hoseyn	2004–8	Tabriz, Adarshahr, and Osku, East Azerbaijan
Fathipur, Arsalan	2004–8	Kaleybar, Hurand, Khoda Afarin, and Abish Ahmad, East Azerbaijan
Fattahi, Abed	2004–8	Urmia, West Azerbaijan
Fayyazbakhsh, Nafiseh	2004–8	Tehran, Tehran
Fazlali, Morteza	2004–8	Tuyserkan, Hamadan
Feda'i-Ashiyani, Hoseyn	2004–8	Tehran, Tehran
Foruzesh, Peyman	2004–8	Zahedan, Sistan and Baluchestan
Fuladgar, Hamid-Reza	2004–8	Isfahan, Isfahan
Gerami-Moqaddam, Esma'il	2004–8	Bojnurd, Jajarm, Maneh and Samalqan, Northern Khorasan
Geranmayeh, Ali-Asghar	2004–8	Aran, Bidgol, and Kashan, Isfahan
Ghafurifard, Hasan	2007–8	Tehran, Tehran
Ghazanfarabadi, Musa	2006–8	Bam, Kerman
Gheyasi-Moradi, Karim	2004–8	Shabestar, East Azerbaijan
Habibi, Bahram	2004–8	Khomeyn, Markazi
Habibzadeh-Bukani, Anvar	2004–8	Bukan, West Azerbaijan
Haddad-Adel, Gholam-Ali	2004–8	Tehran, Tehran
Haji Baba'i, Hamid-Reza	2004–8	Hamadan, Hamadan
Hakimi, Ataollah	2004–8	Rudbar, Gilan
Hamidi, Hushang	2004–8	Divandarreh, Kamyaran, and Sanandaj, Kurdistan
Haqshenas, Hadi	2004–8	Bandar-e Anzali, Gilan
Hasani-Bafrani, Hoseyn	2004–8	Na'in, Isfahan
Hasanvand, Fathollah	2004–8	Khorramabad, Lorestan

Name	Tenure	City and province of constituency
Hasanvand, Fereydun	2004–8	Andimeshk and Shush, Khuzestan
Hasanvand, Mahmud-Reza	2004–8	Delfan and Selseleh, Lorestan
Hashemi, Seyyed Hoseyn	2004–8	Miyaneh, East Azerbaijan
Hashemi-R'iseh, Seyyed Mostafa	2004–8	Shahr-e Babak, Kerman
Hayati, Mohammad-Ali	2004–8	Lamerd and Mohr, Fars
Hedayatkhah, Sattar	2004–8	Buyer Ahmad and Dena, Kohgiluyeh and Buyer Ahmad
Hejazifar, Hashem	2004–8	Khoy, West Azerbaijan
Hemmati, Fereydun	2004–8	Eyvan, Ilam, Malekshahi, Mehran, and Shirvan, Ilam
Heydari, Fakhreddin	2004–8	Saqqez and Baneh, Kurdistan
Heydari-Shelmani, Mohammad-Ali	2004–8	Langarud, Gilan
Heydarpur-Shahrezai, Avaz	2004–8	Semirom and Shahreza, Isfahan
Hoseyni, Seyyed Abdollah	2004–8	Bandar-e Lengeh, Hormozgan
Hoseyni, Seyyed Bohlul	2004–8	Miyaneh, East Azerbaijan
Hoseyni, Seyyed Emad	2006–8	Qorveh, Kurdistan
Hoseyni, Seyyed Hoseyn	2004–8	Fariman, Razavi Khorasan
Hoseyni, Seyyed Jalal	2004–8	Tarom and Zanjan, Zanjan
Hoseyni-Dowlatabad, Seyyed Mahmud	2004–8	Borkhar, Meymeh, and Shahinshahr, Isfahan
Hoseyni-Heydarabadi, Seyyed Sobhan	2004–8	Aq-Qala and Gorgan, Golestan
Hoseyni-Zeydabadi, Seyyed Ahmad	2004–8	Sirjan, Kerman
Imani, Qodratollah	2004–8	Khorramabad, Lorestan
Irannezhad, Abdolghafur	2004–8	Chabahar, Sistan and Baluchestan
Islami, Hoseyn	2004–8	Saveh and Zarandieh, Markazi
Jabbarzadeh, Esma'il	2004–8	Tabriz, East Azerbaijan
Ja'fari, Ali-Morad	2005–8	Basht and Gachsaran, Kohgiluyeh and Buyer Ahmad
Ja'farzadeh, Soleyman	2004–8	Chaldoran and Maku, West Azerbaijan
Jahangirzadeh, Javad	2004–8	Urmia, West Azerbaijan
Jalali, Kazem	2004–8	Shahrud, Semnan
Jalali-Ja'fari, Rashid	2004–8	Eshtehard and Karaj, Tehran
Jamshidi-Ardeshiri, Mohammad-Hasan	2004–8	Behshahr, Mazandaran
Jasemi, Seyyed Heshmatollah	2004–8	Gilan-e Gharb, Qasr-e Shirin, and Sarpol-e Zahab, Kermanshah
Jelowdarzadeh, Sohayla	2006–8	Tehran, Tehran
Joyjeri, Shabib	2006–8	Ahvaz, Khuzestan
Ka'bi, Abdollah	2004–8	Abadan, Khuzestan
Kalhor, Abolfazl	2004–8	Shahriyar, Tehran
Kamran-Dastjerdi, Hasan	2004–8	Isfahan, Isfahan
Karami, Gholam-Reza	2004–8	Kerman and Ravar, Kerman
Karami, Morteza	2004–4	Eyvan, Ilam, Malekshahi, Mehran, and Shirvan, Ilam
Karimi, Mohammad-Ali	2004–8	Marivan, Kurdistan
Karimiyan, Mohammad	2004–8	Sardasht and Piranshahr, West Azerbaijan

Name	Tenure	City and province of constituency
Karkhaneh'i, Ebrahim	2004–8	Famenin and Hamadan, Hamadan
Katuziyan, Hamid-Reza	2004–8	Tehran, Tehran
Kaviyani, Mohammad-Taqi	2004–8	Nahavand, Hamadan
Khadem-Azghadi, Amir-Reza	2004–8	Tehran, Tehran
Khaliltahmasebi, Zadali	2004–8	Lordegan, Chahar Mahal and Bakhtiari
Khasahmadi, Ahmad	2004–8	Torbat-e Jam and Taybad, Razavi Khorasan
Khodadadi, Salman	2004–8	Malekan, East Azerbaijan
Khoshchehreh, Mohammad	2004–8	Tehran, Tehran
Kuchakzadeh, Mehdi	2004–8	Tehran, Tehran
Kuhkan-Rizi, Mohsen	2004–8	Lenjan, Isfahan
Madani-Bajestani, Seyyed Mahmud	2004–8	Gonabad, Razavi Khorasan
Mahdavi-Abhari, Ahmad	2004–8	Abhar, Zanjan
Mahjub, Ali-Reza	2004–8	Tehran, Tehran
Maleki, Vali	2004–8	Meshginshahr, Ardabil
Mansuri-Razi, Moradali	2004–8	Ramiyan and Azadshahr, Golestan
Maqniyan, Mohammad-Ali	2004–8	Bijar, Kurdistan
Marama'i, Mohammad-Qoli	2004–8	Gonbad-e Kavus, Golestan
Marhaba, Shapur	2004–8	Astara, Gilan
Maturzadeh, Mostafa	2004–8	Khorramshahr, Khuzestan
Mesbahi-Moqaddam, Gholam-Reza	2004–8	Tehran, Tehran
Mesri, Abdorreza	2004–6	Kermanshah, Kermanshah
Mir Mohammadi, Seyyed Mohammad	2004–8	Qom, Qom
Mir Morad-Zehi, Hedayatollah	2004–8	Saravan, Sistan and Baluchestan
Mir Tajeddini, Seyyed Mohammad-Reza	2004–8	Tabriz, Osku and Azarshahr, East Azerbaijan
Mirza'i, Gholam-Reza	2004–8	Borujen, Chahar Mahal and Bakhtiari
Mo'addabpur, Seyyed Mojtaba	2004–8	Rasht, Gilan
Mo'allemipur, Ali	2004–8	Minab, Rudan, and Jask, Hormozgan
Moayyedi, Ali	2004–8	Sepidan, Fars
Mofatteh, Mohammad-Mehdi	2004–8	Razan, Hamadan
Mohammadi, Bahman	2004–8	Faridan, Fereydunshahr, and Chadegan, Isfahan
Mohammadi, Mahmud	2004–8	Abadeh, Bavanat, and Khorrambid, Fars
Mohammadi, Mostafa	2004–8	Paveh and Javanrud, Kurdistan
Mohammad-Sadeqi, Shahin	2004–8	Kazerun, Fars
Mohammadyari, Bahman	2004–8	Talesh, Gilan
Mohassel-Hamadani, Seyyed Mohammad-Taqi	2004–8	Taft, Yazd
Mohebbi, Yusef	2004–8	Larestan, Fars
Mohebbinia, Jahanbakhsh	2004–8	Miyandoab, Shahindezh, and Takab, West Azerbaijan
Mohseni-Bandpey, Anushiravan	2004–8	Nowshahr and Chalus, Mazandaran
Mokhtari, Abolqasem	2004–8	Zabol, Sistan and Baluchestan
Molla Nezam-Molla Hoveyzeh, Seyyed Nezam	2004–8	Dasht-e Azadegan, Khuzestan
Moradi, Hasan	2004–8	Arak and Komijan, Markazi
Morovvati, Mehrangiz	2004–8	Khalkhal and Kowsar, Ardabil

Name	Tenure	City and province of constituency
Mortazavi-Farasani, Seyyed Qobad	2004–8	Ardal, Farsan, Kuhrang, and Kiyar, Chahar Mahal and Bakhtiari
Moshiri, Shahriyar	2005–8	Bandar-e Abbas, Qeshm, Abumusa, Hajiabad, and Khamir, Hormozgan
Mo'tamed, Morris	2004–8	Jewish community (minority)
Mottaki, Manouchehr	2004–5	Tehran, Tehran
Movahhed, Seyyed Haji Mohammad	2004–8	Kohgiluyeh, Kohgiluyeh and Buyer Ahmad
Mozaffar, Hoseyn	2004–7	Tehran, Tehran
Mozaffari, Gholam-Hoseyn	2004–8	Neyshabur, Razavi Khorasan
Musavi, Seyyed Ahmad	2004–5	Ahvaz, Khuzestan
Musavi, Seyyed Fazlollah	2004–8	Tehran, Tehran
Musavi, Seyyed Morteza	2004–8	Aligudarz, Lorestan
Musavi, Seyyed Naser	2004–8	Ramhormoz and Ramshir, Khuzestan
Musavi-Sarcheshmeh, Seyyed Yunes	2004–8	Firuzabad, Qir, and Karzi, Fars
Nabizadeh, Mohammad-Ali	2004–4	Gachsaran, Kohgiluyeh and Buyer Ahmad
Naderan, Elyas	2004–8	Tehran, Tehran
Nadimi, Iraj	2004–8	Lahijan and Siyahkal, Gilan
Naseri, Ali-Akbar	2004–8	Babol, Mazandaran
Naserinezhad, Majid	2004–8	Shadegan, Khuzestan
Nasiri, Naser	2004–8	Germi (Moghan), Ardabil
Nateq-Nuri, Ahmad	2004–8	Mahmudabad and Nur, Mazandaran
Nejabat, Hoseyn	2004–8	Tehran, Tehran
Ne'matzadeh-Qarakhiyali, Qorbanali	2004–8	Qaemshahr, Savadkuh, and Juybar, Mazandaran
Nezhad-Fallah, Mohammad-Hoseyn	2004–8	Savojblagh, Nazarabad, and Taleqan, Tehran
Nikfar, Ahmad	2004–8	Eqlid, Fars
Niknam, Kurosh	2004–8	Zoroastrian community (minority)
Nirumand, Seyyed Mohammad-Sadeq	2004–8	Nehbandan and Sarbisheh, South Khorasan
No'i-Aqdam, Nureddin	2004–8	Ardabil, Ardabil
Noushabadi, Hoseyn	2004–8	Varamin, Tehran
Nowruzzadeh, Seyyed Reza	2004–8	Esfarayen, North Khorasan
Paknezhad, Seyyed Abbas	2004–8	Yazd, Yazd
Papi, Hoseyn	2004–8	Dorud and Azna, Lorestan
Pashang, Hamid-Reza	2004–8	Khash, Mirjaveh, Mosratabad, Kurin, and Nokabad, Sistan and Baluchestan
Pirmo'azzen, Nureddin	2004–8	Ardabil, Nir, and Namin, Ardabil
Pishbin, Ahmad	2004–8	Baft, Kerman
Purfatemi, Seyyed Mohammad-Mehdi	2004–8	Dashti and Tangestan, Bushehr
Purzaman, Rasul	2004–8	Naqadeh, West Azerbaijan
Qamari, Daryush	2005–8	Ilam, Eyvan, Mehran, Malekshahi, Shirvan, and Chardavol, Ilam
Qarhekhani-Alustani, Asadollah	2004–8	Aliabad Katul, Golestan
Qasemzadeh, Hoseyn-Ali	2004–8	Babol, Mazandaran
Qobadi-Hamzehkhani, Ali-Akbar	2004–8	Marvdasht and Arsanjan, Fars

Name	Tenure	City and province of constituency
Qomi, Mohammad	2004–8	Pakdasht, Tehran
Qorbani, Musa	2004–8	Qaenat, South Khorasan
Rabbani-Shirazi, Mohammad-Hadi	2004–8	Shiraz, Fars
Rahbar, Fatemeh	2004–8	Tehran, Tehran
Rahbar, Mohammad-Taqi	2004–8	Isfahan, Isfahan
Raheb, Ja'farqoli	2004–8	Tonekabon and Ramsar, Mazandaran
Rahmani, Rajab	2004–8	Takestan, Qazvin
Rahmani, Reza	2004–8	Tabriz, Osku, and Azarshahr, East Azerbaijan
Raja'i, Abbas	2004–8	Arak and Komijan, Markazi
Rastad, Abdolmohammad	2004–8	Darab, Fars
Rasulinezhad, Seyyed Ahmad	2004–8	Damavand and Firuzkuh, Tehran
Rayat, Vali	2004–8	Qaemshahr, Savadkuh, and Juybar, Mazandaran
Razmiyan-Moqaddam, Hasan	2004–8	Dargaz, Razavi Khorasan
Reyaz, Seyyed Ali	2004–8	Tehran, Tehran
Reza'i, Omidvar	2004–8	Masjed Soleyman and Haftkel, Khuzestan
Rostami-Sani, Abbas-Ali	2004–8	Quchan and Faruj, Razavi Khorasan
Rudaki, Mohammad-Nabi	2004–8	Shiraz, Fars
Ruhi, Hojjatollah	2005–8	Babolsar, Mazandaran
Ruhi-Sarokhkala'i, Abolqasem	2004–8	Sari, Mazandaran
Sa'dunzadeh, Javad	2004–8	Abadan, Khuzestan
Sa'adat, Hamid	2004–8	Najafabad, Tiran, and Karvan, Isfahan
Sadat-Musavi, Seyyed Mohammad-Ja'far	2004–8	Mobarakeh, Isfahan
Sadeq-Daqiqi, Kiyanush	2004–8	Astaneh-ye Ashrafiyyeh, Gilan
Sadeqzadeh, Ramezan-Ali	2004–8	Rasht, Gilan
Sadiqi-Bonabi, Rasul	2004–8	Bonab, East Azerbaijan
Sa'edi, Seyyed Jasem	2004–8	Shush, Khuzestan
Sajjadiyan, Mohammad-Reza	2004–8	Khaf and Roshtkhar , Razavi Khorasan
Salehi, Qeysar	2004–8	Deyr, Jam, and Kangan, Bushehr
San'ati-Mehraban, Amir	2004–8	Sarab and Mehraban, East Azerbaijan
Sarafraz-Yazdi, Ali	2004–8	Mashhad and Kalat, Razavi Khorasan
Sarvari, Parviz	2004–8	Tehran, Tehran
Servati, Musarreza	2004–8	Bojnurd, Maneh, Samalqan, and Jajarm, North Khorasan
Seyyed Abadi, Hasan	2004–8	Sabzevar, Razavi Khorasan
Seyyed Hashemi, Seyyed Mostafa	2004–8	Maragheh, East Azerbaijan
Sha'bani, Amin	2004–8	Sanandaj, Divandarreh, and Kamyaran, Kurdistan
Shafei, Karim	2005–8	Marand, East Azerbaijan
Shahbazkhani, Bizhan	2004–8	Malayer, Hamadan
Shahi-Arablu, Mohammad	2004–8	Robat Karim, Tehran
Shahriyari, Hoseyn-Ali	2004–8	Zahedan, Sistan and Baluchestan
Shahrokhi, Seyyed Mohammad-Mehdi	2004–8	Pol-e Dokhtar and Malavi, Lorestan
Shaikh, Mohammad-Ali	2004–8	Shushtar, Khuzestan

Name	Tenure	City and province of constituency
Shaikholislam, Hoseyn	2004–8	Tehran, Tehran
Shari'ati-Kohbani, Effat	2004-8	Mashhad and Kalat, Razavi Khorasan
Shayeq, Eshrat	2004-8	Tabriz, Osku, and Azarshahr, East Azerbaijan
Shoja', Seyyed Abdolmajid	2004-8	Dashtestan, Bushehr
Shoja'ei-Kiyasari, Seyyed Hasan	2004-8	Sari, Mazandaran
Shoja'purian, Valiyollah	2004-8	Behbahan, Khuzestan
Sobhani, Hasan	2004-8	Damghan, Semnan
Sobhaninia, Hoseyn	2004-8	Neyshabur, Razavi Khorasan
Soleymani, Hasan	2004-8	Kangavar, Sahneh, and Harsin, Kermanshah
Soltani, Mohammad	2004-8	Khodabandeh, Zanjan
Sudani, Naser	2004-8	Ahvaz, Khuzestan
Tabataba'i, Seyyed Hadi	2004-8	I'zeh and Baghmalek, Khuzestan
Tabataba'inezhad, Seyyed Mostafa	2004-8	Ardestan, Isfahan
Tabataba'i-Shirazi, Seyyed Mohammad-Mehdi	2004-8	Tehran, Tehran
Tabe'-Miyandoab, Asadollah	2004-8	Miyandoab and Takab, West Azerbaijan
Tabesh, Mohammad-Reza	2004-8	Ardakan, Yazd
Tahmasebi-Sarvestani, Zeynol'abedin	2004-8	Sarvestan and Kavar, Fars
Tahriri-Niksefat, Hajar	2004-8	Rasht, Gilan
Tala'inik, Reza	2004-8	Bahar and Kabudarahang, Hamadan
Tamaddon, Morteza	2004-8	Shahrekord, Chahar Mahal and Bakhtiari
Tavakkoli, Ahmad	2004-8	Tehran, Tehran
Tavassolizadeh, Mohammad-Naser	2004-8	Torbat-e Heydariyyeh, Razavi Khorasan
Torabi, Abdorreza	2006–8	Garmsar, Semnan
Vardan, Gevorg	2004-8	Armenians of northern Iran (minority)
Vaziri, Mokhtar	2004-8	Kahnuj, Kerman
Yahyavi, Seyyed Mohsen	2004-8	Borujerd, Lorestan
Yahyazadeh-Firozabad, Seyyed Jalal	2004-8	Taft and Meybod, Yazd
Yavari, Mansur	2004-8	Golpayegan and Khansar, Isfahan
Yusefiyan-Mola, Ezzatollah	2004-8	Amol, Mazandaran
Zadsar-Jirofti, Ali	2004-8	Jiroft, Kerman
Zakani, Ali-Reza	2004-8	Tehran, Tehran
Zamanifar, Hasan-Reza	2004-8	Malayer, Hamadan
Zangeneh, Hamid	2004-8	Ahvaz, Khuzestan
Zolanvar, Seyyed Hoseyn	2004-8	Shiraz, Fars

Deputies in the Eighth Majlis (2008–12)

Name	Tenure	City and province of constituency
Abbasi, Asadollah	2008–12	Amlash and Rudsar, Gilan
Abbaspur-Tehranifard, Ali	2008–12	Tehran, Tehran
Abdollahi, Reza	2008–12	Mahneshan and Ijrood, Zanjan
Abedi, Mohammad-Karim	2008–12	Ferdows, Sarayan, and Tabas, South Khorasan
Abtahi, Seyyed Mohammad-Javad	2008–12	Khomeinishahr, Isfahan

Name	Tenure	City and province of constituency
Abutorabifard, Seyyed Mohammad-Hasan	2008–12	Qazvin, Qazvin
Adiyanirad, Seyyed Ali	2008–12	Juybar, Qaemshahr, and Savadkuh, Mazandaran
Afshari, Mohammad-Mehdi	2008–12	Darab and Zarrindasht, Fars
Ahmadi-Bighash, Mahmud	2008–12	Shazand, Markazi
Ajorlu, Fatemeh	2008–12	Karaj, Tehran
Akbari-Talarposhti, Ezzatollah	2008–12	Qaemshahr and Savadkuh, Mazandaran
Akbariyan, Aziz	2008–12	Karaj and Eshtehard, Tehran
Akbarnezhad, Shakur	2008–12	Azarshahr, Osku, and Tabriz, East Azerbaijan
Akhavan, Bahman	2008–12	Ashtiyan and Tafresh, Markazi
Akhavan-Bitaraf, Nayyereh	2008–12	Isfahan, Isfahan
Akrami, Seyyed Reza	2008–12	Tehran, Tehran
Alikhani, Qodratollah	2008–12	Qazvin, Qazvin
Alizadeh, Reza	2009–12	Varzaqan, East Azerbaijan
Alya, Fatemeh	2008–12	Tehran, Tehran
Amini, Jahanbakhsh	2008–12	Kermanshah, Kermanshah
Amiri-Kahnuj, Mohammad-Reza	2008–12	Kahnuj, Manujan, Qaleh Ganj, and South Rudbar, Kerman
Amiri-Khamkani, Hoseyn	2008–12	Zarand, Kerman
Ansari, Jamshid	2008–12	Tarom and Zanjan, Zanjan
Aqa Tehrani, Morteza	2008–12	Tehran, Tehran
Aqa Zadeh-Dafsari, Seyyed Ali	2008–12	Rasht, Gilan
Aqa'i-Moghanjuqi, Ali-Akbar	2008–12	Salmas, West Azerbaijan
Ariyanmanesh, Javad	2008–12	Mashhad and Kalat, Razavi Khorasan
Asadi, Yunes	2008–12	Meshginshahr, Ardabil
Asadollahi, Gholam-Reza	2008–12	Torbat-e Jam and Taybad, Razavi Khorasan
Ashtiyani-Araqi, Reza	2008–12	Qom, Qom
Ashuri-Tazyani, Mohammad	2008–12	Abumusa, Bandar-e Abbas, Hajiabad, and Qeshm, Hormozgan
Ava'i, Seyyed Ahmad	2008–12	Dezful, Khuzestan
Babaahmadi-Milani, Abdolmohammad	2009–12	Lordegan, Chahar Mahal and Bakhtiari
Badamchiyan, Asadollah	2008–12	Tehran, Tehran
Bahonar, Mohammad-Reza	2008–12	Tehran, Tehran
Bakhtiari, Mohammad-Taqi	2008–12	Baft, Kerman
Bana'i-Qomi, Ali	2008–12	Qom, Qom
Bashiri, Farhad	2008–12	Pakdasht, Tehran
Bauj-Lahuti, Mehrdad	2008–12	Langarud, Gilan
Beglarian, Robert	2008–12	Armenians of southern Iran (minority)
Betkiliya, Yonaten	2008–12	Assyrians and Chaldeans (minority)
Borna-Boldaji, Sirus	2008–12	Borujen, Chahar Mahal and Bakhtiari
Boroghani, Ali	2008–12	Sabzevar, Razavi Khorasan
Borujerdi, Alaeddin	2008-12	Borujerd, Lorestan
Bozorgvari, Seyyed Ali-Mohammad	2008–12	Bahmai and Kohgiluyeh, Kohgiluyeh and Buyer Ahmad

Name	Tenure	City and province of constituency
Dalqpush, Farhad	2008–12	Astara, Gilan
Dastgheyb [Qom], Seyyed Ahmad-Reza	2008–12	Shiraz, Fars
Dastgheyb [Shiraz], Seyyed Ahmad-Reza	2008–12	Shiraz, Fars
Dehdashti, Seyyed Hoseyn	2008–12	Abadan, Khuzestan
Dehqan, Ezzatollah	2008–12	Dorud, Lorestan
Dehqani, Ali-Reza	2008–12	I'zeh, Khuzestan
Dehqani, Mohammad-Qayyum	2008–12	Iranshahr, Fanuj, Sarbaz, Bent, Lashar, and Ashar, Sistan and Baluchestan
Dehqan-Naserabadi, Gholam-Reza	2008–12	Kazerun, Fars
Dehqani-Nughandar, Mohammad	2008–12	Torqabeh and Chenaran, Razavi Khorasan
Delavar, Mohammad-Ali	2008–12	Dargaz, Razavi Khorasan
Delkhosh-Abatary, Seyyed Kazem	2008–12	Sowme'eh Sara, Gilan
Dogani-Aghchelu, Mohammad-Hasan	2008–12	Fasa, Fars
Ebrahimi, Hoseyn	2008–12	Birjand, South Khorasan
Eftekhari, Laleh	2008–12	Tehran, Tehran
Ekhtiyari, Esfandiyar	2008–12	Zoroastrian community (minority)
Elahiyan, Zohreh	2008–12	Tehran, Tehran
Esma'ili, Ghaffar	2008–12	Hashtrud, East Azerbaijan
Esma'ili, Vali	2008–12	Germi (Moghan), Ardabil
E'zazi-Maleki, Ziyaollah	2008–12	Bonab, East Azerbaijan
Ezzati, Ali	2008–12	Abdanan, Darrehshahr, and Dehloran, Ilam
Faker, Mohammad-Reza	2008–10	Mashhad, Razavi Khorasan
Falahatpisheh, Heshmatollah	2008–12	Islamabad-e Gharb, Kermanshah
Farahmand, Kazem	2008–12	Abarkuh, Bafq, Khatam, and Mehriz, Yazd
Farajzadeh, Mohammad-Amin	2008–12	Abumusa, Bandar-e Abbas, Hajiabad, Khamir, and Qeshm, Hormozgan
Farhangi, Mohammad-Hoseyn	2008–12	Azarshahr, Osku, and Tabriz, East Azerbaijan
Fathipur, Arsalan	2008–12	Kaleybar, Hurand, Khoda Afarin, and Abish Ahmad, East Azerbaijan
Feda'i, Samad	2009–12	Sonqor, Kurdistan
Feda'i-Ashiyani, Hoseyn	2008–12	Tehran, Tehran
Foruzesh, Peyman	2008–12	Zahedan, Sistan and Baluchestan
Fuladgar, Hamid-Reza	2008–12	Isfahan, Isfahan
Garrusi, Hoseyn	2008–12	Shahriyar, Tehran
Geranmayeh, Ali-Asghar	2008–12	Kashan, Aran, and Bidgol, Isfahan
Ghafurifard, Hasan	2008–12	Tehran, Tehran
Ghazanfarabadi, Musa	2008–12	Bam, Kerman
Haddad-Adel, Gholam-Ali	2008–12	Tehran, Tehran
Haji Asghari, Seyyed Mohammad-Reza	2008–12	Miyaneh, East Azerbaijan
Haji Baba'i, Hamid-Reza	2008–9	Hamadan, Hamadan
Hasani, Ali-Asghar	2008–12	Khonj and Larestan, Fars
Hasani-Bafrani, Hoseyn	2008–12	Na'in, Isfahan
Hasanpur-Biglari, Shahbaz	2008–12	Sirjan and Bardsir, Kerman

Name	Tenure	City and province of constituency
Hasanvand, Fereydun	2008–12	Andimeshk and Shush, Khuzestan
Hashemi, Seyyed Enayatolah	2008–12	Sepidan, Fars
Hashemi, Seyyed Hoseyn	2008–12	Miyaneh, East Azerbaijan
Hashemiyan, Hoseyn	2008–12	Rafsanjan, Kerman
Hayati, Mohammad-Ali	2008–10	Lamerd and Mohr, Fars
Hayat-Moqaddam, Khalil	2008–12	Bandar-e Mahshahr, Khuzestan
Hedayatkhah, Sattar	2008–12	Buyer Ahmadazarabad, and Taleqan Tehran
Hejazi, Seyyed Mohammad-Kazem	2008–12	Hamadan, Hamadan
Heydari, Fakhreddin	2008–12	Saqqez and Baneh, Kurdistan
Heydari-Dastena'i, Nurollah	2008–12	Ardal, Chahar Mahal and Bakhtiari
Heydariyan, Mohammad-Hoseyn	2008–8	Sonqor, Kurdistan
Heydarpur-Shahrezai, Avaz	2008–12	Shahreza, Isfahan
Hoseyni, Seyyed Ali	2008–12	Neyshabur, Razavi Khorasan
Hoseyni, Seyyed Emad	2008–12	Qorveh, Kurdistan
Hoseyni, Seyyed Fathollah	2008–12	Paveh and Uramanat, Kermanshah
Hoseyni, Seyyed Hoseyn	2008–12	Sarakhs, Razavi Khorasan
Hoseyni, Seyyed Najib	2008–12	Minudasht, Golestan
Hoseyni, Seyyed Sharif	2008–12	Ahvaz, Khuzestan
Hoseyni-Dowlatabad, Seyyed Mahmud	2008–12	Shahinshahr, Meymeh, and Borkhar, Isfahan
Hoseynipur, Seyyed Qodratollah	2008–12	Gachsaran, Kohgiluyeh and Buyer Ahmad
Hoseyni-Sadr, Mo'ayyed	2008–12	Chaypareh and Khoy, West Azerbaijan
Hoseyniyan, Ruhollah	2008–12	Tehran, Tehran
Hoseynnezhad-Dovin, Mohammad-Reza	2008–12	Shiravan, North Khorasan
Isazadeh, Mehdi	2009–12	Miyandoab, Shahindezh, and Takab, West Azerbaijan
Islami, Hoseyn	2008–11	Saveh and Zarandieh, Markazi
Islamipanah, Ali	2008–12	Anbarabad and Jiroft, Kerman
Jabbari, Ahmad	2008–12	Bandar-e Lengeh, Bastak, and Parsian, Hormozgan
Jadgal, Ya'qub	2008–12	Chabahar, Sistan and Baluchestan
Ja'fari, Behruz	2008–12	Semirom, Isfahan
Ja'fari, Isa	2008–12	Bahar and Kabudarahang, Hamadan
Ja'farzadeh, Soleyman	2008–12	Chaldoran and Maku, West Azerbaijan
Jahangirzadeh, Javad	2008–12	Urmia, West Azerbaijan
Jalali, Kazem	2008–12	Shahrud, Semnan
Jalaliyan, Asgar	2008–12	Deyr, Jam, and Kangan, Bushehr
Jamshidzehi, Abdolaziz	2008–12	Saravan, Sistan and Baluchestan
Jani-Abbaspur, Ruhollah	2008–12	Bu'inzahra, Qazvin
Joygeri, Shabib	2008–12	Ahvaz, Khuzestan
Ka'bi, Abdollah	2008–12	Abadan, Khuzestan
Kaeidi, Ali-Akbar	2008–12	Malavi and Pol-e Dokhtar, Lorestan
Kamaliyan, Nasrollah	2009–12	Faruj and Quchan, Razavi Khorasan
Kamran-Dastjerdi, Hasan	2008–12	Isfahan, Isfahan

Name	Tenure	City and province of constituency
Karami, Abdoljabbar	2008–12	Divandarreh, Kamyaran, and Sanandaj, Kurdistan
Karami, Gholam-Reza	2008–12	Kerman and Ravar, Kerman
Karamirad, Mohammad	2008–12	Kermanshah, Kermanshah
Karimi, Mohammad-Ali	2008–12	Kerman and Ravar, Kerman
Karimi-Firuzjayi, Ali	2008–12	Babol, Mazandaran
Karimi-Qoddusi, Javad	2008–12	Kalat and Mashhad, Razavi Khorasan
Katuziyan, Hamid-Reza	2008–12	Tehran, Tehran
Kavakebiyan, Mostafa	2008–12	Semnan, Semnan
Khabbaz, Mohammad-Reza	2008–12	Kashmar, Razavi Khorasan
Khaleqi, Bashir	2008–12	Khalkhal and Kowsar, Ardabil
Khastehband, Hasan	2008–12	Bandar-e Anzali, Gilan
Kheyri, Ahad	2008–12	Bostanabad, East Azerbaijan
Khodadadi, Salman	2008–12	Malekan, East Azerbaijan
Kikha, Ahmad-Ali	2008–12	Zabol and Zahak, Sistan and Baluchestan
Kowsari, Mohammad-Esma'il	2008–12	Tehran, Tehran
Kuchakinezhad-Eramsadati, Jabar	2008–12	Rasht, Gilan
Kuchakzadeh, Mehdi	2008–12	Tehran, Tehran
Kuhi-Baghanari, Nasrollah	2008–12	Kavar and Sarvestan, Fars
Kuhkan-Rizi, Mohsen	2008–12	Lenjan and Mobarakeh, Isfahan
Larijani, Ali	2008–12	Qom, Qom
Lotfi-Ashtiyani, Seyyed Ahmad	2008–12	Arak and Komijan, Markazi
Mahdavi-Abhari, Ahmad	2008–12	Abhar, Zanjan
Mahjub, Ali-Reza	2008–12	Tehran, Tehran
Mahmudzadeh, Jalal	2008–12	Mahabad, West Azerbaijan
Malekmohammadi, Hasan	2008–12	Damghan, Semnan
Malekshahi, Mohammad-Reza	2008–12	Khorramabad, Lorestan
Mansuri-Razi, Moradali	2008–12	Ramiyan and Azadshahr, Golestan
Marandi, Seyyed Ali-Reza	2008–12	Tehran, Tehran
Mar'ashi, Samad	2008–12	Rudbar, Gilan
Mareh Sedq, Siyamak	2008–12	Jewish community (minority)
Mas'udi-Reyhan, Gholam-Hoseyn	2008–12	Ahar and Haris, East Azerbaijan
Maturzadeh, Mostafa	2008–12	Khorramshahr, Khuzestan
Mehdizadeh, Mehdi	2008–12	Gonabad, Razavi Khorasan
Mesbahi-Moqaddam, Gholam-Reza	2008–12	Tehran, Tehran
Meygolinezhad, Gholam-Ali	2008–12	Bushehr, Genaveh, and Deylam, Bushehr
Mir Khalili, Seyyed Ali	2008–12	Minab, Hormozgan
Mir Tajeddini, Seyyed Mohammad-Reza	2008–9	Tabriz, Osku, and Azarshahr, East Azerbaijan
Mirza'i-Fallahabadi, Ali	2008–12	Fuman and Saft, Gilan
Mofatteh, Mohammad-Mehdi	2008–12	Razan, Hamadan
Mohammadi, Bahman	2008–12	Faridan, Fereydunshahr and Chadegan , Isfahan
Mohammadi, Eqbal	2008–12	Marivan and Sarvabad, Kurdistan
Mohammadi, Mohammad	2008–12	Selseleh and Delfan, Lorestan
Mohammadi, Qasem	2008–12	Ardabil, Namin, and Nir, Ardabil

Name	Tenure	City and province of constituency
Mohammadjani, Davud	2008–12	Abadeh, Bavanat, and Khorrambid, Fars
Mohammadyari, Bahman	2008–12	Talesh, Gilan
Mohebbinia, Jahanbakhsh	2008–12	Miyandoab, Takab, and Shahindezh, West Azerbaijan
Mohseni-Bandpey, Anushiravan	2008–12	Nowshahr and Chalus, Mazandaran
Mohseni-Sani, Mohammad-Reza	2008–12	Sabzevar, Razavi Khorasan
Monadi-Sefidan, Ali-Reza	2008–12	Tabriz, Osku, and Azarshahr, East Azerbaijan
Moqaddasi, Hadi	2008–12	Borujerd, Lorestan
Moqimi, Ahmad-Ali	2008–12	Behshahr, Mazandaran
Moqimi, Mohammad-Hoseyn	2008–12	Khomeyn, Markazi
Moradi, Abdorreza	2008–12	Mamasani, Fars
Moradnia, Bahman	2008–12	Bijar, Kurdistan
Motahhari, Ali	2008–12	Tehran, Tehran
Motahhari-Kuzehkalani, Ali	2008–12	Shabestar, East Azerbaijan
Movahhed, Seyyed Haji Mohammad	2008–12	Behbahan, Khuzestan
Musavi, Seyyed Fazel	2008–12	Khodabandeh, Zanjan
Musavi, Seyyed Kazem	2008–12	Ardabil, Namin, and Nir, Ardabil
Musavi, Seyyed Naser	2008–12	Ramhormoz and Ramshir, Khuzestan
Musavi-Jorf, Seyyed Ali	2008–12	Abadan, Khuzestan
Musavi-Laregani, Seyyed Naser	2008–12	Falavarjan, Isfahan
Musavi-Mobarakeh, Seyyed Ali-Mohammad	2008–12	Mobarakeh, Isfahan
Musavi-Sarcheshmeh, Seyyed Yunes	2008–12	Firuzabad, Farashband, Qir, and Karzin, Fars
Naderan, Elyas	2008–12	Tehran, Tehran
Najafi, Yusef	2008–12	Maragheh and Ajab-Shir, East Azerbaijan
Najafnezhad, Meqdad	2008–12	Babolsar and Fereydunkenar, Mazandaran
Naqavi-Hoseyni, Seyyed Hoseyn	2008–12	Varamin, Tehran
Nariman, Mohsen	2008–12	Babol, Mazandaran
Naseri, Abdolhoseyn	2008–12	Gorgan, Golestan
Naserinezhad, Majid	2008–12	Shadegan, Khuzestan
Nasiri-Qeydari, Sa'dollah	2008–12	Zanjan and Tarom, Zanjan
Nasirpur-Sardeha'i, Majid	2008–12	Sarab, East Azerbaijan
Nateq-Nuri, Ahmad	2008–12	Mahmudabad and Nur, Mazandaran
Nazarimehr, Mohammad-Javad	2008–12	Kordkuy, Torkaman, and Bandar-e Gaz, Golestan
Nejabat, Hoseyn	2008–12	Tehran, Tehran
Nekunam, Mohammad-Ebrahim	2008–12	Golpayegan and Khansar, Isfahan
Nezhad-Fallah, Mohammad-Hoseyn	2008–12	Savojblagh, Nazarabad, and Taleqan, Tehran
Niknam, Abolfath	2008–12	Tonekabon and Ramsar, Mazandaran
Nobaveh, Bizhan	2008–12	Tehran, Tehran
Nowruzi, Hasan	2008–12	Robat Karim, Tehran
Nura, Abbas-Ali	2008–12	Zabol, Sistan and Baluchestan
Osmani, Mohammad-Qasim	2008–12	Bukan, West Azerbaijan
Owlia, Ali-Akbar	2008–12	Yazd and Saduq, Yazd
Papari-Moqaddamfard, Ayyub	2009–12	Dashtestan, Bushehr

Name	Tenure	City and province of constituency
Partovi, Mohammad-Ali	2008–12	Piranshahr, West Azerbaijan
Pashang, Hamid-Reza	2008–12	Khash, Mirjaveh, Nosratabad, Kurin, and Noka-bad, Sistan and Baluchestan
Pezeshkiyan, Mas'ud	2008–12	Tabriz, Osku, and Azarshahr, East Azerbaijan
Puladi, Shapur	2008–12	Ilam, Eyvan, Mehran, Malekshahi, Shirvan, and Chardavol, Ilam
Purfatemi, Seyyed Mohammad-Mehdi	2008–12	Dashti and Tangestan, Bushehr
Qaderi, Ja'far	2008–12	Shiraz, Fars
Qamari, Daryush	2008–12	Ilam, Eyvan, Mehran, Malekshahi, Shirvan, and Chardavol, Ilam
Qarhekhani-Alustani, Asadollah	2008–12	Aliabad Katul, Golestan
Qasemi-Golak, Yusef	2008–12	Lahijan and Siyahkal, Gilan
Qavami, Hadi	2008–12	Esfarayen, North Khorasan
Qazipur, Nader	2008–12	Urmia, West Azerbaijan
Qazizadeh-Hashemi, Seyyed Amir Hoseyn	2008–12	Mashhad and Kalat, Razavi Khorasan
Qorbani, Musa	2008–12	Qaenat, South Khorasan
Rahbar, Fatemeh	2008–12	Tehran, Tehran
Rahbar, Mohammad-Taqi	2008–12	Isfahan, Isfahan
Rahimi, Amin-Hoseyn	2008–12	Malayer, Hamadan
Rahiminasab, Reza	2008–12	Khorramabad, Lorestan
Rahmani, Abolqasem	2008–12	Eqlid, Fars
Rahmani, Hojjatollah	2008–12	Aligudarz, Lorestan
Rahmani, Reza	2008–12	Tabriz, Osku, and Azarshahr, East Azerbaijan
Raja'i, Abbas	2008–12	Arak and Komijan, Markazi
Ramin, Shahrokh	2008–12	Damavand and Firuzkuh, Tehran
Ranjbarzadeh, Akbar	2008–12	Asadabad, Hamadan
Rasa'i, Hamid	2008–12	Tehran, Tehran
Rastegar, Abdollah	2008–12	Gonbad-e Kavus, Golestan
Rezahoseyni-Qotbabadi, Mostafa	2008–12	Shahr-e Babak, Kerman
Reza'i, Mohammad-Ali	2008–12	Torbat-e Heydariyyeh, Razavi Khorasan
Reza'i, Omidvar	2008–12	Masjed Soleyman and Haftkel, Khuzestan
Reza'i-Kuchi, Mohammad-Reza	2008–12	Jahrom, Fars
Sa'adat, Hamid	2008–12	Najafabad, Tiran, and Karvan, Isfahan
Saberi, Mohammad-Reza	2008–12	Nehbandan and Sarbisheh, South Khorasan
Sabur-Aghchekandi, Javad	2008–12	Ardabil, Nir, and Namin, Ardabil
Sadat-Ebrahimi, Seyyed Mohammad	2008–12	Shushtar and Gotvand, Khuzestan
Sadeq, Seyyed Mehdi	2008–12	Astaneh-ye Ashrafiyyeh, Gilan
Sadr, Seyyed Shahabeddin	2008–12	Tehran, Tehran
Sa'edi, Seyyed Jasem	2008–12	Shush, Khuzestan
Safa'i, Tayebeh	2008–12	Tehran, Tehran
Sajjadiyan, Mohammad-Reza	2008–12	Khaf and Roshtkhar, Razavi Khorasan
Salimi, Ali-Reza	2008–12	Mahallat and Delijan, Markazi
Sana'i, Mehdi	2008–12	Nahavand, Hamadan

Name	Tenure	City and province of constituency
Saqqa'i, Mohammad	2008–12	Estahban and Neyriz, Fars
Sarvari, Parviz	2008–12	Tehran, Tehran
Savari, Hashem	2008–12	Dasht-e Azadegan, Khuzestan
Sazdar, Sirus	2008–12	Marand and Jolfa, East Azerbaijan
Sepahajirlu, Vakil	2008–12	Bilehsavar and Parsabad, Ardabil
Servati, Musarreza	2008–12	Bojnurd, Maneh, and Samalqan, and Jajarm, North Khorasan
Sha'bani, Amin	2008–12	Sanandaj, Divandarreh, and Kamyaran, Kurdistan
Sha'bani, Mohammad-Reza	2008–12	Kermanshah, Kermanshah
Sha'banpur, Hasan	2008–12	Marvdasht and Arsanjan, Fars
Shahriyari, Hoseyn-Ali	2008–12	Zahedan, Sistan and Baluchestan
Shahriyari, Mohammad-Mehdi	2008–12	Bojnurd, Maneh, Samalqan, and Jajarm, North Khorasan
Shahrokhi-Qobadi, Ali	2008–12	Kuhdasht, Lorestan
Shahrzad, Mohammad-Karim	2008–12	Isfahan, Isfahan
Shari'ati-Kohbani, Effat	2008–12	Mashhad and Kalat, Razavi Khorasan
Sobhaninia, Hoseyn	2008–12	Neyshabur, Razavi Khorasan
Sudani, Naser	2008–12	Ahvaz, Khuzestan
Tabataba'inezhad, Seyyed Mostafa	2008–12	Ardestan, Isfahan
Tabesh, Mohammad-Reza	2008–12	Ardakan, Yazd
Taheri-Gorgani, Seyyed Ali	2008–12	Gorgan and Aq-Qala, Golestan
Taherkhani, Amir	2008–12	Takestan, Qazvin
Taherpur, Shahriyar	2008–12	Tuyserkan, Hamadan
Tajari, Farhad	2008–12	Qasr-e Shirin, Sarpol-e Zahab, and Gilan-e Gharb, Kermanshah
Ta'mini-Licha'i, Hasan	2008–12	Rasht, Gilan
Tavakkoli, Ahmad	2008–12	Tehran, Tehran
Torabi, Abdorreza	2008–12	Garmsar, Semnan
Torabi-Qahfarrokhi, Nasrollah	2008–12	Shahrekord, Chahar Mahal and Bakhtiari
Vanaei, Hasan	2008–12	Malayer, Hamadan
Vardan, Gevorg	2008–12	Armenians of northern Iran (minority)
Yahyazadeh-Firozabad, Seyyed Jalal	2008–12	Taft and Meybod, Yazd
Yusefiyan-Mola, Ezzatollah	2008–12	Amol, Mazandaran
Yusefnezhad, Ali-Asghar	2008–12	Sari, Mazandaran
Zabeti-Tarqi, Mohammad	2008–12	Natanz and Qamsar, Isfahan
Zakani, Ali-Reza	2008–12	Tehran, Tehran
Zaker, Seyyed Salman	2008–12	Urmia, West Azerbaijan
Zamani, Seyyed Javad	2008–12	Kangavar, Sahneh, and Harsin, Kermanshah
Zanjani-Hasanlu'i, Ali	2008–12	Naqadeh and Oshnaviyyeh, West Azerbaijan
Zare'i, Ali-Asghar	2008–12	Tehran, Tehran
Zolanvar, Seyyed Hoseyn	2008–12	Shiraz, Fars
Zolqadr, Seyyed Mostafa	2008–12	Bandar-e Abbas, Hormozgan

Deputies in the Ninth Majlis (2012–16)

Name	Tenure	City and province of constituency
Abbasi, Soleyman	2012–16	Gonbad-e Kavus, Golestan
Abdi, Iraj	2012–16	Dowreh and Khorramabad, Lorestan
Abdollahi, Reza	2012–16	Mahneshan and Ijrood, Zanjan
Abdollahzadeh, Mohammad-Ali	2012–16	Boshruyeh, Ferdows, Sarayan, and Tabas, South Khorasan
Abutorabi, Abolfazl	2012–16	Karvan, Najafabad, and Tiran, Isfahan
Abutorabifard, Seyyed Mohammad-Hasan	2012–16	Tehran, Tehran
Afkhami, Shahruz	2012–16	Malekan, East Azerbaijan
Afzalifard, Mostafa	2012–16	Ardabil, Namin, Nir, and Sareyn, Ardabil
Aghajari, Habib	2012–16	Bandar-e Mahshahr, Hendijan, and Omidiyeh, Khuzestan
Ahmadi, Ali-Mohammad	2012–16	Dehloran, Ilam
Ahmadi, Musa	2012–16	Deyr, Jam, and Kangan, Bushehr
Ahmadi, Nabiyollah	2012–16	Darab, Fars
Ahmadi, Osman	2012–16	Mahabad, West Azerbaijan
Ahmadi, Vahid	2012–16	Harsin, Kangavar, and Sahneh, Kermanshah
Ahmadi-Lashki, Qasem	2012–16	Chalus and Nowshahr, Mazandaran
Akbariyan, Aziz	2012–16	Karaj, Alborz
Akhavan-Bitaraf, Nayyereh	2012–16	Isfahan, Isfahan
Alavi, Seyyed Ahsan	2012–16	Divandarreh, Kamyaran, and Sanandaj, Kurdistan
Alee, Halimeh	2012–16	Hirmand, Zabol, and Zahak, Sistan and Baluchestan
Alilu, Ali	2012–16	Shabestar, East Azerbaijan
Alimardani, Mohsen	2012–16	Zanjan and Tarom, Zanjan
Alimohammadi, Omran	2013–16	Ilam, Eyvan, Mehran, Malekshahi, and Shirvan, Ilam
Alipur-Khonakdari, Kamal	2012–16	Juybar, Qaemshahr, and Savadkuh, Mazandaran
Alipur-Rahmati, Mohammad	2012–16	Maku, Chaldoran, Poldasht, and Showt, West Azerbaijan
Alya, Fatemeh	2012–16	Tehran, Tehran
Amirabadi-Farahani, Ahmad	2012–16	Qom, Qom
Amiri-Kahnuj, Mohammad-Reza	2012–16	Kahnuj, Manujan, Qaleh Ganj, and South Rudbar, Kerman
Amiri-Khamkani, Hoseyn	2012–16	Zarand, Kerman
Ansari, Mohammad-Sa'id	2012–16	Abadan, Khuzestan
Aqa Mohammadi, Ebrahim	2012–16	Dowreh and Khorramabad, Lorestan
Aqa Tehrani, Morteza	2012–16	Tehran, Tehran
Aqa'i-Moghanjuqi, Ali-Akbar	2012–15	Salmas, West Azerbaijan
Arami, Mansur	2012–16	Bandar-e Abbas, Hormozgan
Arbabi, Mohammad-Sa'id	2012–16	Iranshahr, Sarbaz, Delgan, Fanuj, Bent, Lashar, and Ashar, Sistan and Baluchestan

Name	Tenure	City and province of constituency
Arefi, Farajollah	2012–16	Anbarabad and Jiroft, Kerman
Ariya'inezhad, Ahmad	2012–16	Malayer, Hamadan
Asadi, Yunes	2012–16	Meshginshahr, Ardabil
Asadollahi, Gholam-Reza	2012–16	Torbat-e Jam and Taybad, Razavi Khorasan
Asafari, Mohammad-Hasan	2012–16	Arak, Khondab, and Komijan, Markazi
Ashtiyani-Araqi, Reza	2012–16	Qom, Qom
Ashuri-Qal'erudkhani, Naser	2012–16	Fuman and Shaft, Gilan
Ashuri-Tazyani, Mohammad	2012–16	Abumusa, Bandar-e Abbas, Hajiabad, and Qeshm, Hormozgan
Azin, Hoseyn	2012–16	Anar and Rafsanjan, Kerman
Azizi, Abdorreza	2012–16	Shiravan, North Khorasan
Azizi, Qasem	2012–16	Shazand, Markazi
Azizi-Farsani, Hamid-Reza	2012–16	Ardal, Farsan, Kiyar, and Kuhrang, Chahar Mahal and Bakhtiari
Bahmaei, Shamsollah	2012–16	Ramhormoz and Ramshir, Khuzestan
Bahmani, Mahnaz	2012–16	Sarab, East Azerbaijan
Bahonar, Mohammad-Reza	2012–16	Tehran, Tehran
Bakhshayesh-Ardestani, Ahmad	2012–16	Ardestan, Isfahan
Banihashemi-Chaharom, Seyyed Hashem	2012–16	Mashhad, Razavi Khorasan
Baqeri-Bonabi, Mohammad	2012–16	Bonab, East Azerbaijan
Bashiri, Farhad	2012–16	Pakdasht, Tehran
Bauj-Lahuti, Mehrdad	2012–16	Langarud, Gilan
Bayatiyan, Seyyed Mohammad	2012–16	Bijar, Kurdistan
Bazrpash, Mehrdad	2012–16	Tehran, Tehran
Beglarian, Robert	2012–16	Armenians of southern Iran (minority)
Betkiliya, Yonaten	2012–16	Assyrians and Chaldeans (minority)
Beygi-Eylanlu, Ruhollah	2012–16	Miyandoab, Shahindezh, and Takab, West Azerbaijan
Biglari, Mohsen	2012–16	Saqqez and Baneh, Kurdistan
Biranvand, Bahram	2012–16	Borujerd, Lorestan
Borujerdi, Alaeddin	2012–16	Borujerd, Lorestan
Borumand-Dashqapu, Habib	2012–16	Bilehsavar and Parsabad, Ardabil
Borumandi, Mohammad-Mehdi	2012–16	Arsanjan, Marvdasht, and Pasargad, Fars
Bozorgvari, Seyyed Ali-Mohammad	2012–16	Bahmai and Kohgiluyeh, Kohgiluyeh and Buyer Ahmad
Chardavoli, Ali-Ne'mat	2012–16	Malayer, Hamadan
Damadi, Mohammad	2012–16	Sari and Miandorud, Mazandaran
Dara'ei, Sayd-Isa	2012–16	Andimeshk, Khuzestan
Darvishpur, Hojjatollah	2012–16	Baghmalek and I'zeh, Khuzestan
Dastgheyb, Seyyed Ahmad-Reza	2012–16	Shiraz, Fars
Davatgari, Mehdi	2012–16	Maragheh and Ajab-Shir, East Azerbaijan
Dehdashti, Seyyed Hoseyn	2012–16	Abadan, Khuzestan
Dehqani, Allahverdi	2012–16	Varzaqan and Kharvana, East Azerbaijan
Dehqani-Nughandar, Mohammad	2012–16	Chenaran, Razavi Khorasan

Name	Tenure	City and province of constituency
Dogani-Aghchelu, Mohammad-Hasan	2012–16	Fasa, Fars
Ebadi, Seyyed Mohammad-Baqer	2012–16	Birjand, Darmiyan, and Khoosf, South Khorasan
Eftekhari, Laleh	2012–16	Tehran, Tehran
Ekhtiyari, Esfandiyar	2012–16	Zoroastrian community (minority)
Emami, Isa	2012–16	Aq-Qala and Gorgan, Golestan
Esfanani, Mohammad-Ali	2012–16	Chadegan, Faridan, and Fereydunshahr, Isfahan
Esma'ili, Daryush	2012–16	Kavar, Kherameh, and Sarvestan, Fars
Esma'ili, Mohammad	2012–16	Tarom and Zanjan, Zanjan
Esma'ilniya, Mohammad	2012–16	Kashmar, Khalilabad, and Bardaskan, Razavi Khorasan
Fallahi-Babajan, Abbas	2012–16	Ahar and Heris, East Azerbaijan
Farhangi, Mohammad-Hoseyn	2012–16	Tabriz, Azarshahr, and Osku, East Azerbaijan
Fathipur, Arsalan	2012–16	Kaleybar, Hurand, Khoda Afarin, East Azerbaijan
Fattahi, Abed	2012–16	Urmia, West Azerbaijan
Fattahi, Hoseyn	2012–16	Shahr-e Babak, Kerman
Fayyazi, Abdolvahid	2012–16	Mahmudabad and Nur, Mazandaran
Fereyduni, Nader	2012–16	Farashband, Firuzabad, Karzin, and Qir, Fars
Firuzi, Mohammad	2012–16	Natanz and Qamsar, Isfahan
Fuladgar, Hamid-Reza	2012–16	Isfahan, Isfahan
Garrusi, Hoseyn	2012–16	Shahriyar, Tehran
Ghazanfarabadi, Musa	2012–16	Bam, Kerman
Haddad-Adel, Gholam-Ali	2012–16	Tehran, Tehran
Haji Deligani, Hoseyn-Ali	2012–16	Borkhar, Meymeh, and Shahinshahr, Isfahan
Hakimi, Ataollah	2012–16	Rudbar, Gilan
Haqiqatpur, Mansur	2012–16	Ardabil, Namin, Nir, and Sareyn, Ardabil
Hasannezhad, Mohammad	2012–16	Jolfa and Marand, East Azerbaijan
Hasanpur-Biglari, Shahbaz	2012–16	Sirjan and Bardsir, Kerman
Hashemi, Seyyed Enayatolah	2012–16	Sepidan, Fars
Hashemi, Seyyed Mehdi	2012–16	Tehran, Tehran
Hashemi-Nakhlebrahimi, Seyyed Abdolkarim	2012–16	Bashagard, Jask, Minab, Rudan, and Sirik, Hormozgan
Hashemzehi, Morad	2012–16	Nehbandan and Sarbisheh, South Khorasan
Heravi, Javad	2012–16	Qaenat, South Khorasan
Heydari-Tayeb, Seyyed Sa'id	2012–16	Kermanshah, Kermanshah
Heydarpur-Shahrezai, Avaz	2012–16	Shahreza, Isfahan
Hoseyni, Fathollah	2012–16	Gilan-e Gharb, Qasr-e Shirin, and Sarpol-e Zahab, Kermanshah
Hoseyni, Seyyed Baqer	2012–16	Hirmand, Zabol, and Zahak, Sistan and Baluchestan
Hoseyni, Seyyed Bohlul	2012–16	Miyaneh, East Azerbaijan
Hoseyni, Seyyed Hadi	2012–16	Juybar, Qaemshahr, and Savadkuh, Mazandaran
Hoseyni, Seyyed Morteza	2012–16	Abyek, Alborz, and Qazvin, Qazvin
Hoseyni, Seyyed Sharif	2012–16	Ahvaz, Khuzestan

Name	Tenure	City and province of constituency
Hoseyni-Sadr, Mo'ayyed	2012–16	Khoy and Chaypareh, West Azerbaijan
Hoseyniyan, Ruhollah	2012–16	Tehran, Tehran
Hoseynzadeh, Abdolkarim	2012–16	Naqadeh and Oshnaviyyeh, West Azerbaijan
Hoseynzadeh-Bahreini, Mohammad-Hoseyn	2012–16	Kalat and Mashhad, Razavi Khorasan
Iranpur, Ali	2012–16	Mobarakeh, Isfahan
Isazadeh, Mehdi	2012–16	Miyandoab, Shahindezh, and Takab, West Azerbaijan
Jabbari, Ahmad	2012–16	Bandar-e Lengeh, Bastak, and Parsian, Hormozgan
Jadgal, Ya'qub	2012–16	Chabahar, Sistan and Baluchestan
Ja'fari, Qasem	2012–16	Bojnurd, Garmeh, Jajarm, Maneh, and Samalqan,, North Khorasan
Ja'fari-Baneh Khalkhal, Jalil	2012–16	Khalkhal and Kowsar, Ardabil
Ja'farpur, Jamshid	2012–16	Gerash, Khonj, and Larestan, Fars
Ja'farzadeh-Imanabad, Gholam-Ali	2012–16	Rasht, Gilan
Jahangirzadeh, Javad	2012–16	Urmia, West Azerbaijan
Jalali, Kazem	2012–16	Shahrud, Semnan
Jalili, Esma'il	2012–16	Andika, Haftkel, Lali, and Masjed Soleyman, Khuzestan
Jaliliyan, Ali	2012–16	Dalahu and Islamabad-e Gharb, Kermanshah
Jalil-Sarqal'eh, Majid	2012–16	Lordegan, Chahar Mahal and Bakhtiari
Jani-Abbaspur, Ruhollah	2012–16	Bu'inzahra, Qazvin
Jarareh, Abolqasem	2012–16	Abumusa, Bandar-e Abbas, Hajiabad, Khamir, and Qeshm, Hormozgan
Jomeyri, Abdolkarim	2012–16	Bushehr, Deylam, and Genaveh, Bushehr
Jowkar, Mohammad-Saleh	2012–16	Saduq and Yazd, Yazd
Kaeidi, Ali-Akbar	2012–16	Malavi and Pol-e Dokhtar, Lorestan
Kamran-Dastjerdi, Hasan	2012–16	Isfahan, Isfahan
Karimi-Qoddusi, Javad	2012–16	Kalat and Mashhad, Razavi Khorasan
Karimiyan, Omid	2012–16	Marivan and Sarvabad, Kurdistan
Karkhaneh, Ebrahim	2012–16	Famenin and Hamadan, Hamadan
Kashani, Naser	2012–16	Zahedan, Sistan and Baluchestan
Kateb, Gholam-Reza	2012–16	Aradan and Garmsar, Semnan
Khan Mohammadi-Khorrami, Mohammad-Reza	2012–16	Abhar and Khorramdarreh, Zanjan
Khanlaryan, Karen	2012–16	Armenians of northern Iran (minority)
Khastehband, Hasan	2012–16	Bandar-e Anzali, Gilan
Khezri, Rasul	2012–16	Piranshahr and Sardasht, West Azerbaijan
Khoda'i-Suri, Hojjatollah	2012–16	Delfan, Lorestan
Khojasteh, Amir	2012–16	Hamadan, Hamadan
Khosravi, Ali-Reza	2012–16	Mehdishahr and Semnan, Semnan
Khosravi-Sahlabadi, Abolqasem	2012–16	Mahvelat, Torbat-e Heydariyyeh, and Zaveh, Razavi Khorasan
Khosusi-Sani, Hamid-Reza	2012–16	Sowme'eh Sara, Gilan

Name	Tenure	City and province of constituency
Kiya'inezhad, Mofid	2012–16	Savojblagh, Nazarabad, and Taleqan, Alborz
Kowlivand, Mohammad-Javad	2012–16	Karaj, Alborz
Kowsari, Mohammad-Esma'il	2012–16	Tehran, Tehran
Kuchakinezhad-Eramsadati, Jabar	2012–16	Rasht, Gilan
Kuchakzadeh, Mehdi	2012–16	Tehran, Tehran
Larijani, Ali	2012–16	Qom, Qom
Madadi, Mohammad-Ali	2012–16	Miyaneh, East Azerbaijan
Mahjub, Ali-Reza	2012–16	Tehran, Tehran
Malekshahi, Allahyar	2012–16	Kuhdasht, Lorestan
Mansuri-Arani, Abbas-Ali	2012–16	Kashan, Aran, and Bidgol, Isfahan
Mansuri-Bidakani, Majid	2012–16	Lenjan, Isfahan
Manuchehri, Ne'matollah	2012–16	Paveh, Javanrud, Salase Babajani, and Ravansar, Kermanshah
Manzari-Tavakkoli, Ali-Reza	2012–16	Baft, Rabor, and Arzuiyeh, Kerman
Marandi, Seyyed Ali-Reza	2012–16	Tehran, Tehran
Mareh Sedq, Siyamak	2012–16	Jewish community (minority)
Marvi, Ali	2012–16	Neyshabur, Razavi Khorasan
Mashhadiabbasi, Hamid-Reza	2013–16	Damavand and Firuzkuh, Tehran
Mesbahi-Moqaddam, Gholam-Reza	2012–16	Tehran, Tehran
Mesri, Abdorreza	2012–16	Kermanshah, Kermanshah
Mir Galuye Bayat, Shahla	2012–16	Saveh and Zarandieh, Markazi
Mir Kazemi, Seyyed Mas'ud	2012–16	Tehran, Tehran
Mir Mohammadi, Seyyed Mohammad-Hoseyn	2012–16	Golpayegan and Khansar, Isfahan
Mir Morad-Zehi, Hedayatollah	2012–16	Saravan, Sib, and Suran, Sistan and Baluchestan
Mofatteh, Mohammad-Mehdi	2013–16	Tuyserkan, Hamadan
Mohammadi, Davud	2012–16	Qazvin, Abyek, and Alborz, Qazvin
Mohammad-Sadeqi, Shahin	2012–16	Kazerun, Fars
Mohammadzadeh, Hoseyn	2012–16	Dargaz, Razavi Khorasan
Mohebbi, Mohammad-Ebrahim	2012–16	Sonqor, Kermanshah
Mohseni-Sani, Mohammad-Reza	2012–16	Sabzevar, Razavi Khorasan
Monadi-Sefidan, Ali-Reza	2012–16	Tabriz, Osku, and Azarshahr, East Azerbaijan
Moqimi, Ahmad-Ali	2012–16	Behshahr, Neka, and Galugah, Mazandaran
Moqtada'i, Abbas	2012–16	Isfahan, Isfahan
Moradi, Salar	2012–16	Sanandaj, Divandarreh, and Kamyaran, Kurdistan
Motahhari, Ali	2012–16	Tehran, Tehran
Mozaffar, Hoseyn	2012–16	Tehran, Tehran
Musavi, Seyyed Mohammad-Ali	2012–16	Khodabandeh, Zanjan
Musavi, Seyyed Musa	2012–16	Lamerd and Mehr, Fars
Musavi, Seyyed Shokrekhoda	2012–16	Ahvaz and Bavi, Khuzestan
Musaviasl, Mir Gesmat	2012–16	Germi (Moghan), Ardabil
Musavi-Laregani, Seyyed Naser	2012–16	Falavarjan, Isfahan
Musavinezhad, Seyyed Mehdi	2012–16	Dashtestan, Bushehr
Nabaviyan, Seyyed Mahmud	2012–16	Tehran, Tehran

Name	Tenure	City and province of constituency
Naderan, Elyas	2012–16	Tehran, Tehran
Nadimi, Iraj	2012–16	Lahijan and Siyahkal, Gilan
Na'imi-Raz, Safar	2012–16	Astara, Gilan
Najafnezhad, Meqdad	2012–16	Babolsar and Fereydunkenar, Mazandaran
Naqavi-Hoseyni, Seyyed Hoseyn	2012–16	Varamin, Tehran
Naseri, Ali-Akbar	2012–16	Babol, Mazandaran
Nazarimehr, Mohammad-Javad	2012–16	Kordkuy, Torkaman, and Bandar-e Gaz, Golestan
Negahban-Salami, Mahmud	2012–16	Khaf and Roshtkhar, Razavi Khorasan
Nejabat, Hoseyn	2012–16	Tehran, Tehran
Neku, Ebrahim	2012–16	Robat Karim and Baharestan, Tehran
Ne'mati, Behruz	2012–16	Asadabad, Hamadan
Niazazari, Hoseyn	2012–16	Babol, Mazandaran
Nobaveh, Bizhan	2012–16	Tehran, Tehran
Nowruzi, Rahmatollah	2012–16	Aliabad Katul, Golestan
Nuri-Ghezeljeh, Gholam-Reza	2012–16	Bostanabad, East Azerbaijan
Nuri, Seyyed Razi	2012–16	Shush, Khuzestan
Omrani, Seyyedeh Sakineh	2012–16	Semirom, Isfahan
Osmani, Mohammad-Qasim	2012–16	Bukan, West Azerbaijan
Papizadeh-Palangan, Abbas	2012–16	Dezful, Khuzestan
Pashang, Hamid-Reza	2012–16	Khash, Mirjaveh, Nosratabad, Kurin, and Nokabad, Sistan and Baluchestan
Pezeshkiyan, Mas'ud	2012–16	Tabriz, Osku, and Azarshahr, East Azerbaijan
Pezhmanfar, Nasrollah	2012–16	Mashhad and Kalat, Razavi Khorasan
Pirmo'azzen, Kamaleddin	2012–16	Ardabil, Nir, Namin, and Sareyn, Ardabil
Purebrahimi-Davarani, Mohammad-Reza	2012–16	Kerman and Ravar, Kerman
Purfatemi, Seyyed Mohammad-Mehdi	2012–16	Dashti and Tangestan, Bushehr
Purmokhtar, Mohammad-Ali	2012–16	Bahar and Kabudarahang, Hamadan
Qaderi, Ja'far	2012–16	Shiraz, Fars
Qadermarzi, Hamed	2012–16	Qorveh and Dehgolan, Kurdistan
Qa'edrahmat, Abbas	2012–16	Dorud and Azna, Lorestan
Qavami, Hadi	2012–16	Esfarayen, North Khorasan
Qazipur, Nader	2012–16	Urmia, West Azerbaijan
Qazizadeh-Hashemi, Seyyed Amir-Hoseyn	2012–16	Mashhad and Kalat, Razavi Khorasan
Qorbani, Mohammad-Hoseyn	2012–16	Astaneh-ye Ashrafiyyeh and Bandar-e Kiashahr, Gilan
Qoreh Seyyed Romiyani, Mir Hadi	2012–16	Tabriz, Osku, and Azarshahr, East Azerbaijan
Rahbar, Fatemeh	2012–16	Tehran, Tehran
Rahbari-Amlashi, Mohammad-Mehdi	2012–16	Rudsar, Gilan
Rahmandust, Mojtaba	2012–16	Tehran, Tehran
Rahmani, Rajab	2012–16	Takestan, Qazvin
Rahmani, Reza	2012–16	Tabriz, Osku, and Azarshahr, East Azerbaijan
Rajabi, Abdolkarim	2012–16	Minudasht, Kalaleh, Maraveh Tappeh, and Galikash, Golestan
Raja'i, Abbas	2012–16	Arak and Komijan, Markazi

Name	Tenure	City and province of constituency
Raja'i-Baghsiyaei, Mohammad	2012–16	Gonabad and Bejestan, Razavi Khorasan
Rasa'i, Hamid	2012–16	Tehran, Tehran
Razm, Mohammad	2012–16	Kermanshah, Kermanshah
Reza'i, Mohammad-Ebrahim	2012–16	Khomeyn, Markazi
Reza'i-Kuchi, Mohammad-Reza	2012–16	Jahrom, Fars
Rostamiyan, Abdorrahman	2012–16	Damghan, Semnan
Sa'dunzadeh, Javad	2012–16	Abadan, Khuzestan
Saberi, Reza	2012–16	Ramiyan and Azadshahr, Golestan
Sadat-Ebrahimi, Seyyed Mohammad	2012–16	Shushtar and Gotvand, Khuzestan
Sadeqi, Zargham	2012–16	Shiraz, Fars
Sa'idi, Mohammad-Esma'il	2012–16	Tabriz, Azarshahr, and Osku, East Azerbaijan
Sajjadi, Ahmad	2012–16	Fariman, Sarakhs, Ahmadabad, and Razavieh, Razavi Khorasan
Salahi, Abbas	2012–16	Tafresh, Ashtiyan, and Farahan, Markazi
Salehinasab, Naser	2012–16	Dasht-e Azadegan, Khuzestan
Salek, Ahmad	2012–16	Isfahan, Isfahan
Salimi, Ali-Reza	2012–16	Mahallat and Delijan, Markazi
Sameri, Abdollah	2012–16	Khorramshahr and Mino Island, Khuzestan
Sana'i, Mehdi	2012–13	Nahavand, Hamadan
Saqqa'i, Mohammad	2012–16	Estahban and Neyriz, Fars
Sarrami-Forushani, Mohsen	2012–16	Khomeinishahr, Isfahan
Servati, Musarreza	2012–16	Bojnurd, Maneh, Samalqan, and Jajarm, North Khorasan
Shafi'i, Nowzar	2012–16	Mamasani and Rostam, Fars
Shahriyari, Hoseyn-Ali	2012–16	Zahedan, Sistan and Baluchestan
Shari'ati, Mohammad-Baqer	2012–16	Behbahan, Khuzestan
Shari'atnezhad, Shamsollah	2013–16	Tonekabon, Ramsar, and Abbasabad, Mazandaran
Shiri-Aliabadi, Gholam-Hoseyn	2012–16	Hashtrud and Charuymaq, East Azerbaijan
Shoja'ei-Kiyasari, Seyyed Ramezan	2012–16	Sari and Miandorud, Mazandaran
Shokri, Mahmud	2012–16	Talesh, Rezvanshahr, and Masal, Gilan
Shuhani, Ahmad	2012–16	Ilam, Eyvan, Mehran, Malekshahi, and Shirvan, Ilam
Shushtari, Hadi	2012–16	Quchan and Faruj, Razavi Khorasan
Sobhanifar, Ramezan-Ali	2012–16	Sabzevar, Joghatai, Jowayin, Khoshab, and Davarzan, Razavi Khorasan
Sobhaninia, Hoseyn	2012–16	Neyshabur, Razavi Khorasan
Soleymani, Mohammad	2012–16	Tehran, Tehran
Soltani, Amir-Abbas	2012–16	Borujen, Chahar Mahal and Bakhtiari
Soltani-Sabur, Ataollah	2012–16	Razan, Hamadan
Sudani, Naser	2012–16	Ahvaz, Khuzestan
Tabataba'i-Na'ini, Seyyed Hamid-Reza	2012–16	Na'in, Khur, Biabanak, Isfahan
Tabesh, Mohammad-Reza	2012–16	Ardakan, Yazd

Name	Tenure	City and province of constituency
Tabibzadeh-Nuri, Zohreh	2012–16	Tehran, Tehran
Taheri, Elyas	2012–16	Eqlid, Fars
Taheri-Gorgani, Seyyed Ali	2012–16	Gorgan and Aq-Qala, Golestan
Tajgardun, Gholam-Reza	2012–16	Gachsaran and Basht, Kohgiluyeh and Buyer Ahmad
Tala, Hoseyn	2012–16	Tehran, Tehran
Tamimi, Abdollah	2012–16	Shadegan, Khuzestan
Ta'mini-Licha'i, Hasan	2012–16	Rasht, Gilan
Tavakkoli, Ahmad	2012–16	Tehran, Tehran
Tavakkoli, Mohammad-Taqi	2012–16	Aligudarz, Lorestan
Yahyazadeh-Firozabad, Seyyed Jalal	2012–13	Taft and Meybod, Yazd
Yusefiyan-Mola, Ezzatollah	2012–16	Amol, Mazandaran
Zahedi, Mohammad-Mehdi	2012–16	Kerman and Ravar, Kerman
Zakani, Ali-Reza	2012–16	Tehran, Tehran
Zamaniyan-Dehkordi, Seyyed Sa'id	2012–16	Shahrekord, Chahar Mahal and Bakhtiari
Zare', Rahim	2012–16	Abadeh, Bavanat, and Khorrambid, Fars
Zare'i, Ali-Asghar	2012–16	Tehran, Tehran
Zare'i, Gholam-Mohammad	2012–16	Buyer Ahmad, Kohgiluyeh and Buyer Ahmad
Zare'zadeh-Mehrizi, Dakhil-Abbas	2012–16	Mehriz, Bafq, Abarkuh, Khatam, and Bahabad, Yazd
Zolanvar, Seyyed Hoseyn	2012–16	Shiraz, Fars

Deputies in the Tenth Majlis (2016–20)

Name	Tenure	City and province of constituency
Abbasi, Asadollah	2016–20	Amlash and Rudsar, Gilan
Abdollahi, Beytollah	2017–20	Ahar and Heris, East Azerbaijan
Abedi, Heydar-Ali	2016–20	Isfahan, Isfahan
Abramiyan, Zhorzhik	2016–20	Armenians of southern Iran (minority)
Abtahi, Seyyed Mohammad-Javad	2016–20	Khomeinishahr, Isfahan
Abutorabi, Abolfazl	2016–20	Karvan, Najafabad, and Tiran, Isfahan
Adiyanirad, Seyyed Ali	2016–20	Juybar, Qaemshahr, and Savadkuh, Mazandaran
Afzali, Nazar	2016–20	Nahbandan, South Khorasan
Afzali, Seyyed Hoseyn	2016–20	Eqlid, Fars
Ahmadi, Fereydun	2016–20	Zanjan, Zanjan
Ahmadi-Lashki, Qasem	2016–20	Chalus and Nowshahr, Mazandaran
Akbari [Bojnurd], Ali	2016–20	Bojnurd, Razavi Khorasan
Akbari [Marvdasht], Ali	2016–20	Shiraz, Fars
Akbariyan, Aziz	2016–20	Karaj, Alborz
Alavi, Seyyed Ahsan	2016–20	Divandarreh, Kamyaran, and Sanandaj, Kurdistan
Alavi, Seyyed Mohsen	2016–20	Lamerd, Fars

Name	Tenure	City and province of constituency
Alijani-Zamani, Mohsen	2016–20	Tehran, Tehran
Alireza-Beygi, Ahmad	2016–20	Tabriz, East Azerbaijan
Alizadeh, Reza	2016–20	Varzaqan, East Azerbaijan
Allahqolizadeh, Qoli	2016–20	Hurand and Kaleybar, East Azerbaijan
Almasi, Sakineh	2016–20	Deyr and Kangan, Bushehr
Amini, Salam	2016–20	Ilam, Ilam
Amini, Seyyed Hamzeh	2016–20	Hashtrud, East Azerbaijan
Aminifard, Mohammad-Na'im	2016–20	Iranshahr, Sistan and Baluchestan
Amirabadi-Farahani, Ahmad	2016–20	Qom, Qom
Amir-Hasankhani, Mohammad-Reza	2016–20	Ferdows and Tabas, South Khorasan
Amiri-Khamkani, Hoseyn	2016–20	Zarand, Kerman
Anaraki-Mohammadi, Ahmad	2016–20	Rafsanjan, Kerman
Ansari, Reza	2016–20	Darab and Zarrindasht, Fars
Aqapur-Alishahi, Ma'sumeh	2016–20	Shabestar, East Azerbaijan
Aref, Mohammad-Reza	2016–20	Tehran, Tehran
Asadi, Ali	2016–20	Shahr-e Babak, Kerman
Ashuri-Tazyani, Mohammad	2016–20	Abumusa, Bandar-e Abbas, Hajiabad, and Qeshm, Hormozgan
Azadikhah, Ahad	2016–20	Malayer, Hamadan
Azizi, Abdorreza	2016–20	Shiravan, North Khorasan
Azizi, Mohammad	2016–20	Abhar, Zanjan
Baba'i-Saleh, Ruhollah	2016–20	Bu'inzahra, Qazvin
Badamchi, Mohammad-Reza	2016–20	Tehran, Tehran
Badri, Sadif	2016–20	Ardabil, Ardabil
Bahadori, Seyyed Hadi	2016–20	Urmia, West Azerbaijan
Bahmani, Mahmud	2016–20	Savojblagh, Nazarabad, and Taleqan, Alborz
Bahramnia, Hasan	2016–20	Nahavand, Hamadan
Bakhtiar, Ali	2016–20	Golpayegan and Khansar, Isfahan
Bakhtiari, Ali	2016–20	Baft, Kerman
Bana'i, Hamid	2016–20	Gonabad, Razavi Khorasan
Barzegar-Kalshani, Shahruz	2016–20	Salmas, West Azerbaijan
Bastani, Sa'id	2016–20	Torbat-e Heydariyyeh, Razavi Khorasan
Bauj-Lahuti, Mehrdad	2016–20	Langarud, Gilan
Betkiliya, Yonaten	2016–20	Assyrians and Chaldeans (minority)
Bigdeli, Ahmad	2016–20	Khodabandeh, Zanjan
Biglari, Mohsen	2016–20	Saqqez and Baneh, Kurdistan
Bimeqdar, Shahabeddin	2016–20	Tabriz, East Azerbaijan
Biranvandi, Mohammad	2016–20	Khorramabad, Lorestan
Bonyadi, Behruz	2016–20	Kashmar, Razavi Khorasan
Borujerdi, Alaeddin	2016–20	Borujerd, Lorestan
Borumandi, Mohammad-Mehdi	2016–20	Arsanjan, Marvdasht, and Pasargad, Fars
Chenarani, Hajar	2016–20	Neyshabur, Razavi Khorasan
Dadashi, Vali	2016–20	Astara, Gilan
Dahmardeh, Habibollah	2016–20	Zabol, Sistan and Baluchestan

Name	Tenure	City and province of constituency
Damadi, Mohammad	2016–20	Miandorud and Sari, Mazandaran
Davudi, Yusef	2016–20	Sarab, East Azerbaijan
Dehqani-Firuzabadi, Kamal	2016–20	Taft, Yazd
Dehqani-Nughandar, Mohammad	2016–20	Chenaran, Razavi Khorasan
Delkhosh-Abatary, Seyyed Kazem	2016–20	Sowme'eh Sara, Gilan
Dorrazahi, Mohammad-Baset	2016–20	Saravan, Sistan and Baluchestan
Ebadi, Seyyed Mohammad-Baqer	2016–20	Birjand, Darmiyan, and Khoosf, South Khorasan
Ebrahimi, Ali	2016–20	Shazand, Markazi
Ebrahimi, Ali-Reza	2016–20	Ramiyan, Golestan
Eftekhari, Mohammad-Mehdi	2016–20	Fuman, Gilan
Ekhtiyari, Esfandiyar	2016–20	Zoroastrian community (minority)
Esma'ili, Ali	2016–20	Mahmudabad and Nur, Mazandaran
Esma'ili, Daryush	2016–20	Sarvestan, Kherameh, and Kavar, Fars
E'zazi-Maleki, Ziyaollah	2016–20	Bonab, East Azerbaijan
Falahati, Farhad	2016–20	Qaenat, South Khorasan
Falahatpisheh, Heshmatollah	2016–20	Islamabad-e Gharb, Kermanshah
Farhangi, Mohammad-Hoseyn	2016–20	Tabriz, Azarshahr, and Osku, East Azerbaijan
Farmand, Fardin	2016–20	Miyaneh, East Azerbaijan
Farshadan, Seyyed Mehdi	2016–20	Sanandaj, Kurdistan
Fathi, Mohammad-Javad	2016–20	Tehran, Tehran
Feyzi-Zangir, Mohammad	2016–20	Ardabil, Ardabil
Fuladgar, Hamid-Reza	2016–20	Isfahan, Isfahan
Garmabi, Hamid	2016–20	Neyshabur, Razavi Khorasan
Gilani, Sohrab	2016–20	Shushtar, Khuzestan
Golmoradi, Ali	2016–20	Bandar-e Mahshahr, Khuzestan
Gudarzi, Abbas	2016–20	Borujerd, Lorestan
Gudarzi, Mas'ud	2016–20	Mamasani, Fars
Haji Baba'i, Hamid-Reza	2016–20	Hamadan, Hamadan
Haji Deligani, Hoseyn-Ali	2016–20	Shahinshahr, Meymeh, and Borkhar, Isfahan
Hamzeh, Ahmad	2016–20	Kahnuj, Kerman
Hasanbeygi, Abolfazl	2016–20	Damghan, Semnan
Hasani-Juryabi, Mohammad-Sadeq	2016–20	Rasht, Gilan
Hasannezhad, Mohammad	2016–20	Jolfa and Marand, East Azerbaijan
Hasanpur-Biglari, Shahbaz	2016–20	Bardsir and Sirjan, Kerman
Hasanvand, Fereydun	2016–20	Andimeshk and Shush, Khuzestan
Hashemi, Homayun	2016–20	Miyandoab and Takab, West Azerbaijan
Hashemipur, Adl	2016–20	Kohgiluyeh, Kohgiluyeh and Buyer Ahmad
Hashemi-Takhtinejad, Hoseyn	2016–20	Bandar-e Abbas, Hormozgan
Hashemza'i-Nehbandan, Abdorreza	2016–20	Tehran, Tehran
Hatamiyan, Abdollah	2016–20	Dargaz, Razavi Khorasan
Hazrati, Elyas	2016–20	Tehran, Tehran
Hazratpur, Ruhollah	2016–20	Urmia, West Azerbaijan
Hemmati, Ahmad	2016–20	Semnan, Semnan

Name	Tenure	City and province of constituency
Heydari, Gholam-Reza	2016–20	Tehran, Tehran
Hezarjaribi, Nabi	2016–20	Gorgan, Golestan
Hoseyni, Mohammad	2016–20	Tafresh, Markazi
Hoseyni, Seyyedeh Fatemeh	2016–20	Tehran, Tehran
Hoseyni-Kia, Seyyed Javad	2016–20	Sonqor, Kermanshah
Hoseyni-Shahrudi, Seyyed Hasan	2016–20	Shahrud, Semnan
Hoseynzadeh, Abdolkarim	2016–20	Naqadeh and Oshnaviyyeh, West Azerbaijan
Hoseynzadeh-Bahreini, Mohammad-Hoseyn	2016–20	Kalat and Mashhad, Razavi Khorasan
Irannezhad, Abdolghafur	2016–20	Chabahar, Sistan and Baluchestan
Ja'farpur, Jamshid	2016–20	Larestan, Khonj, and Gerash, Fars
Ja'farzadeh-Imanabad, Gholam-Ali	2016–20	Rasht, Gilan
Jalali, Kazem	2016–20	Tehran, Tehran
Jamali, Manuchehr	2016–20	Rudbar, Gilan
Jamali-Nowbandegani, Mohammad-Javad	2016–20	Fasa, Fars
Jasemi, Seyyed Qasem	2016–20	Kermanshah, Kermanshah
Jelowdarzadeh, Sohayla	2016–20	Tehran, Tehran
Ka'bi, Amer	2016–20	Abadan, Khuzestan
Kabiri, Seyyed Tagi	2016–20	Khoy and Chaypareh, West Azerbaijan
Kamalipur, Yahya	2016–20	Jiroft, Kerman
Kamran-Dastjerdi, Hasan	2017-20	Isfahan, Isfahan
Karampur-Haqiqi, Kurosh	2016–20	Firuzabad, Fars
Karimi, Ali-Akbar	2016–20	Arak, Komijan, and Khondab, Markazi
Karimi, Hamdollah	2016–20	Bijar, Kurdistan
Karimi, Reza	2016–20	Ardabil, Ardabil
Karimi-Qoddusi, Javad	2016–20	Kalat and Mashhad, Razavi Khorasan
Kateb, Gholam-Reza	2016–20	Garmsar and Aradan, Semnan
Kavakebiyan, Mostafa	2016–20	Tehran, Tehran
Kazemi, Mohammad	2016–20	Malayer, Hamadan
Kazemi, Seyyed Hamid-Reza	2016–20	Pol-e Dokhtar, Lorestan
Kazemi-Babaheydari, Ali	2016–20	Ardal, Chahar Mahal and Bakhtiari
Kazemnasab, Javad	2016–20	Ahvaz, Khuzestan
Kazemzadeh, Shadmehr	2016–20	Dehloran, Ilam
Keshtzar, Habibollah	2016–20	Behbahan, Khuzestan
Khadem, Seyyed Alaeddin	2016–20	Sepidan, Fars
Khademi, Hedayatollah	2016–20	I'zeh, Khuzestan
Khaledi-Sardashti, Mohamad	2016–20	Lordegan, Chahar Mahal and Bakhtiari
Khaleqi, Bashir	2016–20	Khalkhal and Kowsar, Ardabil
Khanlaryan, Karen	2016–20	Armenians of northern Iran (minority)
Khastehband, Hasan	2016–20	Bandar-e Anzali, Gilan
Khatami, Seyyed Morteza	2016–20	Ijrood and Mahneshan, Zanjan
Khedri, Abdolhamid	2016–20	Bandar-e Bushehr, Bushehr
Khezri, Rasul	2016–20	Piranshahr and Sardasht, West Azerbaijan
Khodabakhshi, Mohammad	2016–20	Aligudarz, Lorestan

Name	Tenure	City and province of constituency
Khodadadi, Salman	2016–20	Malekan, East Azerbaijan
Khojasteh, Amir	2016–20	Hamadan, Hamadan
Kikha, Ahmad-Ali	2016–20	Zabol and Zahak, Sistan and Baluchestan
Kiyanpur, Majid	2016–20	Dorud, Lorestan
Kosehgharavi, Shahram	2016–20	Minudasht, Golestan
Kowlivand, Mohammad-Javad	2016–20	Karaj, Alborz
Kuchakinezhad-Eramsadati, Jabar	2016–20	Rasht, Gilan
Kuhkan-Rizi, Mohsen	2016–20	Lenjan and Mobarakeh, Isfahan
Kurd, Ali	2016–20	Khash, Mirjaveh, Kurin, and Nosratabad, Sistan and Baluchestan
Larijani, Ali	2016–20	Qom, Qom
Lotfi, Hasan	2016–20	Razan, Hamadan
Mafi, Parvaneh	2016–20	Tehran, Tehran
Mahjub, Ali-Reza	2016–20	Tehran, Tehran
Mahmudi, Somayeh	2016–20	Shahreza, Isfahan
Mahmudi-Shahneshin, Mohammad	2016–20	Shahriyar, Tehran
Mahmudzadeh, Jalal	2016–20	Mahabad, West Azerbaijan
Maleki, Vali	2016–20	Meshginshahr, Ardabil
Malekshahi, Allahyar	2016–20	Kuhdasht, Lorestan
Malekshahi, Mohammad-Reza	2016–20	Khorramabad, Lorestan
Mansuri, Mohammad-Reza	2016–20	Saveh, Markazi
Maqsudi, Hoseyn	2016–20	Sabzevar, Razavi Khorasan
Mareh Sedq, Siyamak	2016–20	Jewish community (minority)
Mas'udi, Asghar	2016–20	Neyriz, Fars
Mazani, Ahmad	2016–20	Tehran, Tehran
Mesri, Abdorreza	2016–20	Kermanshah, Kermanshah
Mirzadeh, Mir Hemayat	2016–20	Germi (Moghan), Ardabil
Mirza'i, Jalal	2016–20	Ilam, Ilam
Mirza'i-Niku, Qasem	2016–20	Damavand, Tehran
Mofatteh, Mohammad-Mehdi	2016–20	Tuyserkan, Hamadan
Mohammadi, Davud	2016–20	Qazvin, Abyek, and Alborz, Qazvin
Mohammadi [Qom], Davud	2016–20	Tehran, Tehran
Mohammadiyan, Eqbal	2016–20	Ramhormoz and Ramshir, Khuzestan
Mohebbinia, Jahanbakhsh	2016–20	Miyandoab, Shahindezh, and Takab, West Azerbaijan
Mokhtar, Jalil	2016–20	Abadan, Khuzestan
Moqaddasi, Seyyed Mehdi	2016–20	Arak, Komijan, and Khondab, Markazi
Moradi, Ahmad	2016–20	Bandar-e Abbas, Hormozgan
Moradi, Ali-Mohammad	2016–20	Qorveh, Kurdistan
Moradi, Mansur	2016–20	Marivan, Kurdistan
Motahhari, Ali	2016–20	Tehran, Tehran
Musavi, Seyyed Farid	2016–20	Tehran, Tehran
Musavi-Boyuki, Seyyed Abolfazl	2016–20	Yazd, Yazd

Name	Tenure	City and province of constituency
Musavi-Laregani, Seyyed Naser	2016–20	Falavarjan, Isfahan
Naderi, Shahab	2016–20	Paveh, Kermanshah
Najafi, Mohammad-Reza	2016–20	Tehran, Tehran
Najafi-Khoshrudi, Ali	2016–20	Babol, Mazandaran
Nano-Kenari, Valiyollah	2016–20	Babolsar, Mazandaran
Naqavi-Hoseyni, Seyyed Hoseyn	2016–20	Varamin, Tehran
Naserinezhad, Majid	2016–20	Shadegan, Khuzestan
Negahban-Salami, Mahmud	2016–20	Khaf and Roshtkhar, Razavi Khorasan
Ne'mati, Behruz	2016–20	Tehran, Tehran
Nikfar, Zabihollah	2016–20	Lahijan, Gilan
Nikzadipanah, Habibollah	2016–20	Bam, Kerman
Niyaz-Azari, Hoseyn	2016–20	Babol, Mazandaran
Nowbakht-Haqiqi, Ali	2016–20	Tehran, Tehran
Nowruzi, Hasan	2016–20	Robat Karim, Tehran
Nuri, Seyyed Razi	2016–20	Shush, Khuzestan
Nuriyan, Ardeshir	2016–20	Shahrekord, Chahar Mahal and Bakhtiari
Nurqolipur, Ramin	2016–20	Kordkuy, Golestan
Osmani, Mohammad-Qasim	2016–20	Bukan, West Azerbaijan
Owladqobad, Farideh	2016–20	Tehran, Tehran
Papizadeh-Palangan, Abbas	2016–20	Dezful, Khuzestan
Parsa'i, Bahram	2016–20	Shiraz, Fars
Pezeshkiyan, Mas'ud	2016–20	Tabriz, Osku, and Azarshahr, East Azerbaijan
Pezhmanfar, Nasrollah	2016–20	Mashhad and Kalat, Razavi Khorasan
Purbafrani, Abbas-Ali	2016–20	Na'in, Isfahan
Purebrahimi-Davarani, Mohammad-Reza	2016–20	Kerman and Ravar, Kerman
Purhoseyn-Shaqlan, Shakur	2016–20	Bilehsavar and Parsabad, Ardabil
Purmokhtar, Mohammad-Ali	2016–20	Bahar and Kabudarahang, Hamadan
Qarhekhani-Alustani, Asadollah	2016–20	Aliabad Katul, Golestan
Qavami, Hadi	2016–20	Esfarayen, North Khorasan
Qazipur, Nader	2016–20	Urmia, West Azerbaijan
Qazizadeh-Hashemi, Seyyed Amir-Hoseyn	2016–20	Mashhad and Kalat, Razavi Khorasan
Qazizadeh-Hashemi, Seyyed Ehsan	2016–20	Fariman, Razavi Khorasan
Qomi, Mohammad	2016–20	Pakdasht, Tehran
Qorbani, Ali	2016–20	Bojnurd, North Khorasan
Qorbani, Mohammad-Hoseyn	2016–20	Astaneh-ye Ashrafiyyeh and Bandar-e Kiashahr, Gilan
Rabi'i-Fardanbeh, Khadijeh	2016–20	Borujen, Chahar Mahal and Bakhtiari
Rahimi, Ali-Reza	2016–20	Tehran, Tehran
Rahimi-Jahanabadi, Jalil	2016–20	Torbat-e Jam, Razavi Khorasan
Rajabi, Farajollah	2016–20	Shiraz, Fars
Ranjbarzadeh, Akbar	2016–20	Asadabad, Hamadan
Raziyan, Abdollah	2016–20	Qaemshahr, Savadkuh, and Juybar, Mazandaran
Reza'i, Mas'ud	2016–20	Shiraz, Fars

Name	Tenure	City and province of constituency
Reza'i, Mohammad-Ebrahim	2016–20	Khomeyn, Markazi
Reza'i-Kuchi, Mohammad-Reza	2016–20	Jahrom, Fars
Rezazadeh, Hoseyn	2016–20	Kazerun, Fars
Rostamiyan, Ali	2016–20	Delfan, Lorestan
Sa'i, Zahra	2016–20	Tabriz, East Azerbaijan
Sa'adat, Mohammad-Baqer	2016–20	Dashtestan, Bushehr
Sabbaghiyan, Mohammad Reza	2016–20	Mehriz, Yazd
Sadatinezhad, Seyyed Javad	2016–20	Kashan, Isfahan
Sadeqi, Mahmud	2016–20	Tehran, Tehran
Sa'edi, Qasem	2016–20	Dasht-e Azadegan, Khuzestan
Safari, Ahmad	2016–20	Kermanshah, Kermanshah
Safari-Natanzi, Morteza	2016–20	Natanz and Qamsar, Isfahan
Sa'idi, Fatemeh	2016–20	Tehran, Tehran
Sa'idi, Mohammad-Esma'il	2016–20	Tabriz, Azarshahr, and Osku, East Azerbaijan
Sa'idi-Mobarekeh, Zahra	2016–20	Mobarakeh, Isfahan
Salahshuri, Parvaneh	2016–20	Tehran, Tehran
Salek, Ahmad	2016–20	Isfahan, Isfahan
Salimi, Ali-Reza	2016–20	Mahallat and Delijan, Markazi
Salimi, Asghar	2016–20	Semirom, Isfahan
Sameri, Abdollah	2016–20	Khorramshahr and Mino Island, Khuzestan
Sari, Ali	2016–20	Ahvaz, Khuzestan
Sha'eri, Ali-Mohammad	2016–20	Behshahr, Mazandaran
Shahriyari, Hoseyn-Ali	2016–20	Zahedan, Sistan and Baluchestan
Shahriyari, Seyyed Kamaleddin	2016–20	Tangestan, Dashti, Kangan, and Deyr, Bushehr
Shaikh, Mehdi	2016–20	Tehran, Tehran
Sharafi, Gholam-Reza	2016–20	Abadan, Khuzestan
Shari'atnezhad, Shamsollah	2016–20	Tonekabon, Ramsar, and Abbasabad, Mazandaran
Sharifpur, Eynollah	2016–20	Maku, West Azerbaijan
Shiran-Khorasani, Reza	2016–20	Mashhad, Razavi Khorasan
Shivyari, Ya'qub	2016–20	Miyaneh, East Azerbaijan
Shokri, Mahmud	2016–20	Talesh, Rezvanshahr, and Masal, Gilan
Shushtari, Hadi	2016–20	Quchan and Faruj, Razavi Khorasan
Siyavashi-Shahenayati, Tayebeh	2016–20	Tehran, Tehran
Sobhanifar, Ramezan-Ali	2016–20	Sabzevar, Khorasan Razavi
Soleymani, Hasan	2016–20	Kangavar, Sahneh, and Harsin, Kermanshah
Sorush, Abolfazl	2016–20	Tehran, Tehran
Tabataba'inezhad, Seyyed Sadeq	2016–20	Ardestan, Isfahan
Tabesh, Mohammad-Reza	2016–20	Ardakan, Yazd
Taherkhani, Bahman	2016–20	Takestan, Qazvin
Tajari, Farhad	2016–20	Qasr-e Shirin, Sarpol-e Zahab, and Gilan-e Gharb, Kermanshah
Tajeddin, Nahid	2016–20	Isfahan, Isfahan

Name	Tenure	City and province of constituency
Tajgardun, Gholam-Reza	2016–20	Gachsaran and Basht, Kohgiluyeh and Buyer Ahmad
Tayyar, Qarjeh	2016–20	Gonbad-e Kavus, Golestan
Torbatinezhad, Nur-Mohammad	2016–20	Gorgan, Golestan
Torki, Akbar	2016–20	Faridan and Fereydunshahr, Isfahan
Vahdati-Helan, Mohammad	2016–20	Bostanabad, East Azerbaijan
Vakili, Mohammad-Ali	2016–20	Tehran, Tehran
Vaqfchi, Ali	2016–20	Zanjan, Zanjan
Yar-Mohammadi, Alim	2016–20	Zahedan, Sistan and Baluchestan
Yusefi, Homayun	2016–20	Ahvaz, Khuzestan
Yusefiyan-Mola, Ezzatollah	2016–20	Amol, Mazandaran
Yusefnezhad, Ali-Asgar	2016–20	Sari, Mazandaran
Zahedi, Mohammad-Mehdi	2016–20	Kerman and Ravar, Kerman
Zaheri, Ali-Asgar	2016–20	Masjed Soleyman, Khuzestan
Zarabadi, Seyyedeh Hamideh	2016–20	Qazvin, Qazvin
Zare', Rahim	2016–20	Abadeh, Bavanat, and Khorrambid, Fars
Zare'i, Gholam-Mohammad	2016–20	Buyer Ahmad, Kohgiluyeh and Buyer Ahmad
Zolanvar, Mojtaba	2016–20	Qom, Qom
Zolqadr, Seyyed Mostafa	2016–20	Minab, Hormozgan
Zolqadr, Seyyedeh Fatemeh	2016–20	Tehran, Tehran

Table 98
Fathers' Professions of Deputies in the First Majlis (1980–84)

Father's profession	Count	Percentage
Clergy	92	28.1%
Farmer/small landowner	75	22.9%
Bazaar tradesman (grocer, shopkeeper, broker)	49	15.0%
Laborer	20	6.1%
Civil servant	13	4.0%
Professionals (teacher, doctor, attorney)	8	2.5%
Unknown	70	21.4%
Total	327	100%

Source: Authors' database.

Note: A total of 327 MPs served in the First Majlis. We identified the father's occupation of 257 (78.6 percent) of the MPs.

Table 99
Women as Percentage of Majlis Candidates and Elected Deputies (1980–2016)

Term of Majlis	Number of registered female candidates	Female candidates as percentage of all registered candidates	Number of female candidates positively vetted in the election	Number of elected female deputies	Female deputies as percentage of all deputies who served in that Majlis session
1980–84	90	2.43%	NA	4	1.2%
1984–88	32	2.01%	25?	4	1.4%
1988–92	47	2.35%	37?	4	1.4%
1992–96	84	2.60%	NA	9[a]	3.3%
1996–2000	351	4.2%	NA	14	5.1%
2000–2004	504	7.35%	NA	13	4.4%
2004–8	857	10.49%	NA	13	4.4%
2008–12	585	7.70%	NA	8	2.8%
2012–16	390	7.38%	249	9	3.1%
2016–20	1,234	10.22%	586	17	5.9%

Note: For sources used in constructing this table, see section titled Data on Majlis Elections (1980–2020).

[a] From 1980 to 1992, all the female MPs were elected from Tehran. In the 1992 election, five female MPs were elected from Isfahan, Kermanshah, Mashhad, and Tabriz.

Table 100
Women Deputies in the Majlis (1980–2020)

Name	Lifespan	Highest educational degree	No. of times elected	City and province of constituency
Alee, Halimeh	1970–	MD	1	Zabol, Zahak, and Hirmand, Sistan and Baluchestan
Ajorlu, Fatemeh	1966–	MA (psychology)	2	Karaj, Tehran
Akhavan-Bitaraf, Nayyereh	1956–	MA (jurisprudence)	4	Isfahan, Isfahan
Alya, Fatemeh	1956–	MA (political science)	3	Tehran, Tehran
Amani-Anganeh, Shahrbanu	1960–	BA (management)	2	Urmia, West Azerbaijan
Aminzadeh, Elham	1964–	PhD (international law)	1	Tehran, Tehran
Amirshaqaqi, Fakhrtaj	1941–	MA (political science)	1	Tabriz, East Azerbaijan
Bahmani, Mahnaz	1970–	MA (management)	1	Sarab, East Azerbaijan
Bayat, Raf'at	1957–	PhD (sociology)	1	Zanjan, Zanjan
Behruzi, Maryam	1945–2012	Pre-diploma	4	Tehran, Tehran
Dastgheyb, Gowharoshshari'eh	1935–	MA (Arabic literature)	3	Tehran, Tehran
Derakhshandeh, Akhtar	1942–	Associate's degree	1	Kermanshah, Kermanshah
Edalat, Hamideh	1956–	PhD (entomology)	1	Dashtestan, Bushehr
Eftekhari, Laleh	1959–	PhD (theology)	3	Tehran, Tehran
Elahiyan, Zohreh	1968–	MD	1	Tehran, Tehran
Fayyazbakhsh, Nafiseh	1964–	PhD (philosophy)	3	Tehran, Tehran
Hadidchi-Dabbagh, Marziyeh	1939–2016	Elementary education	3	Hamadan, Hamadan; Tehran, Tehran
Haqiqatju, Fatemeh	1968–	PhD (counseling)	1	Tehran, Tehran
Hashemi-Bahremani, Fa'ezeh	1962–	MA (international law)	1	Tehran, Tehran
Homayun-Moqaddam, Fatemeh	1945–date unknown	MA (management and planning)	1	Tabriz, East Azerbaijan
Jelowdarzadeh, Sohayla	1959–	BS (textile engineering)	4	Tehran, Tehran
Kadivar, Jamileh	1963–	PhD (political science)	1	Tehran, Tehran
Karrubi, Fatemeh	1947–	Elementary education	1	Tehran, Tehran
Khatami, Seyyedeh Fatemeh	1957–	MD (pediatrics)	1	Mashhad, Razavi Khorasan
Kula'i, Elaheh	1956–	PhD (international relations)	1	Tehran, Tehran
Mir Galuye Bayat, Shahla	1965–	MD (gynecology)	1	Saveh and Zarandieh, Markazi
Morovvati, Mehrangiz	1962–	Associate's degree	2	Khalkhal and Kowsar, Ardabil
Mosavvari-Manesh, Akram	1959–	BA (English literature)	1	Isfahan, Isfahan
Naseripur, A'zam	1965–	MS (architecture/urban planning)	1	Islamabad-e Gharb, Kermanshah
Nowbakht, Monireh	1950–	MA (theology)	2	Tehran, Tehran
Omrani, Seyyedeh Sakineh	1972–	MS (physiology)	1	Semirom, Isfahan
Pishgahifard, Zahra	1955–	PhD (political geography)	1	Isfahan, Isfahan
Rahbar, Fatemeh	1964–	MA (visual communications)	3	Tehran, Tehran
Rake'i, Fatemeh	1954–	PhD (linguistics)	1	Tehran, Tehran

Table 100 (Cont.)
Women Deputies in the Majlis (1980–2020)

Name	Lifespan	Highest educational degree	No. of times elected	City and province of constituency
Ramezanzadeh, Fatemeh	1957–	MD (gynecology)	1	Tehran, Tehran
Rastgu, Elaheh	1962–	MA (educational management)	1	Malayer, Hamadan
Rezazadeh-Shiraz, Tahereh	1960–	BA (political science)	1	Shiraz, Fars
Sadiqi, Ateqeh	1943–	Elementary education	3	Tehran, Tehran
Sadiqi, Marziyeh	1957–	MS (civil engineering)	1	Mashhad, Razavi Khorasan
Safa'i, Tayebeh	1960–	PhD (educational management)	1	Tehran, Tehran
Salihi-Labafinejad, Parvin	1957–	MS (health of mother and child)	1	Tehran, Tehran
Seyyedi Alavi, Bibi Qodsiyyeh	1951–	MD (medicine)	2	Mashhad, Razavi Khorasan
Shari'ati-Kohbani, Effat	1952–	MA (management)	2	Kalat and Mashhad, Razavi Khorasan
Shayeq, Eshrat	1963–	MA (international relations)	1	Azarshahr, Osku, and Tabriz, East Azerbaijan
Tabibzadeh-Nuri, Zohreh	1960–	MD (dentistry)	1	Tehran, Tehran
Tahriri-Niksefat, Hajar	1964–	PhD (educational philosophy)	1	Rasht, Gilan
Taleqani, A'zam	1942–	BA (Persian literature)	1	Tehran, Tehran
Taleqani, Vahideh	1953–	MD (pharmacology)	1	Tehran, Tehran
Vahid-Dastjerdi, Marziyeh	1959–	MD (gynecology)	2	Tehran, Tehran

Source: Authors' database.

Note: This table demonstrates that out of the 1,812 individuals who have served as Majlis deputies between 1980 and 2017, only forty-nine (2.7 percent) have been women.

Table 101
Number and Percentage of Shiite Clerics in the Majlis (1980–2020)

Majlis session	Total number of deputies	Total number of clerics	Percentage of clerics
First	327	170	52.0%
Second	277	155	56.0%
Third	278	86	30.9%
Fourth	274	68	24.8%
Fifth	274	56	20.4%
Sixth	297	39	13.1%
Seventh	294	46	15.7%
Eighth	291	46	15.8%
Ninth	290	36	12.4%
Tenth	290	17	5.9%

Note: For each Majlis session we have counted MPs elected originally and in midterm elections (there may still be such elections for the Tenth Majlis). We used the biographical data on MPs that we have posted at http://irandataportal.syr.edu plus other materials from the Majlis website and the personal websites of the MPs.

Table 102
Sunni Deputies in the Majlis (1980–2020)

Name	City and province of constituency	Majlis session
Ahmadi, Osman	Mahabad, West Azerbaijan	9
Ahmadnezhad, Abdolkarim	Sanandaj, Kurdistan	3, 4
Aminifard, Mohammad-Na'im	Iranshahr, Sistan and Baluchestan	10
Arbabi, Mohammad-Sa'id	Ahoran, Ashar, Bent, Delgan, Fanuj, Iranshahr, Lashar, and Sarbaz, Sistan and Baluchestan	9
A'zami, Maqsud	Naqadeh and Oshnaviyyeh, West Azerbaijan	6
Babakhas, Ali-Mohammad	Paveh and Uramanat, Kermanshah	3
Barmak, Bayromgaldi	Galikash, Kalaleh, Maraveh Tappeh, and Minudasht, Golestan	7
Behmanesh, Rahman	Mahabad, West Azerbaijan	6
Besanjideh, Yusef	Kordkuy, Golestan	3
Biglari, Mohsen	Saqqez and Baneh, Kurdistan	9, 10
Dadgar, Abdolaziz	Chabahar, Sistan and Baluchestan	3
Damani, Hamed	Khash, Sistan and Baluchestan	1, 2
Daseh, Hasel	Piranshahr and Sardasht, West Azerbaijan	6
Dehqani, Mohammad-Qayyum	Ashar, Bent, Fanuj, Iranshahr, Lashar, and Sarbaz, Sistan and Baluchestan	8
Didgah, Nazar-Mohammad	Iranshahr, Sistan and Baluchestan	1
Dorrazahi, Mohammad-Baset	Saravan, Sistan and Baluchestan	10
Dowlati-Bakhshan, Abdolaziz	Saravan, Sistan and Baluchestan	5
Eshaq-Madani, Mohammad	Saravan, Sistan and Baluchestan	1, 2
Farshadan, Seyyed Mehdi	Sanandaj, Kurdistan	10
Fattahi, Abed	Urmia, West Azerbaijan	7, 9
Fattahpur-Mavaneh, Karim	Urmia, West Azerbaijan	6
Foruzesh, Peyman	Zahedan, Sistan and Baluchestan	7, 8
Fotuhi, Mohammad-Sharif	Chabahar and Nik Shahr, Sistan and Baluchestan	5
Golcheshmeh, Naqdi	Gonbad-e Kavus, Golestan	6
Habibzadeh-Bukani, Anvar	Bukan, West Azerbaijan	5, 7
Heydari, Fakhreddin	Saqqez and Baneh, Kurdistan	7, 8
Hoseyni, Seyyed Abdollah	Bandar-e Lengeh, Hormozgan	3, 4, 5, 6, 7
Hoseyni, Seyyed Ali	Sanandaj, Kurdistan	1, 2
Hoseyni, Seyyed Emad	Qorveh, Kurdistan	7, 8
Hoseyni, Seyyed Fathollah	Paveh and Uramanat, Kermanshah	4, 8
Hoseyni, Seyyed Mas'ud	Qorveh, Kurdistan	4, 6
Hoseynzadeh, Abdolkarim	Naqadeh and Oshnaviyyeh, West Azerbaijan	9, 10
Irannezhad, Abdolghafur	Chabahar, Sistan and Baluchestan	4, 6, 7, 10
Jabbari, Ahmad	Bandar-e Lengeh, Bastak, and Parsian, Hormozgan	8, 9
Jadgal, Ya'qub	Chabahar, Sistan and Baluchestan	8, 9
Jalalizadeh, Jalal	Divandarreh, Kamyaran, and Sanandaj, Kurdistan	6
Jamshidzehi, Abdolaziz	Saravan, Sistan and Baluchestan	8
Kahraze'i, Akhtar-Mohammad	Khash, Sistan and Baluchestan	4

Table 102 (Cont.)
Sunni Deputies in the Majlis (1980–2020)

Name	City and province of constituency	Majlis session
Karami, Abdoljabbar	Divandarreh, Kamyaran, and Sanandaj, Kurdistan	8
Karimi, Mohammad-Ali	Marivan, Kurdistan	4, 7
Karimiyan, Mohammad	Piranshahr and Sardasht, West Azerbaijan	4, 5, 7
Karimiyan, Omid	Marivan and Sarvabad, Kurdistan	9
Kashani, Naser	Zahedan, Sistan and Baluchestan	9
Kharmataei, Ali	Saqqez and Baneh, Kurdistan	2
Khasahmadi, Ahmad	Taybad and Torbat-e Jam, Razavi Khorasan	6, 7
Khezri, Rasul	Piranshahr and Sardasht, West Azerbaijan	9, 10
Kosehgharavi, Anehmohammad	Gonbad-e Kavus, Golestan	2
Kosehgharavi, Shahram	Minudasht, Golestan	10
Kurd, Ali	Khash, Kurin, Mirjaveh, and Nosratabad, Sistan and Baluchestan	10
Kurd, Baqer	Zahedan, Sistan and Baluchestan	6
Kurdmandani, Khodabakhsh	Khash, Mirjaveh, and Nosratabad, Sistan and Baluchestan	5
Mahmudzadeh, Jalal	Mahabad, West Azerbaijan	8, 10
Manuchehri, Ne'matollah	Javanrud, Paveh, Ravansar, and Salase Babajani, Kermanshah	9
Mir Morad-Zehi, Hedayatollah	Saravan, Sib, and Suran, Sistan and Baluchestan	7, 9
Mohammadi, Eqbal	Marivan and Sarvabad, Kurdistan	8
Mohammadi, Mostafa	Javanrud and Paveh, Kermanshah	6, 7
Moradi, Ali-Mohammad	Qorveh, Kurdistan	10
Moradi, Mansur	Marivan, Kurdistan	10
Moradi, Salar	Divandarreh, Kamyaran, and Sanandaj, Kurdistan	9
Naderi, Shahab	Paveh, Kermanshah	10
Negahban-Salami, Mahmud	Khaf and Roshtkhar, Razavi Khorasan	9, 10
Nurqolipur, Ramin	Kordkuy, Golestan	10
Osmani, Mohammad-Qasim	Bukan, West Azerbaijan	8, 9, 10
Partovi, Mohammad-Ali	Saqqez and Baneh, Kurdistan; Piranshahr, West Azerbaijan	3, 4, 8
Pashang, Hamid-Reza	Khash, Kurin, Mirjaveh, Nokabad, and Nosratabad, Sistan and Baluchestan	7, 8, 9
Qaderi, Mohammad-Rauf	Javanrud and Paveh, Kermanshah	5
Qadermarzi, Hamed	Dehgolan and Qorveh, Kurdistan	9
Qolizadeh, Yaghmor	Minudasht, Golestan	3
Rahimi, Abdolrahman	Paveh, Kermanshah	2
Rahimi-Jahanabadi, Jalil	Torbat-e Jam, Razavi Khorasan	10
Ra'isi, Khodabakhsh	Bent, Fanuj, Iranshahr, and Lashar, Sistan and Baluchestan	5
Rajabi, Abdolkarim	Galikash, Kalaleh, Maraveh Tappeh, and Minudasht, Golestan	9
Rastegar, Abdollah	Gonbad-e Kavus, Golestan	8
Rezazehi, Fakhreddin	Saravan, Sistan and Baluchestan	3, 4
Sajjadiyan, Mohammad-Reza	Khaf and Roshtkhar, Razavi Khorasan	7, 8
Samadi, Seyyed Ma'ruf	Sanandaj, Kurdistan	4, 5
Sha'bani, Amin	Divandarreh, Kamyaran, and Sanandaj Kurdistan	7, 8

Table 102 (Cont.)
Sunni Deputies in the Majlis (1980–2020)

Name	City and province of constituency	Majlis session
Shaverani, Mohammad	Bukan, West Azerbaijan	1, 2
Sohrabi, Abdollah	Marivan; Kurdistan	6
Sori, Abdollah	Saqqez and Baneh; Kurdistan	1
Tayyar, Atrak	Gonbad-e Kavus; Golestan	4, 6
Tayyar, Qarjeh	Gonbad-e Kavus; Golestan	10
Valipur, Naz-Mohammad	Bandar-e Torkaman, Bandar-e Gaz and Kordkuy; Golestan	6
Yar-Mohammadi, Alim	Zahedan; Sistan and Baluchestan	10

Note: This list has been compiled based on the authors' database. Considering the challenges of information gathering, it is possible that we may have missed a few other Sunni MPs.

Table 103
Deputies Representing Religious Minorities (1980–2020)

Name	Constituency	Majlis session
Abramiyan, Zhorzhik	Armenians of southern Iran	6, 10
Baghumian, Artavaz	Armenians of southern Iran	2,3,4,5
Bat-Oshonagugtappeh, Sergon	Assyrians and Chaldeans	1
Beglarian, Robert	Armenians of southern Iran	7, 8, 9
Betkiliya, Yonaten	Assyrians and Chaldeans	6, 7, 8, 9
Dabestani, Khosrow	Zoroastrian community	6
Davidian, Levon	Armenians of northern Iran	6
Ekhtiyari, Esfandiyar	Zoroastrian community	8, 9, 10
Elyasi, Manuchehr	Jewish community	5
Kalimi-Nikruz, Manuchehr	Jewish community	2, 3
Keyvani, Kuros	Jewish community	4
Khachaturian, Herach	Armenians of southern Iran	1
Khalatian, Hara'i	Armenians of northern Iran	1
Khanansu, Ator	Assyrians and Chaldeans	2, 3
Khanlaryan, Karen	Armenians of northern Iran	9, 10
Malekpur, Parviz	Zoroastrian community	1, 2
Maqsudpursir, Shamshoun	Assyrians and Chaldeans	4, 5
Mareh Sedq, Siyamak	Jewish community	8, 9, 10
Mo'tamed, Morris	Jewish community	6, 7
Naqi, Khosrow	Jewish community	1
Niknam, Kurosh	Zoroastrian community	1
Ravani, Parviz	Zoroastrian community	4, 5
Vardan, Gevorg	Armenians of northern Iran	7, 8
Vartanian, Vartan	Armenians of northern Iran	2, 3, 4, 5
Ziyafat, Aflatun	Zoroastrian community	3

Source: Authors' database.

11
Assembly of Experts

**Members of the Assembly Approving
the Constitution in 1979**[1]

Name	Province/constituency
Afrugh, Ja'far	East Azerbaijan
Akrami, Seyyed Kazem	Hamadan
Angaji, Seyyed Mohammad-Ali	East Azerbaijan
Anvari, Mirza Mohammad	Hormozgan
Arab, Ali-Mohammad	Tehran
Ayat, Seyyed Hasan	Isfahan
Azodi, Hasan	Gilan
Bahonar, Mohammad-Javad	Kerman
Banisadr, Seyyed Abolhasan	Tehran
Barikbin, Hadi	Zanjan
Bat-Oshonagugtappeh, Sergon	Assyrians and Chaldeans
Beheshti, Seyyed Mohammad	Tehran
Besharat, Mohammad-Taqi	Kohgiluyeh and Buyer Ahmad
Daneshrad-Kiyai, Aziz	Jewish community
Dastgheyb, Seyyed Abdolhoseyn	Fars
Falsafi-Tonekaboni, Mirza Ali	Razavi Khorasan
Farsi, Jalaleddin	Razavi Khorasan
Fatehi, Javad	Kurdistan
Fowzi, Mohammad	West Azerbaijan
Golzadeh-Ghafuri, Ali	Tehran
Gorji, Mrs. Monireh	Tehran
Ha'eri-Yazdi, Morteza	Markazi
Haji Tarkhani-Tehrani, Mirza Javad	Razavi Khorasan
Hasheminezhad, Seyyed Habib	Mazandaran
Heydari, Abdorrahman	Ilam
Hojjati-Kermani, Mohammad-Javad	Kerman

1. The Assembly for the Final Examination of the Constitution (AFEC), which is commonly referred to as *Majlis-e Khebregan Qanun-e Asasi* or the Constitution Assembly of Experts, met from Aug. 19 to Nov. 15, 1979. The constitution that they drafted was overwhelmingly ratified in a nationwide referendum held December 2–3, 1979.

Name	Province/constituency
Hoseyni-Alhashemi, Seyyed Monireddin	Fars
Javadi-Amoli, Abdollah	Mazandaran
Karami, Mohammad	Khuzestan
Karimi-Divkolahi, Seyyed Ja'far	Mazandaran
Khademi, Seyyed Hoseyn	Isfahan
Khalatian, Hara'i	Armenians of northern Iran
Khamenei, Seyyed Mohammad	Razavi Khorasan
Khaz'ali, Seyyed Abdolqasem	Semnan
Kiyavash, Seyyed Mohammad	Khuzestan
Madani-Dehkharqani, Mir Asadollah	Hamadan
Makarem-Shirazi, Naser	Fars
Meshkini, Ali-Akbar	East Azerbaijan
Mir Morad-Zehi, Hamidollah	Sistan and Baluchestan
Mollazadeh, Abdolaziz	Sistan and Baluchestan
Montazeri, Hoseyn-Ali	Tehran
Moqaddam-Maragheh'i, Rahmatollah	East Azerbaijan
Moqaddasi-Shirazi, Abdolhasan	Razavi Khorasan
Musavi-Ardabili, Seyyed Abdolkarim	Tehran
Musavi-Jazayeri, Seyyed Mohammad-Ali	Khuzestan
Musavi-Qahderijani, Seyyed Musa	Kermanshah
Musavi-Tabrizi, Seyyed Abolfazl	East Azerbaijan
Musavi-Zanjani, Seyyed Esma'il	Zanjan
Nabavi, Seyyed Mohammad-Hasan	Bushehr
Nurbakhsh, Seyyed Ahmad	Chahar Mahal and Bakhtiari
Parvaresh, Seyyed Ali-Akbar	Isfahan
Qaemi-Amiri, Ali	Mazandaran
Qoreyshi, Mir Ali-Akbar	West Azerbaijan
Rabbani-Amlashi, Mohammad-Mehdi	Gilan
Rabbani-Shirazi, Abdorrahim	Fars
Rahmani, Hoseyn-Ali	Kurdistan
Rashidian, Mohammad	Khuzestan
Ruhani, Mahmud	Razavi Khorasan
Saduqi, Mohammad	Yazd
Safi-Golpayegani, Lotfollah	Markazi
Sahabi, Ezzatollah	Tehran
Shahzadi, Rostam	Zoroastrian community
Sheybani, Abbas	Tehran
Sobhani, Ja'far	East Azerbaijan
Tabataba'i, Seyyed Mohammad-Baqer	Lorestan
Taheri-Gorgani, Seyyed Habibollah	Mazandaran
Taheri-Isfahani, Seyyed Jalal	Isfahan
Taheri-Khorramabadi, Seyyed Hasan	Lorestan

Name	Province/constituency
Taleqani, Seyyed Mahmud	Tehran
Tehrani, Ali-Morad	Razavi Khorasan
Yazdi, Mohammad	Kermanshah
Ziya'iniya, Seyyed Abdollah	Gilan

Table 104
Data on the 1982 Assembly of Experts Election

Date of election	Dec. 10, 1982[a]
Number of eligible voters	23,277,871
Number of actual voters	18,013,061
Voter turnout rate	77.4%
Number of precincts	24
Number of candidates needed	83[b]
Number of registered entrants	168
Number of entrants disqualified	12
Final number of entrants who competed in the election	146
Percentage of all registered entrants who competed in the election	86.9%
Date of inaugural session	Aug. 15, 1983
Total number of deputies who served during the session	86

[a] All data on election date, number of eligible and actual voters, voter turnout rate, and number of registered candidates taken from http://www.moi.ir.
[b] Seventy-six individuals were elected in the first round (Dec. 10, 1982) and seven (two from Gilan, one from Kurdistan, one from East Azerbaijan, one from Isfahan, one from Tehran, and one from Bushehr) had to be elected in the second round (Keyhan, Jan. 9, 1983). Second-round elections were held on Apr. 15, 1984, and May 11, 1984.

Table 105
Breakdown of Votes Based on Province in the 1982 Assembly of Experts Election

Province	Voter turnout rate	Province	Voter turnout rate
Bushehr	85.74%	Khuzestan	76.21%
Chahar Mahal and Bakhtiari	75.03%	Kohgiluyeh and Buyer Ahmad	78.57%
East Azerbaijan	78.76%	Kurdistan	65.24%
Fars	82.20%	Lorestan	89.30%
Gilan	73.37%	Markazi	132.24%[a]
Hamadan	78.63%	Mazandaran	74.00%
Hormozgan	69.91%	Semnan	88.54%
Ilam	99.66%	Sistan and Baluchestan	Nullified[b]
Isfahan	82.86%	Tehran	71.85%
Kerman	76.03%	West Azerbaijan	74.48%
Kermanshah (Bakhtaran)	68.89%	Yazd	Nullified
Khorasan	75.91%	Zanjan	81.79%

[a] In Markazi Province, the number of eligible voters was 521,344, but a total of 689,427 votes were reportedly cast (132.24 percent).
[b] The Guardian Council nullified election results in Sistan and Baluchestan and Yazd Provinces.

Table 106
Data on the 1990 Assembly of Experts Election

Date of election	Oct. 8, 1990[a]
Number of eligible voters	31,280,084
Number of actual voters	11,602,613
Voter turnout rate	37.1%[b]
Number of precincts	24
Number of candidates needed	83
Number of registered entrants	180
Final number of entrants who competed in the election	106
Percentage of all registered entrants who competed in the election	58.9%
Date of inaugural session	Feb. 20, 1991
Total number of deputies who served during the session	85

[a] All data on election date, number of eligible and actual voters, voter turnout rate, and number of registered candidates taken from http://www.moi.ir. Also see *Ettela'at* (5 Aban 1377/October 27, 1998), 2.

[b] This turnout rate was 40% lower than the rate in 1982, which indicates voter disenchantment. This was partly because the Guardian Council imposed an initial written test on the entrants and disqualified many candidates.

Table 107
Breakdown of Votes Based on Province in the 1990 Assembly of Experts Election

Province	Voter turnout rate	Province	Voter turnout rate
Bushehr	Nullified[a]	Khuzestan	40.31%
Chahar Mahal and Bakhtiari	46.89%	Kohgiluyeh and Buyer Ahmad	43.72%
East Azerbaijan	39.63%	Kurdistan	44.77%
Fars	39.02%	Lorestan	46.29%
Gilan	Nullified	Markazi	44.00%
Hamadan	46.69%	Mazandaran	51.98%
Hormozgan	35.98%	Semnan	49.90%
Ilam	77.06%	Sistan and Baluchestan	Nullified
Isfahan	34.08%	Tehran	30.93%
Kerman	41.11%	West Azerbaijan	42.64%
Kermanshah (Bakhtaran)	46.10%	Yazd	48.63%
Khorasan	41.18%	Zanjan	47.38%

[a] The Guardian Council nullified election results in Bushehr, Gilan, and Sistan and Baluchestan Provinces.

Table 108
Data on the 1998 Assembly of Experts Election

Date of election	Oct. 23, 1998[a]
Number of eligible voters	38,570,597
Number of actual voters	17,857,869
Voter turnout rate	46.3%
Number of precincts	28
Number of candidates needed	86
Number of registered entrants	396 (387 male and 9 female)[b]
Number of entrants disqualified	215
Number of entrants approved	160[c]
Number of entrants who withdrew	35
Final number of entrants who competed in the election	146
Percentage of all registered entrants who competed in the election	36.86[d]
Date of inaugural session	Feb. 23, 1999
Total number of deputies who served during the session	90

[a] All data on election date, number of eligible and actual voters, voter turnout rate, and number of registered candidates taken from http://www.moi.ir.

[b] Emboldened by the presidency of Mohammad Khatami, forty-six non-clerics (of which nine were women) registered along with 350 clerics. The Guardian Council, however, did not approve the qualifications of any of the non-clerics. See http://www.bbc.com.

[c] http://www.isna.ir.

[d] *Ettela'at* (5 Aban 1377/October 27, 1998), 2.

Table 109
Breakdown of Votes Based on Province in the 1998 Assembly of Experts Election

Province	Voter turnout rate	Province	Voter turnout rate
Ardabil	44.14%	Khuzestan	41.24%
Bushehr	49.70%	Kohgiluyeh and Buyer Ahmad	69.26%
Chahar Mahal and Bakhtiari	49.71%	Kurdistan	41.65%
East Azerbaijan	41.15%	Lorestan	47.85%
Fars	46.71%	Markazi	47.27%
Gilan	41.20%	Mazandaran	50.75%
Golestan	64.55%	Qazvin	52.44%
Hamadan	44.70%	Qom	58.54%
Hormozgan	48.95%	Semnan	63.54%
Ilam	59.90%	Sistan and Baluchestan	42.79%
Isfahan	41.77%	Tehran	39.45%
Kerman	54.37%	West Azerbaijan	40.74%
Kermanshah	47.33%	Yazd	59.89%
Khorasan	55.12%	Zanjan	48.13%

Table 110
Data on the 2006 Assembly of Experts Election

Date of election	Dec. 15, 2006[a]
Number of eligible voters	46,549,042
Number of actual voters	28,321,270
Voter turnout rate	60.8%
Number of precincts	30
Number of candidates needed	86
Number of registered entrants	493 (483 male and 10 female)[b]
Number of entrants disqualified	209
Number of entrants approved	146[c]
Final number of entrants who competed in the election	167[d]
Percentage of all registered entrants who competed in the election	33.87%
Date of inaugural session	Feb. 20, 2007
Total number of deputies who served during the session	96

[a] All data on election date, number of eligible and actual voters, voter turnout rate, and number of registered candidates taken from http://www.moi.ir. See also www.majlesekhobregan.ir
[b] Mehr News Agency, Oct. 30, 2006.
[c] http://www.isna.ir.
[d] The Guardian Council may have reversed its initial decision to disqualify some candidates.

Table 111
Breakdown of Votes Based on Province in the 2006 Assembly of Experts Election

Province	Voter turnout rate	Province	Voter turnout rate
Ardabil	65%	Kurdistan	52%
Bushehr	72%	Lorestan	58%
Chahar Mahal and Bakhtiari	69%	Markazi	57%
East Azerbaijan	54%	Mazandaran	75%
Fars	64%	North Khorasan	71%
Gilan	68%	Qazvin	71%
Golestan	77%	Qom	58%
Hamadan	57%	Razavi Khorasan	64%
Hormozgan	75%	Semnan	75%
Ilam	83%	Sistan and Baluchestan	75%
Isfahan	54%	South Khorasan	78%
Kerman	80%	Tehran	47%
Kermanshah	57%	West Azerbaijan	56%
Khuzestan	56%	Yazd	68%
Kohgiluyeh and Buyer Ahmad	81%	Zanjan	66%

Table 112
Data on the 2016 Assembly of Experts Election

Date of election	Feb. 26, 2016
Number of eligible voters	54,915,024
Number of actual voters	33,480,548
Voter turnout rate	61.0%
Number of precincts	31
Number of candidates needed	88[a]
Number of registered entrants	801[b] (785 male and 16 female)[c]
Entrants who filled out the applications forms properly	796
Number of entrants who withdrew	158
Number of entrants judged not eligible to compete	111
Number of entrants who did not take the written exam	151[d]
Number of entrants who were disqualified	215
Final number of entrants who competed in the election	161[e]
Percentage of all registered entrants who competed in the election	20.23%
Date of inaugural session	May 25, 2016
Total number of deputies who served during the session (as of Jan. 1, 2018)	88

[a] With the establishment of the province of Alborz, which was assigned two seats, the total number of eligible seats for the Fifth Assembly of Experts increased from 86 to 88.
[b] http://irandataportal.syr.edu.
[c] http://www.bbc.com/persian.
[d] http://www.isna.ir.
[e] http://www.shora-gc.ir.

Table 113
Breakdown of Votes Based on Province in the 2016 Assembly of Experts Election

Province	Voter turnout rate	Province	Voter turnout rate
Alborz	54.07%	Kurdistan	53.43%
Ardabil	61.32%	Lorestan	62.75%
Bushehr	67.68%	Markazi	58.88%
Chahar Mahal and Bakhtiari	67.25%	Mazandaran	72.49%
East Azerbaijan	61.56%	North Khorasan	71.82%
Fars	63.77%	Qazvin	60.86%
Gilan	63.03%	Qom	61.14%
Golestan	71.12%	Razavi Khorasan	62.90%
Hamadan	56.15%	Semnan	65.70%
Hormozgan	68.19%	Sistan and Baluchestan	66.28%
Ilam	74.50%	South Khorasan	72.04%
Isfahan	57.36%	Tehran	53.11%
Kerman	62.87%	West Azerbaijan	65.82%
Kermanshah	59.70%	Yazd	74.22%
Khuzestan	57.81%	Zanjan	67.73%
Kohgiluyeh and Buyer Ahmad	77.22%		

Note: The voter turnout rate was calculated by dividing the actual number of votes cast by the number of eligible voters in each province. See Statistical Yearbook of Iran (2015–16, 914) and https://www.moi.ir.

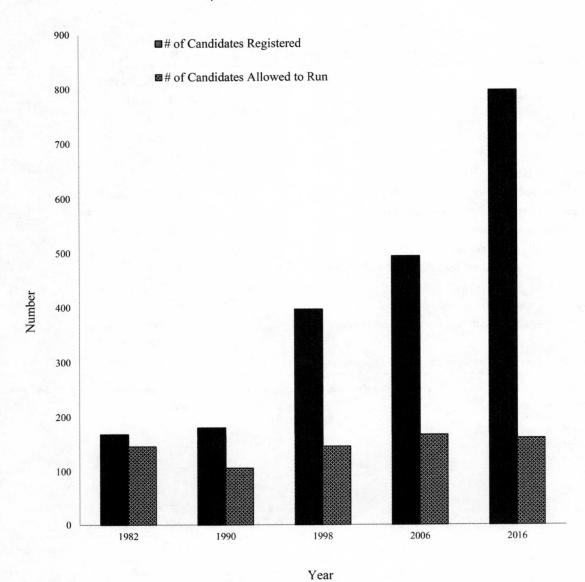

18. Number of Registered Entrants Compared to Number Who Competed in Assembly of Experts Elections. For sources of data, see Chapter 11.

Table 114

Ratio of Final Number of Candidates to Seats in Assembly of Experts Elections (1982–2016)

Session (year)	No. of entrants who competed	No. of seats	Ratio
First (1982)	146	83	1.76
Second (1990)	106	83	1.28
Third (1998)	146	86	1.70
Fourth (2006)	167	86	1.94
Fifth (2016)	161	88	1.83

Note: See the section titled Data on Assembly of Experts Elections (1982–2016) for sources.

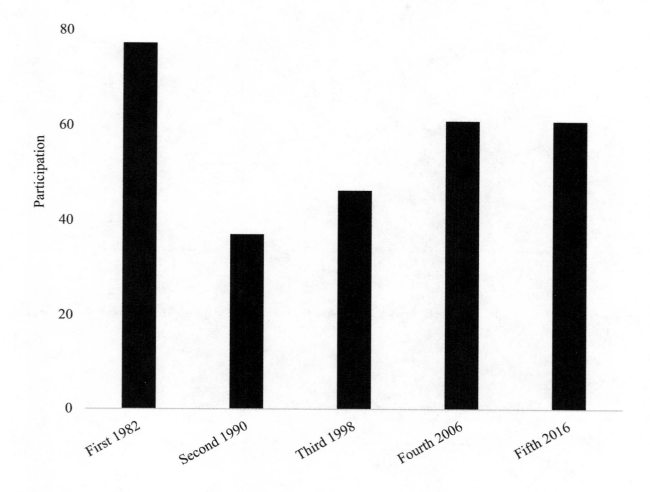

Session and Election Year

19. Average Voter Participation Rate in Assembly of Experts Elections (1982–2016). Source: Ministry of Interior (http://www.moi.ir/portal/File/ShowFile.aspx?ID=30759931-94c9-487d-9368-6426279490c8).

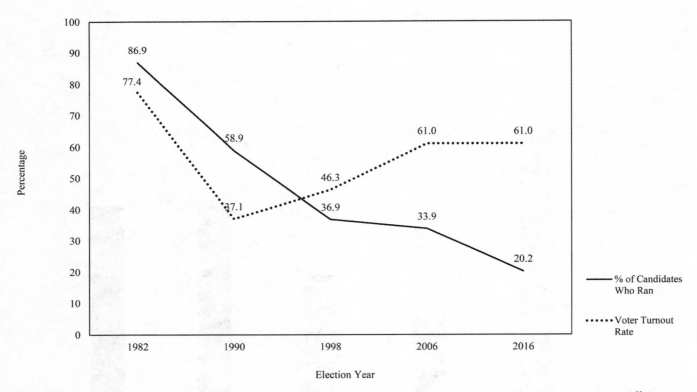

20. Percentage of All Registered Candidates Who Actually Competed in the Election versus Voter Turnout Rates in All Assembly of Experts Elections (1982–2016).

Table 115
Distribution of Seats by Province in Each Assembly of Experts Election

Province	1982	1990	1998	2006	2016
Alborz	*	*	*	*	2
Ardabil	*	*	2	2	2
Bushehr	1	1	1	1	1
Chahar Mahal and Bakhtiari	1	1	1	1	1
East Azerbaijan	7	7	5	5	5
Fars	5	5	5	5	5
Gilan	4	4	4	4	4
Golestan	*	*	2	2	2
Hamadan	2	2	2	2	2
Hormozgan	1	1	1	1	1
Ilam	1	1	1	1	1
Isfahan	5	5	5	5	5
Kerman	3	3	3	3	3
Kermanshah	2	2	2	2	2
Khuzestan	5	5	6	6	6
Kohgiluyeh and Buyer Ahmad	1	1	1	1	1

Table 115 (Cont.)
Distribution of Seats by Province in Each Assembly of Experts Election

Province	1982	1990	1998	2006	2016
Kurdistan	2	2	2	2	2
Lorestan	2	2	2	2	2
Markazi	3	3	2	2	2
Mazandaran	6	6	4	4	4
North Khorasan	*	*	1	1	1
Qazvin	*	*	2	2	2
Qom	*	*	1	1	1
Razavi Khorasan	8	8	6	6	6
Semnan	1	1	1	1	1
Sistan and Baluchestan	2	2	2	2	2
South Khorasan	*	*	1	1	1
Tehran	14	14	16	16	16
West Azerbaijan	3	3	3	3	3
Yazd	1	1	1	1	1
Zanjan	3	3	1	1	1
Total	83	83	86	86	88

Sources: https://www.moi.ir; www.shora-gc.ir.

Table 116
Members of the First Assembly of Experts (1983–90)

Name	Province of constituency	Tenure
Aba'i-Khorasani, Mohammad*	Razavi Khorasan	1988–90
Ahmadi-Miyanji, Ali	West Azerbaijan	1983–90
Amini, Ebrahim*	Chahar Mahal and Bakhtiari	1983–90
Aminiyan, Mokhtar*	Gilan	1983–90
Anvari, Mirza Mohammad	Hormozgan	1983–90
Asadi-Khansari, Seyyed Mohammad-Baqer	Tehran	1983–90
Azari-Qomi, Ahmad	Tehran	1983–90
Banifazl, Morteza	West Azerbaijan	1983–90
Barikbin, Hadi*	Zanjan	1983–90
Dastgheyb, Seyyed Ali-Asghar	Fars	1983–90
Dastgheyb, Seyyed Ali-Mohammad	Fars	1983–90
Ebadi, Seyyed Mehdi	Sistan and Baluchestan	1983–90
Ehsanbakhsh, Sadeq	Gilan	1983–90
Emami-Kashani, Mohammad*	Tehran	1983–88
Eshaq-Madani, Mohammad	Sistan and Baluchestan	1983–90
Fahim-Kermani, Morteza	Kerman	1983–90

Table 116 (Cont.)
Members of the First Assembly of Experts (1983–90)

Name	Province of constituency	Tenure
Fazel-Harandi, Mohyeddin	Fars	1983–90
Fazel-Lankarani, Mohammad	Markazi	1983–90
Ferdowsipur, Esma'il	Razavi Khorasan	1983–90
Feyz-Gilani, Mohammad-Ali	Gilan	1984–90
Gharavi, Abdolhoseyn	East Azerbaijan	1984–90
Gharavian, Abdoljavad	Razavi Khorasan	1983–90
Ha'eri-Shirazi, Mohammad-Sadeq*	Fars	1983–90
Haj Akhund-Kermanshahi, Mojtaba	Kermanshah	1983–90
Hashemi-Rafsanjani, Akbar*	Tehran	1983–90
Hashemiyan, Mohammad*	Kerman	1983–90
Hemmati-Moqaddam, Hasan	Khuzestan	1988–90
Heydari, Abdorrahman	Ilam	1983–86
Hoseyni, Seyyed Ali	Kurdistan	1984–90
Hoseyni-Kashani, Seyyed Mohammad	Isfahan	1984–90
Imani, Asadollah*	Fars	1983–90
Islami-Torbati, Ali-Akbar	Razavi Khorasan	1983–89
Izadi, Abbas	Isfahan	1983–90
Jamal-Yusefi, Ebrahim	Bushehr	1984–90
Jami, Gholam-Hoseyn*	Khuzestan	1983–90
Jannati, Ahmad*	Khuzestan	1983–90
Javadi-Amoli, Abdollah*	Mazandaran	1983–90
Karimi-Divkolahi, Seyyed Ja'far	Mazandaran	1983–90
Khademi, Seyyed Hoseyn	Isfahan	1983–85
Khalilzadeh-Moravvej, Boyuk	East Azerbaijan	1984–90
Khalkhali, Mohammad-Sadeq	Tehran	1984–90
Khamenei, Seyyed Ali*	Tehran	1983–89
Khatami, Seyyed Ruhollah*	Yazd	1983–88
Khaz'ali, Seyyed Abolqasem	Razavi Khorasan	1983–90
Khosrowshahi, Seyyed Hadi	Tehran	1983–90
Mahdavi-Kani, Mohammad-Baqer	Tehran	1983–90
Mahfuzi, Abbas	Gilan	1984–90
Malakuti, Moslem*	East Azerbaijan	1984–90
Ma'sumi, Ali-Asghar*	Razavi Khorasan	1983–90
Meshkini, Ali-Akbar*	Tehran	1983–90
Mohammadi, Abdollah	Kurdistan	1983–90
Mohammadi-Gilani, Mohammad	Tehran	1983–90
Mohammadi-La'ini, Hoseyn	Mazandaran	1983–90
Mohyeddin-Anvari, Mohammad-Baqer	Hamadan	1983–90

Table 116 (Cont.)
Members of the First Assembly of Experts (1983–90)

Name	Province of constituency	Tenure
Mojtahedi-Behbahani, Mohammad-Hoseyn	Khuzestan	1983–90
Mojtahed-Shabestari, Mohsen	East Azerbaijan	1984–90
Mo'men, Mohammad	Semnan	1983–90
Moqaddasi-Shirazi, Abolhasan	Razavi Khorasan	1983–90
Morvarid, Mohammad-Taqi	Ilam	1988–90
Movahhedi-Kermani, Mohammad-Ali*	Kerman	1983–90
Musavi-Ardabili, Seyyed Abdolkarim*	Tehran	1983–90
Musavi-Jazayeri, Seyyed Mohammad-Ali*	Khuzestan	1983–90
Musavi-Kho'iniha, Seyyed Mohammad	Zanjan	1983–90
Musavi-Tabrizi, Seyyed Abolfazl	East Azerbaijan	1984–90
Musavi-Tabrizi, Seyyed Mohsen	East Azerbaijan	1984–90
Musavi-Zanjani, Seyyed Esma'il	Zanjan	1983–90
Nuri-Hamadani, Hoseyn	Hamadan	1983–90
Nurmofidi, Seyyed Kazem*	Mazandaran	1984–90
Qazi-Dezfuli, Seyyed Majdeddin*	Khuzestan	1983–86
Qoreyshi, Mir Ali-Akbar	West Azerbaijan	1983–90
Rabbani-Amlashi, Mohammad-Mehdi	Razavi Khorasan	1983–85
Rasti-Kashani, Hoseyn	Tehran	1983–90
Rezvani, Gholam-Reza	Tehran	1983–90
Ruhani, Seyyed Mehdi	Markazi	1983–90
Ruhani, Hadi	Mazandaran	1983–90
Salehifard, Esma'il	Mazandaran	1983–90
Sane'i, Yusef	Tehran	1983–90
Shahmiri, Qorbanali	Kohgiluyeh and Buyer Ahmad	1983–90
Tabataba'i, Seyyed Mohammad-Baqer	Lorestan	1983–90
Taheri-Isfahani, Seyyed Jalal*	Isfahan	1983–90
Taheri-Khorramabadi, Seyyed Hasan*	Lorestan	1983–90
Taheri-Shams-Golpayegani, Jalal	Markazi	1983–90
Va'ez-Tabasi, Abbas	Razavi Khorasan	1983–90
Yasrebi, Seyyed Mehdi*	Isfahan	1983–90
Yekta'i, Heybatollah*	East Azerbaijan	1984–90
Zarandi-Ma'sumi, Hoseyn*	Kermanshah	1983–90

Source: Authors' database.

Note: An asterisk (*) at the end of an individual's name indicates that he was a Friday prayer leader either before or after serving in the Assembly of Experts. This applies to tables 116 to 119.

Table 117
Members of the Second Assembly of Experts (1991–98)

Name	Province of constituency	Tenure
Ahmadi-Miyanji, Ali	West Azerbaijan	1991–98
Alizadeh, Ali-Akbar	Razavi Khorasan	1991–98
Amini, Ebrahim*	Chahar Mahal and Bakhtiari	1991–98
Aminiyan, Mokhtar*	Gilan	1991–98
Anvari, Mirza Mohammad	Hormozgan	1991–98
Asadi-Khansari, Seyyed Mohammad-Baqer	Tehran	1991–98
Azari-Qomi, Ahmad	Tehran	1991–95
Banifazl, Morteza	East Azerbaijan	1991–98
Barikbin, Hadi*	Zanjan	1991–98
Dorri-Najafabadi, Qorbanali*	Ilam	1991–98
Ebadi, Seyyed Mehdi	Sistan and Baluchestan	1991–98
Emami-Kashani, Mohammad*	Tehran	1991–98
Eshaq-Madani, Mohammad	Sistan and Baluchestan	1991–98
Faqih, Seyyed Mohammad*	Fars	1991–98
Fazel-Harandi, Mohyeddin	Kerman	1991–98
Ferdowsipur, Esma'il	Razavi Khorasan	1991–98
Feyz-Gilani, Mohammad-Ali	Gilan	1991–98
Gharavian, Abdoljavad	Razavi Khorasan	1991–98
Ha'eri-Shirazi, Mohammad-Sadeq*	Fars	1991–98
Haj Akhund-Kermanshahi, Mojtaba	Kermanshah	1991–98
Haqi-Sarabi, Mohammad-Ali	East Azerbaijan	1991–98
Hashemi-Isfahani, Seyyed Esma'il	Isfahan	1991–98
Hashemi-Rafsanjani, Akbar*	Tehran	1991–98
Hojjati-Kermani, Mohammad-Javad	Kerman	1991–98
Hoseyni, Seyyed Ali	Kurdistan	1991–98
Hoseyni-Arsanjani, Seyyed Mohammad-Hoseyn	Fars	1991–98
Imani, Asadollah*	Fars	1991–98
Jabbari, Seyyed Saber*	Mazandaran	1991–98
Jannati, Ahmad*	Khuzestan	1991–98
Javadi-Amoli, Abdollah*	Mazandaran	1991–98
Kazemi-Kermanshahi, Mohammad-Reza	Kermanshah	1991–96
Khalilzadeh-Moravvej, Boyuk	East Azerbaijan	1991–98
Khansari, Abolfazl	Markazi	1991–98
Kharrazi, Seyyed Mohsen	Tehran	1991–98
Khatam-Yazdi, Seyyed Abbas	Yazd	1991–98
Khaz'ali, Seyyed Abolqasem	Razavi Khorasan	1991–98
Khomeini, Seyyed Ahmad	Tehran	1991–94
Khosrowshahi, Seyyed Hadi	Tehran	1991–98
Mahdavi-Kani, Mohammad-Baqer	Tehran	1991–98
Mahfuzi, Abbas	Gilan	1991–98

Table 117 (Cont.)
Members of the Second Assembly of Experts (1991–98)

Name	Province of constituency	Tenure
Malakuti, Moslem*	East Azerbaijan	1991–98
Malekhoseyni, Seyyed Keramatollah*	Kohgiluyeh and Buyer Ahmad	1991–98
Ma'sumi, Ali-Asghar*	Razavi Khorasan	1991–98
Mazaheri, Hoseyn	Isfahan	1991–98
Mehmannavaz, Habibollah*	Razavi Khorasan	1991–98
Mesbah-Yazdi, Mohammad-Taqi	Khuzestan	1991–98
Meshkini, Ali-Akbar*	Tehran	1991–98
Mohammadi, Abdollah	Kurdistan	1991–95
Mohammadi-Araqi, Mohsen*	Khuzestan	1991–98
Mohammadi-Gilani, Mohammad	Tehran	1991–98
Mohammadi-La'ini, Hoseyn	Mazandaran	1991–93
Mohyeddin-Anvari, Mohammad-Baqer	Tehran	1991–98
Mojtahed-Shabestari, Mohsen*	East Azerbaijan	1991–98
Mo'men, Mohammad	Semnan	1991–98
Moqaddasi-Shirazi, Abolhasan	Razavi Khorasan	1991–98
Moqtada'i, Morteza	Isfahan	1991–98
Movahhedi-Kermani, Mohammad-Ali*	Kerman	1991–98
Musavi-Hamadani, Seyyed Abolhasan	Hamadan	1991–98
Musavi-Jazayeri, Seyyed Mohammad-Ali*	Khuzestan	1991–98
Musavipur-Shali, Seyyed Hasan	Zanjan	1991–98
Musavi-Tabrizi, Seyyed Abolfazl	East Azerbaijan	1991–98
Musavi-Zanjani, Seyyed Esma'il	Zanjan	1991–98
Najmi, Mohammad-Sadeq	West Azerbaijan	1991–98
Namazi, Abdolnnabi*	Bushehr	1991–98
Nurmofidi, Seyyed Kazem*	Mazandaran	1991–98
Orumiyan, Ali	East Azerbaijan	1991–98
Qorbani-Panjah, Zeynol'abedin*	Gilan	1991–98
Qoreyshi, Mir Ali-Akbar	West Azerbaijan	1991–98
Rasti-Kashani, Hoseyn	Tehran	1991–98
Rasuli-Mahallati, Seyyed Hashem	Tehran	1991–98
Reyshahri, Mohammad	Tehran	1991–98
Rezvani, Gholam-Reza	Tehran	1991–98
Ruhani, Hadi	Mazandaran	1991–98
Ruhani, Seyyed Mehdi	Markazi	1991–98
Saberi-Hamadani, Ahmad	Hamadan	1991–98
Salehifard, Esma'il	Mazandaran	1991–98
Shafi'i, Seyyed Ali	Khuzestan	1991–98
Shaikhmovahhed, Ali	Fars	1991–98
Tabataba'i, Seyyed Mohammad-Baqer	Lorestan	1991–97
Taheri-Gorgani, Seyyed Habibollah	Mazandaran	1991–98

Table 117 (Cont.)
Members of the Second Assembly of Experts (1991–98)

Name	Province of constituency	Tenure
Taheri-Isfahani, Seyyed Jalal*	Isfahan	1991–98
Taheri-Khorramabadi, Seyyed Hasan*	Lorestan	1991–98
Va'ez-Tabasi, Abbas	Razavi Khorasan	1991–98
Yasrebi, Seyyed Mehdi*	Isfahan	1991–98
Yazdi, Mohammad*	Tehran	1991–98

Table 118
Members of the Third Assembly of Experts (1999–2006)

Name	Province of constituency	Tenure
Abbasifard, Mohammad-Reza	Khuzestan	1999–2006
Ahmadi, Zekrollah	Kermanshah	1999–2006
Ahmadi-Miyanji, Ali	East Azerbaijan	1999–2000
Alemi, Hasan	Razavi Khorasan	1999–2006
Alemi, Mohammad-Ali	Semnan	1999–99
Amini, Ebrahim*	Chahar Mahal and Bakhtiari	1999–2006
Aminiyan, Mokhtar*	Gilan	1999–2006
Ansari, Majid	Tehran	1999–2006
Anvari, Mirza Mohammad	Hormozgan	1999–2002
Asadi-Khansari, Seyyed Mohammad-Baqer	Tehran	1999–2006
Beheshti, Ahmad	Fars	1999–2006
Dastgheyb, Seyyed Ali-Asghar	Fars	1999–2006
Dastgheyb, Seyyed Ali-Mohammad	Fars	1999–2006
Dorri-Najafabadi, Qorbanali*	Tehran	1999–2006
Ebadi, Seyyed Mehdi	Razavi Khorasan	1999–2005
Emami-Kashani, Mohammad*	Tehran	1999–2006
Eshaq-Madani, Mohammad	Sistan and Baluchestan	1999–2006
Fallahiyan, Ali	Khuzestan	1999–2006
Ferdowsipur, Esma'il	Razavi Khorasan	1999–2006
Ghaffari-Qarebagh, Seyyed Akbar	West Azerbaijan	1999–2006
Hashemi-Isfahani, Seyyed Esma'il	Isfahan	1999–99
Hashemi-Rafsanjani, Akbar*	Tehran	1999–2006
Hashemi-Shahrudi, Seyyed Mahmud	Razavi Khorasan	1999–2006
Hashemiyan, Mohammad*	Kerman	1999–2006
Hashemzadeh-Herisi, Hashem	East Azerbaijan	1999–2006
Hoseyni, Seyyed Mojtaba	Sistan and Baluchestan	1999–2006
Hoseyni-Arsanjani, Seyyed Mohammad-Hoseyn	Fars	1999–2006
Imani, Asadollah*	Fars	1999–2006
Jabbari, Seyyed Saber*	Mazandaran	1999–2006

Table 118 (Cont.)
Members of the Third Assembly of Experts (1999–2006)

Name	Province of constituency	Tenure
Jannati, Ahmad*	Tehran	1999–2006
Ka'bi, Abbas	Khuzestan	1999–2006
Karimi-Divkolahi, Seyyed Ja'far	Mazandaran	1999–2006
Khalilzadeh-Moravvej, Boyuk	Ardabil	1999–2001
Kharrazi, Seyyed Mohsen	Tehran	1999–2006
Khatami, Seyyed Ahmad*	Kerman	1999–2006
Khatam-Yazdi, Seyyed Abbas	Yazd	1999–2001
Khaz'ali, Seyyed Abolqasem	Razavi Khorasan	1999–2006
Larijani-Amoli, Sadeq	Mazandaran	1999–2006
Mahdavi, Seyyed Abolhasan*	Isfahan	1999–2006
Mahfuzi, Abbas	Gilan	1999–2006
Malekhoseyni, Seyyed Keramatollah*	Kohgiluyeh and Buyer Ahmad	1999–2006
Ma'sumi, Ali-Asghar*	Razavi Khorasan	1999–2006
Mazaheri, Hoseyn	Isfahan	1999–2006
Mehmannavaz, Habibollah*	Razavi Khorasan	1999–2006
Mesbah-Yazdi, Mohammad-Taqi	Tehran	1999–2006
Meshkini, Ali-Akbar*	Tehran	1999–2006
Mir Mohammadi, Seyyed Abolfazl	Markazi	1999–2006
Mohammadi-Araqi, Mohsen*	Khuzestan	1999–2006
Mohammadi-Gilani, Mohammad	Tehran	1999–2006
Mohammadi-Ilami, Rahim	Ilam	1999–2006
Mohseni-Garakani, Ahmad*	Markazi	1999–2006
Mojtahed-Shabestari, Mohsen*	East Azerbaijan	1999–2006
Moqtada'i, Morteza	Isfahan	1999–2006
Movahhedi-Kermani, Mohammad-Ali*	Kerman	1999–2006
Musavi-Hamadani, Seyyed Abolhasan	Hamadan	1999–2006
Musavi-Jazayeri, Seyyed Mohammad-Ali*	Khuzestan	1999–2006
Musavipur-Shali, Seyyed Hasan	Qazvin	1999–2003
Musavi-Tabrizi, Seyyed Abolfazl	East Azerbaijan	1999–2003
Musavi-Tabrizi, Seyyed Hoseyn	West Azerbaijan	1999–2006
Musavi-Zanjani, Seyyed Esma'il	Zanjan	1999–2002
Najmi, Mohammad-Sadeq	East Azerbaijan	1999–2006
Namazi, Abdolnnabi*	Bushehr	1999–2006
Nurani-Ardabili, Mostafa	Ardabil	1999–2003
Nurmofidi, Seyyed Kazem*	Golestan	1999–2006
Orumiyan, Ali	East Azerbaijan	1999–2006
Ostadi-Moqaddam, Reza*	Tehran	1999–2006
Qomi, Mohsen	Tehran	1999–2006
Qorbani-Panjah, Zeynol'abedin*	Gilan	1999–2006
Qoreyshi, Mir Ali-Akbar	West Azerbaijan	1999–2006

Table 118 (Cont.)
Members of the Third Assembly of Experts (1999–2006)

Name	Province of constituency	Tenure
Reyshahri, Mohammad	Tehran	1999–2006
Rezvani, Gholam-Reza	Tehran	1999–2006
Rouhani, Hassan	Semnan	2000–2006
Ruhani, Hadi	Mazandaran	1999–99
Ruhani, Seyyed Mehdi	Qom	1999–2000
Saberi-Hamadani, Ahmad	Hamadan	1999–2006
Shafi'i, Seyyed Ali	Khuzestan	1999–2006
Shahrokhi, Seyyed Mohammad-Taqi*	Lorestan	1999–2006
Shaikhmohammadi, Ali	Qazvin	1999–2006
Shaikholislami, Mohammad	Kurdistan	1999–2006
Tabarsi, Nurollah*	Mazandaran	1999–2006
Taheri-Gorgani, Seyyed Habibollah	Golestan	1999–2006
Taheri-Isfahani, Seyyed Jalal*	Isfahan	1999–2006
Taheri-Khorramabadi, Seyyed Hasan*	Lorestan	1999–2006
Taskhiri, Mohammad-Ali	Gilan	1999–2006
Tavassoli-Mahallati, Mohammad-Reza	Tehran	1999–2006
Va'ez-Tabasi, Abbas	Razavi Khorasan	1999–2006
Yasrebi, Seyyed Mehdi*	Isfahan	1999–2006
Yazdi, Mohammad*	Tehran	1999–2006
Zahedi, Abdolqader	Kurdistan	1999–2005
Zarandi-Ma'sumi, Hoseyn*	Kermanshah	1999–2006

Table 119
Members of the Fourth Assembly of Experts (2007–16)

Name	Province of constituency	Tenure
Abdollahi, Abdolmahmud	Isfahan	2007–16
Ahmadi-Shahrudi, Mohammad-Hoseyn	Khuzestan	2007–16
Alamolhoda, Seyyed Ahmad*	Razavi Khorasan	2007–16
Alavi, Seyyed Mahmud	Tehran	2009–16
Alemi, Hasan	Razavi Khorasan	2012–16
Ameli-Kalkhoran, Seyyed Hasan*	Ardabil	2007–16
Aminiyan, Mokhtar*	Gilan	2007–14
Bahrami-Khoshkar, Mohammad	Kerman	2007–16
Banifazl, Morteza	East Azerbaijan	2007–7
Barikbin, Hadi*	Qazvin	2007–16
Beheshti, Ahmad*	Fars	2007–16
Dastgheyb, Seyyed Ali-Asghar	Fars	2007–16

Table 119 (Cont.)
Members of the Fourth Assembly of Experts (2007–16)

Name	Province of constituency	Tenure
Dastgheyb, Seyyed Ali-Mohammad	Fars	2007–16
Dirbaz, Asgar	West Azerbaijan	2013–16
Dorri-Najafabadi, Qorbanali*	Tehran	2007–16
Emami-Kashani, Mohammad*	Tehran	2007–16
Faker, Mohammad-Reza	Razavi Khorasan	2007–10
Fallahiyan, Ali	Khuzestan	2007–16
Fayyazi, Gholam-Reza	Zanjan	2007–16
Feyzi-Sarabi, Mohammad	East Azerbaijan	2007–16
Ghaffari-Qarebagh, Seyyed Akbar	West Azerbaijan	2007–12
Ha'eri-Shirazi, Mohammad-Sadeq*	Fars	2007–16
Hashemi-Rafsanjani, Akbar*	Tehran	2007–16
Hashemi-Shahrudi, Seyyed Mahmud	Razavi Khorasan	2007–16
Hashemzadeh-Herisi, Hashem	East Azerbaijan	2008–16
Heydari-Alekasir, Mohsen*	Khuzestan	2007–16
Hoseyni-Bushehri, Seyyed Hashem*	Bushehr	2007–16
Hoseyni-Shahrudi, Seyyed Abdolhadi*	Golestan	2009–16
Imani, Asadollah	Fars	2007–16
Islami, Ali*	Qazvin	2008–16
Islamiyan, Ali-Reza	Chahar Mahal and Bakhtiari	2007–16
Jabbari, Seyyed Saber*	Mazandaran	2007–14
Jannati, Ahmad*	Tehran	2007–16
Ka'bi, Abbas	Khuzestan	2007–16
Kazeruni, Mohsen*	Tehran	2007–16
Kharrazi, Seyyed Mohsen	Tehran	2007–16
Khatami, Seyyed Ahmad*	Kerman	2007–16
Khaz'ali, Seyyed Abolqasem	Razavi Khorasan	2007–15
Khoda'i, Abdorrahman*	Kurdistan	2007–16
Larijani-Amoli, Sadeq	Mazandaran	2007–16
Mahdavi, Seyyed Abolhasan*	Isfahan	2007–16
Mahdavi-Kani, Mohammad-Baqer	Tehran	2007–16
Mahdavi-Kani, Mohammad-Reza	Tehran	2008–14
Mahfuzi, Abbas	Gilan	2007–16
Malekhoseyni, Seyyed Keramatollah*	Kohgiluyeh and Buyer Ahmad	2007–12
Malekhoseyni, Seyyed Sharafeddin*	Kohgiluyeh and Buyer Ahmad	2013–16
Mamduhi, Hasan	Kermanshah	2007–16
Mar'ashi-Shushtari, Mohammad-Hasan	Tehran	2007–8
Ma'sumi, Ali-Asghar*	Razavi Khorasan	2007–16
Mehmannavaz, Habibollah*	North Khorasan	2007–16
Mesbah-Yazdi, Mohammad-Taqi	Tehran	2007–16
Meshkini, Ali-Akbar*	Tehran	2007–7

Table 119 (Cont.)
Members of the Fourth Assembly of Experts (2007–16)

Name	Province of constituency	Tenure
Mir Mohammadi, Seyyed Abolfazl	Markazi	2007–16
Mo'allemi-Juybari, Ali*	Mazandaran	2007–16
Mohammadi-Gilani, Mohammad	Tehran	2007–14
Mohammadi-Hamadani, Gheyaseddin*	Hamadan	2007–16
Mohseni-Garakani, Ahmad*	Markazi	2007–16
Mojtahedi, Hesameddin*	Kurdistan	2012–14
Mojtahed-Shabestari, Mohsen*	East Azerbaijan	2007–16
Mo'men, Mohammad	Qom	2007–16
Moqtada'i, Morteza	Isfahan	2007–16
Movahhedi-Kermani, Mohammad-Ali*	Kerman	2007–16
Musavi-Jazayeri, Seyyed Mohammad-Ali*	Khuzestan	2007–16
Na'imabadi, Gholam-Ali*	Hormozgan	2007–16
Namazi, Abdolnnabi*	Tehran	2007–16
Namazi, Hasan	West Azerbaijan	2007–16
Nurmofidi, Seyyed Kazem*	Golestan	2007–16
Ostadi-Moqaddam, Reza*	Tehran	2007–16
Purmohammadi, Mohammad-Taqi*	East Azerbaijan	2007–16
Qomi, Mohsen	Tehran	2007–16
Qorbani-Panjah, Zeynol'abedin*	Gilan	2007–16
Qoreyshi, Mir Ali-Akbar	West Azerbaijan	2007–16
Ra'isi, Seyyed Ebrahim	South Khorasan	2007–16
Ramezani-Gilani, Reza*	Gilan	2007–16
Razini, Ali	Hamadan	2007–16
Rouhani, Hassan	Tehran	2007–16
Sadati, Seyyed Abdossamad*	Sistan and Baluchestan	2007–16
Salami, Ali-Ahmad	Sistan and Baluchestan	2007–16
Seyyed Hatami, Seyyed Ebrahim	Ardabil	2007–16
Shafi'i, Seyyed Ali	Khuzestan	2007–16
Shahcheraqi, Seyyed Mohammad*	Semnan	2007–16
Shahrokhi, Seyyed Mohammad-Taqi*	Lorestan	2007–16
Shaikholislami, Mohammad	Kurdistan	2007–9
Shari'ati-Niyasar, Hasan Aqa	Isfahan	2007–16
Soleymani-Asbukala'i, Abbas-Ali*	Sistan and Baluchestan	2007–16
Tabarsi, Nurollah*	Mazandaran	2007–16
Tabataba'inezhad, Seyyed Yusef*	Isfahan	2007–16
Taheri-Gorgani, Seyyed Habibollah	Golestan	2007–7
Taheri-Khorramabadi, Seyyed Hasan*	Lorestan	2007–13
Taheri-Khorramabadi, Seyyed Mojtaba	Ilam	2008–16
Va'ezi, Mohammad-Taqi*	Zanjan	2007–16
Va'ez-Musavi, Seyyed Mohammad	East Azerbaijan	2007–16

Table 119 (Cont.)
Members of the Fourth Assembly of Experts (2007–16)

Name	Province of constituency	Tenure
Va'ez-Tabasi, Abbas	Razavi Khorasan	2007–16
Vafi-Yazdi, Abolqasem	Yazd	2007–16
Yazdi, Mohammad*	Tehran	2007–16
Zarandi-Ma'sumi, Hoseyn*	Kermanshah	2007–14

Table 120
Members of the Fifth Assembly of Experts (2016–22)

Name	Province of constituency	Tenure
Abdekhoda'i, Mohammad-Hadi	Razavi Khorasan	2016–22
Abdollahi, Abdolmahmud	Isfahan	2016–22
Abolqasem-Dolabi, Mohammad Haji	Zanjan	2016–22
Ahmadi-Shahrudi, Mohammad-Hoseyn	Khuzestan	2016–22
Alamolhoda, Seyyed Ahmad*	Razavi Khorasan	2016–22
Alavi, Seyyed Mahmud	Tehran	2016–22
Alemi, Hasan	Razavi Khorasan	2016–22
Alimoradi, Amanollah	Kerman	2016–22
Ameli-Kalkhoran, Seyyed Hasan*	Ardabil	2016–22
Amini, Ebrahim*	Tehran	2016–22
Bahrami-Khoshkar, Mohammad	Kerman	2016–22
Bathaie, Seyyed Hashem*	Tehran	2016–22
Beheshti, Ahmad*	Fars	2016–22
Dastgheyb, Seyyed Ali-Asghar	Fars	2016–22
Dirbaz, Asgar	West Azerbaijan	2016–22
Dorri-Najafabadi, Qorbanali*	Tehran	2016–22
Emami-Kashani, Mohammad*	Tehran	2016–22
Esma'ili, Mohsen	Tehran	2016–22
Faqih, Seyyed Mohammad*	Fars	2016–22
Farhani, Abdolkarim	Khuzestan	2016–22
Feyzi-Sarabi, Mohammad	East Azerbaijan	2016–22
Hashemi-Rafsanjani, Akbar*	Tehran	2016–17
Hashemi-Shahrudi, Seyyed Mahmud	Razavi Khorasan	2016–22
Hashemzadeh-Herisi, Hashem	East Azerbaijan	2016–22
Heydari-Alekasir, Mohsen*	Khuzestan	2016–22
Hoseyni, Seyyed Mojtaba	Razavi Khorasan	2016–22
Hoseyni-Bushehri, Seyyed Hashem*	Bushehr	2016–22
Hoseyni-Eshkevari, Seyyed Ali	Gilan	2016–22
Hoseyni-Khorasani, Seyyed Ahmad	Razavi Khorasan	2016–22
Hoseyni-Shahrudi, Seyyed Abdolhadi*	Golestan	2016–22

Table 120 (Cont.)
Members of the Fifth Assembly of Experts (2016–22)

Name	Province of constituency	Tenure
Hoseyni-Shahrudi, Seyyed Mohammad	Kurdistan	2016–22
Imani, Asadollah	Fars	2016–22
Islami, Ali*	Qazvin	2016–22
Islamiyan, Ali-Reza	Chahar Mahal and Bakhtiari	2016–22
Jannati, Ahmad*	Tehran	2016–22
Ka'bi, Abbas	Khuzestan	2016–22
Kalantari, Ali-Akbar	Fars	2016–22
Kazeruni, Mohsen*	Alborz	2016–22
Khatami, Seyyed Ahmad	Kerman	2016–22
Larijani-Amoli, Sadeq	Mazandaran	2016–22
Mahdavi, Seyyed Abolhasan*	Isfahan	2016–22
Malakuti, Ali	East Azerbaijan	2016–22
Malekhoseyni, Seyyed Sharafeddin*	Kohgiluyeh and Buyer Ahmad	2016–22
Mehmannavaz, Habibollah*	North Khorasan	2016–22
Mir Baqeri, Seyyed Mohammad-Mehdi	Alborz	2016–22
Mir Mohammadi, Seyyed Abolfazl	Tehran	2016–22
Mo'allemi-Juybari, Ali*	Mazandaran	2016–22
Mobaleqi, Ahmad	Lorestan	2016–22
Mohammadi-Araqi, Mahmud	Kermanshah	2016–22
Mohammadi-Araqi, Mohsen*	Markazi	2016–22
Mohammadi-Hamadani, Gheyaseddin*	Hamadan	2016–22
Mohseni-Garakani, Ahmad*	Markazi	2016–22
Mojtahed-Shabestari, Javad	West Azerbaijan	2016–22
Mojtahed-Shabestari, Mohsen*	East Azerbaijan	2016–22
Mo'men, Mohammad	Qom	2016–22
Moqtada'i, Morteza	Isfahan	2016–22
Movahhedi-Kermani, Mohammad-Ali*	Tehran	2016–22
Musavi-Faraz, Seyyed Mostafa	Hamadan	2016–22
Musavi-Jazayeri, Seyyed Mohammad-Ali*	Khuzestan	2016–22
Musavi-Nanehkaran, Mir Fakhreddin	Ardabil	2016–22
Namazi, Abdolnnabi*	Isfahan	2016–22
Narimani, Aman*	Kermanshah	2016–22
Niyazi, Hashem	Lorestan	2016–22
Nurmofidi, Seyyed Kazem*	Golestan	2016–22
Parva'i-Rik, Ahmad	Gilan	2016–22
Purmohammadi, Mohammad-Taqi*	East Azerbaijan	2016–22
Qomi, Mohsen	Tehran	2016–22
Qorbani-Panjah, Zeynol'abedin*	Gilan	2016–22
Qoreyshi, Mir Ali-Akbar	West Azerbaijan	2016–22
Ra'isi, Seyyed Ebrahim	South Khorasan	2016–22

Table 120 (Cont.)
Members of the Fifth Assembly of Experts (2016–22)

Name	Province of constituency	Tenure
Ramezani-Gilani, Reza*	Gilan	2016–22
Reyshahri, Mohammad	Tehran	2016–22
Rostami, Fayeq*	Kurdistan	2016–22
Rouhani, Hassan	Tehran	2016–22
Sadrolsadati, Seyyed Ruhollah	Hormozgan	2016–22
Sa'idi-Golpayegani, Seyyed Mohsen	Ilam	2016–22
Salami, Ali-Ahmad	Sistan and Baluchestan	2016–22
Shafi'i, Seyyed Ali	Khuzestan	2016–22
Shahabadi, Nasrollah	Tehran	2016–18
Shahcheraqhi, Seyyed Mohammad*	Semnan	2016–22
Soleymani-Asbukala'i, Abbas-Ali*	Sistan and Baluchestan	2016–22
Tabarsi, Nurollah*	Mazandaran	2016–22
Tabataba'inezhad, Seyyed Yusef*	Isfahan	2016–22
Talkhabi, Majid	Qazvin	2016–22
Taskhiri, Mohammad-Ali	Tehran	2016–22
Tavakkol, Seyyed Rahim	Mazandaran	2016–22
Vafi-Yazdi, Abolqasem	Yazd	2016–22
Zali, Mohammad-Hasan	Tehran	2016–22

Note: The members of the Fifth Assembly of Experts are supposed to serve a six-year term ending in 2022. However, it is quite possible that due to advanced age, resignations, or accidents, some of them will not be able to complete their full term.

Table 121
Sunni Members of the Assembly of Experts

Name	Province of constituency	AE session
Eshaq-Madani, Mohammad	Sistan and Baluchestan	1, 2, 3
Hoseyni, Seyyed Ali	Kurdistan	1, 2
Khoda'i, Abdorrahman	Kurdistan	4
Mir Morad-Zehi, Hamidollah	Sistan and Baluchestan	AFEC
Mohammadi, Abdollah	Kurdistan	1, 2
Mojtahedi, Hesameddin	Kurdistan	4
Mollazadeh, Abdolaziz	Sistan and Baluchestan	AFEC
Rostami, Fayeq	Kurdistan	5
Sadati, Seyyed Abdossamad	Sistan and Baluchestan	4
Salami, Ali-Ahmad	Sistan and Baluchestan	4, 5
Shaikholislami, Mohammad	Kurdistan	3, 4
Zahedi, Abdolqader	Kurdistan	3

Source: Authors' database.

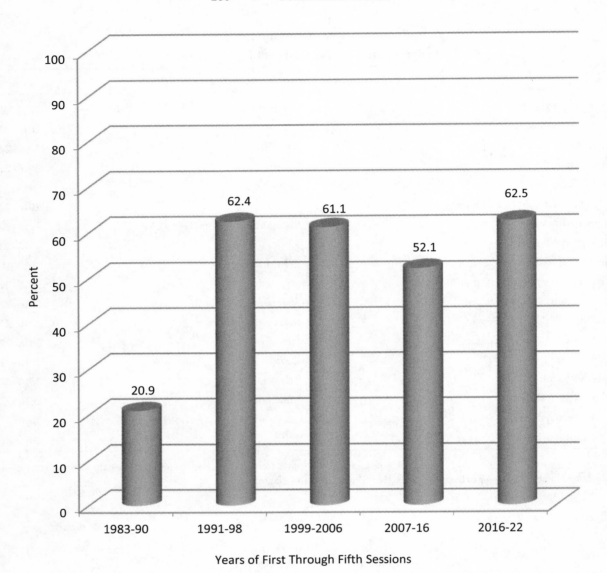

21. Incumbency Rate for Each Assembly of Experts (1983–2022). The Assembly for the Final Examination of the Constitution (AFEC) is generally known as the "Constitutional Assembly of Experts." In this figure the 20.9 percent incumbency rate for the First Assembly of Experts refers to individuals who had also served in the AFEC. Source: Authors' database.

Table 122
Place of Birth of All Assembly of Experts Members (1979–2017)

Province	Number and percentage of deputies from each province	Percentage of deputies born in each provincial capital
Isfahan	34 (12.73%)	Isfahan (32%)
East Azerbaijan	22 (8.24%)	Tabriz (36%)
Razavi Khorasan	20 (7.44%)	Mashhad (74%)
Tehran	17 (6.36%)	Tehran (71%)
Fars	16 (5.99%)	Shiraz (56%)
Qom	16 (5.99%)	Qom (100%)
Mazandaran	12 (4.49%)	Sari (0%)
Kerman	10 (3.75%)	Kerman (30%)
Gilan	10 (3.75%)	Rasht (20%)
Ardabil	9 (3.37%)	Ardabil (33%)
Khuzestan	9 (3.37%)	Ahvaz (22%)
Markazi	9 (3.37%)	Arak (11%)
Lorestan	9 (3.37%)	Khorramabad (44%)
Iraq[a]	9 (3.37%)	Baghdad (0%)
Hamadan	8 (3%)	Hamadan (50%)
Kurdistan	8 (3%)	Sanandaj (13%)
Kermanshah	6 (2.25%)	Kermanshah (50%)
Yazd	6 (2.25%)	Yazd (67%)
Semnan	6 (2.25%)	Semnan (17%)
Qazvin	5 (1.87%)	Qazvin (60%)
Bushehr	5 (1.87%)	Bushehr (40%)
Sistan and Baluchestan	5 (1.87%)	Zahedan (0%)
West Azerbaijan	3 (1.13%)	Urmia (33%)
Zanjan	3 (1.13%)	Zanjan (33%)
South Khorasan	2 (0.75%)	Birjand (0%)
Golestan	2 (0.75%)	Gorgan (100%)
Ilam	2 (0.75%)	Ilam (100%)
Chahar Mahal and Bakhtiari	1 (0.37%)	Shahrekord (0%)
Kohgiluyeh and Buyer Ahmad	1 (0.37%)	Yasouj (0%)
North Khorasan	1 (0.37%)	Bojnurd (0%)
Hormozgan	0 (0%)	0
Alborz	0 (0%)	0
Total	266 (100%)	41%

Source: Authors' database.

Note: This table includes data on 267 individuals who served in the Assembly for the Final Examination of the Constitution (AFEC) and in the First through Fifth Assembly of Experts (1983–2017). The birth province of one individual (Hasan Hemmati-Moqaddam) could not be found and we have not counted him. Numbers have been rounded to the nearest integer.

[a] The following individuals were born in neighboring Iraq: Mohammad-Hoseyn Ahmadi-Shahrudi, Abolhoseyn Gharavi, Seyyed Mahmud Hashemi-Shahrudi, Seyyed Abdolhadi Hoseyni-Shahrudi, Seyyed Mohammad Hoseyni-Shahrudi, Mohammad Karami, Sadeq Larijani-Amoli, Mohsen Mohammadi-Araqi, and Mohammad-Ali Taskhiri.

12
Municipal Councils

Table 123
Data on Municipal Council Elections (1999–2013)

	Date	Number of eligible voters	Number of votes	Turnout rate	Number of candidates
First municipal council elections	Feb. 26, 1999	36,739,982	23,668,739	64.42%	336,138
Second municipal council elections	Feb. 28, 2003	40,501,783	20,235,898	49.96%	218,957
Third municipal council elections	Dec. 15, 2006	43,500,000	28,199,903	64.83%	247,759
Fourth municipal council elections	June 14, 2013	50,483,192	31,627,704	62.65%	259,664

Source: Ministry of Interior (http://www.moi.ir).

Table 124
Number of Urban and Rural Municipal Councils in Each Province in 2003 and 2013

	SECOND MUNICIPAL COUNCILS (2003)			FOURTH MUNICIPAL COUNCILS (2013)		
	Total	Urban areas	Rural areas	Total	Urban areas	Rural areas
Alborz	*	*	*	255	16	239
Ardabil	1,092	20	1,072	995	26	969
Bushehr	410	23	387	415	37	378
Chahar Mahal and Bakhtiari	536	24	512	530	36	494
East Azerbaijan	1,871	53	1,818	1,799	59	1,740
Fars	2,166	69	2,097	2,308	100	2,208
Gilan	2,158	45	2,113	2,094	52	2,042
Golestan	915	22	893	933	26	907
Hamadan	942	25	917	887	29	858
Hormozgan	934	18	916	1,272	38	1,234
Ilam	392	16	376	368	23	345
Isfahan	991	87	904	988	105	883
Kerman	1,513	49	1,464	2,359	70	2,289
Kermanshah	1,662	27	1,635	1,392	30	1,362
Khuzestan	1,682	42	1,640	1,875	76	1,799
Kohgiluyeh and Buyer Ahmad	745	14	731	688	17	671
Kurdistan	1,475	23	1,452	1,352	29	1,323

Table 124 (Cont.)
Number of Urban and Rural Municipal Councils in Each Province in 2003 and 2013

	SECOND MUNICIPAL COUNCILS (2003)			FOURTH MUNICIPAL COUNCILS (2013)		
	Total	Urban areas	Rural areas	Total	Urban areas	Rural areas
Lorestan	1,371	24	1,347	1,160	25	1,135
Markazi	842	24	818	816	32	784
Mazandaran	2,148	47	2,101	2,397	58	2,339
North Khorasan	*	*	*	742	18	724
Qazvin	607	20	587	557	25	532
Qom	117	5	112	136	6	130
Razavi Khorasan	3,980	81	3,899	2,569	73	2,496
Semnan	274	16	258	300	19	281
Sistan and Baluchestan	1,973	31	1,942	2,821	37	2,784
South Khorasan	*	*	*	893	27	866
Tehran	710	44	666	501	42	459
West Azerbaijan	2,085	33	2,052	1,884	42	1,842
Yazd	413	21	392	376	21	355
Zanjan	772	16	756	693	19	674
Total	34,776	919	33,857	36,355	1,213	35,142

Source: Statistical Center of Iran (1394/2015–16, p. 921).

Table 125
Number of Total Candidates Elected in Municipal Council Elections by Province

	First council (1993–2003)	Second council (2003–7)	Third council (2007–13)[a]	Fourth council (2013–17)
Alborz[b]	*	*	*	1,412
Ardabil	5,083	4,696	3,756	4,631
Bushehr	2,080	2,028	1,381	2,212
Chahar Mahal and Bakhtiari	2,574	2,441	1,726	2,622
East Azerbaijan	9,784	8,623	5,893	8,842
Fars	10,822	10,099	7,624	11,356
Gilan	11,233	8,782	6,661	10,225
Golestan	4,608	4,574	2,994	5,104
Hamadan	4,866	4,373	3,223	4,437
Hormozgan	3,597	4,162	3,121	6,463
Ilam	1,945	1,727	1,132	1,817
Isfahan	5,655	5,064	3,211	5,435

[a] The term of the third council was extended by two years.

[b] The votes that were cast in the Alborz region before Alborz Province was established have been counted as part of Tehran Province.

Table 125 (Cont.)
Number of Total Candidates Elected in Municipal Council Elections by Province

	First council (1993–2003)	Second council (2003–7)	Third council (2007–13)[a]	Fourth council (2013–17)
Kerman	6,426	6,752	5,457	11,624
Kermanshah	7,399	7,042	4,942	6,372
Khuzestan	7,651	7,321	5,580	9,317
Kohgiluyeh and Buyer Ahmad	3,356	2,964	2,079	3,154
Kurdistan	7,000	6,529	4,318	6,410
Lorestan	5,921	4,698	3,441	5,294
Markazi	3,972	3,666	2,765	4,032
Mazandaran	10,551	9,459	7,203	12,167
North Khorasan	*	*	2,226	3,708
Qazvin	2,859	2,686	1,854	2,779
Qom	556	557	370	693
Razavi Khorasan	20,076	19,449	8,168	12,913
Semnan	1,387	1,359	901	1,568
Sistan and Baluchestan	5,728	7,999	6,287	13,157
South Khorasan[c]	*	*	2,138	4,302
Tehran	3,897	3,879	2,369	3,000
West Azerbaijan	9,257	8,854	5,748	8,939
Yazd	1,705	2,012	1,319	1,942
Zanjan	3,992	3,524	1,249	3,388
Iran (total)	163,980	155,319	109,136	179,315

Source: Statistical Center of Iran (1394/2015–16), p. 922.
[c] The votes that were cast in the North and South Khorasan regions before North Khorasan Province and South Khorasan Province were established have been counted as part of Razavi Khorasan Province.

Table 126
Number of Male Candidates Elected in Municipal Council Elections by Province (1993–2017)

Province	First council (1993–2003)	Second council (2003–7)	Third council (2007–13)[a]	Fourth council (2013–17)
Alborz[b]	*	*	*	1,344
Ardabil	5,072	4,667	3,734	4,572
Bushehr	2,061	1,971	1,357	2,107
Chahar Mahal and Bakhtiari	2,556	2,424	1,717	2,582
East Azerbaijan	9,751	8,582	5,857	8,741
Fars	10,769	9,993	7,544	10,937
Gilan	11,091	8,628	6,538	9,775
Golestan	4,588	4,452	2,943	4,919
Hamadan	4,842	4,337	3,183	4,336
Hormozgan	3,560	4,085	3,072	6,221
Ilam	1,931	1,713	1,117	1,746
Isfahan	5,578	4,949	3,124	5,225
Kerman	6,282	6,486	5,307	10,787
Kermanshah	7,376	6,995	4,914	6,202
Khuzestan	7,588	7,257	5,513	9,096
Kohgiluyeh and Buyer Ahmad	3,352	2,939	2,065	3,029
Kurdistan	6,976	6,508	4,300	6,356
Lorestan	5,892	4,650	3,411	5,045
Markazi	3,927	3,596	2,699	3,875
Mazandaran	10,459	9,314	7,090	11,717
North Khorasan	*	*	2,206	3,604
Qazvin	2,837	2,653	1,828	2,703
Qom	546	540	362	660
Razavi Khorasan	19,922	19,168	8,059	12,510
Semnan	1,359	1,299	874	1,496
Sistan and Baluchestan	5,655	7,827	6,184	12,659
South Khorasan[c]	*	*	2,108	4,160
Tehran	3,770	3,701	2,296	2,772
West Azerbaijan	9,240	8,819	5,717	8,844
Yazd	1,653	1,940	1,297	1,871
Zanjan	3,972	3,490	1,229	3,328
Total	162,605	152,983	107,645	173,219

Source: Statistical Center of Iran (1394/2015–16), 922.

[a] The term of the third council was extended by two years.

[b] The votes that were cast in the Alborz region before Alborz Province was established have been counted as part of Tehran Province.

[c] The votes that were cast in the North and South Khorasan regions before North Khorasan Province and South Khorasan Province were established have been counted as part of Razavi Khorasan Province.

Table 127
Number of Female Candidates Elected in Municipal Council Elections by Province (1993–2017)

Province	First council (1993–2003)	Second council (2003–7)	Third council (2007–13)[a]	Fourth council (2013–17)
Alborz[b]	*	*	*	68
Ardabil	11	29	22	59
Bushehr	19	57	24	105
Chahar Mahal and Bakhtiari	18	17	9	40
East Azerbaijan	33	41	36	101
Fars	53	106	80	419
Gilan	142	154	123	450
Golestan	20	122	51	185
Hamadan	24	36	40	101
Hormozgan	37	77	49	242
Ilam	14	14	15	71
Isfahan	77	115	87	210
Kerman	144	266	150	837
Kermanshah	23	47	28	170
Khuzestan	63	64	67	221
Kohgiluyeh and Buyer Ahmad	4	25	14	125
Kurdistan	24	21	18	54
Lorestan	29	48	30	249
Markazi	45	70	66	157
Mazandaran	92	145	113	450
North Khorasan	*	*	20	104
Qazvin	22	33	26	76
Qom	10	17	8	33
Razavi Khorasan	154	281	109	403
Semnan	28	60	27	72
Sistan and Baluchestan	73	172	103	498
South Khorasan[c]	*	*	30	142
Tehran	127	178	73	228
West Azerbaijan	17	35	31	95
Yazd	52	72	22	71
Zanjan	20	34	20	60
Iran (total)	1,375	2,336	1,491	6,096

Source: Statistical Center of Iran (1394/2015–16), 923.

[a] The term of the third council was extended by two years.

[b] The votes that were cast in the Alborz region before Alborz Province was established have been counted as part of Tehran Province.

[c] The votes that were cast in the North and South Khorasan regions before North Khorasan Province and South Khorasan Province were established have been counted as part of Razavi Khorasan Province.

Table 128
Voter Turnout by Province in the 1999 Municipal Councils Election

Province	Turnout rate	Province	Turnout rate
Ardabil	74.2%	Khuzestan	68.66%
Bushehr	73.15%	Kohgiluyeh and Buyer Ahmad	99.99%
Chahar Mahal and Bakhtiari	88.77%	Kurdistan	87.21%
East Azerbaijan	65.98%	Lorestan	77.99%
Fars	68.49%	Markazi	64.7%
Gilan	72.57%	Mazandaran	75.25%
Golestan	78.14%	Qazvin	74.98%
Hamadan	65.2%	Qom	50.5%
Hormozgan	79.68%	Semnan	72.02%
Ilam	93.29%	Sistan and Baluchestan	85.82%
Isfahan	54.11%	Tehran	39.03%
Kerman	80.38%	West Azerbaijan	72.34%
Kermanshah	75.36%	Yazd	65.86%
Khorasan	67.23%	Zanjan	70.51%

Source: Ministry of Interior (http://www.moi.ir).

Table 129
Voter Turnout by Province in the 2003 Municipal Councils Election

Province	Turnout rate	Province	Turnout rate
Ardabil	65.27%	Khuzestan	57.89%
Bushehr	55%	Kohgiluyeh and Buyer Ahmad	79.14%
Chahar Mahal and Bakhtiari	64.49%	Kurdistan	53.27%
East Azerbaijan	47.43%	Lorestan	55.28%
Fars	55.98%	Markazi	41.97%
Gilan	66.02%	Mazandaran	66.66%
Golestan	74.85%	Qazvin	55.06%
Hamadan	52.82%	Qom	30.96%
Hormozgan	68.18%	Semnan	56.1%
Ilam	73.09%	Sistan and Baluchestan	78.66%
Isfahan	34.77%	Tehran	23.87%
Kerman	57.75%	West Azerbaijan	61.98%
Kermanshah	60.55%	Yazd	50.54%
Razavi Khorasan	54.68%	Zanjan	63.72%

Source: Ministry of Interior (http://www.moi.ir).

13
Other Important Elite

Table 130
Elites with Highest Number of Influential Positions

Name	Number of positions	Cleric
Habibi, Hasan-Ebrahim	18	No
Hashemi-Rafsanjani, Akbar	17	Yes
Jannati, Ahmad	17	Yes
Movahhedi-Kermani, Mohammad-Ali	17	Yes
Rouhani, Hassan	17	Yes
Dorri-Najafabadi, Qorbanali	15	Yes
Emami-Kashani, Mohammad	13	Yes
Ansari, Majid	12	Yes
Aqa Zadeh, Gholam-Reza	12	No
Hashemi-Shahrudi, Seyyed Mahmud	12	Yes
Mo'men, Mohammad	12	Yes
Musavi, Mir Hoseyn	12	No
Namdar-Zangeneh, Bijan	12	No
Yazdi, Mohammad	12	Yes
Bahonar, Mohammad-Reza	11	No
Larijani, Ali	11	No
Mahdavi-Kani, Mohammad-Reza	10	Yes
Mojtahed-Shabestari, Mohsen	10	Yes
Nabavi, Seyyed Morteza	10	No
Nateq-Nuri, Ali-Akbar	10	Yes
Reyshahri, Mohammad	10	Yes
Velayati, Ali-Akbar	10	No
Amini, Ebrahim	9	Yes
Asgarowladi, Habibollah	9	No
Khaz'ali, Seyyed Abolqasem	9	Yes
Najafi, Mohammad-Ali	9	No
Rezvani, Gholam-Reza	9	Yes
Alavi, Seyyed Mahmud	8	Yes
Aref, Mohammad-Reza	8	No

Table 130 (Cont.)
Elites with Highest Number of Influential Positions

Name	Number of positions	Cleric
Ghafurifard, Hasan	8	No
Haddad-Adel, Gholam-Ali	8	No
Mohammadi-Gilani, Mohammad	8	Yes
Musavi-Kho'iniha, Seyyed Mohammad	8	Yes
Ra'isi, Seyyed Ebrahim	8	Yes
Sheybani, Abbas	8	No
Va'ez-Tabasi, Abbas	8	Yes
Abdollahi, Reza	7	No
Gharazi, Seyyed Mohammad	7	No
Khamenei, Seyyed Ali	7	Yes
Moqtada'i, Morteza	7	Yes
Musavi-Tabrizi, Seyyed Abolfazl	7	Yes
Nabavi, Behzad	7	No
Nateq-Nuri, Ahmad	7	No
Nuri, Abdollah	7	Yes
Parvaresh, Seyyed Ali-Akbar	7	No
Sane'i, Hasan	7	Yes
Taheri-Khorramabadi, Seyyed Hasan	7	Yes
Tavassoli-Mahallati, Mohammad-Reza	7	Yes

Source: Authors' database.
Note: The forty-eight individuals in this table (twenty-nine clerics and nineteen laymen) have held at least seven important political positions in Iran between 1979 and 2017. Each position corresponds to one term in office. For example, because presidents Khatami and Hashemi-Rafsanjani served two back-to-back terms, the count for each as president is two. The same logic has been applied to terms served in the GC, EDA, Majlis, etc. The specific positions held by each individual is listed in Part Two. In conformity with the criteria listed at the beginning of Part Two, the count only refers to positions we have identified as important. For example, Seyyed Ali Khamenei was a deputy defense minister in the early days of the revolution, but we have not counted that in our list of "elite positions" as described elsewhere in this volume.

Table 131
Political Elites Born outside of Iran

Name	Location
Ahmadi-Shahrudi, Mohammad-Hoseyn	Najaf, Iraq
Ahmadzadeh-Heravi, Mahmud	Herat, Afghanistan
Akhundi, Abbas-Ahmad	Najaf, Iraq
Baqeri-Bonabi, Mohammad	Najaf, Iraq
Faqih-Aliabadi, Asgari	Najaf, Iraq
Fazel-Astarabadi, Mohammad	Najaf, Iraq
Gharavi, Abdolhoseyn	Najaf, Iraq
Ha'erizadeh, Seyyed Abolhasan	Karbala, Iraq

Table 131 (Cont.)
Political Elites Born outside of Iran

Name	Location
Hashemi-Golpayegani, Seyyed Mohammad-Reza	Najaf, Iraq
Hashemi-Shahrudi, Seyyed Mahmud	Najaf, Iraq
Hoseyni-Shahrudi, Seyyed Abdolhadi	Najaf, Iraq
Hoseyni-Shahrudi, Seyyed Mohammad	Najaf, Iraq
Iravani, Mohammad-Javad	Najaf, Iraq
Karami, Mohammad	Najaf, Iraq
Karami, Mohammad-Mehdi	Najaf, Iraq
Larijani, Ali	Najaf, Iraq
Larijani, Mohammad-Javad	Najaf, Iraq
Larijani-Amoli, Sadeq	Najaf, Iraq
Mohammadi-Araqi, Mohsen	Najaf, Iraq
Musavi-Bojnurdi, Seyyed Mohammad	Najaf, Iraq
Musavi-Bojnurdi, Seyyed Mohammad-Kazem	Najaf, Iraq
Naseri-Dowlatabadi, Mohammad-Reza	Najaf, Iraq
Nezhad-Hoseyniyan, Ali	Karbala, Iraq
Rahbari-Amlashi, Mohammad-Mehdi	Najaf, Iraq
Reyaz, Seyyed Ali	Karbala, Iraq
Salehi, Ali-Akbar	Karbala, Iraq
Shari'ati-Dehaqani, Mohammad	Najaf, Iraq
Taheri-Gorgani, Seyyed Ali	Najaf, Iraq
Taskhiri, Mohammad-Ali	Najaf, Iraq
Zangeneh, Seyyed Sabah	Karbala, Iraq

Source: Authors' database.

Table 132
Individuals Involved in the Takeover of the United States Embassy in 1979

Name	Future position(s)
Abdi, Abbas	Prominent journalist and managing editor of *Salam*
Aminzadeh, Mohsen	High-level official in the foreign ministry
Asgharzadeh, Mohammad-Ebrahim	MP; secretary-general of IIPF
Baqeri, Mohammad-Hoseyn	Chief of the Armed Forces General Staff
Behzadiyan, Mohammad-Reza	MP; IRIB deputy
Bitaraf, Habibollah	Minister of energy
Dadman, Rahman	Minister of roads and transportation
Dehqan, Hoseyn	VP and head of FMVA; minister of defense and armed forces logistics

Table 132 (Cont.)
Individuals Involved in the Takeover of the United States Embassy in 1979

Name	Future position(s)
Ebtekar, Mrs. Ma'sume	VP and head of the Environmental Protection Organization
Foruzesh, Gholam-Reza	Minister of the Construction Jihad
Ja'fari, Mohammad-Ali	Commander in chief of the IRGC
Khatami, Seyyed Mohammad-Reza	MP (deputy Speaker); secretary-general of IIPF
Hashemi-Isfahani, Seyyed Mohammad	Iranian Oil Company official; husband of Mrs. Ebtekar
Mir Damadi, Mohsen	MP; secretary-general of IIPF
Na'imipur, Mohammad	MP
Nazari, Zohratalsadat	Wife of Rahman Dadman
Nowruzzadeh, Seyyed Reza	MP
Qoddusi, Mohammad-Hasan	Killed in the Iran-Iraq War
Rezazadeh-Shiraz, Mrs. Tahereh	MP; wife of Mohammad-Ebrahim Asgharzadeh
Seyfollahi, Reza	Chief of Law Enforcement Forces
Shaikholislam, Hoseyn	MP; deputy foreign minister for Arab and African affairs; ambassador
Shakurirad, Ali	MP; head of the Party of Islamic Iran's People's Unity
Sharifzadegan, Mohammad-Hoseyn	Minister of welfare and social security
Shirzad, Ahmad	MP
Vahhabi, Seyyed Shamseddin	MP
Zarghami, Seyyed Ezzatollah	Director-general of the IRIB

Source: Authors' database and information available on Iranian media.

Table 133
Supervisors and Director-Generals of the Islamic Republic of Iran Broadcasting (IRIB)[a]

Name	Tenure
Qotbzadeh, Sadeq (managing director)	Feb. 2, 1979–79
Mohtashamipur, Seyyed Ali-Akbar (appointed September 1980) and then Abdollah Nuri (appointed February 1981) (supervisors)	1980–82
Musavi-Kho'iniha, Seyyed Mohammad (supervisor)	1982–84
Hashemi-Bahremani, Mohammad	Aug. 24, 1989–Feb. 13, 1994
Larijani, Ali	Feb. 13, 1994–May 23, 2004
Zarghami, Seyyed Ezzatollah	May 23, 2004–Nov. 8, 2014
Sarafraz, Mohammad	Nov. 8, 2014–May 11, 2016
Aliasgari, Abdolali	May 11, 2016–present

[a] The former name of this organization was National Iranian Radio and Television.

Table 134
Mayors of Tehran

Name	Tenure
Tavassoli, Mohammad	1979–80
Zavareh'i, Seyyed Reza	1980–80
Nikravesh, Seyyed Kamaleddin	1980–81
Delju, Gholam-Hoseyn	1981–82
Seyfiyan, Mohammad-Kazem	1982–83
Bonakdar-Haji Abdolvahhab, Hoseyn	1983–83
Habibi, Mohammad-Nabi	1983–87
Tabataba'i, Seyyed Morteza	1987–89
Karbaschi, Gholam-Hoseyn	1989–98
Alviri, Morteza	1999–2001
Malekmadani, Mohammad-Hasan	2001–2
Ahmadinejad, Mahmoud	2003–5
Qalibaf, Mohammad-Baqer	2005–17
Najafi, Mohammad-Ali	2017–18

Table 135
Governors of the Central Bank

Name	Tenure
Molavi, Mohammad-Ali	Feb. 25–Nov. 5, 1979
Nowbari, Ali-Reza	1980–81
Nurbakhsh, Mohsen	1981–86
Qasemi, Majid	1986–Sept. 1989
Adeli, Seyyed Mohammad-Hoseyn	Sept. 15, 1989–94
Nurbakhsh, Mohsen	1994–2003
Sheybani, Ebrahim	2003–7
Mazaheri, Tahmaseb	2007–8
Bahmani, Mahmud	2008–13
Seyf, Valiyollah	Aug. 25, 2013–present

14
Political Parties

Explanatory Note on Legal Political Parties and Groups

This database was put together based on the following: the Iranian Ministry of Interior's (MI) list of registered political organizations, Internet research, and telephone interviews with a number of secretary-generals of the political parties. The list of founding members is based on Darabi (2009, 599–632), and the list of current and former members is based on Shadlu (2013).

Since the list only includes the officially recognized political parties, a number of important organizations/groupings whose licenses were revoked, that were disbanded, or who never registered with the Ministry of Interior as a political entity do not appear in this list. Some of these groups appear at the end of the list of legal parties.

In addition to the names of the organizations, the database lists the general mandate of the organization, the name of its secretary-general (SG) or leader, the year, city, and province where it was registered, and the names of its founding members.

The categorization of groups has been based on their mandate. Whenever the information was available or needed, we have listed the function and the focus of the group in parenthesis

The political leaning (i.e., reformist, principalist) of each organization is based on the political position of leaders of that party or the party's membership in political coalitions.

The brief description of each organization is based on the history of the organization from the official website of the organization, Internet research, and Shadlu (2013).

To help non-Persian speakers recognize the gender of the individuals, the prefix Mrs. appears before the names of females.

Legal Political Parties and Groups

Alliance of Steadfast Supporters of the Islamic Revolution: Jam'iyyat-e Vafadaran-e Enqelab-e Islami
 2003, Tehran, Tehran
 Mohammad-Mehdi Abdekhoda'i, Ali-Reza Ali-ahmadi, Hoseyn Aliahmadi-Jashfaqani, Mohammad Azimi-Taraqadri, Hoseyn Beygi, Habibollah Burbur, Hasan Ghafurifard, Ali Marvi, Moslem Mirzapur-Keleshter, Javad Shakhs-Tavakkoliyan, Morteza Shamsa'i-Zafarqandi, Abbas Sheybani (SG), Seyyed Ja'far Shobeyri, Mohsen Vafamehr
 Conservative
 This party was formed in response to threats against the regime such as the 1999 student protests. In the 2016 parliamentary election, the party joined the coalition of Principalists in Tehran. Abbas Sheybani, the SG of the party, has been an MP and a presidential candidate.

Alliance of Veterans of the Islamic Revolution (AVIR): Jam'iyyat-e Issargaran-e Enqelab-e Islami
 1997, Tehran, Tehran
 Mahmoud Ahmadinejad, Ali Darabi, Davud Danesh-Ja'fari, Hoseyn Feda'i-Ashtiyani (SG), Ahmad-Ali Moqimi, Abdolhoseyn Ruholamini, Mojtaba Shakeri, Ali Yusefpur
 Other current or former members: Seyyed Ali-Akbar Abutorabifard, Mrs. Nafiseh Fayyazbakhsh, Hadi

Imani, Ahmad Khoshbakhtiyan, Ahmad Nejabat, As-ghar Saburi-Khorasgani, Mohammad-Ali Shamabadi
Conservative

This party was formed in 1997, and though it was not supposed to form a coalition with either reform-ists or conservatives, it got closer to the conservatives. In the 2005 presidential election, the party supported Mohammad-Baqer Qalibaf in the first round and Mahmoud Ahmadinejad in the second round. In the 2009 presidential election, the party again sup-ported Ahmadinejad. The SG of the party, Hoseyn Feda'i-Ashtiyani, was a member of the United Front of Principalists during the Eighth and Ninth Majlis elections.

Alliance of Wayfarers of the Islamic Revolution: Jam'iyyat-e Rahpuyan-e Enqelab-e Islami
2010, Tehran, Tehran
Mrs. Zohreh Elahiyan, Mohammad Dehqan, Fa-rideddin Haddad-Adel, Elyas Naderan, Hamid-Reza Rostami, Malek Shari'ati, Mehdi Ta'eb, Ali-Reza Za-kani (SG),
http://rahpoo.net/
Conservative

This party supported Mahmoud Ahmadinejad during the 2009 presidential election. Gholam-Ali Haddad-Adel's son, Farideddin, is among the founders of the party. Most of the other founders, including the SG, are current or former MPs.

Alumni Assembly of Abureyhan-e Biruni University: Majma'-e Fareghottahsilan-e Daneshgah-e Abureyhan-e Biruni
1999, Tehran, Tehran
Akbar Hakkakan, Mohammad Jariyani (SG), Seyyed Ahmad Musavi, Seyyed Morteza Sahari, Mo-hammad-Reza Sharifniya, Mohammad-Taqi Shirka-vand, Seyyed Abdolhoseyn Vahedi

Amity Association: Jam'iyyat-e Dusti va Mavaddat
2000, Tehran, Tehran
Hoseyn Azimi, Nader Eftekhari-Afshar, Moham-mad-Reza Mohammadi,Mostafa Qasemi (SG)

This association was a member of the Coalition of Moderates (E'telaf-e E'tedalgarayan) during the 2008 parliamentary election in Tehran.

Assembly for Deliberating the Development of Zanjan Province: Majma'-e Hamandishi-ye Towse'eh-ye Ostan-e Zanjan
2013, Zanjan, Zanjan
http://www.majma-htoz.ir/

Assembly of Academics and Educators of Zanjan: Majma'-e Daneshgahiyan va Farhangiyan-e Zanjan
2002, Zanjan, Zanjan
Mahmud Abbasi (SG), Mas'ud Bayat, Tavakkol Ghanilu, Bahram Mohammadi, Mohammad-Naqi Sa-lehi, Seyyed Jabbar Shafi'i, Fereydun Vahedi-Hezarrud
http://mfd-zanjan.blogfa.com/

Assembly of Academics of Golestan Province: Majma'-e Daneshgahiyan-e Ostan-e Golestan
1999, Gorgan, Golestan
Hamid Haqshenas, Ehsan Maktabi, Mr. Mo'meni (SG), Mas'ud Rahnama'i, Yahya Samadinezhad

Assembly of Academics of Hormozgan Province: Majma'-e Daneshgahiyan-e Ostan-e Hormozgan
2003, Bandar-e Abbas, Hormozgan
Abtin Amiri, Ziya Foruqi, Gholam-Abbas Mans-uri, Ali-Reza Nikmanesh, Mrs. Fatemeh Salimi, Mo-hammad Vatanpurhamiyan, Mr. Zakeri-Imani (SG)

Assembly of Alumni of Islamic Iran (India Affiliated): Majma'-e Daneshamukhtegan-e Iran-e Islami (India Affiliated)
1998, Tehran, Tehran
Jalal Bakhtiari (SG), Mir Latif Musavi-Gargari, Abdolhadi Qazviniyan, Mohammad-Javad Rasa'i

Assembly of Combatant Clergy (ACC): Majma'-e Ruhaniyun-e Mobarez
1988, Tehran, Tehran
Seyyed Mohammad-Ali Abtahi, Majid Ansari, Asa-dollah Bayat, Seyyed Mahmud Doa'i, Mehdi Karrubi,

Seyyed Mohammad Khatami, Seyyed Ali-Akbar Mo-htashami[pur], Rasul Montajabniya, Seyyed Mohammad Musavi-Kho'iniha (SG), Seyyed Abdolvahed Musavi-Lari, Sadeq Sadeqi-Givi (Khalkhali), Mohammad-Reza Tavassoli

Other current or former members: Mohammad Aba'i-Khorasani, Qodratollah Alikhani, Mohammad-Ali Ansari, Ali-Akbar Ashtiyani, Seyyed Taqi Dorcheh'i, Hadi Ghaffari, Seyyed Mohammad Hashemi, Akbar Hashemi-Rafsanjani, Hoseyn Hashemiyan, Seyyed Mehdi Imam-Jamarani, Hyedar-Ali Jalali-Khomeni, Gholam-Hoseyn Jami, Mohsen Kadivar, Seyyed Hadi Khamenei, Hojatollah Kiyan-Ersi, Seyyed Mostafa Mohaqqeq-Damad, Seyyed Serajeddin Musavi, Musavi-Ardabili, Seyyed Mohammad Musavi-Bojnurdi, Mohsen Musavi-Tabrizi, Mohammad-Ali Nezamzadeh, Seyyed [Mohammad] Kazem Nurmofidi, Mohammad-Hoseyn Rahimiyan, Mohammad-Ali Rahmani, Mohsen Rohami, Seyyed Hamid Ruhani, Mohammad-Ali Saduqi, Hoseyn Sane'i, Yusef Sane'i, Isa Vela'i, Mohammad-Baqer Zakeri
Reformist

After disagreements emerged among members of the Society of Combatant Clergy (SCC), some of its members who were known as leaning to the left formed the ACC after securing the blessing of Ayatollah Khomeini. Mehdi Karrubi, Seyyed Mohammad Musavi-Kho'iniha, and Seyyed Mohammad Khatami were the prominent figures who introduced the idea of establishing the ACC. While officially a clerical association, the ACC functions like a political party for all practical purposes.

Assembly of Devotees of the Mandate of the Jurist: Majma'-e Asheqan-e Velayat
2000, unknown, Mazandaran
Mehdi Ahmadi-Fuladi, Seyyed Zia' Ma'navi (SG), Naser Taqavi

Assembly of Educators of Islamic Iran: Majma'-e Farhangiyan-e Iran-e Islami
2004, Tehran, Tehran
Seyyed Ali Hoseyni, Mohammad Kheyrkhah, Farajollah Komeijani (SG), Mohammad-Hoseyn Moqaddasi, Mohammad Narm, Mrs. Maryam Zaman

http://farhangiankhabar.ir/
Reformist
Farajollah Komeijani, the SG of this party, was arrested and held for a while during the presidency of Hassan Rouhani.

Assembly of Former MPs: Majma'-e Namayandegan-e Advar-e Mokhtalef-e Majlis-e Showra-ye Islami
1998, Tehran, Tehran
Gholam-Reza Ansari, Asghar Faqih-Aliabadi, Yadollah Islami (SG), Ali-Asghar Rahmani-Khalili, Mohsen Rohami, Zabihollah Safa'i

This reformist group should not be confused with two other conservative rivals: Islamic Society of Former Parliament Deputies (Jame'eh-ye Islami-ye Namayandegan-e Advar-e Mokhtalef-e Majlis) and Society of Former MPs (Kanun-e Namayandegan-e Advar-e Majlis-e Showra-ye Islami).

Assembly of Imam's Line Forces (AILF): Majma'-e Niruha-ye Khat-e Imam
1998, Tehran, Tehran
Ahmad Hakimipur, Seyyed Hadi Khamenei (SG), Rahmatollah Khosravi
http://khateemam.com/
Reformist
Seyyed Hadi Khamenei, the SG of this party, is the brother of the supreme leader of Iran and a former MP. He endorsed Mir Hoseyn Musavi and Hassan Rouhani in the 2009 and 2013 presidential elections respectively. He also criticized the house arrest of Mir Hoseyn Musavi and Mehdi Karrubi.

Assembly of Scholars and Lecturers of Qom Seminary (ASLQS): Majma'-e Modarresin va Mohaqqeqin-e Howzeh-ye Elmiyyeh Qom
2001, Qom, Qom
Mohammad Aba'i-Khorasani, Seyyed Mohammad-Ali Ayyazi, Asadollah Bayat-Zanjani, Mehdi Mahdavihaji, Seyyed Hoseyn Musavi-Tabrizi (SG)
Reformist
This organization was formed during the first presidential term of Mohammad Khatami and endorsed

Mir Hoseyn Musavi in the 2009 presidential election. After the election, the Ministry of Interior suspended the party's license to operate.

Assembly of Seminary Students [following] Imam's Line: Majma'-e Tollab-e Khat-e Imam

2001, Tehran, Tehran

Mohammad-Reza Abdiya'i, Mohammad-Javad Akbarin (SG), Mas'ud Ayyubizadeh, Majid Mohammadi-Sormeh, Mohammad-Reza Nowruzi, Ali Qavibonyeh-Juybari, Yahya Rameshin, Gholam-Ali Vela'i

Reformist

The SG of this party, Mohammad-Javad Akbarin (b. 1975), left the country after the 2009 presidential election.

Assembly of Seminary Students, University Students, and Alumni of Qazvin Province: Majma'-e Tollab va Daneshjuyan va Daneshamukhtegan-e Ostan-e Qazvin

2003, Qazvin, Qazvin

Ali Bahadori, Hoseyn Hashemi, Hoseyn Heydari, Ruhollah Mohammadi, Abolhasan Shirmohammadi (SG)

Assembly of University Students and Academics of Qazvin Province: Majma'-e Daneshjuyan va Daneshgahiyan-e Ostan-e Qazvin

2003, Abyek, Qazvin

Mohsen Badamiyan, Mrs. Mandana Bahrami-Ziyarani, Mohsen Ghaffari, Mrs. Kobra Keshavarziyan, Siyavash Mirza'i (SG), Mrs. Hajar Shir-Mohammadi, Seyyed Ahmad Ya'qubi-Manjin

Assembly of University Students and Alumni from Gilan: Majma'-e Daneshjuyan va Fareghottahsilan-e Gilani

1999, Tehran, Tehran

Sirus Bahramzadeh, Ali Ferdowsi, Seyyed Saber Mir Ata'i, Shahrokh Ramezannezhad, Behzad Ruhi (SG)

This was the first political grouping founded in Gilan Province after the 1979 revolution. *Talesh*, a monthly magazine, is associated with this group.

Assembly of University Students and Alumni from Yazd: Majma'-e Daneshjuyan va Fareghottahsilan-e Yazdi

1999, Yazd, Yazd

Ali Afkhami-Fathabad, Mr. Kafi (SG), Mohammad-Ali Salmaninezhad, Mohammad-Hoseyn Shari'atinasab

Reformist

This group published a statement in support of former interior minister Abdollah Nuri before his trial in 2008.

Assembly of University Students and Alumni of Golestan: Majma'-e Daneshjuyan va Daneshamukhtegan-e Golestan

2002, Tehran, Tehran

Jahangir Arab, Nurbordi Araqi, Abdolkarim Babareza, Ghaffar Kiyani, Aneh-Mohammad Kusehgharavi, Mohammad-Reza Shateri, Mohammad-Ali Tabarra'i (SG)

In the 2016 parliamentary election, this group joined the Front for Deliberation and Islamic Development, which supported moderate candidates whose views were close to that of President Rouhani's administration.

Assembly of Veteran Educators of Yazd: Majma'-e Farhangiyan-e Issargar-e Yazd

2004, Yazd, Yazd

Ali-Reza Ersi, Jalil Ja'fari-Nadushan, Hoseyn Mahdiyan, Sa'id Malakutiyan (SG), Mohammad-Ali Nezhad-Hoseyniyan, Mohammad-Hoseyn Reza'i-Sadrabadi, Hoseyn Shoja'iyan

Assembly of War-Invalids and Veterans of the Islamic Revolution: Majma'-e Janbazan-e va Issargaran-e Enqelab-e Islami

2001, Tehran, Tehran

Hasan Abutalebi, Abbas Ali-Qoli Tayefeh, Amir Aqiqi, Habibollah Azimi, Majid Bana'i-Osku'i, Hamid E'temad, Hamid-Reza Edraki, Hoseyn Esrafili, Azizollah Khansari, Ali-Akbar Mortazavi-Kiyasari (former SG), Gholam-Reza Nejatisalim, Hoseyn Safari, Ali-Akbar Tabidehchi (SG), Yusef Zeynalzadeh

http://www.majmaejanbazan.ir/

This party claims that it is the first NGO associated with veterans in Iran.

Association for Defending the Ideals of the Islamic Revolution in Razavi Khorasan: Jam'iyyate-e Defa' Az Armanha-ye Enqelab-e Islami Khorasan-e Razavi
    Conservative

Association for Defense of the Freedom of the Press: Anjoman-e Defa' Az Azadi-ye Matbu'at
    2000, Tehran, Tehran
    Gholam-Heydar Ebrahim-Baysalami, Ali Hekmat, Abbas Safa'ifar (SG), Rahman-Qoli Qolizadeh
    Other current or former members: Mahmud Alizadeh-Tabataba'i (current chair), Mrs. Fa'ezeh Hashemi (president since 2014), Mostafa Izadi, Mohsen Kadivar (former chair 1999–2014), Mrs. Badrossadat Mofidi (former vice chair), Mohammad-Javad Mozaffar (current vice chair), Isa Saharkhiz, Masha'allah Shamsolva'ezzin (former speaker), Mrs. Marjan Tabataba'i, Reza Tehrani
    Reformist
    This association was formed in 1998 and was officially registered in 2000. It aims to support journalists, and awards a "Golden Pen" prize each year. The organization's activities were halted after the 2009 presidential election but resumed in 2014.

Association for Development and Prosperity of Tehran Province: Jam'iyyat-e Towse'eh va Abadani-ye Ostan-e Tehran
    2008, Tehran, Tehran
    Mohammad Farajollahi (SG)

Association for Development of the Values of Islamic Iran: Jam'iyyat-e Towse'eh-ye Arzeshha-ye Iran-e Islami
    2002, Karaj, Tehran
    Moslem Eskandarihafez, Mansur Ghanizadeh, Asghar Hasanpur, Mahmud Heydari, Hoseyn-Ali Ziya'i (SG)

Association for Safeguarding of National Production: Jam'iyyat-e Defa' Az Towlid-e Melli
    2006, Tehran, Tehran
    Nazar Dahmardeh-Qal'ehnow, Farhad Daneshju (SG), Kamran Daneshju, Ahmad Fatemi, Mohammad Mo'menbellah, Ali-Reza Nezamabadi, Abdorreza Sobhani
    http://tolidemelli.com/
    This association advocates protectionist measures for Iranian industry. The SG of the party, Farhad Daneshju, was rector of Islamic Azad University for less than two years.

Association for Supporting Women's Human Rights: Jam'iyyat-e Hemayat Az Hoquq-e Bashar-e Zanan
    2001, Tehran, Tehran
    Mrs. Ashraf Geramizadehgan, Mrs. Shahindokht Moulaverdi (SG), Mrs. Leila Onsori, Mrs. Shideh Shadlu
    The SG of this party, Mrs. Shahindokht Moulaverdi, served as Iran's vice president for women's and family affairs in President Rouhani's first cabinet.

Association of Academic Modern Thinkers of Bushehr Province: Anjoman-e Nowandishan-e Daneshgahi-ye Ostan-e Bushehr
    2003, Bushehr, Bushehr
    Mrs. Sakineh Almasi, Abdolhoseyn E'temad, Abdolmajid Ejra'i, Mohammad-Amin Heydari, Abdorrasul Moshtaq, Khalil Nikkhah (SG), Javad Parhizkar, Ali Rafi'ipur (former SG)

Association of Advocates of Law and Order: Jam'iyyat-e Tarafdaran-e Nazm va Qanun
    1998, Tehran, Tehran
    Ali Bazmazemun, Ali Muwashshah, Yusef Shaikhinezhad, Hoseyn Tajarlu (SG)
    The SG of this association, Hoseyn Tajarlu, became the SG of the Moderation Front (Jebheh-ye E'tedal) in 2015.

Association of Aficionados of the Islamic Revolution: Jam'iyyat-e Hamian-e Enqelab-e Islami
    2014, Tehran, Tehran
    Ali Keyhaniyan (SG)
    http://www.jhee.ir/
    Conservative
    Along with its official website, the party publishes news on the following blog: http://www.jhee.blogfa.com.

In the 2016 parliamentary election, the party joined the Convergence Council of Principalists (Showra-ye Hamgarayi-e Osulgarayan).

Association of Aides of Imam Mahdi: Jam'iyyat-e Ansar al-Mahdi
1999, Qom, Qom
Abdorrahman Ansari, Mrs. Ozra Ansari (SG), Seyyed Mostafa Hoseyni

Association of Companions of Development: Jam'iyyat-e Hamgaman-e Towse'eh
2006, Tehran, Tehran
Siyavash Daryabar, Ali Hashemi-Bahremani (SG), Mostafa Nasiri, Mrs. Samira Rostami

Association of Devotees of Islam: Jam'iyyat-e Feda'iyan-e Islam
1989, Tehran, Tehran
Mohammad-Mehdi Abdekhoda'i (SG), Ali Bahar-Hamadani, Mohammad-Mehdi Farju, Mohammad-Ali Lavasani, Seyyed Mohammad Mir Damad-Isfahani, Seyyed Hasan Mortazavi, Mohammad-Reza Niknam-Amini, Asghar Omri, Seyyed Javad Vahedi-Badla
The roots of this group date back to 1945, when Mojtaba Navvab-Safavi established it to bring about an Islamic state. The SG of the group, Mohammad-Mehdi Abdekhoda'i, tried to assassinate Seyyed Hoseyn Fatemi (later PM Mosaddeq's foreign minister) on February 15, 1952, when he was only fifteen years old. The activities of the group resumed after the 1979 revolution, though it was halted for a period. The group is loyal to Navvab-Safavi.

Association of Educators of Dashtestan Following the Mandate of the Jurist: Jam'iyyat-e Farhangiyan-e Peyrow-e Velayat-e Faqih-e Dashtestan
1998, Borazjan, Bushehr
Mohammad Abedi, Mas'ud Atashi, Ali Behbahani, Esma'il Hoseyninezhad, Seyyed Akbar Mohajeri, Mr. Saberi (SG)

Association of Industrial and Economic Managers and Professionals of Iran: Anjoman-e Modiran va Motekhassesin-e San'ati va Eqtesadi-ye Iran
1999, Tehran, Tehran
Nurollah Abedi, Morteza Alviri, Morteza Haji, Ebrahim Khaniki (SG), Mr. Mesbahi (former SG), Seyyed Reza Nowruzzadeh, Mohsen Safa'i-Farahani
Reformist

Association of Iranian Jurists Defending Human Rights: Jam'iyyat-e Hoquqdanan-e Irani-ye Modafe'-e Hoquq-e Bashar
1998, Tehran, Tehran
Nabiyollah Ahmadlu (SG), Mansur Alizadeh, Gholam-Reza Amini, Ahmad Arabameri, Hamid-Reza Dehqan-Pudeh, Mrs. Fatemeh Hizomi-Arani, Sa'id Khorshidi, Abazar Mohebbi, Qodratollah Nowruzi
http://www.ngo-jurists.ir/
In 2015, this association sent a letter to UN Secretary-General Ban Ki-moon regarding the humanitarian situation in Yemen.

Association of Justice-Seeking Developers of Islamic Iran: Jam'iyyat-e Abadgaran-e Edalatkhah-e Iran-e Islami
2009, Tehran, Tehran
Bahram Feyzipour (SG), Sa'id Shakuri
Conservative
This party was formed during the presidency of Mahmoud Ahmadinejad and it was reportedly close to him.

Association of Messenger Women: Jam'iyyat-e Zanan-e Payamavar
2004, Tehran, Tehran
Mrs. Zari Baqani, Mrs. Fatemeh Behruzi (SG), Mrs. Qodsiyyeh Derakhshan, Mrs. Fatemeh Kazemi-Jamarani, Mrs. Fatemeh Marvi
Conservative
When Catherine Ashton, first vice president of the European Commission, met Mrs. Narges Mohammadi, a human rights activist, in Iran, this party signed a statement criticizing the meeting.

Association of Modern Muslim Women Thinkers of Iran: Jam'iyyat-e Zanan-e Mosalman-e Nowandish-e Iran

> 2007, Tehran, Tehran
>
> Mrs. Fatemeh Biglari-Bahador, Mrs. Narges Ganji, Mrs. Fatemeh Haqiqatju, Mrs. Fatemeh Rake'i (SG), Mrs. A'zam Sazvar
>
> http://www.zananenoandish.com/index.php/fa/
> Reformist
>
> The SG of this party, Mrs. Fatemeh Rake'i, was a member of IIPF, a reformist party that was banned after the 2009 presidential election. She also supported Hassan Rouhani in the 2013 presidential election.

Association of Modern Thinkers of Green Era: Anjoman-e Nowandishan-e Asr-e Sabz

> 2004, Qom, Qom
>
> Ali-Reza Esma'ili, Hamid-Qasem Feyzabad, Hasan Idrom, Ramezan Mirzapur-Shafi'i (SG), Abdolreza Mohajer
>
> In the 2009 presidential elections, this association supported Mir Hoseyn Musavi.

Association of Muslim Journalists: Anjoman-e Ruznamehnegaran-e Mosalman

> 1997, Tehran, Tehran
>
> Hoseyn Entezami, Seyyed Jalal Fayyazi, Ali-Reza Mokhtarpur, Seyyed Nezam Musavi (SG), Seyyed Morteza Nabavi, Mehdi Nasiri, Mohammad Safizadeh, Abbas Salimi-Namin, Hoseyn Shari'atmadari, Mehdi Shoja'i, Ali Yusefpur (former SG)
>
> Conservative

Association of Producers: Jam'iyyat-e Towlidgarayan

> 2001, Tehran, Tehran
>
> Gholam-Heydar Ali Rashidi, Ebrahim Baysalami, Sohrab Bohluli, Manuchehr Farhang, Abbas Feyz, Abolfazl Razavi, Mojtaba Sadat-Ahmadi, Mehdi Sahra'iyan, Behyar Soleymani, Iraj Yazdanbakhsh, Ali Zafarzadeh (SG), Shahrokh Zahiri, Mostafa Zare'i
>
> http://tolidgarayan.ir/
>
> Ali Zafarzadeh, the SG of this party, was a member of the Sixth Majlis from Mashhad.

Association of Servants of Construction of Khorasan Province: Jam'iyyat-e Khedmatgozaran-e Sazandegi-ye Khorasan

> 1998, Mashhad, Razavi Khorasan
>
> Ali-Asghar A'zami, Mohsen Amiriyan, Javad Ariyanmanesh, Seyyed Jalal Fayyazi (SG), Abdolmajid Helmi, Ghafur Helmi-Torfi, Gholam-Hoseyn Heydari, Abdollah Kupa'i, Seyyed Khalil Mehdizadehgan, Mohammad-Reza Mohseni, Ali-Reza Safari, Ahmad Yarahmadi [-Khorasani], Mostafa Yaqini

Association of Student Movements of Iran: Jam'iyyat-e Advar-e Jonbesh-e Daneshjuyi Keshvar

> 2012, Tehran, Tehran
>
> Mojtaba Ebrahimi (SG), Ahmad Jaberi-Ansari, Seyyed Nezameddin Musavi, Mohsen Omidiyan, Shahram Purjahani, Hoseyn Sharifi, Mohammad Vadud-Heydari
>
> Conservative
>
> One of the founding members of this party, Mohammad Vadud-Heydari, is managing editor of *Javan*, which is associated with the IRGC.

Association of the Leader's Devotees: Jam'iyyat-e Feda'iyan-e Rahbar

> 1998, Shiraz, Fars
>
> Mohammad-Reza Moshfeqiyan, Mohammad-Hoseyn Ruzitalab, Ne'matollah Taqa', Abbas Tuba'i, Mohammad Zare'-Fumani (SG)

Association of [Those] Loyal to the Ideals of Martyrs of Markazi Province: Jam'iyyat-e Vafadaran Beh Arman-e Shahidan-e Ostan-e Markazi

> 2005, Arak, Markazi
>
> Abbas Aqa Nokhustin, Hasan Hoseynabadi, Ali Ja'farmahsuli (SG), Mohammad Karami, Mas'ud-Reza Sameni
>
> In the 2009 and 2013 presidential elections, this group supported Mir Hoseyn Musavi and Hassan Rouhani respectively.

Association of Women of the Islamic Republic of Iran: Jam'iyyat-e Zanan-e Jomhuri-ye Islami-ye Iran

> 1989, Tehran, Tehran

Mrs. Qodsiyeh Firuzan, Mrs. Marziyeh Hadid-chi-Dabbagh, Mrs. Fatemeh Iranmanesh, Mrs. Soheyla Jelowdarzadeh, Mrs. Zahra Mostafavi (SG), Mrs. Sediqeh Moqaddasi, Mrs. Robabeh Rafi'i-Tari (Fayyazbakhsh), Mrs. Fatemeh Tabataba'i

The SG of the party, Mrs. Zahra Mostafavi, is Ayatollah Khomeini's daughter. This party was the first political group to be authorized by the Ministry of Interior. In the 2009 and 2013 presidential elections, the party supported Mir Hoseyn Musavi and Hassan Rouhani respectively. In 2013, when the GC did not approve Hashemi-Rafsanjani to run for the presidency, Mrs. Zahra Mostafavi authored a letter to Iran's supreme leader, Ayatollah Khamenei, asking for his intervention to reverse the decision.

Association of Women of the Islamic Revolution: Jam'iyyat-e Zanan-e Enqelab-e Islami
1999, Tehran, Tehran
Mrs. Mina-Khanom Behzadi, Mrs. Sediqeh-Beygom Hejazi-Taqanaki (SG), Mrs. Hakimeh Ja'farinasab-Kermani, Mrs. Kobra Khaz'ali, Mrs. Zahra Mazlumifard, Mrs. Nayyereh Qavi, Mrs. Sediqeh Taji-Fard

Association of Youth Developers of Islamic Iran: Jam'iyyat-e Abadgaran-e Javan-e Iran-e Islami
2013, Tehran, Tehran
Hoseyn Bayadi (SG), Ahmad-Reza Dabiran-Firuz (SG of the party in Isfahan Province)
http://abadgaranejavan.blogfa.com/
Conservative
The SG of this party, Hoseyn Bayadi, is a conservative figure who served on Tehran's City Council. In the 2009 presidential election, he joined the Perseverance Front of the Islamic Revolution, a group that supported Mohsen Reza'i, and was appointed as its spokesperson.

Association of Youth of Kerman Province: Anjoman-e Javanan-e Ostan-e Kerman
2002, Kerman, Kerman
Jaber Abolhadi, Ali Alizadeh, Ali Barzideh, Hoseyn Da'feh-Ja'fari (SG), Ali-Asghar Esma'ili-Ranjbar, Ataollah Hoseyni, Yaser Nezhadi

Association of Zeynab's [Zeynab bint Ali] Followers: Jam'iyyat-e Peyrowan-e Zeynab
2003, Tehran, Tehran
Mrs. Adeleh Khan Mohammadzadeh-Alamdari, Mrs. Fahimeh Khan Mohammadzadeh-Alamdari (SG), Mrs. Tala Sadeqbeygi, Mrs. Marziyeh Salari

Children of Iran Party: Hezb-e Farzandan-e Iran
1999, Tehran, Tehran
Mohammad-Reza Abolhasani, Mohammad-Taher Ahangari-Osbu'i, Arash Ahmadiyan, Jamshid Irani (SG), Ali Javadi, Behruz Saburi-Sobhani
The SG of this party, Jamshid Irani, was head of the Moderation Front during the 2016 parliamentary elections.

Clean Party of Iran: Hezb-e Pak-e Iran
2001, Tehran, Tehran
Bizhan Esma'ilzadeh (SG), Mrs. Parvindokhat Eftekhar-Khonsari, Shahram Omidvar, Mohammad-Hasan Shahbazi-Monfared, Mrs. Sediqeh Modarresi
This party, formed by a group of young Iranians and students, made a name for itself by inviting Iranians to gather to mourn the victims of the September 11, 2001, terrorist attacks. The party did not endorse anyone during the 2004 parliamentary election, but it did support Akbar Hashemi-Rafsanjani in the second round of the 2005 presidential election.

Coordinating Assembly of Followers of Imam and the Leader in Qom Province: Majma'-e Hamahangi-ye Peyrovan-e Imam va Rahbari-ye Ostan-e Qom
2015
Ali Bana'i-Qomi (SG)
http://mhpir.ir/

Cultural Society of Martyrs' Vows: Kanun-e Farhangi-ye Misaq-e Shohada
1999, Mashhad, Razavi Khorasan
Mrs. Zohreh Erfaniyan, Mrs. Bibi-Qodsiyyeh Seyyedi Alavi (SG), Mrs. Zaqir Parvar-Javan, Mrs. Nayyereh Purjavad

Development and Justice Party of Islamic Iran: Hezb-e Towse'eh va Edalat-e Iran-e Islami

2008, Tehran, Tehran

Sa'id Ahmadiyan, Hoseyn Kan'ani-Moqaddam, Abdolhoseyn Ruholamini (SG), Eskandar Salehi

http://toseevaedalat.ir/

Mohsen Ruholamini, son of party SG Abdolhoseyn Ruholamini, died while in prison after being arrested during the 2009 presidential election demonstrations.

Development of Kermanshah Party: Hezb-e Towse'eh-ye Kermanshah

2001, Kermanshah, Kermanshah

Mehran Beha'in, Mohammad-Reza Ezzati, Peyman Jalilniya, Hasan-Ali Mahdavi (SG), Soheyl Mohammad, Ali-Ashraf Yarahmadi

Reformist

Although this is a reformist party, it broke ranks with the reformist coalition and presented its own slate of candidates during the 2016 parliamentary elections in Kermanshah. The SG of the party has also repeatedly criticized the governor of Kermanshah, even though the party supports President Rouhani's administration. The party deactivated its website in 2016 without any explanation.

Discourse of Reform Assembly: Majma'-e Goftman-e Eslah

2003, Zanjan, Zanjan

Ahmad Abedini (SG), Ali Mir Mohammadlu, Seyyed Sajjad Razaviyan, Mohammad Shafi'i, Nur-Mohammad Shokri (former SG), Behruz Vafa'izadeh, Ayatollah Zangeneh

Fatemiyyun Society: Jame'e-ye Fatemiyyun

2006, Tehran, Tehran

Mrs. Seyyedeh Maryam-Banu Hashemi-Musavi, Mrs. Mina Rahimi, Mrs. Tahereh Rahimi (SG), Mrs. Ma'sumeh Reza'i-Nazari, Mrs. Monir Salehi

The SG of this society is a member of the Islamic Coalition of Women (E'telaf-e Islami-ye Zanan), which includes women from reformist and conservative groups.

Green Party of Iran: Hezb-e Sabz

2000, Tehran, Tehran

Yusef Davudi, Hoseyn Kan'ani-Moqaddam (SG), Mohammad-Ebrahim Maddahi

Omidvar Reza'i

http://greenpartyiran.com/

Despite its title, environmental issues are not among the main concerns of this party.

Homeland Association: Jam'iyyat-e Vatan

2003, Tabriz, East Azerbaijan

Jalal Mohammadi (SG), Khalil Mohammadi, Mostafa Qolizadeh-Aliyar, Mrs. Ameneh Qorban, Mokhtar Sadr-Mohammadi

House of Educators (Instructors) of Iran: Khaneh-ye Farhangiyan (Mo'alleman-e) Iran

2001, Tehran, Tehran

Mrs. Ma'sumeh Ameri, Azim Gol-Mohammadi, Seyyed Hasan Musavilotf, Mr. Sorush

House of the Farmer: Khaneh-ye Keshavarz

2000, Tehran, Tehran

Hoseyn Akbari-Emami, Ali-Akbar Aminzadeh, Mirza Aqa Hoseyni, Mirza Ali Eskavand, Mohammad-Hoseyn Hallajiyan, Bahman Jahani, Isa Kalantari (SG), Ali Mirzadeh-Emami, Abdolhoseyn Mowla'i, Gholam-Ali Sadri, Yusef Vosuqi-Kardekandi

http://www.khanehkeshavarz.ir/

Reformist

After serving as the minister of agriculture for thirteen years (1988–2001), Isa Kalantari founded this NGO and became its SG. In the 2005 and 2009 presidential elections, the party supported Akbar Hashemi-Rafsanjani and Mir Hoseyn Musavi respectively.

House of the Nurse: Khaneh-ye Parastar

2002, Tehran, Tehran

Ramin Ala', Mrs. Kasrineh Mohammad Nazari-Eshtehardi, Mohammad Sharifi-Moqqadam (SG), Mrs. Khorshidkhanom Vosku'i-Ashkevari, Hoseyn Zahedi

http://khp.ir/

This group criticized President Rouhani's administration and his health minister for implementing a plan for transforming the health system.

House of the Worker: Khaneh-ye Kargar
1992, Tehran, Tehran

Mahmud Asadi, Mohammad Daneshvar, Esrafil Ebadati, Hoseyn Kamal, Ali-Reza Mahjub (SG), Reza Mohammad-Vali, Ali Rabi'i

http://www.workerhouse.ir/

The roots of this group date back to more than two decades before the 1979 revolution. The House of the Worker became the labor division of the Rastakhiz party in the mid-1970s. After the revolution, Islamist groups managed to appropriate this entity in competition with leftist groups. Ali Rabi'i, one of founders of the group, was appointed minister of cooperatives, labor, and social welfare in 2013. Though the group is assumed to be close to reformists, its SG claims that it is independent. The Iranian Labor News Agency (ILNA; http://www.ilna.ir/) is associated with the House of the Worker.

Independent Association of Islamic Iran: Jam'iyyat-e Mostaqel-e Iran-e Islami
1999, Tehran, Tehran

Ahmad-Ali Amjadiyan, Javad Baqerzadeh, Ebadollah Fallahi, Mrs. Fereshteh Heshmatiyan, Qodrat-Ali Heshmatiyan (SG)

http://jmiatmostagle.blogfa.com/

In 2016, this group changed its name to the Party of Independence and Moderation of Iran (Hezb-e Mostaqel va Etedal-e Iran). The title of the newspaper published by the group was also changed from Jam'iyyat to Salam Mardom.

Independent Party of Labor: Hezb-e Mostaqel-e Kar
2001, Tehran, Tehran

Ali Ebadi (SG), Abbas Golshani, Seyyed Mojtaba Hashemi, Davud Khamseh, Abolqasem Mowla'i, Gholam-Ali Samadi
Reformist

Iranians' Clarion Party: Hezb-e Neda-ye Iranian
2015, Tehran, Tehran

Mrs. Marziyeh Amiri, Mohsen Barazvan, Isa Chambar, Majid Farahani (SG), Mehdi Ja'fari, Mohammad Keyhani, Peyman Khajavi, Seyyed Mohammad-Sadeq Kharrazi, Sirus Najafi, Kurosh Qaderi, Davud Roshani, Sajad Salek, Seyyed-Hadi Shafi'i, Reza Sharifi, Behruz Shoja'i, Mrs. Saedeh Sima

http://www.nedayeiranian.org/

The most prominent figure in this party is its head of the central council, Mohammad-Sadeq Kharrazi, who was Iran's ambassador to France and is a nephew of former foreign minister Seyyed Kamal Kharrazi. The party claimed that it represented the new generation of reformists, but established reformist groups did not welcome it. In addition to publishing news on its official website, the party publishes at http://irneda.ir/.

Iranian Women Journalists Association: Anjoman-e Ruznamehnegaran-e Zan-e Iran (ROSA)
1999, Tehran, Tehran

Founders: Mrs. Zhaleh Faramarziyan-Borujeni (SG), Mrs. Ashraf Geramizadehgan, Mrs. Homeyra Hoseyni-Yeganeh, Mrs. Jamileh Kadivar (former SG), Mrs. Parvaneh Mohi

Current members of the central council: Mrs. Zhaleh Faramarziyan-Borujeni (SG), Mrs. Ashraf Geramizadegan, Mrs. Forugh Mirtahmaseb, Mrs. Shahindokht Moulaverdi, Mrs. Zahra Nezhad-Bahram

http://www.aroza.ir/
Reformist

This association was formed during the last years of President Khatami's administration and its activities were limited during President Ahmadinejad's administration. The former SG of the society, Mrs. Jamileh Kadivar, was one of the supporters of Mehdi Karrubi in the 2009 presidential elections.

Iranian Youth Party: Hezb-e Javanan Iran-e Islami
1999, Tehran, Tehran

Mehdi Aqa Alikhani (SG), Safiyyeh Aqa Alikhani, Mohammad-Sadeq Inanlu, Ardeshir Sana'i, Gholam-Hoseyn Shaqaqi
Reformist

Iran of Tomorrow Association: Jam'iyyat-e Iran-e Farda
1999, Tehran, Tehran
Mrs. Farah Khosravi (SG), Farrokh Khosravi-Talebi, Mrs. Fereshteh Nasrabadi, Manuchehr Taherkhani

Islamic Assembly for the Ideals of Iranian People: Majma'-e Islami-ye Arman-e Mellat-e Iran
2006, Tehran, Tehran
Abbas Ala'i-Novin, Hoseyn Faryadi (SG), Ja'far Kamani, Abbas Qanbari, Kiya Qarari
http://armanemellat.com/
Conservative
In the last few hours of the campaigning period for the 2013 presidential election, this group endorsed Mohammad-Baqer Qalibaf and asked other conservative candidates to withdraw from the race.

Islamic Assembly of Bank Employees: Majma'-e Islami-ye Karkonan-e Bankha
2003, Tehran, Tehran
Majid Bakhtiari, Hamid-Reza Haj Mo'allemi, Ebrahim Hakimfa'al (SG), Yusef Panahandeh-Nikcheh, Mohsen Safa'iyan, Ja'far Sa'adat
In the 2016 parliamentary election, this association supported a list that included conservative and reformist figures such as Ahmad Tavakkoli and Mohammad-Reza Aref.

Islamic Assembly of Educators of Gilan: Majma'-e Islami-ye Farhangiyan-e Gilan
1999, Rasht, Gilan
Hamid Afa'i, Sorush Akbarzadeh, Hoseyn-Ali Atefi, Ali-Reza Azizi, Gholam-Reza Modirifar (SG), Seyyed Morteza Nikfar, Eshaq Rasti
Reformist

Islamic Assembly of Educators of Kerman: Majma'-e Islami-ye Farhangiyan-e Kerman
1999, Kerman, Kerman
Seyyed Abolqasem Golsorkhi, Hamid Mo'azzenzadeh, Abdolvahed Mostafavi, Nasrollah Nakha'i-Moqaddam, Mohammad Taqizadeh (SG)
Reformist

Islamic Assembly of Engineers: Kanun-e Islami-ye Mohandesin
1990, Tehran, Tehran
Majid Habibiyan, Ali-Asghar Khashehchi, Mokhtar Matinrazm, Gholam-Reza Mehr-Abdollahi (SG), Mohammad-Hasan Najafi-Qodsi, Mostafa Nuri-Latif, Ahmad Rowshanfekr-Rad, Mohammad-Hoseyn Tula'i
The roots of this organization date back to before the 1979 revolution.

Islamic Assembly of Erudite People: Majma'-e Islami-ye Farhikhtegan
2001, Parsabad/Moghan, Ardabil
Ali Baqerzadeh, Valiyollah Fasihi-Pormehr (SG), Naser Hoseynpur, Ali Jalili, Ghafur Sohrabi

Islamic Assembly of Khorasan Guilds: Majma'-e Islami-ye Asnaf-e Khorasan
2001, Mashhad, Razavi Khorasan
Ahmad Zushakiba'i, Ahmad-Ali Zavash-Kiyani, Kazem Bahraini, Mohammad-Reza Purakbar, Mohsen Bahraini, Mohammad-Ali Nikukaran (SG)

Islamic Assembly of Ladies: Majma'-e Islami-ye Banovan
1998, Tehran, Tehran
Mrs. Sohayla Jelowdarzadeh, Mrs. Fatemeh Karrubi (SG), Mrs. Susan Seyf
Reformist
The SG of this party, Mrs. Fatemeh Karrubi, is Mehdi Karrubi's spouse. The association's publication, *Iran Dokht*, became more popular after the 2009 presidential election and was closed down.

Islamic Assembly of Physicians of Fars: Majma'-e Islami-ye Pezeshkan-e Fars
2000, Shiraz, Fars
Abdorrahim Asadi-Lari (SG), Seyyed Mohammad-Reza Hadavi, Bizhan Jahanbakhsh, Sa'id Qazipur, Mohammad-Sa'id Rahiminezhad, Ali-Reza Salehi, Mahmud Shishehgar
Reformist
In the 2016 parliamentary election, this group supported reformist and pro-government candidates in Fars province.

*Islamic Assembly of [Public Sector] Employees
Following Imam's Line: Majma'-e Islami-ye
Karmandan-e Khat-e Imam*
　　1998, Tehran, Tehran
　　Seyyed Hasan Kazemi, Ramezan Mirzapur-Sha-
fi'i, Mrs. Ma'sumeh Mohtarami, Mohammad-Ali Sa-
fari, Ali Tohidlu (SG)
　　Reformist
　　In the 2005 presidential election, this group sup-
ported Mehdi Karrubi.

*Islamic Association of Academics of Isfahan Province:
Anjoman-e Islami-ye Daneshgahiyan-e Ostan-e Isfahan*
　　2001, Isfahan, Isfahan
　　Zabihollah Foruzesh, Mohammad Kermanine-
zhad-Badi, Ali Mehranfar, Javad Nowruzi, Ali
Shari'ati-Moqaddam, Seyyed Mahmud Taheri-Khezri
(SG), Abdollah Varasteh-Badi

*Islamic Association of Aficionados of Tehran Province:
Jam'iyyat-e Islami-ye Hamian-e Ostan-e Tehran*
　　2013, Tehran, Tehran

*Islamic Association of Alumni from Lorestan Province:
Tashakkol-e Islami-ye Fareghottahsilan-e Lorestani*
　　1999, Khorramabad, Lorestan
　　Ebrahim Barani-Beyranvand (SG), Ali-Mikhak
Beyranvand, Forud Hashemi, Aliyar Rashidpur, Majid
Sabbah, Mohammad Sharafi, Bahador Valizadeh
　　This association is one of fewer than twenty active
parties in Lorestan Province. It criticized MPs from
Lorestan because they were not critical enough of a
number of ministers proposed by President Rouhani
in 2013.

*Islamic Association of Alumni of Europe, America,
and Oceania: Anjoman-e Islami-ye Fareghottahsilan-e
Orupa, Amrika, va Oqyanusiyyeh*
　　1992, Tehran, Tehran
　　Ali Asghari, Seyyed Hoseyn Fasihi-Langarudi,
Mehrdad Fuladinezhad (SG), Ali Khoshbaten, Hamid
Mehdiqoli, Ebrahim Ne'matipur, Hoseyn Raqamiza-
deh, Seyyed Amireddin Sadrnezhad

*Islamic Association of Alumni of Shahid Beheshti
University: Anjoman-e Islami-ye Daneshamukhtegan-e
Daneshgah-e Shahid Beheshti*
　　2002, Tehran, Tehran
　　Ali Abadi, Seyyed Mahmud Anjam, Hoseyn
Bigham (SG), Akbar Eftekhari, Hamid-Reza Hoseyni,
Mahmud Morteza'ifard, Ruhollah Owhadi (former SG)
　　http://www.amookhtegan.ir/
　　The roots of this association trace back to the years
before the 1979 revolution, when Shahid Beheshti Uni-
versity was called Melli (National) University.

*Islamic Association of Alumni of Tarbiyat-e Mo'allem
University: Anjoman-e Islami-ye Fareghottahsilan-e
Daneshgah-e Tarbiyat-e Mo'allem*
　　1998, Tehran, Tehran
　　Mrs. Kobra Alipur, Mr. Malekabadi (SG), Abbas
Mirgalu'i-Bayat, Mostafa Monsef, Yusef Niki-Maleki,
Hoseyn Salehi, Ya'qub Siminruy

*Islamic Association of Alumni of Tehran University
and [Tehran] University of Medical Sciences:
Anjoman-e Islami-ye Daneshamukhtegan-e
Daneshgah-e Tehran va Olum-e Pezeshki*
　　2000, Tehran, Tehran
　　Hoseyn-Ali Arab, Gholam-Abbas Bozorgmehr
(SG), Shahriyar Niyazi, Hasan Ra'isiyan-Amiri, Ab-
dolhamid Shahidi

*Islamic Association of Alumni of Universities and Other
Centers of Japan: Anjoman-e Islami-ye Fareghottahsilan-e
Daneshgahha va Sayer-e Marakez-e Zhapon*
　　1999, Tehran, Tehran
　　Vahid Ahmadi, Mohammad-Ali Dustari (SG),
Mahmud Nili-Ahmadabadi, Rahmatollah Qajar, Zi-
ya'eddin Sho'a'i, Adel Torkaman-Rahmani, Seyyed
Hesameddin Zagardi

*Islamic Association of Educators: Jam'iyyat-e Islami-ye
Farhangiyan*
　　2012, Tehran, Tehran
　　Moslem Mirzapur (SG)
　　Conservative

In 2014, this association joined a coalition of conservative groups known as the Front for Followers of the Line of Imam and the Leader.

Islamic Association of Educators of Mahshahr: Anjoman-e Islami-ye Farhangiyan-e Mahshahr

1999, Mahshahr, Khuzestan

Ja'far Behbahani-Islami, Gholam-Hoseyn Delavari, Jalil Heydari, Abdolabbas Mohammadiniya (SG), Ebrahim Sheybani, Seyyed Ja'far Tabataba'i, Ne'matollah Qanavati, Rahim Qanavati

Islamic Association of Educators of Qom Province: Anjoman-e Islami-ye Farhangiyan-e Ostan-e Qom

1999, Qom, Qom

Seyyed Ali-Asghar Borqe'i, Abbas Mohammadi (SG), Taqi Nazeri, Seyyed Yusef Puryazdanparast, Gholam-Reza Reza'iyan-Maleki

Conservative

Islamic Association of Employees of Alborz Insurance Company: Anjoman-e Islami-ye Karkonan-e Bimeh-ye Alborz

1998, Tehran, Tehran

Qorban-Ali Fathi-Gerashini, Mrs. Maryam Karimi, Ali Moqarrab, Hedayat Sadeqi-Arsehgah, Davud-Ali Shirazi (SG)

Islamic Association of Engineers of Khorasan: Anjoman-e Islami-ye Mohandesin-e Khorasan

1992, Mashhad, Razavi Khorasan

Ali-Asghar A'zami, Hasan Alijani-Moqaddam, Abbas Amiripur, Seyyed Hashem Banihashemi-Chaharom, Seyyed Mohsen Banihashemi-Chaharom (SG), Seyyed Khalil Mehdizadehgan, Ahmad Shakhssalim, Ahmad Yarahmadi [-Khorasani]

Islamic Association of Faculty Members of Abualisina University and Hamadan University of Medical Sciences: Anjoman-e Islami-ye A'za-ye Hey'at-e Elmi-ye Daneshgah-e Abualisina va Olum-e Pezeshki-ye Hamadan

1999, Hamadan, Hamadan

Seyyed Mohammad-Mehdi Hazaveh' (Hezaveh'i), Asghar Khancherli, Gholam-Hoseyn Majzubi (SG), Mahmud Nili, Mr. Qal'ehchiyan, Javad Sa'en, Khosrow Sardariyan, Mehdi Sharifiyan, Mohammad-Mehdi Taqdiri

Islamic Association of Geology and Mining Engineers of Iran: Anjoman-e Islami-ye Mohandesan-e Zaminshenasi va Ma'dan-e Iran

1992, Tehran, Tehran

Mohammad-Baqer Farhadiyan, Mohammad Hoseyni-Ekhtiyarabadi, Mohammad-Taqi Kore'i, Hoseyn Mozaffarinezhad (SG), Ne'matollah Rashidnezhad, Ebrahim Rastad, Mohammad-Javad Va'ezipur

Islamic Association of Graduates of Italy: Anjoman-e Islami-ye Fareghottahsilan-e Italiya

1998, Tehran, Tehran

Hasan Haj Najjari, Seyyed Mohammad-Baqer Hoseyni, Qodratollah Karbala'i, Hoseyn Madadi, Hojjat Mehrabi, Fereydun Qadiri-Abyaneh (SG)

After the death of Edoardo Agnelli, an Italian billionaire who had visited Iran, the association published a statement claiming that he was murdered.

Islamic Association of Graduates of the Philippines: Anjoman-e Islami-ye Fareghottahsilan-e Filipin

1998, Tehran, Tehran

Ali Abedzadeh, Rahmatollah Bakhtiari, Mr. Hashemi (SG), Parviz Jeyhuni, Amir-Hoseyn Kambuzia, Ahmad Makhmali, Mohammad-Reza Nezamdust

Islamic Association of Graduates of the Faculty of Judicial Sciences and Administrative Services: Anjoman-e Islami-ye Fareghottahsilan-e Daneshkadeh-ye Olum-e Qaza'i va Khadamat-e Edari

1998, Tehran, Tehran

Mansur Dastgoshadeh, Seyfollah Faqanpur-Azizi, Mohammad-Hasan Mirzabeygi, Ali-Akbar Mollatabar-Elahi, Mohammad-Hasan Pirzadeh, Abdolhashem Ya'qubi (SG), Abbas-Ali Zare'

Islamic Association of Instructors of Mazandaran University of Medical Sciences: Anjoman-e Islami-ye Modarresin-e Daneshgah-e Olum-e Pezeshki-ye Mazandaran

2000, Sari, Mazandaran

Amir Esma'ilnezhad-Moqaddam, Asadollah Farrokhfar, Mohammad-Reza Haqshenas, Abbas-Ali Karimpur-Malekshah, Nadali Musanezhad (SG)

Islamic Association of Iranian Engineers: Anjoman-e Islami-ye Mohandesan-e Iran

1991, Tehran, Tehran

Ali-Mohammad Ahmadi, Seyyed Hasan Alhoseyni, Mohammad-Reza Behzadiyan, Ali-Mohammad Gharibani (SG), Ahmad Kabiri, Rahmatollah Khosravi, Karim Malekasa, Mohsen Nariman, Mohammad Qomi

Reformist

Islamic Association of Iranian Medical Society: Anjoman-e Islami-ye Jame'eh-ye Pezeshki-ye Iran

1993, Tehran, Tehran

Mohammad Farhadi (former SG), Seyyed Hoseyn Fattahi, Hasan Hoseyni-Tudeshki, Ahmad-Ali Nurbala-Tafti, Mohammad-Reza Rahchamani, Omidvar Reza'i, Seyyed Mohammad Sadr, Mohammad-Reza Va'ez-Mahdavi, Mohammad-Reza Zafarqandi (SG)

http://aimsi.ir/

Reformist

Islamic Association of Iranian Nurses: Jam'iyyat-e Islami-ye Parastaran-e Iran

2002, Tehran, Tehran

Siyamak Azizi (SG), Mahmud Karimiasl, Samad Sedaqati

http://www.irnurse.ir/

This association publishes the *Society of Nurses Journal.*

Islamic Association of Iranian Teachers: Anjoman-e Islami-ye Mo'alleman-e Iran

1992, Tehran, Tehran

Mrs. Gowharoshshari'eh Dastgheyb, Abbas Duzduzani, Morteza Katira'i (SG), Mr. Movahhedniya, Asghar Nowruzi

http://www.aemi.ir

Reformist

This association was formed a year before the 1979 revolution (though officially registered many years later) by prominent figures such as Mohammad Beheshti, Mohammad-Ali Raja'i, Mohammad-Javad Bahonar, and Ali Danesh-Monfared.

Islamic Association of Justice-Seeking Educators of Isfahan Province: Jam'iyyat-e Islami-ye Farhangiyan-e Edalatkhah-e Ostan-e Isfahan

2011, Isfahan, Isfahan

http://jamiat.lxb.ir/

News about this association can also be found at http://jfaas.blog.ir/.

Islamic Association of People's Unity of Mazandaran: Jam'iyyat-e Islami-ye Vahdat-e Mardomi-ye Mazandaran

2010, Tehran, Tehran

Esma'il Esma'ili (SG)

Islamic Association of University Instructors: Anjoman-e Islami-ye Modarresin-e Daneshgahha

1991, Tehran, Tehran

Qorban Behzadiyannezhad, Najaf-Qoli Habibi, Mir Fazlollah Musavi, Mohsen Rohami (SG), Ali-Reza Saffariyan, Mahmud Saremi, Davud Soleymani

Reformist

Islamic Association of University Students and Alumni of Lorestan Province: Anjoman-e Islami-ye Daneshjuyan va Daneshamukhtegan-e Ostan-e Lorestan

2003, Aligudarz, Lorestan

Amir-Hoseyn Asadi (SG), Mehrdad Asgari, Sa'id Kheyri, Mehdi Nikumanesh, Hayatollah Sarlak, Ali Selki-Araqi, Ali Tavakkoli

Islamic Association of Women: Jam'iyyat-e Islami-ye Zanan

1998, Tehran, Tehran

Mrs. Fatemeh Azizabadi, Mrs. Zahra Azizabadi-Farahani, Mrs. Maryam Mohseni (SG), Mrs. Batul Ranjbar-Kohan

Islamic Association of Women Following the Path of Noble Zahra: Jam'iyyat-e Islami-ye Zanan-e Peyrow-e Rah-e Hazrat-e Zahra

2001, Tehran, Tehran

Mrs. Fahimeh Ilshahi (former SG), Mrs. Fatemeh Ilshahi (SG), Mrs. Zahra Shaikhhasani

Islamic Association of Workers in Khorasan: Anjoman-e Islami-ye Kargaran-e Khorasan

1998, Mashhad, Razavi Khorasan

Gholam-Abbas Hamidi (SG), Mahmud Mohammadi-Sani, Mohammad Nejati, Hasan Sa'idizadeh, Hasan Sadeqi-Fathabad, Ahmad Tavakkoli-Afshar, Gholam-Hoseyn Torkzadeh

Islamic Bar Association: Jam'iyyat-e Islami-ye Vokalay-e Dadgostari

1997, Tehran, Tehran

Sefatollah Abbasi (SG), Nabiyollah Ahmadlu, Gholam-Reza Amini, Sa'id Baqeri (head), Asadalloh Bayat (former SG), Sa'id Khorshidi, Abazar Mohebbi
http://www.javdan.ir/

Islamic Center of Academics: Markaz-e Islami-ye Daneshgahiyan

1992, Tehran, Tehran

Mr. Reza'i (SG), Reza Dehqani-Farzam, Naser Derakhshan, Ali Hoseynpur, Bahman Nuri, Majid Qa'emiyan, Mrs. Minu Rastmanesh, Mohammad-Reza Shirzad, Asghar Zoka'i

Islamic Civilization Party: Hezb-e Tamaddon-e Islami

1999, Tehran, Tehran

Hamid-Reza Alamolhoda, Mohmmad-Ali Aqa'i, Mojtaba Haratinik, Mohammad Honardust, Moretza Mahmudi, Ali-Reza Manzari, Seyyed-Mohammad Mir Mohammadi-Najafi (SG), Mohammad Motevalliyan, Mir Mehdi Najafi

Other current or former members: Ali Reza'iyan
http://hezbetamaddon.ir/
Conservative

Right before the 2000 parliamentary elections, some relatively lesser-known figures of right-wing groups decided to form a new party called the Islamic Civilization Party.

Islamic Homeland Party: Hezb-e Mihan-e Islami

2000, Tehran, Tehran

Hasan Effati, Rahim Islamparast (SG), Abdollah Khorramdel, Taher Kuhi, Ali-Reza Najafi, Sa'id Sahlani, Javad Soleymani

This party should not be confused with Islamic Homeland Party of Iran (Hezb-e Mihan-e Islami-ye Iran), which announced its existence in April 2016.

Islamic Iran Solidarity Party (IISP): Hezb-e Hambastegi-ye Iran-e Islami

1998, Tehran, Tehran

Ali-Asghar Ahmad (SG), Gholam-Reza Ansari, Gholam-Heydar Ebrahim-Baysalami, Seyyed Mohammad Hashemi, Elyas Hazrati, Seyyed-Mahmud Mirlowhi, Qodratollah Nazariniya, Qorban-Ali Qandehari, Mohammad-Reza Rahchamani, Seyyed Valiollah Tavakkoli

Other current or former members: Gholam-Reza Abdolvand, Mirza Abutalebi, Mohammad-Reza Ali-Hoseyni, Hasan Almasi, Hoseyn Asgari, Ebrahim Asgharzadeh, Mohammad-Reza Bahmani, Manuchehr Behnia, Mrs. Shahrbanu Emami, Kurosh Fuladi, Ja'far Golbaz, Mrs. Marziyeh Hadidchi-Dabbagh, Masha'allah Heydarzadeh, Abdollah Ka'bi, Mostafa Kavakebiyan, Mohammad-Reza Khabbaz, Mohammad-Taqi Khani, Vajihollah Khedmatgozar, Seyyed Ma'ruf Samadi, Karim Malekasa, Mohammad Mir Lowhi, Ali-Mohammad Moslehi, Seyyed Ali Musavi, Mojtaba Musavi-Ojaq, Mohsen Nariman, Ezzatollah Nuri, Mahmud Qanbari, Ali Salehabadi, Fereydun Saliminia, Ali Sohrabi, Parviz Teymurnezhad
Reformist

This party was formed after the 1997 presidential election, though its roots can be traced back to the slight victory of conservatives in the 1997 Majlis elections. Reformist MPs and members of the executive branch formed the party.

Islamic Labor Party: Hezb-e Islami-ye Kar

1998, Tehran, Tehran

Mrs. Soheyla Jelowdarzadeh, Hoseyn Kamali (SG), Ali-Reza Mahjub, Abolqasem Sarhaddizadeh (former SG), Abdorrahman Tajeddin

Other current or former members: Seyyed Abbas Ahmadi, Karamali Ahmadi, Mrs. Forugh Alipu, Mohammad-Reza Badamchi, Mohammad Bakhshali, Mrs. Fahimeh Borz, Davud Darabi, Ali Fallahi, Mrs. Sara Farzad, Seyyed Abutorab Fazel, Mohammad-Hoseyn Golrokhiyan, Esma'il Haqparast, Davud Heydari, Ali Hoseyni-Khatibani, Mohammad-Hoseyn Islami, Kaveh Jaberi, Mehdi Kan'anizadeh, Mohmmad Kazzazlu, Mrs. Maryam Keshavarz, Morteza Lotfi, Ali-Reza Mahmudi, Mohammad-Esma'il Montazeri, Naser Nahid, Parviz Nasiri, Farzin Negarestan, Mrs. Leila Pahlavani, Seyyed Hoseyn Rasuli, Ali Sham'dani-Haq, Mehdi Soleymani, Hamid Soleymani, Mas'ud Tavana, Mrs. Fatemeh Vahdat, Bahman Ya'qubi, Amir Yarahmadi, Ahmad Yarmohammad

Reformist

After the election of Mohammad Khatami as president, the House of the Worker decided to establish a political party. The Islamic Labor Party, which is close to the reformists, was the only reformist group that introduced candidates in the 2012 parliamentary elections.

Islamic Participation of Youth Assembly: Majma'-e Mosharekat-e Islami-ye Javanan

2001, Rey, Tehran

Abbas Abedini, Sa'id Darvishi, Mohammad-Javad Kazemi, Ja'far Khodaqolizadeh (SG), Hasan Khosravi

Reformist

Islamic Party of Farmers: Hezb-e Islami-ye Keshavarz

2000, Tehran, Tehran

Mrs. Zohreh Abtahi-Forushan, Gholam-Hoseyn Aqaya, Mr. Attar, Seyyed Jamal Modarresi-Dorreh, Mohsen Movahhediyan, Mr. Sharifi (SG), Seyyed Abdolhoseyn Vaheditaba'-Zavareh, Gholam-Reza Yavari, Mohammad-Ali Yazdani-Khorasgani

Islamic Party of Land of Iran: Hezb-e Islami-ye Iranzamin

2009, Tehran, Tehran

Khodadad Eqbali, Seyyed Abolqasem Raufiyan (SG), Seyyed Abbas Sajjadi

Islamic Party of Workers' Welfare: Hezb-e Islami-ye Refah-e Kargaran

1999, Tehran, Tehran

Hamid Haqshenas, Ehsan Maktabi, Mas'ud Rahnamayi, Yahya Samadinezhad, Hoseyn Sarafraz (SG)

Other current or former members: Abbas Allahyar, Hasan Faraji-Golhin

This party supported Mir Hoseyn Musavi in the 2009 presidential election.

Islamic Society of Academics of Khorasan: Kanun-e Islami-ye Daneshgahiyan-e Khorasan

1993, Mashhad, Razavi Khorasan

Mohammad-Ali Gandomi, Mehdi Hasanzadeh (SG), Mohammad-Sadeq Javadi-Hesar, Vali Niknam-Shahrak, Mehdi Parsa, Hasan Razmi, Seyyed Mojtaba Sa'adat-Mohammadi (Na'lchian)

Reformist

In 2007, this organization joined the Coalition of Reformists.

Islamic Society of Alumni of Legal Studies: Kanun-e Islami-ye Fareghottahsilan-e Hoquq

1999, Tehran, Tehran

Mehrdad Baradaran-Nasiri (SG), Hasan Faraji-Golchin, Jamshid Manafi, Ahmad Molla'iyan, Hoseyn Sarafraz, Ali Shafi'i

This society was one of the founding members of the Moderate Front for the Development of Islamic Iran (Jebheh-ye Mianeh-ro-ye Towse'eh-ye Iran-e Islami) in 2015.

Islamic Society of Alumni of Shiraz University: Anjoman-e Islami-ye Daneshamukhtegan-e Daneshgah-e Shiraz

2003, Tehran, Tehran

Seyfollah Dad, Mohammad-Javad Haqiqi, Mohammad-Reza Heshmati (SG), Mohammad-Hoseyn Malekahmadi, [Mohandes] Moqimi, Mohammad-Reza Nowtash, Morteza Shahidzadeh, Mr. Shari'ati, Mr. Yusefzadehgan

Islamic Society of Alumni of Tehran University's College of Engineering: Anjoman-e Islami-ye Fareghottahsilan-e Daneshkdeh-ye Fanni-ye Daneshgah-e Tehran

1998, Tehran, Tehran

Ali Asghari (SG), Habibollah Bitaraf, Seyyed Mehdi Fakhra'i, Reza Faraji-Dana, Abdolmajid Shahidi
Reformist

Islamic Society of Athletes: Jame'eh-ye Islami-ye Varzeshkaran

1998, Tehran, Tehran

Eidi Alijani, Mohammad Ansari, Hasan Ghafuri-fard (SG), Mahmud Mashhun, Seyyed Mostafa Mir Salim, Seyyed Amir-Ahmad Mozaffari, Ahmad Nateq-Nuri, Mohammad-Reza Rahimi
Conservative

This society is a member of a coalition of conservative groups known as Front for Followers of the Line of Imam and the Leader.

Islamic Society of Bakhtiaris: Jame'eh-ye Islami-ye Bakhtiariha

1992, Tehran, Tehran

Zabih Karimi, Asadollah Kiyan-Ersi, Mohammad-Reza Mirqayeb, Omidvar Reza'i, Qoli Sheykhi, Qasem Soleymani, Ali Qanbari, Ali Yusefpur (SG)

Islamic Society of Dentists: Jame'eh-ye Islami-ye Dandanpezeshkan

1996, Tehran, Tehran

Mohammad-Sadeq Ahmad-Akhundi (SG), Kazem Ashofteh-Yazdi, Nasrollah Eshqyar, Abbas Monzavi, Ahmad-Hoseyn Nekufar

http://www.idai.ir/

The society was originally formed in 1983 but registered in 1996.

Islamic Society of Educators: Jame'eh-ye Islami-ye Farhangiyan

1992, Tehran, Tehran

Asadollah Badamchiyan, Mrs. Maryam Behruzi, Ezzatollah Dehqan (SG), Mohammad Elahiyan, Ali Farahmandzadeh, Mrs. Mansureh Farahmandzadeh, Mrs. Manizheh Nowbakht, Abolqasem Ra'ufiyan
http://jef.org.ir
Conservative

Islamic Society of Educators of Khorasan Province: Anjoman-e Islami-ye Farhangiyan-e Khorasan

1993, Mashhad, Razavi Khorasan

Gholam-Hoseyn Afzali, Javad Ariyanmanesh (former SG), Seyyed Mohsen Banihashem, Seyyed Ali Fayyazbakhsh, Gholam-Nabi Golestani, Ali-Asghar Khalilzadeh, Nasrollah Mojtahedpur (SG), Azizollah Tavakkoli, Ahmad Yarahmadi [-Khorasani]
Conservative

Islamic Society of Employees: Jame'eh-ye Islami-ye Karmandan

1993, Tehran, Tehran

Rahim Alizadeh-Barogh, Ahmad-Reza Bayat, Mostafa Biglar, Mohammad Bokhara'i, Mohammad-Sadeq Fayyaz, Hesam Kazempur-Dehkordi, Nasrollah Mirza'i-Nasir, Seyyed Kamal Sajjadi (SG)
www.karmandnews.org
Conservative

This society is a member of a coalition of conservative groups known as the Front for Followers of the Line of Imam and the Leader.

Islamic Society of Engineers: Jame'eh-ye Islami-ye Mohandesin

1991, Tehran, Tehran

Gholam-Hoseyn Amiri, Mohammad-Reza Bahonar (SG), Seyyed Mohsen Behfar, Hasan Ghafurifard, Seyyed Morteza Nabavi, Seyyed Mojtaba Samareh-Hashemi

Other current or former members: Mahmoud Ahmadinejad, Ali-Reza Aliahmadi, Mr. Asgari, Davud Danesh-Ja'fari, Mas'ud Derakhshan, Mr. Fuladgar, Rasul Hamediyan, Seyyed Mohammad-Reza Hashemi-Golpayegani, Abdollah Kupa'i, Mohammad-Reza Majidi-Nikfar, Mohammad-Hoseyn Malayeri, Seyyed Mohammad-Ja'far Mar'ashi, Seyyed Mostafa Mir Salim, Mohammad-Hasan Modir-Shanehchi, Mr.

Nejabat, Mohammad Ranjbar, Ali-Akbar Salehi, Seyyed Masih Salim-Bahrami, Seyyed Morteza Saqa'iyannezhad, Mohammad-Kazem Seyfiyan, Seyyed Kamaleddin Shahriyari, Mohammad-Ali Shayestehnia, Seyyed Ahmad Sherafat, Mohamad Soltaniyeh, Seyyed Mohsen Yahyavi, Ali Yusefpur, Ali Zabihi, Mohammad-Sadeq Zabihi

> http://www.mohandesin.ir/
> Conservative

After the dissolution of the IRP, some of the engineer members of the party established the Islamic Society of Engineers in 1988, though formal authorization by the Ministry of Interior was issued in 1991. The SG of the society, Mohammad-Reza Bahonar, was an MP for seven terms. Former president Mahmoud Ahmadinejad was also a member of the society, though the SG announced that the society did not support some of the measures of Ahmadinejad's administration. A number of the society's members are also affiliated with CIC/PCIC.

Islamic Society of Former Parliament Deputies (ISFPD): Jame'eh-ye Islami-ye Namayandegan-e Advar-e Mokhtalef-e Majlis

> 2001, Tehran, Tehran
>
> Mohammad Azimi, Mrs. Maryam Behruzi, Esma'il Feda'i, Seyyed Abdollah, Hejrati-Qazvini (SG), Seyyed Ahmad Hoseyni, Mohsen Kuhkan-Rizi, Mostafa Morseli, Ahmad Nejabat, Ahmad Rasulinezhad, Mrs. Marziyeh Vahid-Dastjerdi, Ali Yusefpur

This conservative group supported Mahmoud Ahmadinejad in the 2009 presidential election. This group should not be confused with the reformist rival group Assembly of Former MPs (Majma'-e Namayandegan-e Advar-e Mokhtalef-e Majlis-e Showra-ye Islami) or the other conservative group Society of Former Parliament Deputies (Kanun-e Namayandegan-e Advar-e Majlis-e Showra-ye Islami).

Islamic Society of Instructors of Teacher Education Centers: Kanun-e Islami-ye Modarresan-e Marakez-e Tarbiyat-e Mo'allem

> 1999, Tehran, Tehran

Mrs. Ruhangiz Dorobati, Mohammad-Reza Hazaveh, Habibollah Jadidi, Mrs. Tahereh Shalchiya, Ayyub Vahdatniya (SG), Mohammad Vakili-Mahallati, Mrs. Tayyebeh Yazdani

This organization supported Mir Hoseyn Musavi in the 2009 presidential election.

Islamic Society of Iranian Academics: Jame'eh-ye Islami-ye Daneshgahiyan-e Iran

> 1993, Tehran, Tehran
>
> Ali Abbaspur-Tehranifard (SG), Reza Maknun, Seyyed Mostafa Mir Salim, Abbas Sheybani, Karim Zare'
>
> http://isiap.ir/main/index.php

Islamic Society of Iranian Physicians: Anjoman-e Islami-ye Pezeshkan-e Iran

> 1993, Tehran, Tehran
>
> Seyyed Shahabeddin Sadr (SG), Mohammad-Karimi Shahrzad, Abbas Sheybani, Ali-Akbar Velayati, Mrs. Marziyeh Vahid-Dastjerdi

In the 2013 presidential election, the society supported Ali-Akbar Velayati.

Islamic Society of Judges: Kanun-e Islami-ye Qozat

> 1999, Tehran, Tehran
>
> Mohammad-Hasan Mirzabeygi (SG), Mohammad Mohammadi, Jamal Qezavati

This society publishes *Soor-e Edalat*.

Islamic Society of Physicians of Iran: Jame'eh-ye Islami-ye Pezeshkan-e Iran

> 1998, Tehran, Tehran
>
> Seyyed-Ahmad Alikazemi, Khosrow Rahmani (SG), Reza Sadeqi, Amir-Mahmud Tafazzoli

Islamic Society of Supporters of Iranian Agriculture: Jame'eh-ye Islami-ye Hameyan-e Keshavarzi-ye Iran

> 2010, Tehran, Tehran
>
> Hoseyn Ravazadeh (SG)
>
> http://hamiyanekeshavarzi.ir/

This society has been critical of genetically modified crops. In the 2013 presidential election, the society supported Ali-Akbar Velayati.

Islamic Society of Tehran University Professors:
Kanun-e Islami-ye Ostadan-e Daneshgah-e Tehran
1998, Tehran, Tehran
Karen Abriniya, Hasan Farhangi, Behzad Moshiri, Mohammad-Hasan Panjehshahi, Seyyed Mohammad-Hoseyn Pishbin, Mojtaba Shari'ati-Niyasar, Reza Shiva (SG), Naser Soltani

Islamic Society of University Students and Alumni of Khorasan: Kanun-e Islami-ye Daneshamukhtegan va Daneshjuyan-e Khorasan
2002, Unknown, Khorasan
Mohammad-Hoseyn Abolbashari (SG), Seyyed Asadollah Asgari-Tabataba'i, Mohammad-Ali Dehqani, Mohammad Pezhman, Hoseyn Shadkam-Torbati

Islamic Society of Veterinarians: Jame'eh-ye Islami-ye Dampezeshkan
1997, Tehran, Tehran
Mohammad-Ali Akhavizadehgan, Hoseyn-Ali Arab (SG), Mohammad-Kazem Kuhim, Mohammad-Ali Rad, Ali-Reza Sediqi

Islamic Society of Women of Isfahan: Jame'eh-ye Islami-ye Zanan-e Isfahan
2003, Kashan, Isfahan
Mrs. Effat Akhbari (SG), Mrs. Atefeh Honardar, Mrs. A'zam Monsef, Mrs. Leila Sha'bani-Moqaddam, Mrs. Soheyla Sha'bani-Moqaddam, Mrs. Maryam Shamakhi, Mrs. Zahra Tamanna'i

Islamic Society of Women of Khorasan: Kanun-e Islami-ye Banovan-e Khorasan
2001, Mashhad, Razavi Khorasan
Mrs. Zahra Amirkhani, Mrs. Bicharanlu, Mrs. Tahereh Farrashbashi, Mrs. Batul Gandomi, Mrs. Akram Hoseynzadeh, Mrs. Mahbubeh Ja'fari, Mrs. Batul Khaza'i, Mrs. Fatemeh Qodrati-Amanat, Mrs. Zahra Sa'idi, Mrs. Fatemeh Zandi

Islamic Society of Workers: Jame'eh-ye Islami-ye Kargaran
1993, Tehran, Tehran
Majid Afshari, Mas'ud Berahman, Mostafa Biglar, Mohammad Eqbal, Abdollah Hamidi (SG), Ali-Reza Saber-Kuchaksara'i (former SG)
http://jekargaran.ir/
Conservative

Islamic Solidarity Association of Tehran Province: Jam'iyyat-e Ensejam-e Islami-ye Ostan-e Tehran
2014, Shahr-e Rey, Tehran
Reza Elahi (SG), Ali Keyhanian (former SG)
http://ensejam-e.ir/
Conservative

Islamic Thought and Unity Assembly of Markazi Province: Majma'-e Andisheh va Vahdat-e Islami-ye Ostan-e Markazi
2013, Arak, Markazi
Reza Azizabadi (SG)
http://maeva.blogfa.com/
Conservative

Justice Party: Hezb-e Edalat
2001, Tehran, Tehran
Farhad Gudarzi, Nabiyollah Mahmudi-Marva'iyeh, Majid Mehdizadeh, Reza Qarebaghi, Hamid-Reza Qasemi, Bizhan Sabeti-Motlaq (SG), Hamid-Reza Shariflu

Justice-Seeking Party: Hezb-e Edalatkhah
2001, Tehran, Tehran
Mohammad-Javad Faza'eli-Aklaq, Hasan Jamshidi, Naser Mohammadi (SG), Hamid-Reza Qandehariyun, Hoseyn Rasa'i, Gholam-Reza Sadiqi-Owra'i, Seyyed Reza Vase'i
Conservative
This party was close to the Good Scent of Service (Rayeheh-ye Khosh-e Khedmat), a conservative political group close to Mahmoud Ahmadinejad.

Kerman Association of Defenders of Justice: Jam'iyyat-e Modafe'in-e Edalat-e Kerman
2006, Kerman, Kerman
Mrs. Mahin Gholamshahi-Fahraji, Mohammad-Reza Kho'i, Mohammad-Reza Mir Hoseynkhani,

Mohammad-Mas'ud Moradzadeh-Fahraji (SG), Ali-Reza Shahmoradzadeh-Fahraji

Liberation Party: Hezb-e Azadi
2001, Tehran, Tehran
Hoseyn Keyhani, Javad Mohtashami, Majid Mohtashami (SG), Mohammad Ra'isi-Nafehchi, Ali Taleblu
Reformist
This party awarded a medal of freedom to former president Hashemi-Rafsanjani.

Life Association: Jam'iyyat-e Zendegi
2001, Tehran, Tehran
Mohsen Ardestani, Faraj-Ali Bayani-Hadesh, Mahmud Bayani-Hadesh, Abdollah Chinichiyan, Mrs. Nilufar Chinichiyan (SG), Mr. Jahanlu (former SG)

Lorestan Free Thinkers Association: Jam'iyyat-e Azadandishan-e Ostan-e Lorestan
2004, Borujerd, Lorestan
Hushang Afshari, Mr. Ahmadi-Tabataba'i, Mr. Ala'i-Ghaffari, Zaker Hoseyni, Mr. Sa'idi, Fathi Yeganeh (SG)

Mahestan Society: Kanun-e Mahestan
2005, Tehran, Tehran
Amir-Hoseyn Amir-Moezzi, Mahyar Pazuki, Mehdi Purnamdari (SG) Mohammad-Ali Rahnama, Siyavash Reza'i, Ali-Reza Setandust, Amir-Peyman Sharifi
Reformist
This society is part of the coordination council of the Reformists' Front. The group also supports the right to work of immigrants such as Afghans.

Martyrs' Assembly of Islamic Iran: Majma'-e Shahed-e Iran-e Islami
2013, Tehran, Tehran
Ja'far Ali-Akbari (SG)
www.isaarpress.com
This group embraces some 3,000 children of martyrs.

Modern Thinkers Party of Islamic Iran: Hezb-e Nowandishan-e Iran-e Islami
2006, Tehran, Tehran

Abolfazl Kalhor, Amir Mohebbiyan (SG), Gholam-Hoseyn Mohammadi, Hoseyn Nushabadi
http://mtpii.com/Fa/
Conservative
This party calls itself a progressive principalist party.

Muslim Graduates Association of America and Canada: Anjoman-e Islami-ye Fareghottahsilan-e Amrika va Kanada
1993, Tehran, Tehran
Davud Bahrami-Siyavashani, Mansur Khodadadi, Hamid Nasrollahizadeh, Farrokh Parsizadeh, Reza Shiva (SG), Naser Soltani
http://www.anjomanonline.com/
This association was active before the 1979 revolution, and some prominent figures such as Mehdi Chamran and Ebrahim Yazdi were among its members.

Muslim People of Iran Party: Hezb-e Mardom-e Mosalman-e Iran
2001, Tehran, Tehran
Fallah Aliverdi, Jahanbakhsh Chenari, Mr. Ganji, Mr. Kazeruni, Mr. Mohammadi, Amrollah Shaikhiyani (SG)
This party supported Mir Hoseyn Musavi in the 2009 presidential election.

Muslim Women Association: Jam'iyyat-e Zanan-e Mosalman
2003, Tehran, Tehran
Mrs. Zohreh Farajzadeh, Mrs. Fereshteh Heshmatiyan, Mrs. Fahimeh Khan Mohammadzadeh-Alamdari, Mrs. Fatemeh Qa'ini (SG), Mrs. Mahnaz Rafi'zadeh-Shahi, Mrs. A'zam Reza'i

National Concord Party: Hezb-e Ettehad-e Melli
2002, Amol, Mazandaran
Qorban-Ali Alitabar, Gholam-Reza Alizadeh, Mohammad-Ali Hadizadeh, Seyyed Mehdi Hoseynnezhad, Sha'ban Keshtkar, Mohsen Mohammadi, Hasan Moradi, Heshmatollah Moslemi, Ali Safarpur, Hasan Safarpur, Mohsen Safarpur (SG)

National Trust Party (NTP): Hezb-e E'temad-e Melli
    2005, Tehran, Tehran

Seyyed Ebrahim Amini, Javad Eta'at, Mohammad-Javad Haqshenas, Elyas Hazrati, Reza Hojjati, Gholam-Reza Islami-Bidgoli, Mehdi Karrubi (SG), Rasul Montajabniya, Esma'il Gerami-Moqaddam, Abdolhoseyn Moqtada'i, Seyyed-Reza Nowruzzadeh, Mrs. A'zam Saqti, Abdorreza Sepahvand, Mahmud Zamani-Qomi

Other current or former members:

Ali-Akbar Abarqu'inezhad, Gholam-Reza Abdolvand, Mohammad-Ali Afshani, Sorush Akbarzadeh, Seyyed Ali-Akbar Anjomani, Reza Ansari, Mehdi Ayati, Azadi Azadmanesh, Hadi Boluki, Esma'il Dusti, Mrs. Najmeh Gudarzi, Seyyed Mohammad Ha'eri, Seyyed Mohammad Hashemi, Seyyed Ahmad Hoseyni, Mohammad Jaliliyan, Reza Janmohammadi, Mohammad-Sadeq Javadi-Hesar, Zabihollah Karimi, Mohammad-Reza Khabbaz, Rahmatollah Khosravi, Rasul Mehrparvar, Mrs. Mehrangiz Morovvati, Mohammad-Ali Moshfeq, Seyyed Rasul Musavi, Ali Ne'matzadeh, Reza Nowruzzadeh, Mohammad-Reza Nuri-Shahrudi, Ruhollah O'Hadi, Seyyed Mohammad-Mehdi Purfatemi, Teymur Qolizadeh, Mohammad Qomi, Vali Ra'yat, Mohammad Shafi'-Jalalvand, Abolfazl Shakuri, Masud Soltanifar, Ali-Mohammad Suri-Laki, Seyyed Kamel Taqavinezhad, Ali Ya'qubi, Abdolmohammad Zahedi, Mohammad-Baqer Zakeri

http://etemadmelli.com/
Reformist

During the 2005 presidential campaign, there was no consensus among the members of ACC about which candidate they should support. One faction supported the candidacy of Mehdi Karrubi, while the other faction favored Mostafa Mo'in. After the 2005 presidential election was over, Karrubi, the second runner-up, resigned from all of his political positions, including membership in ACC and the EDA. Karrubi then established the National Trust Party and ran as its candidate in the 2009 presidential election. The party continued its activities despite the house arrest of its SG. Karrubi resigned from his post as SG in December 2016 due to his indefinite house arrest.

National Unity Party: Hezb-e Vahdat-e Melli
    2001, Tehran, Tehran

Ahmad Barzegar, Mohammad Barzegar (SG), Hoseyn Kameli, Mojtaba Qorbani, Rahim Rostami-Moqaddam

Olive Branch Political and Social Assembly: Majma'-e Siyasi va Ejtema'i-ye Shakheh-ye Zeytun
    2001, Tehran, Tehran

Mehr-Ali Maleki, Mehrdad Reza'i (SG), Abbas Reza'i, Farhad Reza'i, Sharif Reza'i, Sehhatollah Sadeqpur, Mrs. Nayyereh Zulfaqari

Organization for Defense of Iran's National Interest: Sazman-e Defa' Az Manafe'-e Melli-ye Iran
    2003, Tehran, Tehran

Hoseyn Diyanati-Dizjikan, Jamshid Hamidibenam, Abdolkarim Mehdipurmesgar, Shirzad Vojdaninezhad, Sa'id Yari (SG), Ahmad Yusefi-Qal'erudkhani
    Reformist
    The SG of this party, Sa'id Yari, also served as the head of the Reformists' Front (Jebheh-ye Eslahtalaban) in 2015 and 2016.

Organization for Development of Construction of Islamic Iran—Tehran Province: Sazman-e Towse'eh-ye Sazandegi-ye Iran-e Islami-ye—Ostan-e Tehran
    2005, Tehran, Tehran

Mohammad-Reza Aqa'i-Qanjughi, Ayat Asghari, Hadi Dusttalab-Dilamqani (SG), Shirzad Ebrahimi, Reza Mirza-Ahmadi, Ahmad Mohammadzadeh-Fayyaz, Bahman Shirdel, Ali Vatanparast

Organization of Justice and Freedom of Islamic Iran: Sazman-e Edalat va Azadi-ye Iran-e Islami
    2001, Isfahan, Isfahan

Mohammad-Reza Bazmshahi, Ali-Reza Farzanehkhu, Hasan Fayezi, Kurosh Khosravi, Seyyed Mohammad-Lulaki, Mahdi Moghaddari (SG), Ali-Reza Sadeqiyan-Kordabadi
    http://booyebaran.ir/
    This group, previously known as the Solidarity Association of Followers of Imam's Line (Kanun-e Hambastegi-ye Peyrovan-e Khate-Imam), is one of few

reformist parties that has its headquarters outside Tehran. The organization is located mainly in Isfahan and announced its establishment in the office of Ayatollah Taheri, the reform-minded Friday prayer leader of Isfahan from 1979 to 2002.

Organization of Teachers of Iran: Sazman-e Mo'alleman-e Iran
    2000, Tehran, Tehran
    Parviz Dindar-Fumani, Ali-Reza Hashemi-Sanjani (SG), Javad Kheyrabadi-Asl, Kazem Qasemi, Khodayar Rafi'i, Seyyed Abolfazl Razmara, Mohammad Razzaqi, Heydar Zandiyeh
    http://www.iranto.ir/
    Reformist
The SG of this party, Ali-Reza Hashemi-Sanjani, has been arrested several times since the 2009 presidential election.

Organization of University Students and Alumni of Khuzestan Province: Sazman-e Daneshjuyan va Daneshamukhtegan-e Ostan-e Khuzestan (Seda)
    2003, Ahvaz, Khuzestan
    Aqil Daqaqeleh, Mojtaba Dinarvand, Ali Jenadeleh, Ruzbeh Karduni (SG), Human Khorshid, Seyyed Jamal Mahfuziyan, Amin Reza'i, Siyamak Shalu'i
    In the 2016 Majlis election, this party supported the list of reformists in Khuzestan Province. That same year, the party asked the interior minister to appoint a native son as Khuzestan's governor.

Participation and Development Association of Southern Bushehr Province: Anjoman-e Mosharekat va Towse'eh-ye Jonub-e Ostan-e Bushehr
    2001, Bushehr, Bushehr
    Hamzeh E'temad, Abdolhoseyn Eksir, Darab Rafi'ipur (SG), Shapur Raja'i, Mohammad-Hoseyn Mansuri

Party for Defense of Veterans and the Constitution: Hezb-e Defa' Az Issargaran va Qanun-e Asasi
    Hoseyn Kabir, Ali-Reza Matani (SG), Mohammad Rajabalizadeh, Ali Tohidifar
    1999, Karaj, Tehran

The SG of this party was the speaker of the Moderation Front during the 2016 parliamentary elections.

Party for Development of Construction of Islamic Iran—Tehran Province: Hezb-e Towse'eh-ye Sazandegi-ye Iran-e Islami—Ostan-e Tehran
    2005, Tehran, Tehran

Party for Sustainable Development of Iranian Agriculture: Hezb-e Towse'eh-ye Paydar-e Keshavarzi-ye Iran
    2001, Tehran, Tehran
    Hoseyn Alavirad (SG), Mehdi Dehqan, Fereydun Golafra, Ebrahim Pirne'mati, Abdolghaffar Shoja'

Party of Benevolent of Islamic Iran: Hezb-e Nikandishan-e Iran-e Islami
    2006, Tehran, Tehran
    [Ali-] Akbar Asadi, Ali Baghbaniyan, Mohammad-Rasul Darya'ifard-Jahromi, Mrs. Batul Fakharabadi, Mehdi Kiyadarbandsari, Mohammad Nahad, Valiyollah Niki-Maleki, Hojjatollah Niki-Maleki (SG), Abolfath Niknam, Ahmad Rashidi, Mrs. Fatemeh Shakeri-Hoseynabad
    http://www.hezbnikandishan.ir/
    This party, led by HI Niki-Maleki, is close to Mohsen Reza'i.

Party of Civic Reforms of Islamic Iran: Hezb-e Eslahat-e Madani-ye Iran-e Islami
    2001, Tehran, Tehran
    Faramarz Farzadi, Seyyed Eynollah Hoseyni, Mohammad-Taqi Gudarzi, Mrs. Shahrzad Mahmudvand (SG), Rahmatollah Sha'bani

Party of Confederated Islamic Congregations (CIC/PCIC): Hezb-e Mo'talefeh-ye Islami
    1990, Tehran, Tehran
    Habibollah Asgarowladi, Asadollah Badamchiyan, Nabiyollah Habibi (SG), Seyyed Asghar Rokhsefat
    Other current or former members:
    Ali Abbaspur-Tehranifard, Hamid Akbari, Yahya Ale-'Eshaq, Sa'id Amani-Hamadani, Mohammad-Ali

Amani, Mohammad-Kazem Anbarlu'i, Mehdi Araqi, Asadollah Asgarowladi, Raf'at Bayat, Ali Derakhshan, Jalaleddin Farsi, Farrokh Feda'i, Hasan Ghafurifard, Mrs. Shahla Habibi, Human Hasanzadeh, Haji Heydari, Sadeq Islami, Asadollah Khamushi, Asadollah Lajevardi, Seyyed Mostafa Mir Salim, Seyyed Morteza Nabavi, Haj Mohammad-Ali Nazaran, Seyyed Ali-Akbar Parvaresh, Mohsen Rafiqdust, Mrs. Fatemeh Rahbar, Mir Mohammad Sadeqi, Seyyed Ali-Naqi Seyyed Khamushi, Mohammad Shahab, Mr. Sokhansanj, Hamid-Reza Taraqqi, Mr. Tavakkoli-Bina, Abbas Vakil, Seyyed Reza Zavareh'i

http://www.motalefeh.ir/

Conservative

This party has its roots in a coalition of three religious groups that came together in Tehran in 1963 and called themselves the Confederated Islamic Congregations (Hey'atha-ye Mo'talefeh-ye Islami). The group's members, who had deep roots in the Tehran bazaar, forged a close relationship with Ayatollah Khomeini in the years leading up to the revolution. After 1979, the party halted its activities and joined the IRP. However, after the IRP disbanded in 1986, the Confederated Islamic Congregations resumed its activities. The party supported Mahmoud Ahmadinejad in the 2005 and 2009 presidential elections and backed Ali-Akbar Velayati in the 2013 presidential election. The party publishes *Shoma*.

Party of Democracy: Hezb-e Mardomsalari

1999, Tehran, Tehran

Mohammad Aqa Pazuki, Habibollah Dana'i, Mohammad Hoseyni, Abolqasem Kavakebiyan, Mostafa Kavakebiyan (SG), Ali Qasemi

Other current or former members:

Ebrahim Esfandiyari, Jalal Eftekhariyan, Javad Tamimi, Ali-Akbar Ja'fari, Sa'id Haqi, Reza Haqi, Majid Khashe'i, Mrs. Zohreh Zare', Farid Salavati, Gholam-Reza Abdolvand, Seyfollah Ezzeddin, Shahbaz Alizadeh, Ja'far Kandi, Hamid Labbaf, Salim Mar'ashi, Mehrdad Mas'udi, Rajab-Ali Movahhedipur, Mohammad-Reza Homayuni

http://www.hosnanews.ir/

Reformist

This party was established in Semnan by a group of supporters of President Mohammad Khatami and was called Supporters of the Message of Second of Khordad (Modafeine Payam-e Dovvom-e Khordad). The SG of the party ran unsuccessfully for the Ninth Majlis in 2012 and for the presidency in 2013. The party publishes *Mardomsalari*.

Party of Epic Makers of Second of Khordad [in] Kerman: Hezb-e Hemasehsazan-e Dovvom-e Khordad-e Kerman

2002, Kerman, Kerman

Morteza Delavari-Pariz, Mozaffar Eskandarizadeh, Mohammad-Ali Imani, Reza Kamyab-Moqaddas (SG), Ali Panjalizadeh, Bahram Purseyyedi, Mohammad Soltani

Reformist

This was the first party established at a provincial level in Kerman after the 1979 revolution. In the 2005 presidential elections, the party supported Akbar Hashemi-Rafsanjani.

Party of Executives of Construction of Iran (PECI): Hezb-e Kargozaran-e Sazandegi-e Iran

1999, Tehran, Tehran

Reza Amrollahi, Mrs. Fa'ezeh Hashemi-Bahremani, Mohammad Hashemi-Bahremani, Gholam-Hoseyn Karbaschi (SG), Hoseyn Mar'ashi, Seyyed Ataollah Mohajerani, Mohammad-Ali Najafi, Mohsen Nurbakhsh

Other current or former members:

Hedayatollah Agha'i, Morteza Alviri, Majid Ansari, Abolqasem Ashuri, Mohammad Atriyanfar, Gholam-Reza Foruzesh, Seyyed Mohammad Gharazi, Hasan-Ebrahim Habibi, Ali Hashemi-Bahremani, Seyyed Hoseyn Hashemi, Mohsen Hashemi-Bahremani, Seyyed Mostafa Hashemi-Taba, Abdolnaser Hemmati, Esma'il Jabbarzadeh, Eshaq Jahangiri, Seyyed Mohammad Khatami, Reza Malekzadeh, Ali Moslehi, Abdollah Nuri, Mrs. Fatemeh Ramezanzadeh, Gholam-Reza Shafei, Yadollah Tahernejad, Fereydun Verdinejad

Reformist

This party was established a couple of months before the Fifth Majlis election on January 17, 1996, by sixteen figures close to Hashemi-Rafsanjani, including his cabinet ministers. However, Hashemi-Rafsanjani was not officially involved in the party. In the 2009 presidential election, the party supported Mir Hoseyn Musavi, but the SG of the party endorsed another candidate, Mehdi Karrubi. Eshaq Jahangiri, one of the leading members of the party and head of its central council, was appointed first vice president when President Rouhani came to office in 2013. The party has been publishing *Seda Weekly* for the last several years.

Party of Iranian Consensus: Hezb-e Vefaq-e Iran

2001, Qom, Qom

Seyyed Mohammad-Hasan Ayatollahi, Ali Banirazi-Motlaq, Seyyed Reza Borqe'i-Modarres, Ali-Mohammad Davudabadi-Farahani, Faraj Elahi-Moqaddam, Ali-Akbar Fazli, Hoseyn Golyar, Seyyed Mohammad-Hasan Hoseyni (SG), Akbar Karami, Mohammad Mahdabi, Seyyed Hoseyn Moqaddasnezhad, Gholam-Hoseyn Nadi, Mehdi Qasemi, Hasan Qayyumi, Mehdi Safra'i

http://www.hezbevefagh.com/

Party of Iranian Independence: Hezb-e Esteqlal-e Iran

2000, Tehran, Tehran

Mrs. Atefeh Aminniya, Manuchehr Aqa'idusti, Esma'il Asadi, Ahmad Fatemi (SG), Hoseyn Khalili, Hoseyn Mehrdust, Nabiyollah Mohammadi, Sa'id Raja'i-Khorasani, Mahmud Ruhbakhsh-Mehrabani

Party of Iranian People's Will: Hezb-e Eradeh-ye Mellat-e Iran

2000, Tehran, Tehran

Ahmad Hakimipur (SG), Hoseyn Hamidiniya, Seyyed Mehdi Hoseyni-Matin, Mohammad-Taqi Irani, Ali Mollazadeh, Ali-Reza Ruhani, Seyyed Javad Salehi, Ali Shafa'i-Heris

http://www.hamanews.ir/

Reformist

The roots of this party go back to student groups at Tehran University's Faculty of Law and Political Science.

Party of Islamic Civil Society of Hamadan: Hezb-e Jame'eh-ye Madani-ye Islami-ye Ostan-e Hamadan

1999, Hamadan, Hamadan

Mohammad-Hoseyn Faramarzi, Mojtaba Heydari, Ali Lotfalizadeh, Hoseyn Mojahed (SG), Ahmad Moradhaseli, Vajihollah Najafi, Hasan Piri, Mas'ud Rusta'i, Mehran Safari, Bonyad Shahdadi, Ali-Asghar Vafa'i-Basir, Hoseyn Ya'qubi, Peyvand Yasinnabi-Torfi

Reformist

Some of the members of this group, including the SG, were arrested after the 2009 presidential election.

Party of Islamic Enhancement of Lorestan Province: Hezb-e E'telay-e Islami-ye Ostan-e Lorestan

2004, Khorramabad, Lorestan

Mahmud Asadollahi, Mrs. Azar Mohsenizadeh, Kamran Roshnava'i (SG)

Party of Islamic Iran's People's Unity (PIIPU): Hezb-e Ettehad-e Mellat-e Iran-e Islami

2015, Tehran, Tehran

Mrs. Zahra Aghajari, Gholam-Reza Ansari, Amir Aryazand, Reza Bavafa, Mrs. Asharf Borujerdi, Nasim Chalaki, Mostafa Derayati, Hoseyn Ebadi, Mehdi Farahani, Mohammad Fazeli-Kia, Ali-Mohammad Hazeri, Seyyed Mahmud Hoseyni, Hamid-Reza Jala'ipur, Jalal Jalalizadeh, Hoseyn Kashefi, Hadi Khaniki, Emadeddin Khatami, Mohammad Kiyanush-Rad, Mrs. Azar Mansuri, Morteza Mobaleq, Ali-Mohammad Mozaffari, Seyyed Hoseyn Musavinezhad, Hoseyn Naqashi, Mrs. Fatemeh Rake'i, Ali Shakurirad (SG), Hojjat Sharifi, Valiyollah Shoja'purian, Ali Sufi, Ali Tajerniya, Seyyed Shamseddin Vahhabi

http://etehademellat.com/

Reformist

This party held its first congress in 2015 with many reformist figures in attendance. Conservative critics have argued that the party is a new incarnation of the IIPF, which was dissolved after the 2009 presidential election. The SG of the party, Ali Shakurirad, was arrested a few days after the congress, though he was later released.

Party of Islamic Iran's Unity: Hezb-e Vahdat-e Iran-e Islami

　2002, Sowme'eh Sara, Gilan

　Hoseyn Montazerifar, Ahad Mohebbi-Shulami (SG), Hasan Mohebbi-Shulami

　http://vahdatiranislami.blogfa.com/

Party of Justice-Seekers of Islamic Iran: Hezb-e Edalattalaban-e Iran-e Islami

　2011, Tehran, Tehran

　Ne'matollah Hakim (SG)

　Some claim that Esfandiyar Rahimmasha'i, President Ahmadinejad's chief of staff, formed this party. However, the party denied any connection to him and supported Ali-Akbar Velayati in the 2013 presidential election.

Party of Moderation and Development (PMD): Hezb-e E'tedal va Towse'eh

　2001, Tehran, Tehran

　Morteza Mohammadkhan, Ali Musarreza, Mohammad-Baqer Nowbakht-Haqiqi (SG), Mrs. Zahra Pishgahifard, Majid Qasemi, Akbar Torkan, Seyyed Hamed Zarhani

　Other current or former members: Ali-Akbar Aqa'i, Mohammad Ashrafi-Isfahani, Mohammad-Reza Atvari, Morteza Banki, Ali Daneshmandi, Gholam-Ali Dehqan, Abolfazl Ejarehdar, Hamid-Reza Ghal'e, Hamid-Reza Haj Baba'i, Mrs. Fatemeh Hashemi-Bahremani, Seyyed Majid Hoseyni, Mohammad-Javad Iravani, Kazem Jalali, Ali Jannati, Hasan Khastehband, Hoseyn Mala'ek, Samad Mo'men-Bellah, Ali Mobini, Hoseyn Musavian, Mohammad Nahavandian, Mohammad-Ali Najafi, Mohammad Reza Ne'matzadeh, Mahmud Va'ezi, Sabah Zangeneh

　http://www.hezbet.ir/

　This party was established before the 2000 parliamentary elections. It is a moderate party close to President Hassan Rouhani. In the 2001, 2005, and 2009 presidential elections, the party supported Seyyed Mohammad Khatami, Akbar Hashemi-Rafsanjani, and Mir Hoseyn Musavi respectively.

Party of National Unity and Cooperation of Islamic Iran: Hezb-e Vahdat va Hamkari-ye Melli-ye Iran-e Islami

　2013, Tehran, Tehran

　Mr. Fazel-Amirjahani, Seyyed Mohammad Hashemi, Mas'ud Heydarnezhad, Seyyed Sobhan Hoseyni, Seyyed Hasan Mir Qaemi, Mohammad-Hoseyn Moqisi, Seyyed Ali Musavi, Mohammad-Reza Rahchamani (SG), Shahram Sader, Fereydun Saliminia

　http://hamkariemeli.ir/

　Reformist

　This is the first reformist party to be established after the contested 2009 presidential election. Some of the former members of Islamic Iran's Solidarity Party formed this party.

Party of People's Creed: Hezb-e A'in-e Mardom

　2004, Tehran, Tehran

　Shahriyar Heydari, Seyyed Sa'id Jalali (SG), Ali Mohammadzadeh

　Reformist

Party of Veterans of the Islamic Revolution: Hezb-e Issargaran-e Enqelab-e Islami

　2001, Rey, Tehran

　Ali-Reza Asadi, Mohammad Farrokhi, Seyyed Jamshid Oshal (SG), Mostafa Khanzadi, Majid Mohtashami-Khanmoradi, Mohammad-Reza Shahiditabar, Gholam-Reza Yavari

　Conservative

Party of Women of the Islamic Republic of Iran: Hezb-e Zanan-e Jomhuri-ye Islami-ye Iran

　2006, Tehran, Tehran

　Mrs. Fatemeh Alya (SG), Mrs. Zahra Haj Abbas-Qoli, Mrs. Shams Mo'tazedi, Mrs. Monireh Nowbakht, Mrs. Zahra-Beygom Sajjadi, Mrs. Seddiqeh Shakeri

　Conservative

　The SG of this party, Mrs. Fatemeh Alya, was a three-term MP.

People's Participation of Gilan Party: Hezb-e Mosharekatha-ye Mardomi-ye Gilan

　2003, Rasht, Gilan

Mrs. Ameneh Ahmadi, Mrs. Sohayla Hajati-Modara'i (SG), Jamshid Mehrabanrad, Mr. Mo'tamed, Mrs. Ma'sumeh Purhabibiyan, Mrs. Fatemeh Qanbari, Behzad Ruhi, Anushiravan Sana'isadiq
Reformist
The party officially registered in 2003, after already operating for around eight years.

People's Party of Reforms of Islamic Iran: Hezb-e Mardomi-ye Eslahat-e Iran-e Islami
2014, Tehran, Tehran
Mohammad-Reza Fumani (SG)
Reformist
In the 2016 parliamentary elections, this party criticized the List of Hope (*List-e Omid*), a slate of reformist candidates. In the 2016 election for the Majlis Speaker, the party supported Ali Larijani instead of the reformist Mohammad-Reza Aref. In 2015, the party's secretary of education resigned in protest of a meeting between the SG of the party and former president Ahmadinejad.

Pioneers of Development Party: Hezb-e Pishgaman-e Towse'eh
2000, Bonab, East Azerbaijan
Fereydun Azizi, Mehrali Kargar, Abdolmajid Mahdaviniya (SG), Ali Pezeshki, Mehdi Reza'i
Reformist

Progress Party: Hezb-e Taraqqi
2003, Tehran, Tehran
Babak Azarbad (SG), Mohammad Basari-Attar, Ramezan Qolinezhad, Navid Torabi-Safa'i, Hamid-Reza Torkamani
Reformist
The SG of this party is the vice president of Jebheh-ye Eslahtalaban, a coalition of reformist groups. The party also formed a coalition titled the Persian Gulf Watch (Didehban-e Khalij-e Fars).

Prosperity of Iran Party: Hezb-e Sa'adat-e Iran
1999, Tehran, Tehran

Mohammad-Javad Faza'eli-Akhlaqi, Hasan Jamshidi, Naser Mohammadi (SG), Hamid-Reza Qandehariyun, Hoseyn Rasa'i, Gholam-Reza Sadiqi-Owra'i, Seyyed Reza Vase'i

Qom Islamic Society of Admonishers: Jame'eh-ye Islami-ye Nasehin-e Qom
1997, Qom, Qom
Asghar Abdollahi (SG), Ali-Akbar Aghamiri (head of the central council), Ali Ahmadi [Miyanji], Reza Ashtiyani-Araqi, Ja'far Emami, Hoseyn Irani, Mohammad Khalaj, Mohammad-Ali Shar'i

Society for Islamic Education: Kanun-e Tarbiyat-e Islami
1999, Tehran, Tehran
Hoseyn Ahmadi, Ali-Reza Baratiyan, Mahmud Farshidi (SG), Yusef Soltani, Nosratollah Taheri
http://www.kanoonte.ir/
Conservative

Society of Academics of Islamic Iran: Kanun-e Daneshgahiyan-e Iran-e Islami
2005, Tehran, Tehran
Mehdi-Reza Darvishzadeh, Seyyed Mohammad Hoseyni (SG), Ebrahim Kalantari, Gholam-Reza Khajehsarvi, Mohammad-Reza Majidi, Mohammad-Reza Marandi, Mohsen Shaterzadeh-Yazdi
Conservative
Seyyed Mohammad Hoseyni, the SG of this party, served as minister of culture and Islamic guidance from 2009 to 2013.

Society of a Group of Muslim Political Prisoners before the Victory of the Islamic Revolution: Kanun-e Jam'i Az Zendaniyan-e Siyasi-ye Mosalman-e Dowran-e Qabl Az Piruzi-ye Enqelab-e Islami
1999, Tehran, Tehran
Seyyed Kazem Akrami, Mohammad-Reza Alihoseyni-Abbasi (SG), Mostafa Barzegar, Ahmad-Ali Borhanifar, Ahmad Hatami-Yazd, Javad Mansuri, Allahkaram Mirza'i, Jalal Samsamifard, Hoseyn Tusi

Society of Alumni of Islamic Azad University–Tehran: Jame'eh-ye Daneshamukhtegan-e Daneshgah-e Azad-e Islami-ye Tehran
>	2007, Tehran, Tehran
>	Mojtaba Akbari (SG)

Society of Alumni of the Indian Subcontinent: Kanun-e Fareghottahsilan-e Shebhehqarreh-ye Hend
>	1990, Tehran, Tehran
>	Mohammad Asadi-Tari, Anushah Gilaninezhad, Masud Hakim-Javadi (SG), Seyyed Ahmad Mir Ja'far-Tafti, Mas'ud Mohammadzamani, Mehdi Mohtashami, Manuchehr Mottaki (former SG), Seyyed Mehdi Nabizadeh, Javad Salimi, Abbas-Ali Taslimi
>	http://kanoonhend.ir/

This society, which is for alumni of Indian universities, endorsed Ali-Akbar Velayati in the 2013 presidential election. That same year, Manucheher Mottaki, a former foreign minister, resigned from his position as SG of the party.

Society of Alumni of Universities of Tabriz: Kanun-e Daneshamukhtegan-e Daneshgahha-ye Tabriz
>	2005, Tehran, Tehran
>	Hamid-Reza Alipur-Meshkati (SG), Abdorreza Arshadi-Sufiya'i, Mehdi Dehqan-Nayyeri, Jahanbakhsh Khanjani, Ali-Qasem Mazhin, Mohammad Qarehqeyd, Mohammad-Reza Sa'idi, Amin Sadiqi, Ali Tajerniya

Founding member Ali Tajerniya was an MP in the Sixth Majlis and was arrested after the 2009 presidential election.

Society of Alumni of West Azerbaijan: Kanun-e Fareghottahsilan-e Azerbaijan-e Qarbi
>	1998, Unknown, West Azerbaijan
>	Mohsen Baqerzadeh (SG), Amir Islamitabar, Ali Kamyar (former SG), Qasem Moridi, Ali-Reza Siyavashpur

Society of Combatant Clergy of East Azerbaijan: Jame'eh-ye Ruhaniyyat-e Mobarez-e Ostan-e Azerbayjan-e Sharghi
>	2000, Tabriz, East Azerbaijan

Mr. Ahra'i, Seyyed Mohammad-Taqi Al-e Hashem, Ali Elahifard [Qezelje'i], Eshaq Forutan-Sara'i, Mohammad Imani-Yamchi, Hoseyn Nowbari (SG), Mohammad-Taqi Purmohammadi, Musa-Mohammad Sheykhtabasi
Conservative

Society of Combatant Clergy of Tabriz: Jame'eh-ye Ruhaniyyat-e Mobarez-e Tabriz
>	1989, Tabriz, East Azerbaijan
>	Najaf Aqazadeh-Astarkan, Eshaq Forutan-Sara'i, Mohammad Imani-Yamchi, Mohammad Karimi, Ezzat Lahuti, Seyyed Hoseyn Musavi-Tabrizi [Pur-Mir Ghaffari] (SG), Mohammad Ruhanizadeh, Qodrat Shoja'i

In the 2009 presidential election, this society supported Mir Hoseyn Musavi. This organization is closer to the reformists than the Society of Combatant Clergy of East Azerbaijan.

Society of Educators of Gilan Province: Kanun-e Farhangiyan-e Ostan-e Gilan
>	2004, Rasht, Gilan
>	Mohammad Amjadi, Kazem Davudi (deputy head), Ali-Reza Elahi-Rudposhti (SG), Mohammad-Reza Hushangi, Mrs. Fatemeh Jamshidi, Mrs. Fatemeh Khandan-Shadrokh (secretary), Ahmad Ramezanpur-Nargesi (speaker), Kazem Sana'irad, Fariborz Sotudeh (head), Shahram Torabi
Reformist

Society of Former Members of the Islamic Student Associations in Europe: Kanun-e Islami-ye Daneshamukhtegan-e Ozv-e Sabeq-e Ettehadiyyeh-ye Anjomanha-ye Islami-ye Daneshjuyan-e Orupa
>	1999, Tehran, Tehran
>	Mohammad-Taqi Ameli, Seyyed Jamaleddin Arjomand, Seyyed Ramezan Mohsenpur, Ali-Reza Salehi (SG), Morteza Shari'ati-Neyasar, Mohsen Shaterzadeh

Society of Former Parliament Deputies (SFPD): Kanun-e Namayandegan-e Advar-e Majlis-e Showra-ye Islami
>	1998, Tehran, Tehran

Ali Momba'ini-Dehkordi, Mostafa Naseri (SG), Abdollah Nowruzi, Mohammad-Hashem Rahbari, Seyyed Ali-Naqi Seyyed Khamushi, [Gholam-] Hoseyn Sobhaninia (SG)

http://knam.ir/

This conservative organization should not be confused with the reformist rival Assembly of Former MPs (Majma'-e Namayandegan-e Advar-e Mokhtalef-e Majlis-e Showra-ye Islami) or the other conservative competing group Islamic Society of Former Parliament Deputies (*Jame'eh-ye Islami-ye Namayandegan-e Advar-e Mokhtalef-e Majlis*).

Society of Independent University Students and Alumni of Qazvin: Kanun-e Daneshjuyan va Daneshamukhtegan-e Mostaqel-e Qazvin
2001, Qazvin, Qazvin

Majid Garrusi, Mr. Kargar (SG), Mrs. Akram Kho'ini, Mrs. A'zam Kho'ini, Mrs. Narges Mohammadi, Mohammad Nankali-Kharivani

Society of Islamic Associations of Guilds and Bazaar: Jame'eh-ye Anjomanha-ye Islami-ye Asnaf va Bazaar
1993, Tehran, Tehran

Mohammad-Hoseyn Abdolkhaleghi, Sa'id Amani-Hamadani (former SG), Mahmud Faqihi-Reza'i, Masha'allah Javaheriyan, Ahmad Karimi-Isfahani (SG), Morteza Kashani-Zarrin, Ali Rahmani, Mas'ud Zandiyeh

http://www.asnaf-bazar.ir/Fa/Default.aspx
Conservative

This society was formed in 1980 by the direct order of Ayatollah Seyyed Mohammad Beheshti, a prominent politician in the early days of the Islamic Republic.

Society of Islamic Associations of Guilds of Khorasan: Jame'eh-ye Anjomanha-ye Islami-ye Asnaf-e Khorasan
1996, Mashhad, Razavi Khorasan

Mas'ud Akhavizadeh, Mohammad-Ali Ghaffariyan, Naser Moqaddam, Mohammad-Hoseyn Niyazmand, Ali Shamaqdari (SG), Seyyed Ali Shushtari, Mohammad-Ebrahim Vahediyan-Azimi

This society criticized President Hassan Rouhani for the report he presented on his first 100 days in office.

Society of Muslim Artists and Writers: Kanun-e Honarmandan va Nevisandegan-e Mosalman
1989, Tehran, Tehran

Seyyed Mohammad-Baqer Fadavi, Morteza Heydari, Abolqasem Kakhi, Seyyed Amir Mansuri, Farzin Negarestan, Ali-Reza Nowruzi-Talab, Beytollah Sattariyan (SG), Adham Zargham

Society of Physicians of Zanjan Province: Kanun-e Pezeshkan-e Ostan-e Zanjan
2003, Unknown, Zanjan

Majid Ansari, Majid Davudi, Hoseyn Din-Mohammadi, Amir Mansuri (SG), Ali Moqaddam, Parviz Qezelbash, Karim Sa'adati, Mohammad-Reza Sa'ini, Jamshid Vafa

Society of United Islamic Youth: Jame'eh-ye Javanan-e Mottahed-e Islami
2011, Tehran, Tehran
Amir-Meysam Nikfar (SG)
Conservative

This is a conservative party targeting young people. In the 2013 presidential election, the party supported Ali-Akbar Velayati.

Society of University Alumni and Students of Tehran Province and Firuzkuh: Kanun-e Fareghottahsilan va Daneshjuyan-e Ostan-e Tehran va Firuzkuh
2001, Firuzkuh, Tehran

Ramezan Ali-Ahmadi, Mrs. Leila Arab, Fariborz Bateni, Sa'id Ja'fari, Ali-Asghar Ziyari, Mehrdad Ziyari (SG)

Society of University Students and Alumni from Kermanshah: Jame'eh-ye Daneshjuyan va Fareghottahsilan-e Kermanshahi
1999, Kermanshah, Kermanshah

Samad Feda'i, Morad Hasani, Mrs. Marziyeh Mahidashti, Mrs. Nushin Mohammadi (SG), Qodratollah Najafi, Mehdi Ranjbar, Hamid-Reza Samadi-Shohreh

Society of University Students and Alumni of Ardabil Province: Kanun-e Daneshjuyan va Daneshamukhtegan-e Ostan-e Ardabil
2004, Ardabil, Ardabil

Adel Akbari-Majd, Seyyed Hamed Ameli-Kalkhuran (SG), Fattah Musazadeh-Gilandeh, Hoseyn Qadimi-Helabad-Shayeqi, Taqi Reza'i-Moqaddam, Hoseyn Shayeqi-Moqanlu, Hoseyn Vosuqi-Irani

Society of University Students and Alumni of Bushehr: Kanun-e Daneshjuyan va Daneshamukhtegan-e Bushehr

2001, Tehran, Tehran

Ali Bahraini, Mrs. Hamideh Edalat, Seyyed Ja'far Hamidi, Mohammad-Javad Haqshenas (SG), Mehdi Shabankareh

Reformist

This group was one of the founding organizations of the Reformists' Front.

Society of University Students and Alumni of Ilam Province: Kanun-e Daneshjuyan va Daneshamukhtegan-e Ostan-e Ilam

2002, Ilam, Ilam

Ali-Reza Karimiyan, Sa'id Khosravi, Jalal Mirza'i, Ayat Mohammadi (SG), Daryush Qamari

Reformist

This group was one of the founding organizations of the Reformists' Front.

Society of Women of the Islamic Revolution: Jame'eh-ye Zanan-e Enqelab-e Islami

1992, Tehran, Tehran

Mrs. Badrolmoluk Emampur, Mrs. A'zam Taleqani (SG), Mrs. Parvindokht Yazdaniyan

Reformist

This society, which was formed at the beginning of the 1979 revolution by Mrs. A'zam Taleqani, changed its name to the Society of Women of the Islamic Revolution in 1992. The organization is close to nationalist-religious groups such as LMI. The organization increased its activities during the tenure of President Khatami. In the 2009 presidential election, the organization supported Mir Hoseyn Musavi.

Solidarity Clarion of Isfahan: Kanun-e Neda-ye Hambastegi-ye Isfahan

2002, Khansar, Isfahan

Naser Forughi, Mohammad-Reza Ostad-Rahimi, Ali-Akbar Qeysari (SG), Mehdi Qeysari, Hamid-Reza Sami'iyan, Mohammad-Sadeq Sami'iyan, Ja'far Sane'i, Mehdi Seyyedsalehi

After the signing of the nuclear agreement between Iran and P5+1, this organization published a statement supporting the deal.

Solidarity Society of University Students and Alumni: Kanun-e Hambastegi-ye Daneshjuyan va Fareghottahsilan

1999, Islamshahr, Tehran

Mahmud Akbarpur, Farhang Eskandari-Turi, Naser Kasravi-Mavi, Esma'il Sadeqzadeh, Ahmad Sharif-Govashini (SG)

The title of this group has changed to Solidarity Party of University Students and Alumni (Hezb-e Hambastegi-ye Daneshjuyan va Fareqoltahsilan). In the 2016 parliamentary elections, the SG of the party, Ahmad Sharif-Govashini, was head of the central council of the Front for Deliberation and Islamic Development (Jebheh-ye Tadbir va Towse'eh-ye Islami), which supported moderate candidates whose views were close to that of President Rouhani's administration.

Thaqaleyn [Two Precious Gifts] Party: Hezb-e Thaqaleyn

2006, Ahvaz, Khuzestan

Hoseyn Kameli, Mrs. Jamileh Karimi-Hatami, Mrs. Kheiriyyeh Neysi, Seyyed-Mohammad Salaripur, Mohsen Torfi, Hamid Torfi (SG)

The name of this party refers to a hadith attributed to Prophet Mohammad. The party supported Mahmoud Ahmadinejad in the 2009 presidential elections, and claimed that same year to have more than 5,000 members.

Tomorrow's Wayfarers Organization—Khuzestan Province: Sazman-e Rahrovan-e Farda-ye Ostan-e Khuzestan

2003, Masjed Soleyman, Khuzestan

Vahid Bakhshandeh, Jalal Esterki, Hamid-Reza Mohammadi-Abdehvand, Reza Moradi-Aluqareh, Behnud Naderi (SG)

This group joined others in publishing a statement in 2007 asking the government not to fill the Sivand Dam, citing potential threats it posed to historical sites near the dam.

Vali-ye Asr [Mahdi] Society: Kanun-e Vali-ye Asr
    1991, Karaj, Tehran
    Ali-Akbar Amir, Hasan Amiri-Qaryehali, Mohammad-Ali Hakimi, Ramezan Jannati-Razavi (SG), Gholam-Reza Khorasani, Mohammad-Ali Khorasani, Hasan Rashidi-Tashku'i, Mohammad Sohrabi

Verity Party: Hezb-e Rasti
    2015

Welfare of Iranian Nation Party: Hezb-e Refah-e Mellat-e Iran
    2002, Tehran, Tehran
    Rahmatollah Abolfathi, Mohammad-Baqer Ali'i, Khalil Alimohammadzadeh (SG), Majid Mohammad-Hoseyni, Fereydun Sa'ati, Hoseyn Vatanpur, Asghar Yadollahi-Movahhed
    This party supported Akbar Hashemi-Rafsanjani in the 2005 presidential election.

Women's Information Exchange Society: Kanun-e Tabadol-e Ettela'at-e Zanan
    2001, Mashhad, Razavi Khorasan
    Mrs. Bibi-Fatemeh Hoseyni, Mrs. Tahereh Nasiriyan (SG), Mrs. Nayyereh Sabur-Ebrahimzadeh, Mrs. Tahereh Sahebiyan-Naqi, Mrs. Seyyedeh Marziyeh Shafapur, Mrs. Arman Vafadust-Torqabeh'i, Mrs. Fatemeh Zaker-Anbadani

Yazd's Benevolent Group: Majmaolmohsenin-e Yazd
    2000, Yazd, Yazd
    Hoseyn-Ali Hoseyni, Ahmad Mohtashami (SG), Seyyed Ahmad Rashti-Rahmatabadi, Mehdi Taqva'i
    Conservative
    This group, along with a number of other political groups in Yazd, published a statement criticizing the governor of Yazd during the era of President Rouhani for having met with former president Seyyed Mohammad Khatami.

Yazd's Group of the Virtuous: Majmaolarar-e Yazd
    2001, Yazd, Yazd
    Ali-Asghar Amuqadiri, Seyyed Ali Ayatollahi, Haj Mirza-Mohammad Manafzadeh, Hoseyn Mohtashamniya (SG)
    This group is one of fewer than twenty legal parties in Yazd Province that have been active during the last few years.

Youth Association of the Islamic Revolution of Iran: Jam'iyyat-e Javanan-e Enqelab-e Islami-ye Iran
    1999, Tehran, Tehran
    Asghar Abolqasem-Purkiya, Seyyed-Hoseyn Hoseyni, Ali-Asghar Mirza'i, Mohammad-Javad Mohammadi-Nuri (SG)
    http://www.jjeeiran.ir/
    This association supported Mohsen Reza'i during the 2013 presidential election.

Youth Party: Hezb-e Javan
    2006, Tehran, Tehran
    Majid A'inparast (SG), Kambiz Rostamzadehgan, Hamid-Reza Shams

Youth Society of Chahar Mahal and Bakhtiari: Kanun-e Javan-e Chahar Mahal va Bakhtiari
    2001, Borujen, Chahar Mahal and Bakhtiari
    Majid Babadi, Sa'id Derakhshan-Borujeni (former SG), Seyyed Mohammad Fayyazi, Farzad Hadipur-Borujeni, Ali Jangravy (SG), Mohsen Sepehri-Borujeni
    In the 2016 parliamentary election, this party joined the Moderation Front, a political group close to President Rouhani's administration.

Zarrindasht Society: Kanun-e Zarrindasht
    2002, Tehran, Tehran
    Mohammad-Yusef Amirifard, Mohammad Bakhtiarifard, Seyyed Hoseyn Hoseyni, Rahim Mehravar, Seyyed Nasrollah Musavi, Teymur Pazuki, Mr. Velayati (SG)
    In the 2009 presidential election, this group supported Mir Hoseyn Musavi.

Zeynab Society: Jame'eh-ye Zeynab

    1991, Tehran, Tehran

    Mrs. Zahra Abbasqoli (Abbasi), Mrs. Maryam Behruzi (SG), Mrs. Shamsi Mo'tazedi

    Other current or former members:

    Mrs. Nahid A'zami, Mrs. Mir Damadi, Mrs. Nafiseh Fayyazbakhsh, Mrs. Hoseyni, Mrs. Shams Mo'tamedi, Mrs. Mo'tazedi, Mrs. Moqaddam, Mrs. Musavi, Mrs. Monireh Nowbakht, Mrs. A'zam Nushgol, Mrs. Rampanahi, Mrs. Ma'sumeh Reza'i-Nazari, Mrs. Nili Sajjadi, Mrs. Salahshur, Mrs. Parvin Salihi, Mrs. Shakeri, Mrs. Marzieh Vahid-Dastjerdi

    http://jaamezeinab.ir/

    Conservative

The Zeynab Society was formed during the Iran-Iraq War to help the families of veterans. The organization is affiliated with CIC/PCIC, and is a member of the coalition of conservative groups known as the Front for Followers of the Line of Imam and the Leader.

❧

Below we have listed a number of important organizations and groupings whose licenses were revoked, who were disbanded, or who never registered with the Ministry of Interior as political entities and as such do not appear in the list of sanctioned political parties.

Alliance for the Defense of Values of the Islamic Revolution (ADVIR): Jam'iyyat-e Defa' Az Arzeshha-ye Enqelab-e Islami

    1997–98

    Prominent members: Seyyed Ali-Akbar Abutorabifard, Gholam-Hoseyn Elham, Ruhollah Hoseyniyan, Ahmad Purnejati, Ali Razini, Mohammad Reyshahri (SG), Mohammad Shari'atmadari

ADVIR was formed on June 5, 1995, but officially registered with the Ministry of Interior two years later. However, the party members decided to dissolve the organization a year later mainly due to internal discord.

Assembly of Iranian Professionals: Majma'-e Motekhassesin-e Iran

    2002, Tehran, Tehran

    Prominent members: Mahyar Ardeshiri, Mohammad Asali, Mohammad Namazi, Khosrow Nasirizadeh (SG), Jamal Rudaki, Mrs. Maryam Zakeriniya, Karim Zare', Seyyed Mohsen Zarifkarfard

    http://www.isaorg.ir/

This association was formed during the presidency of Mohammad Khatami to support the idea that experts should manage the country. The SG of the party, Khosrow Nasirizadeh, registered to run in the 2013 presidential election but the GC did not approve him.

Developers' Coalition of Islamic Iran (DCII): E'telaf Abadgaran-e Iran-e Islami

    Founder: Hoseyn Feda'i-Ashiyani

    Other members: Parviz Davudi

Islamic Iran Participation Front (IIPF): Hezb-e Jebheh-ye Mosharekat-e Iran-e Islami

    January 17, 1999–2010

    Prominent personalities:

    Mohsen Aminzadeh, Sa'id Hajjarian, Seyyed Mohammad-Reza Khatami (SG), Mohsen Mir Damadi (SG), Ali Shakurirad, Mostafa Tajzadeh

The IIPF was officially formed on January 17, 1999, by some of President Khatami's supporters and confidants. The party supported Mir Hoseyn Musavi in the contested presidential election in 2009 and thereafter was banned. IIPF was the largest party representing the reformist camp.

Organization of Erudite of Islamic Iran: Sazman-e Daneshamukhtegan-e Iran-e Islami

    2001, Tehran, Tehran

    Founders: Mrs. Zohreh Aghajari, Hamid Amin-Esma'ili, Ebrahim Asgharzadeh, Seyyed Ali-Akbar Musavi-Kho'ini (SG from 2001 to 2008), Ali-Reza Nasiri, Seyyed Shamseddin Siyasi-Rad, Davud Soleymani

This graduate organization, better known as *Advar-e Tahkim-e Vahdat*, is different from the Unity Consolidation Bureau (Daftar-e Tahkim-e Vahdat Daneshjuyan), which was a union of students formed in 1979. One hundred individuals who had graduated from different universities issued the group's first statement in 1999. The seven people listed as founders submitted a request to the Ministry of Interior to register the organization. The SG of the organization, Seyyed Ali-Akbar Musavi-Kho'ini, was an MP in the Sixth Majlis and was imprisoned for a while in 2006. Ahmad Zeydabadi, a member of the policymaking council of the group, was elected SG in 2008 and still holds the post, while Abdollah Mo'meni serves as the group's spokesperson. This organization is not currently active, as the Ministry of Interior has suspended its license to operate. The organization has deactivated its website but maintains a Facebook page (https://www.facebook.com/Advarnews/).

Organization of Mojahedin of the Islamic Revolution of Iran (OMIRI): Sazman-e Mojahedin-e Enqelab-e Islami-ye Iran
1979–2010
Reformist
Hashem Aghajari, Mohsen Armin, Behzad Nabavi (founder and SG), Mohammad Salamati (SG from 1991 to 2004), Mostafa Tajzadeh

OMIRI was originally formed in April 1979 and disbanded itself in October 1986 due to ideological differences. Five years later, a number of left-leaning members of the organization added "Iran" to the name of the party and relaunched it as a new party. OMIRI was banned after the controversial 2009 presidential election.

Society of Combatant Clergy (SCC): Jame'eh-ye Ruhaniyyat-e Mobarez Tehran
1977–present
Leading personalities: Seyyed Ahmad Alamolhoda, Abbas-Ali Amid-Zanjani, Mohammad-Javad Bahonar, Seyyed Mohammad-Hoseyn Beheshti, Mohammad Emami-Kashani, Seyyed Ali Ghayuri-Najafabadi, Akbar Hashemi-Rafsanjani, Seyyed Ali Khamenei, Seyyed Hadi Khosrowshahi, Fazlollah Mahallati, Mohammad-Reza Mahdavi-Kani, Gholam-Reza Mesbahi-Moqaddam, Mohammad Mofatteh, Mohammad-Baqer Mohyeddin-Anvari, Mohammad Mojtahed-Shabestari, Morteza Motahhari, Mohammad-Ali Movahhedi-Kermani (SG), Ali-Akbar Nateq-Nuri, Hassan Rouhani, Mehdi Shahabadi, Seyyed Reza Taqavi

The SCC is one of the most important conservative groups in Iranian politics. It was formed before the revolution and has continued its activities up to the present without being pressured to register itself with the Ministry of Interior as a political group. While officially a clerical association, the SCC functions like a political party for all practical purposes. In April 1988, the SCC experienced a split and those who departed formed the rival Assembly of Combatant Clergy.

Society of Qom Seminary Scholars (SQSS): Jame'eh-ye Modarresin-e Howzeh-ye Elmiyyeh-ye Qom
August 19, 1979–present
Founders: Ebrahim Amini, Ahmad Azari-Qomi, Akbar Hashemi-Rafsanjani, Seyyed Ali Khamenei, Ali-Akbar Meshkini, Hoseyn-Ali Montazeri, Abdorrahim Rabbani-Shirazi

Other leading personalities: Ali Ahmadi, Reza Ashtiyani-Araqi, Ahmad Beheshti, Mohammad-Ali Feyz-Gilani, Morteza Ha'eri-Yazdi, Abbas Ka'bi, Mohammad-Sadeq Khalkhali, Abolfazl Khansari, Seyyed Mohsen Kharrazi, Seyyed Ahmad Khatami, Sadeq Larijani-Amoli, Abbas Mahfuzi, Naser Makarem-Shirazi, Moslem Malakuti, Mohammad Mohammadi-Gilani, Abdolnnabi Namazi, Hoseyn Nuri-Hamadani, Mohammad-Mehdi Rabbani-Amlashi, Hoseyn Rasti-Kashani, Seyyed Mehdi Ruhani, Mohammad-Mehdi Shabzendehdar, Mohammad-Ali Shar'i, Seyyed Hasan Taheri-Khorramabadi, Abolqasem Vafi-Yazdi, Mohammad Yazdi (SG)

The SQSS is the most important clerical organization in Iran and articulates policies for all theological seminaries in Iran. Its members have held many of the highest political positions in the country.

Explanatory Note on Banned Parties and Groups

The list below is based on the memoir of Mohammad Reyshahri, who was minister of intelligence (1984–89), prosecutor general (1990–91), and lead prosecutor of the SCFC (1990–98) (Reyshahri 2004, 313–16). By compiling almost 170 groups, Reyshahri provided the most comprehensive list of dissident political groupings after the revolution. It is possible that Reyshahri's list is a bit exaggerated. Many of the groups that he mentioned were really circles made up of a handful of individuals who often just put out a publication. Nonetheless, the list gives the reader a sense of the range of Marxist, Islamic, ethnic, and nationalist groups that opposed the postrevolutionary regime.

Reyshahri divided these groups under the broad headings of "Marxist" and "Non-Marxist." However, the "Marxist" list includes many ethnic and cultural groupings as well, whereas the "non-Marxist" list encompasses not only Islamic but also ethnic, nationalist, and monarchist organizations that the Islamic Republic has closed down.

To help the reader learn about these diverse groups, we have provided not just the name of the organization (in Persian and English) but, when available, the following information as well (in the order listed): Year founded and when the organization became defunct, name of founder or leader, important notes about the organization, and website address. Readers should note the following points:

For the English translation of an organization's name, deference has been given to how it has been written on the website of that organization.

Groups are listed in alphabetical order based on their English titles.

One important Islamic group missing from Reyshahri's list is the Liberation Movement of Iran (LMI; Nehzat-e Azadi-ye Iran), which was a somewhat tolerated opposition group for a while. We have added it to Reyshahri's list.

One important Marxist group missing from Reyshahri's list is the Organization for Struggle on the Path of Working Class Emancipation (OSPWCE; Sazman-e Peykar dar Rah-e Azadi-ye Tabaqeh-ye Kargar). We have added this organization to the list as well because, along with the Tudeh Party and the Organization of Iranian People's Feda'i Guerrillas (OIPFG), it was one of the most popular Marxist organizations.

Front of Arab Warriors (Jebheh-ye Razmandegan-e Arab), which was listed in both the Marxist and non-Marxist lists, has been placed in the latter list.

Organization of Trailblazing Teachers (Sazman-e Mo'alleman-e Pishtaz) and Organization of Pioneering Teachers (Sazman-e Mo'alleman-e Pishgam) have been moved from the non-Marxist list to the Marxist list.

Revolutionary Organization of Masses of Islamic Republic (Sazman-e Enqelabi-ye Tudeh-haye Jomhuri-ye Islami; Satja) has been moved from the Marxist list to the non-Marxist list.

In certain instances we have consulted scholars and activists knowledgeable about some of these groups and have used other sources such as http://www.iran-archive.com/ and http://www.akhbar-rooz.com.

Outlawed Marxist Parties and Groups

Arab Cultural Society of Abadan: Kanun-e Farhangi-ye Arab-e Abadan
1979
This group was active in Khuzestan Province.

Arab Cultural Society of Ahvaz: Kanun-e Farhangi-ye Arab-e Ahvaz
1979
This group was active in Khuzestan Province.

Arab Cultural Society of Mohammareh/Khorramshahr: Kanun-e Farhangi-ye Arab-e Mohammareh/Khorramshahr
1979
This group was active in Khuzestan Province, and there were some clashes between its members and pro-regime forces in 1979.

Association for Defense of the People of Kurdistan: Anjoman-e Defa' Az Jonbesh-e Khalq-e Kurdistan
This group was mostly active in Kurdistan and in a statement issued on March 28, 1979, it invited people to demonstrate in front of Tehran University a day after the assassination of some Kurdish activists in Sanandaj.

Association for Freedom of Women: Anjoman-e Rahayi-ye Zan
This group was associated with the Organization of Communist Unity (Sazman-e Vahdat-e Komunisti) and published a journal titled *Rahayi-e Zan*. They boycotted the election for the Assembly for the Final Examination of the Constitution in 1979.

Center for Coordination of Workers' Syndicates of Iran: Kanun-e Hamahangi-ye Sandikaha-ye Kargaran-e Iran

1979

Combatants Fighting for the Aspirations of the Workers: Mobarezin-e Rah-e Arman-e Kargar

1979

Combatants Fighting for the Freedom of the Iranian People: Mobarezin-e Azadi-ye Khalq-e Iran

1979

This group was against the cultural revolution that began in 1980.

Combatants Fighting for the Freedom of the Working Class: Mobarezin-e Azadi-ye Tabaqeh-ye Kargar

This group was against the cultural revolution that began in 1980.

Combatants of the Path of the Working Class: Mobarezin-e Rah-e Tabaqeh-ye Kargar

This group joined others in holding a conference regarding the Iranian labor force in 1979.

Combatants Paving the Way for the Formation of the Party of the Working Class: Mobarezin-e Rah-e Ijad-e Hezb-e Tabaqeh-ye Kargar

Communist Party of Iran: Hezb-e Komunist-e Iran

1983–present

Ebrahim Alizadeh (SG), Mansur Hekmat (founding leader; real name: Joubin Razani, d. 2002)

This party emerged out of an alliance between Toilers Revolutionary Party of Iranian Kurdistan (Sazman-e Zahmatkeshan-e Kurdistan Iran [Komala]) and the Union of Communist Militants (Ettehad-e Mobarezan-e Komunist [Sahand]) in 1983. However, it has endured numerous splits since then. In 1991, Mansur Hekmat, the leader of the organization, and a few of his colleagues left to form the Workers' Communist Party of Iran (Hezb-e Komunist-e Kargari-ye Iran), and then in 2000 many members of Komala parted ways. What remains of the organization is active mainly in Europe.

http://cpiran.org/index.html

Communist Party of Workers and Peasants: Hezb-e Komunist-e Kargaran va Dehqanan-e Iran

1978

Ali Sa'adati

This group split from the Marxist-Leninist Tufan Organization (Sazman-e Marksisti-Leninisti-ye Tufan) and used to publish *Tufan*.

Communists' League of Iran: Ettehadiyyeh-ye Komunistha-ye Iran (Sar-beh-daran)

1976–83

Morteza Khabaz and Hoseyn Tajmir-Riyahi

This was a splinter group from the Revolutionary Organization of Tudeh Party of Iran (Sazman-e Enqelabi-ye Hezb-e Tudeh-ye Iran; later Hezb-e Ranjbaran-e Iran) which itself splintered off from Hezb-e Tudeh. Before the revolution, this Maoist group used to call itself the Organization of Communist Revolutionaries (Sazman-e Enqelabiyun-e Komunist) and was mainly based in the United States. After the revolution, some of its members moved to Iran. Despite their initial cooperation, this group decided to rebel against the Islamic Republic. In January 1982, the members of Sar-beh-daran attacked the city of Amol in Mazandaran Province. They were defeated by the IRGC and other pro-regime forces and were destroyed by 1983. The remaining members of the organization founded the Communist Party of Iran—Marxist-Leninists-Maoist in 2001 outside Iran.

http://www.cpimlm.com/

Comrades of Heydar Amu Oqli: Goruh-e Yaran-e Heydar Amu Oqli

This group was active during the strikes before the 1979 revolution, and joined OSPWCE in 1979/80.

Confederation of Iranian Students outside Iran: Konfederasyon-e Daneshjuyan-e Irani-ye Kharej Az Keshvar

1958/59

This influential organization represented Iranian students studying abroad and was active against the shah's regime. It was made up of Marxist and non-Marxist members.

Coordinating Council of the Societies of Kurdistan: Showra-ye Hamahangi-ye Jamʻiyyatha-ye Kurdistan

Council of Women of Sanandaj: Showra-ye Zanan-e Sanandaj

Council of Writers and Artists Supporting the Tudeh Party: Havadar-e Hezb-e Tudeh (Showra-ye Nevisandegan va Honarmandan)

In Reyshahri's list, this organization is incorrectly labeled as Ettehadiyyeh-ye Nevisandegan va Honarmandan.

Cultural Center of Arab People: Kanun-e Farhangi-ye Khalq-e Arab
> 1979
> Abujamal Taher Yassin (founder)

This group was active in Khuzestan Province and its members were formerly affiliated with Liberation Front (Jebhat-ol Tahrir).

Democratic Union of Iranian People: Ettehad-e Demokratik-e Mardom-e Iran
> 1978
> Mahmud Eʻtemadzadeh (Behazin)

This group published *Ettehad-e Mardom*, a journal. Its founder, Mahmud Eʻtemadzadeh (Behazin), a well-known literary figure, was inclined to merge the party with the Tudeh Party but Tudeh Party leader Nureddin Kianuri disagreed.

Fedaʼi Path Group: Goruh-e Rah-e Fedaʼi
> 1979
> Mehrdad Babaali (prominent person)

This group split from OIPFG in August/September 1979. At the time of the 1979 revolution, many of its members came back to Iran from abroad. Their position was closer to OIPFG—Minority than OIPFG—Majority. Most of the activists of this group were forced to leave the country after the summer of 1982. In 1984, they united with the Organization of Revolutionary Workers of Iran (Sazman-e Enqelabi-e Kargaran-e Iran [Rah-e Kargar]) but after a few years, they split again. The Fedaʼi Path Group was critical of Stalin and the "decadent workers states" of Eastern Europe and USSR.

Freedom of Labor Group: Goruh-e Azadi-ye Kar
> 1981

This group merged into the Union of Communist Militants (Sahand) (Ettehad-e Mobarezan-e Komunist). It should not be confused with the Freedom of Labor Organization (Sazman-e Azadi-ye Kar), which was a short-lived group that split from OIPFG—Minority in 1983 and later dissolved.

General Staff of Democratic Forces (Mahabad): Setad-e Moshtarak-e Niruha-ye Demokratik (Mahabad)

This group was active in the Mahabad region and was opposed to the 1979 referendum establishing the Islamic Republic.

Group of Struggle for the Freedom of the Working Class: Goruh-e Mobarezeh Baraye Azadi-ye Tabeqeh-ye Kargar
> 1976
> Asghar Amiri (Kak Parviz), Mrs. Susan Amiri (founders), Esmaʼil Pirout-Mohammadi (Kak Esmaʼil)

Related to Arman Khalq group, this group later merged into the Communists' League of Iran (Ettehadiyyeh-ye Komunistha-ye Iran).

Group Struggling for the Freedom of the Working Class: Goruh-e Nabard Baraye Rahayi-ye Tabaqeh-ye Kargar
> 1978
> Amir-Hoseyn Ahmadian

Cadres that split from what became OSPWCE formed this group in 1978. They used to publish a journal titled *Nabard*. Ahmadian was a lieutenant in the Iranian military who helped Taqi Shahram escape from prison. The group was dissolved in the early 1980s and Ahmadian settled in exile in Sweden.

Headquarters of the Torkaman's People: Setad-e Khalq-e Torkaman

This was a short-lived organization front for the other two Torkaman organizations.

Headquarters of Torkaman Sahra Council: Setad-e Showra-ye Torkaman Sahra

International Confederation of Teachers and University Students: Konfederasyon-e Jahani-ye Mo'allemin va Daneshjuyan

This group announced its support for the Islamic Republic in the 1979 referendum.

Iranian People's Feda'i Guerrillas (IPFG): Cherikha-ye Feda'i-ye Khalq-e Iran

1979–present

Mrs. Ashraf Dehqani (leader, 1979–present); Mohammad Hormatipur and Abdorrahim Saburi (leading cadres)

Led by Mrs. Ashraf Dehqani (b. 1949), this group, which is commonly referred to as Ashraf Dehqani's group, split from OIPFG in early 1979 to continue armed struggle against the Islamic Republic. In 1981, IPFG endured its first split when a group calling itself IPFG—Iranian People's Liberation Army, led by Mohammad Hormatipur, left the organization. Hormatipur and a number of his colleagues were killed on March 24, 1982. Subsequently some of the members of IPFG—Iranian People's Liberation Army joined the Communist Party of Iran. Another group calling itself IPFG—the Provincial Committee of Hormozgan (Cherikha-ye Feda'i-ye Khalq-e Iran—Hormozgan) split from Ashraf Dehqani's group in 1982. Both splinter groups later dissolved, and Ashraf Dehqani's group is currently based outside of Iran.

http://www.siahkal.com/

Iranian Turkoman Cultural-Political Organization: Kanun-e Farhangi Siyasi-ye Khalq-e Torkaman

1979–present

This group, which promoted the rights of ethnic Turkoman, became independent from OIPFG—Majority in 1987. Its leaders were assassinated and today it mainly exists as a website from exile.

http://www.turkmenistaniran.com/

Iran Radical Movement: Jonbesh-e Radikal-e Iran

Jungle and Mountain Group: Goruh-e Jangal va Kuhestan

1970–71

As far as we know this was the informal designation of one of the two teams that merged to form OIPFG in 1971 and no such group existed after the revolution. Therefore, HI Reyshahri could not have played a role in suppressing such a group in the 1980s.

Kurdistan Autonomy Council: Showra-ye Khodmokhtari-ye Kurdistan

1979

Ali Hamam Qazi (founder)

Kurdistan Democratic Party—Followers of the Fourth Congress: Qani Boluriyan—Monsha'eb Az Qasemlu va Hamsu ba Hezb-e Tudeh (Hezb-e Demokrat-e Kurdistan-e Iran)

Qani Boluriyan (founder), Mostafa Hejri (SG)

Disagreements between Qani Boluriyan and Abdorrahman Qasemlu caused this group to split from KDPI.

Kurdistan Democratic Party of Iran (KDPI): Hezb-e Demokrat-e Kurdistan (Qasemlu)

1945–present

Khaled Azizi (SG until 2017), Mostafa Mowludi (SG since 2017), Abdorrahman Qasemlu (founder)

Two secretary-generals of this organization, Abdorrahman Qasemlu and Sadeq Sharafkandi, were assassinated by suspected agents of the Iranian government on July 13, 1989 (in Vienna), and September 17, 1992 (in Berlin), respectively. The party advocates for federalism in Iran.

http://www.kurdistanukurd.com/

Labor Group: Goruh-e Kar

Labor's Role Group: Goruh-e Naqsh-e Kar

Left Unity Organization: Sazman-e Ettehad-e Chap

Main Center of Councils of Turkoman Sahra: Kanun-e Markazi-ye Showraha-ye Torkaman Sahra
1979
This group promoted the rights of ethnic Torkaman.

Marxist-Leninist Party of Red Twilight: Hezb-e Marksisti-Leninisti-ye Shafaq-e Sorkh
1979–1981/82
Zavareh Amiri (founder)
This group split from the Marxist-Leninist Tufan Organization (Sazman-e Marksisti-Leninisti-ye Tufan).

Marxist-Leninist Tufan Organization: Sazman-e Marksisti-Leninisti-ye Tufan
1966
Founders: Gholam-Hoseyn Forutan (d. 1998) and Ahmad Qasemi (d. 1974)
This organization split from the Tudeh Party in the mid-1960s. Qasemi and Forutan of the central committee of the Tudeh left the party by supporting China in the Sino-Soviet dispute. The organization started operating under the name of Marxist-Leninist Tufan Organization (Sazman-e Marksisti-Leninisti-ye Tufan) in late 1966. The group was supportive of the Albanian Communist Party. It is currently active outside Iran operating under the title of Party of Labor of Iran.
http://www.toufan.org/

National Congress of Arab People (Marxist and Non-Marxist): Kongereh-ye Melli-ye Khalq-e Arab (Marksist va Qeyr-e Marksist)
This group was purportedly active in Khuzestan Province and was made up of Marxist and non-Marxist members.

National Democratic Front of Iran: Jebheh-ye Demokratik-e Melli-ye Iran
1979
Hedayatollah Matin-Daftari and Shokrollah Paknezhad
This secular leftist group brought Marxist and non-Marxist activists together. In June 1979, it asked the framers of the constitution to ensure adherence to the Universal Declaration of Human Rights and equality of men and women. Then on August 12, 1979, it led a large demonstration in Tehran against the crackdown on press freedom. Paknezhad, the leader of the Palestine Group (Goruh-e Felestin) who had been tried in a famous case before the revolution, was executed by the Islamic regime in 1982. Matin-Daftari settled in exile in France.

National Democratic Society of Iran: Jam'iyyat-e Demokratik-e Melli-ye Iran

Navid Organization: Sazman-e Navid
1974/75
Rahman Hatefi and Mehdi Partovi (Khosrow) (founders)
The Navid Organization (Sazman-e Navid) started as a splinter group from OIPFG during the last years of the shah and the group gravitated towards the Tudeh Party. It folded into the Tudeh Party right after the revolution and worked as its secret branch inside Iran.

New Movement Organization for Liberation of Iran's People: Sazman-e Jonbesh-e Novin-e Rahayibakhsh-e Khalqha-ye Iran

Organization for Struggle on the Path of Working Class Emancipation (OSPWCE): Sazman-e Peykar dar Rah-e Azadi-ye Tabaqeh-ye Kargar
1975
This was a splinter group from PMOI, which in September/October 1975 embraced Marxism-Leninism as its ideology. The new group officially announced its existence under the name of OSPWCE sometime in September/October 1978. Some 560 of its members and supporters were killed in the 1980s at the hands of the Islamic regime. Some of the notable leadership cadres of OSPWCE who were executed were Ali-Reza Sepasi-Astiyani, Hoseyn Ruhani, Mas'ud Jikarehi, Shahram Bajgiran, Ahmad-Hoseyn Ruhani, and Qasem Abedini. OSPWCE disbanded as a major organization in 1982/83 and some of its remaining cadres fled to Europe and the United States, where they set up such

websites as http://peykar.info and http://www.peykar
andeesh.org.

*Organization of Combatant Workers: Sazman-e
Kargaran-e Mobarez*

This group, which was previously known as the
Organization of Toiling Masses of Iran (Sazman-e Tudeh-ye Zahmatkeshan-e Iran), changed its name to the
Organization of Combatant Workers a year after the
1979 revolution.

*Organization of Communist Revolutionaries:
Sazman-e Enqelabiyun-e Komunist*

1970/71

This group, which later formed the Communists'
League of Iran (Ettehadiyyeh-ye Komunistha-ye Iran
[Sar-beh-daran]), was mainly active in the United
States before the revolution.

*Organization of Communist Unity: Sazman-e
Vahdat-e Komunisti*

1979

The roots of this organization can be traced back
to the activities of the Star Group (Goruh-e Setareh),
which was active outside Iran in the early 1970s. Between 1973 and 1977, this group was involved in serious
ideological discussions with OIPFG about a possible
merger. Individuals such as Hasan Masali, Manuchehr
Hamidi, and Kambiz Rusta were involved on behalf of
the Star Group. When this merger did not take place, the
Star Group presented itself as Goruh-e Ettehad-e Komunisti (Communist Unity Group) and following the
1979 revolution changed its name to Organization of
Communist Unity. The activists affiliated with this organization had been very active in the Middle East where
they operated under the name of the Organization of
the National Front Abroad—Middle East Branch. They
used to publish a weekly magazine titled *Rahayi* (and
before that *Bakhtar-e Emrooz* under the name of the
National Front Abroad—Middle East) and were one of
the first Iranian political groups to campaign against

executions. The organization stopped operating after
many of its cadres were arrested in 1990.[1]

http://www.vahdatcommunisti.org/

*Organization of Democrat Women: Sazman-e Zanan-e
Demokrat*

This group supported voting in the referendum to
establish the Islamic Republic in 1979.

*Organization of Democratic Youth and University
Students of Iran: Sazman-e Javanan va Daneshjuyan-e
Demokrat-e Iran*

This group used to publish a journal titled *Arman*.

*Organization of Iranian People's Fedaiyan (Majority):
Sazman-e Feda'i-ye Khalq-e Iran (Aksariyyat); now
Sazman-e Feda'iyan-e Khalq-e Iran (Aksariyyat)*

1980

OIPFG was originally formed in 1971. However, in
June 1980 the organization split into two factions: Majority (Aksariyyat) and Minority (Aqalliyat). The Majority faction dropped the word "guerillas" from their
previous name, became close to the Tudeh Party, and
decided to cooperate with the Islamic regime. However, this group was suppressed in 1983 and forced to
move its operations outside the country.

http://www.fadai.org/

*Organization of People's Feda'i Guerrillas (Hammad
Sheybani): Sazman-e Cherikha-ye Feda'i-ye Khalq-e
Iran (Hammad Sheybani)*

1985

Hammad Sheybani and Mostafa Madani

This group split from the OIPFG—Minority faction in 1985.

*Organization of People's Feda'i Guerrillas—Majority—
Left Wing: Sazman-e Cherikha-ye Feda'i-ye Khalq-e
Iran (Aksariyyat—Jenah-e Chap)*

This organization, which is not mentioned in Reyshahri's list of outlawed Marxist groups, was a splinter

---

1. For more on this organization, see Sadeghi-Boroujerdi (2017).

group from the Majority faction of OIPFG. Two of the leaders of the organization were Naser Mohajer and Mrs. Vida Hajebi (1935–2017), who ended up in exile in France.

Organization of Pioneering High School Students (Supporting OIPFG): Sazman-e Daneshamouzan Pishgam (Havadar-e Feda'iyan-e Khalq)
1979
This was a high school student group supporting the OIPFG.

Organization of Pioneering Teachers (Supporting Feda'iyan-Khalq): Sazman-e Mo'alleman-e Pishgam (Havadar-e Feda'iyan-e Khalq)
The group did not participate in the 1979 referendum on the Islamic Republic.

Organization of Pioneering University Students (Supporting OIPFG): Sazman-e Daneshjuyan-e Pishgam (Havadar-e Feda'iyan-e Khalq)
This university student group supported OIPFG.

Organization of Revolutionary Masses of Students (Setad): Sazman-e Tudeh-ye Enqelabi-ye Daneshjuyan va Daneshamouzan (Setad)
This group was created by the Communists' League of Iran (Ettehadiyyeh-ye Komunistha-ye Iran) and used to publish *Setad*.

Organization of the Workers' Path: Sazman-e Rah-e Kargar
1979–present
Leading cadres: Mehdi Khosrowshahi, Ja'far Riyahi, Hoseyn Qazi-Farhadi, Mohammad-Sadeq Riyahi, Ali-Reza Shokuhi, Heydar Zaqi (all were killed)
This organization was formed before the 1979 revolution by a group of leftist activists in prison who had grown critical of OIPFG's method of armed struggle. After the revolution, they published a number of theoretical pamphlets warning about the emergence of clerical fascism. They were crushed like other oppositional groups in 1981 and lost many of their leading cadres. In 1982, they changed their name to the Organization of

Revolutionary Workers of Iran (Sazman-e Enqelabi-e Kargaran-e Iran) and started their publication outside Iran in 1983. This organization tried to unify with the Feda'i Path Group (Goruh-e Rah-e Feda'i) and a few other Marxist OIPFG splinter groups between 1991 and 1993 but could not reach an agreement.
http://www.rahekargar.net/

Organization of Trailblazing High School Students (Supporting OSPWCE): Sazman-e Daneshamouzan Pishtaz (Havadar-e Peykar)
This student group supported the militant Peykar organization. Reyshahri may have made a mistake here since the organization that supported Peykar was University and High School Students Supporting OSPWCE (Daneshjuyan va Daneshamuzan-e Havadar Sazman-e Peykar dar Rah-e Azadi-ye Tabaqeh-ye Kargar).

Organization of Trailblazing Teachers (Supporting OSPWCE): Sazman-e Mo'alleman-e Pishtaz (Havadar-e Peykar)

Organization of Trailblazing University Students: Sazman-e Daneshjuyan-e Pishtaz
This university student group supported the armed struggle of OIPFG. Reyshahri lists the organization as supporting OSPWCE but as can be seen at http://www.iran-archive.com/node/18913, this group supported OIPFG's method of struggle.

Organization Struggling to Establish an Independent Labor Movement: Sazman-e Mobarezeh Bara-ye Ijad-e Jonbesh-e Mostaqel-e Kargari
This communist organization was active in 1979/80. In addition to their organ, they published a pamphlet titled "Thesis of the Political Office on the Nature of the Iranian Revolution."

People's Democratic Committee: Komiteh-ye Demokratik-e Khalq

People's Warriors Group: Goruh-e Razmandegan-e Khalq
This group opposed the 1979 draft constitution.

Political Organization of Arab People: Sazman-e Siyasi-ye Khalq-e Arab

1979

This group advocated for the rights of ethnic Arabs in Iran, mainly in Khuzestan Province.

Popular Arabic Movement in Iran: Jonbesh-e Mardomi-ye Arabi Dar Iran

This group was active in Khuzestan Province.

Popular Movement of Arab People of Iran: Jonbesh-e Mardomi-ye Khalq-e Arab-e Iran

This group was active in Khuzestan Province.

Preparation Committee for People's Congress: Komiteh-ye Tadarokat-e Kongere-ye Khalq

1979

Proletariat Group: Goruh-e Poroletariya

Fewer than a dozen individuals split from the Marxist-Leninist Party of Red Twilight (Hezb-e Marksisti-Leninisti-ye Shafaq-e Sorkh) to form this group.

Radical Movement of Iran: Nehzat-e Radikal-e Iran

Nader Moqaddam-Maragheh'i (leader), Rahmatollah Moqaddam-Maragheh'i (founder and SG)

This group had a meeting with Ayatollah Khomeini in 1979.

Ranjbaran Party of Iran: Hezb-e Ranjbaran-e Iran

1979–present

Hushang Amirpur, Mohsen Rezvani, Ali Sadeqi, Majid Zarbakhash (leading cadres)

The origin of this Maoist group dates back to the 1960s, when a group calling itself the Revolutionary Organization of Tudeh Party of Iran (Sazman-e Enqelabi-ye Hezb-e Tudeh-ye Iran) split from the Tudeh Party. Ranjbaran initially supported the anti-imperialist stance of the Islamic Republic but by 1980, they sided with President Banisadr, which led to their suppression. The party used to publish *Ranjbar* and the *Khalq* monthly.

http://www.ranjbaran.org/01_ranjbaronline/

Red Organization of Iran's Workers: Sazman-e Sorkh-e Kargaran-e Iran

This group used to publish a journal titled *Zarourat*.

Revolutionary Council of Torkaman's People: Showra-ye Enqelabi-ye Khalq-e Torkaman

This group, which was associated with OIPFG, engaged in clashes with pro-regime forces in 1979 and 1980.

Revolutionary Democratic Organization of Gilan and Mazandaran: Sazman-e Enqelabi-ye Demokratik-e Gilan va Mazandaran

1980

Hasan Masali

This group was active in Mazandaran Province. Masali soon had to leave Iran and continued his opposition to the Iranian regime from exile.

Revolutionary Union of Combatant Women: Ettehadiyyeh-ye Enqelabi-ye Zanan-e Mobarez

1979

This group is associated with the Communist Party of Workers and Peasants (Hezb-e Komunist-e Kargaran va Dehqanan-e Iran). In a statement in 1979, this group condemned granting the right of divorce to men.

Revolutionary Unity of the Arab Masses of Iran: Vahdat-e Enqelabi-ye Khalq-e Arab-e Iran

Socialist Workers Party: Hezb-e Kargaran-e Sosyalist

1974–83

Afsaneh Najmabadi (a.k.a. Azar Tabari), Hormoz Rahimiyan, Maziyar Razi (a.k.a. Hozhabr Khosravi), Babak Zahra'i, Siamak Zahra'i

This Trotskyist group had its origin in two separate groups active in the United States and United Kingdom. Babak Zahra'i, Siamak Zahra'i, and Mahmud Sayrafizadeh led the group in the United States, which was working with the American Socialist Workers Party, among others. Hormoz Rahimiyan and Maziyar Razi led a group of Iranians working in

Britain with the International Marxist Group. They published a journal titled *Kand va Kav* beginning in 1974. After the revolution, most members of these two groups moved to Iran and joined forces to create the Socialist Workers Party (Hezb-e Kargaran-e Sosyalist). They published a paper titled *Kargar* (Worker). Babak Zahra'i ran for the Assembly for the Final Examination of the Constitution from Tehran but received only some 16,000 votes. Eventually there was a split in the group and most of the leadership cadres returned to the United States and United Kingdom. After spending some time in prison, Babak Zahra'i left Iran and gave up on active politics. Razi, however, is still active in Marxist circles in London and works with the Iranian Workers Solidarity Network and the Iranian Revolutionary Marxists' Tendency.

Society for Defense of Liberty and Revolution: Jam'iyyat-e Defa' Az Azadi va Enqelab

This group, which was active in Kurdistan, held a demonstration in 1979 in Sanandaj with some 4,000 participants.

Society for Defense of Toilers and the Rights of Kurdish People: Jam'iyyat-e Defa' Az Zahmatkeshan va Hoquq-e Melli-ye Khalq-e Kurd

1979

This group, which was active in Bukan, opposed the national referendum held on March 30–31, 1979, which approved the formation of the Islamic Republic.

Society for Liberation of Toilers: Jam'iyyat-e Rah-e Rahayi-ye Zahmatkeshan

Kak Foad

This group was associated with Komala and was active in the Mahabad region.

Society of Arab Intellectuals of Iran: Jam'iyyat-e Rowshanfekran-e Arab-e Iran

In a statement issued in 1979, this group, which was active in Khuzestan, supported Sheikh Shobayr-Khaqani.

Society of Combatants for Freedom and Defense of National and Democratic Rights of Kurdish People: Jam'iyyat-e Mobarezin-e Rah-e Azadi va Modafe'-e Hoquq-e Melli va Demokratik-e Khalq-e Kurd

This group, which was active in Baneh, opposed the national referendum held on March 30–31, 1979, to approve the formation of the Islamic Republic.

Society of Combatant Women: Jam'iyyat-e Zanan-e Mobarez

1979

This group published a journal titled *Zan-e Mobarez*.

Society of Women of Turkoman Sahra: Kanun-e Zanan-e Torkaman Sahra

1979

This group was formed after the first round of clashes between Torkaman and pro-regime forces in 1979. It was associated with the Iranian Turkoman Cultural-Political Organization (Kanun-e Farhangi Siyasi-ye Khalq-e Torkaman).

Solidarity Council of Iranian Peoples: Showra-ye Hambastegi-ye Khalqha-ye Iran

Toilers Revolutionary Party of Iranian Kurdistan (Komala): Sazman-e Zahmatkeshan-e Kurdistan Iran

1969–present

Abdollah Mohtadi

Komala was the largest leftist group in Iranian Kurdistan after the revolution. In 1983, Komala and the Union of Communist Militants (Ettehad-e Mobarezan-e Komunist) joined forces to create the Communist Party of Iran (Hezb-e Komunist-e Iran). However, Komala split from the latter group in 2000 and resumed its independent operations under the official name of Komala Party of Iranian Kurdistan (Hezb-e Komala Kurdistan Iran).

http://www.komala.org/

Tudeh Party of Iran: Hezb-e Tudeh-ye Iran

1941–present

Nureddin Kiyanuri (SG), Mohammad Omidvar (current SG)

As the oldest active leftist party in Iran, the Tudeh Party supported the Islamic Republic after the revolution but fell victim to its repression in early 1983. Leading members were paraded on national television denouncing the party and communism. Subsequently, the party continued its operations in exile. In 1984, a splinter group from the Tudeh Party emerged with the name Democratic Party of People of Iran (Hezb-e Demokratik-e Mardom-e Iran).

http://www.tudehpartyiran.org/

Union Group: Goruh-e Peyvand

Union of Communist Militants: Ettehad-e Mobarezan-e Komunist

1978

Iraj Azarin, Mansur Hekmat (real name: Joubin Razani), Mrs. Azar Majed, Hamid Taqva'i

This Maoist group, which was made up largely of activists who lived overseas and known formerly as Sahand Group, officially announced its formation in late 1979. This later group then merged with the Toilers Revolutionary Party of Iranian Kurdistan (Sazman-e Zahmatkeshan-e Kurdistan Iran [Komala]) to form the Communist Party of Iran (Hezb-e Komunist-e Iran) in 1983. Hekmat and Taqva'i later split from this group and went on to form the Workers' Communist Party of Iran (Hezb-e Komunist-e Kargari-ye Iran) in 1991 (http://www.wpiran.org/).

Union of Struggle for Creating the Party of the Working Class: Ettehad-e Mobarezeh Dar Rah-e Ijad-e Hezb-e Tabaqeh-ye Kargar

In 1979, this group merged into the newly formed Ranjbaran Party of Iran (Hezb-e Ranjbaran-e Iran).

Union of Struggle for the Aspirations of the Working Class: Ettehad-e Mobarezeh Dar Rah-e Arman-e Tabaqeh-ye Kargar

1975–78

Javad Qaedi

This was a splinter group from the PMOI-Marxist-Leninist (Sazman-e Mojahedin-e Khalq Marxist-Leninist) (later to become OSPWCE). The members of this group were close to the thinking of Taqi Shahram, who was executed on July 24, 1980. The group endured a split in 1979 and was seriously weakened. Its remaining members later united with the Union of Communist Militants (Ettehad-e Mobarezan-e Komunist).

United Leftist Council for Democracy and Freedom: Showra-ye Mottahed-e Chap (Baray-e Demokrasi va Azadi)

Mehdi Khanbaba-Tehrani

In the early 1980s, this group joined the National Council of Resistance for a few years and then split from it. Their publication was titled *Payam-e Azadi* (Freedom's Message).

Warriors for the Freedom of the Working Class: Razmandegan-e Azadi-ye Tabeqeh-ye Kargar

1977

Dariush Kahedpur

This organization was started by a group of Marxist thinkers who were critical of the Soviet Union and the method of armed struggle. They split from OSPWCE and announced their existence in 1978. Later, they united with the Union of Struggle for the Aspirations of the Working Class (Ettehad-e Mobarezeh Dar Rah-e Arman-e Tabaqeh-ye Kargar) and a few other small groups and eventually formed the Workers' Communist Party of Iran (Hezb-e Komunist-e Kargari-ye Iran).

Warriors of the Arab People: Razmandegan-e Khalq-e Arab

1979

This group was associated with Sheykh Shobayr-Khaqani.

Outlawed Non-Marxist Parties and Groups

Alfaruq group: Goruh-e Alfaruq

This group was active in Kurdistan Province.

Antireactionary Organization: Sazman-e Mobarezeh Ba Erteja' (Samba)

Arab Society: Jame'eh-ye Arab

Arab Warriors Front: Jebheh-ye Razmandegan-e Arab
1979
Maki Feysali, Mr. Al-e Ali, Mr. Mazaripur, Mr. Zobeydi (founders)
This group had the backing of Sheykh Mohammad-Taher Al-e Shobayr-Khaqani, spiritual leader of the Arabs in Khuzestan province.

Arya National Socialist Party: Hezb-e Nasyonal Sosyalist-e Arya
Mehdi Sepehr (leader)

Aspirations of the Oppressed (Organization of Pioneering Warriors of the Iranian Dispossessed): Arman-e Mostaz'afin (Sazman-e Razmandegan-e Pishgam-e Mostaz'afin-e Iran)
1976–82
Mohammad-Baqer Borzou'i (leader)
This group was inspired by the ideas of Ali Shari'ati, and did not support armed struggle.

Association of Free Muslims: Jam'iyyat-e Moslem-e Azad
1951/52
Sheykh Mostafa Rahnama (founder)
This Sunni group had been suppressed before starting its activities again in 1978.

Bakhtar Political Group: Goruh-e Siyasi-ye Bakhtar

Center for Proclamation and Publication of the Thoughts of Dr. Ali Shari'ati: Kanun-e Eblaq va Nashr-e Andisheha-ye Doktor Ali Shari'ati (Ershad)
1980–present
After being suppressed in 1981, this center decided to continue its activities as an underground group.
http://kanoon-eblagh.blogspot.com/
http://www.kanooneblagh.org/

Central Council of Sunnah: Showra-ye Markazi-ye Sonnat (Shams-Moftizadeh)
1981
Ahmad Moftizadeh, Mowlavi Abdolaziz Molla Zadeh, Naser Sobhani (prominent leaders)
This was a Sunni group formed in Tehran.
http://www.shams-iran.org/

Central Organization of the Freedom Movement of Iran: Sazman-e Markazi-ye Nehzat-e Rahayi-ye Iran (Saman)

Corps of Offspring of Lion and Sun: Sepah-e Farzandan-e Shir va Khorshid

Derafsh Kaviyani Organization: Sazman-e Derafsh-e Kaviyani
1986
Sirus Elahi and Manuchehr Ganji (founders)
This was a monarchist organization. Ganji was a former minister of education under the shah. Sirus Elahi, a former professor of political science and one of the other founders of the group, was assassinated in Paris in 1990.

Forqan group: Forqan
1977/78–1980
Akbar Goudarzi (founder and leader)
Forqan was a militant Islamic group that was strongly influenced by the ideas of Ali Shari'ati. It was vehemently opposed to clerical political rule. Forqan assassinated such prominent figures as Major General Valiyollah Qarani (April 23, 1979), Ayatollah Morteza Motahhari (May 1, 1979), and Ayatollah Mohammad Mofatteh (December 18, 1979). The regime executed a number of their members, including the leader of the group, Akbar Goudarzi, in 1980.

Group of Followers of Omar's Path: Goruh-e Peyrovan-e Rah-e Omar
This was a Sunni religious group.

Guardians of Monarchy: Pasdaran-e Shahanshahi
This was a monarchist group.

Hojjatiyyeh [Allah's proof over creation] Society: Anjoman-e Hojjatiyyeh-ye Mahdavi-ye (Anjoman-e Zedd-e Baha'iyyat-e Sabeq)

1953–83

Sheykh Mahmud Zakerzadeh-Tavallaei (Mahmud Halabi) (founder)

This was a conservative association formerly known as the Anti-Baha'i Society. Beginning in the 1950s, they spearheaded an anti-Baha'i campaign. After Ayatollah Khomeini criticized their beliefs, the society announced on July 23, 1983, that it would close all its programs and activities. However, they continued to operate in unofficial ways and many of its members found important posts in the postrevolutionary system.

Iranian People's Party: Hezb-e Mardom-e Iran

This was a splinter group from the Iran Party (Hezb-e Iran), which was formed after the 1953 coup. Mohammad Nakhshab (PhD, 1966, New York University) and Hoseyn Razi led it.

Iranian Writers' Association: Kanun-e Nevisandegan-e Iran

First period: 1968–70. Second period: 1977–81. Third period: 1999–present.

This was the chief organization representing Iranian writers, both Marxist and non-Marxist, before and after the revolution. They held ten nights of poetry reading before the revolution (October 10–19, 1977), where poets read anti-shah poems. After the revolution, the association defended the cause of freedom of speech, which did not sit well with the regime. It was also involved in a controversy when the leadership decided to expel some of their colleagues because of their sympathy for the Tudeh Party.

http://www.kanoon-nevisandegan-iran.org/

Iran's National Front (INF): Jebheh-ye Melli-ye Iran

1949–present

Ali Ardalan, Shapur Bakhtiar, Hoseyn Fatemi, Mohammad Mossadeq, Allahyar Saleh, Karim Sanjabi (prominent personalities)

The National Front was suppressed after the 1953 coup and recommenced its activities in 1960. At this time, the party was known as the Second National Front but it was dissolved in 1964 due to internal disagreements. The Third National Front was established in 1965 and was immediately suppressed. The party started its activities again in 1977. Some of its members held posts in PM Bazargan's provincial government.

http://jebhemeliiran.org/

Iran's Patriots Front: Jebheh-ye Mihanparastan-e Iran

Bahram Aryana, Ardeshir Zahedi (prominent figures)

This was a monarchist group led by prominent officials of the shah's era.

Iran's Patriots Party: Hezb-e Mihandustan-e Iran

After the 1979 revolution, this party campaigned against government confiscation of ordinary citizens' arms.

Islamic Coalition Group: Goruh-e E'telafi-ye Islami (Sanandaj)

This group was mainly active in the Sanandaj region.

Islamic Equality Party: Hezb-e Mosavat-e Islami

1980/81

Ahmad Moftizadeh (founder)

Moftizadeh (1933–93) was a Sunni religious leader who supported the revolution in its early days. In April 1979, Ayatollah Khomeini declared him "the sole religious and political leader of the Kurds." His followers fought antiregime Kurds in 1979/80. He held negotiation meetings with Ayatollah Khomeini's representatives who came to Kurdistan in 1979. However, Moftizadeh was arrested in 1982 and spent ten years in prison. He died a few months after being released from prison.

Islamic Freedom-Seeking Group: Goruh-e Azadikhahan-e Islami

Seyfeddin Nabavi (leader)

This group announced its support for the national referendum that approved the formation of the Islamic Republic in March 1979.

Islamic Movement Party: Hezb-e Harekat-e Islami (Ahl-e Sonnat)

This was a Sunni religious group.

Islamic People's Republican Party of Iran: Hezb-e Jomhuri-ye Khalq-e Mosalman-e Iran

1979

Rahmatollah Moqaddam-Maragheh'i (founder), Seyyed Hadi Khosrowshahi, Seyyed Sadreddin Balaqi

This party was created on February 27, 1979, by Moqaddam-Maragheh'i, who was close to Grand Ayatollah Kazem Shari'atmadari. The judiciary ordered the closure of the party's offices on December 16, 1979. The party's members were tried in a court presided over by HI Mohammad Reyshahri.

Islamic Union of Iranian Baluchestan: Ettehad-e Islami-ye Baluchestan-e Iran

Kurdistan National Union: Ettehadiyyeh-ye Melli-ye Kurdistan

Liberal Union: Ettehad-e Leyberal

Liberation Movement of Iran (LMI): Nehzat-e Azadi-ye Iran

1961

Prominent personalities: Mehdi Bazargan (former SG), Ebrahim Yazdi (SG), Seyyed Mahmud Taleqani, Reza Sadr, Seyyed Ahmad Sadr Haj Seyyed Javadi, Ezzatollah Sahabi, Yadollah Sahabi, Abbas Taj, Mohammad Tavassoli, Mohammad-Hoseyn Baniasadi, Abdolali Espahbodi, Naser Minachi, Ali-Akbar Mo'infar, Hashem Sabbaghiyan

Established in May 1961, LMI formed the backbone of the cabinet of Mehdi Bazargan, who was the first PM of postrevolutionary Iran. The party and its members were gradually pushed aside until the organization was declared illegal. Bazargan headed LMI until he died in 1995. A couple of weeks later, Yazdi replaced him as LMI's leader and held the post until 2017.

Militia Group of the Islamic Movement of Torkaman Youth: Goruh-e Nezami-ye Nehzat-e Islami-ye Javanan-e Torkaman

Mohajerin Organization of Iran: Sazman-e Mohajerin-e Khalq-e Iran

1975

Founders: Hassan Hormozi, Mahmud Rahimkhani, Mohammad-Reza Sardari, Mahmud Jalili-Shabestari

This group, which was mainly active in Khuzestan Province, split from PMOI when a significant segment of PMOI cadres embraced Marxism as their ideology in the mid-1970s. Jalili-Shabestari, Sardari, and Hormozi were killed before the revolution and Rahimkhani died in a car accident a month after the 1979 revolution. The group initially survived the crackdown in the early 1980s but eventually the security forces arrested all members inside the country, including Karim Jokesht. At least two other leadership cadres, Ruhollah Feyli and Reza Ebrahiminezhad, have settled in exile in Europe.

Mojahedin Organization of Arab People of Iran: Sazman-e Mojahedin-e Khalq-e Arab

This group was active in Khuzestan Province and engaged in clashes with pro-regime forces during the early months after the revolution.

Monotheistic Association of Torbat-e Jam (Sunnis): Anjoman-e Towhidi-ye Torbat-e Jam (Ahl-e Sonnat)

Movement for Liberty: Jonbesh Baraye Azadi

Ali-Asghar Haj Seyyed Javadi (leader)

This group introduced candidates for the Assembly for the Final Examination of the Constitution in 1979. Its leader was a well-known public intellectual who wrote critical open letters to Iranian leaders both before and after the revolution.

Movement of Baluchestan Mojahedin: Jonbesh-e Mojahedin-e Baluchestan-e Iran

> 1986–90/91
>
> Mohammadkhan Mir Lashari
>
> This group demanded autonomy for the Baluchestan region and engaged in armed struggle.

Movement of Combatant Muslims: Jonbesh-e Mosalmanan-e Mobarez (JMM)

> 1977–81
>
> Habibollah Peyman (founder and leader)
>
> This group attracted a number of lay religious intellectuals and activists in the early days of the revolution. Peyman was a member of the Revolutionary Council (1979–80), and the group published a magazine titled *Ommat* between 1979 and 1981.

Muslim Brotherhood: Ikhwan-ol-Moslemin

> Naser Sobhani (founder)
>
> This group was active in Kurdistan province and its leader was executed.

Muslims' Reform Party: Hezb-e Eslah-ol-Moslemin (Salaf-e Ettahad-ol-Moslemin)

> This was a Sunni group.

Muslims Unity Party: Hezb-e Ettehad-ol-Moslemin

> Mowlavi Abdolaziz
>
> This was a Sunni group associated with Maki Mosque in Sistan and Baluchestan Province.

National Freedom-Seeking Group: Goruh-e Azadikhahan-e Melli-ye Iran (GAMA)

Nationalist Guerrillas: Cherikha-ye Nasyonalist

Nationalist Warriors of Iran: Razmandegan-e Nasyonalist-e Iran (Rana)

National Movement of Mojahedin: Jonbesh-e Melli-ye Mojahedin

> 1979
>
> Mas'ud Rajavi

This group was formed by members of Sazman-e Mojahedin-e Khalq-e Iran (PMOI) and in less than a year changed its name to PMOI.

National Unity Front: Jebheh-ye Ettehad-e Melli

> http://uip.uipmedia.org/fr/index.html

Organization for Rescuing the Uprising of Great Iran: Sazman-e Neqab (Nejat-e Qiyam-e Iran-e Bozorg)

> This group was made up of a number of military officers who were plotting to carry out a coup, known as the Nojeh coup plot. However, the coup plan was discovered and on July 9, 1980, the ringleaders were arrested and later executed.

Organization of Iranian Muslim University Students outside Iran (supporting PMOI): Sazman-e Daneshjuyan-e Mosalman-e Irani-ye Kharej Az Keshvar (Vabaste be Mojahedin-e Khalq)

Organization of National-Islamic Struggle of Kurdistan Province: Sazman-e Mobarezeh-ye Melli-Islami-ye Kurdistan (Khabat)

> 1979–present
>
> Jalal Hoseyni (leader)
>
> http://www.sazmanixebat.org/sorani/

Pan-Iranist Party: Hezb-e Pan Iranist

> 1947/48
>
> Mohsen Pezeshkpur (founder)
>
> This small secular ultranationalist party has been repressed, but its small cadre of activists continue to operate in Iran.
>
> http://paniranist.org/

Party of the Iranian Nation: Hezb-e Mellat-e Iran

> 1947–present
>
> Daryush Foruhar (SG; 1951–98), Hasan-Ali Saremi-Kalali, Khosrow Seyf (since 1998)
>
> Foruhar, who had been the secretary-general of the party for decades, and who served in PM Bazargan's cabinet, was brutally murdered on November 22, 1998, as part of the "chain murders" of dissident intellectuals.
>
> https://hezbemellateiran.com/

People's Mojahedin Movement of Iran: Nehzat-e Mojahedin-e Khalq-e Iran

1976/77

Lotfollah Meysami (founder) and Mehdi Qani (prominent member)

Meysami was a member of PMOI and became blind in both eyes in 1974 when a bomb he was handling accidently exploded.

People's Mojahedin Organization of Iran (PMOI): Sazman-e Mojahedin-e Khlalq-e Iran

1965–present

Ali-Asghar Badi'zadegan, Mohammad Hanifne-zhad, Sa'id Mohsen (founders); current leader: Mas'ud Rajavi

Along with OIPFG, PMOI has been the main gue-rilla organization that has fought against both the shah and the Islamic Republic. In 1975, the group experienced a split as some members embraced Marxism as their ideology and formed OSPWCE. In 1981, after violent clashes took place between PMOI and pro-regime forces, the organization resorted to a campaign of assassination and its leader, Mas'ud Rajavi, left the country in a clan-destine fashion along with former president Banisadr. Since then, PMOI has operated in exile and views itself as the main opposition group to the Iranian regime.

https://www.mojahedin.org/home/fa

Political Front of Iran's Muslim Arab People: Jebheh-ye Siyasi-ye Khalq-e Arab-e Mosalman-e Iran

The accurate name of this organization may be the Political Organization of Arab People (Sazeman-e Si-yasi-ye Khalq-e Arab). That organization was involved in military clashes with government forces in Abadan and Khorramshahr beginning in 1979 along with an-other group named the Cultural Association of Arab People (Kanun-e Farhangi-ye Khalq-e Arab).

Propaganda Society Group: Goruh-e Jama'at-e Tabliqi (Ahl-e Sonnat)

This was a Sunni religious group.

Razgari's Corp: Sepah-e Razgari

Sheykh Osman Naqshbandi (founder)

This group was established in Kurdistan Province and followed the teachings of its leader.

Republican Party of Iran: Hezb-e Jomhurikhah-e Iran

1979

Abdolhoseyn Baqa'i-Kermani (founder)

Resistance Movement of Iranian Baluchestan: Jonbesh-e Paydari-ye Baluchestan-e Iran

Revolutionary Movement of People of Iran (JAMA): Jonbesh-e Enqelabi-ye Mardom-e Iran

1979–81

Kazem Sami (SG)

In 1963, Kazem Sami and Habibollah Peyman es-tablished the Freedom-Seeking Movement of People of Iran (Jonbesh-e Azadikhahi-ye Mardom-e Iran), which advocated for a more radical strategy of op-posing the shah's regime. In 1965, Sami and Peyman were both arrested and imprisoned and the operation of their organization ended. In February 1979, Sami established the Revolutionary Movement of People of Iran (Jonbesh-e Enqelabi-ye Mardom-e Iran), which had the same acronym but a slightly different name than the previous organization. Sami served as an MP and was health minister in PM Bazargan's provincial government. He also ran in the 1980 presidential elec-tion. He was brutally stabbed in his office on Novem-ber 23, 1988, and died in 1989.

Revolutionary Organization of Masses of Islamic Republic (Satja): Sazman-e Enqelabi-ye Tudeh-haye Jomhuri-ye Islami (Satja)

Mohammad Montazeri (leader)

After the death of its leader, this group joined the Liberation Movement of the Islamic World (Jonbesh-e Azadibakhsh-e Jahan-e Islam).

Sanandaj Union: Ettehadiyyeh-ye Sanandaj

Showra Islamic Organization: Sazman-e Islami-e Showra (Sash)

1979

Society of Muslim Women of Sanandaj: Jame'eh-ye Zanan-e Mosalman-e Sanandaj

Temporary Leadership Group: Goruh-e Qiyade-ye Movaqqat
This group was active in both Iranian and Iraqi Kurdistan.

Toilers Party: Hezb-e Zahmatkeshan-e Mellat-e Iran
1951–79
Mozaffar Baqa'i (founder and leader, 1951–79)
This party split from Iran's National Front. Some former members, such as Seyyed Hasan Ayat and Ebrahim Esrafiliyan, served as MPs after the revolution.

Union of Muslim Student Associations (Supporting PMOI): Ettehadiyyeh-ye Anjomanha-ye Daneshamuzan-e Mosalman (Havadar-e Mojahedin-e Khalq)

Union of Muslim University Student Associations (Supporting PMOI): Ettehadiyyeh-ye Anjomanha-ye Daneshjuyan-e Mosalman (Havadar-e Mojahedin-e Khalq)

Women National Union: Ettehadiyyeh-ye Melli-ye Zanan
This group published a statement criticizing the inequality between rights accorded to men and women in laws passed by the AE.

Youth Organization of PMOI: Sazman-e Javanan-e Mojahed

Youth Organization of the Party of Iranian People's Toilers: Sazman-e Javanan-e Hezb-e Zahmatkeshan-e Mellat-e Iran

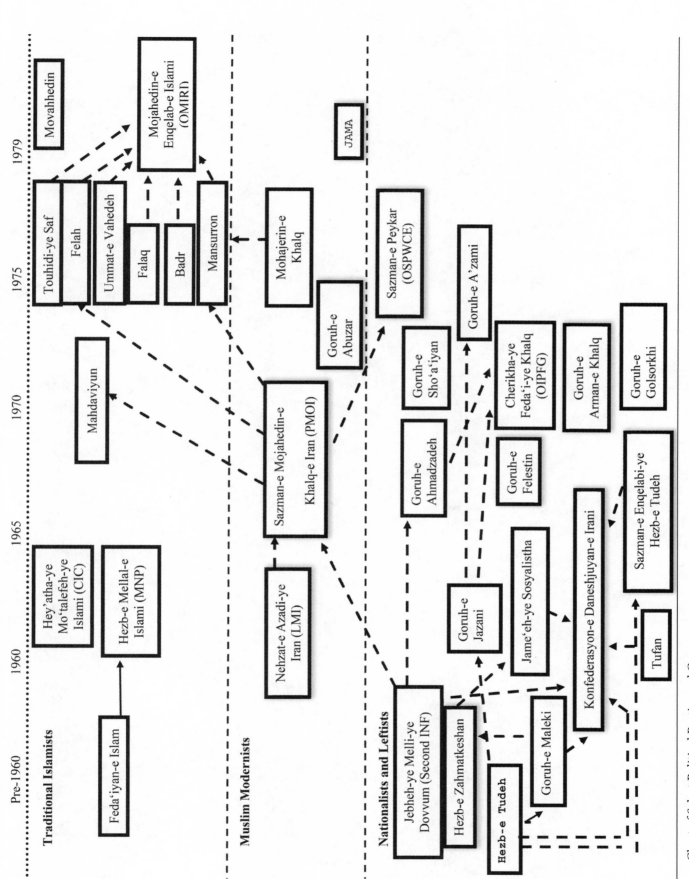

22. Chart of Select Political Parties and Groups.

PART TWO

Political Elite

15

Who Is Who in Postrevolutionary Iran

Codebook

We have assembled the data in this section from numerous sources, including archives, biographies, books, encyclopedias, interviews, journals, obituaries, letters, and websites. We present the information in the following format:

- *Last name, first name of the individual*: First and last names have been listed based on official texts such as lists of MPs put out by the Majlis. Less frequently used elements of a compound personal name appear in brackets, as in [Ardeshir-] Larijani or Musavi [-Khameneh]. If a person is better known by a name other than his or her official name, the official name has been put in brackets, as in Khalkhali [Sadeqi-Givi]. When two or more individuals have the same exact first and last name, the name of the city of birth has been added in brackets for one or two of them to distinguish them, as in Seyyed Mohammad Hoseyni.
- *Elite occupation(s), titles, and years of service*: Occupation refers to a position held by an individual in any of the three branches of government as well as important non-elected bodies identified in the list below. Years of service in that position and location have also been given. When information about exact day and month of tenure were available, we have listed those as well.
- *Years of birth and death*: Years of birth and death were calculated by converting Hijrah solar dates to Common Era (CE) dates. Months and days were added when the data was available. If no end date is listed (e.g., 1950–), it means the person is still alive.

- *City and province of birth*: In instances when an individual was born in a very small village not well known to Iranians, we have listed the nearest large town or city as the birthplace. Also, because the Islamic Republic established some new provinces after the revolution, we have listed the current province as the province of birth rather than the former name. For example, if a person was born in Bojnurd in the 1950s, we have listed the person as being born in North Khorasan rather than Razavi Khorasan. Although this may not be historically correct, it enables us to compare the political weight of provinces currently.
- *Educational degrees*: Educational degrees (or type), academic discipline, institution, country (if outside Iran), year of graduation, and thesis or dissertation title are listed when available. The Iranian State Educational Assessment Organization uses the following four broad groupings for categorizing academic disciplines: mathematics and technological sciences, experimental (and medical) sciences, human sciences, and arts and foreign languages. In cases where the name of a university was changed after the revolution, we have used its most current name (e.g., Sharif University of Technology is listed rather than Aryamehr University of Technology).
- *Father's name and profession*: The name and profession of an individual's father are listed when available.
- *Pre-elite occupation*: The last known occupation is provided for each individual before he or she entered the upper echelons of political elite.
- *Prerevolutionary prison experience*: We have categorized only individuals whom the shah's

regime tried and incarcerated for more than a few months before the 1979 revolution as having had prison experience. We have not included in the category individuals SAVAK questioned or released after a few days nor anyone the Islamic Republic imprisoned after the revolution, as we were attempting to gauge the radicalism of revolutionaries who came to power in 1979.

- *Veteran of the Iran–Iraq War*: We have classified only individuals who fought in the Iran–Iraq War as war veterans. We did not consider those who went to the front for short periods in such capacities as engineers, doctors, or clerics as war veterans. However, if these same individuals spent a good number of months at the front, then we have marked them as war veterans.
- *Member of the Revolutionary Guards (IRGC)*: The category of Revolutionary Guards includes not just IRGC militiamen but also anyone who has been a member of the Basij organization (including Basij student members), which was absorbed into the IRGC in early 1981. In 2008, Basij was fully absorbed into the IRGC's ground forces after some internal restructuring.
- *Member of a martyr's family*: We have defined a martyr as anyone who was killed by the shah's regime (in prison or in revolutionary demonstrations/operations), in the Iran–Iraq War, or in assassinations and bombings carried out by opposition forces. This is consistent with the categories used by the Foundation of Martyrs and Veterans Affairs (FMVA). We have not labeled individuals who were killed in car or plane crashes or belonged to antiregime political forces as martyrs.
- *Political party affiliation and role*: An individual's membership and position held in any political party were recorded to indicate their political leaning and networking ties.
- *Important narrative about the individual*: Based on media reports, official pronouncements, and a host of other sources mentioned elsewhere in this book, we have provided brief narratives about the political life of most individuals included in our database. The personal life of individuals was not our primary concern in this study and we have excluded that type of information unless it could shed some light on the political life of the individual being discussed.

❧

In cases where there was no reliable information about any of the above categories in the database, that particular field does not appear. For example, for many individuals year of graduation, name of university, father's profession, were not available and hence were not included. Similarly, when it came to prison experience, affiliation with the IRGC, war veteran status, and whether an individual was a member of the family of a martyr, we have only included information that was known to us through public sources. To help non-Persian speakers recognize the gender of the individuals, the prefix Mrs. or Ms. appears before the names of females.

We have included individuals in the Who Is Who section that held the following posts:

Cabinet Posts: President, vice president, prime minister, ministerial advisers and all members of the following administrations: Prime Minister Bazargan's cabinet, Revolutionary Council cabinet, Prime Minister Raja'i's cabinet, President Raja'i's cabinet, Interim Prime Minister Mahdavi-Kani's cabinet, Prime Minister Musavi's first and second cabinets, President Hashemi-Rafsanjani's first and second cabinets, President Khatami's first and second cabinets, President Ahmadinejad's first and second cabinets, and President Rouhani's first and second cabinets.

Expediency Discernment Assembly of the System Posts: All members of the First through Eighth Expediency Discernment Assembly.

Assembly of Experts Posts: Members of the Assembly for the Final Examination of the Constitution, all members of the First through Fifth Assembly of Experts.

Guardian Council Posts: All members of the First through Seventh Guardian Councils.

Judicial Posts: Prosecutor-general, chief judge of the Special Court for Clergy, prosecutor-general of the Special Court for Clergy, prosecutor-general of the revolutionary courts, head of State General Inspectorate Organization, head of the judiciary, first deputy to the chief justice, head of the State Supreme Court, head of the Court of Administrative Justice, and members of the High Council of the Judiciary.

Majlis (Parliament) Posts: All members of the First through Tenth Majlis.

Military Posts: Chief of the Armed Forces General Staff, chief of the joint staff of the Islamic Republic of Iran Army, general commander of the army, deputy general commander of the army, commander of the Islamic Republic of Iran Ground Forces, commander of the Islamic Republic of Iran Air Force, commander of the Islamic Republic of Iran Navy, first deputy chief of the Armed Forces General Staff, chief of Law Enforcement Forces, commander in chief of the IRGC, deputy commander in chief of the IRGC, commander of the IRGC Navy, commander of the IRGC's Qods Force, commander of the IRGC's Basij Force, deputy commander of the IRGC's Basij Force, commander of the Khatam al-Anbia Air Defense Base, and deputy chief of the general staff of armed forces in Basij Affairs.

Other Important Posts: Supreme leader, deputy supreme leader, members of the Revolutionary Council, director-general of the Islamic Republic of Iran Broadcasting, rector of Islamic Azad University, governor of the Central Bank, mayor of Tehran, and secretary of the Supreme National Security Council.

List of Political Elite

Aba'i-Khorasani [Va'ez-Aba'i], Mohammad

Member of the First Assembly of Experts, Razavi Khorasan (1988–90); deputy of the Sixth Majlis, Mashhad, Razavi Khorasan (2000–2004)
1939–2004, Mashhad, Razavi Khorasan
Clerical education, Mashhad Seminary
Hoseyn, clergyman
Clergyman
Imprisoned before the revolution
Not a war veteran
Member of the central council of the ACC
Aba'i-Khorasani was the temporary Friday prayer leader of Mashhad for ten years. PMOI wounded him in an assassination attempt. In 1979,

Ayatollah Khomeini appointed him as head of the Qom Seminary Islamic Propaganda Office and he held that post for fifteen years. In 1982, Aba'i-Khorasani took over the Qom Seminary of Ayatollah Seyyed Mohammad-Kazem Shari'atmadari when he was defrocked. He was also a member of the central council of Friday prayer leaders. In 1990, Aba'i-Khorasani refused to stand for elections to the Second Assembly of Experts in protest of the Guardian Council's decision to require a religious test of candidates even though he himself was exempted.

Abbasi, Abbas

Deputy of the First Majlis, Minab, Hormozgan (1980–84); deputy of the Third (1988–92), Fourth (1992–96), and Fifth (1996–2000) Majlis, Bandar-e Abbas, Hormozgan
1941–Sept. 2, 2002, Minab, Hormozgan
Clerical education
Ahmad, farmer
Clergyman
Imprisoned before the revolution
War veteran
Director of Hormozgan branch of the SCC
Ayatollah Khamenei befriended him during their exile in Sistan and Baluchestan before the revolution. After the revolution, he was prosecutor of Hormozgan, as well as the supreme leader's representative in Hormozgan's IRGC.

Abbasi, Asadollah

Deputy of the Seventh (2004–8), Eighth (2008–12), and Tenth (2016–20) Majlis, Rudsar and Amlash, Gilan
1961–, Chaboksar, Gilan
MA, education; PhD, educational science, Islamic Azad University–Tehran
Reza, clergyman
Professor at Payam-e Nur University
No imprisonment
Not a war veteran

Abbasi was the interim minister of cooperatives, labor, and social welfare (February 4–May 5, 2013) and later became a deputy in the Ministry of Cooperatives, Labor, and Social Welfare before returning to the Tenth Majlis.

Abbasi, Mohammad

Deputy of the Seventh Majlis, Gorgan and Aq-Qala, Golestan (2004–6); minister of cooperatives in President Ahmadinejad's first cabinet (November 5, 2006–September 2, 2009); minister of cooperatives (September 3, 2009–August 2, 2011) and then minister of sports and youth (August 3, 2011–August 14, 2013) in President Ahmadinejad's second cabinet
1958–, Gorgan, Golestan
MA, public administration, Islamic Azad University–Tehran; PhD, strategic management, Islamic Azad University–Tehran
Rajab-Ali, farmer
Civil servant, ministries
No imprisonment
War veteran
Abbasi was born in a village near Gorgan. He resigned from the Seventh Majlis to become the minister of cooperatives. The Majlis elected him as minister of cooperatives on November 5, 2006, with 155 positive votes, seventy negative votes, and twenty abstentions, and he was reelected on September 3, 2009, with 163 positive votes, eighty-three negative votes, and thirty-seven abstentions. On August 3, 2011, the MPs confirmed him as minister of sports and youth with 165 positive votes, sixty-one negative votes, and nineteen abstentions. Abbasi was previously rector of Islamic Azad University–Qaemshahr. He received a fake PhD in strategic management from the non-accredited American University of Hawaii.

Abbasi, Seyyed Hasan

Deputy of the Seventh Majlis, Mahallat and Delijan, Markazi (2004–8)

1969–, Delijan, Markazi
BA, political history
Seyyed Mohammad
Civil servant
No imprisonment
Abbasi ran unsuccessfully for the Tenth Majlis.

Abbasi, Soleyman

Deputy of the Ninth Majlis, Gonbad-e Kavus, Golestan (2012–16)
1968–, Gonbad-e Kavus, Golestan
MD, medicine, Kermanshah University of Medical Sciences
Medical doctor and administrator
No imprisonment
A Sunni-populated district elected Abbasi, even though he is neither a Sunni nor a Turkoman.

Abbasi-Davani, Fereydun

VP and head of the Atomic Energy Organization in President Ahmadinejad's second cabinet (February 13, 2011–13)
1958–, Kazerun, Fars
BS, nuclear physics, Shiraz University, 1984; MS, nuclear physics, Ferdowsi University of Mashhad, 1987; PhD, nuclear physics, Amirkabir University of Technology, 2002
Mohammad-Hoseyn
Physics professor at Imam Hoseyn University (since 1993)
No imprisonment
War veteran
IRGC militiaman
A bomb attack on November 29, 2010, seriously wounded Abbasi-Davani. The attack was purportedly related to his work on the Iranian nuclear program. On February 13, 2011, he replaced Ali-Akbar Salehi as the head of AEOI. The United States Treasury Department put Abbasi-Davani on its "Specially Designated Nationals and Blocked Persons List." In 2013, President Rouhani replaced him again with Ali-Akbar Salehi as head

of AEOI. In 2016, he ran unsuccessfully for the Tenth Majlis from Shiraz.

Abbasifard, Mohammad-Reza

Deputy of the First Majlis, Kuhdasht, Lorestan (1980–84); deputy of the Second Majlis, Khorramabad, Lorestan (1984–88); head of the CAJ (1991–93); member of Third (1992–98), and Fourth (1998–2003) Guardian Councils; member of the Third Assembly of Experts, Khuzestan (1999–2006)
1949–, Kuhdasht, Lorestan
Clerical education, Qom Seminary; BA, philosophy, Tehran University; PhD, Islamic Azad University
Ali, farmer
Clergyman
No imprisonment
Not a war veteran
Member of the IRP and NTP
HI Abbasifard was a member of the GC as a lawyer. He was a legal adviser to President Khatami. He resigned from the Fourth GC in 2003 to run for the 2004 Majlis elections but did not win. The GC disqualified him from running in the 2007 and 2016 Assembly of Experts elections.

Abbaspur, Ebrahim

Deputy of the Second Majlis, Kaleybar, East Azerbaijan (1984–88)
1951–, Kaleybar, East Azerbaijan
Clerical education
Hoseyn
Clergyman
No imprisonment

Abbaspur, Mohammad

Deputy of the Fourth (1992–96) and Sixth (2000–2004) Majlis, Maku, West Azerbaijan; deputy of the Seventh Majlis, Urmia, West Azerbaijan (2004–8)
November 26, 1954–, Maku, West Azerbaijan
BA, political science, 1997; MA; pursuing a PhD

Abbas
Civil servant
No imprisonment
IRGC militiaman
Abbaspur was a candidate in the Ninth Majlis election.

Abbaspur-Tehranifard, Ali

Deputy of the Fourth (1992–96), Fifth (1998–2000), Seventh (2004–8), and Eighth (2008–12) Majlis, Tehran, Tehran
1950–, Tehran, Tehran
BS, electrical engineering, Amirkabir University of Technology; MS, nuclear engineering, Tehran University; MS, nuclear engineering, Massachusetts Institute of Technology (USA), 1979; PhD, nuclear engineering, University of California, Berkeley (USA), 1983
Professor of electrical engineering at Sharif University of Technology
Abbas, bazaar tradesman
No imprisonment
Not a war veteran
Secretary-general of the Islamic Society of Iranian Academics
Martyr's family (brother, Hasan)
Abbaspur-Tehranifard is a member of the HCCR. He is the brother-in-law of Abdollah Jasbi, long-time rector of Islamic Azad University and former presidential candidate. His brother, Hasan Abbaspur-Tehranifard, was minister of energy (1979–81) before being killed in the bombing of the IRP headquarters on June 28, 1981. His other brother, Majid, is the husband of one of Morteza Motahhari's four daughters.

Abbaspur-Tehranifard, Hasan

Minister of energy in the Revolutionary Council cabinet (1979–80) and PM Raja'i's cabinet (1980–81)
1944–June 28, 1981, Tehran, Tehran
BS, electrical engineering, Tehran University, 1967; PhD, system analysis, Queen Mary University

of London (England), 1977; dissertation title:
"Integrated Optimization Model for Planning and
Design of Electrical Energy Systems"
Abbas, bazaar tradesman
University professor
No imprisonment
Not a war veteran
Member of the central council of the IRP
Abbaspur-Tehranifard was minister of energy for
   eighteen months (1979–81) before he died in the
   bombing of the IRP headquarters.

Abdekhoda'i, Mohammad-Hadi

Deputy of the First (1980–84), Second (1984–88), and
   Fourth (1992–96) Majlis, Mashhad, Razavi Kho-
   rasan; member of the Fifth Assembly of Experts,
   Razavi Khorasan (2016–22)
1938–, Mashhad, Razavi Khorasan
Clerical education, Mashhad and Qom Seminaries;
   PhD, philosophy and theology, Tehran University
Gholam-Hoseyn [Tabrizi], clergyman (ayatollah)
Clergyman
Imprisoned before the revolution
Not a war veteran
Mohammad-Hadi Abdekhoda'i was imprisoned in
   the 1950s when his brother, Mohammad-Mehdi
   Abdekhoda'i (current secretary-general of the
   Devotees of Islam), tried unsuccessfully to assas-
   sinate foreign minister Hoseyn Fatemi in 1954.
   Mohammad-Hadi teaches at Ferdowsi Univer-
   sity of Mashhad and is a former member of the
   HCCR. He was the first ambassador of the Islamic
   Republic to the Vatican and served in that capac-
   ity for three and a half years.

Abdi, Iraj

Deputy of the Ninth Majlis, Khorramabad and Dow-
   reh, Lorestan (2012–16)
1972–, Khorramabad, Lorestan
MD, Khorramabad University of Medical Sciences
Medical doctor and health official in Lorestan
   province

No imprisonment
War veteran
IRGC militiaman
Martyr's family (brother died at the war front)
Abdi ran unsuccessfully for the Eighth and Tenth Majlis.

Abdolali'zadeh, Ali

Deputy of the Second (1984–88) and Third (1988–92)
   Majlis, Urmia, West Azerbaijan; minister of hous-
   ing and urban development in President Khatami's
   first (August 20, 1997–August 21, 2001) and sec-
   ond (August 22, 2001–August 23, 2005) cabinets
1956–, Urmia, West Azerbaijan
BS, civil engineering, Tabriz University, 1977; MA,
   public administration, Center for Governmental
   Management, 1995; PhD, public administration,
   Center for Governmental Management, 2000
Esma'il, provincial civil servant
Civil servant
No imprisonment
Not a war veteran
Abdolali'zadeh was politically active before the
   revolution and became deputy mayor of Urmia.
   He served as a development deputy in the office
   of the governor-general of West Azerbaijan from
   1981 to 1984. From July 22, 1992, to 1997, he was
   governor-general of West Azerbaijan. He survived
   impeachment on June 2, 2002, while serving as
   minister of housing and urban development. The
   GC rejected him for the Fourth Majlis elections.
   In 2013, he became senior adviser to the interior
   minister on regional development issues.

Abdolkarimi [Kumleh], Seyfollah

Deputy of the First Majlis, Langarud, Gilan (1980–81)
1942–1981, Langarud, Gilan
MA, philosophy, Tehran University, 1971; clerical
   education
Mohammad-Ali, farmer
Academia
No imprisonment
Not a war veteran

Abdolkarimi-Natanzi, Ali

Deputy of the Third Majlis, Qamsar and Natanz,
    Isfahan (1988–92)
1938–, Natanz, Isfahan
High school diploma; some clerical education
Nasrollah
No imprisonment

Abdollahi, Abdolmahmud

Member of the Fourth (2007–16) and Fifth (2016–22)
    Assembly of Experts, Isfahan
1947–, Isfahan, Isfahan
Clerical education
Mohammad-Ali
Clergyman
No imprisonment
HI Abdollahi studied with Ayatollahs Araki, Mesh-
    kini, and Lankarani, and has been a judge in
    Ahvaz (1979–81), Tehran, and Qom. He is a mem-
    ber of the HCRSQ.

Abdollahi, Beytollah

Deputy of the Tenth Majlis, Ahar and Heris, East
    Azerbaijan (2017–20)
1960–, Heris, East Azerbaijan
BS, urban planning, Tabriz University; MA, public
    administration
Father's name unknown, farmer
Governor of Heris, Shabestar, Sarab, and Marand
No imprisonment
Abdollahi has had a long career occupying provincial
    posts in East Azerbaijan. He was finally elected to
    the Tenth Majlis in the 2017 midterm elections,
    after the GC nullified his victory in the second
    round of the 2016 elections.

Abdollahi, Reza

Deputy of the Third (1988–92), Fourth (1992–96),
    Fifth (1996–2000), Sixth (2000–2004), Seventh
(2004–8), Eighth (2008–12), and Ninth (2012–16)
    Majlis, Mahneshan and Ijrood, Zanjan
1955–, Mahneshan, Zanjan
BS, electrical engineering
Hoseyn
Civil servant, state companies
No imprisonment
During the Eighth Majlis, an MP questioned Abdolla-
    hi's credentials; in response, Abdollahi questioned
    the credentials of eighteen other MPs. After a
    while, both sides dropped their charges. He was
    accused of having accepted bribes from business-
    person Shahram Jazayeri.

Abdollahpur, Ali

Deputy of the Second Majlis, Hashtrud, East Azerbai-
    jan (1984–88)
1954–, Hashtrud, East Azerbaijan
Clerical education
Yusef
Clergyman (HI)
No imprisonment

Abdollahpuri-Hoseyni, Mir Ali-Ashraf

Deputy of the Third (1988–92) and Sixth (2000–2004)
    Majlis, Tabriz, East Azerbaijan
1961–, Tabriz, East Azerbaijan
BS, industrial engineering, 1995
Mir Jalal
Academia
No imprisonment
Abdollahpuri-Hoseyni is the president of the Iranian
    Privatization Organization and deputy minister
    of economic affairs.

Abdollahzadeh, Mohammad-Ali

Deputy of the Ninth Majlis, Ferdows, Sarayan, Tabas,
    and Boshruyeh, South Khorasan (2012–16)
1969–, Tabas, South Khorasan
MA, political science, Imam Sadeq University, 1992;
    PhD, international relations

Governor of Tabas
No imprisonment
Not a war veteran
Abdollahzadeh ran unsuccessfully for the Eighth Majlis. He has been rector of Islamic Azad University–Ferdows and Islamic Azad University–Tabas. In 2016, he became IRIB's deputy for parliamentary affairs.

Abdolvand, Gholam-Reza

Deputy of the Fifth (1996–2000) and Sixth (2000–2004) Majlis, Dorud and Azna, Lorestan
1949–, Aligudarz, Lorestan
BA, Persian literature
Rahim
Civil servant
No imprisonment

Abedi, Gholam-Ali

Deputy of the Sixth Majlis, Nehbandan and Sarbisheh, South Khorasan (2000–2004)
1944–, Nehbandan, South Khorasan
BA, law
Nowruz
No imprisonment
The GC disqualified Abedi from running in the 2004 Majlis election.

Abedi, Heydar-Ali

Deputy of the Tenth Majlis, Isfahan, Isfahan (2016–20)
1955–, Fereydunshahr, Isfahan
BS, nursing; MS, nursing, PhD, nursing, University of Technology (Australia)
Associate professor of nursing and midwifery at Islamic Azad University–Khorasgan
Khosrow
No imprisonment
War veteran (wounded)
Member of the AILF
Abedi was a member of the Isfahan City Council.

Abedi, Mohammad-Karim

Deputy of the Eighth Majlis, Ferdows, Sarayan, and Tabas, South Khorasan (2008–12)
1950–, Tabas, South Khorasan
MS, aerospace engineering (not verified)
Abdorrahman, clergyman
Military pilot
No imprisonment
War veteran (wounded)
Abedi underwent training as a pilot in the United States before the revolution and was involved in attacking Kurdish areas in the early days of the revolution. From 1996 to 1999, Abedi was a military attaché in China.

Abedi, Nurollah

Deputy of the Second (1984–88) and Third (1988–92) Majlis, Behbahan, Khuzestan
1955–, Behbahan, Khuzestan
High school diploma
Rahim
Imprisoned before revolution
Founding member of the Society of Industrial Managers and Professionals of Iran

Abedi-Ja'fari, Hasan

Minister of commerce in PM Musavi's first (August 28, 1983–October 27, 1985) and second (October 28, 1985–August 3, 1989) cabinets
June 6, 1951–, Tehran, Tehran
BA, business administration; MA, business administration, Texas A&M University (USA), 1975
Military and security forces
No imprisonment
War veteran
IRGC militiaman (one of the original founders)
Abedi-Ja'fari joined Ayatollah Khomeini in Paris in 1978. He was injured in the IRP headquarters bombing, and the Majlis approved him as minister of commerce on August 28, 1983. In 2009, the regime arrested him for a few weeks for serving as

an adviser to presidential candidate Musavi. Abe-di-Ja'fari is professor of management at Tehran University.

Abedinpur, Abolqasem

Deputy of the Sixth Majlis, Torbat-e Heydariyyeh, Razavi Khorasan (2000–2004)
1961–, Torbat-e Heydariyyeh, Razavi Khorasan
MA, Persian literature
Mohammad-Ali
Academia
No imprisonment
Abedinpur became a civil servant after leaving the Majlis.

Abedinzadeh, Kamel

Deputy of the First (1980–84), Fourth (1992–96), and Fifth (1996–2000) Majlis, Khoy and Chaypareh, West Azerbaijan
1945–, Khoy, West Azerbaijan
BS, physics
Aziz, farmer
Imprisoned before the revolution
IRGC militiaman
Abedinzadeh was the first commander of the IRGC in Khoy after the revolution. The GC disqualified him from running for the Seventh and Eighth Majlis.

Abedi-Shahrekhafri, Asadollah

Deputy of the Third Majlis, Shiraz, Fars (1988–92)
1950–, Jahrom, Fars
MA
Khalil
No imprisonment

Abolqasem-Dolabi [Abolqasemi-Niknam], Mohammad Haji

Member of the Fifth Assembly of Experts, Zanjan (2016–22)

1975–, Mashhad, Razavi Khorasan
Clerical education; PhD, Qur'anic sciences
Mahmud
Clergyman
No imprisonment
Not a war veteran

Abramiyan, Zhorzhik

Deputy of the Sixth (2000–2004) and Tenth (2016–20) Majlis, representing Armenians of southern Iran (as a religious minority)
1952–, Tehran, Tehran
BA, Armenian literature, Isfahan University of Technology
Setrag
Bazaar tradesman
No imprisonment
Not a war veteran

Abtahi, Seyyed Mahmud

Deputy of the Fifth (1996–2000) and Seventh (2004–8) Majlis, Khomeinishahr, Isfahan
1949–October 30, 2013, Homayunshahr, Isfahan
BS, geology
Seyyed Hasan
Civil servant
No imprisonment

Abtahi, Seyyed Mohammad-Ali

VP for parliamentary affairs in President Khatami's second cabinet (2001–4)
January 28, 1960–, Mashhad, Razavi Khorasan
Clerical education, Mashhad Seminary
Seyyed Hasan, clergyman
Civil servant, ministries
Imprisoned before the revolution
Not a war veteran
Martyr's family (maternal uncle Seyyed Habib [Abdolkarim] Hasheminezhad was assassinated by PMOI)
Founding member of the ACC

HI Abtahi worked in IRIB's radio for five years and then went to the Ministry of Culture. The regime imprisoned Abtahi for a while for supporting the 2009 Green Movement.

Abtahi, Seyyed Mohammad-Javad

Deputy of the Eighth (2008–12) and Tenth (2016–20) Majlis, Khomeinishahr, Isfahan
1956–, Homayunshahr, Isfahan
BA, law, Shahid Beheshti University; MA, private law, Islamic Azad University–Khorasan
Seyyed Ne'matollah, clergyman
Academia
No imprisonment
War veteran
Member of the SFIR
Abtahi ran unsuccessfully for the Ninth Majlis in 2012.

Abusa'idi-Manuchehri, Abbas

Deputy of the First Majlis, Jiroft, Kerman (1980–84)
1944–2015, Jiroft, Kerman
BA, Islamic philosophy
Nurali, farmer
Academia
No imprisonment

Abutaleb, Sa'id

Deputy of the Seventh Majlis, Tehran, Tehran (2004–8)
1969–, Tehran, Tehran
BS, chemistry, Tehran University
Yadollah
Producer at IRIB
No imprisonment
War veteran
Abutaleb went to Iraq as a filmmaker in 2003 after the American invasion. American forces detained him for four months. After returning to Iran, he was elected to the Majlis.

Abutorabi, Abolfazl

Deputy of the Ninth (2012–16) and Tenth (2016–20) Majlis, Najafabad, Tiran, and Karvan, Isfahan
1976–, Azizabad, Isfahan
BS, civil engineering, Islamic Azad University–Najafabad; BA, law, University of Judicial Sciences and Administrative Services, 2002
Esma'il
Judiciary official in Isfahan (since 2002)
No imprisonment
Not a war veteran
Martyr's family (father and uncles were killed at the war front)

Abutorabifard, Seyyed Abbas

Deputy of the First Majlis, Qazvin, Qazvin (1980–84)
1916–June 1, 2000, Qazvin, Qazvin
Clerical education, Qom Seminary
Seyyed Abutorab, clergyman
Clergyman
Imprisoned before the revolution
Not a war veteran
HI Abutorabifard had five daughters and three sons; two of the sons—Seyyed Ali-Akbar and Seyyed Mohammad-Hasan—have been MPs. He and his son Seyyed Ali-Akbar died in a car accident.

Abutorabifard, Seyyed Ali-Akbar

Deputy of the Fourth (1992–96) and Fifth (1996–2000) Majlis, Tehran, Tehran
1939–June 1, 2000, Qom, Qom
Clerical education, Qom Seminary
Seyyed Abbas, clergyman
Clergyman
Imprisoned before the revolution
War veteran
Founding member of ADVIR and AVIR
HI Abutorabifard and Seyyed Hasan Andarzgou smuggled weapons into Iran from Lebanon before the revolution. He was a prisoner of war in Iraq for ten years (1980–90) and was an elder of the

POWs. He was a candidate for the Sixth Majlis but was not elected. Abutorabifard had family ties to Mohammad Tavassoli.

Abutorabifard, Seyyed Mohammad-Hasan

Deputy of the Sixth (2000–2004), Seventh (2004–8), and Eighth (2008–12) Majlis, Qazvin, Qazvin; deputy of the Ninth Majlis, Tehran, Tehran (2012–16)
1953–, Qom, Qom
Clerical education, Qom Seminary
Seyyed Abbas, clergyman (HI)
Clergyman
No imprisonment
Not a war veteran
Member of the executive committee of the SCC
Ayatollah Khomeini appointed HI Abutorabifard as head of the ideological-political bureau of the MDAFL. In 2011, Ayatollah Khamenei appointed him as one of the members of a five-person "Dispute Settlement Committee of Branches." Abutorabifard was the deputy speaker of the Majlis from 2004 to 2011, and again from 2012 to 2016. After the Majlis, he took charge of Imam Hoseyn Seminary in Tehran. He registered to run in the 2013 presidential election. In 2017, Khamenei appointed him as one of the Friday prayer leaders of Tehran.

Adab, Bahaeddin

Deputy of the Fifth (1996–2000) and Sixth (2000–2004) Majlis, Sanandaj, Kurdistan
1945–2007, Sanandaj, Kurdistan
MS, civil engineering, Amirkabir University of Technology
Baqer, landowner
No imprisonment
Adab was one of the cofounders of the Karafarin Bank.

Adeli, Seyyed Mohammad-Hoseyn

Governor of the Central Bank (September 15, 1989–94)
1953–, Ahvaz, Khuzestan
BA, business administration; MA, international economics, Tehran University; PhD, economics, 1978 (USA; not confirmed)
Ambassador to Japan
No imprisonment
Not a war veteran
Adeli was active in the Muslim Student Association in the United States before and after the revolution. He returned to Iran in 1980 and joined the Ministry of Foreign Affairs, serving as the director-general for economic affairs, and then the Ministry of Petroleum. He has been the ambassador to Japan (1986–89), Canada (1995–99), and England (2004–5). In addition, he has been deputy foreign minister for economic affairs (1999–2004) and secretary-general of the Gas Exporting Countries Forum (2014–16).

Adiyanirad, Seyyed Ali

Deputy of the Eighth (2008–12) and Tenth (2016–20) Majlis, Qaemshahr, Savadkuh, and Juybar, Mazandaran
1959–, Savadkuh, Mazandaran
BA, Islamic law, Tehran University, 1989; MA, Islamic law, Islamic Azad University–Babol, 1997; PhD, political science, Jamia Hamdard University (India), 2007
Seyyed Jalal
Academia
No imprisonment
War veteran
Adiyanirad ran unsuccessfully for the Ninth Majlis and served for a while as the head of legal affairs of the National Iranian Oil Refining & Distribution Company before being elected to the Tenth Majlis.

Afarideh, Hoseyn

Deputy of the Sixth (2000–2004) and Seventh (2004–5) Majlis, Shiravan, North Khorasan
1954–, Shiravan, North Khorasan
BS, physics, Tehran University, 1980; MS, nuclear physics, University of Birmingham (England), 1985;

PhD, nuclear physics, University of Birmingham (England), 1988; dissertation title: "A Study of Fission in [Superior] 238 U Induced by Monoenergetic Neutrons and Heavy Ions and of Light Particle Emission in [Superior] 252 Cf Spontaneous Fission"
Reza
Civil servant
No imprisonment
Afarideh worked for the government after finishing his term in the Majlis.

Afghahi-Farimani, Ja'far

Deputy of the Sixth Majlis, Fariman, Sarakhs, Ahmadabad, and Razavieh, Razavi Khorasan (2000–2004)
1964–2018, Fariman, Razavi Khorasan
MA, sociology
Eshaq, municipal civil servant
Academia
No imprisonment
Martyr's family (brother)
Afghahi-Farimani worked for the government after finishing his term in the Majlis. He died in a car accident.

Afkhami, Behruz

Deputy of the Sixth Majlis, Tehran, Tehran (2000–2004)
1956–, Tehran, Tehran
Associate's degree, Art, Film Institute
Ali-Akbar
Film Director at IRIB
No imprisonment
Afkhami went into the private sector after finishing his term in the Sixth Majlis. He helped to produce campaign ads for the reformist cleric Mehdi Karrubi during the 2005 presidential campaign.

Afkhami, Shahruz

Deputy of the Ninth Majlis, Malekan, East Azerbaijan (2012–16)
1962–, Malekan, East Azerbaijan

MA, public administration, Institute for Management and Planning Studies
Governor of Kaleybar and teacher
No imprisonment
War veteran (fifty-seven months, wounded)
IRGC militiaman (commander)
Afkhami ran unsuccessfully for the Seventh, Eighth, and Tenth Majlis. He has retired from the teaching profession.

Afqahi, Seyyed Ali-Reza

Deputy of the Fifth Majlis, Sabzevar, Razavi Khorasan (1996–2000)
1953–2017, Shemiran, Razavi Khorasan
Clerical education
Seyyed Fakhreddin, clergyman (ayatollah)
Clergyman (ayatollah)
No imprisonment

Afrazideh, Seyyed Farajollah

Deputy of the Second (1984–88), Third (1988–92), and Fourth (1992–96) Majlis, Nowshahr and Chalus, Mazandaran
1937–, Nowshahr, Mazandaran
BA, theology; clerical education
Seyyed Reza
Clergyman
No imprisonment
Martyr's family (son killed at the war front)
At the beginning of the Second Majlis, some MPs questioned HI Afrazideh's credentials, but ultimately he was approved.

Afrugh, Emad

Deputy of the Seventh Majlis, Tehran, Tehran (2004–8)
1957–, Shiraz, Fars
BA, sociology, Shiraz University, 1986; MA, sociology, Shiraz University, 1990; PhD, sociology, Tarbiyat-e Modarres University, 1997
Kazem

Professor of sociology at Tarbiyat-e Modarres
    University
No imprisonment
IRGC militiaman
Afrugh is a former member of the HCCR (2004–7).

Afrugh [Eshraqi], Ja'far

Member of the Assembly for the Final Examination of
    the Constitution, East Azerbaijan (1979)
1915–2000, Tabriz, East Azerbaijan
Clerical education, Qom Seminary
Hasan, bazaar tradesman
Clergyman (ayatollah)
No imprisonment
Not a war veteran
Afrugh, who studied for a while in Najaf and returned
    to Iran in 1954, was close to Grand Ayatollah
    Seyyed Mohammad-Kazem Shari'atmadari. After
    finishing his work in the AFEC, he returned to
    Tabriz to continue his religious teaching.

Afshar, Ali-Reza

Commander of the IRGC's Basij Force (March 1,
    1990–97)
IRGC militiaman

Afshari, Ali

Deputy of the Seventh Majlis, Semirom, Isfahan
    (2004–8)
1959–, Semirom, Isfahan
MA, geography
Khodakhast
Academia
No imprisonment
Afshari became the Ministry of Energy's deputy for par-
    liamentary affairs after leaving the Seventh Majlis.

Afshari, Mohammad-Mehdi

Deputy of the Eighth Majlis, Darab and Zarrindasht,
    Fars (2008–12)

1961–, Darab, Fars
BA, Persian literature
Eyaz
Civil servant
No imprisonment
After service in the Majlis, Afshari worked for the
    State General Inspectorate Organization.

Afzali, Bahram

Commander of the Islamic Republic of Iran Navy
    (May/June 1980–April 24, 1983)
1938–February 26, 1984, Qom, Qom
BS, military science, Italian Naval Academy, 1961;
    PhD, boat and submarine architecture, Italy,
    1970
No imprisonment
War veteran
The Iranian intelligence services arrested Admi-
    ral Afzali on April 24, 1983, for his clandestine
    membership in the Tudeh Party. On February 26,
    1984, the regime executed Afzali and nine of his
    comrades.

Afzali, Nazar

Deputy of the Tenth Majlis, Nehbandan, South Kho-
    rasan (2016–20)
1958–, Bursafid, South Khorasan
MD, veterinary science, Urmia University, 1983; MS,
    domestic birds, University of Agricultural Sci-
    ences, Bangalore (India); PhD, domestic birds,
    University of Agricultural Sciences, Bangalore
    (India), 1998
Ebrahim, tribal notable/farmer
Professor and administrator at Birjand University
No imprisonment
War veteran
Afzali studied in India for six years in the 1990s, and
    he was dean of the agricultural school at Birjand
    University from 2000 to 2005. He is a conservative
    politician who has been an adviser to the governor-
    general of South Khorasan.

Afzali, Seyyed Hoseyn

Deputy of the Tenth Majlis, Eqlid, Fars (2016–20)
1960–, Eqlid, Fars
BS, civil engineering, Shiraz University; MS, civil
    engineering, Amirkabir University of Technology;
    PhD, civil engineering, Shiraz University
Professor and administrator at Shiraz University
No imprisonment

Afzalifard, Mostafa

Deputy of the Ninth Majlis, Ardabil, Namin, Nir, and
    Sareyn, Ardabil (2012–16)
1961–, Ardabil, Ardabil
BA, educational management, Payam-e Nur Univer-
    sity, Tabriz; MA, Institute for Management and
    Planning Studies
Father's name unknown, bazaar tradesman
No imprisonment
War veteran
IRGC militiaman
Martyr's family (two brothers, father-in-law, and
    brother-in-law killed at the war front)
Afzalifard was a rabid anti-Marxist in the early years
    of the revolution. He ran unsuccessfully for the
    Seventh Majlis.

Aghajari, Habib

Deputy of the Ninth Majlis, Bandar-e Mahshahr,
    Omidiyeh, and Hendijan, Khuzestan (2012–16)
1953–, Bandar-e Mahshahr, Khuzestan
MS, military science
No imprisonment
War veteran
IRGC militiaman (commander of naval operations)
Aghajari was the SFIR nominee in the Ninth Majlis
    election. He ran unsuccessfully for the Tenth Majlis.

Ahadi, Ebrahim

Minister of justice in PM Raja'i's cabinet (November
    5, 1980–December 31, 1980)

1940–, Fuman, Gilan
BA, law, Tehran University, 1969; MA, law, Tehran
    University, 1977
Mohammad-Taqi, bazaar tradesman
Judiciary official
No imprisonment
Not a war veteran
Ahadi spent two years in France before the revolution.
    He resigned as minister of justice in less than two
    months due to lack of any real authority. Ja'far
    Shojuni is his maternal uncle.

Ahani, Esma'il

Deputy of the Second Majlis, Astara, Gilan (1984–88)
1956–, Astara, Gilan
Associate's degree; clerical education
Bahman
No imprisonment

Ahmadi, Ahmad

Deputy of the Seventh Majlis, Tehran, Tehran
    (2004–8)
1933–, Malayer, Hamadan
BA, theology, Tehran University, 1966; MA, philos-
    ophy, Tehran University, 1969; PhD, philosophy,
    Tehran University, 1979; clerical education, Qom
    Seminary
Farajollah, farmer
Clergyman and dean of humanities at Tarbiyat-e
    Modarres University
No imprisonment
Not a war veteran
HI Ahmadi, a moderate, has been a long-time mem-
    ber of the HCCR and played an instrumental
    role in changing the educational curriculum of
    Iranian schools by revising school textbooks.

Ahmadi, Ali

Deputy of the Seventh Majlis, Mamasani, Fars
    (2004–8)
1963–, Mamasani, Fars

BA, political science; MA, international relations, Tehran University, 1993; clerical education
Hasan-Qoli
Academia
No imprisonment
War veteran
IRGC militiaman

Ahmadi, Ali-Asghar

Deputy of the Fifth Majlis, Shahrud, Semnan (1996–2000)
1956–, Shahrud, Semnan
MA
Morteza
Provincial civil servant
No imprisonment
Secretary-general of the Islamic Iran Solidarity Party
Ahmadi has worked in the Red Crescent Society, and he was governor-general of Golestan Province. He worked in President Rouhani's office before becoming the MI's political deputy. He was in charge of the election board for the 2017 presidential and municipal council elections.

Ahmadi, Ali-Mohammad

Deputy of the Third (1988–92) and Sixth (2000–2004) Majlis, Aligudarz, Darrehshahr, Badreh, and Abdanan, Lorestan
1956–, Aligudarz, Lorestan
PhD, strategic management
Yadollah
Academia
No imprisonment
Ahmadi entered the Third Majlis during interim elections held on October 29, 1988. He became governor of Kohgiluyeh and Buyer Ahmad on September 13, 2017.

Ahmadi, Fereydun

Deputy of the Tenth Majlis, Zanjan, Zanjan (2016–20)
1967–, Mahneshan, Zanjan

No imprisonment
Ahmadi worked as a deputy to the minister of industries and an administrative-financial deputy to the minister of commerce before entering the Tenth Majlis.

Ahmadi, Firuz

Deputy of the Fourth Majlis, Germi, Ardabil (1993–96)
1957–, Merallu, East Azerbaijan
BA, Persian literature; clerical education
Mokhtar
No imprisonment
After the Fourth Majlis rejected the credentials of the first candidate from Germi, Habib Borumand-Dashqaplu, Ahmadi became an MP in interim elections in 1993.

Ahmadi, Moradali

Deputy of the Second Majlis, Sonqor, Kermanshah (1984–88)
1954–, Sonqor, Kermanshah
BA; Clerical education
Aziz-Morad
Clergyman
Imprisoned before the revolution

Ahmadi, Musa

Deputy of the Ninth Majlis, Kangan, Deyr, and Jam, Bushehr (2012–16)
1962–, Bonak, Bushehr
Clerical education, Qom Seminary; MA, law, Arak University; PhD, jurisprudence and Islamic law, Islamic Azad University–Mashhad
Clergyman and judge
No imprisonment
War veteran (nine months)
HI Ahmadi ran unsuccessfully for the Eighth Majlis, and he worked for a while as a judge in the Special Court for Clergy (SCFC). He was also a deputy in the State Organization for Registration of Deeds and Properties.

Ahmadi, Nabiyollah

Deputy of the Ninth Majlis, Darab, Fars (2012–16)
1973–, Darab, Fars
BS, civil engineering, Shahid Raja'i Teachers Training
    College; MS, civil engineering, Shahid Bahonar
    University of Kerman, 2003; PhD, civil engineer-
    ing, K. N. Toosi University of Technology
Professor at Shahid Raja'i Teachers Training College
No imprisonment
Not a war veteran
IRGC militiaman (Basij)
Ahmadi was a civil servant in Fars and Tehran
    Provinces.

Ahmadi, Osman

Deputy of the Ninth Majlis, Mahabad, West Azerbai-
    jan (2012–16)
1970–, Mahabad, West Azerbaijan
BA, history, Urmia University, 2009; MA, history,
    Islamic Azad University–Abhar, 2011; pursuing a
    PhD in history
Ahmad, clergyman (mamosta)
Factory owner and executive director of Esteqlal Club
    in Mahabad
No imprisonment
Not a war veteran
Ahmadi, a Sunni MP, followed an independent line
    while in the Majlis.

Ahmadi, Vahid

Deputy of the Third (1988–92) and Ninth (2012–
    16) Majlis, Kangavar, Sahneh, and Harsin,
    Kermanshah
1953–, Kangavar, Kermanshah
Clerical education, Qom Seminary; MA, Islamic law,
    Islamic Azad University–Mashhad
Khodakaram
Clergyman and former ambassador to Morocco
No imprisonment
IRGC militiaman

Ahmadi, Zekrollah

Member of the Third Assembly of Experts, Kerman-
    shah (1999–2006)
1949–, Dehkaboud, Kermanshah
BA, law, Islamic Azad University–Tehran; clerical
    education, Qom Seminary
Soltan-Morad, farmer
Clergyman (ayatollah)
No imprisonment
Not a war veteran
Ahmadi worked for many years in the judiciary
    branch, including as a judge in Hamadan's revolu-
    tionary court.

Ahmadi [Abdanan], Ali-Mohammad

Deputy of the Ninth Majlis, Dehloran, Ilam (2012–16)
1966–, Abdanan, Ilam
BA, economics, Isfahan University of Technology,
    1989; MA, economics, Tarbiyat-e Modarres Uni-
    versity, 1993; PhD, economics, Tarbiyat-e Modar-
    res University, 2003
Professor at Tarbiyat-e Modarres University
No imprisonment
War veteran
After serving in the Majlis, Ahmadi became head of
    the joint commission of the Expediency Council
    and the Office of the Supreme Leader.

Ahmadi [Maku], Ali

Deputy of the Fifth Majlis, Maku, West Azerbaijan
    (1996–2000)
1962–, Maku, West Azerbaijan
BS, agricultural engineering
Musa
No imprisonment

Ahmadi-Miyanji, Ali

Member of the First (1983–90) and Second (1991–98)
    Assembly of Experts, West Azerbaijan; member of

the Third (1999–2000) Assembly of Experts, East Azerbaijan

1927–September 11, 2000, Miyaneh, East Azerbaijan

Clerical education, Qom Seminary

Hoseyn-Ali, clergyman and farmer

Clergyman

No imprisonment

Not a war veteran

IRGC militiaman

Martyr's family (son Ja'far killed at the war front)

Member of the SQSS

Ayatollah Ahmadi-Miyanji was an examiner of clerics wishing to run for the AE.

Ahmadi-Bighash, Mahmud

Deputy of the Eighth Majlis, Shazand, Markazi (2008–12)

1962–, Rey, Tehran

MS, military science (defense management)

Mehdi

No imprisonment

IRGC militiaman

After the GC rejected Ahmadi-Bighash's credentials for the Ninth Majlis, he became governor-general of North Khorasan.

Ahmadi-Danesh-Ashtiyani, Fakhreddin

Minister of education in President Rouhani's first cabinet (November 1, 2016–August 2, 2017)

1955–, Ashtiyan, Markazi

BS, civil engineering, Amirkabir University of Technology; PhD, structural engineering, Imperial College London (England), 1996; dissertation title: "Seismic Behaviour of Steel Frames with Semi-rigid Connections"

Mohammad-Hoseyn, clergyman

University professor and education official

No imprisonment

War veteran

IRGC militiaman

Member of the central council of IIPF

President Rouhani nominated Ahmadi-Danesh-Ashtiyani as the minister of science, research, and technology on November 18, 2014, but he failed to receive enough votes from the Ninth Majlis. In November 2016, the Majlis approved him as minister of education. His father, Mohammad-Hoseyn, was an MP in the First Majlis.

Ahmadi-Danesh-Ashtiyani, Mohammad-Hoseyn

Deputy of the First Majlis, Tafresh, Markazi (1981–84)

1925–, Ashtiyan, Markazi

Clerical education

Hasan, clergyman

Clergyman

No imprisonment

Not a war veteran

HI Ahmadi-Danesh-Ashtiyani, a former teacher, became a member of the First Majlis internal affairs committee. He was also the head of a special appeals court.

Ahmadi-Forushani, Seyyed Mohammad

Deputy of the First (1980–84) and Fourth (1992–96) Majlis, Khomeinishahr, Isfahan

1934–September 2, 2003, Homayunshahr, Isfahan

Clerical education, Isfahan Seminary

Seyyed Mostafa, bazaar tradesman

Clergyman

Imprisoned before the revolution

Not a war veteran

Ahmadi-Forushani spent five months in exile in Saqqez before the revolution. After the revolution, he became the Friday prayer leader of Khomeinishahr.

Ahmadi-Lashki, Qasem

Deputy of the Ninth (2012–16) and Tenth (2016–20) Majlis, Nowshahr and Chalus, Mazandaran

1965–, Nowshahr, Mazandaran

BA, social sciences, Tehran University, 1990; MA, management, cultural affairs, Islamic Azad University–Tehran, 1996; PhD, policy-planning management, Academy of Sciences of the Republic of Tajikistan
Avaz
Governor of Chalus and two-term member of the Nowshahr City Council
No imprisonment
Not a war veteran

Ahmadi-Moqaddam, Esma'il

Chief of Law Enforcement Forces (July 9, 2005–March 9, 2015)
1961–, Tehran, Tehran
Clerical education, Qom, 1977–78; BA, social science, Tehran University; MA, defense management; PhD, strategic science, Supreme National Defense University (degrees could not be verified)
No imprisonment
War veteran (eight years)
IRGC militiaman (joined in 1979)
Brigadier General Ahmadi-Moqaddam was the commander of the Tehran Basij Force and the LEF College. He has held numerous other military-security posts. As chief of the Law Enforcement Forces, he was heavily involved in the suppression of the Green Movement in 2009. Subsequently, the United States Treasury Department placed him on its "Specially Designated Nationals and Blocked Persons List." He is a senior adviser for security affairs to the Chief of the Armed Forces General Staff.

Ahmadinejad, Mahmoud

Mayor of Tehran (2003–5); president (August 3, 2005–August 2, 2013); member of the Seventh (2013–17) and Eighth (2017–22) Expediency Discernment Assembly
October 28, 1956–, Aradan, Semnan
MS, civil engineering, Iran University of Science and Technology, 1989; PhD, transportation engineering, Iran University of Science and Technology, 1997
Ahmad, blacksmith
Civil servant
No imprisonment
War veteran
IRGC militiaman
Founding member of OCU and AVIR
Ahmadinejad was involved in the discussions about storming the American embassy in 1979 but was not among the students who carried out the attack. He claims that during the Iran–Iraq War, he worked as a basiji volunteer in the engineering corps in Kurdistan and West Azerbaijan. Ahmadinejad reportedly became a member of the IRGC in 1986 when he joined the Special Forces division. Later he became governor-general of Khoy and Mako, and governor of Ardabil (1993–97). As a conservative populist politician, he won 61 percent of the vote in a runoff presidential election against former president Hashemi-Rafsanjani in 2005. He was reelected in a disputed vote in 2009 that gave birth to the opposition Green Movement. Ahmadinejad's severe rhetoric about Israel and the United States and his messianic discourse made him a controversial figure in international politics. In 2017, the GC disqualified him from running in the presidential election. He and his wife (A'zamossadat Farahi, b. 1958 in Tehran) were married on June 12, 1980. He has four sisters, two brothers, and three children.

Ahmadiniya, Isaqoli

Deputy of the Sixth Majlis, I'zeh and Baghmalek, Khuzestan (2000–2004)
1949–, I'zeh, Khuzestan
MA, geography
Shahqoli
Civil servant
No imprisonment
He became a civil servant after serving in the Majlis.

Ahmadipur, Mrs. Zahra

VP and head of the Cultural Heritage, Handicrafts and Tourism Organization in President Rouhani's first cabinet (2016–August 13, 2017)
1959–, Malayer, Hamadan
MA, geography and urban planning; PhD, political geography
Professor at Tarbiyat-e Modarres University since 1997
Ahmadipur worked in the MI (1997–2003), and was deputy for women's sports in the Physical Training Organization (2003–5).

Ahmadi-Shahrudi, Mohammad-Hoseyn

Member of the Fourth (2007–16) and Fifth (2016–22) Assembly of Experts, Khuzestan
1958–, Najaf, Iraq
Clerical education, Najaf Seminary (Iraq) and Qom Seminary
Ali-Asghar, clergyman (ayatollah)
Clergyman and judiciary official
No imprisonment
War veteran (wounded in 1982)
After spending some time in Iraqi prisons, Ayatollah Ahmadi-Shahrudi moved to Iran in 1979 and studied at Qom Seminary. He was a combatant in the Iran–Iraq War and later became head of the Khuzestan revolutionary tribunals. In the latter capacity, he ordered the execution of political prisoners in Khuzestan in 1988 and resigned from his post in early 1989. In 1990, Saddam Hussein executed his father after the unsuccessful uprising by Iraqi Shiites. In the early 1990s, Ahmadi-Shahrudi became Ayatollah Khamenei's representative at Islamic Azad University in Khuzestan Province. In 2000, he transferred to the judiciary branch to oversee the selection and hiring of judges for the entire country. Ahmadi-Shahrudi also taught at Ahvaz Seminary and was a judge in the State Supreme Court.

Ahmadiyyeh, Mostafa

Deputy of the Fifth Majlis, Karaj and Eshtehard, Tehran (1996–2000)
1951–, Tehran, Tehran
BA
Abolqasem
Former mayor of Karaj
No imprisonment

Ahmadi-Zadsara'i, Valiyollah

Deputy of the Fourth (1992–96) and Fifth (1996–2000) Majlis, Ahar and Heris, East Azerbaijan
1957–, Tabriz, East Azerbaijan
BS, civil engineering
Jamshid
No imprisonment

Ahmadnezhad, Abdolkarim

Deputy of the Third (1988–92) and Fourth (1994–96) Majlis, Sanandaj, Kurdistan
1940–, Sanandaj, Kurdistan
BA
Abdolaziz
No imprisonment
General secretary of the Front of the Followers of Imam and Leader in Kurdistan
Ahmadnezhad, a conservative Sunni Kurd, had some kinship ties with former vice president Mohammad-Reza Rahimi. In 2014, the governor of Kurdistan appointed him as an adviser.

Ahmadvand, Mohammad-Saleh

Deputy of the Second Majlis, Malayer, Hamadan (1984–88)
1954–, Malayer, Hamadan
Clerical education
Ali-Najaf
Clergyman
No imprisonment

Ahmadzadeh-Heravi, Mahmud

Minister of industries in PM Bazargan's cabinet
(July–November 5, 1979) and the Revolutionary
Council cabinet (November 6, 1979–80); minis-
terial adviser and head of the Iran National Steel
Company in PM Raja'i's cabinet (1980–81)
May 4, 1936–, Herat, Afghanistan
MS, mining engineering, Tehran University, 1956;
PhD, geology, Clausthal University of Technology
(Germany), 1971
Mohammad-Baqer, farmer
Civil servant and university professor
No imprisonment
Not a war veteran
Member of the LMI
Ahmadzadeh-Heravi was ambassador to Yugoslavia
(1982–86), adviser to the minister of mining, and
head of the National Geological Organization
(1989–97).

Ahmadzadeh-Kermani, Ruhollah

VP and head of the Cultural Heritage, Handicrafts and
Tourism Organization in President Ahmadinejad's
second cabinet (2011–January 4, 2012)
1979–, Mashhad, Razavi Khorasan
BS, industrial management, Imam Sadeq University,
2001; MS, industrial management, Imam Sadeq
University, 2005; PhD, media management,
Islamic Azad University–Science and Research
Branch
Tehran, 2010
Governor-general of Fars Province
No imprisonment
Not a war veteran
In 2013, Ahmadzadeh-Kermani registered for the
presidential elections.

A'inparast, Ja'far

Deputy of the Seventh Majlis, Mahabad, West Azerbaijan (2004–8)
1953–, Naqadeh, West Azerbaijan

BA, Persian literature
Hamzeh
Educator and member of the first Mashhad City
Council
No imprisonment
The GC disqualified A'inparast for the Eighth Majlis.

Ajam, Ali

Deputy of the First Majlis, Mashhad, Razavi Kho-
rasan (1981–84)
1949–, Gonabad, Razavi Khorasan
Clerical education
Hasan
Clergyman (HI)
No imprisonment
Member of the IRGC

Ajorlu, Mrs. Fatemeh

Deputy of the Seventh (2004–8) and Eighth (2008–12)
Majlis, Karaj, Tehran
1966–, Rey, Tehran
BS, psychology; MS, psychology
Seyfollah
Academia
No imprisonment
IRGC militiawoman
On September 3, 2009, President Ahmadinejad nom-
inated Ajorlu as minister of welfare and social
security, but she failed to receive enough votes
from the Majlis (seventy-six positive, 181 negative,
and twenty-nine abstentions). She reportedly has
some family ties to Sadeq Mahsuli, who was inte-
rior minister and minister of social welfare under
President Ahmadinejad.

Akbari [Bojnurd], Ali

Deputy of the Tenth Majlis, Bojnurd, Razavi Khorasan (2016–20)
1968–, Bojnurd, Razavi Khorasan
BS, agricultural engineering; MA, international
relations

Provincial civil servant in Tehran and North
    Khorasan
No imprisonment
War veteran

Akbari [Marvdasht], Ali

Deputy of the Tenth Majlis, Shiraz, Fars (2016–20)
1954–, Marvdasht, Fars
BS, geology, Shiraz University, 1977; MA, manage-
    ment, Tehran University, 1994
No imprisonment
He was head of the Tribal Affairs Organization of Iran
    under President Khatami.

Akbari, Saleh

Deputy of the Fifth Majlis, Naqadeh, West Azerbaijan
    (1996–2000)
1956–, Miyandoab, West Azerbaijan
BA, management
Qodrat
No imprisonment

Akbari-Talarposhti, Ezzatollah

Deputy of the Fifth (1996–2000) and Eighth (2008–12)
    Majlis, Qaemshahr and Savadkuh, Mazandaran
1953–, Qaemshahr, Mazandaran
BA, 1985; MA, law, 1999
Akbar
Civil servant
No imprisonment
Akbari-Talarposhti ran unsuccessfully for the Ninth
    Majlis.

Akbariyan, Aziz

Deputy of the Eighth Majlis, Karaj and Eshtehard,
    Tehran (2008–12); deputy of the Ninth (2012–16)
    and Tenth (2016–20) Majlis, Karaj, Alborz
1957–, Hashtrud, East Azerbaijan
BA, political science; MA, political science, Islamic
    Azad University–Karaj

Zolf-Ali, farmer
No imprisonment
War veteran
IRGC militiaman (Karaj commander)
Akbariyan held commanding posts within the
    IRGC (1990–2006) and taught at Imam Hoseyn
    University.

Akbarnezhad, Shakur

Deputy of the Eighth Majlis, Tabriz, Osku, and
    Azarshahr, East Azerbaijan (2008–12)
1960–, Tabriz, East Azerbaijan
MD, Tabriz University, 1996
Bayram-Ali, carpet weaver
Physical therapist
No imprisonment
War veteran (wounded, requires use of a wheelchair)
IRGC militiaman
Akbarnezhad served as chair of the Tabriz City Coun-
    cil for one term.

Akbarzadeh, Ali

Deputy of the Fifth (1998–2000) and Sixth (2000–
    2004) Majlis, Varzaqan and Kharvanagh, East
    Azerbaijan
1956–, Varzaqan, East Azerbaijan
BA, management
Jebre'il
Civil servant, ministries
No imprisonment
IRGC militiaman
Because of accusations of cheating in 1996, the votes
    for the Varzaqan region were invalidated and Ak-
    barzadeh entered the Majlis in interim elections
    in 1998. The GC disqualified Akbarzadeh from
    running in the 2004 Majlis election. He may have
    earned a PhD degree.

Akbarzadeh, Mohammad

Deputy of the Third Majlis, Neyshabur, Razavi Kho-
    rasan (1988–92)

1960–, Neyshabur, Razavi Khorasan
BS, civil engineering, Shahid Beheshti University, 1988
Javad
Member of the central council of Construction Jihad in Neyshabur
No imprisonment
Not a war veteran
There was a dispute over approving Akbarzadeh's credentials for the Third Majlis since he had not completed his military service.

Akhavan, Bahman

Deputy of the Fifth (1996–2000), Sixth (2000–2004), and Eighth (2008–12) Majlis, Tafresh and Ashtiyan, Markazi
1960–, Arak, Markazi
BA, law; MA, sociology
Ramezan
Civil servant
No imprisonment

Akhavan-Bazardeh, Mahmud

Deputy of the Sixth Majlis, Langarud, Gilan (2000–2004)
1951–, Qom, Qom
MA
Hasan
Civil servant of the MI
No imprisonment

Akhavan-Bitaraf, Mrs. Nayyereh

Deputy of the Fifth (1996–2000), Seventh (2004–8), Eighth (2008–12), and Ninth (2012–16) Majlis, Isfahan, Isfahan
1956–, Dorud, Lorestan
BS, psychology, Shiraz University, 1983; MA, jurisprudence
Javad
Civil servant
No imprisonment

Affiliated with the SFIR
Akhavan-Bitaraf and fellow MP Maryam Behruzi hold the record for the most terms served by a woman in the Majlis after the revolution. From 1983 to 1996, Akhavan-Bitaraf was a teacher and headmaster at a number of high schools. After she ran unsuccessfully for the Sixth Majlis, she worked as a deputy for women's affairs in IRIB. Akhavan-Bitaraf has also taught at Islamic Azad University. She is married to another MP from Isfahan, Hasan Kamran-Dastjerdi.

Akhlaqinia [Kamsefidi], Mohammad

Deputy of the First Majlis, Sirjan, Kerman (1981–84)
1952–, Rafsanjan, Kerman
Clerical education
Mirza
Clergyman
No imprisonment
HI Akhlaqinia survived an assassination attempt on April 14, 1984.

Akhtari, Abbas-Ali

Deputy of the First Majlis, Mashhad, Razavi Khorasan (1981–84); deputy of the Seventh Majlis, Tehran, Tehran (2004–8)
1939–, Garmsar, Semnan
Clerical education, Mashhad Seminary
Mohammad-Hoseyn, clergyman
Clergyman
Imprisoned before the revolution
Not a war veteran
Martyr's family (son, Nurollah)
HI Akhtari is the former head of revolutionary committees in Shirvan and Jahrom. In 1981, Ayatollah Khomeini appointed him to be his representative and the Friday prayer leader in Semnan. In 2001, he resigned from this post to become the Friday prayer leader of Shahr-e Rey. Akhtari has been a judge in the State Supreme Court and has taught at various universities. He has been a member of the Friday Prayer Policymaking Council since

2000, and has taught at Mashhad and Qom Seminaries. His two brothers, Ali-Asghar and Mohammad-Hasan, are also clerics. Mohammad-Hasan was the ambassador to Syria for twelve years, and he worked as deputy for foreign relations in the Office of the Supreme Leader.

Akhundi, Abbas-Ahmad

Minister of housing and urban development in President Hashemi-Rafsanjani's second cabinet (August 16, 1993–August 2, 1997); minister of roads and urban development in President Rouhani's first (August 15, 2013–August 13, 2017) and second (August 20, 2017–2021) cabinets
June 6, 1957–, Najaf, Iraq
BS, civil engineering, Tehran University; MS, civil engineering, Tehran University; PhD, geography, Royal Holloway University (England), 2006; dissertation title: "Globalization, the Nation-State and National Economic Policy Making: The Attitudes of Iran's Elites"
Ali-Ahmad, clergyman (ayatollah)
Civil servant
No imprisonment
War veteran
Associated with OMIRI
Akhundi was a member of the first central council of the Construction Jihad, deputy interior minister for political and social affairs (1982–86), head of the Housing Foundation of the Islamic Revolution (1988–93), and deputy manager of IRIB (1997–98). He worked for presidential candidate Mir Hoseyn Musavi's campaign during the 2009 elections.
In 2013, Akhundi was teaching in the School of Global Studies at Tehran University when President Rouhani nominated him as minister of roads and urban development. As a minister, he endured three impeachment attempts (October 5, 2015, February 19, 2017, and March 13, 2018) by the Majlis based on the performance of his ministry. He is the son-in-law of Ayatollah Seyyed Hashem Rasuli-Mahallati and the brother-in-law of Ali-Akbar Nateq-Nuri and Mohammad-Ali Shahidi.

Akhundi, Mohammad-Baqer

Deputy of the Second Majlis, Shabestar, East Azerbaijan (1984–88)
1928–, Tabriz, East Azerbaijan
Clerical education
Mohammad-Taqi
Clergyman
No imprisonment
Not a war veteran

Akrami, Seyyed Kazem

Member of the Assembly for the Final Examination of the Constitution, Hamadan (1979); deputy of the First Majlis, Bahar and Kabudarahang, Hamadan (1981–84); minister of education in PM Musavi's first (October 18, 1984–85) and second (October 28, 1985–88) cabinets
1940–, Hamadan, Hamadan
BS, psychology, Tehran's Higher Teachers Training College, 1963; MA, education, Tehran's Higher Teachers Training College, 1969; PhD, education, Tarbiyat-e Modarres University, 1994
Seyyed Yusef, carpet weaver
Rector of Tarbiyat-e Modarres University
Imprisoned before the revolution (fifty-two months)
Not a war veteran
Martyr's family (son)
Member of the central council of the Islamic Association of Iranian Teachers; founding member of the Society of a Group of Muslim Political Prisoners before the Victory of the Islamic Revolution
In 1988, the Majlis denied Akrami a vote of confidence to continue serving in PM Musavi's second cabinet. He left politics, ran an educational nonprofit organization (Damavand), and taught at Islamic Azad University.

Akrami, Seyyed Reza

Deputy of the Second (1984–88), Third (1988–92), and Fourth (1992–96) Majlis, Semnan, Semnan;

deputy of the Fifth (1996–2000) and Eighth
(2008–12) Majlis, Tehran, Tehran
1942–, Semnan, Semnan
Clerical education, Qom Seminary, 1970
Seyyed Rahmatollah
Clergyman
No imprisonment
Not a war veteran
Martyr's family (son)
Member of the central council of the SCC
HI Akrami was the commissar of the ideological-
political bureau of the Iranian Air Force and
commander of war propagation during the Iran–
Iraq War.

Ala', Eynollah

Deputy of the Third (1988–92) and Fifth (1996–2000)
Majlis, Aliabad Katul, Golestan
1942–, Aliabad Katul, Golestan
MS, accounting
Ali-Asghar
No imprisonment

Alami, Akbar

Deputy of the Sixth (2000–2004) and Seventh (2004–
8) Majlis, Tabriz, Azarshahr, and Osku, East
Azerbaijan
1954–, Tabriz, East Azerbaijan
BA, law, University of Judicial Sciences and Adminis-
trative Services, 1987; MA, economics, Allameh
Tabataba'i University, 1996
Esma'il, civil servant
Civil servant
No imprisonment
War veteran (thirty-two months)
IRGC militiaman
Alami was a journalist working with *Salam*. The
GC disqualified him from running in both the
2008 Majlis election and the 2009 presidential
election.

Alamolhoda, Seyyed Ahmad

Member of the Fourth (2007–16) and Fifth (2016–22)
Assembly of Experts, Razavi Khorasan
September 1, 1944–, Mashhad, Razavi Khorasan
Clerical education
Seyyed Ali, clergyman
Clergyman
No imprisonment
Not a war veteran
Member of the central council of the SCC
In the early days of the revolution, Alamolhoda was in
charge of a revolutionary *komiteh* in Tehran and
arrested many PMOI sympathizers and leftists. As
an archconservative ayatollah, he became a high-
level official at Imam Sadeq University beginning
in 1982. Ayatollah Khamenei appointed him as
the Friday prayer leader of Mashhad in 2005,
and on March 9, 2016, Ayatollah Khamenei gave
him the additional title of representative of the
supreme leader in Razavi Khorasan Province. He
is the father-in-law of HI Seyyed Ebrahim Ra'isi,
a high-level judiciary official and guardian of
Astan-e Qods-e Razavi.

Alamolhoda'i, Bahaeddin

Deputy of the First Majlis, Ardabil, Ardabil (1980–84)
1927–, Ardabil, Ardabil
Clerical education
Abdorrahim, farmer
Clergyman
No imprisonment
Not a war veteran
Member of the IRP

Alavi, Seyyed Ahsan

Deputy of the Ninth (2012–16) and Tenth (2016–20)
Majlis, Sanandaj, Divandarreh, and Kamyaran,
Kurdistan
1959–, Divandareh, Kurdistan
BS, civil engineering; MA, public administration

Seyyed Abbas
Mayor of Sanandaj
No imprisonment

Alavi, Seyyed Mahmud

Deputy of the First (1981–84), Second (1984–88),
    Fourth (1992–96), and Fifth (1996–2000) Majlis,
    Lamerd, Fars; member of Fourth (2009–16) and
    Fifth (2016–22) Assembly of Experts, Tehran;
    minister of intelligence in President Rouhani's
    first (August 15, 2013–August 13, 2017) and second
    (August 20, 2017–2021) cabinets
1954–, Lamerd, Fars
Clerical education; MA, theology, Ferdowsi University
    of Mashhad; PhD, Islamic law, Ferdowsi Univer-
    sity of Mashhad
Seyyed Reza, clergyman
Clergyman
No imprisonment
Not a war veteran
Member of the Perseverance Front of the Islamic
    Revolution
HI Alavi, who lived in Najaf, Iraq, from 1956 to 1970,
    was elected in interim elections (1981) to the First
    Majlis and again in interim elections (2009) to the
    AE (in the latter election he received 35.3 percent
    of the total votes cast). He was Ayatollah Khomei-
    ni's representative in Lamerd (1979–80), a deputy
    in the Ministry of Defense (1989–91), and Ayatol-
    lah Khamenei's representative in the army as head
    of the ideological-political bureau (2000–2009).
    Yet, the GC disqualified him from running in the
    2012 Majlis election. His son, Mohsen, was elected
    to the Tenth Majlis from Lamerd in 2016.

Alavi, Seyyed Mohsen

Deputy of the Tenth Majlis, Lamerd, Fars (2016–20)
1979–, Qom, Qom
Clerical education; pursuing an MA in law at Tehran
    University
Seyyed Mahmud, clergyman and politician

Lawyer
Not a war veteran
Alavi is the son of President Rouhani's minister of
    intelligence, Seyyed Mahmud Alavi. He worked in
    the Iranian embassy in Kuwait.

Alavi-Faradanbeh, Abolqasem

Deputy of the Fourth Majlis, Borujen and Lordegan,
    Chahar Mahal and Bakhtiari (1992–96)
1936–, Borujen, Chahar Mahal and Bakhtiari
MD, surgery
Shokrollah
Medical doctor
No imprisonment
Not a war veteran

Alavi-Hoseyni, Seyyed Mohammad-Hasan

Deputy of the Second (1984–88), Third (1988–92), and
    Fourth (1992–96) Majlis, Gorgan, Golestan
1948–, Qom, Qom
Clerical education
Seyyed Sajjad, clergyman (ayatollah)
Clergyman
No imprisonment
Martyr's family (nephew)
His brother, Seyyed Mohammad-Hoseyn, is a cleric in
    Qom. Ayatollah Habibollah Taheri is his broth-
    er-in-law, and Seyyed Ali Taheri-Gorgani is his
    nephew.

Alee, Mrs. Halimeh

Deputy of the Ninth Majlis, Zabol, Zahak, and Hir-
    mand, Sistan and Baluchestan (2012–16)
1970–, Zabol, Sistan and Baluchestan
MD, internal medicine, 1995
Medical doctor and university professor
No imprisonment
Not a war veteran
Martyr's family (brother)

Alee is the first woman to represent Sistan and Baluchestan Province in the Majlis; she received 61 percent of the vote. Her husband works in the municipality of the city of Zabol.

Ale-'Eshaq, Yahya

Minister of commerce in President Hashemi-Rafsanjani's second cabinet (August 16, 1993–August 2, 1997)
1949–, Qom, Qom
BA, business administration; MS, industrial management; PhD, strategic management, Supreme National Defense University
Mohammad (1924–2016), clergyman (ayatollah)
Civil servant, ministries of commerce and industry
No imprisonment
Not a war veteran
Martyr's family (brother, Abolhassan, killed at the front on March 16, 1985)
Founding member of CIC/PCIC
Ale-'Eshaq was born in Qom, but his birth certificate lists Zanjan as the city of birth. He comes from a big family (two sisters and seven brothers), and his father was imprisoned under the shah for his political activities. Ale-'Eshaq worked in the bazaar when he was a teenager and attended Alavi School. He was the deputy director of the FDWI, and director of the Chamber of Commerce. He was affiliated with *Resalat*, a conservative publication, and he was a presidential candidate in 2013.

Ale-Kazemi [Momondi-Kazem], Ali

Deputy of the First (1980–84) and Fifth (1996–2000) Majlis, Delfan and Selseleh, Lorestan
1946–2015, Harsin, Kermanshah
Clerical education, Qom Seminary
Farajollah, clergyman (ayatollah)
Clergyman (HI)
Imprisoned before the revolution
Not a war veteran

Alemi, Hasan

Member of the Third (1996–2006), Fourth (2012–16), and Fifth (2016–22) Assembly of Experts, Razavi Khorasan
1947–, Sabzevar, Razavi Khorasan
Clerical education, Qom Seminary
Rajabali, clergyman
Clergyman
No imprisonment
Ayatollah Alemi was Ayatollah Khomeini's representative at Sabzevar's Construction Jihad and Ayatollah Khamenei's representative at Qom's Construction Jihad (1990–93), and then Razavi Khorasan's Agricultural Jihad (1993–2004). Since 2004, he has represented Ayatollah Khamenei in the Ministry of Agricultural Jihad. Alemi was elected to the Fourth AE in interim elections.

Alemi [Damghani], Mohammad-Ali

Member of the Third Assembly of Experts, Semnan (1999)
1927–September 8, 1999, Damghan, Semnan
Clerical education, Qom Seminary
Clergyman
Imprisoned before the revolution
Not a war veteran
Ayatollah Alemi was a member of the Third AE for only seven months before he passed away. His replacement was Hassan Rouhani.

Alemi-Nayesi, Abdozzahra

Deputy of the Sixth Majlis, Dasht-e Azadegan, Khuzestan (2000–2004)
1955–, Dasht-e Azadegan, Khuzestan
Associate's degree
Khalaf
Civil servant
No imprisonment
After serving in the Majlis, Alemi-Nayesi worked for the government.

Ale-Seyyed Ghafur, Seyyed Mohammad-Taqi

Deputy of the First Majlis, Shushtar, Khuzestan
    (1981–84)
1955–, Shushtar, Khuzestan
BA, history
Seyyed Morteza
No imprisonment

Alhoseyni, Seyyed Hasan

Deputy of the Third Majlis, Arak, Markazi (1988–92)
1957–, Arak, Markazi
BS, electrical engineering, Babol University, 1979;
    MA, public administration, State Management
    Training Center
Seyyed Taqi, farmer/butcher
Academia
No imprisonment
War veteran
Member of the central council of the AILF and the
    Islamic Association of Iranian Teachers

Aliabadi, Mohammad

VP and head of the Physical Training Organiza-
    tion in President Ahmadinejad's first cabinet
    (2005–9)
1956–, Arak, Markazi
BS, civil engineering, K. N. Toosi University of Tech-
    nology, 1979; MS, architecture, Tehran University,
    1999
Gholam-Abbas
Deputy in the office of the mayor of Tehran (2003–5)
No imprisonment
War veteran
IRGC militiaman
Aliabadi became a deputy to the minister of Agricul-
    tural Jihad after failing to obtain the necessary
    votes to join President Ahmadinejad's second
    cabinet as minister of energy on September 3,
    2009. He is a former head of the National Olym-
    pic Committee of the Islamic Republic of Iran.

In 2011, he served for two months as the acting
    minister of petroleum.

Aliahmadi [-Jashfaqani], Ali-Reza

Minister of education in President Ahmadinejad's
    first cabinet (February 9, 2008–August 2, 2009)
1959–, Isfahan, Isfahan
BS, metallurgy, Iran University of Science and Tech-
    nology, 1986; MS, industrial engineering, Tarbi-
    yat-e Modarres University, 1989; PhD, production
    management, Tarbiyat-e Modarres University
Civil servant
No imprisonment
War veteran
IRGC militiaman (Basij)
Founding member of the Alliance of Steadfast Sup-
    porters of the Islamic Revolution
Aliahmadi was active in basiji circles and as a faculty
    member at Iran University of Science and Tech-
    nology. He was a member of the three-person
    committee that selected President Ahmadine-
    jad's cabinet. On August 24, 2005, Ahmadinejad
    nominated him for the post of minister of coop-
    eratives, but Aliahmadi did not receive enough
    votes from the Majlis. On February 9, 2008, the
    Majlis confirmed him as minister of education
    after receiving 133 positive votes, ninety-two
    negative votes, and twenty-nine abstentions.
    He is the father-in-law of Mehrdad Bazrpash,
    who served in President Ahmadinejad's second
    cabinet as VP and head of the National Youth
    Organization.

Aliasgari, Abdolali

Director-general of IRIB (May 11, 2016–present)
1958–, Shahr-e Rey, Tehran
BS, electrical engineering, Amirkabir University of
    Technology; MA, management, Tehran Univer-
    sity; PhD, industrial engineering, Iran University
    of Science and Technology
Adviser to the chief justice (2014–16)

Imprisoned before the revolution

War veteran

In the early 1980s, Aliasgari was involved with missile research as an employee of the Iran Defense Industries Organization. Later, during the presidency of Hashemi-Rafsanjani, he helped to establish the hugely successful Refah chain stores. Aliasgari has been the executive director of both the Iran Tourism Organization and the Cultural Research Foundation on Occidentalism. He has also worked in high-level positions in IRIB for twenty years. Aliasgari is credited with IRIB's switch from analog to digital broadcasting.

Alihoseyni-Abbasi, Mohammad-Reza

Deputy of the Fifth (1996–2000) and Sixth (2000–2004) Majlis, Nahavand, Hamadan

1956–, Malayer, Hamadan

BS, electrical engineering

Hasan-Ali

Provincial civil servant

Imprisoned before the revolution (1974–78/79)

War veteran (five years, wounded)

Secretary-general of the Society of Prerevolution Muslim Political Prisoners

As a member of the underground Abazar Group (*Goruh-e Abazar*), Alihoseyni-Abbasi was arrested by the shah's regime in 1974 and condemned to life imprisonment. He was in the same prison cell as current Supreme Leader Ayatollah Khamenei, and was released at the time of the revolution. The GC disqualified him after the Sixth Majlis.

Alijani-Zamani, Mohsen

Deputy of the Tenth Majlis, Tehran, Tehran (2016–20)

1969–, Shahr-e Rey, Tehran

MD, medicine

Medical doctor

War veteran (nine months; victim of chemical attack)

Member of the general council of the Islamic Association of Iranian Medical Society

Alijani-Zamani was active in university and medical society Islamic associations.

Alikhani, Mohammad

Deputy of the Seventh Majlis, Qazvin and Abyek, Qazvin (2004–8)

1969–, Qom, Qom

MA, political science, Hawaii University (online program)

Qodratollah, clergyman (HI)

Civil servant

No imprisonment

Alikhani and his father were both MPs from Qazvin Province in the Seventh Majlis.

Alikhani, Qodratollah

Deputy of the Sixth (2000–2004) and Seventh (2004–8) Majlis, Bu'inzahra and Avaj, Qazvin; deputy of the Eighth Majlis, Qazvin, Qazvin (2008–12)

1939–, Takestan, Zanjan

Clerical education, Qazvin Seminary

Zabihollah, farmer

Clergyman

Imprisoned before the revolution

Not a war veteran

HI Alikhani gained his release from prison in early 1977 after taking part in a controversial ceremony praising the shah. He became the director of the central *komiteh* in Qazvin after the revolution. After he failed to enter the Ninth Majlis, he became deputy for parliamentary affairs for Ayatollah Hashemi-Rafsanjani in the EDA. His son, Mohammad, was a deputy in the Seventh Majlis.

Alilu, Ali

Deputy of the Ninth Majlis, Shabestar, East Azerbaijan (2012–16)

1961–, Tehran, Tehran

BA, law, Tehran University

Retired civil servant

No imprisonment

War veteran (POW for nine years)
IRGC militiaman
Alilu ran unsuccessfully for the Sixth and Seventh
    Majlis.

Alimardani, Mohsen

Deputy of the Ninth Majlis, Zanjan and Tarom, Zan-
    jan (2012–16)
1968–, Zanjan, Zanjan
MD, medicine, Zanjan University of Medical Sciences
Medical doctor
No imprisonment
Not a war veteran
IRGC militiaman (Basij)
Martyr's family (brother)
Alimardani, who ran unsuccessfully for the Eighth
    Majlis, was a deputy in the Zanjan Province So-
    cial Welfare Organization.

Alimohammadi, Omran

Deputy of the Ninth Majlis, Ilam, Eyvan, Mehran,
    Malekshahi, and Shirvan, Ilam (2013–16)
1965–, Ilam, Ilam
BA, law
Hasan
Military and security forces
No imprisonment
War veteran (sixty months; wounded)
Alimohammadi entered the Ninth Majlis in interim
    elections held in June 2013.

Alimoradi, Amanollah

Member of the Fifth Assembly of Experts, Kerman
    (2016–22)
1963–, Baft, Kerman
Clerical education, Qom Seminary, 1990; PhD,
    theology
Abdollah
Clergyman (HI)
No imprisonment
Not a war veteran

Alinezhad-Sarkhani, Mohammad

Deputy of the First (1980–June 14, 1981) and Fourth
    (1992–96) Majlis, Tabriz, East Azerbaijan
1938–, Tabriz, East Azerbaijan
MD, medicine
Mohammad-Ali
No imprisonment
Not a war veteran
Alinezhad-Sarkhani resigned from the First Majlis to
    become the governor-general of East Azerbaijan.

Alipur, Ahmad

Deputy of the First Majlis, Piranshahr and Sardasht,
    West Azerbaijan (1983–84)
1926–, Piranshahr and Sardasht, West Azerbaijan
Clerical education
Karim
Clergyman
No imprisonment
Not a war veteran

Alipur, Asadollah

Deputy of the First Majlis, Ilam, Ilam (1980–84)
1943–, Karzan, Ilam
BA, Persian literature
Mohammad-Ali, farmer
Academia
No imprisonment

Alipur-Khonakdari, Kamal

Deputy of the Ninth Majlis, Qaemshahr, Savadkuh,
    and Juybar, Mazandaran (2012–16)
1967–, Qaemshahr, Mazandaran
BS, civil engineering, Islamic Azad University
Hoseyn, farmer
Civil servant, Tehran municipality
No imprisonment
War veteran
Alipur-Khonakdari ran unsuccessfully for the Eighth
    Majlis.

Alipur-Rahmati, Mohammad

Deputy of the Ninth Majlis, Maku, Chaldoran, Pol-dasht, and Showt, West Azerbaijan (2012–16)
September 23, 1962–, Chaldoran, West Azerbaijan
MA, public administration, Institute for Management and Planning Studies
MIIRI officer
No imprisonment
Alipur-Rahmati was in charge of intelligence for the city of Maku and West Azerbaijan Province.

Alireza-Beygi, Ahmad

Deputy of the Tenth Majlis, Tabriz, East Azerbaijan (2016–20)
1964–, Urmia, West Azerbaijan
Governor-general of East Azerbaijan (2008–13)
No imprisonment
War veteran
IRGC militiaman and security official
Alireza-Beygi was involved in stifling the Kurdish unrest in the early 1980s, took part in the Iran–Iraq War, and became a military-security official in East Azerbaijan, Isfahan, and Fars Provinces.

Alireza'i, Ne'matollah

Deputy of the Sixth Majlis, Khomeinishahr, Isfahan (2000–2004)
1951–, Homayunshahr, Isfahan
BS, civil engineering, University of Arkansas (USA)
Rahim
No imprisonment
Alireza'i returned to Iran from the United States at the time of the revolution and was mayor of Ahvaz for a year. After serving in the Majlis, he joined the board of directors of Petropars Company, which is affiliated with the Petroleum Ministry.

Alizadeh, Ahmad

Deputy of the First Majlis, Qaemshahr, Mazandaran (1980–84); member of Second (1989–92), Third (1992–98), and Fourth (1998–2001) Guardian Councils
1939–, Qaemshahr, Mazandaran
MA, law
Mashhad, farmer
No imprisonment
Not a war veteran
Alizadeh and his younger brother, Mohammad-Reza, served together in the GC from 1989 to 2001.

Alizadeh, Mohammad-Reza

Member of Second (1986–92), Third (1992–98), Fourth (1998–2004), Fifth (2004–10), Sixth (2010–16), and Seventh (2016–19) Guardian Councils
1951–, Savadkuh, Mazandaran
BA, law; MA, law
Mashhad, farmer
Judiciary official
No imprisonment
Not a war veteran
Alizadeh is the longest-serving lay lawyer of the GC and is the current deputy secretary. He previously held such other posts as head of the State Organization for Registration of Deeds and Properties, deputy head of the judiciary branch, deputy of the State General Inspectorate Organization, and prosecutor of Qaemshahr. He was also an official responsible for assessing the qualifications of judges. He and his older brother, Ahmad, served together in the GC from 1989 to 2001.

Alizadeh, Reza

Deputy of the Eighth (2009–12) and Tenth (2016–20) Majlis, Varzaqan, East Azerbaijan
1968–, Kasin, East Azerbaijan
BS, phytopathology, 1991; MA, economic
Soltan, farmer
Civil servant, state companies
No imprisonment
Not a war veteran
Due to accusations of cheating, the GC nullified votes from Varzaqan in 2008, and Alizadeh was elected

in interim elections in 2009. He was not elected to
the Seventh and Ninth Majlis.

Alizadeh [-Yazdi], Ali-Akbar

Member of Second Assembly of Experts, Razavi Kho-
rasan (1991–98)
1927–1999, Mashhad, Razavi Khorasan
Clerical education
Clergyman
No imprisonment
Not a war veteran
Ayatollah Alizadeh was the Friday prayer leader of
Ferdows for ten years.

Alizadeh-Barogh, Rahim

Deputy of the Second Majlis, Ardabil, Ardabil
(1984–88)
1950–, Ardabil, Ardabil
Associate's degree
Aziz
No imprisonment
Not a war veteran
Member of the IRP
After serving in the Majlis, Alizadeh-Barogh be-
came a civil servant of the Telecommunications
Ministry.

Allahbedashti, Abolhasan

Deputy of the First Majlis, Nowshahr, Mazandaran
(1981–84)
1950–, Kelardasht, Mazandaran
Clerical education
Yar-Mohammad
Clergyman (ayatollah)
No imprisonment

Allahqolizadeh, Qoli

Deputy of the Fifth (1996–2000), Sixth (2000–2004),
and Tenth (2016–20) Majlis, Kaleybar and Hu-
rand, East Azerbaijan

1960–, Abesh-Ahmad, East Azerbaijan
BA, Arabic literature
Abdollah, farmer
Educational civil servant
No imprisonment
War veteran
Martyr's family (Abolfazl, his brother, and Bayram,
his uncle, were killed at the war front)
Allahqolizadeh ran unsuccessfully for the Fourth and
Seventh Majlis, and the GC rejected his qual-
ifications for the Eighth Majlis. He worked for
some three decades as an administrator in the
education field and retired in 2011. His father also
fought at the war front.

Allahyari, Abbas-Ali

Deputy of the Sixth (2000–2004) and Seventh (2004–
8) Majlis, Kermanshah, Kermanshah
1965–, Kermanshah, Kermanshah
PhD, psychology, Tarbiyat-e Modarres University
Hemmatyar, farmer
Official at the Martyr's Foundation
No imprisonment
Allahyari is a former member of the HCCR.

Allahyari, Reza-Qoli

Deputy of the Fourth Majlis, Mamasani, Fars
(1992–96)
1959–, Mamasani, Fars
Associate's degree
Alinaz
Teacher
No imprisonment
After leaving the Majlis, he worked at the Ministry of
Education.

Almasi, Hasan

Deputy of the Fifth Majlis, Germi, Ardabil (1996–
2000); deputy of the Sixth Majlis, Parsabad and
Bilehsavar, Ardabil (2000–2004)
1965–, Bilehsavar, Ardabil

PhD, public administration
Barat-Ali
No imprisonment

Almasi, Mrs. Sakineh

Deputy of the Tenth Majlis, Deyr and Kangan,
    Bushehr (2016–20)
1978–, Jam, Bushehr
MA, social works; pursuing PhD degree in sociology
Head of the public relations department of the Social
    Welfare Organization
Almasi, a social worker, ran unsuccessfully for the
    Ninth Majlis.

Alviri, Morteza

Deputy of the First Majlis, Damavand, Tehran (1980–
    84); deputy of the Third Majlis, Tehran, Tehran
    (1988–92); mayor of Tehran (1999–2001)
November 23, 1948–, Damavand, Tehran
BS, electrical engineering, Sharif University of Tech-
    nology, 1972
Mohammad-Taqi, academia
Engineer
Imprisoned before the revolution
Not a war veteran
IRGC militiaman (founder and member of the com-
    mand council)
Member of the central council of OMIRI and a found-
    ing member of the Society of Industrial Managers
    and Professionals of Iran
Alviri and his wife were members of the radical un-
    derground Fallah Group before 1979. In the 1980s,
    he was the deputy minister for coordination
    affairs in the Ministry of Planning and Budget.
    On August 30, 1992, President Hashemi-Rafsan-
    jani appointed him as adviser on the affairs of
    free trade zones and later as ambassador to Spain.
    The regime imprisoned Alviri for a while after the
    contested 2009 presidential election. He was close
    to Ayatollah Montazeri and was very active in the
    HKSI.

Alya, Mrs. Fatemeh

Deputy of the Seventh (2004–8), Eighth (2008–12),
    and Ninth (2012–16) Majlis, Tehran, Tehran
1956–, Tehran, Tehran
BA, English translation, Allameh Tabataba'i Uni-
    versity; MA, political science, Islamic Azad
    University
Asghar
IRIB official
No imprisonment
IRGC militiawoman
Martyr's family (brother)
Member of the central council of the Zeynab Soci-
    ety; founding member and secretary-general of
    the Party of Women of the Islamic Republic of
    Iran

Amani [-Hamadani], Sa'id

Deputy of the First (1981–84) and Second (1984–88)
    Majlis, Tehran, Tehran
1915–1999, Hamadan, Hamadan
Pre-diploma (Six years of elementary school)
Ahmad
Bazaar tradesman
No imprisonment
Not a war veteran
Member of the central council of CIC/PCIC; founding
    member of the Society of Islamic Associations of
    Guilds and Bazaars
Amani, the oldest member of the Second Maj-
    lis, was the director of the Society of Islamic
    Guilds of Tehran's Bazaar. One of his brothers,
    Hashem, spent fourteen years in prison under
    the shah. One of his sons, Mohammad-Ali, was
    the executive secretary of CIC/PCIC. His other
    son, Javad, is the son-in-law of Ahmad Qadi-
    riyan, a former Evin Prison official and deputy
    prosecutor-general. Amani is the father-in-law
    of former Tehran MP Asadollah Badamchiyan.
    His brother, Sadeq, was married to the sister of
    Asadollah Ladjvardi.

Amani-Anganeh, Mrs. Shahrbanu

Deputy of the Fifth (1996–2000) and Sixth (2000–2004) Majlis, Urmia, West Azerbaijan
1960–, Urmia, West Azerbaijan
BA, management, 2004
Jamshid
Employee of the State Welfare Organization of Iran in Urmia
No imprisonment
Member of the central council of PECI
Amani-Anganeh did not receive enough votes to enter the Fourth Majlis and the GC rejected her for the Seventh and Tenth Majlis. She was an adviser to the Environmental Protection Organization of Iran on women's and family affairs and became a member of Tehran's City Council.

Ameli-Kalkhoran, Seyyed Hasan

Member of the Fourth (2007–16) and Fifth (2016–22) Assembly of Experts, Ardabil
1962–, Daral Ershad, Ardabil
MA, theology, Tehran University; PhD, theology, Tehran University; clerical education, Qom Seminary
Seyyed Firuzeddin, bazaar tradesman
Clergyman
No imprisonment
Not a war veteran
HI Ameli-Kalkhoran was the Friday prayer leader and Ayatollah Khamenei's representative in Ardabil for many years.

Amid-Zanjani, Abbas-Ali

Deputy of the Third (1988–92) and Fourth (1992–96) Majlis, Tehran, Tehran
1937–2011, Zanjan, Zanjan
Clerical education, Najaf Seminary (Iraq)
Asghar, bazaar tradesman
Clergyman
Imprisoned before the revolution
Not a war veteran

Member of the central council of the SCC
HI Amid-Zanjani enrolled at the Qom Seminary at the age of fifteen (1952) and studied under the guidance of such teachers as Ayatollah Khomeini and Allameh Tabataba'i. In 1962, he left for Najaf to pursue higher-level theological training and returned to Iran in 1969. From 1969 to 1971, he taught at the Qom Seminary and then moved to Tehran to continue his work at mosques and universities. After the victory of the 1979 revolution, he worked closely with the HCCR, and served as Iran's representative at UNESCO. Amid-Zanjani was a member of the committee that emended the constitution, and he was in charge of Lorzadeh Seminary in Tehran. He decided not to run for the Fifth Majlis. He was the son-in-law of Ayatollah Seyyed Shahabeddin Mar'ashi-Najafi.

Amini, Hoseyn

Deputy of the Fourth Majlis, Qaenat, South Khorasan (1992–96)
1953–, Qaenat, South Khorasan
BA, international economics; MA, public administration
Mohammad
Planning deputy in the office of Kurdistan's governor-general (1991–92)
Imprisoned before the revolution
War veteran
IRGC militiaman
Martyr's family (two brothers-in-law killed at the war front)
Amini has held many posts, including governor of Esfarayen (1981–84), governor of Shirvan (1984–88), general manager for social affairs and elections of Khorasan governorate (1988–91), and governor-general of Sistan and Baluchestan (2002–6). He has led foundations close to the reformist camp, and was head of the campaign headquarters of Mir Hoseyn Musavi in Razavi Khorasan Province in 2009.

Amini, Jahanbakhsh

Deputy of the Seventh (2004–8) and Eighth (2008–12)
    Majlis, Kermanshah, Kermanshah
1962–, Kermanshah, Kermanshah
MD, medicine, Kermanshah University of Medical
    Sciences
Morid-Ali
Medical doctor
No imprisonment
War veteran

Amini, Mas'ud

Deputy of the Seventh Majlis, Neyriz and Estahban,
    Fars (2004–8)
1961–, Neyriz, Fars
MD, medicine
Afrasiyab
Academia
No imprisonment

Amini, Salam

Deputy of the Tenth Majlis, Ilam, Ilam (2016–20)
1965–, Mehran, Ilam
BA, social science; MA, sociology; pursuing a PhD in
    sociology
Teacher
No imprisonment
War veteran (wounded)

Amini, Seyyed Hamzeh

Deputy of the Tenth Majlis, Hashtrud, East Azerbai-
    jan (2016–20)
1969–, Hashtrud, East Azerbaijan
BA, Persian literature; MA, Persian literature
Mir Hasan
Teacher/educational administrator for twenty-six
    years; former chair of the Hashtrud City
    Council
No imprisonment

Aminifard, Mohammad-Na'im

Deputy of the Tenth Majlis, Iranshahr, Sistan and
    Baluchestan (2016–20)
1967–, Iranshahr, Sistan and Baluchestan
MD, ophthalmology, Shahid Beheshti University,
    2001
Optometrist and professor at Zahedan University of
    Medical Sciences
No imprisonment
Aminifard, a Sunni, started his career as a medical
    doctor in Iranshahr in 1992, and he was director
    of the health network in Iranshahr from 1993 to
    1997.

Amini-Najafabadi, Seyyed Ebrahim

Deputy of the Sixth Majlis, Mamasani, Fars
    (2000–2004)
1959–, Mamasani, Fars
PhD, law
Seyyed Hasan
Academia
No imprisonment
Founding member of the NTP

*Amini [-Najafabadi] [Haj Amini-Najafabadi],
Ebrahim*

Member of the First (1983–90), Second (1991–98),
    and Third (1999–2006) Assembly of Experts,
    Chahar Mahal and Bakhtiari; member of Fifth
    Assembly of Experts, Tehran (2016–22); member
    of the Fourth (1997–2002), Fifth (2002–7), Sixth
    (2007–12), Seventh (2012–17), and Eighth (2017–
    22) Expediency Discernment Assembly
1925–, Najafabad, Isfahan
Clerical education, Qom Seminary
Hoseyn, farmer
Clergyman
No imprisonment
Not a war veteran
Founding member of the SQSS

Ayatollah Amini was the deputy head of the First AE (1985–90), head of the Office of the Secretariat of the AE, and the Friday prayer leader of Qom until early 2010. He was the oldest member of the EDA, and the second oldest member of the Fifth AE. Amini ran for the position of chair of the Fifth AE in May 2016 and came in a distant second, receiving twenty-one votes compared to Ahmad Jannati's fifty-one votes.

Aminiyan, Mokhtar

Member of the First (1983–90), Second (1991–98), Third (1999–2006), and Fourth (2007–14) Assembly of Experts, Gilan
1926–2014, Langarud, Gilan
Clerical education, Qom Seminary
Abdolhoseyn, landowner
Clergyman (ayatollah)
No imprisonment
Not a war veteran
Ayatollah Khomeini appointed Aminiyan as his representative at Gilan University. He was also the supreme leader's representative and the Friday prayer leader in Astaneh-ye Ashrafiyyeh in Gilan Province.

Aminlu, Hasan

Deputy of the Third (1988–92) and Fourth (1992–96) Majlis, Shabestar, East Azerbaijan
1944–, Shabestar, East Azerbaijan
BA, Persian literature, Tabriz University, 1970; MD, medicine, Shahid Beheshti University, 1980
Ali-Akbar
Medical doctor
No imprisonment
Not a war veteran
After leaving the Majlis, Aminlu worked for eight years at the Management and Planning Organization and officially retired in 2004. He later worked as the health minister's deputy for parliamentary affairs.

Amin-Naseri, Mohammad-Reza

Deputy of the First Majlis, Astaneh-ye Ashrafiyyeh, Gilan (1980–84)
1952–, Astaneh-ye Ashrafiyyeh, Gilan
BS, chemical and petroleum engineering, Amirkabir University of Technology; MS, operational research, Western Michigan University (USA); PhD, industrial engineering, West Virginia University (USA)
Abbas, bazaar tradesman
Professor
No imprisonment
Amini-Naseri is currently a professor at Tarbiyat-e Modarres University.

Aminzadeh, Mrs. Elham

Deputy of the Seventh Majlis, Tehran, Tehran (2004–8); VP for legal affairs in President Rouhani's first cabinet (2013–16)
1964–, Shiraz, Fars
BA, law, Shahid Beheshti University; MA, international law, Shahid Beheshti University; PhD, international law, University of Glasgow (Scotland), 1997; dissertation title: "The United Nations and International Peace and Security: A Legal and Practical Analysis"
Mehdi
Professor at Tehran University's law school
No imprisonment
Aminzadeh, a conservative, was appointed research deputy at Tehran University in 2007, and she has also taught at Imam Sadeq and Allameh Tabataba'i universities. In July 2016, she stepped down from her VP post and became a special assistant to the president on citizenship rights.

Amirabadi-Farahani, Ahmad

Deputy of the Ninth (2012–16) and Tenth (2016–20) Majlis, Qom, Qom
1973–, Farahan, Markazi

BA, management, Tehran University, 1997; MA,
   financial management, Islamic Azad University,
   2001
Father's name unknown, farmer
Member of the Qom City Council and university
   instructor
No imprisonment
War veteran (wounded)
IRGC militiaman
Amirabadi-Farahani went to fight in the Iran–Iraq
   War when he was thirteen and joined the IRGC in
   1990. He was a member of the command council
   of Qom's IRGC.

Amir-Hasankhani, Mohammad-Reza

Deputy of the Seventh (2004–8) and Tenth (2016–20)
   Majlis, Ferdows and Tabas, South Khorasan
1964–, Ferdows, South Khorasan
MD, medicine, Kerman University of Medical Sci-
   ences; specialty in ophthalmology, Mashhad
   University of Medical Sciences, 1994
Abdorrahman, farmer
Medical doctor
No imprisonment
War veteran (wounded in 1985)
Amir-Hasankhani was active in Islamic student asso-
   ciations and was Kerman Province's director-gen-
   eral of the Red Crescent Society of the Islamic
   Republic of Iran.

Amiri, Hoseyn-Ali

Member of the Fifth (2007–10) and Sixth (2010–13)
   Guardian Councils; VP for parliamentary affairs
   in President Rouhani's first (July 12, 2016–August 13, 2017) and second (August 20, 2017–2021)
   cabinets
1967–, Sonqor, Kermanshah
BA, law, University of Judicial Sciences and Administrative Services; MA, law; pursuing a PhD in law
   at Islamic Azad University–Science and Research
   Branch

Malek-Hoseyn
Head of the State Organization for Registration of
   Deeds and Properties
No imprisonment
War veteran
IRGC militiaman
Amiri, a conservative, has held numerous jobs in
   the judiciary branch, and in 2004, Ayatollah
   Hashemi-Shahrudi appointed him as deputy head
   of the judiciary and head of the State Organization for Registration of Deeds and Properties. He
   was also a lawyer in the Fifth GC until he was
   forced to resign from holding two or more simul-
   taneous positions in 2009 (he decided to stay in
   the GC and gave up his judiciary post). As former
   head of the Fars Province justice administration,
   he was the judge in charge of the trial of a number
   of Jews from Shiraz accused of being spies. On
   July 12, 2016, President Rouhani promoted him
   from deputy interior minister to vice president for
   parliamentary affairs.

Amiri-Kahnuj, Mohammad-Reza

Deputy of the Eighth (2008–12) and Ninth (2012–16)
   Majlis, Kahnuj, Manujan, South Rudbar, and
   Qaleh Ganj, Kerman
1968–, Kahnuj, Kerman
Clerical education, Qom Seminary
Amir
Clergyman
No imprisonment
Not a war veteran
HI Amiri-Kahnuj was the Friday prayer leader and
   the supreme leader's representative in Kahnuj
   before entering the Majlis.

Amiri-Khamkani, Hoseyn

Deputy of the Sixth (2000–2004), Seventh (2004–8),
   Eighth (2008–12), Ninth (2012–16), and Tenth
   (2016–20) Majlis, Zarand, Kerman
1958–, Zarand, Kerman

BS, physics, Shahid Bahonar University of Kerman, 1984; MS, physics, University of St. Andrews (Scotland), 1988; PhD, physics, University of Newcastle (England), 1993; dissertation title: "The Visible Consequences of Rising Convective Streams in the Earth"
Akbar
Professor and administrator at Shahid Bahonar University of Kerman
No imprisonment
IRGC militiaman

Amirjahani, Seyyed Fazel

Deputy of the Fourth (1992–96) and Sixth (2000–2004) Majlis, Abhar, Zanjan
1956–, Abhar, Zanjan
Clerical education; BA, philosophy
Seyyed Fakhreddin
Clergyman
No imprisonment

Amirshaqaqi, Mrs. Fakhrtaj

Deputy of the Fourth Majlis, Tabriz, East Azerbaijan (1992–96)
1941–, Hashtrud, East Azerbaijan
BA, French literature; MA, political science
Abdollah
Teacher and school headmaster
No imprisonment
Not a war veteran
Amirshaqaqi retired from the Ministry of Education in 1998.

Amirzadeh-Irani, Mirza Ahmad

Deputy of the Second Majlis, Ardabil, Ardabil (1984–88)
1916–date unknown, Ardabil, Ardabil
Clerical education
Clergyman (HI)
Amir-Ali

No imprisonment
Not a war veteran
Amirzadeh-Irani has passed away (date unknown).

Amrollahi, Reza

VP and head of the Atomic Energy Organization in President Hashemi-Rafsanjani's first (1989–93) and second (1993–97) cabinets
1946–, Yazd, Yazd
BS, physics, Shahid Beheshti University, 1971; MS, electrical engineering, Lamar University (USA), 1976; PhD, nuclear physics, University of Paris (France), 1994
Civil servant, state companies
No imprisonment
Not a war veteran
Founding member of the central council of PECI
Amrollahi was the head of AEOI from 1981 to 1997 and subsequently became a professor in the department of energy engineering and physics at Amirkabir University of Technology.

Anaraki-Mohammadi, Ahmad

Deputy of the Tenth Majlis, Rafsanjan, Kerman (2016–20)
1969–, Anar, Kerman
MS, agricultural engineering
Agricultural engineer
No imprisonment
Anaraki-Mohammadi was elected to the Tenth Majlis as a reformist.

Angaji, Seyyed Javad

Deputy of the Second (1984–88) and Fourth (1992–96) Majlis, Tabriz, East Azerbaijan
1946–, Tabriz, East Azerbaijan
PhD, agricultural engineering
Seyyed Mohammad-Ali, clergyman (ayatollah)
No imprisonment

Angaji's father was a member of parliament before the revolution and in 1979 represented East Azerbaijan in the Assembly for the Final Examination of the Constitution.

Angaji, Seyyed Mohammad-Ali

Member of the Assembly for the Final Examination of the Constitution, East Azerbaijan (1979)
1897–June 5, 1983, Tabriz, East Azerbaijan
Clerical education, Qom Seminary
Seyyed Abolhasan, clergyman (ayatollah)
Clergyman
Imprisoned before the revolution
Not a war veteran
Ayatollah Angaji was one of only a handful of politicians who held a seat in the Majlis before the revolution (Seventeenth Majlis, elected from Azerbaijan) and yet was allowed to serve in a high-level postrevolutionary position. This may be because he was exiled in Kurdistan by the shah's regime for supporting PM Mohammad Mosaddeq. Angaji was elected to represent East Azerbaijan in the First AE as well, but he passed away on June 5, 1983, a month before that assembly was to start its term. His son, Seyyed Javad, twice represented Tabriz in the Majlis.

Anjiri-Motlaq, Ahad

Deputy of the Second Majlis, Mahabad, West Azerbaijan (1984–88)
1938–, Mahabad, West Azerbaijan
BA, English literature
Hoseyn
No imprisonment

Ansari, Fariborz

Deputy of the Fifth Majlis, Mamasani and Doshman Ziari, Fars (1996–2000)
1959–, Mamasani, Fars
BA, theology; clerical education

Khodakaram
No imprisonment
Ansari retired from the Ministry of Petroleum in 2016.

Ansari, Gholam-Reza

Deputy of the Fourth Majlis, Mashhad, Razavi Khorasan (1992–96)
1956–, Mashhad, Razavi Khorasan
MD, medicine
Yusef-Ali
No imprisonment
Member of the central council of PIIPU, founding member of Assembly of Former MPs, and founding member of IISP
After leaving the Majlis, Ansari became head of the State Welfare Organization of Iran (1991–2001) and later a member of the Tehran City Council.

Ansari, Jamshid

Deputy of the Eighth Majlis, Zanjan and Tarom, Zanjan (2008–12); VP and head of the Administrative and Recruitment Organization in President Rouhani's second cabinet (August 20, 2017–2021)
1955–, Zanjan, Zanjan
MS, management
Ali
Governor-general of West Azerbaijan and Urmia
No imprisonment
War veteran
IRGC militiaman
Ansari became the governor-general of Zanjan in 2014.

Ansari, Majid

Deputy of the First (1980–84) and Third (1988–92) Majlis, Zarand, Kerman; deputy of the Fifth (1996–2000) and Sixth (2000–2004) Majlis, Tehran, Tehran; member of the Third Assembly of Experts, Tehran (1999–2006); member of the Fifth

(2002–7), Sixth (2007–12), Seventh (2012–17), and Eighth (2017–22) Expediency Discernment Assembly; VP for parliamentary affairs in President Khatami's second cabinet (2004–5) and President Rouhani's first cabinet (2013–July 12, 2016); VP for legal affairs in President Rouhani's first cabinet (July 12, 2016–August 13, 2017)

March 30, 1954–, Khanuk, Kerman

Clerical education, Qom Seminary, 1978; MA, law, Islamic Azad University–Tehran

Akbar, grocer

Clergyman

No imprisonment

Not a war veteran

IRGC militiaman

Martyr's family (brother, Mahmud, killed in Kurdistan)

Member of the central council and executive director of the ACC

HI Ansari, who was injured in a demonstration before the revolution, handled public relations and general affairs in Ayatollah Khomeini's office. He has held posts such as representative of the High Council of the Judiciary (HCJ) in prisons, first director of the State Prisons and Security and Corrective Measures Organization (1984/85–87), deputy interior minister, planning deputy of the State General Inspectorate Organization, and member of the IRIB policy board. Ansari and his two clerical brothers (Mohammad-Ali and Hamid) all work in the Institute for Compilation and Publication of Imam Khomeini's Work. The GC rejected his qualifications for the Fifth Assembly of Experts.

Ansari, Mohammad-Sa'id

Deputy of the Third (1988–92), Fourth (1992–96), Seventh (2004–8), and Ninth (2012–16) Majlis, Abadan, Khuzestan

1956–, Abadan, Khuzestan

BA, law, Islamic Azad University–Tehran, 2001; MA, law, Islamic Azad University–Tehran, 2005

Abud

Employee of the Ministry of Petroleum

No imprisonment

War veteran

After serving in the Ninth Majlis, he became a member of the board of directors of National Iranian Oil Company Pension Fund.

Ansari, Reza

Deputy of the Tenth Majlis, Darab and Zarrindasht, Fars (2016–20)

1973–, Darab, Fars

BS, mining engineering, Shahid Bahonar University of Kerman; MS, mining engineering; PhD, technology management, Allameh Tabataba'i University, 2011

Professor at Isfahan University of Technology

No imprisonment

Not a war veteran

Ansarirad, Hoseyn

Deputy of the First (1980–84), Fifth (1996–2000), and Sixth (2000–2004) Majlis, Neyshabur, Razavi Khorasan

1937–, Neyshabur, Razavi Khorasan

Clerical education

Gholam-Reza, farmer

Clergyman

No imprisonment

Not a war veteran

HI Ansarirad was a leading figure in the 1978–79 revolutionary activities in Neyshabur and very popular in his city. The GC rejected his qualifications for the Seventh and the Eighth Majlis.

Anvari, Hoseyn

Deputy of the Fifth (1996–2000) and Sixth (2000–2004) Majlis, Sarab, East Azerbaijan

1958–, Sarab, East Azerbaijan

MA, public administration

Yusef
No imprisonment

Anvari, Mirza Mohammad

Member of the Assembly for the Final Examination of
    the Constitution, Hormozgan (1979); member of
    the First (1983–90), Second (1991–98), and Third
    (1999–2002) Assembly of Experts, Hormozgan
1919–2002, Kesnaviyeh, Yazd
Clerical education, Qom Seminary and Najaf Semi-
    nary (Iraq)
Mohammad-Baqer, clergyman
Clergyman (HI)
No imprisonment
Not a war veteran

Aqa Alikhani, Gholam-Abbas

Deputy of the Fifth Majlis, Bu'inzahra and Avaj, Zan-
    jan (1996–2000)
1958–, Takestan, Zanjan
BS, agricultural engineering (USA)
Asadollah, farmer
Civil servant
No imprisonment
Aqa Alikhani registered to run for the Tenth Majlis.

Aqa Hoseyni-Tabataba'i, Seyyed Hasan

Deputy of the First (1981–84), Second (1984–88),
    Fourth (1992–96), and Seventh (2004–8) Majlis,
    Zabol, Sistan and Baluchestan
1934–, Zabol, Sistan and Baluchestan
Clerical education
Seyyed Ali, clergyman
Clergyman
No imprisonment
Not a war veteran
Martyr's family (brother, Mohammad-Taqi
    Hoseyni-Tabataba'i [an MP], killed in the IRP
    bombing)
HI Aqa Hoseyni-Tabataba'i was previously a
    judge and overseer of the Islamic Revolution

Committee. In the First Majlis, he was known
by the last name of Hoseyni-Tabataba'i, like his
brother.

Aqa Mohammadi, Ali

Deputy of the First (1980–84), Second (1984–88), and
    Third (1988–92) Majlis, Hamadan, Hamadan;
    member of the Sixth (2007–12), Seventh (2012–17),
    and Eighth (2017–22) Expediency Discernment
    Assembly
1950–, Hamadan, Hamadan
Associate's degree
Mohammad-Ali, farmer
No imprisonment
Not a war veteran
Aqa Mohammadi previously worked in IRIB, the
    Supreme National Security Council, and in soccer
    management. He was also an adviser to Ayatollah
    Khamenei.

Aqa Mohammadi, Ebrahim

Deputy of the Ninth Majlis, Khorramabad and Dow-
    reh, Lorestan (2012–16)
1962–, Khorramabad, Lorestan
BA, political science; MA, public administration
Civil servant
No imprisonment
War veteran
IRGC militiaman (Lorestan command council)
Aqa Mohammadi worked for the GC and is propri-
    etor of *Aflak Lorestan* weekly. After his retire-
    ment, he became executive director of Melli Shoe
    Company.

Aqa Rahimi, Abdolhamid

Deputy of the First Majlis, Shahr-e Babak, Kerman
    (1980–84)
1947–, Shahr-e Babak, Kerman
BA, Islamic law; MA, public administration
Abbas, farmer
Academia

No imprisonment

Aqa Rahimi worked in the presidential office from 1987 to 1990.

Aqa Tehrani, Morteza

Deputy of the Eighth (2008–12) and Ninth (2012–16) Majlis, Tehran, Tehran

1957–, Isfahan, Isfahan

Clerical education, Qom Seminary, 1986

MA, philosophy, McGill University (Canada), 1996; PhD, philosophy, State University of New York at Binghamton (USA), 1999; dissertation title: "Khajah Nasir al-din Tusi on the Meta-Mysticism of Ibn Sina"

Akbar, stonecutter

Clergyman

No imprisonment

War veteran

Martyr's family (two brothers and one uncle)

Secretary-general of the SFIR

HI Aqa Tehrani was the "moral adviser" for President Ahmadinejad's cabinet (2005–11), and previously represented Ayatollah Khamenei in North America. Aqa Tehrani lived in Canada from 1992 to 1995 and the United States from 1995 to 2000. After returning to Iran, he served in the Majlis, and then went on to teach at the conservative Imam Khomeini Educational and Research Institute.

Aqa Zadeh [-Kho'i], Gholam-Reza

Ministerial adviser for executive affairs in PM Musavi's first cabinet (May 31, 1982–85); minister of petroleum in PM Musavi's second cabinet (October 28, 1985–August 3, 1989) and President Hashemi-Rafsanjani's first (August 29, 1989–August 2, 1993) and second (August 16, 1993–August 2, 1997) cabinets; VP and head of the Atomic Energy Organization in President Khatami's first (1997–2001) and second (2001–5) cabinets, as well as President Ahmadinejad's first cabinet (2005–9); member of the Fourth (1997–2002),

Fifth (2002–7), Sixth (2007–12), Seventh (2012–17), and Eighth (2017–22) Expediency Discernment Assembly

1948–, Khoy, West Azerbaijan

BS, computer programming, Tehran University, 1970

Father's name unknown, bazaar tradesman

Civil servant

No imprisonment

Not a war veteran

Member of the political bureau of the IRP

Aqa Zadeh actively opposed the shah while in the United States (1975/76–78), but he returned to Iran in 1978 before finishing his graduate degree. After the revolution, he was an editor of *Jomhuri Islami*, and in 1982, he became head of the Ministry of Foreign Affairs' finance department. Aqa Zadeh was the head of AEOI from 1997 to 2009.

Aqa Zadeh-Dafsari, Seyyed Ali

Deputy of the Eighth Majlis, Rasht, Gilan (2008–12)

1955–, Dafsar, Gilan

MA, geography

Seyyed Kazem

No imprisonment

War veteran

IRGC militiaman (deputy commander of the Qods Force)

Aqa Zamani (Abusharif), Abbas

Commander in chief of the IRGC (1979–February 1980)

1939–, Tehran, Tehran

BA, theology, Tehran University, 1970; clerical education

Imprisoned before the revolution (1965–67)

War veteran

IRGC militiaman

Martyr's family (brother killed in 1985)

Member of the MNP

Aqa Zamani founded an underground group known as Hezbollah in the late 1960s and underwent military training in Lebanon and PLO camps. After

leaving the IRGC post, he became ambassador
to Pakistan (1981–84). He then studied in Qom
Seminary for a while before returning to Pakistan
to reside there. One of his brothers also belonged
to the MNP.

Aqa'i, Gholam-Hasan

Deputy of the Third Majlis, Hamadan, Hamadan
(1988–92); deputy of the Sixth Majlis, Zabol, Sistan and Baluchestan (2000–2004)
1950–, Mashhad, Razavi Khorasan
MD, Medicine
Qasem
No imprisonment

Aqa'i-Ghiyasabadi, Hedayatollah

Deputy of the Third Majlis, Fasa, Fars (1988–92)
1958–, Fasa, Fars
BS, metallurgy
Javad
No imprisonment
Member of the central council of PECI
The regime arrested Aqa'i-Ghiyasabadi during the
2009 Green Movement and sentenced him to a
five-year prison term.

Aqa'i-Kahlikbolaghi, Khalil

Deputy of the Sixth Majlis, Meshginshahr, Ardabil
(2000–2004)
1960–, Bilehsavar, Ardabil
BS, agricultural engineering
Safar
Civil servant
No imprisonment

Aqa'i-Moghanjuqi, Ali-Akbar

Deputy of the Sixth (2000–2004), Seventh (2004–8),
Eighth (2008–12), and Ninth (2012–15) Majlis, Salmas, West Azerbaijan

1947–2015, Salmas, West Azerbaijan
BS, civil engineering; BA, law; MA, international law;
MA, management
Abdollah
Civil servant, ministries
No imprisonment
Not a war veteran
Aqa'i-Moghanjuqi was a deputy minister for admin-
istrative and financial affairs in the Ministry of
Roads and Transportation in the early days of the
revolution.

Aqapur-Alishahi, Mrs. Ma'sumeh

Deputy of the Tenth Majlis, Shabestar, East Azerbaijan (2016–20)
1970–, Shabestar, East Azerbaijan
BA, accounting, Tehran University, 1995; MA, energy
economics, Islamic Azad University–Tehran,
2004; PhD, labor management, Republic of Azerbaijan, 2014
Qodratollah
Aqapur-Alishahi was an employee of the Ministry of
Information and Communications Technology
from 1988 to 2010, and has been a university professor of economics, accounting, and marketing
since 2005.

Arab, Ali-Mohammad

Member of the Assembly for the Final Examination of
the Constitution, Tehran (1979)
1935–, Varamin, Tehran
Third-grade education
Qorban-Ali, farmer
Civil servant, jihad
Not a war veteran
Arab was a laborer before the revolution and worked
in the Construction Jihad after the revolution. He completed third grade in elementary
school and ten years of religious education in
seminaries.

Arabameri, Yar-Mohammad

Deputy of the Second (1984–88) and Third (1988–92)
     Majlis, Garmsar, Semnan
1952–, Garmsar, Semnan
High school diploma
Rahmatollah
No imprisonment

A'rabi, Mohammad-Ali

Deputy of the Second Majlis, Kashmar, Razavi Kho-
     rasan (1984–88)
1952–, Kashmar, Razavi Khorasan
Clerical education
Qorban-Ali
Clergyman
No imprisonment

Arad, Ali

Member of the First (1980–86), Third (1997–98), and
     Fourth (1998–2001) Guardian Councils
1927–, Azarshahr, East Azerbaijan
PhD, law
Mohammad
Judge
No imprisonment
Not a war veteran
Arad was a criminal courts judge before the revolu-
     tion and became judge of the Disciplinary Court
     for Judges and Public Prosecutors before being
     appointed to the GC. He was elected to the Third
     GC by the Majlis on June 24, 1997, to replace
     Seyyed Reza Zavareh'i.

Arami, Mansur

Deputy of the Ninth Majlis, Bandar-e Abbas, Hor-
     mozgan (2012–16)
1963–, Bandar-e Abbas, Hormozgan
BS, rehabilitation sciences, University of Social
     Welfare and Rehabilitation Sciences; MS,

rehabilitation sciences, University of Social
     Welfare and Rehabilitation Sciences; pursuing a
     PhD in scientific and technological planning in
     Malaysia
Father's name unknown, farmer
MIIRI officer for Hormozgan Province; mayor of
     Bandar-e Abbas (2004–9)
No imprisonment
War veteran

Arasteh, Naser

Deputy general commander of the army (October 14,
     1998–date unknown)
1961–, Hidah, Zanjan
BS, military science, Ground Forces Officers'
     Academy
Military officer (brigadier general)
No imprisonment
War veteran
Arasteh was very close to Ali Sayyad-Shirazi, the
     commander of the army's ground forces and first
     deputy chief of staff of the Iranian Armed Forces.
     He has served in the army for over three decades.
     On June 25, 2000, Ayatollah Khomeini appointed
     him as an adviser on army affairs to the Chief of
     the Armed Forces General Staff.

Arbabi, Abdolkarim

Deputy of the First (1981–84) and Second (1984–88)
     Majlis, Chabahar, Sistan and Baluchestan
1946–, Chabahar, Sistan and Baluchestan
High school (incomplete)
Ebrahim
No imprisonment
Not a war veteran

Arbabi, Mohammad-Sa'id

Deputy of the Ninth Majlis, Iranshahr, Sarbaz,
     Delgan, Fanuj, Bent, Lashar, Ashar, and Ahoran,
     Sistan and Baluchestan (2012–16)

1980–, Sarbaz, Sistan and Baluchestan
BA, business administration, Payam-e Nur University, 2002; MA, executive management, International University of Chabahar, 2011
Bahram, farmer
Civil servant, Ports and Maritime Organization
No imprisonment
Not a war veteran
Arbabi is a Sunni MP.

Arbabifard, Hoseyn

Deputy of the Third Majlis, Ramiyan, Golestan (1988–92)
1957–, Ramiyan, Golestan
Clerical education
Mohammad
Clergyman
No imprisonment
HI Arbabifard is a former employee of IRIB.

Ardakanian, Reza

Minister of Energy in President Rouhani's Second Cabinet (October 29, 2017–21)
1958–, Yazd, Yazd
BS, civil engineering, Sharif University of Technology, 1983; MS, water resources management, McMaster University (Canada); PhD, water resources management, McMaster University (Canada), 1997
Founding Director of the United Nations University's (UNU) Institute for Integrated Management of Material Fluxes and of Resources (2012–17; Dresden, Germany)
No imprisonment
Not a war veteran
Ardakanian held such posts as professor of civil engineering at Yazd University (1998–99) and Sharif University of Technology (since 1999), deputy interior minister for urban development and municipalities (1987–89), deputy energy minister for planning and economic affairs (1989–91), vice minister of energy (1998–2001), deputy energy minister for water affairs (2001–5), and vice rector

of UNU in Europe (2009–11). As an expert in management of water resources, Ardakanian has sat on the boards of such international programs and organizations as the International Hydropower Association, the UNESCO International Hydrological Programme, the UNESCO Institute for Water Education, and the UNU's Institute for Environment and Human Security. He received 225 positive votes, thirty-eight negative votes, and thirteen abstentions on October 29, 2017, when he was confirmed by the Majlis as the minister of energy.

Ardalan, Ali

Minister of economic affairs and finance in PM Bazargan's cabinet (1979)
1914–February 10, 2000, Tehran, Tehran
BA, law, Tehran University; MA, economics and public administration, Tehran University
Mohammad-Vali Khan, tribal chief
Civil servant
Imprisoned before the revolution
Not a war veteran
Member of the central committee of INF
Ardalan completed advanced studies in France and Belgium, and before the revolution, he worked in the Finance Ministry. He began his political activity in the 1940s and was active in journalistic circles. During his tenure as minister of economic affairs and finance, the government nationalized many banks. Ardalan was elected to the First Majlis from Tuyserkan, but the Ministry of Interior did not validate his credentials. The judiciary imprisoned him for thirty months after the revolution for his political activities. Ardalan was the brother-in-law of Karim Sanjabi.

Aref, Mohammad-Reza

Minister of post, telegraph, and telephones (August 20, 1997–August 19, 2000) and then VP and head of the PBO (2000–2001) in President Khatami's first cabinet; first vice president in President

Khatami's second cabinet (2001–5); member of the Fifth (2002–7), Sixth (2007–12), Seventh (2012–17), and Eighth (2017–22) Expediency Discernment Assembly; deputy of the Tenth Majlis, Tehran, Tehran (2016–20)

December 19, 1951–, Yazd, Yazd

BS, electrical engineering, Tehran University, 1975; MS, telecommunications engineering, Stanford University (USA), 1976; PhD, electrical engineering, Stanford University (USA), 1981; dissertation title: "Information Flow in Relay Networks"

Ahmad, rug tradesman

Civil servant

No imprisonment

Not a war veteran

Aref was born into a large family and his father (b. 1927) was a religious man. He lived in the United States from 1975 to 1981 and was active in the Muslim Student Association in the US and Canada. After returning to Iran, Aref taught for more than three decades at Sharif University of Technology and Tehran University, serving as rector of Tehran University from 1994 to 1997. He is the founder and head of Iranians' Hope Foundation and chair of the board of directors of Baran Foundation, which is close to former president Mohammad Khatami. Aref was a candidate during the 2013 presidential election but decided to withdraw in favor of the eventual winner Hassan Rouhani at the request of former president Khatami. During the 2016 Majlis election, he headed the reformist list, known as *Omid* ("Hope"), which swept all thirty seats in Tehran and received the highest number of votes in the capital. He then tried to become the speaker of the parliament but lost the race to Ali Larijani. Aref's wife, Hamideh Moravvej, is a dermatologist who teaches at Tehran University and appeared with him on the campaign trail in 2013.

Arefi, Farajollah

Deputy of the Ninth Majlis, Jiroft and Anbarabad, Kerman (2012–16)

1960–, Jiroft, Kerman

BA, sociology, Payam-e Nur University, 1997; MA, anthropology, Islamic Azad University–Zarand, 2011

Jalal

Provincial civil servant and instructor at Payam-e Nur University

No imprisonment

War veteran (victim of an Iraqi chemical attack)

IRGC militiaman

Martyr's family (brother, Najaf)

Arefi, Seyyed Hasan

Minister of culture and higher education in PM Raja'i's cabinet (1980–81)

1936–, Tehran, Tehran

MD, cardiology

Cardiologist and professor

No imprisonment

Not a war veteran

Arefi completed advanced medical training in New York and in the 1980s was in charge of Ayatollah Khomeini's medical team. He was previously rector of Tehran University (1979), CEO of Shari'ati Hospital, a member of the HCCR, and a faculty member at Tehran University medical school.

Ariya'inezhad, Ahmad

Deputy of the Ninth Majlis, Malayer, Hamadan (2012–16)

1966–, Malayer, Hamadan

MD, medicine, Hamadan University of Medical Sciences

Medical doctor

No imprisonment

Ariya'inezhad ran unsuccessfully for the Tenth Majlis in 2016.

Ariyanmanesh, Javad

Deputy of the Seventh (2004–8) and Eighth (2008–12) Majlis, Mashhad and Kalat, Razavi Khorasan

1953–, Mashhad, Razavi Khorasan
Hasan
MA, education planning
Civil servant
No imprisonment
Head and founding member of the Islamic Society of
Educators of Khorasan Province; founding mem-
ber of the Association of Servants of Construction
of Khorasan [Province]

Arjomand, Seyyed Jamaleddin

Deputy of the Seventh Majlis, Jahrom, Fars (2004–8)
1953–, Jahrom, Fars
MS, architecture; PhD, architecture
Seyyed Hoseyn
Civil servant
No imprisonment
Founding member of the Society of Former Members
of the Islamic Student Associations in Europe

Armin, Mohsen

Deputy of the Sixth Majlis, Tehran, Tehran
(2000–2004)
1954–, Khorramabad, Lorestan
BS, electrical engineering; MA, theology; clerical
education
Ahmad
No imprisonment
War veteran
IRGC militiaman
Member of the central council of OMIRI
Armin joined a radical underground group, Tohidi-ye
Saf, in 1976, and was involved with OMIRI after
1979. Before entering the Majlis, he held posts
such as general manager of publications in the
Ministry of Culture, director of the Center for
Media Studies and Research, Iran's cultural attaché in Lebanon (1986–89), and general manager
of the Foundation for Islamic Thought. Armin
was the editor of *Asr-e ma* (Our Epoch) biweekly,
launched on October 19, 1994. He was disqualified from running in the 1996 Majlis election. The

judiciary imprisoned him for a while in 2010 for
his political activities.

Asadi, Ali

Deputy of the Tenth Majlis, Shahr-e Babak, Kerman
(2016–20)
1964–, Shahr-e Babak, Kerman
MA, public administration
University instructor and education official
No imprisonment
Asadi, who was in charge of the financial affairs for
the Kerman Province department of education
for eleven years, entered the Tenth Majlis as a
reformist.

Asadi, Ne'matollah

Deputy of the Third Majlis, Islamabad-e Gharb, Kermanshah (1988–92)
1957–, Islamabad-e Gharb, Kermanshah
High school diploma
Ja'far
Imprisoned before the revolution (for blowing up
liquor stores in 1978)
Some MPs did not want to approve his credentials due to charges against him such as
embezzlement.

Asadi, Yunes

Deputy of the Eighth (2008–12) and Ninth (2012–16)
Majlis, Meshginshahr, Ardabil
1963–, Meshginshahr, Ardabil
BA, social planning, Allameh Tabataba'i University
Bayram-Ali
Civil servant, lieutenant governor of Meshginshahr
No imprisonment

Asadi-Khansari, Seyyed Mohammad-Baqer

Member of the First (1983–90), Second (1991–98), and
Third (1999–2006) Assembly of Experts, Tehran
1927–2016, Khansar, Markazi

Clerical education
Seyyed Mohammad-Taqi
Clergyman (ayatollah)
No imprisonment
Not a war veteran

Asadiniya, Abdorreza

Deputy of the First (1980–84) and Second (1984–88)
    Majlis, Ahvaz, Khuzestan
1954–, Ahvaz, Khuzestan
Associate's degree
Abdolhoseyn, civil servant
No imprisonment
Not a war veteran

Asadollahi, Gholam-Reza

Deputy of the Eighth (2008–12) and Ninth (2012–
    16) Majlis, Torbat-e Jam and Taybad, Razavi
    Khorasan
1967–, Torbat-e Jam, Razavi Khorasan
BA, law, University of Judicial Sciences and Adminis-
    trative Services; MA, public administration
Habibollah, farmer
Official in the judiciary and the State General Inspec-
    torate Organization
No imprisonment
War veteran
Asadollahi is a former head of revolutionary tribunals
    in Zahedan.

Asafari, Mohammad-Hasan

Deputy of the Ninth Majlis, Arak, Komijan, and
    Khondab, Markazi (2012–16)
1966–, Arak, Markazi
MA, political science
Esma'il
Provincial civil servant
No imprisonment
War veteran (forty-nine months; wounded)
IRGC militiaman (commander in Markazi Province)
Martyr's family (brother)

In addition to fighting in the Iran–Iraq War, Asafari
    also fought in Bosnia and Lebanon. He is the
    former governor of Tafresh and Arak and was
    critical of President Rouhani's foreign policy.

Asgari, Hoseyn

Deputy of the Fifth Majlis, Shahriyar and Robat
    Karim, Tehran (1996–2000)
1955–, Shahriyar, Tehran
BA, education
Ali-Akbar
Teacher
No imprisonment
War veteran

Asgari, Teymurali

Deputy of the Seventh Majlis, Mashhad and Kalat,
    Razavi Khorasan (2004–8)
1960–, Neyshabur, Razavi Khorasan
Clerical education, Qom Seminary
Abbas-Ali
Clergyman
No imprisonment
Not a war veteran
IRGC militiaman
Member of the IRP
HI Asgari was parliamentary deputy to Ayatollah
    Hashemi-Rafsanjani in the EDA and parliamen-
    tary deputy of Islamic Azad University. He was
    a confidant of Abbas Va'ez-Tabasi, the powerful
    guardian of *Astan-e Qods-e Razavi*, and he is also
    close to Ayatollah Khamenei.

Asgarowladi [–Mosalman], Habibollah

Deputy of the First (1980–August 17, 1981) and Fourth
    (1992–96) Majlis, Tehran, Tehran; minister of
    commerce in PM Bahonar's cabinet (August
    17–30, 1981), interim PM Mahdavi-Kani's cabinet
    (September 3–October 18, 1981), and PM Musa-
    vi's first cabinet (November 2, 1981–83); member
    of the Fourth (1997–2002), Fifth (2002–7), Sixth

(2007–12), and Seventh (2012–13) Expediency
  Discernment Assembly
1932–November 5, 2013, Tehran, Tehran
High School (incomplete); religious education, Marvi
  Seminary
Hoseyn, bazaar tradesman
Bazaar merchant
Imprisoned before the revolution
Not a war veteran
Founding member and secretary-general of the CIC/
  PCIC
Asgarowladi was released from prison in early 1977
  after taking part in a controversial ceremony
  praising the shah. After the revolution, in addi-
  tion to being a powerful merchant in the bazaar
  (along with his brother, Assadolah), he also
  became a heavyweight in conservative political
  circles. Asgarowladi survived an assassination
  attempt on July 18, 1981. He resigned from the
  First Majlis to become the minister of commerce.
  Less than two years later, he resigned as minister
  of commerce over policy differences with PM
  Musavi. Asgarowladi ran for the presidency twice
  (1981 and 1985), but the first time he withdrew
  from the race just two days before the vote in
  favor of the eventual president, Mohammad-Ali
  Raja'i. However, his name did appear on the ballot
  and he received around 2 percent of the vote. In
  the 1985 race, he received less than 2 percent of
  the vote. In addition to all his other posts, Asgarowladi was for many years the supreme leader's
  representative on the powerful IKRF, which is the
  largest governmental charity, serving 10 million
  poor people. He was also the brother-in-law of
  Abolfazl Haji-Heydari.

Asghari, Ali-Akbar

Deputy of the First Majlis, Bonab and Malekan, East
  Azerbaijan (1980–October 18, 1981)
1931–October 18, 1981, Bonab, East Azerbaijan
Clerical education
Mohammad
Clergyman

No imprisonment
Not a war veteran
HI Asghari died in a car accident.

Asghari-Bahari, Seyyed Mohammad

Minister of justice in PM Raja'i's cabinet (June 15,
  1981–81), PM Bahonar's cabinet (August 17–30,
  1981), interim PM Mahdavi-Kani's cabinet (September 3–October 18, 1981), and PM Musavi's
  first cabinet (November 2, 1981–84); deputy of
  the Second (1984–88) and Third (1988–92) Majlis,
  Tehran, Tehran
1948–, Bahar, Hamadan
BA, law, Tehran University; MA, law, Tehran
  University
Seyyed Ebrahim, clergyman
Civil servant
No imprisonment
Not a war veteran
Asghari-Bahari replaced Ebrahim Ahadi as minister
  of justice on June 15, 1981. He was previously the
  supreme leader's representative in the *Keyhan*
  media outlet, an ambassador to Bulgaria, and a
  law professor at Tehran University.

Asgharzadeh, Mohammad-Ebrahim

Deputy of the Third Majlis, Tehran, Tehran
  (1988–92)
December 16, 1955–, Khash, Sistan and Baluchestan
BS, electrical engineering, Sharif University of
  Technology, 1978; MA, political science, Tehran
  University
Mohammad-Hoseyn; military officer
No imprisonment
War veteran (commander)
IRGC militiaman
Founding member of OCU; secretary-general of IIPF
Asgharzadeh was the mastermind of the takeover of
  the American embassy and served as a spokes-
  person for the hostage-takers. His wife, Tahereh
  Rezazadeh-Shiraz, who was also involved in
  the hostage takeover, was an MP from Shiraz

in the Sixth Majlis. Asgharzadeh was one of the founders of OCU in 1979. In 1984, he failed to enter the Second Majlis. The judiciary tried him immediately after the Third Majlis ended, and the GC later disqualified him from running in the 1997 and 2001 presidential elections as well as the 1992 and 2004 Majlis election. In 1998, he called for better relations between Iran and the United States. Asgharzadeh, Seyyed Abdolvahed Musavi-Lari, and Abbas Abdi were the first editorial committee of *Salam*. He is the brother-in-law of Mohsen Aminzadeh, who was also involved in the embassy takeover.

Ashrafi, Gholam-Reza

Deputy of the Fifth Majlis, Zabol, Sistan and Baluchestan (1996–2000)
1953–, Zabol, Sistan and Baluchestan
MD, surgery
Mohammad-Hoseyn
Surgeon
No imprisonment

Ashrafi-Isfahani, Mohammad

Deputy of the Second (1984–88) and Third (1988–92) Majlis, Kermanshah, Kermanshah
1944–, Isfahan, Isfahan
Clerical education, Qom Seminary, 1973
Ataollah (1900–1982), clergyman (ayatollah)
Clergyman (HI)
No imprisonment
Not a war veteran
Member of the IRP
Martyr's family (PMOI assassinated his father on October 15, 1982, in Kermanshah)

Ashtari, Hoseyn

Chief of Law Enforcement Forces (March 9, 2015–present)
Date of birth unknown, Isfahan, Isfahan
Morteza

Military official (brigadier general)
War veteran (wounded)
IRGC militiaman
Ashtari, who was previously the chief of LEF's intelligence protection organization, served for nine months as the deputy chief of LEF (May 28, 2014–March 9, 2015) before Ayatollah Khamenei appointed him as its chief.

Ashtiyani-Araqi, Reza

Deputy of the Seventh (2004–8), Eighth (2008–12), and Ninth (2012–16) Majlis, Qom, Qom
1940–, Ashtiyan, Markazi
Clerical education, Qom Seminary
Abbas, farmer
Clergyman (HI)
No imprisonment
Not a war veteran
Founding member of Qom Islamic Society of Admonishers; member and deputy of the SQSS
Ashtiyani-Araqi has been a long-time student of Ayatollah Makarem-Shirazi and was the rector of Payam-e Nur University, Qom. He withdrew from the elections for the Tenth Majlis.

Ashuri-Bandari, Peyman

Deputy of the Sixth Majlis, Bandar-e Mahshahr, Khuzestan (2000–2004)
1967–, Bandar-e Mahshahr, Khuzestan
BA, law
Abossamad
No imprisonment

Ashuri-Qal'erudkhani, Naser

Deputy of the Fifth (1997–2000), Seventh (2004–8), and Ninth (2012–16) Majlis, Fuman and Shaft, Gilan
1958–, Fuman, Gilan
Clerical education (elementary level), Astaneh-ye Ashrafiyyeh Seminary
Abdorrahim, farmer
Civil servant

Imprisoned before the revolution
War veteran
IRGC militiaman (commander in Fuman)
In 2016, Ashuri-Qal'erudkhani became an adviser
  to the minister of cooperatives, labor, and social
  welfare.

Ashuri-Tazyani, Mohammad

Deputy of the Seventh (2004–8), Eighth (2008–12),
  Ninth (2012–16), and Tenth (2016–20) Majlis,
  Bandar-e Abbas, Qeshm, Abumusa, and Hajia-
  bad, Hormozgan
1962–, Bandar-e Abbas, Hormozgan
MA, strategic management; PhD, national security
  studies, Supreme National Defense University
Masha'allah
Political deputy to Hormozgan governor general and
  Bushehr intelligence chief
No imprisonment
IRGC militiaman

Astaneh, Mahmud

Deputy of the Third (1988–92), Fourth (1992–96),
  and Fifth (1996–2000) Majlis, Shazand (Sarband),
  Markazi
1958–, Sarband, Markazi
BA, management, 1992
Ezzatollah
No imprisonment
War veteran
IRGC militiaman

Ata'i, Abdollah

Deputy of the Second Majlis, Sanandaj, Kurdistan
  (1984–June 13, 1986)
1949–June 13, 1986, Rasht, Gilan
High school diploma
Habibollah
No imprisonment
Ata'i died in a car accident.

Atazadeh, Mahmud

Deputy of the Fourth Majlis, Semirom, Isfahan
  (1992–96)
1961–, Shiraz, Fars
BS, agricultural engineering
No imprisonment

Attari, Ahmad

Deputy of the First Majlis, Arak, Markazi (1980–84)
1953–1992, Arak, Markazi
BA, statistics, Tehran University; MS, mathematics,
  University of Southampton (England)
Ali-Akbar, bazaar tradesman
Academia (student)
No imprisonment
Attari was involved with Hojjatiyyeh Society and
  IRP in Arak. Before the revolution, he studied
  for a while in India and England. He was an
  ambassador to Australia, and during President
  Khatami's era, he was a deputy in the Ministry
  of Culture.

Attarzadeh, Shokrollah

Deputy of the Seventh Majlis, Bushehr, Genaveh, and
  Deylam, Bushehr (2004–8)
1960–, Genaveh, Bushehr
BA, law
Taleb
Journalist
No imprisonment
IRGC militiaman

Ava'i, Seyyed Ahmad

Deputy of the Seventh (2004–5) and Eighth (2008–12)
  Majlis, Dezful, Khuzestan
1951–, Dezful, Khuzestan
MA, public administration
Seyyed Asadollah, clergyman
Deputy director of the IRGC's Cooperative
Imprisoned before the revolution (1971–74)

War veteran (1980–84)

IRGC militiaman

Ava'i was a member of the paramilitary Mansurron
group before the revolution, and did not finish his
studies in water engineering at Tehran University.
After being released from prison, he lived underground (1976–77) and then went to Syria and Iraq
(1977–78). He returned to Iran after the revolution
and set up the IRGC in Dezful. Ava'i, who was an
IRGC commander during the Iran–Iraq War, was
sent to Lebanon in 1984 to help train Hezbollah
forces, and stayed there for three years. After Ava'i
completed a program to become a military attaché, the Khuzestan governor-general appointed
him to the post of political-intelligence deputy in
1990. Ava'i then became Iran's military attaché
in Syria (1991–96). Upon returning to Iran, he
became deputy director of the IRGC's Cooperative (1996–2003). The Guardian Council rejected
Ava'i's credentials for the Ninth and Tenth Majlis.
During the tenure of President Rouhani, he became a deputy minister of commerce and in 2016
was appointed SNSC's parliamentary deputy. He
is the older brother of minister of justice Seyyed
Ali-Reza Ava'i.

Ava'i, Seyyed Ali-Reza

Minister of justice in President Rouhani's second
cabinet (August 20, 2017–21)

May 20, 1956–, Dezful, Khuzestan

BA, law, University of Judicial Sciences-Qom; MA,
private law, Tehran University

Seyyed Asadollah, clergyman

No imprisonment

Ava'i joined the Ministry of Justice after the 1979
revolution. He was the prosecutor-general of
Dezful (appointed December 30, 1980) and Ahvaz
(appointed June 8, 1993) and was involved in the
execution of political prisoners. He also served
as the prosecutor of Kurdistan (1983–86), head of
the justice administration in Lorestan (1994–98),
Markazi (1998–2004), Isfahan (2004–5) and
Tehran Provinces (2005–15), and judge of the

State Supreme Court. In 2015, he became deputy
interior minister and head of the State Organization for Registration of Deeds and Properties.
In 2016, President Rouhani appointed him head
of the Special Inspection Bureau at the Office of
President Rouhani until he was chosen as minister of justice. In October 10, 2011, the Council
of the European Union listed Ava'i among some
thirty Iranian officials banned from entering the
European Union on charges of human rights violations. He is the younger brother of former MP
Ahmad Ava'i.

Ayat, Seyyed Hasan

Member of the Assembly for the Final Examination
of the Constitution, Isfahan (1979); deputy of the
First Majlis, Tehran, Tehran (1980–August 5, 1981)

1938–August 5, 1981, Najafabad, Isfahan

BA, education, Tehran's Higher Teachers Training
College; BA, law, Tehran University, 1966; MA,
sociology, Tehran University, 1961; PhD could not
be verified

Seyyed Mohammad-Reza, clergyman and farmer

University lecturer

No imprisonment

War veteran

Member of Toilers Party (before the revolution); head
of the political bureau of the IRP

Ayat, one of the main ideologues of the IRP, was the
party's candidate for the 1980 presidential election
but had to withdraw at the last minute. After the
revolution, he was also involved with the formation of the IRGC and was on the leadership council of the AFEC. Ayat masterminded the campaign
that led to the downfall of President Banisadr, but
PMOI assassinated him on August 5, 1981.

Ayati, Mehdi

Deputy of the Sixth Majlis, Birjand, South Khorasan
(2000–2004)

1957–, Birjand, South Khorasan

MA, architecture and urban planning

Mohammad-Hoseyn
Civil servant
No imprisonment

Ayatollahi, Seyyed Mohammad-Reza

Minister of mining and metals in PM Musavi's second
    cabinet (January 5, 1986–August 3, 1989)
1950–, Qom, Qom
BS, electrical engineering, Tabriz University
Seyyed Fakhrolislam, clergyman
Civil servant
No imprisonment
Not a war veteran

Ayyubi, Mohammad

Deputy of the Second Majlis, Bojnurd, North Kho-
    rasan (1986–88)
1948–, Bojnurd, North Khorasan
Clerical education
Abbas-Ali
Clergyman
No imprisonment

Azadikhah, Ahad

Deputy of the Tenth Majlis, Malayer, Hamadan
    (2016–20)
1975–, Malayer, Hamadan
Clerical education, Qom Seminary
Clergyman and high-level official in the Theological
    Seminaries Center for Services in Qom
No imprisonment
Not a war veteran
HI Azadikhah was director-general of the Islamic
    Propaganda Organization in Hamadan and Kurd-
    istan Provinces, and he was a teacher at Hamadan
    Seminary.

Azadmanesh, Azadi

Deputy of the Sixth Majlis, Gonabad, Razavi Kho-
    rasan (2000–2004)

1943–, Gonabad, Razavi Khorasan
PhD, sociology
Mahmud
Academia
No imprisonment

A'zami, Maqsud

Deputy of the Sixth Majlis, Naqadeh and Oshnavi-
    yyeh, West Azerbaijan (2001–2004)
1965–, Oshnaviyyeh, West Azerbaijan
BA, law
Abdolbani
Academia
No imprisonment
A'zami was a Sunni member of the Majlis who be-
    come a civil servant.

A'zami [-Lorestani], Morteza

Deputy of the First Majlis, Khorramabad, Lorestan
    (1980–84)
1918–1991, Khorramabad, Lorestan
Pre-diploma
Ali-Mardan, landowner
Farmer
Imprisoned before the revolution
Not a war veteran
His son, Dr. Houshang A'zami (1936–76), was killed in
    May 1976 in a shoot-out with security forces.

Azar, Adel

Deputy of the Seventh Majlis, Dehloran, Darrehshahr,
    and Abdanan, Ilam (2004–8)
1966–, Dehloran, Ilam
BS, industrial engineering, Allameh Tabataba'i Uni-
    versity, 1988; MS, industrial engineering, Tarbi-
    yat-e Modarres University, 1991; PhD, industrial
    engineering, Tehran University, 1995
Heydar, farmer
Academia
No imprisonment
War veteran

IRGC militiaman

After leaving the Majlis, Azar, a conservative, held posts such as head of the Statistical Center of Iran and head of the State Audit Court (appointed in 2016).

Azari-Jahromi, Mohammad-Javad

Minister of information and communications technology in President Rouhani's second cabinet (August 20, 2017–21)

1981–, Jahrom, Fars

BS, electrical engineering, Power and Water University of Technology

Deputy minister of information and communications technology (2016–17)

No imprisonment

Not a war veteran

Martyr's family

Azari-Jahromi was a technical expert in the Ministry of Intelligence from 2005 to 2009. He was then head of the security of communication systems for the Communications Regulatory Authority from 2009 to 2014. He was accused of having filtered the internet in Iran in the above capacities. Azari-Jahromi is the first person born after the 1979 revolution to serve as a minister in any cabinet. Of all the ministers who were approved by the Majlis on August 20, 2017, to serve on President Rouhani's second cabinet, he received the fewest positive votes (152 out of 288).

Azari-Qomi [Bigdeli-Azari], Ahmad

Revolutionary prosecutor-general of Tehran (July 2–September 16, 1979); deputy of the Second Majlis, Qom, Qom (1984–88); chief judge of the SCFC (1986–87); member of the First (1983–90) and Second (1991–95) Assembly of Experts, Tehran

1925–February 11, 1999, Qom, Qom

Clerical education, Najaf Seminary (Iraq), 1945

Hoseyn-Ali, clergyman-farmer

Clergyman

Imprisoned and exiled before the revolution

Not a war veteran

Founding member and secretary of the SQSS

Ayatollah Azari-Qomi was Ayatollah Khomeini's representative in Qom's revolutionary court and Ma'sume Shrine, and served for only two and a half months as the first revolutionary prosecutor-general of Tehran before resigning. He was head of the Prophet's Foundation (Bonyad-e Resallat) as well as the first secretary of the Society of Qom Seminary Scholars, but later in life resigned from this society. Azari-Qomi's economic views were close to that of the bazaar but he was a hardliner in terms of application of the Islamic penal code. In the 1980s, he was a harsh critic of the economic policies of PM Mir Hoseyn Musavi. On August 5, 1984, during a Majlis speech, he argued that the supreme leader (Ayatollah Khomeini at the time) had no right to tell the Majlis what to do. Azari-Qomi was a very articulate conservative and the proprietor of *Resalat*, which began publishing on January 9, 1986. By the mid-1990s, Azari-Qomi severed his ties with the newspaper due to differences of opinion. In 1989, as a member of the Council for the Revision of the Constitution, Azari-Qomi strongly advocated for the concept of the absolute mandate of the jurist. In 1995, he also declared that he had resigned from the Second AE. In a thirty-four-page letter to President Khatami dated October 27, 1997, Azari-Qomi openly questioned the credentials of Ayatollah Khamenei as the supreme leader. Khamenei's supporters responded by raiding his house and that of Grand Ayatollah Montazeri. The regime ordered the house arrest of Azari-Qomi, which remained in effect until he passed away from cancer in early 1999.

Azarkish, Madad

Deputy of the Fourth Majlis, Zahedan, Sistan and Baluchestan (1992–96)

1955–, Zabol, Sistan and Baluchestan

BA, theology

Karim

No imprisonment

Azarvash, Vali

Deputy of the Sixth (2000–2004) and Seventh (2004–8) Majlis, Ardabil, Namin, and Nir, Ardabil
1964–, Ardabil, Ardabil
BS, civil engineering; MS, systems management
Behruz
Mayor of Ardabil
No imprisonment
Not a war veteran
Azarvash was in charge of refurbishing the schools in the province of Ardabil and then became mayor of Ardabil before entering the Sixth Majlis. The GC rejected his qualifications for the Eighth Majlis, and then reversed the decision, but he did not manage to receive enough votes. He is a reformist politician who later worked in the municipality of Tehran.

Azimi, Seyyed Ahmad

Deputy of the Sixth Majlis, Shiraz, Fars (2000–2004)
1954–, Abadeh, Fars
MS, physics
Seyyed Abdolali
No imprisonment

Azimi-Taraqdari, Mohammad

Deputy of the Third (1988–92) and Fifth (1996–2000) Majlis, Torqabeh and Chenaran, Razavi Khorasan
1953–, Mashhad, Razavi Khorasan
BA, 1982; MA, management, 1994
Gholam-Reza
No imprisonment
Founding member of the ISFPD

Azin, Hoseyn

Deputy of the Ninth Majlis, Rafsanjan and Anar, Kerman (2012–16)
1966–, Rafsanjan, Kerman
MD, neurologist
Medical doctor and medical school administrator

No imprisonment
War veteran (wounded; POW)
IRGC militiaman (Basij)
Azin was the chief of the Iranian Hospital in Dubai.

Azizi, Abdorreza

Deputy of the Ninth Majlis, Shiravan, North Khorasan (2012–16)
1968–, Shiravan, North Khorasan
MD, medicine, Mashhad University of Medical Sciences, 1998
Civil servant, ministries
No imprisonment
War veteran (wounded)
Azizi finished second in Shiravan and ran unsuccessfully for the Eighth Majlis.

Azizi, Ahmad

Deputy of the Second (1984–88) and Third (1988–92) Majlis, Qazvin, Qazvin
1943–, Qazvin, Qazvin
MA, management
Ebrahim
Civil servant
No imprisonment
Azizi was active in the Muslim Student Association in the United States before the revolution. In the early 1980s, he was an economic deputy in the Ministry of Foreign Affairs. After serving in the Majlis, he became a deputy minister of foreign affairs and served as ambassador to Germany.

Azizi, Ebrahim [Mohammad]

Deputy of the Fifth Majlis, Kermanshah, Kermanshah (1996–2000); member of the Fourth (2001–4) and Fifth (2004–October 2009) Guardian Councils; VP for management and human capital development in President Ahmadinejad's first cabinet (2007–9); VP for planning and strategic supervision (October 2009–May 2012) and later VP for management and human capital development

(May 28, 2012–13) in President Ahmadinejad's
second cabinet
1963–, Kermanshah, Kermanshah
MA, law; PhD, law
Qanbar
No imprisonment
Not a war veteran
Azizi resigned from the Fifth GC in October 2009
to become VP for planning and strategic
supervision.

Azizi, Mohammad

Deputy of the Tenth Majlis, Abhar, Zanjan (2016–20)
1975–, Tehran, Tehran
BA, political science, 1998; MA, urban management,
2009; pursuing a PhD in educational management
at Payam–e Nur University
Deputy district governor in Tehran's municipality
No imprisonment
Not a war veteran
Prior to entering the Majlis, Azizi was an employee of
IRIB (2000–2004), an official in Tehran's mu-
nicipality (2004–5; 2012–15), governor of Abhar
(2005–7), mayor of Zanjan (2007–9), and direc-
tor-general of public relations at the Ministry of
Economic Affairs and Finance (2009–12).

Azizi, Qasem

Deputy of the Sixth (2000–2004), Seventh (2004–8),
and Ninth (2012–16) Majlis, Shazand, Markazi
1955–, Shazand, Markazi
BS, accounting, Islamic Azad University–Arak
Sardar, farmer
Tax controller in Markazi Province
No imprisonment
War veteran

Azizi-Farsani, Hamid-Reza

Deputy of the Ninth Majlis, Ardal, Farsan, Kuhrang,
and Kiyar, Chahar Mahal and Bakhtiari (2012–16)
1970–, Farsan, Chahar Mahal and Bakhtiari

MD, medicine, Shahrekord University of Medical
Sciences, 1995
Nosratollah
Anesthesiologist and medical administrator
No imprisonment
Not a war veteran
Martyr's family (brother)

Azodi, Hasan

Member of the Assembly for the Final Examination of
the Constitution, Gilan (1979)
1946–1981, Rasht, Gilan
BA, journalism, Tehran University; MBA, business
administration, University of Dallas (USA), 1976;
PhD, economics, University of Dallas (unverified)
Mohammad-Ali, bazaar tradesman
Academia
No imprisonment
Not a war veteran
Member of the IRP
Azodi served as head of the State Educational Assess-
ment Organization and as a deputy in the Minis-
try of Culture before he was killed in the bombing
of the IRP headquarters.

Babaahmadi-Milani, Abdolmohammad

Deputy of the Eighth Majlis, Lordegan, Chahar Mahal
and Bakhtiari (2009–12)
1958–, Lordegan, Chahar Mahal and Bakhtiari
BA, law
Ali-Akbar
No imprisonment
Babaahmadi-Milani was elected to the Eighth Majlis
in interim elections but was not elected to the
Ninth Majlis.

Baba'i, Alibaba

Deputy of the First (1982–84) and Second (1984–88)
Majlis, Esfarayen, North Khorasan
1944–, Esfarayen, North Khorasan
Clerical education

Baba
Clergyman
No imprisonment
Not a war veteran
HI Baba'i was the head of a local revolutionary
   komiteh, and was skillful in creating propaganda.

Baba'i-Saleh, Ruhollah

Deputy of the Tenth Majlis, Bu'inzahra, Qazvin
   (2016–20)
1978–, Ardaq, Qazvin
MA, educational management
Political activist
No imprisonment
Not a war veteran

Babakhas, Ali-Mohammad

Deputy of the Third Majlis, Paveh and Uramanat,
   Kermanshah (1988–92)
1954–1997, Paveh, Kermanshah
High school diploma
Mohammad–Ali
No imprisonment
War veteran
IRGC militiaman
Babakhas was a Sunni Kurd who served as mayor of
   Paveh.

Babasafari-Zamani, Mohammad-Reza

Deputy of the First Majlis, Borkhar, Isfahan (1980–84)
1948–, Isfahan, Isfahan
BA, political science
Hasan, civil servant
No imprisonment

Badamchi, Mohammad-Reza

Deputy of the Tenth Majlis, Tehran, Tehran (2016–20)
1941–, Tehran, Tehran
BS, textile engineering, Amirkabir University of Technology, 1965; MA, public administration

War veteran (seven months)
Member of the central council of the Islamic Labor
   Party
Badamchi has established a number of textile companies in Iran, including Shadilon Textile Group
   Co., of which he is the CEO. He was the general
   manager for economic planning in the office of
   the governor-general of East Azerbaijan. In 2000,
   he was a leading campaign organizer for the
   reformist coalition.

Badamchiyan, Asadollah

Deputy of the Second (1984–88) and Eighth (2008–12)
   Majlis, Tehran, Tehran
1941–, Tehran, Tehran
MA, political science; PhD, international relations
Mohammad-Baqer, carpet seller
Political deputy to the head of the judiciary
Imprisoned before the revolution
Not a war veteran
Member of the central council of the CIC/PCIC;
   founding member of the Islamic Society of
   Educators
Badamchiyan, a bazaar merchant, gained his re-
   lease from prison in early 1977 after taking part
   in a controversial ceremony praising the shah.
   The maternal side of the family, including his
   uncle Sa'id Amani [-Hamadani], has been very
   active in the CIC/PCIC. He is the son-in-law of
   Sa'id Amani [-Hamadani]. The Badamchiyan
   and Amani [-Hamadani] families were active in
   both the bazaar and the security sector after the
   revolution.

Badri, Sadif

Deputy of the Tenth Majlis, Ardabil, Ardabil
   (2016–20)
1972–, Germi, Ardabil
BS, civil engineering, Imam Hoseyn University, 1995;
   MS, civil engineering, Tabriz University, 1998
Anamollah
Mayor of Ardabil (2011–15)

Badri has held a variety of provincial government posts in Ardabil and East Azerbaijan Provinces, including mayor of Germi (for seven months) and mayor of Ardabil.

Baghani, Ali-Asghar

Deputy of the First (1980–84) and Fourth (1992–96) Majlis, Sabzevar, Razavi Khorasan
1934–, Sabzevar, Razavi Khorasan
Clerical education
Abbas, clergyman
Clergyman
No imprisonment
Not a war veteran
HI Baghani was an IRP candidate in the First Majlis and was wounded in the June 28, 1981, bombing of the IRP headquarters. He advocated putting the American hostages on trial if the shah was not returned to Iran.

Baghbaniyan, Ali

Deputy of the Fifth (1997–2000), Sixth (2000–2004), and Seventh (2004–8) Majlis, Qamsar, Natanz, and Niyasar, Isfahan
1959–, Natanz, Isfahan
MD, psychology
Ja'far
Psychologist
No imprisonment
In 2016, Baghbaniyan ran for the Tenth Majlis from Natanz but finished second and could not become an MP.

Baghumian, Artavaz

Deputy of the Second (1984–88), Third (1988–92), Fourth (1992–96), and Fifth (1996–2000) Majlis, representing Armenians of southern Iran (as a religious minority)
1953–, Faridan, Isfahan
BS, accounting; MS
Setrak

No imprisonment
Baghumian holds the record, along with fellow Armenian MP Vartan Vartanian, as the MP most frequently elected to represent a religious minority.

Bahadori, Seyyed Hadi

Deputy of the Tenth Majlis, Urmia, West Azerbaijan (2016–20)
1978–, Urmia, West Azerbaijan
BS, civil engineering, Sharif University of Technology, 2000; MS, civil engineering, Tehran University, 2002; PhD, civil engineering, Tehran University, 2008
Father's name unknown, teacher
Engineer and professor at Urmia University
No imprisonment
Not a war veteran

Bahari-Ardeshiri, Abbas-Ali

Deputy of the First (1981–84) and Second (1984–88) Majlis, Sari, Mazandaran
1949–, Sari, Mazandaran
Clerical education; BA, Arabic language and literature, Tehran University
Qasem-Ali
Clergyman
No imprisonment
Not a war veteran
Bahari-Ardeshiri, a former teacher, was involved with propaganda within the IRGC.

Baharvand, Abdorrahim

Deputy of the Sixth Majlis, Khorramabad, Lorestan (2000–2004)
1959–, Khorramabad, Lorestan
PhD, physics
Nurmohammad
University professor
No imprisonment
Baharvand ran unsuccessfully for the Tenth Majlis from Karaj.

Bahmaei, Shamsollah

Deputy of the Ninth Majlis, Ramhormoz and Ramshir, Khuzestan (2012–16)

1970–, Ramhormoz, Khuzestan

MA, public administration; pursuing a PhD in management

University administrator

No imprisonment

Not a war veteran

After serving in the Majlis, Bahmaei was employed at the Petroleum Ministry's Management Development Center.

Bahmani, Mahmud

Governor of the Central Bank (2008–13); deputy of the Tenth Majlis, Savojblagh, Nazarabad, and Taleqan, Alborz (2016–20)

1947–, Fashand, Alborz

BA, economics, Allameh Tabataba'i University; MA, banking, Iran Banking Institute; PhD, business administration

Father's name unknown, farmer

Employee of Bank Melli Iran (since 1968)

No imprisonment

Not a war veteran

Bahmani was the governor of the Central Bank when Iran was facing some of the toughest sanctions due to its nuclear program. He was on the board of directors of Bank Melli from 2000 to 2007, and he has taught courses on banking for over three decades.

Bahmani, Mrs. Mahnaz

Deputy of the Ninth Majlis, Sarab, East Azerbaijan (2012–16)

1970–, Sarab, East Azerbaijan

MA, management, Islamic Azad University–Tabriz

Hushang, military officer

High school teacher

No imprisonment

Martyr's family (father was killed at the war front in 1980)

In 2012, Bahmani won the election to the Ninth Majlis after having lost a son. Four years later, the GC disqualified her from the Tenth Majlis. Bahmani then returned to the Science Ministry, where she worked prior to her term in the Majlis.

Bahme'i, Mohammad-Reza

Deputy of the Third (1988–92), Fourth (1992–96), and Fifth (1997–2000) Majlis, Ramhormoz and Ramshir, Khuzestan

1945–, Ramhormoz, Khuzestan

MS, hydraulics engineering

Hoseyn

No imprisonment

Bahme'i ran unsuccessfully for the Tenth Majlis.

Bahonar, Mohammad-Javad

Member of the Revolutionary Council (1979–80); member of the Assembly for the Final Examination of the Constitution, Kerman (1979); deputy of the First Majlis, Kerman, Kerman (May 20, 1980–May 26, 1981); minister of education in PM Raja'i's cabinet (November 25, 1980–August 1, 1981); prime minister (August 5–August 30, 1981)

1933–1981, Kerman, Kerman

BA, literature, Tehran University, 1958; MA, education, Tehran University; PhD, theology, Tehran University; clerical education, Qom Seminary

Ali-Asghar, tradesman

Clergyman

Imprisoned before the revolution

Not a war veteran

Founding member and secretary-general of the IRP; founding member of the SCC

HI Bahonar, a former student of Ayatollah Khomeini, was active in writing school textbooks before the revolution. In mid-1979, he became deputy minister of education. He became secretary-general of the IRP after the assassination of Ayatollah

Beheshti. Bahonar was also a member of the Headquarters for Cultural Revolution. The Majlis approved PM Bahonar's cabinet on August 17, 1981, but Bahonar was killed in a bombing assassination along with President Raja'i on August 30, 1981. The University of Kerman was renamed Shahid Bahonar University of Kerman in his memory.

Bahonar, Mohammad-Reza

Deputy of the Second Majlis, Baft, Kerman (1984–88); deputy of the Third (1988–92), Fourth (1992–96), Fifth (1996–2000), Eighth (2008–12), and Ninth (2012–16) Majlis, Tehran, Tehran; deputy of the Seventh (2004–8) Majlis, Kerman, Kerman; member of the Fifth (2002–7), Sixth (2007–12), Seventh (2012–17), and Eighth (2017–22) Expediency Discernment Assembly

1952–, Kerman, Kerman
BS, architecture, Iran University of Science and Technology; MA, economics, Allameh Tabataba'i University
Ali-Asghar, laborer
Civil servant
No imprisonment
Not a war veteran
Martyr's family (brother, Mohammad-Javad)
Member of the central council of the IRP; founder and member of the central council of the Islamic Society of Engineers
Bahonar, the younger brother of slain former PM Mohammad-Javad Bahonar, was an MP for seven terms. He was elected to the Second Majlis after his brother was killed in a bombing assassination that also killed President Raja'i. He was only unsuccessful in the elections for the Sixth Majlis when the reformists won by a landslide. Bahonar, a powerful conservative politician, was the deputy speaker of the Majlis from 2004 to 2010 and again from 2011 to 2016. He and like-minded colleagues founded the influential Islamic Society of Engineers in 1991. In 2013, he registered to run in the presidential election. His son married the granddaughter of Ali-Akbar Mohtashamipur.

Bahrami, Ahmad

Deputy of the First Majlis, Paveh, Kermanshah (1981–84)
1950–, Paveh, Kermanshah
Clerical education
Mostafa
Clergyman
No imprisonment
Bahrami was a Sunni MP.

Bahrami, Mohammad-Baqer

Deputy of the Second (1984–88), Fourth (1992–96), and Seventh (2004–8) Majlis, Asadabad, Hamadan
1955–, Asadabad, Hamadan
Associate's degree, 1978; BA, management, 1990; PhD, law
Alidad
Academia
No imprisonment

Bahrami, Mohammad-Kazem

Head of CAJ (April 10, 2016–present)
Clerical education
Clergyman
HI Bahrami was head of the Judicial Organization of the Armed Forces before becoming head of CAJ. On October 10, 2011, the Council of the European Union put Bahrami on its list of sanctioned individuals and wrote that he was "complicit in the repression of peaceful demonstrators" during the 2009 protests.

Bahrami-Ahmadi, Hamid

Deputy of the Seventh Majlis, Rafsanjan, Kerman (2004–8)
1942–, Rafsanjan, Kerman

BA, law, Tehran University; MA, law, Tehran University; PhD, law, Tehran University
Hoseyn, farmer
Academia
Imprisonment before the revolution (1971–73)
Bahrami-Ahmadi was affiliated with PMOI before the revolution. He became the first governor of Kerman after the revolution and then governor of Sistan and Baluchestan for a few months. Bahrami-Ahmadi spent six years in the Netherlands representing Iran in legal cases at the International Court of Justice in The Hague. He was elected to the Fifth Majlis, but the GC rejected his credentials.

Bahrami-Hasanabadi, Qahreman

Deputy of the Sixth Majlis, Mobarakeh, Isfahan (2000–2004)
1947–, Mobarakeh, Isfahan
BA, management
Mohammad
Civil servant
No imprisonment

Bahrami-Khoshkar, Mohammad

Member of the Fourth (2007–16) and Fifth (2016–22) Assembly of Experts, Kerman
1962–, Baft, Kerman
PhD, law; clerical education
Hoseyn, farmer
Academia
No imprisonment

Bahramnia, Hasan

Deputy of the Tenth Majlis, Nahavand, Hamadan (2016–20)
1964–, Nahavand, Hamadan
BS, civil engineering, Tabriz University, 1995; MA, geography and urban planning, 2009; pursuing a PhD degree in geography and urban planning

No imprisonment
War veteran
IRGC militiaman
Bahramnia, the commander of an IRGC division during the Iran–Iraq War, joined the NIOC in 1989. He has since held various municipal posts in Hamadan Province, including that of governor of Tuyserkan, as well as the political-security deputy for the border province of Ilam.

Bakhshayesh-Ardestani, Ahmad

Deputy of the Ninth Majlis, Ardestan, Isfahan (2012–16)
1961–, Ardestan, Isfahan
MA, political science, Imam Sadeq University, 1988; PhD, political science, University of New South Wales (Australia), 1995; dissertation title: "The Nature of Shiite State: An Attempt at Defining an Ethical Theory of State and Its Dilemmas in Modern World"
Father's name unknown, farmer
Professor of political science at Tehran University
No imprisonment
War veteran
IRGC militiaman

Bakhshi [-Nowaab], Hoseyn

Deputy of the First Majlis, Ramhormoz, Khuzestan (1981–84)
1948–, Saveh, Markazi
Clerical education
Dust-Ali
Clergyman
No imprisonment
Not a war veteran

Bakhtiar, Ali

Deputy of the Tenth Majlis, Golpayegan and Khansar, Isfahan (2016–20)
1973–, Tehran, Tehran

BS, electrical engineering; MS, management information systems, Tarbiyat-e Modarres University
Mostafa
Employee of the State General Inspectorate Organization (since 1998)
Not a war veteran

Bakhtiari, Ali

Deputy of the Tenth Majlis, Baft, Kerman (2016–20)
1957–, Baft, Kerman
BS, engineering; MA, public administration
Civil servant
No imprisonment
Bakhtiari was active in the Agricultural Jihad in Baft, and he was executive director of a pasteurized milk company in Kerman from 2004 to 2010. He entered the Tenth Majlis as a reformist.

Bakhtiari, Mohammad-Taqi

Deputy of the Eighth Majlis, Baft, Kerman (2008–12)
1960–, Baft, Kerman
BS, civil engineering; MA, public administration
Hamzeh
Civil servant
No imprisonment

Bakhtiari, Seyyed Morteza

Minister of justice in President Ahmadinejad's second cabinet (September 3, 2009–August 3, 2013)
1952–, Mashhad, Razavi Khorasan
Clerical education
Provincial civil servant
No imprisonment
Not a war veteran
Bakhtiari was in charge of the State Prisons Organization (until June 2004) and then became governor-general of Isfahan Province before becoming a minister. After serving in the cabinet, he became deputy prosecutor-general. In October 10, 2011, the Council of the European Union put Bakhtiari on its sanctioned list and wrote: "As Minister of Justice, he has played a key role in threatening and harassing the Iranian diaspora by announcing the establishment of a special court to deal specifically with Iranians who live outside the country."

Bameri, Golmohammad

Deputy of the Seventh Majlis, Iranshahr and Sarbaz, Sistan and Baluchestan (2005–8)
1962–, Iranshahr, Sistan and Baluchestan
Khodabakhsh
No imprisonment
Bameri was elected in interim elections in June 2005, and he became a political-security deputy to the governor-general of Hormozgan for a couple of years after leaving the Majlis.

Bana'i, Hamid

Deputy of the Tenth Majlis, Gonabad, Razavi Khorasan (2016–20)
1967–, Gonabad, Razavi Khorasan
BS, civil engineering, University of Sistan and Baluchestan; MS, agricultural engineering, Islamic Azad University–Gonabad; pursuing a PhD in management
War veteran
IRGC militiaman (Basij)
Bana'i was active in the Construction Jihad in Sistan and Baluchestan and Gonabad, and served twice as the mayor of Gonabad.

Bana'i-Qomi, Ali

Deputy of the Seventh (2004–8) and Eighth (2008–12) Majlis, Qom, Qom
1959–, Qom, Qom
Clerical education
Asadollah
Clergyman (HI) and political-security deputy of Qom Province

No imprisonment

Not a war veteran

Secretary-general of the Association for Coordination of the Followers of Imam and the Leader in Qom Province

Bana'i-Qomi ran unsuccessfully for the Ninth Majlis.

Baniasadi, Mohammad-Hoseyn

Ministerial adviser for revolutionary affairs (1979) and then ministerial adviser for executive affairs (September 28–November 5, 1979) in PM Bazargan's cabinet

1942–, Isfahan, Isfahan

BS, engineering sciences, Purdue University (USA), 1965; MS, industrial engineering, Illinois Institute of Technology (USA), 1967; PhD, systems management, University of Pennsylvania (USA), 1983

Mohammad-Baqer, textile merchant

Management consultant (1970–79)

Imprisoned before the revolution

Not a war veteran

Member of the central council of the LMI

Baniasadi taught at the University of Isfahan from 1967 to 1970. He was in charge of the cultural section of *Mizan* (the organ of the LMI) before the judiciary closed it down. He is the son-in-law of former PM Mehdi Bazargan.

Banifazl, Morteza

Member of the First Assembly of Experts, West Azerbaijan (1983–90); member of the Second (1991–98) and Fourth (2007) Assembly of Experts, East Azerbaijan

1933–2007, Tabriz, East Azerbaijan

Clerical education, Qom Seminary

Seyfali, bazaar tradesman

Clergyman (ayatollah)

No imprisonment

Not a war veteran

Member of the SQSS

Ayatollah Khomeini appointed Banifazl, his former student, as his representative in the Azerbaijan region.

Banihashemi-Chaharom, Seyyed Hashem

Deputy of the Third (1988–92), Fourth (1992–96), and Ninth (2012–16) Majlis, Mashhad, Razavi Khorasan

1949–, Mashhad, Razavi Khorasan

BS, civil engineering, Iran University of Science and Technology, 1976

Seyyed Hasan

Civil servant, Construction Jihad

Imprisoned before the revolution

War veteran

Founding member of the Islamic Society of Khorasan Engineers

Banihashemi-Chaharom was mayor of Mashhad from 2003 to 2007, and was the first governor of Qom.

Banisadr, Seyyed Abolhasan

Member of the Revolutionary Council (1979–80); member of the Assembly for the Final Examination of the Constitution, Tehran (1979); minister of economic affairs and finance in the Revolutionary Council cabinet (November 11, 1979–February 4, 1980); president (February 4, 1980–June 21, 1981)

1933–, Hamadan, Hamadan

BA, Islamic studies, Tehran University, 1956; BA, economics, Tehran University, 1960

Seyyed Nasrollah, clergyman (ayatollah)

Imprisoned before the revolution (for a few months)

Not a war veteran

Member of INF

The son of an ayatollah, Banisadr married his wife, Ozra Hoseyni, in September 1961. He went to Europe in 1963 to study economics, but he never defended his PhD dissertation, which was on foreign private investment in Iran. While living in France, he was very active in opposition to the shah's regime. In August 1979, he received the second highest number of votes in Tehran in the election for the Assembly for the Final Examination of the Constitution, where he opposed the principle of *velayat-e faqih*. He was elected Iran's first postrevolutionary president on January 25, 1980, with 75.7 percent of the popular vote, and he functioned in that capacity until the Majlis dismissed him on June 21, 1981. After his dismissal, Banisadr was forced to flee the country and has been living in exile outside of Paris since then. Iraq's invasion of Iran happened on his watch and augmented his differences with the clerical establishment.

Banisadr, Seyyed Fathollah

Prosecutor-general (1979–80)
1921–October 21, 1997, Hamadan, Hamadan
BA, law
Seyyed Nasrollah, clergyman (ayatollah)
Lawyer and judge
Imprisoned before the revolution
Not a war veteran
Seyyed Fathollah Banisadr, the older brother of former president Abolhasan Banisadr, was an experienced judge before the revolution. He helped draft the first text of the postrevolutionary Constitution, and ran unsuccessfully for the First Majlis.

Banki, Mohammad-Taqi

Ministerial adviser and head of the PBO in PM Bahonar's cabinet (August 17–30, 1981), interim PM Mahdavi-Kani's cabinet (September 3–October 18, 1981), and PM Musavi's first cabinet (November 2, 1981–October 27, 1985); minister of energy in PM Musavi's second cabinet (October 28, 1985–June 12, 1987)
1946–, Tehran, Tehran
BS, civil engineering, Tehran University, 1971; MS, civil engineering, North Carolina State University (USA), 1973; PhD, civil engineering, University

of Missouri (USA), 1980; dissertation title: "The Relationship Between the Mental Environment of Workers and the Incidence of Injuries"
Reza, medical doctor (eye specialist)
Civil servant
No imprisonment
Not a war veteran
Banki graduated from Alavi High School and went to the United States in 1971 to pursue graduate studies. In the early 1980s, he was deputy minister for administrative and financial affairs in the Labor Ministry and adviser to the supervisor of the FDWI. He was chiefly responsible for the first postrevolutionary five-year development plan. After he finished his term as energy minister, he became the CEO of the Steel Company of Iran in 1989. Banki is a former chairman of the Organization of National Industries of Iran, and was a professor (now retired) at Amirkabir University. His wife is the daughter of well-known preacher Mohammad-Taqi Falsafi. The philosopher Abdolkarim Soroush was married to Banki's sister for a while.

Baqa'i, Habib

Commander of the Islamic Republic of Iran Air Force (January 26, 1995–May 27, 2001); deputy general commander of the army (May 26, 2004–September 26, 2005)
1950–, Shiraz, Fars
Military pilot
BS, military science, Ground Forces Officers' Academy
No imprisonment
War veteran
Brigadier General Baqa'i entered the Ground Forces Officers' Academy in 1969 and completed training as a pilot in the United States.

Baqa'i, Hamid

VP and head of the Cultural Heritage, Handicrafts, and Tourism Organization (2009–11) and then

VP for executive affairs (2011–13) in President
   Ahmadinejad's second cabinet
1969–, Hamadan, Hamadan
BS, information technology (online degree)
Civil servant
No imprisonment
Not a war veteran
Baqa'i worked in IRIB before retiring from his post
   on October 23, 2011. He was part of Ahmadinejad's team in Tehran and served as chief of staff
   of Esfandiyar Rahimmasha'i's office there. Baqa'i
   was appointed by President Ahmadinejad as a
   special envoy for Asia in addition to heading the
   Iran Cultural Heritage, Handcrafts, and Tourism
   Organization. He is also a former director of Iran
   Free and Special Economic Zones. The judiciary
   imprisoned Baqa'i for some seven months in 2015
   for financial wrongdoings until he was released
   on the order of Ayatollah Khamenei, only to be
   rearrested in early 2018. The GC disqualified him
   from running in the 2017 presidential election.

Baqeri, Amir-Bahman

Commander of the Islamic Republic of Iran Air Force
   (August 15, 1979–June 3, 1980)
Major General Baqeri was a decorated pilot before the
   revolution and was appointed by President Banisadr as commander of the Iranian Air Force. He
   resigned from his post on June 3, 1980, and was
   appointed by Banisadr as the head of the Civil
   Aviation Organization of the Islamic Republic of
   Iran. While serving in this post, Baqeri was arrested for a period of time on the unsubstantiated
   charge of supporting former PM Shapur Bakhtiar
   and participating in the Nojeh coup attempt.
   However, President Banisadr ordered his release.

Baqeri [Afshordi], Mohammad-Hoseyn

Chief of the Armed Forces General Staff (June 28,
   2016–present); Member of the Eighth Expediency
   Discernment Assembly (2017–22)
1958–, Tehran, Tehran

PhD, political geography, Tarbiyat-e Modarres
   University
War veteran
IRGC militiaman
Martyr's family (brother, Gholam-Hoseyn [known as
   Hasan Baqeri], was the deputy commander of the
   IRGC's ground forces and was killed at the war
   front in 1982)
Major General Baqeri was among the students
   who attacked the American embassy, and after
   joining the IRGC in 1980, he became IRGC's
   first intelligence and operations deputy during
   the Iran–Iraq War. Like his brother, Hasan, he
   was considered the most informed IRGC official
   when it came to assessing the military strength of
   the Iraqi Army. Before becoming the most senior
   military official in the country, Baqeri served as
   head of AFGS's Intelligence and Operations Directorate, and chief of the Armed Forces Services
   and Joint Affairs.

Baqeri-Bonabi, Abdolhamid

Deputy of the Fifth Majlis, Tabriz, East Azerbaijan
   (1996–2000)
1937–, Bonab, East Azerbaijan
Clerical education, Najaf Seminary (Iraq), 1962
Yusef, clergyman (ayatollah)
Clergyman (HI)
Imprisoned before the revolution
Not a war veteran

Baqeri-Bonabi, Mohammad [Shaikh Reza]

Deputy of the Ninth Majlis, Bonab, East Azerbaijan
   (2012–16)
1971–, Najaf, Iraq
Clerical education, Qom Seminary; BA, political sci-
   ence, Imam Khomeini Educational and Research
   Institute
Mosaffa, clergyman (HI)
Clergyman and director of Bonab seminary
No imprisonment
War veteran (wounded)

Baqeri-Bonabi's grandfather and father were both clerics, and he came to Iran from Iraq in 1975. He was in charge of the Friday Prayer Headquarters in Bonab in 2007. He ran unsuccessfully for the Tenth Majlis.

Baqeri-Lankarani, Kamran

Minister of health and medical education in President Ahmadinejad's first cabinet (August 24, 2005–9)
1965–, Tehran, Tehran
MD, medicine, Shiraz University of Medical Sciences, 1989
Manuchehr, aluminum factory owner
Medical doctor and professor at Shiraz University
No imprisonment
War veteran
Baqeri-Lankarani was a candidate in the 2013 presidential elections.

Baqeri-Nezhadiyanfard, Mohammad-Baqer

Deputy of the Third (1988–92) and Sixth (2000–2004) Majlis, Kazerun, Fars
1950–, Shiraz, Fars
BS, mathematics, Tabriz University, 1977; MA, management, 1995
Sohrab
Academia
Imprisoned before the revolution
The shah's regime imprisoned Baqeri-Nezhadiyanfard in 1972 on the charge of armed struggle. His mother and two brothers died in a car accident while returning from visiting him in prison. The GC rejected Baqeri-Nezhadiyanfard's qualifications for the Fourth Majlis, despite his forceful protests. His daughter, Fatemeh, was abducted and killed in 2011—he claims the current regime is responsible.

Baqerzadeh, Seyyed Javad

Deputy of the Fifth Majlis, Zanjan and Tarom, Zanjan (1997–2000)

1960–, Zanjan, Zanjan
BA
Bashir
No imprisonment

Baradaran-Shoraka, Hamid-Reza

VP and head of the Management and Planning Organization in President Khatami's second cabinet (2004–5)
1953–, Torbat-e Heydariyyeh, Razavi Khorasan
BA, economics, Allameh Tabataba'i University; MA, economics, University of Florida (USA); PhD, economics, University of Florida (USA), 1992; dissertation title: "Essays in Cross-Country Economic Growth"
Economic deputy of the Management and Planning Organization (2002–4)
No imprisonment
Not a war veteran
Baradaran-Shoraka began teaching economics at Allameh Tabataba'i University in 1975, and he was the dean of its school of economics from 1993 to 2002.

Barikbin, Hadi

Member of the Assembly for the Final Examination of the Constitution, Zanjan (1979); member of the First (1983–90) and Second (1991–98) Assembly of Experts, Zanjan; member of the Fourth Assembly of Experts, Qazvin (2007–16)
1930–April 8, 2017, Qazvin, Qazvin
Clerical education, Qom Seminary
Abolqasem, bazaar tradesman
Clergyman (ayatollah)
No imprisonment; spent six months in internal exile
Not a war veteran
Martyr's family (son, Morteza, died at the war front in 1982)
Barikbin escaped an assassination attempt in June 1979. He was the Friday prayer leader of Qazvin from 1981 to 2009. He was also the supreme leader's representative in Qazvin. Barikbin played an

important role in making Qazvin an independent province in 1997.

Barmak, Bayromgaldi

Deputy of the Seventh Majlis, Minudasht, Ka-
laleh, Maraveh Tappeh, and Galikash, Golestan
(2004–8)
1970–, Kalaleh, Golestan
BA, law
Ghardarvi
No imprisonment
IRGC militiaman (Basij)
Barmak is a Sunni Turkoman.

Barzegar [Forughinia], Gholam-Hoseyn

Deputy of the Sixth Majlis, Sepidan, Fars (2000–2004)
1957–, Sepidan, Fars
BA, public administration
Mohammad-Ali
No imprisonment
After serving in the Majlis, Barzegar became head of
human resources of South Zagros Oil and Gas
Production Company.

Barzegar-Kalshani, Shahruz

Deputy of the Tenth Majlis, Salmas, West Azerbaijan
(2016–20)
1975–, Salmas, West Azerbaijan
MA, political science
Shahriyar
University professor
No imprisonment
Not a war veteran

Barzegar-Tekmehdash, Taher Aqa

Deputy of the Fifth (1996–2000), Sixth (2000–2004),
and Seventh (2004–8) Majlis, Bostanabad, East
Azerbaijan
1955–, Tabriz, East Azerbaijan
BS, mechanical engineering; MS, energy engineering

Hasan
Military and security official
No imprisonment

Bashiri, Farhad

Deputy of the Eighth (2008–12) and Ninth (2012–16)
Majlis, Pakdasht, Tehran
1963–, Rey, Tehran
BA, counseling, Allameh Tabataba'i University
Mohammad
Civil servant, ministries
No imprisonment
Bashiri was a conservative MP.

Bastani, Sa'id

Deputy of the Tenth Majlis, Torbat-e Heydariyyeh,
Razavi Khorasan (2016–20)
1971–, Torbat-e Heydariyyeh, Razavi Khorasan
BS, polymer engineering, Amirkabir University of
Technology; MS, polymer engineering; possible
PhD (unverified)
Mohammad, bazaar tradesman
University professor
No imprisonment

Bathaie, Seyyed Mohammad

Minister of education in President Rouhani's second
cabinet (August 20, 2017–2021)
1963–, Tehran, Tehran
BA, educational planning, 1987; MA, public administration, 1999
Seyyed Mohsen
No imprisonment
Bathaie spent three decades of his career in the Ministry of Education, and was affiliated with the PBO.

Bathaie [-Golpayegani], Seyyed Hashem

Member of the Fifth Assembly of Experts, Tehran
(2016–22)
1941–, Golpayegan, Isfahan

Clerical education, Qom Seminary; BA, philosophy, Tehran University, 1968; MA, philosophy, Tehran University, 1973; PhD, theology, Tehran University, 2001
Seyyed Abbas
Clergyman (ayatollah)
Imprisoned before the revolution
Bathaie was a long-time student of Ayatollah Khomeini and Ayatollah Mohammad-Reza Golpayegani. He went to Egypt in 1976 to pursue religious studies. Bathaie was the first governor-general and Ayatollah Khomeini's representative in Chahar Mahal and Bakhtiari after the revolution. He was also Ayatollah Khamenei's representative and the Friday prayer leader of Golpayegan from 1994 to 1997. Bathaie, who teaches at both Tehran University and Qom Seminary, was disqualified from running in the 2017 presidential election.

Bat-Oshonagugtappeh, Sergon

Member of the Assembly for the Final Examination of the Constitution, representing Assyrians and Chaldeans (as a religious minority) (1979); deputy of the First Majlis, representing Assyrians and Chaldeans (1980–84)
1927–1988, Urmia, West Azerbaijan
MD, medicine
Pulis, laborer
Medical doctor
No imprisonment
Not a war veteran
Bat-Oshonagugtappeh was arrested toward the end of the First Majlis for cooperating with the Tudeh Party and was expelled from the Majlis. He was released from prison because of a medical condition and died a few years later.

Bauj-Lahuti, Mehrdad

Deputy of the Eighth (2008–12), Ninth (2012–16), and Tenth (2016–20) Majlis, Langarud, Gilan
1961–, Kumeleh, Gilan

BA, public administration, Institute for Management and Planning Studies
Manuchehr
Mayor of Divandareh, Damghan, and Langarud
No imprisonment
Bauj-Lahuti is a conservative MP.

Bayanak, Amin

Deputy of the Third (1988–92) and Fifth (1996–2000) Majlis, Ahvaz, Khuzestan
1956–, Ahvaz, Khuzestan
BS, electrical engineering, 1990; PhD, electrical engineering, Amirkabir University of Technology
Abdolhoseyn
No imprisonment
Bayanak has been mayor of several cities, including Ahvaz, Andimeshk, and Behbahan. He was also an adviser to ministers of road and transportation as well as commerce and has held leadership roles in the petrochemical industry.

Bayani, Salaheddin

Deputy of the First Majlis, Khaf, Razavi Khorasan (1980–84)
1938–, Khaf, Razavi Khorasan
BA, law
Habibollah, farmer
Civil servant
No imprisonment

Bayat, Gholam-Reza

Deputy of the Second Majlis, Mahneshan and Ijrood, Zanjan (1984–88)
1937–, Zanjan, Zanjan
Clerical education
Yahya
Clergyman
No imprisonment

Bayat, Mrs. Raf'at

Deputy of the Seventh Majlis, Zanjan, Zanjan (2004–8)

1957–, Zanjan, Zanjan
PhD, sociology
Abbas
Civil servant
No imprisonment
Bayat registered for the 2009 presidential election but
was disqualified by the GC.

Bayatiyan, Seyyed Mohammad

Deputy of the Ninth Majlis, Bijar, Kurdistan (2012–16)
1973–, Bijar, Kurdistan
MS, architecture; MA, management
Seyyed Mansur, IRGC commander
Former director of public relations for the Imam Kho-
meini International University in Qazvin
No imprisonment
Not a war veteran
Martyr's family (father)
Bayatiyan, who was previously the executive director
of Alborz Industrial City Company, ran unsuc-
cessfully in the 2013 presidential election. The GC
disqualified him from running in the 2016 Majlis
election. He is currently development deputy of
Pars Oil and Gas Company.

Bayat-Zanjani, Asadollah

Deputy of the First Majlis, Mahneshan and Ijrood,
Zanjan (1980–84); deputy of the Second (1984–88)
and Third (1988–92) Majlis, Zanjan and Tarom,
Zanjan
1941–, Mahneshan, Zanjan
Clerical education, Qom Seminary
Hashem, farmer
Clergyman (ayatollah)
Imprisoned before the revolution (1972–73)
Not a war veteran
Martyr's family (brother, nephew, and brother-in-law
killed at the war front)
Member of the central council of the ACC; founding
member of ASLQS
In the early 1980s, Bayat-Zanjani advocated for the
exportation of the revolution and the purging of

Iranian embassy staffs. He was a member of the
committee that reassessed the constitution in
1989 and served as a deputy speaker in the Third
Majlis. However, the GC disqualified him from
the Fourth Majlis. In 1998, the SCFC prosecuted
him and he spent three and a half months in
prison. He currently resides in Qom and continues his clerical duties.

Bazargan, Mehdi

Member of the Revolutionary Council (1979–1980);
prime minister (February 11–November 5,
1979); deputy of the First Majlis, Tehran, Tehran
(1980–84)
1907–January 20, 1995, Tehran, Tehran
BS, mechanical engineering, École Centrale des Arts
et Manufactures (France), 1933
Abbas-Qoli, bazaar tradesman
University professor
Imprisoned before the revolution
Not a war veteran
Member of INF; founder and secretary-general of the
LMI
Bazargan lived in France from 1928 to 1935, and
served as the associate dean and then dean of the
college of engineering at Tehran University from
1942 to 1951. He was a deputy minister under
Premier Mohammad Mossadeq, who appointed
him as head of the NIOC after nationalizing the
Iranian oil industry. In 1961, Bazargan founded
the LMI and played a crucial role in the Islamic
intellectual circles before the revolution. He was
in prison from 1962 to 1967. On February 4,
1979, Ayatollah Khomeini appointed Bazargan as
prime minister of the provisional Revolutionary
government. A week later, he began his legal term
as Iran's first postrevolutionary prime minister.
Bazargan was in office for 275 days until he and
his entire cabinet resigned on November 5, 1979,
in protest of the takeover of the American embassy the day before. In a famous speech before
his resignation, Bazargan distinguished his style
from Ayatollah Khomeini by saying: "Don't expect

me to act in the manner of Khomeini, who, head down, moves ahead like a bulldozer crushing rocks, roots, and stones in his path. I am a delicate passenger car and must ride on a smooth, as-phalted road." The GC disqualified him from running in the 1985 presidential race on account of his support for Abbas Amir-Entezzam. Bazargan died in 1995 in Switzerland. He was the father-in-law of Mohammad-Hoseyn Baniasadi, and his niece was married to Ezzatollah Sahabi.

Bazqandi, Hoseyn

Deputy of the First Majlis, Dorud, Lorestan (1981–84)
1950–, Bazqand, Lorestan
Clerical education
Gholam-Reza
Clergyman
No imprisonment
HI Bazqandi, Friday prayer leader of Azna, was elected in interim elections after the previous candidate, HI Mohammad-Hoseyn Sadeqi, was killed in the bombing of the IRP headquarters.

Bazrpash, Mehrdad

VP and head of the National Youth Organization in President Ahmadinejad's second cabinet (2009–10); deputy of the Ninth Majlis, Tehran, Tehran (2012–16)
1980–, Tehran, Tehran
BS, industrial engineering, Sharif University of Technology, 2004; MA, executive management, Allameh Tabataba'i University, 2006
Civil servant, state companies
Mansur
No imprisonment
Not a war veteran
IRGC militiaman
Martyr's family (father)
Member of Good Scent of Service
At a very young age, Bazrpash was appointed director-general and head of the board of directors of Pars Khordo, an automobile company. After

President Ahmadinejad dismissed Bazrpash, IRGC Commander Ja'fari appointed him as a deputy in the IRGC Cooperative Foundation. Bazrpash is the proprietor of *Vatan Emrouz*. He headed the National Youth Organization during Ahmadinejad's presidency, and he was part of the leadership team during the Ninth Majlis. After his unsuccessful run for the Tenth Majlis from Tehran in 2016, Bazrpash worked in IRIB. He is the son-in-law of Ali-Reza Aliahmadi-Jashfaqani, who was minister of education under President Ahmadinejad.

Beglarian, Robert

Deputy of the Seventh (2004–8), Eighth (2008–12), and Ninth (2012–16) Majlis representing Armenians of southern Iran (as a religious minority)
1961–, Tehran, Tehran
MA, economics, Isfahan University of Technology
Sampat
Civil servant, ministries
No imprisonment
In 2012, Beglarian received 100 percent of his constituency's votes, the highest of any MP. He did not run for the Tenth Majlis in 2016.

Behbahani, Hamid

Minister of roads and transportation in President Ahmadinejad's first (August 12, 2008–August 2, 2009) and second (September 3, 2009–February 1, 2011) cabinets
1941–, Shiraz, Fars
BS, civil engineering, Iran University of Science and Technology; MS, civil engineering, University of Florida (USA), 1974; PhD, civil engineering, University of Florida (USA), 1977; dissertation title: "Econocrete-Design and Properties"
University professor
No imprisonment
Not a war veteran
Behbahani was the chairman of the civil engineering department at the Iran University of Science

and Technology from 1979 to 1998, and served as Mahmoud Ahmadinejad's dissertation adviser. When Ahmadinejad became the mayor of Tehran, he hired Behbahani as one of his deputies. Behbahani was the oldest member of President Ahmadinejad's cabinet and the Majlis successfully impeached him on February 1, 2011. Later on, Behbahani was also accused of plagiarizing an academic paper.

Behbahani, Mohammad-Zeyd

Deputy of the First Majlis, Bandar-e Mahshahr, Khuzestan (1980)
1929–April 5, 2017, Bandar-e Mahshahr, Khuzestan
Ya'qub
Imprisoned before the revolution
Not a war veteran
Behbahani was Behbahan's revolutionary prosecutor-general in the early days of the revolution. He resigned from the First Majlis five months after it started on September 2, 1980, due to medical reasons.

Beheshti, Ahmad

Deputy of the First (1980–84) and Second (1984–88) Majlis, Fasa, Fars; member of the Third (1999–2006), Fourth (2007–16), and Fifth (2016–22) Assembly of Experts, Fars
1935–, Fasa, Fars
Clerical education, Shiraz and Qom Seminaries; BA, theology, Tehran University, 1963; PhD, philosophy, Tehran University, 1966
Abdolmajid, clergyman (HI)
Clergyman
No imprisonment
Not a war veteran
Martyr's family (son, Mohsen)
Member of the SQSS
HI Beheshti's initial election to the Second Majlis in 1984 was invalidated after a rival complained of vote rigging. He was reelected in September 1984 in midterm elections. His dissertation advisers

were Morteza Motahhari and Mehdi Ha'eri-Yazdi. He wrote for the influential religious journal *Maktab-e Islam* before the revolution. Beheshti became chairman of Tehran University's philosophy department in 1988 and the Friday prayer leader of Miyanshahr in 2014.

Beheshti, Seyyed Mohammad

Member of the Revolutionary Council (1979–80); member and deputy head of the Assembly for the Final Examination of the Constitution, Tehran (1979); head of the Revolutionary Council cabinet (1979–80); head of the State Supreme Court (February 23, 1980–June 28, 1981)
October 24, 1928–June 28, 1981, Isfahan, Isfahan
Clerical education, Qom Seminary, 1951; BA, theology, Tehran University, 1951; PhD, theology, Tehran University, 1959
Seyyed Fazlollah [Hoseyni-Beheshti], clergyman (HI)
Clergyman
Imprisoned before the revolution
Not a war veteran
Founder and secretary-general of the IRP; founding member of the SCC
Ayatollah Beheshti was an Islamic missionary in Hamburg, Germany, from 1965 to 1970, and he worked in the Ministry of Education before the revolution. He was one of Ayatollah Khomeini's most trusted and powerful students and clerical allies during and immediately after the revolution. Beheshti negotiated with American emissaries on behalf of Ayatollah Khomeini before the revolution. Ayatollah Khomeini appointed him as head of the State Supreme Court, and in that post, he played a crucial role in forming the judiciary after 1979. Some considered it "unconstitutional" that he was simultaneously heading a political party (IRP). Beheshti presided over the meetings of both the Revolutionary Council (after the death of Ayatollah Taleqani) and the AFEC that drafted the Islamic Republic's constitution. He also chaired the HCJ while serving as head of the State Supreme Court. Beheshti was favored by the IRP

for the first presidential election but did not run after Ayatollah Khomeini declared, "The ulama should not seek the presidency." Beheshti died in the bombing of the IRP headquarters on June 28, 1981, and one of Tehran's most prestigious universities was named after him. He was conversant in Arabic, English, and German.

Beheshtinezhad, Seyyed Hoseyn

Deputy of the First Majlis, Isfahan, Isfahan (1981–84)
1953–, Isfahan, Isfahan
Clerical education, Isfahan Seminary; BA, human sciences, University of Judicial Sciences-Qom
Seyyed Mostafa
Clergyman (HI)
No imprisonment
Member of the IRGC

Behmanesh, Rahman

Deputy of the Sixth Majlis, Mahabad, West Azerbaijan (2000–2004)
1953–, Mahabad, West Azerbaijan
BA, education
Rahim
Civil servant, Ministry of Education
No imprisonment
Behmanesh, a Sunni Muslim, was a member of the central council of PECI in West Azerbaijan. He was among the 139 members of the Sixth Majlis who staged a sit-in in early 2004 to protest the massive disqualification of candidates for the Seventh Majlis.

Behnia, Manuchehr

Deputy of the Fifth Majlis, Kermanshah, Kermanshah (1996–2000)
1952–, Kermanshah, Kermanshah
MD, cardiology
Ja'far
Cardiologist
No imprisonment

Behruzi [-Za'farani], Mrs. Maryam

Deputy of the First (1981–84), Second (1984–88), Third (1989–92), and Fourth (1992–96) Majlis, Tehran, Tehran
1945–February 18, 2012, Tehran, Tehran
Pre-diploma (six years of elementary school)
Mohammad-Ali
Imprisoned before the revolution (one month)
Martyr's family (PMOI assassinated his teenage son, Mehdi Haji Abbasi, in 1981)
Member of the IRP; founding member and secretary-general of Zeynab Society; founding member of the Islamic Society of Educators; founding member of the ISFPD
Behruzi and fellow MP Nayyereh Akhavan-Bitaraf hold the record for the most terms served by a woman in the Majlis after the revolution. She was not elected to the Fifth Majlis, and the GC disqualified her from running in the Ninth Majlis election. Behruzi, who was married to a cleric, was involved with the committee welcoming Ayatollah Khomeini back to Iran. She died of cancer.

Behzadiyan, Mohammad-Reza

Deputy of the Third Majlis, Qaenat, South Khorasan (1988–92)
1957–, Qaenat, South Khorasan
BS, textile engineering, Amirkabir University of Technology
Zabihollah
Civil servant, ministries
No imprisonment
Not a war veteran
IRGC militiaman
Behzadiyan, who was involved in the takeover of the American embassy in Tehran, later became a deputy in IRIB. During the presidency of Mohammad Khatami, he was the MI's deputy for administrative and financial affairs. He was chair of the Tehran Chamber of Commerce from 2002 to 2005.

Besanjideh, Yusef

Deputy of the Third Majlis, Kordkuy, Golestan
(1990–92)
1961–, Bandar-e Torkaman, Golestan
BS, electrical engineering
Tavaqdurdi
No imprisonment
Besanjideh, a Sunni Muslim, is the former director
of economic affairs for the office of Golestan's
governor-general.

Besharat, Mohammad-Taqi

Member of the Assembly for the Final Examination of
the Constitution, Kohgiluyeh and Buyer Ahmad
(1979); deputy of the First Majlis, Semirom, Isfa-
han (1980–December 28, 1981)
1945–December 28, 1981, Dehaqan, Isfahan
Clerical education, Qom Seminary
Haji Baba, bazaar tradesman
Clergyman
No imprisonment
Not a war veteran
Member of the IRP
HI Besharat was Ayatollah Khomeini's representative
in Gachsaran and was director of the Martyr's
Foundation in Kohgiluyeh and Buyer Ahmad. A
court judge who sentenced many to death, he was
assassinated by PMOI.

Besharati [-Jahromi], Ali-Mohammad

Deputy of the First Majlis, Jahrom, Fars (1980–84); in-
terior minister in President Hashemi-Rafsanjani's
second cabinet (August 16, 1993–August 2, 1997)
1944–, Jahrom, Fars
BA, political science, University of Judicial Sciences
and Administrative Services
Fazlollah, bazaar tradesman
Deputy minister of foreign affairs
Imprisoned before the revolution
Not a war veteran

IRGC militiaman
Besharati was one of the founders of the IRGC and
was in charge of its intelligence unit for a while.
He was the main individual behind the arrest
of Ayatollah Taleqani's children soon after the
revolution, and he was reportedly involved in a
series of unlawful killings that took place in his
birthplace of Jahrom. For some time in the 1980s,
he served as the first deputy minister of foreign
affairs.

Betkiliya, Yonaten

Deputy of the Sixth (2000–2004), Seventh (2004–8),
Eighth (2008–12), Ninth (2012–16), and Tenth
(2016–20) Majlis, representing Assyrians and
Chaldeans (as a religious minority)
1951–, Urmia, West Azerbaijan
Associate's degree, hotel management, Allameh Taba-
taba'i University
Eliyeh
Bazaar tradesman
No imprisonment
Not a war veteran
Betkiliya, the executive director of a construction
company, was also previously the secretary-gen-
eral of the Assyrian Universal Alliance.

Beygi-Eylanlu, Ruhollah

Deputy of the Ninth Majlis, Miyandoab, Takab,
and Shahindezh, West Azerbaijan (2012–16)
1973–, Baroogh, West Azerbaijan
Clerical education, Qom Seminary, 2002; MA,
theology, Islamic Schools of Thought Educational and Research Institute; PhD, jurisprudence, 2011
Beyg Mirza
Clergyman (HI) and director of the Pious Endowments Organization of West Azerbaijan
(2008–11)
No imprisonment
Not a war veteran

Beygmoradi, Hemmat

Deputy of the Fifth Majlis, Qasr-e Shirin, Sarpol-e Zahab, and Gilan-e Gharb, Kermanshah
(1996–2000)
1953–, Qasr-e Shirin, Kermanshah
BS, agricultural engineering, Tabriz University, 1995
Beyg Mirza
No imprisonment

Bigdeli, Ahmad

Deputy of the Tenth Majlis, Khodabandeh, Zanjan
(2016–20)
1976–, Khodabandeh, Zanjan
MD, dentistry, 2003; advanced training in
orthodontics
Dentist
No imprisonment
Not a war veteran

Biglari, Mohsen

Deputy of the Ninth (2012–16) and Tenth (2016–20)
Majlis, Saqqez and Baneh, Kurdistan
1974–, Saqqez, Kurdistan
BS, mechanical engineering, Shahid Raja'i Teach-
ers Training College; MS, natural resources,
Islamic Azad University–Karaj; PhD, public
administration
Head of a number of technical-vocational schools
No imprisonment
Not a war veteran
Biglari, an independent Sunni MP, has worked in
various factories.

Bimeqdar, Shahabeddin

Deputy of the First (1981–84) and Second (1984–88)
Majlis, Varzaqan, East Azerbaijan; deputy
of the Tenth Majlis, Tabriz, East Azerbaijan
(2016–20)
1953–, Varzaqan, East Azerbaijan

BS, mechanical engineering
Mohammad-Hasan
No imprisonment
Not a war veteran
Bimeqdar previously held such posts as Ayatollah
Khomeini's representative in the Construction
Jihad of Varzaqan, founder of the Office of Heavy
Industries in East Azerbaijan, and adviser to the
minister of heavy industries.

Biranvand, Bahram

Deputy of the Ninth Majlis, Borujerd, Lorestan
(2012–16)
1965–, Shaikh Miri, Lorestan
BS, electrical engineering, Isfahan University of Tech-
nology, 1995; MA, public administration
Tahmaseb, farmer
Director of the FDWI in Borujerd
No imprisonment
War veteran (lost a leg)
Martyr's family (two brothers, Bahman and Borzu,
killed at the war front)
Biranvand was in charge of the FDWI in Borujerd.
He returned to farming after serving in the
Majlis.

Biranvandi, Mohammad

Deputy of the Ninth Majlis, Khorramabad, Lorestan
(2012–16)
1970–, Khorramabad, Lorestan
PhD, Persian language and literature
University professor
Biranvandi, a reformist, was an educational administrator in Lorestan Province.

Bitaraf, Habibollah

Minister of energy in President Khatami's first (August 20, 1997–August 1, 2001) and second (August
22, 2001–August 2, 2005) cabinets
1956–, Yazd, Yazd

BS, civil engineering, Tehran University, 1981; MS, civil engineering, Tehran University, 1986
Civil servant
No imprisonment
War veteran (wounded)
IRGC militiaman
Founding member of OCU and the Islamic Society of Alumni of Tehran University's College of Engineering
Bitaraf was one of the three main architects of the takeover of the American embassy. He was the coordinator of the reformist camp in several municipal council elections. Bitaraf was the governor of Yazd from 1986 to 1989, as well as the deputy minister of energy (1990–94), head of Tehran Province Construction Engineering Organization, and deputy minister of petroleum. As minister of energy, he was responsible for the construction of several dams that have proven controversial in terms of their environmental impact. On August 20, 2017, the Majlis rejected Bitaraf as President Rouhani's proposed minister of energy.

Bizhani, Khosrow

Member of the First (1983–86), Second (1986–89), and Third (1992–98) Guardian Councils
1936–, Babol, Mazandaran
PhD
Abdoljavad
Judiciary official
No imprisonment
Not a war veteran

Bodaghi, Mrs. Fatemeh

VP for legal affairs in President Ahmadinejad's second cabinet (2009–13)
1966–, Tehran, Tehran
BA, theology; MA, judicial law: PhD, law
Judiciary official
No imprisonment
Bodaghi filed legal cases against many of Ahmadinejad's critics. Her husband, Mohammad-Ali Hejazi, was a member of the Council for the Implementation of the Constitution.

Bohluli-Qashqa'i, Sohrab

Deputy of the Fifth (1996–2000) and Sixth (2000–2004) Majlis, Firuzabad, Fars
1953–, Firuzabad, Fars
MS, mining engineering
Masih
No imprisonment

Bolfath, Ali

Deputy of the Fourth Majlis, Pol-e Dokhtar and Malavi, Lorestan (1992–96)
1962–, Pol-e Dokhtar, Lorestan
High school diploma; pursuing a law degree
Alijan
No imprisonment
War veteran (lost a hand and a leg)
IRGC militiaman (commander during the Iran–Iraq War)

Bolukiyan, Ahmad

Deputy of the Third (1988–92) and Seventh (2004–8) Majlis, Kashmar, Razavi Khorasan
1957–, Gonabad, Razavi Khorasan
BA, management; MA, political science
Mohammad-Ali
Civil servant
No imprisonment
Bolukiyan was a conservative MP.

Bonakdar-Haji Abdolvahhab, Hoseyn

Mayor of Tehran (1983)
1938–, Tehran, Tehran
Nasrollah, bazaar tradesman
Imprisoned before the revolution (freed in 1979)
Not a war veteran
Member of the CIC/PCIC

Bonakdar-Haji Abdolvahhab is a former ambassador to Italy and the Vatican, and he was mayor of Tehran for only five months in 1983.

Bonyadi, Behruz

Deputy of the Tenth Majlis, Kashmar, Razavi Khorasan (2016–20)
1970–, Kabodan, Razavi Khorasan
MD, pediatric specialization, Mashhad University of Medical Sciences
Medical doctor
No imprisonment
Bonyadi, a reformist, is a former member of the Kashmar City Council (elected in 1999). He was also a professor at Islamic Azad University–Kashmar from 1998 to 2000 and Bojnurd University of Medical Sciences from 2012 to 2014.

Borna-Boldaji, Sirus

Deputy of the Eighth Majlis, Borujen, Chahar Mahal and Bakhtiari (2008–12)
1968–, Boldaji, Chahar Mahal and Bakhtiari
BA, political science; pursuing a PhD in political science
Mohammad
Civil servant, ministries
No imprisonment
Borna-Boldaji was not elected to the Ninth Majlis.

Boroghani, Ali

Deputy of the Eighth Majlis, Sabzevar, Razavi Khorasan (2008–12)
1959–, Boroghan, Razavi Khorasan
BS, mathematics; MA, social sciences
Morteza
Teacher and member of the Sabzevar City Council
No imprisonment
War veteran
Martyr's family (brother, Abbas)
Boroghani ran but was not elected to the Ninth or the Tenth Majlis.

Borqe'i, Seyyed Amir-Mansur

VP and head of the Management and Planning Organization in President Ahmadinejad's first cabinet (November 16, 2006–July 9, 2007)
1957–, Qom, Qom
BS, mechanical engineering, Iran University of Science and Technology
Civil servant, ministries
No imprisonment
War veteran
IRGC militiaman
Borqe'i is a former planning deputy in the Ministry of Energy, CEO of Sepasad (IRGC's dam-building arm), and ambassador to Japan (appointed in 2011). President Ahmadinejad abolished the Management and Planning Organization while Borqe'i was in charge of it. During President Rouhani's administration, Borqe'i was arrested for financial impropriety.

Borujerdi, Alaeddin

Deputy of the Sixth (2000–2004), Seventh (2004–8), Eighth (2008–12), Ninth (2012–16), and Tenth (2016–20) Majlis, Borujerd, Lorestan
1950–, Lar, Fars
BS, laboratory science, 1977; MA, international relations, Tehran University
Mohammad-Ebrahim, clergyman (ayatollah)
Civil servant, ministries
Imprisoned before the revolution
Not a war veteran
According to some reports, Borujerdi was born in Najaf, Iraq, and it is certain that he completed his elementary and high school education in Najaf. He was a laboratory technician in the Dubai Red Crescent Society before the revolution and became Iran's first counsel-general in Dubai after the revolution. Borujerdi was an employee of the Ministry of Foreign Affairs for fifteen years and functioned as chief of the Persian Gulf, Iraq, Arabian Peninsula department and as deputy to former minister of foreign affairs Ali-Akbar Velayati.

In the 1980s, Borujerdi was ambassador to China and his brother was ambassador to Japan. In the Majlis, Borujerdi chaired the important Foreign Policy and National Security Committee. His sister, Ashraf Borujerdi, was the interior minister's social deputy under President Khatami.

Borumand, Mohammad-Hadi

Deputy of the First Majlis, Borujerd, Lorestan (1980–84)
1938–, Borujerd, Lorestan
MA, Islamic philosophy
Mohammad-Hasan, bazaar tradesman
Academia
No imprisonment

Borumand-Dashqapu, Habib

Deputy of the Third Majlis, Germi, Ardabil (1988–92); deputy of the Ninth Majlis, Parsabad and Bilehsavar, Ardabil (2012–16)
1961–, Dashqapu, Ardabil
Clerical education; BA, theology, Islamic Azad University–Tehran; MA, Arabic language
Ali-Hoseyn
Clergyman
No imprisonment
War veteran (wounded)
IRGC militiaman and head of Germi's revolutionary committee
Although HI Borumand-Dashqapu was previously a commander of the revolutionary committee of Parsabad and a member of the Third Majlis, the GC rejected his credentials to take the seat he won in the Fourth Majlis. He also failed to win in the elections for the Seventh Majlis. Borumand-Dashqapu worked for a while in the legal commission of the EDA.

Borumandi, Mohammad-Mehdi

Deputy of the Ninth (2012–16) and Tenth (2016–20) Majlis, Marvdasht, Pasargad, and Arsanjan, Fars

1973–, Marvdasht, Fars
MS, agricultural engineering, Islamic Azad University–Arsanjan; MA, political science, Shiraz University
Ebrahim
Civil servant, Ministry of Economic Affairs and Finance and Tehran Tax Organization; governor of Bavanat
No imprisonment
War veteran (wounded)
IRGC militiaman (Basij)

Bozorgiyan, Ahmad

Deputy of the Seventh Majlis, Sabzevar, Razavi Khorasan (2004–8)
1960–, Sabzevar, Razavi Khorasan
MA, theology
Mohammad-Reza
MDAFL official for twenty-four years
No imprisonment
War veteran

Bozorgvari, Seyyed Ali-Mohammad

Deputy of the Eighth (2008–12) and Ninth (2012–16) Majlis, Kohgiluyeh and Bahmai, Kohgiluyeh and Buyer Ahmad
1957–, Dehdasht, Kohgiluyeh and Buyer Ahmad
Clerical education, Qom Seminary, 1989
Seyyed Habibollah, farmer
Clergyman (HI)
No imprisonment
War veteran (twenty-four months; victim of a chemical attack)
Martyr's family (brother)
Member of ADVIR
Bozorgvari worked for over twenty years as a high school and university teacher in Kohgiluyeh and Buyer Ahmad, and he was the supreme leader's representative at Yasouj University. One of Bozorgvari's brothers was killed in the war, and another brother was a prisoner of war.

Burqani-Farahani, Ahmad

Deputy of the Sixth Majlis, Tehran, Tehran (2000–2004)

1959–2008, Tehran, Tehran

BA, geography, Shahid Beheshti University, 1983

Mohammad-Ali, laborer

Civil servant

No imprisonment

Not a war veteran

Before entering the Majlis, Burqani was a journalist and editor at Islamic Republic of Iran News
Service, spokesperson for the War Information
Headquarters, media deputy to the minister of
culture and Islamic guidance, and adviser to the
interior minister.

Chamran [-Saveh'i], Mostafa

Ministerial adviser for revolutionary affairs and then
minister of national defense in PM Bazargan's
cabinet (September 29–November 5, 1979);
minister of national defense in the Revolutionary
Council cabinet (November 6, 1979–80); deputy of
the First Majlis, Tehran, Tehran (1980–81)

1933–June 21, 1981, Tehran, Tehran

BS, electrical engineering, Tehran University, 1957;
PhD, electrical engineering, University of Cal-
ifornia, Berkeley (USA), 1963; dissertation title:
"Electron Beam in the Cold-Cathode Magnetron"

Hasan, laborer

No imprisonment

War veteran

Chamran left Iran for the United States in the early
1950s. After getting his doctorate, he went to
Egypt in January 1965 to undergo military training. Afterward, he went to Lebanon, where he
helped to found the AMAL organization and
worked with Imam Musa Sadr. After living for
more than two decades abroad, Chamran returned
to Iran on February 26, 1979, and used his military
background in training the Revolutionary Guards.
Seven months later, on September 29, 1979, he became the minister of defense, and at that time Ayatollah Khamenei was his deputy in the ministry.

Chamran was killed in the war against Iraq two
years later while serving as commander of uncon-
ventional warfare. In his memory, the University
of Ahvaz was renamed Shahid Chamran University of Ahvaz. Chamran's brother, Mehdi, has been
chair of the Tehran City Council for many years.

Chardavoli, Ali-Ne'mat

Deputy of the Ninth Majlis, Malayer, Hamadan
(2012–16)

1967–, Malayer, Hamadan

BA, counseling, Shahid Beheshti University; MA,
counseling, Tarbiyat-e Mo'allem University

Father's name unknown, farmer

Teacher and educational administrator in Hamadan
Province

No imprisonment

War veteran

Chardavoli ran unsuccessfully for the Tenth Majlis.

Chehregani-Anzabi, Mohammad-Hoseyn

Deputy of the First (1980–84), Second (1984–88), and
Third (1988–92) Majlis, Tabriz, East Azerbaijan

1920–January 10, 2000, Tabriz, East Azerbaijan

Clerical education

Morteza, clergyman

Clergyman

Imprisoned before the revolution

Not a war veteran

Member of the IRP and the SCC

HI Chehregani-Anzabi was the oldest member of the
Third Majlis. He was opposed to land reform and
strongly anti-Soviet. After serving in the Majlis,
he joined the Office of the Supreme Leader.

Chenarani, Mrs. Hajar

Deputy of the Tenth Majlis, Neyshabur, Razavi Khorasan (2016–20)

1978–, Chenaran, Razavi Khorasan

MA, sociology, Alzahra University

University teacher and administrator

Cheraghzadeh-Dezfuli, Ali-Reza

Deputy of the First Majlis, Ramhormoz, Khuzestan
(1980–June 28, 1981)
1953–June 28, 1981, Ahvaz, Khuzestan
BS, accounting
Mohammad-Ali, laborer
Civil servant
No imprisonment
Cheraghzadeh-Dezfuli was killed in the bombing of
the IRP headquarters in June 1981.

Chitchiyan, Hamid

Deputy of the Third Majlis, Tabriz, East Azerbaijan
(1988–92); minister of energy in President Rou-
hani's first cabinet (August 15, 2013–August 13,
2017)
1957–, Tabriz, East Azerbaijan
BS, mechanical engineering, Amirkabir University
of Technology, 1985; MS, industrial engineering,
Amirkabir University of Technology, 1995; PhD,
industrial engineering, Tarbiyat-e Modarres University, 2005
Boyuk, clergyman (HI) and bookseller
Civil servant, ministries
No imprisonment
War veteran
IRGC militiaman
Martyr's family (brother, Mohsen, killed at the war
front)
Chitchiyan was a member of the Construction Jihad
in East Azerbaijan and IRGC's intelligence com-
mander in Tabriz. He joined the MIIRI in 1983.
From 1992 to 2013, he worked in the Ministry of
Energy, including as deputy minister, as well as in
the private energy sector.

Dabestani, Khosrow

Deputy of the Sixth Majlis, representing the Zoroastrian
community (as a religious community) (2000–2004)
1940–, Ardakan, Yazd

MD, medicine
Ardeshir
Medical doctor
No imprisonment

Dabestani, Majid

Deputy of the Third (1988–92), Fourth (1992–96), and
Fifth (1996–2000) Majlis, Bam, Kerman
1951–, Bam, Kerman
BS, business administration, 1985; MS, management,
1995
Mohammad-Taqi
No imprisonment
The GC disqualified Dabestani from running in the
2016 Majlis election.

Dadashi, Vali

Deputy of the Tenth Majlis, Astara, Gilan (2016–20)
1981–, Astara, Gilan
MA, theology, Shahid Beheshti University; pursuing a
PhD in jurisprudence at Qom Seminary
Eskandar
Instructor at universities and seminaries
Not a war veteran
Dadashi entered the Tenth Majlis as an independent
candidate.

Dadbin, Ahmad

Commander of the Islamic Republic of Iran Ground
Forces (October 25, 1994–October 1, 1997)
1955–, Tehran, Tehran
BS, military science, Ground Forces Officers' Acad-
emy, 1977
Yadollah, military officer
Military official
No imprisonment
War veteran
Brigadier General Dadbin, a religiously orthodox offi-
cer, was involved in fighting Kurdish rebel groups
in the early years of the revolution. In 2005, he

was badly injured in a mountain climbing fall and was in a coma for some time.

Dadfar, Mohammad

Deputy of the Sixth Majlis, Bushehr, Genaveh, and Deylam, Bushehr (2000–2004)
1963–, Tangestan, Bushehr
MA, Persian literature, Islamic Azad University–Bushehr; PhD, Tajik State National University (Tajikistan)
Hoseyn, landowner
Academia
No imprisonment
Dadfar came from a wealthy family, and after leaving the Majlis, he became active in the private sector selling paper products in Iran and Central Asia.

Dadgar, Abdolaziz

Deputy of the Third Majlis, Chabahar, Sistan and Baluchestan (1988–92)
1946–October 15, 2005, Chabahar, Sistan and Baluchestan
High school diploma
Abubakr
Teacher
No imprisonment
Dadgar was a Sunni MP.

Dadgar, Hoseyn

Public prosecutor-general of Tehran (1980–84)
Hamadan, Hamadan
Judiciary official
Dadgar has served in such roles as adviser to the HCJ, adviser to the chief justice, and judicial deputy of the State Supreme Court. In 1981, he was a member of an investigative committee sent by the head of the judiciary to investigate the practice of torture in Iranian prisons. In July 1989, Dadgar failed to get enough votes from the Majlis to be elected as a lawyer for the Guardian Council. In early 1991, Ayatollah Khamenei appointed him to a three-member committee to review the conduct of the judiciary branch and issue a report to him within three months.

Dadman, Rahman

Minister of roads and transportation in President Khatami's first cabinet (January 14–May 17, 2001)
1956–May 17, 2001, Ardabil, Ardabil
BS, civil engineering, Tehran University, 1983; MS, civil engineering, Tehran University, 1986; PhD, civil engineering, University of Manchester (England), 1996; dissertation title: "Flow around Normal and Yawed Cylinders Oscillating over a Plane Bed"
Father's name unknown, grain seller
Managing director of the Islamic Republic of Iran Railways
No imprisonment
War veteran
IRGC militiaman (commander of the IRGC in East Azerbaijan)
Member of PMOI before the revolution
Dadman was expelled from Tehran University before the revolution for his political activities. He and his wife, Zohratalsadat Nazari, were both involved in the takeover of the American embassy, and he took some of the hostages to Tabriz after the failed Tabas rescue mission. Dadman was elected to the First Majlis from Tabriz on August 23, 1981, but the GC did not approve his qualifications because of his affiliation with PMOI before the revolution. In 1987, he was one of the leaders of the Mecca pilgrims' protests, which led to the death of some 400 pilgrims. Dadman was a minister for only four months before he died in a plane crash. Abbas Palizar, a member of the judicial inquiry and review commission of the Majlis, claimed some years later that the plane crash involved foul play.

Dadras, Mohammad-Hoseyn

Commander of the Islamic Republic of Iran Ground Forces (September 26, 2005–August 25, 2008);

coordinating deputy and chief of the joint staff of the Islamic Republic of Iran Army (August 26, 2008–present); deputy general commander of the army (November 5, 2017–present)

BS, military science, Ground Forces Officers' Academy; PhD, military science, Supreme National Defense University

War veteran (wounded)

Brigadier General Dadras joined the military in 1979 after spending a few months in the Construction Jihad. He was deputy commander of the Islamic Republic of Iran Ground Forces before being promoted to commander in 2005.

Dadvar, Khalil

Deputy of the Fourth Majlis, Neyriz and Estahban, Fars (1992–96)

1950–, Neyriz, Fars

BA, philosophy

Mohammad-Ebrahim

No imprisonment

Dadvar is the brother-in-law of Seyyed Abufazel Razavi-Ardakani.

Dahgan, Hasan

Deputy of the Fifth Majlis, Langarud, Gilan (1996–2000)

1958–, Langarud, Gilan

MS, management

Mohammad-Hoseyn

No imprisonment

Dahmardeh, Habibollah

Deputy of the Tenth Majlis, Zabol, Sistan and Baluchestan (2016–20)

1952–, Zabol, Sistan and Baluchestan

BS, mathematics, Isfahan University of Technology, 1977; MS, mathematics, University of Oxford (England), 1978; PhD, mathematics, University of Oxford (England), 1980; dissertation title: "Some Problems in Numerical Integration"

University professor

No imprisonment

Not a war veteran

Dahmardeh was a professor and rector of the University of Sistan and Baluchestan from 1989 to 1998 and rector of the University of Zabol from 1999 to 2005. He has also served as governor-general of Sistan and Baluchestan (2005–8), Kerman (2008–10), and Lorestan (appointed in 2010). When Dahmardeh, who is a Shiite Sistani, became the governor-general of the predominantly Sunni Baluchi province of Sistan and Baluchestan in 2005, two MPs from the province turned in their resignation letters; they subsequently withdrew their resignations.

Dalqpush, Farhad

Deputy of the Eighth Majlis, Astara, Gilan (2008–12)

1968–, Astara, Gilan

BA, educational management, Payam-e Nur University, Ardabil; MA, educational science, Islamic Azad University–Tehran

Mohrram-Ali

Civil servant

No imprisonment

War veteran

IRGC militiaman

Damadi, Mohammad

Deputy of the Ninth (2012–16) and Tenth (2016–20) Majlis, Sari and Miandorud, Mazandaran

1979–, Sari, Mazandaran

MS, civil engineering, Babol Noshirvani University of Technology

Ezzatollah, Majlis deputy

University instructor and member of the Sari City Council

No imprisonment

Not a war veteran

Damadi's father also represented Sari in the Third and Fourth Majlis.

Damadi-Kohnehdeh, Ezzatollah

Deputy of the Third (1988–92) and Fourth (1992–96)
    Majlis, Sari, Mazandaran
1950–2001, Sari, Mazandaran
Associate's degree, agricultural engineering
Valiyollah
No imprisonment
His son, Mohammad, became an MP from Sari in the
    Ninth Majlis.

Damani, Hamed

Deputy of the First (1981–84) and Second (1984–88)
    Majlis, Khash, Sistan and Baluchestan
1945–2007, Khash, Sistan and Baluchestan
Clerical education, Karachi (Pakistan)
Abdolghafur
Clergyman (Sunni)
No imprisonment
Not a war veteran
Damani, who worked in a power facility before the
    revolution, was put in charge of Iranshahr's water
    bureau after he left the Majlis and stayed in that
    post for ten years. He then represented the Office
    of the Supreme Leader in the affairs of Sunnis in
    Iranshahr.

Dana, Seyyed Mohammad-Hoseyn

Deputy of the Fourth (1992–96) and Fifth (1996–2000)
    Majlis, Abadeh, Fars
1958–, Abadeh, Fars
BS, metallurgy, 1989; MS, industrial engineering, 1996
Seyyed Ziyaeddin
No imprisonment

Danesh, Jahanshah

Deputy of the Third Majlis, Masjed Soleyman, Khuz-
    estan (1988–92)
1936–, Chahar Mahal, Chahar Mahal and Bakhtiari
High school diploma
Kheybar

Head of the agricultural office in Masjed Soleyman
No imprisonment
Martyr's family

Danesh, Seyyed Mohammad-Kazem

Deputy of the First Majlis, Andimeshk and Shush,
    Khuzestan (1980–81)
1939–1981, Dezful, Khuzestan
Clerical education
Seyyed Mahmud, clergyman
Clergyman (HI)
No imprisonment
Danesh was a member of the paramilitary group
    Mansurron and was killed in the bombing of the
    IRP headquarters on June 28, 1981.

Danesh-Ashtiyani, Gholam-Reza

Deputy of the First Majlis, Tafresh and Ashtiyan,
    Markazi (1980–81)
1930–1981, Ashtiyan, Markazi
Clerical education, Qom Seminary; PhD, theology,
    Tehran University
Abolfazl, bazaar tradesman
Clergyman (HI)
Imprisoned before the revolution
Not a war veteran
IRGC militiaman (early commander)
Martyr's family (seventeen-year-old daughter, Mah-
    bubeh, died during a revolutionary demonstration
    on September 8, 1978)
Member of the IRP
Ayatollah Khomeini appointed Danesh-Ashtiyani
    as the Friday prayer leader of Ashtiyan in 1980.
    Danesh-Ashtiyani was killed in the bombing of the
    IRP headquarters on June 28, 1981. His brother, Ali
    Danesh-Monfared, represented Ashtiyan and later
    Tafresh in the Fourth and Seventh Majlis.

Danesh-Ja'fari, Davud

Deputy of the Fifth (1996–2000) and Seventh (2004–
    August 28, 2005) Majlis, Tehran, Tehran; minister

of economic affairs and finance in President Ahmadinejad's first cabinet (August 24, 2005–August 6, 2008); member of the Sixth (2007–12), Seventh (2012–17), and Eighth (2017–22) Expediency Discernment Assembly

1954–, Tehran, Tehran

BS, civil engineering, University of Kashmir (India), 1979; MA, economics, Tehran University, 1992; PhD, economics, Allameh Tabataba'i University, 2001; dissertation title: "Factors Affecting Fluctuations in Iran's Macroeconomics"

Ebrahim, civil servant (companies)

Civil servant

No imprisonment

War veteran

IRGC militiaman

Martyr's family

Member of AVIR

Danesh-Ja'fari was a member of the radical underground Badr group before 1979. He lived in India for five years in the 1970s. During the years of the Iran–Iraq War, he was the commander of the war engineering office in Abadan, and later was a member of the high council of reconstruction of war-torn regions. Danesh-Ja'fari resigned from the Seventh Majlis to become minister of economic affairs and finance. He was also a member of the central council of the Construction Jihad and the high council for money and credit, and head of the Supervision Commission in the Office of the EDA. Danesh-Ja'fari served as an adviser to Qazizadeh-Hashemi, the minister of health, during President Rouhani's tenure, and was an economic deputy in the headquarters of the Supreme National Security Council. His wife is the cousin of Morteza Nabavi.

Daneshju, Farhad

Rector of Islamic Azad University (January 17, 2012–September 26, 2013)

1957–, Damghan, Semnan

BS, civil engineering; MS, information systems, Queen Mary University of London (England); PhD, civil engineering (seismology), Polytechnic of Central London (currently known as the University of Westminster) (England)

Mas'ud, judiciary civil servant

Professor of civil and environmental engineering at Tarbiyat-e Modarres University

No imprisonment

Not a war veteran

Secretary-general of the Association for Safeguarding of National Production

Daneshju was rector of Tarbiyat-e Modarres University from 2005 to 2010. He was a deputy to his brother Kamran Daneshju, the minister of science, research, and technology, before he was appointed rector of Islamic Azad University.

Daneshju, Kamran

Minister of science, research, and technology in President Ahmadinejad's second cabinet (September 3, 2009–August 3, 2013)

1957–, Damghan, Semnan

BS, mechanical engineering, Queen Mary University of London (England); MS, mechanical engineering, Imperial College of London (England); PhD, mechanical engineering, Amirkabir University of Technology, 1989

Mas'ud, judiciary civil servant

Civil servant, ministries

No imprisonment

Not a war veteran

IRGC militiaman

Founding member of the Association for Safeguarding of National Production

Daneshju lived in England from 1977 to 1989, when the British government expelled him over the Salman Rushdie issue. Between 1989 and 2005, Daneshju was working for the IRGC and the MDAFL in different capacities. In 1994, he also became a faculty member at Iran University of Science and Technology, and in 1999, he was one of the four plaintiffs against *Salam*, alongside Mahmoud Ahmadinejad. In 2005, Daneshju became the governor-general of Tehran and later deputy interior minister. In late 2008, he became the caretaker of MI after the Majlis impeached the former minister. During the contested 2009 presidential election, he was the political deputy of MI in charge of the election. Afterward, he became the minister of science, research, and technology. There were doubts about his academic degrees and in September 2009, the scientific magazine *Nature* accused him of having plagiarized an earlier academic paper by a South Korean scholar. He is the brother of Farhad Daneshju.

Danesh-Monfared, Ali

Commander in chief of the IRGC (March–May 1979); deputy of the Fourth Majlis, Tafresh and Ashtiyan, Markazi (1992–96); deputy of the Seventh Majlis, Tafresh, Markazi (2004–8)
1941–, Ashtiyan, Markazi
BS, mathematics, Tehran University
Abolfazl, bazaar tradesman
Civil servant
Imprisoned before the revolution
IRGC militiaman (founding member)
Member of the LMI (resigned after the revolution)
Martyr's family (brother, HI Gholam-Reza Danesh-Ashtiyani, killed in the IRP headquarters bombing; niece Mahbubeh died during a revolutionary demonstration on September 8, 1978)
Danesh-Monfared was a member of PMOI but left the organization. In 1979, he was the executive manager of the welcoming committee for Ayatollah Khomeini upon his return to Iran. Danesh-Monfared, along with Mohsen Rafiqdust, Mohammad Gharazi, Javad Mansuri, and Asghar Baghbanian, was one of the founders of the IRGC. He was the governor of Fars (1979–80 and 1989–93), Hamadan, and Markazi Provinces and ran unsuccessfully for the First Majlis from

Tehran. In the 1980s, he was deputy for administrative and financial affairs and deputy for coordination of provincial affairs in the Ministry of Industries.

Daneshrad-Kiyai, Aziz

Member of the Assembly for the Final Examination of the Constitution, representing the Jewish community (as a religious minority) (1979)
1920–1991, Golpayegan, Isfahan
BS, electrical engineering, Tehran University
Haqnazar, bazaar merchant and Jewish cleric
Retired civil servant
No imprisonment
Not a war veteran
There were rumors about his affiliation with the Tudeh Party.

Daneshyar, Kamal

Deputy of the Fourth (1992–96), Fifth (1996–2000), and Seventh (2004–8) Majlis, Bandar-e Mahshahr, Khuzestan
1956–, Behbahan, Khuzestan
BS, mathematics; MS, industrial management
Morad-Ali
Civil servant
No imprisonment
War veteran

Dara'ei, Sayd-Isa

Deputy of the Ninth Majlis, Andimeshk, Khuzestan (2012–16)
1963–, Sad-e Dez, Khuzestan
BA, policing, Police Academy
Law enforcement official
No imprisonment
War veteran
IRGC militiaman
Dara'ei was wounded at the war front and spent thirty-two months as a prisoner of war. He fought

against the Kurdistan Democratic Party in Kurdistan in 1993.

Darvishpur, Hojjatollah

Deputy of the Ninth Majlis, I'zeh and Baghmalek, Khuzestan (2012–16)
1961–, Ardal, Chahar Mahal and Bakhtiari
MA, political science, Imam Sadeq University; PhD, political science, University of Pune (India)
Father's name unknown, farmer
University professor
No imprisonment
War veteran
Darvishpur ran unsuccessfully for the Seventh Majlis and is now a professor at Islamic Azad University.

Darvishzadeh, Mehdi-Reza

Deputy of the Fifth Majlis, Dezful, Khuzestan (1996–2000)
1956–, Dezful, Khuzestan
PhD, mathematics
Abdolmohammad
Professor of mathematics at Tehran University
No imprisonment
Darvishzadeh was one of the four individuals, including future president Mahmoud Ahmadinejad, who filed a lawsuit against *Salam* in 1999.

Daseh, Hasel

Deputy of the Sixth Majlis, Piranshahr and Sardasht, West Azerbaijan (2000–2004)
1967–, Piranshahr, West Azerbaijan
BS, agricultural engineering
Ahmad-Beyk
Civil servant
No imprisonment
After finishing his term in the Majlis, Daseh, who is a Sunni, went back to work for the government. The GC disqualified him from running in the 2016 Majlis election.

Dashti-Tolier, Motalleb

Deputy of the Second Majlis, Germi, Ardabil (1984–88)
1952–, Germi, Ardabil
Associate's degree
Bohlul
No imprisonment

Dastgheyb, Mrs. Gowharoshshari'eh

Deputy of the First (1980–84), Second (1984–88), and Third (1988–92) Majlis, Tehran, Tehran
1935–, Shiraz, Fars
MA, Arabic literature
Abbas-Ali, clergyman
High school and college teacher and administrator
No imprisonment
Founding member of the Islamic Association of Iranian Teachers
Dastgheyb failed to receive enough votes for the Fifth and Sixth Majlis, and she did not run for the Seventh Majlis in protest of the massive disqualification of reformist candidates. Her husband, Hasan Asadi-Lari (d. 1990), who had a doctorate in theology from Tehran University and was imprisoned a number of times under the shah, was Iran's ambassador to India in the early 1980s. After the revolution, he became Iran's cultural attaché in Pakistan. She is the niece of Ayatollah Seyyed Abdolhoseyn Dastgheyb, and the mother-in-law of Mostafa Mo'in.

Dastgheyb, Seyyed Abdolhoseyn

Member of the Assembly for the Final Examination of the Constitution, Fars (1979)
1913–December 11, 1981, Shiraz, Fars
Clerical education, Najaf Seminary (Iraq), 1942
Seyyed Mohammad-Taqi, clergyman (HI)
Clergyman
Imprisoned before the revolution
Not a war veteran

Ayatollah Dastgheyb was the Friday prayer leader of Shiraz from 1979 until December 11, 1981. A young female PMOI activist assassinated him in a suicide attack.

Dastgheyb, Seyyed Ali-Asghar

Member of the First (1983–90), Third (1999–2006), Fourth (2007–16), and Fifth (2016–22) Assembly of Experts, Fars
1945–, Shiraz, Fars
Clerical education, Qom Seminary
Seyyed Ali-Akbar, clergyman
Clergyman
Imprisoned before the revolution
Not a war veteran
Martyr's family (uncle)
Ayatollah Seyyed Ali-Asghar Dastgheyb is the nephew of Ayatollah Seyyed Abdolhoseyn Dastgheyb, who was assassinated by PMOI. His own son, Seyyed Ahmad-Reza Dastgheyb, became a representative in the Eighth Majlis.

Dastgheyb, Seyyed Ali-Mohammad

Member of the First (1983–90), Third (1999–2006), and Fourth (2007–16) Assembly of Experts, Fars
1935–, Shiraz, Fars
Clerical education, Najaf Seminary (Iraq)
Seyyed Ali-Akbar, clergyman
Clergyman
Imprisoned before the revolution
Not a war veteran
Martyr's family (uncle)
Ayatollah Seyyed Ali-Mohammad Dastgheyb was Ayatollah Khomeini's representative at Shiraz University and head of the revolutionary tribunal in Fars Province. To protest the mandatory clerical competency exam, he did not take part in the elections for the Second AE. He supported Mir Hoseyn Musavi in the 2009 presidential election. He is the nephew of Ayatollah Seyyed Abdolhoseyn Dastgheyb, whom PMOI assassinated, and the brother of Seyyed Ali-Asghar Dastgheyb.

Dastgheyb [Qom], Seyyed Ahmad-Reza

Deputy of the Eighth (2008–12) and Ninth (2012–16) Majlis, Shiraz, Fars
1976–, Qom, Qom
PhD, political science
Seyyed Ali-Asghar, clergyman (ayatollah)
University professor and adviser to the governor-general
No imprisonment
Not a war veteran
Dastgheyb was the youngest member of the Eighth Majlis, where he was active in the Culture Commission. His father, Seyyed Ali-Asghar, is a three-time member of the AE.

Dastgheyb [Shiraz], Seyyed Ahmad-Reza

Deputy of the Eighth Majlis, Shiraz, Fars (2008–12)
1964–, Shiraz, Fars
BS, industrial management, Shiraz University
Seyyed Fakhreddin
Law enforcement official
No imprisonment
There were two representatives in the Eighth Majlis from Shiraz named Seyyed Ahmad-Reza Dastgheyb. This one is a reformist politician who was disqualified by the GC when he ran for the Ninth Majlis.

Davatgari, Mehdi

Deputy of the Ninth Majlis, Maragheh and Ajab-Shir, East Azerbaijan (2012–16)
1966–, Maragheh, East Azerbaijan
BA, public administration; MA, public law, Islamic Azad University–Tehran, 2001; pursuing a PhD in international law
Javad, craftsman
Judiciary official
No imprisonment
Davatgari went back to the judiciary as a judge in 2016, but in 2017 he ran in midterm elections for the Tenth Majlis.

Davidian, Levon

Deputy of the Sixth Majlis, representing Armenians of
　　northern Iran (as a religious minority) (2000–2004)
1944–2009, Hamadan, Hamadan
MD, medicine
David
Medical doctor
No imprisonment
Davidian died in a plane crash.

Davudi, Mohammad-Baqer

Deputy of the Second Majlis, Kordkuy, Golestan
　　(1984–88)
1943–, Kordkuy, Golestan
Clerical education
Mohammad
Clergyman
No imprisonment

Davudi, Parviz

First vice president in President Ahmadinejad's first
　　cabinet (2005–9); member of the Sixth (2007–12),
　　Seventh (2012–17), and Eighth (2017–22) Expedi-
　　ency Discernment Assembly
1952–, Tehran, Tehran
MA, economics, Iowa State University (USA); PhD,
　　economics, Iowa State University (USA), 1981;
　　dissertation title: "Money Supply Determination
　　and a Lagged Reserve Accounting System"
Davud
Professor of economics
No imprisonment
Not a war veteran
Member of the central council of DCII
Davudi was head of the economics department at
　　Tarbiyat-e Modarres University until 1991, when
　　he began teaching at Shahid Beheshti University.
　　In addition, from 1989 to 1997, he was an eco-
　　nomic deputy at the Ministry of Economic Affairs
　　and Finance. He ran unsuccessfully for the Tenth
　　Majlis from Tehran in 2016.

Davudi, Yusef

Deputy of the Fifth Majlis, Najafabad, Isfahan
　　(1997–2000)
1961–, Farsan, Chahar Mahal and Bakhtiari
BS, industrial engineering; clerical education
Ali-Asghar
No imprisonment

Davudi [Sarab], Yusef

Deputy of the Tenth Majlis, Sarab, East Azerbaijan
　　(2016–20)
1964–, Sarab, East Azerbaijan
MD, veterinary science
Davudi is the former rector of Islamic Azad
　　University–Sarab.

Davudi-Shamsi, Seyyed Esma'il

Deputy of the Third (1988–92) and Fourth (1992–96)
　　Majlis, Ardakan, Yazd
1946–, Yazd, Yazd
BA, 1976; MS, management, 1991
Seyyed Mahmud
No imprisonment

Davudolmusavi-Damghani, Seyyed Abolqasem

Deputy of the Second Majlis, Ramhormoz and Ram-
　　shir, Khuzestan (1984–February 20, 1986)
1944–February 20, 1986, Damghan, Semnan
Clerical education
Seyyed Mohammad, farmer
Clergyman and Friday prayer leader of Ramhormoz
　　(1981–84)
No imprisonment
HI Davudolmusavi-Damghani was killed when Iraqi
　　forces shot down his plane.

Dehdashti, Seyyed Hoseyn

Deputy of the Eighth (2008–12) and Ninth (2012–16)
　　Majlis, Abadan, Khuzestan

1967–, Abadan, Khuzestan

MD, medicine, Shahid Chamran University of Ahvaz

Seyyed Mohammad-Kazem, clergyman (ayatollah)

Medical doctor; university professor and
administrator

No imprisonment

War veteran

After serving in the Majlis, Dehdashti served as an
adviser to the minister of health, and in January
2017 the VP for parliamentary affairs, Hoseyn-Ali
Amiri, appointed him as one of his deputies.

Dehqan, Ali-Akbar

Deputy of the First Majlis, Torbat-e Jam, Razavi Khorasan (1980–81)

1948–June 28, 1981, Torbat-e Jam, Razavi Khorasan

Associate's degree

Mohammad-Javad, laborer

High school teacher

No imprisonment

Not a war veteran

IRGC militiaman

Member of the IRP

Dehqan, who was active in anti-Baha'i activities
beginning in the mid-1960s, was killed in the
bombing of the IRP headquarters in 1981.

Dehqan [Dehqani-Pudeh], Hoseyn

VP and head of FMVA in President Khatami's second
cabinet (2004–5) and President Ahmadinejad's
first cabinet (2005–9); minister of defense and
armed forces logistics in President Rouhani's first
cabinet (August 15, 2013–August 13, 2017)

1957–, Shahreza, Isfahan

PhD, management, Tehran University, 2000

Yadollah

No imprisonment

War veteran

IRGC militiaman (brigadier general)

Dehqan was involved in the takeover of the American
embassy and then spent some time in Lebanon.
He has served in many important posts, including

commander of the IRGC's Sarollah base (1984–
86), deputy head and head of the IRGC's air force
(April 24, 1990–1992), deputy joint chief of the
IRGC (1992–96), head of the IRGC's cooperative
foundation (1996–97), deputy minister of defense
(1997–2003), and head of the political, defensive,
and intelligence committee of the EDA (2010–13).

Dehqan[i], Ezzatollah

Deputy of the First (1981–84) and Second (1984–88)
Majlis, Torbat-e Jam and Taybad, Razavi Khorasan; deputy of the Eighth Majlis, Dorud, Lorestan (2008–12)

1951–, Aligudarz, Lorestan

BA, Islamic law, Ferdowsi University of Mashhad,
1978; MA, theology, Tehran University, 1987;
PhD, theology, 1994

Seyfollah

Academia

Imprisoned before the revolution

Not a war veteran

Founding member of the Islamic Society of Educators

Dehqani, Ali-Reza

Deputy of the Eighth Majlis, I'zeh and Baghmalek,
Khuzestan (2008–12)

1966, I'zeh, Khuzestan

MA, physical training

Esma'il

Sports anchor at IRIB

No imprisonment

Dehqani ran unsuccessfully for the Ninth Majlis from
Tehran.

Dehqani, Allahverdi

Deputy of the Ninth Majlis, Varzaqan and Kharvana,
East Azerbaijan (2012–16)

1969–, Varzaqan, East Azerbaijan

BS, chemistry, Tabriz University, 1995; MA, political
science, Islamic Azad University–Karaj, 2004

Isa

Chemist and adviser to various industrial and mining firms

No imprisonment

War veteran

IRGC militiaman

Dehqani's wife and two children died in a car accident in November 2012, and he himself was injured.

Dehqani, Mohammad-Qayyum

Deputy of the Eighth Majlis, Iranshahr, Fanuj, Sarbaz, Bent, Lashar, and Ashar, Sistan and Baluchestan (2008–12)

1970–, Iranshahr, Sistan and Baluchestan

BS, mathematics

Mir Khan

Academia

No imprisonment

Dehqani, who is a Sunni, was not elected to the Ninth Majlis.

Dehqani, Yadollah

Deputy of the First Majlis, Ahar, East Azerbaijan (1980–84)

1933–May 29, 2012, Mehtarlu, East Azerbaijan

Clerical education, Qom Seminary

Mohammad, farmer

Clergyman (HI)

No imprisonment

Not a war veteran

After Majlis he became head of the teacher training center in Ahar.

Dehqani-Firuzabadi, Kamal

Deputy of the Tenth Majlis, Taft, Yazd (2016–20)

1964–, Meybod, Yazd

BA, law; MA, political science and Islamic studies, Imam Sadeq University; PhD, international relations, Islamic Azad University–Science and Research Branch

Diplomat

No imprisonment

War veteran (fifteen months; wounded)

Dehqani-Firuzabadi previously served as an official in the Ministry of Foreign Affairs, where he toured as a diplomat in Morocco. He was also an official in Tehran municipality and a political-security deputy in Fars Province.

Dehqani-Nughandar, Mohammad

Deputy of the Seventh (2004–8), Eighth (2008–12), Ninth (2012–16), and Tenth (2016–20) Majlis, Torqabeh and Chenaran, Razavi Khorasan

1963–, Torqabeh, Razavi Khorasan

BA, law, Tehran University; MA, law, Tehran University; PhD, private law, Tehran University, 2003

Rajab

No imprisonment

War veteran (twenty-two months; POW in Iraq for sixty-four months)

IRGC militiaman (engineering commander in Marivan IRGC)

Member of the SFIR

Dehqan-Naserabadi, Gholam-Reza

Deputy of the Eighth Majlis, Kazerun, Fars (2008–12)

1969–, Kazerun, Fars

BA, law, Islamic Azad University–Shiraz, 1993; MA, law (penal and criminal), Shahid Chamran University of Ahvaz

Reza

Judiciary official

No imprisonment

Not a war veteran

After the Eighth Majlis, Dehqan-Naserabadi became an inspector in the State General Inspectorate Organization. The GC disqualified him from running in the 2016 Majlis election.

Delavar, Mohammad-Ali

Deputy of the Eighth Majlis, Dargaz, Razavi Khorasan (2008–12)

1957–, Dargaz, Razavi Khorasan

BS, mathematics
Sohrab, farmer
Civil servant
No imprisonment
Not a war veteran
Delavar was involved in the city council of his district but he was not elected to the Ninth Majlis.

Delbari, Mohammad-Esma'il

Deputy of the Third (1988–92) and Fourth (1992–96) Majlis, Bostanabad, East Azerbaijan
1955–, Bostanabad, East Azerbaijan
High school diploma
Ne'matollah
No imprisonment

Delju, Gholam-Hoseyn

Mayor of Tehran (1981–82)
1944–
MA, public administration, Iranian National Tax Administration School, 1975; PhD, public administration, Allameh Tabataba'i University, 2006
Delju was the CEO of Iran Insurance Company from September 15, 1990, to April 4, 1994, and he retired from Allameh Tabataba'i University's management school in 2009.

Delkhosh-Abatary, Seyyed Kazem

Deputy of the Seventh (2004–8), Eighth (2008–12), and Tenth (2016–20) Majlis, Sowme'eh Sara, Gilan
1961–, Sowme'eh Sara, Gilan
BA, public administration; MA, economics; pursuing a PhD in economics
Seyyed Torab
Civil servant
No imprisonment
IRGC militiaman (Basij)
Delkhosh-Abatary, who used to read poems (often humorous) in the Majlis, was not elected to the Ninth Majlis and worked as a deputy in the

government-owned Iran Insurance Company before being reelected to the Tenth Majlis.

Derakhshandeh, Mrs. Akhtar

Deputy of the Fourth Majlis, Kermanshah, Kermanshah (1992–96)
1942–, Kermanshah, Kermanshah
Associate's degree
Ahmad
Teacher and school administrator
No imprisonment
Not a war veteran
Derakhshandeh was the first female MP elected from Kermanshah Province. She retired from the Ministry of Education in 1998 and set up a cultural foundation.

Dialameh, Seyyed Abdolhamid

Deputy of the First Majlis, Mashhad, Razavi Khorasan (1980–81)
1954–June 28, 1981, Tehran, Tehran
MD, pharmacy, Ferdowsi University of Mashhad, 1980
Hamid
Imprisoned before the revolution
Not a war veteran
IRGC militiaman (member of the command council in Mashhad)
Dialameh died in the bombing of the IRP headquarters.

Didgah, Nazar-Mohammad

Deputy of the First Majlis, Iranshahr, Sistan and Baluchestan (1980–84)
1932–, Iranshahr, Sistan and Baluchestan
Clerical education
Mazar, farmer
Clergyman
No imprisonment
Not a war veteran
Didgah was a Sunni MP and is currently in charge of a religious school near Iranshahr.

Dini, Valiyollah

Deputy of the Seventh Majlis, Ahar, East Azerbaijan
(2004–8)
1972–, Ahar and Heris, East Azerbaijan
BA, mechanical engineering and public administra-
tion, Petroleum University of Technology, 1994;
MA, human resource management, Petroleum
University of Technology
Mohammad, farmer
Civil servant, state companies
No imprisonment
Not a war veteran
After leaving the Majlis, Dini worked in the gas in-
dustry in various capacities.

Dirbaz, Ali

Deputy of the Sixth (2001–4) and Seventh (2004–8)
Majlis, Bandar-e Abbas, Hormozgan
1952–, Bandar-e Abbas, Qeshm, Abumusa, and Hajia-
bad, Hormozgan
BA, business administration; MA, public
administration
Mohammad
Civil servant
No imprisonment
After serving in the Majlis, Dirbaz became a civil
servant.

Dirbaz, Asgar

Member of the Fourth (2013–16) and Fifth (2016–22)
Assembly of Experts, West Azerbaijan
1959–, Miyaneh, East Azerbaijan
MA, theology, Qom University, 1992; PhD, theology,
Tarbiyat-e Modarres University, 2003; clerical
education, Qom Seminary
Nowruz-Ali
Clergyman and rector of Qom University (appointed
in 2012)
No imprisonment

HI Dirbaz was elected to the Fourth AE in interim
elections in June 2013. He was previously head of
the ideological-political bureau of the Ministry of
Defense.

Doa'i, Seyyed Mahmud

Deputy of the First (1981–84), Second (1984–88), Third
(1988–92), Fourth (1992–96), Fifth (1996–2000),
and Sixth (2000–2004) Majlis, Tehran, Tehran
1941–, Yazd, Yazd
Clerical education, Qom Seminary and Najaf Semi-
nary (Iraq)
Seyyed Mohammad
Clergyman
Imprisoned before the revolution
Not a war veteran
Founding member of the ACC
HI Doa'i was responsible for an arson attack on a
newspaper in Kerman for having insulted Ayatol-
lah Khomeini before the revolution. In the 1960s,
he collaborated with such religious journals as
Enteqam and *Besat*. Doa'i lived in Iraq from 1967
to 1979 and ran "Radio Nehzat-e Ruhaniyyat"
(Movement of Clergy Radio) from 1968 to 1974.
He underwent military training in PLO camps.
A close confidant of Ayatollah Khomeini, Doa'i
became Iran's first ambassador to Iraq (February
1979–80) before the outbreak of the war. Khomeini appointed him as the editor of the daily
Ettela'at in May 1980.

Dogani-Aghchelu, Mohammad-Hasan

Deputy of the Seventh (2004–8), Eighth (2008–12),
and Ninth (2012–16) Majlis, Fasa, Fars
1956–, Fasa, Fars
PhD, mathematics
Ali
No imprisonment
University professor and administrator
Dogani-Aghchelu ran unsuccessfully for the Tenth
Majlis.

Dorrazahi, Mohammad-Baset

Deputy of the Tenth Majlis, Saravan, Sistan and Balu-
    chestan (2016–20)
1980–, Saravan, Sistan and Baluchestan
MA, English language, University of Pune (India)
University professor
No imprisonment
Not a war veteran
Dorrazahi, a Sunni, studied in India for eight years,
    and has taught at Islamic Azad University and
    Payam-e Nur University.

Dorri-Najafabadi, Qorbanali [Hoseyn-Ali]

Deputy of the First Majlis, Ardal, Chahar Mahal and
    Bakhtiari (1980–84); deputy of the Second (1984–
    88), Fourth (1992–96), and Fifth (1996–August 20,
    1997) Majlis, Tehran, Tehran; member of the Sec-
    ond Assembly of Experts, Ilam (1991–98); mem-
    ber of the Third (1999–2006), Fourth (2007–16),
    and Fifth (2016–22) Assembly of Experts, Tehran;
    member of the Fourth (1997–2002), Fifth (2002–
    7), Sixth (2007–12), Seventh (2012–17), and Eighth
    (2017–22) Expediency Discernment Assembly;
    minister of intelligence in President Khatami's
    first cabinet (August 20, 1997–February 10, 1999);
    head of the CAJ (1999–August 15, 2004), prosecu-
    tor-general (August 15, 2004–August 25, 2009)
1945–, Najafabad, Isfahan
Clerical education, Qom Seminary
Asadollah, farmer
Clergyman (ayatollah)
No imprisonment
Not a war veteran
Member of the SCC and the central council of the IRP
Dorri-Najafabadi has been an influential political
    actor in the Islamic Republic of Iran. He resigned
    from the Fifth Majlis in 1997 to become the
    minister of intelligence. During his tenure, MIIRI
    officers carried out the extrajudicial killings of
    dissident intellectuals (known as "chain mur-
    ders"), including former labor minister Daryush

Foruhar and his wife. Dorri-Najafabadi was
forced to resign his post over this matter. As prosecutor-general during the 2009 protests, he supervised the televised "show trials" of protesters that
summer. In addition, Dorri-Najafabadi also held
the following positions: Friday prayer leader of
Shahrekord and Arak and interim Friday prayer
leader of Shahr-e Rey, director of the Center for
Strategic Research, member of the high council of
the Ahlulbeyt World Assembly, supreme leader's
representative in Markazi Province, and overseer
of Ayatollah Montazeri's office during his tenure
as deputy supreme leader. Dorri-Najafabadi's son-
in-law, Hesameddin Ashna, is the main cultural
adviser to President Rouhani.

Dowlatabadi, Mohammad-Reza

Deputy of the Sixth Majlis, Neyshabur, Razavi Kho-
    rasan (2000–2004)
1956–, Neyshabur, Razavi Khorasan
Clerical education
Ramezan-Ali
Clergyman
No imprisonment
HI Dowlatabadi was disqualified by the GC from
    running for the Tenth Majlis.

Dowlati-Bakhshan, Abdolaziz

Deputy of the Fifth Majlis, Saravan, Sistan and Balu-
    chestan (1996–2000)
1962–, Saravan, Sistan and Baluchestan
BA, Persian literature
Shahmorad
No imprisonment
Dowlati-Bakhshan was a Sunni MP.

Dusti, Esma'il

Deputy of the Fifth Majlis, Kuhdasht, Lorestan
    (1996–2000)
1958–, Kuhdasht, Lorestan

BA, Persian literature; BA, management
Asad
No imprisonment
IRGC militiaman
Dusti is a former member of the Tehran City Council.

Dustmohammadi, Hadi

Deputy of the Seventh Majlis, Semnan, Semnan
(2004–8)
1956–, Semnan, Semnan
Clerical education, Qom Seminary; PhD, theology,
Qom Seminary and Tehran University
Ebrahim
Clergyman (HI)
No imprisonment
After serving in the Majlis, Dustmohammadi became
a history professor at Tehran University.

Duzduzani, Abbas

Commander in chief of the IRGC (February–July 1980);
minister of Islamic guidance in PM Raja'i's cabinet
(1980–81); deputy of the First Majlis, Tabriz, East
Azerbaijan (1981–84); deputy of the Second (1984–
88) and Third (1988–92) Majlis, Tehran, Tehran
1942–, Tabriz, East Azerbaijan
High school diploma; clerical education
Haji Baba
Imprisoned before the revolution (6 years)
War veteran
IRGC militiaman
Member of the MNP before the revolution; founding
member of the Islamic Association of Iranian
Teachers
Duzduzani was one of the founders of the IRGC, and
Ayatollah Khomeini appointed him its commander in chief in February 1980. He became
minister of Islamic guidance on September 10,
1980, and on October 1, 1980, announced the
closure of his ministry until further notice. After
serving three terms in the Majlis, he became head
of the Tehran City Council. He was close to PM

Mir Hoseyn Musavi and continues to be active as
a political reformist.

Ebadi, Seyyed Ali-Reza

Deputy of the Fifth (1996–2000) and Seventh
(2004–8) Majlis, Birjand and Nehbandan, South
Khorasan
1939–, Khoosf, South Khorasan
Clerical education
Seyyed Heydar, clergyman and farmer (HI)
Clergyman
No imprisonment
Martyr's family (three nephews)
Ebadi was commissar of the ideological-political
bureau of the armed forces. His brother, Seyyed
Mehdi Ebadi, was a member of the AE for three
terms. His son, Seyyed Mohammad-Baqer Ebadi,
represented Birjand in the Ninth Majlis.

Ebadi, Seyyed Mehdi

Member of the First (1983–90) and Second (1991–98)
Assembly of Experts, Sistan and Baluchestan;
member of the Third Assembly of Experts, Razavi
Khorasan (1999–2005)
1936–2005, Khoosf, South Khorasan
Clerical education, Qom Seminary
Seyyed Heydar, clergyman and farmer (HI)
Clergyman (ayatollah)
No imprisonment
Not a war veteran
Martyr's family (sons Seyyed Mohsen and Seyyed
Mohammad-Ali killed at the war front)
Ebadi studied in Mashhad (thirteen years), Najaf
(three years), and Qom (fifteen years). Ayatollah
Vahid Khorasani sent him to Kuwait before the
revolution. He was appointed by Ayatollah Kho-
meini as the Friday prayer leader of Zahedan and
appointed by Ayatollah Khamenei as the Friday
prayer leader of Mashhad, where he served until
2005. His brother, Seyyed Ali-Reza Ebadi, and his
nephew, Seyyed Mohammad-Baqer, both represented Birjand in the Majlis.

Ebadi, Seyyed Mohammad-Baqer

Deputy of the Ninth (2012–16) and Tenth (2016–20)
    Majlis, Birjand, Darmiyan, and Khoosf, South
    Khorasan
1970–, Khoosf, South Khorasan
Clerical education, Qom Seminary; BA, theology,
    Ferdowsi University of Mashhad; MA, theology,
    Tarbiyat-e Modarres University
Seyyed Ali-Reza, clergyman
Clergyman (HI) and Friday prayer leader of Birjand
No imprisonment
War veteran
Martyr's family (three cousins)

Ebrahim-Baysalami, Gholam-Heydar

Deputy of the Fifth (1996–2000) and Sixth (2000–2004)
    Majlis, Khaf and Roshtkhar, Razavi Khorasan
1965–, Khaf, Razavi Khorasan
PhD, sociology
Qorban-Ali
Academia
No imprisonment
Founding member of the Islamic Iran Solidarity Party
    and of the Association for Defense of the Free-
    dom of the Press; member of the Association of
    Producers
He later became CEO of the Tourism Holding of So-
    cial Security Organization.

Ebrahimi, Ali

Deputy of the Tenth Majlis, Shazand, Markazi
    (2016–20)
1967–, Shazand, Markazi
MS, genetics
Ebrahimi has been involved with the Agricultural Jihad
    and was an adviser to the head of that organization.

Ebrahimi, Ali-Asghar

Deputy of the Sixth Majlis, Aliabad Katul, Golestan
    (2001–4)

1966–, Aliabad Katul, Golestan
MD, medicine
Abdolhoseyn
Medical doctor
No imprisonment

Ebrahimi, Ali-Reza

Deputy of the Tenth Majlis, Ramiyan, Golestan
    (2016–20)
1976–, Rezaabad, Golestan
BA, Islamic philosophy and theology, Islamic Azad
    University–Tehran; MA, Islamic philosophy and
    theology, Islamic Azad University–Tehran
Provincial civil servant
No imprisonment
Not a war veteran
Ebrahimi entered the Tenth Majlis after serving as a
    local governor and working for local governments.

Ebrahimi, Hoseyn

Deputy of the Second Majlis, Varamin, Tehran
    (1984–88); deputy of the Eighth Majlis, Birjand,
    South Khorasan (2008–12)
1945–, Hasanabad, South Khorasan
Clerical education, Qom Seminary
Abbas-Ali
Clergyman (HI)
Imprisoned before the revolution
Not a war veteran
Member of the executive committee of the SCC
Ebrahimi is a former ideological-political commissar
    in the army and was Ayatollah Khamenei's repre-
    sentative in Afghanistan.

Ebrahimiyan, Nejatollah

Member of the Sixth (June 14, 2013–16) and Seventh
    (2016–19) Guardian Councils
1965–, Tonekabon, Mazandaran
BA, law, University of Judicial Sciences and Admin-
    istrative Services, 1988; MA, law, Tehran Univer-
    sity; PhD, law (France; unverified)

Judiciary official
No imprisonment
Not a war veteran
Ebrahimiyan started working in the judiciary in 1991
and became a member of the GC on June 14, 2013
upon the approval of the Majlis. He then became
spokesperson for the GC. Ebrahimiyan also
teaches at Shahid Beheshti University.

Ebrahimnezhad, Ja'far

Deputy of the Fourth Majlis, Quchan, Razavi Kho-
rasan (1992–96)
1953–, Quchan, Razavi Khorasan
Clerical education
Abdollah, clergyman
Clergyman (HI)
No imprisonment
Not a war veteran
Member of the IRP
Ebrahimnezhad was a member of the IKRF's supervi-
sory council for four years.

Ebrahimzadeh, Akbar

Deputy chief of the General Staff of Armed Forces in
Basij Affairs (May 23, 2010–present)
IRGC militiaman (brigadier general)

Ebtekar, Mrs. Ma'sume (Nilofar)

VP and head of the Environmental Protection Orga-
nization in President Khatami's first (1997–2001)
and second (2001–5) cabinets, as well as in
President Rouhani's first cabinet (2013–August
13, 2017); VP for women's and family affairs in
President Rouhani's second cabinet (2017–21)
1960–, Tehran, Tehran
BS, medical technology, Shahid Beheshti University,
1986; MS, immunology, Tarbiyat-e Modarres
University, 1989; PhD, immunology, Tarbiyat-e
Modarres University, 1996
Taqi, engineer
Academia

No imprisonment
In 1997, Ebtekar became the first female vice president
in postrevolutionary Iran. She and her husband,
Seyyed Mohammad Hashemi-Isfahani, were both
involved in the takeover of the American embassy. Ebtekar, who grew up in the United States,
became spokesperson for the hostage takers and
was known to the American television audience
as "Sister Mary." She and her husband got married in 1981 and he worked for the NIOC. Her
father, who has a PhD in energy engineering, was
director of the Iranian Environmental Protection
Organization from 1979 to 1981. Her mother,
Fatemeh Barzegar, is in charge of Zeynab Kobra
Charity Foundation. Ebtekar represented Iran at
the World Women's Conferences in Nairobi and
Beijing. She is the daughter-in-law of Ayatollah
Seyyed Esma'il Hashemi-Isfahani, who was a
member of the First and Second AE.

Edalat, Mrs. Hamideh

Deputy of the Sixth Majlis, Dashtestan, Bushehr
(2000–2004)
1956–, Khorramshahr, Khuzestan
BS, soil science, Shiraz University; PhD, entomology,
Tehran University
Hasan
Academia
No imprisonment
Member of the Alliance of the Women of the Islamic
Republic
In 2000, Edalat won the only available seat from
Dashtestan to get elected to the Sixth Majlis. She
decided not to run for the Seventh Majlis, and
started working for the government. She is a
faculty member at Tehran University of Medical
Sciences.

Efri [Torfi], Mohammad-Amin

Deputy of the Second Majlis, Abadan, Khuzestan
(1984–88)
1952–, Dasht-e Azadegan, Khuzestan

High school diploma
Isa
No imprisonment

Eftekhari, Mrs. Laleh

Deputy of the Seventh (2004–8), Eighth (2008–12),
    and Ninth (2012–16) Majlis, Tehran, Tehran
1959–, Shahrud, Semnan
BA, theology, Ferdowsi University of Mashhad; MA,
    theology, Tehran University; PhD, theology, Teh-
    ran University, 2001
Mohammad-Hoseyn, medical doctor
Professor at Shahed University
No imprisonment
IRGC militiawoman
Martyr's family (father and husband were both killed
    at the war front in 1986)
Member of DCII

Eftekhari, Mohammad-Hoseyn

Deputy of the Third Majlis, Fuman, Gilan (1988–June
    27, 1990)
1950–June 27, 1990, Fuman, Gilan
Clerical education
Clergyman (HI)
No imprisonment
Eftekhari died in a helicopter crash while helping
    the victims of the Rudbar earthquake. His son,
    Mohammad-Mehdi, later represented Fuman in
    the Tenth Majlis.

Eftekhari, Mohammad-Mehdi

Deputy of the Tenth Majlis, Fuman, Gilan (2016–20)
1973–, Rasht, Gilan
Clerical education; BA, law
Mohammad-Hoseyn, MP
Clergyman (HI)
No imprisonment
Not a war veteran
Eftekhari, a reformist, served as head of cultural af-
    fairs for the port authority of Gilan Province. His

father who was a member of the Majlis, died in a
    helicopter crash in 1990.

Eftekhar-Jahromi, Gudarz

Member of the First (1980–83) and Second (1986–92)
    Guardian Councils
1943–, Jahrom, Fars
BA, law, Tehran University, 1966; MA, commercial
    law, University of Paris (France), 1972; PhD, law,
    University of Paris (France), 1977
Akbar, farmer
Judiciary official
No imprisonment
Not a war veteran
Eftekhar-Jahromi was dean of the law school at Sha-
    hid Beheshti University for thirty-two years.

Ehsanbakhsh, Sadeq

Member of the First Assembly of Experts, Gilan
    (1983–90)
1930–June 4, 2001, Leyf, Gilan
Clerical education, Qom Seminary; BA, theology,
    Tehran University, 1957
Gholam-Reza
Clergyman (HI)
No imprisonment
Not a war veteran
Martyr's family (son-in-law)
Ehsanbakhsh was Ayatollah Khomeini's representa-
    tive and the Friday prayer leader of Rasht. He was
    imprisoned for only eleven days under the shah
    and survived two assassination attempts after the
    revolution, in mid-1981 and on April 15, 1982. He
    was the father-in-law of Ayatollah Mohammad
    Mofatteh, and grandfather of Mohammad-Mehdi
    Mofatteh.

Ekhtiyari [-Kesnaviyyeh-Yazd], Esfandiyar

Deputy of the Eighth (2008–12), Ninth (2012–16), and
    Tenth (2016–20) Majlis, representing the Zoroas-
    trian community (as a religious minority)

1966–, Yazd, Yazd
PhD, textile engineering, Amirkabir University of
    Technology, 2001; postdoctorate in management
Bahman, bank employee
Academia
No imprisonment
Not a war veteran
Ekhtiyari is member of the National Elites Founda-
    tion, Iran Nanotechnology Initiative Council, and
    Iran Inventors Association.

Elahiyan, Mrs. Zohreh

Deputy of the Eighth Majlis, Tehran, Tehran
    (2008–12)
1968–, Kermanshah, Kermanshah
MD, medicine, Tehran University of Medical Sciences
Mohammad
Medical doctor
No imprisonment
IRGC militiawoman
Member of the central council of the Alliance of Way-
    farers of the Islamic Revolution
Elahiyan was in charge of the Basij for women in
    Iranian universities. She did not accept President
    Ahmadinejad's proposal to become the minister
    of social welfare. Elahiyan, who headed both the
    human rights committee and the women's faction
    in the Eighth Majlis, did not secure enough votes
    to get into the Ninth Majlis.

Ela'i, Salaheddin

Deputy of the Sixth Majlis, Saqqez and Baneh, Kurd-
    istan (2001–4)
1954–2008, Saqqez, Kurdistan
High school diploma; clerical education
Najmeddin
Academia
No imprisonment
After service in the Majlis, Ela'i, a Kurd, became a
    civil servant. He received a six-month prison term
    but did not seem to have served it. He ran unsuc-
    cessfully for the Eighth Majlis.

Elham, Gholam-Hoseyn

Member of the Fifth Guardian Council (2004–10);
    minister of justice in President Ahmadinejad's
    first cabinet (2007–9)
1959–, Andimeshk, Khuzestan
BA, law, Tehran University; MA, penal law, Tarbiyat-e
    Modarres University; PhD, penal law and crimi-
    nology, Tarbiyat-e Modarres University; disserta-
    tion title: "Multiplicity of Crimes from Legal and
    Jurisprudential View"
Nezam, bazaar tradesman
Judiciary spokesperson (2002–4)
No imprisonment
Not a war veteran
IRGC militiaman
Elham became minister of justice with a low vote
    total (130 positive, 101 negative, and twenty-three
    abstentions). He served as spokesperson for
    President Ahmadinejad's cabinet. While serving
    as minister, he held many other positions, which
    earned him the nickname of "abolmashaqel" (Mr.
    Many Jobs). He has also aided in the Office of the
    Supreme Leader. Elham's wife, Fatemeh Rajabi,
    who is the daughter of a well-known cleric named
    Ali Davani, is an archconservative journalist.

Elyasi, Bahman

Deputy of the Seventh Majlis, Sonqor and Koliyayi,
    Kermanshah (2004–8)
1962–, Hamadan, Hamadan
MS, management
Hoseyn
Civil servant
No imprisonment
The GC rejected Elyasi's qualifications for the Tenth
    Majlis in 2016.

Elyasi, Golmohammad

Deputy of the Fourth (1992–96) and Seventh (2004–8)
    Majlis, Varzaqan, East Azerbaijan
1957–, Ahar, East Azerbaijan

BS, business administration, 2000
Elyas
Bank official
No imprisonment
Elyasi ran unsuccessfully for the Third, Fourth, and
    Fifth Majlis.

Elyasi, Manuchehr

Deputy of the Fifth Majlis, representing the Jewish
    community (as a religious minority) (1996–2000)
1941–, Sanandaj, Kurdistan
MD, medicine
Mansur
No imprisonment

Emadi, Seyyed Keramatollah

Deputy of the Sixth Majlis, Semirom, Isfahan
    (2000–2004)
February 18, 1940–, Semirom, Isfahan
Clerical education
Seyyed Ne'matollah
Clergyman (HI)
No imprisonment
He ran unsuccessfully for the Ninth Majlis.

Emami, Abdollah

Deputy of the First Majlis, Torbat-e Heydariyyeh,
    Razavi Khorasan (1980–83)
1914–1983, Torbat-e Heydariyyeh, Razavi Khorasan
Clerical education, Najaf Seminary
Zabihollah, farmer
Clergyman (HI)
No imprisonment
Not a war veteran

Emami, Baqer

Deputy of the Sixth Majlis, Marand and Jolfa, East
    Azerbaijan (2000–2004)
1959–, Marand, East Azerbaijan
MA, international law

Mohammad
No imprisonment
After serving in the Majlis, Emami became a civil
    servant.

Emami, Isa

Deputy of the Ninth Majlis, Gorgan and Aq-Qala,
    Golestan (2012–16)
1964–, Kordkuy, Golestan
BA, judicial law, 1994; MA, international law, 1998
Father's name unknown, farmer
Civil servant
No imprisonment
War veteran
IRGC militiaman (Basij)
Emami worked in the banking industry for some
    twenty years, including as the manager of Bank
    Mellat in Golestan Province, and was a member
    of the Gorgan City Council from 2002 to 2006.

Emami-Kashani, Mohammad

Deputy of the First Majlis, Kashan, Isfahan (1980–
    June 10, 1982); head of the CAJ (June 10, 1982–
    July 1983); member of the First (1983–88), Second
    (1991–98), Third (1999–2006), Fourth (2007–16),
    and Fifth (2016–22) Assembly of Experts, Tehran;
    member of the First (1983–86), Second (1986–92),
    Third (1992–98), and Fourth (1998–August 3,
    1999) Guardian Councils; member of the Fourth
    (1997–2002), Fifth (2002–7), and Sixth (2007–12)
    Expediency Discernment Assembly
October 3, 1931–, Kashan, Isfahan
Clerical education, Qom Seminary
Abutorab, clergyman
Clergyman
No imprisonment
Not a war veteran
Ayatollah Emami-Kashani, former chairman and
    member of the central council of the SCC, has
    been an influential political actor in postrevolu-
    tionary Iran, as judged by the number of positions
    he has held. Exiled before the revolution, he was

in charge of Ayatollah Khomeini's Qom office. Emami-Kashani resigned from the First Majlis in 1982 to become head of the CAJ but had to resign from the latter in July 1983 to take up his seat in the GC. He was also the Friday prayer leader of Qom and Tehran and was a member of the Council for Revision of the Constitution in 1989. Emami-Kashani resigned from the Fourth GC in August 1999. For almost four decades, he has run the Sepahsalar (renamed Shahid Motahhari) Seminary in Tehran, which is one of the oldest and most prestigious seminaries in the capital.

Emami-Rad, Ali

Deputy of the Fourth (1992–96), Sixth (2000–2004), and Seventh (2004–8) Majlis, Kuhdasht and Chegini, Lorestan
1957–, Kuhdasht, Lorestan
Associate's degree, 1980; BA, political science, 1999
Ali
Civil servant
No imprisonment

Emammusavi, Seyyed Mohammad-Kazem

Deputy of the Second (1984–88) and Third (1988–92) Majlis, Shushtar, Khuzestan
1926–, Shushtar, Khuzestan
Clerical education, Qom Seminary
Seyyed Mohammad-Ali
Clergyman (HI)
No imprisonment
Not a war veteran

Emamzadeh-Vaqfi, Seyyed Mohammad-Reza

Deputy of the Second (1984–88) and Third (1988–January 7, 1990) Majlis, Isfahan, Isfahan
1949–, Isfahan, Isfahan
BS, mechanical engineering
Seyyed Mo'ineddin
No imprisonment

Emamzadeh-Vaqfi underwent military training in Lebanon before the 1979 revolution. He resigned from the Third Majlis to become the governor-general of Isfahan.

Enayat, Ali

Deputy of the Third Majlis, Khorramabad, Lorestan (1988–92)
1951–, Aleshtar, Lorestan
PhD, electrical engineering, University of Manchester (England), 1979
Rostam-Beyk
Professor and dean of engineering at Shahid Chamran University of Ahvaz
No imprisonment
Enayat was the founder of the University of Lorestan and Lorestan University of Medical Sciences. He returned to academia after completing his term as an MP.

Erfani, Seyyed Mojtaba

Deputy of the First (1981–84), Second (1984–88), and Fourth (1992–96) Majlis, Talesh, Gilan
1955–, Qom, Qom
BS, management
Seyyed Yunes, clergyman
No imprisonment
Not a war veteran
Erfani is the son of Seyyed Yunes Erfani.

Erfani, Seyyed Yunes

Deputy of the First Majlis, Talesh, Gilan (1980–July 25, 1982)
1934–July 25, 1982, Talesh, Gilan
Clerical education
Mir Fazel, farmer
Clergyman (ayatollah)
No imprisonment
Not a war veteran
Member of the SCC

Erfani was in charge of one of the revolutionary committees in Tehran in the early years of the revolution. After he died in a car accident, his son, Seyyed Mojtaba Erfani, took over his seat.

Esfanani, Mohammad-Ali

Deputy of the Ninth Majlis, Faridan, Fereydunshahr, and Chadegan, Isfahan (2012–16)
1968–, Faridan and Fereydunshahr, Isfahan
BA, law, University of Judicial Sciences and Administrative Services; MA, law, Islamic Azad University–Khorasgan
Father's name unknown, construction worker
Judiciary official
No imprisonment
War veteran (forty-five months)
IRGC militiaman (navy diver)
Esfanani came from a poor background and lost his father when he was twelve. After the war, he became a judge, panegyrist, and professor.

Esfandiyarpur, Ali-Asghar

Deputy of the Second Majlis, Kuhdasht, Lorestan (1984–88)
1955–, Kuhdasht, Lorestan
Associate's degree
Azizollah
No imprisonment
Esfandiyarpur was elected to the Second Majlis with the highest votes in his district. He was also elected to the Third Majlis, but the GC rejected his credentials based on the objections of HI Shahrokhi-Qobadi.

Eshaq-Madani, Mohammad

Deputy of the First (1981–84) and Second (1984–88) Majlis, Saravan, Sistan and Baluchestan; member of the First (1983–90), Second (1991–98), and Third (1999–2006) Assembly of Experts, Sistan and Baluchestan

1946–, Saravan, Sistan and Baluchestan
Clerical education, Pakistan; BA (unconfirmed)
Pir-Mohammad
Sunni clergyman and former teacher
No imprisonment
Not a war veteran
Molavi Eshaq-Madani, a Sunni, was associated with land reform in Sistan and Baluchestan in the 1980s, and later became an adviser to President Ahmadinejad on Sunni affairs.

Eshraqi, Morteza

Revolutionary prosecutor-general of Tehran (1986–89)
Golpayegan, Isfahan
BA, Law
Prosecutor-general of Isfahan
Eshraqi entered the judiciary after the 1979 revolution. He was a member of a special committee, nicknamed the "death committee," that oversaw the extrajudicial execution of thousands (estimates vary between 2,800 and 5,000) of political prisoners following Ayatollah Khomeini's edict in 1988. He later headed one of the branches of the State Supreme Court and worked as an attorney.

Eskandari, Mohammad-Reza

Minister of agriculture in President Ahmadinejad's first cabinet (August 24, 2005–August 2, 2009)
1959–, Ahvaz, Khuzestan
BS, agricultural engineering, Shahid Chamran University of Ahvaz, 1985; MS, public administration, State Management Training Center
Abdollah
Civil servant
No imprisonment
War veteran
Martyr's family (brother)
Eskandari held positions in the Construction Jihad from 1979 to 1999, and he was in charge of the

Organization for Tribal Affairs. He became the minister of agriculture with 214 positive, forty-five negative, and twenty-four abstaining votes, and he survived impeachment on October 22, 2006. After leaving the cabinet, he became chairman of the Kowsar Economic Foundation, which is a subsidiary of the Martyr's Foundation and controls over thirty companies.

Esma'ili, Ali (Safar)

Deputy of the Tenth Majlis, Nur and Mahmudabad, Mazandaran (2016–20)

1961–, Dinkuh, Mazandaran

BA, economics, University of Mazandaran; MA, public administration; pursuing a PhD in strategic management

Retired MIIRI officer and instructor at Islamic Azad University–Qaemshahr

Father's name unknown, farmer

No imprisonment

War veteran

Esma'ili ran unsuccessfully for the Eighth Majlis and was initially disqualified for the Tenth Majlis, but the GC reversed the decision and allowed him to run.

Esma'ili, Daryush

Deputy of the Ninth (2012–16) and Tenth (2016–20) Majlis, Sarvestan, Kherameh, and Kavar, Fars

1966–, Kherameh, Fars

BS, geology (petrology), Tarbiyat-e Modarres University, 1989; MS, geology (petrology), Tehran University, 1992; PhD, geology (petrology), Tarbiyat-e Modarres University, 2001

University professor

No imprisonment

IRGC militiaman (deputy commander in Zanjan)

Esma'ili was in charge of the Tehran University dormitories from December 2009 until he was elected to the Majlis in 2012. During this time, as a hardliner, he enacted policies that harmed students.

Esma'ili, Farzad

Commander of the Khatam al-Anbia Air Defense Base (January 25, 2011–present)

1971–, Rudsar, Gilan

BS, command and control technology, Air Force Academy, 1993; MS, military science, Iranian Army Command and General Staff College, 2007

Father's name unknown, teacher

Military official (brigadier general)

No imprisonment

Not a war veteran

Esma'ili was in charge of the radar division of Khatam al-Anbia Air Defense Base from 2008 to 2009 and the intelligence and reconnaissance unit from 2009 to September 7, 2010.

Esma'ili, Ghaffar

Deputy of the Third (1988–92), Fourth (1992–96), Seventh (2004–8), and Eighth (2008–12) Majlis, Hashtrud, East Azerbaijan

1953–, Hashtrud, East Azerbaijan

BS, physics, 1980; MS, management, 1991

Mohammad-Baqer

Academia

No imprisonment

IRGC militiaman

After serving in the Majlis, Esma'ili became an official in the National Development Funds of Iran. Esma'ili ran unsuccessfully for the Ninth and Tenth Majlis.

Esma'ili, Mohammad

Deputy of the Ninth Majlis, Zanjan and Tarom, Zanjan (2012–16)

1960–, Miyaneh, East Azerbaijan

MS, strategic management

Mohammad-Shafie, clergyman and farmer

No imprisonment

War veteran (sixty-two months)

IRGC militiaman

Martyr's family (two brothers killed at the war front)

Esma'ili, Mohsen

Member of the Fourth (2001–4), Fifth (2004–10), Sixth
    (2010–16), and Seventh (2016–19) Guardian Coun-
    cils; member of the Fifth Assembly of Experts,
    Tehran (2016–22)
1966–, Tehran, Tehran
MA, Tarbiyat-e Modarres University; PhD, law, Tar-
    biyat-e Modarres University, 1999; clerical educa-
    tion, Marvi Seminary
Azizollah
Dean of Imam Sadeq University's law school
No imprisonment
War veteran
Ayatollah Hashemi-Shahrudi recommended Esma'ili
    for the GC, and in 2001, he became the youngest
    person elected to the council. He was a student in
    Ayatollah Khamenei's religious courses as well.
    He received 237 out of 260 votes when approved
    by the Majlis to serve in the GC. Esma'ili was the
    only non-cleric elected to the Fifth AE in 2016.
    His brother, Parviz Esma'ili, was President Rou-
    hani's communications deputy.

Esma'ili, Vali

Deputy of the Eighth Majlis, Germi, Ardabil
    (2008–12)
1971–, Germi, Ardabil
BS, management
Boyuk
Civil servant, ministries
No imprisonment
He ran unsuccessfully for the Ninth Majlis.

Esma'ili-Moqaddam, Mohammad-Reza

Deputy of the Sixth Majlis, Qom, Qom (2000–2004)
1951–, Qom, Qom
BS, chemistry
Hydar
Academia
No imprisonment
War veteran (injured)

After the GC disqualified Esma'ili-Moqaddam from
    running for the Seventh Majlis, he became a civil
    servant.

Esma'ilniya, Mohammad

Deputy of the Ninth Majlis, Kashmar, Khalilabad,
    and Bardaskan, Razavi Khorasan (2012–16)
1957–, Kashmar, Razavi Khorasan
BS, forestry; MS, forestry; PhD, forestry, Tarbiyat-e
    Modarres University
Civil servant and professor of forestry
No imprisonment
War veteran (fourteen months)
Esma'ilniya, a conservative, was the head of rural
    affairs in the office of Razavi Khorasan's gover-
    nor-general before he was elected to the Majlis.

Esma'ilzadeh, Habibollah

Deputy of the Fifth (1996–2000), Sixth (2000–2004),
    and Seventh (2004–8) Majlis, Falavarjan, Isfahan
1952–, Falavarjan, Isfahan
BS, management
Ne'matollah
Civil servant
No imprisonment

Espahbodi, Abdolali

Minister of labor and social affairs in PM Bazargan's
    cabinet (September 30–November 5, 1979)
1939–, Mashhad, Razavi Khorasan
PhD
Not a war veteran
Member of the LMI
Espahbodi translated Peter Mansfield's *History of the
    Middle East* and Halil İnalcık's *The Ottoman Em-
    pire: The Classical Age 1300 to 1600* into Persian.

Esrafiliyan, Ebrahim

Deputy of the Second Majlis, Tehran, Tehran
    (1984–88)

1935–, Najafabad, Isfahan

BS, mathematics, Tehran's Higher Teachers Training
College, 1960; PhD, mathematics, University of
Southampton (England), 1975; dissertation title:
"Normal Structures on Manifolds"

Gholam-Reza, carpenter

Academia

No imprisonment

Not a war veteran

Member of the Toilers Party and IRP

Esrafiliyan is a former rector of Science and Technology University (1979–80), Imam Sadeq University
(1980–83), and Tarbiyat-e Modarres University.
He was also a deputy minister of culture and
Islamic guidance.

Estaki, Fereydun

Deputy of the First (1982–84) and Second (1984–88)
Majlis, Shahrekord, Chahar Mahal and
Bakhtiari

1954–, Shahrekord, Chahar Mahal and Bakhtiari

Associate's degree

Reza, bazaar tradesman

No imprisonment

Not a war veteran

Martyr's family (two brothers, Rahman and Mojtaba)

Fereydun Estaki's brother Rahman was killed in the
bombing of the IRP headquarters in June 1981.
His brother Mojtaba replaced Rahman in the First
Majlis but PMOI assassinated him on December
22, 1981. Fereydun Estaki then finished his brother's term in the First Majlis.

Estaki, Mohammad-Hoseyn

Deputy of the Seventh Majlis, Isfahan, Isfahan
(2004–8)

1961–, Tehran, Tehran

PhD, mechanical engineering

Javad

Academia

No imprisonment

Estaki, Mojtaba

Deputy of the First Majlis, Shahrekord, Chahar Mahal
and Bakhtiari (1981)

1955–December 22, 1981, Shahrekord, Chahar Mahal
and Bakhtiari

Associate's degree

Reza, bazaar tradesman

No imprisonment

Martyr's family (brother, Rahman)

After his brother Rahman was killed in the bombing
of the IRP headquarters, Mojtaba replaced Rahman in the First Majlis. Mojtaba was then assassinated by PMOI on December 22, 1981.

Estaki, Rahman

Deputy of the First Majlis, Shahrekord, Chahar Mahal
and Bakhtiari (1980–June 28, 1981)

1950–June 28, 1981, Shahrekord, Chahar Mahal and
Bakhtiari

BA, physical training, Tehran University, 1978

Reza, bazaar tradesman

Civil servant

No imprisonment

Not a war veteran

Martyr's family (brother, Mojtaba)

Member of the IRP

Estaki was killed in the bombing of the IRP headquarters in June 1981.

Etaa't, Javad

Deputy of the Sixth Majlis, Darab and Zarrindasht,
Fars (2001–4)

1963–, Darab, Fars

BA, political science, Shahid Beheshti University; MA,
political science, Tehran University; PhD, political
science, Tehran University

Hoseyn

University professor

No imprisonment

Founding member of the NTP

After serving in the Majlis, Etaa't returned to his university teaching position.

Eydi-Goltapeh'i, Gazanfar

Deputy of the Fifth Majlis, Arak, Markazi
   (1996–2000)
1946–, Arak, Markazi
BS, engineering
Ali-Akbar
No imprisonment

Eyri, Mohammad-Qoli Haji

Deputy of the Seventh Majlis, Kordkuy and Bandar-e
   Torkaman, and Bandar-e Gaz, Golestan (2004–8)
1961–, Bandar-e Torkaman, Golestan
MD, medicine, Tehran University
Khodaqoli
Medical doctor
No imprisonment

E'zazi-Maleki, Ziyaollah

Deputy of the Eighth (2008–12) and Tenth (2016–20)
   Majlis, Bonab, East Azerbaijan
1965–, Miyandoab, West Azerbaijan
BA, history, Tabriz University
Abutaleb
No imprisonment
War veteran (wounded)
IRGC militiaman
E'zazi-Maleki was a carpet-weaver in the 1970s and
   went to night school. He was wounded at the
   war front in 1986. Afterward, he was in charge of
   security in East Azerbaijan and Ardabil and the
   medical school in Tabriz. He ran unsuccessfully
   for the Ninth Majlis but managed to get reelected
   to the Tenth Majlis.

Ezheh'i, Mehdi

Deputy of the First (1982–84) and Fourth (1992–96)
   Majlis, Isfahan, Isfahan

1950–, Isfahan, Isfahan
Clerical education; BS, psychology
Ali-Mohammad, clergyman (ayatollah)
Clergyman (HI)
No imprisonment

Ezheh'i, Mohammad-Javad

Ministerial adviser and head of the Public Health
   Organization in PM Musavi's first cabinet (November 9, 1982–85)
1948–, Isfahan, Isfahan
Clerical education, Isfahan Seminary; BA, theology,
   Isfahan University of Technology, 1971; PhD, psychology, University of Vienna (Austria), 1981
Ali-Mohammad, clergyman (ayatollah)
Clergyman and civil servant (ministries)
No imprisonment
Not a war veteran
Martyr's family (brother and father-in-law)
Member of the central council of the IRP
HI Ezheh'i, who speaks German, worked in the
   Ministry of Education under the shah. After the
   revolution, he worked in the Ministry of Foreign
   Affairs, and is the founder of several schools for
   talented students and of the Organization for
   Talented Students. On April 23, 1990, the supreme
   leader appointed him as his representative for
   liaison with Iranian Islamic student associations
   in Europe. He is the son-in-law of Ayatollah
   Mohammad Beheshti. Ezheh'i's younger brother,
   HI Ali-Akbar Ezheh'i (b. 1952), who was involved
   with paramilitary groups before the revolution
   and became chairman of the IRP in Isfahan, was
   killed in the bombing of the IRP headquarters in
   1981.

Ezzati, Ali

Deputy of the Eighth Majlis, Dehloran, Darrehshahr,
   and Abdanan, Ilam (2008–12)
1963–, Darreshahr, Ilam
BA, educational management
Baranazar

Civil servant
No imprisonment
Not a war veteran

Fadavi, Ali

Commander of the IRGC Navy (May 3,
    2010–present)
1961–
BS, electrical engineering, Isfahan University of
    Technology; MS, strategic management, Isfahan
    University of Technology
No imprisonment
War veteran
IRGC commander
Rear Admiral Fadavi joined the IRGC in 1983 and
    served in IRGC Qods Force. He held sensitive
    intelligence posts and was deputy commander of
    the IRGC navy from 1997 to 2010.

Fahimi-Giglu, Soleyman

Deputy of the Seventh Majlis, Parsabad and Bilehsa-
    var, Ardabil (2004–8)
1958–, Parsabad, Ardabil
BS, mechanical engineering; MS, industrial
    management
Ali-Hoseyn
Capitalist
No imprisonment
The GC disqualified Fahimi-Gilgu from running in
    the election for the Ninth Majlis.

Fahim-Kermani, Morteza

Deputy of the First (1981–84) and Second (1984–88)
    Majlis, Kerman, Kerman; member of the First
    Assembly of Experts, Kerman (1983–90)
1934–, Kerman, Kerman
Clerical education
Gholam-Reza, farmer
Clergyman
Imprisoned before the revolution
Not a war veteran

HI Fahim-Kermani was Friday prayer leader and head
    judge of the Islamic revolutionary tribunal in
    Kerman (1979–81). He then became a deputy to
    Assadolah Ladjvardi, the notorious prison warden
    and former revolutionary prosecutor-general of
    Tehran. When Admiral Ahmad Madani could
    not take his seat in the First Majlis, Fahim-Ker-
    mani was elected to replace him in a midterm
    election. In 1984, he called on Ayatollah Kho-
    meini to retract women's suffrage. In the late
    1980s, he was arrested and tried in the SCFC.
    Fahim-Kermani, who was one of the founders of
    the Islamic Propaganda Organization, currently
    resides and teaches in Qom.

Faker, Mohammad-Reza

Deputy of the Fifth (1996–2000), Seventh (2004–8),
    and Eighth (2008–February 10, 2010) Majlis,
    Mashhad, Razavi Khorasan; member of the
    Fourth Assembly of Experts, Razavi Khorasan
    (2007–February 10, 2010)
1945–February 10, 2010, Mashhad, Razavi Khorasan
Clerical education, Qom Seminary
Gholam-Hoseyn
Clergyman (HI)
Imprisoned before the revolution
IRGC militiaman
Member of the SQSS
In 1979, Faker started the Bureau for Islamic Publica-
    tions (*Daftar-e Entesharat-e Islami*) with capital
    allocated by Ayatollah Khomeini. In 1982, he
    became Ayatollah Khomeini's representative to
    the IRGC.

Fakheri, Hasan

Member of the First (July 17, 1983–86), Second
    (1986–92), and Third (1992–July 16, 1995) Guard-
    ian Councils
1923–September 22, 2016, Tehran, Tehran
MA, law
Mohammad-Taqi
First deputy to the prosecutor-general

No imprisonment

Not a war veteran

Fakheri did not receive enough votes from the Majlis on July 16, 1995, or July 8, 1998, to be reelected to the GC.

Fakuri, Javad

Commander of the Islamic Republic of Iran Air Force (June 19, 1980–September 29, 1981); minister of national defense in PM Raja'i's cabinet (1980–September 29, 1981)

1938–September 29, 1981, Tabriz, East Azerbaijan

BS, military science

Father's name unknown, tradesman

Military pilot

No imprisonment

War veteran

Fakuri completed training in the United States flying F-4 fighter jets before the revolution. He was defense minister and commander of the Islamic Republic of Iran Air Force simultaneously for slightly more than a year before dying in a plane crash.

Falahati, Farhad

Deputy of the Tenth Majlis, Qaenat, South Khorasan (2016–20)

1972–, Qaenat, South Khorasan

MA, Persian literature

No imprisonment

Not a war veteran

Falahati was active in the education field in South Khorasan and served as governor of Zirkuh. He was the conservative coalition's candidate for the Tenth Majlis.

Falahatpisheh, Heshmatollah

Deputy of the Seventh (2004–8), Eighth (2008–12), and Tenth (2016–20) Majlis, Islamabad-e Gharb, Kermanshah

1971–, Islamabad-e Gharb, Kermanshah

BA, political science, Tehran University, 1993; MA, political science, Tehran University, 1996; PhD, political science, Tarbiyat-e Modarres University; dissertation title: "Human Development and Political Development Relations"

Khodakaram, farmer

Journalist

No imprisonment

Not a war veteran

Falahatpisheh ran unsuccessfully for the Ninth Majlis and taught at Allameh Tabataba'i University for a while. He survived an assassination attempt on July 10, 2016.

Falasiri, Seyyed Fakhreddin

Deputy of the Second Majlis, Neyriz and Estahban, Fars (1984–88)

1929–2008, Shiraz, Fars

Clerical education

Seyyed Mohyeddin

Clergyman (HI)

No imprisonment

Not a war veteran

Fallahhojjat-Ansari, Arsalan

Deputy of the First Majlis, Lahijan, Gilan (1980–84)

1940–, Komachal, Gilan

BS, psychology

Fattah, farmer

Laborer

No imprisonment

Fallahi, Valiyollah

Commander of the Islamic Republic of Iran Ground Forces (ca. March 1979–June 19, 1980); chief of the joint staff of the Islamic Republic of Iran Army (June 19, 1980–September 30, 1981)

1931–September 30, 1981, Taleqan, Tehran

BS, military science, Ground Forces Officers' Academy

Army officer

Imprisoned before the revolution

War veteran

In 1979, when Fallahi was commander of the army's
ground forces, he was imprisoned a number
of times by the revolutionary committees on
charges of participating in military training
in Vietnam. During the first year of the Iran–
Iraq War, he and Qasem-Ali Zahirnezhad, the
commander of the army's ground forces, had
disagreements over whether Iraqi forces were
aiming to conquer Ahvaz or hold on to the
northern parts of Khuzestan Province. Fallahi also believed in militarily suppressing the
Iranian Kurds. After the dismissal of President
Banisadr, Ayatollah Khomeini appointed Fallahi
as chief of JSIRIA. Fallahi died three months
later in a plane crash.

Fallahi-Babajan, Abbas

Deputy of the Ninth Majlis, Ahar and Heris, East
Azerbaijan (2012–16)
1967–, Ahar, East Azerbaijan
BA, political geography, Tehran University; MS,
urban planning, Islamic Azad University–Ma-
rand, 2004
No imprisonment
War veteran (forty-eight months as a commander)
IRGC militiaman and university professor

Fallahiyan, Ali

Prosecutor-general of the SCFC (June 12, 1987–Janu-
ary 3, 1990); minister of intelligence in President
Hashemi-Rafsanjani's first (August 29, 1989–Au-
gust 2, 1993) and second (August 16, 1993–August
2, 1997) cabinets; member of the Third (1999–
2006) and Fourth (2007–16) Assembly of Experts,
Khuzestan
1949–, Najafabad, Isfahan
Clerical education, Haqqani Seminary
Abdollah, judiciary civil servant
Clergyman
Imprisoned before the revolution

War veteran

Member of the IRP

From 1982 to 1985, HI Fallahiyan was commander
of all Islamic revolutionary *komitehs*. He held
various judiciary and intelligence jobs, including chief magistrate in Abadan, Mashhad, and
Kermanshah. He was among the initial founders of the MIIRI, serving as deputy minister of
intelligence from 1984 to 1989. In 1990, Fallahiyan resigned his post as prosecutor-general of
the SCFC to become minister of intelligence. In
1996, a German court indicted Fallahiyan for
involvement in the 1992 assassination of leaders of
the Kurdistan Democratic Party in the Mykonos
restaurant in Berlin. Fallahiyan was also in charge
of MIOS when its agents were reportedly involved
in the bombing of a Jewish community center in
Argentina in 1994. He ran in the 2001 presidential election but received 0.2 percent of the vote.
He also registered to run in the 2013 presidential
election.

Falsafi-Tonekaboni, Mirza Ali

Member of the Assembly for the Final Examination of
the Constitution, Razavi Khorasan (1979)
1921–2005, Tehran, Tehran
Clerical education, Najaf Seminary (Iraq)
Mohammad-Reza, clergyman
Clergyman (ayatollah)
No imprisonment
Not a war veteran

Fani, Ali-Asghar

Minister of education in President Rouhani's first
cabinet (October 27, 2013–October 19, 2016)
1954–, Tehran, Tehran
BS, civil engineering, Tehran University; MS, civil
engineering, Tehran University; MA, public administration, State Management Training Center;
PhD, human resource management, Tarbiyat-e
Modarres University
Father's name unknown, lathe operator

Professor at Tarbiyat-e Modarres University
No imprisonment
Not a war veteran
IRGC militiaman
Fani entered the Ministry of Education in 1980 and has subsequently held the following posts: general manager of education in Kurdistan (1981–85); associate dean of humanities at Tarbiyat-e Modarres University (1989–93); cultural deputy of FMVA (1993–97); deputy minister of education (1997–2005); and professor at Tarbiyat-e Modarres University (2005–13). The Majlis approved him as minister of education on October 27, 2013, with 183 positive votes, fifty-three negative votes, and twenty-four abstentions. Fani survived impeachment by the Majlis on August 20, 2014, when he received the support of 167 lawmakers. Fani left the cabinet in October 2016.

Faqih, Seyyed Mohammad

Member of the Second (1991–98) and Fifth (2016–22) Assembly of Experts, Fars
1942–, Neyriz, Fars
Clerical education, Qom Seminary
Hedayatollah, clergyman (ayatollah)
Clergyman (ayatollah)
Imprisoned before the revolution (spent five months in exile in Ferdows)
Not a war veteran
Faqih became the Friday prayer leader of Neyriz after the revolution.

Faqih-Aliabadi, Asgari

Deputy of the Fourth Majlis, Qaemshahr and Savadkuh, Mazandaran (1993–96)
1952–, Najaf, Iraq
Clerical education
Hasan
Clergyman (HI)
No imprisonment
Founding member of the Assembly of Former Parliament MPs

Farahmand, Kazem

Deputy of the Eighth Majlis, Mehriz, Bafq, Abarkuh, and Khatam, Yazd (2008–12)
1959–, Abarkuh, Yazd
MA, public administration
Reza
Civil servant
No imprisonment

Faraji-Dana, Reza

Minister of science, research, and technology in President Rouhani's first cabinet (October 27, 2013–August 13, 2014)
1960–, Qom, Qom
BS, electrical engineering, Tehran University, 1986; MS, electrical engineering, University of Waterloo (Canada), 1989; PhD, electrical engineering, University of Waterloo (Canada), 1993; dissertation title: "An Efficient and Accurate Green's Function Analysis of Packaged Microwave Integrated Circuits"
Mohammad, tradesman
Professor of electrical engineering at Tehran University
No imprisonment
IRGC militiaman (1980–82)
Founding member of the Islamic Society of Alumni in Tehran University's College of Engineering
Faraji-Dana, the former rector of Tehran University (2002–5), became minister of science, research, and technology in October 2013 with 159 positive votes, seventy negative votes, and thirty-two abstentions. However, the Majlis successfully impeached him on August 20, 2014, by a vote of 110–145–15.

Farajzadeh, Mohammad-Amin

Deputy of the Eighth Majlis, Bandar-e Abbas, Qeshm, Abumusa, Hajiabad, and Khamir, Hormozgan (2008–12)
1941–, Bandar-e Abbas, Hormozgan
BS, mathematics
Mohammad-Rafih

Civil servant

No imprisonment

Farajzadeh ran unsuccessfully for the Ninth Majlis.

Farbod, Naser

Chief of the joint staff of the Islamic Republic of Iran
　　Army (March 26–July 19, 1979)
1922–, Tehran, Tehran
BS, military science, Ground Forces Officers' Acad-
　　emy, 1943
Military officer (retired as of 1975)
No imprisonment
Not a war veteran
Member of the central council of INF
PM Bazargan appointed Major General Farbod as
　　chief of JSIRIA, replacing Major General Qa-
　　rani, and accepted his resignation less than four
　　months later. Farbod, who completed military
　　training in the United States before the revolu-
　　tion, has also authored a number of books.

Farhadi, Mohammad

Minister of higher education in PM Musavi's second
　　cabinet (October 28, 1985–August 3, 1989): min-
　　ister of health and medical education in President
　　Khatami's first cabinet (August 20, 1997–Au-
　　gust 1, 2001); minister of science, research, and
　　technology in President Rouhani's first cabinet
　　(November 26, 2014–August 13, 2017)
1949–, Shahrud, Semnan
MD, nose/ear/throat specialist, Ferdowsi University of
　　Mashhad, 1980
Ali-Asghar, telecommunications office employee
Rector of Tehran University (1985)
No imprisonment
Not a war veteran
Founding member of the Islamic Association of Ira-
　　nian Medical Society
Farhadi has held posts such as rector of Shiraz Univer-
　　sity (1981–82) and deputy of the Red Crescent So-
　　ciety of the Islamic Republic of Iran (1982–83), and
　　he was a member of the HCCR for fourteen years.

He was the fifth candidate introduced by President
Rouhani for the post of minister of science, research, and technology and during his confirmation
on November 26, 2014, received 197 positive votes,
twenty-eight negative votes, and ten abstentions.

Farhang, Mansur

Permanent representative of Iran to the UN (Decem-
　　ber 17, 1979–April 26, 1980)
1935–, Sari, Mazandaran
BA, political science, University of Arizona, 1965;
　　PhD, political science, Claremont Graduate
　　School, 1969
Professor of political science at California State Uni-
　　versity at Sacramento
Imprisonment before the revolution (two months in
　　1954)
Not a war veteran
Farhang, who was an academic and human rights ac-
　　tivist in the United States, agreed to become Iran's
　　first ambassador to the UN after the revolution so
　　that he could help a United Nations Commission
　　of Inquiry to settle the hostage crisis. On Decem-
　　ber 10, 1979, he met with Ayatollah Khomeini in
　　Qom and received his support for the creation
　　of the commission. However, the commission
　　retuned from Iran empty-handed in March 1980.
　　Farhang resigned from his post in protest and
　　left Iran as a dissident in June 1981. He returned
　　to the United States and taught first at Princeton
　　University (1981–83) and then as a professor of
　　international relations and Middle Eastern studies
　　at Bennington College (1983–2014). Farhang has
　　been a human rights activist since his undergrad-
　　uate years and is the author of *U.S. Imperialism*
　　and coauthor of *The US Press and Iran: Foreign
　　Policy and the Journalism of Deference.*

Farhangi, Mohammad-Hoseyn

Deputy of the Seventh (2004–8), Eighth (2008–12),
　　Ninth (2012–16), and Tenth (2016–20) Majlis,
　　Tabriz, Azarshahr, and Osku, East Azerbaijan

1961–, Tabriz, East Azerbaijan

MA, theology, Tehran University; PhD, jurisprudence, Tehran University

Farzali, clergyman (ayatollah)

No imprisonment

War veteran (four years)

IRGC militiaman (commander of Ashura 31 Brigade)

After the war, Farhangi became director of the Organization for the Mobilization of University Students. While serving in the Majlis, he was a conservative legislator who became a member of the leadership team. Farhangi teaches at Islamic Azad University.

Farhani, Abdolkarim

Member of the Fifth Assembly of Experts, Khuzestan (2016–22)

1964–, Ahvaz, Khuzestan

Clerical education, Qom Seminary, 1987

Balasem

Clergyman (ayatollah) and deputy director of High Council of Religious Seminaries

No imprisonment

War veteran

IRGC militiaman

Farid, Akbar

Deputy of the Fourth Majlis, Khorramabad, Lorestan (1992–96)

1942–, Khorramabad, Lorestan

MD, surgery

Papi

Medical doctor

No imprisonment

Farmand, Fardin

Deputy of the Tenth Majlis, Miyaneh, East Azerbaijan (2016–20)

1956–, Miyaneh, East Azerbaijan

BS/BA, physics and Near Eastern studies, New York University (USA); PhD, New York University

(USA), 1992; dissertation title: "Technology Transfer and Economic Development: The Role of Industrial Research Base in Newly Industrializing Countries: Lessons from Iran"

Farhad

University professor

No imprisonment

Not a war veteran

Farmand went to the United States in 1976 and conducted postdoctoral research at Rensselaer Polytechnic Institute in Troy, New York.

Farrokhi, Mohammad

Deputy of the Sixth Majlis, Jiroft, Kerman (2001–4)

1950–2009, Jiroft, Kerman

MD, medicine

Hoseyn

Medical doctor

No imprisonment

Secretary of the Kerman branch of the NTP

Farshadan, Seyyed Mehdi

Deputy of the Tenth Majlis, Sanandaj, Kurdistan (2016–20)

September 23, 1974–, Sanandaj, Kurdistan

MD, Tabriz University of Medical Sciences

Seyyed Mohammad-Ali, farmer

Medical doctor and health official in Kurdistan

No imprisonment

Not a war veteran

Farshadan is a Sunni.

Farshidi, Mahmud

Minister of education in President Ahmadinejad's first cabinet (November 9, 2005–December 1, 2007)

1951–, Mashhad, Razavi Khorasan

MS, chemical engineering, Shiraz University, 1975 (unverified)

Abolhasan

Head of IRIB in Kerman and director of the education department in East Azerbaijan

Imprisoned before the revolution (8 months)

Not a war veteran

Secretary-general of the Society for Islamic Education

Farshidi survived impeachment on May 16, 2007, but he resigned from his post on December 1, 2007.

Farsi, Jalaleddin

Member of the Assembly for the Final Examination of the Constitution, Razavi Khorasan (1979); deputy of the Second Majlis, Tehran, Tehran (1984–88)

1934–, Mashhad, Razavi Khorasan

High school diploma

Mohammad-Ali, bazaar tradesman

Political activist

Imprisoned before the revolution

Not a war veteran

Member of the central council of the IRP

Farsi went to Iraq in 1960 and was arrested by the Iraqi regime. He then went to Syria and upon his return to Iran in 1961 was arrested by the shah's regime. In the 1970s, he went to Lebanon and Libya and trained many Iranian revolutionaries there. He returned to Iran in the company of Yasser Arafat in 1979. Farsi was a candidate for the first presidential election in 1980, but dropped out over charges that he was of Afghan and not Iranian parentage. A few months later, Ayatollah Khomeini appointed him to the Headquarters for Cultural Revolution. Farsi's claim to have a BA degree in theology from Ferdowsi University of Mashhad has been questioned by his peers. In 1992, Farsi killed a man in a personal dispute but the court ruled it was accidental and he was freed.

Farugh, Seyyed Mostafa

Deputy of the Second (1984–88) and Third (1988–92) Majlis, Dezful, Khuzestan

1932–March 4, 2014, Dezful, Khuzestan

Clerical education

Seyyed Hoseyn

Clergyman (HI)

No imprisonment

Not a war veteran

Martyr's family (son, Mas'ud)

Farzad, Ali-Reza

Deputy of the Third Majlis, Taft, Yazd (1988–92)

1956–, Taft, Yazd

PhD

Mohammad-Ali

No imprisonment

War veteran

Farzad ran unsuccessfully for the Tenth Majlis.

Farzpor-Machiyani, Mohammad

Deputy of the First (1980–84) and Third (1988–92) Majlis, Astara, Gilan

1951–July 22, 2015, Astara, Gilan

BA, law, Tehran University; advanced studies in England

Hoseyn, farmer

Lawyer and judiciary official

No imprisonment

Not a war veteran

Farzpor-Machiyani was very active in the Iranian Association of Jurists.

Fatehi, Javad

Member of the Assembly for the Final Examination of the Constitution, Kurdistan (1979)

1934–, Hamadan, Hamadan

Clerical education

Ali, clergyman and teacher

Clergyman

Not a war veteran

Fatehi, a Shiite HI, was elected by a small number of votes in a largely Sunni region. After finishing his term in the AFEC, Fatehi devoted himself only to religious teaching.

Fathi, Mohammad-Javad

Deputy of the Tenth Majlis, Tehran, Tehran (2016–20)

1965–, Ramhormoz, Khuzestan
BA, law, University of Judicial Sciences–Tehran, 1988;
    MA, law, Shahid Beheshti University, 1991; PhD,
    law, Tehran University, 2008
Cheragh, teacher
Lawyer and a director-general at the Ministry of Sci-
    ence, Research, and Technology
No imprisonment
War veteran (twelve months)
Fathi worked in the outreach office of President Hash-
    emi-Rafsanjani (1990–93), and was an instructor
    at Qom University and Tehran University, assistant
    dean of Tehran University's law school, dean of the
    law school at Tehran University–Pardis-e Farabi
    (2008–12), and a director-general at the Ministry
    of Science, Research, and Technology (2014–16).

Fathipur, Arsalan

Deputy of the Seventh (2004–8), Eighth (2008–12),
    and Ninth (2012–16) Majlis, Kaleybar, Hu-
    rand, Khoda Afarin, and Abish Ahmad, East
    Azerbaijan
1965–, Tabriz, East Azerbaijan
BA, economics, Islamic Azad University–Tehran; MS,
    cultural planning, Islamic Azad University–Sci-
    ence and Research Branch
Mohrram
Civil servant, ministries
No imprisonment
War veteran
Fathipur served in Iran's military for sixteen years.
    Even though he was a conservative politician, the
    GC disqualified him from running in the 2016
    Majlis election.

Fattah [-Qarabaghi], Seyyed Parviz

Minister of energy in President Ahmadinejad's first
    cabinet (August 24, 2005–August 2, 2009)
1961–, Urmia, West Azerbaijan
BS, civil engineering, Sharif University of Technology,
    1989; MS, industrial engineering, Imam Hoseyn
    University, 2003

Mir Shakur
No imprisonment
War veteran (many years as a commander)
IRGC militiaman
Fattah was deputy head of the IRGC's dam construc-
    tion company, SepaSad, for eleven years. After
    President Ahmadinejad did not choose him to
    serve in his second cabinet, Fattah first became
    the executive director of Ansar al-Mojahedin
    Bank, a bank owned by the IRGC cooperative
    foundation, and was then appointed the director
    of the IRGC cooperative foundation. In April
    2015, Ayatollah Khamenei appointed Fattah as
    director of the IKRF.

Fattahi, Abed

Deputy of the Seventh (2004–8) and Ninth (2012–16)
    Majlis, Urmia, West Azerbaijan
1958–, Narqi, West Azerbaijan
MD, ophthalmology, Istanbul University (Turkey)
Fattah, tribesman
Medical doctor
No imprisonment
Fattahi is a Sunni Kurd who supported Mohsen Rezai
    in the 2009 presidential election. His brother
    was a member of the Urmia City Council for two
    terms.

Fattahi, Hoseyn

Deputy of the Ninth Majlis, Shahr-e Babak, Kerman
    (2012–16)
1965–, Shahr-e Babak, Kerman
MA, defense management, Imam Hoseyn University
Abdolhoseyn, farmer
No imprisonment
War veteran (eight years as a commander)
IRGC militiaman and employee of MI
Fattahi earned his high school diploma after the war.
    He later became an IRGC commander in Sis-
    tan and Baluchestan and now teaches at Imam
    Hoseyn University.

Fattahi-Ma'sum, Seyyed Hoseyn

Deputy of the Fourth Majlis, Mashhad, Razavi Kho-
rasan (1992–96)
1948–, Mashhad, Razavi Khorasan
Mir Sattar
MD, surgery
Medical doctor
No imprisonment

Fattahpur-Mavaneh, Karim

Deputy of the Sixth Majlis, Urmia, West Azerbaijan
(2000–2004)
1959–, Urmia, West Azerbaijan
MD, pharmacy
Mohammad
Medical doctor
No imprisonment
The GC disqualified Fattahpur-Mavaneh, a Sunni,
from running in the 2016 Majlis election.

Fayyazbakhsh, Mohammad-Ali

Ministerial adviser and head of the Public Health
Organization in PM Raja'i's cabinet (1980–June
28, 1981)
1938–June 28, 1981, Tehran, Tehran
MD, surgery, Tehran University, 1972
Qasem, bazaar tradesman
Surgeon
No imprisonment
Not a war veteran
Fayyazbakhsh, who used to work in IKRF and as a
surgeon at Sina Hospital, was killed in the bomb-
ing of the IRP headquarters in 1981. His daugh-
ter, Nafiseh, later became a Majlis deputy from
Tehran.

Fayyazbakhsh, Mrs. Nafiseh

Deputy of the Fourth (1992–96), Fifth (1996–2000),
and Seventh (2004–8) Majlis, Tehran, Tehran
1964–, Tehran, Tehran

MA, philosophy; PhD, philosophy, Islamic Azad Uni-
versity, 1996
Mohammad-Ali, MD
Academia
No imprisonment
Martyr's family (brother, Mohammad-Ali)
Founding member of the Zeynab Society; member
of the Association of Veterans of the Islamic
Revolution
When elected to the Fourth Majlis at the age of 28,
Fayyazbakhsh became the youngest woman
elected to any of the first ten postrevolutionary
parliaments. She has worked as a writer, translator,
university professor, and member of the editorial
board of *Shahed* magazine. Her father, Moham-
mad-Ali, was ministerial adviser and head of the
Public Health Organization in PM Raja'i's cabinet.

Fayyazi, Abdolvahid

Deputy of the Ninth Majlis, Nur and Mahmudabad,
Mazandaran (2012–16)
1965–, Nur, Mazandaran
MA, educational management, State Management
Training Center
Hoseyn, clergyman (HI)
Provincial civil servant
No imprisonment
War veteran
Martyr's family (brother)
Fayyazi was close to President Ahmadinejad, who
appointed him as head of the education bureau
of Mazandaran Province. One of his brothers, HI
Mofid Fayyazi, was the Friday prayer leader of
Nur for twenty years.

Fayyazi, Gholam-Reza

Member of the Fourth Assembly of Experts, Zanjan
(2007–16)
1949–, Qom, Qom
Clerical education, Qom Seminary
Asadollah, mason
Clergyman (HI)

No imprisonment
Not a war veteran
Member of the SQSS
Fayyazi is a follower of the conservative Ayatollah
Mesbah-Yazdi.

Faza'eli, Ataollah

Deputy of the Second (1984–88) and Third (1988–92)
Majlis, Semirom, Isfahan
1935–, Semirom, Isfahan
BS, psychology
Mohammad-Ebrahim
No imprisonment
Not a war veteran

Fazel, Iraj

Minister of culture and higher education in PM
Musavi's first cabinet (August 20, 1984–October
27, 1985); minister of health and medical education in President Hashemi-Rafsanjani's first
cabinet (August 29, 1989–January 13, 1991)
1939–, Ardestan, Fars
MD, medicine, Tehran University, 1964; specialty in
surgery, 1974
Reza, civil servant
Medical doctor
No imprisonment
Not a war veteran
Fazel became the minister of higher education in 1984.
He was the first postrevolutionary minister forced
to leave a cabinet after the Majlis impeached him
on January 13, 1991, while he was serving as minister of health and medical education. As a surgeon, he has operated on both Ayatollah Khomeini
and Ayatollah Khamenei. In August 2017, Fazel
was elected to a four-year term as head of the
Islamic Republic of Iran Medical Council.

Fazel-Astarabadi, Mohammad

Deputy of the First Majlis, Babol, Mazandaran
(1980–84)

1935–November 26, 2016, Najaf, Iraq
Clerical education, Najaf Seminary (Iraq)
Najafali, clergyman (ayatollah)
Clergyman
No imprisonment
Not a war veteran
Martyr's family (son, HI Mohammad-Mehdi, was
killed at the war front)
Ayatollah Fazel-Astarabadi moved to Iran with his
family in 1947 but returned to Najaf in 1951 to
attend seminary and ended up staying until 1975.
In 1984, he founded the Feyziyyeh Seminary of
Mazandaran in Babol.

Fazel-Harandi, Mohyeddin

Deputy of the First Majlis, Eqlid, Fars (1981–84); dep-
uty of the Second (1984–88) and Third (1988–92)
Majlis, Isfahan, Isfahan; member of the First As-
sembly of Experts, Fars (1983–90); member of the
Second Assembly of Experts, Kerman (1991–98)
1934–2006, Harand, Isfahan
Clerical education, Qom Seminary
Yahya, clergyman (ayatollah)
Clergyman (ayatollah)
Imprisoned before the revolution (a few months in
1978)
Not a war veteran
Member of the central council of the IRP
In 1980, Ayatollah Khomeini appointed Fazel-Harandi as his representative in the seven-member
committee for land distribution. In this capacity,
he played a significant role in postrevolutionary
land distribution. He was also a revolutionary
court judge. Fazel-Harandi held the post of
supreme leader's representative until his death in
2006. In the 1980s, Ayatollah Montazeri—at that
time the deputy supreme leader—appointed him
as his representative in Europe. He survived an
assassination attempt in July 1981. Fazel-Harandi
is the uncle of both former minister of culture
Mohammad-Hoseyn Saffar-Harandi and former
deputy interior minister Mostafa Tajzadeh, a leading critic of Ayatollah Khamenei.

Fazel-Lankarani [Movahhedi], Mohammad

Member of the First Assembly of Experts, Markazi
    (1983–90)
1931–June 16, 2007, Qom, Qom
Clerical education, Qom Seminary
Abdollah, clergyman (ayatollah)
Clergyman
Imprisoned before the revolution
Not a war veteran
Secretary of the SQSS
Ayatollah Fazel-Lankarani's father was born in Lan-
    karan, in the present-day Republic of Azerbaijan.
    His mother was an ethnic Hazara from Afghan-
    istan. Ayatollah Khomeini appointed Ayatollah
    Fazel-Lankarani head of the Islamic Revolu-
    tion Court of Qom. Like his former mentors
    Ayatollah Borujerdi and Ayatollah Khomeini,
    Fazel-Lankarani became a source of emulation.
    In November 2006, Ayatollah Fazel-Lankarani
    issued a fatwa calling for two journalists in the
    neighboring country of Azerbaijan to be killed
    for writing and publishing an allegedly blasphe-
    mous article. In 2011, the author of that article,
    Rafiq Tagi, was stabbed multiple times and died
    after four days. Fazel-Lankarani, who died in
    London, was the brother-in-law of Ayatollah
    Mar'ashi-Najafi.

Fazlali, Morteza

Deputy of the First Majlis, Garmsar, Semnan (1980–
    84); deputy of the Fifth (1996–2000) and Seventh
    (2004–8) Majlis, Tuyserkan, Hamadan
1949–, Tuyserkan, Hamadan
BA, English literature and management; clerical
    education
Khodaverdi, farmer
Academia
No imprisonment
IRGC militiaman
Fazlali was wounded in the bombing of the IRP
    headquarters on June 28, 1981, while serving as
    an MP. He ran unsuccessfully for the Fourth and

Ninth Majlis, and after leaving the Majlis, Fazlali
    became a civil servant.

Fazli, Ali

Deputy commander of the IRGC's Basij Force (De-
    cember 10, 2009–present)
1961–, Tuyserkan, Hamadan
War veteran (wounded in one eye)
IRGC militiaman (commander)
Fazli joined the IRGC in 1979 and became one of its
    most popular and brave commanders. He led the
    IRGC's Seyyed al-Shohada Corps of Tehran Prov-
    ince until February 2010, and has so far been the
    only person to hold the position of deputy com-
    mander of the IRGC's Basij Force. He is on the US
    Treasury Office of Foreign Assets Control's Spe-
    cially Designated Nationals and Blocked Persons
    List because of his role in the 2009 crackdown
    and Basij's cyberattacks.

Feda'i, Esma'il

Deputy of the First (1980–84) and Second (1984–88)
    Majlis, Shazand (Sarband), Markazi
1941–, Arak, Markazi
BA, Arabic literature; clerical education
Jamaleddin, clergyman
Academia
No imprisonment
Not a war veteran
Founding member of the ISFPD

Feda'i, Samad

Deputy of the Eighth Majlis, Sonqor, Kurdistan
    (2009–12)
1971–, Sonqor, Kurdistan
BA, education, Shahid Beheshti University; MA,
    education, Tehran University; PhD educational
    management, Islamic Azad University
Academia
Bahram-Ali
No imprisonment

Not a war veteran

Founding member of the Society of University Students and Alumni from Kermanshah

After he lost the election for the Ninth Majlis, Feda'i worked in the Ministry of Cooperatives, Labor, and Social Welfare in Tehran.

Feda'i-Araqi, Gholam-Reza

Deputy of the Second (1984–88), and Third (1988–92) Majlis, Arak, Markazi

1945–, Arak, Markazi

MS, library science; PhD, library science

Morteza

No imprisonment

After serving in the Majlis, Feda'i-Araqi received a PhD and became a faculty member at Tehran University.

Feda'i-Ashiyani, Hoseyn

Deputy of the Seventh (2004–8) and Eighth (2008–12) Majlis, Tehran, Tehran

1955–, Rey, Tehran

Associate's degree

Abolfath

Imprisoned before the revolution

War veteran

IRGC militiaman

Secretary-general of AVIR; Founder of DCII

Feda'i-Ashiyani was a founding member of the paramilitary group Tohidi-ye Badr before the revolution, for which the shah's regime imprisoned him in 1976. He joined OMIRI in 1979. He is a former secretary-general of the FDWI of Tehran Province. In October 2017, he was appointed head of the supervision and audit bureau of the Office of the Supreme Leader by Ayatollah Khamenei.

Ferdowsipur, Esma'il

Deputy of the First (1980–84), Second (1984–88), and Third (1988–92) Majlis, Mashhad, Razavi Khorasan; member of the First (1984–90), Second (1991–98), and Third (1999–2006) Assembly of Experts, Razavi Khorasan; head of the CAJ (December 5, 1993–July 16, 1997)

1938–2007, Ferdows, South Khorasan

Clerical education

Gholam-Ali, farmer

Clergyman (HI)

No imprisonment

Not a war veteran

Member of the IRP and SCC

Ferdowsipur traveled with Ayatollah Khomeini to Iraq and France, where he was in charge of telephone contact with Iran. He returned with Ayatollah Khomeini to Iran. He received paramilitary training in Lebanon and Syria before the revolution. On October 29, 1979, Ayatollah Khomeini appointed him as the judge of the revolutionary court in Mashhad. He was injured in the June 28, 1981, bombing of the IRP headquarters. On February 21, 1984, the Majlis rejected him as the candidate for minister of intelligence. In addition to serving in the Majlis and the AE, Ferdowsipur has held the following positions: Ayatollah Khomeini's representative in Ferdows, Ayatollah Montazeri's representative at Tarbiyat-e Modarres University, member of the oversight committee of IRIB, adviser to the head of the judiciary, and member of the policy council of Friday prayer leaders.

Fereyduni, Nader

Deputy of the Ninth Majlis, Firuzabad, Farashband, Qir, and Karzin, Fars (2012–16)

1962–, Firuzabad, Fars

BS, physics, Arak University; MS, physics, Tarbiyat-e Mo'allem University

Physics instructor

No imprisonment

War veteran (wounded)

Feyz-Gilani, Mohammad-Ali

Member of the First (1984–90) and Second (1991–98) Assembly of Experts, Gilan; head of the CAJ (1986–89)

1925–, Lahijan, Gilan
Clerical education, Qom Seminary
Father's name unknown, farmer
Clergyman (ayatollah)
No imprisonment
Not a war veteran
Member of the SQSS
Feyz-Gilani was head or deputy head of the CAJ for eight years. He was a member of the Council for Selection of Judges and briefly served as Ayatollah Khomeini's representative at Alzahra University. He was elected to the First AE in interim elections held on April 15, 1984.

Feyzi-Sarabi, Mohammad

Member of the Fourth (2007–16) and Fifth (2016–22) Assembly of Experts, East Azerbaijan
1928–, Zarnaq, East Azerbaijan
Clerical education, Qom Seminary
Mohammad-Qoli
Clergyman (HI)
No imprisonment
Not a war veteran

Feyzi-Zangir, Mohammad

Deputy of the Tenth Majlis, Ardabil, Ardabil (2016–20)
April 26, 1981–, Ardabil, Ardabil
BA, public administration, Payam-e Nur University, Khalkhal, 2003; MA, public administration, Islamic Azad University–Tehran, 2005; PhD, public administration, Islamic Azad University–Science and Research Branch, 2012
University professor
IRGC militiaman (Basij)

Firuzabadi, Seyyed Hasan

Chief of the Armed Forces General Staff (September 26, 1989–June 28, 2016); member of the Fourth (1997–2002), Fifth (2002–7), Sixth (2007–12), Seventh (2012–17), and Eighth (2017–22) Expediency Discernment Assembly
1951–, Mashhad, Razavi Khorasan
MD, veterinary medicine, Ferdowsi University of Mashhad
Military and security official
Imprisoned before the revolution
Not a war veteran
IRGC militiaman
Major-General Firuzabadi knew Ayatollah Khamenei from before the revolution in Mashhad and followed him uncritically. He was one of the founders of the Construction Jihad in Khorasan Province, and then became the president of the Red Crescent Society of the Islamic Republic of Iran. During the years of the Iran–Iraq War, he was deputy commander of Khatam al-Anbia Construction Headquarters, defense deputy for the prime minister, and deputy to the chief of JSIRIA. Ayatollah Khamenei promoted him to major general in 1995, and his twenty-seven-year tenure as chief of the Armed Forces General Staff (AFGS) finally ended in 2016. Firuzabadi was the first chief of AFGS not to have a military background. Ayatollah Khamenei subsequently appointed him as a senior military adviser. On October 10, 2011, the Council of the European Union put Firuzabadi on its sanctioned list and wrote that "forces under his formal chain of command brutally suppressed peaceful protestors and perpetrated mass detentions" in 2009.

Firuzi, Mohammad

Deputy of the Ninth Majlis, Qamsar and Natanz, Isfahan (2012–16)
1976–, Badrood, Isfahan
BA, Persian literature, Kashan University, 1998; MA, Persian literature, Islamic Azad University–Kashan, 2011
Teacher and educational official in Badrood
No imprisonment
Not a war veteran

After serving in the Ninth Majlis, Firuzi was put in charge of overseeing the development plans of oil-rich regions.

Forughi, Mohammad

Deputy of the First Majlis, Masjed Soleyman, Khuzestan (1981–84)
1952–, Naraq, Markazi
Clerical education
Hoseyn, clergyman
Clergyman (HI)
No imprisonment
War veteran
Martyr's family (brother, Ali-Asghar, killed at the war front)
Forughi was a member of the Construction Jihad.

Foruhar, Daryush

Minister of labor and social affairs (1979) and later ministerial adviser (without portfolio) in PM Bazargan's cabinet (September 28–November 5, 1979)
1928–November 22, 1998, Isfahan, Isfahan
BA, law, Tehran University (incomplete)
Sadeq, military
Imprisoned before the revolution
Not a war veteran
Member of the Pan-Iranist Party and secretary-general of the Party of the Iranian Nation
In the early 1950s, Foruhar published a newspaper titled *Arman-e Mellat*. In 1979, before the victory of the revolution, he survived a bomb blast at his house. PM Bazargan appointed Foruhar roving minister (*vazir-e sayar*) on September 28, 1979, and in that capacity he dealt with the unrest in Kurdistan. Foruhar ran in the 1980 presidential election, but received less than 1 percent of the vote. In 1981, he was imprisoned for five months and upon his release became involved in the nationalist opposition movement. He and his wife, Parvaneh, were both brutally murdered on November 22, 1998, by regime assailants as part of the "chain murder" of dissident intellectuals.

Forutan-Pishbijari, Hoseyn

Deputy of the Third Majlis, Tehran, Tehran (1988–92)
1948–, Rudsar, Gilan
MD, medicine
Mohammad
Professor and rector of Tehran University
No imprisonment

Foruzandeh, Mohammad

First deputy chief of the Armed Forces General Staff (October 1, 1989–93); minister of defense and armed forces logistics in President Hashemi-Rafsanjani's second cabinet (August 16, 1993–August 2, 1997); member of the Sixth (2007–12), Seventh (2012–17), and Eighth (2017–22) Expediency Discernment Assembly
1960–, Tehran, Tehran
BA
No imprisonment
War veteran
IRGC militiaman
Foruzandeh, who was an engineering commander for the IRGC during the war, became the youngest person to serve as minister of defense at thirty-three years old. He served for a while as the governor of Khuzestan Province, and he headed the FDWI from July 22, 1999, to 2014. He married the widow of fellow IRGC commander Mohammad Jahanara after Jahanara died in the war. Foruzandeh's brother, Ahmad, is one of the major commanders of the IRGC's Qods Force.

Foruzandeh-Dehkordi, Lotfollah

VP for management and human capital development (2009–12) and then VP for parliamentary affairs (May 28, 2012–13) in President Ahmadinejad's second cabinet

1961–, Shahrekord, Chahar Mahal and Bakhtiari

BS, business administration, Isfahan University of
Technology; PhD, strategic management, Tehran
University, 1999

Civil servant

No imprisonment

War veteran

IRGC militiaman

Spokesperson and deputy secretary-general of the
Alliance of Veterans of the Islamic Revolution

Foruzandeh-Dehkordi was a deputy to MP Ahmad
Tavakkoli in the Islamic Majlis Research Center,
and he ran the State Management Training Center for a short while. He ran unsuccessfully for the
Tenth Majlis from Tehran in 2016.

Foruzesh, Gholam-Reza

Minister of the Construction Jihad in PM Musavi's
second cabinet (September 20, 1988–August 3,
1989), as well as President Hashemi-Rafsanjani's
first (August 29, 1989–August 2, 1993) and second
(August 16, 1993–August 2, 1997) cabinets

1955–, Dezful, Khuzestan

BS, mining engineering, Tehran University

Father's name unknown, shopkeeper

No imprisonment

War veteran (victim of a chemical attack)

Martyr's family (brother)

Member of the central council of PECI

Foruzesh was one of the radical students who took
over the American embassy. After he finished
serving in the cabinet, he became a member of
the Tehran City Council.

Foruzesh, Peyman

Deputy of the Seventh (2004–8) and Eighth (2008–12)
Majlis, Zahedan, Sistan and Baluchestan

1973–, Mashhad, Razavi Khorasan

MS, agricultural engineering

Abdorrahman

Academia

No imprisonment

Not a war veteran

The qualifications of Foruzesh, a reformist Sunni and
one of the youngest MPs in the Seventh Majlis,
were rejected for the Ninth Majlis.

Fotuhi, Mohammad-Sharif

Deputy of the Fifth Majlis, Chabahar and Nikshahr,
Sistan and Baluchestan (1996–2000)

1960–, Chabahar, Sistan and Baluchestan

High school diploma

Fattah-Mohammad

No imprisonment

Fotuhi was a Sunni MP.

Fowzi, Mohammad

Member of the Assembly for the Final Examination of
the Constitution, West Azerbaijan (1979)

1925–2007, Urmia, West Azerbaijan

Clerical education

Ali-Asghar, clergyman

Clergyman (HI)

Not a war veteran

Fowzi was the representative of Grand Ayatollah
Seyyed Mohammad-Kazem Shari'atmadari in
Urmia. He helped to set up revolutionary committees in Urmia. After the attacks on Shari'atmadari, Fowzi became a bookseller in Qom.

Fuladgar, Hamid-Reza

Deputy of the Seventh (2004–8), Eighth (2008–12),
Ninth (2012–16), and Tenth (2016–20) Majlis,
Isfahan, Isfahan

1960–, Isfahan, Isfahan

BS, mechanical engineering, Iran University of
Science and Technology, 1986; MS, industrial
engineering, Islamic Azad University–Najafabad,
1995; PhD, industrial engineering, 2015

Mohammad, craftsman

University professor and engineer

No imprisonment

War veteran

IRGC militiaman

Member of the central council of the Islamic Society of Engineers

Fuladgar was active in the Islamic council of the Iran University of Science and Technology before the revolution.

Fuladi, Kurosh

Deputy of the Fifth Majlis, Khorramabad, Lorestan (1996–2000)

1963–, Khorramabad, Lorestan

PhD, English literature

Mehdi

No imprisonment

In 1979, the British police arrested Fuladi on terrorism charges, and he spent the next ten years in British jails. Upon his release in 1989, he returned to Iran.

Fumani-Ha'eri, Mostafa

Deputy of the First Majlis, Fuman, Gilan (1980–84)

1950–, Tehran, Tehran

Clerical education

Javad, clergyman

Clergyman

No imprisonment

HI Fumani-Ha'eri became ambassador to UAE in 1985 and in September 2014 became a special assistant to foreign minister Mohammad-Javad Zarif.

Garmabi, Hamid

Deputy of the Tenth Majlis, Neyshabur, Razavi Khorasan (2016–20)

1961–, Neyshabur, Razavi Khorasan

BS, chemical engineering, Sharif University of Technology, 1986; MS, chemical engineering, Amirkabir University of Technology, 1990; PhD, chemical engineering, McGill University (Canada), 1997; dissertation title: "Development of Laminar Morphology in Sheet Extrusion of Polymer Blends"

Professor and dean at Amirkabir University of Technology

No imprisonment

Garmabi lived in Canada from 1991 to 1997.

Garrusi, Hoseyn

Deputy of the Eighth (2008–12) and Ninth (2012–16) Majlis, Shahriyar, Tehran

1964–, Bijar, Kurdistan

BA, philosophy, Shahid Beheshti University, 1991; MA, public administration

Mahmud

Civil servant of the Martyr's Foundation

No imprisonment

War veteran

Martyr's family (father, Mahmud, and brother, Abolfazl)

Garrusi was previously a member of the city council, lieutenant governor, and governor of Bijar. As an expert in martial arts, he served as head of the Kung Fu Federation of the Islamic Republic of Iran. He ran unsuccessfully for the Seventh Majlis.

Garshasebi, Ghafur

Deputy of the First Majlis, Bandar-e Lengeh, Hormozgan (1981–84)

1955–, Tehran, Tehran

BS, public health

Mohammad-Taqi

No imprisonment

Garshasenbi was the managing director of the reformist newspaper *Asr-e-Azdegan* before the judiciary banned it.

Gerami-Moqaddam, Esma'il

Deputy of the Seventh Majlis, Bojnurd, Maneh and Samalqan, and Jajarm, North Khorasan (2004–8)

1967–, Bojnurd, North Khorasan

BS, aerospace engineering, Imam Hoseyn University, 1996; MS, financial management, Center for

Governmental Management, 2006; PhD, economics, University of Pune (India), 2011
Hoseyn, bazaar tradesman
MI's parliamentary deputy
No imprisonment
War veteran (wounded)
IRGC militiaman
Founding member and spokesperson for the NTP
After the contested 2009 presidential election, Gerami-Moqaddam, who was an adviser to Mehdi Karrubi, left Iran to reside in Malaysia and India. Upon his return to Iran from India in 2015, the judiciary arrested Gerami-Moqaddam, who is almost blind.

Geranmayeh[pur], Ali-Asghar

Deputy of the Seventh (2004–8) and Eighth (2008–12) Majlis, Kashan, Aran, and Bidgol, Isfahan
1952–, Kashan, Isfahan
BS, mathematics; MA, public administration
Abbas
Civil servant
Imprisoned before the revolution
Not a war veteran
Geranmayeh is a former governor of Yazd, Mazandaran, and Chahar Mahal and Bakhtiari (served between 1984 and 1989). He was not elected to the Ninth Majlis.

Ghaffari, Hadi

Deputy of the First (1980–84), Second (1984–88), and Third (1988–92) Majlis, Tehran, Tehran
June 25, 1950–, Azarshahr, East Azerbaijan
Clerical education; BA, theology, Tehran University, 1971
Hoseyn, clergyman
Clergyman
Imprisoned before the revolution
Not a war veteran
IRGC militiaman
Martyr's family (father was killed in shah's prison on December 27, 1975)

Member of the central council of the ACC and the AILF
HI Ghaffari, who was active in the anti-shah movement, was accused of killing former PM Hoveyda on April 7, 1979, while he was on trial. He was a judge in Mazandaran Province courts before being elected to the First Majlis, and he was the youngest member of the Second Majlis. A moderate MP unsuccessfully challenged his credentials for the Second Majlis. He had a reputation as a fiery cleric in the early years of the revolution and used to organize street mobs known as *hezbollahis* to attack opposition forces. Ghaffari also had a well-armed private army. He was rewarded for his hooliganism by being granted ownership of the stocking factory Star Light, which he directed for a while. Ghaffari, who escaped an assassination attempt in March 1981, was affiliated with *Sobh-e Azadegan*, which was closed by the judiciary in 1985. He was disqualified from running for Majlis on three separate occasions starting in 1992. Ghaffari criticized Ayatollah Khamenei for his denunciation of the 2009 protests. His maternal grandfather was Ayatollah Mirza Ali Moqaddas-Tabrizi, and his brother-in-law is Ahmad Mollazadeh.

Ghaffari, Mohammad

Deputy of the First Majlis, Salmas, West Azerbaijan (1980–84)
1933–, Maku, West Azerbaijan
Clerical education, Qom Seminary
Gholam-Reza, farmer
Clergyman (HI)
No imprisonment
Not a war veteran
Ghaffari was the Friday prayer leader of Salmas.

Ghaffari-Qarebagh[i], Seyyed Akbar [Mir Akbar]

Deputy of the First Majlis, Urmia, West Azerbaijan (1980–84); member of the Third (1999–2006) and Fourth (2007–12) Assembly of Experts, West Azerbaijan

1936–2012, Qarabagh, West Azerbaijan

Clerical education, Qom Seminary

Mir Jalil, farmer

Clergyman (ayatollah)

No imprisonment

Not a war veteran

Ghafurifard, Hasan

Deputy of the First Majlis, Mashhad, Razavi Khorasan (May 28, 1981–August 17, 1981); minister of energy in PM Bahonar's cabinet (August 17–30, 1981), interim PM Mahdavi-Kani's cabinet (September 3–October 18, 1981), and PM Musavi's first cabinet (November 2, 1981–85); VP and head of the Physical Training Organization in President Hashemi-Rafsanjani's first cabinet (1990–93); deputy of the Fifth (1996–2000), Seventh (2007–8), and Eighth (2008–12) Majlis, Tehran, Tehran

August 5, 1943–, Tehran, Tehran

BS, physics, Tehran University, 1965; MS, seismology, University of Tokyo (Japan), 1966; MS, physics, Tehran University, 1968; MS, nuclear physics, University of Kansas (USA), 1971; PhD, nuclear physics, University of Kansas (USA), 1976

Mohammad, laborer

Governor of Khorasan

Imprisoned before the revolution

Not a war veteran

Member of the central council of CIC/PCIC and IRP; founding member of the Islamic Society of Engineers; secretary-general of both the Islamic Society of Athletes and the Alliance of Steadfast Supporters of the Islamic Revolution

Ghafurifard resigned from the First Majlis after less than three months to become the minister of energy in PM Bahonar's cabinet but served for only six days before Bahonar and President Raja'i were assassinated. He ran in the third (1981) and eighth (2001) presidential elections but received less than 1 percent of the vote each time. He has

held posts such as professor at Amirkabir University, governor-general of Razavi Khorasan, head of the Physical Training Organization, and head of the House of [Political] Parties. In 2016 he ran unsuccessfully for the Tenth Majlis. Ghafurifard is a member of the HCCR.

Ghanizadeh, Ali-Reza

Deputy of the Fifth Majlis, Urmia, West Azerbaijan (1996–2000)

1964–, Urmia, West Azerbaijan

BS, management

Cheragh-Ali

No imprisonment

IRGC militiaman

Ghanizadeh later became director-general of financial affairs for Islamic Azad University.

Gharavi, Abdolhoseyn

Member of the First Assembly of Experts, East Azerbaijan (1984–90)

1907–1994, Najaf, Iraq

Clerical education, Qom Seminary

Morteza, clergyman

Clergyman (ayatollah)

No imprisonment

Not a war veteran

Gharavi is the son-in-law of Ayatollah Seyyed Hasan Angaji.

Gharavian, Abdoljavad

Member of the First (1983–90) and Second (1991–98) Assembly of Experts, Razavi Khorasan

1926–2015, Neyshabur, Razavi Khorasan

Clerical education, Mashhad Seminary

Mohammad-Reza, laborer

Clergyman

No imprisonment

Not a war veteran

HI Gharavian was the Friday prayer leader of Neyshabur from 1981 to 2009.

Gharazi, Seyyed Mohammad

Deputy of the First Majlis, Isfahan, Isfahan (1981);
minister of petroleum in PM Bahonar's cabinet
(August 17–30, 1981), interim PM Mahdavi-Kani's
cabinet (September 3–October 18, 1981), and PM
Musavi's first cabinet (November 2, 1981–August
14, 1985); minister of post, telegraph, and tele-
phones in PM Musavi's second cabinet (October
28, 1985–August 3, 1989) and President Hash-
emi-Rafsanjani's first (August 29, 1989–August
2, 1993) and second (August 16, 1993–August 2,
1997) cabinets
February 12, 1942–, Isfahan, Isfahan
BS, electrical engineering, Tehran University, 1965;
MS, electrical engineering, Tehran University,
1967
Seyyed Reza, proprietor and merchant
Civil servant
Imprisoned before the revolution
Not a war veteran
IRGC militiaman (commander)
Member of PMOI (before the revolution)
The Ministry of Energy sent Gharazi to France in
1967 to study electrical engineering but he did
not finish his studies. He was imprisoned for his
affiliation with PMOI, but was released in 1972
and left Iran in 1975 to go to Turkey and then
Iraq. Between 1975 and 1978, he was involved
in revolutionary activities in Iraq, Syria, Egypt,
Lebanon, Pakistan, and Turkey. Gharazi joined
Ayatollah Khomeini in Paris in 1978 and became
an IRGC commander in 1979. He resigned from
the First Majlis on August 17, 1981, to accept the
position of minister of post, telegraph, and telephones. He also served as the deputy provincial
governor of Kurdistan, deputy to the governor
of Khuzestan (Ahmad Madani), and governor of
Khuzestan. Gharazi did not receive the backing of
the Majlis on October 27, 1981, to become President Khamenei's prime minister. He was involved
with Resalat from the very beginning, and the GC
approved him to run for the presidency in 2013,
but he received only 446,015 votes (1.2 percent). In
2016, he ran unsuccessfully for the Tenth Majlis,
and in 2017, the GC disqualified him from running in the presidential race.

Ghayuri-Najafabadi, Seyyed Ali

Deputy of the Fourth Majlis, Tehran, Tehran
(1992–96)
1930–2014, Najafabad, Isfahan
Clerical education, Qom Seminary
Seyyed Mostafa, bazaar tradesman
Clergyman
Imprisoned before the revolution (internally exiled)
Not a war veteran
Martyr's family (son Seyyed Hasan died from being
exposed to chemical weapons during the Iran–
Iraq War)
Member of the central council of the SCC; founding
member of ADVIR
HI Ghayuri-Najafabadi held such posts as the Fri-
day prayer leader of Shahr-e Rey and Ayatollah
Khomeini's representative in Africa. He was also
Ayatollah Khamenei's representative in charge of
financial affairs for the Free University and the
Red Crescent Society. Ghayuri-Najafabadi, who
was one of the two oldest members of the Fourth
Majlis, did not run for the Fifth Majlis. He was a
distant relative of Ayatollah Montazeri (son-in-
law of Mrs. Montazeri's maternal uncle).

Ghazanfarabadi, Musa

Deputy of the Seventh (2006–8), Eighth (2008–12),
and Ninth (2012–16) Majlis, Bam, Kerman
1966–, Bam, Kerman
MA, private law, Islamic Azad University–Khorasgan
Hoseyn
Clergyman (HI) and judge
No imprisonment
After Ghazanfarabadi, a conservative, was not elected
to the Tenth Majlis, he became the judge of Teh-
ran's Revolutionary Court.

Ghazanfari [-Khansari], Mehdi

Minister of commerce (September 3, 2009–August 2, 2011) and then minister of industry, mining, and trade (August 3, 2011–August 3, 2013) in President Ahmadinejad's second cabinet

1960–, Aligudarz, Lorestan

BS, industrial engineering, Iran University of Science and Technology, 1986; MS, industrial engineering, Amirkabir University of Technology, 1989; PhD, industrial engineering, University of New South Wales (Australia), 1996

Employee of the Ministry of Commerce and professor at Iran University of Science and Technology

No imprisonment

War veteran

IRGC militiaman

On August 3, 2011, Ghazanfari received 218 positive votes, twenty negative votes, and seven abstentions to become minister of industry, mining, and trade. He was subject to a new vote after the Ministries of Industries and Commerce merged on June 29, 2011.

Ghazanfarpur, Ahmad

Deputy of the First Majlis, Lenjan, Isfahan (1980–January 17, 1982)

1942–, Lenjan, Isfahan

MD, dentistry, University of Paris (France), 1972

Karim, landowner

Dentist

No imprisonment

Not a war veteran

Ghazanfarpur began his political life as a Maoist. When Ayatollah Khomeini first went to Paris, he stayed at Ghazanfarpur's apartment for a few days. After the events of summer 1981 that led to the ouster of his friend and political ally President Banisadr, Ghazanfarpur stopped attending Majlis sessions. Therefore, the Majlis voted on January 7, 1982, that he had indeed resigned his post. After President Banisadr escaped Iran, Ghazanfarpur did the same. However, he changed his mind and decided to return to Iran. After he and his wife were imprisoned, he gave up on politics and concentrated on his dentistry work. The Ministry of Education recognized Ghazanfarpur's degree as equal to an MD because he worked for two years outside Tehran.

Gheyasi-Moradi, Karim

Deputy of the Sixth (2000–2004) and Seventh (2004–8) Majlis, Shabestar, East Azerbaijan

1957–, Shabestar, East Azerbaijan

BS, biological sciences

Mirza Ali-Akbar

Civil servant

No imprisonment

After serving in the Majlis, Gheyasi-Moradi became a civil servant.

Gheybparvar, Gholam-Hoseyn

Commander of the IRGC's Basij Force (December 7, 2016–present)

1962–, Shiraz, Fars

No imprisonment

War veteran

IRGC militiaman

Commander of the IRGC's Imam Hoseyn headquarters (2015–16)

Brigadier General Gheybparvar was in charge of the IRGC forces in Fars Province for eleven years and helped suppress Green Movement supporters in 2009. He has also been the training deputy of the IRGC's ground forces. In 2015, Gheybparvar became the commander of the IRGC's Imam Hoseyn base in Syria.

Gholami, Mansur

Minister of science, research, and technology in President Rouhani's second cabinet (October 29, 2017–21)

1953–, Hamedan, Hamedan
BS, agricultural extension, Hamedan Agricultural
    College, 1976; MS, agricultural engineering,
    Tarbiyat-e Modarres University, 1985; PhD,
    agricultural engineering, University of Adelaide
    (Australia), 1996
Rector of Bu-Ali Sina University
No imprisonment
Not a war veteran
Gholami has been a member of the Construction
    Jihad and University Jihad and served as a profes-
    sor (since 1987), dean of the school of agriculture,
    deputy rector for administration and finance and
    finally rector (1997–2004 and 2014–17) of Bu-
    Ali Sina University. He lived in Australia from
    1991 to 1996 when doing his doctoral studies.
    He received 180 positive votes, eighty-two nega-
    tive votes and fourteen abstentions when he was
    confirmed by the Majlis as minister of science,
    research, and technology on October 29, 2017.

Gilani, Sohrab

Deputy of the Tenth Majlis, Shushtar, Khuzestan
    (2016–20)
1961–, Dimcheh, Khuzestan
MA, management, Imam Hoseyn University
War veteran
IRGC commander
Martyr's family (brother)
Gilani was a high-level IRGC officer in Khuzestan
    Province and a member of Ayatollah Khamenei's
    security team before joining the Majlis. He ran
    unsuccessfully for the Ninth Majlis in 2012.

Gol, Azim

Deputy of the Sixth Majlis, Bandar-e Torka-
    man, Kordkuy and Bandar-e Gaz, Golestan
    (2000–2001)
1962–May 17, 2001, Bandar-e Torkaman, Golestan
MD, medicine
Alti
Medical doctor

No imprisonment
Gol was killed in a plane crash along with the minis-
    ter of roads and transportation, Rahman Dad-
    man, among others.

Golbaz, Ja'far

Deputy of the Fifth (1996–2000), and Sixth (2000–
    2004) Majlis, Savojblagh, Nazarabad, and Tale-
    qan, Tehran
1957–, Savojblagh, Tehran
MA, penal law and criminology; clerical education
Safar
Civil servant
No imprisonment

Golcheshmeh, Naqdi

Deputy of the Sixth Majlis, Gonbad-e Kavus, Goles-
    tan (2001–4)
1946–2015, Gonbad-e Kavus, Golestan
Associate's degree
Ash
No imprisonment
Golcheshmeh, who was a Sunni Turkoman, became a
    civil servant after leaving the Majlis.

Golmoradi, Ali

Deputy of the Tenth Majlis, Bandar-e Mahshahr,
    Khuzestan (2016–20)
1971–, Darreshahr, Ilam
BA, business administration, Islamic Azad Univer-
    sity–Abadan, 1999; MA, executive management;
    pursuing a PhD degree in human resource
    management
Hashem, laborer
Mayor of Bandar-e Imam Khomeini
Not a war veteran
Golmoradi has been a farmer, street vendor, and civil
    servant in the Ports and Maritime Organization.
    He served as mayor of Bandar-e Mahshahr from
    2007 to 2009 and Bandar-e Imam Khomeini from
    2011 to 2015.

Golshani, Faramarz

Deputy of the Fourth (1992–96) and Fifth (1996–2000)
    Majlis, Rudbar, Gilan
1952–, Rudbar, Gilan
BS, electrical engineering; MS, electrical engineering;
    PhD, management
Hoseyn
Civil servant, state companies
No imprisonment
Golshani was a candidate for the Ninth Majlis.

Golzadeh-Ghafuri, Ali

Member of the Assembly for the Final Examination
    of the Constitution, Tehran (1979); deputy of the
    First Majlis, Tehran, Tehran (1980–82)
1923–January 1, 2010, Qazvin, Qazvin
Clerical education, Qom Seminary; MA, law, Tehran
    University, 1969; PhD, Islamic law, University of
    Paris (France) 1972
Gholam-Ali, bazaar tradesman
Clergyman
No imprisonment
Not a war veteran
HI Golzadeh-Ghafuri, who used to collaborate with
    Ayatollah Beheshti and HI Bahonar on school
    textbooks before the revolution, received the
    fourth highest number of votes in the 1979 elec-
    tion for the AFEC. In 1980, Tehran voters elected
    him as their tenth deputy in the Majlis. However,
    Golzadeh-Ghafuri stopped attending Majlis
    meetings as of June 10, 1981, in protest of poli-
    cies adopted by the new regime. The other MPs
    voted on January 7, 1982, that his absenteeism
    signaled his resignation from the Majlis. His son
    Mohammad-Sadeq was executed on September
    19, 1981, and his second son Mohammad-Kazem
    was executed on October 5, 1981, for their par-
    ticipation in PMOI. Golzadeh-Ghafuri staged a
    sit-in in the First Majlis after his sons were killed.
    His daughter Maryam was executed on July 26,
    1988, and her husband, Ali-Reza Haj-Samadi, was
    executed one or two months later. Toward the

end of his life, Golzadeh-Ghafuri abandoned his
    clerical robe.

Gonabadi, Mohammad-Shahab

Minister of housing and urban development in PM
    Raja'i's cabinet (1980–81), PM Bahonar's cabinet
    (August 17–30, 1981), interim PM Mahdavi-Kani's
    cabinet (September 3–October 18, 1981), and PM
    Musavi's first cabinet (November 2, 1981–83)
1942–, Tehran, Tehran
BS, civil engineering, Iran University of Science and
    Technology, 1970
Civil servant, ministries
No imprisonment
Not a war veteran
Gonabadi survived impeachment by the Majlis on
    November 4, 1982. After serving in various
    cabinets, he remained active in the construction
    business.

Gorji [Fard], Mrs. Monireh

Member of the Assembly for the Final Examination of
    the Constitution, Tehran (1979)
1929–, Tehran, Tehran
Seminary education
Qur'an researcher and orator
Mohammad, farmer
No imprisonment
In 1979, Gorji, a candidate of the IRP, made history
    by becoming the only female member of the
    AFEC. Some of the elected male members in the
    assembly threatened to resign if she was allowed
    to take her seat but Gorji was not deterred. After
    serving in the AFEC, she taught theology in a
    women's seminary and did not accept any politi-
    cal posts.

Gorzin, Gholam-Reza

Deputy of the Sixth Majlis, Qaemshahr, Savadkuh
    and Juybar, Mazandaran (2000–2004)
1962–, Savadkuh, Mazandaran

BA, law
Davud
Civil servant, judiciary
No imprisonment
IRGC militiaman
After serving in the Majlis, Gorzin worked in the
military establishment.

Gudarzi, Abbas

Deputy of the Tenth Majlis, Borujerd, Lorestan
(2016–20)
1977–, Borujerd, Lorestan
BS, physics, Arak University; MA, political science
IRGC militiaman (Basij)
Martyr's family (two brothers, Ebrahim and Moham-
mad, killed at the war front)
Gudarzi was active in university Basij and worked
previously in the Office of Supreme Leader at
Arak University, the Borujerd City Council
(2006–11), and the Cultural Heritage and Tourism
Organization.

Gudarzi, Mahmud

Minister of sports and youth in President Rouhani's first
cabinet (November 16, 2013–October 18, 2016)
1955–, Malayer, Hamadan
PhD, management and planning, Tehran University
Head of the School of Physical Training at Tehran
University (2008–13)
No imprisonment
War veteran
IRGC militiaman (1979–82)
Gudarzi, a wrestler and wrestling coach, was President Rouhani's fourth nominee for the post of
minister of sports and youth. The Majlis approved
him by 199 positive votes, forty-four negative
votes, and twenty-four abstentions. He resigned
from his post in October 2016.

Gudarzi, Mas'ud

Deputy of the Tenth Majlis, Mamasani, Fars (2016–20)

1975–, Mamasani, Fars
BS, agricultural engineering, University of Sistan and
Baluchestan, 1998; MA, political science, Shahid
Beheshti University, 2004; PhD, political science,
Islamic Azad University–Science and Research
Branch
Foreign policy expert and professor
No imprisonment
Not a war veteran

Habibi, Abutaleb

Deputy of the Second (1984–88) and Third (1988–92)
Majlis, Qaemshahr, Mazandaran
1948–2014, Qaemshahr, Mazandaran
Clerical education; BA, law
Ya'qub
Clergyman
No imprisonment
HI Habibi was in charge of the legal office of Shahid
Beheshti University and was head of Shahr-e Rey
Seminary.

Habibi, Ahmad

Deputy of the Sixth Majlis, Bandar-e Abbas, Qeshm,
Abumusa, and Hajiabad, Hormozgan (2001–4)
1960–, Bandar-e Abbas, Hormozgan
BA, Persian literature; MA, public administration
Mohammad
Civil servant
No imprisonment
After leaving the Majlis, Habibi became a civil
servant.

Habibi, Bahram

Deputy of the Seventh Majlis, Khomeyn, Markazi
(2004–8)
1966–, Khomeyn, Markazi
MS, management
Ali-Akbar
Civil servant
No imprisonment

Habibi, Habibollah

Deputy of the Fourth Majlis, Khaf, Razavi Khorasan
    (1992–96)
1944–, Khaf, Razavi Khorasan
Clerical education, Mashhad Seminary, 1969
Esma'il
Clergyman (HI)
No imprisonment

Habibi, Hasan-Ebrahim

Minister of higher education in the Revolutionary
    Council (1979–80); minister of Islamic guidance
    in PM Bazargan's cabinet (September 30–No-
    vember 5, 1979); minister of culture and higher
    education in the Revolutionary Council cabinet
    (1979–80); deputy of the First Majlis, Tehran, Teh-
    ran (1980–84); minister of justice in PM Musavi's
    first (August 15, 1984–85) and second (October 28,
    1985–August 3, 1989) cabinets; first vice president
    in President Hashemi-Rafsanjani's first (August
    29, 1989–August 2, 1993) and second (August 16,
    1993–August 2, 1997) cabinets; first vice president
    in President Khatami's first cabinet (1997–2001);
    member of the Second (1989–92), Third (1992–
    98), and Fourth (1998–2001) Guardian Councils;
    member of the Second (May 8, 1991–92), Third
    (1992–97), Fourth (1997–2002), Fifth (2002–7),
    Sixth (2007–12), and Seventh (2012–13) Expedi-
    ency Discernment Assembly
1937–January 21, 2013, Tehran, Tehran
BA, law, Tehran University; PhD, sociology, Tehran
    University
Baqer, bazaar tradesman
No imprisonment
Not a war veteran
Member of the LMI (resigned after the revolution),
    IRP, and PECI
Habibi was active in student demonstrations in the
    early 1960s. He went to France toward the end of
    1964 and studied in Paris, Strasburg and Aix-en-
    Provence. He attended the classes of well-known
    professors like Jacques Burke and even chose a

dissertation title but did not finish the dissertation. Years later, Tehran University's School of
Social Sciences granted him a doctoral degree
in recognition of his extensive publications. In
1978, Habibi joined Ayatollah Khomeini in France
and helped to draft the first constitution of the
Islamic Republic. He ran in the 1980 presidential
election but received less than 5 percent of the
vote. However, on October 28, 1985, he received
the highest number of votes (241 out of 258) when
the MPs were casting their votes for PM Musavi's
second cabinet. Habibi became the first ever first
vice president after the post was created in 1989.
Between 1979 and 2013, Habibi held a record
number of eighteen high-level positions in the
Islamic Republic. Habibi's wife, Shafiqeh Rahi-
deh, who has a doctorate in economics from the
Sorbonne, was in charge of emergency drugs and
medical equipment for the Red Crescent Society
of the Islamic Republic of Iran.

Habibi, Mohammad-Nabi

Mayor of Tehran (1983–87)
1945–, Varamin, Tehran
BA, Tarbiyat-e Modarres University; MA, sociology,
    Tehran University
Mohammad-Mehdi
Civil servant
No imprisonment
Not a war veteran
Secretary-general of the CIC/PCIC
Habibi has held many government posts, including
    governor-general of Fars, Khorasan, and Tehran
    Provinces, head of the Iranian postal service,
    head of the Iran Airline Organization, deputy of
    the FDWI, deputy minister of commerce, and
    mayor of Tehran (for forty-four months) until in-
    terior minister Seyyed Ali-Akbar Mohtashamipur
    terminated his term. Despite becoming the sec-
    retary-general of the CIC/PCIC in 2004, Habibi
    ran unsuccessfully for the Ninth Majlis. His wife,
    Fatemeh Fakhr, is also a member of the central
    council of the CIC/PCIC.

Habibi, Najafqoli

Deputy of the Third Majlis, Tehran, Tehran (1988–92)
1941–, Khansar, Isfahan
PhD, Islamic philosophy, Tehran University; clerical education
Ali-Qoli
Professor and dean at Tehran University
No imprisonment
Not a war veteran
Founding member of the Islamic Association of University Scholars
Habibi, who was a member of the HCCR, failed to enter the Second Majlis in 1984, and a year later, he was appointed as dean of Tehran University's School of Law and Political Science. During his career, he was also rector of three universities—Alzahra, Tarbiyat-e Modarres, and Allameh Tabataba'i.

Habibiyan, Ahmad

Deputy of the Fourth Majlis, Hamadan, Hamadan (1992–96)
1945–, Hamadan, Hamadan
MA, Islamic civilization; clerical education
Hoseyn
No imprisonment

Habibzadeh-Bukani, Anvar

Deputy of the Fifth (1996–2000) and Seventh (2004–8) Majlis, Bukan, West Azerbaijan
1957–, Bukan, West Azerbaijan
BA, public administration
Mostafa
Civil servant
No imprisonment
Habibzadeh-Bukani was a Sunni member of the Majlis.

Hadavi, Mehdi

Prosecutor-general of the revolutionary courts (February 28–August 6, 1979); member of the First Guardian Council (1980–83)

1926–
BA, law, Tehran University
Judiciary official
No imprisonment
Not a war veteran
Hadavi was a judge in charge of Qom's justice administration at the time of the June 5, 1963 (15 Khordad 1342) uprising. The shah's regime relieved Hadavi of his duty when he did not cooperate in the arrest and exile of Ayatollah Khomeini. After the revolution, Hadavi, who had permission for *ejtehad*, was appointed by Ayatollah Khomeini as the first prosecutor-general of the revolutionary courts on February 28, 1979. He became a lay lawyer in the first GC, and was also one of the managers of Hoseyniyyeh-ye Ershad. His son, Mohammad-Amin, was in charge of irregular warfare under Chamran in the Iran–Iraq War. The government arrested Mohammad-Amin in 2011.

Hadavi, Mohsen

Member of the First Guardian Council (1980–83)
1928–, Tehran, Tehran
PhD, law
Attorney
No imprisonment
Not a war veteran

Haddad-Adel, Gholam-Ali

Deputy of the Sixth (2000–2004), Seventh (2004–8), Eighth (2008–12), and Ninth (2012–16) Majlis, Tehran, Tehran; member of the Fifth (2002–7), Sixth (2007–12), Seventh (2012–17), and Eighth (2017–22) Expediency Discernment Assembly
1945–, Tehran, Tehran
BS, physics, Tehran University, 1965; MS, physics, Tehran University, 1968; MA, philosophy, Tehran University, 1972; PhD, philosophy, Tehran University, 1974
Reza (1924–1995), garage and truck company owner
Academia
Imprisoned before the revolution (two to three months)

Not a war veteran

Martyr's family (brother, Majid)

Haddad-Adel is an influential conservative politician close to Ayatollah Khamenei. He was born into a family involved in the transportation business, and his father was PM Raja'i's representative in ports and customs affairs. After the revolution, Haddad-Adel, who has advanced degrees in physics and philosophy, wrote a number of middle school and high school textbooks on religion and social studies. In the 1980s, he was deputy for planning and research in the Ministry of Education. In 2000, he managed to get into the Sixth Majlis as one of the last MPs from Tehran after the GC nullified over 700,000 votes of another candidate (Ali-Reza Raja'i). Many lawmakers objected to Haddad-Adel's qualifications but he managed to hold his seat. In 2004, he was elected as the speaker of the Seventh Majlis, becoming the first non-cleric to hold the post. In addition to serving in the Majlis and the EDA, he was the head of the Iranian Language Academy, Sa'di Foundation, and a member of the HCCR. On June 28, 2008, the supreme leader appointed him as a senior adviser. In 2013, he became a presidential candidate but withdrew from the race without any explanation four days before the election. In 2016, he failed to enter the Tenth Majlis and afterward became the managing director of the Encyclopedia of Islam Foundation. Haddad-Adel married his wife, Tayebeh Mahruzadeh (b. 1950), in 1972 and they have one son and three daughters. One of his daughters, Zahra (b. 1979), is married to Ayatollah Khamenei's son Mojtaba. His brother Majid, who was a deputy in the office of the governor-general of Bakhtaran, was killed by Iraqi forces on September 30, 1981, during a visit to the war front.

Hadidchi-Dabbagh, Mrs. Marziyeh [Tahereh]

Deputy of the Second (1984–88) and Third (1988–92) Majlis, Tehran, Tehran; deputy of the Fifth Majlis (1996–2000), Hamadan, Hamadan

1939–2016, Hamadan, Hamadan

Pre-diploma (six years of elementary school)

Ali-Pasha, bookseller

Imprisoned before the revolution (two years total)

IRGC militiawoman

Deputy director of the Alliance of the Women of the Islamic Republic

Hadidchi-Dabbagh got married in 1954 and spent a few years in prison for revolutionary activities. She left Iran in the mid-1970s to go to Lebanon (for military training), Syria, England, and France. While Ayatollah Khomeini was in Paris, Hadidchi-Dabbagh was one of his bodyguards and also helped with housekeeping tasks at his residence. After the revolution, Hadidchi (also known as Tahereh Dabbagh) was in charge of Tehran women's prisons and later became the first female IRGC commander, leading the IRGC force in Hamadan until 1981. She was a member of the delegation Ayatollah Khomeini sent to deliver a message to Mikhail Gorbachev, the last leader of the Soviet Union. She ran unsuccessfully for the Fourth Majlis.

Hadi-Najafabadi, Mohammad-Ali

Deputy of the First (1980–84) and Second (1984–88) Majlis, Tehran, Tehran

1938–, Najafabad, Isfahan

MA, international relations; PhD; clerical education

Gholam-Hoseyn, farmer

Academia

No imprisonment

Not a war veteran

Hadi-Najafabadi translated Ayatollah Khomeini's speeches into Arabic while the ayatollah resided in Paris in 1978. In the early days of the revolution, he was in charge of *Keyhan* and served on the supervisory council of IRIB. He was close to Ayatollah Montazeri and took part in the negotiations with Robert McFarlane during the Iran-Contra affair. It is rumored that he was the one who told Ayatollah Montazeri about the Iran-Contra affair, and that he was also involved

in the assassination of Kazem Rajavi (brother of
Mas'ud Rajavi, the leader of PMOI) in Europe.
He was deputy foreign minister and ambassador
to Saudi Arabia and UAE before retiring when
President Ahmadinejad came to office.

Hadizadeh, Ali-Asghar

Deputy of the Fifth (1996–2000) and Sixth (2000–
    2004) Majlis, Mahallat and Delijan, Markazi
1957–, Mahallat, Markazi
Associate's degree, 1978; BA, 2000
Mohammad
No imprisonment
IRGC militiaman

Ha'eri, Seyyed Mohammad

Deputy of the Third Majlis, Dehloran, Darrehshahr,
    and Badreh, Ilam (1988–92)
1952–, Mehran, Ilam
BA, theology (unverified)
Seyyed Qasem
No imprisonment
Ha'eri is a reformist who is affiliated with NTP.

Ha'eri-Shirazi, Mohammad-Sadeq [Mohyeddin]

Deputy of the First Majlis, Shiraz, Fars (1980–82);
    member of the First (1983–90), Second (1991–
    98), and Fourth (2007–16) Assembly of Experts,
    Fars
February 1, 1937–December 20, 2017, Shiraz, Fars
Clerical education, Qom Seminary
Abdolhoseyn, clergyman (ayatollah)
Clergyman
Imprisoned before the revolution
Not a war veteran
Ayatollah Ha'eri-Shirazi ran seminars for students
    who occupied the American embassy. He resigned
    from the First Majlis on April 27, 1982, to become
    the Friday prayer leader of Shiraz (1981–2009) and
    the supreme leader's representative in Shiraz after
    PMOI assassinated Ayatollah Dastgheyb. In 1989,

he voiced strong opposition to the idea of having
a leadership council instead of a single supreme
leader. Ha'eri-Shirazi continued as Ayatollah
Khamenei's representative in Fars Province and
then worked in the Office of the Supreme Leader.
He was a member of the Rifling Federation of
Iran and was accused of taking over lands ille-
gally. He decided not to run for the Fifth AE. He
was the son-in-law of Ayatollah Seyyed Nurred-
din Hoseyni-Alhashemi-Shirazi.

Ha'eri-Yazdi, Morteza

Member of the Assembly for the Final Examination of
    the Constitution, Markazi (1979)
1917–March 16, 1986, Arak, Markazi
Clerical education
Abdolkarim, clergyman (ayatollah)
Clergyman
No imprisonment
Not a war veteran
Ayatollah Ha'eri-Yazdi, who was opposed to mixing
    religion and politics, voted against the principle
    of *velayat-e faqih* in the AFEC. After finishing his
    term in the AFEC, he returned to teaching at the
    Qom Seminary, which his father founded. His
    oldest daughter, Masumeh, was the wife of Mo-
    stafa Khomeini, and his brother was the philoso-
    pher Mehdi Ha'eri-Yazdi.

Ha'erizadeh, Seyyed Abolhasan

Deputy of the First (1980–84), Second (1984–88), and
    Third (1988–92) Majlis, Birjand, South Khorasan
1947–2008, Karbala, Iraq
Clerical education; BS, mechanical engineering
Seyyed Kazem, clergyman
Clergyman
No imprisonment
Not a war veteran
HI Ha'erizadeh was a reformist. The GC rejected his
    qualifications for the Fourth Majlis. He worked
    for the government and died in 2008 of a heart
    attack.

Haj Akhund-Kermanshahi, Mojtaba

Member of the First (1983–90) and Second (1991–98)
    Assembly of Experts, Kermanshah
1929–2001, Kermanshah, Kermanshah
Clerical education, Qom Seminary
Hasan, clergyman (ayatollah)
Clergyman (ayatollah)
Imprisoned before the revolution
Not a war veteran
Haj Akhund-Kermanshahi was Ayatollah Khomei-
    ni's representative in the Construction Jihad and
    served as ideological-political commissar for the
    army in the western region of Iran.

Haj Aliakbari, Mohammad-Javad

VP and head of the National Youth Organization in
    President Ahmadinejad's first cabinet (2005–9)
1964–, Damavand, Tehran
MA, theology; clerical education
Clergyman (HI)
No imprisonment
War veteran
IRGC militiaman
HI Haj Aliakbari is the supreme leader's representa-
    tive in the Union of Students' Islamic Students'
    Associations. On January 6, 2018, Ayatollah
    Khamenei also appointed him as the chair of the
    Friday Prayer Policymaking Council.

Haji, Morteza

Minister of cooperatives in President Khatami's first
    cabinet (August 20, 1997–August 1, 2001); min-
    ister of education in President Khatami's second
    cabinet (August 22, 2001–August 2, 2005)
1948–, Tehran, Tehran
BS, mathematics, Tarbiyat-e Modarres University,
    1976; received a fake graduate degree from the
    non-accredited American University of Hawaii
Taqi, civil servant
Journalist
Imprisoned before the revolution

Not a war veteran
IRGC militiaman (commander of the IRGC in Babol)
Member of the MNP; founding member of the Society
    of Industrial Managers and Professionals of Iran
Haji was involved with the radical MNP in his youth,
    and taught mathematics in high schools. In the
    1980s and 1990s, he served as governor-general of
    Mazandaran, deputy minister of heavy industries,
    deputy to the minister of culture and Islamic
    guidance, and director-general of *Hamshahri*.
    Haji is a former member of the HCCR. In 1997, he
    was in charge of Mohammad Khatami's election
    headquarters. He survived impeachment as min-
    ister of education on August 31, 2003.

Haji Asghari, Seyyed Mohammad-Reza

Deputy of the Eighth Majlis, Miyaneh, East Azerbai-
    jan (2008–12)
1972–, Miyaneh, East Azerbaijan
BS, agricultural engineering
Seyyed Taqi
Civil servant
No imprisonment
Not a war veteran

Haji Baba'i, Hamid-Reza

Deputy of the Fifth (1996–2000), Sixth (2000–2004),
    Seventh (2004–8), Eighth (2008–November 15,
    2009), and Tenth (2016–20) Majlis, Hamadan,
    Hamadan; minister of education in President
    Ahmadinejad's second cabinet (November 15,
    2009–August 3, 2013)
1959–, Maryanaj-e Hamadan, Hamadan
BA, theology, Tehran University, 1988; MA, theology,
    Islamic Azad University–Karaj, 1993; PhD, theol-
    ogy, Islamic Azad University–Tehran, 1998
Jalal
Academia
No imprisonment
Not a war veteran
Haji Baba'i resigned from the Eighth Majlis on
    November 15, 2009, after receiving 217 positive,

thirty-three negative, and thirteen abstaining votes during his confirmation as the new minister of education. In 2017, he became the leader of YEKTA Front (the Front of Comrades for the Effectiveness and Transformation of Islamic Iran).

Haji Deligani, Hoseyn-Ali

Deputy of the Ninth (2012–16) and Tenth (2016–20) Majlis, Shahinshahr, Meymeh, and Borkhar, Isfahan
1962–, Isfahan, Isfahan
MA, public administration, Higher Institute of Training and Research for Planning and Management
No imprisonment
War veteran
IRGC militiaman (commander of the IRGC Basij Force in Zarinshahr)
Member of the SFIR
Haji Deligani was formerly the governor of Kashan and deputy governor of Isfahan.

Haji Naseri, Davud

Deputy of the Third Majlis, Zanjan and Tarom, Zanjan (1988–92)
1953–, Zanjan, Zanjan
BS, biological sciences; clerical education
Gholam-Hoseyn
No imprisonment

Haji Tarkhani-Tehrani, Mirza Javad

Member of the Assembly for the Final Examination of the Constitution, Razavi Khorasan (1979)
1904–1989, Tehran, Tehran
Clerical education, Najaf Seminary (Iraq)
Taqi, bazaar tradesman
Clergyman (ayatollah)
Not a war veteran

Hajiyani, Abdollah

Deputy of the Fifth Majlis, Tangestan, Deyr, Kangan, and Dashti, Bushehr (1996–2000); deputy

of the Sixth Majlis, Deyr and Kangan, Bushehr (2000–2004)
1955–, Deyr, Bushehr
Clerical education
Kamal
Clergyman (HI)
No imprisonment

Hakimi, Ataollah

Deputy of the Seventh (2004–8) and Ninth (2012–16) Majlis, Rudbar, Gilan
1963–, Rudbar, Gilan
MA, business administration, Islamic Azad University–Rasht; pursuing a PhD in business administration
Jamshid, farmer
University instructor; director-general of state companies
No imprisonment
War veteran
IRGC militiaman

Hakimipur, Ahmad

Deputy of the Fourth Majlis, Zanjan and Tarom, Zanjan (1992–96)
1963–, Zanjan, Zanjan
MA, political science, Tehran University
Morad-Ali
No imprisonment
War veteran (fifty months; victim of a chemical attack)
Secretary-general of the Party of Iranian People's Will; founding member of the AILF
Hakimipur has served a number of times on the Tehran City Council.

Hamidi, Hushang

Deputy of the Seventh Majlis, Sanandaj, Divandarreh, and Kamyaran, Kurdistan (2004–8)
1973–, Sanandaj, Kurdistan
MA, law
Mohammad-Aref, driver

Attorney
No imprisonment
Not a war veteran

Hamidi, Seyyed Hashem

Deputy of the First (1980–84) and Second (1984–88)
    Majlis, Hamadan, Hamadan
1930–, Hamadan, Hamadan
Clerical education, Qom Seminary
Seyyed Abolqasem, clergyman
Clergyman
No imprisonment
Not a war veteran
Member of the central council of the SCC
Martyr's family (son, Seyyed Mohammad-Reza, killed
    at the war front)
Ayatollah Hamidi is a professor at Imam Sadeq Univer-
    sity, and was Ayatollah Khamenei's representative at
    Science and Technology University. In 2016, he ran
    unsuccessfully for the Fifth AE from Tehran.

Hamidzadeh-Givi, Ali-Akbar

Deputy of the First (1982–84) and Second (1984–86)
    Majlis, Bu'inzahra, Zanjan
1948–, Bu'inzahra, Zanjan
Clerical education
Ghaffar
Clergyman
Imprisoned before the revolution
Not a war veteran
Member of the IRP
HI Hamidzadeh-Givi was on the list of people not
    allowed to leave Iran before the revolution. He
    used to run the revolutionary prosecutor-gener-
    al's public relations office, and also headed the
    ideological-political office of the Gendarmerie. He
    resigned from the Second Majlis.

Hamtaei, Ali-Akbar

Deputy of the Third Majlis, Neyriz and Estahban, Fars
    (1988–92)

1949–, Neyriz, Fars
High school diploma
Mohammad
No imprisonment

Hamzeh, Ahmad

Deputy of the Tenth Majlis, Kahnuj, Kerman
    (2016–20)
1961–, Jiroft, Kerman
MD
Medical doctor and health official in Kerman
    Province
No imprisonment
Hamzeh entered the Tenth Majlis as a reformist.

Hamzeh'i, Ali

Deputy of the First Majlis, Asadabad, Hamadan
    (1981–84)
1946–, Asadabad, Hamadan
Pre-diploma
Abolhasan
No imprisonment

Haqiqat-Afshar, Ali

Deputy of the First Majlis, Urmia, West Azerbaijan
    (1980–84)
1927–date unknown, Urmia, West Azerbaijan
BA, philosophy
Mirza Ali, bazaar tradesman
Academia
No imprisonment
Not a war veteran
After serving in the Majlis, Haqiqat-Afshar became
    an educational administrator. He has since passed
    away (date unknown).

Haqiqatju, Ms. Fatemeh

Deputy of the Sixth Majlis, Tehran, Tehran
    (2000–2004)
1968–, Tehran, Tehran

BA, counseling, Tarbiyat-e Modarres University, 1992; MA, counseling, Tarbiyat-e Modarres University, 1996; PhD, counseling, Tarbiyat-e Modarres University, 2005

Orshan, driver for the Red Crescent Society

Researcher and university professor

No imprisonment

Member of the central council of IIPF; founding member of the Alliance of Modern Muslim Women Thinkers of Iran

In 2004, Haqiqatju resigned from the Sixth Majlis to protest the mass disqualification of reformist candidates from running in the Seventh Majlis election. In 2005, she moved to the United States.

Haqiqatpur, Mansur

Deputy of the Ninth Majlis, Ardabil, Namin, Nir, and Sareyn, Ardabil (2012–16)

1959–, Ardabil, Ardabil

BA, sociology, Tehran University; MS, defense management, Ground Forces Officers' Academy; PhD, strategic management, Ground Forces Officers' Academy

No imprisonment

War veteran

IRGC militiaman (joined in 1980; commander of Karaj IRGC)

Haqiqatpur was active in storming a number of institutions in the revolutionary days of February 1979. He became a high-level official in the IRGC and the Qods Force. In 1985, in the midst of several airplane hijackings, he was put in charge of airport security for the entire country. Starting in 1987, he carried out missions in Central Asia and later Iraq for the IRGC and the Qods Force, serving for two years as the military attaché in the Republic of Azerbaijan. From 2009 to 2010 he was the governor-general of Ardabil, after which he began teaching at IRGC's Imam Hoseyn University and a few other universities. He was not elected to the Tenth Majlis.

Haqi-Sarabi, Mohammad-Ali

Deputy of the Third Majlis, Sarab, East Azerbaijan (1988–92); member of the Second Assembly of Experts, East Azerbaijan (1991–98)

1927–1998, Sarab, East Azerbaijan

Clerical education, Najaf Seminary (Iraq)

Abdollah, clergyman (ayatollah)

Clergyman (ayatollah)

No imprisonment

Not a war veteran

Haqqani, Gholam-Hoseyn

Deputy of the First Majlis, Bandar-e Abbas, Hormozgan (1980–June 28, 1981)

1941–June 28, 1981, Qom, Qom

Clerical education, Qom Seminary

Mohammad, clergyman

Clergyman (HI)

Imprisoned before the revolution

Not a war veteran

Member of the IRP

Haqqani was Ayatollah Khomeini's representative in Hormozgan Province before being elected to the First Majlis. He died in the bombing of the IRP headquarters.

Haqshenas, Hadi

Deputy of the Seventh Majlis, Bandar-e Anzali, Gilan (2004–8)

1967–, Sowme'eh Sara, Gilan

BS, electrical engineering; MS, electrical engineering

Mehdi

Civil servant, state companies

No imprisonment

Haqshenas-Kuddehi, Mazaher

Deputy of the First Majlis, Aliabad Katul, Golestan (1980–84)

1938–, Sowme'eh Sara, Gilan

High school diploma
Gholam, civil servant
No imprisonment
After serving in the Majlis, Haqshenas-Kuddehi became a civil servant.

Harati, Hoseyn

Deputy of the First (1980–84), Second (1984–88), and Third (1988–92) Majlis, Sabzevar, Razavi Khorasan
1945–, Sabzevar, Razavi Khorasan
Associate's degree
Ramezan-Ali, farmer
No imprisonment
Not a war veteran
After serving in the Majlis, Harati joined the Ministry of Education.

Harizavi, Abdozzahra

Deputy of the Fifth Majlis, Abadan, Khuzestan (1996–2000)
1953–, Bostan, Khuzestan
BA
Hasan
No imprisonment

Hasanbeygi, Abolfazl

Deputy of the Third (1988–92), Fourth (1992–96), and Tenth (2016–20) Majlis, Damghan, Semnan
1958–, Damghan, Semnan
High school diploma, 1986; BA, political science, Allameh Tabataba'i University; MA, political science, Farabi University
Baqer, farmer
No imprisonment
War veteran (eight years as a commander; wounded in a chemical attack)
IRGC militiaman
Martyr's family (two brothers, Ali and Mohsen, killed at the war front)

Ayatollah Khamenei appointed Hasanbeygi as an adviser to the chair of the AFGC in 2000, and he was in charge of security for the Petroleum Ministry for a while. He also worked for the Ministry of Agriculture and the Office of the Joint Chiefs of Staff and was a member of the board of directors of the National Iranian Gas Company. He ran unsuccessfully for the Ninth Majlis.

Hasani, Ali

Deputy of the Sixth Majlis, Arak, Markazi (2001–4)
1960–, Arak, Markazi
BS, mathematics, Arak University, 1985; MA, economics, Allameh Tabataba'i University, 1993; PhD, economics (tourism planning), National University of Malaysia, 2010
Abolfazl
Governor of Arak; military and security forces
No imprisonment
After serving in the Majlis, Hasani returned to the academic world.

Hasani, Ali-Asghar

Deputy of the Eighth Majlis, Larestan and Khonj, Fars (2008–12)
1958–, Gerash, Fars
MA, public administration
Mohammad-Ali
Civil servant
No imprisonment
The GC disqualified Hasani from running in the 2012 Majlis election, and he now works for the Red Crescent Society of the Islamic Republic of Iran.

Hasani, Mohammad

Deputy of the Fourth Majlis, Dehloran, Ilam (1992–96)
1950–2015, Ilam, Ilam
BA, economics
Ali

Teacher
No imprisonment

Hasani, Seyyed Mohammad-Amin

Deputy of the First Majlis, Sanandaj, Kurdistan
(1981–84)
1925–date unknown (deceased), Sanandaj, Kurdistan
Clerical education
Seyyed Shokrollah, clergyman
Clergyman (HI)
No imprisonment
Not a war veteran

Hasani [-Bozorgabad], Gholam-Reza

Deputy of the First Majlis, Urmia, West Azerbaijan
(1980–August 5, 1982)
1927–, Urmia, West Azerbaijan
Clerical education, Qom Seminary
Ali, farmer
Clergyman
No imprisonment
Not a war veteran
HI Hasani ran a notary public registering marriages
and divorces in Urmia before the revolution. He
was also involved in demonstrations against the
shah's regime and was harassed by SAVAK. After
the revolution, he headed the Islamic Revolutionary Committee in West Azerbaijan. He survived
two assassination attempts on August 4, 1981, and
August 13, 1982. In August 1982, he resigned from
the First Majlis to become the Friday prayer leader
of Urmia, a position he held until 2014 when
he stepped down due to age and health issues.
Hasani played an important role in putting down
the uprising in Naqadeh in the early days of the
revolution. One of his sons was wounded at the
war front. In 1981, he revealed the whereabouts of
his oldest son (Rashid), a member of OIPFG, who
was subsequently executed by the regime. The
CIA's directory of Iranian clerics (1987) describes
him as a "ruthless egoist."

Hasani-Bafrani, Hoseyn

Deputy of the Seventh (2004–8) and Eighth (2008–12)
Majlis, Na'in, Isfahan
1967–, Bafran, Isfahan
MD
Davud
Cardiologist
No imprisonment
Hasani-Bafrani ran unsuccessfully for the Sixth and
Ninth Majlis.

Hasani-Juryabi, Mohammad-Sadeq

Deputy of the Tenth Majlis, Rasht, Gilan (2016–20)
1965–, Lashtenesha, Gilan
PhD, economics
Father's name unknown, farmer
Civil servant, Ministry of Economic Affairs and
Finance
No imprisonment
Hasani-Juryabi is a reformist.

Hasani-Sa'di, Abbas

Deputy of the Third Majlis, Kerman, Kerman (1988–
March 24, 1989)
1933–March 24, 1989, Sa'di, Kerman
Clerical education, Qom Seminary
Ramezan, farmer
Clergyman (HI)
No imprisonment
Not a war veteran
Member of the SCC
Hasani-Sa'di was Ayatollah Khomeini's represen-
tative in Kerman Province and the temporary
Friday prayer leader of Kerman. He died in a car
accident.

Hasani-Sa'di, Hoseyn

Commander of the Islamic Republic of Iran Ground
Forces (August 2, 1986–May 8, 1991)

BS, military science (artillery), Ground Forces Officers' Academy
No imprisonment
War veteran
Military officer
Major General Hasani-Sa'di is a battle-tested artillery officer from the prerevolutionary era who
also played a key role as a commander during
the Iran–Iraq War. He served as commander of
the army's most powerful brigade (21 Hamzeh)
for a while. Hasani-Sa'di stepped down as the
commander of the army's ground forces on May
8, 1991, and became a military adviser to the
supreme leader. From 1999 to 2016, Hasani-Sa'di
served as the coordinating deputy of AFGS. In
2001, he became a major general. In July 2016,
Hasani-Sa'di was appointed as deputy commander of the Central Khatam al-Anbia Headquarters, which in the event of a war is the lead
body for coordinating war efforts.

Hasannezhad, Mohammad

Deputy of the Ninth (2012–16) and Tenth (2016–20)
Majlis, Marand and Jolfa, East Azerbaijan
1981–, Ahar, East Azerbaijan
BA, business administration, University of Mazan-
daran, 2002; MA, Financial Management,
University of Mazandaran, 2004; PhD, finan-
cial management, Shahid Beheshti University,
2011
University professor; CEO of a company associated
with *Astan-e Qods-e Razavi*
No imprisonment (born after the revolution)
Not a war veteran
Hasannezhad was one of the youngest members of the
Ninth Majlis.

Hasanpur-Biglari, Shahbaz

Deputy of the Eighth (2008–12), Ninth (2012–16),
and Tenth (2016–20) Majlis, Sirjan and Bardsir,
Kerman

1961–, Bardsir, Kerman
BA, public administration, Shahid Bahonar Univer-
sity of Kerman
Mokhtar
Official in the office of the governor-general of Ker-
man Province
No imprisonment
War veteran
IRGC militiaman (commander)
Hasanpur-Biglari was wounded by a bullet during the
1979 revolutionary demonstrations, and he was
very active in Basij after the revolution. He was
also mayor of Sirjan.

Hasanvand, Fatollah

Deputy of the Seventh Majlis, Khorramabad, Lorestan
(2004–8)
1960–, Khorramabad, Lorestan
MS, mathematics
Hoseyn-Ali
Academia
No imprisonment

Hasanvand, Fereydun

Deputy of the Sixth (2000–2004), Seventh (2004–8),
Eighth (2008–12), and Tenth (2016–20) Majlis,
Andimeshk and Shush, Khuzestan
1965–, Dorud, Khuzestan
MA, political science (unverified)
Taqi
MIIRI officer (deputy intelligence officer in Dezful)
No imprisonment
War veteran
IRGC militiaman
Hasanvand had a high school diploma when he first
entered the Majlis, but later claimed to have a
master's degree. After he was not elected to the
Ninth Majlis, he became the governor of Bushehr
Province for a year (2012–13). Fereydun is not re-
lated to the other two individuals on this list with
the last name of Hasanvand.

Hasanvand, Mahmud-Reza

Deputy of the Seventh Majlis, Delfan and Selseleh, Lorestan (2004–8)
1965–, Aleshter, Lorestan
MA, public administration
Mohammad-Reza
Civil servant
No imprisonment

Hasanzadegan-Rudsari, Davud

Deputy of the Sixth Majlis, Rudsar and Amlash, Gilan (2000–2004)
1960–, Rudsar, Gilan
BS, military science; MA, international law
Mahmud
No imprisonment
Hasanzadegan-Rudsari joined the military establishment after serving in the Majlis.

Hasanzadeh-Mirabadi, Hasan

Deputy of the First Majlis, Kashmar, Razavi Khorasan (1981–84)
1947–, Kashmar, Razavi Khorasan
Clerical education
Ramezan
Clergyman (HI)
No imprisonment
IRGC militiaman (commander and *komiteh* leader in Kashmar)

Hashemi, Homayun

Deputy of the Tenth Majlis, Miyandoab and Takab, West Azerbaijan (2016–20)
1966–, Takab, West Azerbaijan
MD, Urmia University of Medical Sciences
Head of the Social Welfare Organization of Iran (2011–15)
No imprisonment
War veteran

Hashemi was active in the medical services field in West Azerbaijan for many years, and was an adviser to the minister of cooperatives, labor, and social welfare.

Hashemi, Seyyed Baqer

Deputy of the First Majlis, Falavarjan, Isfahan (1981–84)
1933–, Qahderijan, Isfahan
Clerical education
Seyyed Ebrahim, farmer
Clergyman (HI)
No imprisonment
Not a war veteran
IRGC militiaman
Hashemi is a former Friday prayer leader of Mobarekeh.

Hashemi, Seyyed Enayatolah

Deputy of the Eighth (2008–12) and Ninth (2012–16) Majlis, Sepidan, Fars
1953–, Sepidan, Fars
BA, judicial law, University of Judicial Sciences-Qom
Seyyed Aqa
Civil servant; governor of Jahrom and Kazerun
No imprisonment
IRGC militiaman

Hashemi, Seyyed Fakhreddin

Deputy of the Second (1984–88) and Third (1988–92) Majlis, Jahrom, Fars
1946–, Jahrom, Fars
Clerical education
Seyyed Mohammad-Ali, clergyman
Clergyman
No imprisonment
Not a war veteran
HI Hashemi's father was the oldest Friday prayer leader in Iran until he died in 2016.

Hashemi, Seyyed Hoseyn

Deputy of the Fourth (1992–96), Fifth (1996–2000),
    Sixth (2000–2004), Seventh (2004–8), and Eighth
    (2008–12) Majlis, Miyaneh, East Azerbaijan
1953–, Sarab, East Azerbaijan
MS, industrial engineering
Mir Ma'sum, clergyman
Manager in the Ministry of Industries
No imprisonment
Hashemi was governor-general of Tehran from
    September 8, 2013, to October 2, 2017, and then
    became deputy minister of interior. In 2016, the
    media criticized him for his exorbitant salary (17
    million tomans a month).

Hashemi, Seyyed Mehdi

Deputy of the Ninth Majlis, Tehran, Tehran (2012–16)
1963–, Tehran, Tehran
BS, architecture, Islamic Azad University; MA, archi-
    tecture, 1990; pursuing a PhD in civil engineering
University instructor
No imprisonment
War veteran (113 months; wounded and left 50 per-
    cent paralyzed)
IRGC militiaman
On August 24, 2005, President Ahmadinejad intro-
    duced Hashemi as his candidate for the post of
    minister of social welfare, but he did not receive
    enough votes in the Majlis. Hashemi then served
    as an official in the MI. He is a hardliner who the
    SFIR supported in the 2012 Majlis election. After
    serving in the Majlis, he became the chairman of
    the board of a housing company affiliated with
    the Social Welfare Organization, as well as presi-
    dent of Iran's Shooting Federation.

Hashemi, Seyyed Mohammad

Deputy of the Fifth (1996–2000) and Sixth (2000–
    2004) Majlis, Sirjan and Bardsir, Kerman
1951–, Sirjan, Kerman

BA, theology
Seyyed Hoseyn
No imprisonment
Founding member of the Islamic Iran Solidarity
    Party

Hashemi, Seyyed Mohammad-Reza

Deputy of the Second Majlis, Aligudarz, Lorestan
    (1984–88)
1936–, Aligudarz, Lorestan
Clerical education
Seyyed Hebatollah
Clergyman (HI)
No imprisonment
Not a war veteran

Hashemi, Seyyed Mojtaba

Deputy of the Fourth Majlis, Shahreza, Isfahan
    (1992–96)
1944–2014, Shahreza, Isfahan
BS, chemistry; clerical education
Seyyed Esma'il
No imprisonment

Hashemi-Bahremani, Ali

Deputy of the Sixth Majlis, Rafsanjan, Kerman
    (2000–2004)
1961–, Rafsanjan, Kerman
BS, geology; MA, political science
Qasem
No imprisonment
Member of PECI
After serving in the Majlis, Hashemi-Bahremani
    became a civil servant.

Hashemi-Bahremani, Mrs. Fa'ezeh

Deputy of the Fifth Majlis, Tehran, Tehran
    (1996–2000)
1962–, Qom, Qom

BA, political science, Islamic Azad University–Tehran, 1993; BA, business administration, Alzahra University; MA, international law, Islamic Azad University–Tehran; MA, human rights, University of Central England (United Kingdom)

Deputy head of the National Olympics Committee

Akbar, clergyman

No imprisonment

Founding member of PECI and head of its women's division

In 2000, Hashemi-Bahremani started Iran's first newspaper for women (*Zan*), but the judiciary banned it after a few months for publishing a statement by the former empress Farah Pahlavi. While she received the second highest number of votes in Tehran in elections for the Fifth Majlis, Fa'ezeh was not elected to the Sixth Majlis. She lived in England for four and a half years starting in March 2003. She was arrested in September 2012 and spent six months in prison on the charge of anti-regime propagation. She is the daughter of Akbar Hashemi-Rafsanjani. In 1979, Fa'ezeh married Hamid Lahuti, a medical doctor, who is the son of the late Ayatollah Hasan Lahuti-Eshkevari.

Hashemi-Bahremani [Rafsanjani], Mohammad

Director-general of IRIB (August 24, 1989–February 13, 1994); VP for executive affairs in President Hashemi-Rafsanjani's second cabinet (1995–97) and President Khatami's first cabinet (1997–2001); member of the Fourth (1997–2002), Fifth (2002–7) and Sixth (2007–12) Expediency Discernment Assembly

1942–, Rafsanjan, Kerman

MA, management, USA (unverified); religious education

Mirza Ali, small landowner and clergyman

Civil servant

Imprisoned before the revolution

Not a war veteran

Founding member and head of the political bureau of PECI

Hashemi-Bahremani is a former deputy minister of agriculture. He is the brother of Akbar Hashemi-Rafsanjani and the uncle of Fa'ezeh Hashemi-Bahremani. His daughter-in-law is a niece of both Ayatollah Musavi-Ardabili and Ayatollah Javadi-Amoli.

Hashemi-Golpayegani, Seyyed Mohammad-Reza

Minister of higher education in President Hashemi-Rafsanjani's second cabinet (August 16, 1993–August 2, 1997)

January 4, 1947–, Najaf, Iraq

MS, electrical engineering, Tehran Polytechnic University (later renamed Amirkabir University of Technology); MS, electrical engineering (USA); PhD, electrical engineering, Amirkabir University of Technology

Seyyed Ahmad, clergyman (ayatollah)

University professor

No imprisonment

Not a war veteran

After serving in the cabinet, Hashemi-Golpayegani returned to being a professor at Amirkabir University of Technology. His uncle was Ayatollah Seyyed Ali Hashemi-Golpayegani (1932–2011), and his grandfather was Ayatollah Seyyed Jamaleddin Hashemi-Golpayegani.

Hashemi-Isfahani, Seyyed Esma'il

Member of the Second (1991–98) and Third (1999) Assembly of Experts, Isfahan

1903–September 11, 1999, Semirom, Isfahan

Clerical education, Qom Seminary

Seyyed Mohammad-Hasan Musavi, clergyman (ayatollah)

Clergyman (ayatollah)

No imprisonment

Not a war veteran

Hashemi-Isfahani was the oldest person elected to the Second and Third AE. His son, Seyyed Mohammad Hashemi-Isfahani, was involved in the takeover of the American embassy, and later married fellow hostage-taker (and future VP) Mas'sume (Nilofar) Ebtekar.

Hashemi-Nakhlebrahimi, Seyyed Abdolkarim

Deputy of the Ninth Majlis, Minab, Rudan, Jask, Sirik, and Bashagard, Hormozgan (2012–16)
1966–, Minab, Hormozgan
MA, development planning
Yusef
Civil servant in Hormozgan Province
No imprisonment

Hasheminezhad, Seyyed Habib [Abdolkarim]

Member of the Assembly for the Final Examination of the Constitution, Mazandaran (1979)
1933–September 29, 1981, Behshahr, Mazandaran
Clerical education, Qom Seminary, 1961
Seyyed Hasan, bazaar tradesman
Clergyman
Imprisoned before the revolution
War veteran
Secretary-general of the IRP in Khorasan Province
A seventeen-year-old PMOI militant assassinated HI Hasheminezhad three days before the third presidential election in 1981. He was the uncle of Seyyed Mohammad-Ali Abtahi.

Hashemipur, Adl

Deputy of the Tenth Majlis, Kohgiluyeh, Kohgiluyeh and Buyer Ahmad (2016–2020)
July 28, 1961, Dehdasht, Kohgiluyeh and Buyer Ahmad
BS, mechanical engineering, Behbahan University
War veteran (injured)
IRGC militiaman
Hashemipur is a former mayor of Dehdasht and Masjed Soleyman.

Hashemi-Rafsanjani [Bahremani], Akbar

Member of the Revolutionary Council (1979); interior minister in the Revolutionary Council cabinet

(November 12, 1979–February 27, 1980); deputy of the First (1980–84), Second (1984–88), and Third (1988–August 15, 1989) Majlis, Tehran, Tehran; president (August 17, 1989–August 2, 1997); member of the First (1983–90), Second (1991–98), Third (1999–2006), Fourth (2007–16), and Fifth (2016–January 8, 2017) Assembly of Experts, Tehran; member of the First (1988–89), Fourth (1997–2002), Fifth (2002–7), Sixth (2007–12), and Seventh (2012–January 8, 2017) Expediency Discernment Assembly
August 25, 1934–January 8, 2017, Bahreman, Kerman
Clerical education, Qom Seminary
Mirza Ali, small landowner and clergyman
Clergyman
Imprisoned before the revolution
Not a war veteran
Founding member and deputy head of the central council of the IRP; founding member of the central council of the SCC
Nicknamed "the shark" because his smooth-skinned face did not have a long beard, HI Hashemi-Rafsanjani emerged as one of the most powerful and politically skillful members of the postrevolutionary elite. He spent some time in exile in Najaf in the 1970s and was also imprisoned by the shah's regime for over four years. In 1979, he became one of the first clerics to enter the government when he became deputy interior minister. Hashemi-Rafsanjani was one of the Friday prayer leaders of Tehran, and survived an assassination attempt on May 25, 1979. Upon the assassination of President Mohammad-Ali Raja'i on August 30, 1981, Ayatollah Khomeini appointed Hashemi-Rafsanjani as a member of an interim presidential commission. On October 13, 1981, he was appointed as Ayatollah Khomeini's representative in the Supreme Defense Council, and on June 2, 1988, he was appointed deputy chief of the armed forces. In addition, he was the speaker of the Majlis from 1980 to 1989 and headed its war committee, which played a major policymaking role. He was chosen by the Second AE to be a member of a committee overseeing the

eventual implementation of Ayatollah Khomeini's will. Hashemi-Rafsanjani also sat on such bodies as IRGC's command council and the Cultural Revolution Headquarters. In 1989, he resigned from the Third Majlis to serve two consecutive terms as president. He was elected president with the highest number of votes in his political career (94 percent of the vote cast by 15.5 million voters). Hashemi-Rafsanjani was deputy-secretariat of the AE from 1982 to 2006 and secretariat from 2007 until March 8, 2011. In 2004 the GC disqualified him from running for the Seventh Majlis, and in 2005, Mahmoud Ahmadinejad soundly defeated him in the presidential election. He entered the 2013 presidential race but the GC disqualified him even though he was head of the EDA. Hashemi-Rafsanjani played a central role in building the Tehran subway system and establishing the Islamic Azad University system. He served as chair of the founding committee of the latter until his death in 2017. He was also the driving force behind the formation of PECI. He and his family received widespread criticism for being pistachio tycoons and having accumulated ill-gotten wealth. Two of his daughters married two sons of Ayatollah Hasan Lahuti-Eshkevari.

Hashemi-R'iseh, Seyyed Mostafa

Deputy of the Fifth (1996–2000) and Seventh (2004–8) Majlis, Shahr-e Babak, Harat, Marvdast, and Raviz, Kerman
1958–, Shahr-e Babak, Kerman
BS, physics
Seyyed Ali
Civil servant, state companies
No imprisonment

Hashemi-Sanjani, Ali

Deputy of the First Majlis, Arak, Markazi (1980–June 28, 1981)
1911–June 28, 1981, Sanjan, Markazi
Clerical education

Mahmud, farmer
Clergyman
No imprisonment
Not a war veteran
HI Hashemi-Sanjani was killed in the bombing of the IRP headquarters.

Hashemi-Shahrudi, Seyyed Mahmud

Member of the Third (1995–98), Fourth (1998–99), Fifth (2009–10), Sixth (2010–16), and Seventh (2016–19) Guardian Councils; chief justice (August 14, 1999–August 14, 2009); member of the Third (1999–2006), Fourth (2007–16), and Fifth (2016–22) Assembly of Experts, Razavi Khorasan; member of the Sixth (2009–12), Seventh (2012–17), and Eighth (2017–22) Expediency Discernment Assembly
1948–, Najaf, Iraq
Clerical education, Najaf Seminary (Iraq)
Seyyed Mohammad-Ali, clergyman
Clergyman (ayatollah)
Imprisoned before the revolution
Not a war veteran
Member of the SQSS
Hashemi-Shahrudi studied with Ayatollah Khomeini and Seyyed Mohammad-Baqer Sadr in Iraq. He reached the status of *ejtehad* in 1965. The Iraqi government imprisoned Hashemi-Shahrudi for a number of years. They deported him to Iran along with his father and the rest of his family in April 1980. As head and speaker of the Supreme Council of Islamic Revolution in Iraq (SCIRI), Hashemi-Shahrudi played a crucial role in the formation of SCIRI's Badr brigade. In early 1991, Ayatollah Khamenei appointed him as the founding director of the Institute for Encyclopedia of Islamic Fiqh. Hashemi-Shahrudi resigned from the GC in July 1999 to become the head of the judiciary, and stepped down from this post in August 2009. He was the deputy head of the Fourth AE and second deputy head of the Fifth AE. In 2011, Ayatollah Khamenei appointed him a member of

the five-person "Dispute Settlement Committee of Branches." On August 14, 2017, Khamenei appointed him head of the Expediency Discernment Assembly. He was appointed a member of the HCCR in 1999 and is the most religiously learned member of the Expediency Discernment Assembly. His daughter is married to the son of Ayatollah Musavi-Ardabil.

Hashemi-Taba, Seyyed Mostafa

Minister of industries in PM Bahonar's cabinet (August 17–30, 1981), interim PM Mahdavi-Kani's cabinet (September 3–October 18, 1981), and PM Musavi's first cabinet (November 2, 1981–August 14, 1984); VP and head of the Physical Training Organization in President Hashemi-Rafsanjani's second cabinet (1993–97) and President Khatami's first cabinet (1997–2001)

May 22, 1946–, Isfahan, Isfahan

MS, textile engineering, Tehran Polytechnic University (later renamed Amirkabir University of Technology)

Seyyed Abolqasem

Civil servant

No imprisonment

Not a war veteran

Member of the central council of PECI

Hashemi-Taba did not receive enough votes from MPs on August 14, 1984, to continue as minister of industries. He served for many years as the president of Iran's National Olympic Committee. He ran in the 2001 presidential election but received 0.1 percent of the vote. Hashemi-Taba later became an adviser to the minister of sports and youth under President Rouhani. In 2017, he ran as the oldest of six presidential candidates and received 0.5 percent of the vote.

Hashemi-Takhtinejad, Hoseyn

Deputy of the Tenth Majlis, Bandar-e Abbas, Hormozgan (2016–2020)

1961–, Takht, Hormozgan

Ahmad, farmer

Hashemi-Takhtinejad served previously as a political security deputy in Bushehr Province and governor-general of Hormozgan Province (2009–12).

Hashemi-Toghroljerdi, Seyyed Taha

Deputy of the Fifth Majlis, Qom, Qom (1996–2000)

1958–, Zarand, Kerman

Clerical education; MD, medicine

Clergyman

Seyyed Akbar, mercer

No imprisonment

HI Hashemi-Toghroljerdi is a rare cleric who also has a medical degree.

Hashemiyan, Hoseyn

Deputy of the First (1980–84), Second (1984–88), Third (1988–92), Fourth (1992–96), and Eighth (2008–12) Majlis, Rafsanjan, Kerman

1936–, Rafsanjan, Kerman

Clerical education, Qom Seminary

Abbas, clergyman and farmer

Clergyman

Imprisoned before the revolution

Not a war veteran

HI Hashemiyan was a deputy speaker of the Majlis from 1988 to 1992, and is a former Friday prayer leader of Rafsanjan. The SCFC summoned him in 1991, when Hashemi-Rafsanjani was president, for visiting Ayatollah Montazeri along with ninety-nine other MPs when Montazeri was under house arrest. He was board chairman of the Rafsanjan pistachio cooperative. Hashemiyan is the cousin of Akbar Hashemi-Rafsanjani.

Hashemiyan, Mohammad

Member of the First (1983–90) and Third (1999–2006) Assembly of Experts, Kerman

1928–2012, Nuq, Kerman

Clerical education, Qom Seminary

Abbas, clergyman and farmer
Clergyman
No imprisonment
Not a war veteran
HI Mohammad Hashemiyan was the Friday prayer
leader and supreme leader's representative in
Rafsanjan for thirty years. He is the brother of
Hoseyn Hashemiyan, and cousin and brother-in-
law of Akbar Hashemi-Rafsanjani. He is the son-
in-law of Ayatollah Mohammad-Ali Saduqi.

Hashemizadeh, Faramand

Deputy of the Fifth Majlis, Ahvaz, Khuzestan
(1996–2000)
1953–, Bostan, Khuzestan
MS, architecture and urban planning
Delavi
Provincial civil servant
No imprisonment
Hashemizadeh held a variety of posts before and
after serving in the Majlis, including mayor of
Ahvaz and manager of petrochemical facilities in
Abadan and Khorasan.

Hashemzadeh-Herisi, Hashem

Deputy of the Third (1988–92) and Fifth (1996–2000)
Majlis, Tabriz, East Azerbaijan; member of the
Third (1999–2006), Fourth (2008–16), and Fifth
(2016–22) Assembly of Experts, East Azerbaijan
1938–, Heris, East Azerbaijan
Clerical education, Qom Seminary; PhD, theology
Qorban, farmer
Clergyman
No imprisonment
Not a war veteran
Martyr's family (brother)
Ayatollah Hashemzadeh-Herisi was Ayatollah Kho-
meini's representative in the IRGC and the
supreme leader's representative in University
Basij. He was elected to the Fourth AE in interim
elections. Hashemzadeh-Herisi has a certificate
in human rights from the European Institute of

Human Rights. His son was a prisoner of war
during the Iran–Iraq War.

Hashemza'i-Nehbandan, Abdorreza

Deputy of the Second Majlis, Ferdows and Tabas,
South Khorasan (1984–88); deputy of Tenth Maj-
lis, Tehran, Tehran (2016–20)
1944–, Na'in, Isfahan
Hasan
BS, physics
Civil servant
No imprisonment
Member of the central council of HKSI
Hashemza'i-Nehbandan was a high school teacher
before the revolution and then worked in the
Ministry of Energy. He was on the leadership
team of the Second Majlis and has held many
other posts, including governor of Ferdows,
political-administrative deputy in the office of the
Khorasan governor-general, research deputy in
the Ministry of Post, Telegraph, and Telephones,
adviser to the minister of industry and mining
(2001–5), and director-general for economic affairs at the Martyr's Foundation.

Hashemzehi, Mas'ud

Deputy of the Third (1988–92) and Sixth (2000–2002)
Majlis, Khash, Sistan and Baluchestan
1953–October 30, 2002, Khash, Sistan and Baluchestan
BS, public health, 1978; MS, public health
Afzal
Civil servant
No imprisonment
Hashemzehi died in a car accident along with fellow
MP Ali-Reza Nuri.

Hashemzehi, Morad

Deputy of the Ninth Majlis, Nehbandan and Sarbisheh, South Khorasan (2012–16)
1959–, Nehbandan, South Khorasan
MD, surgery, Ferdowsi University of Mashhad, 1991

Surgeon
No imprisonment
War veteran
Martyr's family (brother)
Hashemzehi is a former member of the medical
school faculty in Razavi Khorasan and was rector
of Birjand Medical University from 2005 to 2010.

Hatami, Amir

Minister of defense and armed forces logistics in
President Rouhani's second cabinet (August 20,
2017–2021)
1966–, Zanjan, Zanjan
No imprisonment
War veteran
Brigadier General Hatami joined the Basij Force after
the 1979 revolution and then entered the Iranian
Army. He was the deputy defense minister before
being appointed as the minister. Prior to these
posts, Hatami served for seven years as the intelligence deputy and five years as the human resource
deputy of the army. He fought against PMOI and
Kurdish opposition groups in western and northwestern regions of Iran. On August 20, 2017, he
received the highest number of positive votes (261
out of 288) of all ministers approved by the Majlis
to serve in President Rouhani's second cabinet.

Hatamiyan, Abdollah

Deputy of the Tenth Majlis, Dargaz, Razavi Khorasan
(2016–20)
1970–, Dargaz, Razavi Khorasan
MA, agricultural economics
No imprisonment
Hatamiyan, a reformist, has worked in the Construction Jihad since 1998. He also teaches agricultural
economics at Dargaz University.

Hatefi, Nosratollah

Deputy of the First Majlis, Qorveh, Kurdistan (1981–84)
1952–, Khomeyn, Markazi

Clerical education
Mohammad-Ali, clergyman
Clergyman (HI) and teacher
No imprisonment
Not a war veteran

Hayati, Mohammad-Ali

Deputy of the Seventh (2004–8) and Eighth (2008–
June 6, 2010) Majlis, Lamerd and Mohr, Fars
1954–June 6, 2010, Lamerd, Fars
BS, business administration, Rasht School of Business,
1978; MA, educational management, Allameh
Tabataba'i University, 1994
Mohammad
Member of the Lamerd City Council
No imprisonment
War veteran
Hayati died while serving in the Eighth Majlis.

Hayat-Moqaddam, Khalil

Deputy of the Eighth Majlis, Bandar-e Mahshahr,
Khuzestan (2008–12)
1962–, Hendijan, Khuzestan
BA, law, Yasouj University, 1991; pursuing MA in law
at Islamic Azad University–Tehran
Ebrahim, farmer
Judiciary official in Bushehr
No imprisonment
War veteran (seventy-eight months)
IRGC militiaman
Hayat-Moqaddam was one of the founders of the
IRGC in Abadan. He held a number of positions
in the judiciary of Khuzestan and Kohgiluyeh and
Buyer Ahmad. Hayat-Moqaddam was not elected
to the Ninth Majlis.

Hazrati, Elyas

Deputy of the Third (1988–92), Fourth (1992–96), and
Fifth (1996–2000) Majlis, Rasht, Gilan; deputy of
the Sixth (2000–2004) and Tenth (2016–20) Majlis, Tehran, Tehran

1961–, Idehlu, East Azerbaijan
BA, 1990; MA, public administration, 2000
Seyfollah
No imprisonment
War veteran (fifty-four months; wounded)
IRGC militiaman
Founder and member of the central council of the Islamic Iran Solidarity Party for ten years; founding member of the central council of the NTP
Hazrati was a high-level IRGC member who served in such capacities as commander of Gilan division. After serving for ten years in the IRGC, he left in 1987 to run for the Majlis. He was the proprietor of *E'temad* and led the Martial Arts Federation of the Islamic Republic of Iran from 1995 to 2003.

Hazratpur, Ruhollah

Deputy of the Tenth Majlis, Urmia, West Azerbaijan (2016–20)
1983–, Urmia, West Azerbaijan
MA, international relations
Not a war veteran
Martyr's family (father killed at the war front)

Hedayati-Sichani, Seyyed Abbas

Deputy of the Third Majlis, Faridan and Fereydunshahr, Isfahan (1988–92)
February 18, 1940–, Isfahan, Isfahan
BA; clerical education
Seyyed Mohammad-Hoseyn
Clergyman (HI)
No imprisonment
Not a war veteran

Hedayatkhah, Sattar

Deputy of the Seventh (2004–8) and Eighth (2008–12) Majlis, Buyer Ahmad and Dena, Kohgiluyeh and Buyer Ahmad
1962–, Buyer Ahmad, Kohgiluyeh and Buyer Ahmad

MA, Islamic law; PhD, theology, Ferdowsi University of Mashhad
Shahbaz
Academia
No imprisonment
Hedayatkhah, a conservative, ran unsuccessfully for the Ninth Majlis.

Hejazi, Fakhreddin

Deputy of the First (1980–84), Second (1984–88), and Third (1988–92) Majlis, Tehran, Tehran
1929–2007, Sabzevar, Razavi Khorasan
BA, Persian literature
Mohammad, clergyman
Notary public
Imprisoned before the revolution
Not a war veteran
Hejazi, a great orator and preacher, ran unsuccessfully for a seat in the AFEC in 1979. A year later, however, he received the highest number of votes in Tehran during the First Majlis election. Hejazi was the founder and director of Besat Publishing.

Hejazi, Seyyed Mohammad-Kazem

Deputy of the Eighth Majlis, Hamadan, Hamadan (2008–12)
1966–, Hamadan, Hamadan
BA, theology; MA, Islamic studies
Seyyed Javad
Civil servant
No imprisonment
War veteran

Hejazi [Hoseynzadeh], Seyyed Mohammad

Commander of the IRGC's Basij Force (March 11, 1998–2007); chief of the joint staff of the IRGC (September 20, 2007–May 2008); deputy commander in chief of the IRGC (May 22, 2008–October 4, 2009)
1956–, Isfahan, Isfahan

MA, public administration, Tehran University; pursuing a PhD in strategic management, Supreme National Defense University

No imprisonment

War veteran

IRGC militiaman

Hejazi was involved in putting down uprisings in Kurdistan and West Azerbaijan soon after the revolution. In 2008, he became commander of Sarallah Corp, a powerful military unit in the IRGC. In 2009, Hejazi, who is close to Ayatollah Khamenei, became deputy for industrial research of the joint staff of the Islamic Republic of Iran Army. He also was a member of the faculty at Imam Hoseyn University. On October 10, 2011, the Council of the European Union put Hejazi on its sanctions list for the central role he played in the 2009 postelection crackdown. The Council wrote: "Hejazi was the author of a letter sent to the Ministry of Health on 26 June 2009 forbidding the disclosure of documents or medical records of anyone injured or hospitalised during post-election events, implying a cover up."

Hejazifar, Hashem

Deputy of the First (1981–84) Majlis, Maku, West Azerbaijan; deputy of the Second (1984–88), Third (1988–92), and Seventh (2004–8) Majlis, Khoy and Chaypareh, West Azerbaijan

1942–, Maku, West Azerbaijan

Clerical education

Karim, laborer

Clergyman

No imprisonment

Not a war veteran

HI Hejazifar is the former head of the *komiteh* and the city council of Khoy, and was associated with the Literacy Jihad. Later he worked at the National Library.

Hejazi-Kamsari, Seyyed Abutaleb

Deputy of the Second Majlis, Rasht, Gilan (1984–88)

1942–, Rasht, Gilan

Clerical education, Qom Seminary

Seyyed Sadeq

Clergyman (HI)

No imprisonment

Not a war veteran

Hejrati-Qazvini, Seyyed Abdollah

Deputy of the Second (1984–88) and Third (1988–92) Majlis, Qazvin, Qazvin

1940–September 5, 2006, Qazvin, Qazvin

BA, communications

Seyyed Abdolqani

No imprisonment

War veteran

Secretary-general of the ISFPD

Hemmati, Ahmad

Deputy of the First (1980–84), Second (1984–88), Third (1988–92), and Fourth (1992–96) Majlis, Meshginshahr, Ardabil

1934–, Meshginshahr, Ardabil

Clerical education

Naqi, farmer

Clergyman

No imprisonment

Not a war veteran

Hemmati, Fereydun

Deputy of the Seventh Majlis, Ilam, Eyvan, Mehran, Malekshahi, and Shirvan, Ilam (2004–8)

1960–, Ilam, Ilam

MA, public administration

Mohammad-Ali

Civil servant

No imprisonment

After leaving the Majlis, Hemmati became an adviser to the interior minister. During the tenure of President Rouhani, Hemmati became governor-general of Qazvin and Hormozgan (appointed on September 13, 2017).

Hemmati-Moqaddam, Hasan

Member of the First Assembly of Experts, Khuzestan
    (1988–90)
Clerical education
Clergyman
No imprisonment
HI Hemmati-Moqaddam was elected to the first AE
    in interim elections held on April 8, 1988. The GC
    disqualified him from running in the election for
    the Second Assembly of Experts.

Hemmati [Semnan], Ahmad

Deputy of the Tenth Majlis, Semnan, Semnan
    (2016–20)
1962–, Semnan, Semnan
MD, pediatrics
Abbas-Ali
Medical doctor and university professor
No imprisonment
War veteran (wounded)
IRGC militiaman (Basij)
Hemmati was elected as a reformist.

Heravi, Javad

Deputy of the Ninth Majlis, Qaenat, South Khorasan
    (2012–16)
1966–, Qaenat, South Khorasan
BA, history, Ferdowsi University of Mashhad; PhD,
    history, Islamic Azad University–Science and
    Research Branch
Mohammad-Hoseyn
University professor
No imprisonment
Not a war veteran
Heravi is a former head of the Iran Cultural Her-
    itage and Tourism branch of eastern Iran.
    Hoseyn-Ali Amiri, the VP for parliamentary
    affairs, appointed Heravi as his adviser in
    2016, and in 2017 appointed him as one of his
    deputies.

Hesari, Mohammad

Deputy of the Second Majlis, Kangavar, Kermanshah
    (1984–88)
1953–, Neyshabur, Razavi Khorasan
Clerical education
Qasem
Clergyman (HI) and Friday prayer leader
No imprisonment

Heshmatiyan, Qodrat-Ali

Deputy of the Fifth Majlis, Sonqor and Koliyayi, Ker-
    manshah (1996–2000)
1953–, Sonqor and Koliyayi, Kermanshah
BS, military science, Ground Forces Officers' Acad-
    emy; MA, public administration, State Manage-
    ment Training Center
Fathali, farmer
Military/security official
Imprisoned before the revolution (4 months)
War veteran (sixty-two months; wounded)
Secretary-general of the Independent Association of
    Islamic Iran

Heydari, Abbas

Deputy of the First Majlis, Bandar-e Bushehr, Bushehr
    (1980–June 28, 1981)
1944–June 28, 1981, Shiraz, Fars
Associate's degree
Borzu, laborer
Civil servant
No imprisonment
Not a war veteran
Heydari was killed in the bombing of the IRP
    headquarters.

Heydari, Abdorrahman

Member of the Assembly for the Final Examination of
    the Constitution, Ilam (1979); member of the First
    Assembly of Experts, Ilam (1983–January 1, 1987)
1925–January 1, 1987, Ilam, Ilam

Clerical education, Najaf Seminary (Iraq)
Baba, farmer
Clergyman
No imprisonment
War veteran
Ayatollah Heydari was Ayatollah Khomeini's repre-
sentative in Ilam Province.

Heydari, Fakhreddin

Deputy of the Seventh (2004–8) and Eighth (2008–12)
Majlis, Saqqez and Baneh, Kurdistan
1973–, Baneh, Kurdistan
BS, nursing
Omar
Civil servant
No imprisonment
Not a war veteran
Heydari, a Sunni, was not elected to the Ninth Majlis.

Heydari, Gholam-Reza

Deputy of the Second (1984–88) and Third (1988–92)
Majlis, Tafresh, Markazi; deputy of the Tenth
Majlis, Tehran, Tehran (2016–20)
1955–, Chalus, Mazandaran
BS, electrical engineering; Amirkabir University,
1980; PhD, policy management
Mohammad-Ali
Civil servant, Ministry of Energy
No imprisonment
War veteran
Heydari entered the Ministry of Energy in 1983 and
has held high-level posts including adviser to
the minister. He was the dean of the School of
Management and Economics at the University of
Water and Electrical Industry, and he has taught
at the Niroo Research Institute, which is affiliated
with the Ministry of Energy.

Heydari, Kiyumars

Commander of the Islamic Republic of Iran Ground
Forces (November 15, 2016–present)

1964–, Sahneh, Kermanshah
No imprisonment
War veteran
IRGC militiaman
Brigadier General Heydari joined the Basij Force in
1982 and the army in 1984. He held positions in
the security and intelligence branch of the army
from 1988 to 1998 before serving as a base commander (1998–2005) and deputy commander of
the army (2007–16).

Heydari, Mohammad-Ali

Deputy of the First Majlis, Nahavand, Hamadan
(1980–June 28, 1981)
1936–June 28, 1981, Qom, Qom
Clerical education
Mohammad-Vali, clergyman
Clergyman (HI)
Imprisoned before the revolution
Not a war veteran
Heydari was killed in the bombing of the IRP
headquarters.

Heydari-Alekasir, Mohsen

Member of the Fourth (2007–16), and Fifth (2016–22)
Assembly of Experts, Khuzestan
September 26, 1957–, Shush, Khuzestan
Clerical education, Qom Seminary; BA, theology, Tehran
University; MA, theology, Tehran University, 1992
Obeid, farmer
Clergyman
War veteran
IRGC militiaman
HI Heydari-Alekasir has been the Friday prayer leader
of Ahvaz since 1992. He did not get elected to the
Third AE.

Heydari-Darani, Gholam-Reza

Deputy of the Fifth Majlis, Faridan and Fereydunshahr, Isfahan (1996–2000)
1949–, Fereydunshahr, Isfahan

BA, management
Hasan
No imprisonment
Martyr's family

Heydari-Dastena'i, Nurollah

Deputy of the Eighth Majlis, Ardal, Chahar Mahal
and Bakhtiari (2008–12)
1960–, Dastena, Chahar Mahal and Bakhtiari
MA, educational management
Abdollah
Civil servant
No imprisonment
Heydari-Dastena'i ran unsuccessfully for the Ninth
Majlis.

Heydari-Moqaddam, Masha'allah

Deputy of the Third Majlis, Delfan and Selseleh, Lor-
estan (1988–92)
1949–, Selseleh, Lorestan
BA, law
Ahmad-Beyk
Judiciary official
No imprisonment
Heydari-Moqaddam was elected in an election
marred by tribal violence.

Heydari-Shelmani, Mohammad-Ali

Deputy of the Seventh Majlis, Langarud, Gilan (2004–8)
1954–, Langarud, Gilan
BS, geology
Gholam-Hoseyn
Teacher and civil servant
No imprisonment
Heydari-Shelmani ran unsuccessfully for the Eighth
and Ninth Majlis.

Heydari-Tayeb, Seyyed Sa'id

Deputy of the Ninth Majlis, Kermanshah, Kermanshah (2012–16)

1970–, Kermanshah, Kermanshah
BA, law, Islamic Azad University–Tehran, 1997; MA,
private law, Islamic Azad University–Kerman-
shah; pursuing a PhD
Father's name unknown, farmer
Judiciary official
No imprisonment
Not a war veteran
Martyr's family (brother, sister, and nephew were
killed in an Iraqi aerial bombardment in 1988)
After finishing his term in the Ninth Majlis, Hey-
dari-Tayeb became an appointee of the minister of
petroleum.

Heydariyan, Mohammad-Hoseyn

Deputy of the Eighth Majlis, Sonqor, Kurdistan (2008)
1958–June 27, 2008, Sonqor, Kermanshah
BA, educational management
Ali-Hoseyn
Academia
No imprisonment
Heydariyan died of cancer in the first year of his term
in the Eighth Majlis.

Heydarizadi, Abdorreza

Deputy of the Sixth Majlis, Ilam, Eyvan, Mehran,
Chardavol, and Shirvan, Ilam (2000–2004)
1953–, Chardavol, Ilam
MD, medicine
Ali-Akbar
Medical doctor
No imprisonment
After the Sixth Majlis, Heydari decided not to run
for office again. He has since mainly worked as a
medical doctor in UAE.

Heydarpur-Shahrezai, Avaz

Deputy of the Seventh (2004–8), Eighth (2008–12),
and Ninth (2012–16) Majlis, Shahreza and Semirom, Isfahan

1954–, Shahreza, Isfahan
MD, anesthesiology, Isfahan University of
    Medical Sciences
Rasul
Anesthesiologist
No imprisonment
War veteran
IRGC militiaman
Martyr's family (brother killed at the war front)

Hezarjaribi, Gholam-Ali

Deputy of the Sixth Majlis, Gorgan, Golestan
    (2000–May 17, 2001)
1953–May 17, 2001, Gorgan, Golestan
BS; MA, management
Qorban
No imprisonment
Martyr's family
Hezarjaribi died in a plane crash along with
    minister of roads and transportation Rahman
    Dadman and a few other MPs.

Hezarjaribi, Nabi

Deputy of the Tenth Majlis, Gorgan, Golestan
    (2016–20)
1975–, Gorgan, Golestan
BS, agricultural engineering, Islamic Azad Uni-
    versity–Gorgan; MBA, State Management
    Training Institute–Gorgan; pursuing an MA
    in political science at Islamic Azad University-
    Azadshahr
Gholam-Ali, MP
Civil servant, Iranian Tobacco Company in
    Golestan Province
No imprisonment
Not a war veteran
Hezarjaribi worked as a civil servant in the
    PBO and served on the Gorgan City Council
    before joining the Majlis. His father, Gholam-
    Ali, represented Gorgan briefly in the Sixth
    Majlis.

Hojaji, Seyyed Sajjad

Deputy of the First (1980–84) and Third (1988–92)
    Majlis, Miyaneh, East Azerbaijan
1928–, Miyaneh, East Azerbaijan
Clerical education, Qom Seminary
Mir Hoseyn, clergyman (ayatollah)
Clergyman (HI) and Friday prayer leader of Miyaneh
Imprisoned before the revolution
Not a war veteran
Member of the IRP

Hojjati, Aziz

Deputy of the Second Majlis, Maku, West Azerbaijan
    (1984–88)
1944–, Maku, West Azerbaijan
BA, education; clerical education
Abdollah
Clergyman
No imprisonment

Hojjati [-Najafabadi], Mahmud

Minister of roads and transportation (August 20,
    1997–2000) and then minister of Agricultural
    Jihad (January 14, 2001–August 1, 2001) in Pres-
    ident Khatami's first cabinet; minister of agricul-
    tural jihad in President Khatami's second cabinet
    (August 22, 2001–August 2, 2005); minister of
    agricultural jihad in President Rouhani's first
    (August 15, 2013–August 13, 2017) and second
    (August 20, 2017–2021) cabinets
October 10, 1955–, Najafabad, Isfahan
BS, civil engineering, Isfahan University of Technol-
    ogy, 1987
Gholam-Reza, clergyman (HI)
Executive director of Karkeh Dam
No imprisonment
War veteran
Martyr's family
Member of the central council of IIPF
Hojjati was governor-general of Sistan and Baluches-
    tan from 1989 to 1994, and was also in charge of

the Chabahar Free Zone (appointed on August 30, 1992).

Hojjati-Kermani, Mohammad-Javad

Member of the Assembly for the Final Examination of the Constitution, Kerman (1979); deputy of the First Majlis, Tehran, Tehran (1980–84); member of the Second Assembly of Experts, Kerman (1991–98)
1932–, Kerman, Kerman
Clerical education, Qom Seminary, 1957
Abdolhoseyn, clergyman (HI)
Clergyman
Imprisoned before the revolution (1965–75)
Not a war veteran
Founding member of the MNP
HI Hojjati-Kermani was active in the anti-shah movement and was involved with the publication of the journal *Besat* before the revolution. He voted against the principle of *velayat-e faqih* in the AFEC. After the revolution, he became the first Friday prayer leader of Kerman (1979–80). He also held such posts as President Khamenei's cultural adviser (1984–89), cultural adviser to the Iranian Ministry of Foreign Affairs (1989–98), and member of the board of trustees of the Great Islamic Encyclopedia. The GC rejected his qualifications to run for the Fifth Assembly of Experts.

Hojjat-Kashfi, Seyyed Ja'far

Deputy of the First Majlis, Neyriz and Estahban, Fars (1980–84)
1946–, Estahban, Fars
Clerical education
Seyyed Mohammad, clergyman
Clergyman
No imprisonment
HI Hojjat-Kashfi, who is an expert in calligraphy, went to Iraq in 1966 and stayed there for more than a decade. After the revolution, he was deputy head of the Martyr's Foundation cultural organization and a cultural attaché in Sweden.

Holaku, Mo'ami

Deputy of the Fourth (1993–96) Majlis, Ramiyan, Golestan; deputy of the Fifth (1996–2000) Majlis, Gonbad-e Kavus, Golestan
1954–May 17, 2001, Gonbad-e Kavus, Golestan
Associate's degree
Qoli
No imprisonment
Holaku worked in the Iranian railroad sector after the Majlis before dying in a plane crash.

Homayun-Moqaddam, Mrs. Fatemeh

Deputy of the Fourth Majlis, Tabriz, East Azerbaijan (1992–96)
1945–date unknown, Azarshahr, East Azerbaijan
BA, theology; MA, management and planning
Yusef-Ali, notary public
No imprisonment
Martyr's family (son and son-in-law)
Member of the IRP and Zeynab Society
After serving in the Majlis, Homayun-Moqaddam worked for the Ministry of Education and taught at universities until she died in a car accident (date unknown).

Hoseyni, Esfandiyar

Commander of the Islamic Republic of Iran Navy (April 30, 1983–June 27, 1985)
Naval officer (captain)
War veteran

Hoseyni, Fathollah

Deputy of the Ninth Majlis, Qasr-e Shirin, Sarpol-e Zahab, and Gilan-e Gharb, Kermanshah (2012–16)
1963–, Sarpol-e Zahab, Kermanshah
BA, political science, Tehran University, 2009; MA, sociology, Islamic Azad University–Rudhen
Heybatollah, farmer
Director-general of Mazandaran Physical Training Organization

No imprisonment
War veteran
IRGC militiaman
Fathollah Hoseyni is not the same as Seyyed Fathol-
    lah Hoseyni, who represented Paveh in the Fourth
    and Eighth Majlis. His father, Heybatollah, also
    fought in the Iran–Iraq War.

Hoseyni, Mohammad

Deputy of the Tenth Majlis, Tafresh, Markazi
    (2016–20)
1968–, Tafresh, Markazi
BA, industrial management; MA, public
    administration
Planning director-general of the State Audit Court, an
    arm of the Majlis
No imprisonment
Hoseyni held auditing positions at provincial and
    national levels before joining the Majlis.

Hoseyni, Seyyed Abdollah

Deputy of the Third (1988–92), Fourth (1992–96),
    Fifth (1996–2000), Sixth (2000–2004), and
    Seventh (2004–8) Majlis, Bandar-e Lengeh,
    Hormozgan
1958–, Bandar-e Lengeh, Hormozgan
BA, law, 1984; MA, management, 1996
Seyyed Isa
Attorney
No imprisonment
Member of PECI and HKSI
Hoseyni holds the record as the Sunni MP most
    elected to the Majlis.

Hoseyni, Seyyed Abolhasan

Deputy of the First (1980–84) and Second (1984–88)
    Majlis, Minudasht, Golestan
1923–, Gorgan, Golestan
Clerical education; BA, theology
Seyyed Abbas, farmer
Clergyman (HI)

No imprisonment
Not a war veteran

Hoseyni, Seyyed Abolqasem

Deputy of the Third (1988–92), Fourth (1992–96), and
    Sixth (2000–2004) Majlis, Bojnurd, North Khorasan
1951–, Bojnurd, North Khorasan
Degree unknown, mechanical engineering
Seyyed Ahmad
No imprisonment

Hoseyni, Seyyed Ahmad

Deputy of the First Majlis, Marvdasht, Fars (1980–84)
1925–, Arsanjan, Fars
PhD, Arabic literature; clerical education
Seyyed Ali-Akbar, clergyman
No imprisonment
Not a war veteran
Founding member of the ISFPD

Hoseyni, Seyyed Ali

Deputy of the First (1981–84) and Second (1984–88)
    Majlis, Sanandaj, Kurdistan; member of the First
    (1984–90) and Second (1991–98) Assembly of
    Experts, Kurdistan
1919–date unknown, Sardasht, Kurdistan
Clerical education
Seyyed Abdollah, farmer
Clergyman
No imprisonment
Not a war veteran
Komelah fighters attacked and wounded Mamosta
    Hoseyni, a Sunni who was the Friday prayer
    leader of Sanandaj. He was elected to the First
    Assembly of Experts in interim elections held on
    April 15, 1984.

Hoseyni, Seyyed Baqer

Deputy of the Ninth Majlis, Zabol, Zahak, and Hir-
    mand, Sistan and Baluchestan (2012–16)

1969–, Zabol, Sistan and Baluchestan
PhD, theology, Tehran University
Professor and administrator at Zabol University
No imprisonment
War veteran
IRGC militiaman (Basij)

Hoseyni, Seyyed Bohlul

Deputy of the Seventh (2004–8) and Ninth (2012–16)
    Majlis, Miyaneh, East Azerbaijan
1961–, Miyaneh, East Azerbaijan
BS, civil engineering, Amirkabir University of Tech-
    nology, 1990; MS, project management, Tarbiyat-e
    Modarres University, 1998
Father's name unknown, clergyman
Civil servant, Tehran municipality (under Mayor
    Mahmud Ahmadinejad)
No imprisonment
War veteran (two years)
IRGC militiaman (deputy commander of Ashura
    brigade)
After leaving the Seventh Majlis, Hoseyni worked in
    the office of President Ahmadinejad.

Hoseyni, Seyyed Emad

Deputy of the Seventh (2006–8) and Eighth (2008–12)
    Majlis, Qorveh, Kurdistan
July 18, 1972–, Qorveh, Kurdistan
BS, petrochemical engineering, Amirkabir University
    of Technology; MS, petrochemical engineering,
    Calgary University (Canada), 2000
Seyyed Reza
University professor
No imprisonment
Not a war veteran
Hoseyni, a conservative Sunni, had the credentials
    to become the minister of petroleum but was not
    chosen. He was also not elected to the Ninth Ma-
    jlis. He was a professor at the Petroleum Research
    Center before President Rouhani designated him
    as deputy minister of petroleum. Hoseyni is a
    cousin of Seyyed Mas'ud Hoseyni.

Hoseyni, Seyyed Fathollah

Deputy of the Fourth (1992–96) and Eighth (2008–12)
    Majlis, Paveh and Uramanat, Kermanshah
1961–, Javanrud, Kermanshah
BA, law
Seyyed Hasan, farmer
Civil servant, state companies
No imprisonment
Not a war veteran
Martyr's family (father and brother killed at the war
    front)
Hoseyni, a Sunni, served for fourteen years in the
    Martyr's Foundation. The GC disqualified him
    from running in the 2012 Majlis election.

Hoseyni, Seyyed Hadi

Deputy of the Ninth Majlis, Qaemshahr, Savadkuh,
    and Juybar, Mazandaran (2012–16)
1963–, Savadkuh, Mazandaran
MA, sociology, Tehran University
Seyyed Mohammad
MIIRI officer
No imprisonment
War veteran (wounded)
IRGC militiaman
Hoseyni was in charge of Mazandaran Province's
    physical training department.

Hoseyni, Seyyed Jalal

Deputy of the Seventh Majlis, Zanjan and Tarom,
    Zanjan (2004–8)
1965–, Zanjan, Zanjan
PhD, developmental management
Seyyed Khalil
Civil servant
No imprisonment

Hoseyni, Seyyed Javad

Deputy of the Second (1984–88) and Fourth (1992–96)
    Majlis, Aliabad Katul, Golestan

1939–September 5, 2013, Aliabad Katul, Golestan

Seyyed Mahmud, clergyman

Clerical education, Qom and Najaf Seminaries

No imprisonment

Not a war veteran

HI Hoseyni was the Friday prayer leader of Rudbar and Safa Shahr, and was in charge of the ideological-political bureau of Mehrabad Airport.

Hoseyni, Seyyed Mansur

Deputy of the Sixth Majlis, Minudasht, Golestan (2000–2001)

1952–May 17, 2001, Qom, Qom

BS, physics

Seyyed Hoseyn

No imprisonment

After Hoseyni died in a plane crash, his brother, Seyyed Najib, took over his seat in the Sixth Majlis.

Hoseyni, Seyyed Mas'ud

Deputy of the Fourth (1992–96) and Sixth (2000–2004) Majlis, Qorveh, Kurdistan

1958–, Qorveh, Kurdistan

BA, political science

Seyyed Ala'eddin

Civil servant

No imprisonment

Hoseyni is a Sunni.

Hoseyni, Seyyed Mohammad

Deputy of the Fifth Majlis, Rafsanjan, Kerman (1996–2000); minister of culture and Islamic guidance in President Ahmadinejad's second cabinet (September 3, 2009–August 3, 2013)

1961–, Rafsanjan, Kerman

BS, mining engineering (possibly incomplete); MA, theology, Imam Sadeq University; PhD, theology, Tehran University, 1994

Seyyed Ali, bazaar tradesman

Civil servant, ministries

Imprisoned before the revolution

War veteran

IRGC militiaman

Martyr's family (sister's teenage son killed at the war front)

Secretary-general of the Society of Academics of Islamic Iran

Hoseyni was one of the main people behind the impeachment of culture minister Ataollah Mohajerani in the Fifth Majlis (1999). Later he became a deputy to the minister of science, research, and technology. On October 10, 2011, the Council of the European Union put Hoseyni on its sanctioned list and charged him with being "complicit in the repression of journalists" as minister of culture and Islamic guidance. After finishing his term as minister, Hoseyni taught at Tehran University's Faculty of Theology. His brother, Seyyed Hamid Hoseyni, is a reformist close to former president Akbar Hashemi-Rafsanjani. He ran unsuccessfully for the Tenth Majlis from Rafsanjan in 2016. His brother is married to one of the daughters of Mohammad-Sadeq Khalkhali.

Hoseyni, Seyyed Mojtaba

Member of the Third Assembly of Experts, Sistan and Baluchestan (1999–2006); member of the Fifth Assembly of Experts, Razavi Khorasan (2016–22)

1954–, Mashhad, Razavi Khorasan

Clerical education, Qom Seminary

Seyyed Jalil, clergyman (ayatollah)

Clergyman

No imprisonment

Not a war veteran

Ayatollah Hoseyni's family is originally from Sistan, but he was born in Khorasan. He is fluent in Arabic and has connections to Lebanese groups such as Hezbollah and Amal. He was the supreme leader's representative in Baluchestan and later in Iraq and Syria. He also served as head of the Bureau of Sunni Brethren in Baluchestan from September 9, 1996, to 2003.

Hoseyni, Seyyed Morteza

Deputy of the Ninth Majlis, Qazvin, Abyek, and Alborz, Qazvin (2012–16)
1957–, Shal, Qazvin
Clerical education, Qom Seminary, 1992
Seyyed Hasan, farmer
Clergyman and IRGC militiaman
No imprisonment
War veteran
HI Seyyed Morteza Hoseyni, a conservative who closely follows Ayatollah Khamenei, was the supreme leader's representative in IRGC branches in Karaj and Qazvin.

Hoseyni, Seyyed Najib

Deputy of the Sixth Majlis, Minudasht, Golestan (2001–4); deputy of the Eighth Majlis, Minudasht, Golestan (2008–12)
1967–, Minudasht, Golestan
BS, agricultural engineering; MA, public administration
Seyyed Hasan
Civil servant
No imprisonment
Hoseyni took over the seat of his deceased brother, Seyyed Mansur, in the Sixth Majlis.

Hoseyni, Seyyed Safdar

Minister of labor and social affairs (August 22, 2001–April 24, 2004) and then minister of economic affairs and finance (April 25, 2004–August 2, 2005) in President Khatami's second cabinet
1954–, I'zeh, Khuzestan
BS, agricultural economics, Shiraz University, 1978; MS, agricultural economics, Shiraz University, 1988; PhD, agricultural economics, University of Saskatchewan (Canada), 1995; dissertation title: "The Aggregate Impact of the Whole-Farm Approach to Farm Income Support Programs"
Seyyed Ali-Akbar, village elder

Deputy in the Management and Planning Organization (2000–2001)
No imprisonment
War veteran
Member of IIPF
Seyyed Safdar Hoseyni was a consultant to the PBO (1996–97), the governor-general of Chahar Mahal and Bakhtiari (1997–2000), and professor of economics at Tehran University (since 1995). On August 22, 2001, he received the highest number of votes (221 out of 263) of any of ministers in President Khatami's second cabinet to become the minister of labor and social affairs. He was the chairman of the board of the National Development Fund of Iran until 2016, when he had to resign after being criticized in the media for the exorbitant salary he was receiving. That same year, Hoseyni's daughter, Seyyedeh Fatemeh, was elected to the Tenth Majlis from Tehran.

Hoseyni, Seyyed Shamseddin

Minister of economic affairs and finance in President Ahmadinejad's first (August 12, 2008–August 2, 2009) and second (September 3, 2009–August 3, 2013) cabinets
1967–, Tonekabon, Mazandaran
BA, economics, Allameh Tabataba'i University, 1989; MA, economics, Tehran University, 1992; PhD, economics, Islamic Azad University–Science and Research Branch, 2005
Academia
No imprisonment
Not a war veteran
Seyyed Shamseddin Hoseyni was in charge of the Economic Studies Bureau of the Ministry of Commerce. As minister of economic affairs and finance, he survived an impeachment on November 1, 2011.

Hoseyni, Seyyed Sharif

Deputy of the Eighth (2008–12) and Ninth (2012–16) Majlis, Ahvaz, Khuzestan

1968–, Abadan, Khuzestan
BA, business administration, Shahid Chamran University of Ahvaz; MA, executive management
Seyyed Shabil
Civil servant, state companies
No imprisonment
In 2016, Hoseyni became an adviser to the minister of petroleum.

Hoseyni, Mrs. Seyyedeh Fatemeh

Deputy of the Tenth Majlis, Tehran, Tehran (2016–20)
1985–, Kohgiluyeh and Buyer Ahmad
MA, executive management; pursuing a PhD degree in financial management at Tehran University
Seyyed Safdar, university professor and former chair of the board of the National Development Fund of Iran
Financial consultant to various companies
Hoseyni is the daughter of Seyyed Safdar Hoseyni, who was minister of labor and social affairs and then minister of economic affairs and finance in President Khatami's second cabinet. She was the youngest person elected to the Tenth Majlis.

Hoseyni [Buyer Ahmad], Seyyed Mas'ud

Deputy of the Fourth Majlis, Buyer Ahmad, Kohgiluyeh and Buyer Ahmad (1992–96)
1955–, Buyer Ahmad, Kohgiluyeh and Buyer Ahmad
Associate's degree, 1977; BA, 1996
Seyyed Khodakaram
No imprisonment
Hoseyni served for a while as the governor of Kohgiluyeh and Buyer Ahmad Province, starting on October 19, 2005.

Hoseyni [Dehsorkh], Seyyed Hoseyn

Deputy of the Seventh (2004–8) and Eighth (2008–12) Majlis, Fariman and Sarakhs, Razavi Khorasan
1956–, Dehsorkh, Razavi Khorasan
BA, public administration

Mohammad-Ayub
Civil servant, state companies
No imprisonment

Hoseyni [Mahabad], Seyyed Mohammad

Deputy of the Third Majlis, Mahabad, West Azerbaijan (1988–92)
1953–, Mahabad, West Azerbaijan
High school diploma
Seyyed Saleh
No imprisonment

Hoseyni [Neyshabur], Seyyed Ali

Deputy of the Eighth Majlis, Neyshabur, Razavi Khorasan (2008–12)
May 8, 1971–, Neyshabur, Razavi Khorasan
Clerical education; BA, philosophy, Tehran University; MA, international relations, Tehran University; PhD, international law
Seyyed Asghar, clergyman
Clergyman and teacher
No imprisonment
War veteran (wounded)
IRGC militiaman (Basij)
HI Hoseyni ran unsuccessfully for the Ninth Majlis.

Hoseyni [Qaenat], Seyyed Hoseyn

Deputy of the Second Majlis, Qaenat, South Khorasan (1984–88)
1951–2015, Qaenat, South Khorasan
Clerical education, Mashhad Seminary
Seyyed Mahmud, farmer
Clergyman
Imprisoned before the revolution
Not a war veteran
IRGC militiaman
Secretary-general of the Youth Alliance of the Iranian Islamic Revolution
HI Hoseyni knew Ayatollah Khamenei from their prerevolutionary days in Mashhad. He was the Friday prayer leader of Shandiz (Razavi

Khorasan) from 1998 to 2009, and he died in the 2015 stampede in Mecca, Saudi Arabia.

Hoseyni [Torbat-e Jam], Seyyed Mohammad

Deputy of the Fourth (1992–96) and Fifth (1996–2000) Majlis, Torbat-e Jam and Taybad, Razavi Khorasan
March 21, 1952–, Torbat-e Jam, Razavi Khorasan
BS, chemical engineering, Sharif University of Technology, 1976; PhD, chemical engineering, University of Manchester (England)
Seyyed Mirza Aqa, farmer
University professor and food science and technology expert
No imprisonment
Not a war veteran

Hoseyni-Alhashemi, Seyyed Monireddin

Member of the Assembly for the Final Examination of the Constitution, Fars (1979)
1943–March 2, 2001, Shiraz, Fars
Clerical education, Najaf Seminary (Iraq)
Seyyed Nureddin, clergyman (ayatollah)
Clergyman
No imprisonment
Not a war veteran
HI Hoseyni-Alhashemi was an intellectual mentor to members of the paramilitary group Mansurron in the last couple of years leading up to the revolution. He was the founder of the Academy of Islamic Sciences in Qom.

Hoseyni-Almadini, Seyyed Razi

Deputy of the Third Majlis, Lamerd, Fars (1988–92)
1957–, Lamerd, Fars
Clerical education; BA
Seyyed Ali
Clergyman
No imprisonment
HI Hoseyni-Almadini, who is a former Friday prayer leader of Ashkana, registered to run for the Tenth Majlis.

Hoseyni-Arsanjani, Seyyed Mohammad-Hoseyn

Member of the Second (1991–98) and Third (1999–2006) Assembly of Experts, Fars
1922–2014, Arsanjan, Fars
Clerical education, Qom Seminary
Clergyman
Imprisoned before the revolution
Not a war veteran
Ayatollah Hoseyni-Arsanjani was the Friday prayer leader of Fasa, Fars Province, from 1980 to 2002.

Hoseyni-Barzanji, Abdorrahman

Deputy of the Third Majlis, Naqadeh, West Azerbaijan (1988–92)
1953–, Oshnaviyyeh, West Azerbaijan
BA, law
Ma'ruf
No imprisonment

Hoseyni-Brameh'i, Seyyed Fazlollah

Deputy of the First (1981–84) and Second (1984–88) Majlis, Dargaz, Razavi Khorasan
1947–, Behshahr, Mazandaran
Clerical education; BA, theology
Seyyed Ja'far, clergyman
Clergyman
No imprisonment
Not a war veteran
HI Hoseyni-Brameh'i, who worked for the Ministry of Education before the revolution and taught at Qom Seminary, became a revolutionary court judge in Quchan and Dargaz after the revolution. He was in leadership posts in the First and Second Majlis.

Hoseyni-Bushehri, Seyyed Hashem

Member of the Fourth (2007–16) and Fifth (2016–22) Assembly of Experts, Bushehr
1956–, Bordokhan, Bushehr
Clerical education, Qom Seminary

Seyyed Mohammad, clergyman and farmer
Clergyman
No imprisonment
Not a war veteran
Member of the SQSS; secretary of the HCRSQ
Ayatollah Hoseyni-Bushehri has been the editor of
    various Islamic journals. His tenure as the secre-
    tary of the HCRSQ ended in 2016. He was also the
    Friday prayer leader of Qom.

Hoseyni-Dowlatabad[i], Seyyed Mahmud

Deputy of the Seventh (2004–8) and Eighth (2008–12)
    Majlis, Shahinshahr, Meymeh, and Borkhar,
    Isfahan
1961–, Dowlatabad, Isfahan
Clerical education
Seyyed Hasan
Clergyman (HI)
No imprisonment
Hoseyni-Dowlatabad[i] was not elected to the Ninth
    Majlis.

Hoseyni-Eshkevari, Seyyed Ali

Member of the Fifth Assembly of Experts, Gilan
    (2016–22)
1958–, Mashhad, Razavi Khorasan
Clerical education, Qom Seminary
Seyyed Mohammad, clergyman (ayatollah)
Clergyman
Martyr's family (son, Ali, killed at the war front)
Ayatollah Hoseyni-Eshkevari lived in Iraq for many
    years, where Saddam Hussein's regime tortured
    him.

Hoseyni-Heydarabadi, Seyyed Sobhan

Deputy of the Sixth (2001–4) and Seventh (2004–8)
    Majlis, Gorgan and Aq-Qala, Golestan
1957–, Gorgan, Golestan
MA, counseling
Mohammad-Reza
Academia

No imprisonment
IRGC militiaman
The GC rejected Hoseyni-Heydarabadi's qualifica-
    tions to run in the election for the Tenth Majlis.

Hoseyni-Kashani [Kashi], Seyyed Mohammad

Member of the First Assembly of Experts, Isfahan
    (1984–90)
1934–, Kashan, Isfahan
Clerical education, Qom Seminary
Seyyed Hasan, laborer
Clergyman (ayatollah)
No imprisonment
Not a war veteran
Martyr's family (son, Seyyed Mohammad-Mehdi,
    killed at the war front)
On September 28, 1979, Ayatollah Khomeini ap-
    pointed Hoseyni-Kashani as the judge of the
    revolutionary court in Kazerun. He was elected to
    the First AE in interim elections held on April 15,
    1984.

Hoseyni-Khorasani, Seyyed Ahmad

Member of the Fifth Assembly of Experts, Razavi
    Khorasan (2016–22)
1959–, Fajrabad, North Khorasan
Clerical education
Mirza Arab
Clergyman (ayatollah)
No imprisonment
Member of the SQSS

Hoseyni-Kia, Seyyed Javad

Deputy of the Tenth Majlis, Sonqor, Kermanshah
    (2016–20)
1972–, Sonqor, Kermanshah
Clerical education, Qom Seminary; BA, philosophy
Seyyed Mohammad
Clergyman and educational director-general of Imam
    Khomeini and Islamic Revolution Research
    Institute

No imprisonment

Not a war veteran

Before entering the Majlis, HI Hoseyni-Kia worked in the Construction Jihad in Kermanshah Province and in the Office of the Supreme Leader at Razi University. He has worked at the Imam Khomeini and Islamic Revolution Research Institute since 1998.

Hoseyni-Kuhestani, Seyyed Rasul

Deputy of the Third Majlis, Behshahr, Mazandaran (1988–92)

1939–, Behshahr, Mazandaran

Clerical education

Mir Ali-Asghar

Clergyman

No imprisonment

Martyr's family (son)

He ran unsuccessfully for the Fourth Majlis.

Hoseyni-Lavasani, Seyyed Mohammad-Baqer

Deputy of the First Majlis, Tehran, Tehran (1980–81)

1944–June 28, 1981, Tehran, Tehran

MD, medicine, Tehran University, 1974

Seyyed Mohammad-Reza, clergyman

Medical doctor and Ministry of Health official

No imprisonment

Not a war veteran

Member of the IRP

Hoseyni-Lavasani was killed in the bombing of the IRP headquarters.

Hoseyni-Na'ini, Seyyed Shamseddin

Deputy of the First Majlis, Na'in, Isfahan (1980–81)

1933–June 28, 1981, Soltannasir, Isfahan

BA, theology, Tehran University; MA, theology, Tehran University; PhD, theology, Aligarh Muslim University (India)

Seyyed Reza, clergyman

Academia

No imprisonment

Not a war veteran

Hoseyni-Na'ini was killed in the bombing of the IRP headquarters.

Hoseyninasab, Seyyed Rajab

Deputy of the Sixth Majlis, Dehloran, Darrehshahr, and Abdanan, Ilam (2000–2004)

1962–, Dehloran, Ilam

MA, theology

Hasan

No imprisonment

After serving in the Majlis, Hoseyninasab became a civil servant.

Hoseyninezhad, Seyyed Akbar

Deputy of the Fifth Majlis, Ardakan and Meybod, Yazd (1996–2000)

1949–, Ardakan, Yazd

MD, medicine, Isfahan University of Technology, 1978

Seyyed Mehdi, clergyman (HI)

Pediatrician and hospital administrator

No imprisonment

Hoseyninezhad, Seyyed Mehdi

Deputy of the Second Majlis, Nur and Mahmudabad, Mazandaran (1984–88)

1943–, Nur, Mazandaran

Clerical education

Seyyed Ali-Asghar

Clergyman (HI)

No imprisonment

After serving in the Majlis, Hoseyninezhad set up a religious foundation.

Hoseyninezhad, Seyyed Mohammad

Deputy of the Second Majlis, Ardakan, Yazd (1984–88)

1942–, Ardakan, Yazd

Clerical education

Seyyed Mehdi
Clergyman
No imprisonment
HI Hoseyninezhad's brother, Seyyed Akbar, also rep-
resented Ardakan in the Fifth Majlis.

Hoseyni-Niya-Kajidi, Mohammad [Amin]

Deputy of the First Majlis, Rudsar, Gilan (1981–84)
1946–, Kajid, Gilan
Clerical education
Ali-Asghar
Clergyman
No imprisonment
HI Hoseyni-Niya-Kajidi was active in the Martyr's
Foundation and IKRF in the 1980s.

Hoseynipur, Seyyed Qodratollah

Deputy of the Eighth Majlis, Gachsaran, Kohgiluyeh
and Buyer Ahmad (2008–12)
1955–, Gachsaran, Kohgiluyeh and Buyer Ahmad
BA, educational management
Seyyed Soleyman
No imprisonment
IRGC militiaman
Hoseynipur ran unsuccessfully for the Ninth
Majlis.

Hoseyni-Sadr, Mo'ayyed

Deputy of the Eighth (2008–12) and Ninth (2012–16)
Majlis, Khoy and Chaypareh, West Azerbaijan
1970–, Khoy, West Azerbaijan
BS, chemistry, Urmia University, 1993; MS, chemis-
try, Bu-Ali Sina University, 1996; PhD, chemistry,
Shahid Chamran University of Ahvaz, 2001
Gholam-Hoseyn, farmer and beekeeper
University professor and administrator
No imprisonment
Not a war veteran
After leaving the Majlis, Hoseyni-Sadr became an
adviser to the minister of petroleum, minister of
industry, and VP for planning and budget.

Hoseyni-Shahrudi, Seyyed Abdolhadi

Member of the Fourth (2009–16) and Fifth (2016–22)
Assembly of Experts, Golestan
1947–, Najaf, Iraq
Clerical education, Najaf Seminary (Iraq)
Seyyed Mohammad, clergyman (ayatollah)
Clergyman
No imprisonment
Not a war veteran
Ayatollah Hoseyni-Shahrudi, the Friday prayer leader
of Aliabad Katul (1980–98), was one of the found-
ers of that city's university and taught there as
well. He was elected to the Fourth AE in interim
elections in 2009, having received 43 percent of
the vote. His father, Seyyed Mohammad Hoseyni-
Shahrudi, served concurrently with him in the
Fifth AE representing Kurdistan Province.

Hoseyni-Shahrudi, Seyyed Hasan

Deputy of the Tenth Majlis, Shahrud, Semnan
(2016–20)
1962–, Shahrud, Semnan
BA, management; MA, public administration, Univer-
sity of Mazandaran; pursuing a PhD in cultural
engineering at Imam Hoseyn University
Seyyed Mahmud, bazaar merchant
Civil servant
No imprisonment
War veteran
IRGC militiaman
Hoseyni-Shahrudi was governor of Minudasht
(1991–94) and Babolsar (1994–97), and he was a
deputy of the Islamic Propaganda Organization.
His older brother, HI Seyyed Hoseyn, represented
Shahrud in the Second, Third, and Fourth Majlis.

Hoseyni-Shahrudi, Seyyed Mohammad

Member of the Fifth Assembly of Experts, Kurdistan
(2016–22)
1925–, Najaf, Iraq
Clerical education, Najaf Seminary (Iraq)

Seyyed Mahmud, clergyman (ayatollah)

Clergyman

No imprisonment

Not a war veteran

Ayatollah Hoseyni-Shahrudi lived the first fifty-five
years of his life in Iraq. Saddam Hussein's regime
expelled him to Iran in 1980. He was the representative of the supreme leader, Ayatollah Khamenei, in Kurdistan Province. His son, Seyyed
Abdolhadi Hoseyni-Shahrudi, also served in the
Fourth and Fifth AE.

*Hoseyni-Shahrudi [Chitsaz-Mohammadi], Seyyed
Hoseyn*

Deputy of the Second (1984–88), Third (1988–92), and
Fourth (1992–94) Majlis, Shahrud, Semnan

1950–1994, Shahrud, Semnan

Clerical education

Seyyed Mahmud, bazaar merchant

Clergyman

No imprisonment

Not a war veteran

In the Second Majlis, HI Hoseyni-Shahrudi was
known by the last name of Chitsaz-Mohammadi.
He sought cancer treatment in England and
Germany but finally died on October 11, 1994.
His younger brother, Seyyed Hasan, represented
Shahrud in the Tenth Majlis.

Hoseyni-Tabataba'i, Seyyed Mohammad-Taqi

Deputy of the First Majlis, Zabol, Sistan and Baluchestan (1980–81)

1928–June 28, 1981, Zabol, Sistan and Baluchestan

Clerical education; MA, theology, Tehran University

Seyyed Ali, clergyman

Clergyman

No imprisonment

Not a war veteran

HI Hoseyni-Tabataba'i was killed in the bombing of
the IRP headquarters. His brother, Seyyed Hasan
Aqa Hoseyni-Tabataba'i, represented Zabol four
times in the Majlis.

Hoseyni-Vae'z, Seyyed Mahmud

Deputy of the Fifth Majlis, Ramiyan, Golestan
(1996–2000)

1952–, Shahrud, Semnan

Clerical education

Seyyed Hoseyn, clergyman and MP

Clergyman

No imprisonment

HI Hoseyni-Vae'z's father represented Ramiyan in the
First Majlis.

Hoseyni-Vae'z-Ramiyani, Seyyed Hoseyn

Deputy of the First Majlis, Ramiyan, Golestan
(1980–84)

1921–1993, Ramiyan, Golestan

Clerical education, Qom Seminary

Seyyed Sadeq, farmer

Clergyman

No imprisonment

Not a war veteran

After leaving the Majlis, HI Hoseyni-Vae'z-Ramiyani was in charge of Ramiyan's Martyr's
Foundation.

Hoseyniyan, Ruhollah

Deputy of the Eighth (2008–12) and Ninth (2012–16)
Majlis, Tehran, Tehran

1955–, Shiraz, Fars

Clerical education, Haqqani Seminary

Qodratollah, farmer

Clergyman and judiciary official

Imprisoned before the revolution

War veteran (wounded)

Martyr's family (brother)

Founding member of ADVIR; member of the SFIR

HI Hoseyniyan, an archconservative, was both a
judge and a prosecutor-general in the revolutionary tribunal of Tehran and SCFC. He has headed
the Islamic Revolution Documentation Center
for many years. He did not register to run for the
Tenth Majlis.

Hoseynizadeh, Seyyed Ali

Deputy of the Second Majlis, Borujen and Lordegan, Chahar Mahal and Bakhtiari (1984–88)
1953–, Silab, Chahar Mahal and Bakhtiari
Clerical education
Seyyed Esma'il
Clergyman
No imprisonment

Hoseyni-Zeydabadi, Seyyed Ahmad

Deputy of the Second (1984–88), Third (1988–92), Fourth (1992–96), and Seventh (2004–8) Majlis, Sirjan, Kerman
1950–, Sirjan, Kerman
Clerical education
Seyyed Kazem
Clergyman
No imprisonment
HI Hoseyni-Zeydabadi was previously an adviser to the secretary of the HCCR.

Hoseynnezhad-Dovin, Mohammad-Reza

Deputy of the Eighth Majlis, Shiravan, North Khorasan (2008–12)
1965–, Shiravan, North Khorasan
MS, civil engineering
Ramezan-Ali
Civil servant
No imprisonment
Hoseynnezhad-Dovin ran unsuccessfully for the Ninth Majlis.

Hoseynzadeh, Abdolkarim

Deputy of the Ninth (2012–16) and Tenth (2016–20) Majlis, Naqadeh and Oshnaviyyeh, West Azerbaijan
1980–, Naqadeh, West Azerbaijan
MS, urban planning, Iran University of Science and Technology
Executive director of a private construction company

No imprisonment (born after the revolution)
Not a war veteran
Hoseynzadeh is a Sunni Kurd.

Hoseynzadeh, Javad

Deputy of the Third Majlis, Dargaz, Razavi Khorasan (1988–92)
1958–, Dargaz, Razavi Khorasan
High school diploma
Soltan-Ali
No imprisonment

Hoseynzadeh-Bahreini, Mohammad-Hoseyn

Deputy of the Ninth (2012–16) and Tenth (2016–20) Majlis, Mashhad and Kalat, Razavi Khorasan
1963–, Mashhad, Razavi Khorasan
Clerical education, Mashhad Seminary; BA, economics, Ferdowsi University of Mashhad, 1993; MA, economics, Allameh Tabataba'i University, 1995; PhD, economics, Allameh Tabataba'i University, 2003; dissertation title: "Economic Security and Investment in Iran"
Clergyman and professor of economics at Ferdowsi University of Mashhad
No imprisonment
War veteran
HI Hoseynzadeh-Bahreini is a former official in the Office of the Supreme Leader. He is the son-in-law of Ayatollah Mehdi Noqani, who lives in Mashhad.

Hoseynzadeh-Taqiabadi, Shahbaz

Deputy of the Sixth Majlis, Miyandoab, Takab, and Shahindezh, West Azerbaijan (2000–2004)
1967–, Miyandoab, West Azerbaijan
BA, law
Ebrahim
Judiciary official
No imprisonment
After serving in the Majlis, Hoseynzadeh-Taqiabadi worked for the government.

Imani, Asadollah

Member of the First (1983–90), Second (1991–98),
   Third (1999–2006), Fourth (2007–16), and Fifth
   (2016–) Assembly of Experts, Fars
1947–, Kazerun, Fars
Clerical education, Qom Seminary
Mohammad-Sadeq, clergyman
Clergyman
No imprisonment
Not a war veteran
Ayatollah Imani was the Friday prayer leader of Ka-
   zerun from 1979 to 2001 and Bushehr from 2001
   to 2009. In early 2009, he became the representa-
   tive of the supreme leader and the Friday prayer
   leader of Shiraz.

Imani, Qodratollah

Deputy of the Seventh Majlis, Khorramabad, Lorestan
   (2004–8)
1956–, Khorramabad, Lorestan
MA, political science; PhD, international law
Ali, farmer
Academia
No imprisonment
IRGC militiaman
Member of the IRP
Imani, who has retired from the Ministry of Edu-
   cation, registered to run in the elections for the
   Eighth and Tenth Majlis.

Imaniyan, Asghar

Commander of the Islamic Republic of Iran Air Force
   (February 25–August 15, 1979)
August 9, 1929–April 17, 2015, Mashhad, Razavi
   Khorasan
BS, military science, Ground Forces Officers' Acad-
   emy, 1954
Father's name unknown, bazaar merchant
Military pilot (brigadier general)
No imprisonment
Not a war veteran

Imaniyan joined the Iranian military in 1950 and
   underwent flight training in Germany and the
   United States. He resigned from his post as air force
   commander in August 1979 after serving for six
   months.

Irani, Hoseyn

Deputy of the Fourth (1992–96) and Fifth (1996–2000)
   Majlis, Qom, Qom
1944–2009, Qom, Qom
Clerical education
Mohammad
Clergyman (HI)
No imprisonment
War veteran
IRGC militiaman
Founding member of the Qom Islamic Society of
   Admonishers

Irannezhad, Abdolghafur

Deputy of the Fourth (1992–96), Sixth (2000–2004),
   Seventh (2004–8), and Tenth (2016–20) Majlis,
   Chabahar, Sistan and Baluchestan
1956–, Chabahar, Sistan and Baluchestan
High school diploma
Sadiq
Civil servant
No imprisonment
War veteran
IRGC militiaman (Basij)
Irannezhad, a Sunni, was active in Basij and in the
   Agricultural Jihad.

Iranpur, Ali

Deputy of the Ninth Majlis, Mobarakeh, Isfahan
   (2012–16)
August 25, 1980–, Mobarakeh, Isfahan
BA, law; PhD, veterinary sciences, Islamic Azad
   University–Shahrekord
Father's name unknown, teacher (retired)
Journalist and IRIB official in Isfahan

No imprisonment

Not a war veteran

In the Ninth Majlis, Iranpur was accused by other MPs of embezzlement and claiming false academic credentials but managed to keep his seat.

Iravani, Mohammad-Javad

Minister of economic affairs and finance in PM Musavi's second cabinet (January 5, 1986–August 3, 1989); member of the Fifth (2002–7), Sixth (2007–12), Seventh (2012–17), and Eighth (2017–22) Expediency Discernment Assembly

1953–, Najaf, Iraq

MA, business administration; PhD, management, Tehran University, 1997

Yusef, clergyman

Ministry of Commerce official

No imprisonment

Not a war veteran

Iravani, the son of a famous conservative cleric in Tehran, was active in the Muslim Student Association in California before the revolution. In the early 1980s, he was an employee of Bank Mellat and then worked in the Ministry of Economic Affairs and Finance from 1985 to 1989. From 1989 to 2007, he was a member and chair of the board of directors of Esteqlal Sporting Club, which owns one of the most popular soccer teams. From November 11, 1997, to 2007, he was director of the Headquarters for Implementation of Imam's Order, and then he became deputy inspector for the Office of the Supreme Leader. Iravani, a professor of finance at Tehran University, was also deputy director of the Construction Jihad under President Hashemi-Rafsanjani. His daughter is married to the son of Gholam-Hoseyn Mohammadi-Golpayegani, who is in charge of the Office of the Supreme Leader.

Isazadeh, Mehdi

Deputy of the Eighth (2009–12) and Ninth (2012–16) Majlis, Miyandoab, Shahindezh, and Takab, West Azerbaijan

1962–, Miyandoab, West Azerbaijan

BS, agricultural engineering, Tabriz University; MS, military science, Imam Hoseyn University; PhD, military science

Ahmad-Ali

No imprisonment

War veteran

IRGC militiaman

Isfahani, Reza

Deputy of the First Majlis, Varamin, Tehran (1980–84)

1935–2002, Tehran, Tehran

Clerical education

Mohammad-Sadeq, bazaar tradesman

Clergyman

No imprisonment

Not a war veteran

HI Isfahani was deputy minister of agriculture under Abbas Sheybani in the Revolutionary Council. He had semi-socialist views on economic issues and his plans faced strong opposition from many individuals, including Ayatollah Khomeini.

Islamdust-Karbandi, Askar

Deputy of the Sixth Majlis, Talesh, Gilan (2000–2004)

1956–, Talesh, Gilan

BS, industrial management; MA, public administration

Molla Qoli

Provincial civil servant

No imprisonment

After leaving the Majlis, Islamdust-Karbandi was governor of Talesh and later governor of Lahijan.

Islami, Ali

Member of the Fourth (2008–16) and Fifth (2016–22) Assembly of Experts, Qazvin

1947–, Shal, Qazvin

Clerical education, Najaf Seminary (Iraq)

Ahmad

Clergyman (ayatollah)
No imprisonment
Not a war veteran
Islami, who lived in Iraq for many years and speaks
fluent Arabic, worked for a while in the Pilgrimage Office of the Supreme Leader. He was the Friday prayer leader of Takestan, and he was elected
to the Fourth AE in interim elections.

Islami, Hoseyn

Deputy of the Seventh (2004–8) and Eighth (2008–11)
Majlis, Saveh and Zarandieh, Markazi
1966–September 2, 2011, Saveh, Markazi
Clerical education; PhD in philosophy (incomplete)
Mohammad-Ali
Clergyman (HI)
No imprisonment
War veteran (victim of a chemical attack)

Islami, Mohammad-Hasan

Minister of post, telegraph, and telephones in PM Ba-
zargan's cabinet (February 22–November 4, 1979)
1934–, Tehran, Tehran
PhD, electrical engineering, University of Karlsruhe
(Germany), 1964
Alhaq, civil servant
Civil servant, ministries
No imprisonment
Not a war veteran
Member of the executive committee of INF-European
Branch
Islami served as minister of post, telegraph, and
telephones for less than nine months. He lived in
Germany from 1956 to 1964 and migrated with
his family to Canada in the 2000s.

Islami, Yadollah

Deputy of the Third Majlis, Baft, Kerman (1988–92)
1956–, Baft, Kerman
MD, optometry

Farajollah
Optometrist
No imprisonment
War veteran (wounded)
Secretary-general of the Assembly of Former MPs
Yadollah Islami, a leading optometrist, was the editor
of the banned *Fateh*. The GC rejected his qualifi-
cations to run in the Fourth Majlis in 1992, and in
1998, he formed the ISFPD. The judiciary impris-
oned him for a month in 2011.

Islami-Kheramehi, Ebrahim

Deputy of the Second Majlis, Eqlid, Fars (1984–88)
1949–, Eqlid, Fars
Clerical education
Mohammad-Hasan
Clergyman (HI)
No imprisonment

Islamipanah, Ali

Deputy of the Eighth Majlis, Jiroft and Anbarabad,
Kerman (2008–12)
1960–, Jiroft, Kerman
PhD, law
Morad
Academia
No imprisonment
Islamipanah was not elected to the Ninth Majlis.

Islami-Torbati, Ali-Akbar

Member of the First Assembly of Experts, Razavi
Khorasan (1983–89)
1906–1989, Torbat-e Heydariyyeh, Razavi Khorasan
Clerical education
Sadr
Clergyman
No imprisonment
Not a war veteran
Islami-Torbati worked in Ayatollah Khomeini's office
before the revolution.

Islamiyan, Ali-Reza

Member of the Fourth (2007–16) and Fifth (2016–
  22) Assembly of Experts, Chahar Mahal and
  Bakhtiari
1958–, Qom, Qom
Clerical education, Qom Seminary
Abdolhoseyn, glassware seller
Clergyman (HI)
Imprisoned before the revolution (2 months in 1972)
Member of the SQSS

Izadi, Abbas

Member of the First Assembly of Experts, Isfahan
  (1983–90)
1922–1992, Najafabad, Isfahan
Clerical education, Qom Seminary
Father's name unknown, bazaar tradesman
Clergyman
Imprisoned before the revolution
Not a war veteran
Martyr's family (son, Ahmad, killed at the war front
  in 1986)
Ayatollah Izadi was the Friday prayer leader of Naja-
  fabad from 1979 to 1992 and headed Najafabad's
  seminary for some thirty years. He was a candi-
  date for the Second AE. He was close to Ayatollah
  Montazeri, who gave the sermon at his funeral.

Izadi, Ali-Mohammad

Minister of agriculture in PM Bazargan's cabinet
  (1979)
1927–, Shiraz, Fars
PhD, agricultural economics, Oregon State Univer-
  sity (USA), 1975; dissertation title: "An Economic
  Evaluation of Irrigation Water Pricing on Farm
  Incomes and Cropping Patterns, Marvdasht Plain
  in Fars, Iran"
Father's name unknown, farmer
Agricultural engineer
No imprisonment

Not a war veteran
Izadi returned to Iran from the United States after the
  revolution to serve as a minister. After his unsuccessful run for the First Majlis from Shiraz, he
  returned to the United States before settling down
  in Canada.

Jabbari, Ahmad

Deputy of the Eighth (2008–12) and Ninth (2012–16)
  Majlis, Bandar-e Lengeh, Bastak, and Parsian,
  Hormozgan
1967–, Bastak, Hormozgan
BA, judicial law and civil engineering
Abdollah
Civil servant in the education bureau (seventeen
  years) and the Red Crescent Society of the Islamic
  Republic of Iran (twelve years)
No imprisonment
Not a war veteran
After Jabbari, a Sunni, ended his term, his nephew,
  Naser Sharifi, managed to occupy his seat and
  represent the same constituency.

Jabbari, Seyyed Saber

Member of the Second (1991–98), Third (1999–2006),
  and Fourth (2007–14) Assembly of Experts,
  Mazandaran
1938–2014, Behshahr, Mazandaran
Clerical education, Qom Seminary
Seyyed Mohammad, clergyman
Clergyman
No imprisonment
Not a war veteran
HI Seyyed Saber Jabbari was the Friday prayer leader
  of Behshahr for many years.

Jabbarzadeh, Esma'il

Deputy of the Fourth (1992–96), Fifth (1996–2000),
  Sixth (2000–2004), and Seventh (2004–8) Majlis,
  Tabriz, East Azerbaijan

1960–, Khoy, West Azerbaijan
Fathollah
MD, laboratory science
Medical professional
No imprisonment
War veteran (fifty months)
IRGC militiaman
Jabbarzadeh served as governor-general of East Azerbaijan until he became deputy interior minister for political affairs in September 2017.

Jaberi-Bonab, Mir Yusef

Deputy of the First Majlis, Bonab and Malekan, East Azerbaijan (1983–84)
1946–, Bonab, East Azerbaijan
Clerical education
Mir Mahmud
Clergyman
No imprisonment
HI Jaberi-Bonab was a clerical representative in the Construction Jihad and was associated with the IRGC and military forces.

Jadgal, Ya'qub

Deputy of the Eighth (2008–12) and Ninth (2012–16) Majlis, Chabahar, Sistan and Baluchestan
1969–, Chabahar, Sistan and Baluchestan
BA, elementary education, Farhangian University–Zahedan
Ali
Teacher and member of the Chabahar City Council
No imprisonment
After serving in the Majlis, Jadgal, who is a Sunni, retired from the teaching profession.

Jadri, Jasem

Deputy of the Third (1988–92), Fourth (1992–96), and Fifth (1996–2000) Majlis, Dasht-e Azadegan, Khuzestan
March 21, 1957–, Susangerd, Khuzestan
BA, 1985; MA, management, 1992

Yunes
Official in Khatam al-Anbia Construction Headquarters
No imprisonment
War veteran
IRGC militiaman
Jadri was active in the Construction Jihad for many years. After leaving the Majlis, Jadri became a deputy to the minister of mining and then the minister of energy. In 2013, he was in charge of Hassan Rouhani's campaign headquarters in Khuzestan and was rewarded with the post of governor of Hormozgan.

Ja'fari, Ali-Akbar

Deputy of the Sixth Majlis, Saveh, Markazi (2000–2004)
1954–, Saveh, Markazi
BA, economics; MA, management
Nazarali
Civil servant
No imprisonment

Ja'fari, Ali-Morad

Deputy of the Seventh Majlis, Gachsaran and Basht, Kohgiluyeh and Buyer Ahmad (2005–8)
1957–, Gachsaran, Kohgiluyeh and Buyer Ahmad
PhD, political science
Allah-Morad
No imprisonment
War veteran
Martyr's family (two bothers killed at the war front)
Ja'fari was elected to the Majlis in a midterm election on July 17, 2005. He did not get elected to the Tenth Majlis.

Ja'fari, Behruz

Deputy of the Eighth Majlis, Semirom, Isfahan (2008–12)
1958–, Semirom, Isfahan
BA, educational management

Soltan-Ali

Provincial civil servant, Isfahan Province

No imprisonment

Behruz Ja'fari ran unsuccessfully for the Tenth Majlis.

Ja'fari, Beytollah

Deputy of the Third (1988–92) and Fourth (1992–96) Majlis, Urmia, West Azerbaijan

1953–, Urmia, West Azerbaijan

BA

Arab

No imprisonment

Ja'fari was involved in armed attacks on the shah's regime before the revolution.

Ja'fari, Hasan

Deputy of the Second (1984–88) and Third (1988–92) Majlis, Shahr-e Babak, Kerman

1939–, Shahr-e Babak, Kerman

Clerical education

Gholam-Reza

Clergyman (HI)

No imprisonment

Ja'fari, Hoseyn

Deputy of the First Majlis, Kermanshah, Kermanshah (1981–84)

1927–, Hamadan, Hamadan

MD, medicine

Ali

No imprisonment

Not a war veteran

Ja'fari, Isa

Deputy of the Eighth Majlis, Bahar and Kabudarahang, Hamadan (2008–12)

1961–, Kabudarahang, Hamadan

BA, theology

Yusef

Civil servant, ministries

Ja'fari was governor of Kabudarahang for five years and worked in the State Audit Court. He ran unsuccessfully for the Ninth and Tenth Majlis.

Ja'fari, Mohammad-Ali [Aziz]

Commander in chief of the IRGC (September 1, 2007–present); commander of the IRGC's Basij Force (2008)

1957–, Yazd, Yazd

BS, architecture, Tehran University; MS, military science, Imam Hoseyn University, 1993

No imprisonment

War veteran (wounded)

Martyr's family (two sons of his aunt)

IRGC militiaman

Major General Ja'fari went from Yazd to Tehran in 1977 to study architecture at Tehran University. After the revolution, he was involved in the takeover of the American embassy and joined the ranks of the IRGC in 1981. During the Iran–Iraq War, he held various leadership roles and was badly injured. After the war, he completed his BS degree in architecture. Ja'fari was commander of the IRGC's ground forces from July 12, 1992, to 2005. As commander of Sarollah base from 2005 to 2007, he was responsible for the security of Tehran in emergency situations. Ayatollah Khamenei appointed him commander in chief of the IRGC on September 1, 2007. The United States government put Ja'fari on the US Treasury Office of Foreign Assets Control's Specially Designated Nationals and Blocked Persons List in 2011.

Ja'fari, Qasem

Deputy of the Ninth Majlis, Bojnurd, Maneh and Samalqan, Jajarm, and Garmeh, North Khorasan (2012–16)

1968–, Raz, North Khorasan

Clerical education, Qom Seminary, 1997; BA, law, Tehran University, 1996; MA, theology, Tehran University, 2002; PhD, theology, Islamic Azad University–Science and Research Branch, 2006

Ebrahim
Clergyman
No imprisonment
War veteran (wounded; prisoner of war for eighty-
seven months)
IRGC militiaman
HI Qasem Ja'fari was the supreme leader's represen-
tative in the affairs of prisoners of war from 1995
to 2000. Saudi Arabia imprisoned Ja'fari for one
month for propagating Shiism.

Ja'fari, Seyyed Mohammad-Mehdi

Deputy of the First Majlis, Dashtestan, Bushehr
(1980–84)
September 28, 1939–, Borazjan, Bushehr
BA, Persian literature, Shiraz University, 1961; MA,
Arabic language and literature, Tehran University,
1975; PhD, Arabic literature, Tehran University,
1988
Seyyed Ebadollah, clergyman
Professor and researcher in the Iranian Language
Academy
Imprisoned before the revolution
Member of the LMI
Ja'fari is a translator and a scholar of Islamic studies.
In the late 1960s, he assisted PMOI for a while.
He taught at Shiraz University from 1988 until his
retirement in 2006.

Ja'fari-Baneh Khalkhal, Jalil

Deputy of the Ninth Majlis, Khalkhal and Kowsar,
Ardabil (2012–16)
1967–, Kowsar, Ardabil
BS, mechanical engineering, Tabriz University; MS,
nuclear engineering, Sharif University of Tech-
nology; PhD, nuclear engineering, Amirkabir
University of Technology
Father's name unknown, farmer
Nuclear scientist and research deputy at AEOI (since
2003)
No imprisonment

Not a war veteran
After serving in the Ninth Majlis, Ja'fari-Baneh
Khalkhal became a member of the board of direc-
tors of the Iranian Fuel Conservation Company.

Ja'fari-Chenijani, Mohammad

Deputy of the First Majlis, Langarud, Gilan (1981–84)
1938–, Rudsar, Gilan
Clerical education
Mohammad-Hoseyn
Clergyman
No imprisonment
HI Ja'fari-Chenijani was affiliated with the Qom Sem-
inary Islamic Propaganda Office.

Ja'fari-Dowlatabadi, Abbas

Public and revolutionary prosecutor-general of Tehran (August 30, 2009–present)
1957–, Isfahan, Isfahan
MA, law; PhD, penal law, 2010
Father's name unknown, baker
No imprisonment
War veteran (wounded)
Ja'fari-Dowlatabadi, who was previously the head of
the judiciary in Khuzestan Province and chief
of the Basij Force, ordered the arrest of many
protesters and politicians during the 2009 protests
and banned two political parties in 2010. The
Council of the European Union put him on its
sanctions list on April 12, 2011.

Ja'fari-Hesarlu, Seyyed Mir Heydar

Deputy of the Second Majlis, Bonab and Malekan,
East Azerbaijan (1984–88)
July 1, 1956–, Miyandoab, West Azerbaijan
Clerical education
Mir Ghaffar
Clergyman
No imprisonment
Ja'fari-Hesarlu ran unsuccessfully for the Tenth Majlis.

Ja'fari-Nasab-Jori, Seyyed Mohammad-Reza

Deputy of the Fifth Majlis, Zarand, Kerman
    (1996–2000)
1957–, Kerman, Kerman
BA, political science
Seyyed Ahmad
No imprisonment

Ja'farpur, Jamshid

Deputy of the Ninth (2012–16) and Tenth (2016–20)
    Majlis, Larestan, Khonj, and Gerash, Fars
1963–, Lar, Fars
BA, theology, Shahid Motahhari University, 1986;
    MA, theology, Shahid Motahhari University,
    1990; PhD, jurisprudence, Tehran University,
    1996; clerical education
Professor of theology
No imprisonment
War veteran (ten months; wounded)
IRGC militiaman
Ja'farpur was a member of the HCCR for twenty
    years.

Ja'farzadeh, Soleyman

Deputy of the Seventh (2004–8) and Eighth
    (2008–12) Majlis, Maku and Chaldoran, West
    Azerbaijan
1965–, Maku, West Azerbaijan
MA, history
Abbas-Qoli
No imprisonment
IRGC militiaman
After serving in the Majlis, Ja'farzadeh returned to
    working in the military establishment.

Ja'farzadeh-Imanabad, Gholam-Ali

Deputy of the Ninth (2012–16) and Tenth (2016–20)
    Majlis, Rasht, Gilan
1967–, Imanabad, Gilan

BS, civil engineering, Gilan University, 1997; MS, civil
    engineering, Gilan University–Pardis Anzali, 2011
Mohammad-Ja'far
Professor at Gilan University and FMVA official
No imprisonment
War veteran (wounded in 1987)
IRGC militiaman (Basij)
Ja'farzadeh-Imanabad, who has to use a wheelchair
    because of his severe wartime wounds, is a con-
    servative MP. He was head of the FMVA in Gilan
    Province, and an adviser to the vice president on
    veterans' affairs.

Jahandideh, Gholam-Mohammad

Deputy of the Sixth Majlis, Saravan, Sistan and Balu-
    chestan (2000–2004)
1952–, Saravan, Sistan and Baluchestan
BA, English literature
Dad-Mohammad
No imprisonment

Jahangiri, Mohammad-Hoseyn

Deputy of the Third Majlis, Qasr-e Shirin, Kerman-
    shah (1988–92)
1953–, Qasr-e Shirin, Kermanshah
High school diploma
Abbas
No imprisonment

Jahangiri [-Kuhshahi], Eshaq

Deputy of the Second (1984–88) and Third (1988–92)
    Majlis, Jiroft, Kerman; minister of mining and
    metals (August 20, 1997–January 14, 2001) and
    then minister of industries and mining (January
    14–August 1, 2001) in President Khatami's first
    cabinet; minister of industries and mining in
    President Khatami's second cabinet (August 22,
    2001–August 2, 2005); first vice president in Pres-
    ident Rouhani's first (2013–August 13, 2017) and
    second (2017–21) cabinets

January 21, 1958–, Sirjan, Kerman

BS, physics, Shahid Bahonar University of Kerman, 1984; MS, industrial engineering, Sharif University of Technology, 1993; PhD, industrial engineering, Islamic Azad University–Science and Research Branch

Hasan, miner

Official in the Construction Jihad

No imprisonment

Not a war veteran

Martyr's family (two brothers, Mohammad and Ya'qub)

Founding member of the central council of PECI

Jahangiri was wounded before the revolution in the anti-shah demonstrations. After the revolution, he held such posts as head of the Construction Jihad in Jiroft (1980–82), member of the council of Construction Jihad in Kerman Province (1982–84), governor-general of Isfahan (1992–97), and faculty member at Industrial Management Organization (2005–13). During President Khatami's first term, he switched posts from minister of mining and metals to the minister of industries. During the 2013 presidential elections, he was in charge of former president Hashemi-Rafsanjani's election headquarters, but once the GC disqualified Hashemi-Rafsanjani, Jahangiri became an adviser to Hassan Rouhani, who later chose him as his vice president. In 2017, Jahangiri was one of six candidates in the presidential race but withdrew in favor of Rouhani.

Jahangirzadeh, Javad

Deputy of the Seventh (2004–8), Eighth (2008–12), and Ninth (2012–16) Majlis, Urmia, West Azerbaijan

1966–, Urmia, West Azerbaijan

BA, sociology, Tabriz University; MA, sociology, Shiraz University; pursuing a PhD in political sociology at Allameh Tabataba'i University

Nurali

MIIRI officer and researcher at the Center for Strategic Research

No imprisonment

Not a war veteran

Martyr's family (brother, Mohammad-Reza)

In 2016, after Jahangirzadeh ran unsuccessfully for the Tenth Majlis, foreign minister Zarif appointed him as Iran's ambassador to the Republic of Azerbaijan.

Jahromi, Seyyed Mohammad [Alinaqi]

Minister of labor and social affairs in President Ahmadinejad's first cabinet (August 24, 2005– August 2, 2009)

1958–, Tehran, Tehran

BA, public administration, 1993; MA, public administration, 1997; PhD, strategic management, 2005

Seyyed Reza

Civil servant

No imprisonment

War veteran (twenty-six months)

IRGC militiaman

From 1982 to 1997, Jahromi was the governor-general of five different provinces—Zanjan, Lorestan, Hamadan, Semnan, and Fars. After finishing his term as minister, he became head of Bank Sadarat but was later dismissed after a huge financial scandal.

Jalali, Abdolhoseyn

Deputy of the First Majlis, Neyshabur, Razavi Khorasan (1980–84)

1951–, Shahrud, Semnan

BA, law

Ali-Asghar, civil servant

Revolutionary prosecutor-general of Neyshabur

No imprisonment

Jalali was the first person to serve as prosecutor-general of Neyshabur after the 1979 revolution.

Jalali, Ahmad

Member of the Revolutionary Council (1979–80)

1949–, Shahrud, Semnan

BA, mechanical engineering, Shiraz University; pursued PhD in political philosophy at the University of Oxford (England)

Not a war veteran

At age 30, Jalali, who had a program on the Qur'an on national television, became the youngest person appointed to the Revolutionary Council. Since then, he has held many posts, including deputy director of IRIB, adviser to Iran's Ministry of Foreign Affairs, ambassador and permanent delegate of the Islamic Republic of Iran to UNESCO (1997–2007), head of the Iranian Majlis Library, and cultural adviser to the Speaker of the Majlis. Jalali is also a professor at Allameh Tabataba'i University.

Jalali, Kazem

Deputy of the Sixth (2000–2004), Seventh (2004–8), Eighth (2008–12), and Ninth (2012–16) Majlis, Shahrud, Semnan; deputy of the Tenth Majlis, Tehran, Tehran (2016–20)

1967–, Shahkuh Aliya, Golestan

MA, political science, Imam Sadeq University, 1993; PhD, political science, Imam Sadeq University, 2001

Karam, farmer

Television reporter and producer

No imprisonment

War veteran

IRGC militiaman (Basij)

Martyr's family (two brothers-in-law)

Jalali has served in many positions, including head of the Basij committee at Imam Sadeq University, Ministry of Foreign Affairs official, university professor, and member of the supreme leader's inspection office (1997–2000). While serving in the Majlis, he became very close to Speaker Ali Larijani. Jalali headed the Islamic Parliament Research Center, in the Ninth and Tenth Majlis.

Jalali, Khodakaram

Deputy of the Second (1984–88), Third (1988–92), and Fourth (1992–96) Majlis, Firuzabad, Fars

1956–, Firuzabad, Fars

BS, agricultural engineering, 1980; MA, management, 1991

Jalal

No imprisonment

Jalali is a former manager at the Construction Jihad, and he headed the Iran Fisheries Organization and the Forests, Range, and Watershed Management Organization for twenty months.

Jalali, Mohammad-Hoseyn

Minister of defense in PM Musavi's second cabinet (1985–89)

Military science

Military pilot and commander of Iran Army Aviation

No imprisonment

War veteran

IRGC militiaman

Brigadier General Jalali was commander of Iran Army Aviation before becoming minister of defense. In April 1987, Ayatollah Khomeini promoted him from colonel to brigadier general. On January 18, 1992, Ayatollah Khamenei appointed Jalali commander of the IRGC's air force; he served in that post for five years. On February 3, 2015, he became an adviser to the Red Crescent Society of the Islamic Republic of Iran on air rescue missions.

Jalali-Ja'fari, Rashid

Deputy of the Seventh Majlis, Karaj and Eshtehard, Tehran (2004–8)

1958–, Varamin, Tehran

MA, geography

Ali

Civil servant

No imprisonment

War veteran

IRGC militiaman

Jalali-Ja'fari was a candidate in the election for the Tenth Majlis.

Jalaliyan, Asgar

Deputy of the Eighth Majlis, Deyr, Kangan, and Jam, Bushehr (2008–12)
1967–, Kangan, Bushehr
PhD, communications
Malek
Civil servant, ministries
No imprisonment
After Jalaliyan was not elected to the Ninth Majlis, he became director of the parliamentary and planning division of Payam-e Nur University.

Jalalizadeh, Jalal

Deputy of the Sixth Majlis, Sanandaj, Divandarreh, and Kamyaran, Kurdistan (2000–2004)
1960–, Golban, Kurdistan
BA, theology, Tehran University, 1987; MA, theology, 1989; PhD, theology, 1997
Ali, clergyman
University professor and member of the Sanandaj City Council
No imprisonment
Martyr's family (father and brother)
Member of the central council of IIPF and the Party of Iranian People's Unity
In 1981, Jalalizadeh's father and brother, who were both clerics, were killed and he himself was wounded when gunmen attacked their home in Kurdistan. When Jalalizadeh was elected to a leadership post in the Sixth Majlis, he faced objections from Shiite MPs who did not want such a post to go to a Sunni. The GC then disqualified him from running in any subsequent election for the Majlis. Jalalizadeh was the only Sunni member of the central council of IIPF during his term. He is now a professor of theology at Tehran University.

Jalili, Esma'il

Deputy of the Ninth Majlis, Masjed Soleyman, Lali, Haftkel, and Andika, Khuzestan (2012–16)

1967–, Abadan, Khuzestan
BA, public administration, Islamic Azad University; MS, systems management, Tarbiyat-e Modarres University; PhD, strategic management, Tarbiyat-e Modarres University
Father's name unknown, laborer
University instructor and civil servant
No imprisonment
War veteran (wounded)
Jalili ran unsuccessfully for the Tenth Majlis.

Jalili, Sa'id

Secretary of the Supreme Council for National Security (June 28, 2008–October 9, 2013); member of Seventh (2013–17) and Eighth (2017–22) Expediency Discernment Assembly
1965–, Mashhad, Razavi Khorasan
PhD, political science, Imam Sadeq University; dissertation title: "Political Thought in the Qur'an"
Mohammad-Hasan, teacher (retired)
Civil servant
No imprisonment
War veteran (lost his right leg in 1987)
IRGC militiaman
Jalili started working in the Iranian Ministry of Foreign Affairs in 1989 and rose through the ranks to become head of the Europe and North America Bureau. In 2001, he worked in the Office of the Supreme Leader, and in 2007, he became the secretary of the SCNS. Under President Ahmadinejad, Jalili was Iran's chief nuclear negotiator with Western powers from October 21, 2007, to August 16, 2013). He was the youngest member of the Sixth EDA. As a candidate in the 2013 presidential election, he received 11 percent of the vote. He decided not to run for the presidency in 2017 after failing to reach a consensus among the conservatives. His brother, Vahid Jalili, is an IRGC commander.

Jalili-Shishvan, Ali

Deputy of the Tenth Majlis, Maragheh and Ajab-Shir, East Azerbaijan (2017–20)

October 6, 1969–, Ajab-Shir, East Azerbaijan
PhD, psychology, Allameh Tabataba'i University
University professor and tae kwon do coach
No imprisonment
Jalili, who has a black belt in tae kwon do, was elected in
    midterm elections to fill the seat of elected MP Mo-
    hammad-Ali Hoseynzadeh, who died in May 2016
    a few weeks before the Tenth Majlis was to begin.

Jaliliyan, Ali

Deputy of the Ninth Majlis, Islamabad-e Gharb and
    Dalahu, Kermanshah (2012–16)
1962–, Islamabad-e Gharb, Kermanshah
BA, law, Tehran University; MA, law, Islamic Azad
    University–Khorramabad; pursuing a PhD in law
Father's name unknown, farmer
Judiciary official in Kermanshah
No imprisonment
War veteran

Jalilkhani, Gholam-Hoseyn

Deputy of the Fifth Majlis, Zanjan and Tarom, Zanjan
    (1997–2000)
1957–, Zanjan, Zanjan
MA, management
Mohammad-Hoseyn
No imprisonment

Jalil-Sarqal'eh, Majid

Deputy of the Ninth Majlis, Lordegan, Chahar Mahal
    and Bakhtiari (2012–16)
1964–, Lordegan, Chahar Mahal and Bakhtiari
BS, electrical engineering; MA, jurisprudence and
    Islamic law, Shahid Mahalati University; pursuing
    a PhD in crisis management
University professor; civil servant, state companies
No imprisonment
War veteran (twenty-six months)
IRGC militiaman (1983–2003)
Jalil-Sarqal'eh decided not to run for the Tenth Majlis.
    He works as a civil servant.

Jama'ati-Malvani, Rasul

Deputy of the Sixth Majlis, Fuman, Gilan
    (2000–2004)
1968–, Fuman, Gilan
BA, public administration
Reza
Civil servant
No imprisonment
After leaving the Majlis, Jama'ati-Malvani went to the
    private sector.

Jamali, Mahmud

Deputy of the Third (1989–92), Fourth (1992–96), and
    Fifth (1996–2000) Majlis, Kashan, Isfahan
1946–, Kashan, Isfahan
BS, mechanical engineering
Abbas
No imprisonment

Jamali, Manuchehr

Deputy of the Tenth Majlis, Rudbar, Gilan (2016–20)
1965–, Rudbar, Gilan
MD
Father's name unknown, farmer
Medical doctor and hospital administrator; member
    of the Rasht City Council
No imprisonment

Jamali-Nowbandegani, Mohammad-Javad

Deputy of the Tenth Majlis, Fasa, Fars (2016–20)
1963–, Nowbandegan, Fars
MD, Shiraz University of Medical Sciences, 1989;
    general surgery, Tehran University of Medical
    Sciences, 1996
Hospital chief
No imprisonment
IRGC militiaman (joined in 1981)
Jamali was formerly chief of Iran Hospital in Shiraz
    (2001–3), Valiasr Hospital in Tehran (2003–7), and
    Iranian medical centers in Dubai (2007–10). He

has been chief of Najmiyeh Hospital in Tehran since 2010.

Jamal-Yusefi [Dashti], Ebrahim

Deputy of the Second Majlis, Dashti and Tangestan, Bushehr (1984–88); member of the First Assembly of Experts, Bushehr (1984–90)
1939–, Khormuj, Bushehr
Clerical education
Javad
Clergyman and Friday prayer leader of Bushehr
No imprisonment
Not a war veteran
HI Jamal-Yusefi, the former Friday prayer leader of Bushehr, was a founder of the central council of Friday prayer leaders. As a radical, he unsuccessfully challenged the credentials of Ayatollah Azari-Qomi in the Second Majlis. He was elected to First AE in interim elections held on April 15, 1984. After his term ended, he devoted himself fully to his clerical duties.

Jami, Asadollah

Deputy of the Third Majlis, Torbat-e Jam and Taybad, Razavi Khorasan (1988–92)
1961–, Torbat-e Jam, Razavi Khorasan
High school diploma; religious education
Nasrollah
No imprisonment
In 2003–4, Jami was director-general of print and publishing for the Ministry of Culture. He registered to run for the Tenth Majlis.

Jami, Gholam-Hoseyn

Member of the First Assembly of Experts, Khuzestan (1983–90)
1925–2008, Bandar-e Bushehr, Bushehr
Clerical education, Najaf Seminary (Iraq)
Father's name unknown, clergyman
Clergyman
Imprisoned before the revolution

War veteran
HI Jami, who was active in the anti-shah movement, became Friday prayer leader and Ayatollah Khomeini's representative in Abadan in 1980.

Jamshidi-Ardeshiri, Mohammad-Hasan

Deputy of the Fourth (1992–96), Fifth (1996–2000), and Seventh (2004–8) Majlis, Behshahr, Mazandaran
1941–, Neka, Mazandaran
Clerical education
Mohammad-Hasan
Clergyman
No imprisonment
War veteran (POW for nine years)
IRGC militiaman
Martyr's family (son; another son wounded)
He ran unsuccessfully for the Tenth Majlis.

Jamshidinezhad, Iraj

Deputy of the Fifth Majlis, Islamabad-e Gharb, Kermanshah (1996–2000)
1950–, Islamabad-e Gharb, Kermanshah
BS, electrical engineering
Qasem-Ali
No imprisonment

Jamshidzehi, Abdolaziz

Deputy of the Eighth Majlis, Saravan, Sistan and Baluchestan (2008–12)
1969–, Saravan, Sistan and Baluchestan
MD, medicine
Tajmohammad
Medical doctor
No imprisonment
Jamshidzehi, a Sunni, ran unsuccessfully for the Ninth Majlis.

Jandaqi, Abbas

Deputy of the Fifth Majlis, Garmsar, Semnan (1996–2000)

1961–, Garmsar, Semnan
MD, medicine
Qorban-Ali
Medical doctor
No imprisonment

Jani-Abbaspur, Ruhollah

Deputy of the Eighth (2008–12) and Ninth (2012–16)
    Majlis, Bu'inzahra, Qazvin
1960–, Bu'inzahra, Qazvin
BA, educational management; pursuing an MA in
    political science
Nabiyollah, farmer
Governor of Alborz Industrial City
No imprisonment
War veteran (twenty-two months)
Martyr's family (brother; another brother wounded)
Secretary-general of the Islamic Society of Iranian
    Academics

Jannati, Ahmad

Member of the First (1980–86), Second (1986–92),
    Third (1992–98), Fourth (1998–2004), Fifth
    (2004–10), Sixth (2010–16), and Seventh (2016–19)
    Guardian Councils; member of the First (1983–
    90) and Second (1991–98) Assembly of Experts,
    Khuzestan; member of the Third (1999–2006),
    Fourth (2007–16), and Fifth (2016–22) Assembly
    of Experts, Tehran; member of the Fourth (1997–
    2002), Fifth (2002–7), Sixth (2007–12), Seventh
    (2012–17), and Eighth (2017–22) Expediency
    Discernment Assembly
February 23, 1927–, Ladan, Isfahan
Clerical education, Qom Seminary
Hashem, clergyman (molla)
Clergyman (ayatollah)
Imprisoned before the revolution
Not a war veteran
Member of the SQSS
Jannati is one of the most important political person-
    alities in postrevolutionary Iran. An archconser-
    vative cleric, he was born into a clerical family

also known for producing good quality quince
and pear. Before the revolution, he was one of the
directors of the conservative Haqqani Seminary
in Qom. After the revolution, Jannati held several
positions including revolutionary court judge in
Ahvaz, Isfahan, and Tehran; temporary Friday
prayer leader of Kermanshah, Ahvaz, Qom, and
Tehran (appointed in March 1992); and head of
the Islamic Propaganda Organization. Ayatollah
Khomeini appointed him to the founding board
for the women's seminary in Qom, and he headed
the provincial Friday prayer leaders' committee.
Jannati was also Ayatollah Khamenei's representative in Balkan affairs, and chaired the central
council of the Office of Representatives of the
Supreme Leader in Universities. Jannati is the longest-serving member of the GC, with seven terms
so far, and has served as its secretary since July
1992. In 2007, he failed to garner enough votes
to become the chairman of the Fourth AE, but he
was elected to that post in the Fifth Assembly in
May 2016 with fifty-one yes votes out of eighty-six
total votes. As such, he was concurrently in charge
of two important political institutions. Jannati's
son Hoseyn joined the opposition PMOI and was
killed in a battle with security forces in 1982. Another son, Ali, was minister of culture and Islamic
guidance for three years under President Rouhani.

Jannati, Ali

Minister of culture and Islamic guidance in President
    Rouhani's first cabinet (August 15, 2013–October
    19, 2016)
1949–, Isfahan, Isfahan
Clerical education, Haqqani Seminary
Ahmad, clergyman
Civil servant, ministries
Imprisoned before the revolution
Not a war veteran
Until 1973, Ali Jannati was a cleric and was affiliated
    with PMOI. He left Iran in 1975 for Lebanon and
    worked with Imam Musa Sadr's AMAL orga-
    nization before returning to Iran in February

1979. Jannati, who also lived in Kuwait before the revolution, has held several positions including head of Khuzestan IRIB (1980), governor-general of Khuzestan (1984–87), HI Hashemi-Rafsanjani's chief of staff during his term as Majlis Speaker (1987–88), governor-general of Khorasan (1989–92), deputy for international affairs in the Ministry of Culture and Islamic Guidance (1992–98), and ambassador to Kuwait (1998–2010). Jannati was a political deputy at MI and knew Hassan Rouhani from their time together in the oversight committee of IRIB. He resigned from his post as minister in October 2016.

Jarareh, Abolqasem

Deputy of the Ninth Majlis, Bandar-e Abbas, Qeshm, Abumusa, Hajiabad, and Khamir, Hormozgan (2012–16)
1981–, Bandar-e Abbas, Hormozgan
BA, law, Islamic Azad University–Bandar-e Abbas, 2004; MA, Law, Islamic Azad University–Bandar-e Abbas
University instructor and researcher
No imprisonment
Not a war veteran
Jarareh was the youngest person elected to the Ninth Majlis.

[Ja'far-Ali] Jasbi, Abdollah

Rector of Islamic Azad University (April 1982–January 17, 2012)
October 26, 1944–, Tehran, Tehran
BS, industrial engineering, Iran University of Science and Technology 1966; MS, industrial management, Aston University (England); PhD, production management and technology, Aston University (England)
Eskandar, confectioner
No imprisonment
Not a war veteran
Deputy secretary of the IRP (appointed in 1983)
Jasbi was a member of an underground militant group before the revolution and was also active in the

Muslim Student Organization in Birmingham, England. He helped to found Islamic Azad University, one of the world's largest free universities, in April 1982, and served as its first rector for thirty years. Jasbi has held such other posts as adviser to interior minister Hashemi-Rafsanjani (1979), deputy PM (under PM Raja'i, PM Bahonar, interim PM Mahdavi-Kani, and PM Musavi), member and secretary of the HCCR (appointed in 1990), professor at Iran University of Science and Technology, and member of the board of trustees of the National Elites Foundation. PM Raja'i proposed him as minister of commerce but President Banisadr did not approve his appointment. Jasbi has also been the proprietor of such journals, magazines, and newspapers as *International Journal of Management and Business Research*, *Farhikhtegan* (Enlightened), and *Afarinesh* (Creation). He was a presidential candidate in 1993 and 2001 and respectively received 8.9 and 0.92 percent of the vote. Jasbi was very close to former president Hashemi-Rafsanjani and is the brother-in-law of Ali Abbaspur-Tehranifard.

Jasemi, Seyyed Heshmatollah

Deputy of the Seventh Majlis, Qasr-e Shirin, Sarpol-e Zahab, and Gilan-e Gharb, Kermanshah (2004–8)
1960–, Sarpol-e Zahab, Kermanshah
Associate's degree
Seyyed Hasan
Civil servant
No imprisonment

Jasemi, Seyyed Qasem

Deputy of the Tenth Majlis, Kermanshah, Kermanshah (2016–20)
1965–, Kermanshah, Kermanshah
MA, geography and urban planning
Seyyed Ali
No imprisonment
War veteran (wounded in a chemical attack during Iran–Iraq War)
IRGC militiaman (commander)

Javadi-Amoli [Va'ez-Javadi], Abdollah

Member of the Assembly for the Final Examination of
    the Constitution, Mazandaran (1979); member of
    the HCJ (July 13, 1980–January 6, 1983); member
    of the First (1983–90) and Second (1991–98) As-
    sembly of Experts, Mazandaran
1933–, Amol, Mazandaran
Clerical education, Qom Seminary, 1968
Mirza Abolhasan, clergyman
Clergyman
No imprisonment
Not a war veteran
Member of the SQSS
Ayatollah Javadi-Amoli, who has a strong interest
    in Islamic philosophy, was the Friday prayer
    leader of Qom for almost thirty years before
    resigning on November 27, 2009. He was the
    head of revolutionary tribunals, and in 1988,
    he delivered Ayatollah Khomeini's message to
    Soviet leader Mikhail Gorbachev. His daughter
    is married to the son of Ayatollah Musavi-Ard-
    abili. His granddaughter (daughter of the above
    marriage) is married to the son of Mohammad
    Hashemi-Bahremani.

Jelowdarzadeh, Mrs. Sohayla

Deputy of the Fifth (1996–2000), Sixth (2000–2004),
    Seventh (2006–8), and Tenth (2016–20) Majlis,
    Tehran, Tehran
1959–, Tehran, Tehran
BS, textile engineering, Amirkabir University of
    Technology
Mohammad, glazier
High school teacher; minister of labor's representative
    in the Women's Cultural and Social Council
No imprisonment
Founding member of the Islamic Association of La-
    dies and the Association of Women of the Islamic
    Republic of Iran; founding member of the central
    council of the Islamic Labor Party
In the Sixth Majlis, Jelowdarzadeh became the first
    woman in the postrevolutionary period to become

a member of the leadership team. She did not
    receive enough votes to get elected to the Ninth
    Majlis. Jelowdarzadeh, who has an extensive
    background in social and labor issues, became an
    adviser to the minister of industries on women's
    issues under President Rouhani. She has also been
    an adviser on women and family issues in the EDA.

Jomeyri, Abdolkarim

Deputy of the Ninth Majlis, Bushehr, Genaveh, and
    Deylam, Bushehr (2012–16)
1960–, Bandar-e Bushehr, Bushehr
BA, law, Shahid Beheshti University; MA, public law,
    Islamic Azad University–Fars
High school teacher and provincial civil servant
No imprisonment
Not a war veteran
IRGC militiaman
Jomeyri ran unsuccessfully for the Eighth Majlis.

Joneydi, La'ya

VP for legal affairs in President Rouhani's second
    cabinet (2017–21)
1968–, Babol, Mazandaran
BA, law, Tehran University, 1989; MA, law, Tehran Uni-
    versity, 1994; PhD, law, Tehran University, 2000
Professor of law at Tehran University
No imprisonment
Not a war veteran
In 2002–3, Joneydi was a visiting fellow at Harvard
    Law School and worked on a research project
    titled "A Comparative Study of Commercial Arbi-
    tration in Islamic Law and Other Major Contem-
    porary Legal Systems."

Jowkar, Mohammad-Saleh

Deputy of the Ninth Majlis, Yazd and Saduq, Yazd
    (2012–16)
1957–, Yazd, Yazd
BS, biological sciences, Isfahan University of Medical
    Sciences, 1984; MS, biological sciences, Isfahan

University of Medical Sciences, 1991; PhD, national security, Ground Forces Officers' Academy
Baqer, construction foreman
No imprisonment
War veteran
IRGC militiaman
Jowkar is a former IRGC commander in Yazd, Hormozgan, and Chahar Mahal and Bakhtiari. He has also been the head of Imam Hoseyn University in Yazd since 1999. On December 10, 2017, the IRGC commander appointed him as the organization's legal and parliamentary deputy.

Joygeri, Shabib

Deputy of the Seventh (2006–8) and Eighth (2008–12) Majlis, Ahvaz, Khuzestan
1967–, Ahvaz, Khuzestan
MD, medicine, Ahvaz University
Abdolhamid, clergyman
Office of the Supreme Leader
No imprisonment
Joygeri, a former ambassador to Sudan, registered to run in the Tenth Majlis election.

Ka'bi, Abdollah

Deputy of the Fifth (1996–2000), Sixth (2000–2004), Seventh (2004–8), and Eighth (2008–12) Majlis, Abadan, Khuzestan
1953–, Khorramshahr, Khuzestan
Associate's degree
Bahador
Civil servant
No imprisonment
Ka'bi ran unsuccessfully for the Ninth Majlis and then became an adviser on parliamentary affairs to the minister of petroleum.

Ka'bi, Amer

Deputy of the Tenth Majlis, Abadan, Khuzestan (2016–20)

1971–, Abadan, Khuzestan
BS, mathematics, Shahid Bahonar University of Kerman, 1994; MS, mathematics, Tarbiyat-e Modarres University, 1997; PhD, mathematics, Ferdowsi University of Mashhad, 2005
Father's name unknown, clergyman
Professor at Khorramshahr University of Marine Science and Technology since 2006
No imprisonment

Ka'bi [-Nasab], Abbas

Member of the Third (1999–2006), Fourth (2007–16), and Fifth (2016–22) Assembly of Experts, Khuzestan; member of the Fifth Guardian Council (2004–10)
1962–, Ahvaz, Khuzestan
BA, law, Qom Higher Education Complex; MA, public law, Tehran University; clerical education, Qom Seminary
Mohammad
Clergyman
No imprisonment
War veteran (forty-six months; wounded)
IRGC militiaman
Martyr's family (brother)
Member of the SQSS
Ayatollah Ka'bi went to Lebanon in 1981 and helped to set up Hezbollah forces there. He was elected to the Fifth GC as a lawyer and not as a cleric. He is the secretary of the specialized school of jurisprudence at the World Center for Islamic Sciences.

Kabiri, Qanbar [Ahmad]

Deputy of the Second (1984–88) and Third (1988–92) Majlis, Marvdasht, Fars
1952–, Marvdasht, Fars
BS, agricultural engineering
Ja'far
No imprisonment
After serving in the Majlis, Kabiri, who is a reformist, became a civil servant.

Kabiri, Seyyed Taqi

Deputy of the Tenth Majlis, Khoy and Chaypareh, West Azerbaijan (2016–20)
1965–, Khoy, West Azerbaijan
MA, Qur'anic sciences, Islamic Azad University–Khoy, 1993; PhD, Qur'anic sciences, Islamic Azad University–Science and Research Branch
University professor and administrator
No imprisonment
IRGC militiaman (Basij)

Kadivar, Mrs. Jamileh

Deputy of the Sixth Majlis, Tehran, Tehran (2000–2004)
1963–, Shiraz, Fars
BA, political science, Tehran University, 1988; MA, international relations, 1992; PhD, political science, Tehran University, 1999; dissertation title: "The Evolution of the Political Discourse of Shiism in Iran"
Manuchehr, academia
Journalist
No imprisonment
Secretary-general of the Iranian Women Journalists Association
Before being elected to the Sixth Majlis, Kadivar held several posts including professor at Alzahra University, adviser to President Khatami, member of the Tehran City Council, and member of the editorial board of *Ettela'at*. In the 2000 Majlis elections, she received the second highest percentage of votes (47 percent) from Tehran. During the contested 2009 presidential election, she was Mehdi Karrubi's adviser on women's affairs. Kadivar is the wife of former culture minister Ataollah Mohajerani and the sister of dissident cleric Mohsen Kadivar. She and her husband now live in England and her brother is in the United States.

Kadkhoda'i [-Elyaderani], Abbas-Ali

Member of the Fourth (2001–4), Fifth (2004–10), Sixth (2010–13), and Seventh (2016–22) Guardian Councils
1961–, Isfahan, Isfahan
BA, law, Tehran University; MA, law, University of Hull (England), 1992; PhD, law, University of Leeds (England), 1997
Ali-Reza
Civil servant
No imprisonment
Not a war veteran
Kadkhoda'i's service in the Fifth GC was interrupted, as he served from 2004 until July 2007 and then again from November 2009 to July 2010. He was spokesperson of the GC for many years. In 2011, Ayatollah Khamenei appointed him to the five-person Dispute Settlement Committee of Branches. In 2013, he failed to secure enough votes from the Ninth Majlis to continue serving on the GC. Kadkhoda'i subsequently became an adviser to the head of the GC, Ayatollah Ahmad Jannati. In 2016, he was elected to the GC for the fourth time.

Kaeidi, Ali-Akbar

Deputy of the Eighth (2008–12) and Ninth (2012–16) Majlis, Pol-e Dokhtar and Malavi, Lorestan
1959–, Pol-e Dokhtar, Lorestan
MD, medicine
Malek-Mohammad
Medical doctor (general practice)
No imprisonment
Martyr's family (father and brother killed at the war front)
Kaeidi was elected to the Eighth Majlis in an election marred by violence between his supporters and those of his chief rival HI Ali Shahrokhi-Qobadi.

Kahraze'i, Akhtar-Mohammad

Deputy of the Fourth Majlis, Khash, Sistan and Balu-
chestan (1992–96)
1948–, Khash, Sistan and Baluchestan
High school diploma
Ashur
No imprisonment
Kahraze'i, a Sunni, was born in the village of Sangan,
close to Khash.

Kalantari, Ali-Akbar

Member of the Fifth Assembly of Experts, Fars
(2016–22)
1962–, Arsanjan, Fars
Clerical education, Qom Seminary, 1999; MS, the-
ology, Qom University; PhD, Qur'anic sciences,
Qom University, 2002
Gholam-Abbas, farmer
No imprisonment
Not a war veteran
Ayatollah Kalantari was head of the faculty of
theology at Shiraz University from 2013 to
2014.

Kalantari, Isa

Minister of agriculture in PM Musavi's second cabinet
(September 20, 1988–August 3, 1989), President
Hashemi-Rafsanjani's first (August 29, 1989–August 2, 1993) and second (August 16, 1993–August
2, 1997) cabinets, and President Khatami's first
cabinet (August 20, 1997–2001); VP and head of
the Environmental Protection Organization in
President Rouhani's second cabinet (August 20,
2017–2021)
1952–, Marand, East Azerbaijan
BS, agricultural engineering; MS, agricultural engineering; PhD, agricultural engineering, Iowa State
University (USA), 1981; dissertation title: "Stimu-
lation of Corn Seedling Growth by Allelochemi-
cals from Soybean Residue"
Mohammad-Hoseyn, farmer

Civil servant, ministries
No imprisonment
Not a war veteran
Martyr's family (older brother Musa was killed in the
bombing of the IRP headquarters)
The GC disqualified Kalantari from running in
the 2008 Majlis election. After leaving office,
he founded the NGO House of the Farmer. On
August 28, 1983, he failed to receive enough votes
from the Majlis to become the minister of agriculture (seventy-four in favor, fifty-seven opposed,
and fifty-eight in abstention). He is a leading
expert on agricultural issues, and he has consis-
tently warned the government about agricultural
issues including water usage.

Kalantari, Musa

Minister of roads and transportation in PM Raja'i's
cabinet (September 10, 1980–June 28, 1981)
1948–June 28, 1981, Marand, East Azerbaijan
MS, civil engineering, Amirkabir University of
Technology
Mohammad-Hoseyn, farmer
Civil servant
No imprisonment
Not a war veteran
Member of the IRP
Kalantari, who took part in an armed struggle in the
days leading up to the 1979 revolution, became
general director of roads and transportation
in West Azerbaijan Province before becoming
minister. He was killed in the bombing of the IRP
headquarters.

Kalateh'i, Mohammad

Deputy of the Second Majlis, Bojnurd, North Kho-
rasan (1984–February 20, 1986)
1947–February 20, 1986, Bojnurd, North Khorasan
Pre-high school diploma
Ebrahim
No imprisonment
Kalateh'i died when Iraqis shot down his plane.

Kalhor, Abolfazl

Deputy of the Seventh Majlis, Shahriyar, Tehran
    (2004–8)
1954–2017, Shahriyar, Tehran
BA, public administration
Ali
Civil servant, state companies
No imprisonment

Kalimi-Nikruz, Manuchehr

Deputy of the Second (1984–88) and Third (1988–92)
    Majlis, representing the Jewish community (as a
    religious minority)
September 17, 1946–January 31, 1995, Isfahan, Isfahan
PhD, pharmacology, Tabriz University, 1971
Ebrahim
No imprisonment

Kamali, Hoseyn

Deputy of the First (1981–84), Second (1984–88), and
    Third (1988–August 29, 1989) Majlis, Tehran, Teh-
    ran; minister of labor and social affairs in President
    Hashemi-Rafsanjani's first (August 29, 1989–Au-
    gust 2, 1993) and second (August 16, 1993–August
    2, 1997) cabinets and President Khatami's first
    cabinet (August 20, 1997–August 1, 2001)
1953–, Dorud, Lorestan
BA, political science, Tehran University; MA, political
    science, 1997
Hasan
Journalist
No imprisonment
Not a war veteran
Secretary-general of the Islamic Labor Party starting
    in 2001
Kamali was a founding member of House of the
    Worker. He resigned from the Third Majlis to
    become the minister of labor and social affairs.
    At that time, he only had a high school diploma.
    He later was an adviser to Ayatollah Hashemi-
    Rafsanjani as head of the EDA.

Kamaliniya, Mohammad-Taqi

Deputy of the First Majlis, Quchan, Razavi Khorasan
    (1980–June 22, 1981)
1944–June 22, 1981, Quchan, Razavi Khorasan
MA, Islamic law; clerical education
Gholam-Hasan, farmer
Academia
No imprisonment
Not a war veteran
Kamaliniya died in 1981 when a building collapsed
    due to structural flaws.

Kamalipur, Yahya

Deputy of the Tenth Majlis, Jiroft, Kerman (2016–20)
1969–, Jiroft, Kerman
MA, law
Judiciary official in Kerman Province
No imprisonment
War veteran (wounded; POW)
Kamalipur was a high-level official in the justice
    administration of Jiroft and Bam and a judicial
    deputy of revolutionary courts in Kerman. He ran
    unsuccessfully for the Ninth Majlis.

Kamaliyan, Nasrollah

Deputy of the Eighth Majlis, Quchan and Faruj, Ra-
    zavi Khorasan (2009–12)
1950–, Quchan, Razavi Khorasan
BS, physics, Ferdowsi University of Mashhad, 1973;
    MS, geophysics, Tehran University, 1980; PhD,
    geology, Indian Institute of Technology (India),
    1994
Mahmud
Academia
Imprisoned before the revolution
Not a war veteran
Kamaliyan has served in such roles as governor of
    Zahedan and Khash, rector of Sistan and Baluch-
    estan University, and director of the Geophysics
    Institute at Tehran University (1985–89). He ran
    unsuccessfully for the Ninth Majlis.

Kambuzia, Ja'far

Deputy of the Sixth Majlis, Zahedan, Sistan and Balu-
    chestan (2000–2004)
1960–, Zahedan, Sistan and Baluchestan
PhD, agricultural engineering
Amir-Tavakol
Civil servant
No imprisonment
After leaving the Majlis, Kambuzia became a civil
    servant.

Kamran-Dastjerdi, Hasan

Deputy of the Fourth (1992–96), Fifth (1999–2000),
    Seventh (2004–8), Eighth (2008–12), Ninth (2012–
    16), and Tenth (2017–20) Majlis, Isfahan, Isfahan
1954–, Dastjerd, Isfahan
PhD, political geography
Mohammad-Ali
No imprisonment
IRGC militiaman
Kamran-Dastjerdi headed the Majlis Commission on
    National Security and Foreign Policy in the Ninth
    Majlis. His wife is MP Nayyereh Akhavan-Bitaraf.
    He was elected to the Tenth Majlis in 2017 mid-
    term elections.

Kamyar, Ali

Deputy of the Second (1984–88), Third (1988–92), and
    Fourth (1992–96) Majlis, Urmia, West Azerbaijan
1957–, Urmia, West Azerbaijan
BA, theology, 1988
Jamshid
No imprisonment
During the Third Majlis, questions were raised about
    Kamyar's cooperation with outlawed groups in
    Urmia but he managed to keep his seat.

Karamatlu, Abbas-Ali

Deputy of the Fifth Majlis, Minudasht, Golestan
    (1996–2000)

1951–, Minudasht, Golestan
Clerical education; six years of elementary school
Mohsen
Clergyman (HI)
No imprisonment

Karami, Abdoljabbar

Deputy of the Eighth Majlis, Sanandaj, Divandarreh,
    and Kamyaran, Kurdistan (2008–12)
1969–, Behbahan, Khuzestan
MD, medicine, Kurdistan University of Medical Sci-
    ences, 1998
Mohammad-Karim, army officer
Medical doctor
No imprisonment
Not a war veteran
After serving in the Majlis, Karami, a Sunni, went on
    to manage a private medical clinic.

Karami, Ali Mir

Deputy of the Fourth Majlis, Qasr-e Shirin, Kerman-
    shah (1992–96)
1954–, Sarpol-e Zahab, Kermanshah
High school diploma
Hasan
No imprisonment

Karami, Gholam-Reza

Deputy of the Seventh (2004–8) and Eighth (2008–12)
    Majlis, Kerman and Ravar, Kerman
1957–, Kerman, Kerman
MS, defense management
Ali
No imprisonment
IRGC militiaman
After running unsuccessfully for the Ninth Majlis,
    Karami rejoined the military establishment.

Karami, Mohammad

Member of the Assembly for the Final Examination of
    the Constitution, Khuzestan (1979)

1921–2003, Najaf, Iraq
Clerical education, Najaf Seminary (Iraq)
Mohammad-Taha, clergyman
Clergyman
No imprisonment
Not a war veteran
Ayatollah Karami was in charge of revolutionary committees in Ahvaz. After finishing his work in the AFEC, he returned to Ahvaz to continue his religious teaching. His brother, Mohammad-Mehdi, was an MP for a year in the First Majlis.

Karami, Mohammad-Mehdi

Deputy of the First Majlis, Dasht-e Azadegan, Khuzestan (1980–January 7, 1982)
1948–, Najaf, Iraq
Clerical education
Mohammad-Taha, clergyman
No imprisonment
The Majlis voted on January 7, 1982, that Karami's absenteeism meant that he had resigned from his post. He left the First Majlis and joined the military establishment.

Karami, Morteza

Deputy of the Seventh Majlis, Ilam, Eyvan, Mehran, Malekshahi, and Shirvan, Ilam (2004)
1963–December 19, 2004, Ilam, Ilam
MA, educational management
Karam-Reza
Academia
No imprisonment
IRGC militiaman
Karami died in a car accident.

Karamirad, Mohammad

Deputy of the Eighth Majlis, Kermanshah, Kermanshah (2008–12)
1960–, Kermanshah, Kermanshah
PhD, political science; clerical education, Isfahan Seminary

Esma'il
Imprisoned before the revolution
War veteran
IRGC militiaman
Karamirad was one of the founders of the IRGC in Kermanshah.

Karampur-Haqiqi, Kurosh

Deputy of the Tenth Majlis, Firuzabad, Fars (2016–20)
1958–, Firuzabad, Fars
Imprisoned before the revolution
War veteran (seventy-two months, wounded)
IRGC militiaman
Martyr's family (two brothers and a brother-in-law)
Karampur-Haqiqi is a former governor of Masjed Soleyman (2006).

Karbaschi [-Tehrani], Gholam-Hoseyn

Mayor of Tehran (1989–98)
1953–, Qom, Qom
BS, mathematics, Tehran University (incomplete); Clerical education, Qom Seminary
Mohammad-Sadeq, clergyman (ayatollah)
Governor of Isfahan
Imprisoned before the revolution
Not a war veteran
Secretary-general of PECI
The son of an ayatollah, Karbaschi studied theology at Qom Seminary and mathematics at Tehran University, but he did not finish his BA degree because he was arrested by the shah's regime. He traded in his clerical robe for civilian clothes and had a successful political career, serving in the IRIB, Gendarmerie Force (as Ayatollah Khomeini's representative), as the governor of Isfahan, and finally as the mayor of Tehran. Karbaschi garnered a great deal of attention in this latter post for skillfully transforming the reputation of Tehran as a mega-city. In 1992, while serving as Tehran's mayor, he founded the popular *Hamshahri*. On April 4, 1998, Karbaschi, a reformist ally of

President Khatami, was arrested on corruption charges and his televised "show trial" captivated the Iranian public. The SCFC sentenced him to five years in prison for mismanagement of state funds but acquitted him on a bribery charge. The Court of Appeals later reduced his sentence from five years to two.

Karbasiyan, Mas'ud

Minister of economic affairs and finance in President Rouhani's second cabinet (August 20, 2017–2021)
1956–, Isfahan, Isfahan
BS, planning; MA, management; PhD, business administration
Head of the Iran Customs Administration (2013–17)
Ahmad
No imprisonment
From 1989 to 2001, Karbasiyan served as a deputy in such ministries as the Ministry of Heavy Industries, Ministry of Commerce, and Ministry of Petroleum. He was also a senior adviser to Tehran's mayor.

Karimi, Ali-Akbar

Deputy of the Tenth Majlis, Arak, Komijan, and Khondab, Markazi (2016–20)
1968–, Arak, Markazi
BA, economics, Tehran University, 1990; MA, economics, Islamic Azad University–Arak, 1995; PhD, strategic management, Supreme National Defense University, 2003
Director-general of a housing company
No imprisonment
War veteran (five years)
IRGC militiaman (Basij)
Karimi was an official in the Office of the President (beginning in 1991) and the FDWI, and he was mayor of Arak from 2007 to 2009. He has also occupied high-level administrative posts in Zanjan and East Azerbaijan Provinces.

Karimi, Foad

Deputy of the First (1980–84) and Second (1984–88) Majlis, Ahvaz, Khuzestan
1951–, Khorramshahr, Khuzestan
Associate's degree; clerical education
Abdolali, bazaar tradesman
No imprisonment
Not a war veteran
IRGC militiaman
After serving in the Majlis, Karimi worked in the Ministry of Welfare, where he became a deputy minister during the tenure of President Khatami. He has since retired from the ministry.

Karimi, Hamdollah

Deputy of the Tenth Majlis, Bijar, Kurdistan (2016–20)
1980–, Bijar, Kurdistan
Nabiyollah
Governor of Bijar (appointed December 6, 2012)
Not a war veteran
Martyr's family
Karimi's father was killed in 1981 while fighting opposition Kurdish forces.

Karimi, Hamid

Deputy of the Fifth Majlis, Ilam, Eyvan, and Chardavol, Ilam (1996–2000)
1957–, Mehran, Ilam
MA, management
Hoseyn
Provincial governor
No imprisonment
Karimi later became a manager in the Iranian oil company.

Karimi, Hoseyn

Head of the State Supreme Court (August 23, 2014–)
1951–, Mahneshan, Zanjan
Clerical education

Clergyman
Judiciary chief Sadeq Larijani appointed HI Karimi
   as head of the State Supreme Court on August 23,
   2014.

Karimi, Mohammad-Ali

Deputy of the Fourth (1992–96) and Seventh (2004–8)
   Majlis, Marivan, Kurdistan
1949–, Zhanin, Kurdistan
BA, political science, 1996
Asadollah
Civil servant, Agricultural Jihad
No imprisonment
Karimi is a Sunni.

Karimi, Reza

Deputy of the Second Majlis, Marand, East Azerbai-
   jan (1984–88)
November 24, 1943–September 26, 1999, Marand,
   East Azerbaijan
Clerical education, Qom Seminary, 1969
Mohammad, clergyman and farmer
Clergyman (HI)
No imprisonment

Karimi, Zabihollah

Deputy of the Fourth Majlis, Shushtar, Khuzestan
   (1992–96)
1963–, Farsan, Chahar Mahal and Bakhtiari
Associate's degree
Sardar
No imprisonment

Karimi [Bojnurd], Mohammad-Ali

Deputy of the Second Majlis, Bojnurd, North Khorasan (1984–88)
1956–, Bojnurd, North Khorasan
Clerical education
Abbas-Ali

No imprisonment
Not a war veteran
IRGC militiaman

Karimi [Kerman], Mohammad-Ali

Deputy of the Eighth Majlis, Kerman and Ravar, Ker-
   man (2008–12)
1958–, Kerman, Kerman
BS, physics, Shahid Bahonar University of Kerman;
   MS, physics, Shahid Bahonar University of
   Kerman
Mohammad-Ebrahim, clergyman (HI)
No imprisonment
Not a war veteran
IRGC militiaman
Mohammad-Ali Karimi was governor-general of
   Kerman under President Khatami. His wife is the
   daughter of HI Seyyed Reza Khoshro and sister of
   Seyyed Hasan Khoshro.

Karimi [Namin], Reza

Deputy of the Tenth Majlis, Ardabil, Ardabil
   (2016–20)
1970–, Namin, Ardabil
BS, agricultural engineering, University of Mohaqqeq
   Ardabili; MA, public administration
Khaleq
Civil servant, Office of the Ardabil Governor-General
No imprisonment
War veteran (eighteen months)
Karimi worked in the Office of the Ardabil Gover-
   nor-General for eighteen years as an expert. He
   ran unsuccessfully for the Ninth Majlis.

Karimi-Bizhaninezhad, Emadeddin

Deputy of the First Majlis, Nowshahr, Mazandaran
   (1980–June 28, 1981)
August 1, 1932–June 28, 1981, Nowshahr,
   Mazandaran
Clerical education, Qom Seminary

Mohammad, clergyman
Clergyman (HI)
No imprisonment
Not a war veteran
Member of IRP
Karimi-Bizhaninezhad was killed in the bombing of
    the IRP headquarters.

Karimi-Divkolahi, Seyyed Ja'far

Member of the Assembly for the Final Examination of
    the Constitution, Mazandaran (1979); member of
    the First (1983–90) and Third (1999–2006) Assem-
    bly of Experts, Mazandaran
1930–, Babol, Mazandaran
Clerical education, Najaf Seminary (Iraq)
Seyyed Reza, farmer
Clergyman (ayatollah)
No imprisonment
Not a war veteran
Member of the SQSS
Ayatollah Karimi-Divkolahi joined the radical para-
    military group Devotees of Islam in 1948, and
    then lived in Iraq from 1955 to 1978. He headed
    Ayatollah Khomeini's office of responding to
    correspondence from followers (1968–89), and
    then he did the same type of work for Ayatollah
    Khamenei. Karimi-Divkolahi was a member of
    the High Council of Religious Seminaries of Qom
    from 1979 to 1990, and he also headed the Disci-
    plinary Court for Judges and Public Prosecutors
    (December 30, 1982–94).

Karimi-Firuzjayi, Ali

Deputy of the Eighth Majlis, Babol, Mazandaran
    (2008–12)
1972–, Babol, Mazandaran
MA, linguistics
Mohammad
Civil servant, ministries
No imprisonment
Not a war veteran
Secretary-general of the Islamic Society of Engineers

Karimi-Munjermo'i, Ebrahim

Deputy of the Fifth Majlis, Borujen and Lordegan,
    Chahar Mahal and Bakhtiari (1996–2000)
1965–, Lordegan, Chahar Mahal and Bakhtiari
Clerical education
Karim
Clergyman
No imprisonment

Karimi-Qoddusi, Javad

Deputy of the Eighth (2008–12), Ninth (2012–16),
    and Tenth (2016–20) Majlis, Mashhad and Kalat,
    Razavi Khorasan
1956–, Mashhad, Razavi Khorasan
MA, law, Shiraz University
Abolqasem, tailor
No imprisonment
War veteran
IRGC militiaman

Karimirad, Jamal

Minister of justice in President Ahmadinejad's first
    cabinet (August 24, 2005–December 28, 2006)
1956–December 28, 2006, Qazvin, Qazvin
BA, law, University of Judicial Sciences and Admin-
    istrative Services, 1986; MA, international law,
    Tehran University, 2000; MA, public administra-
    tion, State Management Training Center
Fakhrollah
Prosecutor in the Disciplinary Court for Judges and
    Public Prosecutors (2003–5)
No imprisonment
Not a war veteran
Karimirad died in a car accident.

Karimiyan, Mohammad

Deputy of the Fourth (1993–96), Fifth (1996–2000),
    and Seventh (2004–8) Majlis, Sardasht and Piran-
    shahr, West Azerbaijan
1954–, Sardasht, Kurdistan

High school diploma
Ali
Civil servant
No imprisonment
War veteran (victim of a chemical attack)
Karimiyan is a Sunni.

Karimiyan, Omid

Deputy of the Ninth Majlis, Marivan and Sarvabad,
    Kurdistan (2012–16)
1975–, Marivan, Kurdistan
BA, public administration, Tehran University, 1998;
    MA, executive management, Tehran University,
    2011
Mohammad, laborer
Provincial civil servant and university instructor
No imprisonment
Not a war veteran
The GC disqualified Karimiyan, a Sunni, from run-
    ning in the 2016 Majlis election.

Karimpur-Natanzi, Mas'ud

Deputy of the Fourth Majlis, Qamsar and Natanz,
    Isfahan (1994–96)
1956–, Natanz, Isfahan
BA, law
Qorban-Ali
Judiciary official
No imprisonment
Karimpur-Natanzi ran unsuccessfully for the Tenth
    Majlis.

Karkhaneh, Ebrahim

Deputy of the Seventh (2004–8) and Ninth (2012–16)
    Majlis, Hamadan and Famenin, Hamadan
1950–, Gangavar, Kermanshah
MS, nuclear science; PhD, chemistry
Mohammad
University professor and administrator
No imprisonment
War veteran

Karkhaneh is a member of the conservative SFIR, and
    he was an archcritic of the 2015 nuclear deal with
    Western powers. He is a former director of the
    Iranian National Standards Organization.

Karrubi, Mrs. Fatemeh

Deputy of the Fifth Majlis, Tehran, Tehran
    (1999–2000)
1947–, Aligudarz, Lorestan
Pre-high school diploma
Reza, bazaar tradesman
Head of Khatam al-Anbia and Mostafa Khomeini
    Hospitals
No imprisonment
Secretary-general of the Islamic Association of Ladies;
    member of the National Trust Party; founder
    of the Alliance of the Women of the Islamic
    Republic
Fatemeh Sharifi (maiden name) married her husband,
    Mehdi Karrubi, in 1962 at the age of fifteen. She
    was in charge of *Irandokht* weekly magazine. She
    is the mother of four sons, one of whom, Mo-
    hammad-Taqi, lost a leg in the Iran–Iraq War.
    After the contested 2009 presidential election, the
    regime put her under house arrest along with her
    husband but she was released.

Karrubi, Mehdi

Deputy of the First Majlis, Aligudarz, Lorestan
    (1980–84); deputy of the Second (1984–88), Third
    (1988–92), and Sixth (2000–2004) Majlis, Tehran,
    Tehran; member of the Fifth Expediency Discern-
    ment Assembly (2004–7)
1937–, Aligudarz, Lorestan
Clerical education, Qom Seminary; BA, theology,
    Tehran University, 1972
Ahmad, clergyman
Clergyman
Imprisoned before the revolution
Not a war veteran
Founding member of the ACC; founder and secre-
    tary-general of the NTP (2005–16)

Mehdi Karrubi has been hugely influential in post-revolutionary Iranian politics. The son of a cleric whom the shah sent into exile, Mehdi was also imprisoned before the revolution. He gained his release from prison in early 1977 after taking part in a controversial ceremony praising the shah. After the revolution, he became a trusted lieutenant of Ayatollah Khomeini, who put him in charge of the Martyr's Foundation (April 1980–August 4, 1992) and the Pilgrimage Affairs (July 1985–90). Karrubi also headed IKRF for a period of time. He was involved in the secretive Iran-Contra negotiations that took place between Iranian and American officials in the 1980s, and he was also a member of the Council for Revision of the Constitution in 1989. He was the deputy Speaker (1985–89) and then Speaker of the Majlis (1989–92 and 2000–2004). After serving for sixteen years as a member of Majlis, he ran for president in 2005 and 2009. Both times, he accused the regime of rigging the vote. In 2005, Karrubi, who had been the leader of the ACC, broke with his colleagues over his election protest and founded the NTP. In 2009, he and Mir Hoseyn Musavi emerged as the two most prominent leaders of the Green Movement. The government claimed that Karrubi had only received 0.87 percent of the vote in the 2009 presidential election, whereas in the first round of the 2005 presidential election he had garnered 17.2 percent of the vote. He has been under house arrest with no official trial since 2011, and he has undergone numerous medical operations.

Kashani, Naser

Deputy of the Ninth Majlis, Zahedan, Sistan and Baluchestan (2012–16)
1971–, Mashhad, Razavi Khorasan
MD, medicine, Zahedan University of Medical Sciences
Medical doctor
No imprisonment
Not a war veteran

Kashani, a Sunni, comes from an important tribe in Sistan and Baluchestan.

Kashfi, Seyyed Mansur

Deputy of the Sixth Majlis, Larestan, Fars (2000–2004)
1960–, Lar, Fars
MD, medicine
Seyyed Mohammad-Hoseyn
Medical doctor
No imprisonment
IRGC militiaman

Kateb, Gholam-Reza

Deputy of the Ninth (2012–16) and Tenth (2016–20) Majlis, Garmsar and Aradan, Semnan
1962–, Garmsar, Semnan
BA, theology; MA, public administration; PhD, human resource management, Jamia Millia Islamia University (India)
Mohammad
Civil servant
No imprisonment
War veteran
IRGC militiaman
Kateb worked for FMVA and for the Management and Planning Organization. His credentials were called into question by a fellow MP in the Ninth Majlis but he responded by questioning the credentials of thirty other lawmakers. In the end, both sides dropped their charges.

Katira'i, Morteza

Deputy of the First Majlis, Malayer, Hamadan (1980–84); deputy of the Third Majlis, Tehran, Tehran (1988–92)
1931–May 21, 2012, Malayer, Hamadan
BS, physics, Tehran University
Hoseyn, bazaar tradesman
High school teacher and principal
No imprisonment

Not a war veteran

Founding member and secretary-general of the Islamic Association of Iranian Teachers

Katira'i was a member of the committee welcoming Ayatollah Khomeini back to Iran. Besides being an MP, he was also a deputy minister of education and deputy in the Institute for Compilation and Publication of Imam Khomeini's Work. His brother, Mostafa, was minister of housing and urban development in PM Bazargan's cabinet.

Katira'i, Mostafa

Member of the Revolutionary Council (1979); minister of housing and urban development in PM Bazargan's cabinet (1979) and the Revolutionary Council cabinet (1979)

1928–February 3, 2016, Malayer, Hamadan

MS, civil engineering, Tehran University, 1951

Hoseyn, bazaar tradesman

Civil engineer in the Ministry of Housing and Urban Development (for more than twenty years)

No imprisonment

Not a war veteran

Founding member of the Islamic Society of Engineers

Katira'i was one of the founders of the Islamic Society of Engineers in 1957. He worked as an engineer in the Ministry of Housing and Urban Development for more than twenty years before the revolution, and in 1978, he was one of the coordinators of the oil workers' strike. He left the Revolutionary Council to join Bazargan's cabinet, but after the cabinet resigned on November 5, 1979, he stayed on as minister of housing and urban development in the Revolutionary Council cabinet for two weeks, until November 20, 1979. A plan to assassinate him failed on October 13, 1979. After his time as minister, Katira'i, a civil engineer, worked as director of the Administrative and Recruitment Organization and for the judiciary dealing with construction issues. While Katira'i was not a member of the LMI, his political views were very close to that of its founder, Mehdi Bazargan. His brother, Morteza, served two terms in the Majlis.

Katuziyan, Hamid-Reza

Deputy of the Seventh (2004–8) and Eighth (2008–12) Majlis, Tehran, Tehran

1959–, Tehran, Tehran

BS, mechanical engineering, Amirkabir University of Technology; MS, mechanical engineering, Amirkabir University of Technology; PhD, mechanical engineering, Case Western Reserve University (USA), 1993; dissertation title: "Three Dimensional Design Optimization of Femoral Components of Total Hip Endoprostheses"

Mohammad-Reza

Professor at Amirkabir University of Technology

No imprisonment

War veteran

Martyr's family (brother)

Member of the Islamic Society of Engineers

In the Ninth Majlis elections, Katuziyan went to the second round but then withdrew his candidacy before the runoff elections were held. He is a former president of the Research Institute of Petroleum Industry and an adviser to the minister of petroleum.

Kavakebiyan, Mostafa

Deputy of the Eighth Majlis, Semnan, Semnan (2008–12); deputy of the Tenth Majlis, Tehran, Tehran (2016–20)

March 1, 1962–, Semnan, Semnan

Clerical education; BA, political science, Imam Sadeq University, 1982; MA, political science, Imam Sadeq University; PhD, political science, Tarbiyat-e Modarres University, 1997; dissertation title: "Legitimacy in the System of Velayat-e Faqih"

Haj Aqa, laborer (cloth-weaver)

Journalist and owner of Mardomsalari

No imprisonment

War veteran (wounded)

Martyr's family (brother and brother-in-law)

Member of the IRP; member of the Islamic Iran Solidarity Party; secretary-general of the Party of Democracy

Kavakebiyan ran unsuccessfully for the Ninth Majlis in 2012 and was disqualified from running in the presidential races in 2013 and 2017. He is a professor at Allameh Tabataba'i University.

Kaviyani[pur], Mohammad-Taqi

Deputy of the Seventh Majlis, Nahavand, Hamadan (2004–8)
1958–, Nahavand, Hamadan
MA, public administration
Nader
Civil servant
No imprisonment

Kavusi, Nader

Deputy of the Third Majlis, Tuyserkan, Hamadan (1988–92)
1955–, Tuyserkan, Hamadan
BS, civil engineering, Tehran University
Mehdi
No imprisonment
The GC deemed Kavusi, a reformist, unqualified to run for the Fourth Majlis.

Kazem-Dinan, Seyyed Mahmud

Deputy of the Third (1988–92), Fourth (1992–96), and Sixth (2000–2004) Majlis, Amol, Mazandaran
1939–2007, Amol, Mazandaran
BA, management, 1997
Seyyed Zia'
No imprisonment
IRGC militiaman
Martyr's family (two of his sons were killed at the war front)

Kazemi, Mohammad

Deputy of the Sixth (2000–2004) and Tenth (2016–20) Majlis, Malayer, Hamadan
1959–, Malayer, Hamadan
BA, law, Tehran University; MA, law

Mansur, farmer
Judiciary official (prosecutor)
No imprisonment
Not a war veteran
Kazemi, a reformist, was formerly the prosecutor of Hamadan, Kermanshah, and Ilam Provinces, representative of the State General Inspectorate Organization in Hamadan, deputy of the Justice Administration of Tehran Province, and legal director-general of the Social Security Organization.

Kazemi, Parviz

Minister of welfare and social security in President Ahmadinejad's first cabinet (November 9, 2005–October 2006)
1958–, Tehran, Tehran
MA, business administration, Tehran University, 1999
Darvish
CEO of Saipa and the Investment Company of Iran Khodro
No imprisonment
War veteran
IRGC militiaman
Martyr's family (brother, Naser)
Kazemi was in office for only ten months before he became the first minister to be dismissed by President Ahmadinejad. He was disqualified by the GC from running in the 2013 presidential election and ran unsuccessfully as an independent for the Tenth Majlis from Tehran in 2016.

Kazemi, Seyyed Hamid-Reza

Deputy of the Tenth Majlis, Pol-e Dokhtar, Lorestan (2016–20)
1964–, Pol-e Dokhtar, Lorestan
High school diploma
Seyyed Azizollah
Security/intelligence official
War veteran (wounded)
IRGC militiaman (Basij)
Kazemi joined the Basij in 1981 and fought at the war front until he was wounded in 1983. In 1984, he

joined the newly established MIIRI and was active in various cities in Lorestan Province. Kazemi has worked for the judiciary, the Islamic Culture and Communication Organization (on the committee selecting cultural attachés), and as head of security for the Ministry of Justice.

Kazemi, Seyyed Motahhar

Deputy of the Second (1984–88), Third (1988–92), Fourth (1992–96), and Fifth (1996–2000) Majlis, Khalkhal, Ardabil
1947–2006, Khalkhal, Ardabil
Clerical education
Seyyed Reza
Clergyman (HI)
No imprisonment
Kazemi was elected to the Sixth Majlis but could not occupy his seat because other lawmakers rejected his credentials. He died in a car accident.

Kazemi-Babaheydari, Ali

Deputy of the Tenth Majlis, Ardal, Chahar Mahal and Bakhtiari (2016–20)
1967–, Baba-Heydar, Chahar Mahal and Bakhtiari
BS, chemistry, Bu-Ali Sina University, 1991; MS, chemistry, Islamic Azad University–Arak, 1994; PhD, physical chemistry, Islamic Azad University–Science and Research Branch, 2008
Ruz-Ali
Professor at Islamic Azad University–Shahrekord
No imprisonment
Not a war veteran

Kazemi-Kermanshahi, Mohammad-Reza

Member of the Second Assembly of Experts, Kermanshah (1991–96)
1906–1997, Delfan, Lorestan
Clerical education, Najaf Seminary (Iraq)
Clergyman (ayatollah)
No imprisonment
Not a war veteran

Kazemnasab, Javad

Deputy of the Tenth Majlis, Ahvaz, Khuzestan (2016–20)
1965–, Albaji, Khuzestan
BA, political science, Islamic Azad University–Ahvaz; MA, political science, Islamic Azad University–Ahvaz
No imprisonment
Kazemnasab was head of the Ahvaz City Council, and worked for Khuzestan Telecommunications Company.

Kazempur-Ardabili, Hoseyn

Minister of commerce in PM Raja'i's cabinet (1981)
1952–, Tehran, Tehran
BA, business administration, Allameh Tabataba'i University (known at the time as Madreseh Ali-ye Bazargani), 1974; MA, business administration, Oklahoma State University (USA)
Civil servant, state companies
No imprisonment
Not a war veteran
Member of the IRP
Kazempur-Ardabili went to the United States in 1974 and later became Iranian minister of commerce on March 11, 1981. He survived the explosion at the IRP headquarters. He was the Ministry of Foreign Affairs' deputy for economic and international affairs during the premiership of Mir Hoseyn Musavi. He joined the Petroleum Ministry in 1985, and eventually became Iran's OPEC governor and deputy minister of petroleum. From 1990 to 1995, Kazempur-Ardabili was Iran's ambassador to Japan. In 1995, he became adviser to the foreign minister, and in 1996, he was elected chairman of OPEC's Board of Governors, a position he kept until 1999. President Ahmadinejad replaced Kazempur-Ardabili as Iran's OPEC governor in 2008, but in 2013, President Rouhani once again reappointed him to this position. His OPEC role made him an important player in the Iranian economy.

Kazemzadeh, Shadmehr

Deputy of the Tenth Majlis, Dehloran, Ilam (2016–20)
1970–, Darrehshahr, Ilam
MA, civil engineering
Engineer and civil servant
War veteran
Kazemzadeh ran unsuccessfully for the Ninth Majlis.

Kazeruni, Mohsen

Member of the Fourth (2007–2016) Assembly of
    Experts, Tehran; member of the Fifth (2016–22)
    Assembly of Experts, Alborz
1960–, Tehran, Tehran
BA, law; clerical education, Qom Seminary
Ali-Reza
Clergyman (HI)
No imprisonment
War veteran
Member of the SCC
Kazeruni has been the supreme leader's representative
    in Karaj since 2005, and was the Friday prayer
    leader of Karaj. He ran unsuccessfully for the
    Ninth Majlis.

Kazeruni, Serajeddin

Minister of housing and urban development in PM
    Musavi's first (August 15, 1984–85) and second
    (October 28, 1985–August 3, 1989) cabinets and
    President Hashemi-Rafsanjani's first cabinet (Au-
    gust 29, 1989–August 2, 1993)
1946–January 10, 2006, Isfahan, Isfahan
BS, Shahid Chamran University of Ahvaz; MS, archi-
    tecture, Tehran University, 1976
Abbas
Civil servant, ministries
No imprisonment
Not a war veteran
The Majlis rejected Kazeruni as minister of hous-
    ing and urban development on August 28, 1983
    (sixty-six in favor, sixty-eight opposed, and

forty-eight abstentions). However, he finally ob-
    tained the post on August 15, 1984.

Kermani, Hoseyn

Deputy of the First Majlis, Abadeh, Fars (1980–No-
    vember 26, 1981)
1930–, Darab, Fars
Clerical education
Najmali, farmer
Clergyman (HI)
No imprisonment
Not a war veteran
Kermani resigned from the First Majlis.

Keshtzar, Habibollah

Deputy of the Tenth Majlis, Behbahan, Khuzestan
    (2016–20)
1960–, Behbahan, Khuzestan
BS, agricultural engineering; MA, social science
Mayor of Sardasht (for fourteen years)
No imprisonment
Keshtzar became a civil servant in the MI beginning
    in 1985.

Keyvani, Kuros

Deputy of the Fourth Majlis, representing the Jewish
    community (as a religious minority) (1992–96)
1939–, Hamadan, Hamadan
MD, medicine, University of Bordeaux (France), 1973
Al'azar, MD
Dentist
No imprisonment
Keyvan moved to the United States in 2006.

Khabbaz, Mohammad-Reza

Deputy of the Fourth (1992–96), Fifth (1996–2000),
    Sixth (2000–2004), and Eighth (2008–12) Majlis,
    Kashmar, Razavi Khorasan
1954–, Kashmar, Razavi Khorasan

BA, Arabic literature, 1979; MA, political science, 1996; PhD, political science

Abdolhoseyn, baker

Civil servant

No imprisonment

Member of the central council of the NTP

Khabbaz was a teacher for some thirty years. He ran unsuccessfully for the Ninth and Tenth Majlis. In 2016, President Rouhani's cabinet appointed him governor-general of Semnan.

Khachaturian, Herach

Deputy of the First Majlis, representing Armenians of southern Iran (as a religious minority) (1980–84)

1948–, Isfahan, Isfahan

MD, medicine

Golestan, laborer

Medical doctor

No imprisonment

Not a war veteran

There were rumors about Khachaturian's sympathy for the Tudeh Party. After serving in the Majlis, he worked in the private sector.

Khadem, Seyyed Alaeddin

Deputy of the Tenth Majlis, Sepidan, Fars (2016–20)

1955–, Sepidan, Fars

BS, agricultural engineering; MA, management

Father's name unknown, farmer

Provincial civil servant

War veteran

Khadem has worked with the Construction Jihad.

Khadem-Arabbaghi, Mohsen

Deputy of the Fifth Majlis, Urmia, West Azerbaijan (1996–2000)

1948–, Urmia, West Azerbaijan

BS, mechanical engineering

Hoseyn

No imprisonment

In 2013, the government appointed Khadem-Arabbaghi as director-general of Aras Free Zone.

Khadem-Azghadi, Amir-Reza

Deputy of the Seventh Majlis, Tehran, Tehran (2004–8)

1969–, Mashhad, Razavi Khorasan

MA, public administration

Mohammad

Faculty member at Shahid Beheshti University

No imprisonment

Khademi, Hedayatollah

Deputy of the Tenth Majlis, I'zeh, Khuzestan (2016–20)

1959–, I'zeh, Khuzestan

BS, mechanical engineering

Engineer

War veteran (POW)

Khademi was an employee of the Iran National Steel Industrial Group and the National Iranian Drilling Company from 1988 to 2009. He served as executive director of the North Drilling Company from 2009 to 2015.

Khademi [Majlisi-Khademi], Seyyed Hoseyn

Member of the Assembly for the Final Examination of the Constitution, Isfahan (1979); member of the First Assembly of Experts, Isfahan (1983–85)

November 15, 1901–March 11, 1985, Isfahan, Isfahan

Clerical education, Najaf Seminary (Iraq)

Seyyed Ja'far, clergyman (ayatollah)

Clergyman

No imprisonment

Not a war veteran

Ayatollah Khademi was head of Isfahan Seminary before and after the revolution. He was active in the anti-shah movement and was named as the "age leader" (an honorific title of respect for an elder)

of the AFEC. Khademi considered land reform a violation of the sanctity of private property under Islam. He and Ayatollah Seyyed Jalal[eddin] Taheri-Isfahani were two rival high-ranking clerics in Isfahan. In the 1980s, Khademi's son served as ambassador to East Germany.

Khajehpur, Mohammad

Deputy of the Fourth (1992–96) and Fifth (1996–2000) Majlis, Bushehr and Genaveh, Bushehr
1950–, Ahvaz, Khuzestan
MS, electrical engineering
Abdorrasul
No imprisonment
Khajehpur has been a high-level deputy in the Communications Ministry for many years.

Khak-Aji-Bozeh, Ali-Reza

Deputy of the Third Majlis, Rasht, Gilan (1988–92)
1956–, Rasht, Gilan
Clerical education
Fathollah
No imprisonment
After serving in the Majlis, Khak-Aji-Bozeh worked in the Ministry of Energy.

Khalatian, Hara'i

Member of the Assembly for the Final Examination of the Constitution, representing Armenians of northern Iran (as a religious minority) (1979); deputy of the First Majlis, representing Armenians of northern Iran (as a religious minority) (1980–84)
1929–1988, Kermanshah, Kermanshah
Associate's degree, accounting
Gregori, laborer
Journalist (editor of an Armenian journal)
No imprisonment
Not a war veteran
Khalatian was a socialist and survived an assassination attempt on August 28, 1981.

Khaledi-Sardashti, Mohammad

Deputy of the Tenth Majlis, Lordegan, Chahar Mahal and Bakhtiari (2016–20)
1974–, Monjar Mui, Chahar Mahal and Bakhtiari
BS, chemistry, Yazd University; MS, inorganic chemistry, Isfahan University of Technology; PhD, inorganic chemistry, Isfahan University of Technology, 2008
Professor at Islamic Azad University–Shahrekord (since 2010)
No imprisonment
Not a war veteran
Khaledi-Sardashti was rector of Payam-e Nur University, Lordegan from 2007 to 2010. He is an expert in nanotechnology.

Khaleqi, Bashir

Deputy of the Eighth (2008–12) and Tenth (2016–20) Majlis, Khalkhal and Kowsar, Ardabil
1949–, Khalkhal, Ardabil
MD, medicine, Tabriz University, 1976; pediatric specialization, Shahid Beheshti University, 1991
Rajabali
Medical doctor
No imprisonment
War veteran
Khaleqi, who treated patients during the Iran–Iraq War, specialized in children's health at Shahid Beheshti University. He ran unsuccessfully for the Ninth Majlis.

Khaleqi, Naser

Deputy of the Fifth (1997–2000) and Sixth (2000–2004) Majlis, Isfahan, Isfahan; minister of labor and social affairs in President Khatami's second cabinet (April 25, 2004–August 2, 2005)
1949–, Shahreza, Isfahan
BS, mechanical engineering, 1978
Iraj
Civil servant, state companies
Imprisoned before the revolution

War veteran (POW for ten years)

Khaleqi resigned early from the Sixth Majlis to become minister of labor and social affairs. His niece, Minoo Khaleqi, was elected to the Tenth Majlis from Isfahan but the GC disqualified her after she had won her seat.

Khalili, Mohammad

Deputy of the First Majlis, Baft, Kerman (1980–84)

1939–2014, Baft, Kerman

MD, medicine

Hoseyn, farmer

Medical doctor

No imprisonment

Not a war veteran

Khalili worked for *Ettela'at* for many years.

Khalili-Ardakani, Mohammad-Hoseyn

Deputy of the Sixth Majlis, Karaj, Tehran (2000–2004)

1954–, Ardakan, Yazd

MA, public administration

Mohammad

Academia

No imprisonment

After serving in the Majlis, Khalili-Ardakani became a civil servant.

Khaliliyan, Sadeq

Minister of agricultural jihad in President Ahmadinejad's second cabinet (September 3, 2009–August 2, 2013)

1959–, Ahvaz, Khuzestan

BS, agricultural engineering, Shahid Chamran University of Ahvaz, 1984; MA, agricultural economics, Tarbiyat-e Modarres University, 1989; PhD, agricultural economics, Tarbiyat-e Modarres University, 1996

Planning deputy to the minister of Agricultural Jihad

No imprisonment

War veteran

IRGC militiaman

Khaliliyan was disqualified by the GC from running for president in 2013. In 2016 he ran unsuccessfully for the Tenth Majlis from Tehran.

Khaliltahmasebi, Zadali

Deputy of the Seventh Majlis, Lordegan, Chahar Mahal and Bakhtiari, (2004–8)

1963–, Lordegan, Chahar Mahal and Bakhtiari

BA, theology

Mohammad-Hoseyn

Academia

No imprisonment

Khalilzadeh-Moravvej, Boyuk

Member of the First (1984–90) and Second (1991–98) Assembly of Experts, East Azerbaijan; member of the Third Assembly of Experts, Ardabil (1999–2001)

1930–2001, Ardabil, Ardabil

Clerical education, Qom Seminary

Mohammad-Reza, bazaar tradesman

Clergyman (ayatollah)

No imprisonment

Not a war veteran

Khalilzadeh-Moravvej was the Friday prayer leader of Ardabil from 1981 to 2001. He was also Ayatollah Khomeini's and then Ayatollah Khamenei's representative in Ardabil.

Khalkhali [Sadeqi-Givi], Mohammad-Sadeq

Deputy of the First (1980–84), Second (1984–88), and Third (1988–92) Majlis, Qom, Qom; member of the First Assembly of Experts, Tehran (1984–90)

1925–2003, Givi, Ardabil

Clerical education, Qom Seminary

Yadollah, farmer and bazaar tradesman

Clergyman

Imprisoned before the revolution

Not a war veteran

Member of the central council of the ACC; member of the SQSS

Ayatollah Khomeini appointed HI Khalkhali as head judge of the revolutionary tribunals two days after the revolution, and in that position Khalkhali ordered the execution of hundreds of individuals, including Amir-Abbas Hoveyda, a long-serving prime minister under the shah. In May 1980, Khalkhali was put in charge of the antinarcotics campaign and ordered the executions of hundreds of drug addicts and peddlers. As a roving executioner, he acquired the nickname of the "hanging judge." In 1979, he ran unsuccessfully for a seat in the AFEC. In 1980, he resigned from his judiciary post to run for the Majlis, where he served three consecutive terms. He was elected to the First AE in interim elections held on April 15, 1984. However, the GC rejected his qualifications for the Fourth Majlis in 1992. He did not play an active political role in the last dozen years of his life. He is the brother of former MP Ghafur Sadeqi-Givi and the father-in-law of HI Asadollah Kiyan-Ersi. Khalkhali was married to the sister of Seyyed Hashem Rasuli-Mahallati.

Khamenei, Seyyed Ali

Member of the Revolutionary Council (1979–80); deputy of the First Majlis, Tehran, Tehran (1980–October 13, 1981); president (October 13, 1981–August 16, 1989); member of the First Assembly of Experts, Tehran (1983–89); member of the First Expediency Discernment Assembly (1988–89); supreme leader (June 4, 1989–present)

July 16, 1939–, Mashhad, Razavi Khorasan

Clerical education, Mashhad Seminary, 1968

Seyyed Javad, clergyman (HI)

Clergyman (ayatollah)

Imprisoned before the revolution

Not a war veteran

Founder, member of the central council, and secretary-general of the IRP; founding member of the SCC

Khamenei was born in Mashhad and studied theology there and in Qom, where he was exposed to Ayatollah Khomeini's ideas. On January 14, 1980, Ayatollah Khomeini appointed him as the Friday prayer leader of Tehran. He was one of the first clerics to enter government service in mid-1979 as deputy defense minister, and in that position became very familiar with the IRGC. However, on February 24, 1980, Khamenei resigned from his post as deputy defense minister. In March 1980, he came in fifth among Tehran candidates elected to the first Majlis, receiving 1,405,976 votes. An assassination attempt on June 27, 1981, left him paralyzed in the right hand. He was a member of a Majlis committee that considered terms for releasing the American hostages. Khamenei served in such other roles as member of the prayer leaders' central council, member of the Headquarters for Cultural Revolution, and supervisor of IRIB. He resigned from the First Majlis to become Iran's first clerical president, receiving 16,008,579 votes. Khamenei was reelected in 1985 to a second term, and was a wartime president for seven of his eight years. In 1989, after Ayatollah Khomeini's death, the AE selected him as the new supreme leader, and he officially resigned from his post as president on August 16, 1989. Khamenei married his wife, who is from a merchant family from Mashhad, in 1964 when she was 17. He has six children. His son Seyyed Mas'ud is married to the daughter of Ayatollah Seyyed Mohsen Kharrazi. Another son, Seyyed Mojtaba, is married to the daughter of Haddad-Adel. His third son, Seyyed Mostafa, is married to the daughter of Ayatollah Khoshvaqt. His daughter is married to the son of HI Mohammadi-Golpayegani. Sadeq Va'ezzadeh-Khorasani, a former VP who also sits on the EDA, is the son of Khamenei's maternal aunt. Khamenei also has three brothers, one sister, and three half-sisters, two of whom have passed away. One of his brothers, Seyyed Hasan, is a non-cleric who works in the Petroleum Ministry.

[Hoseyni-] Khamenei, Seyyed Hadi

Deputy of the First Majlis, Fariman, Razavi Khorasan (1981–84); deputy of the Second (1984–88) and Third (1988–92) Majlis, Mashhad, Razavi

Khorasan; deputy of the Sixth Majlis, Tehran,
Tehran (2000–2004)

1947–, Mashhad, Razavi Khorasan

Clerical education, Mashhad Seminary

Seyyed Javad, clergyman

Clergyman

Imprisoned before the revolution

Not a war veteran

Member of the IRP and the ACC; founder and secretary-general of the AILF

HI Khamenei is the younger brother of Supreme
Leader Ayatollah Khamenei, but he is a critic of his
brother and his policies. He was the founder and
publisher of several newspapers, including *Sobh-e
Azadegan*, *Jahan-e Islam*, and *Hayat-e Now*, all of
which the judiciary banned on charges of castigating political leaders. On March 26, 1987, Khamenei was injured in a grenade attack by PMOI. In
1992, the GC rejected his qualifications for the
Fourth Majlis, and in 1998, they rejected him as a
candidate for the AE, even though his brother was
the supreme leader. In 1998, Khamenei founded
the Assembly of Imam's Line Forces and was an
adviser to President Khatami. He endorsed Hassan
Rouhani during the 2013 presidential election.

[Hoseyni-] Khamenei, Seyyed Mohammad

Member of the Assembly for the Final Examination of
the Constitution, Razavi Khorasan (1979); deputy
of the First (1980–84) and Second (1984–88) Majlis, Mashhad, Razavi Khorasan

December 25, 1935–, Mashhad, Razavi Khorasan

Clerical education, Qom Seminary; BA, law, Tehran
University, 1968

Seyyed Javad, clergyman

Clergyman

No imprisonment

Not a war veteran

Secretary-general of the AILF

Before the revolution, HI Seyyed Mohammad Khamenei worked as a lawyer and teacher, all while being
a cleric. In 1979, he was in charge of the former
SAVAK organization responsible for intelligence

gathering. He was also a revolutionary prosecutor. Even though he was a member of the Constitutional Assembly of Experts, the GC did not
approve his qualifications for the first AE. Yet
Khamenei, who survived an assassination attempt
on January 10, 1982, was part of the Council for
Revision of the Constitution in 1989. He has been
the head of the Bonyad Hekmat Islami Sadra for
many years. He is the older brother of Supreme
Leader Ayatollah Khamenei.

Khan Mohammadi-Khorrami, Mohammad-Reza

Deputy of the Ninth Majlis, Abhar and Khorramdarreh, Zanjan (2012–16)

1964–, Khorramdarreh, Zanjan

BS, chemistry, Shahid Beheshti University, 1991; MS,
analytical chemistry, Tehran University; PhD, analytical chemistry, Shahid Beheshti University, 2002

Baqer, clergyman

Professor of chemistry at Imam Khomeini University
of Qazvin

No imprisonment

War veteran

IRGC militiaman

Khan Mohammadi-Khorrami ran unsuccessfully for
the Eighth Majlis.

Khanansu, Ator

Deputy of the Second (1984–88) and Third (1988–92)
Majlis, representing Assyrians and Chaldeans (as
a religious minority)

1941–, Urmia, West Azerbaijan

BA, French literature

Yulyuz

No imprisonment

Khanlaryan, Karen

Deputy of the Ninth (2012–16) and Tenth (2016–20)
Majlis, representing Armenians of northern Iran
(as a religious minority)

1964–, Tehran, Tehran

BS, civil engineering, Tehran University, 1988; MS,
seismology, Islamic Azad University–Tehran,
2000; PhD, seismology, Islamic Azad University,
2006; PhD, history, National Academy of Sciences
of the Republic of Armenia (Armenia)
Hrant
Professor at Islamic Azad University–Tehran; engineer at Iran Rock Wool Company
No imprisonment
Not a war veteran
In the 2012 elections, Khanlaryan received the second
highest percentage of votes, having garnered 91
percent of the vote of Armenians of northern Iran.

Khansari, Abolfazl

Member of the Second Assembly of Experts, Markazi
(1991–98)
1917–2001, Isfahan, Isfahan
Clerical education, Najaf Seminary (Iraq), 1950
Ahmad, clergyman
Clergyman (ayatollah)
No imprisonment
Not a war veteran
Founding member of the SQSS
Khansari, who lived in Najaf from 1934 to 1950, was
the Friday prayer leader of Arak and Ayatollah
Khomeini's representative in Markazi Province
from 1979 to 1992.

Khanzadeh, Mostafa

Deputy of the Sixth Majlis, Damavand and Firuzkuh,
Tehran (2001–4)
1958–, Damavand, Tehran
PhD, civil engineering
Fazlollah
Civil servant
No imprisonment

Khanzadi, Hoseyn

Commander of the Islamic Republic of Iran Navy
(November 5, 2017–present)

1967–, Gorgan, Golestan
BS, naval sciences, Imam Khomeini Naval University
of Nowshahr; MS, naval defense management,
Iranian Army's Command and General Staff
College; thesis: "Use of Hovercraft to Deal with
Threats in Future Missions of the Iranian Navy"
Deputy for design, planning and budget of the Islamic
Republic of Iran Navy
No imprisonment
Rear Admiral Khanzadi has undergone naval warfare
training in Pakistan and is a hovercraft pilot.

Kharestani, Ahmad

Deputy of the Third Majlis, Sarvestan, Fars (1988–92)
1955–, Kharestan, Fars
Associate's degree
Kahzad
High school teacher
No imprisonment

Kharmataei, Ali

Deputy of the Second Majlis, Saqqez and Baneh,
Kurdistan (1984–88)
1924–, Saqqez, Kurdistan
Clerical education
Obeydollah
No imprisonment
Clergyman
Not a war veteran
Martyr's family
In 1980, in an attempt to assassinate Mamosta Khar-
mataei, leftist forces killed his daughter. At that
time Kharmataei, a Sunni, was the Friday prayer
leader of Saqqez.

Kharrazi, Seyyed Kamal [Ali-Naqi]

Permanent representative of Iran to the UN (September 13, 1989–1997); minister of foreign affairs in
President Khatami's first (August 20, 1997–August 1, 2001) and second (August 22, 2001–August
2, 2005) cabinets

1944–, Tehran, Tehran

BA, Persian literature, Tehran University, 1969; MA, education, Tehran University, 1971; PhD, educational management, University of Houston (USA), 1976

Seyyed Mehdi, bazaar tradesman

Head of the War Information Headquarters (1980s)

No imprisonment

Not a war veteran

Kharrazi is a professor at Tehran University, and in 2006 Ayatollah Khamenei appointed him head of the Strategic Council on Foreign Relations. He is the brother of Ayatollah Seyyed Mohsen Kharrazi, who is in the AE. His nephew, Mohammad-Baqer Kharrazi, is secretary-general of Hezbollah Iran and publisher of *Hezbollah*. His niece is married to Seyyed Mas'ud [Hoseyni-] Khamenei.

Kharrazi [Mir Mohammad-Ali], Seyyed Mohsen

Member of the Second (1991–98), Third (1999–2006), and Fourth (2007–16) Assembly of Experts, Tehran

1937–, Tehran, Tehran

Clerical education, Qom Seminary

Seyyed Mehdi, bazaar merchant

Clergyman (ayatollah)

No imprisonment

Not a war veteran

Member of the SQSS

Seyyed Mohsen Kharrazi, the son of a powerful merchant in Tehran bazaar, founded In the Righteous Path Institute in 1964 to battle Muslims converting to Christianity. Seyyed Kamal Kharrazi is his brother and Seyyed Mohammad-Sadeq Kharrazi is his son. His other son, Mohammad-Baqer Kharrazi, is secretary-general of Hezbollah Iran. His daughter is married to Seyyed Mas'ud [Hoseyni-] Khamenei, and his grandson is married to the daughter of Mohammad-Reza Khatami.

Khasahmadi, Ahmad

Deputy of the Sixth (2000–2004) and Seventh (2004–8) Majlis, Torbat-e Jam and Taybad, Razavi Khorasan

1958–, Torbat-e Jam, Razavi Khorasan

MD, medicine

Nurmohammad

Medical doctor

No imprisonment

Khasahmadi is a Sunni.

Khastehband, Hasan

Deputy of the Sixth (2000–2004), Eighth (2008–12), Ninth (2012–16), and Tenth (2016–20) Majlis, Bandar-e Anzali, Gilan

1957–, Bandar-e Anzali, Gilan

MA, public administration, University of Gilan

Farajollah

Provincial civil servant

No imprisonment

Khastehband is a conservative member of the Majlis and was close to former president Mahmud Ahmadinejad. Between the Sixth and Eighth Majlis he served as Iran's commercial attaché in Russia.

Khatami, Hadi

Deputy of the Fourth (1992–96) and Fifth (1996–August 11, 1999) Majlis, Borujerd, Lorestan

1942–August 11, 1999, Borujerd, Lorestan

Clerical education

Hasan

Clergyman

No imprisonment

HI Khatami was elected in midterm elections to the Third Majlis but could not occupy his seat after the Majlis rejected his credentials.

Khatami, Seyyed Ahmad

Member of Third (1999–2006), Fourth (2007–16), and Fifth (2016–) Assembly of Experts, Kerman

1960–, Semnan, Semnan

Clerical education, Qom Seminary

Seyyed Mehdi, clergyman

Clergyman (ayatollah)

No imprisonment

Not a war veteran

Member of the SQSS and the SCC

Khatami, an archconservative, was a temporary Friday prayer leader of Tehran and a member of the
HCRSQ.

Khatami, Seyyed Mohammad

Deputy of the First Majlis, Ardakan, Yazd (1980–November 9, 1982); minister of [culture and] Islamic
guidance in PM Musavi's first (November 9,
1982–85) and second (October 28, 1985–August 3,
1989) cabinets and President Hashemi-Rafsanjani's first cabinet (August 29, 1989–May 24, 1992);
president (August 3, 1997–August 2, 2005)

October 14, 1943–, Ardakan, Yazd

BA, Western philosophy, Isfahan University of Technology, 1969; MA, education, Tehran University;
clerical education, Qom Seminary

Seyyed Ruhollah, clergyman (ayatollah)

Clergyman

No imprisonment

Not a war veteran

Martyr's family (nephew)

Member of the central council of the ACC

HI Khatami has held a variety of posts, including
administrator of an Islamic center in Hamburg,
head of a government publishing house, member
of the Majlis, and minister of culture and Islamic
guidance. He was the acting director of Kayhan
publications from November 1980 to November
1982. He resigned from the first Majlis to become
the culture minister. On August 29, 1989, Khatami received the highest number of votes (246
out of 260) when the Majlis voted on President
Hashemi-Rafsanjani's first cabinet. However, less
than three years later, on May 24, 1992, Khatami
was forced to resign as culture minister after
protesting increasing censorship imposed by
hardliners. On August 30, 1992, he became head
of the National Library. Khatami went on to win
landslide victories in the 1997 and 2001 presidential elections—69 percent and 77 percent of
the vote, respectively. He advocated the concept

of a "Dialogue of Civilizations" and pursued
domestic and foreign policies that somewhat
improved Iran's image during his term in office.
He withdrew from the tenth presidential race on
March 16, 2009. In 2015, the Iranian government
banned the media from quoting or mentioning
Khatami and prohibited him from traveling
outside Iran, a result of his outspoken support
of opposition leaders Mir Hoseyn Musavi and
Mehdi Karrubi. His wife, Zohreh Sadeqi, is the
cousin of Ayatollah Khomeini's daughter-in-law,
Seyyedeh Fatemeh Tabataba'i [Soltani]. His sister,
Maryam, is the wife of Mohammad-Ali Saduqi.
His brother is Seyyed Mohammad-Reza Khatami. The son of his other sister, Fatemeh, was
killed in the war.

Khatami, Seyyed Mohammad-Reza

Deputy of the Sixth Majlis, Tehran, Tehran
(2000–2004)

1959–, Ardakan, Yazd

MD, internal medicine, Tehran University

Seyyed Ruhollah, clergyman (ayatollah)

Medical doctor and deputy in the Ministry of Health

No imprisonment

War veteran (wounded)

IRGC militiaman

Martyr's family (nephew)

Secretary-general of IIPF

Seyyed Mohammad-Reza Khatami, the younger
brother of former president Mohammad Khatami, was involved in the takeover of the American embassy. He served in the IRGC in the
1980s, and in the 2000 Majlis elections, he received the highest percentage of votes (61.2 percent) from Tehran. He was the deputy Speaker
of the Sixth Majlis and head of the Islamic
Parliament Research Center from 2000 to 2004.
Despite his high-level position in the Sixth Majlis, the GC disqualified Khatami from running
in the 2004 Majlis election. Afterward, he went
back to practicing medicine while staying close
to the reformist camp. His wife, Zahra Eshraqi,

is the granddaughter of Seyyed Ruhollah Khomeini, and he is related to the Kharrazi family.

Khatami, Seyyed Morteza

Deputy of the Tenth Majlis, Mahneshan and Ijrood,
    Zanjan (2016–20)
1963–, Ijrood, Zanjan
MD, Tehran University
Ali, clergyman
War veteran
Khatami held various managerial positions in the
    medical field before he was elected to the Tenth
    Majlis as an independent.

Khatami, Seyyed Ruhollah

Member of the First Assembly of Experts, Yazd
    (1983–88)
1906–October 27, 1988, Ardakan, Yazd
Clerical education, Isfahan Seminary
Clergyman
Mohammad-Reza
No imprisonment
Not a war veteran
Martyr's family (grandson)
Ayatollah Khatami was the founder of Ardakan Sem-
    inary. A moderate, he was Ayatollah Khomeini's
    representative and the Friday prayer leader of
    Yazd from 1982 to 1988. Khatami was the oldest
    member of the First AE. He was the father of for-
    mer president Seyyed Mohammad Khatami and
    Seyyed Mohammad-Reza Khatami, as well as the
    father-in-law of Mohammad-Ali Saduqi.

Khatami, Mrs. Seyyedeh Fatemeh

Deputy of the Sixth Majlis, Mashhad, Razavi Kho-
    rasan (2000–2004)
1957–, Birjand, South Khorasan
MD, pediatrics
Mohammad-Hoseyn
Medical doctor and professor
No imprisonment

Khatami has worked for more than two decades in
    the Ministry of Health and is a faculty member at
    the Mashhad University of Medical Sciences. She
    ran unsuccessfully for the Seventh Majlis from
    Birjand. She is not related to former president
    Mohammad Khatami.

Khatam-Yazdi, Seyyed Abbas

Member of the Second (1991–98) and Third (1999–
    2001) Assembly of Experts, Yazd
1930–2001, Yazd, Yazd
Clerical education, Najaf Seminary (Iraq)
Seyyed Yahya, clergyman
Clergyman (ayatollah)
No imprisonment
Not a war veteran
Member of the SQSS
Khatam-Yazi was secretary of the policy board for
    Friday prayer leaders.

Khayyati, Taleb

Deputy of the Second Majlis, Dasht-e Azadegan, Khu-
    zestan (1984–88)
1954–, Susangerd, Khuzestan
High school diploma
Na'im
No imprisonment

Khayyer [-Habibollahi], Musa

Ministerial adviser and head of the PBO in PM Ra-
    ja'i's cabinet (September 25, 1980–81)
1941–, Ardabil, Ardabil
BS, electrical engineering, Tehran University, 1965
Father's name unknown, bookstore owner
Adviser to the governor-general of Khuzestan
No imprisonment
Not a war veteran
Khayyer worked at Isfahan's Mobarakeh Steel Com-
    pany from 1967 to 1972. After the revolution,
    he purged over seventy PBO civil servants on
    the charge of being Baha'i or Freemasons. On

September 25, 1980, he became the ministerial adviser and head of the PBO and then first deputy minister of petroleum.

Khaza'i, Abdolazim

Deputy of the Third Majlis, Bandar-e Mahshahr, Khuzestan (1988–92)
1952–, Bandar-e Mahshahr, Khuzestan
High school diploma
Hamdollah
No imprisonment

Khaza'i, Mohammad-Mehdi

Deputy of the Fourth (1992–96) and Fifth (1996–2000) Majlis, Fariman, Sarakhs, Ahmadabad, Marzdaran, and Razavieh, Razavi Khorasan
1945–, Sarakhs, Razavi Khorasan
BS, chemistry, Tarbiyat-e Mo'allem University, 1970; MA, political science, 1996
Mohammad-Hasan
No imprisonment
War veteran
IRGC militiaman

Khaza'i [-Torshizi], Mohammad

Deputy of the First (1980–84) and Second (1984–88) Majlis, Rasht, Gilan; Permanent Representative of Iran to the UN (July 25, 2007–March 9, 2014)
1953–, Kashmar, Razavi Khorasan
BA, business administration, University of Gilan; MA, international transactions, George Mason University (USA), 1993
Ali-Asghar, civil servant
Academia
No imprisonment
Not a war veteran
Khaza'i has held such posts as governor of OPEC Fund, alternate governor for the Islamic Development Bank, and Iran's representative at the World Bank (1988–2002). Since July 12, 2014, he has served as deputy minister of economy and chair

of the Organization for Investment, and Economic, and Technical Assistance of Iran.

Khaz'ali, Seyyed Abolqasem

Member of the Assembly for the Final Examination of the Constitution, Semnan (1979); member of the First (1981–86), Second (1986–92), Third (1992–98), and Fourth (1998–August 3, 1999) Guardian Councils; member of the First (1983–90), Second (1991–98), Third (1999–2006), and Fourth (2007–15) Assembly of Experts, Razavi Khorasan
1925–2015, Borujerd, Lorestan
Clerical education, Qom Seminary
Gholam-Reza, laborer
Clergyman
Imprisoned before the revolution
Not a war veteran
Martyr's family (son, Hoseyn, killed in revolutionary demonstrations in 1978)
Member of the SQSS
Ayatollah Khaz'ali joined the first GC after Ayatollah Mahadavi-Kani resigned to become interior minister. He was one of the founders of *Resalat* in 1985. Khaz'ali resigned from the GC in August 1999. He was a staunch supporter of President Ahmadinejad, and he was the founder and secretary of Qadir International Foundation (2000–2015). His son, Mehdi, publicly denounced his father's views and spent some time in prison after the contested 2009 presidential election for questioning the accuracy of the results. Khaz'ali was the son-in-law of Shaikh Mahmud Kalbasi and father-in-law of Mohammad-Hadi Marvi.

Khedri, Abdolhamid

Deputy of the Tenth Majlis, Bandar-e Bushehr, Bushehr (2016–20)
1978–, Genaveh, Bushehr
Clerical education, Qom Seminary; MA, law, Islamic Judicial Law Educational Research Institute
Father's name unknown, farmer
Clergyman (HI) and judiciary official in Gachsaran

No imprisonment
Not a war veteran

Kheyrabadi, Morteza

Deputy of the Sixth Majlis, Sabzevar, Razavi Kho-
    rasan (2000–2004)
1963–, Tehran, Tehran
MD, medicine
Abbas-Ali
No imprisonment

Kheyri, Ahad

Deputy of the Eighth Majlis, Bostanabad, East Azer-
    baijan (2008–12)
1969–, Bostanabad, East Azerbaijan
BS, nursing; MA, management
Rahim
Civil servant
No imprisonment
Kheyri was not elected to the Ninth Majlis and went
    on to work in the Welfare Ministry.

Kheyrkhah, Kamel

Deputy of the Second (1984–88), Third (1988–92), and
    Fifth (1996–2000) Majlis, Lahijan, Gilan
1938–, Lahijan, Gilan
Clerical education
Gholam-Ali
Clergyman (HI)
No imprisonment

Khezri, Rasul

Deputy of the Ninth (2012–16) and Tenth (2016–20)
    Majlis, Piranshahr and Sardasht, West Azerbaijan
1968–, Piranshahr, West Azerbaijan
MD, medicine, Shahid Beheshti University of Medical
    Sciences, 1995
Medical doctor and clinic administrator
No imprisonment
Not a war veteran

Khezri, a Sunni doctor, founded a medical clinic in
    Piranshahr.

Khodabakhshi, Mohammad

Deputy of the Tenth Majlis, Aligudarz, Lorestan
    (2016–20)
1971–, Zolqi, Lorestan
BS, applied mathematics, Isfahan University of Tech-
    nology, 1995; MS, applied mathematics, Tarbi-
    yat-e Mo'allem University, 1998; PhD, applied
    mathematics
Professor at Shahid Beheshti University
No imprisonment
Khodabakhshi did doctoral research at McGill
    University in Canada and has taught at Shahid
    Beheshti University as well as other universities in
    Lorestan.

Khodadadi, Salman

Deputy of the Fifth Majlis, Bonab and Malekan, East
    Azerbaijan (1996–2000); deputy of the Sixth
    (2000–2004), Seventh (2004–8), Eighth (2008–12),
    and Tenth (2016–20) Majlis, Malekan, East
    Azerbaijan
1962–, Malekan, East Azerbaijan
BA, 1996; MA, political science; PhD, international
    relations (unverified)
Ebrahim
MIIRI officer
No imprisonment
IRGC commander
Khodadadi's credentials were called into question by
    others MPs in the Eighth Majlis on account of
    ethical violations (rape and sexual harassment),
    but he managed to keep his seat.

Khoda'i, Abdorrahman

Member of the Fourth Assembly of Experts, Kurdis-
    tan (2007–16)
1941–, Baneh, Kurdistan
Clerical education

Mostafa, farmer
Clergyman
No imprisonment
Not a war veteran
Mamosta Khoda'i, a Sunni cleric, has been the Friday
　　prayer leader of Baneh (1983–2014) and Sanandaj
　　(2014–present).

Khoda'i-Suri, Hojjatollah

Deputy of the Ninth Majlis, Delfan, Lorestan (2012–16)
1964–, Selseleh, Lorestan
BA, political science, Islamic Azad University–Karaj
MIIRI officer and prison warden
No imprisonment
War veteran (wounded)
Martyr's family (brother)
Khoda'i-Suri spent twenty-five years in the judiciary
　　and the prison system, serving at times as a warden.

Khojasteh, Amir

Deputy of the Ninth (2012–16) and Tenth (2016–20)
　　Majlis, Hamadan, Hamadan
1959–, Hamadan, Hamadan
MA, theology
Father's name unknown, farmer
Civil servant, department of veterans and former
　　POWs
No imprisonment
War veteran (fourteen months; wounded; POW for
　　eight years)
IRGC militiaman (Basij)
Khojasteh ran for the Sixth and Seventh Majlis but
　　was defeated both times. He also served on the
　　Hamadan City Council.

Khomeini, Seyyed Ahmad

Member of the First (1988–89), Second (1989–92), and
　　Third (1992–95) Expediency Discernment Assem-
　　bly; member of the Second Assembly of Experts,
　　Tehran (1991–94)
1946–March 16, 1995, Qom, Qom

Clerical education
Seyyed Ruhollah, clergyman (ayatollah)
Clergyman
No imprisonment
Not a war veteran
HI Seyyed Ahmad was the son, spokesperson, and
　　intermediary of Ayatollah Khomeini. In the mid-
　　1980s, President Banisadr recommended Seyyed
　　Ahmad Khomeini for the post of prime minis-
　　ter but Ayatollah Khomeini rejected the idea. In
　　addition to the above posts, he served in the SCNS,
　　the HCCR (appointed on December 11, 1992), and
　　the board of trustees of the IKRF. His wife was the
　　daughter of Ayatollah Seyyed Mohammad-Baqer
　　Tabataba'i [Soltani] and sister of Seyyed Sadeq Ta-
　　bataba'i [Soltani], the second director of the FDWI.

Khomeini, Seyyed Ruhollah

Supreme leader (December 3, 1979–June 3, 1989)
1902–1989, Khomeyn, Markazi
Clerical education, Qom Seminary, 1926
Seyyed Mostafa, clergyman (HI)
Clergyman
Imprisoned before the revolution
Not a war veteran
Born into a clerical family, Ayatollah Khomeini grew
　　increasingly critical of the shah's regime, which
　　then sent him into exile in Iraq. He continued his
　　revolutionary activism during sixteen years of
　　exile in Najaf, where he articulated the doctrine
　　of the mandate of the jurist as a theory of state-
　　craft. At the age of seventy-three, he witnessed
　　the realization of his dream and deposed one
　　of the US's strongest allies in the Middle East.
　　Khomeini was officially the leader of the Islamic
　　Republic from December 3, 1979, to June 3, 1989.
　　His followers refer to him as "Imam," an honorific
　　title. He had two sons and three daughters. One
　　of his sons-in-law was Ayatollah Shahabeddin
　　Eshraqi, who directed his office in exile and died
　　on September 11, 1981. One of Ayatollah Khomei-
　　ni's great-granddaughters is married to the son of
　　Mohsen Reza'i.

Khorram, Ahmad

Minister of roads and transportation in President
    Khatami's second cabinet (August 22, 2001–
    October 3, 2004)
1950–, Isfahan, Isfahan
BS, civil engineering, Tabriz University, 1979; MA,
    public administration, 1998
Father's name unknown, civil servant (state
    companies)
Civil servant
No imprisonment
Not a war veteran
IRGC militiaman
Khorram's term as minister ended in 2004 when the
    Majlis successfully impeached him.

Khoshchehreh [-Jamali], Mohammad

Deputy of the Seventh Majlis, Tehran, Tehran (2004–8)
1953–, Tehran, Tehran
PhD, economics, University of Strathclyde (Scotland),
    1996; dissertation title: "The Role of Free Zones in
    the Regional and National Development of Iran"
Hasan
Professor of economics at Tehran University
No imprisonment
Khoshchehreh was head of independent principalists
    in the Seventh Majlis. He retired from Tehran
    University in 2010. He ran unsuccessfully for the
    Eighth and Tenth Majlis.

Khoshnevis, Esma'il

Deputy of the First Majlis, Ardabil, Ardabil (1980–84)
1948–, Ardabil, Ardabil
MA, Persian literature
Ebrahim, civil servant
Director of the education department in Ardabil
No imprisonment
Not a war veteran
Khoshnevis was an activist in his student days at
    Tabriz University before the revolution. After the
    First Majlis, he returned to his teaching career.

For a while, he was rector of Islamic Azad Univer-
    sity–Ardabil. He supported Mir Hoseyn Musavi
    and the reformists in 2009.

Khoshro, Gholam-Ali

Permanent representative of Iran to the UN (February
    17, 2015–present)
January 16, 1955–
BA, sociology, Tehran University; MA, sociology,
    Tarbiyat-e Modarres University
Ambassador to Switzerland (2014–15)
No imprisonment
Khoshro has served in such capacities as dean (1981–
    89 and 1995–97) of the School of International Re-
    lations (affiliated with Iran's Ministry of Foreign
    Affairs), ambassador and deputy of the Perma-
    nent Mission of the Islamic Republic of Iran to
    the United Nations (1989–95), deputy foreign
    minister for research and training (1997–99), am-
    bassador to Australia (1999–2002), deputy foreign
    minister for legal and international affairs (2002–
    5), and assistant secretary-general of the Asian
    Parliamentary Assembly (2005–14). Khoshro has
    undertaken graduate studies at the New School
    for Social Research. He is the father-in-law of
    President Rouhani's niece, Maryam Fereydun.

Khoshro, Seyyed Hasan

Deputy of the Sixth Majlis, Kerman, Kerman
    (2000–2004)
1960–, Kerman, Kerman
PhD, mining engineering
Seyyed Reza, clergyman
Academia
No imprisonment
After serving in the Majlis, HI Khoshro became a
    civil servant.

Khosravi, Ali-Reza (Javad)

Deputy of the Ninth Majlis, Semnan and Mehdishahr,
    Semnan (2012–16)

1962–, Semnan, Semnan
BS, electrical engineering, Semnan University; MS, defense management
Abbas-Ali, railroad employee
Mayor of Semnan (2007–11)
No imprisonment
War veteran (sixty-eight months; wounded)
IRGC militiaman
Khosravi taught at Imam Hoseyn University.

Khosravi, Mohammad-Ali

Deputy of the First Majlis, Miyandoab, West Azerbaijan (1981–84)
1955–, Takab, West Azerbaijan
Clerical education
Azizollah
Clergyman
No imprisonment
Member of the central council of the ACC
HI Khosravi was a revolutionary court judge, *komiteh* head, and Friday prayer leader. He later served as editor of a number of magazines and was cultural deputy in the Pious Endowments and Charity Affairs Organization.

Khosravi, Rahmatollah

Deputy of the Third Majlis, Abadeh, Fars (1988–92)
1950–, Abadeh, Fars
BS, civil engineering; MA, management
Hasan
Civil servant, state companies
No imprisonment
Founding member of the AILF
After leaving the Majlis, Khosravi became the housing deputy of the FMVA and then a member of the first Tehran City Council. He is a reformist close to the NTP.

Khosravi-Sahlabadi, Abolqasem

Deputy of the Ninth Majlis, Torbat-e Heydariyyeh, Mahvelat, and Zaveh, Razavi Khorasan (2012–16)

1965–, Zaveh, Razavi Khorasan
BA, education, Farhangian University; MA, theology, Islamic Azad University–Torbat-e Heydariyyeh
Father's name unknown, farmer
High school instructor
No imprisonment
War veteran

Khosrowshahi, Seyyed Hadi

Member of the First (1983–90) and Second (1991–98) Assembly of Experts, Tehran
1938–, Tabriz, East Azerbaijan
Clerical education, Qom Seminary
Seyyed Morteza, clergyman (ayatollah)
Clergyman
Imprisoned before the revolution
Not a war veteran
Member of the SCC
HI Khosrowshahi was a child prodigy at the Qom Seminary, and in the 1970s he edited publications put out by Hoseyniyyeh-ye Ershad. After the revolution, he served for two years as Ayatollah Khomeini's representative in the Ministry of Culture and Islamic Guidance and escaped an assassination attempt in August 1979. HI Khosrowshahi then served for five years as postrevolutionary Iran's first ambassador to the Vatican (June 1981–March 1986). He played an active role both before and after the revolution in introducing the Iranian public to the works of Arab scholars, including by translating works by Seyyed Qutb, and engaging in Sunni-Shiite dialogues. Khosrowshahi was close to Grand Ayatollah Seyyed Mohammad-Kazem Shari'atmadari and was affiliated with the Islamic People's Republican Party of Iran. He is the former son-in-law of Ayatollah Seyyed Sadeq Ruhani.

Khosusi-Sani, Hamid-Reza

Deputy of the Ninth Majlis, Sowme'eh Sara, Gilan (2012–16)

1960–, Sowme'eh Sara, Gilan
MS, construction engineering, Islamic Azad
    University–Takestan
Provincial civil servant and university instructor
No imprisonment
Member of the IRP
Khosusi-Sani ran unsuccessfully for the Majlis five
    times before he was finally elected in 2012. Once
    in office, he was accused of appointing his family
    members to a good number of posts.

Kia, Mohammad-Qasem

Deputy of the Fourth Majlis, Kordkuy and Torkaman,
    Golestan (1992–96)
1950–, Kordkuy, Golestan
BS, health
Qoli
No imprisonment

Kikha, Ahmad-Ali

Deputy of the Eighth (2008–12) and Tenth
    (2016–20) Majlis, Zabol and Zahak, Sistan and
    Baluchestan
1967–, Zabol, Sistan and Baluchestan
PhD, agricultural economics
Gholam
Professor
No imprisonment
Not a war veteran

Kiyafar, Mohammad

Deputy of the Sixth Majlis, Miyaneh, East Azerbaijan
    (2000–2004)
1951–, Miyaneh, East Azerbaijan
MS, industrial engineering; MA, public
    administration
Mohammad-Ebrahim
No imprisonment
After serving in the Majlis, Kiyafar became a civil
    servant.

Kiya'i, Seyyed Mostafa

Deputy of the First Majlis, Tuyserkan, Hamadan
    (1981–84)
1947–2009, Tuyserkan, Hamadan
BS, medical science
Seyyed Naqi
Director of a health facility in Tuyserkan; MD in
    Tehran
No imprisonment
Kiya'i was politically active against the shah's regime
    before the revolution. In 2009, he died of a heart
    attack while delivering a speech supporting the
    presidential candidate Mir Hoseyn Musavi.

Kiya'inezhad, Mofid

Deputy of the Third (1988–92) and Fourth (1992–96)
    Majlis, Savojblagh, Nazarabad, and Taleqan, Teh-
    ran; deputy of the Ninth (2012–16) Majlis, Savo-
    jblagh, Nazarabad, and Taleqan, Alborz
1952–, Taleqan, Tehran
Clerical education, Qom Seminary
Mohammad, clergyman (ayatollah)
Clergyman
Imprisoned before the revolution
Not a war veteran
HI Kiya'inezhad has been in charge of screening
    candidates for IRIB and the Iranian Air Force.
    He was a representative of the supreme leader at
    Islamic Azad University–Tehran South Campus,
    where he also headed the Islamic sciences depart-
    ment. As a conservative MP, he was opposed to
    the Iranian nuclear deal.

Kiyan-Ersi, Asadollah

Deputy of the First (1980–84), Second (1984–88),
    Fourth (1992–96), and Sixth (2000–2004) Majlis,
    Faridan and Fereydunshahr, Isfahan
1938–, Faridan, Isfahan
Clerical education, Najaf Seminary (Iraq), 1970
Khodakaram, farmer
Clergyman (HI)

No imprisonment

Not a war veteran

Member of the central council of the ACC; founding member of the Islamic Society of Bakhtiaris

Kiyan-Ersi was the supreme leader's representative in the IRGC. He is the son-in-law of Mohammad-Sadeq Khalkhali.

Kiyani-Falavarjani, Hoseyn

Deputy of the Fourth Majlis, Falavarjan, Isfahan (1992–96)

1941–, Falavarjan, Isfahan

Clerical education

Mohammad-Ali

Clergyman (HI)

No imprisonment

Kiyanpur, Majid

Deputy of the Tenth Majlis, Dorud, Lorestan (2016–20)

1973–, Dorud, Lorestan

Lorestan governor's deputy for development (2013–14)

Kiyanush-Rad, Mohammad

Deputy of the Sixth Majlis, Ahvaz, Khuzestan (2000–2004)

1959–, Ahvaz, Khuzestan

MA, political science

Abdolmajid

Civil servant and university professor

No imprisonment

Member of the central council of the Party of Iranian People's Unity

Kiyavash [Alavitbar], Seyyed Mohammad

Member of the Assembly for the Final Examination of the Constitution, Khuzestan (1979); deputy of the First Majlis, Ahvaz, Khuzestan (1980–84); deputy of the Second Majlis, Abadan, Khuzestan (1984–88)

1921–, Zanjan, Zanjan

BA, Persian literature, Daneshsara-ye Ali-ye Tehran, 1955; clerical education

Seyyed Hasan, bazaar tradesman

Academia

No imprisonment

Not a war veteran

After the revolution, Kiyavash became governor of Abadan and head of Khuzestan's educational system. He was wounded in the bombing of the IRP headquarters in 1981. He supported presidential candidate Mir Hoseyn Musavi during the 2009 elections.

Kohram, Hamid

Deputy of the Sixth Majlis, Ahvaz, Khuzestan (2000–2004)

1958–, Tehran, Tehran

PhD, animal science

Mohammad-Ali

University professor

No imprisonment

Kohram has been a professor of animal science at Tehran University and director of Razi Vaccine and Serum Research Institute (2013–April 12, 2017). In 2017, he was head of Hassan Rouhani's presidential campaign headquarters in Khuzestan.

Kolahduz, Yusef

Deputy commander in chief of the IRGC (date unknown–September 29, 1981)

December 22, 1946–September 29, 1981, Quchan, Razavi Khorasan

BS, Military Science, Ground Forces Officers Academy

No imprisonment

IRGC militiaman

Kolahduz was a member of the shah's Imperial Guard and played an influential role in setting up the IRGC. He was slightly injured in the 1981 bombing that claimed the lives of President Raja'i and

PM Bahonar. Kolahduz died later that year in a plane crash.

Kordan, Ali [Avazali]

Interior minister in President Ahmadinejad's first cabinet (August 12–November 4, 2008)
October 23, 1958–November 22, 2009, Sari, Mazandaran
Associate's degree, English language, Daneshsara-ye Fani-ye Sari
Kamal, farmer
Civil servant
No imprisonment
War veteran
IRGC militiaman
Kordan became the interior minister by receiving 169 positive, sixty-four negative, and thirty-six abstention votes. However, his tenure only lasted for three months before the Majlis impeached him for falsely claiming to have a graduate degree from University of Oxford.

Kosehgharavi, Anehmohammad

Deputy of the Second Majlis, Gonbad-e Kavus, Golestan (1984–88)
1955–, Gonbad-e Kavus, Golestan
BS, metallurgy
Mohammad
No imprisonment
Kosehgharavi was a Sunni deputy.

Kosehgharavi, Shahram

Deputy of the Tenth Majlis, Minudasht, Golestan (2016–20)
1969–, Kalaleh, Golestan
BS, civil engineering; MBA; pursuing a PhD in business administration
Ilmohammad, teacher and high school headmaster
Engineer and owner of a construction company
No imprisonment

Kosehgharavi, a Sunni, entered the Tenth Majlis as an independent.

Kowlivand, Mohammad-Javad

Deputy of the Ninth (2012–16) and Tenth (2016–20) Majlis, Karaj, Alborz
1967–, Tuyserkan, Hamadan
BA, industrial management, Islamic Azad University–Karaj, 1994; MA, industrial management, Islamic Azad University–Semnan, 1998
Pasha, farmer
Civil servant, ministries; instructor at Islamic Azad University–Karaj
No imprisonment
War veteran (wounded)
Martyr's family (two brothers, Mohammad-Safa and Mohammad-Baqer)
Kowlivand worked at the Telecommunications Company of Iran, Post Bank Iran, and the Ministry of Foreign Affairs. In 2013, he was head of the election supervisory board overseeing the nationwide municipal elections.

Kowsari, Mohammad-Esma'il

Deputy of the Eighth (2008–12) and Ninth (2012–16) Majlis, Tehran, Tehran
1955–, Tehran, Tehran
BA, political geography; MS, defense management, Imam Hoseyn University; PhD, defense management, Imam Hoseyn University, 2015
Mohammad-Baqer
No imprisonment
War veteran (eighty-four months; wounded)
IRGC militiaman
Kowsari was a member of the radical Touhidi-ye Saf Group before the revolution. For sixteen years, he was the commander of a major IRGC brigade. He was also in charge of the intelligence bureau of the General Command of the Armed Forces. Kowsari was briefly arrested in 1989 for occupying agricultural lands. He was a major critic of the nuclear deal with the West during

the Ninth Majlis. After the Majlis, he returned to the IRGC and taught at Imam Hoseyn University. In July 2017, almost a month after an ISIS attack on the Majlis and Khomeini's mausoleum, Kowsari became commander of Sarollah base, which is in charge of providing security for the capital.

Kuchaki-Badelani, Sajjad

Commander of the Islamic Republic of Iran Navy (September 26, 2005–August 20, 2007)
1955–
War veteran
Commodore Kuchaki-Badelani was in charge of various naval units during the Iran–Iraq War. Before becoming commander of the navy in 2005, he was deputy chief for design, planning, and budget of the Armed Forces General Staff.

Kuchaki-Borujeni, Mansur-Mirza

Deputy of the Sixth Majlis, Borujen, Chahar Mahal and Bakhtiari (2000–2004)
1964–, Borujen, Chahar Mahal and Bakhtiari
MD, medicine
Medical doctor
No imprisonment

Kuchakinezhad-Eramsadati, Jabar

Deputy of the Eighth (2008–12), Ninth (2012–16), and Tenth (2016–20) Majlis, Rasht, Gilan
1961–, Eramsadat, Gilan
BA, pedology; MA, public administration
Hafez
Lawyer, university instructor, and adviser to the director of the Pious Endowments and Charity Affairs Organization
No imprisonment
War veteran (seventy-two months)
IRGC militiaman
Member of the central council of AVIR in Gilan Province

Kuchakinezhad-Eramsadati held high-level posts in the IRGC General Command for sixteen years.

Kuchakzadeh, Mehdi

Deputy of the Seventh (2004–8), Eighth (2008–12), and Ninth (2012–16) Majlis, Tehran, Tehran
1958–, Tehran, Tehran
BS, hydraulics and irrigation engineering, Tehran University, 1985; MS, hydraulics and irrigation engineering, International Institute for Hydraulic and Environmental Engineering (The Netherlands), 1989; PhD, irrigation engineering, Tarbiyat-e Modarres University, 1997
Hoseyn
Faculty member at Tarbiyat-e Modarres University
No imprisonment
War veteran (wounded)
IRGC militiaman
While an MP, Kuchakzadeh continued to teach at Tarbiyat-e Modarres University. He returned to that position full time after his terms in the Majlis. His daughter is married to the son of Hoseyn Mozaffar.

Kuhi-Baghanari, Nasrollah

Deputy of the Eighth Majlis, Sarvestan and Kavar, Fars (2008–12)
1959–, Shiraz, Fars
BA, social science
Asadollah
Civil servant, state companies
No imprisonment
Kuhi-Baghanari held the record for absenteeism in the Eighth Majlis and later owned a gas station in Tehran.

Kuhkan-Rizi, Mohsen

Deputy of the Fourth (1992–96), Seventh (2004–8), Eighth (2008–12), and Tenth (2016–20) Majlis, Lenjan and Mobarakeh, Isfahan
1957–, Lenjan, Isfahan

BA, law; MA, law
Nasir
Civil servant
No imprisonment
IRGC militiaman
Founding member and secretary-general of the
    ISFPD; member of the SFIR
Kuhkan-Rizi, a conservative MP, was in charge of the
    IRP in Lenjan. He was governor of Borujen and
    Farsan, as well as a lawyer.

Kuhsari, Ali

Deputy of the Sixth Majlis, Ramiyan and Azadshahr,
    Golestan (2000–2001)
1969–May 17, 2001, Azadshahr, Golestan
BS, agricultural engineering
Jalal
Member of the Azadshahr City Council
No imprisonment
Kuhsari died in a plane crash.

Kuhsari, Gholam-Ali

Deputy of the Sixth Majlis, Ramiyan and Azadshahr,
    Golestan (2001–4)
1971–, Azadshahr, Golestan
BS, agricultural engineering
Jalal
No imprisonment
Not a war veteran
Gholam-Ali Kuhsari became the youngest MP in
    the Sixth Majlis when he replaced his deceased
    brother, Ali.

Kula'i, Mrs. Elaheh

Deputy of the Sixth Majlis, Tehran, Tehran
    (2000–2004)
1956–, Tehran, Tehran
PhD, international relations, Tarbiyat-e Modarres
    University, 1988
Mohammad-Hoseyn, bazaar tradesman
Professor of political science at Tehran University

No imprisonment
Member of the central council and deputy secre-
    tary-general of IIPF

Kurd, Ali

Deputy of the Tenth Majlis, Khash, Mirjaveh,
    Kurin, and Nosratabad, Sistan and Baluchestan
    (2016–20)
1966–, Sangan, Razavi Khorasan
Father's name unknown, farmer
Kurd, a Sunni, was a district mayor for sixteen years
    in Sistan and Baluchestan.

Kurd, Baqer

Deputy of the Sixth Majlis, Zahedan, Sistan and Balu-
    chestan (2000–2004)
1955–, Khash, Sistan and Baluchestan
BS, mechanical engineering; MS, industrial
    engineering
Mohammad
Professor and engineer
No imprisonment
Kurd, a Sunni, became a civil servant after serving in
    the Majlis.

Kurdmandani, Khodabakhsh

Deputy of the Fifth Majlis, Khash, Nosratabad, and
    Mirjaveh, Sistan and Baluchestan (1996–2000)
1957–, Khash, Sistan and Baluchestan
BA, Persian literature
Abdollah
No imprisonment
Kurdmandani was a Sunni MP.

Kuzehgar, Mohammad-Ali

Deputy of the Sixth Majlis, Shahriyar and Qods, Teh-
    ran (2000–2004)
1965–, Nur, Mazandaran
MD, medicine
Ali

Medical doctor

No imprisonment

Kuzehgar went into the private sector after leaving the Majlis.

Ladjvardi, Asadollah

Revolutionary prosecutor-general of Tehran (September 11, 1980–December 1984)

1935–August 23, 1998, Tehran, Tehran

High school (incomplete)

Ali-Akbar, logs seller

Imprisoned before the revolution (three times)

War veteran

Founding member of the CIC/PCIC

The shah's regime arrested Ladjvardi for the first time in 1965 after the assassination of PM Hassan-Ali Mansur. He was last freed from prison in 1977 and was involved with the committee welcoming Ayatollah Khomeini back to Iran. He ran unsuccessfully for the First Majlis on the joint slate of CIC and IRP. In 1980, Ladjvardi was the court prosecutor trying members of the Forqan group. He subsequently became the warden of Evin Prison and was so notorious that the HCJ dismissed him in 1984. He then worked as a tradesman in the bazaar and also went to the war front. The last position Ladjvardi held before he was assassinated by PMOI was chief of the State's Prisons Organization (1989–97). Ladjvardi's sister was married to the brother of Sa'id Amani [-Hamadani].

Lahuti-Eshkevari, Hasan

Deputy of the First Majlis, Rasht, Gilan (1980–October 29, 1981)

1927–October 29, 1981, Rudsar, Gilan

Clerical education

Nasrollah, clergyman

Clergyman

Imprisoned before the revolution

Not a war veteran

Ayatollah Lahuti-Eshkevari, who was active in the anti-shah movement, was very much influenced by the ideas of Ali Shari'ati. Ayatollah Khomeini appointed him as his representative in the IRGC in February 1979 but he resigned on November 19, 1979. He was also the Friday prayer leader of Rasht and Ayatollah Khomeini's representative in Gilan. He supported President Banisadr during his term in office and was critical of the IRP. Lahuti-Eshkevari's two sons, Hamid and Sa'id, married Faezeh and Fatemeh Hashemi-Bahremani. His third son, Vahid, was a leftist (PMOI). Lahuti-Eshkevari reportedly died of a heart attack after he was questioned about his son Vahid at Evin Prison.

Larijani, Ali

Minister of culture and Islamic guidance in President Hashemi-Rafsanjani's first (August 11, 1992–August 2, 1993) and second (August 16, 1993–February 11, 1994) cabinets; director-general of IRIB (February 13, 1994–May 23, 2004); member of the Fourth (1997–2002), Fifth (2002–7), Sixth (2007–12), Seventh (2012–17), and Eighth (2017–22) Expediency Discernment Assembly; secretary of the Supreme Council for National Security (May 25, 2004–June 27, 2008); deputy of the Eighth (2008–12), Ninth (2012–16), and Tenth (2016–20) Majlis, Qom, Qom

1957–, Najaf, Iraq

BS, computer science and mathematics, Sharif University of Technology, 1979; MA, philosophy, Tehran University; PhD, philosophy, Tehran University

Mirza Hashem [Amoli], clergyman (ayatollah)

No imprisonment

War veteran

IRGC militiaman

Larijani was a high-level official in IRIB from 1979 to 1982. He joined the IRGC in 1982, becoming parliamentary deputy to the IRGC commander. He also served as deputy minister for legal and parliamentary affairs in the Ministry of Post, Telegraph, and Telephones in the 1980s. President Hashemi-Rafsanjani appointed Larijani as culture minister on August 11, 1992, after Seyyed Mohammad Khatami resigned. Larijani held the post until February 11, 1994, when Ayatollah Khamenei decided to appoint him as head of IRIB. Larijani became the Speaker of the Eighth Majlis, even though he had no prior experience as an MP. He continued as the Speaker in the Ninth and Tenth Majlis as well. Larijani was Iran's chief nuclear negotiator from August 16, 2005, to October 20, 2007, and he was the supreme leader's representative in the SCNS. Larijani received only 5.8 percent of the vote in the first round of the 2005 presidential election. However, in the 2008 Majlis election, he received the highest number of votes in Qom and immediately became the Majlis Speaker. He is the son of Ayatollah Mirza Hashem Amoli and son-in-law of Ayatollah Morteza Motahhari. MP Ali Motahhari, Morteza Motahhari's son, is his brother-in-law. He is also related to Ahmad Tavakkoli.

[Ardeshir-] Larijani, Mohammad-Javad

Deputy of the Fourth (1992–96) and Fifth (1996–2000) Majlis, Tehran, Tehran
1951–, Najaf, Iraq
BS, electrical engineering, Sharif University of Technology, 1974; unfinished doctoral studies at the University of California, Berkeley (USA)
Mirza Hashem [Amoli], clergyman (ayatollah)
No imprisonment
Not a war veteran
Larijani is an institution builder in Iran. In 1989, he founded the Institute for Studies in Theoretical Physics and Mathematics (later renamed the Institute for Research in Fundamental Sciences), which is affiliated with the Ministry of Science, Research, and Technology. He also founded the Islamic Majlis Research Center, an advisory arm of the Majlis, which he headed from 1992 to 2000 (the center officially started its work in 1995). Larijani has held other positions including university professor, deputy foreign minister, and head of the Ministry of Foreign Affairs' Center for Political and International Studies. He was a member of the delegation Ayatollah Khomeini sent to deliver a message to the Soviet leader Mikhail Gorbachev.

Larijani-Amoli, Sadeq

Member of the Third (1999–2006), Fourth (2007–16), and Fifth (2016–22) Assembly of Experts, Mazandaran; member of the Fourth (2001–4) and Fifth (2004–9) Guardian Councils; chief justice (August 14, 2009–present)
1960–, Najaf, Iraq
Clerical education, Qom Seminary, 1989
Mirza Hashem [Amoli], clergyman (ayatollah)
Clergyman
No imprisonment
Not a war veteran
Member of the SQSS
Ayatollah Larijani-Amoli started as a theology student in 1977, and Ayatollah Khamenei appointed him judiciary chief in August 2009. He was in charge of the judiciary when the regime put the leaders of the Green Movement under house arrest and killed some of its activists in 2009 and when it arrested and killed protesters in early January 2018. On January 12, 2018, the US government put Larijani-Amoli on its list of sanctioned individuals. He is the younger brother of Majlis Speaker Ali Larijani and son-in-law of Ayatollah Hoseyn Vahid-Khorasani, a source of emulation in Qom. His other brothers are Mohammad-Javad, a conservative theoretician and judiciary official, Baqer, rector of the University of Medical Sciences, and Fazel, Iran's cultural attaché in Canada). Larijani-Amoli is also related to the influential MP Ahmad Tavakkoli.

Latifiyan, Hedayat

Chief of Law Enforcement Forces (February 15, 1997–June 27, 2000)
War veteran
IRGC militiaman
Brigadier General Latifiyan was the commander of Hamzeh military base, which was responsible for

the northwest region of Iran during the Iran–Iraq War. He has a background in the intelligence service, and was the IRGC's deputy for planning and budget. He became commander of LEF in 1997, but was sacked by the regime in 2000 due to public pressure regarding his harsh handling of the 1999 student riots in Tehran.

Loqmaniyan, Hoseyn

Deputy of the Sixth Majlis, Hamadan, Hamadan (2000–2004)
1953–, Hamadan, Hamadan
BA, Persian literature
Safar-Ali
Academia
No imprisonment
In the course of delivering a speech in the Majlis in 2006, Loqmaniyan criticized the judiciary for its crackdown on the press. After the judiciary arrested Loqmaniyan, Majlis Speaker Mehdi Karrubi threatened that he would not attend any more Majlis meetings until Loqmaniyan was released. Loqmaniyan was quickly released but was handed a ten-month prison term. However, Ayatollah Khamenei pardoned him. After finishing his term in the Majlis, Loqmaniyan worked as a civil servant.

Lotfi, Hasan

Deputy of the Tenth Majlis, Razan, Hamadan (2016–20)
1971–, Razan, Hamadan
MA, law
Head of the Hamadan governor-general's administrative office
No imprisonment

Lotfi, Mohammad-Taqi

Deputy of the Second Majlis, Ilam, Ilam (1984–88)
1955–, Ilam, Ilam
Clerical education, Qom Seminary
Kheirollah

Clergyman
Imprisoned before the revolution
Not a war veteran
IRGC militiaman
HI Lotfi was the Friday prayer leader of Ilam from 2002 to 2010.

Lotfi-Ashtiyani, Seyyed Ahmad

Deputy of the Eighth Majlis, Arak and Komijan, Markazi (2008–12)
1960–, Ashtiyan, Markazi
BA, public administration
Seyyed Baqer
Civil servant
No imprisonment
Lotfi-Ashtiyani was not elected to the Ninth Majlis.

Madadi, Mohammad-Ali

Deputy of the Ninth Majlis, Miyaneh, East Azerbaijan (2012–16)
1959–, Miyaneh, East Azerbaijan
BS, mathematics, Tehran University, 1979; MA, educational management, Institute for Management and Planning Studies, 2002; PhD, Iranology, Yerevan State University (Armenia), 2006
Abdolghaffar
Member of the Miyaneh City Council; professor at Payam-e Nur University
No imprisonment

Madani, Seyyed Ahmad

Commander of the Islamic Republic of Iran Navy (February–March 2, 1979); minister of national defense in PM Bazargan's cabinet (March 6–31, 1979)
1929–February 12, 2006, Kerman, Kerman
BS, military science, Royal Naval College (England); PhD, international law, Tehran University
Father's name unknown, clergyman
Academia
No imprisonment
Not a war veteran

Member of the central council of INF

Madani, a retired rear admiral before the revolution, became commander of the Islamic Republic of Iran Navy in 1979. While he was in that post, PM Bazargan appointed him as minister of national defense, where Khamenei was his deputy. The government reversed the decision on March 2, 1979, and said he couldn't hold both posts simultaneously. He then became governor of Khuzestan, from which he resigned on November 3, 1979. In the first presidential election held in January 1980, Madani became the first runner-up by garnering 15.7 percent of the vote and winning a number of provinces including Hormozgan, Kerman, Kurdistan, Sistan and Baluchestan, and Zanjan. Later that year, Madani was elected to the first Majlis as Kerman's representative but, knowing that his credentials would not be approved, he resigned. Madani left Iran in 1980 and lived in self-imposed exile first in France and then in the United States until he died.

Madani-Bajestani, Seyyed Mahmud

Deputy of the Seventh Majlis, Gonabad, Razavi Khorasan (2004–8)

1964–, Gonabad, Razavi Khorasan

Clerical education, Qom Seminary

Seyyed Javad, clergyman (ayatollah)

Clergyman (HI)

No imprisonment

War veteran

Martyr's family (brother Seyyed Mohammad)

Madani-Dehkharqani, Mir Asadollah

Member of the Assembly for the Final Examination of the Constitution, Hamadan (1979)

1914–September 11, 1981, Azarshahr, East Azerbaijan

Clerical education, Najaf Seminary (Iraq)

Mir Ali, bazaar tradesman

Clergyman

Imprisoned before the revolution

Not a war veteran

Ayatollah Khomeini appointed Ayatollah Madani-Dehkharqani as his personal representative and the Friday prayer leader of Tabriz on November 3, 1979. He was assassinated by PMOI twenty-two months later.

Madani-Kermani, Seyyed Jalaleddin

Member of the First (1983–86) and Second (1986–89) Guardian Councils

1937–, Kerman, Kerman

MA, law; PhD, political science

Jamaleddin

Judiciary official

No imprisonment

Not a war veteran

Madani-Kermani served as a lawyer in the GC. He has also been an adviser to the head of the judiciary, a university professor, a judge, and the director of the education branch of the Justice Administration.

Maddahi, Mohammad-Ebrahim

Deputy of the Fifth Majlis, Aligudarz, Lorestan (1996–2000)

1961–, Aligudarz, Lorestan

MS, psychology

Mohammad-Taqi

No imprisonment

Founding member of the Green Party

Mafi, Mrs. Parvaneh

Deputy of the Tenth Majlis, Tehran, Tehran (2016–20)

1957–, Kermanshah

MA, management

No imprisonment

Member of the central council of HKSI and the Alliance of the Women of the Islamic Republic

Mafi, who has retired from the MI, was also an adviser to the minister of education, an economics expert for the secretariat of the EDA, and an editor of a number of periodicals. During the reformist era of President Khatami, she became the first deputy governor of Shemiranat district in postrevolutionary Iran. When she was elected to the Tenth Majlis at the age of 59, she became the oldest female ever elected to the Majlis.

[Mehdizadeh-] Mahallati, Fazlollah

Deputy of the First Majlis, Mahallat, Markazi (1980–84)
1930–February 20, 1986, Mahallat, Markazi
Clerical education, Qom Seminary
Gholam-Hoseyn, bazaar tradesman and farmer
Clergyman
Imprisoned before the revolution
Not a war veteran
HI Mahallati joined the paramilitary group Devotees of Islam in 1948. He was a member of the committee welcoming Ayatollah Khomeini back to Iran. Mahallati was Ayatollah Khomeini's representative in the IRGC's command council from June 1980 to February 1986 before being elected to the Majlis. In July 1980, he resigned his post in the Pilgrimage and Pious Endowment Foundation to pursue other duties. He was killed when the Iraqi Air Force shot down an aircraft he was on.

Mahallati, Mohammad-Ja'far (Amir)

Permanent Representative of Iran to the UN (1987–89)
1952–, Tehran, Tehran
BA, economics, National University (Shahid Beheshti University), 1975; BS, civil engineering, University of Kansas, 1978; MA, political economy, University of Oregon (USA), 1980; PhD, Islamic studies, McGill University (Canada), 2006
Majdeddin, clergyman (ayatollah)
Ministry of Foreign Affairs official
No imprisonment
Not a war veteran
Mahallati served in such capacities as chair of the economic department at Kerman University (1980) and director-general for economic and international affairs in the foreign ministry (1981–87).

He was very important in getting UN Resolution 598 accepted to end the Iran–Iraq War. His father, Ayatollah Majdeddin Mahallati (1925–2000), was part of the "quiet" opposition to some of the clerical rule policies. Mahallati is currently a presidential scholar in the department of religion at Oberlin College.

Mahbudi, Borzu

Deputy of the Second Majlis, Kazerun, Fars (1984–88)
1955–, Kazerun, Fars
Associate's degree
Ali-Baba
No imprisonment

Mahdavi, Seyyed Abolhasan

Member of the Third (1999–2006), Fourth (2007–16), and Fifth (2016–22) Assembly of Experts, Isfahan
1962–, Isfahan, Isfahan
Clerical education, Isfahan Seminary
Seyyed Bahaeddin, clergyman
Clergyman (ayatollah)
No imprisonment
Not a war veteran
Mahdavi was formerly the temporary Friday prayer leader of Isfahan.

Mahdavi Haji, Mehdi

Deputy of the Second Majlis, Babolsar and Bandpay, Mazandaran (1984–88)
1942–, Babol, Mazandaran
Clerical education
Heydar
Clergyman
No imprisonment
Not a war veteran

Mahdavi-Abhari, Ahmad

Deputy of the Fifth (1996–2000), Seventh (2004–8), and Eighth (2008–12) Majlis, Abhar, Zanjan

1957–, Qom, Qom
BS, electrical engineering
Habibollah
Civil servant
No imprisonment
After serving in the Majlis, Mahdavi-Abhari became
    head of the Association of Petrochemical Industry
    Corporations.

Mahdavi-Kani [Baqeri], Mohammad-Reza

Member of the Revolutionary Council (1979–80);
    interior minister in the Revolutionary Council
    cabinet (1980), PM Raja'i's cabinet (1980–81), and
    PM Bahonar's cabinet (August 17–30, 1981); mem-
    ber of the First Guardian Council (1980; 1982–83);
    interim prime minister (September 2–October 18,
    1981); member of the Second (1989–97) and Third
    (1997–2002) Expediency Discernment Assembly;
    member of the Fourth Assembly of Experts, Teh-
    ran (2008–14)
August 6, 1931–October 21, 2014, Kan, Tehran
Clerical education, Qom Seminary
Asadollah, small landowner
Clergyman
Imprisoned before the revolution (sent to internal
    exile in Bukan in 1975)
Not a war veteran
Secretary-general of the SCC (for decades)
Ayatollah Mahdavi-Kani was in charge of Marvi Sem-
    inary before and after the revolution. Ayatollah
    Khomeini appointed him to the Revolutionary
    Council in 1978. In the chaotic early days after
    the revolution, he was in charge of all revolution-
    ary committees (komitehs) and served as acting
    Friday prayer leader in Tehran. He was one of
    the first clerics to enter government service when
    he became deputy interior minister in July 1979.
    Mahdavi-Kani signed up for the first presidential
    election in January 1980, but he could not get
    the support of the powerful IRP, which he never
    joined. Later that year, he headed the GC from
    July to December 1980. Mahdavi-Kani resigned
    from the first GC on December 3, 1980, to take

on the role of interior minister. At 48, he was the
oldest member in both President Banisadr and
President Raja'i's cabinets. After Raja'i's assassination, Mahdavi-Kani served forty-five days as
interim prime minister in 1981. He also termi-
nated his presidential candidacy in October 1981.
On February 10, 1982, Mahdavi-Kani returned to
the first GC upon the death of Ayatollah Rabbani-Shirazi. He was appointed to the Headquarters
for Cultural Revolution in December 1984. Mahdavi-Kani, an influential conservative politician,
ran unsuccessfully for the chairmanship of the
Second AE, but finally replaced Hashemi-Rafsanjani as the chairman of the Fourth AE in
an election held on March 8, 2011. He founded
Imam Sadeq University in 1983 and served as its
rector until his death in 2014. His wife, Qodsiyyeh Sorkhehi (daughter of Ayatollah Sorkhehi),
whom he married when she was less than twelve
years old, is in charge of Imam Sadeq University's
Women's Bureau. His son, HI Mohammad-Sa'id
Mahdavi-Kani, replaced his father as rector of
Imam Sadeq University in September 2015. The
ayatollah's daughter, Maryam, is married to
HI Mir Lohi and is also a high-level official at
the university. His brother, Mohammad-Baqer
Baqeri-Kani, was the vice rector of the university.

Mahdavi-Kani [Baqeri-Kani], Mohammad-Baqer

Member of the First (1983–90), Second (1991–98), and
    Fourth (2007–16) Assembly of Experts, Tehran
1926–, Tehran, Tehran
Clerical education, Qom Seminary
Asadollah, small landowner
Clergyman
Imprisoned before the revolution
Not a war veteran
Ayatollah Mohammad-Baqer Mahdavi-Kani is the
    older brother of Ayatollah Mohammad-Reza Mah-
    davi-Kani. In the early days of the revolution, he
    was a deputy to his brother, who was in charge of
    all revolutionary committees. A longtime member
    of the AE, he was not elected to the Fifth AE from

Tehran in 2016. He was also a professor and his brother's deputy at Imam Sadeq University.

Mahdavi-Khanaki, Seyyed Mohammad-Baqer

Deputy of the Fourth Majlis, Kerman, Kerman (1992–96)
1930–2011, Kerman, Kerman
MA, theology; clerical education
Seyyed Ali
Clergyman
No imprisonment
Not a war veteran
HI Mahdavi-Khanaki was the oldest member of the Fourth Majlis.

Mahfuzi, Abbas

Member of the First (1984–90), Second (1991–98), Third (1999–2006), and Fourth (2007–16) Assembly of Experts, Gilan
1928–, Rudsar, Gilan
Clerical education, Qom Seminary
Isa, farmer and tradesman
Clergyman
Imprisoned before the revolution
Not a war veteran
Member of the SQSS
Ayatollah Mahfuzi was elected to the First AE in interim elections held on April 15, 1984. He was Ayatollah Khamenei's representative at Tehran University for a while. Mahfuzi's son, Ali-Reza (b. 1956), who has lived in exile in France since the early 1980s, was a high-ranking member of the Marxist OIPFG.

Mahjub, Ali-Reza

Deputy of the Fifth (1996–2000), Sixth (2001–4), Seventh (2004–8), Eighth (2008–12), Ninth (2012–16), and Tenth (2016–20) Majlis, Tehran, Tehran
1958–, Karaj, Tehran
BA, history, Tehran University
Gholam-Reza
Workers' representative in the High Council of Labor

No imprisonment
War veteran
Secretary-general of the House of the Worker; founder of the Islamic Labor Party
Mahjub has been an adviser on labor affairs to various prime ministers and presidents.

Mahlujchi [Mahluji], Hoseyn

Deputy of the First (1982–84), Second (1984–88), and Third (1988–89) Majlis, Kashan, Isfahan; minister of mining and metals in President Hashemi-Rafsanjani's first (August 29, 1989–August 2, 1993) and second (August 16, 1993–August 2, 1997) cabinets
1947–, Kashan, Isfahan
BS, mechanical engineering, Amirkabir University of Technology, 1971
Ali-Akbar
Governor-general of Lorestan
No imprisonment
No war veteran
Mahlujchi was a member of PMOI before the revolution, but he parted ways with them in the early 1970s. While serving in the Majlis in the 1980s, Speaker Hashemi-Rafsanjani appointed him to oversee weapons production in factories, and he held the chairmanship of the Industries Committee. He resigned from the Third Majlis on August 29, 1989, to become the minister of mining and metals, and he held that post for eight years, surviving an impeachment on December 14, 1994. He is considered to have been a competent minister who improved the Iranian mining sector. After leaving politics, Mahlujchi led the Persepolis Club for eight or nine years and then founded the Kashan Cultural Foundation. His maternal uncle is Ayatollah Seyyed Mehdi Yasrebi, who served in the AE for many years.

Mahmudi, Morteza

Deputy of the First Majlis, Qasr-e Shirin, Kermanshah (1980–84)

1943–, Islamabad-e Gharb, Kermanshah
BA, philosophy
Fattah, farmer
Academia
No imprisonment
Not a war veteran
After leaving the Majlis, Mahmudi became a civil
    servant.

Mahmudi, Mrs. Somayeh

Deputy of the Tenth Majlis, Shahreza, Isfahan
    (2016–20)
1984–, Vanak, Isfahan
BA, sociology, Isfahan University of Technology; MA,
    Islamic Azad University–Dehagan
Gholam-Reza
Martyr's family (father killed at the war front)

Mahmudi-Golpayegani, Seyyed Abutaleb

Deputy of the First (1980–84), Second (1984–88), and
    Third (1988–92) Majlis, Golpayegan and Khansar,
    Isfahan
1926–September 5, 1993, Golpayegan, Isfahan
Clerical education
Seyyed Hoseyn, farmer
Clergyman
No imprisonment
Not a war veteran
HI Mahmudi-Golpayegani, who was the Friday prayer
    leader of Golpayegan and Arak, died in a car
    accident.

Mahmudi-Sartangi, Seyyed Shahab

Deputy of the First Majlis, Borujen, Chahar Mahal
    and Bakhtiari (1980–84)
1930–, Borujen, Chahar Mahal and Bakhtiari
BA, Arabic literature
Seyyed Ali-Akbar, clergyman
Academia
No imprisonment
Not a war veteran

After serving in the Majlis, Mahmudi-Sartangi be-
    came a civil servant.

Mahmudi-Shahneshin, Mohammad

Deputy of the Tenth Majlis, Shahriyar, Tehran (2016–20)
1964–, Shahneshin, Ardabil
BS, electrical engineering; MA, executive education
Nasrollah
No imprisonment
War veteran (thirty months)

Mahmudiyan, Seyyed Nurmohammad

Deputy of the Second Majlis, Buyer Ahmad, Kohgi-
    luyeh and Buyer Ahmad (1984–88); deputy of
    the Third Majlis, Yasouj, Kohgiluyeh and Buyer
    Ahmad (1988–92)
1953–2014, Kohgiluyeh, Kohgiluyeh and Buyer Ahmad
Clerical education
Seyyed Ahmad
Clergyman (HI)
No imprisonment

Mahmud-Robati, Ahmad

Deputy of the Third Majlis, Shahriyar and Robat
    Karim, Tehran (1988–92)
1955–, Karaj, Tehran
BA
Shirali
No imprisonment
After leaving the Majlis, Mahmud-Robati became a
    deputy to the minister of cooperatives.

Mahmudzadeh, Jalal

Deputy of the Eighth (2008–12) and Tenth (2016–20)
    Majlis, Mahabad, West Azerbaijan
1966–, Mahabad, West Azerbaijan
MS, agricultural engineering
Ali
Civil servant
No imprisonment

Mahmudzadeh was the coordinator of Sunni lawmakers in the Eighth Majlis. In 2010, he survived an assassination attempt after revealing corruption by the mayor and city council of Mahabad. He was a director of the Agricultural Jihad in Mahabad. The GC disqualified him from running in the 2012 Majlis election.

Mahsuli, Sadeq

Interior minister in President Ahmadinejad's first cabinet (November 18, 2008–August 2, 2009); minister of welfare and social security in President Ahmadinejad's second cabinet (November 15, 2009–May 14, 2011)
1959–, Urmia, West Azerbaijan
BS, civil engineering, Iran University of Science and Technology; MA, business administration, Tehran University
Father's name unknown, bazaar tradesman
Military and security forces
No imprisonment
War veteran
IRGC militiaman
On November 9, 2005, Mahsuli, who had been governor of Urmia and deputy to the governor-general of West Azerbaijan, withdrew his name from consideration as minister of petroleum. On November 18, 2008, he became the interior minister, and in that capacity, he oversaw the controversial 2009 presidential election. On November 15, 2009, Mahsuli received 149 positive votes, ninety-five negative votes, and twenty-one abstentions to become minister of welfare and social security. However, in May 2011 his old friend President Ahmadinejad ended his term by claiming that he wanted to reduce the number of ministries. In October 10, 2011, the Council of Europe put Mahsuli on its sanctioned list and wrote that as interior minister, he "had authority over all police forces, interior ministry security agents, and plainclothes agents. The forces under his direction were responsible for attacks on the dormitories of Tehran University on 14 June 2009 and the torture of students in the basement of the Ministry (the notorious basement level 4). Other protestors were severely abused at the Kahrizak Detention Center, which was operated by police under Mahsouli's control." He is also on the US Treasury Office of Foreign Assets Control's Specially Designated Nationals and Blocked Persons List because of his role in the 2009 crackdown. Mahsuli and former foreign minister Ali-Akbar Velayati are married to two sisters.

Majdara, Mohammad

Deputy of the Third (1988–92), Fourth (1992–96), and Fifth (1996) Majlis, Babolsar and Bandpay, Mazandaran
1954–September 20, 1996, Babol, Mazandaran
MS, mechanical engineering
Esma'il
No imprisonment
Majdara died of an illness.

Majidi, Mohammad-Reza

Deputy of the Fourth (1993–96) and Fifth (1996–2000) Majlis, Fasa, Fars
1943–, Fasa, Fars
BS, electrical engineering; MA, management, 1995
Abbas-Qoli
No imprisonment

Makarem-Shirazi, Naser

Member of the Assembly for the Final Examination of the Constitution, Fars (1979)
1926–, Shiraz, Fars
Clerical education, Najaf Seminary (Iraq), 1950
Ali-Mohammad, laborer and trader
Clergyman (ayatollah)
Imprisoned before the revolution
Not a war veteran
Founding member of the SQSS
Before the revolution, theologian Makarem-Shirazi started a magazine titled *Maktab-e Islam* that

appealed to educated Muslims. A prolific writer and articulate debater, he defended more conservative Islamic positions against lay thinkers such as Ali Shari'ati before the revolution and Abdolkarim Soroush after the revolution. After serving in the Assembly for the Final Examination of the Constitution, Makarem-Shirazi did not hold any political posts. In 1979 he was strongly opposed to the idea of rule by a supreme jurisconsult. He founded the Amir Al-Mo'menin Institute in 1986. As a conservative source of emulation, he issued a fatwa objecting to women attending stadiums to watch soccer games.

Makhzan-Musavi, Seyyed Abolhasan

Deputy of the Second Majlis, Rudbar, Gilan (1984–88)
1950–, Rudbar, Gilan
MA
Seyyed Fazlollah
No imprisonment
Makhzan-Musavi is a former rector of Ahlulbeyt International University.

Malakuti, Ali

Deputy of the First (1980–84) and Second (1984–88) Majlis, Sarab, East Azerbaijan; member of the Fifth Assembly of Experts, East Azerbaijan (2016–22)
1948–, Qom, Qom
Clerical education
Moslem, clergyman (ayatollah)
Clergyman
No imprisonment
Not a war veteran
HI Malakuti's father was also a member of the Assembly of Experts.

Malakuti, Moslem

Member of the First (1984–90) and Second (1991–98) Assembly of Experts, East Azerbaijan
1924–2014, Sarab, East Azerbaijan
Clerical education, Najaf Seminary (Iraq)

Father's name unknown, farmer
Clergyman
No imprisonment
Not a war veteran
Member of the SQSS
Ayatollah Malakuti studied in Najaf from 1955 to 1966 before returning to Qom. In November 1981, Ayatollah Khomeini appointed him as his representative in Azerbaijan and the Friday prayer leader of Tabriz. He served in this post for some thirteen years. In 1982, Malakuti became a member of the central council of Friday prayer leaders, and in March 1983, Ayatollah Khomeini appointed him as a mediator between the GC and the Majlis. From 1994 until he passed away, Malakuti resided in Qom as a source of emulation.

Malekasa, Karim

Deputy of the Second (1986–88) and Third (1988–92) Majlis, Pol-e Dokhtar, Lorestan
1948–, Khorramabad, Lorestan
MS, chemistry
Sadeq
No imprisonment
Malekasa was elected to the Second Majlis in interim elections to replace Seyyed Nureddin Rahimi, who died in a plane crash in early 1986. The GC disqualified Malekasa, a reformist, from running in elections for the Fourth, Seventh and Tenth Majlis, and he did not receive enough votes for the Sixth Majlis.

Malekhoseyni, Seyyed Keramatollah

Member of the Second (1991–98), Third (1999–2006), and Fourth (2007–12) Assembly of Experts, Kohgiluyeh and Buyer Ahmad
1924–2012, Buyer Ahmad, Kohgiluyeh and Buyer Ahmad
Clerical education, Qom Seminary, 1961
Seyyed Sadreddin, clergyman
Clergyman
Imprisoned before the revolution

Not a war veteran

Ayatollah Malekhoseyni was the representative of
Supreme Leader Ayatollah Khamenei in Kohgi-
luyeh. After he died, his son replaced him in the
Fourth AE.

Malekhoseyni, Seyyed Sharafeddin

Member of the Fourth (2013–16) and Fifth (2016–22)
Assembly of Experts, Kohgiluyeh and Buyer
Ahmad

1962–, Shiraz, Fars

Clerical education, Qom Seminary

Seyyed Keramatollah, clergyman (ayatollah)

Clergyman

No imprisonment

Not a war veteran

HI Malekhoseyni was elected to the Fourth AE in
midterm elections held in June 2013, replacing
his father, who passed away in 2012. On March
4, 2013, Ayatollah Khamenei appointed Seyyed
Sharafeddin as his representative in Kohgiluyeh, a
position his father also held.

Maleki, Vali

Deputy of the Seventh (2004–8) and Tenth (2016–20)
Majlis, Meshginshahr, Ardabil

1957–, Meshginshahr, Ardabil

BS, food industry engineering, Tabriz University; MS,
industrial engineering, Islamic Azad University–
Science and Research Branch

Ali

Civil servant, state companies

No imprisonment

Not a war veteran

Maleki was a member of Meshginshahr's Construction Jihad between 1979 and 1981. He headed
many industrial state companies between 1985
and 2004.

Malekmadani, Mohammad-Hasan

Mayor of Tehran (2001–2)

1954–, Meybod, Yazd

BA, engineering

Ali, landowner

Official in the office of Tehran's mayor

Malekmadani was active in the Construction Jihad and
courts in the early days of the revolution, before
culture minister Khatami put Malekmadani in
charge of *Keyhan*'s administrative and financial affairs department. He and Khatami knew each other
as sons of two well-known families in the Ardakan
and Yazd regions. Malekmadani was mayor of Isfahan from 1983 to 1990 and then became a deputy
to Tehran Mayor Gholam-Hoseyn Karbaschi. He
became the mayor of Tehran in early 2002.

Malekmohammadi, Hasan

Deputy of the Eighth Majlis, Damghan, Semnan
(2008–12)

1961–, Damghan, Semnan

Clerical education, Qom Seminary, 1982

Musa

Clergyman

No imprisonment

War veteran (fifty-three months; wounded)

HI Malekmohammadi studied with Ayatollah Khamenei for sixteen years, and he was put in charge of
Ghadir International Foundation in 1992. After his
unsuccessful run for the Ninth Majlis, he became
parliamentary deputy of Azad University.

Malekpur, Parviz

Deputy of the First (1980–84) and Second (1984–88)
Majlis, representing the Zoroastrian community
(as a religious minority)

1947–, Rafsanjan, Kerman

MS, research process

Sorush, civil servant

Civil servant

No imprisonment

Not a war veteran

After serving in the Majlis, Malekpur went back to
work as a civil servant.

Malekshahi, Allahyar

Deputy of the Ninth (2012–16) and Tenth (2016–20)
  Majlis, Kuhdasht, Lorestan
1962–, Kuhdasht, Lorestan
BA, judicial law, Tehran University, 1989; MA, crim-
  inal law, Islamic Azad University–Khorramabad;
  PhD, law, (UAE; unverified)
Judiciary official
No imprisonment
War veteran
IRGC militiaman
Malekshahi, a conservative, served as head of the jus-
  tice administration for Lorestan and Kermanshah
  Provinces and was a judge in the CAJ.

Malekshahi [Rad], Mohammad-Reza

Deputy of the Eighth (2008–12) and Tenth (2016–20)
  Majlis, Khorramabad, Lorestan
1957–, Aleshtar, Lorestan
BA, management, Tehran University, 1995; MA, edu-
  cational management, 1999
Jozeali
Deputy director of IRIB in Hamadan
No imprisonment
Malekshahi is a former teacher and IRIB deputy in
  Lorestan Province. He was appointed as head of
  the education department in Lorestan Province in
  2005.

Malekzadeh, Mohammad-Sharif

Vice president and head of the Cultural Heritage
  Organization in President Ahmadinejad's second
  cabinet (December 2, 2012–13)
1966–, Zabol, Sistan and Baluchestan
PhD
Director of the Office of Iranians Abroad
No imprisonment
While Malekzadeh was in charge of the Office of Ira-
  nians Abroad, he was accused of financial fraud.
  Ayatollah Khamenei pardoned him. President
  Ahmadinejad appointed him as a VP in 2012 and

later he became an adviser to the former head of
  the judiciary, Ayatollah Hashemi-Shahrudi.

Malekzadeh, Reza

Minister of health and medical education in Presi-
  dent Hashemi-Rafsanjani's first cabinet (March 5,
  1991–August 2, 1993)
1951–, Kazerun, Fars
MD, gastroenterology (England)
Javad, farmer
Medical doctor
No imprisonment
Not a war veteran
Member of the central council of PECI
Malekzadeh, a former rector of Shiraz University,
  became head of the Ministry of Health after the
  Majlis impeached Iraj Fazel on January 13, 1991.
  He officially became the minister of health and
  medical education on March 5, 1991.

Malekzadehgan, Mohammad-Hoseyn

Commander of the Islamic Republic of Iran Navy
  (June 27, 1985–October 30, 1989)
1944–, Ardabil, Ardabil
Commodore Malekzadehgan underwent training at
  the Italian Naval Academy, as well as in England
  and Pakistan. After his retirement, he became a
  military adviser to the supreme leader. Malekzadehgan is currently in charge of the Jask Free
  Zone in Hormozgan Province.

Mamduhi, Hasan

Member of the Fourth Assembly of Experts, Kerman-
  shah (2007–16)
1939–, Kermanshah, Kermanshah
Clerical education, Qom Seminary
Mohammad-Hoseyn, bazaar tradesman
Clergyman (ayatollah)
Imprisoned before the revolution
Not a war veteran
Member of the SQSS

Manafi, Hadi

Minister of health in PM Raja'i's cabinet (1980–81), PM Bahonar's cabinet (August 17–30, 1981), interim PM Mahdavi-Kani's cabinet (September 3–October 18, 1981), and PM Musavi's first cabinet (November 2, 1981–84); VP and head of the Environmental Protection Organization in President Hashemi-Rafsanjani's first (1989–93) and second (1993–97) cabinets

1941–, Tabriz, East Azerbaijan

MD, medicine, Istanbul University (Turkey)

Surgeon

No imprisonment

Not a war veteran

Martyr's family (teenage son)

In the August 14, 1984, vote of confidence, Manafi failed to receive enough votes to continue as minister of health, with only 102 positive votes. He was in charge of the Environmental Protection Organization from 1984 to 1997 and the Islamic Republic of Iran Medical Council from 1986 to 1992. As a physician, he was also in charge of Ayatollah Khomeini's medical team. Manafi was the founder of Iran's Hypnosis Association, and after leaving his political posts, he continued his career as a medical doctor.

Mansuri, Javad

Commander in chief of the IRGC (1979)

1945–, Kashan, Isfahan

BA, economics, Tehran University

Masha'allah, watch seller

Imprisoned before the revolution (four years; released in November 1978)

Not a war veteran

IRGC militiaman

Member of the MNP (joined in 1964); member of the central council of the IRP; founder of the Society of Prerevolution Muslim Political Prisoners

Mansuri was appointed by the Revolutionary Council as the IRGC's commander in chief in May 1979 and served in that post for a short time. He

entered the Ministry of Foreign Affairs in 1981 and retired from it in 2009. During this time, his posts included deputy foreign minister for cultural and consular affairs, deputy foreign minister for Asia-Pacific affairs, ambassador to Pakistan and China, and adviser to the foreign minister.

Mansuri, Mohammad-Reza

Deputy of the Tenth Majlis, Saveh, Markazi (2016–20)

1966–, Saveh, Markazi

BS, electrical engineering

Member of the Saveh City Council (until 2015); university teacher

Mansuri has taught electrical engineering and aerospace engineering at various universities. He ran unsuccessfully for the Ninth Majlis in 2012.

Mansuri-Arani, Abbas-Ali

Deputy of the Ninth Majlis, Kashan, Aran, and Bidgol, Isfahan (2012–16)

1960–, Aran and Bidgol, Isfahan

BS, military science, Ground Forces Officers' Academy, 1983; MA, political science, Farabi University; pursuing a PhD in strategic management at Supreme National Defense University

MIIRI officer

No imprisonment

War veteran

IRGC militiaman

Mansuri-Arani retired from military service in 2011 after a long career serving as director of army's intelligence bureau, member of the SCNS, military attaché in Saudi Arabia, and rector of Ground Forces Officers' Academy. The GC rejected his qualifications to run for the Tenth Majlis.

Mansuri-Bidakani, Majid

Deputy of the Ninth Majlis, Lenjan, Isfahan (2012–16)

1967–, Masjed Soleyman, Khuzestan

BS, industrial management; MS, industrial management, Islamic Azad University–Najafabad

Adviser to the director-general of Isfahan Steel
    Company
No imprisonment
Mansuri-Bidakani, who is a Bakhtiari, was elected in
    round two of elections for the Ninth Majlis. The
    GC rejected his qualifications to run for the Tenth
    Majlis.

Mansuri-Razi, Moradali

Deputy of the Seventh (2004–8) and Eighth (2008–12)
    Majlis, Ramiyan and Azadshahr, Golestan
1964–, Ramiyan, Golestan
MA, demography
Ali
Civil servant
No imprisonment

Manuchehri, Ne'matollah

Deputy of the Ninth Majlis, Paveh, Javanrud, Salase
    Babajani, and Ravansar, Kermanshah (2012–16)
1962–, Javanrud, Kermanshah
MD, medicine, Baqiyatollah University of Medical
    Sciences, 2001
Tofiq, education official
Medical doctor
No imprisonment
Not a war veteran
IRGC militiaman
Manuchehri, a Sunni, established a clinic for treating
    drug addicts in Sanandaj in 2011.

Manzari-Tavakkoli, Ali-Reza

Deputy of the Ninth Majlis, Baft, Rabor, and Arzui-
    yeh, Kerman (2012–16)
1957–, Baft, Kerman
BS, psychology, Shiraz University, 1993; MS, psychol-
    ogy, Shiraz University, 1997; PhD, pedagogical
    philosophy, Shiraz University, 2004
Rector of Azad University–Baft and Azad
    University–Kerman
No imprisonment

War veteran (sixty-five months)
IRGC militiaman

Maqniyan, Mohammad-Ali

Deputy of the Fourth (1992–96) and Seventh (2004–8)
    Majlis, Bijar, Kurdistan
1955–, Bijar, Kurdistan
BA, law (allegedly a forged degree)
Abolfazl
Civil servant
No imprisonment

Maqsudi, Hoseyn

Deputy of the Tenth Majlis, Sabzevar, Razavi Kho-
    rasan (2016–20)
1974–, Sabzevar, Razavi Khorasan
MA, educational management; PhD, business ad-
    ministration, University of Applied Science and
    Technology
Hasan, farmer
Provincial civil servant
IRGC militiaman (Basij)
Maqsudi began his career as a laborer in the Sabzevar
    municipality and moved on to the education depart-
    ment. He was elected to the Sabzevar City Council
    and then became mayor of Sabzevar (2011–13).

Maqsudpursir, Shamshoun

Deputy of the Fourth (1992–96) and Fifth (1996–2000)
    Majlis, representing Assyrians and Chaldeans (as
    a religious minority)
1930–, Urmia, West Azerbaijan
MA, public administration
Yukhneh
No imprisonment
Not a war veteran

Marama'i, Mohammad-Qoli

Deputy of the Seventh Majlis, Gonbad-e Kavus, Go-
    lestan (2004–8)

1961–, Gonbad-e Kavus, Golestan
BS, public health
Ata
Civil servant
No imprisonment

Marandi, Seyyed Ali-Reza

Minister of health and public health in PM Musavi's
    first (August 20, 1984–85) cabinet; minister of
    health and medical education in PM Musavi's
    second (October 28, 1985–August 3, 1989) cabinet,
    as well as President Hashemi-Rafsanjani's second
    cabinet (August 16, 1993–August 2, 1997); dep-
    uty of the Eighth (2008–12) and Ninth (2012–16)
    Majlis, Tehran, Tehran
1939–, Isfahan, Isfahan
MD, medicine, Tehran University, 1964; advanced
    training in pediatrics (USA)
Seyyed Mahmud, civil servant, Isfahan's
    governor-general
Medical doctor and university professor
Imprisoned before the revolution (six months)
Not a war veteran
Marandi went to the United States in 1966 to gain
    expertise in pediatric medicine in Richmond,
    Virginia, and Dayton, Ohio, and returned to
    Iran in November 1979. On August 16, 1993, he
    received the highest number of votes (246 out of
    261) when the Majlis voted on President Hash-
    emi-Rafsanjani's second cabinet. Marandi was
    the oldest member of the Ninth Majlis and did
    not register to run for the Tenth Majlis elections,
    citing his age.

Mar'ashi, Salim

Deputy of the Sixth Majlis, Rudbar, Gilan
    (2000–2004)
1960–2005, Manjil, Gilan
MD
Salman
Medical doctor
No imprisonment

Mar'ashi, Samad

Deputy of the Eighth Majlis, Rudbar, Gilan (2008–12)
1964–, Talesh, Gilan
BA, public administration
Salman
Civil servant
No imprisonment
Samad Mar'ashi is the younger brother of Salim
    Mar'ashi, who also represented Rudbar in the
    Majlis.

Mar'ashi, Seyyed Hoseyn

Deputy of the Fifth (1996–2000) and Sixth (2000–
    2004) Majlis, Kerman, Kerman; VP and head of
    the Cultural Heritage and Tourism Organization
    in President Khatami's second cabinet (2004–5)
July 29, 1958–, Rafsanjan, Kerman
BA, economics, Tehran University, 2000
Seyyed Mohammad-Taqi, farmer
Director of the Office of President
    Hashemi-Rafsanjani
No imprisonment
Not a war veteran
Founder, member of the central council, and spokes-
    person of PECI
Mar'ashi was governor-general of Kerman from 1985
    to 1994, and then he became director of Presi-
    dent Hashemi-Rafsanjani's office (1994–95). He
    resigned from the Sixth Majlis to become VP
    and head of the Cultural Heritage Organiza-
    tion (CHO). CHO was established in 2003, and
    Mar'ashi was the first person to hold this title.
    He is the brother-in-law of former president
    Hashemi-Rafsanjani (his wife is Farideh Hashem-
    inejad). The judiciary imprisoned Mar'ashi for a
    while after the contested 2009 election.

Mar'ashi-Shushtari, Mohammad-Hasan

Member of the HCJ (1985–89); member of the Fourth
    Assembly of Experts, Tehran (2007–8)
1937–August 8, 2008, Shushtar, Khuzestan

Clerical education
Soltan-Mohammad, clergyman
Clergyman (ayatollah)
No imprisonment
Not a war veteran
Ayatollah Mar'ashi-Shushtari entered judicial service
in 1982 and rose to the level of judiciary deputy
under Ayatollah Hashemi-Shahrudi.

Mareh Sedq, Siyamak

Deputy of the Eighth (2008–12), Ninth (2012–16), and
Tenth (2016–20) Majlis, representing the Jewish
community (as a religious minority)
1965–, Shiraz, Fars
MD, surgery, Shiraz University
Jahangir
Surgeon and university professor
No imprisonment
Not a war veteran
In the 2012 election, Mareh Sedq received 82 percent
of the vote of the Jewish community, and in the
2016 election he received 71 percent of the vote.
He is affiliated with the Dr. Sapir Charity Hospital.

Marhaba, Shapur

Deputy of the Fourth (1992–96), Fifth (1997–2000),
and Seventh (2004–8) Majlis, Astara, Gilan
1957–, Astara, Gilan
BA, law, 2001; MA, law
Mohammad-Baqer
Civil servant
No imprisonment

Marvi, Ali

Deputy of the Fourth (1992–96), Fifth (1996–2000),
and Ninth (2012–16) Majlis, Neyshabur, Razavi
Khorasan
1958–, Neyshabur, Razavi Khorasan
BS, psychology, Ferdowsi University of Mashhad, 1988; MA, political science, Islamic Azad
University–Tehran, 1991; PhD (unverified)

Mohammad
Head of the education department in Neyshabur
No imprisonment
Not a war veteran
Founding member of the Alliance of Steadfast Sup-
porters of the Islamic Revolution
Marvi has previously served in IRIB, in the Petroleum
Ministry, and as deputy to ministers of labor and
petroleum. He ran unsuccessfully for the Sixth
Majlis. After serving in the Ninth Majlis, he be-
came head of the board of directors of Petropars
Company.

Marvi, Mohammad-Hadi

First deputy to the chief justice (1999–2004)
April 4, 1946–September 9, 2007, Mashhad, Razavi
Khorasan
Clerical education, Qom Seminary
Yahya, bazaar merchant
Clergyman
No imprisonment
Not a war veteran
HI Marvi served as Ayatollah Khomeini's represen-
tative in Masjed Soleyman and Behbahan (1979),
deputy of the State General Inspectorate Organi-
zation (1981), and head of the Disciplinary Court
for Judges and Public Prosecutors (1983–2007). He
was the son-in-law of Ayatollah Seyyed Abolqa-
sem Khaz'ali.

Marvi-Samavarchi, Mahmud

Deputy of the First (1980–84) and Second (1984–
88) Majlis, Torqabeh and Chenaran, Razavi
Khorasan
1944–, Mashhad, Razavi Khorasan
Clerical education
Ahmad, laborer
Clergyman
No imprisonment
Not a war veteran
HI Marvi-Samavarchi was injured in the bombing of
the IRP headquarters on June 28, 1981.

Mashhadiabbasi, Hamid-Reza

Deputy of the Ninth Majlis, Damavand and Firuzkuh, Tehran (2013–16)
1970–, Damavand, Tehran
BS, mathematics; MA, educational research
Civil servant, ministries
No imprisonment
War veteran (wounded)
Secretary of the CIC/PCIC in Damavand
Mashhadiabbasi was elected in midterm election held in June 2013.

Masjed-Jame'i, Ahmad

Minister of culture and Islamic guidance in President Khatami's first (January 14–August 1, 2001) and second (August 22, 2001–August 2, 2005) cabinets
1956–, Tehran, Tehran
BA, geography, Tehran University; MS, urban planning, Tehran University
Mostafa, clergyman (ayatollah)
Civil servant, ministries
No imprisonment
Not a war veteran
Masjed-Jame'i was deputy minister of culture and Islamic guidance under Mohajerani and then replaced him after Mohajerani resigned. After leaving the cabinet, Masjed-Jame'i served on the Tehran City Council for many years.

Mas'udi, Ali-Asghar

Member of the Revolutionary Council (1979–80)
BS, military science
Military officer (brigadier general)
Mas'udi was the managing director of the Bank Sepah from April 9, 1979, until September 23, 1979.

Mas'udi, Asghar

Deputy of the Tenth Majlis, Neyriz, Fars (2016–20)
1965–, Neyriz, Fars

MA, philosophy/theology, Baqir al-Olum University, 2005; PhD, theology, 2007; clerical education, Qom Seminary
Amir
Rector of Al-Mostafa International University
No imprisonment
Mas'udi is a former professor and official at the Islamic Propaganda Organization.

Mas'udi-Reyhan, Gholam-Hoseyn

Deputy of the Eighth Majlis, Ahar and Heris, East Azerbaijan (2008–12)
1961–, Ahar, East Azerbaijan
MA, educational management
Mohammad-Ali
Academia
No imprisonment
Mas'udi-Reyhan was not elected to the Ninth Majlis.

Ma'sumi, Ali-Akbar

Deputy of the First Majlis, Shahrud, Semnan (1980–84)
1951–, Shahrud, Semnan
Clerical education
Mohammad-Hoseyn, farmer
Clergyman (HI)
No imprisonment
Not a war veteran

Ma'sumi, Ali-Asghar

Member of the First (1983–90), Second (1991–98), Third (1999–2006), and Fourth (2007–16) Assembly of Experts, Razavi Khorasan
1926–September 17, 2017, Shahrud, Semnan
Clerical education, Najaf Seminary (Iraq)
Abbas, clergyman and farmer
Clergyman
Imprisoned before the revolution
Not a war veteran
Ma'sumi lived in Najaf, Iraq, for fourteen years (1947–61). He was the supreme leader's representative and the Friday prayer leader of Torbat-e

Heydariyyeh (1982–2002), as well as rector of
Islamic Azad University–Torbat-e Heydariyyeh.

Matin, Abbas

Deputy of the First (1981–84) and Second (1984–88)
    Majlis, Bandar-e Abbas, Hormozgan
1949–, Bandar-e Abbas, Hormozgan
Clerical education
Gholam-Abbas
Clergyman
Imprisoned before the revolution
Not a war veteran
Head of the IRP branch in Bandar-e Abbas
HI Matin was Friday prayer leader of Bandar-e Abbas
    and was associated with the Islamic Propaganda
    Organization.

Matori, Ali

Deputy of the Fourth Majlis, Ahvaz, Khuzestan
    (1992–96)
1959–, Ahvaz, Khuzestan
PhD, theology
Shavi
No imprisonment
Matori became Iran's cultural attaché in UAE and
    dean of the school of theology at Shahid Chamran
    University of Ahvaz.

Maturzadeh, Mostafa

Deputy of the Fifth (1996–2000), Seventh (2004–8), and
    Eighth (2008–12) Majlis, Khorramshahr, Khuzestan
1956–, Khorramshahr, Khuzestan
BA, economics, Shahid Chamran University of Ahvaz
Sharif
No imprisonment
War veteran (eight years)
The GC disqualified Maturzadeh for the Ninth Majlis.

Mazaheri, Hoseyn

Member of the Second (1991–98) and Third (1999–
    2006) Assembly of Experts, Isfahan

1923–, Tiran, Isfahan
Clerical education, Qom Seminary
Hasan, clergyman
Clergyman (ayatollah)
No imprisonment
Not a war veteran
Member of the SQSS

Mazaheri [-Khuzani], Tahmaseb

Minister of economic affairs and finance in President
    Khatami's second cabinet (August 22, 2001–4);
    governor of the Central Bank (2007–8)
1953–, Tehran, Tehran
BS, civil engineering, Tehran University, 1976; MA,
    management, Tehran University
Father's name unknown, military and security forces
Civil servant, ministries
No imprisonment
Not a war veteran
Mazaheri worked for four years in the PBO during
    Mir Hoseyn Musavi's premiership. He was su-
    pervisor of the FDWI from 1984 to 1989, and was
    President Khatami's economic adviser before be-
    coming a minister. Mazaheri was pursuing a PhD
    in economics when President Khatami nominated
    him to become the finance minister. Khatami
    dismissed him from that post in 2008. He was
    disqualified from running in the 2013 presidential
    election.

Mazani, Ahmad

Deputy of the Tenth Majlis, Tehran, Tehran
    (2016–20)
1961–, Nokandeh, Golestan
Clerical education; MA, public administration
Clergyman
Imprisoned before the revolution (three months)
Not a war veteran
Martyr's family (brother)
Member of the IRP and the NTP
HI Mazani was affiliated with the Martyr's Foun-
    dation from 1980 to 2014, and he held many

high-level positions including research deputy. He was one of the youngest political prisoners under the shah. Mazani, who is a reformist, has also been the editor of several periodicals.

Mazare'i, Jamshid

Deputy of the Second Majlis, Bandar-e Mahshahr, Khuzestan (1986–88)
1953–, Bandar-e Mahshahr, Khuzestan
High school diploma
Qarib
No imprisonment

Mazru'i, Rajab-Ali

Deputy of the Sixth Majlis, Isfahan, Isfahan (2000–2004)
October 7, 1957–, Isfahan, Isfahan
BS, physics, Isfahan University of Technology, 1980; MA, planning economic systems, Shahid Beheshti University, 1996
Ramezan, municipal laborer
Journalist
No imprisonment
War veteran (seven months as a basiji volunteer)
Founding member of the central council of IIPF; member of OMIRI (joined in 1991)
Mazru'i was economic adviser to President Khatami from 1997 to 2000. He was a member of Mir Hoseyn Musavi's presidential election campaign in 2009.

Mehdizadeh, Mehdi

Deputy of the Second (1984–88), Third (1988–92), Fourth (1992–96), Fifth (1996–2000), and Eighth (2008–12) Majlis, Gonabad, Razavi Khorasan
1939–, Gonabad, Razavi Khorasan
PhD, mathematics (France), 1981
Mahmud
University professor
No imprisonment
Not a war veteran

Mehmannavaz, Habibollah

Member of the Second (1991–98) and Third (1999–2006) Assembly of Experts, Razavi Khorasan; member of the Fourth (2007–16), and Fifth (2016–22) Assembly of Experts, North Khorasan
1926–, Neyshabur, Razavi Khorasan
Clerical education, Mashhad Seminary
Morad-Ali, farmer
Clergyman
No imprisonment
Not a war veteran
Martyr's family (sons killed at the war front)
HI Mehmannavaz was the Friday prayer leader of Bojnurd and Neyshabur.

Mehrabiyan, Ali-Akbar (Gholam-Hoseyn)

Minister of industries and mining in President Ahmadinejad's first (November 14, 2007–August 2, 2009) and second (September 3, 2009–May 14, 2011) cabinets
1969–, Khansar, Isfahan
BS, civil engineering, Iran University of Science and Technology; PhD, organizational behavior, Tehran University, 1995
Civil servant
No imprisonment
Not a war veteran
Mehrabiyan was a student of Ahmadinejad's at Iran University of Science and Technology. He became minister of industries and mining on November 14, 2007. In May 2011, President Ahmadinejad ended his term by saying that he wanted to reduce the number of ministries. Afterward, President Ahmadinejad appointed Mehrabiyan as one of his senior advisers. He has family ties to former MPs Ahmad and Hoseyn Nejabat.

Mehr-Alizadeh, Mohsen

VP and head of the Physical Training Organization in President Khatami's second cabinet (2001–5)
1956–, Maragheh, East Azerbaijan

BS, mechanical engineering, Tabriz University, 1977;
MS, mechanical engineering, Tabriz University,
1983; claimed to be studying toward a PhD in
econometrics at Tilburg University (Netherlands)
Father's name unknown, bazaar tradesman
Civil servant
No imprisonment
War veteran
IRGC militiaman
Mehr-Alizadeh has held such posts as director of the
Kish Free Trade Zone and governor-general of
Khorasan. The GC disqualified him from running
in the 2005 presidential election, but Ayatollah
Khamenei ordered his reinstatement. However,
in the first round of that election, he received the
lowest percentage of votes (4.4 percent). In 2017,
he was a candidate for the municipal council elec-
tions but decided to withdraw at the last minute.

Mehrparvar, Rasul

Deputy of the Sixth Majlis, Dargaz, Razavi Khorasan
(2000–2004)
1957–November 18, 2017, Dargaz, Razavi Khorasan
BS, agricultural engineering
Yahyaqoli
Civil servant
No imprisonment
Founding member of the National Trust Party

Mehrpur-Mohammadabadi, Hoseyn

Member of the First (1980–86) and Second (1986–92)
Guardian Councils
1943–, Mohammadabad, Yazd
BA, law, Tehran University, 1971; MA, law, Tehran
University, 1973; PhD, law, Tehran University,
1988; clerical education, Qom Seminary
Gholam-Reza
Attorney and head of the Office of the State Supreme
Court
No imprisonment
Not a war veteran
Martyr's family (younger brother)

Mehrpur-Mohammadabadi entered the judiciary
branch in 1972, and before being elected to the
First GC, he was a practicing attorney. He has been
a professor of law at Shahid Beheshti University
since 1990, was a legal adviser to President Khatami (1997–2005), and has also served in the HCJ.

Mehrzad-Sedqiyani, Qasem

Deputy of the Second (1984–88), Third (1988–92),
and Fifth (1999–2000) Majlis, Salmas, West
Azerbaijan
1944–, Salmas, West Azerbaijan
BA, law, 1983
Abbas
No imprisonment
Mehrzad-Sedqiyani, a reformist politician, was a
supporter of Ayatollah Montazeri. He registered
to run for the Tenth Majlis.

Me'mari, Qasem

Deputy of the Second (1984–88), Third (1988–92), and
Sixth (2000–2004) Majlis, Ahar, East Azerbaijan
1935–, Ahar, East Azerbaijan
BA, French literature
Isa
Academia
No imprisonment
Not a war veteran

Mesbahi-Moqaddam, Gholam-Reza

Deputy of the Seventh (2004–8), Eighth (2008–12),
and Ninth (2012–16) Majlis, Tehran, Tehran;
member of the Seventh (2012–17) and Eighth
(2017–22) Expediency Discernment Assembly
1951–, Mashhad, Razavi Khorasan
MA, economics, 1983; PhD, theology, Qom Seminary,
1995
Esma'il
Clergyman
No imprisonment
War veteran (six months)

Member and spokesperson of the central council of
the SCC

Mesbahi-Moqaddam was head of the Islamic Research Center of the IRGC, dean of faculty of
theology at Tehran University (1996–98), and
research deputy of Imam Sadeq University. He is
considered an expert in Islamic economics.

Mesbah-Yazdi, Mohammad-Taqi

Member of the Second Assembly of Experts, Khuzestan (1991–98); member of the Third (1999–2006)
and Fourth (2007–16) Assembly of Experts,
Tehran

January 31, 1935–, Yazd, Yazd

Clerical education, Qom Seminary, 1960

Baqer, bazaar tradesman

Clergyman

No imprisonment

Not a war veteran

Member of the SQSS

Mesbah-Yazdi is an ultraconservative senior ayatollah
who serves as the spiritual leader of many conservative clerics and politicians. Despite being
from the same province (Yazd) as Mohammad
Khatami, he and his disciples created constant
problems for the president during his tenure.
He also headed the main opposition to Akbar
Hashemi-Rafsanjani in the AE. Mesbah-Yazdi is a
former member of the HCCR, where he served as
the representative of Supreme Leader Khamenei.
He also heads the well-funded Imam Khomeini
Educational and Research Institute. He did not
receive enough votes to enter the Fifth AE. His
son-in-law is Mahmud Mohammadi-Araq.

Meshkini [Feyz-Ani], Ali-Akbar

Member of the Assembly for the Final Examination of
the Constitution, East Azerbaijan (1979); member
of the First (1983–90), Second (1991–98), Third
(1999–2006), and Fourth (2007) Assembly of
Experts, Tehran

1921–2007, Meshginshahr, Ardabil

Clerical education, Qom Seminary

Ali, clergyman

Clergyman

Imprisoned before the revolution

Not a war veteran

Founding member and secretary of the SQSS; member of the central council of the SCC

Ayatollah Meshkini was the secretariat of the AE
for twenty-four years, from its inception in 1983
until he died in 2007. Born into a clerical family
from the Ardabil Province, he studied theology
at the Qom Seminary with Ayatollahs Borujerdi
and Khomeini. Meshkini, who wrote a booklet
on land reform, was heavily involved in the land
reform legislation after the revolution. He was
the Friday prayer leader of Qom for many years,
starting in 1981. Meshkini was a member of
the central council of Friday prayer leaders, the
Islamic Propaganda Organization, and a board
to found a seminary for women in Qom. He was
named by the Second AE to a committee tasked
with overseeing the eventual implementation of
Ayatollah Khomeini's will. Meshkini and Mohammad Yazdi were the oldest members elected
to the Fourth AE.

Mesri, Abdorreza

Deputy of the Seventh (2004–6), Ninth (2012–16), and
Tenth (2016–20) Majlis, Kermanshah, Kermanshah; minister of welfare and social security in
President Ahmadinejad's first cabinet (October
29, 2006–8)

1956–, Kermanshah, Kermanshah

BS, geology, Tarbiyat-e Mo'allem University, 1990;
MS, geology, Tarbiyat-e Mo'allem University,
1995; PhD, geology, 2001 (unverified)

Ali

Civil servant

No imprisonment

Not a war veteran

IRGC militiaman

Mesri resigned from the Seventh Majlis to become
minister of social welfare with 191 positive votes,

forty-two negative votes, and eleven abstentions. After he left the cabinet, Mesri became ambassador to Venezuela, and then he was elected to the Ninth Majlis from Kermanshah. He has also worked in IKRF and the judiciary branch.

Meydari, Ahmad

Deputy of the Sixth Majlis, Abadan, Khuzestan (2000–2004)
1963–, Abadan, Khuzestan
PhD, economics, Tehran University
Hoseyn
Academia
No imprisonment
Not a war veteran
After serving in the Majlis, Meydari became deputy for social affairs in the Ministry of Labor and Social Welfare.

Meygolinezhad, Gholam-Ali

Deputy of the Eighth Majlis, Bushehr, Genaveh, and Deylam, Bushehr (2008–12)
1955–, Bandar-e Bushehr, Bushehr
BS, civil engineering; MA, public administration
Mohammad
Provincial civil servant
No imprisonment
War veteran
Martyr's family (brother, who was a war commander)
Meygolinezhad was not elected to the Ninth Majlis.

Meyqani, Ahmad

Commander of the Islamic Republic of Iran Air Force (October 29, 2006–August 31, 2008); commander of the Khatam al-Anbia Air Defense Base (August 31, 2008–January 25, 2011)
1957–, Shahrud, Semnan
Military academy; PhD, military science, Supreme National Defense University, 1997
Military pilot (brigadier general)
No imprisonment

War veteran
Meyqani joined the Iranian Air Force in 1975 and underwent pilot training in the United States in the late 1970s.

Milani-Hoseyni, Seyyed Mohammad

Deputy of the First Majlis, Tabriz, East Azerbaijan (1980–84)
1939–, Tabriz, East Azerbaijan
MD, pediatrics
Seyyed Ahmad, bazaar tradesman
Pediatrician
Imprisoned before the revolution (four years)
Not a war veteran
Milani-Hoseyni was a member of PMOI before the revolution.

Milani-Hoseyni, Seyyed Mohammad-Reza

Deputy of the Fifth Majlis, Tabriz, East Azerbaijan (1996–2000)
1951–, Tabriz, East Azerbaijan
PhD, chemistry
Seyyed Ahmad, bazaar tradesman
No imprisonment
Milani-Hoseyni's brother, Seyyed Mohammad, also represented Tabriz in the Majlis.

Minachi, Naser [Hasan]

Minister of Islamic guidance in PM Bazargan's cabinet (1979) and the Revolutionary Council cabinet (1979–1980)
1931–January 25, 2014, Tehran, Tehran
MA, law and economics, Tehran University; unfinished doctoral studies in economics
Father's name unknown, bazaar tradesman
Attorney
Imprisoned before the revolution
Not a war veteran
Member of the LMI
Minachi was one of the founders of Hoseyniyeh-ye Ershad in the 1960s and managed it until he died.

He helped to compose the first draft of the postrevolutionary constitution. In early 1979, he met with John D. Stempel, a United States foreign service officer in Tehran, to provide an update on the discussions between Mehdi Bazargan and General Abbas Gharabachi, chief of the joint staff of the Islamic Republic of Iran Army at the time. On February 6, 1980, he was arrested for twenty-four hours after the students who took over the American embassy accused him of having inappropriate ties with the United States. Minachi was close to Grand Ayatollah Seyyed Mohammad-Kazem Shari'atmadari, and his son was affiliated with PMOI.

Mir, Amir

Deputy of the Second (1984–88) and Third (1988–92) Majlis, Zahedan, Sistan and Baluchestan
1956–, Zabol, Sistan and Baluchestan
Associate's degree
Mohammad-Hasan
No imprisonment

Mir Baqeri, Seyyed Mohammad-Mehdi

Member of the Fifth Assembly of Experts, Alborz (2016–22)
1961–, Qom, Qom
Clerical education, Qom Seminary
Seyyed Hasan
Clergyman
HI Mir Baqeri was director of the Islamic Sciences Academy of Qom before he was elected to the Fifth Assembly of Experts.

Mir Damadi [-Najafabadi], Mohsen

Deputy of the Sixth Majlis, Tehran, Tehran (2000–2004)
1955–, Najafabad, Isfahan
PhD, international relations, University of Cambridge (England), 1998; dissertation title: "The European Community Policy and the Persian Gulf, 1973–1991"
Mostafa
Professor of political science at Tehran University
No imprisonment
War veteran
IRGC militiaman
Founding member of OCU; secretary-general of IIPF
Mir Damadi was one of the three masterminds of the takeover of the American embassy. He then joined the IRGC and was responsible for its international relations bureau. In 1984, he failed to enter the Second Majlis. Mir Damadi has held such posts as governor-general of Khuzestan (in the late 1980s), deputy of the Center for Strategic Research, and university professor. During the Sixth Majlis, he was chairman of the National Security and Foreign Policy Committee. The regime imprisoned him after the disputed 2009 presidential election and forced him to take part in televised trials. The judiciary sentenced him to a six-year prison term.

Mir Emadi, Seyyed Ziya'eddin

Public prosecutor-general of Tehran (1984–88)
Mashhad, Razavi Khorasan
Clerical education
Clergyman and lawyer
HI Mir Emadi had worked as the prosecutor-general of Shiraz and Bandar-e Abbas. A number of former political prisoners have accused Mir Emadi of brutal treatment. In 2002, he was arrested on corruption charges.

Mir Galuye Bayat, Mrs. Shahla

Deputy of the Ninth Majlis, Saveh and Zarandieh, Markazi (2012–16)
1965–, Tehran, Tehran
MD, gynecology, Hamadan University of Medical Sciences, 1996
Nasrollah, bazaar tradesman
Gynecologist and hospital administrator
No imprisonment
War veteran

Mir Galuye Bayat served for twenty years as a medical
doctor in Saveh before being elected to the Ninth
Majlis, receiving 36 percent of the vote. She ran
unsuccessfully for the Seventh and Eighth Majlis.

Mir Ghaffari-Marya'i, Seyyed Ebrahim

Deputy of the Third Majlis, Talesh, Gilan (1988–92)
1942–, Talesh, Gilan
BA, law
Mir Salman
No imprisonment

Mir Heydari, Abbas

Deputy of the Second Majlis, Shahriyar, Tehran
   (1984–88)
1952–, Varamin, Tehran
High school diploma
Seyyed Ali
No imprisonment

Mir Hoseyni, Abbas

Deputy of the Fourth (1992–96) and Fifth (1996–2000)
   Majlis, Zabol, Sistan and Baluchestan
1956–, Zabol, Sistan and Baluchestan
BA, educational science, 1995
Morad-Ali
No imprisonment
War veteran
IRGC militiaman
Martyr's family (brother, Qasem)

Mir Ja'fari, Seyyed Mojtaba

Deputy of the First (1981–84) and Second (1984–88)
   Majlis, Arak, Markazi
1930–March 16, 1991, Arak, Markazi
Clerical education
Seyyed Abdollah
Clergyman
No imprisonment
Not a war veteran

HI Mir Ja'fari became the Friday prayer leader
of Arak in 1981, and was affiliated with the
Martyr's Foundation and other revolutionary
organizations.

Mir Kazemi, Seyyed Mas'ud

Minister of commerce in President Ahmadinejad's
first cabinet (August 24, 2005–August 2, 2009);
minister of petroleum in President Ahmadinejad's second cabinet (September 3, 2009–May 14,
2011); deputy of the Ninth Majlis, Tehran, Tehran
(2012–16)
1960–, Tehran, Tehran
BS, industrial engineering, Iran University of Science
and Technology, 1986; MS, industrial engineering, Iran University of Science and Technology,
1989; PhD, industrial engineering, Tarbiyat-e
Modarres University, 1997
Seyyed Hasan, bazaar tradesman
University professor
No imprisonment
War veteran
IRGC militiaman
Mir Kazemi was an adviser to the minister of defense
and served as rector of Shahed University. In May
2011, President Ahmadinejad ended his term by
stating that he wanted to reduce the number of
ministries. Mir Kazemi ran unsuccessfully for the
Tenth Majlis from Tehran.

Mir Khalili, Seyyed Ali

Deputy of the Fourth (1992–96), Fifth (1996–2000),
   Sixth (2001–4), and Eighth (2008–12) Majlis,
   Minab, Hormozgan
1949–, Taft, Yazd
Clerical education, Yazd Seminary
Seyyed Javad
Clergyman
Imprisoned before the revolution
War veteran
HI Mir Khalili is a member of the policy council for
   Friday prayer leaders.

Mir Mohammadi, Seyyed Mohammad-Hoseyn

Deputy of the Ninth Majlis, Golpayegan and Khansar,
    Isfahan (2012–16)
1962–, Tehran, Tehran
MA, public law, Imam Hoseyn University
Judiciary official
No imprisonment
IRGC militiaman (Basij for fourteen years)
Mir Mohammadi, who worked for the FDWI,
    ran unsuccessfully for the Seventh and Eighth
    Majlis. In 2016, he returned to the legal
    profession.

Mir Mohammadi [-Zarandi], Seyyed Abolfazl

Member of the HCJ (May 1983–June 1985); member of
    the Third (1999–2006) and Fourth (2007–16) As-
    sembly of Experts, Markazi; member of the Fifth
    Assembly of Experts, Tehran (2016–22)
1923–, Zarand, Markazi
Clerical education, Qom Seminary
Seyyed Hoseyn, farmer
Clergyman
No imprisonment
Not a war veteran
Member of the central council of the SQSS
Ayatollah Mir Mohammadi was the dean of Tehran
    University's faculty of theology from 1985 to 1996.
    Before that, he was head of Qom's revolutionary
    tribunal. He did not receive enough votes in the
    second round of elections to the HCJ and was re-
    placed by Mohammad-Hasan Mar'ashi-Shushtari.
    Mir Mohammadi was the oldest member of the
    Fourth and Fifth AE. He is the son-in-law of Aya-
    tollah Seyyed Ahmad Zanjani and brother-in-law
    of Musa Shobeyri-Zanjani. Mir Mohammadi's
    son, Seyyed Mohammad, served twice as Qom's
    deputy in the Majlis.

Mir Mohammadi [-Zarandi], Seyyed Mohammad

Deputy of the Sixth (2000–2004) and Seventh
    (2004–8) Majlis, Qom, Qom; Member of the

Eighth Expediency Discernment Assembly
    (2017–22)
1948–, Qom, Qom
MA, international economics, Tehran University;
    PhD, Management, Tehran University
Seyyed Abolfazl, clergyman (ayatollah)
Civil servant
No imprisonment
Not a war veteran
Member of the central council of the IRP; secre-
    tary-general of the Party of Islamic Civilization
Mir Mohammadi was in charge of the offices of
    Presidents Khamenei (1981–89) and Hashemi-
    Rafsanjani (1989–93). He was deputy for oversight
    and accounting in the Office of Supreme Leader
    Ayatollah Khamenei for fourteen years. He was
    a member of the board of trustees of the Head-
    quarters for Implementation of Imam's Order and
    a professor at Allameh Tabataba'i University. He
    later became governor-general of Yazd Province.
    Mir Mohammadi is the son of Seyyed Abolfazl
    Mir Mohammadi, a longtime member of the AE,
    and the nephew of Grand Ayatollah Seyyed Musa
    Shobeyri-Zanjani. Mir Mohammadi's son-in-law
    is Masih Borujerdi, who is a grandchild of Ayatol-
    lah Khomeini.

Mir Mohammad-Sadeqi, Mohammad

Minister of labor and social affairs in PM Raja'i's
    cabinet (November 5, 1980–81), PM Bahonar's
    cabinet (August 17–30, 1981), and interim PM
    Mahdavi-Kani's cabinet (September 3–October
    18, 1981)
1946–, Isfahan, Isfahan
BS, systems analysis, 1976; PhD, management, Tehran
    University
Mojtaba, laborer
Civil servant, state companies
Imprisoned before the revolution
Not a war veteran
Member of the MNP
Mir Mohammad-Sadeqi later became deputy chair of
    the Tehran Chamber of Commerce.

Mir Morad-Zehi, Hamidollah

Member of the Assembly for the Final Examination of
the Constitution, Sistan and Baluchestan (1979)
1949–, Saravan, Sistan and Baluchestan
MA, law
Ahmad, farmer
Attorney
No imprisonment
Not a war veteran
Mir Morad-Zehi, a Sunni Baluch, was a private attorney practicing in Zahedan before he was elected
to the AFEC at the age of thirty. He was one of a
handful members of the AFEC who opposed the
principle of *velayat-e faqih*.

Mir Morad-Zehi, Hedayatollah

Deputy of the Seventh (2004–8) and Ninth (2012–16)
Majlis, Saravan, Sib, and Suran, Sistan and
Baluchestan
1960–, Saravan, Sistan and Baluchestan
BS, water engineering, Shiraz University
Gahram
Military and security forces
No imprisonment
Martyr's family (brother, Mohammad-Amin, who
was a pilot, was killed at the war front)
Mir Morad-Zehi, a Sunni, was active in the Agricul-
tural Jihad and became governor of Nikshahr in
2010.

[Aqa] Mir Salim, Seyyed Mostafa

Minister of culture and Islamic guidance in President
Hashemi-Rafsanjani's second cabinet (February
22, 1994–97); member of the Fourth (1997–2002),
Fifth (2002–7), Sixth (2007–12), Seventh (2012–17),
and Eighth (2017–22) Expediency Discernment
Assembly
June 10, 1947–, Tehran, Tehran
MS, mechanical engineering, University of Poitiers
(France), 1970
Seyyed Jalal

Civil servant
No imprisonment
Not a war veteran
Member of the central council of the IRP; member
and chair of the central council of the CIC/PCIC;
founding member of the Islamic Society of Iranian Academics as well as the Islamic Society of
Athletes
Mir Salim graduated from the highly regarded Alborz
High School in 1965. Before 1979, he was the
manager of a section of Tehran's railway. In the
early days of the revolution, he was in charge
of the national police force and was a political
deputy in MI. In September 1993, he became the
secretary of the HCCR. As minister of culture
and Islamic guidance, he ordered the closure of
numerous newspapers and periodicals. In 2017,
he ran for the presidency as the candidate of CIC/
PCIC but received only 1.1 percent of the vote.

Mir Shams-Shahshani, Abolfazl

Public prosecutor-general of Tehran (1979–October
31, 1979)
Attorney
Mir Shams-Shahshani was arrested in 1990 after he
and some ninety other activists published an
open letter criticizing violations of human rights
in Iran. He was a signatory to many other open
letters critical of the Iranian regime.

Mir Tajeddini, Seyyed Mohammad-Reza

Deputy of the Seventh (2004–8) and Eighth (2008–
November 15, 2009) Majlis, Tabriz, Osku, and
Azarshahr, East Azerbaijan; VP for parliamentary
affairs (2009–12) and VP for implementation of
the constitution (May 28, 2012–13) in President
Ahmadinejad's second cabinet
1962–, Tabriz, East Azerbaijan
Clerical education, Qom Seminary; MA, theology,
Tarbiyat-e Modarres University–Qom, 1993
Mir Ahmad
Clergyman

No imprisonment

Not a war veteran

HI Mir Tajeddini taught theology for twelve years at a university. He resigned from the Eighth Majlis to become VP for parliamentary affairs. On May 28, 2012, President Ahmadinejad appointed him to the newly created post of VP for implementation of the constitution.

Mir Valad, Seyyed Kazem

Deputy of the Third (1988–92) and Fourth (1992–96) Majlis, Malayer, Hamadan

1955–, Malayer, Hamadan

BS, civil engineering, Tabriz University; MA, management, 1992

Seyyed Hasan

Head of the high council for reconstruction of Ilam Province

No imprisonment

Mir Valad has held other positions, such as political deputy to the governor-general of Kermanshah and Hormozgan, head of the State Audit Court (appointed in 1997), chair of the board of directors of Pasargad Bank, and deputy interior minister (2013–May 2014).

Mir Yunesi, Seyyed Abbas

Deputy of the First Majlis, Kangavar, Kermanshah (1980–84)

1933–, Arak, Markazi

Clerical education

Seyyed Abolfazl, clergyman

Clergyman

No imprisonment

Not a war veteran

HI Mir Yunesi is a former Friday prayer leader of Kangavar.

Mirza Abutalebi, Abbas

Deputy of the Third Majlis, Bu'inzahra and Avaj, Zanjan (1988–92)

1954–, Karaj, Tehran

BA

Qasem

No imprisonment

Mirza Abutalebi was in prison for almost two months after the contested 2009 presidential election.

Mirzadeh, Hamid

VP for executive affairs in President Hashemi-Rafsanjani's first cabinet (1989–93); VP for executive affairs (1993–95) and VP and head of the Management and Planning Organization in President Hashemi-Rafsanjani's second cabinet (August 2, 1995–97); rector of Islamic Azad University (September 26, 2013–May 2, 2017)

1950–, Sirjan, Kerman

BS, chemistry, Ferdowsi University of Mashhad, 1973; MS, polymer engineering, Amirkabir University of Technology, 1978; PhD, polymer engineering, University of New South Wales (Australia), 1994

Mir Abolqasem

Executive assistant to the prime minister; professor of polymer engineering

No imprisonment

Not a war veteran

Member of the central council of PECI

Mirzadeh has held such posts as governor of Sirjan (1980–81), governor-general of Kerman (1981–85), executive assistant to PM Musavi (1985–89), and member of the board of trustees of Islamic Azad University (since 2007). Mirzadeh, who was very close to Akbar Hashemi-Rafsanjani, has also taught at Shahid Bahonar University in Kerman (1979–94) and Amirkabir University of Technology (since 1994).

Mirzadeh, Mir Hemayat

Deputy of the Tenth Majlis, Germi, Ardabil (2016–20)

1962–, Germi, Ardabil

MA, sociology

Mir Aziz

Education official in East Azerbaijan

War veteran

Mirzadeh has been a teacher and educational deputy in Ardabil, East Azerbaijan, and Tehran for almost three decades. He ran unsuccessfully for the Ninth Majlis.

Mirza'i, Gholam-Reza

Deputy of the Seventh Majlis, Borujen, Chahar Mahal and Bakhtiari (2004–8)

1962–, Borujen, Chahar Mahal and Bakhtiari

MA, history

Zalam Khan

Military and security forces

No imprisonment

IRGC militiaman

Mirza'i, Jalal

Deputy of the Tenth Majlis, Ilam, Ilam (2016–20)

1973–, Shirvan, Ilam

PhD, political science, Tehran University

Professor at Shahid Bahonar University of Kerman

No imprisonment

Not a war veteran

Mirza'i was a reformist candidate.

Mirza'i-Ataabadi, Eydimohammad

Deputy of the Second Majlis, Falavarjan, Isfahan (1984–87?)

1953–, Qomsheh, Isfahan

Clerical education

Ja'far-Qoli

Clergyman

No imprisonment

HI Mirza'i-Ataabadi, who was popular with IRGC forces in Isfahan, was arrested by the regime while serving as an MP. This was perhaps due to his affiliation with Seyyed Mehdi Hashemi, the brother of Ayatollah Montazeri's son-in-law who was executed in 1987. He did not complete his full term in the Second Majlis.

Mirza'i-Fallahabadi, Ali

Deputy of the Eighth Majlis, Fuman and Saft, Gilan (2008–12)

1956–, Fuman, Gilan

BS, agricultural engineering

Ahmad

Civil servant

No imprisonment

Mirza'i-Fallahabadi was not elected to the Ninth Majlis.

Mirza'i-Niku, Qasem

Deputy of the Tenth Majlis, Damavand, Tehran (2016–20)

1955–, Kilan, Tehran

BA, urban planning, Allameh Tabataba'i University; MA, architecture and urban planning, Tehran University

War veteran (thirty months; wounded)

IRGC militiaman

Mirza'i-Niku worked in the IRGC's intelligence bureau and the Ministry of Intelligence until 1989, and has taught at Imam Hoseyn University and Imam Baqer University. He is also a former civil servant of the Ministry of Foreign Affairs and the Ministry of Roads and Transportation. He worked as an inspector and adviser in President Khatami's office. From 2003 to 2005 Mirza'i-Niku was based in the United Arab Emirates, where he helped to set up the local branch of the Trade Promotion Organization of Iran.

Mirzapur-Kleshtari, Moslem

Deputy of the First (1980–84) and Third (1988–92) Majlis, Rudbar, Gilan

1942–, Rudbar, Gilan

Associate's degree

Baba, bazaar tradesman

Academia

No imprisonment

War veteran

Founding member of the Alliance of Steadfast Supporters of the Islamic Revolution

Mo'in [-Najafabadi], Mostafa

Deputy of the First Majlis, Shiraz, Fars (1982–84); deputy of the Third Majlis, Tehran, Tehran (1988–August 29, 1989); minister of higher education in President Hashemi-Rafsanjani's first cabinet (August 29, 1989–August 2, 1993); deputy of the Fifth Majlis, Isfahan, Isfahan (June–August 1997); minister of higher education in President Khatami's first cabinet (August 20, 1997–August 1, 2001); minister of science, research, and technology in President Khatami's second cabinet (August 22, 2001–June 23, 2003)

April 1, 1951–, Najafabad, Isfahan

MD, pediatrics, Shiraz University, 1979

Mehdi, bazaar tradesman and farmer

Pediatrician and rector of Shiraz University

No imprisonment

Not a war veteran

Mo'in, who entered Shiraz University in 1969 as an undergraduate, became its rector in 1981, at the age of thirty. A year later, he entered the First Majlis through interim elections. He did not receive enough votes to get into the Second Majlis but did get into the Third Majlis, from which he resigned to become the minister of higher education. After serving for only two months in the Fifth Majlis, he had to resign yet again on August 20, 1997, to become the minister of higher education for a second time. Mo'in tried to resign his post on July 9, 1999, after the attack on Tehran University students, but President Khatami did not accept his resignation. Mo'in resorted once again to resignation on June 23, 2003, while serving as minister of science, research, and technology and this time President Khatami accepted his resignation. The GC disqualified Mo'in from running in the 2005 presidential election, but Ayatollah Khamenei ordered his reinstatement. Afterward, in the first

round of the 2005 presidential election, he placed fifth out of seven and received 13.8 percent of the vote. He was also a member of the HCCR for two decades (1983–2003) and was a professor at Tehran University of Medical Sciences. Mo'in is the son-in-law of Gowharoshshari'eh Dastgheyb.

Mo'infar, Ali-Akbar

Ministerial adviser and head of the PBO in PM Bazargan's cabinet (February 13–September 23, 1979); minister of petroleum in PM Bazargan's cabinet (September 30–November 5, 1979); member of the Revolutionary Council (1979–1980); minister of petroleum in the Revolutionary Council cabinet (1979–1980); deputy of the First Majlis, Tehran, Tehran (1980–84)

1928–January 2, 2018, Tehran, Tehran

BS, civil engineering, Tehran University, 1951; MS, seismology, Waseda University (Japan), 1960

Hoseyn, bazaar tradesman

Civil servant

No imprisonment

Not a war veteran

Member of INF and LMI; founding member of the Islamic Society of Engineers

Mo'infar was head of the Technical Research and Standards Bureau of the PBO from 1975 to February 1979, and PM Bazargan appointed him as the first minister of petroleum. He registered to run in the 1997 presidential election but was disqualified. He was one of the pioneers in the field of seismology in Iran.

Mo'inipur, Mohammad-Hasan

Commander of the Islamic Republic of Iran Air Force (October 1, 1981–November 25, 1983)

Date of birth unknown–June 21, 2014

BS, military science, Ground Forces Officers' Academy

Military pilot

No imprisonment

War veteran

Brigadier General Mo'inipur joined the Iranian military in 1952 and underwent flight training in England and United States.

Mo'azzenzadeh, Seyyed Mostafa

Deputy of the Third Majlis, Kerman, Kerman (1988–92)

1954–, Kerman, Kerman

BS, engineering

Morteza

No imprisonment

Mo'ezi, Mohammad

Deputy of the Second (1984–88) and Third (1988–92) Majlis, Isfahan, Isfahan

1949–, Isfahan, Isfahan

BS, agricultural engineering

Morteza

No imprisonment

Not a war veteran

Mo'addabpur, Seyyed Mohammad

Deputy of the Sixth Majlis, Rasht, Gilan (2000–2002)

1947–November 19, 2002, Rasht, Gilan

Clerical education

Seyyed Mehdi

Clergyman

No imprisonment

Mo'addabpur, Seyyed Mojtaba

Deputy of the Seventh Majlis, Rasht, Gilan (2004–8)

1968–, Rasht, Gilan

Clerical education

Seyyed Mohammad, clergyman

Clergyman (HI)

No imprisonment

Mo'addabpur was a member of the Rasht City Council.

Mo'adikhah, Abdolmajid

Deputy of the First Majlis, Tehran, Tehran (1980–August 20, 1981); minister of Islamic guidance in PM Bahonar's cabinet (August 17–30, 1981), interim PM Mahdavi-Kani's cabinet (September 3–October 18, 1981), and PM Musavi's first cabinet (November 2, 1981–1982)

1942–, Tehran, Tehran

Clerical education, Qom Seminary

Hoseyn, bazaar tradesman

Clergyman

Imprisoned before the revolution

Not a war veteran

HI Mo'adikhah, who was active in the anti-shah movement, worked in the revolutionary courts after the revolution. Before being elected to the First Majlis, he was Ayatollah Khomeini's representative in Kurdistan Province. While serving in the First Majlis, Mo'adikhah was also the deputy supervisor of the nationwide literacy campaign. He survived an assassination attempt in Hamadan in mid-1981. Mo'adikhah resigned from the first Majlis to become the minister of Islamic guidance. He was minister for less than two years when he resigned after a raid by security forces found him in an illicit relationship with a woman. After a few years in prison, he became the general manager of the Foundation for the History of the Islamic Revolution in Iran. He started publishing a periodical titled *Yad* in 1983.

Mo'allemi-Juybari, Ali

Deputy of the Fifth Majlis, Qaemshahr and Savadkuh, Mazandaran (1996–2000); member of the Fourth (2007–16) and Fifth (2016–22) Assembly of Experts, Mazandaran

1943–, Juybar, Mazandaran

Clerical education, Najaf Seminary (Iraq)

Gholam-Hoseyn, schoolmaster and Qur'an teacher

Clergyman

Imprisoned before the revolution

Not a war veteran

Martyr's family (two sons, Gholam-Ali and Gholam-Reza, killed at the war front)

Ayatollah Mo'allemi-Juybari lived in Iraq from 1965
to 1971, and after the revolution, he was active in
the Mazandaran Province judiciary as well as in
the Islamic Propaganda Organization. He was
also the Friday prayer leader of Qaemshahr and of
Juybar, where he served for fourteen years.

Mo'allemipur, Ali

Deputy of the Seventh Majlis, Minab, Rudan, and
Jask, Hormozgan (2004–8)

December 23, 1955–, Minab, Hormozgan

BS, water engineering, Shahid Chamran University of
Ahvaz; MS, water resource engineering (France);
PhD, hydraulics (France)

Mohammad, farmer

Civil servant and university professor

No imprisonment

Mo'allemipur is highly involved in water resource
management issues in Iran.

Moarrefi'zadeh, Ali

Deputy of the First (1980–84) and Second (1984–February 20, 1986) Majlis, Khorramshahr and Shadegan, Khuzestan

1948–February 20, 1986, Shadegan, Khuzestan

High school diploma, 1984

Esma'il, bazaar tradesman

Civil servant

No imprisonment

Not a war veteran

Moarrefi'zadeh was killed when Iraqi forces shot
down his plane.

Moayyedi, Ali

Deputy of the Seventh Majlis, Sepidan, Fars (2004–8)

1959–, Sepidan, Fars

BA, public administration

Reza

Civil servant

No imprisonment

Mobaleqi, Ahmad

Member of the Fifth Assembly of Experts, Lorestan
(2016–22)

1959–, Kuhdasht, Lorestan

Clerical education, Qom Seminary

Masha'allah Moravveji, clergyman (ayatollah)

Clergyman

Imprisoned before the revolution

War veteran

HI Mobaleqi was head of the Islamic Research Center
of the Majlis before he was elected to the Fifth AE.

Mobasheri [-Monfared], Asadollah

Minister of justice in PM Bazargan's cabinet (February–
June 20, 1979)

1907–1990, Tehran, Tehran

BA, law, Tehran University, 1935; PhD, law, University
of Paris (France), 1952; dissertation title: "La morale islamique et son application en droit penal"

Mobasher, civil servant

Attorney

No imprisonment

Not a war veteran

Member of INF

Mobasheri entered the Iranian judiciary in 1928/29
and was active in it until the time of the revolution. He received a diploma d'état in Paris under
the name Mobachery. Mobasheri resigned his
post on June 20, 1979, and thereafter involved
himself mainly in cultural activities.

Mobini-Dehkordi, Ali

Deputy of the Fourth Majlis, Shahrekord, Chahar
Mahal and Bakhtiari (1992–96)

1955–, Shahrekord, Chahar Mahal and Bakhtiari

BS, agricultural engineering; MA, political science;
PhD, strategic management, Supreme National
Defense University

Haj Aqa

Civil servant

No imprisonment

Not a war veteran

Founding member of the Society of Former MPs

Mobini-Dehkordi was a civil servant in the International Institute for Energy Studies and a member of one of the special commissions of the EDA. He was also the first native-born governor-general of Chahar Mahal and Bakhtiari.

Modarresi-Yazdi, Seyyed Mohammad-Reza

Member of the Fifth (2004–10), Sixth (2010–16), and Seventh (2016–19) Guardian Councils

1955–, Yazd, Yazd

Clerical education

Seyyed Javad, clergyman (ayatollah)

Clergyman

No imprisonment

Not a war veteran

Member of the SQSS

Ayatollah Modarresi-Yazdi was Ayatollah Khomeini's representative in Yazd before the revolution. He was the Friday prayer leader of Shahedieh in Yazd Province after the revolution. He was also a trustee of the National Elites Foundation.

Moezzi, Esma'il

Deputy of the First Majlis, Malayer, Hamadan (1980–84)

1923–2008, Malayer, Hamadan

Clerical education

Qasem, farmer

Clergyman

No imprisonment

Not a war veteran

In 1981, the judiciary arrested two of HI Moezzi's sons for supporting PMOI. At least one of his sons was executed.

Mofatteh, Mohammad

Member of the Revolutionary Council (1979)

1928–December 18, 1979, Hamadan, Hamadan

Clerical education, Qom Seminary; PhD, theology, Tehran University

Mahmud, clergyman (HI)

Clergyman

Imprisoned before the revolution

The Forqan group assassinated Ayatollah Mofatteh, a close aide to Ayatollah Khomeini, on December 18, 1979. At the time, he was in charge of the faculty of theology at Tehran University.

Mofatteh, Mohammad-Mehdi

Deputy of the Fourth (1993–96), Fifth (1996–2000), Seventh (2004–8), and Eighth (2008–12) Majlis, Razan, Hamadan; deputy of the Ninth (2013–16) and Tenth (2016–20) Majlis, Tuyserkan, Hamadan

1956–, Qom, Qom

BS, industrial engineering, Sharif University of Technology; MS, industrial engineering, Amirkabir University of Technology; MA, economics, Allameh Tabataba'i University; PhD, economics, Islamic Azad University–Tehran, 2003

Mohammad, clergyman (ayatollah)

Manager

No imprisonment

Not a war veteran

Martyr's family (father)

Mofatteh was not elected to the Ninth Majlis in the first round but was elected in interim elections held in June 2013. Mofatteh, a conservative, also served in the Tehran City Council. He is the son of Ayatollah Mohammad Mofatteh, who was a member of the Revolutionary Council and was assassinated by the Forqan group in 1979. He is the grandson of Sadeq Ehsanbakhsh, who was a member of the First AE.

Mofid, Hoseyn

Head of the State Supreme Court (August 15, 2004–August 25, 2009)

Clerical education

Clergyman (ayatollah)

Mofid entered the judiciary branch in 1979 and spent some twenty-seven years working in the State Supreme Court.

Mohajerani, Seyyed Ataollah

Deputy of the First Majlis, Shiraz, Fars (1980–84); VP for parliamentary affairs in President Hashemi-Rafsanjani's first (1989–93) and second (1993–97) cabinets; minister of culture and Islamic guidance in President Khatami's first cabinet (August 20, 1997–December 14, 2000)
1954–, Arak, Markazi
BA, history, Isfahan University of Technology, 1977; MA, history, Shiraz University, 1982; PhD, history, Tarbiyat-e Modarres University, 1996
Seyyed Aqa Nur, laborer
University student
No imprisonment
Not a war veteran
Member of the central council of PECI
In addition to the above posts, Mohajerani was also legal and parliamentary deputy to PM Mir Hoseyn Musavi. In the mid-1980s, he criticized secular political forces. He published a weekly journal, *Bahman*, from January 1995 to April 1996. As culture minister, Mohajerani survived impeachment on May 1, 1999, but finally resigned his post in December 2000. He then headed the Center for the Dialogue of Civilizations for two years but had to resign for personal reasons. Mohajerani later settled in London with his wife, Jamileh Kadivar, a former MP.

Mohammad Khan, Morteza

Minister of economic affairs and finance in President Hashemi-Rafsanjani's second cabinet (October 6, 1993–August 2, 1997)
January 1, 1946–, Tehran, Tehran
BS, industrial engineering, San Jose State University (USA), 1972; MA, economics, San Jose State University (USA), 1975; PhD, technology transfer, University of Pune (India)

Civil servant, customs
No imprisonment
Not a war veteran
Member of the central council of the IRP; founding member of the PMD
Mohammad Khan was active in the Muslim Student Association in the United States before 1979, and he was injured in the bombing of the IRP headquarters in June 1981. He was in charge of the customs bureau for four years before becoming a minister (receiving 151 positive votes, forty-six negative votes, and twenty-six abstentions). An economist at K. N. Toosi University of Technology, he was also in charge of the economic bureau of the EDA.

Mohammad-Gharibani, Ali

Deputy of the Second (1984–88), Third (1988–92), Fourth (1992–96), and Sixth (2000–2004) Majlis, Ardabil, Ardabil
1944–, Ardabil, Ardabil
BS, civil engineering
Mohrram
Civil servant, ministries
No imprisonment
Not a war veteran
Martyr's family (three brothers)
Mohammad-Gharibani was elected to the Second Majlis in a wave of sympathy votes after PMOI assassinated one of his brothers, who was the prosecutor of Ardabil. He lost two more brothers at the war front. After serving in the Majlis, he became the governor-general of Ardabil and was close to the reformists.

Mohammadi, Abdollah

Member of the First (1983–90) and Second (1991–95) Assembly of Experts, Kurdistan
1917–1995, Sardasht, Kurdistan
Clerical education
Mahmud, farmer
Clergyman

No imprisonment
Not a war veteran
Mohammadi, a Sunni mamosta, was the Friday prayer
leader of Saqqez.

Mohammadi, Bahman

Deputy of the Seventh (2004–8) and Eighth (2008–12)
Majlis, Faridan, Fereydunshahr, and Chadegan,
Isfahan
1957–, Faridan, Isfahan
BA, business administration
Asgar
Academia
No imprisonment
Mohammadi was not elected to the Ninth Majlis.

Mohammadi [Qazvin], Davud

Deputy of the Ninth (2012–16) and Tenth (2016–20)
Majlis, Qazvin, Abyek, and Alborz, Qazvin
1963–, Qazvin, Qazvin
BA, law, University of Judicial Sciences and Adminis-
trative Services, 1986; MA, criminal law, Islamic
Azad University–Tehran, 1994
Judiciary official in Zanjan Province
No imprisonment
Not a war veteran
Mohammadi was elected to the Seventh Majlis but the
GC nullified his votes. He is a judge, athlete, and
university lecturer.

Mohammadi [Qom], Davud

Deputy of the Tenth Majlis, Tehran, Tehran (2016–20)
1950–, Qom, Qom
BS, physics; MA, political science
Morad
Teacher and political law enforcement manager of the
Fars governor-general's office
No imprisonment
War veteran
Mohammadi was active in the Islamic Association of
Iranian Teachers.

Mohammadi, Eqbal

Deputy of the Eighth Majlis, Marivan and Sarvabad,
Kurdistan (2008–12)
1963–, Marivan, Kurdistan
BS, water engineering, Tehran University; MS, water
engineering, Tarbiyat-e Modarres University,
1994
Mohammad-Aziz, farmer
Academia
No imprisonment
Not a war veteran
Mohammadi, a Sunni, was not elected to the Ninth
Majlis.

Mohammadi, Hoseyn

Member of the Seventh (2012–17) and Eighth (2017–
22) Expediency Discernment Assembly
Civil servant, supreme leader
Member of the IRP
Mohammadi worked in Khamenei's campaign headquarters when he ran for the presidency in the
1980s. He then worked in the PBO while Khamenei was president and followed him to the Office
of the Supreme Leader when Khamenei occupied
the post. Mohammadi worked for a while as a
political deputy in IRIB under Ali Larijani before
returning to the Office of the Supreme Leader
to work as Khamenei's deputy on cultural and
media-related issues. His brother, HI Hamid
Mohammadi, is deputy head of the Council to
Expand Qur'anic Culture.

Mohammadi, Mahmud

Deputy of the Seventh Majlis, Abadeh, Bavanat, and
Khorrambid, Fars (2004–8)
1953–, Abadeh, Fars
PhD, international relations, Orientale University of
Naples (Italy)
Mohammad
Ambassador to Tunisia
No imprisonment

Mohammadi served in such capacities as spokesperson of the Iranian Ministry of Foreign Affairs (1991–98) and ambassador to Tunisia (1999–2003) before entering the Majlis. After the Majlis, he was an adviser to the foreign minister from 2008 to 2009.

Mohammadi, Mohammad

Deputy of the Second (1984–88), Fourth (1992–96), Sixth (2000–2004), and Eighth (2008–12) Majlis, Selseleh and Delfan, Lorestan
1937–, Delfan, Lorestan
Clerical education
Karamollah
Clergyman
No imprisonment
HI Mohammadi was elected to the Second Majlis in an election marked by tribal violence. He ran unsuccessfully for the Ninth Majlis.

Mohammadi, Mostafa

Deputy of the Sixth (2000–2004) and Seventh (2004–8) Majlis, Paveh and Javanrud, Kermanshah
1962–, Javanrud, Kermanshah
Associate's degree
Ahmad
Military and security forces
No imprisonment
IRGC militiaman
Mohammadi, a Sunni, joined the military establishment after leaving the Majlis.

Mohammadi, Qasem

Deputy of the Eighth Majlis, Ardabil, Namin, and Nir, Ardabil (2008–12)
1967–, Moqan, Ardabil
BS, agricultural engineering; MA, educational planning
Mirza Khan
Director of public relations for the Ministry of Agriculture

No imprisonment
Not a war veteran
Mohammadi got the highest votes for Ardabil in the Eighth Majlis but was not elected to the Ninth Majlis. He was close to President Ahmadinejad's faction and served for a while as the director of public relations and adviser to the minister of economy.

Mohammadi, Seyyed Mohammad-Hoseyn

Deputy of the First Majlis, Dashti and Tangestan, Bushehr (1981–84)
1938–, Rudbaran, Bushehr
Clerical education
Seyyed Abdollah
Clergyman
No imprisonment

Mohammadi, Yunes

Deputy of the First (1980–84), Second 1984–88), Third (1988–92), and Fourth (1993–96) Majlis, Khorramshahr and Shadegan, Khuzestan
1949–, Khorramshahr, Khuzestan
Associate's degree
Karim, farmer
Teacher
No imprisonment
Not a war veteran

Mohammadi-Araqi, Mahmud

Member of the Seventh (2012–17) and Eighth (2017–22) Expediency Discernment Assembly; member of the Fifth Assembly of Experts, Kermanshah (2016–22)
1952–, Kangavar, Kermanshah
Clerical education, Qom Seminary
Bahaeddin, clergyman
Clergyman
Imprisoned before the revolution (1975–78)
IRGC militiaman
Martyr's family (father, Bahaeddin)

Member of the central council of the SCC

Ayatollah Mohammadi-Araqi's father was a Friday prayer leader in Kermanshah whom PMOI assassinated in 1981. Mohammadi-Araqi served as the supreme leader's deputy representative to the IRGC before becoming the lead representative from June 26, 1990 to February 17, 1992. On June 28, 1992, Ayatollah Khamenei appointed him director of the Islamic Propaganda Organization. He is a member of the HCCR. Mohammadi-Araqi was a student of Ayatollahs Beheshti and Khamenei. He is also the son-in-law of Ayatollah Mesbah-Yazdi.

Mohammadi-Araqi (Araki), Mohsen

Member of the Second (1991–98) and Third (1999–2006) Assembly of Experts, Khuzestan (1999–2006); member of the Fifth Assembly of Experts, Markazi (2016–22)

1955–, Najaf, Iraq

Clerical education, Qom Seminary; PhD, philosophy, University of Portsmouth (England; unverified)

Habibollah, clergyman (ayatollah)

Clergyman

No imprisonment

Not a war veteran

Ayatollah Mohammadi-Araqi, also known as Mohsen Araki, lived in Iraq from 1955 to 1975. After residing in Qom, he became affiliated with the Haqqani Seminary run by Ayatollah Qoddusi. In 1980, Qoddusi appointed him head of the revolutionary courts in Abadan and Khorramshahr, and a year later, at age twenty-six, he became head of the revolutionary tribunals and the judiciary in the Khuzestan Province. In these posts, he signed off on the execution orders of numerous Arab political activists. In 1983, Mohammadi-Araqi helped set up the military wing of the High Council for Islamic Revolution (later known as the Ninth Badr brigade), and from 1987 to 1996, he served as the supreme leader's representative in that brigade. From 1986 to 1988, Mohammadi-Araqi was the Friday prayer leader and

Ayatollah Khomeini's representative in Dezful. At thirty-six years old, he was the youngest member entering the Second AE. From 1994 to 2005 he lived in England as the supreme leader's representative in that country and helped establish a good number of Islamic institutions there, including the Islamic College for Advanced Studies and the Sakina Trust Mosque. On August 10, 2012, Ayatollah Khamenei appointed Mohammadi-Araqi as the secretary-general of WFPIST.

Mohammadiazar, Seyyed Hoseyn

Deputy of the Second Majlis, Takestan, Zanjan (1984–88)

1954–, Qazvin, Qazvin

Clerical education

Seyyed Hamzeh, clergyman

Clergyman (HI)

No imprisonment

Not a war veteran

Mohammadifar, Baratali

Deputy of the Fourth Majlis, Sonqor, Kermanshah (1992–96)

1957–, Asadabad, Hamadan

Clerical education

Ezzatali

No imprisonment

Mohammadifar was elected to the Sixth Majlis but could not occupy his seat after his credentials were called into question by other MPs.

Mohammadifar, Naser

Commander of the Islamic Republic of Iran Ground Forces (February 7, 2001–September 25, 2005)

Date of birth unknown, Khalkhal, Ardabil

Military officer (brigadier general)

War veteran

After stepping down from his post, Brigadier General Mohammadifar served as a military adviser to the supreme leader.

Mohammadi-Gilani, Mohammad

Member of the First (1983–90), Second (1991–98), Third (1999–2006), and Fourth (2007–14) Assembly of Experts, Tehran; member of the First (July 1983–86), Second (1986–92), and Third (1992–March 1995) Guardian Councils; head of the State Supreme Court (August 28, 1994–August 15, 2004)
Clerical education, Qom Seminary
1928–July 9, 2014, Rudsar, Gilan
Mohammad-Ja'far, farmer
Clergyman
No imprisonment
Not a war veteran
Member of the SQSS
Ayatollah Mohammadi-Gilani was in charge of all revolutionary courts until 1983 and was opposed to absorbing them into the Ministry of Justice. In this capacity, he ordered the execution of many people in the early days of the revolution, and especially after the PMOI uprising of 1981. He was known as an advocate of the on-the-spot execution of dissidents. Two of his sons were affiliated with PMOI and were killed by the regime. Mohammadi-Gilani presided over the trial of Abbas Amir-Entezam, the former deputy and spokesperson for PM Bazargan. He also appeared on a television program where he explained the intricacies of the Islamic penal code. In November 1984, he was appointed by Ayatollah Montazeri to a committee investigating prison conditions. Mohammadi-Gilani headed the GC from July 1988 to July 1992 and was a member of the Council for Revision of the Constitution in 1989. He resigned from the GC in March 1995 to become head of the State Supreme Court.

Mohammadi [-Gorgani], Mohammad

Deputy of the First Majlis, Gorgan, Golestan (1980–84)
1943–, Gorgan, Golestan
BA, law, Tehran University; MA, law, Tehran University; PhD, law, University of Bradford (England), 1998; dissertation title: "Legitimacy of Power in the Constitution of the Islamic Republic of Iran"

Mohammad-Hadi, civil servant
Political party activist
Imprisoned before the revolution (1973–78)
Not a war veteran
Mohammadi was originally a member of PMOI but broke with the organization in 1977. While imprisoned, he was a cellmate of future prime minister and president Mohammad-Ali Raja'i. He retired as a professor from Allameh Tabataba'i University. Mohammadi is close to the National-Religious forces, and he is the father-in-law of dissident journalist Ahmad Zeydabadi.

Mohammadi-Hamadani [Taha-Mohammadi], Gheyaseddin

Member of the Fourth (2007–16) and Fifth (2016–22) Assembly of Experts, Hamadan
1947–, Famenin, Hamadan
Clerical education, Qom Seminary, 1975
Abbas-Ali
Clergyman
Imprisoned before the revolution
Not a war veteran
Ayatollah Mohammadi-Hamadani worked in the office of Ayatollah Khomeini in Qom and was the Friday prayer leader of Famenin from 1982 to 2004. In 2004, he was appointed by Ayatollah Khamenei as the Friday prayer leader of Hamadan and as his representative in Hamadan Province. His son, Mehdi, was the victim of a chemical attack during the Iran–Iraq War.

Mohammadi-Ilami, Rahim

Member of the Third Assembly of Experts, Ilam (1999–2006)
1962–, Ilam, Ilam
Father's name unknown, farmer
Clerical education, Qom Seminary
Clergyman (HI)
No imprisonment
War veteran (wounded)

Mohammadi-Jezzi, Amrollah

Deputy of the Sixth Majlis, Borkhar and Meymeh,
Isfahan (2000–2004)
1958–, Borkhar, Isfahan
MA, management
Ali
No imprisonment
After leaving the Majlis, Mohammadi-Jezzi became a
civil servant.

Mohammadi-Kaftarkari, Abbas

Deputy of the Fifth Majlis, Kordkuy and Torkaman,
Mazandaran (1996–2000)
1953–, Kordkuy, Golestan
BA, management
Rahim
No imprisonment

Mohammadi-La'ini, Hoseyn

Member of the First (1983–90) and Second (1991–93)
Assembly of Experts, Mazandaran
1922–1993, La'in, Mazandaran
Clerical education, Najaf Seminary (Iraq), 1960
Mohammad-Ali, clergyman
Clergyman (ayatollah)
No imprisonment
Not a war veteran

Mohammadiyan, Ali-Karam

Deputy of the Third Majlis, Ilam, Shirvan, and Char-
davol, Ilam (1988–92)
1956–, Shirvan, Ilam
BS, agricultural engineering
Ali-Nazar, farmer
Director-general of tribal affairs in Ilam Province
No imprisonment
War veteran
IRGC militiaman
After leaving the Majlis, Mohammadiyan worked for
the Ministry of Agriculture.

Mohammadiyan, Eqbal

Deputy of the Tenth Majlis, Ramhormoz and Ram-
shir, Khuzestan (2016–20)
1965–, Ramhormoz, Khuzestan
BA, public administration, Islamic Azad Univer-
sity–Shushtar; MA, public administration; PhD,
strategic management
Administrative deputy of Ahvaz
No imprisonment
IRGC militiaman
Mohammadiyan is a former teacher, university ad-
ministrator, and high-level official of the Foun-
dation for Dispossessed and War-Invalids in
Khuzestan Province. He also served as mayor of
Ramhormoz.

Mohammadizadeh, Mohammad-Javad

VP and head of the Environmental Protection Or-
ganization in President Ahmadinejad's second
cabinet (2009–13)
1955–, Dezful, Khuzestan
MS, environmental health, Tehran University School
of Medical Sciences
Civil servant
No imprisonment
War veteran
IRGC militiaman
Mohammadizadeh was the governor of Razavi
Khorasan Province during President Ahmadine-
jad's first term in office, and before that, he was
Ahmadinejad's deputy in the office of Tehran's
mayor.

Mohammadjani, Davud

Deputy of the Eighth Majlis, Abadeh, Bavanat, and
Khorrambid, Fars (2008–12)
1967–, Bavanat, Fars
Clerical education
Hoseyn-Ali
Clergyman
No imprisonment

After the GC did not approve his credentials for the
Ninth Majlis, HI Mohammadjani worked as a
notary public registering marriages and divorces
in Tehran.

Mohammadkhani-Shahrudi, Hoseyn

Deputy of the Second Majlis, Darab, Fars (1984–88)
1949–, Shahrud, Semnan
BA, educational sciences; clerical education
Mohammad
Clergyman (HI)
No imprisonment

Mohammad-Najjar, Mostafa

Minister of defense and armed forces logistics in
President Ahmadinejad's first cabinet (August 24,
2005–August 2, 2009); interior minister in Presi-
dent Ahmadinejad's second cabinet (September 3,
2009–August 2, 2013) cabinets
1956–, Tehran, Tehran
BS, mechanical engineering, K. N. Toosi University
of Technology, 1984; MA, executive management,
Industrial Management Organization, 2004
Mohammad
Military and security forces
No imprisonment
War veteran
IRGC militiaman
Mohammad-Najjar has been involved with the IRGC
and the defense industry, including the Defense
Industries Organization, since 1979. For a while,
he was in charge of the IRGC's cooperative unit.
He is on the US Treasury Office of Foreign Assets
Control's Specially Designated Nationals and
Blocked Persons List because of his role in the
1999 suppression of student protesters.

Mohammad-Reza'i, Mohammad

Deputy of the Sixth Majlis, Bijar, Kurdistan
(2000–2004)

1958–, Bijar, Kurdistan
Associate's degree
Ali-Pasha
Civil servant
No imprisonment
IRGC militiaman

Mohammad-Sadeqi, Shahin

Deputy of the Seventh (2004–8) and Ninth (2012–16)
Majlis, Kazerun, Fars
1963–, Kazerun, Fars
MD, medicine, Shiraz University of Medical Sciences,
1990
Gholam-Ali
Medical doctor
No imprisonment
War veteran
Mohammad-Sadeqi, a former dean of Kohgiluyeh
and Buyer Ahmad University's medical school,
did a fellowship in surgery at Imperial Col-
lege (London), and in 2008, he became dean of
Shahid Beheshti University's medical school.
During the war in Bosnia, he served as a medical
professional.

Mohammadyari, Bahman

Deputy of the Fifth (1996–2000), Seventh (2004–8),
and Eighth (2008–12) Majlis, Talesh, Gilan
1962–, Masal, Gilan
BA, public administration
Heyatollah, shop owner
Provincial civil servant
No imprisonment
War veteran
IRGC militiaman (joined in 1980)
Mohammadyari ran unsuccessfully for the Fourth
and Sixth Majlis. He had previously worked at the
Iranian customs office and Alborz Insurance. He
was also an adviser to Hoseyn Namazi, the minis-
ter of economy.

Mohammadzadeh, Hoseyn

Deputy of the Ninth Majlis, Dargaz, Razavi Khorasan
   (2012–16)
1965–, Bojnurd, North Khorasan
BS, civil engineering, University of Sistan and
   Baluchestan
Civil servant
No imprisonment
Mohammadzadeh is a former mayor of Dargaz and
   governor of Torqabeh.

Mohaqqar, Ali

Deputy of the Third Majlis, Bojnurd, North Khorasan
   (1988–92)
1957–, Bojnurd, North Khorasan
BS, industrial engineering, Sharif University of
   Technology, 1980; MS, system planning, Isfahan Industrial University, 1986; PhD, industrial
   engineering, Tarbiyat-e Modarres University,
   2001
Hoseyn
No imprisonment
After serving in the Majlis, Mohaqqar went to MI,
   and after earning his doctorate, he became a faculty member at Tehran University.

Mohaqqeq-Banki, Hoseyn

Deputy of the Second Majlis, Karaj, Tehran
   (1984–88)
1937–, Qom, Qom
Clerical education
Esma'il
Clergyman
No imprisonment

Mohaqqeq-Damad [Ahmadabadi], Seyyed Mostafa

Head of the State General Inspectorate Organization
   (October 10, 1981–94)
1945–, Qom, Qom

Clerical education, Qom Seminary; MA, law and
   Islamic philosophy, Tehran University; PhD, law,
   Catholic University of Louvain (Belgium); disser-
   tation title: "Protection of Individuals in Times of
   Armed Conflict under International and Islamic
   Laws"
Seyyed Mohammad, clergyman (ayatollah)
No imprisonment
Not a war veteran
In 1981, HI Mohaqqeq-Damad became deputy justice
   minister and helped to rewrite the legal code. He
   was also a professor of jurisprudence and law at
   Shahid Beheshti University and a fellow of the
   Academy of Sciences of the Islamic Republic of
   Iran.

Mohassel-Hamadani, Seyyed Mohammad-Taqi

Deputy of the Fourth (1992–96), Fifth (1996–2000),
   and Seventh (2004–8) Majlis, Taft, Yazd
1935–, Yazd, Yazd
Clerical education
Seyyed Hoseyn
Clergyman
No imprisonment
Not a war veteran
HI Mohassel-Hamadani was a judiciary official before
   being elected to the Majlis.

Mohebbi, Mohammad-Ebrahim

Deputy of the Ninth Majlis, Sonqor, Kermanshah
   (2012–16)
1963–, Qarehtapeh, Kermanshah
MD, medicine, Tehran University of Medical Sci-
   ences, 1994; clerical education
Father's name unknown, farmer
Medical doctor and health official in Sonqor
No imprisonment
Not a war veteran
Mohebbi was not elected to the Seventh Majlis. After
   serving in the Ninth Majlis, he became an official
   in the oil industry.

Mohebbi, Yusef

Deputy of the Seventh Majlis, Larestan, Fars (2004–8)
1947–, Larestan, Fars
BA, production management
Mohammad-Ja'far
Civil servant
No imprisonment

Mohebbinia, Jahanbakhsh

Deputy of the Fifth (1997–2000), Sixth (2000–2004),
    Seventh (2004–8), Eighth (2008–12), and Tenth
    (2016–20) Majlis, Miyandoab, Takab, and Shahin-
    dezh, West Azerbaijan
1962–, Shahindezh, West Azerbaijan
BA, 1995; MA, political science, 2000; PhD, political
    science
Gholam-Hasan
Civil servant
No imprisonment
IRGC militiaman
Mohebbinia is a former rector of Farhangian Uni-
    versity and was a member of the leadership team
    during the Seventh and Eighth Majlis. He was not
    elected to the Ninth Majlis.

Mohseni-Bandpey, Anushiravan

Deputy of the Sixth (2000–2004), Seventh (2004–8),
    and Eighth (2008–12) Majlis, Nowshahr and Cha-
    lus, Mazandaran
1956–, Nowshahr, Mazandaran
BS, agricultural engineering, University of Mazan-
    daran, 1979; MS, health engineering, Tarbiyat-e
    Modarres University; PhD, health engineering,
    Newcastle University (England), 1996; disserta-
    tion title: "Nitrate Removal from Groundwater
    Using a Rotating Biological Contactor with Alter-
    native Carbon Sources"
Abolfath
University professor
No imprisonment
War veteran

Mohseni-Bandpey, a reformist, was not elected to
    the Ninth Majlis. On April 13, 2015, he became a
    deputy in the Ministry of Health and head of the
    State Welfare Organization of Iran.

Mohseni-Ezheh'i, Gholam-Hoseyn

Prosecutor-general of the SCFC (December 16, 1998–
    September 24, 2005); minister of intelligence in
    President Ahmadinejad's first cabinet (August 24,
    2005–July 25, 2009); prosecutor-general (August
    25, 2009–August 23, 2014); member of the Sixth
    (2007–12), Seventh (2012–17), and Eighth (2017–
    22) Expediency Discernment Assembly; first dep-
    uty to the chief justice (August 23, 2014–present)
1956–, Ezhe, Isfahan
Clerical education, Qom Seminary; MA, international
    law, Islamic Azad University–Tehran
Father's name unknown, clergyman
Clergyman
Judiciary official
No imprisonment
Not a war veteran
HI Mohseni-Ezheh'i is a hardliner and feared cleric
    who has been intimately connected to MIIRI and
    the judiciary. He moved from MIIRI to become
    the SCFC prosecutor-general in Tehran (1995–97)
    before being promoted to prosecutor-general of
    the SCFC. In the latter capacity, he tried Gholam-
    Hoseyn Karbaschi, then-mayor of Tehran, in
    a closely watched trial. President Ahmadine-
    jad dismissed Mohseni-Ezheh'i as intelligence
    minister a few days before his term was over, but
    Ayatollah Sadeq Larijani, the head of the judi-
    ciary, rewarded him with the post of prosecutor-
    general. Mohseni-Ezheh'i was heavily involved
    in the postelection crackdown and show trials of
    2009. He is on the US Treasury Office of Foreign
    Assets Control's Specially Designated Nationals
    and Blocked Persons List because of his role in the
    2009 crackdown. He is also on the sanctions list
    of the Council of the European Union. In 2014,
    Larijani appointed him first deputy of the judi-
    ciary as well as spokesperson of the judiciary.

Mohseni-Garakani, Ahmad

Member of the Third (1999–2006), Fourth (2007–16), and Fifth (2016–22) Assembly of Experts, Markazi; head of the State Supreme Court (August 25, 2009–August 20, 2014)
1926–, Garakan, Markazi
Clerical education, Qom Seminary
Ali-Asghar, farmer
Clergyman
No imprisonment
Not a war veteran
Ayatollah Khomeini appointed HI Mohseni-Garakani as the Friday prayer leader of Torbat-e Heydari-yyeh and Tuyserkan in 1983. Ayatollah Khamenei appointed him as the Friday prayer leader of Arak, where he served from 1993 to 2009. For a while, he was responsible for the examination of students in the Qom Seminary.

Mohseni-Sani, Mohammad-Reza

Deputy of the Eighth (2008–12) and Ninth (2012–16) Majlis, Sabzevar, Razavi Khorasan
1952–, Sabzevar, Razavi Khorasan
BS, chemical engineering, Middlesbrough University (England); MA, public administration, Institute for Management and Planning Studies
Mohammad-Hasan, bazaar tradesman
Civil servant
No imprisonment
War veteran
IRGC militiaman
Mohseni-Sani returned to Iran from England after the revolution. He became the first commander of the IRGC in Sabzevar and then governor of Amol. From 1989 to 1992, he was an assistant to Asadollah Ladjvardi in the State Prisons Organization. Afterward, he served as governor or governor-general of Qom, Damghan, Mashhad, and Lorestan until he was elected to the Majlis. Because of his background in running prisons, Mohseni-Sani was assigned to the Majlis committee investigating the torture, rape, and killing of protestors after the contested 2009 presidential election. He denied any serious wrongdoing on the part of prison wardens. Mohseni-Sani's daughter is married to the son of Va'ez-Tabasi.

Mohtaj, Abbas

Commander of the Islamic Republic of Iran Navy (August 27, 1997–September 25, 2005)
Date of birth unknown, Qom, Qom
War veteran (leading commander)
IRGC militiaman
Mohtaj, a high-level IRGC commander, became deputy commander of the IRGC's ground forces after the war. He served as deputy commander of the Islamic Republic of Iran Navy from 1990 to 1997 before becoming commander. After he left the navy, Commodore Mohtaj became the governor-general of Qom (2005–7), security deputy of MI, and adviser to the supreme leader.

Mohtashamipur, Seyyed Ali-Akbar

Interior minister in PM Musavi's second cabinet (October 28, 1985–August 3, 1989); deputy of the Third (1989–92) and Sixth (2000–2004) Majlis, Tehran, Tehran
1946–, Tehran, Tehran
Clerical education, Najaf Seminary (Iraq)
Seyyed Hoseyn, bazaar tradesman
Clergyman (HI)
No imprisonment
Not a war veteran
Founder and member of the central council of the ACC
Mohtashamipur moved to Lebanon in 1966 and went with Ayatollah Khomeini to France in 1978. Between September 1980 and September 1981, he was Ayatollah Khomeini's representative in IRIB. A radical who believed in the export of the revolution, he served as ambassador to Syria from September 1981 to October 1985 and played an important role in the formation of the Lebanese Hezbollah. On February 15, 1984, while

serving as an ambassador, he was injured in an assassination attempt when a book containing a bomb blew up in his hands, causing him to go deaf in one ear. His family has long been active in the CIC/PCIC. Indeed, his brothers Hoseyn and Mahmud were members of the central committee of the CIC/PCIC, but he himself severed ties with the organization after the revolution. The judiciary closed the daily *Bayan*, which he edited, in 2000, and he was tried by the SCFC. Mohtashamipur was a social adviser to former president Khatami. Mostafa Tajzadeh and Morteza Rafiqdust are married to two of his nieces, and his granddaughter is married to the son of Mohammad-Reza Bahonar.

Mohyeddin-Anvari, Mohammad-Baqer

Deputy of the First Majlis, Razan, Hamadan (1980–84); deputy of the Second Majlis, Tehran, Tehran (1984–88); member of First Assembly of Experts, Hamadan (1983–90); member of Second Assembly of Experts, Tehran (1991–98)
1926–October 14, 2012, Qom, Qom
Clerical education, Marvi Seminary
Zeynol'abedin, clergyman (ayatollah)
Clergyman
Imprisoned before the revolution (1964–77)
Not a war veteran
Member of the IRP; member and head of the central council of the SCC
The shah's regime imprisoned Ayatollah Mohyeddin-Anvari for thirteen years before the revolution for being involved with the military wing of the CIC/PCIC. He finally gained his release from prison in early 1977 after taking part in a controversial ceremony praising the shah. Mohyeddin-Anvari played a big role in the committee welcoming Ayatollah Khomeini back to Iran. He was the imam of the Narmak mosque, and in 1979, he became Ayatollah Khomeini's representative for pilgrimage affairs. He also was Ayatollah Khomeini's representative in the gendarmerie force in the 1980s. After leaving the

AE, he became director of the Center for Supervision of Mosque Affairs. He also taught at Imam Sadeq University. Mohyeddin-Anvari's son was in charge of the IKRF. His wife is the daughter of Ayatollah Abbas Ansari.

Mojtahedi, Hesameddin

Member of Fourth Assembly of Experts, Kurdistan (March 2012–April 2014)
1924–April 26, 2014, Sanandaj, Kurdistan
Clergyman
Molla Mohammad-Sadiq, clergyman
No imprisonment
Not a war veteran
Mamosta Mojtahedi, a Sunni cleric, was elected in interim elections in March 2012 to replace Mohammad Shaikholislami, who was assassinated. He became the Friday prayer leader of Baneh on February 11, 1983, and he served as Friday prayer leader of Sanandaj from 2004 to 2014.

Mojtahedi-Behbahani, Mohammad-Hoseyn

Member of the First Assembly of Experts, Khuzestan (1983–90)
1918–January 2013, Behbahan, Khuzestan
Clerical education
Abdolhadi, clergyman
Clergyman (ayatollah)
No imprisonment
Not a war veteran
Mojtahedi-Behbahani became the first Friday prayer leader of Behbahan in February 1982.

Mojtahed-Shabestari, Javad

Member of the Fifth Assembly of Experts, West Azerbaijan (2016–22)
1967–, Qom, Qom
Clerical education, Qom Seminary
Mohsen, clergyman (ayatollah)
No imprisonment
War veteran

HI Mojtahed-Shabestari and his father, Mohsen,
    served together in the Fifth AE.

Mojtahed-Shabestari, Mohammad

Deputy of the First Majlis, Shabestar, East Azerbaijan
    (1980–84)
1936–, Shabestar, East Azerbaijan
Clerical education, Qom Seminary, 1969
Mirza Kazem, clergyman (ayatollah)
Clergyman
No imprisonment
Not a war veteran
From 1969 to 1978, HI Mojtahed-Shabestari lived in
    Germany, where he directed the Islamic Center
    of Hamburg. Upon returning to Iran, he briefly
    published a biweekly titled *Andisheh-ye Islami*.
    After the First Majlis, he did not run for any other
    political offices. Instead, he devoted himself to
    being a professor of theology at Tehran University
    and emerged as one of the leading intellectual
    voices of postrevolutionary Iran. He has also been
    a member of the Academy of Sciences. Over time,
    he grew more and more estranged from the politi-
    cal establishment and even abandoned his clerical
    robe. His younger brother, Mohsen, remained a
    very well-positioned conservative ayatollah.

Mojtahed-Shabestari, Mohsen

Deputy of the First (1980–84), Second (1984–88),
    Fourth (1992–96), and Fifth (1996–2000) Majlis,
    Tehran, Tehran; member of the First (1984–90),
    Second (1991–98), Third (1999–2006), Fourth
    (2007–16), and Fifth (2016–22) Assembly of
    Experts, East Azerbaijan; Member of the Eighth
    Expediency Discernment Assembly (2017–22)
1937–, Shabestar, East Azerbaijan
Clerical education, Qom Seminary
Mirza Kazem, clergyman (ayatollah)
Clergyman
No imprisonment
Not a war veteran
Member of the central council of the SCC

Ayatollah Mojtahed-Shabestari entered the Qom
    Seminary in 1952. He and his brother, Moham-
    mad, were MPs in the First Majlis simultaneously.
    He was Ayatollah Khamenei's representative in
    East Azerbaijan as well as the Friday prayer leader
    of Tabriz from 1995 to 2017.

Mojtahedzadeh, Mrs. Maryam

VP for women's and family affairs in President Ah-
    madinejad's second cabinet (August 3–October 8,
    2013)
1957–, Sari, Mazandaran
MS, nursing, Tarbiyat-e Modarres University, 1989
Faculty member at Shahid Beheshti University of
    Medical Sciences
No imprisonment
War veteran
IRGC militiaman
Mojtahedzadeh studied electrical engineering in
    Georgia (USA), and she was a member of the
    Muslim Student Association there. However, she
    did not finish her studies and returned to Iran
    after the revolution. Her husband, Seyyed Mohsen
    Musavi, was an Iranian chargé d'affaires who
    disappeared in Lebanon in 1982. She became VP
    for women's and family affairs on August 3, 2013,
    the last day of President Ahmadinejad's second
    term. Two months later, on October 8, 2013,
    President Rouhani replaced her with Shahindokht
    Moulaverdi.

Mokhtar, Jalil

Deputy of the Tenth Majlis, Abadan, Khuzestan
    (2016–20)
1974–, Abadan, Khuzestan
BA, sociology, Payam-e Nur University, Ahvaz; MA,
    sociology, Islamic Azad University
Civil servant, State Welfare Organization (Abadan
    branch)
Mokhtar was elected to the Abadan City Council in
    2003. He taught at various universities beginning
    in 2006, and in 2016 switched from the State

Welfare Organization to the Ministry of Petroleum before being elected to the Tenth Majlis.

Mokhtari, Abolqasem

Deputy of the Sixth (2000–2004) and Seventh (2004–8) Majlis, Zabol, Sistan and Baluchestan
1956–, Zabol, Sistan and Baluchestan
MD, optometry
Gholam-Hoseyn
Optometrist
No imprisonment
Mokhtari is a former head of the Islamic Republic of Iran Medical Council.

Mokhtari, Hasan

Deputy of the Third (1988–92) and Fourth (1992–96) Majlis, Najafabad, Isfahan
1950–, Najafabad, Isfahan
BS, mechanical engineering
Mostafa
No imprisonment

Molavi, Mohammad-Ali

Governor of the Central Bank (February 25–November 5, 1979)
Date of birth unknown, Tabriz, East Azerbaijan
PhD, economics, University of Paris (France), 1957
No imprisonment
Not a war veteran
Member of the central council of INF
Molavi was Iran's ambassador to the European Commonwealth before the revolution. During his term as governor of the Central Bank, Iran adopted the dual exchange rate system. A confidential cable from the American embassy, dated May 10, 1979, and published by WikiLeaks, described Molavi as beholden to President Banisadr, having no support from Khomeini, and dependent politically solely on Grand Ayatollah Seyyed Mohammad-Kazem Shari'atmadari. Molavi resigned from his post in early November 1979.

Molla Nezam-Molla Hoveyzeh, Seyyed Nezam

Deputy of the Seventh Majlis, Dasht-e Azadegan, Khuzestan (2004–8)
1965–, Dasht-e Azadegan, Khuzestan
PhD, Oriental studies
Seyyed Mobarak
Journalist
No imprisonment
IRGC militiaman

Molla Zehi, Hamidaddin

Deputy of the Second (1984–88) and Third (1988–92) Majlis, Iranshahr, Sistan and Baluchestan
1951–, Iranshahr, Sistan and Baluchestan
High school diploma
Shamseddin
No imprisonment

Mollazadeh, Abdolaziz (Molavi)

Member of the Assembly for the Final Examination of the Constitution, Sistan and Baluchestan (1979)
1916–1987, Iranshahr, Sistan and Baluchestan
Clerical education
Abdollah, clergyman
Clergyman
Not a war veteran
Mollazadeh, a Sunni cleric, became the Friday prayer leader of Zahedan in February 1982. He was head of the Islamic Unity Party and encouraged the Baluchis to vote in the AE elections.

Mollazadeh, Ahmad

Deputy of the First Majlis, Gonabad, Razavi Khorasan (1980–84)
1946–, Gonabad, Razavi Khorasan
Clerical education
Hoseyn, farmer
Clergyman
Imprisoned before the revolution
Not a war veteran

IRGC militiaman
Martyr's family (father-in-law, Hoseyn Ghaffari)
HI Mollazadeh was the managing director of *Farhang va towse'eh*, a pioneer left-leaning magazine. He is the son-in-law of Ayatollah Hoseyn Ghaffari, whom SAVAK killed in 1975. He is also the brother-in-law of Hadi Ghaffari.

Mo'men [-Daneshzadeh], Mohammad

Member of the HCJ (October 4, 1981–January 6, 1983); member of the First (1983–90) and Second (1991–98) Assembly of Experts, Semnan; member of the Fourth (2007–16) and Fifth (2016–22) Assembly of Experts, Qom; member of the First (1983–86), Second (1986–92), Third (1992–98), Fourth (1998–2004), Fifth (2004–10), Sixth (2010–16), and Seventh (2016–19) Guardian Councils
1938–, Qom, Qom
Clerical education, Qom Seminary, 1974
Abbas, farmer
Clergyman
Imprisoned before the revolution
Not a war veteran
Member of the SQSS
Ayatollah Mo'men has been appointed to seven consecutive terms in the GC. He has also been deputy chair of the AE, member of the High Policy-Planning Council, head of Qom Seminary, head of Ahlulbeyt World Assembly, and member of the board of trustees of Qom University. In the early 1980s, he was entrusted with the task of recruiting revolutionary court judges.

Mo'meni, Eskandar

Deputy chief of Law Enforcement Forces (April 4, 2015–present)
1962–, Qaemshahr, Mazandaran
PhD, national security
Head of Traffic Police (2008–15)
No imprisonment
War veteran (fifty-six months)
IRGC militiaman

Brigadier General Mo'meni was an IRGC commander during the Iran–Iraq War, and had also been in charge of security for the Khorasan Province.

Monadi-Sefidan, Ali-Reza

Deputy of the Eighth (2008–12) and Ninth (2012–16) Majlis, Tabriz, Osku, and Azarshahr, East Azerbaijan
1969–, Tabriz, East Azerbaijan
PhD, veterinary sciences, Islamic Azad University, 1995
Ali
University professor and administrator
No imprisonment
Not a war veteran
Monadi-Sefidan is a former member of the Tabriz City Council. He became the rector of Islamic Azad University–Zanjan at the age of thirty-two. He was elected to the Tenth Majlis, but the GC ruled that there was human error in counting the vote and he could not take his seat. In May 2017, he became Islamic Azad University's deputy for parliamentary affairs.

Montajabniya, Rasul

Deputy of the First Majlis, Andimeshk and Shush, Khuzestan (1981–84); deputy of the Second (1984–88) and Third (1988–92) Majlis, Shiraz, Fars
1948–, Shiraz, Fars
Clerical education, Qom Seminary
Qanbar-Ali [Adlband], laborer
Clergyman
Imprisoned before the revolution
Not a war veteran
Deputy secretary-general and founding member of the NTP; founding member of the ACC
HI Montajabniya, who was active in the anti-shah movement, is a former Friday prayer leader of Khomein and Dezful. He was Ayatollah Khomeini's representative and commissar of the ideological-political bureau of Iran's police force and was active in revolutionary and military courts. He later became an adviser to President Khatami.

Monesan, Ali-Asghar

VP and head of the Cultural Heritage, Handicrafts
and Tourism Organization in President Rouhani's
second cabinet (August 2017–2021)

1970–, Tehran, Tehran

BS, civil engineering, Sharif University of Tech-
nology; MBA, Industrial Management Or-
ganization; MS, construction management,
Amirkabir University of Technology; pursuing a
PhD in civil engineering at Sharif University of
Technology

Monesan has worked in Tehran Municipality and
for companies affiliated with the FDWI. He was
also the director of the Kish Free Trade Zone. In
2014, the minister of youth and sports appointed
him to the board of directors of the popular
soccer club Persepolis.

Montazeri, Mohammad-Ja'far

Head of the CAJ (August 26, 2009–April 10, 2016);
chief judge of the SCFC (May 2, 2012–present);
prosecutor-general (April 3, 2016–present)

1949–, Qom, Qom

Clerical education, Qom Seminary

Father's name unknown, clergyman

Clergyman

No imprisonment

Not a war veteran

Member of the central council of the SCC

HI Montazeri entered the judiciary branch in
1980. Over three decades, he held such posts
as founder and head of the Judicial Organization of the Armed Forces, deputy prosecutor-
general (for four years), adviser to Chief Justice
Ayatollah Hashemi-Shahrudi, parliamentary
deputy of the minister of justice (1989), and
judiciary's inspector. In early 2016, Ayatollah
Sadeq Larijani appointed him prosecutor-
general. Montazeri's father was Ayatollah Borujerdi's representative in Ashtiyan and later head
of the Office of Ayatollah Mohammad-Reza
Golpayegani.

Montazeri [-Najafabadi], Hoseyn-Ali

Member of the Assembly for the Final Examination of
the Constitution, Tehran (1979); deputy supreme
leader (November 23, 1985–March 26, 1989)

1922–December 20, 2009, Najafabad, Isfahan

Clerical education, Qom Seminary, 1955

Ali, farmer and small landowner

Clergyman

Imprisoned before the revolution (four different
occasions)

Not a war veteran (son Sa'id was a wounded veteran)

Martyr's family (son, Mohammad-Ali)

Founding member of the SQSS

Ayatollah Montazeri, one of Ayatollah Khomeini's chief lieutenants, was severely tortured by
SAVAK. In November 1978, the shah's regime
freed him from prison, and soon after, he went to
visit Khomeini in Paris. In the early days of the
revolution, he was the target of jokes calling him
a simpleton. He was a Friday prayer leader in both
Tehran and Qom between 1979 and 1981. In the
August 3, 1979, election for the AFEC, he received
1,663,423 of the 2,525,381 votes cast in Tehran. On
June 10, 1980, Ayatollah Khomeini asked him to
select the candidates for the State Supreme Court.
On November 23, 1985, the AE appointed him
deputy supreme leader. However, his opposition
to the mass execution of dissidents in 1988 cost
him his position; Ayatollah Khomeini dismissed
him on March 26, 1989. Montazeri spent the next
twenty years of his life in Qom under pressure
but continued to speak out against the regime
and its human rights record as its leading clerical
dissident. On November 14, 1998, he delivered a
critical speech in Qom that led to his house arrest,
which lasted until January 30, 2003. Montazeri,
who was initially an enthusiastic advocate of
the theory of mandate of the jurist, later became
one of its archcritics. He also questioned the
qualifications of Ali Khamenei as the supreme
leader. The fact that, despite his house arrest,
Montazeri's theological standing was greater than
Supreme Leader Ayatollah Khamenei was not

lost on anyone. In May 2008, in a radical break with other Shiite clerics, he defended the rights of Baha'is as citizens. One of his sons, Ahmad, is married to the daughter (Zahra) of Ayatollah Mohammad-Mehdi Rabbani-Amlashi.

Montazeri [-Najafabadi], Mohammad-Ali

Deputy of the First Majlis, Najafabad, Isfahan (1980–81)
1944–June 28, 1981, Najafabad, Isfahan
Clerical education, Qom Seminary
Hoseyn-Ali, clergyman (ayatollah)
Clergyman
Imprisoned before the revolution (1966–68)
Not a war veteran
HI Montazeri, the eldest son of Ayatollah Hoseyn-Ali Montazeri, was severely tortured by SAVAK. After serving his prison term, he left Iran in 1971 and lived for six years in Afghanistan, Pakistan, Iraq, Syria, and Lebanon. He underwent military training in Palestinian camps in Lebanon and became a strong champion of revolutionary causes in the region. Montazeri had one of the earliest ideas to form a force akin to the IRGC. In the early years of the revolution, Ayatollah Khomeini appointed him to investigate torture in prisons and then look into the war efforts of the Supreme Defense Council. Montazeri, a zealous revolutionary, was a thorn in the side of PM Bazargan's moderate government. In the summer of 1979, he and his armed gang closed Tehran's international airport for a day after airport officials tried to prevent his illegal departure. Ayatollah Montazeri disclaimed responsibility for his actions. He was given the nickname "Ringo" for his cowboy-style behavior. Mohammad-Ali was killed in the bombing of the IRP headquarters in 1981.

Moqaddam-Firuz, Mohammad-Reza

Deputy of the Fourth Majlis, Arak, Markazi (1992–96)
1955–, Tehran, Tehran

MS, physics
Hojjatollah
No imprisonment

Moqaddamizad, Isa

Deputy of the Fourth (1992–96), Fifth (1996–2000), and Sixth (2000–2004) Majlis, Shadegan, Khuzestan
1960–, Shadegan, Khuzestàn
MA, theology; PhD, Islamic law, Tehran University, 1995; clerical education
Ebrahim
No imprisonment
After serving in the Majlis, Moqaddamizad held several high-level positions in the Petroleum Ministry.

Moqaddam-Maragheh'i, Rahmatollah

Member of the Assembly for the Final Examination of the Constitution, East Azerbaijan (1979)
1921–, Maragheh, East Azerbaijan
BA, geography and journalism (France)
Fathollah
Civil servant
Imprisoned before the revolution
Not a war veteran
Founder and secretary-general of the Radical Movement of Iran (1977)
Moqaddam-Maragheh'i came from a prominent Azerbaijani family and attended the Ground Forces Officers' Academy before the military sent him to France to continue his education. He obtained the rank of colonel but became active against the shah's regime. He was one of a handful of politicians who served in a prerevolutionary Majlis (elected to the Twentieth Majlis from Miyandoab and Takab) and also served in a postrevolutionary assembly. Moqaddam-Maragheh'i was a member of the Iranian Writers' Association. Agents of the shah's regime bombed his office before the revolution. In the AFEC, he was one of eight deputies who opposed the notion

of *velayat-e faqih*. For a few months in 1979, he was the governor-general of East Azerbaijan. In February 1979, Moqaddam-Maragheh'i founded the Islamic People's Republican Party of Iran, which was close to Grand Ayatollah Seyyed Mohammad-Kazem Shari'atmadari and operated until December 1979. After the judiciary closed down the party, he left Iran and lived in self-imposed exile for fifteen years. He returned in 1994 and stayed away from political activity.

Moqaddasi, Hadi

Deputy of the Eighth Majlis, Borujerd, Lorestan (2008–12)
1961–, Borujerd, Lorestan
MA, international relations
Mohammad
Civil servant, ministries
No imprisonment
Moqaddasi's claim that he had a PhD in economics from the University of Oxford proved to be a falsehood.

Moqaddasi, Seyyed Mehdi

Deputy of the Tenth Majlis, Arak, Komijan, and Khondab, Markazi (2016–20)
1963–, Arak, Markazi
MA, management
Bank official
No imprisonment
Moqaddasi, a reformist, has been city governor of Arak (1987–2001), Hamadan, and Khomeyn, and mayor of Karaj (2007–9). He later held high-level posts in Bank Mellat and Bank Parsian.

Moqaddasi-Shirazi, Abolhasan

Member of the Assembly for the Final Examination of the Constitution, Razavi Khorasan (1979); member of the First (1983–90) and Second (1991–98) Assembly of Experts, Razavi Khorasan

1914–August 6, 2000, Darab, Fars
Clerical education, Najaf Seminary (Iraq)
Mehdi-Qoli, landowner
Clergyman
No imprisonment
Not a war veteran
On June 17, 1980, Ayatollah Khomeini appointed Ayatollah Moqaddasi-Shirazi as the first Friday prayer leader of Mashhad after the revolution.

Moqimi, Ahmad-Ali

Deputy of the Eighth (2008–12) and Ninth (2012–16) Majlis, Behshahr, Neka, and Galugah, Mazandaran
1957–, Behshahr, Mazandaran
BA, law, Tehran University; MA, private law, Gilan University; PhD, international relations, Gilan University
Gholam-Reza
Civil servant
No imprisonment
War veteran (sixty-one months; treated for his wounds in Iran and Germany)
IRGC militiaman
Member of the central council of the Alliance of Veterans of the Islamic Revolution
Moqimi has worked for IRIB, the FDWI, and the State Welfare Organization of Iran. He was the deputy director of *Jam-e Jam*, and he ran unsuccessfully for the Tenth Majlis.

Moqimi, Mohammad-Hoseyn

Deputy of the Eighth Majlis, Khomeyn, Markazi (2008–12)
1950–, Khomeyn, Markazi
MS, mechanical engineering, Shiraz University; MS, industrial engineering, 1996
Mohammad-Ali, bazaar tradesman
Governor-general of Kermanshah
No imprisonment
Founding member of the Islamic Society of Alumni of Shiraz University

Moqimi was mayor of Khomeyn in 1979 and an executive deputy to President Hashemi-Rafsanjani in 1989. He was the interim mayor of Tehran for four months in 2003, and he was governor-general of Khuzestan (1993–97) and Kermanshah (1997–2001) before entering the Eighth Majlis. After serving in the Majlis, he became governor-general of Markazi Province (2013–14) and then political deputy to the interior minister (2014–16). During the 2016 Majlis and AE elections, he was the head of MI's election headquarters. In September 2016, Moqimi became deputy interior minister and on October 2, 2017, he became the governor-general of Tehran.

Moqtada'i, Abbas

Deputy of the Ninth Majlis, Isfahan, Isfahan (2012–16)
1967–, Isfahan, Isfahan
MA, political science, Imam Sadeq University, 1996; PhD, international relations, Islamic Azad University, 2008
Abolqasem
Professor at Islamic Azad University–Shahreza
No imprisonment
In the Ninth Majlis, Moqtada'i was affiliated with the conservative SFIR. He is a close relative of Morteza Moqtada'i.

Moqtada'i, Abdolhasan

Deputy of the Third (1988–92) and Fourth (1992–96) Majlis, Abadan, Khuzestan
1955–, Abadan, Khuzestan
High school diploma
Behruz
No imprisonment
Founding member of the NTP

Moqtada'i, Morteza

Member of the HCJ (October 4, 1981–July 1989); head of the State Supreme Court (1989–94); prosecutor-general (August 28, 1994–98); member of the Second (1991–98), Third (1999–2006), Fourth (2007–16), and Fifth (2016–22) Assembly of Experts, Isfahan
1925–, Isfahan, Isfahan
Clerical education, Qom Seminary
Mahmud, clergyman (ayatollah)
Clergyman
No imprisonment
Not a war veteran
Deputy head of the Society of Qom Seminary Scholars
Ayatollah Moqtada'i was a judge and supervisor of revolutionary courts after the revolution. He also served as spokesperson for the HCJ and was a member and secretary of the HCRSQ. Moqtada'i was known for his judicial knowledge.

Moradi, Abdorreza

Deputy of the Eighth Majlis, Mamasani, Fars (2008–12)
1968–, Mamasani, Fars
BA, judicial law, 1995; MA, law
Bahram, farmer
Judiciary official
No imprisonment
After the GC rejected Moradi's credentials for the Ninth Majlis, he was put in charge of legal affairs for the State Organization for Registration of Deeds and Properties.

Moradi, Ahmad

Deputy of the Fourth (1993–96) and Sixth (2000–2004) Majlis, Torqabeh and Chenaran, Razavi Khorasan
1965–, Chenaran, Razavi Khorasan
BA, 1990; MA, sociology
Ali-Asghar
No imprisonment
Moradi was the youngest member of the Fourth Majlis.

Moradi, Ali-Mohammad

Deputy of the Tenth Majlis, Qorveh, Kurdistan
    (2016–20)
1962–, Qorveh, Kurdistan
BA, law
Father's name unknown, farmer
Teacher and lieutenant governor of Dehkalan (one
    year)
No imprisonment
Moradi is a Sunni.

Moradi, Behruz

VP for planning and strategic supervision in Pres-
    ident Ahmadinejad's second cabinet (May 28,
    2012–13)
Date of birth unknown, Kermanshah, Kermanshah
MA, management; PhD, public administration
Provincial civil servant
No imprisonment
War veteran
IRGC militiaman (commander, Ninth Brigade of the
    IRGC)
Moradi has held such posts as head of the board
    of directors of Basij Cooperative, governor-
    general of Hamadan Province (2005–10), and
    head of the Organization of Targeted Subsidies.
    On December 27, 2011, while serving in the last
    post, he hit an MP in the face during a Majlis
    session and was thrown out of the chamber.
    On May 28, 2012, President Ahmadinejad
    appointed Moradi as VP for planning and
    strategic supervision.

Moradi, Hasan

Deputy of the Seventh Majlis, Arak and Komijan,
    Markazi (2004–8)
1957–, Arak, Markazi
PhD, international business
Esma'il
Civil servant
No imprisonment

Moradi was elected to the Sixth Majlis but could not
    occupy his seat because other lawmakers rejected
    his credentials.

Moradi, Mansur

Deputy of the Tenth Majlis, Marivan, Kurdistan
    (2016–20)
1977–, Sarvabad, Kurdistan
BA, accounting, Zanjan University, 2003; MA, ac-
    counting, Islamic Azad University–Borujerd, 2011
Bank official and university teacher
Not a war veteran
Moradi, a Sunni, ran unsuccessfully for the Ninth Majlis.

Moradi, Salar

Deputy of the Ninth Majlis, Sanandaj, Divandarreh,
    and Kamyaran, Kurdistan (2012–16)
1979–, Kamyaran, Kurdistan
BA, political science, Allameh Tabataba'i University;
    MA, political science, Allameh Tabataba'i Univer-
    sity, 2004
Father's name unknown, farmer
Professor at Payam-e Nur University, Sanandaj
No imprisonment
Not a war veteran
Moradi, a Sunni, was disqualified from running in
    the election for the Tenth Majlis.

Moradi [Bandar-e Abbas], Ahmad

Deputy of the Tenth Majlis, Bandar-e Abbas, Hor-
    mozgan (2016–20)
September 27, 1968–, Bandar-e Abbas, Hormozgan
BA, law; MA, law; pursuing a PhD in business
    administration
Governor of Bandar-e Abbas
No imprisonment
War veteran (wounded)

Moradnia, Bahman

Deputy of the Eighth Majlis, Bijar, Kurdistan (2008–12)

1965–, Bijar, Kurdistan
MA, public administration
Morad
Civil servant
No imprisonment
Moradnia, who was not elected to the Ninth Majlis,
　became governor of Kurdistan.

Moravveji, Mohammad-Karim

Deputy of the Third Majlis, Borujerd, Lorestan
　(1989–92)
1949–, Kuhdasht, Lorestan
Clerical education
Asadollah
Clergyman (HI)
No imprisonment

Morovvati, Mrs. Mehrangiz

Deputy of the Sixth (2002–4) and Seventh (2004–8)
　Majlis, Khalkhal and Kowsar, Ardabil
1962–, Khalkhal, Ardabil
Associate's degree
Ahmad
Civil servant
No imprisonment

Morseli, Mostafa

Deputy of the Third Majlis, Abhar, Zanjan
　(1988–92)
1957–, Abhar, Zanjan
Clerical education
Ali
No imprisonment
Clergyman
Founding member of the ISFPD

Mortazavi, Sa'id

Public and revolutionary prosecutor-general of Teh-
　ran (2003–August 29, 2009)
1967–, Taft, Yazd

BA, Islamic Azad University–Taft; PhD, criminal law,
　Islamic Azad University–Tehran
No imprisonment
Mortazavi entered the judiciary branch in 1990 and
　rose through the ranks. As judge of the press
　court, he ordered the mass closure of some 120
　newspapers and magazines. He became even
　more notorious for handing out harsh sentences
　and imprisoning many of the protestors during
　the contested 2009 presidential election, where
　some died while in custody. Chief Justice Sadeq
　Larijani-Amoli appointed Mortazavi as deputy
　prosecutor-general on August 30, 2009, and he
　served in that post for a few months. On Decem-
　ber 16, 2009, President Ahmadinejad appointed
　Mortazavi as head of the anti-smuggling task
　force, and on March 18, 2012, he appointed
　Mortazavi as the executive director of the Iranian
　Social Security Organization. On August 18, 2013,
　the labor minister dismissed Mortazavi from this
　post on charges of financial embezzlement, and
　on December 13, 2014 the State Supreme Court
　permanently barred him from serving as a judge.
　He is on the US Treasury Office of Foreign Assets
　Control's Specially Designated Nationals and
　Blocked Persons List because of his role in the
　2009 crackdown.

Mortazavi, Seyyed Fatah

Deputy of the Fourth (1992–96) and Fifth (1996–2000)
　Majlis, Qazvin, Qazvin
1953–, Qazvin, Qazvin
Clerical education; MA, theology
Seyyed Hadi
Clergyman (HI)
No imprisonment

Mortazavi, Seyyed Mohammad-Kazem

Deputy of the Sixth Majlis, Mehriz, Bafq, Abarkuh,
　and Khatam, Yazd (2000–2004)
1953–, Abarkuh, Yazd
MA, law

Seyyed Mostafa
No imprisonment
After serving in the Majlis, Mortazavi became a judge
in the judiciary.

Mortazavifar [Ja'fari-Isfahani], Ali-Asghar

Deputy of the Second (1984–88) and Third (1988–92)
Majlis, Lenjan, Isfahan
1925–, Zarinshahr, Isfahan
Clerical education
Mohammad-Ali
Clergyman
Imprisoned before the revolution
Not a war veteran
HI Mortazavifar spent two years studying in Najaf in
the early 1950s and was affiliated with PMOI for a
period of time in the early 1970s.

Mortazavi-Farasani, Seyyed Qobad

Deputy of the Seventh Majlis, Ardal, Farsan, Kuhrang,
and Kiyar, Chahar Mahal and Bakhtiari (2004–8)
1963–, Farsan, Chahar Mahal and Bakhtiari
MA, law; PhD, international law
Nureddin
Judiciary official
No imprisonment

Morvarid, Mohammad-Taqi

Member of the First Assembly of Experts, Ilam
(1988–90)
1921–2012, Mashhad, Razavi Khorasan
Clerical education, Qom Seminary, 1948
Ali, clergyman
Clergyman
Imprisoned before the revolution
Not a war veteran
HI Morvarid was elected to the First AE in interim
elections held on April 8, 1988. His brother, Ali-
Asghar Morvarid (b. 1924), was also a follower of
Ayatollah Khomeini.

Mosavvari-Manesh, Mrs. Akram

Deputy of the Sixth Majlis, Isfahan, Isfahan
(2000–2004)
1959–, Isfahan, Isfahan
BA, English literature, Isfahan University of
Technology
Rahim
Teacher at various schools in Isfahan
No imprisonment
Member of the central council of the Party of Islamic
Iran's People's Unity

Mosbet [Fazel-Hamadani], Ali

Deputy of the Second (1984–88) and Third (1988–91)
Majlis, Bahar and Kabudarahang, Hamadan
1945–, Qom, Qom
Clerical education
Yahya
Clergyman (HI)
No imprisonment
Mosbet resigned from the Third Majlis to protest the
arbitrary use of power by the governor of Hama-
dan Province and became a Friday prayer leader.

Moshiri, Shahriyar

Deputy of the Seventh Majlis, Bandar-e Abbas,
Qeshm, Abumusa, Hajiabad, and Khamir, Hor-
mozgan (2005–8)
1957–, Bandar-e Abbas, Hormozgan
PhD, architecture
Kahzad
Civil servant
No imprisonment

Moslehi, Heydar

Minister of intelligence in President Ahmadinejad's
second cabinet (September 3, 2009–August 3,
2013)
1957–, Shahreza, Isfahan

Clerical education, Qom Seminary; MA, theology,
    Imam Khomeini Educational and Research
    Institute
Clergyman
No imprisonment
War veteran
Member of the SQSS
HI Moslehi was Ayatollah Khamenei's representative
    in various branches of the IRGC and in the Pious
    Endowments and Charity Affairs Organization
    before he became minister of intelligence. Pres-
    ident Ahmadinejad dismissed Moslehi from his
    post on April 17, 2011, apparently for wiretap-
    ping the office of Ahmadinejad's chief of staff,
    Esfandiyar Rahimmasha'i. However, in an open
    letter dated April 19, 2011, Ayatollah Khamenei
    overruled the decision and Moslehi stayed in
    the cabinet until 2013. To show his displeasure,
    Ahmadinejad stayed at his home for eleven days
    and did not report for work. On October 10, 2011,
    the Council of the European Union put Moslehi
    on its sanctioned list for taking part in the ongo-
    ing abuse of protesters and dissidents in Iranian
    prisons. He is also on the US Treasury Office of
    Foreign Assets Control's Specially Designated
    Nationals and Blocked Persons List because of
    his role in the 2009 crackdown. After leaving the
    cabinet, Moslehi worked as an adviser to the head
    of the IKRF and was involved in a publishing
    venture.

Mostafavi-Kashani, Seyyed Ahmad

Deputy of the First (1980–84) and Second (1984–86)
    Majlis, Qamsar and Natanz, Isfahan
1947–, Tehran, Tehran
MS, civil engineering
Seyyed Abolqasem, clergyman (ayatollah)
No imprisonment
Not a war veteran
Mostafavi-Kashani is the son of Ayatollah Seyyed
    Abolqasem Kashani, who played an influential role
    in Iranian politics in the 1950s, including during

the oil nationalization campaign. He was head of
    candidate Hasan Ayat's campaign headquarters
    during the first presidential election. In 1986, the
    regime arrested him for fomenting discord be-
    tween the army and the IRGC and he was forced to
    resign from the Second Majlis. Mostafavi-Kashani
    was imprisoned for twenty-eight months from
    1987 to 1989. He ran in the 2001 presidential elec-
    tion but received less than 1 percent of the vote. He
    was disqualified from running in the 2016 Majlis
    election. His brother, Seyyed Mahmud Kashani, a
    former judge representing Iran in The Hague, ran
    in the 1985 presidential election but received less
    than 10 percent of the vote.

Mostafavi-Siyahmazgi, Seyyed Davud

Deputy of the First (1982–84) and Second (1984–88)
    Majlis, Rasht, Gilan
1940–, Shaft, Gilan
Clerical education, Qom Seminary; MA, theology
Mir Abutaleb
Clergyman and teacher
No imprisonment
Not a war veteran
HI Mostafavi-Siyahmazgi was the Friday prayer
    leader of Anzali from 1989 to 2001.

Motahhari, Ali

Deputy of the Eighth (2008–12), Ninth (2012–16), and
    Tenth (2016–20) Majlis, Tehran, Tehran
1957–, Tehran, Tehran
PhD, Islamic philosophy, Tehran University
Morteza, clergyman (ayatollah)
University professor
No imprisonment
Not a war veteran
Martyr's family (father)
Motahhari, who is the son of Ayatollah Morteza
    Motahhari, started his academic career studying
    mechanical engineering but switched to Islamic
    philosophy. In 2016, he was elected as deputy

Speaker of the Majlis. One of his sisters is married to Ali Larijani.

Motahhari, Morteza

Member of the Revolutionary Council (1979)
1920–May 1, 1979, Fariman, Razavi Khorasan
Clerical education, Qom Seminary, 1951
Mohammad-Hoseyn, clergyman
Clergyman
No imprisonment
Founding member of the SCC
Ayatollah Motahhari was a leading theologian, ideologue, political activist, and cleric from Khorasan Province whom many considered Ayatollah Khomeini's favorite disciple. A member of the faculty of theology at Tehran University before the revolution, he emerged as the chair of the Revolutionary Council. The Forqan group assassinated him on May 1, 1979. Ayatollah Khomeini provided his most famous eulogy on the occasion of Motahhari's death. He is the father of Ali Motahhari, brother of Mohammad-Taqi Motahhari [–Farimani], and father-in-law of Ali Larijani.

Motahhari [-Farimani], Mohammad-Taqi

Deputy of the First Majlis, Fariman, Razavi Khorasan (May 28–July 7, 1980)
1928–, Fariman, Razavi Khorasan
Clerical education
Mohammad-Hoseyn, clergyman
Clergyman
No imprisonment
Not a war veteran
Martyr's family (brother, Morteza)
HI Motahhari, who is the brother of Morteza Motahhari, resigned from the First Majlis after only five weeks on the job.

Motahhari [Zarand], Ali

Deputy of the Second (1984–88) and Fourth (1992–96) Majlis, Zarand, Kerman

1954–, Zarand, Kerman
Clerical education
Hoseyn
Clergyman
No imprisonment

Motahhari-Kuzehkalani, Ali

Deputy of the Eighth Majlis, Shabestar, East Azerbaijan (2008–12)
1965–, Kuzehkonan, East Azerbaijan
BS, electrical engineering
Kazem
Civil servant, state companies
No imprisonment
Motahhari-Kuzehkalani was not elected to the Ninth Majlis.

Mo'tamed, Morris

Deputy of the Sixth (2000–2004) and Seventh (2004–8) Majlis, representing the Jewish community (as a religious minority)
1944–, Hamadan, Hamadan
MS, civil engineering
Mahmud
Civil servant, ministries
No imprisonment
Not a war veteran

Mo'tamedi, Seyyed Ahmad

Minister of post, telegraph, and telephones in President Khatami's first (January 14–August 1, 2001) and second (August 22, 2001–August 2, 2005) cabinets
1953–, Tehran, Tehran
BS, electrical engineering, Amirkabir University of Technology, 1978; MS, electrical engineering, Pierre and Marie Curie University (France), 1980; PhD, electrical engineering, Pierre and Marie Curie University (France), 1983
Civil servant
Imprisoned before the revolution

Not a war veteran

Mo'tamedi was a member of the Union of Islamic Associations of Students in Europe. After returning to Iran, he served for several years as head of the war committee of the Ministry of Science and Higher Education. In 1986, he became deputy minister of science and higher education and head of the Organization for Scientific and Industrial Research. On November 5, 2003, while serving as minister, Mo'tamedi survived an impeachment attempt by the Majlis. He has been a professor of electrical engineering at Amirkabir University since 1983. On May 3, 2010, he was seriously injured in a machete attack on the campus of Amirkabir University.

Mo'tamediniya, Gholam-Reza

Deputy of the Third (1988–92), Fourth (1992–96), and Fifth (1996–2000) Majlis, Kahnuj, Kerman
1939–2017, Manujan, Kerman
Clerical education
Ebrahim
Clergyman (HI)
No imprisonment
Not a war veteran

Mottaki, Manouchehr

Deputy of the First Majlis, Kordkuy, Golestan (1980–84); deputy of the Seventh Majlis, Tehran, Tehran (2004–August 24, 2005); minister of foreign affairs in President Ahmadinejad's first (August 24, 2005–August 2, 2009) and second (September 3, 2009–December 13, 2010) cabinets
1953–, Bandar-e Gaz, Golestan
BA, social sciences, Al-Ameen Bangalore University (India), 1976
Mohammad-Ali, bazaar tradesman
Academia
No imprisonment
Not a war veteran
Secretary-general of the Society of Alumni of the Indian Subcontinent

Mottaki served as chief of the Southeast Asia department and as a legal deputy in the Ministry of Foreign Affairs. He was also an ambassador to Turkey and Japan. He resigned from the Seventh Majlis to become foreign minister. On December 13, 2010, while he was on an official trip to Africa as foreign minister, President Ahmadinejad fired him. In 2013, he registered to run in the presidential election but was disqualified by the GC. Questions have been raised about his master's degree in international relations from Tehran University. Mottaki appointed his wife, Tahereh Nazarimehr, who has a doctorate in pharmacology, as deputy for human rights and women's affairs while he served as foreign minister. His wife ran unsuccessfully for the Ninth Majlis from Tehran.

Moulaverdi, Mrs. Shahindokht

VP for women's and family affairs in President Rouhani's first cabinet (2013–August 13, 2017)
1965–, Khoy, West Azerbaijan
BA, law, Shahid Beheshti University, 1988; MA, international law, Allameh Tabataba'i University; MA thesis title: "International standards for women's rights"
Father's name unknown, military forces
Notary public (starting in 2007/8)
No imprisonment
Member of IIPF; secretary-general of the Association for Supporting Women's Human Rights
Moulaverdi has been a strong advocate for women's rights.

Movahhed, Seyyed Haji Mohammad

Deputy of the Fourth (1992–96) and Fifth (1996–2000) Majlis, Gachsaran, Kohgiluyeh and Buyer Ahmad; deputy of the Sixth (2000–2004) and Seventh (2004–8) Majlis, Kohgiluyeh, Kohgiluyeh and Buyer Ahmad; deputy of the Eighth (2008–12) Majlis, Behbahan, Khuzestan
1952–, Kohgiluyeh, Kohgiluyeh and Buyer Ahmad
Clerical education

Seyyed Mozaffar
Clergyman
No imprisonment
It is claimed that HI Movahhed does not have much
    education, clerical or otherwise.

Movahhedi-Kermani, Mohammad-Ali

Deputy of the First Majlis, Kerman, Kerman (1980–84);
    deputy of the Second (1984–88), Third (1989–92),
    Fourth (1992–96), and Fifth (1996–2000) Majlis,
    Tehran, Tehran; member of the First (1983–90),
    Second (1991–98), Third (1999–2006), and Fourth
    (2007–16) Assembly of Experts, Kerman; member
    of the Fifth Assembly of Experts, Tehran (2016–22);
    member of the Second (1989–92) Third (1992–97),
    Fourth (1997–2002), Fifth (2002–7), Sixth (2007–
    12), Seventh (2012–17), and Eighth (2017–22)
    Expediency Discernment Assembly
1931–, Kerman, Kerman
Clerical education, Najaf Seminary (Iraq)
Abbas, clergyman
Clergyman
No imprisonment
Not a war veteran
Founder and member of the central council of the
    IRP; founding member (1976) and secretary-gen-
    eral (appointed in 2014) of the SCC
Ayatollah Movahhedi-Kermani was active in the an-
    ti-shah movement. Ayatollah Khomeini appointed
    him as his representative in the national police in
    June 1981 and then as his representative and the
    Friday prayer leader of Kermanshah in November
    1982. Ayatollah Khamenei appointed him as his
    representative in the IRGC on February 17, 1992,
    and he stayed in that post until 2005. Movahhe-
    di-Kermani was a deputy Speaker of the Majlis
    (1993–94 and 1995–2000) and became deputy
    head of the Fifth AE in 2016. Ayatollah Khame-
    nei appointed him as one of Tehran's Friday
    prayer leaders in December 2012. In early 2017,
    Movahhedi-Kermani, who has one of the longest
    tenures in the EDA, became its temporary head
    after the death of Ayatollah Hashemi-Rafsanjani.

Movahhedi-Kermani's brother, Ayatollah Mohammad-Mehdi Movahhedi-Kermani (d. 2015),
was Ayatollah Khomeini's representative in the
police force and commissar of the ideological-political bureau of the military's central command.

Movahhedi-Savoji, Ali

Deputy of the First (1980–84), Second (1984–88), and
    Third (1988–92) Majlis, Saveh, Markazi; deputy
    of the Fourth (1992–96) and Fifth (1996–2000)
    Majlis, Tehran, Tehran
1943–2000, Saveh, Markazi
Clerical education, Mashhad Seminary
Mehdi, farmer
Clergyman
Imprisoned before the revolution (badly tortured)
Not a war veteran
Member of the IRP and the SCC
HI Movahhedi-Savoji was the Friday prayer leader
    and Ayatollah Khomeini's representative in Saveh,
    as well as a revolutionary judge there. During the
    1999 municipal elections, Movahhedi-Savoji, an
    archconservative, was head of the central election
    supervisory board.

Movallizadeh, Seyyed Mohammad-Reza

Deputy of the Fourth (1992–96) and Fifth (1996–2000)
    Majlis, Ahvaz, Khuzestan
1960–, Khorramshahr, Khuzestan
MD, medicine
Seyyed Shebl
Medical doctor
No imprisonment

Movashah, Seyyed Khalil

Deputy of the Third Majlis, Bandar-e Anzali, Gilan
    (1988–92)
1940–, Bandar-e Anzali, Gilan
High school diploma
Seyyed Eshaq
No imprisonment

Mowla'i, Ahmad

Deputy of the First Majlis, Tehran, Tehran (1982–84)
1924–May 23, 1995, Tehran, Tehran
Clerical education
Abbas
Clergyman
No imprisonment
Not a war veteran
HI Mowla'i was part of the clerical council of the CIC/
PCIC before the revolution and served as a notary
public. In the early 1980s, he was a guardian of
Shah-Abdolazim Shrine.

Mozaffar, Abbas

Deputy of the First Majlis, Bojnurd, North Khorasan
(1980–84)
1953–, Bojnurd, North Khorasan
BS, industrial engineering
Nasrollah, laborer
No imprisonment
Not a war veteran

Mozaffar, Hoseyn

Minister of education in President Khatami's first
cabinet (August 20, 1997–August 1, 2001); mem-
ber of the Fifth (2002–7), Sixth (2007–12), Seventh
(2012–17), and Eighth (2017–22) Expediency
Discernment Assembly; deputy of the Seventh
(2004–7) and Ninth (2012–16) Majlis, Tehran,
Tehran
1952–, Malayer, Hamadan
MA, management, Allameh Tabataba'i University;
PhD, cultural planning
Rahmkhoda, baker
Academia
No imprisonment
War veteran (wounded)
IRGC militiaman
Martyr's family (three brothers, Hasan, Ali, and Reza,
were killed at the war front in 1988)
Member of the Developers' Coalition of Islamic Iran

Mozaffar was a member of Tohidi-ye Saf, an armed
guerilla group, before the revolution. Mozaffar,
his father, and four of his brothers all fought in
the Iran–Iraq War. At that time, his mother was
active in Ahvaz garrison. Mozaffar was a member
of the HCCR and was head of Mohammad-Baqer
Qalibaf's campaign headquarters during the 2013
presidential election. He taught at Shahid Raja'i
Teachers Training College and was a deputy to
Majlis Speaker Ali Larijani. His son is married to
the daughter of Mehdi Kuchakzadeh.

Mozaffari, Gholam-Hoseyn

Deputy of the Seventh Majlis, Neyshabur, Razavi
Khorasan (2004–8)
1968–, Neyshabur, Razavi Khorasan
MA; pursuing a PhD in developmental management
Gholam-Reza
Governor of Neyshabur
No imprisonment
Not a war veteran
Mozaffari ran unsuccessfully for the Eighth and
Ninth Majlis.

Mozaffarinezhad, Hoseyn

Deputy of the Third Majlis, Tehran, Tehran (1988–92)
1944–, Kerman, Kerman
BA
Ali-Akbar
Academia
Imprisoned before the revolution
Not a war veteran
Mozaffarinezhad was a deputy to Mohammad-Ali
Raja'i in the Ministry of Education and a geology
deputy in the Ministry of Mining.

Musavi, Seyyed Abbas

Deputy of the Second Majlis, Dorud and Azna, Lorestan (1984–88)
1954–, Azna, Lorestan
High school diploma

Seyyed Nosrat
No imprisonment

Musavi, Seyyed Abdorrahim

Chief of the joint staff of the Islamic Republic of Iran
Army (September 26, 2005–August 25, 2008);
deputy general commander of the army (August
26, 2008–July 5, 2016); first deputy chief of the
Armed Forces General Staff (July 5, 2016–August
21, 2017); general commander of the army (August 21, 2017–)
1960–, Qom, Qom
BS, military science, Ground Forces Officers' Academy; PhD, military science, Supreme National
Defense University
Military official
No imprisonment
War veteran (ninety-six months)
Brigadier General Musavi entered the Ground
Forces Officers' Academy in 1979 and rose
through the ranks. He was in charge of the
army's center for strategic studies for many
years. Ayatollah Khamenei promoted Musavi
to major general on August 21, 2017, when he
appointed him as the new general commander
of the army.

Musavi, Seyyed Abdorrasul

Deputy of the Third Majlis, Mamasani, Fars
(1988–92)
1946–, Mamasani, Fars
Clerical education, Qom Seminary; BA, physics, Sha-
hid Beheshti University
Seyyed Reza
Clergyman and teacher
No imprisonment
Not a war veteran
IRGC militiaman
HI Musavi taught math and physics for over two
decades. He ran unsuccessfully for the First and
Second Majlis.

Musavi, Seyyed Afzal

Deputy of the Sixth Majlis, Zanjan and Tarom, Zan-
jan (2000–2004)
1954–, Zanjan, Zanjan
BS, civil engineering, Amirkabir University of
Technology
Seyyed Sajjad
Civil servant
No imprisonment
Member of the central council of PECI

Musavi, Seyyed Ahmad

Deputy of the Third (1988–92), Fourth (1992–96), and
Seventh (2004–5) Majlis, Ahvaz, Khuzestan; VP
for parliamentary affairs in President Ahmadine-
jad's first cabinet (2005–7)
1961–, Bostan, Khuzestan
BA, law, Shahid Beheshti University; PhD, theology;
clerical education, Qom Seminary
Seyyed Ja'far, clergyman
Clergyman (HI)
No imprisonment
War veteran (served for five years; wounded)
Martyr's family
Musavi has served in such capacities as university
professor, head of the political bureau of the
Iranian Air Force, and member of the consultative bureau of the Office of the Supreme Leader.
He resigned from the Seventh Majlis to become
VP for parliamentary affairs. After leaving Ah-
madinejad's cabinet, Musavi, who speaks Arabic,
became ambassador to Syria in 2007. He ran un-
successfully for the Ninth Majlis. Musavi's family
includes two freed prisoners of war, one martyr,
and two wounded veterans.

Musavi, Seyyed Amrollah

Deputy of the Sixth Majlis, Khomeyn, Markazi
(2000–2004)
1953–, Khomeyn, Markazi
BA, Arabic literature

Seyyed Fazlollah
No imprisonment
IRGC militiaman (leadership council)

Musavi, Seyyed Farid

Deputy of the Tenth Majlis, Tehran, Tehran (2016–20)
1980–, Maragheh, East Azerbaijan
PhD, operational management
University professor
No imprisonment
Not a war veteran
Member of the Party of Islamic Iran's People's Unity
Musavi is an expert in industrial quality control.

Musavi, Seyyed Fazel

Deputy of the Eighth Majlis, Khodabandeh, Zanjan
   (2008–12)
1960–, Khodabandeh, Zanjan
BA, judicial law
Seyyed Ebrahim
MIIRI officer
No imprisonment

Musavi, Seyyed Fazlollah

Deputy of the Seventh Majlis, Tehran, Tehran (2004–
   8); member of the Seventh Guardian Council
   (2016–19)
1953–, Isfahan, Isfahan
BA, law, Tehran University, 1976; MA, private law,
   Tehran University, 1983; PhD, international law,
   University of Liverpool (England), 1991; disser-
   tation title: "Examination of the Applicability of
   the Joint Sovereignty Method to the Arvand-Rood
   (Shatt-al-Arab)"
Hoseyn
Professor at Tehran University
No imprisonment
IRGC militiaman (Basij commander)
Musavi lived in England from 1985 to 1991, and in
   1992, he became a professor at the school of law
   and political science at Tehran University. His

term as dean of the school of law and political
   science ended in 2015.

Musavi, Mir Hasan

VP and head of the Cultural Heritage, Handicrafts,
   and Tourism Organization in President Ah-
   madinejad's second cabinet (2012)
Date of birth unknown, Savadkuh, Mazandaran
Civil servant, state companies
No imprisonment
IRGC militiaman
Musavi served in Mazandaran's provincial office,
   Semnan's industrial park cities, Martyr's Founda-
   tion in Tehran, and SAIPA Yadak Car Company
   (2004–7). In December 2012, President Ah-
   madinejad appointed Musavi as his chief of staff.

Musavi, Seyyed Heshmat

Deputy of the Fourth Majlis, Ilam, Ilam (1992–96)
1955–, Ilam, Ilam
High school diploma
Seyyed Mohammad
No imprisonment

Musavi, Seyyed Jalal

Deputy of the Sixth Majlis, Lamerd, Fars (2000–2004)
1950–, Lamerd, Fars
Clerical education
Seyyed Hoseyn
Clergyman (HI)
No imprisonment
Not a war veteran

Musavi, Seyyed Kazem

Deputy of the Eighth Majlis, Ardabil, Namin, and Nir,
   Ardabil (2008–12)
1968–, Germi, Ardabil
Clerical education; pursuing an MA in criminology
Mir Mahbub
Clergyman (HI)

No imprisonment

Not a war veteran

Musavi is a conservative who spent money lavishly in his election campaign. He owns a marriage and divorce registration office.

Musavi, Seyyed Mir Taher

Deputy of the Sixth Majlis, Karaj and Eshtehard, Tehran (2000–2004)

1961–, Tehran, Tehran

BA, Tehran University; MA, sociology, Allameh Tabataba'i University; PhD, sociology

Mir Yusef

Governor of Karaj

No imprisonment

War veteran (fourteen months)

IRGC militiaman (1979–95)

Musavi, Seyyed Mohammad-Ali

Deputy of the Fourth (1992–96), Fifth (1996–2000), and Ninth (2012–16) Majlis, Khodabandeh, Zanjan

1952–, Qom, Qom

Clerical education, Qom Seminary

Seyyed Ne'matollah, clergyman

Clergyman

Judiciary official

No imprisonment

War veteran

After leaving the Fifth Majlis, Musavi worked in the CAJ and held other judicial posts.

Musavi, Seyyed Morteza

Deputy of the Seventh Majlis, Aligudarz, Lorestan (2004–8)

1949–, Aligudarz, Lorestan

MA, law

Seyyed Naqi, pots and pans seller

Civil servant, judiciary

No imprisonment

Martyr's family (brother)

Musavi is reputed to have been a taxi driver before the revolution. It is rumored that he was involved in the execution of a good number of people under HI Sadeq Khalkhali while employed in the judiciary.

Musavi, Seyyed Musa

Deputy of the Ninth Majlis, Lamerd and Mehr, Fars (2012–16)

1958–, Lamerd, Fars

MD, medicine (surgery), Shiraz University of Medical Sciences

Surgeon and university professor

No imprisonment

War veteran

IRGC militiaman (founder of the IRGC in Lamerd)

Musavi entered Shiraz University in 1976 but left in 1977. He returned to finish his degree there sometime in the 1980s. At one point, he was rector of Shiraz University of Medical Sciences.

Musavi, Seyyed Naser

Deputy of the Sixth (2000–2004), Seventh (2004–8), and Eighth (2008–12) Majlis, Ramhormoz and Ramshir, Khuzestan

1951–2017, Baghmalek, Khuzestan

Clerical education

Seyyed Taher

Clergyman (HI)

No imprisonment

IRGC militiaman

Musavi, who was head of Khorramshahr's justice administration, was not elected to the Ninth Majlis.

Musavi, Seyyed Rasul

Deputy of the Second (1984–88) and Third (1988–92) Majlis, Ahvaz, Khuzestan

1948–, Bostan, Khuzestan

BA, Persian literature

Seyyed Abrash

Teacher and education official

No imprisonment

Musavi is the proprietor of *Asr-e Karun*.

Musavi, Seyyed Shokrekhoda

Deputy of the Ninth Majlis, Ahvaz and Bavi, Khuzestan (2012–16)

1963–, I'zeh, Khuzestan

MA, public administration, Institute for Management and Planning Studies

Father's name unknown, farmer

Instructor at Imam Hoseyn University

No imprisonment

War veteran

IRGC militiaman

Musavi was the commander of the IRGC forces in Ahvaz for four years.

Musavi, Seyyed Yunes

Deputy of the Fourth Majlis, Abadan, Khuzestan (1992–96)

1958–, Abadan, Khuzestan

High school diploma

Seyyed Hashem

No imprisonment

Musavi [Baghmalek], Seyyed Abbas

Deputy of the Third (1988–92) and Fifth (1996–2000) Majlis, I'zeh, Khuzestan

1956–, Baghmalek, Khuzestan

Clerical education

Seyyed Moheb

Clergyman

No imprisonment

Musavi [-Khameneh], Mir Hoseyn

Member of the Revolutionary Council (1979–80); minister of foreign affairs in PM Raja'i's cabinet (July 5, 1981–August 1981), PM Bahonar's cabinet (August 17–30, 1981), and interim PM Mahdavi-Kani's cabinet (September 3–October 18, 1981);

prime minister (October 29, 1981–August 3, 1989); member of the First (1988–89), Second (1989–97), Third (1997–2002), Fourth (2002–7), and Fifth (2007–12) Expediency Discernment Assembly

March 2, 1942–, Khameneh, East Azerbaijan

MS, architecture, Melli University, 1969

Mir Esma'il (1908–2011), tea merchant

Architect and university professor

No imprisonment

Not a war veteran

Member of the central council and head of the political bureau of the IRP

Mir Hoseyn Musavi came to Tehran in 1962. In 1969, he earned his MS degree and married his wife, Zahra Rahnavard (b. 1945), who later became rector of Alzahra University. He was active in the Islamic Student Association at his university and after graduation, with the help of his colleagues, set up a company named Samarqand. He started teaching at the university in 1974 and after the revolution served on the central council of the IRP. Musavi was also the chief editor of the party's newspaper, *Jomhuri-ye Islami*, from 1979 to 1980. He became foreign minister a few weeks after President Banisadr was impeached by the Majlis but while PM Raja'i was still in charge. Because of Musavi's left-wing reputation, the new President Ali Khamenei did not want Musavi as his PM, despite the two being distant relatives (Musavi's grandmother is Ayatollah Khamenei's paternal aunt). On October 22, 1981, Khamenei introduced Ali-Akbar Velayati for the PM role, but the Majlis did not approve him. Khamenei then offered the role of PM to Musavi who, at the age of thirty-nine, became Iran's youngest postrevolutionary prime minister and also its longest-serving. In 1985, at the beginning of his second term as president, Khamenei again was determined to replace Musavi as prime minister. However, after sensing strong opposition from Ayatollah Khomeini, he reintroduced Musavi as prime minister. On October 13, 1985, the Majlis reconfirmed Musavi as prime minister with 162 positive votes, seventy-three negative votes, and twenty-six abstentions. Musavi continued to have frequent disagreements with President Khamenei, and on September 7, 1988, he tried to resign from the post, but Ayatollah Khomeini did not accept his resignation. Musavi is generally credited with competent management of the country during the course of the Iran–Iraq War. In addition to being prime minister, Musavi was Ayatollah Khomeini's representative to the FDWI for some years, and from 1989 to 2009, he served as an adviser to Presidents Hashemi-Rafsanjani and Khatami. He was also a member of the HCCR from 1996 to 2010. In 2009, Musavi claimed to have won the presidential election and fiercely contested President Ahmadinejad's declared victory. The regime, however, claimed that Musavi had only received 34 percent of the popular vote. His charge of election fraud, along with that of presidential candidate Mehdi Karrubi, gave rise to the opposition Green Movement, and the regime put him and his wife under house arrest from that point on.

Musavi [Tabriz], Seyyed Mir Taher

Deputy of the Sixth Majlis, Tabriz, Azarshahr, and Osku, East Azerbaijan (2000–2004)
1955–, Tabriz, East Azerbaijan
BS, civil engineering
Seyyed Ebrahim
No imprisonment
IRGC militiaman
Musavi was arrested during the 2009 Green Movement protests.

Musavi-Abrbekuh, Mir Morteza

Deputy of the Second Majlis, Andimeshk and Shush, Khuzestan (1984–88)
1950–, Qom, Qom
Clerical education
Mir Aziz
Clergyman (HI)
No imprisonment

Musavi-Ardabili, Seyyed Abdolkarim

Member of the Assembly for the Final Examination of the Constitution, Tehran (1979); member of the Revolutionary Council (1979–80); prosecutor-general (February 23, 1980–June 29, 1981); head of the State Supreme Court (June 29, 1981–June 30, 1989); member of the First Assembly of Experts, Tehran (1983–90); member of the First Expediency Discernment Assembly (1988–89)
January 28, 1926–November 23, 2016, Ardabil, Ardabil
Clerical education, Qom Seminary, 1960
Seyyed Abdolrahim, clergyman
Clergyman
No imprisonment
Not a war veteran
Founding member of the IRP and the SCC
Ayatollah Musavi-Ardabili studied in Najaf from 1945 to 1947. He was on the editorial board of *Maktab-e Islam* magazine before the revolution, and he met with the American ambassador William Sullivan in Tehran a couple of weeks before the victory of the revolution. Musavi-Ardabili was a member of the three-person committee mediating between President Banisadr and his opponents. Ayatollah Khomeini appointed him head of the Foundation for Dispossessed and War-Invalids (1979–December 1981) and prosecutor-general (appointed February 23, 1980). After Ayatollah Beheshti's death, on June 29, 1981, Khomeini promoted Musavi-Ardabili to the post of head of the State Supreme Court, where he served two terms. He also began acting as the occasional Friday prayer leader of Tehran (June 1981), supervisor of IRIB (May 1982), member of a board to found a seminary for women (August 1984), and member of the Headquarters for Cultural Revolution (December 1984). Musavi-Ardabili escaped two assassination attempts in August and December of 1981. Following the assassination of President Mohammad-Ali Raja'i on August 30, 1981, Ayatollah Khomeini appointed Musavi-Ardabili a member of an interim presidential commission.

As head of the State Supreme Court, Musavi-Ardabili also presided over the HCJ from 1981 to 1989. His term ended on June 30, 1989, after new Supreme Leader Ayatollah Khamenei decided to name Ayatollah Mohammad Yazdi to the newly created position of judiciary chief. As compensation, President Hashemi-Rafsanjani offered Musavi-Ardabili the directorship of the Center for Strategic Research. Musavi-Ardabili has also been a member of the HCCR. In 1989, he was a member of the council that revised the constitution. In 1994, he left Tehran for Qom and abandoned active political life. Musavi-Ardabili published a religious treatise that established him as a source of emulation. He also founded the influential Mofid University and Mofid schools. Toward the end of his life, Musavi-Ardabili's political views became close to that of the reformists. Musavi-Ardabili's wife was the sister of General Qasemali Zahirnezhad, chief of the joint staff of the Iranian Army. One of his sons is married to the daughter of Ayatollah Seyyed Mahmud Hashemi-Shahrud, another son is married to the daughter of Ayatollah Javadi-Amoli, and a third son is married to the daughter of Ayatollah Shahrestani, who is Ayatollah Sistani's representative in Iran.

Musaviasl, Mir Gesmat

Deputy of the Sixth (2000–2004) and Ninth (2012–16) Majlis, Germi, Ardabil
1961–, Germi, Ardabil
Clerical education, Qom Seminary; BA, theology, Baqir al-Olum University
Mir Heydar, farmer
Clergyman (HI)
No imprisonment
War veteran
Musaviasl has served in such posts as Friday prayer leader of Germi and Namin, the supreme leader's representative at Islamic Azad University–Tehran, head of the ideological-political bureau of Law Enforcement Forces, and adviser to the Pious Endowments and Charity Affairs Organization.

Musavi-Bojnurdi, Seyyed Mohammad

Member of the HCJ (May 1983–July 1989)
1943–, Najaf, Iraq
Seyyed Hasan, clergyman (ayatollah)
No imprisonment
Not a war veteran
Member of the ACC
Ayatollah Musavi-Bojnurdi was in charge of the Disciplinary Court for Judges and Public Prosecutors in 1980. His judicial expertise was widely recognized within the clerical community. Musavi-Bojnurdi is active in the Great Islamic Encyclopedia, which his brother Seyyed Mohammad-Kazem runs. The GC rejected his qualifications for the Fifth Assembly of Experts even though Ayatollah Khomeini had given him permission for *ejtehad*. He is the father-in-law of Seyyed Hasan Khomeini, Ayatollah Khomeini's grandson.

Musavi-Bojnurdi, Seyyed Mohammad-Kazem

Deputy of the First Majlis, Tehran, Tehran (1980–84)
1942–, Najaf, Iraq
High school diploma; clerical education, Najaf Seminary (Iraq)
Seyyed Hasan, clergyman (ayatollah)
Civil servant
Imprisoned before the revolution (fourteen years)
Not a war veteran
Founder of the MNP; member of the central committee of the IRP
Musavi-Bojnurdi came to Iran in 1960 and founded the radical MNP in 1962. He spent fourteen years in prison for the group's militant activities and was released on the eve of the revolution. After the revolution, he held such posts as governor-general of Isfahan, head of the Confiscated Properties Organization, founder of the Center for the Great Islamic Encyclopedia (1983), and head of the National Library (1997–2005). His father was a conservative grand ayatollah who resided in Najaf. His brother is also affiliated with the Center for the Great Islamic Encyclopedia.

Musavi-Boyuki, Seyyed Abolfazl

Deputy of the Tenth Majlis, Yazd, Yazd (2016–20)
1963–, Yazd, Yazd
BS, civil engineering, Iran University of Science and
    Technology, 1989; MS, civil engineering, Amirk-
    abir University of Technology, 1994
War veteran
IRGC militiaman (1982–88)
Musavi-Boyuki has worked in the office of the prime
    minister, at Amirkabir University, in the MI
    (1998–2005), and in the Ministry of Housing
    and Urban Development (2005–9). He was also a
    senior adviser to the director-general of Tehran
    Renewal Organization from 2009 to 2016.

Musavi-Faraz, Seyyed Mostafa

Member of the Fifth Assembly of Experts, Hamadan
    (2016–22)
1944–, Isfahan, Isfahan
Clerical education, Qom Seminary
Seyyed Akbar, mercer
Clergyman (HI)
No imprisonment

Musavi-Hamadani [Dabestani], Seyyed Abolhasan

Member of the Second (1991–98) and Third (1999–
    2006) Assembly of Experts, Hamadan
1929–October 31, 2007, Shorin, Hamadan
Clerical education, Qom Seminary
Seyyed Mohammad, clergyman
Clergyman (ayatollah)
No imprisonment
War veteran
Member of the SCC
In 1984, Ayatollah Khomeini appointed Musavi-Hama-
    dani as his representative in Hamadan Province.

Musavi-Hoseyni, Seyyed Ali-Akbar

Deputy of the Fourth (1992–96) and Fifth (1996–2000)
    Majlis, Tehran, Tehran
1939–, Tehran, Tehran
Clerical education
Seyyed Javad, laborer
Clergyman
No imprisonment
Not a war veteran
HI Musavi-Hoseyni used to have a popular televi-
    sion program titled *Ethics in Family* when he was
    elected to the Fourth Majlis. He became the first
    television personality to be elected to the Majlis.
    Musavi-Hoseyni has held such posts as member
    of the HCCR, general manager of Tehran's edu-
    cation department, and faculty member at Imam
    Sadeq University.

Musavi-Jahanabad, Seyyed Baqer

Deputy of the Fifth (1996–2000) and Sixth (2000–
    2004) Majlis, Yasouj, Kohgiluyeh and Buyer
    Ahmad
1962–, Buyer Ahmad, Kohgiluyeh and Buyer Ahmad
MA, political science
Seyyed Nosratollah
Military and security forces
No imprisonment

Musavi-Jahanabadi, Seyyed Hoseyn

Deputy of the First Majlis, Mashhad, Razavi Kho-
    rasan (1980–84)
1941–, Mashhad, Razavi Khorasan
Clerical education
Seyyed Ali-Asghar, farmer
Clergyman
No imprisonment
Not a war veteran

Musavi-Jazayeri, Seyyed Mohammad-Ali

Member of the Assembly for the Final Examination
    of the Constitution, Khuzestan (1979); member
    of the First (1983–90), Second (1991–98), Third
    (1999–2006), Fourth (2007–16), and Fifth (2016–
    22) Assembly of Experts, Khuzestan

1943–, Shushtar, Khuzestan

Clerical education, Qom Seminary, 1974

Seyyed Mohammad, clergyman (ayatollah)

Clergyman (ayatollah)

No imprisonment

Not a war veteran

Musavi-Jazayeri, who returned to Iran from Najaf in 1971, was a judge in Khuzestan's special military court from 1979 to 1980. He became the Friday prayer leader of Ahvaz in April 1981 and held that post for more than three decades. During the deliberations of the AFEC, he argued that the idea of mandate of the jurist was undemocratic. He has also been the supreme leader's representative in Khuzestan Province for many years. Musavi-Jazayeri escaped an assassination attempt in October 1981.

Musavi-Jorf, Seyyed Ali

Deputy of the Eighth Majlis, Abadan, Khuzestan (2008–12)

1969–, Khorramshahr, Khuzestan

BS, botany, Shahid Chamran University of Ahvaz, 1992; MS, botany, Shahid Chamran University of Ahvaz, 1996; PhD, botany, Tarbiyat-e Modarres University–Tehran, 2000; dissertation title: "Histopathological Studies of Wheat Infected by Tilletia indica and Cytology of Its Causal Agent"

Seyyed Hoseyn

Professor

No imprisonment

Musavi-Kho'ini, Seyyed Ali-Akbar

Deputy of the Sixth Majlis, Tehran, Tehran (2000–2004)

1969–, Garrus, Zanjan

BS, electrical engineering, K. N. Toosi University of Technology; MS, information technology, K. N. Toosi University of Technology

Seyyed Aqa, clergyman

Academia

No imprisonment

War veteran

Secretary-general of the Organization of the Erudite of Islamic Iran

Musavi-Kho'ini has no relationship with Seyyed Mohammad Musavi-Kho'iniha. He added Kho'ini to his last name during the Sixth Majlis election to distinguish himself from another candidate. He is an expert on communications technology in Iran and was active in this field before becoming an MP. The judiciary imprisoned Musavi-Kho'ini for a while in 2006. He later settled in the United States.

Musavi-Kho'iniha, Seyyed Mohammad

Deputy of the First Majlis, Tehran, Tehran (1980–84); supervising director-general of IRIB (1982–84); member of the First Assembly of Experts, Zanjan (1983–90); prosecutor-general (July 10, 1985–August 1989); member of the First (1988–89), Second (1989–92), Third (1992–97), and Fourth (1997–2002) Expediency Discernment Assembly

1941–, Qazvin, Qazvin

Clerical education

Seyyed Hoseyn, bazaar tradesman

Clergyman

Imprisoned before the revolution

Not a war veteran

Secretary of the ACC

Ayatollah Musavi-Kho'iniha was active in the anti-shah movement and was expelled from Iraq for his political activities in 1968. He came back from France with Ayatollah Khomeini and was his representative in evaluating the credentials of all candidates in the first presidential election (solely by himself). He was also Ayatollah Khomeini's representative in IRIB, for Pilgrimage Affairs (1982–85), and in dealing with the Muslim Students Followers of the Imam's Line who took over the American embassy in Tehran when he served as their "guide" from 1979 to 1981. Musavi-Kho'iniha was the deputy Speaker of the Majlis (1980–81 and 1983–84), and from 1985 to 1989 he served as prosecutor-general. He was also on the High Council of the Judiciary. He was the prosecutor-general when the mass execution of political prisoners began in 1988. In addition to the above posts, he was a member of the Council for Revision of the Constitution and the director of the Center for Strategic Research (1990–92). Musavi-Kho'iniha was one of the thirteen original members of the EDA. In 1990, Musavi-Kho'iniha refused to stand for elections to the Second Assembly of Experts in protest of the Guardian Council's decision to require a religious test of candidates even though he himself was exempt. In the 1990s, he was the publisher of the influential *Salam*, which the regime banned after it released a secret governmental document that led to the student riots in July 1999. He received a suspended year prison term after the riots, and his views became closer to the reformist faction in Iran.

Musavi-Kuzehkonani, Seyyed Ali

Deputy of the Fifth Majlis, Shabestar, East Azerbaijan (1996–2000)
1956–, Kuzehkonan, East Azerbaijan
BS, agricultural engineering
Mir Karim
No imprisonment

Musavi-Laregani, Seyyed Naser

Deputy of the Eighth (2008–12), Ninth (2012–16), and Tenth (2016–20) Majlis, Falavarjan, Isfahan
1963–, Falavarjan, Isfahan
Clerical education, Isfahan Seminary, 1988; BA, theology, Islamic Azad University–Najafabad
Seyyed Mehdi, clergyman
Clergyman
No imprisonment
War veteran
IRGC militiaman
For six months in 1982, Musavi-Laregani was an IRGC guard at Ayatollah Khomeini's residence. A year later, he resigned from the IRGC and

returned to the Isfahan Seminary to continue his clerical studies.

Musavi-Lari, Seyyed Abdolvahed

Deputy of the First Majlis, Larestan, Fars (1981–84); deputy of the Third Majlis, Tehran, Tehran (1988–92); VP for parliamentary affairs (1997–98) and interior minister (July 22, 1998–August 21, 2001) in President Khatami's first cabinet; interior minister in President Khatami's second cabinet (August 22, 2001–August 23, 2005)
1954–, Larestan, Fars
Clerical education, Qom Seminary
Seyyed Ahmad, farmer
Clergyman
Imprisoned before the revolution (1974–76)
Not a war veteran
Founding member of the ACC
In late 1984, HI Musavi-Lari became deputy for parliamentary and public relations in the Ministry of Islamic Guidance. Musavi-Lari, Mohammad-Ebrahim Asgharzadeh, and Abbas Abdi made up the first editorial committee of *Salam*. He was one of few ministers who received a higher confidence vote from the MPs in 2001 than in 1997 (203 compared to 177).

Musavi-Mobarakeh, Seyyed Ali-Mohammad

Deputy of the Eighth Majlis, Mobarakeh, Isfahan (2008–12)
1952–, Masjed Soleyman, Khuzestan
MA, planning management
Seyyed Abdorrasul
Civil servant
No imprisonment
Musavi-Mobarakeh was not elected to the Ninth Majlis.

Musavi-Nanehkaran, Mir Fakhreddin

Deputy of the First (1980–84), Third (1988–92), and Fifth (1996–2000) Majlis, Ardabil, Ardabil;

member of the Fifth Assembly of Experts, Ardabil
(2016–22)
1930–, Nanehkaran, Ardabil
Clerical education, Najaf Seminary (Iraq)
Mir Mohammad, farmer
Clergyman (HI)
No imprisonment
Not a war veteran
Member of the NTP
Musavi-Nanehkaran escaped an assassination attempt
in September 1981. He worked in the State Supreme
Court after leaving the Majlis. He ran unsuccess-
fully for the Assembly of Experts in 1982 general
elections and 2007 midterm elections from Tehran.

Musavinasab [Avvazzadeh], Seyyed Ali

Deputy of the Second (1984–88), Third (1988–92),
and Fifth (1996–2000) Majlis, Shiravan, North
Khorasan
1954–, Shiravan, North Khorasan
BA, 1993; MA, management, 1996
Seyyed Hoseyn
No imprisonment
Musavinasab was known in the Second and Third
Majlis with the last name of Avvazzadeh.

Musavinezhad, Seyyed Isa

Deputy of the Sixth Majlis, Khorramabad, Lorestan
(2000–2004)
1956–, Khorramabad, Lorestan
MA, educational management
Seyyed Elias
No imprisonment

Musavinezhad, Seyyed Mehdi

Deputy of the Ninth Majlis, Dashtestan, Bushehr
(2012–16)
1975–, Dashtestan, Bushehr
Clerical education, Qom Seminary
Seyyed Hoseyn, farmer
Clergyman (HI)

No imprisonment
Not a war veteran
IRGC militiaman
Musavinezhad, who is close to Ayatollah Khamenei,
was engaged in anti-Wahhabi activities. He was
active in the Bushehr branch of the IRGC, and the
GC disqualified him from running in the Tenth
Majlis election.

Musavi-Ojaq [Vazmaleh], Seyyed Ayatollah

Deputy of the Fourth Majlis, Kermanshah, Kerman-
shah (1992–December 5, 1994)
1953–December 5, 1994, Kermanshah, Kermanshah
Clerical education
Seyyed Ezzatollah
Clergyman (HI)
No imprisonment
Not a war veteran
Musavi-Ojaq died in a car accident.

Musavi-Ojaq [Vazmaleh], Seyyed Mojtaba

Deputy of the Fifth (1996–2000) and Sixth (2000–
2004) Majlis, Kermanshah, Kermanshah
1962–, Kermanshah, Kermanshah
BS, agricultural engineering
Seyyed Ezzatollah
No imprisonment
War veteran
IRGC militiaman
Musavi-Ojaq won his brother's seat after he died in a
car accident. The GC did not approve his qual-
ifications for the Eighth Majlis, and he was not
elected to the Tenth Majlis.

Musavipur, Seyyed Hasan

Deputy of the Second Majlis, Abhar, Zanjan (1984–88)
1951–, Abhar, Zanjan
Clerical education
Seyyed Abdolvahhab
Clergyman (HI)
No imprisonment

Musavipur-Shali, Seyyed Hasan

Member of the Second Assembly of Experts, Zanjan
(1991–98); member of the Third Assembly of Ex-
perts, Qazvin (1999–2003)
1915–2003, Shal, Zanjan
Clerical education, Najaf Seminary (Iraq), 1934–57
Seyyed Mohammad, clergyman
Clergyman
No imprisonment
Not a war veteran
Ayatollah Khamenei appointed Ayatollah Musavipur-
Shali as the Friday prayer leader and as his repre-
sentative in Takestan.

Musavi-Qahderijani, Seyyed Musa

Member of the Assembly for the Final Examination of
the Constitution, Kermanshah (1979)
1948–, Qahderijan, Isfahan
Clerical education
Seyyed Hoseyn, clergyman
Clergyman
Ayatollah Musavi-Qahderijani was Ayatollah Khomeini's representative in western Iran and deputy
secretary-general of WFPIST.

Musavi-Sarcheshmeh, Seyyed Yunes

Deputy of the Seventh (2004–8) and Eighth (2008–12)
Majlis, Firuzabad, Farashband, Qir, and Karzin, Fars
1956–, Karzin, Fars
Clerical education
Rasul
Clergyman (HI)
No imprisonment
Musavi-Sarcheshmeh was not elected to the Ninth
Majlis, and he now lives in Qom.

Musavi-Shahrudi, Seyyed Mohammad

Deputy of the Fourth Majlis, Shahrud, Semnan
(1995–96)
1940–, Shahrud, Semnan

PhD, economics
Seyyed Abbas
No imprisonment
Not a war veteran

Musavi-Tabrizi [Pur-Mir Ghaffari], Seyyed Hasan

Deputy of the First Majlis, Hashtrud, East Azerbaijan
(October 19, 1981–1984)
1954–, Tabriz, East Azerbaijan
Clerical education
Mir Jabbar, clergyman and grocer
Clergyman
No imprisonment
Not a war veteran
Member of the ASLQS
Musavi-Tabrizi's real name is Seyyed Hasan Pur-Mir
Ghaffari. The Majlis MPs approved his creden-
tials as a member on October 19, 1981, after some
discussion about his history of support for PMOI.
Musavi-Tabrizi was active in Tabriz's revolution-
ary courts and prosecutor's office.

Musavi-Tabrizi [Pur-Mir Ghaffari], Seyyed Hoseyn

Deputy of the First (1980–May 26, 1981) and Third
(1988–92) Majlis, Tabriz, East Azerbaijan; pros-
ecutor-general of the revolutionary courts (Sep-
tember 7, 1981–January 28, 1984); member of
the Third Assembly of Experts, West Azerbaijan
(1999–2006)
1947–, Tabriz, East Azerbaijan
Clerical education, Qom Seminary
Mir Jabbar, clergyman and grocer
Clergyman (ayatollah)
No imprisonment
Not a war veteran
Secretary-general of the ASLQS; secretary-general of
the Society of Combatant Clergy of Tabriz
Musavi-Tabrizi was active in the anti-shah movement.
In 1979, he became the revolutionary tribunal's
prosecutor in East Azerbaijan and prosecuted
Grand Ayatollah Seyyed Mohammad-Kazem
Shari'atmadari's supporters. In November 1980,

Musavi-Tabrizi condemned Kazem Saadati, a high-ranking member of PMOI, to a long prison term for being a Soviet spy. He resigned from the First Majlis to become the prosecutor-general of the revolutionary courts on September 30, 1981. The mass execution of political prisoners in 1982 happened while he was prosecutor-general. He resigned from the post of prosecutor-general of the revolutionary courts in January 1984 after the position was merged with that of the prosecutor-general. He served twice as the head of the House of Parties. Musavi-Tabrizi supported Mir Hoseyn Musavi during the tenth presidential elections and now considers himself among the reformists. He is the son-in-law of Ayatollah Hoseyn Nuri-Hamadani and brother of Seyyed Mohsen and Seyyed Hasan Musavi-Tabrizi.

Musavi-Tabrizi [Pur-Mir Ghaffari], Seyyed Mohsen

Deputy of the First Majlis, Tabriz, East Azerbaijan (1981–84); member of the First Assembly of Experts, East Azerbaijan (1984–90)
1951–, Tabriz, East Azerbaijan
Clerical education
Mir Jabbar, clergyman and grocer
Clergyman
Imprisoned before the revolution
Not a war veteran
Member of the ASLQS
Ayatollah Musavi-Tabrizi held a wide range of posts in the judiciary in the first decade after the revolution, including in the revolutionary courts and land reform courts. However, he did not hold any major posts after Ayatollah Khamenei became the supreme leader. Musavi-Tabrizi nominated himself for the Fourth Majlis (1992) and the Fourth Assembly of Experts (2006) from Qom, but the GC disqualified him.

Musavi-Tabrizi [Seyyed Reyhani], Seyyed Abolfazl

Member of the Assembly for the Final Examination of the Constitution, East Azerbaijan (1979); deputy of the First (1980–84) and Second (1984–88) Majlis, Tabriz, East Azerbaijan; member of the First (1984–90), Second (1991–98), and Third (1999–2003) Assembly of Experts, East Azerbaijan; prosecutor-general (1991–94)
1935–2003, Tabriz, East Azerbaijan
Clerical education, Qom Seminary
Seyyed Reza, clergyman
Clergyman
No imprisonment
Not a war veteran
Member of the IRP and the SQSS
Ayatollah Seyyed Abolfazl Musavi-Tabrizi was a student of Grand Ayatollah Seyyed Mohammad-Kazem Shari'atmadari but abandoned him after the revolution. A fellow MP who claimed Musavi-Tabrizi supported the shah unsuccessfully challenged his credentials in the Second Majlis. Musavi-Tabrizi became the prosecutor-general under Ayatollah Khamenei and headed the CAJ from 1989 to 1991 and again from 1997 to 1999. When Ayatollah Hashemi-Shahrudi became the judiciary chief, Musavi-Tabrizi became one of his advisers.

Musavi-Tareh, Seyyed Mohammad

Deputy of the First Majlis, Dasht-e Azadegan, Khuzestan (1982–84)
1953–1985, Abadan, Khuzestan
Clerical education
Seyyed Salem
Clergyman
No imprisonment
HI Musavi-Tareh was associated with revolutionary *komitehs* in Abadan and Ahvaz and translated materials into Arabic for IRIB.

Musaviyani, Seyyed Hoseyn

Minister of mining and metals in PM Bahonar's cabinet (August 17–30, 1981), interim PM Mahdavi-Kani's cabinet (September 3–October 18, 1981), and PM Musavi's first cabinet (November

2, 1981–83); deputy of the Second Majlis, Tehran, Tehran (1984–88)

1946–, Kashan, Isfahan

MS, mechanical engineering, Tehran Polytechnic University (later renamed Amirkabir University of Technology)

Seyyed Ali

Civil servant, state companies

No imprisonment

Not a war veteran

Musaviyani and Hoseyn Mahlujchi, who also was minister of mining, are both from Kashan and were classmates.

Musavi-Zanjani, Seyyed Esma'il (Mir-Aqa)

Member of the Assembly for the Final Examination of the Constitution, Zanjan (1979); member of the First (1983–90), Second (1991–98), and Third (1999–December 18, 2002) Assembly of Experts, Zanjan

1928–December 18, 2002, Pari, Zanjan

Clerical education, Qom Seminary

Seyyed Abbas, laborer

Clergyman

No imprisonment

Not a war veteran

Martyr's family (son Seyyed Mehdi killed in 1976; son Seyyed Mohammad-Sadeq killed at the war front in 1982)

Ayatollah Musavi-Zanjani was a judge in revolutionary tribunals in such prisons as Qasr and Evin after 1979. In 1982, Ayatollah Khomeini appointed him as the Friday prayer leader of Zanjan, and on July 27, 1983, he became Ayatollah Khomeini's representative in Zanjan Province.

Nabavi, Behzad

Ministerial adviser for executive affairs in PM Raja'i's cabinet (1980–81), PM Bahonar's cabinet (August 17–30, 1981), interim PM Mahdavi-Kani's cabinet (September 3–October 18, 1981), and PM Musavi's first cabinet (November 2, 1981–May 31, 1982);

minister of heavy industries in PM Musavi's first (May 31, 1982–October 27, 1985) and second (October 28, 1985–July 20, 1989) cabinets; deputy of the Sixth Majlis, Tehran, Tehran (2000–2004)

1942–, Tehran, Tehran

MS, electrical engineering, Amirkabir University of Technology, 1964

Hasan, academia

Imprisoned before the revolution (1971–78)

Not a war veteran

Founder and secretary-general of OMIRI

Nabavi was a Marxist who, during his six-year prison term, became a devoted Muslim. He helped to found OMIRI in April 1979 and was a spokesperson for PM Bahonar's government. In 1980–81, Nabavi was Iran's chief negotiator with the United States in the deal known as the Algiers Accord that led to the release of the American hostages. Nabavi survived an impeachment attempt by the Majlis as minister of heavy industries on July 20, 1989. He has held other posts such as presidential adviser and logistical deputy of the command headquarters of the armed forces. The Guardian Council disqualified Nabavi from running for Majlis elections in 1992 and 2004. However, he was the deputy Speaker of the Majlis from 2000 to 2001 and again from 2002 to 2004. The judiciary imprisoned him for a while after the contested 2009 presidential election.

Nabavi, Seyyed Mohammad-Hasan

Member of the Assembly for the Final Examination of the Constitution, Bushehr (1979); deputy of the First (1981–84), Second (1984–88), and Third (1988–92) Majlis, Bandar-e Bushehr, Bushehr

1924–November 7, 2002, Khormuj, Bushehr

Clerical education, Najaf Seminary (Iraq); BA, theology, Tehran University

Seyyed Mohammad-Sadeq, teacher

Clergyman and high school principal

No imprisonment

Not a war veteran

HI Nabavi studied in Najaf, Iraq. The shah's regime exiled him to Ahvaz before the revolution. He was in charge of the education bureau of Bushehr Province after the revolution.

Nabavi, Seyyed Morteza

Minister of post, telegraph, and telephones in PM Bahonar's cabinet (August 17–30, 1981), interim PM Mahdavi-Kani's cabinet (September 3–October 18, 1981), and PM Musavi's first cabinet (November 2, 1981–85); deputy of the Fourth (1992–96) and Fifth (1996–2000) Majlis, Tehran, Tehran; member of the Fourth (1997–2002), Fifth (2002–7), Sixth (2007–12), Seventh (2012–17), and Eighth (2017–22) Expediency Discernment Assembly

November 28, 1947–, Qazvin, Qazvin

BS, electrical engineering, Tehran University; MS, electrical engineering, Tehran University, 1973

Seyyed Ahmad, tradesman

Civil servant, state companies

Imprisoned before the revolution

Not a war veteran

IRGC militiaman

Member of the CIC/PCIC, the IRP, and the Islamic Society of Engineers

Nabavi was the chief editor of the conservative *Resalat* and a founding member of the Society of Muslim Journalists. He resigned as minister of post, telegraph, and telephones in 1985 in disagreement with the policies of PM Mir Hoseyn Musavi. Nabavi was a faculty member at Islamic Azad University, and in 2011, Ayatollah Khamenei appointed him as a member of the five-person "Dispute Settlement Committee of Branches." His cousin is the wife of Davud Danesh-Ja'fari.

Nabaviyan, Seyyed Mahmud

Deputy of the Ninth Majlis, Tehran, Tehran (2012–16)

1965–, Babol, Mazandaran

Clerical education, Qom Seminary; MA, philosophy, Imam Khomeini Educational and Research Institute; PhD, philosophy, Imam Khomeini Educational and Research Institute

Clergyman

No imprisonment

War veteran

HI Nabaviyan returned to teaching at the conservative Imam Khomeini Educational and Research Institute after his term in the Majlis. He is close to Ayatollah Mesbah-Yazdi, and he has been a critic of the philosopher Abdolkarim Soroush.

Nabizadeh, Mohammad-Ali

Deputy of the Sixth (2001–4) and Seventh (2004) Majlis, Gachsaran, Kohgiluyeh and Buyer Ahmad

1950–October 15, 2004, Gachsaran, Kohgiluyeh and Buyer Ahmad

MA, theology

Gholam-Hoseyn

Academia

No imprisonment

War veteran

Martyr's family (two brothers killed at the war front)

Nabizadeh died of an illness.

Nabovvati, Mohammad

Deputy of the Fourth (1992–96) and Fifth (1996–2000) Majlis, Saveh, Markazi

1943–, Saveh, Markazi

MA, business banking

Abbas

No imprisonment

Nabovvati worked at the State Audit Court.

Naderan, Elyas

Deputy of the Seventh (2004–8), Eighth (2008–12), and Ninth (2012–16) Majlis, Tehran, Tehran

1955–, Shahrud, Semnan

BA, economics, Tehran University, 1985; MA, economics, Tehran University, 1988; PhD, economics, Pierre Mendès-France University (France), 1996;

dissertation title: "Les facteurs de la mobilisation fiscale en Iran"

Heydar-Ali

Professor at Tehran University

No imprisonment

War veteran

IRGC militiaman

Member of the central council of the Alliance of Veterans of the Islamic Revolution; founding member of the Alliance of Wayfarers of the Islamic Revolution

Naderan, who had some contacts with the paramilitary group Mansurron before the revolution, was wounded in 1978 when handling dynamite. After leaving the Majlis, he returned to teaching economics at Tehran University.

Naderi, Majid

Deputy of the Fourth Majlis, Bu'inzahra and Avaj, Zanjan (1992–96)

1961–, Tehran, Tehran

Clerical education

Nazarali

Clergyman

No imprisonment

Naderi, Shahab

Deputy of the Tenth Majlis, Paveh, Kermanshah (2016–20)

1975–, Salase Babajani, Kermanshah

BA, economics, Tehran University, 2000; MA, management, Islamic Azad University–Arak

University professor

No imprisonment

Not a war veteran

Naderi, a Sunni, was a civil servant of the Ministry of Economic Affairs and Finance.

Nadi [-Najafabadi], Gholam-Hoseyn

Deputy of the First (1981–84) and Second (1984–88) Majlis, Najafabad, Isfahan

1949–, Najafabad, Isfahan

Clerical education

Rajabali

Clergyman

No imprisonment

Not a war veteran

HI Nadi is a former head of the Najafabad komiteh and Isfahan court. In the Majlis, he was in favor of strengthening the private sector.

Nadimi, Iraj

Deputy of the Sixth (2000–2004), Seventh (2004–8), and Ninth (2012–16) Majlis, Lahijan and Siyahkal, Gilan

1957–, Lahijan, Gilan

MA, economics; MA, public administration

Ali

MIIRI officer and director-general in the Ministry of Industries

No imprisonment

War veteran (wounded)

Martyr's family (two brothers killed at the war front)

Nadimi was a reformist politician whom the GC disqualified for the Eighth Majlis. He then became a conservative. He worked as an adviser to the VP and head of PBO Mohammad-Baqer Nowbakht-Haqiqi after finishing his term in the Ninth Majlis.

Na'imabadi, Gholam-Ali

Member of the Fourth Assembly of Experts, Hormozgan (2007–16)

1944–, Damghan, Semnan

Clerical education, Qom Seminary

Boyuk-Mohammad, clergyman

Clergyman (HI)

Imprisoned before the revolution

Not a war veteran

Na'imabadi was the Friday prayer leader of Damghan for eleven years. He then became the supreme leader's representative and the Friday prayer leader of Bandar-e Abbas. He took part in the elections for the Fifth Assembly of Experts but did not receive enough votes.

Na'imipur, Mohammad

Deputy of the Sixth Majlis, Tehran, Tehran (2000–2004)
1955–, Tehran, Tehran
BS, chemistry
Abdorrasul
No imprisonment
IRGC militiaman (1980s)
Na'imipur was involved in the takeover of the American embassy in Tehran. Before entering the Majlis, he held managerial posts at the Center for Strategic Research and in Tehran Province.

Na'imi-Raz, Safar

Deputy of the Ninth Majlis, Astara, Gilan (2012–16)
1959–, Raz, Gilan
BA, law, Zanjan University, 1997; MA, law, Islamic Azad University–Tehran, 1999
Father's name unknown, farmer
No imprisonment
War veteran (served for forty-four months; wounded)
IRGC militiaman (retired as a commander in 2004)

Najafi, Abdollah

Commander of the Islamic Republic of Iran Ground Forces (May 8, 1991–October 25, 1994)
1951–, Razan, Hamadan
BS, military science, Ground Forces Officers' Academy
Habibollah, farmer and gardener
No imprisonment
War veteran
Brigadier General Najafi entered military service in 1967. From 1985 to 1989 he was in charge of a group of military advisers to President Khamenei. For a while, he was responsible for the exchange of POWs between Iran and Iraq.

Najafi, Mohammad-Ali

Minister of culture and higher education in PM Bahonar's cabinet (August 17–30, 1981), interim PM Mahdavi-Kani's cabinet (September 3–October 18, 1981), and PM Musavi's first cabinet (November 2, 1981–August 14, 1984); minister of education in PM Musavi's second cabinet (September 20, 1988–August 3, 1989) and President Hashemi-Rafsanjani's first (August 29, 1989–August 2, 1993) and second (August 16, 1993–August 2, 1997) cabinets; VP and head of the Management and Planning Organization in President Khatami's first cabinet (1997–2000); VP and head of the Cultural Heritage, Handicrafts, and Tourism Organization in President Rouhani's first cabinet (2013–14); mayor of Tehran (June 5, 2017–present)
January 14, 1952–, Tehran, Tehran
BS, mathematics, Sharif University of Technology, 1974; MS, mathematics, Massachusetts Institute of Technology (USA), 1977
Ahmad-Ali, military
Academia
No imprisonment
Not a war veteran
Founding member of PECI
Najafi and Bizhan Namdar-Zangeneh hold the record for the number of terms served in postrevolutionary cabinets (eight so far). Najafi did graduate work at MIT from 1974 to 1978 and was active in the Muslim Student Association. In 1978, he abandoned his doctoral studies in mathematics to join the revolution. After serving as a deputy to Mostafa Chamran, the ministerial adviser for revolutionary affairs and then minister of defense, Najafi became rector of Isfahan University of Technology (1980–81). In 1981, he was tapped to become minister of higher education and served in that post in various cabinets until August 14, 1984, when he was ousted after failing to secure a confidence vote from the Majlis. Najafi then became a professor at Sharif University of Technology and in 1988 PM Musavi chose him as minister of education. He served in that capacity for nine years and managed to survive an impeachment on April 24, 1991. Najafi was a member of the Tehran City Council from 2006 to 2013 and was Mehdi Karrubi's adviser during the contested 2009 presidential election. He met with Ayatollah Khamenei on Karrubi's behalf

to try to resolve the issues. On August 15, 2013, he did not receive enough votes to become President Rouhani's minister of education. Instead, Rouhani appointed him as VP and head of the Cultural Heritage, Handicrafts, and Tourism Organization, but Najafi resigned from this post in January 2014, citing health reasons. President Rouhani then appointed him as an economic adviser. In 2017, he replaced Qalibaf as mayor of Tehran but resigned his post on April 10, 2018.

Najafi, Mohammad-Reza

Deputy of the Tenth Majlis, Tehran, Tehran (2016–20)
1969–
MA, industrial engineering
No imprisonment
War veteran (wounded)
Najafi was the secretary of the Islamic Association of Students at Amirkabir University and served as director-general of a number of industrial firms.

Najafi, Qodratollah

Deputy of the First (1980–84) and Fifth (1996–2000) Majlis, Shahreza, Isfahan
1940–, Shahreza, Isfahan
Clerical education, Qom Seminary
Abbas, bazaar tradesman
Clergyman
No imprisonment
Not a war veteran
Founding member of the Society of University Students and Alumni from Kermanshah
HI Najafi was injured in the June 28, 1981, bombing of the IRP headquarters. He was director-general for cultural affairs in the Ministry of Foreign Affairs.

Najafi, Yusef

Deputy of the Eighth Majlis, Maragheh and Ajab-Shir, East Azerbaijan (2008–12)
1971–, Maragheh, East Azerbaijan

PhD, anthropology
Ya'qub
Academia
No imprisonment
Not a war veteran
Najafi was not elected to the Ninth Majlis.

Najafi-Khoshrudi, Ali

Deputy of the Tenth Majlis, Babol, Mazandaran (2016–20)
1970–, Babol, Mazandaran
BA, political science, Tehran University; MA, diplomacy and international organizations, School of International Relations (affiliated with Iran's Ministry of Foreign Affairs)
Ambassador to Kyrgyzstan (appointed in 2012)
No imprisonment
Najafi-Khoshrudi has been affiliated with the Iranian Ministry of Foreign Affairs since 1994, and he was first deputy of the Iranian embassy in Armenia from 2002 to 2006. The GC originally approved him to run for the Tenth Majlis from Tehran but then switched his electoral district to Babol.

Najafi-Rahnani, Hasan-Ali

Deputy of the Second Majlis, Gachsaran, Kohgiluyeh and Buyer Ahmad (1984–88)
1958–, Isfahan, Isfahan
Clerical education
Mohammad
Clergyman
No imprisonment
HI Najafi-Rahnani is a former Friday prayer leader of Gachsaran.

Najafi-Sani-Rashtkhari, Hoseyn

Deputy of the Third Majlis, Khaf and Rashtkhar, Razavi Khorasan (1988–92)
1955–, Khaf, Razavi Khorasan
High school diploma

Akbar
No imprisonment

Najafnezhad, Meqdad

Deputy of the Fifth (1997–2000), Sixth (2000–2004),
    Eighth (2008–12), and Ninth (2012–16) Ma-
    jlis, Babolsar, Bandpay, and Fereydunkenar,
    Mazandaran
1961–, Babolsar, Mazandaran
BA, political science, 1995; MA, public administra-
    tion, Islamic Azad University–Sari
Gholam-Abbas
No imprisonment
War veteran
IRGC militiaman (Mazandaran commander)
Najafnezhad, a conservative politician, was the di-
    rector of the popular Esteqlal [Esteghlal] Tehran
    football club for a while.

Najmi, Mohammad-Sadeq

Member of the Second Assembly of Experts, West
    Azerbaijan (1991–98); member of the Third As-
    sembly of Experts, East Azerbaijan (1999–2006)
1936–2011, Heris, East Azerbaijan
Clerical education, Qom Seminary; PhD, 1985
Mirza Ahmad, clergyman
Clergyman
No imprisonment
Not a war veteran
Ayatollah Khomeini appointed Ayatollah Najmi as his
    representative and as Friday prayer leader of Khoy
    in 1982, and he held that post until 2001. One of
    his sons was wounded at the war front. Najmi
    founded Islamic Azad University–Khoy in 1985,
    and headed it until 2001. His son, Ahmad, runs
    the "manbar net" blog.

Namazi, Abdolnnabi

Member of the Second (1991–98) and Third
    (1999–2006) Assembly of Experts, Bushehr;

prosecutor-general (1998–August 14, 2004);
    member of the Fourth Assembly of Experts, Teh-
    ran (2007–16); member of the Fifth Assembly of
    Experts, Isfahan (2016–22)
1945–, Bandar-e Bushehr, Bushehr
Clerical education, Qom Seminary
Ahmad, clergyman (HI)
Clergyman (HI)
Imprisoned before the revolution
War veteran (wounded, victim of a chemical attack)
IRGC militiaman
Member of the SQSS
Namazi was a judge in revolutionary tribunals
    shortly after the revolution. He has held such
    posts as Friday prayer leader of Kashan, Ayatol-
    lah Khamenei's representative in Kashan, and
    director of the ideological-political seminars of
    the IRGC. He was the prosecutor-general when
    the "chain murder" of dissidents and the 1999
    attack on Tehran University students took place.
    He and his son, Hasan, simultaneously served in
    the Fourth AE.

Namazi, Ali-Mohammad

Deputy of the Sixth Majlis, Lenjan, Isfahan
    (2000–2004)
1954–, Lenjan, Isfahan
BA, educational science
Avazali
Civil servant
No imprisonment

Namazi, Hasan

Member of the Fourth Assembly of Experts, West
    Azerbaijan (2007–16)
1976–, Qom, Qom
Clerical education, Qom Seminary
Abdolnnabi, clergyman (HI)
Clergyman (HI)
No imprisonment
Not a war veteran

Namazi's father is a member of the AE, and he was in charge of his father's office before being elected to the AE himself. Namazi was the youngest member of the Fourth AE, and he threated to resign due to a dispute with Ayatollah Ahmad Jannati.

Namazi, Hoseyn

Minister of economic affairs and finance in PM Raja'i's cabinet (appointed March 11, 1981), PM Bahonar's cabinet (August 17–30, 1981), interim PM Mahdavi-Kani's cabinet (September 3–October 18, 1981), PM Musavi's first cabinet (November 2, 1981–85), and President Khatami's first cabinet (August 20, 1997–August 1, 2001)

1944–, Shiraz, Fars

BA, economics, University of Innsbruck (Austria), 1969; MA, economics, University of Innsbruck (Austria), 1971; PhD, economics, University of Innsbruck (Austria), 1973

University professor

No imprisonment

Not a war veteran

Namazi went to Austria in 1963 and returned to Iran in 1975. He became the minister of economics under PM Raja'i on March 11, 1981. After serving as minister, Namazi worked for the Iranian Academy of Science.

Namdar-Zangeneh, Bizhan

Minister of the Construction Jihad in PM Musavi's first (February 21, 1984–85) and second (October 28, 1985–September 20, 1988) cabinets; minister of energy in PM Musavi's second cabinet (September 20, 1988–August 3, 1989) and President Hashemi-Rafsanjani's first (August 29, 1989–August 2, 1993) and second (August 16, 1993–August 2, 1997) cabinets; minister of petroleum in President Khatami's first (August 20, 1997–August 1, 2001) and second (August 22, 2001–August 2, 2005) cabinets and President Rouhani's first (August 15, 2013–August 13, 2017) and second (August 20, 2017–2021) cabinets; member of the Fourth (1997–2002), Fifth (2002–7), and Sixth (2007–12) Expediency Discernment Assembly

1952–, Kermanshah, Kermanshah

BS, civil engineering, Tehran University, 1975; MS, civil engineering, Shahid Beheshti University, 1977

Father's name unknown, state companies

Civil servant, ministries

No imprisonment

Not a war veteran

Member of PECI

Namdar-Zangeneh is one of the two longest-serving ministers in the Islamic Republic, having served in eight cabinets, from 1984 to 2005 and again from 2013 to 2017. From 1978 to 1979, he taught at K. N. Toosi University of Technology. After the revolution, he worked first as a cultural deputy in the Ministry of Culture, and then he became the first minister of the Construction Jihad. Namdar-Zangeneh officially retired from K. N. Toosi University of Technology in 2006. He was a supporter of Mir Hoseyn Musavi during the 2009 election and served as Musavi's representative in a meeting with Ayatollah Khamenei after the contested election to complain about the vote.

Nami, Mohammad-Hasan

Minister of information and communications technology in President Ahmadinejad's second cabinet (February 26–August 14, 2013)

1953–, Delijan, Markazi

BS, defense management, Officers College, 1974; MS, defense management, Iranian Army Command and General Staff College, 1999; PhD, political geography, Islamic Azad University–Tehran, 2012

Army officer (brigadier general)

No imprisonment

War veteran (served for 110 months; wounded three times)

Nami was the first regular army officer in the postrevolutionary era to become a minister on February 26, 2013, with 177 positive votes out of 243. He served for the last few months of President Ahmadinejad's second administration. He had previously been a deputy defense minister and military attaché in North Korea.

Namju, Majid

Minister of energy in President Ahmadinejad's second cabinet (November 15, 2009–August 3, 2013)
1962–, Kerman, Kerman
BS, civil engineering, Shahid Bahonar University of Kerman, 1991; MS, hydraulics engineering, Shahid Bahonar University of Kerman, 1996
Father's name unknown, landowner
No imprisonment
War veteran
IRGC militiaman
Martyr's family (two brothers killed at the war front)
Namju served at the war front under the command of Parviz Fattah and did various engineering projects for the IRGC. When the latter became the energy minister, he made Namju his deputy. Namju became minister of energy with 210 positive votes, thirty-six negative votes, and nineteen abstentions. He survived an impeachment on March 6, 2011, with the narrowest of margins.

Namju, Rahman

Deputy of the Sixth Majlis, Bukan, West Azerbaijan (2000–2004)
1965–, Bukan, West Azerbaijan
BS, psychology
Mohammad-Amin
No imprisonment

Namju, Seyyed Musa

Minister of national defense in PM Bahonar's cabinet (August 17–30, 1981) and interim PM Mahdavi-Kani's cabinet (September 3–27, 1981)
1938–September 27, 1981, Bandar-e Anzali, Gilan
BS, military science, Ground Forces Officers' Academy, 1961
Father's name unknown, tradesman
Army officer

No imprisonment
War veteran
Colonel Namju became head of the Ground Forces Officers' Academy and Ayatollah Khomeini's representative in the Supreme Defense Council after the revolution. He died in a plane crash.

Nano-Kenari, Valiyollah

Deputy of the Tenth Majlis, Babolsar, Mazandaran (2016–20)
1958–, Fereydunkenar, Mazandaran
BA, social science; BS, military science; MA, public administration
Yusef
No imprisonment
War veteran
IRGC militiaman
Martyr's family (brother, Kheirollah)

Naqavi, Seyyed Ali-Naqi

Deputy of the First Majlis, Qaenat, South Khorasan (1980–84)
1937–February 23, 2000, Qaenat, South Khorasan
BS, physics, Tehran University; MA, social science
Seyyed Baqer, farmer
Civil servant
No imprisonment
Not a war veteran
Naqavi, who retired from the State Organization for Registration of Deeds and Properties in 1983, died in a car accident in 2000.

Naqavi-Hoseyni, Seyyed Hoseyn

Deputy of the Eighth (2008–12), Ninth (2012–16), and Tenth (2016–20) Majlis, Varamin, Tehran
1960–, Varamin, Tehran
BA, political science, Tehran University, 1985; MA, political science, Tehran University, 1991; PhD, political science, Islamic Azad University–Science and Research Branch
Seyyed Baqer

University rector and professor
No imprisonment
Not a war veteran
IRGC militiaman (Basij)
In both 2005 and 2009, Naqavi-Hoseyni was a member of Mahmud Ahmadinejad's election headquarters.

Naqdi, Mohammad-Reza

Commander of the IRGC's Basij Force (October 4, 2009–December 7, 2016)
1961–, Tehran, Tehran (some sources mention Najaf, Iraq, as his birth place)
BS, military science, Iranian Army Command and General Staff College
Ali-Akbar Samani, bazaar merchant and pistachio farmer
No imprisonment
War veteran
Martyr's family
IRGC militiaman; head of the intelligence unit of the Basij
Naqdi joined the IRGC in 1979 and was active in intelligence units. In early 1987, he became the commander of the Badr brigade, which was made up of Iraqi POWs and defectors. He fought for less than a year in Bosnia. Naqdi played an important role in the prosecution of Tehran Mayor Gholam-Hoseyn Karbaschi and his colleagues in 1998 and in the interrogation of those arrested during the postelection crackdown in 2009. He was in charge of the intelligence unit of LEF, and from 2005 to 2007, he was in charge of the Headquarters for Combating Contraband Goods and Currency. The UN Security Council put Naqdi on its sanctions list in 2006. He is also on the US Treasury Office of Foreign Assets Control's Specially Designated Nationals and Blocked Persons List because of his role in the 2009 crackdown.

Naqi, Khosrow

Deputy of the First Majlis, representing the Jewish community (as a religious minority) (1981–84)

1946–, Tehran, Tehran
BA, law, Tehran University; MA, law
Habibollah, lawyer
Lawyer
No imprisonment
Not a war veteran
After serving in the Majlis, Naqi returned to the legal profession.

Nariman, Mohsen

Deputy of the Third (1988–92), Fourth (1992–96), Sixth (2000–2004), and Eighth (2008–12) Majlis, Babol, Mazandaran
1952–, Babol, Mazandaran
BS, civil engineering
Morad
IRIB civil servant
No imprisonment
Deputy secretary-general of the Islamic Iran Solidarity Party
After finishing his term in the Majlis, Nariman became a deputy to the minister of energy.

Narimani, Aman

Deputy of the Fourth Majlis, Islamabad-e Gharb, Kermanshah (1992–96); member of the Fifth Assembly of Experts, Kermanshah (2016–22)
1955–, Islamabad-e Gharb, Kermanshah
Clerical education
Nariman
Clergyman
No imprisonment
In 1997, Ayatollah Narimani became the Friday prayer leader of Qorveh. He was also a high-level official at the State General Inspectorate Organization. In 2007, he ran for the Fourth Assembly of Experts but was not elected.

Nari'zadeh, Ali

Deputy of the First Majlis, Marivan, Kurdistan (1981–84)
1947–, Marivan, Kurdistan

Pre-diploma
Abdollah, tailor
No imprisonment
Not a war veteran

Naru'i, Hatam

Deputy of the Second (1984–88) and Sixth (2000–
    2004) Majlis, Bam, Kerman
1946–, Bam, Kerman
Associate's degree
Dad-Mohammad
Civil servant
No imprisonment

Naseri, Abdolhoseyn

Deputy of the Sixth Majlis, Gorgan and Aq-Qala,
    Golestan (2001–4); deputy of the Eighth Majlis,
    Gorgan, Golestan (2008–12)
1964–, Gonbad-e Kavus, Golestan
PhD, biological sciences, Shahid Beheshti University,
    1991
Ebrahim
Medical professional
No imprisonment
War veteran
Naseri was in charge of the Construction Jihad's bureau
    of Shahid Beheshti University. He was elected to
    Eighth Majlis in interim elections. After serving in
    the Majlis, he went to teach at Tehran University.

Naseri, Mostafa

Deputy of the First (1981–84), Second (1984–88), and
    Fourth (1992–96) Majlis, Zanjan, Zanjan
1951–, Zanjan, Zanjan
Clerical education
Gol Mirza
Clergyman
No imprisonment
Not a war veteran
Head of the IRP branch in Zanjan; secretary-general
    of the Society of Former MPs

HI Naseri was head of the ideological-political bureau
    of the police force in Zanjan in the 1980s. He later
    became Iran's cultural attaché in Turkmenistan,
    and in 2013, he became the legal and parliamen-
    tary deputy of the Ministry of Education.

Naseri-Salehabadi, Mohammad

Public prosecutor-general of Tehran (date
    unknown-1994)
Date of birth unknown, Semnan, Semnan
Clerical education
Clergyman
Ayatollah Naseri-Salehabadi has been the prosecutor
    general of Isfahan and headed branch 20 of the
    State Supreme Court.

Naseri[zadeh], Ali-Akbar

Deputy of the Seventh (2004–8) and Ninth (2012–16)
    Majlis, Babol, Mazandaran
1956–, Babol, Mazandaran
Clerical education, Qom Seminary
Aqajan
Clergyman
Imprisoned before the revolution
Not a war veteran
Martyr's family (brother killed during the revolution-
    ary uprisings in 1978)
HI Naseri was active in Ayatollah Khomeini's head-
    quarters at the Alavi School in 1979, and he was
    the Friday prayer leader in Mahmudabad and
    Hamburg, Germany. Before entering the Seventh
    Majlis, he was promoting Islam in overseas mis-
    sions, and later became ambassador to the Vatican.

Naseri-Dowlatabadi, Mohammad-Reza

Deputy of the Fourth Majlis, Borkhar and Meymeh,
    Isfahan (1992–96)
1957–, Najaf, Iraq
Clerical education, Qom Seminary, 1984
Mohammad-Ali, clergyman
Clergyman

No imprisonment
War veteran (wounded)
IRGC militiaman (member of the Qods Force)
HI Naseri-Dowlatabadi went to Lebanon with the
    Qods Force after the revolution.

Naserigahar, Ahmad

Deputy of the Fifth Majlis, Dehloran, Mehran, Darre-
    hshahr, and Abdanan, Ilam (1996–2000)
1964–, Malekshahi, Ilam
High school diploma
Hoseyn
Bank employee
No imprisonment

Naserinezhad, Majid

Deputy of the Seventh (2004–8), Eighth (2008–12),
    and Tenth (2016–20) Majlis, Shadegan, Khuzestan
1967–, Shadegan, Khuzestan
Clerical education, Qom Seminary
Eyad
Clergyman (HI) and judiciary official in Ahvaz
No imprisonment
War veteran

Naseripur, Ms. A'zam

Deputy of the Sixth Majlis, Islamabad-e Gharb, Ker-
    manshah (2001–4)
1965–, Islamabad-e Gharb, Kermanshah
MS, architecture/urban planning
Parviz
No imprisonment
Not a war veteran
Naseripur was the second single woman to enter the
    Majlis, after Ms. Fatemeh Haqiqatju. She nom-
    inated herself for the Seventh Majlis from Ker-
    manshah but did not receive enough votes.

Nasiri, Naser

Deputy of the Seventh Majlis, Germi, Ardabil (2004–8)

1968–, Germi, Ardabil
BS, electrical engineering; MS, industrial engineering
Ya'qub
Civil servant
No imprisonment
Nasiri resigned from his post as district governor of
    Parsabad.

Nasiri-Lari, Mehdi

Deputy of the First Majlis, Larestan, Fars (1980–June
    28, 1981)
1933–June 28, 1981, Baft, Kerman
BA, education
Habib, farmer
Academia
No imprisonment
Not a war veteran
Nasiri-Lari was killed in the bombing of the IRP
    headquarters in June 1981.

Nasiri-Qeydari, Sa'dollah

Deputy of the Eighth Majlis, Zanjan and Tarom, Zan-
    jan (2008–12)
1959–, Khodabandeh, Zanjan
BS, physics, Shiraz University, 1984; MS, physics, Shi-
    raz University, 1988; PhD, physics, Shiraz Univer-
    sity, 1992
Ebrahim
Physics professor
No imprisonment
In 2014, Nasiri-Qeydari, a reformist, became the par-
    liamentary and legal deputy for the Ministry of
    Science. He did not participate in the election for
    the Ninth Majlis.

Nasirpur-Sardeha'i, Majid [Mohammad]

Deputy of the Eighth Majlis, Sarab, East Azerbaijan
    (2008–12)
1968–, Tehran, Tehran
BA, political science
Ebrahim

Civil servant, ministries
No imprisonment
War veteran (wounded)
IRGC militiaman

Nasri, Seyyed Ahmad

Deputy of the Fourth Majlis, Qazvin, Qazvin
    (1992–96)
1949–, Qazvin, Qazvin
BS, chemistry, Tehran University
Seyyed Mohammad
Civil servant
Imprisoned before the revolution
Nasri served as governor of Sistan and Baluches-
    tan from 1981 to 1993. He was also governor of
    Bushehr and Qazvin.

Nasrollahi, Mohammad

Deputy of the First Majlis, Abadan, Khuzestan
    (1980–84)
1952–date unknown, Abadan, Khuzestan
High school diploma
Nasrollah, laborer
No imprisonment
Not a war veteran
Nasrollahi joined the military establishment after
    leaving the Majlis. He died in a car accident (date
    unknown).

Nateq-Nuri, Abbas-Ali

Deputy of the First Majlis, Nur and Mahmudabad,
    Mazandaran (1980–81)
1935–June 28, 1981, Nur, Mazandaran
High school diploma
Abolqasem, clergyman
Bazaar tradesman
Imprisoned before the revolution
Not a war veteran
Nateq-Nuri was killed in the bombing of the IRP
    headquarters in June 1981. He was the brother of
    Ahmad and Ali-Akbar Nateq-Nuri. He was the

father-in-law of Seyyed Mohammad Jahromi's
    brother.

Nateq-Nuri, Ahmad

Deputy of the First (1981–84), Third (1988–92), Fourth
    (1992–96), Fifth (1996–2000), Sixth (2000–2004),
    Seventh (2004–8), and Eighth (2008–12) Majlis,
    Nur and Mahmudabad, Mazandaran
1937–, Nur, Mazandaran
Associate's degree
Abolqasem, clergyman
IRIB civil servant
No imprisonment
Not a war veteran
Martyr's family (brother, Abbas-Ali, killed in the
    bombing of the IRP headquarters)
Founding member of the Society of Islamic Athletes
Ahmad Nateq-Nuri was the longest-serving member
    of the Majlis, but he did not receive enough votes
    for either the Ninth or Tenth Majlis. He was in
    charge of the Iranian Boxing Federation from
    1990 to 2017.

Nateq-Nuri, Ali-Akbar

Deputy of the First Majlis, Tehran, Tehran (1980–
    December 15, 1981); interior minister in PM
    Musavi's first cabinet (December 15, 1981–
    85); deputy of the Second (1986–88), Third (1988–
    92), Fourth (1992–96), and Fifth (1996–2000) Maj-
    lis, Tehran, Tehran; member of the Fifth (2002–7),
    Sixth (2007–12), Seventh (2012–17), and Eighth
    (2017–22) Expediency Discernment Assembly
1943–, Nur, Mazandaran
Clerical education, Qom Seminary; BA, theology,
    Tehran University
Abolqasem, clergyman
Clergyman
Imprisoned before the revolution
Not a war veteran
Martyr's family (brother, Abbas-Ali, killed in the
    bombing of the IRP headquarters)
Member of the central council of the IRP and SCC

HI Nateq-Nuri was Ayatollah Khomeini's representative in the Construction Jihad until January 1982 and he built a national power base for himself in that role. In October 1980, President Banisadr rejected him as a candidate for interior minister. However, a year later Nateq-Nuri became the interior minister in PM Musavi's first cabinet. He survived an impeachment by the Majlis on November 6, 1983. Nateq-Nuri was a member of the editorial board of the conservative *Resalat*, a member of the Supreme Council for reconstruction of war-torn areas, and a member of the SCNS. He was the Speaker of the Fourth and Fifth Majlis (1992–2000). Nateq-Nuri ran as a candidate in the 1997 presidential race but lost to Mohammad Khatami by a 44 percent margin. Afterward, he decided not to run for any other office. During the 2005 presidential election, he was tasked with trying to unify the conservative camp but his efforts failed; three conservative candidates—Mahmoud Ahmadinejad, Mohammad-Baqer Qalibaf, and Ali Larijani—all decided to compete in the election and ended up splitting the vote. Realizing that he could not lead the conservative camp, Nateq-Nuri then dedicated himself to his regular job of heading the supervision and audit bureau of the Office of the Supreme Leader, where he worked until 2017. During the 2009 televised presidential debates, President Ahmadinejad accused Nateq-Nuri and his sons of corruption. Nateq-Nuri, Seyyed Mohammad-Ali Shahidi-Mahallati, and Abbas-Ahmad Akhundi married three daughters of Seyyed Hashem Rasuli-Mahallati.

Nazari, Ali

Deputy of the Sixth Majlis, Arak, Markazi (2000–2004)
1964–, Tehran, Tehran
BA, law
Karim
Journalist

No imprisonment
After serving in the Majlis, Nazari worked in the private sector.

Nazarimehr, Mohammad-Javad

Deputy of the Eighth (2008–12) and Ninth (2012–16) Majlis, Kordkuy, Torkaman, and Bandar-e Gaz, Golestan
1966–, Bandar-e Gaz, Golestan
MD, dentistry, Shahid Beheshti University
Yusef, teacher
Dentist and medical administrator
No imprisonment
War veteran
Martyr's family (father killed at the war front)
Nazarimehr was not elected to the Seventh Majlis.

Nazari-Monfared, Ali

Deputy of the First (1982–84) and Second (1984–88) Majlis, Abadeh, Fars
1947–, Qom, Qom
Clerical education
Abolqasem
Clergyman
No imprisonment
Not a war veteran
HI Nazari-Monfared is a former revolutionary and SCFC judge in Qom.

Nazariniya, Qodratollah

Deputy of the Fifth (1996–2000) and Sixth (2000) Majlis, Kangavar, Kermanshah
1960–September 29, 2000, Kangavar, Kermanshah
Clerical education
Hoseyn
Clergyman (HI)
No imprisonment
Not a war veteran
Founding member of the Islamic Iran Solidarity Party
Nazariniya died in a car accident.

Nazemi-Ardakani, Mohammad

Minister of cooperatives in President Ahmadinejad's
first cabinet (November 9, 2005–2006)
1955–, Ardakan, Yazd
BS, telecommunications engineering, K. N. Toosi
University of Technology, 1979; MA, executive
management, Industrial Management Organiza-
tion, 2000
Ebrahim
Head of the Organization for Standards and Scientific
Research
No imprisonment
Not a war veteran
IRGC militiaman
Nazemi-Ardakani is a former deputy in the Housing
Foundation, deputy minister of industries, and
head of the Civil Registration Organization. After
serving for fourteen months in the cabinet, he
resigned and returned to his previous position
as head of the Organization for Standards and
Scientific Research. He became the governor of
Qom in 2008 and then became a deputy minis-
ter. Nazemi-Ardakani ran unsuccessfully for the
Tenth Majlis from Tehran in 2016.

Nazri, Ali-Reza

Deputy of the Second Majlis, Mahallat and Delijan,
Markazi (1984–88)
1956–, Delijan, Markazi
Clerical education; BA, law
Fathali
Clergyman (HI)
No imprisonment

Nazripur, Ahmad-Ali

Deputy of the Third Majlis, Darab, Fars (1988–92)
1946–, Darab, Fars
Associate's degree
Ali-Asghar
No imprisonment

Negahban-Salami, Mahmud

Deputy of the Ninth (2012–16) and Tenth (2016–20)
Majlis, Khaf and Roshtkhar, Razavi Khorasan
1977–, Khaf, Razavi Khorasan
BA, educational management, Birjand University;
MS, educational psychology, Tehran University,
2005; pursuing a PhD in educational psychology
at Tarbiyat-e Mo'allem University
Gholam-Hoseyn, farmer
University instructor
No imprisonment
Not a war veteran
Negahban-Salami, a Sunni, was an educational ad-
viser in Alborz Province.

Nejabat, Ahmad

Deputy of the Fourth (1992–96) and Fifth (1996–2000)
Majlis, Shiraz, Fars
August 21, 1944–November 13, 2015, Shiraz, Fars
MD, surgery
Heydar-Ali
Surgeon
No imprisonment
Founder and member of the central council of the
ISFPD
Nejabat's brother, Hoseyn, has also been an MP.

Nejabat, Hoseyn

Deputy of the Seventh (2004–8), Eighth (2008–12),
and Ninth (2012–16) Majlis, Tehran, Tehran
1953–, Shiraz, Fars
BS, physics, Shiraz University, 1975; MS, physics,
Durham University (England), 1977; PhD, Nu-
clear Physics, Durham University (England),
1980; dissertation title: "Study of High Energy
Particles in Extensive Air Showers"
Heydar-Ali
University professor
No imprisonment
IRGC militiaman (Basij commander)

After his unsuccessful run for the Tenth Majlis, Nejabat went to teach at Islamic Azad University–Qom. His older brother Ahmad was an MP before him.

Neku, Ebrahim

Deputy of the Ninth Majlis, Robat Karim and Baharestan, Tehran (2012–16)
1968–, Malekan, East Azerbaijan
MA, educational management, Islamic Azad University–Science and Research Branch
High school and university teacher; member of city council
No imprisonment
Not a war veteran
After serving in the Majlis, Neku returned to the teaching profession.

Nekunam, Mohammad-Ebrahim

Deputy of the Eighth Majlis, Golpayegan and Khansar, Isfahan (2008–12)
1958–, Golpayegan, Isfahan
Clerical education
Qanbar-Ali
Clergyman (HI)
No imprisonment
As an SCFC prosecutor, Nekunam tried two former interior ministers—Abdollah Nuri in 1999 and Seyyed Ali-Akbar Mohtashamipur in 2000.

Ne'mati, Behruz

Deputy of the Ninth Majlis, Asadabad, Hamadan (2012–16); deputy of the Tenth Majlis, Tehran, Tehran (2016–20)
1968–, Asadabad, Hamadan
BA, theology, Razi University; MBA
Ali-Hashem
Governor of Bijar
No imprisonment
War veteran (thirty-two months; wounded)

Ne'mati was one of the handful of moderate conservatives on the reformist Majlis ballot for Tehran in 2016, and he won easily.

Ne'matzadeh, Ali

Deputy of the Fifth Majlis, Saqqez and Baneh, Kurdistan (1996–2000)
1958–, Saqqez, Kurdistan
MA, management
Mohammad-Sharif
No imprisonment

Ne'matzadeh, Mohammad-Reza

Minister of labor and social affairs in the Revolutionary Council cabinet (1979–80); minister of industries in PM Raja'i's cabinet (1980–81) and President Hashemi-Rafsanjani's first (August 29, 1989–August 2, 1993) and second (August 16, 1993–August 2, 1997) cabinets; minister of industry, mining, and trade in President Rouhani's first cabinet (August 15, 2013–August 13, 2017)
1945–, Tabriz, East Azerbaijan
BS, environmental engineering, California State Polytechnic University (USA), 1968; unfinished MA in industrial management at University of California, Berkeley (USA)
Father's name unknown, capitalist
Civil servant
No imprisonment
Not a war veteran
Founding member of the PMD
Ne'matzadeh, who withdrew from theological studies in 1977 to join Ayatollah Khomeini's movement, was in charge of an inspection committee at the Ministry of Labor and Social Affairs after the revolution. He has also held the following posts: director of the Iran National Company, and CEO of Tavanir (February–August 1989). Ne'matzadeh was a petrochemical deputy under minister of petroleum Namdar-Zangeneh during President Khatami's era, and then he held another deputy

post in the same ministry during President Ahmadinejad's era. He was the head of Hassan Rouhani's presidential campaign headquarters in 2013. Before becoming minister in 2013, he was CEO of a commercial company related to oil and gas that was doing lucrative business. He was also on the board of directors of some two dozen other companies.

Ne'matzadeh-Qarakhiyali, Qorbanali

Deputy of the Seventh Majlis, Qaemshahr, Savadkuh, and Juybar, Mazandaran (2004–8)
1954–, Qaemshahr, Mazandaran
PhD, genetics
Ne'mat
Civil servant
No imprisonment

Nezamolesalmi, Abdolmohammad

Deputy of the Sixth Majlis, Borujerd, Lorestan (2000–2004)
1953–2009, Borujerd, Lorestan
BS, agricultural engineering
Karam-Ali
No imprisonment

Nezhad-Fallah, Mohammad-Hoseyn

Deputy of the Seventh (2004–8) and Eighth (2008–12) Majlis, Savojblagh, Taleqan, and Nazarabad, Tehran
1968–, Savojblagh, Tehran
MA, political science
Abbas-Ali
IRIB civil servant
No imprisonment

Nezhad-Hoseyniyan, Mohammad-Hadi

Minister of roads and transportation in interim PM Mahdavi-Kani's cabinet (September 3–October 18, 1981) and PM Musavi's first cabinet (November 2, 1981–85); minister of heavy industries in President Hashemi-Rafsanjani's first (August 29, 1989–August 2, 1993) and second (August 16, 1993–October 5, 1994) cabinets; permanent representative of Iran to the UN (1997–2002)
1946–, Karbala, Iraq
BS, civil engineering, Tehran University, 1970; MS, civil engineering, George Washington University (USA), 1976; unfinished PhD in civil engineering, George Washington University (USA)
Civil servant, ministries
No imprisonment
Not a war veteran
Nezhad-Hoseyniyan went to the United States in 1975 and was a leader of the Iranian Muslim Students Association. He was in charge of the FDWI of New York—later known as the Alavi Foundation—after the revolution. He has also held such posts as deputy in the PBO (1980–81), deputy minister of petroleum (1985–89), and Iran's representative to OPEC. He also worked as deputy minister of petroleum for international affairs (1995–97).

Niazazari, Hoseyn

Deputy of the Ninth Majlis, Babol, Mazandaran (2012–16)
1957–, Firuzjah, Mazandaran
MA, public administration, Institute for Management and Planning Studies
Aqa Bozorg, farmer
Governor of Babolsar and Babol; water official in Mazandaran and Tehran
No imprisonment
Not a war veteran
Martyr's family (two brothers and two cousins killed at the war front)
While Niazazari was in the Construction Jihad, he was mainly supporting the needs of those fighting at the war front.

Nikfar, Ahmad

Deputy of the Third (1988–92), Fourth (1992–96), and
    Seventh (2004–8) Majlis, Eqlid, Fars
1951–, Eqlid, Fars
BS, agricultural engineering
Morad-Qoli
Civil servant
No imprisonment

Nikfar, Zabihollah

Deputy of the Tenth Majlis, Lahijan, Gilan (2016–20)
1966–, Lahijan, Gilan
MD, Gilan University of Medical Sciences
Medical doctor
No imprisonment
Nikfar, a conservative, was a university instructor and
    a civil servant in Gilan's ports and maritime office
    before he was elected to the Majlis.

Niknam, Abolfath

Deputy of the Fourth (1992–96) and Eighth (2008–12)
    Majlis, Tonekabon and Ramsar, Mazandaran
1947–, Tonekabon, Mazandaran
BA, economics
Javad
Civil servant, state companies
No imprisonment
Niknam, a factory owner, was elected to the Ninth
    Majlis from Ramsar, but the GC nullified the
    election results.

Niknam, Kurosh

Deputy of the Seventh Majlis, representing the Zoroas-
    trian community (as a religious minority) (2004–8)
1954–, Yazd, Yazd
PhD, Zoroastrian philosophy, Zorastrian College
    (India), 2001
Khodarahm
University professor
No imprisonment

Nikravesh [-Yadavar], Seyyed Kamaleddin

Mayor of Tehran (1980–81); interior minister in
    interim PM Mahdavi-Kani's cabinet (September
    3–October 18, 1981) and PM Musavi's first cabinet
    (November 2–December 1981); deputy of the Sec-
    ond Majlis, Tehran, Tehran (1984–88)
1944–, Borujerd, Lorestan
BS, electrical engineering, Amirkabir University of
    Technology, 1967; MS, electrical engineering, Uni-
    versity of Missouri (USA), 1970; PhD, electrical
    engineering, University of Missouri (USA), 1973
Seyyed Morteza
University professor
No imprisonment
Not a war veteran
Nikravesh was the governor-general of Kohgiluyeh
    and Buyer Ahmad in 1979. As rector of Amirk-
    abir University of Technology, he purged many
    faculty and staff. He later became Tehran's mayor,
    serving for only seven months. He resigned as
    interior minister in December 1981, having been
    on the job for only a few months. Nikravesh later
    returned to university teaching.

Nikzad, Ali

Minister of housing and urban development (Sep-
    tember 3, 2009–June 25, 2011) and then minister
    of roads and urban development (June 26, 2011–
    2013) in President Ahmadinejad's second cabinet
1965–, Ardabil, Ardabil
BS, civil engineering, Iran University of Science and
    Technology; MA, public administration, Tehran
    University
Governor-general of Ardabil
No imprisonment
Not a war veteran
Prior to becoming a minister in 2009, Nikzad was
    general manager for housing, planning deputy in
    the Lorestan governorate, and governor-general of
    Ardabil. In June 2011, he became the first per-
    son to head the newly created Ministry of Roads
    and Urban Development, which was created by

the merger of Ministry of Roads and Transportation and the Ministry of Housing and Urban Development. Nikzad received 205 positive votes, sixteen negative votes, and sixteen abstentions when reconfirmed as a minister on June 26, 2011, but the GC disqualified him from running in the 2013 presidential election. In 2017, he was the campaign manager of presidential candidate HI Seyyed Ebrahim Ra'isi.

Nikzadipanah, Habibollah

Deputy of the Tenth Majlis, Bam, Kerman (2016–20)
1953–, Khash, Sistan and Baluchestan
BS, agricultural engineering; MA, public administration
Civil servant, agricultural bank of Sistan and Baluchestan (since 1981)
No imprisonment
Nikzadipanah entered the Tenth Majlis as a reformist.

Nili [-Ahmadabadi], Hoseyn

Minister of mining and metals in PM Musavi's first cabinet (December 7, 1983–85)
1946–October 26, 1989, Isfahan, Isfahan
BS, electrical engineering, Shiraz University, 1975
Manager of Isfahan's Mobarakeh Steel Company
No imprisonment
Not a war veteran
Member of the IRP and the central committee of the SFIR
Nili became the minister of mining in 1983 but did not receive enough votes on October 28, 1985, to serve in PM Musavi's second cabinet. President Rouhani nominated his brother, Mahmud Nili [-Ahmadabadi], for the post of minister of science, research, and technology on October 29, 2014, but the Majlis rejected him and he subsequently became rector of Tehran University. Another brother, Sadeq, was a journalist for Fars News who was killed when his plane crashed in 2005. Hoseyn Nili's son, Maysam, is in charge of the ultraconservative *Raja News*. Nili died in an accident.

Nirumand, Seyyed Mohammad-Sadeq

Deputy of the Seventh Majlis, Nehbandan and Sarbisheh, South Khorasan (2004–8)
1965–, Mashhad, Razavi Khorasan
BA, law
Seyyed Javad
Head of the supreme leader's office for Sunni affairs in Sistan and Baluchestan Province
No imprisonment

Niyaz-Azari, Hoseyn

Deputy of the Tenth Majlis, Babol, Mazandaran (2016–20)
1957–, Ari, Mazandaran
MA, public administration
Bozorg, farmer
Civil servant
No imprisonment
War veteran
IRGC militiaman (Basij)
Martyr's family (two brothers, Ramazan and Esrafil, and two cousins, Ahmad and Behzad)
Niyaz-Azari was active in Babol's Construction Jihad.

Niyazi, Mahmud

Deputy of the Third Majlis, Bijar, Kurdistan (1988–92)
1950–, Bijar, Kurdistan
BA, accounting
Khalil
No imprisonment

Niyazi, Mohammad

Head of the State General Inspectorate Organization (2004–June 28, 2008)
1958–, Qom, Qom
Clerical education, Qom Seminary; BA, Imam Khomeini Educational and Research Institute; MA, law, Islamic Azad University
Father's name unknown, clergyman
Clergyman

No imprisonment

Not a war veteran

HI Niyazi, who entered the judiciary in 1982, was head of the Judicial Organization of the Armed Forces in Khuzestan Province (1986–1988), Tehran's military prosecutor (1989–99), and head of the national Judicial Organization of the Armed Forces (1999–2004).

Niyazi [Khorramabadi], Hashem

Member of the Fifth Assembly of Experts, Lorestan (2016–22)

1946–, Khorramabad, Lorestan

Clerical education, Qom Seminary

Gholam-Reza

Clergyman

No imprisonment

Ayatollah Niyazi was head of Supreme Leader Khamenei's office responding to correspondence from followers.

Nobaveh [-Vatan], Bizhan

Deputy of the Eighth (2008–12) and Ninth (2012–16) Majlis, Tehran, Tehran

1959–, Tehran, Tehran

MA, broadcasting, IRIB University

Ali-Akbar

Director of IRIB's political bureau in New York, London, and the UN

No imprisonment

War veteran (victim of a chemical attack)

Nobaveh, a retiree of IRIB, is the proprietor of *Siyasta-e Ruz*.

No'i-Aqdam [-Shamasbi], Nureddin [Hasan]

Deputy of the Fourth (1992–96) and Seventh (2004–8) Majlis, Ardabil, Ardabil

1957–, Ardabil, Ardabil

BS, mathematics, Isfahan University of Technology, 1979; MA, economics, 1997; PhD, economics

Ahmad

Academia

No imprisonment

Not a war veteran

Martyr's family (two brothers)

No'i-Aqdam, a conservative, held a leadership post in the Majlis. One of his brothers is an IRGC commander.

Nokhbeh-Alfuqha'i, Mohammad-Hoseyn

Deputy of the Fourth (1992–96) and Fifth (1996–2000) Majlis, Larestan, Fars

1952–2013, Lar, Fars

BA, law, 1991; MA, political science, 1995

Mohammad-Baqer

No imprisonment

Nokhbeh-Alfuqha'i worked in the Ports and Maritime Organization and later at the antidrug agency. He died of a heart attack.

Noqaba'i, Seyyed Mohammad

Deputy of the Fourth Majlis, Tuyserkan, Hamadan (1992–96)

1961–, Tuyserkan, Hamadan

Associate's degree

Teacher

No imprisonment

War veteran

Noqaba'i ran unsuccessfully for the Fifth Majlis, and the GC disqualified him from running in the elections for the Seventh and Eighth Majlis. During the 2009 presidential elections, he was a supporter of Mehdi Karrubi.

Nosratirad, Ahmad

Deputy of the Fourth Majlis, Rasht, Gilan (1992–96)

1951–, Rasht, Gilan

MA, business administration

Sattar

No imprisonment

Noushabadi, Hoseyn

Deputy of the Sixth (2000–2004) and Seventh (2004–
8) Majlis, Varamin, Tehran
1963–, Varamin, Tehran
BS, psychology
Civil servant
No imprisonment
After serving in the Majlis, Noushabadi held a gov-
ernment post.

Nowbakht, Mrs. Monireh

Deputy of the Fourth (1992–96) and Fifth (1996–2000)
Majlis, Tehran, Tehran
1950–, Tehran, Tehran
MA, theology
Abbas
Teacher at Tarbiyat-e Mo'allem University
No imprisonment
Founding member of Zeynab Society, the Party of
Women of the Islamic Republic of Iran, and the
Islamic Society of Educators; secretary-general
of the Women's Organization of the Islamic
Revolution

Nowbakht-Haqiqi, Ali

Deputy of the Tenth Majlis, Tehran, Tehran (2016–20)
1948–, Rasht, Gilan
MD, Isfahan University of Technology, 1978; med-
ical residency at the Iran University of Medical
Sciences, Tehran
Morteza, bazaar tradesman
Medical doctor (nephrology); professor of medicine at
Shahid Beheshti University of Medical Sciences
Member of the PMD
Nowbakht-Haqiqi has served in such capacities as
deputy in the Ministry of Health, deputy in the
Islamic Republic of Iran Medical Council, mem-
ber and secretary of the Academy of Medical Sci-
ences of the Islamic Republic of Iran, and medical
adviser and representative of President Rouhani

in the Red Crescent Society of the Islamic Republic of Iran. He is the older brother of Mohammad-Baqer Nowbakht-Haqiqi.

Nowbakht-Haqiqi, Mohammad-Baqer

Deputy of the Third (1988–92), Fourth (1992–96),
Fifth (1996–2000), and Sixth (2000–2004) Maj-
lis, Rasht, Gilan; VP for planning and strategic
supervision in President Rouhani's first cabinet
(2013–August 13, 2017); VP and head of the Plan
and Budget Organization in President Rouhani's
second cabinet (August 20, 2017–2021)
1950–, Rasht, Gilan
BA, 1987; MA, management, 1991; PhD, management,
Islamic Azad University–Tehran; PhD, economics, University of the West of Scotland (Scotland),
1995
Morteza, bazaar tradesman
Academia
No imprisonment
War veteran
Secretary-general of the PMD
Nowbakht-Haqiqi became the first secretary-general
of the Party of Moderation and Development
when it was founded in 1999. In addition to
being a vice president, he has also been spokesperson for President Rouhani's cabinet. He was
previously deputy for economic research at the
research center of the EDA, as well as general
manager for education of Kermanshah Province.
Nowbakht-Haqiqi is the grandson of Ayatollah
Abolqasem Hojjati (a cleric in Gilan), and his
brother Ali was elected as a deputy to the Tenth
Majlis.

Nowbari, Ali-Reza

Governor of the Central Bank (1980–81)
1947–, Tehran, Tehran
MS, mathematics, University of Paris (France); MA,
economics, Stanford University (USA)
No imprisonment before the revolution

Not a war veteran

Nowbari, who is the son-in-law of former president
Abolhasan Banisadr, was active in the Muslim
Student Association in California before the revolution. In the early 1980s, he became the editor in
chief of *Enqelab-e Islami*, which was the mouthpiece of President Banisadr. He fled Iran in 1981,
after President Banisadr had fled, and has been
living in Europe ever since.

Nowruzi, Asghar

Deputy of the Third Majlis, Damavand, Tehran
(1988–92)
1944–, Damavand, Tehran
Associate's degree
No imprisonment
Member of the Islamic Association of Iranian
Teachers

Nowruzi, Esma'il

Deputy of the Fourth Majlis, Sarvestan and Karbal,
Fars (1992–96)
1948–, Shiraz, Fars
Clerical education
Mohammad-Ebrahim
Clergyman (HI)
No imprisonment

Nowruzi, Hasan

Deputy of the Eighth (2008–12) and Tenth (2016–20)
Majlis, Robat Karim, Tehran
1960–, Mashhad, Razavi Khorasan
Clerical education; MA, Arabic literature; pursuing a
PhD in international law
Esma'il
Clergyman
Imprisoned before the revolution
War veteran (POW 1980–90; wounded and left 50
percent paralyzed)
HI Nowruzi has been the Friday prayer leader of sev-
eral cities, including Robat Karim and Torqabeh,

and has founded a number of seminaries. He ran
unsuccessfully for the Ninth Majlis.

Nowruzi, Kazem

Deputy of the First Majlis, Amol, Mazandaran
(1980–84)
1947–, Amol, Mazandaran
Clerical education
Reza-Qoli, farmer
Clergyman (HI)
No imprisonment
Not a war veteran

Nowruzi, Mohammad

Deputy of the First Majlis, Gonbad-e Kavus, Golestan
(1980–84)
1941–, Gonbad-e Kavus, Golestan
High school diploma
Qasem, bazaar tradesman
No imprisonment
Not a war veteran

Nowruzi, Rahmatollah

Deputy of the Ninth Majlis, Aliabad Katul, Golestan
(2012–16)
1974–, Aliabad Katul, Golestan
MA, history of ancient Iran, Islamic Azad University
Hoseyn-Ali
Provincial education official
No imprisonment
Not a war veteran

Nowruzi-Mishani, Abdollah

Deputy of the Third (1988–92) and Fourth (1992–96)
Majlis, Malayer, Hamadan
1947–, Malayer, Hamadan
BS, civil engineering, 1980; MA, management, 1991
Hasan
No imprisonment
Founding member of the ISFPD

Nowruzzadeh, Seyyed Reza

Deputy of the Third (1988–92), Fourth (1992–96), Fifth (1996–2000), Sixth (2000–2004), and Seventh (2004–8) Majlis, Esfarayen, North Khorasan
1952–, Esfarayen, North Khorasan
BS, chemistry, 1987; MS, industrial engineering, 1995; MA, public administration
Seyyed Aqa Qashamsham
Civil servant
No imprisonment
Founding member of the NTP
Nowruzzadeh was involved in the takeover of the American embassy. He served for five terms in the Majlis, but the GC rejected his qualifications for the Eighth Majlis. He was one of the founding members of the Society of Industrial Managers and Professionals of Iran.

Nowzari, Gholam-Hoseyn

Deputy of the Fourth (1992–96) and Fifth (1996–2000) Majlis, Kazerun, Fars; minister of petroleum in President Ahmadinejad's first cabinet (November 14, 2007–September 2, 2009)
1954–, Kazerun, Fars
BS, petroleum engineering; MS, industrial management, Tehran University, 1996
Ahmad
NIOC official
No imprisonment
War veteran

Nura, Abbas-Ali

Deputy of the Fifth (1996–2000) Majlis, Zahedan, Sistan and Baluchestan; deputy of the Eighth (2008–12) Majlis, Zabol, Sistan and Baluchestan
1953–January 2, 2018, Zabol, Sistan and Baluchestan
BS, mathematics, Isfahan University of Technology, 1975; MS, mathematics, University of Manchester (England), 1977; PhD, mathematics, University of Exeter (England), 1980; dissertation title: "Some

Contributions to the Analysis of Survival Data with Co-variates"
Esma'il
University professor and administrator
No imprisonment
Not a war veteran

Nurani-Ardabili, Mostafa

Member of the Third Assembly of Experts, Ardabil (1999–October 30, 2003)
1926–October 30, 2003, Taqedizej, Ardabil
Clerical education, Najaf Seminary (Iraq)
Shokrollah, clergyman
Clergyman (ayatollah)
Imprisoned before the revolution
Not a war veteran

Nurbakhsh, Abdorrahim

Deputy of the Fourth (1992–96) and Fifth (1996–2000) Majlis, Mahabad, West Azerbaijan
1954–, Urmia, West Azerbaijan
BA, Persian literature, 1991; MA, political science, 1995; clerical education
Najmeddin
No imprisonment

Nurbakhsh, Mohsen

Governor of the Central Bank (1981–86); deputy of the Third Majlis, Tehran, Tehran (1988–August 29, 1989); minister of economic affairs and finance in President Hashemi-Rafsanjani's first cabinet (August 29, 1989–August 2, 1993); governor of the Central Bank (1994–2003); member of the Fourth Expediency Discernment Assembly (1997–2002)
1948–March 22, 2003, Isfahan, Isfahan
BA, economics, National University (later renamed Shahid Beheshti University); PhD, economics, University of California, Davis (USA), 1978; dissertation title: "Dynamic Consideration of Trade Agreements Case Study: Iran"
Hoseyn, army colonel

Economics professor at Shahid Beheshti University

No imprisonment

Not a war veteran

Founder and member of the central council of PECI

Nurbakhsh was active in the Muslim Student Association in California before the revolution. In 1980, PM Raja'i recommended Nurbakhsh as minister of economics to President Banisadr but the latter did not accept him. Between 1980 and 1981, he was the deputy governor of the Central Bank. After stepping down as governor of the Central Bank, he went back to university teaching but was soon elected to the Third Majlis. Nurbakhsh resigned from the Third Majlis to become the minister of economics and as such the architect of President Hashemi-Rafsanjani's economic policies. However, in 1993, Nurbakhsh failed to receive enough votes from the Majlis to continue as minister of economics, and President Hashemi-Rafsanjani appointed him as his deputy.

Nurbakhsh, Seyyed Ahmad

Member of the Assembly for the Final Examination of the Constitution, Chahar Mahal and Bakhtiari (1979)

1944–, Shahrekord, Chahar Mahal and Bakhtiari

PhD, mechanical engineering

Seyyed Kamal, university professor

Nurbakhsh voted against the principle of *velayat-e faqih* in the AFEC.

Nuri, Abdollah

Deputy of the Second Majlis, Isfahan, Isfahan (1984–88); member of the Second Expediency Discernment Assembly (1989–97); interior minister in President Hashemi-Rafsanjani's first cabinet (August 29, 1989–August 2, 1993); deputy of the Fifth Majlis, Tehran, Tehran (1996–August 20, 1997); interior minister in President Khatami's first cabinet (August 20, 1997–June 21, 1998); member of the Second (1989–92), Third (1992–97),

and Fourth (1997–2002) Expediency Discernment Assembly

1950–, Isfahan, Isfahan

Clerical education, Qom Seminary

Mohammad-Ali

Clergyman

Civil servant, Office of the Supreme Leader

No imprisonment

Not a war veteran

Martyr's family

IRGC militiaman

Member of the central council of PECI

HI Nuri has held the following additional posts after the revolution: Ayatollah Khomeini's representative in the election of members of HCJ (appointed May 18, 1980), his representative in IRIB (appointed in February 1981), his representative in the Construction Jihad (appointed January 3, 1982), and his representative in the IRGC (March 9, 1989–June 26, 1990); member of the SCNS; deputy foreign minister; and member of the Council for Revision of the Constitution. In the late 1980s, Nuri was the messenger between Ayatollah Khomeini and Ayatollah Montazeri when the latter was being dismissed. At that time, Nuri was Ayatollah Khomeini's representative in the IRGC. Nuri, who was leader of the minority (reformist) faction in the Fifth Majlis, resigned from his post on August 20, 1997, to become interior minister. He proceeded to create a unified police force called the Law Enforcement Forces. However, the Majlis successfully impeached him as interior minister on June 21, 1998, making him the first minister to be removed during President Khatami's administration. Nuri then started a reformist daily newspaper titled *Khordad* and was subsequently elected to the Tehran City Council and became its chairman. The conservative SCFC put him on trial in November 1999 for material published in *Khordad*. Nuri's open trial became one of Iran's most sensational postrevolutionary legal cases as he proceeded to challenge the legality of the SCFC and declared, "I do not accept the court's competence." He was condemned to a five-year prison term but was released early in 2002 after serving three years of his sentence. Afterward, he did not openly involve himself with politics.

Nuri, Ali-Reza

Deputy of the Sixth Majlis, Tehran, Tehran (2000–October 30, 2002)
1963–October 30, 2002, Isfahan, Isfahan
MD, surgery, Isfahan University of Medical Sciences
Mohammad-Ali
Medical doctor and university professor
No imprisonment
War veteran
Ali-Reza Nuri was a member of the HCCR. The younger brother of Abdollah Nuri, he was killed in a car accident along with fellow MP Mas'ud Hashemzehi.

Nuri, Ezzatollah

Deputy of the Fifth Majlis, Qorveh, Kurdistan (1996–2000)
1954–, Qorveh, Kurdistan
BA, theology
Yadollah
No imprisonment
IRGC militiaman

Nuri, Seyyed Razi

Deputy of the Ninth (2012–16) and Tenth (2016–20) Majlis, Shush, Khuzestan
1967–, Dasht-e Azadegan, Khuzestan
MD, Ahvaz University of Medical Sciences
Medical doctor and administrator in Shush
No imprisonment
Nuri, a conservative, ran unsuccessfully for the Eighth Majlis in 2008.

Nuri-Ghezeljeh, Gholam-Reza

Deputy of the Ninth Majlis, Bostanabad, East Azerbaijan (2012–16)
1970–, Ghezeljeh, East Azerbaijan
BS, 1992; MS, agricultural management, Islamic Azad University–Miyaneh
Salman
Official in the Agricultural Jihad in East Azerbaijan for twenty years
No imprisonment
Not a war veteran
Nuri-Ghezeljeh ran unsuccessfully for the Eighth Majlis in 2008.

Nuri-Hamadani, Hoseyn

Member of the First Assembly of Experts, Hamadan (1983–90)
1925–, Hamadan, Hamadan
Clerical education, Qom Seminary
Ebrahim, clergyman
Clergyman (ayatollah)
Imprisoned and exiled before the revolution
Not a war veteran
Member of the SQSS
Before the revolution, Nuri-Hamadani was on the editorial board of *Maktab-e Islam* magazine. In 1979–80, he was Ayatollah Khomeini's representative in Europe. As a conservative source of emulation, Nuri-Hamadani is known for his opposition to Sufi groups and Jews, as well as to the UN Convention to Eliminate All Forms of Discrimination against Women. His son-in-law is Seyyed Hoseyn Musavi-Tabrizi [Pur-Mir-Ghaffari].

Nuriyan, Ardeshir

Deputy of the Tenth Majlis, Shahrekord, Chahar Mahal and Bakhtiari (2016–20)
1966–, Shahrekord, Chahar Mahal and Bakhtiari
BA, political science, Tehran University, 1993; MA, diplomacy and international organizations, School of International Relations (affiliated with Iran's Ministry of Foreign Affairs), 1997; pursuing a PhD in national security at the Supreme National Defense University
Mayor of Shahrekord (starting in 2009)

No imprisonment
Not a war veteran
Nuriyan was an official in the governorate general of
    Chahar Mahal and Bakhtiari from 1995 to 1998
    and a political secretary in the Iranian embassy in
    Sarajevo, Bosnia-Herzegovina from 2002 to 2005.

Nurizadeh, Seyyed Mahmud

Deputy of the Fifth Majlis, Meshginshahr, Ardabil
    (1996–2000)
1927–, Meshginshahr, Ardabil
Clerical education, Qom Seminary
Mir Moslem
Clergyman
No imprisonment
Not a war veteran
Ayatollah Nurizadeh, whom the shah's regime sent
    into exile before the revolution, was the oldest
    member of the Fifth Majlis.

Nurmofidi, Seyyed [Mohammad] Kazem

Member of the First (1984–90) and Second (1991–98)
    Assembly of Experts, Mazandaran; member of
    the Third (1999–2006), Fourth (2007–16), and
    Fifth (2016–22) Assembly of Experts, Golestan
1940–, Gorgan, Golestan
Clerical education, Qom Seminary
Seyyed Mehdi, civil servant
Clergyman
Imprisoned before the revolution
Not a war veteran
In 1981, Ayatollah Khomeini appointed Ayatollah
    Nurmofidi as the Friday prayer leader and his rep-
    resentative in Gorgan. Nurmofidi held these posts
    for more than three decades. PMOI targeted him
    for an assassination attempt in August 1981 that
    resulted in the death of two of his bodyguards.
    Nurmofidi was elected to the First AE in interim
    elections held on April 15, 1984. He played an
    important role in the establishment of Golestan
    Province. Nurmofidi is the son-in-law of Ayatol-
    lah Mohammad Fazel-Lankarani.

Nurqolipur, Ramin

Deputy of the Tenth Majlis, Kordkuy, Golestan
    (2016–20)
1971–, Bandar-e Torkaman, Golestan
BS, range and watershed management, Gorgan Univer-
    sity of Agricultural Sciences and Natural Resources,
    1998; MS, Tehran University; PhD, geomatics engi-
    neering, University Putra Malaysia (Malaysia), 2011
Water management official in North Khorasan
No imprisonment
Nurqolipur, a Sunni, entered the Tenth Majlis as a
    reformist.

Okhovvatiyan, Abolqasem

Deputy of the First Majlis, Sari, Mazandaran (1980–84)
1927–2014, Sari, Mazandaran
MD, surgery
Mohammad-Ali, civil servant
Surgeon
No imprisonment
Not a war veteran
After his term ended, Okhovvatiyan returned to the
    medical profession for the rest of his life.

Omid-Najafabadi, Fathollah

Deputy of the First Majlis, Isfahan, Isfahan (1980–84)
1943–December 7, 1988, Najafabad, Isfahan
Clerical education; BA, law
Mahmud, bazaar tradesman
Clergyman
Imprisoned and exiled before the revolution
Not a war veteran
HI Omid-Najafabadi spent two years (1975–77) in
    internal exile under the shah. He became head of
    the revolutionary court in Isfahan in 1979 before
    entering the Majlis. Omid-Najafabadi, who was
    close to Ayatollah Montazeri, was arrested on
    November 30, 1988, on charges of connection
    with Mehdi Hashemi's gang and sexual miscon-
    duct. Ayatollah Montazeri, however, maintained
    that he was executed because of the role he played

in revealing the secret negotiations that became known as the Iran-Contra affair. The SCFC condemned Omid-Najafabadi to death and he was executed on December 7, 1988.

Omrani, Mrs. Seyyedeh Sakineh

Deputy of the Ninth Majlis, Semirom, Isfahan (2012–16)
1972–, Semirom, Isfahan
BS, biological sciences, Shiraz University, 1995; MS, physiology, Shahid Beheshti University, 2000
Father's name unknown, farmer
High school and university instructor
No imprisonment

Orumiyan, Ali

Deputy of the First (1980–84) and Second (1984–88) Majlis, Maragheh, East Azerbaijan; member of the Second (1991–98) and Third (1996–2000) Assembly of Experts, East Azerbaijan
1932–, Maragheh, East Azerbaijan
Clerical education, Najaf Seminary (Iraq)
Esma'il, bazaar tradesman
Clergyman
Imprisoned before the revolution
Not a war veteran
Martyr's family (three sons killed at the war front; one son wounded in an attack by PMOI)
Ayatollah Orumiyan, who lived in Najaf from 1954 to 1973, was the Friday prayer leader of Maragheh and later worked in the Office of the Supreme Leader under Ayatollah Khamenei.

Osmani, Mohammad-Qasim

Deputy of the Eighth (2008–12), Ninth (2012–16), and Tenth (2016–20) Majlis, Bukan, West Azerbaijan
1969–, Bukan, West Azerbaijan
BA, accounting, Shahid Beheshti University; MA, accounting, Shahid Beheshti University, 1995; PhD, accounting, Allameh Tabataba'i University, 2003
Jasim, clergyman
Professor at Shahid Beheshti University

No imprisonment
War veteran
As a professional accountant, Osmani, a Sunni Kurd, sits on the board of a number of companies. He has been the chair of the Kurdish caucus in the Majlis and was a member of the Tenth Majlis leadership team from 2016 to 2017.

Ostadi-Moqaddam [-Tehrani], Reza

Member of the Third (1999–2006) and Fourth (2007–16) Assembly of Experts, Tehran; member of the Fourth Guardian Council (1999–2001)
1937–, Tehran, Tehran
Clerical education, Qom Seminary
Khodadad, bazaar tradesman
Clergyman
No imprisonment
Not a war veteran
Member of the SQSS; member and secretary of the HCRSQ
Ayatollah Ostadi-Moqaddam's family has been prominent in the conservative CIC/PCIC; his brother Mehdi was a member before the revolution. Reza Ostadi-Moqaddam was head of the Qom Seminary from 1995 to 1998 and sits on the board of the Great Islamic Encyclopedia.

Owladqobad, Mrs. Farideh

Deputy of the Tenth Majlis, Tehran, Tehran (2016–20)
1970–, Kuhdasht, Lorestan
MA, anthropology, Tehran University, 2000
High school teacher and headmistress
Martyr's family (father and husband)
Owladqobad was elected as a reformist candidate. Her husband, Sadeq, was killed in 1988 during Operation Mersad against PMOI forces, who had entered Iran from Iraq.

Owlia, Ali-Akbar

Deputy of the Eighth Majlis, Yazd and Saduq, Yazd (2008–12)

1956–, Yazd, Yazd
BS, civil engineering, Amirkabir University of
    Technology
Mahmud
Civil servant
No imprisonment
Owlia has worked in IRIB, Yazd governorate, MI, and
    the Ministry of Energy.

Paknezhad, Seyyed Abbas

Deputy of the Fourth (1992–96), Fifth (1996–2000),
    and Seventh (2004–8) Majlis, Yazd, Yazd
1930–, Yazd, Yazd
MD, surgery, Tehran University
Seyyed Abolqasem, clergyman
Surgeon
No imprisonment
Not a war veteran
Martyr's family (two brothers killed in the bombing
    of the IRP headquarters)
Member of the IRP
Paknezhad was a POW in Iraq for many years after
    Iraqi forces captured him while he was visiting the
    front with minister of petroleum Mohammad-Ja-
    vad Tondguyan. He was one of the two oldest
    members of the Fourth Majlis and the oldest mem-
    ber of the Seventh Majlis. He was also a presiden-
    tial adviser and head of the IRGC's health services.

Paknezhad, Seyyed Reza

Deputy of the First Majlis, Yazd, Yazd (1980–81)
1924–June 28, 1981, Yazd, Yazd
MD, Tehran University, 1957
Seyyed Abolqasem, clergyman
Medical doctor
No imprisonment
Not a war veteran
Martyr's family (brother)
Paknezhad was involved in anti-Baha'i activities
    before the revolution. He and his brother, Seyyed
    Mohammad, were killed in the bombing of the

IRP headquarters in 1981. He was related to Ayatollah Mohammad Saduqi on his father's side.

Panahandeh, Ali

Deputy of the Second (1984–88) and Third (1988–92)
    Majlis, Borkhar, Isfahan
1944–, Borkhar and Meymeh, Isfahan
Clerical education
Gholam-Reza
Clergyman (HI)
No imprisonment

Papari-Moqaddamfard, Ayyub

Deputy of the Eighth Majlis, Dashtestan, Bushehr
    (2009–12)
1964–, Kazerun, Fars
BS, agricultural education, Shahid Chamran Univer-
    sity of Ahvaz, 1993; MS, agricultural engineering,
    Shiraz University, 2000
Baqer
Civil servant
No imprisonment
War veteran
IRGC militiaman
In 1985, Papari-Moqaddamfard fought for six months
    along with Hezbollah forces in Lebanon.

Papi, Hoseyn

Deputy of the Seventh Majlis, Dorud and Azna, Lor-
    estan (2004–8)
1968–, Dorud, Lorestan
MA, law
Heydar
Civil servant
No imprisonment

Papizadeh-Palangan, Abbas

Deputy of the Ninth (2012–16) and Tenth (2016–20)
    Majlis, Dezful, Khuzestan

1981–, Dezful, Khuzestan
MS, agricultural management
Expert in the Ministry of Agriculture
No imprisonment (born after the revolution)
Not a war veteran

Pardis, Seyyed Reza

Commander of the Islamic Republic of Iran Air Force
(May 27, 2001–October 5, 2004)
1947–, Qazvin, Qazvin
PhD, military science, Supreme National Defense
University, 2000
Father's name unknown, grocer
Military pilot (brigadier general)
War veteran
Pardis joined the Iranian Air Force in 1965 and un-
derwent radar and flight training in the United
States in the late 1960s and early 1970s.

Parhizkar, Akbar

Deputy of the Second Majlis, Tabriz, East Azerbaijan
(1984–September 20, 1987)
1949–, Khoy, West Azerbaijan
MS, civil engineering
Reza
No imprisonment
Parhizkar resigned from the Second Majlis to become
the governor-general of East Azerbaijan.

Pari'zad, Ali

Deputy of the Second Majlis, Naqadeh, West Azerbai-
jan (1984–88)
1949–, Naqadeh, West Azerbaijan
Pre-diploma
Moslem
No imprisonment

Parsa'i, Bahram

Deputy of the Tenth Majlis, Shiraz, Fars (2016–20)

1970, Mamasani, Fars
MD, dentistry, University of Rafsanjan
Dentist; owner of a bottled water company
No imprisonment
War veteran (one year)
Parsa'i, a reformist, was a member of the Shiraz City
Council for two years.

Partovi, Mohammad-Ali

Deputy of the Third (1988–92) and Fourth (1992–96)
Majlis, Saqqez and Baneh, Kurdistan; deputy of
the Eighth Majlis, Piranshahr, West Azerbaijan
(2008–12)
1953–, Baneh, Kurdistan
Associate's degree
Mohammad
IRIB civil servant
Partovi, a Sunni, was not elected to the Ninth
Majlis.

Partow, Morovvatollah

Deputy of the Third (1988–92) and Sixth (2000–2004)
Majlis, Khodabandeh, Zanjan
1948–, Khodabandeh, Zanjan
BS, engineering, 1980; MS, 2000
No imprisonment
Partow joined the military establishment after leaving
the Majlis.

Parva'i-Rik, Ahmad

Member of the Fifth Assembly of Experts, Gilan
(2016–22)
1982–, Talesh, Gilan
Clerical education, Qom Seminary
Qoli
Clergyman
No imprisonment
Not a war veteran
HI Parva'i-Rik was the second-youngest person
elected to the Fifth AE.

Parvaresh, Seyyed Ali-Akbar

Member of the Assembly for the Final Examination
of the Constitution, Isfahan (1979); deputy of the
First (1980–August 17, 1981), Third (1988–92), and
Fourth (1992–96) Majlis, Isfahan, Isfahan; minis-
ter of education in PM Bahonar's cabinet (August
17–30, 1981), interim PM Mahdavi-Kani's cabinet
(September 3–October 18, 1981), and PM Musavi's
first cabinet (November 2, 1981–August 14, 1984)
1942–December 27, 2013, Isfahan, Isfahan
BA, Persian literature, Isfahan University of Technol-
ogy, 1977; MA, teachers' training, Daneshsara-ye
Ali-ye Tehran; clerical education
Seyyed Hoseyn, laborer
Academia
Imprisoned before the revolution
Not a war veteran
Member of the central council and deputy secretary-general of CIC/PCIC; member of the central
committee and deputy secretary-general of the
IRP
Parvaresh, a skilled orator, joined the radical Tohidi-ye Saf group in 1975, and before that he was
active in CIC/PCIC. He was freed from prison
before the revolution after writing a letter of
repentance. Two days before the first 1981 presidential election, held on July 24, 1981, Parvaresh
withdrew from the race in favor of the eventual
winner, Mohammad-Ali Raja'i. He resigned
from the First Majlis a month later to become the
minister of education. After President Raja'i was
assassinated, Parvaresh ran in the second presidential election held on October 2, 1981, but lost
to Seyyed Ali Khamenei by a lopsided margin.
He became minister of education in PM Musavi's
first administration but could not secure enough
votes from the Majlis in 1984 to continue. Parvaresh was intimately involved with the launching
of the conservative *Resalat* in January 1986 and
was a member of the Supreme Defense Council.
He served as deputy secretary-general of CIC/
PCIC until 2001 and twice served as deputy
Speaker of the Majlis.

Pashang [Rigi], Hamid-Reza

Deputy of the Seventh (2004–8), Eighth (2008–12),
and Ninth (2012–16) Majlis, Khash, Mirjaveh,
Nosratabad, Kurin, and Nokabad, Sistan and
Baluchestan
1966–, Ladiz, Sistan and Baluchestan
BS, civil engineering, University of Sistan and Baluch-
estan, 1995
Mohammad-Reza Rigi, farmer
Teacher and provincial civil servant
No imprisonment
Not a war veteran
Pashang is a Sunni politician.

Peyman, Habibollah

Member of the Revolutionary Council (1979–80)
1935–, Shiraz, Fars
MA, sociology, Tehran University; MD, dentistry,
Tehran University, 1960
Dentist
Imprisoned before the revolution
Not a war veteran
Founder of the Movement of Combatant Muslims
In 1963, Peyman and Kazem Sami established the
Freedom Seeking Movement of People of Iran,
which advocated for a more radical strategy of op-
posing the shah's regime. They were both arrested
in 1965. In 1977, Peyman founded the Movement
of Combatant Muslims by himself. In 1979, he
joined the Revolutionary Council but left it a year
later after feeling that he could not be effective
there. Peyman ran unsuccessfully for a seat in the
Assembly for the Final Examination of the Constitution in 1979. The GC disqualified him from
running in the 1997 presidential election and the
2000 Majlis election.

Pezeshki, Hokmollalh

Deputy of the Second Majlis, Miyaneh, East Azerbaijan (1984–88)
1935–, Miyaneh, East Azerbaijan

BA
Ja'far-Qoli
Deputy governor-general of Miyaneh
No imprisonment
Not a war veteran

Pezeshkiyan, Mas'ud

Minister of health and medical education in President
　Khatami's second cabinet (August 22, 2001–
　August 2, 2005); deputy of the Eighth (2008–12),
　Ninth (2012–16), and Tenth (2016–20) Majlis,
　Tabriz, Osku, and Azarshahr, East Azerbaijan
1954–, Mahabad, West Azerbaijan
MD, Tabriz University, 1985; MD, heart surgery, Teh-
　ran University of Medical Sciences, 1993
Mohammad-Ali, civil servant
Heart surgeon
No imprisonment
War veteran
IRGC militiaman (Basij)
Pezeshkiyan survived impeachment on June 17, 2003,
　while serving as health minister. After his term
　ended, he returned to Tabriz to continue work-
　ing as a heart surgeon and was then elected to
　consecutive terms in the Majlis. In 2013, the GC
　disqualified him from running in the presidential
　election, but in 2016, he was elected to the Majlis
　and became a deputy Speaker.

Pezhmanfar, Nasrollah

Deputy of the Ninth (2012–16) and Tenth (2016–20)
　Majlis, Mashhad and Kalat, Razavi Khorasan
1964–, Tehran, Tehran
Clerical education, Mashhad Seminary
Clergyman and educational deputy of Mashhad Semi-
　nary (starting in 2009)
No imprisonment
War veteran (wounded)
HI Pezhmanfar was also the director of Martyr
　Saduqi Seminary in Mashhad and a member
　of the Office of Representatives of the Supreme
　Leader in Universities.

Piran, Mohammad

Deputy of the Sixth Majlis, Razan, Hamadan
　(2000–2004)
1944–, Razan, Hamadan
MA, Persian literature
Ali-Akbar
Civil servant
Imprisoned before the revolution
Member of MNP
Piran was an early member of the MNP, for which
　he was sentenced to life imprisonment under the
　shah. The GC disqualified him from running in
　the Seventh Majlis election.

Pirmo'azzen, Kamaleddin

Deputy of the Ninth Majlis, Ardabil, Nir, Namin, and
　Sareyn, Ardabil (2012–16)
1959–, Ardabil, Ardabil
MS, urban planning, Islamic Azad University–Tabriz,
　1991
Yusef, bazaar tradesman
Provincial civil servant
No imprisonment
War veteran
Martyr's family (brother, Bahaeddin, plus ten other
　family members)
Pirmo'azzen, who comes from a well-known family in
　Ardabil, was the mayor of Sarab and then mayor
　of Ardabil. The GC rejected his qualifications
　to run for the Eighth and Tenth Majlis, but he
　did manage to get elected to the Ninth Majlis. In
　2009, he ran the office of presidential candidate
　Mir Hoseyn Musavi in Ardabil.

Pirmo'azzen, Nureddin

Deputy of the Sixth (2000–2004), and Seventh
　(2004–8) Majlis, Ardabil, Nir, and Namin,
　Ardabil
1958–, Ardabil, Ardabil
MD, surgery, Tabriz University, 1986
Yusef, bazaar tradesman

Thoracic surgeon
No imprisonment
War veteran
Martyr's family (brother, Bahaeddin, plus ten other family members)
Pirmo'azzen, a thoracic surgeon, moved to the United States after serving in the Majlis and underwent further training at Harvard Medical School before relocating to California. His younger brother, Kamaleddin, later took his seat in the Majlis.

Pirne'mati, Ebrahim

Deputy of the Fifth Majlis, Ardabil, Ardabil (1996–2000)
1959–2006, Ardabil, Ardabil
BS, agricultural engineering, Tabriz University
Ayyub
Civil servant, Agricultural Jihad
No imprisonment
Pirne'mati was the executive director of Pars Melli Agricultural, Industrial, and Livestock Company until his death in a car accident.

Pirzadeh, Seyyed Ahmad

Deputy of the Fourth Majlis, Dargaz, Razavi Khorasan (1992–96)
1953–, Dargaz, Razavi Khorasan
MS, engineering
Seyyed Abdolhoseyn
No imprisonment

Pishbin, Ahmad

Deputy of the Fourth (1992–96), Fifth (1996–2000), Sixth (2000–2004), and Seventh (2004–8) Majlis, Baft, Kerman
1949–, Baft, Kerman
BS, chemistry; MA, political science, 2000
Reyhan
Civil servant
No imprisonment
War veteran

Pishgahifard, Mrs. Zahra

Deputy of the Fifth Majlis, Isfahan, Isfahan (1997–2000)
1955–, Isfahan, Isfahan
BA, geography, 1984; PhD, political geography, Islamic Azad University–Tehran, 1992
Mehdi, mechanic
No imprisonment
Not a war veteran
Founder and member of the central council of the PMD
Pishgahifard and her husband, Sharifkhani, underwent military training in Lebanon before the revolution. They traveled to Israel and brought maps from there to give to the PLO. She is a former director of the Center for Women's Studies at Tehran University. In 2016, the GC rejected her qualifications for the Tenth Majlis. Pishgahifard is currently a professor of geography at Tehran University. Her husband, who was a student of Ayatollah Beheshti and a member of the central council of the IRP, was later in charge of the Alavi Foundation. Ayatollah Seyyed Mohammad Beheshti was the husband of Pishgahifard's maternal aunt. Her brother, Mohammad, was a high-level official in IRIB and married the daughter of Ayatollah Mohammad Mofatteh.

Pudineh, Mohammad-Hoseyn

Deputy of the Third Majlis, Zabol, Sistan and Baluchestan (1988–92)
1962–, Pudineh, Sistan and Baluchestan
High school diploma
Ali-Asghar, farmer
No imprisonment
War veteran (wounded seven times; victim of a chemical attack)
IRGC militiaman (commander)
Pudineh later worked in the Office of the President.

Puladi, Shapur

Deputy of the Eighth Majlis, Ilam, Eyvan, Mehran, Malekshahi, Shirvan, and Chardavol, Ilam (2008–12)

1969–, Chardavol, Ilam
BS, civil engineering, Islamic Azad University–Dezful
Mansur
Civil servant, ministries
No imprisonment
Puladi later became development deputy to the
    governor-general of Ilam.

Purbafrani, Abbas-Ali

Deputy of the Tenth Majlis, Na'in, Isfahan (2016–20)
1972–, Bafran, Isfahan
Associate's degree, Tehran University of Medical
    Sciences, 1994
Mohammad-Hasan, mason and architect
Not a war veteran
IRGC militiaman
Purbafrani, who is a Qur'an reciter, ran unsuccess-
    fully for the Ninth Majlis. Before being elected to
    the Tenth Majlis, he was a security deputy for the
    Ministry of Health.

Purdastan, Ahmad-Reza

Commander of the Islamic Republic of Iran Ground
    Forces (August 25, 2008–November 15, 2016);
    deputy general commander of the army (Novem-
    ber 19, 2016–November 5, 2017)
1956–, Masjed Soleyman, Khuzestan
No imprisonment
War veteran (100 months)
Purdastan served as head of the Ground Forces Officers'
    Academy and was the army's chief commander in
    Fars and Kohgiluyeh and Buyer Ahmad Provinces.

Purebrahimi-Davarani, Mohammad-Reza

Deputy of the Ninth (2012–16) and Tenth (2016–20)
    Majlis, Kerman and Ravar, Kerman
1970–, Rafsanjan, Kerman
BA, business administration, Isfahan University of
    Technology, 1994; MA, business administration,
    Shahid Beheshti University; PhD, financial man-
    agement, Tehran University

No imprisonment
War veteran (1985–88)
IRGC militiaman (Basij)
Purebrahimi-Davarani, a conservative, is an expert on
    Iran's stock market, and he has been a professor at
    Shahid Beheshti University and Tehran University.

Purfatemi, Seyyed Mohammad-Mehdi

Deputy of the Sixth (2000–2004), Seventh (2004–8),
    Eighth (2008–12), and Ninth (2012–16) Majlis,
    Dashti and Tangestan, Bushehr
1962–, Dashti, Bushehr
Clerical education, Qom Seminary
Seyyed Hoseyn, clergyman (ayatollah)
Clergyman and employee of the Pious Endowments
    and Charity Affairs Organization
No imprisonment
War veteran
The GC disqualified HI Purfatemi from running
    in the 2016 Majlis election. He was then put in
    charge of prayers and cultural affairs of residen-
    tial camps of the Ministry of Petroleum.

Purgol, Mohammad-Mehdi

Deputy of the First (1981–84) and Second (1984–88)
    Majlis, Bandar-e Anzali, Gilan
1932–2010, Bandar-e Anzali, Gilan
BA, Arabic literature; MA, Arabic literature; PhD,
    theology
Hasan
No imprisonment
Not a war veteran
Member of CIC/PCIC
After serving in the Majlis, Purgol became ambas-
    sador to Norway and then dean of the school of
    theology at Ferdowsi University of Mashhad.

Purhoseyn-Shaqlan, Shakur

Deputy of the Tenth Majlis, Parsabad and Bilehsavar,
    Ardabil (2016–20)
1977–, Parsabad, Ardabil

PhD, law, Shahid Beheshti University
Esma'il
Judge
No imprisonment
Not a war veteran
Martyr's family (brother, Rahim)

Purjazayeri, Samir

Deputy of the Sixth Majlis, Khorramshahr, Khuzestan
(2000–2004)
1950–, Khorramshahr, Khuzestan
PhD, chemistry
Kazem
No imprisonment

Purmohammadi, Mohammad-Taqi

Member of the Fourth (2007–16) and Fifth (2016–22)
Assembly of Experts, East Azerbaijan
1956–, Marand, East Azerbaijan
Clerical education, Qom Seminary
Soltan-Ali
Clergyman
No imprisonment
War veteran
IRGC militiaman
HI Purmohammadi, commander of the Ardabil IRGC
during the Iran–Iraq War, became the Friday
prayer leader of Maragheh.

Purmohammadi, Mostafa

Interior minister in President Ahmadinejad's first
cabinet (August 24, 2005–April 2008); head of the
State General Inspectorate Organization (July 2,
2008–August 2013); minister of justice in President Rouhani's first cabinet (August 15, 2013–August 13, 2017)
1959–, Qom, Qom
Clerical education, Haqqani Seminary
Hoseyn, tailor
Head of the social-political bureau in the Office of the
Supreme Leader (2002–5)

No imprisonment
Not a war veteran
HI Purmohammadi attended the Haqqani Seminary
in Qom, which trained many of the leading judicial and intelligence officials of postrevolutionary
Iran, beginning in 1971. After the revolution, at
only twenty years old, he became a revolutionary
prosecutor in Masjed Soleyman. He later held
this post in Hormozgan and Khorasan (1979–86).
He was a high-level official in MIIRI from 1987
to the late 1990s and served as head of the State
General Inspectorate Organization from July 2,
2008 to August 2013. During his tenure as head of
the MIIRI Counterintelligence Directorate and its
representative in Evin Prison (1987–90), Purmohammadi was a member of a special committee
(nicknamed the "death committee") that oversaw
the extrajudicial execution of thousands (estimates vary between 2,800 and 5,000) of political
prisoners following Ayatollah Khomeini's edict in
1988. President Ahmadinejad dismissed him as
interior minister in April 2008. In 2013, he registered to run in the presidential election. In 2015,
the GC rejected his qualifications to run for the
Assembly of Experts. Purmohammadi's nephew,
Ali-Asghar Purmohammadi, is the director of
IRIB's Channel 3 television network.

Purmohammadi-Fallah, Ali

Deputy of the Third Majlis, Astaneh-ye Ashrafiyyeh,
Gilan (1988–92)
1947–, Astaneh-ye Ashrafiyyeh, Gilan
BA
Mohammad-Ali
No imprisonment

Purmokhtar, Mohammad-Ali

Deputy of the Ninth (2012–16) and Tenth (2016–20)
Majlis, Bahar and Kabudarahang, Hamadan
1962–, Bahar, Hamadan
MA, law, Islamic Azad University–Tehran
No imprisonment

War veteran (served for seventy-five months;
    wounded)
IRGC militiaman
Martyr's family
Purmokhtar, a high-level commander within the
    IRGC, became deputy chief of Law Enforcement
    Forces.

Purnejati, Ahmad

Deputy of the Sixth Majlis, Tehran, Tehran
    (2000–2004)
1954–, Qom, Qom
MD, dentistry, Tehran University, 1985
Hoseyn, pastry seller
Imprisoned before the revolution
Founding member of ADVIR
Purnejati, who was among the initial founders of the
    MIIRI, has held other posts such as head of the
    medical committee of the Construction Jihad,
    head of the political bureau of MI, member of the
    HCCR, political deputy of the prosecutor-general,
    deputy representative of the supreme leader for
    pilgrimage affairs, media deputy for the Ministry
    of Culture, and deputy director of IRIB.

Purostad, Ali-Akbar

Deputy of the First Majlis, Tehran, Tehran (1981–84)
1929–, Tehran, Tehran
Clerical education
Gholam-Ali
No imprisonment
Not a war veteran
Purostad was a representative of the MDAFL looking
    into foreign contracts before being elected to the
    First Majlis.

Purqorban, Khan Ali

Deputy of the Fourth Majlis, Kaleybar, East Azerbai-
    jan (1992–96)
1950–, Kaleybar, East Azerbaijan
High school diploma

Nazarali
No imprisonment

Pursalari, Hoseyn

Deputy of the First (1982–84) and Second (1984–88)
    Majlis, Kahnuj, Kerman
1942–, Kahnuj, Kerman
Clerical education
Ali
Clergyman
No imprisonment
Not a war veteran
HI Pursalari is a former local komiteh head and revo-
    lutionary prosecutor.

Purshasb, Abdolali

Commander of the Islamic Republic of Iran Ground
    Forces (October 1, 1997–February 7, 2001); chief
    of the joint staff of the Islamic Republic of Iran
    Army (February 5, 2001–September 25, 2005)
Military school (Pakistan)
War veteran
Brigadier General Purshasb was the deputy inspectorate
    of the chief of the Armed Forces General Staff from
    September 26, 2005, to November 10, 2013.

Purzaman, Rasul

Deputy of the Fourth (1992–96) and Seventh (2004–8)
    Majlis, Naqadeh, West Azerbaijan
1953–, Naqadeh, West Azerbaijan
BA, Persian literature
No imprisonment

Qaderi, Ja'far

Deputy of the Eighth (2008–12) and Ninth (2012–16)
    Majlis, Shiraz, Fars
1964–, Lamerd, Fars
BA, economics, Shiraz University; MA, economics,
    Shiraz University; PhD, economics, Tarbiyat-e
    Modarres University

Heydar
Provincial civil servant
No imprisonment
War veteran
Qaderi has been a rector and faculty member at
    Shiraz University since 1994. He was mayor of
    Shiraz from 2005 to 2007. He was not elected to
    the Tenth Majlis.

Qaderi, Mohammad-Rauf

Deputy of the Fifth Majlis, Paveh and Javanrud, Ker-
    manshah (1996–2000)
1963–, Ravansar, Kermanshah
BA, management
Mohammad
No imprisonment
Qaderi is a Sunni politician.

Qaderi, Mostafa

Deputy of the Second Majlis, Piranshahr and Sar-
    dasht, West Azerbaijan (1984–88)
1956–, Piranshahr, West Azerbaijan
BA, accounting
Ebrahim
No imprisonment

Qadermarzi, Hamed

Deputy of the Ninth Majlis, Qorveh and Dehgolan,
    Kurdistan (2012–16)
1979–, Dehgolan, Kurdistan
BS, urban planning, Tabriz University; MS,
    rural planning, Tarbiyat-e Modarres Univer-
    sity; PhD, rural planning, Shahid Beheshti
    University, 2009
Hasan, clergyman
Professor of urban planning at Payam-e Nur Univer-
    sity, Sanandaj
No imprisonment
Not a war veteran
The GC disqualified Qadermarzi, a Sunni, from run-
    ning in the 2016 Majlis election.

Qadiri, Mohammad-Hasan

Member of the Fourth Guardian Council (2001–4)
1938–2008, Isfahan, Isfahan
Clerical education, Najaf Seminary (Iraq)
Ali, clergyman (ayatollah)
Clergyman
No imprisonment
Not a war veteran
HI Qadiri went to Najaf in 1958. He has worked in the
    offices of Ayatollahs Khomeini, Araki, Khame-
    nei, and Behjat, responding to religious questions
    from pious followers and matters concerning
    fatwas.

Qa'edrahmat, Abbas

Deputy of the Ninth Majlis, Dorud and Azna, Lor-
    estan (2012–16)
1969–, Dorud, Lorestan
BS, Isfahan University of Technology; MS, psychol-
    ogy, Islamic Azad University–Rudhen; PhD,
    geography, Shahid Beheshti University
Azizollah
Civil servant, state companies; professor at Payam-e
    Nur University, Kurdistan
No imprisonment
War veteran (wounded)
IRGC militiaman (Basij)

Qaemi-Amiri, Ali

Member of the Assembly for the Final Examination of
    the Constitution, Mazandaran (1979); deputy of
    the First Majlis, Babolsar and Bandpay, Mazanda-
    ran (1980–84)
1937–, Babol, Mazandaran
BA, Tehran's Higher Teachers Training College; PhD,
    sociology and educational science; clerical educa-
    tion, Qom Seminary
Nasrollah, clergyman
Professor and author
No imprisonment
Not a war veteran

Qaemifar [Mollay-e Semnani], Mehdi

Deputy of the First Majlis, Buyer Ahmad and Dena,
    Kohgiluyeh and Buyer Ahmad (1981–84); deputy
    of the Second Majlis, Sarvestan, Fars (1984–88)
1954–, Shahr-e Rey, Tehran
Clerical education
Ali-Akbar
Clergyman
No imprisonment
Not a war veteran
HI Qaemifar's name in the First Majlis was Mollay-e
    Semnani.

Qahremani, Mohammad-Mehdi

Deputy of the Fifth Majlis, Shiraz, Fars (1996–2000)
1956–, Abadan, Khuzestan
BS, civil engineering
Avaz
No imprisonment

Qalibaf, Mohammad-Baqer

Chief of Law Enforcement Forces (June 27, 2000–
    April 4, 2005); mayor of Tehran (September
    2005–17); member of the Eighth Expediency
    Discernment Assembly (2017–22)
August 23, 1961–, Torqabeh, Razavi Khorasan
BA, political geography, Tehran University; MA, po-
    litical geography, Tarbiyat-e Modarres University,
    1996; PhD, political geography, Tarbiyat-e Modar-
    res University, 2001
Hoseyn, baker
Military and security official
No imprisonment
War veteran
IRGC militiaman (brigadier general)
Martyr's family (brother killed at the war front)
Qalibaf joined the IRGC in 1980 and was one of
    its youngest commanders during the Iran–Iraq
    War. A pilot by training, he has held such posts
    as commander of Khatam al-Anbia Construc-
    tion Headquarters (1994–97), commander of the

IRGC's air force (October 29, 1997–2000), and
commander of LEF, and he has been Tehran's
longest-serving mayor. In 1999, after the student
uprising at Tehran University, Qalibaf was one
of the twenty-four IRGC commanders who sent
a threatening letter to President Mohammad
Khatami urging a crackdown. He was also not on
good terms with President Ahmadinejad because
Ahmadinejad prevented Qalibaf from attending
cabinet meetings. Qalibaf received 13.9 percent of
the vote in the first round of the 2005 presidential election, and he finished second in the 2013
presidential election with 16.5 percent of the vote.
He was approved by the GC as one of six candidates positively vetted for the presidency in 2017
but withdrew a few days before the race in favor of
fellow candidate Seyyed Ebrahim Ra'isi.

Qamari, Daryush

Deputy of the Seventh (2005–8) and Eighth (2008–12)
    Majlis, Ilam, Eyvan, Mehran, Malekshahi,
    Shirvan, and Chardavol, Ilam
1970–, Ilam, Ilam
PhD, political science
Ne'mat
Academia
No imprisonment
Not a war veteran

Qanbari-Adivi, Ali

Deputy of the Fifth (1996–2000) and Sixth (2000–
    2004) Majlis, Ardal, Farsan, and Kiyar, Chahar
    Mahal and Bakhtiari
1955–, Kuhrang, Chahar Mahal and Bakhtiari
PhD, economics
Fattah
Civil servant
No imprisonment

Qanbari-Maman, Jamshid

Deputy of the Fourth (1992–96) and Fifth (1996–2000)
    Majlis, Miyaneh, East Azerbaijan

1950–, Miyaneh, East Azerbaijan
BS, electrical engineering, 1985; MS, aviation engineering, 1995
Ahmad-Ali
No imprisonment

Qanbari-Qazikolahi, Abdolali

Deputy of the Second Majlis, Qaemshahr, Mazandaran (1984–88)
1950–, Qaemshahr, Mazandaran
Clerical education
Hoseyn, farmer
Clergyman
No imprisonment
HI Qanbari-Qazikolahi was a judge in revolutionary and army courts in Hormozgan, Fars, and Mazandaran Provinces. He also represented Ayatollah Khomeini in the Construction Jihad in Qaemshahr.

Qandehari, Qorbanali

Deputy of the Fifth (1996–2000) and Sixth (2000–2001) Majlis, Gorgan, Golestan
1958–May 17, 2001, Gorgan, Golestan
Clerical education; MA, management
Gholam-Hoseyn
Clergyman (HI)
No imprisonment
Founding member of the Islamic Iran Solidarity Party
Qandehari died in a plane crash.

Qandi, Mahmud

Minister of post, telegraph, and telephones in the Revolutionary Council cabinet (November 29, 1979–80) and PM Raja'i's cabinet (1980–81)
1944–June 28, 1981, Tehran, Tehran
BS, electrical engineering, Tehran University, 1966; PhD, electrical engineering, University of California, Davis (USA), 1971; dissertation title: "Energy Spectrum of Electrons in Non-Crystalline Materials"
Ahmad, bazaar tradesman
Professor of electronics
No imprisonment
Not a war veteran
Member of the IRP
Qandi, who was active in the Muslim Student Association in the United States before the revolution, was killed in the bombing of the IRP headquarters.

Qarani, Valiyollah

Member of the Revolutionary Council (February 11–March 26, 1979); chief of the joint staff of the Islamic Republic of Iran Army (February 11–March 26, 1979)
1913–April 23, 1979, Tehran, Tehran
BS, military science, Ground Forces Officers' Academy
Mirza Aqa Jan, civil servant, Iranian Tobacco Company
Military officer
Imprisoned before the revolution
Not a war veteran
Lieutenant General Qarani entered the Ground Forces Officers' Academy in 1930 and took an active part in the 1953 coup against Premier Mosaddeq. He became a major general in 1957 and was in charge of the Iranian Army's intelligence staff (G-2). In February 1958, while in the latter post, the shah's regime arrested him for plotting a coup and sentenced him to three years' imprisonment, but released him early. In the days leading to the revolution, he held talks with American diplomats stationed at the American embassy in Tehran and tried to alleviate their concerns about the revolution and Ayatollah Khomeini. After the revolution, PM Bazargan appointed Qarani chief of JSIRIA, but Qarani left the post in less than two months. The Forqan group assassinated Qarani on April 23, 1979, less than a month after he left the post.

Qarayi-Ashtiyani, Mohammad-Reza

Deputy general commander of the army (September 26, 2005–August 25, 2008)
BS, military science, Ground Forces Officers' Academy; PhD, military science, Supreme National Defense University
War veteran
On November 10, 2013, Ayatollah Khamenei appointed Brigadier General Qarayi-Ashtiyani as deputy inspectorate of the chief of staff of the Iranian Armed Forces.

Qarhekhani-Alustani, Asadollah

Deputy of the Seventh (2004–8), Eighth (2008–12), and Tenth (2016–20) Majlis, Aliabad Katul, Golestan
1959–, Aliabad Katul, Golestan
BA, Islamic studies; MA, management
Mohammad
Education official in Mazandaran Province
No imprisonment
Qarhekhani-Alustani, a conservative, was not elected to the Ninth Majlis. He then became an adviser to the managing director of the National Iranian Gas Company.

Qasemi, Abdolvahhab

Deputy of the First Majlis, Sari, Mazandaran (1980–81)
1933–June 28, 1981, Savadkuh, Mazandaran
Clerical education, Mashhad Seminary
Azizollah, clergyman
Clergyman
Imprisoned before the revolution
Not a war veteran
HI Qasemi was killed in the bombing of the IRP headquarters and was buried in Qom.

Qasemi, Fereydun

Deputy of the Third Majlis, Varzaqan, East Azerbaijan (1988–92)

1943–date unknown, Varzaqan, East Azerbaijan
High school diploma; clerical education (elementary level)
Qasem
No imprisonment
Qasemi, who was absent from many Majlis sessions, has passed away (date unknown).

Qasemi, Khodanazar

Deputy of the Third (1988–92) and Fifth (1996–2000) Majlis, Dashtestan, Bushehr
1955–, Dashtestan, Bushehr
BA, law
Hoseyn
No imprisonment
Not a war veteran

Qasemi, Majid

Governor of the Central Bank (1986–September 1989)
1952–, Tehran, Tehran
PhD, economics, University of Southampton (England), 2001; dissertation title: "Estimation of Urban Household Demand in Iran"
Ali-Hoseyn
No imprisonment
Not a war veteran
Founding member of the PMD

Qasemi, Rostam

Minister of petroleum in President Ahmadinejad's second cabinet (August 13, 2011–August 3, 2013)
1964–, Mohr, Fars
BS, civil engineering, 1995
No imprisonment
War veteran
IRGC Militiaman (brigadier general, commander of Khatam al-Anbia Construction Headquarters)
The Majlis elected Qasemi as minister of petroleum with 216 positive votes, twenty-two negative votes, and seven abstentions. During the

presidency of Hassan Rouhani, he became an adviser to the First VP. He is on the US Treasury Office of Foreign Assets Control's Specially Designated Nationals and Blocked Persons List because he is charged with supporting terrorism and trying to acquire weapons of mass destruction.

Qasemi[pur], Abdollah

Deputy of the Fifth Majlis, Marivan, Kurdistan
    (1996–2000)
1952–, Marivan, Kurdistan
BA
Mohammad-Saleh, local nobility
Academia
No imprisonment

Qasemi-Golak, Yusef

Deputy of the Eighth Majlis, Lahijan and Siyahkal,
    Gilan (2008–12)
1963–, Lahijan, Gilan
BA, international law
Mohsen
No imprisonment
IRGC militiaman
Qasemi-Golak teaches at the IRGC's Imam Hoseyn
    University.

Qasempur, Samad

Deputy of the Fifth Majlis, Tabriz, East Azerbaijan
    (1996–2000)
1958–, Tabriz, East Azerbaijan
BA, Persian literature
Qader
Warden of Tabriz Prison
No imprisonment
War veteran
IRGC militiaman
After the war, Qasempur was in charge of the Tabriz
    IRGC's cooperative foundation. He then became
    the warden of Tabriz Prison before entering the

Majlis. After serving in the Majlis, he worked for six years as an adviser to the minister of commerce. In 2012, Qasempur was sentenced to death for drug trafficking but the supreme leader pardoned him.

Qasemzadeh, Hoseyn-Ali

Deputy of the Fifth (1996–2000), Sixth (2000–2004),
    and Seventh (2004–8) Majlis, Babol, Mazandaran
1959–, Babol, Mazandaran
PhD, theology; clerical education
Ali-Asghar
Academia
No imprisonment

Qashqavi, Hasan

Deputy of the Fourth Majlis, Shahriyar and Robat
    Karim, Tehran (1992–96); deputy of the Sixth
    Majlis, Robat Karim, Tehran (2000–2004)
1957–, Babol, Mazandaran
BA, law
Mohammad-Ali
No imprisonment
After leaving the Majlis, Qashqavi became the fifth
    spokesperson of the Ministry of Foreign Affairs,
    ambassador to Switzerland, and deputy counselor
    of the Ministry of Foreign Affairs.

Qatmiri, Seyyed Hoseyn

Deputy of the Second Majlis, Shiraz, Fars (1984–88)
1944–, Shiraz, Fars
BS, mathematics
Seyyed Ja'far
No imprisonment

Qavami, Hadi

Deputy of the Eighth (2008–12), Ninth (2012–16),
    and Tenth (2016–20) Majlis, Esfarayen, North
    Khorasan
1967–, Esfarayen, North Khorasan

BA, economics, Allameh Tabataba'i University, 1991;
MA, economics, Tarbiyat-e Modarres University,
1995; PhD, economics, Tarbiyat-e Modarres Uni-
versity, 2003
Ebrahim
Governor of Esfarayen; professor at Ferdowsi Univer-
sity of Mashhad
No imprisonment
Not a war veteran

Qavami, Karim

Commander of the Islamic Republic of Iran Air Force
(October 5, 2004–October 29, 2006)
1950–, Ardabil, Ardabil
BS, military science, Ground Forces Officers' Acad-
emy, 1973; MS, military science, Iranian Army
Command and General Staff College
Military pilot (brigadier general)
No imprisonment
War veteran
Qavami underwent military flight training overseas
in the 1970s.

Qavami, Seyyed Naser

Deputy of the Sixth Majlis, Qazvin, Qazvin
(2000–2004)
1943–, Qazvin, Qazvin
Clerical education
Seyyed Dadash, farmer
Clergyman (HI)
No imprisonment
Qavami, a reformist, was close to former Speaker
Mehdi Karrubi.

Qaza'i-Niyyari, Ahad

Deputy of the Fifth Majlis, Ardabil, Ardabil (1996–2000)
1950–, Ardabil, Ardabil
MA, political science
Reza
No imprisonment
War veteran

Qaza'i-Niyyari, a reformist, has worked in the Ministry of Foreign Affairs, as counsel general in India,
and as ambassador to Azerbaijan.

Qazi-Dezfuli, Seyyed Majdeddin

Member of the First Assembly of Experts, Khuzestan
(1983–February 2, 1986)
1900–February 2, 1986, Dezful, Khuzestan
Clerical education
Seyyed Abdolhoseyn, clergyman
Clergyman
No imprisonment
Not a war veteran
Ayatollah Qazi-Dezfuli was the Friday prayer leader
of Dezful and stayed in the city during the years
of the Iran–Iraq War despite the heavy bombard-
ment of the city.

Qazipur, Mir Naqi

Deputy of the Third (1988–92) and Fourth (1992–96)
Majlis, Ardabil, Ardabil
1943–, Ardabil, Ardabil
Clerical education
Mir Aqa
Clergyman
Head of Ardabil's revolutionary tribunals
No imprisonment
Not a war veteran
After leaving the Majlis, HI Qazipur worked as a
judge in the CAJ.

Qazipur, Nader

Deputy of the Eighth (2008–12), Ninth (2012–16), and
Tenth (2016–20) Majlis, Urmia, West Azerbaijan
1958–, Urmia, West Azerbaijan
BS, physics, Urmia University; MA, public adminis-
tration, Urmia University
Shobeyr
Civil servant in West Azerbaijan; lieutenant governor
of Piranshahr
No imprisonment

War veteran (forty-two months)

IRGC militiaman

Qazipur was in charge of Ayatollah Khamenei's campaign headquarters in West Azerbaijan during the 1981 and 1985 presidential elections. He was affiliated with the Imam Sadeq's 83 Brigade (Qom), the IRGC's military unit composed of clerics, which was formed during the Iran–Iraq War and provides protection for the supreme leader. The GC rejected his credentials for the Seventh Majlis. Qazipur is the son-in-law of Seyyed Hasan Va'ez-Musavi-Anzabi.

Qazizadeh-Hashemi, Seyyed Amir-Hoseyn

Deputy of the Eighth (2008–12), Ninth (2012–16), and Tenth (2016–20) Majlis, Mashhad and Kalat, Razavi Khorasan

1971–, Fariman, Razavi Khorasan

MD, surgery (ear, nose, and throat), 2002

Seyyed Hasan

Surgeon

No imprisonment

War veteran (wounded)

Martyr's family (cousin, Ali)

Spokesperson of the SFIR

Qazizadeh-Hashemi, a former rector of Semnan University of Medical Sciences, is a faculty member at Shahid Beheshti University. He and his younger brother, Seyyed Ehsan, were elected to the Tenth Majlis together. He is also the cousin of Seyyed Hasan Qazizadeh-Hashemi, the health minister in President Rouhani's first cabinet, and Seyyed Hoseyn Qazizadeh-Hashemi, a former MP from Fariman.

Qazizadeh-Hashemi, Seyyed Ehsan

Deputy of the Tenth Majlis, Fariman, Razavi Khorasan (2016–20)

1976–, Fariman, Razavi Khorasan

Pursuing a PhD in international law

Seyyed Hasan

No imprisonment

Not a war veteran

Martyr's family (cousin, Ali)

Qazizadeh-Hashemi worked in the Ministry of Culture and Islamic Guidance and was Iran's cultural attaché in Croatia for a while. He is the younger brother of Seyyed Amir-Hoseyn Qazizadeh-Hashemi and the cousin of Seyyed Hasan Qazizadeh-Hashemi and Seyyed Hoseyn Qazizadeh-Hashemi.

Qazizadeh-Hashemi, Seyyed Hasan

Minister of health and medical education in President Rouhani's first (August 15, 2013–August 13, 2017) and second (August 20, 2017–2021) cabinets

1959–, Fariman, Razavi Khorasan

MD, medicine, Mashhad University of Medical Sciences, 1986; MD, ophthalmology, Mashhad University of Medical Sciences, 1989

Seyyed Ahmad, grocer

Ophthalmologist and university professor

No imprisonment

War veteran (thirty-three months)

IRGC militiaman

Martyr's family (brother, Ali, died in 1993 as a victim of Iraqi chemical attacks)

Qazizadeh-Hashemi was a member of the central committee of the Construction Jihad from 1981 to 1983. He was also a professor of ophthalmology at Shahid Beheshti University of Medical Sciences. His older brother, Seyyed Hoseyn, and two of his cousins, Seyyed Amir-Hoseyn and Seyyed Ehsan Qazizadeh-Hashemi, have been MPs. His wife is a professor of oncology at Tehran University of Medical Sciences.

Qazizadeh-Hashemi, Seyyed Hoseyn

Deputy of the Second (1984–88) and Third (1988–92) Majlis, Fariman, Razavi Khorasan

1952–, Fariman, Razavi Khorasan

High school diploma

Seyyed Ahmad, grocer

No imprisonment

War veteran
Martyr's family (brother, Ali, died in 1993 as a victim
    of Iraqi chemical attacks)

Qermezi, Shahriyar

Deputy of the Fifth Majlis, Semirom, Isfahan
    (1996–2000)
1959–, Kazerun, Fars
BA, educational sciences
Sohrab
No imprisonment

Qobadi, Khodadad

Deputy of the Fifth (1996–2000) and Sixth (2000–
    2004) Majlis, Eqlid, Fars
1957–, Eqlid, Fars
MA, management
Ali-Karam
Civil servant
No imprisonment

Qobadi-Hamzehkhani, Ali-Akbar

Deputy of the Seventh Majlis, Marvdasht and Arsan-
    jan, Fars (2004–8)
1955–, Kayforouz, Fars
MS, geology
Darab
Civil servant
No imprisonment

Qoddusi, Ali

Prosecutor-general of the revolutionary courts (Au-
    gust 6, 1979–September 5, 1981); member of the
    HCJ (July 13, 1980–September 5, 1981)
1927–September 5, 1981, Nahavand, Hamadan
Clerical education, Qom Seminary, 1962
Ahmad, clergyman (molla)
Clergyman
Imprisoned before the revolution
Not a war veteran

Martyr's family (son, Mohammad-Hasan, killed at the
    war front)
Member of the SQSS
For a decade before the revolution, Ayatollah Qoddusi
    was in charge of the influential Haqqani Sem-
    inary where many of the future elites of the Is-
    lamic Republic were educated. He was a member
    of the committee welcoming Ayatollah Khomeini
    back to Iran. Ayatollah Khomeini appointed
    Qoddusi as prosecutor-general of the revolution-
    ary courts on August 6, 1979, and he wrote the
    bylaws for the revolutionary courts. He tried to
    resign from that post in March 1980, but Ayatol-
    lah Khomeini did not accept his resignation. His
    son, Mohammad-Hasan Qoddusi (b. 1957), was
    involved in the takeover of the American embassy
    and was killed at the war front on January 6, 1981.
    PMOI assassinated Qoddusi on September 5,
    1981. Qoddusi was the son-in-law of the famous
    philosopher-theologian Allameh Tabataba'i.

Qoli, Mohammad-Hasan

Deputy of the Fourth Majlis, Aligudarz, Lorestan
    (1992–96)
1963–, Aligudarz, Lorestan
BA
Hoseyn-Ali
No imprisonment

Qolizadeh, Rahman-Qoli

Deputy of the Fifth Majlis, Bojnurd, North Khorasan
    (1996–2000)
1954–, Bojnurd, North Khorasan
MA
Hasan
No imprisonment
Qolizadeh is a reformist.

Qolizadeh, Yaghmor

Deputy of the Third Majlis, Minudasht, Golestan
    (1988–92)
1959–, Minudasht, Golestan

BA
Vardi Khan
No imprisonment
Qolizadeh, a Sunni Turkoman, later became the director-general of an Iranian automobile company in Turkmenistan.

Qomi, Mohammad

Deputy of the Third (1988–92), Fourth (1992–96), and Fifth (1996–2000) Majlis, Varamin, Tehran; deputy of the Sixth (2000–2004), Seventh (2004–8), and Tenth (2016–20) Majlis, Pakdasht, Tehran
1952–, Shahr-e Rey, Tehran
MA, educational planning, PhD, international relations
Hoseyn, farmer
Teacher and education official
Imprisoned before the revolution
War veteran
Martyr's family (three brothers—Hasan, Ali, and Valiyollah—and a nephew, Vahid, were killed at the war front or assassinated)
Member of the central council of the NTP
Mohammad Qomi was one of Ayatollah Khomeini's bodyguards and later became rector of Islamic Azad University–Parand. He was a member of the Majlis leadership from 1999 to 2003 but was not elected to the Eighth or Ninth Majlis. His brother, Mohsen, is a member of the AE.

Qomi, Mohsen

Member of the Third (1999–2006), Fourth (2007–16), and Fifth (2016–22) Assembly of Experts, Tehran
1960–, Varamin, Tehran
Clerical education, Qom Seminary; BA, educational sciences, University of Judicial Sciences–Qom; MA, philosophy, Tehran University; PhD, philosophy, Tehran University; dissertation title: "The Theoretical Foundations of Post-Modernism: A Case Study of Jean-François Lyotard"
Hoseyn, farmer
Clergyman
War veteran (wounded)

Martyr's family (three brothers—Hasan, Ali, and Valiyollah—and a nephew, Vahid, were killed at the war front or assassinated)
Member of the central council of the SCC
HI Qomi has been deputy for international communications in the Office of the Supreme Leader since 2005. He was a member of the HCCR and served as head of the headquarters representing the supreme leader in universities from November 24, 1998, to January 10, 2006. Qomi was under consideration for the minister of intelligence post when President Rouhani came to office.

Qorbani, Ali

Deputy of the Tenth Majlis, Bojnurd, North Khorasan (2016–20)
1972–, Maneh and Samalqan, North Khorasan
PhD, geography and rural planning, Ferdowsi University of Mashhad
Father's name unknown, farmer
Provincial civil servant in North Khorasan
No imprisonment
Not a war veteran

Qorbani, Mohammad-Hoseyn

Deputy of the Ninth (2012–16) and Tenth (2016–20) Majlis, Astaneh-ye Ashrafiyyeh and Bandar-e Kiashahr, Gilan
1965–, Astaneh-ye Ashrafiyyeh, Gilan
MD, dentistry, Shahid Beheshti University of Medical Sciences, 1996
Dentist
No imprisonment
War veteran (five years; wounded three times)
Martyr's family (brother killed at the war front)
Qorbani, a conservative, was spokesperson for the health committee in the Majlis.

Qorbani, Musa

Deputy of the Fifth (1996–2000), Sixth (2000–2004), Seventh (2004–8), and Eighth (2008–12) Majlis, Qaenat, South Khorasan

September 11, 1960–, Qaenat, South Khorasan

BA, judicial law, Qom University, 1983; clerical education, Qom Seminary

Hasan, farmer

Clergyman

No imprisonment

Not a war veteran

Martyr's family (brother killed at the war front)

HI Qorbani has been active in the judiciary branch, holding such posts as deputy justice minister, head of the Penitentiary Organization (1994–95), and head of the justice administration in Mazandaran, Kermanshah, and Sistan and Baluchestan Provinces. He did not take part in the elections for the Ninth Majlis and instead worked in the State Supreme Court.

Qorbani-Panjah, Zeynol'abedin

Deputy of the Second Majlis, Astaneh-ye Ashrafiyyeh, Gilan (1984–88); member of the Second (1991–98), Third (1999–2006), Fourth (2007–16), and Fifth (2016–22) Assembly of Experts, Gilan

1933–, Lahijan, Gilan

Clerical education, Qom Seminary

Gholam-Hasan, farmer

Clergyman

Imprisoned before the revolution (first time in 1963)

Not a war veteran

After the revolution, Ayatollah Qorbani held positions such as judge in the revolutionary tribunals of Gilan Province, Friday prayer leader and Khomeini's representative in Lahijan (1981–1999), and Friday prayer leader of Rasht. He has been the supreme leader's representative in Gilan since 2001.

Qoreh Seyyed Romiyani, Mir Hadi

Deputy of the Ninth Majlis, Tabriz, Osku, and Azarshahr, East Azerbaijan (2012–16)

1975–, Azarshahr, East Azerbaijan

BA, judicial law, University of Judicial Sciences and Administrative Services; MA, international law, Mofid University

Judiciary official

No imprisonment

Not a war veteran

Qoreh Seyyed Romiyani returned to the judiciary after finishing his term in the Majlis.

Qoreyshi, Mir Ali-Akbar

Member of the Assembly for the Final Examination of the Constitution, West Azerbaijan (1979); member of the First (1983–90), Second (1991–98), Third (1999–2006), Fourth (2007–16), and Fifth (2016–22) Assembly of Experts, West Azerbaijan

1928–, Bonab, East Azerbaijan

Clerical education, Qom Seminary

Mir Mohammad, clergyman

Clergyman

Imprisoned before the revolution (released from internal exile on August 30, 1978)

Not a war veteran

Martyr's family (son-in-law)

Ayatollah Qoreyshi, a long-time resident of Orumiyeh, was head of the city's clerical association. He was Ayatollah Khomeini's representative in the Construction Jihad of East Azerbaijan and Ayatollah Khamenei's representative in Orumiyeh University. His son, Mir Mehdi, is the supreme leader's representative and the Friday prayer leader of Orumiyeh.

Qoreyshi, Seyyed Mohammad-Ali

Deputy of the Second (1984–88), Third (1988–92), and Fifth (1998–2000) Majlis, Khomeyn, Markazi

1934–2016, Khansar, Isfahan

Clerical education, Qom Seminary

Seyyed Jamal, clergyman

Clergyman and teacher

Imprisoned before the revolution

Not a war veteran

Martyr's family (brother, HI Seyyed Mohammad-Kazem Qoreyshi, killed by the shah's regime)

Qoreyshi taught for twenty years and retired in 1973. He was suffering from Parkinson's disease before he died.

Qotbzadeh, Sadeq

Member of the Revolutionary Council (1979–80);
 managing director of the National Iranian Radio
 and Television (later renamed IRIB) (1979); minister of foreign affairs in the Revolutionary Council
 cabinet (November 30, 1979–November 7, 1980)
1936–September 15, 1982, Isfahan, Isfahan
BA, Notre Dame University (Canada), 1969
Hoseyn, lumber merchant
Political activist
Imprisoned before the revolution
Not a war veteran
Qotbzadeh was involved in anti-shah activities in the
 1950s, for which he was arrested several times.
 He went to the United States to study in 1958 but
 did not finish his studies at Georgetown University due to his political activism. He was expelled
 from the United States in 1962 and again in 1967,
 and he spent time in the Middle East (Algeria,
 Iraq, Libya, and Syria), Europe, and Canada. He
 met Ayatollah Khomeini in Iraq, became one of
 his roving ambassadors, and in 1978, joined him
 in Paris as one of his closest advisers. Qotbzadeh
 was appointed as the caretaker of the National
 Iranian Radio and Television (NIRT) on February
 2, 1979, during the tenure of PM Bazargan. A few
 months later, he became its first managing director. His attempts to control program content and
 purge some NIRT personnel proved controversial.
 He became foreign minister of the Revolutionary
 Council cabinet on November 30, 1979, replacing
 Banisadr, who was caretaker. This appointment
 came a few weeks after the takeover of the American embassy, and he had to defend the position
 of the Iranian regime on the issue while trying to
 negotiate the release of the hostages. Qotbzadeh
 was a candidate in the first presidential election
 in January 1980 but finished last among seven
 candidates, receiving less than 1 percent of the
 vote. He was dismissed as foreign minister on
 November 7, 1980, and was arrested for a few
 days for criticizing the clergy's growing political

power, but Ayatollah Khomeini ordered him to
 be freed. Qotbzadeh was arrested a second time
 on April 6, 1982, and had to confess on television
 to the charge of plotting to assassinate Ayatollah
 Khomeini and topple the government. During his
 trial, however, he denied the charge of trying to
 kill Ayatollah Khomeini. On September 15, 1982,
 Qotbzadeh was executed, becoming the only postrevolutionary minister to have faced such a fate.

Rabbani-Amlashi [Rabbani-Rankuhi], Mohammad-Mehdi

Member of the Assembly for the Final Examination
 of the Constitution, Gilan (1979); member of
 the HCJ (July 13, 1980–January 6, 1983); prosecutor-general (June 29, 1981–January 6, 1983);
 member of the First Guardian Council (January
 18–July 16, 1983); member of the First Assembly
 of Experts, Razavi Khorasan (1983–85); deputy of
 the Second Majlis, Tehran, Tehran (1984–85)
1934–July 1985, Qom, Qom
Clerical education, Qom Seminary
Abolmakarem, clergyman
Clergyman
Imprisoned before the revolution
Not a war veteran
Member of the central council of the IRP; founding
 member of the SQSS
Ayatollah Khomeini appointed Ayatollah Rabbani-Amlashi, who was active in the anti-shah
 movement, as the prosecutor-general on June 29,
 1981. Two months later, he had to lead the investigation into the bombing that killed President Raja'i and PM Bahonar. Beginning in 1982, he called
 for bringing the revolutionary courts under the
 jurisdiction of the Ministry of Justice but failed to
 do so. Rabbani-Amlashi survived an assassination
 attempt by PMOI a few months later. He left the
 post of prosecutor-general in 1983. Rabbani-Amlashi became a member of the original Headquarters for Cultural Revolution in 1980. He was
 deputy Speaker of the Second Majlis, deputy head

of the First AE (1983–85), and temporary Friday prayer leader of Tehran, starting in June 1981. There were rumors that the group associated with Mehdi Hashemi killed him. His daughter was married to Ahmad Montazeri, the son of Ayatollah Hoseyn-Ali Montazeri.

Rabbani-Shirazi, Abdorrahim

Member of the Assembly for the Final Examination of the Constitution, Fars (1979); member of the First Guardian Council (1980–82)
1924–March 8, 1982, Shiraz, Fars
Clerical education, Qom Seminary
Beman-Ali, bazaar tradesman
Clergyman
Imprisoned before the revolution
Not a war veteran
Member of the SQSS
Ayatollah Rabbani-Shirazi was active against the shah's regime, the Tudeh Party, and Baha'is before the revolution. He served as Ayatollah Khomeini's representative in Fars Province from June 1980 to March 1982. He was opposed to the regime's land reform program. On March 29, 1981, Rabbani-Shirazi survived an assassination attempt by Forqan. He died in a car accident in 1982. He is the father of Mohammad-Hadi Rabbani-Shirazi.

Rabbani-Shirazi, Mohammad-Hadi

Deputy of the Seventh Majlis, Shiraz, Fars (2004–8)
1958–, Qom, Qom
BA, law, Tehran University
Clerical education, Qom Seminary
Abdorrahim, clergyman (ayatollah)
Clergyman
No imprisonment
Not a war veteran
HI Rabbani-Shirazi was the Friday prayer leader of Estahban from 1999 to 2009. He was appointed as Friday prayer leader in Zarqan in 2016. He is the son of Ayatollah Abdorrahim Rabbani-Shirazi.

Rabi'i, Abolfazl

Deputy of the Fourth Majlis, Garmsar, Semnan (1992–96)
1952–, Garmsar, Semnan
BA, Arabic literature
Gholam-Ali
No imprisonment

Rabi'i, Ali

Minister of cooperatives, labor, and social welfare in President Rouhani's first (August 15, 2013–August 13, 2017) and second (August 20, 2017–2021) cabinets
1955–, Tehran, Tehran
BA, public administration, Tehran University; MA, social sciences, Allameh Tabataba'i University; PhD, strategic management, Allameh Tabataba'i University
Father's name unknown, laborer
MIIRI officer
No imprisonment
War veteran
IRGC militiaman
Member of the IRP; member of the central council of the House of the Worker
Rabi'i was in charge of the workers' bureau of the IRP in the early days of the revolution and was among the initial founders of MIIRI in 1984. He was a deputy in MIIRI under Reyshahri, and later directed the main office of the SCNS. He was an adviser to Mohammad Khatami during his presidency.

Rabi'i-Fardanbeh, Mrs. Khadijeh

Deputy of the Tenth Majlis, Borujen, Chahar Mahal and Bakhtiari (2016–20)
1980–, Borujen, Chahar Mahal and Bakhtiari
BS, chemistry, Yazd University; MS, chemistry, Kashan University; PhD, chemistry, Kashan University
Gholam-Hoseyn

Professor of chemistry at Qom University of
Technology
No imprisonment

Radan, Ahmad-Reza

Deputy chief of Law Enforcement Forces (October 11,
2008–May 26, 2014)
1963–, Isfahan, Isfahan
No imprisonment
IRGC militiaman
Radan served with Basij and IRGC in Sistan and Baluchestan and Kurdistan for over two decades. He
played an important role in suppressing the 2009
protests. On April 12, 2011, the Council of the European Union put Radan on its list of sanctioned
individuals and wrote that as deputy chief of LEF
he "was responsible for beatings, murder, and
arbitrary arrests and detentions against protestors
that were committed by the police forces" in 2009.

Rafi'iyan, Esma'il

Deputy of the First Majlis, Marand, East Azerbaijan
(1980–84)
1923–July 1, 2008, Marand, East Azerbaijan
BA, Tehran's Higher Teachers Training College, 1942;
PhD, literature, Tehran University
Mohammad-Hasan, clergyman
Professor and researcher
No imprisonment
Not a war veteran
Rafi'iyan returned to teaching and research after leav-
ing the Majlis.

Rafiqdust, Mohsen

Minister of revolutionary guards in PM Musavi's first
(November 9, 1982–85) and second (October 28,
1985–88) cabinets
1940–, Tehran, Tehran
High school diploma, 1957
Mirza Abdollah, bazaar tradesman
IRGC militiaman (commander)

Imprisoned before the revolution
War veteran
Member of the CIC/PCIC
Rafiqdust was a tradesman before the revolution. He
was in the military branch of the CIC/PCIC and
reportedly underwent training in PLO camps before the revolution. He started his career as Ayatollah Khomeini's bodyguard and then became
responsible for obtaining the needed weapons for
the IRGC during the early stages of the Iran–Iraq
War. In 1982, he became the first IRGC minister.
In 1988, Rafiqdust did not receive a vote of confidence from the Majlis to continue serving in PM
Musavi's second cabinet. He subsequently headed
the FDWI (September 6, 1989–July 21, 1999) and
then the Noor Foundation, which is involved in
such varied activities as construction and impor-
tation of pharmaceutical drugs. Rafiqdust refers
to himself as the "father of Iran's missile program." He was affiliated with *Resalat*. One of his
brothers, Javad, is a member of the central committee of the CIC/PCIC. In 1995, Rafiqdust, his
brother Morteza, and a friend, Fazel Khodadad,
were accused of embezzling 123 billion tomans.
Khodadad was executed and Morteza Rafiqdust
was sentenced to a fifteen-year prison sentence
for corruption, but Mohsen Rafiqdust was not
charged.

Rahbar, Farhad

VP and head of the Management and Planning Orga-
nization in President Ahmadinejad's first cabinet
(September 20, 2005–November 2006)
October 7, 1959–, Semnan, Semnan
BA, economics, Tehran University, 1984; MA, eco-
nomics, Tehran University, 1996; PhD, economics,
Tehran University, 2000
MIIRI officer
No imprisonment
Not a war veteran
Rahbar was an economic deputy in MIIRI during
President Hashemi-Rafsanjani's era. He became
VP and head of the Management and Planning

Organization in September 2005, but President Ahmadinejad fired him in November 2006. Rahbar was rector of Tehran University from 2008 to 2014. President Ahmadinejad ordered his dismissal in 2013 but it did not happen. Rahbar then worked as an economic deputy to Seyyed Ebrahim Ra'isi in *Astan-e Qods-e Razavi* and in July 2017 he was appointed rector of the Islamic Azad University system.

Rahbar, Mrs. Fatemeh

Deputy of the Seventh (2004–8), Eighth (2008–12), and Ninth (2012–16) Majlis, Tehran, Tehran
1964–, Tehran, Tehran
MA, visual communications, Islamic Azad University
Ali-Akbar
IRIB official
No imprisonment
Member of the central council of the CIC/PCIC

Rahbar, Mohammad-Taqi

Deputy of the Seventh (2004–8) and Eighth (2008–12) Majlis, Isfahan, Isfahan
December 9, 1935–, Zarrinshahr, Isfahan
Clerical education, Qom Seminary
Hoseyn
Clergyman
Imprisoned before the revolution
Not a war veteran
Member of the central council of the SCC
HI Rahbar worked in the Ministry of Culture and the Islamic Propaganda Organization before entering the Majlis. He was the oldest member of the Eighth Majlis and did not take part in the election for the Ninth Majlis. He then became the Friday prayer leader of Isfahan.

Rahbar, Ahmad

Deputy of the Third Majlis, Razan and Famenin, Hamadan (1988–92)
1948–, Razan, Hamadan

MA
Hoseyn-Ali
No imprisonment
Rahbari is affiliated with the reformist camp.

Rahbari, Mohammad-Hashem

Deputy of the First (1982–84), Second (1984–88), and Fourth (1992–96) Majlis, Tehran, Tehran
1948–2013, Tehran, Tehran
MS, architecture
Naser
Member of the cultural council of the Martyr's Foundation
No imprisonment
Not a war veteran
Founding member of the Society of Former MPs
After leaving the Majlis, Rahbari worked mainly in the judiciary and was briefly head of the Islamic Republic of Iran Customs.

Rahbari [Garmsar], Ahmad

Deputy of the Sixth Majlis, Garmsar, Semnan (2000–2004)
1953–, Garmsar, Semnan
MS, industrial engineering
Ali-Mohammad
No imprisonment

Rahbari-Amlashi, Mohammad-Mehdi

Deputy of the Second (1984–88), Third (1988–92), Fourth (1992–96), Fifth (1996–2000), and Ninth (2012–16) Majlis, Rudsar, Gilan
1951–, Najaf, Iraq
BA, English language; MA, theology
Hasan, clergyman
Adviser to the director of the PBO and the Management and Planning Organization
Imprisoned before the revolution
Not a war veteran
Rahbari-Amlashi began studying medicine before the revolution but never finished his studies.

Rahbarpur, Gholam-Hoseyn

Deputy of the Second Majlis, Tuyserkan, Hamadan
  (1984–88)
1952–, Nahavand, Hamadan
Clerical education, Haqqani Seminary
Hoseyn-Morad
Clergyman
No imprisonment
After leaving the Majlis, HI Rahbarpur worked for
  the judiciary and held posts in Gilan and Tehran,
  including head of Tehran's revolutionary court.

Rahchamani, Mohammad-Reza

Deputy of the Second (1984–88), Third (1988–92),
  Fourth (1992–96), and Fifth (1996–2000) Majlis,
  Sabzevar, Razavi Khorasan
1952–, Sabzevar, Razavi Khorasan
MD, medicine
Gholam-Hoseyn
Medical doctor
No imprisonment
Not a war veteran
Founding member of the Islamic Iran Solidarity Party
After serving in the Majlis, Rahchamani became head of
  the Social Welfare Organization of Iran (2001–5).

Raheb, Ja'farqoli

Deputy of the Fifth (1996–2000) and Seventh (2004–8)
  Majlis, Tonekabon and Ramsar, Mazandaran
1951–2015, Ramsar, Mazandaran
MS, agricultural engineering
Mohammad-Mehdi
Military official
No imprisonment
Raheb was a director-general of the Construction
  Jihad in Mazandaran and Gilan.

Rahimi, Abdorrahman

Deputy of the Second Majlis, Paveh, Kermanshah
  (1984–88)

1951–, Paveh, Kermanshah
Clerical education
Hedayat
Clergyman
No imprisonment
Mamosta Rahimi, a Sunni cleric, ran unsuccessfully
  for the Third Majlis.

Rahimi, Ali-Reza

Deputy of the Tenth Majlis, Tehran, Tehran (2016–20)
1968–, Ahvaz, Khuzestan
BA, Shahid Beheshti University; MA, international
  law (Scotland)
War veteran (POW; wounded—lost a leg)
Rahimi was a child soldier in the Iran–Iraq War and
  became a POW in 1982 at the age of fourteen.
  He spent two years in Iraqi prisoner camps and
  became famous in Iran when, as a POW, he told
  a female television interviewer to cover her head.
  Rahimi, who ran unsuccessfully for the Sixth
  and Eighth Majlis, is a reformist and served as an
  adviser to President Khatami's minister of commerce and President Rouhani's VP for executive
  affairs.

Rahimi, Amin-Hoseyn

Deputy of the Eighth Majlis, Malayer, Hamadan
  (2008–12)
1968–, Malayer, Hamadan
MA, law
Mohammad-Karim
Judiciary official
No imprisonment
After leaving the Majlis, Rahimi became a prosecutor
  in the judiciary. He is a former director of the
  State Audit Court.

Rahimi, Mohammad-Reza

Deputy of the Second (1984–88) and Third (1988–92)
  Majlis, Qorveh, Kurdistan; deputy of the Fourth
  Majlis, Sanandaj, Kurdistan (1992–October 5,

1993); VP for parliamentary affairs in President
Ahmadinejad's first cabinet (2008–9); first vice
president in President Ahmadinejad's second
cabinet (2009–13)

1954–, Qorveh, Kurdistan

BA, law, Tehran University, ca. 1976; MA, sociology,
Islamic Azad University, 2000

Hasan, farmer

IRIB official

No imprisonment

Not a war veteran

Member of AVIR; founding member of the Society of
Islamic Athletes

Rahimi was a prosecutor in Sanandaj and Qorveh in
the 1980s. He became a law professor at Islamic
Azad University and head of the State Audit
Court. He resigned from the Fourth Majlis to become the governor-general of Kurdistan (1993–
97). After an investigation in 2010, the Majlis
rejected the validity of his doctoral degree from
an institute in France. In 2014, he was condemned
to a five-year prison term for embezzlement.

Rahimi, Seyyed Fakhreddin

Deputy of the First Majlis, Malavi, Lorestan (1980–
June 28, 1981)

1944–June 28, 1981, Khorramabad, Lorestan

Clerical education

Seyyed Ali-Akbar, clergyman

Clergyman

Imprisoned before the revolution (internal exile)

Not a war veteran

HI Rahimi was killed in the bombing of the IRP
headquarters. Five years later, his brother, who
had replaced him in the Majlis, died when Iraqi
forces shot down his plane.

Rahimi, Seyyed Nureddin

Deputy of the First (1981–84) and Second (1984–February 29, 1986) Majlis, Pol-e Dokhtar and Malavi,
Lorestan

1935–February 29, 1986, Khorramabad, Lorestan

Clerical education

Seyyed Ali-Akbar, clergyman

Clergyman

No imprisonment

Not a war veteran

Martyr's family (brother, Seyyed Fakhreddin, killed
in the bombing of the IRP headquarters)

HI Seyyed Nureddin Rahimi replaced his brother in
1981 interim elections for the First Majlis. He was
later killed when Iraqi forces shot down his plane.

Rahimi-Haji Abadi, Abbas

Deputy of the Second Majlis, Dashtestan, Bushehr
(1984–88)

1947–, Najafabad, Isfahan

Clerical education

Gholam-Ali, clergyman

Clergyman

No imprisonment

Not a war veteran

HI Rahimi-Haji Abadi was the Friday prayer leader of
Mobarakeh from 1996 to 2009.

Rahimi-Haji Abadi, Gholam-Reza

Deputy of the First (1981–84) and Second (1984–
January 3, 1986) Majlis, Bandar-e Mahshahr,
Khuzestan

1944–January 3, 1986, Najafabad, Isfahan

Clerical education

Gholam-Ali, clergyman

Clergyman

No imprisonment

Not a war veteran

HI Rahimi-Haji Abadi and his brother Abbas served
on the Second Majlis concurrently until he died in
a car accident on January 3, 1986.

Rahimi-Jahanabadi, Jalil

Deputy of the Tenth Majlis, Torbat-e Jam, Razavi
Khorasan (2016–20)

1972–, Torbat-e Jam, Razavi Khorasan

BA, political science, Isfahan University of Technology; MA, international relations, Islamic Azad University–Tehran; PhD, international relations, Islamic Azad University–Science and Research Branch

Professor of political science at Islamic Azad University–Mashhad

No imprisonment

Not a war veteran

Before entering the Majlis, Rahimi-Jahanabadi, a Sunni, was a member of the cultural council of Torbat-e Jam, a social and political consultant to the Islamic council of Razavi Khorasan, and a professor at Islamic Azad University–Kabul, Afghanistan (2010–14).

Rahiminasab, Reza

Deputy of the Eighth Majlis, Khorramabad, Lorestan (2008–12)

1966–, Khorramabad, Lorestan

BA, philosophy; MA, public administration

Seyyed Ahmad, clergyman

No imprisonment

War veteran

IRGC militiaman

Rahimmasha'i, Esfandiyar

VP and head of the Cultural Heritage, Handicrafts, and Tourism Organization (2005–9) and first vice president (2009) in President Ahmadinejad's first cabinet

January 1, 1951–, Ramsar, Mazandaran

BS, electrical engineering, Isfahan University of Technology; pursuing an MA in international relations at Payam-e Nur University

No imprisonment

War veteran

IRGC militiaman

Rahimmasha'i became a member of the IRGC in 1981 and fought in the Kurdistan region against Kurdish and PMOI forces as an intelligence officer.

He was in MI from 1993 to 1997, and then Mayor Ahmadinejad hired him in Tehran municipality. In 2009, President Ahmadinejad appointed Rahimmasha'i as his First VP, which caused negative reactions from some of his ministers. On July 18, 2009, the supreme leader asked Ahmadinejad in an open letter to withdraw the appointment. A week later Rahimmasha'i resigned from the post. To show his displeasure with Khamenei's directive, President Ahmadinejad appointed Rahimmasha'i as his chief of staff (2009–12), and in December 2012 appointed him to the additional post of head of the Non-Aligned Movement's office in Iran. It was rumored that Ahmadinejad wanted to see Rahimmasha'i as his replacement in the 2013 presidential election, but the GC disqualified him. Numerous political analysts considered Rahimmasha'i architect of many of President Ahmadinejad's policies. Rahimmasha'i's controversial ideas about closeness to the Hidden Imam and his emphasis on nationalist cultural features of Iranian society did not sit well with various quarters. Not only was Rahimmasha'i one of President Ahmadinejad's closest confidants, but in 2008, his daughter married Mahmud Ahmadinejad's oldest son.

Rahimnezhad-Baqcheh-Joqi, Bakhshali

Deputy of the Third Majlis, Maku, West Azerbaijan (1988–92)

1961–, Maku, West Azerbaijan

High school diploma

Rahim

No imprisonment

Rahmandust, Mojtaba

Deputy of the Ninth Majlis, Tehran, Tehran (2012–16)

1954–, Hamadan, Hamadan

BS, civil engineering, Tehran University, 1979; PhD, Arabic literature, Islamic Azad University, 1994; clerical education, Qom Seminary

Morteza

Faculty member at Tehran University

No imprisonment

War veteran (lost a leg and a hand)

Martyr's family (brother-in-law)

Secretary-general of the Society for Defense of the Rights of Palestinian People

Rahmandust was a high official in the FDWI. From 1997 to 2010, he was an adviser to Presidents Khatami and Ahmadinejad on the affairs of wounded veterans, but Ahmadinejad dismissed Rahmandust after he criticized some of the president's friends. After serving in the Majlis, Rahmandust returned to teaching at Tehran University. He is also a former director-general at the Ministry of Culture.

Rahmani, Abolqasem

Deputy of the Eighth Majlis, Eqlid, Fars (2008–12)

1947 (or 1949)–, Eqlid, Fars

BS, civil engineering, K. N. Toosi University of Technology, 1976

Keravqoli, farmer

Deputy for executive affairs of the National Water and Wastewater Engineering Company

No imprisonment

After serving in the Majlis, Rahmani became executive director of the Iranian Offshore Engineering and Construction Company. He was also previously an IRIB civil servant.

Rahmani, Hojjatollah

Deputy of the Eighth Majlis, Aligudarz, Lorestan (2008–12)

1965–, Aligudarz, Lorestan

BA (equivalent), educational management

Ezzatollah

No imprisonment

Rahmani later became an adviser to the head of the Forests, Range, and Watershed Management Organization.

Rahmani, Hoseyn-Ali

Member of the Assembly for the Final Examination of the Constitution, Kurdistan (1979); deputy of the First (1980–84) and Second (1984–88) Majlis, Bijar, Kurdistan

1926–April 7, 1996, Bijar, Kurdistan

Clerical education

Mohammad-Karim, bazaar tradesman

Clergyman

No imprisonment

Not a war veteran

Martyr's family (son, an IRGC commander, killed in the Kurdistan war in 1979)

HI Rahmani was elected three times from a region generally dominated by Sunnis thanks to low turnout rates.

Rahmani, Mohammad-Ali

Commander of the IRGC's Basij Force (March 11, 1983–March 1, 1990)

1953–, Quchan, Razavi Khorasan

Clerical education

Clergyman (HI)

IRGC militiaman

Rahmani made the Basij into a real force, and later became the supreme leader's representative in the Basij. He worked in Ayatollah Khomeini's office for several years.

Rahmani, Qahreman

Deputy of the First (1980–84) and Third (1988–92) Majlis, Takestan, Zanjan

1954–, Takestan, Zanjan

Associate's degree

Hoseyn-Ali, farmer

No imprisonment

War veteran (a few months)

Member of the Basij

In the early days after the revolution, Rahmani, who used to teach mathematics in middle schools, was put in charge of revolutionary committees in Takestan. He also worked in the MI.

Rahmani, Rajab

Deputy of the Fourth (1992–96) Majlis, Takestan, Zanjan; deputy of the Fifth (1996–2000), Sixth (2000–2004), Seventh (2004–8), and Ninth (2012–16) Majlis, Takestan, Qazvin
1953–, Takestan, Zanjan
BS, agricultural engineering, Karaj Agricultural University, 1980; MA, private law and public administration, Islamic Azad University–Tehran, 1992
Qorban-Ali, farmer in a vineyard
Civil servant
No imprisonment
War veteran (a few months)
Martyr's family (brother, Ali, killed at the war front)
Member of the Basij
Rahmani was a teacher before the revolution. After the revolution, he created a party in Takestan named Abuzar. He became governor of Takestan (1981), head of Takestan education bureau (1986), and a deputy in the Ministry of Education before being elected to the Majlis. He has also worked in the Petroleum Ministry and State Audit Court.

Rahmani, Reza

Deputy of the Seventh (2004–8), Eighth (2008–12), and Ninth (2012–16) Majlis, Tabriz, Osku, and Azarshahr, East Azerbaijan
1966–, Marand, East Azerbaijan
BA, law; MA, human resources management; pursuing a PhD in strategic management
Abdollah
Civil servant, state companies
No imprisonment
Rahmani did not run for the Tenth Majlis.

Rahmaniasl, Abolfazl

Deputy of the Second Majlis, Razan, Hamadan (1984–88)

1945–, Tehran, Tehran
BS, physics
Hasan
No imprisonment

Rahmani-Fazli, Abdorreza

Deputy of the Fourth Majlis, Shiravan, North Khorasan (1992–96); interior minister in President Rouhani's first (August 15, 2013–August 13, 2017) and second (August 20, 2017–2021) cabinets
1959–, Shiravan, North Khorasan
BA, geography, Ferdowsi University of Mashhad; MA, geography, Ferdowsi University of Mashhad; PhD, geography, Tarbiyat-e Modarres University, 1992
Yadollah
University professor
No imprisonment
IRGC militiaman
Rahmani-Fazli has been a deputy of the SCNS, a political deputy of IRIB (1996–2006), professor of geography at Shahid Beheshti University (2003–13), and head of the State Audit Court (2008–13).

Rahmani-Khalili, Ali-Asghar

Deputy of the First (1981–84), Second (1984–88), and Sixth (2000–2004) Majlis, Behshahr, Mazandaran
November 5, 1944–, Behshahr, Mazandaran
Clerical education; BA
Abdorrahman
Clergyman and teacher
No imprisonment
Not a war veteran
Founding member of the Assembly of Former MPs
HI Rahmani-Khalili is a former member of the Ministry of Education's legal and parliamentary relations office. His brother was head of the Iranian Tobacco Company for a while.

Rahmati, Mohammad

Minister of roads and transportation in President Khatami's second cabinet (February 2–August 2,

2005) and President Ahmadinejad's first cabinet (August 24, 2005–8)

1958–, Yazd, Yazd

BS, civil engineering, Sharif University of Technology; MS, civil engineering, Tehran University, 1993

Abbas

Head of the Islamic Republic of Iran Railways

No imprisonment

Not a war veteran

Rahmati, who was active in University Jihad from 1981 to 1999, became the minister of roads and transportation for the last six months of President Khatami's second cabinet. He was the only minister from the outgoing administration who stayed on to serve in President Ahmadinejad's cabinet in the same post. However, Rahmati resigned from Ahmadinejad's cabinet after three years.

Rahmati, Rahmatollah

Deputy of the Second (1984–88) Majlis, Qomsheh, Isfahan; deputy of the Third (1988–92) Majlis, Shahreza, Isfahan

1951–, Qomsheh, Isfahan

Associate's degree

Mohammad-Ali

No imprisonment

Rahmati is a high-level official in the Ministry of Education.

Rahpeyk, Siyamak

Member of the Sixth Guardian Council (2010–16)

1963–, Tehran, Tehran

PhD, private law, Tarbiyat-e Modarres University, 1995

Gholam-Hoseyn

Academia

No imprisonment

Rahpeyk received 114 (out of 228) votes from the Eighth Majlis to enter the GC. Prior to that post, he was the head of the University of Judicial Sciences and Administrative Services, editor in chief of *Didgahhay-e Hoquqi* (Legal Perspectives)

quarterly, editor of *Motale'eat Rahbordi* (Strategic Studies) quarterly, and head of the Center for Strategic Research, which is affiliated with the security and intelligence forces. The chief justice did not nominate him for the next round of the GC.

Ra'isi, Khodabakhsh

Deputy of the Fifth Majlis, Iranshahr, Bent, Lashar, and Fanuj, Sistan and Baluchestan (1996–2000)

1953–, Nikshahr, Sistan and Baluchestan

BA, theology

Karimbakhsh

No imprisonment

Ra'isi was a Sunni member of the Majlis.

Ra'isi [-Alsadati], Seyyed Ebrahim

Revolutionary prosecutor-general of Tehran (1989–94); head of the State General Inspectorate Organization (1994–2004); first deputy to the chief justice (2004–August 23, 2014); member of the Fourth (2007–16) and Fifth (2016–22) Assembly of Experts, South Khorasan; prosecutor-general of the SCFC (June 16, 2012–present); prosecutor-general (August 23, 2014–March 6, 2016); member of the Eighth Expediency Discernment Assembly (2017–22)

December 14, 1960–, Noqab, Razavi Khorasan

Clerical education, Qom Seminary; MA, law, 2001; PhD, theology, Shahid Motahhari University

Seyyed Haji, clergyman

Clergyman

No imprisonment

Not a war veteran

Member of the central council of the SCC (since 1997)

HI Ra'isi was the prosecutor of the city of Karaj from 1980 to 1982, and then Hamadan from 1982 to 1985. In 1983, Ra'isi married Jamileh-Sadat Alamolhoda, daughter of Ayatollah Seyyed Ahmad Alamolhoda. In 1985, he became the deputy prosecutor-general of Tehran. In 1988, while serving as deputy prosecutor-general, he was a member of a special committee, nicknamed the "death committee," that oversaw the extrajudicial execution of thousands (estimates vary between 2,800 and 5,000) of political prisoners following Ayatollah Khomeini's edict. From 1989 to 1994 he was the prosecutor-general of Tehran, and from 1994 to 2004 he served as head of the State General Inspectorate Organization. From 2004 to 2014 Ra'isi was the first deputy of the judiciary; while holding this post, he was appointed by Ayatollah Khamenei as the prosecutor-general of the SCFC on June 7, 2012. In 2007 and 2016, he received 68.6 percent and 75.4 percent of the vote, respectively, when he was elected to the Fourth and Fifth AE from South Khorasan. In 2014, he became the prosecutor-general. To cap his meteoric rise, on March 6, 2016, Ayatollah Khamenei appointed him the guardian of *Astan-e Qods-e Razavi*. A former student of Ayatollah Khamenei, he is also a member of the governing board of the AE. In 2017, Ra'isi was the first runner-up in the presidential race and received 38.2 percent of the vote.

Ra'isi-Dehkordi, Asghar

Deputy of the Fifth Majlis, Shahrekord, Chahar
    Mahal and Bakhtiari (1996–2000)
1959–, Shahrekord, Chahar Mahal and Bakhtiari
MS, physics
Haj Aqa
Rector of Islamic Azad University–Shahrekord
    (1989–96 and 2006–9)
No imprisonment

Ra'isi-Naf'chi, Mohammad

Deputy of the Third (1988–92) and Sixth (2000–2004)
    Majlis, Shahrekord, Chahar Mahal and Bakhtiari
1957–, Shahrekord, Chahar Mahal and Bakhtiari
BA, 1994; MA, law, 1997
Mehdi-Qoli
Academia
No imprisonment
After serving in the Majlis, Ra'isi-Naf'chi became a
    civil servant.

Rajabi, Abdolkarim

Deputy of the Ninth Majlis, Minudasht, Kalaleh, Maraveh Tappeh, and Galikash, Golestan (2012–16)
1972–, Maraveh Tappeh, Golestan
BS, Tehran University of Medical Sciences; MA, international law, Payam-e Nur University
Rajabali
Civil servant, medical insurance
No imprisonment
Not a war veteran
Rajabi was a Sunni Turkoman MP.

Rajabi, Farajollah

Deputy of the Tenth Majlis, Shiraz, Fars (2016–20)
1961–, Shiraz, Fars
BS, civil engineering, Shiraz University, 1985; MA,
    public administration; MS, urban planning
Rajabi held various managerial positions in Fars
    Province before he was elected mayor of Shiraz in
    1997. He later became the executive director of the
    Shiraz metro system.

Raja'i, Abbas

Deputy of the Seventh (2004–8), Eighth (2008–12),
    and Ninth (2012–16) Majlis, Arak and Komijan,
    Markazi
1960–, Arak, Markazi
BS, Shiraz University, 1986; MS, construction management, Tehran University, 1987; MS, industrial engineering, Amirkabir University of Technology, 1987
Hoseyn, railroad worker
Civil servant, Construction Jihad
No imprisonment
Not a war veteran
Martyr's family (three brothers killed at the war front)

Raja'i, Mohammad-Ali

Member of the Revolutionary Council (1979–80);
    minister of education in the Revolutionary

Council cabinet (November 16, 1979–80); deputy of the First Majlis, Tehran, Tehran (1980–August 9, 1980); prime minister (August 11, 1980–August 1, 1981); president (August 2–30, 1981)

1933–August 30, 1981, Qazvin, Qazvin

BS, mathematics, Daneshsara-ye Ali-ye Tehran, 1959

Abdossamad, shopkeeper

Teacher

Imprisoned before the revolution

Not a war veteran

Former member of the LMI; member of the central council of the IRP and the Islamic Association of Iranian Teachers

Raja'i came from a humble background and held such jobs as bazaar tradesman, air force technician, and high school mathematics teacher before the revolution. While in prison, he switched from sympathizing with PMOI to becoming a staunch supporter of the clergy. He resigned from the First Majlis to become the minister of education. On August 11, 1980, he was elected prime minister with 153 positive, twenty-four negative, and nineteen abstaining votes. He also held the post of foreign minister for a few months while serving as PM. Raja'i was forced upon President Banisadr as the prime minister and the two had serious differences of opinion. These differences delayed the confirmation process for Raja'i's proposed ministers; they were eventually confirmed on September 10, 1980. Raja'i won the presidential election on July 24, 1981, with 90 percent of the vote, becoming the only person in postrevolutionary Iran to serve as both PM and president. However, he only served in the later capacity for twenty-eight days before he was killed in a bomb explosion. Shahid Raja'i Teachers Training College is named after him.

Raja'i-Baghsiyaei, Mohammad

Deputy of the Ninth Majlis, Gonabad and Bejestan, Razavi Khorasan (2012–16)

1958–, Gonabad, Razavi Khorasan

Clerical education, Qom Seminary; PhD, economics, Durham University (England), 2011; dissertation title: "The Contribution of Islamic Banking to Economic Development: The Case of the Islamic Republic of Iran"

Father's name unknown, clergyman

Clergyman

No imprisonment

War veteran

IRGC militiaman

Martyr's family (brother killed at the war front)

HI Raja'i-Baghsiyaei is a professor at Imam Khomeini Educational and Research Institute.

Raja'i-Khorasani, Sa'id

Permanent Representative of Iran to the UN (1981–87); Deputy of the Third (1988–92) and Fourth (1992–96) Majlis, Tehran, Tehran

1936–2013, Kerman, Kerman

BA, philosophy, Tehran University, 1960; MA, educational philosophy, American University of Beirut (Lebanon), 1967; PhD, philosophy, Durham University (England), 1976; dissertation title: "Mulla Sadra's Philosophy and Its Epistemological Implications"

Mahmud

Civil servant, ministries

No imprisonment

Not a war veteran

Founding member of the Party of Iranian Independence

Raja'i-Khorasani taught at Tabriz University and Kerman University, eventually becoming vice rector of the former and rector of the latter. He was also director of Iran's radio network. In 1993, in a private letter to Ayatollah Khamenei, he recommended the resumption of ties between Iran and the United States.

Raja'iyan, Mohammad

Deputy of the First Majlis, Zanjan, Zanjan (1980–84)

1936–, Zanjan, Zanjan

MS, mathematics

Zeynol'abedin, bazaar tradesman

Education deputy in the Ministry of Culture and
   Islamic Guidance
No imprisonment
Raja'iyan started teaching at universities in 1967,
   and he was in charge of the nationwide University Entrance Examination (*Konkur*) after the
   revolution.

Raji, Nabiyollah

Deputy of the Second (1984–88) and Third (1988–92)
   Majlis, Na'in, Isfahan
1950–, Na'in, Isfahan
Clerical education
Ne'matollah
Clergyman
No imprisonment
HI Raji failed to get elected to the Fourth Majlis.

Rake'i, Mrs. Fatemeh

Deputy of the Sixth Majlis, Tehran, Tehran
   (2000–2004)
1954–, Zanjan, Zanjan
PhD, linguistics, Tarbiyat-e Modarres University
Abdollah
Poet; professor and administrator at Alzahra
   University
No imprisonment
Secretary-general of the Alliance of New Thinking
   Muslim Women of Iran; member of IIPF; member
   of the central council of the Party of Islamic Iran's
   People's Unity (elected in 2015)
Rake'i did not participate in the election for the
   Seventh Majlis, and the GC disqualified her from
   running in the 2016 Majlis election.

Ramezanianpur, Hasan

Deputy of the Sixth Majlis, Shahreza, Isfahan
   (2000–2004)
1944–, Tehran, Tehran
MS, statistics and infomatics
Mohammad

Academia
No imprisonment

Ramezani-Gilani, Reza

Member of the Fourth (2007–16) and Fifth (2016–22)
   Assembly of Experts, Gilan
1964–, Rasht, Gilan
Clerical education, Qom Seminary; MA, philosophy,
   Qom University, 1994
Abbas
Clergyman
No imprisonment
Not a war veteran
HI Ramezani-Gilani was the supreme leader's rep-
   resentative and the Friday prayer leader of Karaj
   (2001–5), director of Imam Ali Islamic Center in
   Vienna, Austria (2006–9), and director of the Is-
   lamic Center of Hamburg, Germany (2009–pres-
   ent). He speaks German.

Ramezani-Khorshiddust, Reza

Deputy of the First Majlis, Rasht, Gilan (1980–84)
1954–, Rasht, Gilan
BS, mechanical engineering; PhD, systems and
   control engineering, Case Western Reserve
   University (USA), 1991; dissertation title: "A
   Multiattribute Approach to General Flowshop
   Problems" (under the name Reza Ramazani
   Khorshid-Doust)
Hoseyn, bazaar tradesman
No imprisonment
Ramezani-Khorshiddust is a professor in Amirkabir
   University of Technology's department of indus-
   trial engineering and management systems.

Ramezanpur-Nargesi, Ahmad

Deputy of the Fifth (1996–2000) and Sixth (2000–
   2004) Majlis, Rasht, Gilan
1954–, Sowme'eh Sara, Gilan
MA, management
Ali

Provincial civil servant
No imprisonment
Not a war veteran
Martyr's family (brother, Naser)

Ramezanpur-Nargesi, Qasem

Deputy of the Fourth (1992–96) and Fifth (1996–2000)
    Majlis, Sowme'eh Sara, Gilan
1958–, Sowme'eh Sara, Gilan
BS, physics, Tehran University; MS, industrial engi-
    neering, Amirkabir University of Technology;
    PhD, public administration, Tehran University
Civil servant, state companies
No imprisonment
Not a war veteran
Martyr's family (brother, Naser)
Qasem Ramezanpur-Nargesi and his brother Ahmad
    were both MPs in the Fifth Majlis.

Ramezanzadeh, Mrs. Fatemeh

Deputy of the Fifth Majlis, Tehran, Tehran
    (1996–2000)
1957–, Yazd, Yazd
MD, gynecology
Mohammad-Ali
Gynecologist and university professor
No imprisonment
Member of the central council of PECI
Before being elected to the Fifth Majlis, Ramezan-
    zadeh was a general manager in the Ministry of
    Health.

Ramin, Shahrokh

Deputy of the Eighth Majlis, Damavand and Firuz-
    kuh, Tehran (2008–12)
1967–, Tehran, Tehran
MD, Shahid Beheshti University
Jalal
Eye surgeon
No imprisonment
War veteran

Ranjbar-Chubeh, Mohammad-Taqi

Deputy of the First (1980–84), Second (1984–88),
    Third (1988–92), and Sixth (2000–2004) Majlis,
    Sowme'eh Sara, Gilan
1942–, Sowme'eh Sara, Gilan
BA, Arabic literature, Tehran School of Translation,
    1974
Zakariya, farmer
Civil servant
No imprisonment
Not a war veteran
IRGC militiaman
Member of the IRP and the CIC/PCIC
After leaving the Majlis, Ranjbar-Chubeh became a
    civil servant.

Ranjbarzadeh, Akbar

Deputy of the Eighth (2008–12) and Tenth (2016–
    2020) Majlis, Asadabad, Hamadan
1965–, Asadabad, Hamadan
MD
Ezzatollah
Medical doctor
No imprisonment

Rasa'i, Hamid

Deputy of the Eighth (2008–12) and Ninth (2012–16)
    Majlis, Tehran, Tehran
1968–, Tehran, Tehran
Clerical education, Qom Seminary
Kasali
Clergyman
No imprisonment
War veteran (sixteen months; wounded)
HI Rasa'i has worked with the IRGC's research center
    since 1992, and he has held other posts such as
    general manager of culture and Islamic guidance
    in Qom Province, adviser to the culture minister,
    and director of the Bureau for Understanding
    Contemporary Currents. He was a very conserva-
    tive MP. He lived in Africa from 1997 to 1999.

Rashed, Mohammad-Reza

Deputy of the First Majlis, Germi, Ardabil (1981–84)
1952–, Gachsar, Mazandaran
High school diploma
Ghayur
No imprisonment
Rashed is in charge of the radical *9 Day* weekly maga-
zine, which the authorities have closed repeatedly
for its radical content.

Rashid [Alinur], Gholam-Ali

First deputy chief of the Armed Forces General Staff
(August 15, 1999–July 5, 2016)
1953–, Dezful, Khuzestan
BA, political geography, Tehran University; MA, political geography, Tehran University; PhD, political
geography, Tarbiyat-e Modarres University, 2008
Father's name unknown, bazaar tradesman
Imprisoned before the revolution (eighteen months)
War veteran
IRGC militiaman (leading commander)
Major General Rashid became involved with underground Islamic activities in 1969 and joined
the paramilitary group Mansurron before the
revolution. He was arrested once in 1971 and a
second time in 1976. He joined the IRGC after the
revolution and formed its branch in Dezful. On
July 5, 2016, he was appointed commander of the
Central Khatam al-Anbia Headquarters, which in
the event of a war is the leading body for coordinating war efforts.

Rashidi, Hoseyn

Deputy of the Fourth Majlis, Darab, Fars (1992–96)
1941–, Darab, Fars
BA, English language and literature, Tehran University,
1970; BA, law, Shahid Beheshti University, 1978
Ali
Civil servant in State Audit Court
No imprisonment
Not a war veteran

Rashidi worked for many years as a financial expert
in the Ministry of Economic Affairs and Finance
and retired in 2002.

Rashidian, Mohammad

Member of the Assembly for the Final Examination
of the Constitution, Khuzestan (1979); deputy
of the First (1980–84), Second (1984–88), Third
(1988–92), and Sixth (2000–2004) Majlis, Abadan,
Khuzestan
1938–2013, Behbahan, Khuzestan
BA, sociology
Nasir, bazaar tradesman
Academia
No imprisonment
Not a war veteran
Member of the IRP

Rashidi-Kuchi, Habibollah

Deputy of the Fourth (1995–96) and Fifth (1996–2000)
Majlis, Marvdasht, Fars
1960–, Marvdasht, Fars
BA, theology
Shanbehali
No imprisonment
Martyr's family (two brothers, Majid and Karim,
killed at the war front)
After his brother Jalil died in a car accident, Habibol-
lah Rashidi-Kuchi replaced him in the Majlis.

Rashidi-Kuchi, Jalil

Deputy of the Fourth Majlis, Marvdasht, Fars (1992–
October 11, 1994)
1954–October 11, 1994, Marvdasht, Fars
BA, Persian literature, Shiraz University
Shanbehali
Provincial civil servant
No imprisonment
War veteran (wounded)
Martyr's family (two brothers, Majid and Karim,
killed at the war front)

Rashidi-Kuchi died in a car accident while serving as an MP.

Rasi [-Gol], Mohsen

Deputy of the First (1981–84), Second (1984–88), and Fourth (1992–96) Majlis, Miyandoab and Takab, West Azerbaijan
1952–, Maragheh, East Azerbaijan
MA, Persian literature; PhD, Persian literature, 1991
Mohammad-Ali
No imprisonment
Not a war veteran

Rastad, Abdolmohammad

Deputy of the Fifth (1996–2000) and Seventh (2004–8) Majlis, Darab, Fars
1953–, Darab, Fars
Clerical education; MA, theology
Gholam-Abbas
Clergyman (HI)
No imprisonment
Rastad became the Friday prayer leader of Zarrindasht in May 2017.

Rastegar, Abdollah

Deputy of the Eighth Majlis, Gonbad-e Kavus, Golestan (2008–12)
1968–, Gonbad-e Kavus, Golestan
MS, architecture, Iran University of Science and Technology, 1994
Rahmanbordi
Architect
No imprisonment
Not a war veteran
Rastegar was a Sunni Turkoman MP.

Rastgu, Mrs. Elaheh

Deputy of the Fifth Majlis, Malayer, Hamadan (1997–2000)
1962–, Malayer, Hamadan

BA, management and planning, Allameh Tabataba'i University; MA, educational management, Allameh Tabataba'i University, 1996
Nosratollah, engineer
Civil servant
No imprisonment
Member of the central council and spokesperson of the Islamic Labor Party
Rastgu has worked for many years in the educational field. After finishing her term in the Fifth Majlis, she worked in the Labor Ministry from 2000 to 2002. In 2013, she was elected to the Tehran City Council as a reformist and cast the decisive vote to elect Qalibaf mayor again, over the son of Ayatollah Hashemi-Rafsanjani. This vote led to her dismissal from the Islamic Labor Party.

Rasti-Kashani, Hoseyn

Member of the First (1983–90) and Second (1991–98) Assembly of Experts, Tehran
1927–September 20, 2017, Kashan, Isfahan
Clerical education, Najaf Seminary (Iraq)
Ali, silk weaver
Clergyman
No imprisonment
Not a war veteran
Member of the SQSS
Ayatollah Rasti-Kashani lived in Najaf for twenty-five years. He then worked in Ayatollah Khomeini's office and was his representative to OMIRI from 1979 to October 1986, when the organization disbanded itself due to ideological differences. He was a member of the High Council of Religious Seminaries of Qom and was affiliated with the conservative *Resalat* from its very beginning in 1985.

Rasti-Lari, Mohammad-Javad

Deputy of the Second (1984–88) and Third (1988–92) Majlis, Larestan, Fars
1948–, Larestan, Fars
BS, electrical engineering

Mohammad-Ebrahim
No imprisonment

Rasuli, Jalal

Deputy of the Fourth Majlis, Miyandoab and Takab,
   West Azerbaijan (1992–96)
1955–, Miyandoab, West Azerbaijan
MD, pharmacy
Majid
Medical doctor
No imprisonment

Rasuli-Mahallati, Seyyed Hashem

Member of the Second Assembly of Experts, Tehran
   (1991–98)
1932–, Mahallat, Markazi
Clerical education, Qom Seminary
Seyyed Hoseyn, clergyman
Clergyman
No imprisonment
Not a war veteran
Ayatollah Rasuli-Mahallati was a close friend of Ayatollah Khomeini and worked in his office starting
   in the early 1960s. In this capacity, he controlled
   access to the ayatollah and distributed funds to
   theology students and charities. He traveled with
   Khomeini to Iraq and France. He also taught at
   Alzahra University. Rasuli-Mahallati now works
   in the office of Ayatollah Khamenei, where he is
   in charge of religious funds and correspondence.
   He retired from the directorship of the policy
   planning council of Friday prayer leaders in 2000.
   One of Rasuli-Mahallati's sons was in charge
   of AEOI in Isfahan, while two others worked
   in the Ministry of Foreign Affairs; one of them,
   Mohammad-Javad, was Iran's ambassador to
   Saudi Arabia under Presidents Ahmadinejad and
   Rouhani. Rasuli-Mahallati is the father-in-law of
   Ali-Akbar Nateq-Nuri, whom he recommended
   as interior minister, Abbas-Ahmad Akhundi, a
   two-time minister, HI Mohammad-Ali Shahidi-Mahallati, the VP and head of FMVA, and HI

Mohammad-Hasan Qarhi (d. 2017), who worked
   in the office of Supreme Leader Khamenei. Rasuli-Mahallati's sister was the wife of HI Sadeq
   Khalkhali.

Rasulinezhad, Seyyed Ahmad

Deputy of the Fourth (1992–96), Fifth (1996–2000),
   and Seventh (2004–8) Majlis, Damavand and
   Firuzkuh, Tehran
1963–, Firuzkuh, Tehran
Associate's degree
Seyyed Abolqasem
Civil servant
No imprisonment
Founding Member of the ISFPD

Ravani, Parviz

Deputy of the Fourth (1994–96) and Fifth (1996–2000)
   Majlis, representing the Zoroastrian community
   (as a religious minority)
1952–, Ardakan, Yazd
MS, architecture
Ardehsir
Architect
No imprisonment

Rayat, Vali

Deputy of the Sixth (2000–2004) and Seventh (2004–
   8) Majlis, Qaemshahr, Savadkuh, and Juybar,
   Mazandaran
1961–, Qaemshahr, Mazandaran
BA, law
Ahmad
Judiciary official
No imprisonment

Razavi, Morteza

Deputy of the Second Majlis, Tabriz, East Azerbaijan
   (1984–88)

1945–, Naqadeh, West Azerbaijan
Clerical education
Clergyman
No imprisonment
HI Razavi ran for the Third Majlis from Tehran and
made it to the second round but withdrew after
the GC questioned his qualifications.

Razavi, Seyyed Abolfazl

Deputy of the Fourth (1992–96), Fifth (1996–2000),
and Sixth (2000–2004) Majlis, Na'in, Isfahan
1956–, Khomeyn, Markazi
MS, geology
Seyyed Karim
Civil servant
No imprisonment

Razavi [-Mahv-Marvi], Seyyed Mohammad

Deputy of the Third (1988–92) and Sixth (2000–2004)
Majlis, Yazd, Yazd
1952–, Qom, Qom
Clerical education, Qom Seminary; BA, law, Shahid
Beheshti University (unverified)
Seyyed Kazem, clergyman
Clergyman (HI)
Imprisoned before the revolution (one year)
Not a war veteran
Member of the ACC

Razavi-Ardakani, Seyyed Abufazel

Deputy of the First (1980–84), Fourth (1992–96), and
Fifth (1996–2000) Majlis, Sepidan, Fars
1949–, Sepidan, Fars
Clerical education, Qom Seminary
Seyyed Jalal, clergyman
Clergyman (HI)
No imprisonment
Not a war veteran
Razavi-Ardakani is the brother-in-law of former MP
Khalil Dadvar.

Razavi-Rashtipur, Asadalloh

Deputy of the Third (1989–92), Fourth (1992–96), and
Fifth (1996–2000) Majlis, Kerman, Kerman
1945–, Kerman, Kerman
MS, mechanical engineering; PhD, mathematics, 1991
Mahmud
No imprisonment

Razeqi, Gholam-Reza

Deputy of the Fourth Majlis, Dashtestan, Bushehr
(1992–96)
1958–, Dashtestan, Bushehr
BS, agricultural engineering
Khodakaram
No imprisonment

Razini, Ali

Revolutionary prosecutor-general of Tehran (1985–
86); chief judge of the SCFC (June 15, 1987–June
2012); head of the CAJ (August 17, 2004–August
19, 2009); member of the Fourth Assembly of
Experts, Hamadan (2007–16)
1953–, Razan, Hamadan
Clerical education, Qom Seminary; BA, law, Tehran
University; MA, law, Shahid Beheshti University;
PhD, law, Islamic Azad University–Science and
Research Branch
Mahmud (d. 2011), clergyman (HI)
Judiciary official
No imprisonment
Not a war veteran
Martyr's family (brothers, Abbas and Morteza, killed
at the war front)
Founding member of ADVIR
Razini became head of the Haqqani Seminary in Qom
in 1979 and entered the judiciary in 1980. In 1981,
he was a judge in Khorasan Province, where he
handed out harsh sentences to the regime's oppo-
nents. Ayatollah Khomeini appointed him as the
chief judge of the SCFC and he held that post for
twenty-five years. In that position, he ordered the

execution of many political prisoners, including Seyyed Mehdi Hashemi on September 28, 1987. Razini was injured in an assassination attempt by PMOI on January 5, 1999. He has held such other positions as head of the ideological-political bureau of the IRGC, head of Tehran's justice department, head of the judicial organization of the armed forces, and legal deputy of the judiciary (since August 19, 2009).

Raziyan, Abdollah

Deputy of the Tenth Majlis, Qaemshahr, Savadkuh, and Juybar, Mazandaran
1967–, Arteh, Mazandaran
BA, law; MA, law; PhD, law
University professor
War veteran (eighteen months; wounded)
Raziyan, a reformist, was head of the justice administration in Behshahr, Amol, and Babol, and has held other judicial posts.

Razm, Mohammad

Deputy of the Ninth Majlis, Kermanshah, Kermanshah (2012–16)
1967–, Delfan, Lorestan
MA, criminal law, Qom University
Ahmad, IKRF civil servant
Judiciary official in Harsin
No imprisonment
War veteran
After serving in the Majlis, Razm returned to work in the judiciary.

Razmiyan-Moqaddam, Hasan

Deputy of the Fifth (1996–2000) and Seventh (2004–8) Majlis, Dargaz, Razavi Khorasan
1958–, Dargaz, Razavi Khorasan
BA, theology; pursuing an MA in management
Reza-Qoli
Civil servant
No imprisonment

Razzaqi, Abolqasem

Deputy of the Second Majlis, Tonekabon and Ramsar, Mazandaran (1984–February 20, 1986)
1952–February 20, 1986, Taleqan, Tehran
Clerical education, Qom Seminary
Ahmad
Clergyman (HI)
No imprisonment
Not a war veteran
Razzaqi died when Iraqi forces shot down his plane.

Rebosheh, Mohammad

Deputy of the Fourth (1992–96) and Sixth (2000–2004) Majlis, Iranshahr, Sistan and Baluchestan
1960–, Iranshahr, Sistan and Baluchestan
BA, Persian literature
Rostam
Civil servant
No imprisonment
War veteran

Reyaz, Seyyed Ali

Deputy of the Seventh Majlis, Tehran, Tehran (2004–8)
1958–, Karbala, Iraq
MD, dentistry, Tehran University
Seyyed Ahmad
Dentist and administrator at Shahid Beheshti University of Medical Sciences
No imprisonment
Reyaz has worked for the Red Crescent Society of the Islamic Republic of Iran and as a legal and parliamentary deputy for the Islamic Republic of Iran Medical Council.

Reyshahri [Mohammadinik], Mohammad

Minister of intelligence in PM Musavi's first (August 15, 1984–85) and second (October 28, 1985–August 3, 1989) cabinets; prosecutor-general (August 21, 1989–91); prosecutor-general of the SCFC

(January 3, 1990–December 16, 1998); member of the Second (1991–98), Third (1999–2006), and Fifth (2016–22) Assembly of Experts, Tehran; member of the Fourth (1997–2002), Fifth (2002–7), and Sixth (2007–12) Expediency Discernment Assembly

October 26, 1946–, Shahr-e Rey, Tehran

Clerical education, Qom Seminary

Esma'il, baker

Clergyman; head of the revolutionary military courts

Imprisoned before the revolution

Not a war veteran

Secretary-general and founding member of ADVIR

Reyshahri was born with the family name of Daronparvar. He changed his last name to Mohammadinik but is better known as Reyshahri. Soon after the revolution, he became a revolutionary court judge. He later became head of the revolutionary military courts, where he oversaw the trials of members of the Islamic People's Republican Party of Iran, officers plotting the Nojeh coup, members of the Tudeh Party, Sadeq Qotbzadeh, Seyyed Mehdi Hashemi (brother of the son-in-law of Ayatollah Montazeri), and Grand Ayatollah Seyyed Mohammad-Kazem Shari'atmadari. In 1984, Reyshahri became the first minister of intelligence in postrevolutionary Iran, and in 1990, Ayatollah Khamenei appointed him the prosecutor-general of the SCFC. He ran in both the 1989 and 1997 presidential elections but received a negligible percentage of votes. He was the supreme leader's representative for pilgrimage affairs from April 26, 1991 to 2010, and has been in charge of Shah-Abdolazim Shrine in Shahr-e Rey since April 9, 1990. In addition to these posts, he has been head of Dar-al-Hadith Cultural Institute since November 13, 1995. That same year, on June 5, 1995, Reyshahri also formed his political party, Alliance for the Defense of the Values of the Islamic Revolution. However, the judiciary suspended the party three years later, on November 15, 1998. He is the son-in-law of Ayatollah Ali Meshkini, who issued Reyshahri's permission for *ejtehad*.

Rezahoseyni-Qotbabadi, Mostafa

Deputy of the Eighth Majlis, Shahr-e Babak, Kerman (2008–12)

1970–, Tehran, Tehran

MS, architecture and urban planning, Iran University of Science and Technology

Gholam-Abbas

Provincial civil servant

No imprisonment

War veteran

Martyr's family (brother)

Reza'i, Mas'ud

Deputy of the Tenth Majlis, Shiraz, Fars (2016–20)

1957–, Shiraz, Fars

BA, Persian language and literature, Shiraz University; MA, law, Shiraz University

Academia

No imprisonment

Not a war veteran

Member of PECI in Fars Province

Reza'i, Mohammad-Ali

Deputy of the Eighth Majlis, Torbat-e Heydariyyeh, Razavi Khorasan (2008–12)

1948–, Torbat-e Heydariyyeh, Razavi Khorasan

Clerical education

Naser

Clergyman; supreme leader's representative in the Friday prayer policy council

No imprisonment

Not a war veteran

IRGC militiaman

HI Reza'i knew Supreme Leader Khamenei from their time in Mashhad Seminary before the revolution.

Reza'i, Mohammad-Ebrahim

Deputy of the Ninth (2012–16) and Tenth (2016–20) Majlis, Khomeyn, Markazi

1962–, Khomeyn, Markazi

MA, defense management, Imam Hoseyn University
Mohammad-Ali, farmer
No imprisonment
War veteran (lost a hand and a leg; victim of a chemical attack)
IRGC militiaman (commander of military and law enforcement forces in northwestern Iran)

Reza'i, Morteza

Commander in chief of the IRGC (July 19, 1980–81); deputy commander in chief of the IRGC (April 30, 2006–May 22, 2008)
No imprisonment
War veteran
IRGC militiaman
President Banisadr appointed Reza'i as the IRGC commander in chief in July 1980, which Ayatollah Khomeini approved. Once the Majlis dismissed Banisadr, Reza'i was replaced. In 1993, Ayatollah Khamenei appointed him as head of the IRGC's intelligence protection unit.

Reza'i, Seyyed Abolqasem

Deputy of the Fourth (1992–96) and Fifth (1996–2000) Majlis, Bojnurd, North Khorasan
1954–, Bojnurd, North Khorasan
BS, civil engineering
Seyyed Mohsen
No imprisonment

Reza'i [-Mir Qaed], Mohsen

Commander in chief of the IRGC (1981–September 9, 1997); member of the Fourth (September 9, 1997–2002), Fifth (2002–7), Sixth (2007–12), Seventh (2012–17), and Eighth (2017–22) Expediency Discernment Assembly
1954–, Masjed Soleyman, Khuzestan
BA, economics, Tehran University, 1974; MA, economics, Tehran University; PhD, economics, Tehran University, 2000

Najaf (1887–1999), oil worker
Imprisoned before the revolution
War veteran
IRGC militiaman
Major General Reza'i was a member of the paramilitary Mansurron group and was involved in a number of political assassinations before the revolution. Ayatollah Khomeini appointed him as the IRGC's commander in chief at the age of twenty-seven. On April 29, 1987, he tried to resign from his post, but Ayatollah Khomeini did not accept his resignation and he stayed on the job until 1997. Reza'i is the longest-serving IRGC commander in chief with sixteen years on the job. He ran unsuccessfully for the Sixth Majlis in 1999 and for the presidency in 2005, 2009, and 2013. In the 2009 and 2013 presidential races, he received 1.7 percent and 10.5 percent of the vote, respectively. His string of defeats in the face of his appetite for power led to much ridicule in the public arena. INTERPOL issued a warrant for Reza'i's arrest in 2007 for his alleged involvement in the bombing of a Jewish center (Asociación Mutual Israelita Argentina) in Argentina in July 1994. He presently serves as the secretary of the EDA and in 2015 he rejoined the IRGC. One of his sons married a relative of Ayatollah Khomeini. Another son, Ahmad, denounced the Islamic Republic and died under suspicious circumstances in a hotel room in Dubai, UAE.

Reza'i [-Mir Qaed], Omidvar

Deputy of the Fifth (1996–2000), Sixth (2000–2004), Seventh (2004–8), and Eighth (2008–12) Majlis, Masjed Soleyman and Haftkel, Khuzestan
1957–, Masjed Soleyman, Khuzestan
MD, surgery, Shahid Beheshti University
Najaf (1887–1999), oil worker
Medical doctor
No imprisonment
Founding member of the Islamic Society of Bakhtiaris, the Islamic Association of Iranian Medical Society, and the Green Party of Iran

Reza'i has been a faculty member of the Shahid
    Beheshti University since 1989, head of Loqman
    Hospital in Tehran, and a member of the HCCR
    (2004–8). He was not elected to the Ninth Majlis,
    but Speaker Ali Larijani appointed him to a legal
    deputy position.

Reza'i-Darshaki, Fathollah

Deputy of the Fourth Majlis, Salmas, West Azerbaijan
    (1992–96)
1957–, Mahabad, West Azerbaijan
Associate's degree
Hasan
No imprisonment

Reza'i-Dobandari, Hasan

Deputy of the Third Majlis, Andimeshk and Shush,
    Khuzestan (1988–92)
1952–, Andimeshk, Khuzestan
BA, law
Mirza, farmer
Laborer
No imprisonment
Reza'i-Dobandari earned his law degree after leaving
    the Majlis.

Reza'i-Henji, Mahmud

Deputy of the First Majlis, Karaj, Tehran (1980–84)
1926–, Kashan, Isfahan
PhD, theology
Hasan, farmer
Academia
No imprisonment
Not a war veteran

Reza'i-Kuchi, Mohammad-Reza

Deputy of the Eighth (2008–12), Ninth (2012–16), and
    Tenth (2016–20) Majlis, Jahrom, Fars
1971–, Jahrom, Fars

MD, Shiraz University of Medical Sciences
Khanold
Mayor of Jahrom; medical doctor and university
    administrator
No imprisonment
War veteran (wounded)

Reza'i-Sardareh, Mohammad

Deputy of the Fourth (1996) and Fifth (1996–2000)
    Majlis, Bandar-e Abbas, Hormozgan
1948–, Bandar-e Abbas, Hormozgan
BS, physics
Hoseyn
Provincial educational official
No imprisonment

Rezazadeh, Hoseyn

Deputy of the Tenth Majlis, Kazerun, Fars (2016–20)
September 21, 1968–, Qaemiyeh, Fars
BA, law, University of Judicial Sciences and Adminis-
    trative Services; MA, law
Judge in the justice administration of Kohgiluyeh and
    Buyer Ahmad Province
No imprisonment
War veteran (nine months)
Martyr's family (brother, Farajollah, killed at the war
    front)

Rezazadeh-Shiraz, Mrs. [Seyyedeh] Tahereh

Deputy of the Sixth Majlis, Shiraz, Fars (2000–2004)
1960–, Shiraz, Fars
BA, political science, Tehran University
Seyyed Mohammad
Academia
No imprisonment
Not a war veteran
Rezazadeh-Shiraz was involved in the takeover of the
    American embassy and later married fellow hos-
    tage-taker (and future MP) Mohammad-Ebrahim
    Asgharzadeh.

Rezazehi, Fakhreddin

Deputy of the Third (1988–92) and Fourth (1992–96)
    Majlis, Saravan, Sistan and Baluchestan
1948–, Saravan, Sistan and Baluchestan
Clerical education
Pati-Mohammad
Clergyman
No imprisonment
Mamosta Rezazehi is a Sunni cleric.

Rezvani, Ali-Akbar

Deputy of the First Majlis, Firuzabad, Fars
    (1981–84)
1940–, Firuzabad, Fars
Clerical education; high school diploma
Mahmud
Clergyman (HI)
No imprisonment

Rezvani, Gholam-Reza

Member of the First (1980–83), Second (1989–92),
    Third (1992–98), Fourth (1998–2004), Fifth
    (2004–10), and Sixth (2010–13) Guardian Coun-
    cils; member of the First (1983–90), Second
    (1991–98), and Third (1999–2006) Assembly of
    Experts, Tehran
1930–2013, Khomeyn, Markazi
Clerical education, Najaf Seminary (Iraq)
Mohammad-Karim
Clergyman
No imprisonment
Not a war veteran
Ayatollah Rezvani spent twenty years in Najaf until
    Saddam's regime expelled him in 1980. That
    same year, Ayatollah Khomeini appointed him to
    the GC. Rezvani was Ayatollah Khomeini's and
    Ayatollah Khamenei's representative in the bazaar
    as well. He was head of the CAJ from July 1983
    to 1985 and oversaw the Fourth Majlis election
    in 1992. Rezvani was highly respected within the
    clerical community.

Riyahi, Mohammad-Taqi

Minister of national defense in PM Bazargan's cabinet
    (March 31–September 18, 1979)
1910–August 5, 1988, Isfahan, Isfahan
BS, hydraulics engineering and artillery, École Poly-
    technique (France)
Retired military officer
Imprisoned before the revolution
Not a war veteran
Brigadier General Riyahi was chief of the joint staff
    of the Islamic Republic of Iran Army under PM
    Mossadeq until the coup of August 19, 1953,
    and he spent two or three years in prison under
    the shah. He was sixty-nine years old when he
    became minister of national defense and served
    for only six months before resigning. Riyahi later
    went to Paris and formed a topography company
    in Paris.

Roghani-Zanjani, Mas'ud

Minister of planning and budget in PM Musavi's
    second cabinet (October 30, 1985–February 9,
    1989); VP and head of the PBO in President
    Hashemi-Rafsanjani's first (1989–93) and second
    (1993–95) cabinets
1953–, Zanjan, Zanjan
MA, economics (USA)
Reza, bazaar tradesman
Civil servant, state companies
No imprisonment
Not a war veteran
Martyr's family (brother)
Roghani-Zanjani was involved in anti-Baha'i activ-
    ities from 1965, and was a religious activist at
    the National University from 1974. He did some
    graduate work in the United States and then
    joined Ayatollah Khomeini in France before
    heading back to Iran and teaching business
    administration at Allameh Tabataba'i University.
    Roghani-Zanjani then had the longest tenure
    in charge of the PBO; he joined in 1983 and
    served for ten years. He was the PM's deputy in

PBO (1983–85), minister of planning and budget (1985–89), and finally VP and head of the PBO until he resigned in the summer of 1995. Roghani-Zanjani first informed PM Musavi in a letter in 1986 that the government did not have enough funds to continue fighting Iraq. This letter played an important role in convincing Ayatollah Khomeini to finally end the war. After leaving government posts, Roghani-Zanjani worked as an economics professor at Allameh Tabataba'i University.

Rohami, Mohsen

Deputy of the First (1980–84) and Second (1984–88) Majlis, Khodabandeh, Zanjan
1952–, Khodabandeh, Zanjan
Clerical education
Mirza Ali, clergyman
Clergyman (HI)
No imprisonment
Not a war veteran
Founding member of the Assembly of Former MPs; secretary-general of the Islamic Association of University Instructors

Roshancheragh, Hoseyn

Deputy of the Fifth Majlis, Borkhar and Meymeh, Isfahan (1996–2000)
1941–, Borkhar and Meymeh, Isfahan
BS, chemistry
High school teacher
Ali
No imprisonment

Rostami, Ali-Reza

Deputy of the Third Majlis, Sonqor and Koliyayi, Kermanshah (1988–92)
1952–, Sonqor, Kermanshah
Associate's degree
Hoseyn-Ali
No imprisonment

Rostami, Fayeq

Member of the Fifth Assembly of Experts, Kurdistan (2016–22)
1948–, Marivan, Kurdistan
Clerical education
Abdolqader
Mamosta Rostami, a Sunni cleric, was formerly the temporary Friday prayer of Marivan.

Rostami, Shahram

Chief of the joint staff of the Islamic Republic of Iran Army (date unknown–February 5, 2001)
June 8, 1948–, Ahar, East Azerbaijan
BS, military sciences, Air Force Academy
Father's name unknown, employee of a sugar company
Military pilot
No imprisonment
War veteran
Brigadier General Rostami entered the air force in 1967 and underwent pilot training in Pakistan for two years. In 1975/76, he underwent further pilot training at the Naval Air Station Oceana in Virginia Beach, Virginia. He was in charge of one of Iran's airfields during the Iran–Iraq War and was involved in combat missions.

Rostami-Qarahquz, Asghar

Deputy of the First Majlis, Naqadeh, West Azerbaijan (1981–84)
1951–, Urmia, West Azerbaijan
Associate's degree
Hoseyn
No imprisonment

Rostami-Sani, Abbas-Ali

Deputy of the Seventh Majlis, Quchan and Faruj, Razavi Khorasan (2004–8)
1960–, Quchan, Razavi Khorasan
Clerical education, Qom Seminary; MA

Mohammad
Clergyman (HI)
No imprisonment

Rostamiyan, Abdorrahman

Deputy of the Ninth Majlis, Damghan, Semnan
(2012–16)
1960–, Damghan, Semnan
MD, rheumatology, Tehran University of Medical
Sciences, 1992
Father's name unknown, farmer
Medical doctor; university professor and adminis-
trator at Tehran University of Medical Sciences
(since 1995)
No imprisonment
War veteran

Rostamiyan, Ali

Deputy of the Tenth Majlis, Delfan, Lorestan (2016–20)
1968–, Ashrafabad, Lorestan
BA, history, Tehran University; MA, history
Dowlatmorad, farmer
War veteran (more than two years; victim of chemical
attack)
IRGC militiaman (Basij)
Rostamiyan went to fight in the war when he was
just twelve years old. A conservative, he has been
governor of Divandareh (Kurdistan), an IRIB
deputy in Ilam Province (1997–99), director-gen-
eral of the IKRF in Lorestan (1999–2005) and
Hormozgan Provinces, and head of the Labor and
Social Affairs Organization in Kurdistan.

Rouhani, Hassan

Deputy of the First Majlis, Semnan, Semnan
(1980–84); deputy of the Second (1984–88), Third
(1988–92), Fourth (1992–96), and Fifth (1996–
2000) Majlis, Tehran, Tehran; secretary of the
Supreme Council for National Security (November 13, 1989–2005); member of the Second (May
8, 1991–92), Third (1992–97), Fourth (1997–2002),

Fifth (2002–7), Sixth (2007–12), Seventh (2012–17),
and Eighth (2017–22) Expediency Discernment
Assembly; member of the Third Assembly of
Experts, Semnan (2000–2006); member of the
Fourth (2007–16) and Fifth (2016–22) Assembly of
Experts, Tehran; president (August 3, 2013–2021)
November 12, 1948–, Sorkheh, Semnan
Clerical education, Qom Seminary; BA, judicial law,
Tehran University, 1973; MPhil, law, Glasgow
Caledonian University (Scotland), 1995 (thesis
title: "The Islamic Legislative Power with Ref-
erence to the Iranian Experience"); PhD, con-
stitutional law, Glasgow Caledonian University
(Scotland), 1999 (dissertation title: "The Flexibility
of Shariah (Islamic Law), with Reference to the
Iranian Experience") (both degrees earned under
the name Hassan Feridon)
Asadollah, shopkeeper (imprisoned before the
revolution)
Clergyman (HI)
Imprisoned before the revolution (first time in 1964)
Not a war veteran
Member of the central council of the SCC since 1977
Rouhani, whose real last name is Fereydun, has held
the following additional posts in postrevolutionary Iran: member of the Supreme Defense
Council; commissar of the ideological-political
bureau of the armed forces, where he played a
prominent role in launching the bureau; Ayatollah Montazeri's liaison in dealing with Islamic student associations in Europe (starting
January 1983); supervisor of IRIB; deputy war
commander (1983–85); head of Central Khatam
al-Anbia Construction Headquarters (1985–88);
commander of the Khatam al-Anbia Air Defense
Base (1985–91); secretary of the SCNS; Iran's chief
nuclear negotiator (October 6, 2003–August 15,
2005); deputy Speaker of the Majlis (1992–2000);
and director of the EDA's Center for Strategic
Research (1992–2013). In 2003, he reached a deal
with European powers over Iran's nuclear activities that led to the signing of the 2003 agreement.
Rouhani won the 2013 and the 2017 presidential
elections, capturing 50.6 percent and 57.1 percent

of all votes cast, respectively. His brother, Hoseyn Fereydun, has held such posts as governor of Karaj, ambassador to Malaysia, member of Iran's mission to the UN, and member of the Iranian nuclear team negotiating the 2015 deal. Hoseyn Fereydun's daughter, Maryam, is married to the son of Gholam-Ali Khoshro. Rouhani's son committed suicide.

Rudaki, Mohammad-Nabi

Deputy of the Seventh Majlis, Shiraz, Fars (2004–8)
1958–, Shiraz, Fars
BA, law
Karim
No imprisonment
War veteran
IRGC commander
Martyr's family (brother, Samad)
After leaving the Seventh Majlis, Rudaki became a special adviser to Tehran's mayor.

Ruhani, Mahmud

Member of the Assembly for the Final Examination of the Constitution, Razavi Khorasan (1979); ministerial adviser and head of the Public Health Organization in PM Bahonar's cabinet (August 17–30, 1981), interim PM Mahdavi-Kani's cabinet (September 3–October 18, 1981), and PM Musavi's first cabinet (November 2, 1981–August 1982)
1937–, Mashhad, Razavi Khorasan
MD, epidemiology, University of Brussels (Belgium)
Mokhtar, clergyman
Epidemiologist and professor
No imprisonment
Not a war veteran
Ruhani was in charge of the Public Health Organization of Iran from August 1981 to August 1982.

Ruhani, Seyyed Mehdi

Member of the First (1983–90) and Second (1991–98) Assembly of Experts, Markazi; member of the
Third (1999–November 23, 2000) Assembly of Experts, Qom
1924–November 23, 2000, Qom, Qom
Clerical education, Qom Seminary
Seyyed Abolhasan, clergyman (ayatollah)
Clergyman (ayatollah)
No imprisonment
Not a war veteran
Martyr's family (son, HI Ali Ruhani, killed at the war front)
Member of the SQSS; founding member of the Qom Islamic Society of Admonishers

Ruhani, Seyyed Mostafa

Deputy of the Fourth Majlis, Mahallat and Delijan, Markazi (1992–96)
1944–, Mahallat, Markazi
Clerical education; MA, Islamic philosophy
Seyyed Abolfazl
Clergyman (HI)
No imprisonment

Ruhani [-rad], Hadi

Member of the First (1983–90), Second (1991–98), and Third (1999) Assembly of Experts, Mazandaran
1924–1999, Babolsar, Mazandaran
Clerical education, Qom Seminary
Father's name unknown, clergyman
Clergyman
No imprisonment
Not a war veteran
Ayatollah Ruhani was Ayatollah Khomeini's representative in Mazandaran Province and the Friday prayer leader of Babol.

Ruhanifard, Ali-Akbar

Deputy of the Second Majlis, Dehloran, Ilam (1984–88)
1935–, Golpayegan, Isfahan
Clerical education
Ali-Asghar

Clergyman (HI)
No imprisonment
Not a war veteran

Ruhaniniya, Ramezan

Deputy of the Second (1984–88) and Third (1988–92)
    Majlis, Sepidan, Fars
1955–, Darab, Fars
Clerical education
Ahmad
Clergyman
No imprisonment

Ruhanizadeh-Qadikolahi, Saleh

Deputy of the Third (1988–92) and Fourth (1992–96)
    Majlis, Qaemshahr and Savadkuh, Mazandaran
1958–, Qaemshahr, Mazandaran
High school diploma
Mofid, clergyman
No imprisonment
Ruhanizadeh-Qadikolahi's father was the Friday
    prayer leader of Qaemshahr and Sari.

Ruhbakhsh-Mehraban, Mahmud

Deputy of the Fourth Majlis, Sarab, East Azerbaijan
    (1992–96)
1953–, Tehran, Tehran
BA, industrial management
Farrokh
No imprisonment

Ruhi, Hojjatollah

Deputy of the Seventh Majlis, Babolsar and Ferey-
    dunkenar, Mazandaran (2005–8)
1970–, Fereydunkena, Mazandaran
BS, electrical engineering, Sharif University of Tech-
    nology; MS, electrical engineering, K. N. Toosi
    University of Technology; PhD, electrical engi-
    neering, K. N. Toosi University of Technology
No imprisonment

Ruhi, a reformist, was elected to the Seventh Majlis
    in midterm elections and lost the election for the
    Eighth Majlis. He sits on the board of directors of
    Omid Iranian Foundation.

Ruhi-Sarokhkala'i, Abolqasem

Deputy of the Fifth (1996–2000) and Seventh (2004–8)
    Majlis, Sari, Mazandaran
1961–, Sari, Mazandaran
MA, law
Ahmad
Judiciary official
No imprisonment
Ruhi-Sarokhkala'i ran unsuccessfully for the Tenth
    Majlis.

Rustatasuji, Sa'dollah

Deputy of the Sixth Majlis, Sarvestan, Kherameh, and
    Karbal, Fars (2000–2004)
1957–, Karbal, Fars
BS, agricultural engineering
Qoli
Military and security official
No imprisonment
War veteran

Ruzbehi, Hoseyn

Deputy of the Sixth Majlis, Sari, Mazandaran
    (2000–2004)
1947–, Bandar-e Torkaman, Golestan
BA, management
Academia
No imprisonment

Sa'dunzadeh, Javad

Deputy of the Seventh (2004–8) and Ninth (2012–16)
    Majlis, Abadan, Khuzestan
1959–, Abadan, Khuzestan
BA, law, Islamic Azad University–Abadan, 2011; MA,
    Arabic literature, Shahid Beheshti University,

1990; PhD, Arabic literature, Shahid Beheshti
University, 1995
Professor of Arabic language and literature
Musa
No imprisonment
War veteran
Sa'dunzadeh, a conservative, has worked as a pro-
pagandist and translator in the Office of the
Supreme Leader. He is a former deputy to the
minister of science, and he earned a BA in law
after having earned a PhD in Arabic literature.

Sa'i, Mrs. Zahra

Deputy of the Tenth Majlis, Tabriz, East Azerbaijan
(2016–20)
1980–, Tabriz, East Azerbaijan
BA, Persian language and literature; MA, political
geography; pursuing a PhD in political geography
at Kharazmi University
Ahad
University lecturer and researcher at the EDA's research center
No imprisonment (born after the revolution)
Martyr's family (father)

Sa'adat, Hamid

Deputy of the Seventh (2004–8), and Eighth
(2008–12) Majlis, Najafabad, Tiran, and Karvan,
Isfahan
1952–, Rafsanjan, Kerman
PhD, mathematics
Ali
IRIB civil servant
No imprisonment
Sa'adat was not elected to the Ninth Majlis.

Sa'adat, Mohammad-Baqer

Deputy of the Tenth Majlis, Dashtestan, Bushehr
(2016–20)
1955–, Shabankareh, Bushehr
MA, Persian Gulf studies, Persian Gulf University

Senior adviser to the governor of Bushehr
No imprisonment
Sa'adat was active in Bushehr Province and was lieutenant governor of Bandar-e Rig for a while. He
headed the campaign headquarters of President
Khatami in Shabankareh and President Rouhani
in Bushehr Province.

Sa'adatiyan, Seyyed Jalal

Deputy of the Fourth Majlis, Hamadan, Hamadan
(1992–96)
1952–, Tehran, Tehran
MA, political science
Seyyed Ali-Akbar
No imprisonment
Sa'adatiyan served as director of Far East and Ocea-
nia in Iran's Ministry of Foreign Affairs and was
Iran's chargé d'affaires in London.

Sabbaghiyan, Hashem

Ministerial adviser for revolutionary affairs (1979) and
interior minister (June 20–November 5, 1979) in
PM Bazargan's cabinet; deputy of the First Majlis,
Tehran, Tehran (1980–84)
1937–, Tehran, Tehran
MS, civil engineering, Tehran University, 1961
Taqi, medical professional
Civil engineer
Imprisoned before the revolution
Not a war veteran
Member of the central council of the LMI
Sabbaghiyan was a member of the oil strike commit-
tee appointed by Ayatollah Khomeini before the
revolution and was the chair of the committee
welcoming him back to Iran in 1979. He was also
PM Bazargan's chief of staff. The GC rejected his
qualifications to run in the Sixth Majlis.

Sabbaghiyan, Mohammad-Reza

Deputy of the Tenth Majlis, Mehriz, Yazd (2016–20)
1968–, Bafq, Yazd

BA, history, Yazd University; MA, political science, Islamic Azad University–Qom
Akbar
Teacher and provincial official
No imprisonment
Sabbaghiyan was elected to the Bafq City Council in 1998, and he was mayor of Bafq from 2001 to 2004. He ran unsuccessfully for the Ninth Majlis in 2012.

Saber-Hamishegi, Mahmud

Deputy of the Fourth Majlis, Tehran, Tehran (1992–96)
1951–, Lahijan, Gilan
BS, mathematics
Mohammad
Governor of Shahr-e Ray (1980–89)
No imprisonment
Saber-Hamishegi is a former governor of Shahr-e Rey. He also worked as director of Iran's Tea Company and IRIB's deputy for parliamentary affairs. He has retired from the Ministry of Education.

Saberi, Fakhreddin

Deputy of the Sixth Majlis, Tonekabon and Ramsar, Mazandaran (2000–2004)
1961–, Nowshahr, Mazandaran
Clerical education
Mohammad-Hadi
Clergyman (HI)
No imprisonment

Saberi, Mohammad-Reza [Nasrollah]

Deputy of the Eighth Majlis, Nehbandan and Sarbisheh, South Khorasan (2008–12)
1951–, Birjand, South Khorasan
BS, civil engineering
Ali-Akbar
Retired
No imprisonment
Saberi was not elected to the Ninth Majlis.

Saberi, Reza

Deputy of the Ninth Majlis, Ramiyan and Azadshahr, Golestan (2012–16)
1966–, Seyd Abad Nili, Golestan
BA, anthropology, Allameh Tabataba'i University; MA, anthropology, Tehran University; PhD, anthropology, University of Pune (India), 2008; dissertation title: "Ethnicity and Ethnic Relations in Golestan Province of Iran with Special Reference to Turkmen"
Father's name unknown, farmer
University professor
No imprisonment
War veteran
Saberi, a conservative MP, is an expert in tribal affairs and was a member of the city council.

Saberi-Hamadani, Ahmad

Member of the Second (1991–98) and Third (1999–2006) Assembly of Experts, Hamadan
1923–May 13, 2017, Boyukabad, Hamadan
Clerical education, Qom Seminary
Qiyas-Ali, landowner
Clergyman (ayatollah)
No imprisonment
Not a war veteran
Member of the SQSS
Saberi-Hamadani preached in Turkey and Syria before the revolution. He later became Ayatollah Khomeini's representative in Istanbul and Ayatollah Khamenei's representative in Baku.

Sabur-Aghchekandi, Javad

Deputy of the Eighth Majlis, Ardabil, Nir, and Namin, Ardabil (2008–12)
1955–, Ardabil, Ardabil
BA, public administration, School of Public Administration
Yadollah, bazaar tradesman
No imprisonment
War veteran

IRGC commander

Martyr's family (brother killed at the war front)

Sabur-Aghchekandi was governor of Ardabil. He
was not elected to the Ninth Majlis and has now
retired from the IRGC.

Saburi, Mohammad-Kazem

Deputy of the First Majlis, Shiravan, North Khorasan
(1981–84)

1951–, Shiravan, North Khorasan

BS, mathematics

Ali-Akbar

No imprisonment

Sa'da'i-Jahromi, Mohammad-Ali

Deputy of the Sixth Majlis, Jahrom, Fars (2000–2004)

1955–2008, Shiraz, Fars

BS, agricultural engineering

Mohammad

Military and security official

No imprisonment

Member of the central council of IIPF

Sadat-Ebrahimi, Seyyed Mohammad

Deputy of the Eighth (2008–12) and Ninth (2012–16)
Majlis, Shushtar and Gotvand, Khuzestan

1971–, Shushtar, Khuzestan

Clerical education, Shushtar Seminary; BA, history,
Islamic Azad University–Shushtar

Seyyed Qopani

Clergyman (HI); head of the ideological-political
bureau of the Law Enforcement Forces

No imprisonment

Not a war veteran

Sadati, Seyyed Abdossamad

Member of the Fourth Assembly of Experts, Sistan
and Baluchestan (2007–16)

1949–, Saravan, Sistan and Baluchestan

Clerical education, Jamia Darul Uloom Karachi
(Pakistan)

Abdolaziz, clergyman (mowlana)

Clergyman

No imprisonment

War veteran

Sadati, a Sunni, was the Friday prayer leader of
Saravan.

Sadatinezhad, Seyyed Javad

Deputy of the Tenth Majlis, Kashan, Isfahan (2016–20)

1972–, Sefidshahr, Isfahan

BS, natural resource engineering, University of
Mazandaran, 1995; MS, water engineering, Tarbi-
yat-e Modarres University, 1998; PhD, hydrology,
Moscow State University (Russia), 2003

No imprisonment

Not a war veteran

IRGC militiaman (Basij)

Sadatinezhad has held such posts as rector of Kashan
University (2007–11), legal and parliamentary
deputy of the Ministry of Science, Research, and
Technology (2011–13), head of Tehran University
basiji faculty (2013–15), and faculty member at
Tehran University.

Sadat-Musavi, Seyyed Mohammad-Ja'far

Deputy of the Seventh Majlis, Mobarakeh, Isfahan
(2004–8)

1957–, Rostamabad, Tehran

Clerical education

Hasan

Clergyman

No imprisonment

Sadat-Musavi was a judge in regular courts and revolutionary tribunals.

Sadeq, Seyyed Mehdi

Deputy of the Eighth Majlis, Astaneh-ye Ashrafiyyeh,
Gilan (2008–12)

1952–, Tehran, Tehran

BS, physics; MS, electrical engineering; MS, industrial
    engineering
Seyyed Taqi
University professor
No imprisonment

Sadeq-Daqiqi, Kiyanush

Deputy of the Seventh Majlis, Astaneh-ye Ashrafi-
    yyeh, Gilan (2004–8)
1962–, Astaneh-ye Ashrafiyyeh, Gilan
MD
Ebrahim
Medical doctor
No imprisonment

Sadeqi, Mahmud

Deputy of the Tenth Majlis, Tehran, Tehran (2016–20)
1962–, Qom, Qom
BA, law, Tehran University–Pardis Qom, 1990; MA,
    private law, Tarbiyat-e Modarres University, 1993;
    PhD, private law, Tarbiyat-e Modarres University,
    2000; clerical education, Qom Seminary
Lawyer and law professor at Tarbiyat-e Modarres
    University
Mohammad-Hoseyn, clergyman
No imprisonment
War veteran (wounded)
Martyr's family (father killed in the bombing of the
    IRP headquarters)
Member of the central council of the Islamic Associa-
    tion of University Scholars
Sadeqi ran unsuccessfully for the Sixth Majlis from
    Azna while he was a cleric. He was an adviser
    to the minister of science from 2013 to 2015. In
    November 2016, the judiciary tried to arrest him
    after he questioned financial irregularities involv-
    ing Chief Justice Sadeq Larijani-Amoli.

Sadeqi, Mohammad-Hoseyn

Deputy of the First Majlis, Dorud and Azna, Lorestan
    (1980–81)

1923–June 28, 1981, Aligudarz, Lorestan
Clerical education
Mohammad, clergyman
Clergyman
No imprisonment
Not a war veteran
HI Sadeqi, the Friday prayer leader of Azna, was killed
    in the bombing of the IRP headquarters in June
    1981. His son, Mahmud, became a deputy in the
    Tenth Majlis.

Sadeqi, Mohammad-Sadeq

Deputy of the Sixth Majlis, Aliabad Katul, Golestan
    (2000–2001)
1960–May 17, 2001, Aliabad Katul, Golestan
MD
Mohammad-Baqer, clergyman
Medical doctor
No imprisonment
War veteran
Martyr's family
Sadeqi died in a plane crash.

Sadeqi, Qasem

Deputy of the First Majlis, Mashhad, Razavi Kho-
    rasan (1980–June 28, 1981)
1936–June 28, 1981, Garmeh, North Khorasan
Clerical education; PhD, theology
Esfandiyar, farmer
Clergyman (HI)
No imprisonment
Not a war veteran
Sadeqi was killed in the bombing of the IRP head-
    quarters in June 1981.

Sadeqi, Zargham

Deputy of the Ninth Majlis, Shiraz, Fars (2012–16)
1965–, Mamasani, Fars
MD, Shiraz University of Medical Sciences; MA,
    public law
Medical doctor

No imprisonment
War veteran (wounded; POW in Iraq for sixty-two
    months)
Martyr's family (father and uncle killed at the war front)
While a POW, Sadeqi taught himself a number of
    foreign languages. He held the post of director in
    the Office of the President and has worked for the
    NIOC.

Sadeqi-Azad, Mas'ud

Deputy of the Third Majlis, Kaleybar, East Azerbaijan
    (1988–92)
1945–, Tehran, Tehran
MA
Yahya
No imprisonment
As an employee of the office of PM, Sadeqi-Azad was in-
    jured in the bombing of IRP headquarters in 1981.

Sadeqi-Givi [Khalkhali], Ghafur

Deputy of the First Majlis, Khalkhal, Ardabil (1980–84)
1930–2015, Khalkhal, Ardabil
Pre-diploma
Yadollah, farmer and bazaar tradesman
Bazaar tradesman
No imprisonment
Not a war veteran
After leaving the Majlis, Sadeqi-Givi returned to the
    private sector. He is the younger brother of Sadeq
    Khalkhali.

Sadeqlu, Hasan

Deputy of the Second Majlis, Ramiyan, Golestan
    (1984–88)
1957–, Ramiyan, Golestan
BA
No imprisonment

Sadeqzadeh, Ramezan-Ali

Deputy of the Seventh Majlis, Rasht, Gilan (2004–8)

1958–, Rasht, Gilan
PhD, telecommunications engineering
Mohammad-Ali
Civil servant, state companies
No imprisonment
Sadeqzadeh has worked as a development deputy
    in the Industrial Development and Renovation
    Organization of Iran. He was a member of the
    telecommunications security committee of the
    Supreme Council of Security and an adviser to
    the minister of commerce.

Sadiq, Hushang

Commander of the Islamic Republic of Iran Air Force
    (November 25, 1983–January 30, 1987)
No imprisonment
War veteran (pilot)
Long after the Iran–Iraq War ended, Major General
    Sadiq became the executive director of Chabahar
    Airlines and Zagros Airlines.

Sadiq, Jahanshah

Deputy of the Fourth Majlis, Dorud and Azna, Lor-
    estan (1992–96)
1955–, Arak, Markazi
BA; pursuing an MS in agricultural engineering
Hoseyn
No imprisonment
Sadiq served as head of the Tribal Affairs Organiza-
    tion of Iran from 1995 to 1999 and again from
    2005 to 2013.

Sadiqi, Mrs. Marziyeh

Deputy of the Fifth Majlis, Mashhad, Razavi Kho-
    rasan (1996–2000)
1957–, Tehran, Tehran
BS, civil engineering (USA), MS, civil engineering
    (USA)
Mohammad-Hasan
Transportation expert
No imprisonment

Not a war veteran
Sadiqi got married at the age of thirteen, and she is
    now the executive director of a transportation
    company.

Sadiqi [Raja'i], Mrs. Ateqeh

Deputy of the First (1980–84), Second (1984–88), and
    Third (1988–92) Majlis, Tehran, Tehran
1943–, Qazvin, Qazvin
Pre-diploma (six years of elementary school)
Mohammad-Sadeq
No imprisonment
Member of the central council of the Islamic Society
    of Teachers
Sadiqi received the highest number of votes of any
    deputy in the First Majlis when she was elected
    in the second round on May 9, 1980. Thirteen
    months later, her husband, Mohammad-Ali Raja'i,
    who was serving as president at the time, was as-
    sassinated. The GC disqualified her from running
    in the 1996 Majlis election.

Sadiqi-Bonabi, Rasul

Deputy of the Third (1988–92), Fourth (1992–96),
    Sixth (2000–2004), and Seventh (2004–8) Majlis,
    Bonab and Malekan, East Azerbaijan
1952–, Bonab, East Azerbaijan
PhD, physics
Hoseyn
Academia
No imprisonment

Sadr, Reza

Minister of commerce in PM Bazargan's cabinet (1979)
    and the Revolutionary Council cabinet (1979–80)
1933–, Kashan, Isfahan
PhD, chemistry, University of Miami (USA), 1958
Business manager
No imprisonment
Not a war veteran
Member of the LMI

Before joining Bazargan's cabinet, Sadr was the busi-
    ness manager of one of the Khosrowshahi Group's
    companies in the United States. Later on, he
    became head of the political bureau of the LMI.

Sadr, Seyyed Mohammad

Member of the Eighth Expediency Discernment As-
    sembly (2017–22)
1951–, Qom, Qom
Seyyed Reza, clergyman (ayatollah)
PhD, pharmaceutical, Tehran University, 1976
Senior researcher at the Ministry of Foreign Affairs'
    research center
No imprisonment
Not a war veteran
Founding member of Islamic Iran's Participation Front
Sadr was the Interior Ministry's political deputy from
    1985 to 1989. He has held senior-level positions in
    the Iranian Ministry of Foreign Affairs for many
    years, including as deputy foreign minister for
    European and American affairs and deputy foreign
    minister for Arab and African affairs (1997–2004),
    and was an adviser to foreign minister Javad Zarif
    and former president Khatami. Sadr is the nephew
    of Seyyed Musa Sadr and the father-in-law of Yaser
    Khomeini, the grandson of Ayatollah Khomeini.

Sadr, Seyyed Shahabeddin

Deputy of the Fourth (1992–96), Fifth (1996–2000),
    and Eighth (2008–12) Majlis, Tehran, Tehran
1961–, Tehran, Tehran
MD, physiology, Tehran University
Seyyed Abdollah, clergyman (ayatollah)
Medical doctor
No imprisonment
Not a war veteran
Founding member of the Islamic Society of Iranian
    Physicians
Sadr is a former deputy health minister and fac-
    ulty member at Tehran University. Although
    Sadr served three terms in the Majlis, including
    as deputy Speaker from 2008 to 2012, the GC

disqualified him from running in the Ninth Majlis election.

Sadr Haj Seyyed Javadi, Seyyed Ahmad

Interior minister (February 13–June 20, 1979) and
    minister of justice (1979) in PM Bazargan's
    cabinet; member of the Revolutionary Council
    (1979–80); deputy of the First Majlis, Qazvin,
    Qazvin (1980–84)
May 24, 1917–March 31, 2013, Qazvin, Qazvin
BA, law, Tehran University, 1942; PhD, Law
    (unverified)
Seyyed Ali, landowner
Attorney
No imprisonment
Not a war veteran
Member of the central council of the LMI
Sadr Haj Seyyed Javadi served as Tehran's prosecutor
    (1959–61), a judge, and an attorney before the rev-
    olution. In the latter capacity, he defended many
    of the revolutionaries fighting the shah's regime.
    As interior minister, he was in charge of holding
    the national referendum that took place on March
    30–31, 1979, approving the formation of the
    Islamic Republic. On June 20, 1979, he switched
    posts from interior minister to minister of justice
    after Asadollah Mobasheri-Monfared resigned
    from that post. He was involved with the *Ency-
    clopedia of Shiism* for many years. His brother is
    the well-known public intellectual Ali-Asghar Haj
    Seyyed Javadi. Seyyed Ahmad Sadr Haj Seyyed
    Javadi and his brother's brother-in-law, the jurist
    Naser Katuziyan, were two of the authors of
    the preliminary draft of the Constitution of the
    Islamic Republic.

Sadra, Ali-Reza

Deputy of the Fourth Majlis, Dezful, Khuzestan
    (1992–96)
1958–, Dezful, Khuzestan
BA, political science, Tehran University, 1981; MA,
    political science, Tarbiyat-e Modarres University;
PhD, political science, Tarbiyat-e Modarres Uni-
    versity, 1987
University professor
Mohammad-Ali
No imprisonment

Sadrolsadati, Seyyed Ruhollah

Member of the Fifth Assembly of Experts, Hor-
    mozgan (2016–22)
1983–, Qom, Qom
Clerical education, Qom Seminary
Seyyed Mehdi, clergyman
Clergyman (HI)
Sadrolsadati was the youngest person elected to the
    Fifth AE.

Sadr-Tabataba'i, Seyyed Jalil

Deputy of the Second Majlis, Yazd, Yazd (1984–88)
December 31, 1943–, Mehriz, Yazd
Clerical education, Qom Seminary
Seyyed Ahmad
Clergyman (HI)
No imprisonment
Not a war veteran
Sadr-Tabataba'i ran unsuccessfully a number of times
    for the Majlis and the AE.

Saduqi, Mohammad

Member of the Assembly for the Final Examination of
    the Constitution, Yazd (1979)
1909–July 2, 1982, Yazd, Yazd
Clerical education, Qom Seminary
Mirza Abutaleb, clergyman
Clergyman
No imprisonment
Not a war veteran
Member of the central council of the ACC
Ayatollah Saduqi, a defender of the paramilitary
    group Devotees of Islam, was a long-time ally of
    Ayatollah Khomeini, who appointed him his rep-
    resentative in Yazd from May 1980 to July 1982.

Furthermore, Khomeini chose him to supervise presidential and Majlis elections. Saduqi, who was also the Friday prayer leader of Yazd and a revolutionary court judge, ordered many executions. He escaped an assassination attempt in January 1980; PMOI assassinated him in 1982. Saduqi's students included Ayatollahs Motahhari, Qoddusi, and Mohammad Fazel-Lankarani. He is the father of Mohammad-Ali Saduqi.

Saduqi, Mohammad-Ali

Deputy of the First Majlis, Yazd, Yazd (1981–84); deputy of the Third Majlis, Tehran, Tehran (1988–92); VP for parliamentary affairs in President Khatami's first cabinet (1998–2001)
1949–2011, Abbasabad, Qom
Clerical education, Qom Seminary
Mohammad, clergyman (ayatollah)
Clergyman
No imprisonment
Not a war veteran
Martyr's family (father assassinated by PMOI)
Member of the IRP and the ACC
HI Saduqi was with Ayatollah Khomeini in Paris. He was appointed as the Friday prayer leader of Yazd after the assassination of his father in 1982. He also held such posts as member of the IRGC's command council in Yazd, supervisor for the election of members of the HCJ (appointed by Ayatollah Khomeini on January 25, 1983, and May 26, 1985), deputy to the HCJ, and deputy prosecutor-general. Saduqi was President Khatami's brother-in-law and served as his VP for parliamentary affairs for three years. He was also the father-in-law of HI Mohammad Hashemiyan.

Sa'edi, Mohammad-Reza [Meysam]

Deputy of the Sixth Majlis, Tehran, Tehran (2000–2004)
1969–, Quchan, Razavi Khorasan

MS, chemistry
Yahya
Sa'edi was a student activist and the reformists put him on their list for Tehran's election.

Sa'edi, Qasem

Deputy of the Tenth Majlis, Dasht-e Azadegan, Khuzestan (2016–20)
1965–, Na'meh, Khuzestan
BA, sociology, Tehran University; MA sociology, Islamic Azad University–Shushtar
Father's name unknown, farmer
Head of the education department in Dasht-e Azadegan
No imprisonment
War veteran
IRGC militiaman

Sa'edi, Seyyed Jasem

Deputy of the Fourth (1992–96), Fifth (1996–2000), Sixth (2000–2004), Seventh (2004–8), and Eighth (2008–12) Majlis, Shush and Andimeshk, Khuzestan
1959–, Ahvaz, Khuzestan
BA, social planning
Seyyed Abdollah
Civil servant
No imprisonment
Sa'edi was not elected to the Ninth Majlis.

Safa'i, Mrs. Tayebeh

Deputy of the Eighth Majlis, Tehran, Tehran (2008–12)
1960–, Urmia, West Azerbaijan
MA, educational management, Alzahra University; PhD, educational management, Islamic Azad University–Tehran
Ja'far, civil servant
University professor
No imprisonment

IRGC militiawoman (women's Basij in West Azerbaijan)
Member of the IRP
In the Eighth Majlis, Safa'i headed the women's caucuses. She did not receive enough votes to get elected to the Ninth Majlis. Her husband has been governor of West Azerbaijan and was Mahmoud Ahmadinejad's planning deputy when he was Tehran's mayor.

Safa'i, Zabihollah

Deputy of the Third (1988–92), Fifth (1996–2000), and Sixth (2000–2004) Majlis, Asadabad, Hamadan
1955–, Asadabad, Hamadan
BA, 1985; MA, management, 1995
Valiyollah
No imprisonment
War veteran
IRGC militiaman
Founding member of the Assembly of Former MPs

Safa'i-Farahani, Mohsen

Deputy of the Sixth Majlis, Tehran, Tehran (2000–2004)
1948–, Tehran, Tehran
MS, civil engineering, Tehran University, 1971
Mohammad-Hasan
Civil servant
No imprisonment
Not a war veteran
Member of the central council of Islamic Iran Participation Front
Safa'i-Farahani held the following positions before being elected to the Majlis: adviser to Tehran municipality, deputy minister of heavy industries (in the 1980s), deputy of the Organization for Expansion and Renewal of Iranian Industries, chair of the board of directors of the Sugar Cane Development Corporation, head of the state power company (Tavanir), and head of Iran's soccer federation (1997–2002). He was imprisoned for a while after the contested 2009 presidential election.

Safa'ipur-Zamani, Arsalan

Deputy of the First (1983–84), Second (1984–88), and Third (1988–92) Majlis, Kermanshah, Kermanshah
1939–, Kermanshah, Kermanshah
BA, law; clerical education
Gholam-Reza
No imprisonment
Safa'ipur-Zamani worked hard in the late 1980s to change the name of his province from Bakhtaran to its previous name of Kermanshah.

Safari, Ahmad

Deputy of the Tenth Majlis, Kermanshah, Kermanshah (2016–20)
1971–, Mahidasht, Kermanshah
BS, Islamic Azad University–Kermanshah
Shahin
Lieutenant governor of Kuzaran-e Sanjabi
No imprisonment
Not a war veteran
Martyr's family (father and father-in-law)
Safari held various military-security posts in Kermanshah Province.

Safari, Latif

Deputy of the First (1980–84) and Second (1984–88) Majlis, Islamabad-e Gharb, Kermanshah
1945–, Islamabad-e Gharb, Kermanshah
MS, biological sciences
Khalifeh, farmer
Academia
No imprisonment
Not a war veteran
Safari was the managing director of the reformist *Neshat* until the judiciary banned it.

Safari, Mahmud

Deputy of the Second Majlis, Damavand, Tehran (1984–88)

1945–, Damavand, Tehran
BA; clerical education
Habibollah
No imprisonment
Safari became rector of Islamic Azad University–
    Damavand after leaving the Majlis.

Safari-Natanzi, Morteza

Deputy of the Tenth Majlis, Qamsar and Natanz,
    Isfahan (2016–20)
1956–, Natanz, Isfahan
BA, insurance management, Tehran's Higher Institute
    of Insurance; MA, economics, Bucharest Univer-
    sity of Economic Studies (Romania), 1984; PhD,
    economics, Bucharest University of Economic
    Studies (Romania), 1987
Diplomat
No imprisonment
Not a war veteran
Safari-Natanzi was chargé d'affaires in Romania from
    1981 to 1987. He has been ambassador to Hungary
    (1991–95), Khazakistan (2000–2004), and Spain
    (2010–14).

Safavi, Seyyed Yahya [Rahim]

Deputy commander in chief of the IRGC (September
    24, 1989–September 1997); commander in chief of
    the IRGC (September 10, 1997–September 1, 2007)
1952–, Lenjan, Isfahan
BS, geology, Tabriz University, 1975; MA, geography,
    Imam Hoseyn University, 1995; PhD, geography,
    Tarbiyat-e Modarres University, 2001
Seyyed Abbas, farmer
IRGC commander
No imprisonment
War veteran
Martyr's family (two brothers killed at the war front)
Major General Safavi underwent military training
    in Syria before the revolution and served in the
    shah's army from 1975 to 1977. He was com-
    mander of the IRGC's ground forces from 1985
    to 1989, and started teaching at Imam Hoseyn

University in 1993. In 1997, Safavi replaced
Mohsen Reza'i as the IRGC's commander in
chief. After his term ended, the supreme leader
appointed him as his senior military assistant. He
is on the list of Iranian individuals sanctioned by
the United States government.

Safavi-Kuhesareh, Mir Abbas

Deputy of the Second Majlis, Fuman, Gilan (1984–88)
1956–, Ardabil, Ardabil
Clerical education
Mir Reza
Clergyman
No imprisonment

Saffar-Harandi, Mohammad-Hoseyn

Minister of culture and Islamic guidance in President
    Ahmadinejad's first cabinet (August 24, 2005–Au-
    gust 2, 2009); member of the Seventh (2012–17)
    and Eighth (2017–22) Expediency Discernment
    Assembly
1953–, Tehran, Tehran
MS, defense management, Supreme National Defense
    University, 1993
Ali-Asghar
No imprisonment
War veteran
IRGC militiaman
Saffar-Harandi did not complete his BA in civil engi-
    neering at Iran University of Science and Technol-
    ogy, nor did he finish his doctoral dissertation. He
    held high positions within the IRGC from 1980
    to 1993, and he was deputy editor of *Keyhan* from
    1994 to 2005. President Ahmadinejad dismissed
    him on July 26, 2009, but then realized that the
    cabinet needed to seek another vote of confidence
    from the Majlis for its remaining week, due to
    the high turnover in the cabinet. As such, Ah-
    madinejad kept Saffar-Harandi on his post until
    the end. After finishing his term in the cabinet,
    Saffar-Harandi became the IRGC's director of
    cultural affairs. The shah's regime executed his

relative, Reza Saffar-Harandi, for involvement in the assassination of PM Hassan-Ali Mansur and a number of army officers in 1964. His maternal cousin is Fakhrolsadat Mohtashamipur, the wife of reformist politician Mostafa Tajzadeh.

Safi-Golpayegani, Lotfollah

Member of the Assembly for the Final Examination of the Constitution, Markazi (1979); member of the First (February 1980–86) and Second (1986–June 1988) Guardian Councils
1919–, Golpayegan, Isfahan
Clerical education, Qom Seminary, 1942 (also studied in Najaf)
Mohammad-Javad, clergyman (molla)
Clergyman (ayatollah)
No imprisonment
Not a war veteran
In the era of Ayatollah Borujerdi, Safi-Golpayegani was in charge of examination of theology students. Ayatollah Khomeini appointed him as the secretary of the Guardian Council in December 1981, and he held that post until June 1988, when he resigned from the second GC to return to Qom and become a *marja'*. Ayatollah Safi-Golpayegani, a prolific writer, has very conservative views on artistic (i.e., musical concerts) and cultural issues and has often criticized the executive branch on these grounds. He is the son-in-law of Grand Ayatollah Seyyed Mohammad-Reza Golpayegani.

Sahabi, Ezzatollah

Member of the Revolutionary Council (1979–80); member of the Assembly for the Final Examination of the Constitution, Tehran (1979); ministerial adviser and head of the PBO in PM Bazargan's cabinet (1979) and the Revolutionary Council cabinet (1979–80); deputy of the First Majlis, Tehran, Tehran (1980–84)
May 9, 1930–May 31, 2011, Tehran, Tehran
BS, mechanical engineering, Tehran University, 1952; MS, electrical engineering, Tehran University

Yadollah, academia
Engineer
Imprisoned before the revolution
Not a war veteran
Member of the central council of the LMI
Sahabi took charge of the PBO on September 23, 1979, and led it for some ten months. He was one of eight deputies in the AFEC who opposed the notion of *velayat-e faqih*. Sahabi's wife is the niece of Mehdi Bazargan. Despite this family tie, Sahabi was the one member of the LMI who forcefully opposed the organization's nomination of Bazargan as the party's candidate for the first presidential election in 1980. That same year he left the LMI to form a coalition of nationalist-religious activists. In 1981, Sahabi's son was arrested for supporting PMOI. Altogether, he spent fifteen years in prison, almost equally before and after the revolution. Sahabi launched the *Iran Farda* magazine in May 1992, and he was its editor until the judiciary closed it down in 2000. The GC disqualified Sahabi from running in the 1997 presidential election and the 2000 Majlis election. His daughter Haleh died of a heart attack during her father's funeral.

Sahabi, Yadollah

Member of the Revolutionary Council (1979); ministerial adviser for revolutionary affairs and ministerial adviser for education and research in PM Bazargan's cabinet (1979); deputy of the First Majlis, Tehran, Tehran (1980–84)
1906–April 11, 2002, Tehran, Tehran
BS, natural sciences, Daneshsara-ye Ali-ye Tehran, 1931; PhD, geology, University of Lille (France), 1936
Ali, farmer
Academia
Imprisoned before the revolution
No war veteran
Founder and member of the central council of the LMI
Sahabi founded LMI alongside Mehdi Bazargan and Ayatollah Mahmud Taleqani in 1961. Before the

revolution, he worked as a civil servant, helped to establish religiously inclined high schools and a publishing house, and was a political prisoner for many years. On January 18, 1979, Ayatollah Khomeini appointed him to a committee supporting and coordinating revolutionary demonstrations. He was a member of PM Bazargan's cabinet and changed his portfolio on September 28, 1979. He coordinated the writing of the first draft of the postrevolutionary constitution. Sahabi was the oldest member serving in the First Majlis. He spent the rest of his time as a member of the political opposition. He was the father of Ezzatollah Sahabi.

Sahebozzamani, Fathali

Deputy of the First Majlis, Asadabad, Hamadan (1980–October 25, 1981)
1922–October 25, 1981, Razan, Hamadan
Clerical education
Ramezan, clergyman
Clergyman
Imprisoned before the revolution
Not a war veteran
Before the revolution, the shah's regime exiled HI Sahebozzamani to Kurdistan; they later permitted his return on August 30, 1978. He died in a car accident.

Sahebozzamani, Mohammad-Ali

Deputy of the Second Majlis, Urmia, West Azerbaijan (1984–88)
1936–, Urmia, West Azerbaijan
Clerical education, Qom Seminary
Esma'il
Clergyman
No imprisonment
HI Sahebozzamani was in charge of a revolutionary komiteh in the early days of the revolution, and also served for a while as the supreme leader's representative in the IRGC.

Sahmihesari, Esma'il

Deputy of the Second (1986–88) and Third (1988–92) Majlis, Torbat-e Heydariyyeh, Razavi Khorasan
1934–, Torbat-e Heydariyyeh, Razavi Khorasan
Clerical education
Ali-Mohammad
Clergyman (HI)
No imprisonment
Not a war veteran
Martyr's family (son, Javad)

Sa'idi, Abdollah-e Sani

Deputy of the Fourth Majlis, Minudasht, Golestan (1992–96)
1958–, Minudasht, Golestan
MD, medicine
Abdolahad
Medical doctor
No imprisonment

Sa'idi, Mrs. Fatemeh

Deputy of the Tenth Majlis, Tehran, Tehran (2016–20)
1963–, Tehran, Tehran
MA, educational management
High school teacher and headmistress
Member of the Tehran Province council of the HKSI
Sa'idi was long active in the educational field in Kerman Province, and she was elected to the Majlis as a reformist.

Sa'idi, Mohammad-Esma'il

Deputy of the Ninth (2012–16) and Tenth (2016–20) Majlis, Tabriz, Azarshahr, and Osku, East Azerbaijan
1961–, Azarshahr, East Azerbaijan
BA, management, Tabriz University; MA, public administration, Tehran University
No imprisonment
War veteran
IRGC militiaman

Sa'idi became commander of the Azarshahr IRGC at the age of twenty-one and was deputy commander of Ashura 31 Brigade. He managed to enter the Tenth Majlis in 2016 after the GC decided that he was the last elected MP from Tabriz instead of Ali-Reza Monadi-Sefidan.

Sa'idi-Golpayegani, Seyyed Mohsen

Member of the Fifth Assembly of Experts, Ilam (2016–22)
1962–, Qom, Qom
Clerical Education, Qom Seminary
Seyyed Mohammad-Reza, clergyman (ayatollah)
Clergyman (HI)
No imprisonment
Martyr's family (father)
Prison authorities tortured Sa'idi-Golpayegani's father to death before the revolution. In 2016, he ran for the AE from Ilam as a non-native candidate.

Sa'idi-Kiya, Mohammad

Minister of roads and transportation in PM Musavi's second cabinet (October 28, 1985–August 3, 1989) and President Hashemi-Rafsanjani's first cabinet (August 29, 1989–August 2, 1993); minister of Construction Jihad in President Khatami's first cabinet (August 20, 1997–2000); minister of housing and urban development in President Ahmadinejad's first cabinet (August 24, 2005–August 2, 2009)
1946–, Isfahan, Isfahan
BS, civil engineering, Amirkabir University of Technology; MS, civil engineering, Amirkabir University of Technology, 1969
Ali, oil worker
Civil servant, ministries
No imprisonment
Not a war veteran
As a cabinet minister, Sa'idi-Kiya has worked under four different heads of government. He began his career as a provincial civil servant, working in the Hormozgan Province roads and transportation department in 1980. While serving as the minister of roads and transportation, he survived impeachment on March 2, 1993. From 1993 to 1997, he worked as an official of the FDWI, and he later became an adviser to President Khatami (2000–2005). Sa'idi-Kiya has the distinction of having received the highest number of positive votes for any minister on two occasions when ministers were introduced to the Majlis: On August 20, 1997, when he became minister of the Construction Jihad in President Khatami's first cabinet, and on August 24, 2005, when he became minister of housing and urban development in President Ahmadinejad's first cabinet. When he joined the latter administration, he was also the cabinet's most experienced minister. However, the GC disqualified Sa'idi-Kiya from running in the 2013 presidential election. On July 22, 2014, Ayatollah Khamenei appointed him head of the FDWI as compensation.

Sa'idi-Mobarekeh, Mrs. Zahra

Deputy of the Tenth Majlis, Mobarakeh, Isfahan (2016–20)
1983–, Mobarakeh, Isfahan
BS, biochemistry; MS, industrial engineering
Provincial civil servant
Sa'idi-Mobarekeh is a Qur'an researcher and reciter. Her father was wounded at the war front.

Sa'idiyanfar, Mohammad-Ja'far

Deputy of the Second (1984–88) and Third (1988–92) Majlis, Khomeinishahr, Isfahan
1952–, Homayunshahr, Isfahan
Clerical education
Heydar
Clergyman (HI) and university lecturer
Imprisoned before the revolution
Member of the ASLQS
Sa'idiyanfar was one of the supporters of Ayatollah Montazeri.

Sa'idlu, Ali

VP for executive affairs in President Ahmadinejad's
   first cabinet (August 24, 2005–August 2, 2009);
   VP and head of the Physical Training Organization in President Ahmadinejad's second cabinet
   (2009–10)
1952–, Tabriz, East Azerbaijan
BS, geology, Tabriz University, 1974; MS, geology, 1978
Mohammad
Civil servant
No imprisonment
War veteran
Sa'idlu became the director of Iran's Tea Company in
   1980. He worked for eight years as a deputy minister of industries. Sa'idlu obtained a phony PhD
   from Hartford University, registered in the Pacific
   island of Vanuatu, while working as a deputy in
   the office of Tehran's mayor in 2003. In 2005, the
   Majlis rejected him as President Ahmadinejad's
   first choice for minister of petroleum (101 positive votes, 133 negative votes, and thirty-eight
   abstentions). Ahmadinejad then restored the
   post of VP for executive affairs, which had been
   abolished during Khatami's second term in office
   due to interference with the tasks of the first VP,
   and appointed Sa'idlu to it. In his second cabinet,
   Ahmadinejad appointed Sa'idlu as the last head
   of the Physical Training Organization before the
   organization was dissolved on December 29, 2010.

Sajjadi, Ahmad

Deputy of the Ninth Majlis, Fariman, Sarakhs,
   Ahmadabad, and Razavieh, Razavi Khorasan
   (2012–16)
1966–, Sarakhs, Razavi Khorasan
BA, elementary education, Farhangian
   University–Mashhad
Teacher and member of the Sarakhs City Council
No imprisonment
War veteran
IRGC militiaman (Basij commander)

After the Ninth Majlis, Sajjadi who is a conservative,
   went to work for the Iranian Central Oil Fields
   Company.

Sajjadiyan, Mohammad-Reza

Deputy of the Seventh (2004–8) and Eighth
   (2008–12) Majlis, Khaf and Roshtkhar, Razavi
   Khorasan
1972–, Tehran, Tehran
MS, mining engineering
Abbas-Ali
Civil servant
No imprisonment
Not a war veteran
Sajjadiyan was a Sunni MP.

Sajjadnezhad, Seyyed Mir Ghaffar

Deputy of the First (1981–84) and Second (1984–88)
   Majlis, Bostanabad, East Azerbaijan
1930–, Tabriz, East Azerbaijan
Clerical education
Mir Sadeq
Clergyman
No imprisonment
Not a war veteran
HI Sajjadnezhad is a former head of the Special Civil
   Courts branch 5, Tehran. He was also very active
   in delivering support material to the front during
   the war with Iraq.

Salahi, Abbas

Deputy of the Ninth Majlis, Tafresh, Ashtiyan, and
   Farahan, Markazi (2012–16)
1964–, Tafresh, Markazi
MD, physiology and rehabilitation, Shiraz University
   of Medical Sciences, 1995
Medical doctor
No imprisonment
Martyr's family
In 2016, Salahi returned to the private sector.

Salahshuri, Mrs. Parvaneh

Deputy of the Tenth Majlis, Tehran, Tehran (2016–20)
1964–, Masjed Soleyman, Khuzestan
BA, sociology; MA, sociology; PhD, sociology
Professor at Islamic Azad University
No imprisonment
Member of the Organization of the Erudite of Islamic Iran
Salahshuri wrote many articles for reformist newspapers, and she was head of the women's headquarters in Chahar Mahal and Bakhtiari Province. She worked in the Office of the VP for Women's and Family Affairs under President Rouhani. Her husband, Barat Qobadiyan, also tried to run for the Tenth Majlis, but the GC disqualified him.

Salamati, [Seyyed] Mohammad

Minister of agriculture in PM Raja'i's cabinet (September 10, 1980–81), PM Bahonar's cabinet (August 17–30, 1981), interim PM Mahdavi-Kani's cabinet (September 3–October 18, 1981), and PM Musavi's first cabinet (November 2, 1981–83); deputy of the Third Majlis, Tehran, Tehran (1988–92)
1946–, Kashmar, Razavi Khorasan
BA, economics, Tehran University, 1973
Seyyed Mehdi
Civil servant, ministries
Imprisoned before the revolution (three years)
Not a war veteran
Secretary-general of OMIRI (1991–2004)
In addition to being minister of agriculture in four cabinets in the early years of the revolution (1980–84) and being an MP from Tehran, Salamati was also a deputy minister for cultural affairs in the Labor Ministry. After the dissolution of OMIRI in 2009, he continued his political activities as a reformist.

Salamatiyan, Seyyed Ahmad

Deputy of the First Majlis, Isfahan, Isfahan (1980–82)
April 18, 1944–, Isfahan, Isfahan
BA, law, Tehran University, 1964; MA (diploma d'etudes superieures [DES]), political science, University of Paris (France), 1967; MA thesis title: "History of the Political Role of the Military in Iran"
Seyyed Hoseyn, bazaar tradesman
Academia
Imprisoned before the revolution
Not a war veteran
Member of INF
Salamatiyan was a member of the INF until 1971 and the Committee for Defense of Human Rights in Iran until 1978. He and Banisadr knew each other from their student days in France. Salamatiyan resigned from his post as the political deputy of foreign minister Karim Sanjabi in 1979. He ran Banisadr's presidential office and was in charge of the legal section of Enqelab-e Islami, published by Banisadr. Salamatiyan left the First Majlis after serving for fourteen months. The Majlis voted on January 7, 1982, that his absenteeism meant that he had resigned from his post. Salamatiyan went into exile in Paris, where he owns a bookstore and is a political commentator on Iranian affairs.

Salami, Ali-Ahmad

Member of the Fourth (2007–16) and Fifth (2016–22) Assembly of Experts, Sistan and Baluchestan
1945–, Sarbaz, Sistan and Baluchestan
Clerical education, Jamia Darul Uloom Karachi (Pakistan); MA, economics, University of Karachi (Pakistan)
Ali-Mohammad, clergyman
Clergyman
No imprisonment
Not a war veteran
Salami, a Sunni cleric, teaches theology and Hanafi law at Islamic Schools of Thought Educational and Research Institute. He has also been a member of the high council of the World Forum for Proximity of Islamic Schools of Thought.

Salami, Hoseyn

Deputy commander in chief of the IRGC (October 4, 2009–present)
1960–, Golpayegan, Isfahan
BS, Iran University of Science and Technology; MS, military science, Iranian Army Command and General Staff College
No imprisonment
IRGC militiaman
Brigadier General Salami joined the IRGC in 1980 and fought in Kurdistan and in the Iran–Iraq War. He was the operations deputy of the IRGC's joint staff from 1997 to 2005, and is considered one of the IRGC's best strategic thinkers. Salami also teaches at the Supreme National Defense University.

Salavati [-Khozani], Fazlollah

Deputy of the First Majlis, Isfahan, Isfahan (1980–84)
1938–, Isfahan, Isfahan
BA, Arabic language and literature, Isfahan University of Technology, 1965; MA, Arabic language and literature, Tehran University, 1970; PhD, theology, 2001; clerical education
Heydar, clergyman
Governor of Isfahan
Imprisoned and exiled before the revolution
Salavati was very active against the shah's regime before the revolution. After leaving the Majlis, Salavati published a weekly magazine (*Navid-e Isfahan*) and served as an adviser to the mayor of Isfahan. The GC disqualified him from running in any more parliamentary elections. Salavati was close to national-religious forces. He is the son-in-law of the learned cleric Mohammad-Taqi Ja'fari.

Salehabadi, Qorbanali

Deputy of the Third Majlis, Mashhad, Razavi Khorasan (1988–92)
1952–, Salehabad, Razavi Khorasan
BS, engineering
Ebrahim

No imprisonment
Member of IISP
The revolutionary court sentenced Salehabadi to two years' imprisonment in October 1992, and the GC rejected his qualifications for the Fourth Majlis.

Salehi [Saleh-Shari'ati], Abbas

Minister of culture and Islamic guidance in President Rouhani's second cabinet (August 20, 2017–2021)
1964–, Mashhad, Razavi Khorasan
Clerical education, Mashhad and Qom Seminaries; PhD, Islamic theology, Qom University
Hasan, clergyman (ayatollah)
Deputy minister of culture and Islamic guidance
No imprisonment
Salehi, a cleric who does not wear his religious robe, was appointed deputy minister of culture and Islamic guidance in 2013; in 2016, he served for a while as the caretaker of the ministry after the resignation of Ali Jannati and the appointment of Reza Salehi-Amiri as the new minister. He has taught Islamic theology and jurisprudence at universities and religious seminaries since 1991 and has been the editor of a number of publications. In 1997, Ayatollah Khamenei appointed Salehi to the board of trustees of Qom Seminary Islamic Propaganda Office and he served in that capacity until 2017.

Salehi, Ali-Akbar

VP and head of the Atomic Energy Organization (2009–11) and then minister of foreign affairs (January 30, 2011–August 3, 2013) in President Ahmadinejad's second cabinet; VP and head of the Atomic Energy Organization in President Rouhani's first (2013–August 13, 2017) and second (August 20, 2017–2021) cabinets
March 24, 1949–, Karbala, Iraq
BS, physics, American University of Beirut (Lebanon), 1971; PhD, nuclear engineering, Massachusetts Institute of Technology (USA), 1977; dissertation title: "Resonance Region Neutronics of Unit Cells in Fast and Thermal Reactors"

Seyyed Ahmad, bazaar tradesman
Deputy secretary-general of the Organization of Islamic Conference (2007–9)
No imprisonment
Not a war veteran
Salehi went to MIT in fall 1972 and graduated in 1977. He then returned to Iran and taught at Sharif University of Technology, serving as rector from 1982 to 1984 and again from 1989 to 1993. In the mid-1980s, he was deputy for education affairs in the Ministry of Culture. Salehi was also Iran's representative to the IAEA in Vienna from 1997 to 2005. MPs confirmed him as foreign minister in 2011 with 60 percent of the vote.

Salehi, Mohammad

Member of the First Guardian Council (1980–86)
1932–, Qom, Qom
PhD, law
Abdolvahhab
Judiciary official
No imprisonment
Not a war veteran
Before Ayatollah Khomeini appointed him to the first GC, Salehi held posts such as head of the Qom and Kerman justice administrations and revolutionary prosecutor-general of Qom.

Salehi, Qeysar

Deputy of the Seventh Majlis, Deyr, Kangan, and Jam, Bushehr (2004–8)
1968–, Kangan, Bushehr
BA, educational management
Gholam-Ali
Academia
No imprisonment

Salehi, Seyyed Ataollah

General commander of the army (September 11, 2005–August 21, 2017); first deputy chief of

the Armed Forces General Staff (August 21, 2017–present)
1950–, Rudsar, Gilan
BS, military science (artillery), Ground Forces Officers' Academy, 1970
Army commander
War veteran
Major General Salehi has spent half a century in Iran's military. After the revolution, he served as commander of the army's most powerful brigade (21 Hamzeh), rector of the Ground Forces Officers' Academy, and AFGS's deputy for inspection and human capital. Salehi is the brother-in-law of Mohammad Shari'atmadari, the former minister of commerce and VP of executive affairs.

Salehi, Yavar

Deputy of the Fourth Majlis, I'zeh, Khuzestan (1992–96)
1957–, I'zeh, Khuzestan
Associate's degree
Hajatmorad
No imprisonment

Salehi-Amiri, Seyyed Reza

Minister of culture and Islamic guidance in President Rouhani's first cabinet (November 1, 2016–August 13, 2017)
1961–, Babol, Mazandaran
BA, political science, Islamic Azad University–Tehran; MA, political science, Tehran University; PhD, public administration, Islamic Azad University–Science and Research Branch; dissertation title: "Managing Ethnic Diversity in Iran and the World"
No imprisonment
War veteran
Salehi-Amiri was an official in the MIIRI, including as director-general of MIIRI in Khuzestan Province, and later he worked alongside Hassan Rouhani in the Center for Strategic Research. During the 2013 presidential race, he was a cultural deputy in

Rouhani's election headquarters. On October 27, 2013, he failed to receive enough votes (107 positive, 141 negative, and thirteen abstentions) from the Ninth Majlis to become minister of sports and youth after being the caretaker for that ministry. In February 2014, President Rouhani appointed him head of the National Library, and on November 1, 2016, the Tenth Majlis approved him as the minister of culture and Islamic guidance with 180 positive votes, eighty-nine negative votes, and six abstentions.

Salehifard [Salehi-Mazandarani], Esma'il

Member of the First (1983–90) and Second (1991–98)
   Assembly of Experts, Mazandaran
1933–2001, Qaemshahr, Mazandaran
Clerical education, Qom Seminary
Rahmatollah, clergyman and farmer
Clergyman (ayatollah)
Imprisoned before the revolution
Not a war veteran

Salehi-Haji Abadi, Nasrollah

Deputy of the Second Majlis, Isfahan, Isfahan
   (1984–88)
1924–, Najafabad, Isfahan
Clerical education
Farajollah
Clergyman (HI)
No imprisonment
Not a war veteran

Salehi-Khansari, Seyyed Morteza

Deputy of the Fifth Majlis, Golpayegan and Khansar,
   Isfahan (1996–2000)
1939–, Khansar, Isfahan
Clerical education
Seyyed Jamal
Clergyman (HI)
Imprisoned before the revolution (for a short period
   of time)

Salehinasab, Naser

Deputy of the Ninth Majlis, Dasht-e Azadegan, Khuz-
   estan (2012–16)
1968–, Dasht-e Azadegan, Khuzestan
BS, agricultural engineering, Shahid Chamran Uni-
   versity of Ahvaz; MS, agricultural engineering,
   Shahid Chamran University of Ahvaz
Civil servant
No imprisonment

Salehi-Salhchini, Golmohammad

Deputy of the Sixth Majlis, Lordegan, Chahar Mahal
   and Bakhtiari (2000–2004)
1963–, Lordegan, Chahar Mahal and Bakhtiari
Pursuing a degree in public administration
Mohammad
Civil servant
No imprisonment
IRGC militiaman

Saleh-Jalali, Reza

Deputy of the Sixth Majlis, Astaneh-ye Ashrafiyyeh,
   Gilan (2000–2004)
1955–, Astaneh-ye Ashrafiyyeh, Gilan
MA, Persian literature
Mohammad-Ali
Civil servant
No imprisonment
IRGC militiaman

Salek [-Kashani], Ahmad

Commander of the IRGC's Basij Force (1980–81);
   deputy of the First (1981–84), Third (1992), Fourth
   (1992–96), Ninth (2012–16), and Tenth (2016–20)
   Majlis, Isfahan, Isfahan
1946–, Isfahan, Isfahan
Clerical education, Qom Seminary
Mahmud, clergyman (ayatollah)
Clergyman
Imprisoned before the revolution

Not a war veteran

IRGC militiaman

Member of the central council (1997–present), deputy head, and spokesperson (2008–12) of the SCC

HI Salek was the founder and commander of the Isfahan IRGC (1979), commander of the Islamic Revolution Committee (1985–87), head of the Bureau of Islamic Movements in the Ministry of Foreign Affairs, and the supreme leader's representative in the IRGC's Qods Force (1990–2000) and the IRGC's intelligence organization (2001–6). In the 1980s, he also served as the first deputy interior minister. Salek, a conservative cleric who is very close to Ayatollah Khamenei, was also a member of the HCCR and was in charge of screening candidates for various high-level positions in the country.

Salihi-Labafinejad, Mrs. Parvin

Deputy of the Fourth Majlis, Tehran, Tehran (1992–96)

1957–, Isfahan, Isfahan

BS, health; MS, health of mother and child, Isfahan University of Medical Sciences

Hasan

Nursing school official

Imprisoned before the revolution

Member of the IRP; founder and member of the central council of Zeynab Society

Salihi-Labafinejad's husband, Morteza Labafinejad, was a high-ranking member of PMOI whom SAVAK killed in 1975. Salihi-Labafinejad, who was barely twenty years old, was arrested by SAVAK and spent two years in prison. After the revolution, she became a consultant on women's affairs for IRIB.

Salim-Bahrami, Seyyed Masih

Deputy of the Sixth Majlis, Sari, Mazandaran (2000–2004)

1955–February 11, 2004, Salim-Bahram, Mazandaran

BS, forest and pasture engineering, University of Mazandaran, 1977

Seyyed Ali, farmer

Civil servant

No imprisonment

After leaving the Majlis, Salim-Bahrami worked for the government.

Salimi, Ali-Reza

Deputy of the Eighth (2008–12), Ninth (2012–16), and Tenth (2016–20) Majlis, Mahallat and Delijan, Markazi

1964–, Mahallat, Markazi

Clerical education, Qom Seminary; BA, Arabic literature, Tehran University; BA, law, Tehran University; MA, law, Tehran University; PhD, jurisprudence, Islamic Azad University–Science and Research Branch

Ali-Asghar

Clergyman

No imprisonment

War veteran

IRGC militiaman

HI Salimi is a former head of the Mahallat Seminary, and he teaches at Islamic Azad University–Mahallat.

Salimi, Asghar

Deputy of the Tenth Majlis, Semirom, Isfahan (2016–20)

1971–, Semirom, Isfahan

MD, Isfahan University of Medical Sciences, 2002; MA, political science

Father's name unknown, farmer

Medical doctor

No imprisonment

Not a war veteran

IRGC militiaman (Basij)

Salimi was previously a member of the Semirom City Council.

Salimi, Mohammad

Minister of national defense in PM Musavi's first cabinet (November 2, 1981–August 14, 1984); general

commander of the army (May 21, 2000–September 11, 2005)
BS, military science, Ground Forces Officers' Academy, 1960
1938–2016, Mashhad, Razavi Khorasan
Army officer
No imprisonment
War veteran
Active member of the Hojjatiyyeh Society (since 1960)
Major General Salimi was an officer in the counterintelligence directorate of the army under the shah in Shiraz, and he underwent military training in the United States in the early 1970s. He was arrested for a brief period before the revolution for his anti-Baha'i activities. Salimi was the head of Khamenei's office when the latter was serving as Ayatollah Khomeini's representative in the MDAFL in the early days of the revolution. Salimi and Khamenei knew each other from their prerevolutionary days in Mashhad. In 1980, Salimi became a member of the Supreme Defense Council, and on November 2, 1981, he became the minister of defense. However, Salimi did not manage to receive enough votes to continue as defense minister in the August 14, 1984, round of confidence voting by the Majlis. In April 1987, Ayatollah Khomeini promoted him from colonel to brigadier general. On May 21, 2000, Ayatollah Khamenei appointed Salimi general commander of the army and promoted him from brigadier general to major general. Salimi served in that post until tendering his resignation on September 11, 2005. After that, he continued as a member of Ayatollah Khamenei's circle of military advisers.

Salimi [Hamadan], Mohammad

Member of the Fifth (2004–10) and Sixth (2010–16) Guardian Councils; prosecutor-general of the SCFC (September 24, 2005–May 1, 2012)
1954–, Hamadan, Hamadan
Clerical education, Haqqani Seminary
Zabihollah, farmer
Clergyman and judiciary official
No imprisonment
Not a war veteran
HI Salimi has been a judge in Tehran, Khorasan, Fars, and Hamadan Provinces. He also served as head of the judicial organization of the armed forces in Hamadan Province and head of branch 31 of the State Supreme Court. As prosecutor-general of the SCFC, he was involved in the trials of clerics such as Abdollah Nuri, Seyyed Mohammad Musavi-Kho'iniha, and Mohsen Kadivar. Salimi was elected as a lay lawyer of the GC in 2004, receiving 162 of the 228 votes cast. He also teaches law at various universities. The chief justice did not nominate him for the next round of the GC.

Salimi-Gamini, Musa

Deputy of the First (1981–84), Second (1984–88), and Third (1988–92) Majlis, Miyaneh, East Azerbaijan
1933–, Miyaneh, East Azerbaijan
Clerical education, Qom Seminary
Sattar
Clergyman and revolutionary court judge in Miyaneh
No imprisonment
Not a war veteran
Martyr's family (two sons died at the war front)
HI Salimi-Gamini was a judge in Miyaneh's revolutionary and special civil courts, and he was involved with the city's Construction Jihad. After serving in the Majlis, Salimi-Gamini returned to the judiciary.

Salimi-Mahmudjayq [Saliminia], Fereydun

Deputy of the Second (1984–88) and Fifth (1997–2000) Majlis, Miyandoab and Takab, West Azerbaijan
1956–, Mahmudabad, Mazandaran
BS, agricultural engineering
No imprisonment

Salmani-Zarji [Rahimi], Mohammad-Hoseyn

Deputy of the First Majlis, Sonqor and Koliyayi, Kermanshah (1980–84)

1934–, Yazd, Yazd
Clerical education
Javad, farmer
Clergyman (HI)
No imprisonment
Not a war veteran

Samadi, Seyyed Ma'ruf

Deputy of the Fourth (1992–94) and Fifth (1996–2000)
    Majlis, Sanandaj, Kurdistan
1963–, Sanandaj, Kurdistan
BA, business administration, 1990; MA, political
    science
Seyyed Tajeddin, farmer
No imprisonment
Samadi, a Sunni, became governor of Mahabad after
    leaving the Majlis.

Samadzadeh, Nosrat

Deputy of the Fourth Majlis, Urmia, West Azerbaijan
    (1992–96)
1949–, Urmia, West Azerbaijan
BS, mechanical engineering
Ebrahim
No imprisonment

Samarghandi, Balal

Deputy of the Fifth Majlis, Tabriz, East Azerbaijan
    (1996–2000)
1952–, Ajab-Shir, East Azerbaijan
MS, civil engineering
Hasan
No imprisonment

Sameri, Abdollah

Deputy of the Ninth (2012–16) and Tenth (2016–20)
    Majlis, Khorramshahr and Mino Island,
    Khuzestan
1971–, Khorramshahr, Khuzestan
BA, social science, Payam-e Nur University

MIIRI official
No imprisonment
Not a war veteran
IRGC militiaman (Basij)

Sami, Kazem

Minister of health in PM Bazargan's cabinet (1979);
    deputy of the First Majlis, Tehran, Tehran
    (1980–84)
1935–1989, Mashhad, Razavi Khorasan
PhD, psychology, Tehran University
Gholam-Reza, laborer
Psychologist
Imprisoned before the revolution
Not a war veteran
Secretary-general of JAMA (1979–81)
Sami left the minister of health post on October 27,
    1979, eight days before PM Bazargan's full cab-
    inet was to tender its resignation, citing chaos,
    lack of revolutionary resolve of the cabinet, and
    monopolization of power. He was a candidate
    in the 1980 presidential election and received
    less than 1 percent of the vote. On November 23,
    1988, Sami was brutally attacked with a knife in
    his office. After being in a coma for a while, he
    passed away.

Sana'i, Mehdi

Deputy of the Eighth (2008–12) and Ninth (2012–De-
    cember 1, 2013) Majlis, Nahavand, Hamadan
1968–, Nahavand, Hamadan
BA, political science, Tehran University, 1992; MA,
    political science, Tehran University, 1995; PhD,
    political science, Russian Academy of Sciences
    (Russia), 2001; clerical education, Qom Seminary
Nurollah
University professor
No imprisonment
War veteran
Sana'i resigned from the Ninth Majlis to become
    ambassador to Russia. Interim elections to fill his
    seat were not held in Nahavand.

San'ati-Mehraban[i], Amir

Deputy of the Seventh Majlis, Sarab and Mehraban,
    East Azerbaijan (2004–8)
1963–, Tehran, Tehran
MA, management
Abdolali
Civil servant, state companies
No imprisonment
San'ati–Mehraban was in charge of security for the
    FDWI.

Sane'i, Hasan

Member of the Second (1989–92), Third (1992–97),
    Fourth (1997–2002), Fifth (2002–7), Sixth (2007–
    12), Seventh (2012–17), and Eighth (2017–22)
    Expediency Discernment Assembly
1937–, Shahreza, Isfahan
Clerical education
Mohammad-Ali, clergyman
Clergyman
No imprisonment
Not a war veteran
Member of the central council of the ACC
Ayatollah Sane'i was a close follower of Ayatollah
    Khomeini and worked in his office before and
    after the revolution. He has been in charge of the
    Fifteenth of Khordad Foundation since 1983. This
    foundation put a bounty on the head of Salman
    Rushdie, the author of *The Satanic Verses*. He is
    the brother of Yusef Sane'i.

Sane'i, Yusef

Member of the First Guardian Council (July 17, 1980–
    January 9, 1983); prosecutor-general (January 9,
    1983–July 10, 1985); member of the First Assembly
    of Experts, Tehran (1983–90); member of the Sec-
    ond Expediency Discernment Assembly (1989–92)
1937–, Isfahan, Isfahan
Clerical education, Qom Seminary, 1959
Mohammad-Ali, clergyman
Clergyman

Imprisoned before the revolution
Not a war veteran
Member of the SQSS
Ayatollah Sane'i earned his credentials for *ejtehad* at
    the very young age of twenty-two. He was active
    in the anti-shah movement. In 1983, he resigned
    from the First GC to become the prosecutor-gen-
    eral. Occupying the post of prosecutor-general
    made him a juristic member of the HCJ as well.
    Sane'i was Ayatollah Khomeini's representative
    in the intelligence unit of the prime minister's
    office and in the Supreme Council for War Zone
    Reconstruction. He also occasionally acted as the
    Friday prayer leader of Qom. On May 11, 1985,
    Sane'i tried to resign as the prosecutor-general
    but Ayatollah Khomeini did not initially accept
    his resignation. Sane'i, who had been a radical
    cleric, changed his political views after the 2009
    presidential election and as a source of emula-
    tion issued more progressive views regarding the
    rights of women and religious minorities. He is
    the brother of Hasan Sane'i.

Sanjabi, Karim

Member of the Revolutionary Council (1979); minister
    of foreign affairs in PM Bazargan's cabinet (1979)
1904–July 4, 1995, Kermanshah, Kermanshah
PhD, law, University of Paris (France), 1934; disserta-
    tion title: "Essai sur l'economie rurale et le regime
    agraire de l'Iran"
Qasem, landowner and tribal chief
Academia
Imprisoned before the revolution
Not a war veteran
Secretary-general of INF
Sanjabi went to Europe in 1928, and he became minis-
    ter of culture under PM Mossadeq and a member
    of the Seventeenth Majlis before the revolution.
    In 1978, as the leader of INF, he visited Ayatollah
    Khomeini in Paris, and upon his return to Iran the
    shah's regime arrested him. Khomeini appointed
    Sanjabi as a member of the Revolutionary Council,
    and he resigned his post as foreign minister on

April 15, 1979, after serving only fifty-five days in PM Bazargan's cabinet (he was the oldest member of the cabinet). Sanjabi was elected to the first post-revolutionary Majlis, but was denied a seat when his credentials were rejected. After Ayatollah Khomeini lashed out against INF in 1981, Sanjabi went into hiding for more than a year and settled in exile first in France and then in the United States. Ali Ardalan, the minister of economics in PM Bazargan's cabinet, was his brother-in-law.

Saqqa'i, Mohammad

Deputy of the Fifth (1996–2000), Sixth (2000–2004), Eighth (2008–12), and Ninth (2012–16) Majlis, Neyriz and Estahban, Fars
1949–, Estahban, Fars
BS, civil engineering
Ahmad-Ali
Director-general of the roads and transportation department in various provinces
No imprisonment
Saqqa'i ran unsuccessfully for the Tenth Majlis and then became an adviser to the minister of petroleum.

Sarafraz, Mohammad

Director-general of IRIB (November 8, 2014–May 11, 2016)
1961–, Tehran, Tehran
BA, Imam Sadeq University; PhD, political science (both degrees unverified)
Abolfazl, clergyman (HI)
IRIB official
No imprisonment
War veteran (wounded)
Martyr's family (one brother, Javad [head of Ayatollah Beheshti's office], killed in the bombing of the IRP headquarters; another brother, Ali, killed at the war front)
Sarafraz was injured at the war front and underwent medical treatment in Iran and England. He was a writer and editor of the conservative *Resalat*, and he was an IRIB civil servant for more than two decades

before becoming its director. As IRIB's deputy chief for external services, Sarafraz helped to set up the English-language (Press TV) and Arabic-language (Al-Alam) channels for IRIB. His father was the supreme leader's representative at Iran Air.

Sarafraz-Yazdi, Ali

Deputy of the Seventh Majlis, Mashhad and Kalat, Razavi Khorasan (2004–8)
1950–2017, Mashhad, Razavi Khorasan
BS, chemistry, Mashhad University, 1975; PhD, chemistry, University of Birmingham (England), 1980
Abdorrahim
Professor, dean, and rector of Mashhad University (1996–98)
No imprisonment
Not a war veteran
Sarafraz-Yazdi was rector of Urmia University from 1981 to 1998.

Sarhaddizadeh, Abolqasem

Minister of labor and social affairs in PM Musavi's first (August 28, 1983–85) and second (October 28, 1985–August 3, 1989) cabinets; deputy of the Third (1990–92), Fifth (1996–2000), and Sixth (2000–2004) Majlis, Tehran, Tehran
1945–, Tehran, Tehran
Pre-diploma (fifth grade)
Ali-Akbar, clergyman
Civil servant, state companies
Imprisoned before the revolution (thirteen years)
Not a war veteran
IRGC militiaman
Member of the MNP and the central committee of the IRP (resigned in 1984); secretary-general and founding member of the Islamic Labor Party (1998–2001)
Sarhaddizadeh joined the militant MNP in 1963 and was arrested in 1965. He spent more than thirteen years in prison and was released a few months before the revolution. After the revolution, he functioned in capacities such as overseer of the

FDWI, publisher of *Sobh-e Azadegan* (closed in
1985), warden of Tehran's Qasr Prison, member of
the overseeing council for prisons, and founding
member of the House of the Worker. The Majlis
approved Sarhaddizadeh as labor minister in 1983
with 121 positive votes, seventeen negative votes,
and forty-seven abstentions. During Hassan
Rouhani's presidency, he served as an adviser to
the minister of labor, cooperatives, and welfare,
Ali Rabi'i.

Sari, Ali

Deputy of the Tenth Majlis, Ahvaz, Khuzestan (2016–20)
1976–, Rofaye, Khuzestan
BS, electrical engineering, Isfahan University of
Technology, 2000; MS, Amirkabir University of
Technology, 2001; pursuing a PhD in electrical
engineering at the University of Semnan
Hasan
Engineer and university professor
Not a war veteran
Sari worked as an engineer at Fajr Petrochemical
Company from 2002 to 2014 and taught at various universities in Khuzestan beginning in 2006.

Sarraf, Ebrahim

Deputy of the Fourth Majlis, Marand, East Azerbaijan
(1992–96)
1941–, Marand, East Azerbaijan
BS, electrical engineering
Ali-Akbar
No imprisonment
Sarraf unsuccessfully ran for the Eighth Majlis.

Sarrami-Forushani, Mohsen

Deputy of the Ninth Majlis, Khomeinishahr, Isfahan
(2012–16)
1970–, Homayunshahr, Isfahan
BS, biology, Isfahan University of Technology
Teacher; head of the educational bureau of
Khomeinishahr

No imprisonment
War veteran (victim of a chemical attack)

Sarvari, Parviz

Deputy of the Seventh (2004–8) and Eighth (2008–12)
Majlis, Tehran, Tehran
1960–, Hamadan, Hamadan
BA, public administration, Tehran University; MA,
defense management
Ramezan-Ali
No imprisonment
War veteran (thirty-one months)
IRGC militiaman
Member of the Alliance of Wayfarers of the Islamic
Revolution
Sarvari is a former IRGC commander who carried
out missions in Syria and Lebanon. He was also
a member of the Tehran City Council. He is in
charge of the conservative Jahan News website.

Sattari, Mansur

Commander of the Islamic Republic of Iran Air Force
(January 30, 1987–January 5, 1995)
August 21, 1948–January 5, 1995, Varamin, Tehran
BS, military science, Ground Forces Officers' Academy, 1969
Major General Sattari joined the Iranian Air Force in
1969 and underwent training as a radar officer in
the United States in 1972. In 1975, he entered Tehran University to study electrical engineering but
did not finish his studies because of the revolution
and the war. Sattari, who was a brilliant military
planner during the Iran–Iraq War, was killed in
a plane crash on January 5, 1995. After his death,
the air force academy was named after him. Sattari was very close to Ayatollah Khamenei and is
the father of Sourena Sattari.

Sattari, Sourena

VP for scientific and technological affairs in President
Rouhani's first (2013–August 13, 2017) and second
(August 20, 2017–2021) cabinets

1972–, Tehran, Tehran

BS, mechanical engineering, Sharif University of Technology, 1994; MS, mechanical engineering, Sharif University of Technology, 1997; PhD, mechanical engineering, Sharif University of Technology, 2006

Mansur, pilot

University professor

No imprisonment

Not a war veteran

Martyr's family (father)

Sattari is the youngest minister in President Rouhani's cabinet.

Sattarifar, Mohammad

VP and head of the Management and Planning Organization in President Khatami's second cabinet (2001–May 9, 2004)

1952–, Isfahan, Isfahan

PhD, economics, University of Illinois at Urbana-Champaign (USA) (unverified)

Shirali

Civil servant

No imprisonment

Not a war veteran

Member of IIPF

Sattarifar was a deputy in the PBO in the 1980s. He was head of the social security organization of Iran from 1997 to 2001 before becoming a VP. He left the latter post in 2004, but not before playing an important role in establishing the Ministry of Welfare and Social Security.

Savadkuhifar, Sam

Member of the Sixth (2013–16) and Seventh (2016–19) Guardian Councils

1957–, Tehran, Tehran

BA, law, Tehran University, 1980; MA, law, Shahid Beheshti University, 1989; PhD, law, Jean Monnet University (France), 1995

Nariman

Judiciary official

No imprisonment

Savadkuhifar was head of the justice administration in Islamshahr, deputy head of Tehran's justice administration, and manager of the Persian-language *Journal of Private Law*. He received 147 positive votes in July 2013 when he was first elected to the Guardian Council as a lay lawyer.

Savari, Hashem

Deputy of the Eighth Majlis, Dasht-e Azadegan, Khuzestan (2008–12)

1958–, Dasht-e Azadegan, Khuzestan

MA, public administration

Ali

Civil servant

No imprisonment

Savari ran unsuccessfully for the Ninth Majlis in 2012.

Saveh, Abdolhoseyn

Deputy of the Second Majlis, Kerman, Kerman (1984–88)

April 17, 1940–2000, Kerman, Kerman

BS, chemistry

Masha'allah

Head of the education department in Kerman

No imprisonment

Saveh, a teacher, was one of the main organizers of demonstrations in Kerman before the revolution. After serving in the Majlis, he worked in the Ministry of Defense.

Sayyad-Shirazi, Ali

Commander of the Islamic Republic of Iran Ground Forces (October 1, 1981–August 2, 1986); first deputy chief of the Armed Forces General Staff (September 11, 1993–April 10, 1999)

1944–April 10, 1999, Dargaz, Razavi Khorasan

BS, military science, Ground Forces Officers' Academy, 1967

Zyad, military officer

Military commander (brigadier general)

Imprisoned before the revolution

War veteran

Sayyad-Shirazi underwent infantry training in Oklahoma in 1972 and played an instrumental role in crushing the Kurdish uprising in the early years of the revolution. As commander of the army's ground forces, he had serious differences of opinion over war strategy and tactics with the Mohsen Reza'i, the commander in chief of the IRGC. Sayyad-Shirazi then became one of Ayatollah Khomeini's representatives in the Supreme Defense Council, and in April 1987, Ayatollah Khomeini promoted him from colonel to lieutenant general. In July 1988, he was in charge of the operation against PMOI forces, which had invaded Iran from Iraq and were defeated. PMOI assassinated Sayyad-Shirazi a decade later.

Sayyari, Habibollah

Commander of the Islamic Republic of Iran Navy (August 20, 2007–November 5, 2017); chief of the joint staff of the Islamic Republic of Iran Army (November 5, 2017–present)

1955–, Fasa, Fasa

BS, military science, Ground Forces Officers' Academy; MS, military science, Iranian Army Command and General Staff College; PhD, military science, Supreme National Defense University

Deputy commander of the Islamic Republic of Iran Navy (2005–7)

No imprisonment

War veteran (seventy-five months; wounded)

Rear Admiral Sayyari was commissioned in the Iranian military in 1974, and he has worked for the joint headquarters of the army. He was a member of the naval commandos in Khorramshahr who fought heroically against Iraqi forces.

Sazdar, Sirus

Deputy of the Eighth Majlis, Marand and Jolfa, East Azerbaijan (2008–12)

1955–, Jolfa, East Azerbaijan

BS, metallurgy

Hoseyn, teacher

Employee of the National Iranian Gas Company

No imprisonment

Sazegarnezhad, Jalil

Deputy of the Sixth Majlis, Shiraz, Fars (2000–2004)

1954–, Shiraz, Fars

MA, management and planning

Mohammad-Hasan, bazaar tradesman

Teacher

No imprisonment

Sazegarnezhad's brother, Mohammad-Amin, was also an MP from Fars in the First Majlis.

Sazegarnezhad, Mohammad-Amin

Deputy of the First Majlis, Sarvestan, Fars (1980–84)

1952–, Shiraz, Fars

Associate's degree

Mohammad-Hasan, bazaar tradesman

No imprisonment

After serving in the Majlis, Sazegarnezhad joined the military establishment.

Sefati-Dezfuli, Iraj

Deputy of the First (1980–84) and Fifth (1996–2000) Majlis, Abadan, Khuzestan

1939–, Khorramshahr, Khuzestan

BS, mathematics

Amir, laborer

Academia

Imprisoned before the revolution

Sefati-Dezfuli was injured in the June 28, 1981, bombing of the IRP headquarters. During the Second and Third Majlis, he was the head of the State Audit Court, an arm of the Majlis.

Sepahajirlu, Vakil

Deputy of the Eighth Majlis, Parsabad and Bilehsavar, Ardabil (2008–12)

1966–, Parsabad, Ardabil

BS, agricultural engineering
Amin Aqa
Civil servant
No imprisonment
Sepahajirlu was not elected to the Ninth Majlis.

Sepahvand, Abdorreza

Deputy of the Fifth Majlis, Khorramabad, Lorestan
    (1996–2000)
1958–, Khorramabad, Lorestan
MS, industrial engineering
Masqali
No imprisonment
Founding member of the NTP

Seraj, Naser

Head of State General Inspectorate Organization (August 21, 2013–present)
Judge
Seraj presided as judge in a number of controversial
    cases, including the trial of Mehdi Hashemi,
    son of Ayatollah Hashemi-Rafsanjani. He was
    appointed as the political-security deputy of the
    prosecutor-general on September 11, 2006. In
    2010, chief justice Larijani-Amoli appointed Seraj
    as the judiciary's representative on the committee
    overseeing the press.

Servati, Musarreza

Deputy of the Seventh (2004–8), Eighth (2008–12),
    and Ninth (2012–16) Majlis, Bojnurd, Maneh and
    Samalqan, and Jajarm, North Khorasan
1957–, Bojnurd, North Khorasan
BS, mathematics, Allameh Tabataba'i University; MA,
    public administration, Mashhad Management
    Institute
Mohammad-Rahim, farmer
Academia
No imprisonment (claims he was arrested twice before the revolution)
War veteran

Martyr's family (brother)
Servati was governor of Birjand and Bojnurd.

Seyf, Valiyollah

Governor of the Central Bank (August 25, 2013–present)
1952–, Nahavand, Hamadan
BA, accounting, Tehran Oil College; MA, accounting,
    Tehran Oil College; PhD, accounting, Allameh
    Tabataba'i University
No imprisonment
Not a war veteran
Seyf has been the CFO of the Industrial Development
    and Renovation Organization of Iran, a member
    of the board of directors of Sepah Bank, CEO of
    Bank Melli Iran, and director of Future Bank in
    Bahrain. In 1995, when he was serving as CEO of
    Bank Sadarat, a number of important embezzlement cases took place.

Seyfiyan, Mohammad-Kazem

Mayor of Tehran (1982–83); deputy of the Fourth Majlis, Tehran, Tehran (1992–96)
1935–May 27, 2016, Tehran, Tehran
MS, architectural engineering
Gholam-Ali
Civil servant
Imprisoned before the revolution
Not a war veteran
Member of the MNP
Seyfiyan was the first director of the Housing Foundation of the Islamic Revolution, and served for
    a while as governor of Markazi Province. He ran
    unsuccessfully for the Second Majlis.

Seyfollahi, Reza

Chief of Law Enforcement Forces (September 24,
    1992–February 15, 1997)
1957–, Isfahan, Isfahan
BS, physics, Sharif University of Technology
War veteran (senior IRGC commander)
IRGC militiaman

Brigadier General Seyfollahi was the founder of the IRGC and Construction Jihad in Isfahan. He was among the students who stormed the American embassy, and later he was in charge of the IRGC's intelligence directorate. In 2013, he became deputy for domestic security at the Supreme Council for National Security.

Seyqali-Kumeleh, Parviz

Deputy of the Third (1988–92) and Fourth (1992–96) Majlis, Langarud, Gilan
1957–, Langarud, Gilan
BS, mathematics
Qasem
No imprisonment
Seyqali-Kumeleh ran unsuccessfully for the Fifth Majlis, and the GC disqualified him from running in the 2008 Majlis election. He worked at the Iran Fisheries Organization and was a provincial civil servant.

Seyyed Abadi, Hasan

Deputy of the Sixth (2000–2004) and Seventh (2004–8) Majlis, Sabzevar, Razavi Khorasan
1962–, Sabzevar, Razavi Khorasan
BA, law, Tehran University; MA, public administration
Qodratollah
Civil servant

Seyyed Aqa Miri, Seyyed Ali

Deputy of the Sixth Majlis, Dezful, Khuzestan (2000–2004)
1955–, Dezful, Khuzestan
Associate's degree
Seyyed Asadollah
Teacher
No imprisonment

Seyyed Hashemi, Seyyed Mostafa

Deputy of the Fourth (1992–96), Fifth (1996–2000), Sixth (2000–2004), and Seventh (2004–8) Majlis, Maragheh, East Azerbaijan

1953–, Maragheh, East Azerbaijan
BS, industrial engineering, 1990; MA, economics
Seyyed Sajjad
Civil servant
No imprisonment

Seyyed Hatami, Seyyed Ebrahim

Member of the Fourth Assembly of Experts, Ardabil (2007–16)
1924–, Ardabil, Ardabil
Clerical education, Qom Seminary, 1964
Mir Javad, clergyman
Clergyman (ayatollah)
No imprisonment
Not a war veteran
Martyr's family (son killed at the war front)
Seyyed Hatami was in charge of Ardabil Seminary for a while.

Seyyed Khamushi, Seyyed Ali-Naqi

Deputy of the Fourth Majlis, Tehran, Tehran (1992–96)
1939–, Tehran, Tehran
BS, textile engineering
Seyyed Abdollah
No imprisonment
Not a war veteran
Founding member of the Society of Former MPs
Seyyed Khamushi was the first director of the FDWI, and he headed the Chamber of Commerce office for twenty-seven years. His family was active in the CIC/PCIC but one of his brothers, Seyyed Mohsen, was affiliated with PMOI and was killed.

Seyyed Khamushi, Seyyed Taqi

Deputy of the First Majlis, Tehran, Tehran (1981–84)
1937–2006, Tehran, Tehran
Pre-high school diploma; clerical education
Seyyed Abdollah
No imprisonment
Seyyed Khamushi is the brother of Seyyed Ali-Naqi Seyyed Khamushi. Seyyed Taqi's son, HI Seyyed

Mehdi Khamushi, is head of the Islamic Propaganda Organization.

Seyyed Khavari-Langarudi, Seyyed Mir Ali-Naqi

Deputy of the Second Majlis, Langarud, Gilan (1984–88)
1948–1988, Langarud, Gilan
Clerical education
Seyyed Ashraf
Clergyman (HI)
No imprisonment
He was executed on the charge of connection with Mehdi Hashemi's group.

Seyyed Mahdavi-Aqdam, Seyyed Hamid

Deputy of the Sixth Majlis, Tabriz, Azarshahr, and Osku, East Azerbaijan (2000–2004)
1952–, Tabriz, East Azerbaijan
Clerical education, Qom Seminary
Clergyman (HI)
No imprisonment
War veteran (wounded)
In 2014, he was sentenced to a seven-month prison term for his political views.

Seyyed Zadeh [Yazdi], Seyyed Jalil

Deputy of the First (1981–84), Second (1984–88), and Third (1988–92) Majlis, Kermanshah, Kermanshah
1950–, Kermanshah, Kermanshah
BS, mathematics; clerical education
Seyyed Ali-Asghar
No imprisonment
Not a war veteran

Seyyedi Alavi, Mrs. [Seyyedeh] Bibi Qodsiyyeh

Deputy of the Fourth (1992–96) and Fifth (1996–2000) Majlis, Mashhad, Razavi Khorasan
1951–, Mashhad, Razavi Khorasan
MD, medicine, Mashhad University

Seyyed Hoseyn
Gynecologist and medical school professor
No imprisonment
Not a war veteran

Seyyedin, Mohsen

Deputy of the First Majlis, Khomeyn, Markazi (1980–84)
1945–, Khomeyn, Markazi
BA, education
Mohammad, civil servant
Academia
No imprisonment
After serving in the Majlis, Seyyedin became a civil servant.

Seyyedzadeh-Galehban, Seyyed Hoseyn

Deputy of the Fifth Majlis, Marand, East Azerbaijan (1996–2000)
1956–, Marand, East Azerbaijan
BA, English literature, 1990
Mir Ali
No imprisonment

Sha'bani, Amin

Deputy of the Seventh (2004–8) and Eighth (2008–12) Majlis, Sanandaj, Divandarreh, and Kamyaran, Kurdistan
1971–, Divandarreh, Kurdistan
BA, business administration
Sirus, landowner
Provincial civil servant
No imprisonment
Sha'bani was a Sunni MP.

Sha'bani, Mohammad-Reza

Deputy of the Eighth Majlis, Kermanshah, Kermanshah (2008–12)
1957–, Harsin, Kermanshah
BA, theology
Cheragh-Ali
Civil servant

No imprisonment

Sha'bani was in charge of Hassan Rouhani's campaign headquarters in Kermanshah; afterward, he worked in Rouhani's administration.

Sha'banpur, Hasan

Deputy of the Sixth (2000–2004) and Eighth (2008–12) Majlis, Marvdasht and Arsanjan, Fars

1959–, Marvdasht, Fars

BA, public administration

Ali

Civil servant, state companies

No imprisonment

IRGC militiaman

Sha'banpur was defeated in the Ninth Majlis elections, but was then put in charge of legal affairs for the National Iranian Oil Refining and Distribution Company.

Shabzendehdar, Mohammad-Mehdi

Member of the Sixth (2013–16) and Seventh (2016–19) Guardian Councils

1943–, Darab, Fars

Clerical education, Qom Seminary

Hoseyn, clergyman (ayatollah)

Clergyman

No imprisonment

Not a war veteran

Member of the central council of the SQSS

HI Shabzendehdar is a former member of the High Council of Religious Seminaries of Qom and was director of Baqiollah institute and school. He was a student of Ayatollah Mo'men, who simultaneously served with him on the GC.

Shadidzadeh, Jasem

Deputy of the Sixth Majlis, Ahvaz, Khuzestan (2000–2004)

1962–, Ahvaz, Khuzestan

BA, theology

Mohammad

Civil servant

No imprisonment

Shadmehr, Mohammad-Hadi

Chief of the joint staff of the Islamic Republic of Iran Army (December 22, 1979–June 19, 1980)

1920–December 11, 2008, Tehran, Tehran

Major General Shadmehr was a deputy chief of JSIRIA before serving for seven months as its chief.

Sha'eri, Ali-Mohammad

Deputy of the Tenth Majlis, Behshahr, Mazandaran (2016–20)

1959–, city unknown, Mazandaran

BS, agricultural engineering, University of Mazandaran, 1981; MS, agricultural engineering, Tarbiyat-e Modarres University, 1992; PhD, agricultural engineering, Islamic Azad University–Science and Research Branch, 1998

No imprisonment

War veteran

Sha'eri was mayor of Tehran's District 22 when Ahmadinejad was Tehran's mayor; he was appointed governor-general of Golestan Province when Ahmadinejad became president in 2005. Sha'eri has held such other posts as deputy interior minister, deputy minister of Construction Jihad, and head of the Environmental Protection Organization.

Shafei, Gholam-Reza

Minister of industries in PM Musavi's first (August 20, 1984–85) and second (October 28, 1985–August 3, 1989) cabinets; minister of cooperatives in President Hashemi-Rafsanjani's first (December 31, 1991–August 2, 1993) and second (August 16, 1993–August 2, 1997) cabinets; minister of industries in President Khatami's first cabinet (August 20, 1997–August 1, 2001)

1951–, Marand, East Azerbaijan

BS, mechanical engineering, Sharif University of Technology, 1975

Abdollah

Civil servant

Imprisoned before the revolution (arrested in 1975)

Not a war veteran

Shafei has held such posts as head of Iran National Industries Organization, deputy of the PBO, presidential adviser, and ambassador to Russia. He is the brother of Karim Shafei.

Shafei, Karim

Deputy of the Third (1988–92) and Seventh (2005–8) Majlis, Marand, East Azerbaijan

1961–, Marand, East Azerbaijan

BA, law; MA, management

Abdollah

Deputy to Tehran's governor

No imprisonment

War veteran (thirty months; wounded)

IRGC militiaman

Shafei has served as the PM's representative in the Ministry of Interior, and was a legal adviser to various state bodies. He is the brother of Gholam-Reza Shafei.

Shafi'i, Nowzar

Deputy of the Ninth Majlis, Mamasani and Rostam, Fars (2012–16)

1968–, Mamasani, Fars

PhD, political science, Tehran University

Father's name unknown, farmer

University professor and Ministry of Foreign Affairs expert

No imprisonment

Not a war veteran

The GC disqualified Shafi'i from running in the 2016 Majlis election.

Shafi'i, Seyyed Ali

Member of the Second (1991–98), Third (1999–2006), Fourth (2007–16), and Fifth (2016–22) Assembly of Experts, Khuzestan

1940–, Dezful, Khuzestan

Clerical education, Najaf Seminary (Iraq)

Seyyed Mohammad-Reza, clergyman

Clergyman

No imprisonment

Not a war veteran

Martyr's family (son, Morteza)

Ayatollah Shafi'i has held positions such as Friday prayer leader of Ahvaz, head of the ideological-political bureau for Army Division 92, and head of the justice administration for Khuzestan Province. He is close to Supreme Leader Ayatollah Khamenei.

Shafi'i, Seyyed Mohsen

Deputy of the Third Majlis, Dorud and Japlaq, Lorestan (1988–92)

1957–, Tarom, Gilan

Associate's degree

Seyyed Mohammad

No imprisonment

Shafi'i-Kas-Ahmadani, Mohammad-Reza

Deputy of the Third (1990–92) and Fourth (1992–96) Majlis, Fuman, Gilan

1942–, Fuman, Gilan

Clerical education

Valiyollah

Clergyman (HI)

No imprisonment

He ran unsuccessfully for the Tenth Majlis.

Shahabadi, Mehdi

Deputy of the First Majlis, Tehran, Tehran (1980–April 26, 1984)

1930–April 26, 1984, Tehran, Tehran

Clerical education, Qom Seminary

Mohammad-Ali, clergyman (ayatollah)

Clergyman

Imprisoned before the revolution

Not a war veteran

HI Shahabadi was active in armed guerilla organizations before the revolution and spent time in prison and exile. He was involved with the IRGC and *komitehs*, and was killed at the war front just after reelection to the Second Majlis.

Shahabadi, Nasrollah

Member of the Fifth Assembly of Experts, Tehran (2016–18)
September 24, 1930–March 12, 2018, Qom, Qom
Clerical education, Najaf Seminary (Iraq)
Mohammad-Ali, clergyman (ayatollah)
Clergyman
No imprisonment
Not a war veteran
Ayatollah Shahabadi lived in Iraq from 1950 to 1970. His father was Ayatollah Khomeini's teacher in mysticism.

Shahbazi, Ali

Chief of the joint staff of the Islamic Republic of Iran Army (May 3, 1988–September 29, 1998); general commander of the army (September 30, 1998–May 21, 2000)
Date of birth unknown, Qom, Qom
BS, military science, Ground Forces Officers' Academy
War veteran
Shahbazi acquired the rank of colonel in 1984 and major general in 1989. On September 22, 1989, Ayatollah Khamenei appointed Major General Shahbazi as head of the Joint Headquarters of the Army, and on May 29, 2000, Khamenei appointed him as head of his circle of military advisers. Shahbazi was a religiously orthodox officer.

Shahbazkhani, Bizhan

Deputy of the Sixth (2000–2004) and Seventh (2004–8) Majlis, Malayer, Hamadan
1963–, Malayer, Hamadan
MD, gastroenterology
Hushang
Medical doctor
No imprisonment

Shahcheraqi, Seyyed Hasan

Deputy of the First (1980–84) and Second (1984–86) Majlis, Damghan, Semnan
January 29, 1953–February 20, 1986, Damghan, Semnan
Clerical education, Haqqani Seminary
Seyyed Masih, clergyman (HI)
Chief of staff for the revolutionary prosecutor
No imprisonment
Not a war veteran
Before being elected to the First Majlis, Shahcheraqi was the chief of staff to Ayatollah Qoddusi when he was serving as prosecutor-general of the Revolutionary Courts. Shahcheraqi was put in charge of *Keyhan* in 1982 and founded *Keyhan Farhangi* monthly. He was killed when Iraqi forces shot down his plane.

Shahcheraqi, Seyyed Mohammad

Member of the Fourth (2007–16) and Fifth (2016–22) Assembly of Experts, Semnan
1934–, Damghan, Semnan
Clerical education, Qom Seminary
Seyyed Hasan
Clergyman
No imprisonment
Not a war veteran
Ayatollah Shahcheraqi has held such posts as revolutionary tribunal judge, general manager of FMVA and the IKRF in Semnan Province, and Friday prayer leader of Semnan (2001–9). He is the uncle of Seyyed Hasan Shahcheraqi, who served in the First and Second Majlis.

Shahhoseyni, Hoseyn

Ministerial adviser and head of the Physical Training Organization in PM Bazargan's cabinet (1979)
1927–December 24, 2017, Tehran, Tehran
BS (incomplete), chemistry, Tehran's Higher Teachers Training College
Zeynol'abedin, clergyman

Farm owner and herder

Imprisoned before the revolution

Not a war veteran

Member of the central committee of INF

Shahhoseyni was a member of the welcoming committee for Ayatollah Khomeini upon his return to Iran. He stayed on as head of the Physical Training Organization under the Revolutionary Council cabinet until he resigned on September 9, 1980. He also resigned from his post as head of the National Olympic Committee of the Islamic Republic of Iran in July or August of 1981.

Shahi-Arablu, Mohammad

Deputy of the Fifth (1996–2000) and Sixth (2000–2004) Majlis, Hashtrud, East Azerbaijan; deputy of the Seventh Majlis, Robat Karim, Tehran (2004–8)

1963–, Miyaneh, East Azerbaijan

Clerical education; BA, law

Hoseyn

Clergyman

No imprisonment

HI Shahi-Arablu was previously head of the political bureau of western Tehran's police force.

Shahidi-Mahallati, Seyyed Mohammad-Ali

Deputy of the Third Majlis, Mahallat and Delijan, Markazi (1988–92); VP and head of FMVA in President Rouhani's first (2013–August 13, 2017) and second (August 20, 2017–2021) cabinets

1949–, Mahallat, Markazi

Clerical education

Seyyed Hashem, clergyman

Clergyman (HI)

No imprisonment

War veteran

IRGC militiaman

Member of the IRP

Shahidi-Mahallati was Hassan Rouhani's adviser on clerical affairs during the 2013 presidential election campaign thanks to his solid ties to the clerical establishment. He was a deputy in the Ministry of Foreign Affairs before Rouhani appointed him as a VP. On September 18, 2013, Ayatollah Khamenei appointed him as the supreme leader's representative in FMVA. In the 1980s, he was deputy for legal and parliamentary affairs of the IRGC ministry. He, Ali-Akbar Nateq-Nuri, and Abbas-Ahmad Akhundi have married three daughters of Seyyed Hashem Rasuli-Mahallati. He is also the father-in-law of Mohammad-Sa'id, who is the son of Mohammad-Reza Mahdavi-Kani.

Shahmiri, Qorbanali

Member of the First Assembly of Experts, Kohgiluyeh and Buyer Ahmad (1983–90)

1939–, Neyshabur, Razavi Khorasan

Clerical education, Mashhad Seminary

Father's name unknown, farmer

Clergyman (HI)

No imprisonment

Not a war veteran

Shahmiri was the Friday prayer leader of Zabol (1979–80), Yasouj (1980–88), and Kashmar (1988–2009).

Shahraki, Gholam-Ali

Deputy of the First (1980–84), Second (1984–88), and Third (1988–92) Majlis, Zabol, Sistan and Baluchestan

1948–, Zabol, Sistan and Baluchestan

BS, civil engineering

Ebrahim, farmer

No imprisonment

Not a war veteran

After serving in the Majlis, Shahraki became a civil servant.

Shahriyari, Hoseyn-Ali

Deputy of the Seventh (2004–8), Eighth (2008–12), Ninth (2012–16), and Tenth (2016–20) Majlis, Zahedan, Sistan and Baluchestan

1951–, Zabol, Sistan and Baluchestan
MD, surgery, Shahid Beheshti University, 1986
Abbas
Eye surgeon and medical school administrator
No imprisonment
Not a war veteran
Shahriyari is a member of the HCCR.

Shahriyari, Mir Behzad

Deputy of the First Majlis, Dashti and Tangestan,
　　Bushehr (1980–June 28, 1981)
1954–June 28, 1981, Khormuj, Bushehr
BA, Islamic law
Seyyed Mohammad-Taher, civil servant
Academia
No imprisonment
Not a war veteran
Shahriyari was killed in the bombing of the IRP head-
　　quarters in June 1981.

Shahriyari, Mohammad-Mehdi

Deputy of the Eighth Majlis, Bojnurd, Maneh
　　and Samalqan, and Jajarm, North Khorasan
　　(2008–12)
1964–, Maneh and Samalqan, North Khorasan
BA, international relations
Abbas-Ali
Counsel-general in Frankfurt, Germany
No imprisonment
In 2017, President Rouhani's administration ap-
　　pointed Shahriyari governor of West Azerbaijan.

Shahriyari, Seyyed Kamaleddin

Deputy of the Third (1988–92), Fourth (1992–96), and
　　Tenth (2016–20) Majlis, Tangestan, Dashti, Kan-
　　gan, and Deyr, Bushehr
1952–, Tehran, Tehran
MS, architecture
Seyyed Hoseyn
No imprisonment

Shahrokhi, Seyyed Mohammad-Mehdi

Deputy of the Fifth (1996–2000), Sixth (2000–2004),
　　and Seventh (2004–8) Majlis, Pol-e Dokhtar and
　　Malavi, Lorestan
1960–, Qom, Qom
Clerical education
Seyyed Shamsollah
Clergyman (HI)
No imprisonment

Shahrokhi, Seyyed Mohammad-Taqi

Deputy of the First Majlis, Khorramabad, Lorestan
　　(1980–84); member of the Third (1999–2006) and
　　Fourth (2007–16) Assembly of Experts, Lorestan
1934–November 25, 2016, Khorramabad, Lorestan
Clerical education, Qom Seminary
Seyyed Ali-Naqi, bazaar tradesman
Clergyman
Imprisoned before the revolution
Not a war veteran
HI Shahrokhi was appointed by Ayatollah Khomeini as
　　the judge of the revolutionary court in Borujerd on
　　July 23, 1979. Shahrokhi, who later became the Fri-
　　day prayer leader of Khorramabad (appointed Au-
　　gust 1981), was close to Ayatollah Khamenei and as
　　his representative traveled for over two decades to
　　South and East Asia (Bangladesh, India, Myanmar,
　　Sri Lanka, and Thailand) to promote Islam.

Shahrokhi-Qobadi, Ali

Deputy of the Eighth Majlis, Kuhdasht, Lorestan
　　(2008–12)
1950–, Khorramabad, Lorestan
Clerical education; BA, judicial law
Roshan-Ali
Clergyman and judiciary official
No imprisonment
HI Shahrokhi-Qobadi was elected to the Third Majlis
　　from Kuhdasht in a midterm election where riots
　　led to the death of seventeen people in Kuhdasht.

However, the GC rejected his credentials just as they had done previously to the credentials of his main rival, Ali-Asghar Esfandiyarpur. Thus, Kuhdasht did not have any representatives in the Third Majlis. Shahrokhi-Qobadi was banned from political activities for four years, and went on to hold numerous jobs in the judiciary branch until being elected to the Eighth Majlis. He failed to enter into the Ninth Majlis.

Shahrzad, Mohammad-Karim

Deputy of the Third (1988–92), Fourth (1992–96), and Eighth (2008–12) Majlis, Isfahan, Isfahan
1949–, Tuyserkan, Hamadan
MD, medicine, Tabriz University, 1976
Hasan
Medical doctor
Imprisoned before the revolution
War veteran (wounded)
Shahrzad ran in midterm elections for the Tenth Majlis in 2017.

Shahsafi, Hasan

Commander of the Islamic Republic of Iran Air Force (August 31, 2008–present)
1964–, Damavand, Tehran
BS, military science, Air Force Academy; MS, military science, Iranian Command Staff College (DAFOOS), 1999
Military pilot (brigadier general)
No imprisonment
Shahsafi joined the Iranian Air Force in 1982 and was deputy commander of the air force before becoming commander in 2008.

Shahzadi, Rostam

Member of the Assembly for the Final Examination of the Constitution, representing the Zoroastrian community (1979)
1912–1999, Yazd, Yazd

BA, law
Dinyar, Zoroastrian priest
Academia
Not a war veteran

Shaikh, Mehdi

Deputy of the Tenth Majlis, Tehran, Tehran (2016–20)
1966–, Tehran, Tehran
Clerical education, Qom Seminary; pursuing a PhD in Islamic studies at Allameh Tabataba'i University
Clergyman
War veteran (wounded)
IRGC militiaman (Basij)
HI Shaikh has taught at various Iranian universities, and he has held executive posts in the ideological-political bureau of Law Enforcement Forces (retired in 2009) and free zone organizations. During the war in Bosnia-Herzegovina, he went there as a propagandist and stayed until 1997.

Shaikh [-Shushtari], Mohammad-Ali

Deputy of the Fifth (1996–2000), Sixth (2000–2004), and Seventh (2004–8) Majlis, Shushtar, Khuzestan
1929–2017, Shushtar, Khuzestan
Clerical education; PhD, law, Tehran University
Mohammad-Taqi, clergyman
University professor
No imprisonment
Not a war veteran
Before the revolution, Shaikh was a faculty member at National University (now known as Shahid Beheshti University). He was a former member of the HCCR, and the oldest member of both the Sixth and the Seventh Majlis.

Shaikhi, Qoli

Deputy of the Second Majlis, I'zeh, Khuzestan (1984–88)
1952–2011, I'zeh, Khuzestan

Associate's degree
Ali Aqa
No imprisonment
After leaving the Second Majlis, Shaikhi became a
deputy to the labor minister and was the manag-
ing director of *Towse'eh*.

Shaikhmohammadi [Mohammadi-Takandi], Ali

Member of the Third Assembly of Experts, Qazvin
(1999–2006)
1933–, Takand, Qazvin
Clerical education, Qom Seminary
Ali-Asghar, clergyman
Clergyman (ayatollah)
No imprisonment
Not a war veteran

Shaikhmovahhed, Ali

Member of the Second Assembly of Experts, Fars
(1991–98)
1946–, Shiraz, Fars
Clerical education
Mohammad-Ali, clergyman
Clergyman
No imprisonment
Ayatollah Shaikhmovahhed was Ayatollah Khomeini's representative in the Construction Jihad of
Fars Province, rector of Islamic Azad University–Shiraz (1987–99), and Ayatollah Khamenei's
representative in Islamic Azad University. His
brother Mohammad, who converted to the Baha'i
faith before the revolution, was abducted in 1979
and was never heard from again.

Shaikholislam, Hoseyn

Deputy of the Seventh Majlis, Tehran, Tehran
(2004–8)
1952–, Isfahan, Isfahan
BS, computer science
Mohammad-Ali

Ambassador to Syria (1998–2003)
No imprisonment
Not a war veteran
Shaikholislam was active in the Muslim Student
Association in the United States from 1978 to
1979, and it is not clear whether he finished any
academic degrees while in the United States. He
was involved in the takeover of the American
embassy, and was a spokesperson for the hostage-takers. Later on, Shaikholislam held the post
of deputy foreign minister for Arab and African
affairs for sixteen years and was ambassador to
Syria for five years.

Shaikholislami, Abdorreza

Minister of cooperatives, labor, and social welfare in
President Ahmadinejad's second cabinet (Septem-
ber 3, 2009–February 3, 2013)
1967–, Kachur-e Nowshahr, Mazandaran
MS, civil engineering, Iran University of Science and
Technology, 1995; PhD, civil engineering, Iran
University of Science and Technology
Civil servant
No imprisonment
War veteran
IRGC militiaman
Shaikholislami was governor-general of Hormozgan
before becoming Ahmadinejad's chief of staff
when he was mayor of Tehran. During Ahmadinejad's first term as president, he was the
chief of his presidential office. Shaikholislami
held the post of minister of labor and social affairs from September 3, 2009 to August 3, 2011.
On August 3, 2011, after the merger of the ministries of cooperatives, labor and social welfare,
and social security into one unified ministry,
he became the minister of cooperatives, labor,
and social welfare. Shaikholislami held this post
until February 3, 2013, when the Majlis successfully impeached him. He served in the cabinet
together with the adviser of his master's thesis,
Hamid Behbahani.

Shaikholislami, Mohammad

Member of the Third (1999–2006) and Fourth (2007–
 September 17, 2009) Assembly of Experts, Kurdistan
1934–September 17, 2009, Baneh, Kurdistan
Clerical education
Mohammad
Clergyman
No imprisonment
Not a war veteran
Mamosta Shaikholislami, a Sunni, taught Sunni law
 and theology at various universities. He was
 assassinated.

Shaker, Mohammad-Hoseyn

Chief of the joint staff of the Islamic Republic of Iran
 Army (July 21–December 22, 1979)
Date of birth unknown, Shiraz, Fars
BS, military science, Ground Forces Officers' Academy, 1952
Military officer
Shaker completed a number of military training programs in the United States. He was in the intelligence directorate of the army under the shah, and
 the new regime imprisoned him for two months
 after the revolution. He replaced Farbod as chief
 of JSIRIA.

Shakhesi, Hasan

Deputy of the Fourth (1992–96) and Fifth (1996–2000)
 Majlis, Astaneh-ye Ashrafiyyeh, Gilan
1960–, Astaneh-ye Ashrafiyyeh, Gilan
BA, 1995; MA, political science
Hoseyn
No imprisonment
Shakhesi ran for the Sixth and the Tenth Majlis.

Shakibi, Seyyed Masha'allah

Deputy of the Fifth (1996–2000) and Sixth (2000–
 August 2004) Majlis, Tabas and Ferdows, South
 Khorasan
1951–August 2014, Tabas, South Khorasan

BS, civil engineering, University of Oklahoma (USA)
Seyyed Abbas
Engineer and water official in Khorasan and Tehran
No imprisonment
Not a war veteran
When Shakibi was reelected in 2000, Tabas was a part
 of Khorasan Province, but in 2001, it became a
 part of Yazd Province. Shakibi did not receive
 enough votes for the Seventh Majlis, and the GC
 disqualified him from the Eighth Majlis. He died
 in a plane crash in August 2014.

Shakuri, Abolfazl

Deputy of the Sixth Majlis, Zanjan, Zanjan (2000–2004)
1955–, Zanjan, Zanjan
Clerical education, Qom Seminary; PhD, political
 science, Tarbiyat-e Modarres University
Lotfali
Clergyman (HI)
Imprisoned before the revolution
Not a war veteran
Shakuri is the editor of E'temad Melli.

Shakurirad, Ali

Deputy of the Sixth Majlis, Tehran, Tehran
 (2000–2004)
1962–, Tehran, Tehran
MD, radiology, Tehran University, 1994
Mohammad, clergyman
Medical doctor and university professor
No imprisonment
Not a war veteran
Member of the central council of IIPF; secretary-
 general of the Party of Islamic Iran's People's Unity
Shakurirad joined the students taking over the American embassy after a few months. He was a general
 manager of the Ministry of Health's inspectorate
 before being elected to the Sixth Majlis. In 2010,
 the judiciary arrested Shakurirad for criticiz-
 ing the banning of IIPF. In 2015, he became the
 secretary-general of the newly formed Party of
 Islamic Iran's People's Unity.

Shamkhani, Ali

Deputy commander in chief of the IRGC (1985–88); minister of revolutionary guards in PM Musavi's second cabinet (September 20, 1988–August 3, 1989); commander of the Islamic Republic of Iran Navy (October 31, 1989–August 26, 1997); minister of defense and armed forces logistics in President Khatami's first (August 20, 1997–August 1, 2001) and second (August 22, 2001–August 2, 2005) cabinets; secretary of the Supreme Council for National Security (October 9, 2013–present)
1955–, Ahvaz, Khuzestan
BS, agricultural engineering, Shahid Chamran University of Ahvaz, 1986; military science, Iranian Army Command and General Staff College, 1990
Saleh, bazaar merchant
Military official
No imprisonment
War veteran
Martyr's family (two brothers killed at the war front; another brother, also a veteran, died in 2001)
Vice Admiral Shamkhani, an ethnic Arab, was a member of the paramilitary Mansurron group before the revolution. He became one of the founders of the IRGC and its commander in Khuzestan. Shamkhani was the deputy commander of the IRGC and the commander of its ground forces during the Iran–Iraq War. In 1989, Ayatollah Khamenei appointed him commander of the Islamic Republic of Iran Navy and for a while, Shamkhani was simultaneously commander of the IRGC's naval forces as well. In 2001, while serving as President Khamati's defense minister, he ran against his boss in the presidential election but received only 2.6 percent of the vote. Nonetheless, Khatami retained him as defense minister in his second cabinet. In 2006, Ayatollah Khamenei appointed him to the Strategic Council on Foreign Relations. Shamkhani directed the Center for Strategic Defensive Studies (affiliated with the armed forces) until his appointment as secretary and representative of the supreme leader in the SCNS in 2013. During Shamkhani's tenure, the SCNS played an active role in Iran's nuclear negotiations with world powers.

Shamlu-Mahmudi, Mehdi

Deputy of the Second Majlis, Malayer, Hamadan (1984–88)
1941–, Malayer, Hamadan
BA, law
Abdollah
No imprisonment
He served as ambassador to Libya and the Netherlands and ran unsuccessfully for the Third and Fifth Majlis.

Shaqaqiyan, Javad

Deputy of the Second Majlis, Shiraz, Fars (1984–88)
1951–, Shiraz, Fars
Clerical education
Mohammad-Ali
No imprisonment
In 2009, Shaqaqiyan was chair of the Fars Province campaign headquarters of presidential candidate Mir Hoseyn Musavi.

Sharafi, Gholam-Reza

Deputy of the Tenth Majlis, Abadan, Khuzestan (2016–20)
1964–, Abadan, Khuzestan
MA, business administration
University professor
War veteran
No imprisonment
IRGC militiaman
Sharafi, who has retired from the IRGC, is a conservative who ran unsuccessfully for the Ninth Majlis.

Shar'i, Abdolkarim

Deputy of the First Majlis, Darab, Fars (1980–84)
1949–, Darab, Fars
Clerical education; BA, sociology
Gholam-Hoseyn, clergyman

Clergyman (HI)
No imprisonment
Martyr's family (nephew, HI Mohammad-Taqi Shar'i,
    killed at the war front)

Shar'i, Mohammad-Ali

Deputy of the Third (1988–92) and Fourth (1992–96)
    Majlis, Qom, Qom
1936–January 1, 2017, Qom, Qom
Clerical education, Qom Seminary
Gholam-Hoseyn, clergyman
Clergyman
Imprisoned before the revolution
Not a war veteran
Martyr's family (son, HI Mohammad-Taqi Shar'i,
    killed at the war front)
Member of the SQSS; founding member of the Qom
    Islamic Society of Admonishers
HI Shar'i was head of the headquarters for Islamic
    revolution in Qom in the early days of the revolu-
    tion, and was named by Khomeini to the founding
    committee for the women's seminary in 1984. In
    May 1984, he withdrew after the first round of
    Majlis elections in Qom in favor of Ayatollah Azar-
    Qomi. Shar'i was affiliated with *Resalat*, of which
    Azari-Qomi was the proprietor, from its inception in
    1985. He was also affiliated with the Qom Seminary
    Islamic Propaganda Office. His brother, Abdolkarim,
    represented Darab before him in the First Majlis.

Shari'ati, Mohammad-Baqer

Deputy of the Ninth Majlis, Behbahan, Khuzestan
    (2012–16)
1953–, Behbahan, Khuzestan
MA, public administration; clerical education
Mayor of Behbahan
No imprisonment

Shari'ati-Dehaqani, Mohammad

Deputy of the First Majlis, Semirom, Isfahan (1981–84)
1948–, Najaf, Iraq

Clerical education
Mohammad-Baqer
Clergyman
No imprisonment
HI Shari'ati-Dehaqani held such posts as deputy
    Islamic guidance minister for international affairs
    (resigned February 1985), deputy interior minister
    for legal and parliamentary affairs, and deputy
    director for provincial affairs in IRIB.

Shari'ati-Kohbani, Mrs. Effat

Deputy of the Seventh (2004–8) and Eighth (2008–12)
    Majlis, Mashhad and Kalat, Razavi Khorasan
1952–, Kerman, Kerman
BA, history; MA, planning
Academia
No imprisonment
Not a war veteran
Deputy secretary-general of Zeynab Society
After Shari'ati-Kohbani did not receive enough votes
    to get into the Ninth Majlis, she became an ad-
    viser to culture minister Ali Jannati.

Shari'ati-Niyasar, Hasan Aqa

Member of the Fourth Assembly of Experts, Isfahan
    (2007–16)
1933–, Niyasar, Isfahan
Clerical education, Najaf Seminary (Iraq), beginning
    in 1956
Ali, clergyman
Clergyman
No imprisonment
Not a war veteran
Martyr's family (son Mohammad-Hoseyn killed in
    Iran-Iraq War)
Ayatollah Shari'ati-Niyasar has held various judicial
    posts, including serving in the State Supreme Court.

Shari'atmadari, Ali

Minister of culture and higher education in PM Ba-
    zargan's cabinet (February 22–September 28, 1979)

1923–2017, Shiraz, Fars

BA, education, Tehran University, 1953; MA, education (teachers' training), University of Michigan (USA), 1957; PhD, education (teachers' training), University of Tennessee (USA), 1959; dissertation title: "The Professional Preparation of Elementary School Teachers in Iran"

Jalal, clergyman

University professor

Imprisoned before the revolution

Not a war veteran

Member of JAMA

Upon finishing his doctoral studies, Shari'atmadari returned to Iran and taught for five years at Isfahan University of Technology before returning to the United States to teach at Indiana University and the University of Tennessee. He returned to Iran after the revolution and became minister of culture and higher education (until he resigned) as well as a professor at Tehran University. Shari'atmadari was a member of the HCCR from its inception and was responsible for the humanities.

Shari'atmadari, Mohammad

Minister of commerce in President Khatami's first (August 20, 1997–August 1, 2001) and second (August 22, 2001–August 2, 2005) cabinets; VP for executive affairs in President Rouhani's first cabinet (2013–August 13, 2017); minister of industry, mining, and trade in President Rouhani's second cabinet (August 20, 2017–2021)

1957–, Tehran, Tehran

MA, business administration, 2003; pursuing graduate studies in political science at Tehran University

Nureddin, clergyman

Director of the Headquarters for Implementation of Imam's Order

No imprisonment

Not a war veteran

Martyr's family (brother)

Founder and member of the central council of ADVIR

Shari'atmadari, who comes from a family of ayatollahs, entered Kerman University in 1977 to study electrical engineering but did not finish his studies as the revolution occurred. In 1981, he joined the Office of the Prime Minister, working in the unit dealing with the affairs of the revolution. In 1984, he worked alongside Mohammad Reyshahri and others to establish MIIRI. In 1989, Shari'atmadari became a deputy minister of commerce, and from 1990 to 1997, he was in charge of the supervision and accounting bureau of the Office of the Supreme Leader. In 1990, Ayatollah Khamenei appointed him as the special representative for supervising pilgrims and made him a trustee of the committee overseeing properties under the control of the supreme leader. In 1994, Ayatollah Khamenei put Shari'atmadari in charge of the Headquarters for Implementation of Imam's Order, and in 1997, he became an adviser to the Office of the Supreme Leader. In 2006, Ayatollah Khamenei appointed him to the Strategic Council on Foreign Relations. Throughout the last three decades, Shari'atmadari has remained very close to Ayatollah Khamenei and former intelligence minister Mohammad Reyshahri. The latter appointed him as a member of the board of trustees and his plenipotentiary representative in the affairs of Shah-Abdolazim Shrine near Tehran. Shari'atmadari has been intimately involved in the economic activities of this religious foundation and its subsidiaries. In 2017, he was head of the campaign headquarters of President Rouhani. He is the brother-in-law of Ataollah Salehi, the former chief of the Armed Forces General Staff.

Shari'atnezhad, Shamsollah

Deputy of the Ninth (2013–16) and Tenth (2016–20) Majlis, Tonekabon, Ramsar, and Abbasabad, Mazandaran

1957–, Tonekabon, Mazandaran

BS, forestry and pasture engineering, Gorgan University of Agricultural Sciences and Natural

Resources, 1983; MS, Tehran University, 1995;
PhD, sociology, Tarbiyat-e Modarres University
Mohammad-Baqer
Civil servant, state companies
No imprisonment
Shari'atnezhad, who ran unsuccessfully for the Fifth
and Sixth Majlis, was elected to the Ninth Majlis
in interim elections in June 2013.

Sharifi, Naser

Deputy of the Tenth Majlis, Bandar-e Lengeh, Bastak,
and Parsian, Hormozgan (2017–20)
January 5, 1978–, Bastak, Hormozgan
Ali
MA, public law
Provincial official and university instructor in
Hormozgan
No imprisonment
Not a war veteran
Sharifi served for seventeen years in various provin-
cial posts in Hormozgan before being elected
to the Tenth Majlis in midterm elections. Sharifi
is the nephew of Ahmad Jabbari, who repre-
sented the same constituency for eight years
before him.

Sharifi, Seyyed Hoseyn

Deputy of the Fourth (1992–96) and Fifth (1996–2000)
Majlis, Arak, Markazi
1953–, Arak, Markazi
BS, physics; MA, political science, 1995
Seyyed Ali
No imprisonment

Sharifpur, Eynollah

Deputy of the Tenth Majlis, Maku, West Azerbaijan
(2016–20)
February 20, 1957–, Chaldoran, West Azerbaijan
MA, research management
Provincial civil servant
No imprisonment

Sharifzadegan, Mohammad-Hoseyn

Minister of welfare and social security in President Khatami's second cabinet (July 3, 2004–August 2, 2005)
1954–, Hamadan, Hamadan
PhD, economics, University of London (England)
(unverified)
Civil servant
No imprisonment
War veteran
Sharifzadegan was involved in the takeover of the
American embassy and later became an adviser
to PM Musavi, his brother-in-law, on agricultural
issues. The regime arrested Sharifzadegan in 2011
for his political activities.

Sharifzadeh, Qader

Deputy of the Third Majlis, Sardasht and Piranshahr,
West Azerbaijan (1988–92)
1955–, Sardasht, West Azerbaijan
High school diploma
Sharif
No imprisonment

Shar'pasand, Abdolmajid

Deputy of the Second (1986–88) and Third (1988–July
9, 1989) Majlis, Karaj, Tehran
1959–, Karaj, Tehran
Associate's degree
Mohammad-Ali
Teacher
No imprisonment
War veteran (wounded)
Martyr's family (two brothers killed at the war front)
Shar'pasand was elected to the Second Majlis in
interim elections and was its youngest member.
During the Third Majlis, he delivered a fiery
speech on the concentration of power in a few
hands and violations of democratic rights. This
speech, on July 2, 1989, came less than a month
after the death of Ayatollah Khomeini, and
other MPs strongly objected to it. Shar'pasand

was arrested a couple of days after delivering his
speech and was interrogated for forty days. In the
meantime, while he was under arrest, the Majlis
approved his resignation/expulsion on July 9,
1989. He returned to teaching until he retired,
and could not hold any other posts. In addition
to the two brothers killed in the war, his father
sustained damage to his eyes during the war.

Shaverani, Mohammad

Deputy of the First (1981–84) and Second (1984–88)
    Majlis, Bukan, West Azerbaijan
1947–, Mahabad, West Azerbaijan
Clerical education
Mohammad-Sharif
Clergyman (mamosta)
No imprisonment
Not a war veteran
Shaverani, a Sunni, is a former Friday prayer leader of
    Bukan and was associated with the IRGC in that
    city.

Shayeq, Mrs. Eshrat

Deputy of the Seventh Majlis, Tabriz, Osku, and
    Azarshahr, East Azerbaijan (2004–8)
1963–, Bam, Kerman
Clerical education, Qom and Kerman Seminaries;
    MA, international relations
Azizollah
Civil servant
No imprisonment
Not a war veteran
IRGC militiawoman
Member of the central council of ASIR
Shayeq was the director of the Historical-Cultural
    Collection of Sadabad (a former palace of the
    shah) and a member of the board of directors of
    Tehran's Esteqlal, a popular soccer team.

Shayesteh, Morteza

Deputy of the Fourth (1992–96) and Sixth (2000–
    2004) Majlis, Golpayegan and Khansar, Isfahan

1942–, Golpayegan, Isfahan
BS, agricultural engineering; clerical education
Mohammad-Ja'far
Civil servant
No imprisonment
IRGC militiaman

Shehnimostafa, Mohammad

Deputy of the Second Majlis, Masjed Soleyman, Khu-
    zestan (1984–88)
1951–2012, Abadan, Khuzestan
BA
Ali-Baqer
No imprisonment
IRGC militiaman

Sherafat, Seyyed Mohammad-Javad

Deputy of the First Majlis, Shushtar, Khuzestan
    (1980–June 28, 1981)
1927–June 28, 1981, Shushtar, Khuzestan
BA, Persian literature, Daneshsara-ye Ali-ye Tehran
Seyyed Javad, clergyman
Academia
No imprisonment
Not a war veteran
Sherafat was killed in the bombing of the IRP head-
    quarters in June 1981.

Sherdust, Ali-Asghar

Deputy of the Sixth Majlis, Tabriz, Azarshahr, and
    Osku, East Azerbaijan (2000–2004)
1961–, Tabriz, East Azerbaijan
PhD, philology
Mohammad
No imprisonment
Sherdust became ambassador to Tajikistan in 2007.

Sheybani, Abbas

Member of the Revolutionary Council (1979–80); mem-
    ber of the Assembly for the Final Examination of the
    Constitution, Tehran (1979); minister of agriculture

in the Revolutionary Council cabinet (February 9–May 28, 1980); deputy of the First (1981–84), Second (1984–88), Third (1988–92), Fourth (1992–96), and Fifth (1996–2000) Majlis, Tehran, Tehran

January 23, 1932–, Tehran, Tehran

MD, medicine, Tehran University, 1969

Hedayatollah, civil servant

Medical doctor

Imprisoned before the revolution (thirteen years)

Not a war veteran

Founding member of the LMI, the Islamic Society of Iranian Physicians, and the Islamic Society of Iranian Academics; member of the central council of the IRP

Sheybani started his political career with LMI before the revolution. A physician by training, he had no background in agriculture when he became the minister of agriculture in the Revolutionary Council cabinet in 1979. Sheybani was the first runner-up in the 1981 and 1989 presidential elections, receiving less than 5 percent and 4 percent of the vote, respectively. In the 1980s, he also served in other capacities such as head of the Islamic Republic of Iran Medical Council and interim rector of Tehran University. Sheybani has been a member of the Tehran City Council since 2002.

Sheybani, Ebrahim

Governor of the Central Bank (2003–7)

1948–, Khor and Biyabanak, Isfahan

BA, economics, Tehran University; MA, economics, Tehran University, 1976; MA, economics, Indiana University (USA), 1981; PhD, economics, Indiana University, 1983 (under the name Ebrahim Sheibani)

Economics professor at Tehran University (since 1991)

No imprisonment

Not a war veteran

Sheybani did graduate work at Indiana University from August 1978 to May 1983. Before becoming the governor of the Central Bank, he chaired the Money and Credit Council, the Stock Exchange Council, and the Banks High Council of Iran.

Sheybani became ambassador to Austria in 2008. His wife, Zahra Afshari, is also a full professor of economics at Alzahra University.

Shiran-Khorasani, Reza

Deputy of the Tenth Majlis, Mashhad, Razavi Khorasan (2016–20)

1963–, Mashhad, Razavi Khorasan

PhD, international law, Allameh Tabataba'i University

No imprisonment

War veteran (wounded)

Shiran-Khorasani, a conservative, has been a long-time adviser to Mohammad-Baqer Qalibaf, the mayor of Tehran. He has held managerial posts in Tehran municipality and was an adviser to the MI's inspectorate in 2013.

Shiraziyan, Javad

Deputy of the First Majlis, Qaemshahr, Mazandaran (1980–84)

1929–, Qom, Qom

MD, pediatrics, Tehran University

Ebrahim, farmer

Medical doctor

No imprisonment

Not a war veteran

Shiraziyan was rector of Islamic Azad University–Qom for a while.

Shiraziyan, Seyyed Gholam-Reza

Deputy of the Fifth Majlis, Mashhad, Razavi Khorasan (1996–2000)

1951–, Mashhad, Razavi Khorasan

BS, civil engineering, Shiraz University, 1975; MS, civil engineering, Iowa State University (USA), 1977; PhD, civil engineering, Auburn University (USA), 1981

Seyyed Ali-Akbar

Civil servant

No imprisonment

Not a war veteran

Shiri-Aliabadi, Gholam-Hoseyn

Deputy of the Ninth Majlis, Hashtrud and Charuy-
maq, East Azerbaijan (2012–16)
1961–, Hashtrud, East Azerbaijan
MA, Islamic history, 2004
Abdolali, clergyman
Civil servant; mayor of Hashtrud (one term)
No imprisonment
War veteran
Shiri-Aliabadi ran unsuccessfully for the Fourth,
Fifth, Eighth, and Tenth Majlis from Hashtrud.

Shirzad, Ahmad

Deputy of the Sixth Majlis, Isfahan, Isfahan
(2000–2004)
1958–, Isfahan, Isfahan
BS, physics, Sharif University of Technology, 1984;
MS, physics, Sharif University of Technology,
1988; PhD, physics, Sharif University of Technol-
ogy, 1992
Mostafa, laborer
Professor of nuclear physics
No imprisonment
Not a war veteran
Member of IIPF
Shirzad was involved in the takeover of the American
embassy in Tehran.

Shirzadi, Morteza

Deputy of the Second (1984–88) and Sixth (2000–
2004) Majlis, Qasr-e Shirin, Sarpol-e Zahab, and
Gilan-e Gharb, Kermanshah
1948–, Gilan-e Gharb, Kermanshah
BA, theology, 1998
Jahanbakhsh
Civil servant
No imprisonment

Shivyari, Ya'qub

Deputy of the Tenth Majlis, Miyaneh, East Azerbaijan
(2016–20)

1969–, Miyaneh, East Azerbaijan
MD, Tabriz University of Medical Sciences
Yadollah
Medical doctor
IRGC militiaman (Basij)
Martyr's family (father killed at the war front in
1986)
Not a war veteran
Shivyari ran unsuccessfully for the Ninth Majlis.

Shoja', Abdolghaffar

Deputy of the Fourth (1992–96) and Fifth (1996–2000)
Majlis, Bandar-e Anzali, Gilan
1945–, Bandar-e Anzali, Gilan
BS, natural resources engineering; MS, agricultural
engineering
Safar-Ali
No imprisonment
Member of the central committee of the PMD
In 2013, Shoja' was head of Rouhani's campaign head-
quarters in Gilan Province. He was also head of
the Iran Tea Company.

Shoja', Seyyed Abdolmajid

Deputy of the Seventh Majlis, Dashtestan, Bushehr
(2004–8)
1961–, Dashtestan, Bushehr
MD, psychology
Seyyed Musa
Civil servant
No imprisonment
Shoja' has been the dean of Bushehr University Med-
ical School and deputy of the Ministry of Health
in Bushehr.

Shoja'eifard, Mohammad-Mehdi

Deputy of the Fourth (1992–96) and Fifth (1996–2000)
Majlis, Jahrom, Fars
1947–, Jahrom, Fars
BA, 1992; MA, planning, 2000
Hoseyn

Civil servant
No imprisonment
War veteran

Shoja'ei-Kiyasari, Seyyed Hasan

Deputy of the Second (1984–88), Third (1988–92),
    Fourth (1992–96), and Seventh (2004–8) Majlis,
    Sari, Mazandaran
1941–2014, Kiyasar, Mazandaran
Clerical education
Seyyed Aqa Mir
Clergyman
No imprisonment
Not a war veteran
HI Shoja'ei-Kiyasari was head of a branch of the CAJ.
    He is the cousin of Seyyed Ramezan Shoja'ei-
    Kiyasari, who also served in the Majlis.

Shoja'ei-Kiyasari, Seyyed Ramezan

Deputy of the Eighth (2008–12) Majlis, Sari, Mazan-
    daran; deputy of the Ninth (2012–16) Majlis, Sari
    and Miandorud, Mazandaran
1965–, Sari, Mazandaran
BA, law, University of Judicial Sciences-Qom, 1991;
    MA, theology, Islamic Azad University–Babol,
    1996; PhD, Oriental studies, Yerevan State Uni-
    versity (Armenia)
Seyyed Ebrahim, farmer
Civil servant and university instructor
No imprisonment
Shoja'ei-Kiyasari has worked in IRIB and is in charge
    of the MI's communications and international af-
    fairs bureau. The GC disqualified him from run-
    ning in the 2016 Majlis election. In 2017, he was a
    member of the election board for the presidential
    and municipal elections.

Shoja'i, Mohammad

Deputy of the First Majlis, Zanjan, Zanjan (1980–
    April 22, 1982)

1940–2015, Zanjan, Zanjan
Clerical education
Ali, clergyman
Clergyman
No imprisonment
Not a war veteran
Disgusted with political conflicts, Shoja'i resigned
    from the First Majlis and went back to teaching in
    the seminary.

Shoja'iyan, Samad

Deputy of the First (1980–84) and Second (1984–88)
    Majlis, Mamasani, Fars
1948–, Mamasani, Fars
Associate's degree
Mohammad, farmer
Teacher in tribal regions
No imprisonment
Not a war veteran

Shoja'purian, Valiyollah

Deputy of the Sixth (2000–2004) and Seventh (2004–
    8) Majlis, Behbahan, Khuzestan
1962–, Behbahan, Khuzestan
BA, Arabic literature, Tehran University, 1988; MA,
    Arabic literature, Tehran University, 1990; PhD,
    Arabic literature, Tehran University, 1994
Mehrab, farmer
University professor
No imprisonment
War veteran (wounded)
Member of the central council of the PIIPU
After leaving the Majlis, Shoja'purian, a reformist,
    became a professor at Shahid Chamran Uni-
    versity of Ahvaz. However, after the 2009 pro-
    tests, he was dismissed because he was head of
    Mir Hoseyn Musavi's campaign headquarters
    in Khuzestan Province. Subsequently, he was
    elected to the Tehran City Council (2013–17).
    The GC disqualified Shoja'purian for the Eighth
    Majlis and he decided not to run for the Ninth
    Majlis.

Shojuni [-Javadi], Ja'far

Deputy of the First Majlis, Karaj, Tehran (1980–84)
1932–2016, Fuman, Gilan
Clerical education, Qom Seminary, 1956
Mohammad, clergyman (HI)
Clergyman (HI)
Imprisoned before the revolution
Not a war veteran
Member of the central council of the SCC and CIC/
    PCIC
Shojuni, an archconservative, was a follower of
    Mojtaba Navvab-Safavi (1923–56), leader of the
    paramilitary group Devotees of Islam, during the
    shah's era. Before the revolution, SAVAK set up a
    trap to film him having sex with a prostitute. He
    was in charge of confiscating Pahlavi family as-
    sets and palaces in Karaj, and a picture appeared
    in a foreign newspaper of him holding up a pair
    of women's underwear for auction in the looted
    Pearle Palace. Shojuni supported President Ah-
    madinejad, opposed President Rouhani, and was
    on record saying that Mir Hoseyn Musavi could
    only receive the votes of street women. Shojuni
    was the maternal uncle of Ebrahim Ahadi, who
    was justice minister in PM Raja'i's cabinet.

Shokri, Mahmud

Deputy of the Ninth (2012–16) and Tenth (2016–20)
    Majlis, Talesh, Rezvanshahr, and Masal, Gilan
1959–, Siyahdaran, Gilan
BA, public administration, Payam-e Nur University,
    Rasht; MA, public administration, School of Pub-
    lic Administration; pursuing a PhD in strategic
    management at Tarbiyat-e Mo'allem University
Father's name unknown, farmer
Adviser to the minister of economy
No imprisonment
War veteran (ten months)
Shokri, a conservative, worked at various state eco-
    nomic and financial organizations from 1982 to
    2011, and then he became an adviser to the minis-
    ter of economy.

Shokuhi, Gholam-Hoseyn

Minister of education in PM Bazargan's cabinet (Feb-
    ruary–September 1979)
June 26, 1926–May 6, 2016, Khoosf, South Khorasan
BA, Persian literature, Daneshsara-ye Ali-ye Tehran,
    1956; PhD, education, University of Geneva (Swit-
    zerland), 1962
Ali-Akbar, tailor
Professor of education at Tehran University
    (1967–93)
No imprisonment
Not a war veteran
Shokuhi went to Switzerland in 1957 and studied
    with clinical psychologist Jean Piaget. He was
    minister of education for less than seven months
    and resigned due to ill health in September 1979.

Sho'lehsa'di, Qasem

Deputy of the Third (1988–92) and Fourth (1992–96)
    Majlis, Shiraz, Fars
1954–, Shiraz, Fars
BA, judicial law, Shahid Beheshti University, 1976;
    MA, political science, University of Paris (France);
    PhD, political science, University of Paris
    (France), 1983
Jaber, farmer
Attorney
No imprisonment
Not a war veteran
Martyr's family (brother, Asghar, killed at the war
    front)
After serving in the Majlis, Sho'lehsa'di wrote a
    number of courageous open letters to the supreme
    leader and was arrested in 2011. The GC disquali-
    fied him from running in the 2009, 2013, and 2017
    presidential elections.

Shuhani, Ahmad

Deputy of the Ninth Majlis, Ilam, Eyvan, Mehran,
    Malekshahi, and Shirvan, Ilam (2012–16)
1972–, Mehran, Ilam

BA, political science, Isfahan University of Technology, 1994; MA, political science, Tehran University, 1997; PhD, political science
Father's name unknown, farmer
Professor of political science
No imprisonment
War veteran

Shushtari, Ali

Deputy of the Second Majlis, Neyshabur, Razavi Khorasan (1984–88)
1950–, Neyshabur, Razavi Khorasan
Clerical education
Rahmatollah
Clergyman
No imprisonment
IRGC militiaman
HI Shushtari was commander of the IRGC and head of the ideological-political bureau of the police force in Neyshabur after the revolution. He ran unsuccessfully for the Third Majlis.

Shushtari, Hadi

Deputy of the Ninth (2012–16) and Tenth (2016–20) Majlis, Quchan and Faruj, Razavi Khorasan
1971–, Quchan, Razavi Khorasan
BA, law; MA, law, Tehran University
Adineh-Mohammad
Governor of Dargaz
No imprisonment
Not a war veteran
Shushtari previously worked as a judge and deputy governor.

Shushtari, Mohammad-Esma'il

Deputy of the First (1981–84) and Second (1984–88) Majlis, Quchan, Razavi Khorasan; minister of justice in President Hashemi-Rafsanjani's first (August 29, 1989–August 2, 1993) and second (August 16, 1993–August 2, 1997) cabinets and President Khatami's first (August 20, 1997–August 1, 2001)

and second (August 22, 2001–August 2, 2005) cabinets
1949–, Quchan, Razavi Khorasan
Clerical education, Qom Seminary
Fazlollah, clergyman
Clergyman
No imprisonment
Not a war veteran
Martyr's family (two brothers)
HI Shushtari entered the judiciary in 1979, and he was head of Iran's Prison Organization from 1987 to 1989, when thousands of political prisoners were executed. He is a former Friday prayer leader of Shirvan. In addition to being the justice minister for sixteen years, he was also head of the inspectorate bureau in President Rouhani's office. His brother, Nur-Ali Shushtari, was deputy commander of the IRGC's ground forces. Baluchi rebel groups assassinated Nur-Ali in Sarbaz, Sistan and Baluchestan, on October 18, 2009.

Siyavashi-Shahenayati, Mrs. Tayebeh

Deputy of the Tenth Majlis, Tehran, Tehran (2016–20)
1966–, Shemiranat, Tehran
BA, political science, Tehran University; MA, international relations, School of International Relations (affiliated with Iran's Ministry of Foreign Affairs)
No imprisonment
Siyavashi-Shahenayati is a former Ministry of Foreign Affairs official. She also founded a childcare center and was a member of the editorial board of *Payetakht-e Kohan* magazine.

Sobhani, Hasan

Deputy of the Fifth (1996–2000), Sixth (2000–2004), and Seventh (2004–8) Majlis, Damghan, Semnan
1953–, Damghan, Semnan
BA, economics, Shahid Beheshti University, 1979; MA, economics, Tarbiyat-e Modarres University, 1986; PhD, economics, Tehran University, 1993
Mohammad-Ebrahim, sweeper

Professor of economics at Tehran University (since 1992/93)

No imprisonment

Not a war veteran

Sobhani was active in revolutionary committees, and his doctoral dissertation dealt with Islam's economic system. The GC disqualified him from running in the 2013 and 2017 presidential elections.

Sobhani [Eqbal-Sobhani], Ja'far

Member of the Assembly for the Final Examination of the Constitution, East Azerbaijan (1979)

1930–, Tabriz, East Azerbaijan

Clerical education, Qom Seminary

Mohammad-Hoseyn, clergyman

Clergyman (ayatollah)

No imprisonment

Not a war veteran

Member of the SQSS

Sobhani went to Qom Seminary in 1946, and he became one of the founders of the influential *Maktab-e Islam* magazine. He was close to Grand Ayatollah Seyyed Mohammad-Kazem Shari'atmadari, and he wrote many articles against Wahhabis. Ayatollah Sobhani, who is now a *marja'* in Qom, established the Imam Sadeq Institute in 1991.

Sobhanifar, Ramezan-Ali

Deputy of the Ninth (2012–16) and Tenth (2016–20) Majlis, Sabzevar, Joghatai, Jowayin, Khoshab, and Davarzan, Razavi Khorasan

1965–, Sabzevar, Razavi Khorasan

MA, theology, Islamic Azad University

Deputy director of Iran Communications Company

No imprisonment

IRGC militiaman

Sobhaninia, Hoseyn [Gholam-Hoseyn]

Deputy of the Second (1984–88), Third (1988–92), Fourth (1992–96), Seventh (2004–8), Eighth (2008–12), and Ninth (2012–16) Majlis, Neyshabur, Razavi Khorasan

1954–, Neyshabur, Razavi Khorasan

Clerical education, Tehran Seminary; BA, political science, Tehran University, 1978; MA, international relations, Tehran University, 1991; PhD, political science, Mashhad Seminary School of Human Sciences

Abdorrahim

Clergyman (HI)

No imprisonment

Not a war veteran

Member of the IRP; secretary-general of the Society of Former MPs

The IRP endorsed Sobhaninia, a conservative, for the Second Majlis. During the Third Majlis, he had to defend his credentials against the charge of using state assets for his election campaign. He ran unsuccessfully for the Fifth and Sixth Majlis. He is a former employee of the Ministry of Foreign Affairs and was ambassador to Morocco. He is reportedly close to Ayatollah Khamenei.

Sobhanollahi, Mohammad-Ali

Deputy of the First (1980–84), Second (1984–88), Third (1988–92), and Fourth (1992–96) Majlis, Tabriz, East Azerbaijan

1948–, Tabriz, East Azerbaijan

BS, mathematics, Tabriz University, 1975; MS, mathematics, Tabriz University, 1975; PhD, industrial engineering, Swinburne University of Technology (Australia), 1996

Yahya, bazaar tradesman

Supreme leader's representative in the Construction Jihad of East Azerbaijan

No imprisonment

Not a war veteran

Sobhanollahi was governor-general of East Azerbaijan from 2001 to 2005 and became rector of Kharazmi University on February 23, 2016.

Sohrabi, Abdollah

Deputy of the Sixth Majlis, Marivan, Kurdistan (2000–2004)

1963–, Marivan, Kurdistan
MA, public administration
Mohammad
Employee of the Literacy Movement Organization of
    Iran in Marivan
No imprisonment
The GC disqualified Sohrabi, a Sunni, from running
    in the 2004 Majlis election.

Sohrabi, Ali

Deputy of the Fifth Majlis, Shiraz, Fars
    (1996–2000)
1954–, Shiraz, Fars
MA, law; clerical education
Khodayar
No imprisonment

Sohrabi, Esma'il

Chief of the joint staff of the Islamic Republic of Iran
    Army (October 25, 1984–May 3, 1988)
Date of birth unknown, Mahidasht, Kermanshah
Military official (brigadier general)
In April 1987, Ayatollah Khomeini promoted Sohrabi
    from colonel to brigadier general.

Sohrabi, Mohammad

Chief of Law Enforcement Forces (April 1, 1991–Sep-
    tember 24, 1992)
1940–, Tabas, South Khorasan
BS, military science, Ground Forces Officers'
    Academy
Military officer
Sohrabi became chief of the Gilan Province gendar-
    merie in February 1979, and he was chief of the
    national gendarmerie from February 9, 1985, until
    April 1, 1991, when he became the first chief of the
    newly formed LEF. In that capacity, he oversaw
    the unification of LEF. He retired from this post
    just over a year later with the rank of brigadier
    general.

Sohrabi, Naser

Deputy of the Fourth Majlis, Masjed Soleyman, Khu-
    zestan (1992–96)
1958–, Naftshahr, Kermanshah
High school diploma
Employee of the revolutionary court
Ja'far-Qoli
No imprisonment
Sohrabi is an official in the judiciary of Tehran.

Soleymani, Behyar

Deputy of the Sixth Majlis, Fasa, Fars (2000–2004)
1960–, Shiraz, Fars
MA, history
Alibaz
Civil servant
No imprisonment

Soleymani, Davud

Deputy of the Sixth Majlis, Tehran, Tehran
    (2000–2004)
1957–, Shemiranat, Tehran
PhD, theology, Tehran University
Professor at Tehran University
No imprisonment
Martyr's family (brother)
Founding member of OMIRI
Soleymani, a reformist, was a research deputy at the
    University Jihad and an alternate member of the
    Tehran City Council before being elected to the
    Sixth Majlis. The regime imprisoned him for a
    while after the contested 2009 presidential election.

Soleymani, Hasan

Deputy of the Fourth (1992–96), Sixth (2001–4),
    Seventh (2004–8), and Tenth (2016–20) Majlis,
    Kangavar, Sahneh, and Harsin, Kermanshah
December 1, 1953–, Sahneh, Kermanshah
BA, law, Tehran University, 1975
Abbas, farmer

Judiciary official (since 1979)
No imprisonment
War veteran (six months)
Soleymani was a judge and a civil servant of the State
    Supreme Court.

Soleymani, Mohammad

Minister of information and communications tech-
    nology in President Ahmadinejad's first cabinet
    (August 24, 2005–August 2, 2009); deputy of the
    Ninth Majlis, Tehran, Tehran (2012–16)
1954–, Kazerun, Fars
BS, electrical engineering, Shiraz University, 1978;
    MS, electrical engineering, Pierre and Marie
    Curie University (France); PhD, electrical en-
    gineering, Laboratory of Signals and Systems
    (France), 1982
Gholam-Hoseyn
University professor and deputy to the science minister
No imprisonment
Not a war veteran
Martyr's family (two brothers, Asghar and Baqer,
    killed at the war front)
Member of the SFIR
Soleymani started teaching at Iran University of
    Science and Technology in 1983 and eventually
    became its rector; he and Ahmadinejad knew
    each other from their days at this university. An
    award-winning professor and researcher, he also
    headed the Scientific and Industrial Research Or-
    ganization. He ran unsuccessfully for the Tenth
    Majlis from Tehran in 2016, and then he returned
    to being a full-time faculty member at Iran Uni-
    versity of Science and Technology.

Soleymani, Qasem

Commander of the IRGC's Qods Force (1997–present)
1957–, Rabor, Kerman
No imprisonment
IRGC militiaman (major general)
Martyr's family (brother, Ahmad, killed at the war
    front in 1984)

Before the revolution, Major General Soleymani
    worked as a mason and later a contractor in the
    water department of Kerman. He joined the IRGC
    in 1979 and led its First Division (Sarollah) during
    the Iran–Iraq War. After the war, he returned to
    Kerman and led the IRGC's activities at Iran's
    eastern borders. In 1997, he was appointed as the
    commander of the IRGC's elite Qods Force. In
    1999, Soleymani was one of the twenty-four IRGC
    commanders who penned a threatening letter to
    President Khatami. In 2005, Ayatollah Khamenei
    referred to Soleymani as a "living martyr," and on
    January 24, 2011, promoted him from brigadier
    general to major general, the highest rank that
    can be bestowed on a serving officer. Soleymani
    has been credited with masterminding important
    battlefield victories in Iraq and Syria. He is on
    the US Treasury Office of Foreign Assets Con-
    trol's Specially Designated Nationals and Blocked
    Persons List.

Soleymani-Asbukala'i, Abbas-Ali

Member of the Fourth (2007–16) and Fifth (2016–22)
    Assembly of Experts, Sistan and Baluchestan
1947–, Amirkala, Mazandaran
Clerical education, Qom Seminary
Alijan, farmer
Clergyman
No imprisonment
Not a war veteran
HI Soleymani-Asbukala'i has held such positions as
    Friday prayer leader of Babolsar (1980–2001),
    supreme leader's representative at various univer-
    sities in Mazandaran Province (1981–96), Friday
    prayer leader of Zahedan, Ayatollah Khamenei's
    representative in Sistan and Baluchestan (2001–
    present), and supreme leader's representative in
    the affairs of the Sunnis (2003–present).

Soleymani-Meymandi, Mansur

Deputy of the Fourth (1992–96) and Sixth (2000–
    2004) Majlis, Shahr-e Babak, Kerman

1951–, Shahr-e Babak, Kerman
BS, mechanical engineering, 1978; MS, industrial
    engineering, 1998
Mohammad
Civil servant
No imprisonment

Soltani, Amir-Abbas

Deputy of the Ninth Majlis, Borujen, Chahar Mahal
    and Bakhtiari (2012–16)
1958–, Borujen, Chahar Mahal and Bakhtiari
MA, history of Shiism, Payam-e Nur University, Qom
Mayor of Borujen
No imprisonment
Soltani was one of the MPs who doggedly pursued
    a famous embezzlement case involving Babak
    Zanjani in the Ninth Majlis. After serving in the
    Majlis, he became a high official of the Iranian
    Offshore Oil Company.

Soltani, Gholam-Reza

Deputy of the Second Majlis, Karaj, Tehran (1984–
    February 20, 1986)
1943–February 20, 1986, Karaj, Tehran
Clerical education
Ataollah
Clergyman and Friday prayer leader of Eshtehard,
    Tehran
No imprisonment
Not a war veteran
HI Soltani was Ayatollah Montazeri's representative
    in the humanities department at Tehran Univer-
    sity. He was killed when Iraqi forces shot down
    his aircraft.

Soltani, Hoseyn [Yahya]

Deputy of the Second Majlis, Ardestan, Isfahan
    (1984–88)
1940–, Ardestan, Isfahan
Clerical education
Mohammad

Clergyman
No imprisonment
HI Soltani is a former head of the education depart-
    ment in the Ministry of Foreign Affairs, and
    former head of the FMVA in Ilam Province.

Soltani, Mohammad

Deputy of the Seventh Majlis, Khodabandeh, Zanjan
    (2004–8)
1954–, Khodabandeh, Zanjan
BA, Persian literature
Gheyollah
Civil servant
No imprisonment

Soltanifar, Mas'ud

VP and head of the Cultural Heritage, Handicrafts,
    and Tourism Organization in President Rouhani's
    first cabinet (January 30, 2014–16); minister of
    sports and youth in President Rouhani's first
    (November 1, 2016–August 13, 2017) and second
    (August 20, 2017–2021) cabinets
1959–, Tehran, Tehran
BA, political science; MA, political science
Member of the Tehran City Council
No imprisonment
Not a war veteran
Member of the NTP
Soltanifar was previously governor of Markazi (1992–
    96), Zanjan (1997–2001), and Gilan (2001–5) Prov-
    inces, and he worked alongside Hassan Rouhani
    in the Center for Strategic Research. He was in
    charge of the executive bureau of the National
    Trust Party during the contested 2009 presiden-
    tial election. On August 15, 2013, the MPs re-
    jected him as the proposed minister of sports and
    youth (117 positive votes, 148 negative votes, and
    eighteen abstentions). He then became a member
    of the Tehran City Council, and President Rou-
    hani appointed him to the VP post on January 30,
    2014. On November 1, 2016, the Majlis approved
    him for his second nomination as the minister of

sports and youth (193 positive votes, seventy-two negative votes, and nine abstentions).

Soltani-Sabur, Ataollah

Deputy of the Ninth Majlis, Razan, Hamadan (2012–16)
1969–, Razan, Hamadan
BA, Islamic theosophy, Tehran University, 1990; MA, Qur'anic sciences, Islamic Azad University–Karaj, 2010
Fathollah
University instructor at Bu-Ali Sina University and Islamic Azad University–Razan
No imprisonment

Soltankhah, Mrs. Nasrin

VP for scientific and technological affairs in President Ahmadinejad's second cabinet (2009–13)
1961–, Tehran, Tehran
BS, mathematics, Sharif University of Technology, 1986; MS, mathematics, Sharif University of Technology, 1988; PhD, mathematics, Sharif University of Technology, 1994
Head of the State Management Training Center (2005–9)
No imprisonment
Not a war veteran
Soltankhah has been professor of mathematics at Alzahra University since 1994. She was a member of the Tehran City Council from 2003 to 2007 and served as presidential adviser and director of the president's bureau for women's and family affairs in 2005.

Sori, Abdollah

Deputy of the First Majlis, Saqqez and Baneh, Kurdistan (1983–84)
1921–1995, Baneh, Kurdistan
Clerical education
Ahmad, farmer
Clergyman

No imprisonment
Not a war veteran
Mamosta Sori, a Sunni Kurdish cleric, was born in the village of Varchak near Baneh and was the city's Friday prayer leader from 1980 to 1995, except for 1983 to 1984, when he served in the Majlis. On June 5, 1984, he was injured when Iraqi planes bombed the city of Baneh as he was delivering a sermon. He was a member of the central council of the Literacy Jihad.

Sorush, Abolfazl

Deputy of the Tenth Majlis, Tehran, Tehran (2016–20)
1969–, Neka, Mazandaran
MD
Medical doctor
No imprisonment
War veteran (twenty-one months; wounded)
Member of the central council of the Islamic Association of Iranian Medical Society
Sorush was a leader in various university and medical Islamic associations, and he was an official in Tehran municipality.

Sudani, Naser

Deputy of the Seventh (2004–8), Eighth (2008–12), and Ninth (2012–16) Majlis, Ahvaz, Khuzestan
1960–, Howeyzeh, Khuzestan
PhD, Qur'anic sciences, Tehran University, 1991
Ali
University professor and administrator
No imprisonment
War veteran
IRGC militiaman
Sudani worked in the Water and Electricity Organization in Khuzestan Province.

Sufi, Ali

Minister of cooperatives in President Khatami's second cabinet (August 22, 2001–August 2, 2005)

1950–, Langarud, Gilan
BS, physics, Tabriz University, 1978; MA, public administration, Tehran University, 1998
Civil servant
No imprisonment
Not a war veteran
Member of PIIPU
Sufi has been the governor-general of three provinces (Gilan, Bushehr, and Kohgiluyeh and Buyer Ahmad), adviser to the interior minister, legal deputy in the Ministry of Housing and Urban Development, director-general of telecommunications for East Azerbaijan Province, and a member of the board of directors of Iranians' Hope Foundation. In 2016, Sufi was in charge of the campaign headquarters of reformist forces.

Suri-Laki, Ali-Mohammad

Deputy of the Third Majlis, Khorramabad, Lorestan (1988–92)
1953–, Kuhdasht, Lorestan
BA
Hoseyn-Ali
No imprisonment
War veteran
IRGC militiaman
Suri-Laki, a reformist, became a civil servant after his Majlis term ended.

Tabarsi, Nurollah

Member of the Third (1999–2006), Fourth (2007–16), and Fifth (2016–22) Assembly of Experts, Mazandaran
1940–, Neka, Mazandaran
Clerical education
Hasan, clergyman (ayatollah)
Clergyman
No imprisonment
Not a war veteran
Ayatollah Tabarsi was the Friday prayer leader of Sari from 1980 to 2009 and was Ayatollah Khamenei's representative in Mazandaran Province.

Tabataba'i, Seyyed Hadi

Deputy of the Seventh Majlis, I'zeh and Baghmalek, Khuzestan (2004–8)
1958–, Baghmalek, Khuzestan
BA, law (unverified)
Seyyed Fakhreddin
Judiciary official
No imprisonment

Tabataba'i, Seyyed Mehdi

Deputy of the Sixth Majlis, Abadeh, Bavanat, and Khorrambid, Fars (2000–2004)
1954–, Abadeh, Fars
MS, statistics
Seyyed Qasem
No imprisonment

Tabataba'i [Soltani], Seyyed Mohammad-Baqer

Member of the Assembly for the Final Examination of the Constitution, Lorestan (1979); member of the First (1983–90) and Second (1991–97) Assembly of Experts, Lorestan
1910–1997, Borujerd, Lorestan
Clerical education, Najaf Seminary (Iraq), 1939
Seyyed Ali-Asghar, clergyman
Clergyman
No imprisonment
Not a war veteran
One of Tabataba'i's sons served as a cabinet minister and another as mayor of Tehran in the first decade of the revolution. He was the son-in-law of Ayatollah Seyyed Sadreddin Sadr, a leading *marja'* in Qom, and the father-in-law of Seyyed Ahmad Khomeini.

Tabataba'i [Soltani], Seyyed Morteza [Javad]

Mayor of Tehran (November 1987–89)
Date unknown, Qom, Qom
BS, urban planning
Seyyed Mohammad-Baqer, clergyman (ayatollah)
Ambassador to Mexico (1982–86)

No imprisonment
Not a war veteran
In the mid-1970s, Tabataba'i left Iran and went to
Germany and Lebanon. He returned to Iran after
the revolution and in 1979 became governor of
Khorasan Province. Tabataba'i is the brother-in-
law of Seyyed Ahmad Khomeini, the nephew of
Musa Sadr (leader of Lebanese Shiites), cousin
of President Seyyed Mohammad Khatami's wife,
brother of Seyyed Sadeq Tabataba'i, and husband
of Ayatollah Khomeini's nephew (Fereshteh A'rabi).

Tabataba'i [Soltani], Seyyed Sadeq

Ministerial adviser for executive affairs in PM Bazargan's cabinet (1979)
1943–February 21, 2015, Qom, Qom
PhD, biochemistry, Ruhr University Bochum (Germany), 1973
Seyyed Mohammad-Baqer Tabataba'i [Soltani], clergyman (ayatollah)
Academia
No imprisonment
Not a war veteran
Tabataba'i was active in opposition circles in Europe
and Lebanon before the revolution. He was the
nephew of Musa Sadr, leader of Lebanese Shiite, and got entangled in the Lebanese civil war
through that connection. In June 1979, he became
the ministerial adviser for executive affairs and
government spokesperson. In 1979–80, he was
involved in negotiations with the Carter administration to release the American hostages. From
November 1979, when the Bazargan cabinet
resigned, to September 1980, when PM Raja'i
started his term, Tabataba'i was the caretaker of
the Office of the Prime Minister. He ran for the
1980 presidential election but received a negligible
number of votes. In the early 1980s, Tabataba'i
was a special envoy for Iran in purchasing arms
thanks to his wide contacts in Europe and Lebanon. In January 1983, German customs agents
arrested him at the airport in Dusseldorf, when
agents discovered four pounds of raw opium in

his suitcase. Tabataba'i fled Germany before the
court was to sentence him to a three-year prison
term. He was not given any other assignment after
this case and worked in the Office of Ayatollah
Khomeini, which was run by his brother-in-law
Seyyed Ahmad Khomeini. Tabataba'i was also the
cousin of President Khatami's wife.

Tabataba'i-Na'ini, Seyyed Hamid-Reza

Deputy of the Ninth Majlis, Na'in, Khur, and Bi-
abanak, Isfahan (2012–16)
1967–, Isfahan, Isfahan
BA, law, Tehran University, 1989; MA, private law,
Islamic Azad University–Khorasan, 2006
Judiciary official
No imprisonment
War veteran
Tabataba'i-Na'ini has held positions in the judiciary
in Isfahan, Tehran and Karaj, including being
appointed Isfahan's state prosecutor in 2005. He
has also taught at various universities. He ran
unsuccessfully for the Eighth Majlis.

Tabataba'inezhad, Seyyed Abbas

Deputy of the First Majlis, Ardestan, Isfahan
(1981–84)
1936–2001, Ardestan, Isfahan
Clerical education
Seyyed Ali, clergyman
Clergyman
No imprisonment
Not a war veteran
Martyr's family (brother, Seyyed Nurollah, killed in
the bombing of the IRP headquarters in 1981)
When his younger brother was killed in the IRP
bombing, Seyyed Abbas finished his term as Ard-
estan's MP.

Tabataba'inezhad, Seyyed Mostafa

Deputy of the Seventh (2004–8) and Eighth (2008–12)
Majlis, Ardestan, Isfahan (2008–12)

1954–, Ardestan, Isfahan
Clerical education
Seyyed Mohammad
Clergyman (HI)
No imprisonment
Seyyed Mostafa Tabataba'inezhad was not elected to
the Ninth Majlis.

Tabataba'inezhad, Seyyed Nurollah

Deputy of the First Majlis, Ardestan, Isfahan (1980–
June 28, 1981)
1940–June 28, 1981, Ardestan, Isfahan
Clerical education
Seyyed Ali, clergyman
Clergyman
Imprisoned before the revolution (1977–78)
Not a war veteran
Member of IRP
HI Seyyed Nurollah Tabataba'inezhad died in the
bombing of the IRP headquarters in June 1981. He
was the first member of the prominent Tabataba'in-
ezhad family to represent Ardestan in the Majlis.

Tabataba'inezhad, Seyyed Sadeq

Deputy of the Tenth Majlis, Ardestan, Isfahan (2016–20)
1981–, Qom, Qom
Clerical education; MA, Qur'anic sciences, University
of Qur'anic Sciences and Education
Clergyman (HI)
Seyyed Yusef, clergyman (ayatollah)
Not a war veteran
Martyr's family (uncle, Seyyed Nurollah, killed in the
bombing of the IRP headquarters in 1981; brother,
Seyyed Ali, killed at the war front in 1986)
Tabataba'inezhad's father and two of his uncles have
represented Ardestan in the Majlis. His father has
also been a member of the AE.

Tabataba'inezhad, Seyyed Yusef

Deputy of the Third (1988–92) and Fourth (1992–96)
Majlis, Ardestan, Isfahan; member of the Fourth

(2007–16) and Fifth (2016–22) Assembly of Experts, Isfahan
1944–, Ardestan, Isfahan
Clerical education, Najaf Seminary (Iraq)
Seyyed Ali, clergyman
Clergyman
No imprisonment
Not a war veteran
Martyr's family (brother, Seyyed Nurollah Nureddin,
killed in the bombing of the IRP headquarters in
1981; son, Seyyed Ali, killed at the war front in
1986; five nephews also killed in the Iran–Iraq War)
Ayatollah Tabataba'inezhad was the Friday prayer
leader of Isfahan and the supreme leader's representative in Syria, returning to Iran in 2001. His
brothers, Seyyed Abbas and Seyyed Nurollah, and
his son, Seyyed Sadeq, have all been MPs as well.

Tabataba'i-Shirazi, Seyyed Mohammad-Mehdi

Deputy of the Second (1984–88) and Third (1988–92)
Majlis, Mashhad, Razavi Khorasan; deputy of the
Seventh Majlis, Tehran, Tehran (2004–8)
1936–, Rafsanjan, Kerman
Clerical education
Seyyed Mohammad-Hoseyn
Clergyman (HI)
No imprisonment
Not a war veteran
Tabataba'i-Shirazi, a famous preacher, was a judge and
former executive secretary of the SCC.

Tabe'-Miyandoab, Asadollah

Deputy of the Third (1988–92) and Seventh (2004–8)
Majlis, Miyandoab and Takab, West Azerbaijan
1948–, Miyandoab, West Azerbaijan
BS, mathematics
Hatam
Provincial civil servant
No imprisonment
War veteran (wounded)
Tabe'-Miyandoab was the first governor of Miyandoab,
serving from December 22, 1979 to January 1, 1983.

Tabesh, Mohammad-Reza

Deputy of the Sixth (2000–2004), Seventh (2004–8), Eighth (2008–12), Ninth (2012–16), and Tenth (2016–20) Majlis, Ardakan, Yazd
1958–, Ardakan, Yazd
BS, natural resources engineering, Tehran University; MS, natural resources engineering, Tehran University; PhD, natural resources engineering, Islamic Azad University–Science and Research Branch
Mohammad
University instructor, civil servant, ministries
No imprisonment
War veteran (twenty months)
Member of the central council of IIPF
Tabesh was in charge of Ayatollah Ruhollah Khatami's office in Yazd. He is a nephew of former president Seyyed Mohammad Khatami. His brother, Ali-Reza Tabash, was President Khatami's chief of staff.

Tabibzadeh-Nuri, Mrs. Zohreh

Deputy of the Ninth Majlis, Tehran, Tehran (2012–16)
1960–, Tehran, Tehran
MD, dentistry, Shahid Beheshti University, 1994
Professor and dean of Shahid Beheshti University's Dental School (2009–11)
No imprisonment
Tabibzadeh-Nuri was head of the Center for Women's and Family Affairs in the Office of President Ahmadinejad. As a conservative, she was opposed to women serving as ministers. She returned to teaching dentistry full time at Shahid Beheshti University in 2016.

Tabrizi, Mostafa

Deputy of the First Majlis, Bojnurd, North Khorasan (1980–84)
1945–, Bojnurd, North Khorasan
MA, education; PhD, psychology and counseling, Allameh Tabataba'i University
Mohammad-Ali, bazaar tradesman

Academia
No imprisonment
Tabrizi became a professor of psychology at Allameh Tabataba'i University and was the editor of *Farhang va Towse'eh* journal for a while.

Ta'eb, Hoseyn [real first name may be Hasan]

Commander of the IRGC's Basij Force (July 12, 2008–October 4, 2009)
1963–, Tehran, Tehran
Clerical education
Clergyman
IRGC militiaman
Martyr's family (brother, Hoseyn, killed at the war front)
HI Ta'eb joined the IRGC in 1982, and he has worked in Supreme Leader Khamenei's office as a deputy coordinator. In March 2008, the UN Security Council stated "forces under his command participated in mass beatings, murders, detentions and tortures of peaceful protestors." As head of the Basij organization, he played a leading role in suppressing the protestors after the contested 2009 presidential election. He was in charge of the IRGC's Imam Hoseyn University for a while. In 2009, he was put in charge of the newly formed Intelligence Organization of the IRGC. The European Union has alleged that Ta'eb has assisted in suppressing protests not just in Iran but in Syria as well. He is also on the US Treasury Office of Foreign Assets Control's Specially Designated Nationals and Blocked Persons List.

Taha, Ahmad

Deputy of the Third (1988–92) and Fourth (1992–96) Majlis, Bukan, West Azerbaijan
1942–2014, Mahabad, West Azerbaijan
BA, English literature, Tehran University; MA, political science, 2007
Mohammad, clergyman and poet
Teacher and provincial education official
No imprisonment

Taha, a Kurd, was governor of Piranshahr from 1996
    to 2000. He then became an adviser to the gov-
    ernor-general of West Azerbaijan. He retired
    from the teaching profession. The GC rejected his
    credentials for the Seventh Majlis.

Taha'i, Seyyed Ali-Akbar

Deputy of the Third Majlis, Tonekabon and Ramsar,
    Mazandaran (1988–92)
1953–, Chalus, Mazandaran
BS, industrial engineering
Seyyed Ahmad
No imprisonment
On July 19, 1992, Taha'i became governor-general
    of Gilan, and on December 15, 2013, he became
    deputy for legal and parliamentary affairs in the
    Labor Ministry.

Taheri, Ali

Deputy of the First Majlis, I'zeh, Khuzestan (1981–84)
1950–, I'zeh, Khuzestan
High school diploma
Mostafa
No imprisonment

Taheri, Elyas

Deputy of the Ninth Majlis, Eqlid, Fars (2012–16)
1960–, Eqlid, Fars
BA, management, Shahid Raja'i Teachers Training
    College; MA, educational management, State
    Management Training Center
Governor of Darab
No imprisonment
War veteran (wounded)
IRGC militiaman
Taheri is a former rector of Jahrom University and
    governor of Sepidan.

Taheri, Nader

Deputy of the Third Majlis, Maragheh, East Azerbai-
    jan (1988–92)

1956–, Maragheh, East Azerbaijan
High school diploma
Ahmad
No imprisonment

Taheri, Rajab-Ali

Deputy of the First Majlis, Kazerun, Fars (1980–84)
1936–2013, Kazerun, Fars
MS, civil engineering, Tehran University, 1961
Mahmud, bazaar tradesman
Civil servant, ministries
Imprisoned before the revolution (four years)
Not a war veteran
IRGC militiaman
Member of the central council of the IRP
Taheri had some connections with PMOI before the
    revolution and was close to Ayatollah Taleqani.
    After the revolution, he became the first IRGC
    commander in Fars Province. After serving in the
    Majlis, he worked in the Ministry of Roads and
    Transportation until he retired. Taheri became the
    governor-general of Tehran during President Hash-
    emi-Rafsanjani's first term in office. He ran unsuc-
    cessfully in the 1993 presidential election, receiving
    2.3 percent of the vote. Taheri also ran unsuccess-
    fully in a number of other Majlis and AE elections.

Taheri, Seyyed Taher

Deputy of the Fifth (1996–2000) and Sixth (2000–
    2004) Majlis, Semnan, Semnan
1951–, Semnan, Semnan
BS, industrial management, Gilan School of Man-
    agement, 1973; MS, industrial management, Iran
    University of Science and Technology, 1995
Seyyed Hasan
Director-general of Industrial Towns Company in
    Semnan Province
No imprisonment
Taheri is a former legal and parliamentary deputy
    in the Ministry of Industries. He became gov-
    ernor-general of Alborz Province in September
    2013. He has also worked in various companies.

Taheri-Gorgani, Seyyed Ali

Deputy of the Eighth (2008–12) and Ninth (2012–16)
    Majlis, Gorgan and Aq-Qala, Golestan
1969–, Najaf, Iraq
Clerical education; MA, theology; pursuing a PhD
    degree in theology at Islamic Azad University–
    Science and Research Branch
Seyyed Habibollah, clergyman (ayatollah)
Clergyman and university instructor
No imprisonment
War veteran (1986–88)
Martyr's family (brother, HI Seyyed Mohammad-
    Taher, killed at the war front)
HI Taheri-Gorgani, a conservative, ran unsuccessfully
    for the Sixth Majlis. His father served in the AE
    for many years, and his paternal uncle, Seyyed
    Mohammad-Hasan Alavi-Hoseyni, was an MP
    from Gorgan.

Taheri-Gorgani, Seyyed Habibollah

Member of the Assembly for the Final Examina-
    tion of the Constitution, Mazandaran (1979);
    member of the Second Assembly of Experts,
    Mazandaran (1991–98); member of the Third
    (1999–2006) and Fourth (2007) Assembly of
    Experts, Golestan
1930–2007, Gorgan, Golestan
Clerical education, Najaf Seminary (Iraq), 1962
Seyyed Kazem, civil servant
Clergyman
Imprisoned before the revolution
Not a war veteran
Martyr's family (son, HI Seyyed Mohammad-Taher,
    killed at the war front)
Member and spokesperson of the SCC in Mazandaran
Ayatollah Taheri-Gorgani, a member of a prominent
    family from Gorgan, was wounded when PMOI
    attempted to assassinate him on September 28,
    1981. He was the representative of Qadir Interna-
    tional Foundation in Golestan Province. His son,
    Seyyed Ali, became an MP in the Eighth and
    Ninth Majlis. He was the son-in-law of Ayatollah

Seyyed Sajad Alavi and brother-in-law of Seyyed
    Mohammad-Hasan Alavi-Hoseyni.

Taheri-Isfahani [Hoseynabadi], Seyyed Jalal[eddin]

Member of the Assembly for the Final Examination
    of the Constitution, Isfahan (1979); member of
    the First (1983–90), Second (1991–98), and Third
    (1999–2006) Assembly of Experts, Isfahan
1926–2013, Isfahan, Isfahan
Clerical education, Qom Seminary
Seyyed Abdolkhaleq, clergyman
Clergyman
Imprisoned before the revolution
Not a war veteran
Martyr's family (son, Seyyed Ali, killed at the war
    front in 1982)
Ayatollah Khomeini appointed Ayatollah Taheri-Is-
    fahani as the first Friday prayer leader of Isfahan
    in January 1979. He held that post for twen-
    ty-three years, until he resigned on July 8, 2002,
    by publishing a strongly worded letter in which
    he criticized the violations of human rights in
    Iran and the conservatives' monopoly of power.
    The next day, the SCNS banned the media from
    reporting on Taheri's letter. Ayatollah Taheri
    strongly opposed the house arrest of Ayatollah
    Montazeri, and he supported Mohammad Kha-
    tami in the 1997 presidential election and Mir
    Hoseyn Musavi in the 2009 presidential election.
    He sided with the Green Movement in 2009 and
    declared President Ahmadinejad's government to
    be illegitimate. In 1982, he was appointed a mem-
    ber of the prayer leaders' central council. Taheri's
    daughter-in-law is Na'imeh Eshraqi, a niece of
    Ayatollah Khomeini (the daughter of Ayatollah
    Shahabeddin Eshraqi).

Taheri-Khorramabadi, Seyyed Hasan

Member of the Assembly for the Final Examination
    of the Constitution, Lorestan (1979); member
    of the First (1983–90), Second (1991–98), Third
    (1999–2006), and Fourth (2007–13) Assembly of

Experts, Lorestan; member of the Fourth Guardian Council (1999–2001)

1938–2013, Khorramabad, Lorestan

Clerical education, Qom Seminary

Seyyed Heydar, clergyman

Clergyman

Imprisoned before the revolution

Not a war veteran

Founding member of the SQSS (1977); member of the IRP

Ayatollah Taheri-Khorramabadi was one of the five individuals appointed by Ayatollah Khomeini as his representatives for pilgrimage affairs in 1981, and he also represented Ayatollah Khomeini at the IRGC's command council (beginning in November 1981) and in Pakistan (appointed in August 1982). He was chosen by the Second AE to be a member of a committee overseeing the eventual implementation of Ayatollah Khomeini's will. In 1989, he was a member of the Council for Revision of the Constitution, and he resigned from the GC in 2001. Taheri-Khorramabadi was the Friday prayer leader of Tehran from 2003 to 2009.

Taheri-Khorramabadi, Seyyed Mohammad-Saleh

Deputy of the Second (1984–88) and Fourth (1992–96) Majlis, Khorramabad, Lorestan

1939–, Khorramabad, Lorestan

BA, Islamic philosophy; Clerical education

Seyyed Abutaleb

Clergyman

Imprisoned before the revolution

HI Taheri-Khorramabadi was Ayatollah Khomeini's representative in Khuzestan Province and the Friday prayer leader of Ahvaz. He resigned from his post due to illness in April 1981.

Taheri-Khorramabadi, Seyyed Mojtaba

Member of the Fourth Assembly of Experts, Ilam (2008–16)

1959–, Khorramabad, Lorestan

Clerical education, Qom Seminary

Seyyed Hasan, clergyman (ayatollah)

Clergyman

No imprisonment

Not a war veteran

HI Seyyed Mojtaba Taheri-Khorramabadi was elected to the Fourth AE in interim elections. His father served with him concurrently in that assembly as the representative of Lorestan.

Taheri-Musavi, Seyyed Abdossaheb

Deputy of the Second (1986–88) and Third (1988–92) Majlis, Khorramshahr and Shadegan, Khuzestan

1950–, Shadegan, Khuzestan

Clerical education

Seyyed Mohammad

Clergyman

No imprisonment

HI Taheri-Musavi, an ethnic Arab, has been the supreme leader's representative for promotion of Shiism in Syria and Lebanon.

Taheri-Najafabadi, Mostafa

Deputy of the Sixth Majlis, Najafabad, Tiran, and Karvan, Isfahan (2000–2004)

1949–, Najafabad, Isfahan

BS, electrical engineering; MA, management

Hasan

Civil servant

No imprisonment

Taheri-Najafabadi became the director-general of the National Petrochemical Company after leaving the Majlis.

Taheri [-Qazvini], Yusef

Minister of roads and transportation in PM Bazargan's cabinet (May 16–November 5, 1979) and the Revolutionary Council cabinet (November 6–December 26, 1979)

1927–, Qom, Qom

BS, civil engineering, Tehran University, 1950

Mohammad-Sadeq, bazaar tradesman

Official in the Ministry of Roads and Transportation
Imprisoned before the revolution
Not a war veteran
Member of the Islamic Society of Engineers
Taheri was a close friend of Abbas Taj, Mostafa
    Katira', and Ali-Akbar Mo'infar, who all served
    with him in PM Bazargan's cabinet. He resigned
    from being a minister on December 26, 1979, and
    he retired from the Ministry of Roads and Trans-
    portation in 1981.

Taheri-Shams-Golpayegani, Jalal

Member of the First Assembly of Experts, Markazi
    (1983–90)
1927–1995, Golpayegan, Isfahan
Clerical education, Qom Seminary
Abdossamad
Clergyman (ayatollah)
No imprisonment
Not a war veteran
Member of the SQSS
Taheri-Shams-Golpayegani was a member of the
    leadership council of Qom Seminary. He died in a
    car accident.

Taherizadeh, Mostafa

Deputy of the Third Majlis, Falavarjan, Isfahan
    (1988–92)
1951–, Isfahan, Isfahan
BS, electrical engineering
Javad
No imprisonment

Taherkhani, Amir

Deputy of the Eighth Majlis, Takestan, Qazvin
    (2008–12)
1962–, Takestan, Zanjan
MA, theology
Eynollah, farmer and landowner
Academia
No imprisonment

Not a war veteran
Taherkhani was not elected to the Ninth Majlis.

Taherkhani, Bahman

July 27, 1961–, Takestan, Zanjan
Deputy of the Tenth Majlis, Takestan, Qazvin (2016–20)
BA, judicial sciences, Tehran University; MA, judi-
    cial sciences, University of Judicial Sciences and
    Administrative Services, 1989
Lawyer and judiciary official in Alborz Province
No imprisonment
War veteran (twenty-two months)
IRGC militiaman (Basij)

Tahernezhad, Yadollah

Deputy of the Fifth Majlis, Nowshahr, Mazandaran
    (1996–2000)
1957–, Kelardasht, Mazandaran
BS, agrology
Sadrollah
No imprisonment
Member of the central council of PECI
Tahernezhad was the head of the campaign head-
    quarters of PECI for a while. The GC rejected his
    qualifications for the Tenth Majlis in 2016.

Taherpur, Shahriyar

Deputy of the Eighth Majlis, Tuyserkan, Hamadan
    (2008–12)
1958–, Tuyserkan, Hamadan
BS, industrial engineering, Sharif University of Tech-
    nology, 1985; MS, industrial engineering, Iran
    University of Science and Technology, 1995
Bahram
University instructor; owner of a dairy factory
No imprisonment
Taherpur ran unsuccessfully for the Fifth and Sixth
    Majlis and did not become a candidate for the
    Ninth Majlis. In July 2015, the minister of indus-
    tries appointed Taherpur as his deputy for legal
    and parliamentary affairs.

Tahmasebi, Ali-Reza

Minister of industries and mining in President Ahmadinejad's first cabinet (August 24, 2005–October 2007)
1961–, Shiraz, Fars
BS, mechanical engineering, Shiraz University, 1987; MS, mechanical engineering, Shiraz University, 1990; PhD, mechanical engineering, Université Laval (Canada), 1996
Abdorrazaq
No imprisonment
War veteran
IRGC militiaman
Tahmasebi was involved with the IRGC and Construction Jihad for many years, and prior to becoming minister, he worked at the Islamic Majlis Research Center. He was the first minister to quit President Ahmadinejad's cabinet.

Tahmasebi-Sarvestani, Zeynol'abedin

Deputy of the Seventh Majlis, Sarvestan and Kavar, Fars (2004–8)
1958–, Shiraz, Fars
PhD, agricultural engineering
Mohammad-Ali
Rector of Ilam University
No imprisonment
In 2015, Tahmasebi-Sarvestani became director-general of planning for the Iranian Research Organization for Science and Technology.

Tahriri-Niksefat, Mrs. Hajar

Deputy of the Seventh Majlis, Rasht, Gilan (2004–8)
1964–, Rasht, Gilan
BA, elementary education, Islamic Azad University–Rasht; MA, educational philosophy, Islamic Azad University–Tehran; PhD, educational philosophy, Islamic Azad University–Science and Research Branch
Hadi
University professor and administrator

No imprisonment
Tahriri-Niksefat started working for the education department in Gilan Province in 1983, and she is a professor at Islamic Azad University–Rasht.

Taj, Abbas

Minister of energy in PM Bazargan's cabinet (February 17, 1979–1979)
1917–1990, Kashan, Isfahan
BS, electrical engineering, Tehran University, 1941
Father's name unknown, clergyman
Engineer at the Ministry of Energy (railroad system)
No imprisonment
Not a war veteran
Member of the LMI and Islamic Society of Engineers
Taj was a deputy minister before the revolution. He was a minister for nine months in 1979 and after leaving the cabinet, he worked in the private sector. He had memorized the Qur'an and used to teach it.

Tajari, Farhad

Deputy of the Eighth (2008–12) and Tenth (2016–20) Majlis, Qasr-e Shirin, Sarpol-e Zahab, and Gilan-e Gharb, Kermanshah
1968–, Sarpol-e Zahab, Kermanshah
MA, penal law and criminology
Ali-Morad
Judiciary official
No imprisonment
Tajari was not elected to the Ninth Majlis.

Tajeddin, Nahid

Deputy of the Tenth Majlis, Isfahan, Isfahan (2016–20)
1976–, Isfahan, Isfahan
BS, microbiology, Isfahan University of Technology; MS, genetics, Tarbiyat-e Modarres University; pursuing a PhD in genetics at Islamic Azad University–Science and Research Branch
Professor at Islamic Azad University–Falavarjan

Martyr's family (father, brother, brother-in-law, and two cousins)

Tajeddin was elected to the Tenth Majlis on the re-formist slate.

Tajeddin-Khuzani, Abdorrahman

Deputy of the Fifth (1997–2000) and Sixth (2000–2004) Majlis, Isfahan, Isfahan

1955–, Isfahan, Isfahan

High school diploma

Zeynol'abedin

No imprisonment

Founding member of the Islamic Labor Party

Tajeddin-Khuzani became the legal and parliamentary deputy of the Social Security Organization after leaving the Majlis.

Tajerniya, Ali

Deputy of the Sixth Majlis, Mashhad, Razavi Khorasan (2000–2004)

1969–, Qom, Qom

MD, dentistry, Mashhad University of Medical Sciences

Ali-Reza, clergyman

No imprisonment

Not a war veteran

Member of the central council of the Party of Iranian People's Unity; founding member of the Society of Alumni of Universities of Tabriz

The judiciary imprisoned Tajerniya for a while after the contested 2009 presidential election.

Tajgardun, Bahram

Deputy of the First (1980–84) and Third (1988–92) Majlis, Gachsaran, Kohgiluyeh and Buyer Ahmad

1946–, Kohgiluyeh, Kohgiluyeh and Buyer Ahmad

BS, biological sciences

Bahman, farmer

Civil servant, education department

No imprisonment

Tajgardun and Seyyed Kamaleddin Nikravesh, the governor-general of Kohgiluyeh and Buyer Ahmad, did not get along in Kohgiluyeh. Tajgardun was injured in the June 28, 1981, bombing of the IRP headquarters.

Tajgardun, Gholam-Reza

Deputy of the Ninth (2012–16) and Tenth (2016–20) Majlis, Gachsaran and Basht, Kohgiluyeh and Buyer Ahmad

1966–, Dogonbadan, Kohgiluyeh and Buyer Ahmad

BA, economics, Shahid Beheshti University, 1988; MA, economic planning, 1991; PhD, management, Global Business Academy–Belgium (online program), 2008

Civil servant

No imprisonment

War veteran (wounded)

Martyr's family (brother, Ahmad-Reza)

Tajgardun worked in the PBO for many years. His cousin, Bahram, was also a representative from Kohgiluyeh and Buyer Ahmad in the First Majlis.

Takaffoli, Gholam-Hoseyn

Deputy of the Sixth Majlis, Mashhad, Razavi Khorasan (2000–2004)

1959–, Ferdows, South Khorasan

MA, public administration

Gholam-Ali

Governor of Qaenat (1988–91)

No imprisonment

Takaffoli registered to run for the Tenth Majlis.

Tala, Hoseyn

Deputy of the Ninth Majlis, Tehran, Tehran (2012–16)

1969–, Tehran, Tehran

MD, medicine, Shahid Beheshti University of Medical Sciences; pursuing a PhD in economics

Deputy governor-general of Tehran province (until September 2010)

No imprisonment

War veteran

Member of the Steadfastness Front of the Islamic Revolution

Tala was deputy governor-general of Tehran during the 2009 presidential election protests. On October 10, 2011 the Council of the European Union put him on its sanctions list and wrote that Tala was "in particular responsible for the intervention of police forces and therefore for the repression of demonstrations. He received a prize in December 2010 for his role in the post-election repression." On August 23, 2017, he was elected as mayor of Islamshahr. Tala is also a former head of the governing board of the Iranian Tobacco Company and was a deputy in the Ministry of Industries.

Tala'inik, Reza

Deputy of the Sixth (2000–2004) and Seventh (2004–8) Majlis, Bahar and Kabudarahang, Hamadan

1963–, Bahar, Hamadan

MA, sociology

Safiollah

No imprisonment

IRGC militiaman

Secretary-general of the PMD (2007–9)

Tala'inik worked as an expert on youth issues in the EDA.

Taleqani, Seyyed Mahmud

Member of the Assembly for the Final Examination of the Constitution, Tehran (1979); member of the Revolutionary Council (1979)

1911–September 10, 1979, Taleqan, Tehran

Clerical education, Qom Seminary, 1939

Seyyed Abolhasan, watchmaker and clergyman

Clergyman

Imprisoned before the revolution

Not a war veteran

Member of the Second Iran National Front (INF)

Ayatollah Taleqani, who came from a poor family, was a supporter of PM Mossadeq and was a very open-minded cleric who had good relations with guerrilla groups such as PMOI. He was released from prison on October 30, 1978, and became the chair of the Revolutionary Council after the assassination of Ayatollah Motahhari. Taleqani was the first postrevolutionary Friday prayer leader of Tehran and delivered his first sermon on July 27, 1979. In August 1979, he received the highest number of votes (over two million) in Tehran in the election for the AFEC. However, Taleqani died a month later and did not get to see the final draft of the constitution. His death happened five months after two of his sons were detained on account of belonging to leftist opposition groups. Taleqani was opposed to the principle of mandate of the jurist.

[Ala'i-] Taleqani, Mrs. A'zam

Deputy of the First Majlis, Tehran, Tehran (1980–84)

1942–, Tehran, Tehran

BA, Persian literature

Seyyed Mahmud, clergyman (ayatollah)

Teacher

Imprisoned before the revolution (1975–77)

Secretary-general of the Society of Women of the Islamic Revolution

The shah's regime arrested Taleqani, a school principal, in 1975 and condemned her to a life sentence. She ran unsuccessfully for the AFEC in 1979, presidential elections in 1997, 2009, and 2017, Majlis elections in 2000 and 2016, and the AE in 2016. In all instances, the GC rejected her qualifications. Taleqani established the Society of Women of the Islamic Revolution in 1992, and was the proprietor of *Payam-e Hajar* magazine, which the judiciary banned. She returned to teaching after leaving the Majlis. She is the daughter of Ayatollah Seyyed Mahmud Taleqani and the sister of Mrs. Vahideh [Ala'i-] Taleqani.

[Ala'i-] Taleqani, Mrs. Vahideh

Deputy of the Sixth Majlis, Tehran, Tehran (2000–2004)

1953–, Tehran, Tehran

MD, pharmacology, Tehran University
Seyyed Mahmud, clergyman (ayatollah)
Health official in Tehran Province
Taleqani worked as a civil servant in the pharmacol-
ogy field, and her husband worked in the Minis-
try of Industries. She is the daughter of Ayatollah
Seyyed Mahmud Taleqani and the younger sister
of Mrs. A'zam [Ala'i-] Taleqani.

Talkhabi, Majid

Member of the Fifth Assembly of Experts, Qazvin
(2016–22)
1981–, Farahan, Markazi
Clerical education, Qom Seminary; BA, theology,
Imam Khomeini and Islamic Revolution Research
Institute; MA, theology, Tehran University–Pardis
Qom; PhD, theology, Imam Khomeini and Is-
lamic Revolution Research Institute
Ghazanfar, farmer
Clergyman
No imprisonment (born after the revolution)
Not a war veteran

Tamaddon, Morteza

Deputy of the Seventh Majlis, Shahrekord, Chahar
Mahal and Bakhtiari (2004–8)
1959–, Shahrekord, Chahar Mahal and Bakhtiari
MA, management
Hasan
Civil servant
No imprisonment
IRGC militiaman
During the 2009 Green Movement protests, Tamad-
don was the IRGC governor-general of Tehran
Province, and head of Tehran provincial Public
Security Council. On October 10, 2011, the Coun-
cil of the European Union put Tamaddon on its
list of sanctioned individuals and wrote that "in
his capacity as governor and head of Tehran pro-
vincial Public Security Council, he bears overall
responsibility for all repressive activities, including cracking down on political protests since June

2009. He is known for being personally involved
in the harassing of opposition leaders Karrubi and
Musavi."

Tamimi, Abdollah

Deputy of the Ninth Majlis, Shadegan, Khuzestan
(2012–16)
1964–, Khorramshahr, Khuzestan
BA, theology
No imprisonment
War veteran (seventy-nine months; wounded)
IRGC militiaman
Tamimi retired from military service in 2010 and
after leaving the Majlis became the head of the Oil
Industry Pension Fund.

Ta'mini-Licha'i, Hasan

Deputy of the Eighth (2008–12) and Ninth (2012–16)
Majlis, Rasht, Gilan
1966–, Rasht, Gilan
MS, health education, Tehran University of Medical
Sciences; PhD, health education, Tehran Univer-
sity of Medical Sciences
Morteza
Medical professional and university professor
No imprisonment
Not a war veteran
Martyr's family (two brothers killed at the war front)

Taqavi, Seyyed Reza

Deputy of the Second Majlis, Damghan, Semnan
(1986–88); deputy of the Fourth (1992–96) and
Fifth (1996–2000) Majlis, Tehran, Tehran
1946–, Damghan, Semnan
Clerical education; BA or diploma in Persian
literature
Seyyed Ali
Clergyman
No imprisonment
Member of the central council, deputy leader, and
Speaker of the SCC

HI Taqavi was the Friday prayer leader of Shahrekord and deputy director of the Islamic Propaganda Organization. The supreme leader appointed him chair of the Friday prayer policymaking council on May 30, 2000, and he served until January 6, 2018.

Taqipur [-Anvari], Reza

Minister of information and communications technology in President Ahmadinejad's second cabinet (September 3, 2009–December 1, 2012)

1957–, Maragheh, East Azerbaijan

BS, computer engineering, Shahid Beheshti University, 1985; MS, industrial engineering, Iran University of Science and Technology, 2000; MA, management, University of Bordeaux (France), 2007

Civil servant, ministries

No imprisonment

War veteran

IRGC militiaman

Taqipur, whom President Ahmadinejad dismissed in 2012, was on the United States sanctions list and promoted setting up a "national internet." He is a member of the Supreme Council of Cyberspace and a former member of the Tehran City Council.

Taqi'zadeh, Ali

Deputy of the Sixth Majlis, Khoy and Chaypareh, West Azerbaijan (2001–4)

1962–, Maku, West Azerbaijan

PhD, law, University of Paris (France)

Hasan

No imprisonment

After serving in the Majlis, Taqi'zadeh, a reformist, became a law professor at Islamic Azad University–Tehran.

Taraqqi, Hamid-Reza

Deputy of the Fifth Majlis, Mashhad, Razavi Khorasan (1996–2000)

1955–, Neyshabur, Razavi Khorasan

BA, management

Abbas, civil servant

Imprisoned before the revolution

Martyr's family (brother, Sa'id, killed at the war front)

Tariqat-Monfared, Mohammad-Hasan

Minister of health and medical education in President Ahmadinejad's second cabinet (March 17–August 2, 2013)

1946–, Tehran, Tehran

MD, optometry, Germany

Head of Imam Hoseyn Hospital; professor at Shahid Beheshti University (since 1986)

No imprisonment

Not a war veteran

Tariqat-Monfared lived in Germany from 1965 until after the revolution. He received the lowest confidence vote for any minister in President Ahmadinejad's cabinet (113 positive votes, ninety-nine negative votes, and twelve abstentions out of 224 votes cast on March 17, 2013).

Taskhiri, Mohammad-Ali

Member of the Third Assembly of Experts, Gilan (1999–2006); member of the Fifth Assembly of Experts, Tehran (2016–22)

1944–, Najaf, Iraq

Clerical education, Qom Seminary

Ali-Akbar, clergyman (ayatollah)

Clergyman

No imprisonment

Not a war veteran

Member of the central council of the SCC

Ayatollah Taskhiri, who was born and lived for many years in Najaf, spent time in Iraqi prisons for being a member of the Al-Dawah Party. He was involved with Iran's propaganda activities beginning in the early 1980s. On December 25, 1990, he became the secretary-general of Ahlulbeyt World Assembly, then director of the Islamic Propaganda Organization (1994–2001), and finally, on

September 22, 2001, Ayatollah Khamenei's representative and head of WFPIST.

Taslimi, Mohammad-Sa'id

Deputy of the Third Majlis, Tehran, Tehran (1988–92)
1954–, Tehran, Tehran
PhD, management, United States International University, 1980; dissertation title: "A Study on the Role of Informal Relationships among the Service Employees of a Work Organization"
Abdollah
Civil servant
No imprisonment
Taslimi, a reformist, has been the director-general of the Ministry of Education's international bureau, vice rector of Tarbiyat-e Modarres University, deputy to the culture minister (Farhadi), and dean of the school of management at Tehran University.

Tatali, Abdollah

Deputy of the Second (1984–88) and Third (1988–92) Majlis, Marivan, Kurdistan
1941–, Marivan, Kurdistan
Pre-high school diploma
Fathollah, farmer
Carpet and rug merchant in Marivan
No imprisonment
War veteran
Tatali did not get elected to the Fourth Majlis.

Tatari, Esma'il

Deputy of the Fourth (1992–96) and Sixth (2000–2004) Majlis, Kermanshah, Kermanshah
1952–2010, Malesorkh, Kermanshah
Pre-high school diploma
Ali
Civil servant, Kermanshah's telecommunications department
No imprisonment
War veteran

Founding member of the NTP
Tatari was involved in mobilizing the tribes during the Iran–Iraq War and conducting guerrilla attacks inside Iraq. As an MP, he managed to change the name of his province back to Kermanshah from Bakhtaran. After leaving the Majlis, he became an adviser to the minister of petroleum. Tatari was an NTP activist until he died of a heart attack.

Tatari, Mohammad-Ali

Deputy of the First Majlis, Zahedan, Sistan and Baluchestan (1980–84)
1942–, Zabol, Sistan and Baluchestan
BS, electrical engineering; BA, law
Reza, bazaar tradesman
Civil servant
No imprisonment

Tavakkol, Seyyed Rahim

Member of the Fifth Assembly of Experts, Mazandaran (2016–22)
1952–, Babol, Mazandaran
Clerical education, Qom Seminary
Seyyed Taqi
Clergyman (ayatollah)
No imprisonment
Not a war veteran

Tavakkoli, Ahmad

Deputy of the First Majlis, Behshahr, Mazandaran (1980–October 29, 1981); minister of labor and social affairs in PM Musavi's first cabinet (November 2, 1981–83); deputy of the Seventh (2004–8), Eighth (2008–12), and Ninth (2012–16) Majlis, Tehran, Tehran; member of the Eighth Expediency Discernment Assembly (2017–22)
1951–, Behshahr, Mazandaran
BA, economics, Shahid Beheshti University; MA, economics, Isfahan University of Technology; PhD, economics, University of Nottingham (England),

1996; dissertation title: "Causes of Inflation in the Iranian Economy, 1972–1990"

Abolhasan, bazaar tradesman

Judiciary official

Imprisoned before the revolution

Not a war veteran

Tavakkoli studied electrical engineering at Shiraz University from 1969 to 1972, but the university expelled him in his junior year. He resigned from the First Majlis to become minister of labor, and then resigned from that post in 1983 due to policy differences with PM Mir Hoseyn Musavi. Tavakkoli was a presidential candidate in the 1993, 1997, and 2001 elections, and he was the first runner-up in his first and third tries, receiving 24 percent and 16 percent of the vote, respectively. He was one of the founders of *Resalat* in 1986, and he started the political website "Alef" in 2005. Tavakkoli also headed the Islamic Parliament Research Center from 2004 to 2012. He is a maternal cousin to the influential Larijani brothers, and his son is married to the oldest daughter of prominent political scientist Sadeq Zibakalam.

Tavakkoli, Mohammad-Baqer

Deputy of the Fourth Majlis, Khomeyn, Markazi (1992–96)

1953–, Golpayegan, Isfahan

MD, medicine

Mohammad-Hoseyn

Medical doctor

No imprisonment

Tavakkoli, Mohammad-Taqi

Deputy of the Ninth Majlis, Aligudarz, Lorestan (2012–16)

1957–, Aligudarz, Lorestan

BS, water resources; MA, executive management, Institute for Management and Planning Studies

Father's name unknown, academia

Civil servant, Iran Water and Power Resources Development Company and Ministry of Energy

No imprisonment

IRGC militiaman (Basij)

Tavakkoli has worked in a variety of posts as an expert in water issues.

Tavakkoli-Tabazavareh, Seyyed Valiyollah

Deputy of the Fifth (1996–2000) and Sixth (2000–2004) Majlis, Ardestan, Isfahan

1947–, Ardestan, Isfahan

MA, planning

Seyyed Hoseyn

Civil servant

No imprisonment

Founding member of the Islamic Iran Solidarity Party

Tavassoli, Mohammad-Reza

Deputy of the Third (1988–92) and Fourth (1992–96) Majlis, Ferdows and Tabas, South Khorasan

1956–, Ferdows, South Khorasan

BS, civil engineering; MA, industrial management, Tehran University

Gholam-Reza

Official in Construction Jihad in Khorasan

No imprisonment

Tavassoli [-Hojjati], Mohammad

Mayor of Tehran (1979–80)

May 15, 1938–, Tehran, Tehran

BS, civil engineering, Tehran University, 1961; MS, transportation engineering, University of Illinois at Urbana-Champaign (USA), 1965

Reza, bazaar tradesman (hat maker)

Engineer

Imprisoned before the revolution

Not a war veteran

Martyr's family (brother, Majid, killed in a clash with SAVAK agents in 1977)

Head of the political bureau and member of the central council of the LMI

Tavassoli lived in the United States from 1963 to 1965. He then underwent military training in Egypt before moving to Iraq and then returning to Iran in 1967. He wrote the first draft of the IRGC constitution after the revolution, and he was mayor of Tehran for twenty-two months. The GC rejected Tavassoli's qualifications to run in the Sixth Majlis. In 2011, he was arrested on charges of anti-regime activities. In September 2017, Tavassoli became the secretary-general of LMI after the passing of his brother-in-law, Ebrahim Yazdi, who had held the post before him. Tavassoli has family ties to Seyyed Ali-Akbar Abutorabifard.

Tavassoli-Mahallati, Mohammad-Reza

Member of the First (1988–89), Second (1989–92), Third (1992–97), Fourth (1997–2002), Fifth (2002–7), and Sixth (2007–8) Expediency Discernment Assembly; member of the Third Assembly of Experts, Tehran (1999–2006)
1930–2008, Mahallat, Markazi
Clerical education, Qom Seminary
Clergyman
Imprisoned before the revolution
Not a war veteran
Founding member of the ACC
Ayatollah Tavassoli-Mahallati was head of Ayatollah Khomeini's office and influenced the selection of Friday prayer leaders and Khomeini's representatives. He was Khomeini's representative for pilgrimage affairs in 1981, and was named to the board establishing a seminary for women in Qom in 1984. Tavassoli-Mahallati was also a member of the Council for Revision of the Constitution. In 1990, Tavassoli-Mahallati refused to stand for elections to the Second Assembly of Experts in protest of the GC's decision to require a religious test of candidates even though he himself was exempt. He was the father-in-law of HI Isa Vela'i, who was in charge of Khatami's legal office during his presidency.

Tavassolizadeh, Mohammad-Naser

Deputy of the Second Majlis, Khaf, Razavi Khorasan (1984–88); deputy of the Fourth (1992–96), Fifth (1996–2000), and Seventh (2004–8) Majlis, Torbat-e Heydariyyeh, Razavi Khorasan
1950–, Torbat-e Heydariyyeh, Razavi Khorasan
MA, Islamic law
Asghar
No imprisonment
Tavassolizadeh, a hardliner, ran unsuccessfully for the Eighth Majlis. Afterward, he went to teach at Shahid Beheshti University.

Tayyar, Atrak

Deputy of the Fourth (1993–96) and Sixth (2000–2001) Majlis, Gonbad-e Kavus, Golestan
1955–May 17, 2001, Gonbad-e Kavus, Golestan
High school diploma
Qarjeh
Civil servant
No imprisonment
Tayyar, a Sunni, died in a plane crash.

Tayyar, Qarjeh

Deputy of the Tenth Majlis, Gonbad-e Kavus, Golestan (2016–20)
1976–, Gonbad-e Kavus, Golestan
BA, theology, Islamic Azad University–Azadshahr; MA, Political Science, Islamic Azad University–Azadshahr; pursuing an MA in private law at Islamic Azad University–Gorgan
Atrak, Majlis deputy
Bank official
Not a war veteran
Tayyar, a Sunni reformist, followed in the footsteps of his father by representing Gonbad-e Kavus.

Tayyeb, Mehdi

Deputy of the First Majlis, Na'in, Isfahan (1981–84)
1952–, Tehran, Tehran
MS, architecture, 1976
Yadollah
Academia
No imprisonment

Tayyeb, and expert in mysticism, was forced to retire from university teaching in 2008.

Tayyebi, Mohammad-Hasan

Deputy of the First Majlis, Esfarayen, North Khorasan (1980–June 28, 1981)
1931–June 28, 1981, Esfarayen, North Khorasan
Clerical education
Rahman, clergyman
Clergyman
No imprisonment
Not a war veteran
HI Tayyebi died in the bombing of the IRP headquarters.

Tayyebniya, Ali

Minister of economic affairs and finance in President Rouhani's first cabinet (August 15, 2013–August 13, 2017)
April 5, 1960–, Isfahan, Isfahan
BA, economics, Tehran University, 1985; MA, economics, Tehran University, 1988 (thesis title: "Inflation Model in Iran"); PhD, economics, Tehran University, 1993 (dissertation title: "Structural Inflation in Iran")
Professor of economics at Tehran University
No imprisonment
Tayyebniya spent one year at the London School of Economics while working on his Tehran University doctorate. He had previously worked in the Office of the President and as an economic adviser at PBO. Tayyebniya received the highest positive votes from the Majlis during the confirmation of President Rouhani's first cabinet.

Tehrani [Khani-Arangeh] (Shaikh Ali Tehrani), Ali-Morad

Member of the Assembly for the Final Examination of the Constitution, Razavi Khorasan (1979)
1930–, Tehran, Tehran
Clerical education
Ezzatollah, farmer
Clergyman
Imprisoned before the revolution
Not a war veteran
HI Tehrani was in charge of the revolutionary tribunals in Mashhad and Ahvaz in the early days of the revolution. He defected to Iraq in early 1984 and spoke out against the Iranian government on Iraqi radio's Farsi-language service. He returned to Iran in 1995. The regime condemned him to a twenty-year prison term, but he was released in 2005. Tehrani is the brother-in-law of Supreme Leader Khamenei.

Tofiqi, [Seyyed] Hasan

Deputy of the Sixth Majlis, Kashan, Aran, and Bidgol, Isfahan (2000–2004)
1950–, Kashan, Isfahan
BS, Shiraz University; MS, University of California, Davis (USA); PhD, agricultural engineering, University of California, Davis, 1980
Professor and agricultural expert in the Ministry of Agriculture
Seyyed Hoseyn
No imprisonment
Not a war veteran

Tofiqi [-Dariyan], Ja'far

Minister of science, research, and technology in President Khatami's second cabinet (October 8, 2003–August 2, 2005)
1955–, Tehran, Tehran
MS, chemistry, Shiraz University, 1981; PhD, chemistry, Polytechnic Institute of Bucharest (Romania), 1986
Ahmad, bazaar tradesman
University professor
No imprisonment
Not a war veteran
Tofiqi was Mohammad-Reza Aref's campaign chief during the 2013 presidential election until Aref withdrew from the race. Tofiqi was in charge of the Ministry of Science, Research, and Technology for sixty-seven days under President Rouhani.

Subsequently, the minister of science, research, and technology appointed him as his senior adviser, but Tofiqi resigned from his post in 2014.

Tohidi, Davud

Deputy of the Third Majlis, Borujen and Lordegan, Chahar Mahal and Bakhtiari (1988–92)
1961–, Borujen, Chahar Mahal and Bakhtiari
BA, political science; MA, public administration; PhD, management
Fazlollah, farmer
No imprisonment
War veteran
IRGC militiaman
Martyr's family (two brothers killed at the war front)

Tondguyan, Mohammad-Javad

Minister of petroleum in PM Raja'i's cabinet (September 25–August 1981)
1950–1989, Tehran, Tehran
BS, engineering, Abadan Oil College, 1972; MA, management, Iran School of Management, 1978
Ja'far, shoe shop owner
Supervisor of oil-rich regions
Imprisoned before the revolution (eleven months)
War veteran
Tondguyan was one of the youngest ministers in Iran's history. However, Iraqi forces captured him and housing minister Seyyed Mohsen Yahyavi on October 31, 1980, during a visit to the front. Tondguyan died in captivity and his body was returned to Iran in 1991. His son, Mohammad-Mehdi, has been a member of the Tehran City Council.

Torabi, Abdorreza

Deputy of the Seventh (2006–8) and Eighth (2008–12) Majlis, Garmsar, Semnan
1956–, Tehran, Tehran
BS, civil engineering, University of Kashmir (India), 1984; MA, political science, 2012

Mohammad-Reza
Civil servant, Construction Jihad
No imprisonment

Torabipur, Mostafa

Chief of the joint staff of the Islamic Republic of Iran Army (October 14, 1998–date unknown)
Army official (brigadier general)
Torabipur was at one time the highest-ranking counterintelligence officer in the Iranian Army.

Torabi-Qahfarrokhi, Nasrollah

Deputy of the Eighth Majlis, Shahrekord, Chahar Mahal and Bakhtiari (2008–12)
1958–, Farrokhshahr, Chahar Mahal and Bakhtiari
BS, mechanical engineering, Isfahan University of Technology, 1983; MA, public administration
Mohammad, mason
Civil servant
No imprisonment
IRGC militiaman
Torabi-Qahfarrokhi was not elected to the Ninth Majlis.

Torabizadeh, Heshmatollah

Deputy of the Fifth Majlis, Lenjan and Mobarakeh, Isfahan (1996–2000)
1960–, Lenjan, Isfahan
BA, management
Ali
No imprisonment

Torang, Enayatollah

Deputy of the Fifth Majlis, Amol, Mazandaran (1996–2000)
1956–, Amol, Mazandaran
BS, agricultural engineering, Sari Agricultural Sciences and Natural Resources University, 1979; MA, economic development, Tehran University
Abbas

Official in the Construction Jihad (including serving in Tanzania)

No imprisonment

War veteran (fifty months; wounded)

Torang worked in the Construction Jihad before and after the Majlis.

Torbatinezhad, Nur-Mohammad

Deputy of the Tenth Majlis, Gorgan, Golestan (2016–20)

1956–, Kolajanghajar, Golestan

PhD, animal nutrition, University of Adelaide (Australia), 1995

University professor and administrator

No imprisonment

War veteran (fourteen months)

Torbatinezhad became rector of Gorgan University of Agricultural Sciences and Natural Resources in 1999. In 2013, he became adviser to the rector and a member of the board of trustees of this university. He has also cooperated with the Construction Jihad.

Torkan, Akbar

Minister of defense and armed forces logistics in President Hashemi-Rafsanjani's first cabinet (August 29, 1989–August 2, 1993); minister of roads and transportation in President Hashemi-Rafsanjani's second cabinet (August 16, 1993–August 2, 1997)

1952–, Tehran, Tehran

BS, mechanical engineering, Sharif University of Technology, 1974; MA, management

Civil servant, state companies

No imprisonment

Not a war veteran

Martyr's family (one brother killed in Kurdistan in 1979; another brother killed at the war front)

Founding member of the PMD

Torkan has been the governor-general of Ilam (1981–82) and Hormozgan (1983–85), deputy of the FDWI, and CEO of the Defense Industries Organization (1985–89). In 1989, he became the only non-military person to become defense minister in postrevolutionary Iran. After leaving the cabinet, he became the CEO of Pars Oil and Gas Company. Under President Ahmadinejad, he was a deputy in the Petroleum Ministry (2005–9). During the 2013 presidential election, Torkan was deputy director of Rouhani's electoral headquarters, and after the election, he became a senior adviser to President Rouhani and was the director of the Coordinating Council of Free Trade and Industrial Zones.

Torkashvand, Mohsen

Deputy of the Sixth Majlis, Tuyserkan, Hamadan (2000–2004)

1962–, Tuyserkan, Hamadan

BA, political science

Mohammad-Vali

No imprisonment

War veteran (wounded)

IRGC militiaman (Basij)

Member of the central council of OMIRI

Torkashvand was an IRGC commander during the Iran–Iraq War. He ran unsuccessfully for the Fifth Majlis and was disqualified by the GC for the Seventh Majlis. He took part in the 2004 sit-in by MPs protesting the massive disqualification of candidates for the Seventh Majlis.

Torki, Akbar

Deputy of the Tenth Majlis, Faridan and Fereydunshahr, Isfahan (2016–20)

1963–, Faridan, Isfahan

MD, Shahid Beheshti University of Medical Sciences, 1995; advanced training in radiology, Isfahan University of Medical Sciences, 2001

Asadollah, farmer

Medical doctor and hospital CEO

No imprisonment

War veteran

IRGC militiaman (since 1979)

Torki ran unsuccessfully for the Ninth Majlis.

Va'ezi, Farajollah

Deputy of the First Majlis, Abhar, Zanjan (1980–84)
1925–date unknown, Abhar, Zanjan
Clerical education
Abdolbaqi, farmer
Clergyman
Imprisoned before the revolution
Not a war veteran
HI Va'ezi's son, Mohammad-Taqi, served in the
    Fourth AE.

Va'ezi, Mahmud

Minister of information and communications tech-
    nology in President Rouhani's first cabinet (Au-
    gust 15, 2013–August 13, 2017)
1953–, Tehran, Tehran
BS, electrical engineering, Sacramento State Univer-
    sity (USA), 1976; MS, electrical engineering, San
    Jose State University (USA), 1978; MA, interna-
    tional relations, Tehran University; PhD, inter-
    national relations, Warsaw University (Poland),
    2003
High-level official in the Ministry of Foreign Affairs
No imprisonment
Not a war veteran
Member of the central council of HET
Va'ezi went to the United States in 1971 and returned
    in 1979 before finishing his PhD in telecommuni-
    cations at Louisiana State University. He was the
    managing director and chairman of the board of
    directors of the Telecommunications Company of
    Iran from 1979 to 1986 and also served as deputy
    minister of post, telegraph, and telephones. He
    joined the Ministry of Foreign Affairs in 1987 and
    held various posts, including deputy foreign min-
    ister in economic affairs and deputy of foreign
    policy and international relations at the Center for
    Strategic Research, where he worked with Hassan
    Rouhani. On August 20, 2017, Rouhani appointed
    Va'ezi as his chief of staff as he started his second
    term as president. Va'ezi's wife, Parvin [Zahra]

Dadandish (PhD, political science), was Rouhani's
    women's affairs adviser during the 2013 presiden-
    tial campaign.

Va'ezi, Mohammad-Taqi

Member of the Fourth Assembly of Experts, Zanjan
    (2007–16)
1951–, Tehran, Tehran
Clerical education, Qom Seminary
Farajollah, clergyman (HI)
Clergyman (HI)
No imprisonment
Not a war veteran
Ayatollah Khamenei appointed Va'ezi as the Friday
    prayer leader of Zanjan and the supreme lead-
    er's representative in Zanjan Province, where he
    served from 2003 to 2011. His father, Farajollah,
    was a deputy in the First Majlis.

Va'ez-Javadi [Amoli], Mrs. Fatemeh

VP and head of the Environmental Protection Orga-
    nization in President Ahmadinejad's first cabinet
    (October 2005–9)
1966–, Tehran, Tehran
BS, geology, Tarbiyat-e Modarres University, 1990;
    MS, geology, Tehran University, 1995; PhD, geol-
    ogy, Tarbiyat-e Modarres University, 2001
Esma'il, academia
Professor of geology at Shiraz University
No imprisonment
Not a war veteran
Va'ez-Javadi, the niece of Ayatollah Abdollah Java-
    di-Amoli, was a university professor and an ex-
    pert at the Research Center for Natural Disasters
    in Iran before becoming a VP. She ran unsuccess-
    fully for the Tenth Majlis from Tehran in 2016.

Va'ez-Musavi, Seyyed Mohammad

Member of the Fourth Assembly of Experts, East
    Azerbaijan (2007–16)

1964–, Shabestar, East Azerbaijan
Clerical education, Qom Seminary
Seyyed Ahmad, clergyman (HI)
Clergyman (HI)
No imprisonment
War veteran
IRGC militiaman (Basij)
Va'ez-Musavi was one of the youngest members of the
   Fourth AE. The GC rejected his qualifications for
   the Fifth AE.

Va'ez-Musavi-Anzabi, Seyyed Hasan

Deputy of the First Majlis, Urmia, West Azerbaijan
   (1982–84)
1922–, Anzab, Ardabil
Clerical education, Qom Seminary
Mir Davud
Clergyman
No imprisonment
Not a war veteran
HI Va'ez-Musavi-Anzabi was, among other roles, head
   of the ideological-political bureau of the police
   force and the cultural deputy of the governor-gen-
   eral of West Azerbaijan. He is the father-in-law of
   Nader Qazipur.

Va'ez-Tabasi, Abbas

Member of the First (1983–90), Second (1991–98),
   Third (1999–2006), and Fourth (2007–16) Assem-
   bly of Experts, Razavi Khorasan; member of the
   Fourth (1997–2002), Fifth (2002–7), Sixth (2007–
   12), and Seventh (2012–March 4, 2016) Expedi-
   ency Discernment Assembly
1936–March 4, 2016, Mashhad, Razavi Khorasan
Clerical education, Mashhad Seminary
Gholam-Reza, clergyman
Clergyman
Imprisoned before the revolution
Not a war veteran
IRGC militiaman
Member of the central council of the IRP

In the early days of the revolution, Ayatollah Khomeini appointed Ayatollah Va'ez-Tabasi, who was
   active in the anti-shah movement, as the supreme
   leader's representative in Khorasan Province.
   Va'ez-Tabasi was also a representative of the IRP
   in Mashhad, and head of the IRGC in Khorasan
   Province. On April 13, 1980, Ayatollah Khomeini
   officially appointed him as the custodian of
   Astan-e Qods-e Razavi. He escaped two assassination attempts in November 1981 and on February
   13, 1983. Upon becoming the supreme leader, Ayatollah Khamenei reappointed Va'ez-Tabasi as the
   guardian of Astan-e Qods-e Razavi, and in 2004,
   when Khorasan Province was divided into three
   provinces (North, South, and Razavi Khorasan),
   Va'ez-Tabasi was recognized as the supreme leader's representative in all three provinces. He held
   the above posts until he passed away. During his
   tenure, the size and economic power of Astan-e
   Qods-e Razavi, which was exempt from pay-
   ing any taxes, increased significantly. Ayatollah
   Va'ez-Tabasi was also the head of Mashhad Seminary until his death. Two of his sons were accused
   of embezzlement and fraud but were exonerated
   by the courts. Va'ez-Tabasi's son is married to the
   daughter of Mohammad-Reza Mohseni-Sani.

Va'ezzadeh-Khorasani, Sadeq

VP for scientific and technological affairs in President
   Ahmadinejad's first cabinet (2005–9); member of
   the Seventh (2012–17) and Eighth (2017–22) Expe-
   diency Discernment Assembly
1959–, Mashhad, Razavi Khorasan
BS, electrical engineering, Iran University of Science
   and Technology, 1985; MS, electrical engineering,
   Queen's University (Canada), 1993; PhD, electrical
   engineering, Queen's University, 1997 (Canada)
Mohammad, clergyman (ayatollah) and professor at
   Mashhad University's faculty of theology
Professor of electrical engineering at Tehran
   University
No imprisonment

Not a war veteran

Va'ezzadeh-Khorasani is Ayatollah Khamenei's maternal cousin. He was a candidate in the 2013 presidential election.

Vafi-Yazdi, Abolqasem

Deputy of the First (1980–84) and Second (1984–88) Majlis, Taft, Yazd; member of the Fourth (2007–16) and Fifth (2016–22) Assembly of Experts, Yazd

1935–, Hoseynabad, Kerman

Clerical education, Qom Seminary

Mahmud, farmer

Clergyman

No imprisonment

Not a war veteran

Member of the SQSS

HI Vafi-Yazdi is in charge of the famous Jamkaran mosque. His term on the seven-member HCRSQ ended in 2016.

Vahaji, Abdolhoseyn

Minister of commerce in President Hashemi-Rafsanjani's first cabinet (August 29, 1989–August 2, 1993)

BA, business management, California State University (campus not identified, USA), 1975; MA, business management, Shahid Beheshti University, 1996; PhD, strategic management, Islamic Azad University–Tehran, 2004

Civil servant, ministries

No imprisonment

Not a war veteran

Vahaji joined the Ministry of Commerce in 1980, where he was deputy for purchases. He then became deputy minister of commerce in 1986, and minister of commerce in 1989. He was deputy minister for the Ministry of Economic Affairs and Finance and chief of the Customs Administration (1993–97), deputy minister for foreign trade of the Ministry of Commerce (1997–2001), and deputy minister for international affairs of the Ministry of Commerce (2001–5). In August 2014, he

became Iran's ambassador to Australia. His 1996 master's thesis was on the GATT trade agreement and was supervised by Mohsen Nurbakhsh, who had previously served with him in President Hashemi-Rafsanjani's first cabinet.

Vahdati-Helan, Mohammad

Deputy of the Tenth Majlis, Bostanabad, East Azerbaijan (2016–20)

1960–, Bostanabad, East Azerbaijan

MD (Turkey), 1991

Medical doctor and health official

No imprisonment

IRGC militiaman (Basij)

Vahhabi, Seyyed Shamseddin

Deputy of the Sixth Majlis, Tehran, Tehran (2000–2004)

1955–, Behbahan, Khuzestan

MS, mining engineering

Abutaleb

Professor at Tehran University; general manager of the Institute for Mining Research

No imprisonment

War veteran

Member of the central council of the Unity Consolidation Office; member of IIPF; member of the central council of the Party of Iranian People's Unity

Vahhabi was involved in the takeover of the American embassy in Tehran and was in charge of the public relations bureau set up by the occupying students. After serving in the Majlis, he went back to teaching mining engineering at Tehran University.

Vahid, Motlleb

Deputy of the First Majlis, Kaleybar, East Azerbaijan (1981–84)

1927–, Kaleybar, East Azerbaijan

Clerical education

Mehdi
Clergyman
No imprisonment
Not a war veteran
HI Vahid used to teach at Qom Seminary.

Vahid[i]-Mehrjerdi, Sarajeddin

Deputy of the Sixth Majlis, Taft and Meybod, Yazd
   (2000–2004)
1957–, Meybod, Yazd
MD, urology, Shahid Beheshti University
Yahya, clergyman
Urologist
No imprisonment
Vahid-Mehrjerdi was a member of the Construction
   Jihad in Meybod.

Vahid-Dastjerdi, Mrs. Marziyeh

Deputy of the Fourth (1992–96) and Fifth (1996–2000)
   Majlis, Tehran, Tehran; minister of health and
   medical education in President Ahmadinejad's
   second cabinet (September 3, 2009–December 27,
   2012)
1959–, Tehran, Tehran
MD, gynecology, Tehran University of Medical Sciences, 1988
Seyfollah, medical doctor
Medical doctor and university professor
No imprisonment
Founding member of the ISFPD; member of Zeynab
   Society; secretary-general of the United Front of
   Principalist and Skilled Women; spokesperson of
   the Popular Front of Islamic Revolution Forces
In 2009, Vahid-Dastjerdi became the first female
   minister in the Islamic Republic and third female
   minister in Iranian history. President Ahmadine-
   jad dismissed her from her post in December
   2012 after she had served for forty months.
   Vahid-Dastjerdi, who is on the board of trustees
   of the IKRF, ran unsuccessfully for the Sixth and
   Tenth Majlis. Her father was president of the Red
   Crescent Society of the Islamic Republic of Iran

and a founding member of the Islamic Society of
   Iranian Physicians.

Vahidi, Ahmad

Commander of the IRGC's Qods Force (1990s; exact
   dates unknown); minister of defense and armed
   forces logistics in President Ahmadinejad's second cabinet (September 3, 2009–August 3, 2013);
   member of the Seventh (2012–17) and Eighth
   (2017–22) Expediency Discernment Assembly
1958–, Shiraz, Fars
BS, electrical engineering, Shiraz University; MS,
   industrial engineering
Military and security official
No imprisonment
War veteran
IRGC militiaman
Vahidi was a high-level official in both the IRGC
   and the Ministry of Defense before becoming
   minister of defense. His name appeared in a
   warrant issued by INTERPOL in 2007 accusing
   him of involvement in the bombing of a Jewish
   center (Asociación Mutual Israelita Argentina)
   in Argentina in July 1994 when he was serving as
   commander of the IRGC's Qods Force. He was
   among the twenty-seven individuals named in
   the UN's Security Council resolution 1747 (March
   24, 2007), which asked member countries to
   curtail trade with those involved in Iran's nuclear
   program. On September 3, 2009, Vahidi received
   the highest positive votes (227 out of 286) from
   the Majlis during the confirmation of President
   Ahmadinejad's second cabinet. In 2013, the chief
   of the Armed Forces General Staff appointed him
   director of the Center for Strategic Defense Studies. He is also a member of the Strategic Council
   on Foreign Relations that advises the supreme
   leader on foreign policy issues.

Vahidi, Ramezan

Deputy of the Sixth Majlis, Bojnurd and Jajarm,
   North Khorasan (2000–2004)

1951–, Bojnurd, North Khorasan
MS, energy engineering
Abbas-Ali
Civil servant
No imprisonment
Vahidi, who is involved in environmental protection
projects, ran for the Tenth Majlis.

Vakili, Mohammad-Ali

Deputy of the Tenth Majlis, Tehran, Tehran (2016–20)
1965–, Yasouj, Kohgiluyeh and Buyer Ahmad
PhD, theology; PhD, political science; clerical
education
No imprisonment
War veteran (thirty months; wounded)
Vakili was the cultural deputy in the Bureau of Repre-
sentatives of the Supreme Leader in Universities.
He is the managing director of *Ebtekar.*

Valipur, Naz-Mohammad

Deputy of the Sixth Majlis, Bandar-e Torkaman, Ban-
dar-e Gaz, and Kordkuy, Golestan (2001–4)
1963–, Bandar-e Torkaman, Golestan
BA
Abdorrahman
Academia
No imprisonment
Valipur was a Sunni MP.

Vanaei, Hasan

Deputy of the Eighth Majlis, Malayer, Hamadan
(2008–12)
1968–, Malayer, Hamadan
BA, business administration; PhD, industrial
management
Gholam-Ali
Civil servant, ministries
No imprisonment
After the Eighth Majlis, Vanaei worked in the office of
the VP for management and human capital development. He ran unsuccessfully for the Tenth Majlis.

Vaqfchi, Ali

Deputy of the Tenth Majlis, Zanjan, Zanjan (2016–20)
1966–, Tarom, Zanjan
MD, veterinary science
Veterinarian and university professor
No imprisonment

Vardan, Gevorg

Deputy of the Seventh (2004–8) and Eighth (2008–12)
Majlis, representing Armenians of northern Iran
(as a religious minority)
1969–, Tehran, Tehran
BS, metallurgy, Iran University of Science and Tech-
nology, 1994; MS, metallurgy, State Engineering
University of Armenia (Armenia)
Engineer
No imprisonment
Not a war veteran

Vartanian, Vartan

Deputy of the Second (1984–88), Third (1988–92),
Fourth (1992–96), and Fifth (1996–2000) Majlis,
representing Armenians of northern Iran (as a
religious minority)
1942–, Isfahan, Isfahan
MS, mechanical engineering
Ebrahim
No imprisonment
Not a war veteran
Vartanian and fellow Armenian MP Artavaz Baghu-
mian hold the record as the MP most frequently
elected to represent a religious minority.

Vaziri, Mokhtar

Deputy of the Sixth (2000–2004) and Seventh (2004–
8) Majlis, Kahnuj, Kerman
1961–, Abadan, Khuzestan
Clerical education
Fatollah
Clergyman (HI)
No imprisonment

Vaziri-Hamaneh, Seyyed Kazem

Minister of petroleum in President Ahmadinejad's first cabinet (December 11, 2005–August 12, 2007)

1945–, Hamaneh, Yazd

BS, mechanical engineering, Iran University of Science and Technology, 1970; MS, systems management, 1973

Father's name unknown, farmer

Petroleum Ministry official

No imprisonment

Not a war veteran

Vaziri-Hamaneh joined the NIOC in 1973 and worked there for thirty-seven years. In 2005, he was the fourth candidate suggested by President Ahmadinejad for the post of minister of petroleum, and he received 172 positive votes, fifty-three negative votes, and thirty-four abstentions. President Ahmadinejad dismissed Vaziri-Hamaneh on August 12, 2007.

Vela'i, Isa

Deputy of the Second Majlis, Amol, Mazandaran (1984–88); deputy of the Third Majlis, Tehran, Tehran (1988–92)

1950–, Amol, Mazandaran

Clerical education

Yadollah

Clergyman

No imprisonment

Not a war veteran

Member of the central council of the ACC

In 2013, President Rouhani's VP for parliamentary affairs appointed HI Vela'i as head of the Center for Research and Information. Vela'i is the son-in-law of Ayatollah Mohammad-Reza Tavassoli-Mahallati.

Velayati, Ali-Akbar

Deputy of the First Majlis, Tehran, Tehran (1980–December 15, 1981); minister of foreign affairs in PM Musavi's first (December 15, 1981–85) and second (October 28, 1985–August 3, 1989) cabinets and President Hashemi-Rafsanjani's first (August 29, 1989–August 2, 1993) and second (August 16, 1993–August 2, 1997) cabinets; member of the Fourth (1997–2002), Fifth (2002–7), Sixth (2007–12), Seventh (2012–17), and Eighth (2017–22) Expediency Discernment Assembly

June 25, 1945–, Tehran, Tehran

MD, pediatrics, Tehran University, 1971

Ali-Asghar (1900–80), civil servant

Pediatrician and deputy in the Ministry of Health

No imprisonment

Not a war veteran

Member of the central council of the IRP; founding member of the Islamic Society of Iranian Physicians

As a pediatrician, Velayati completed a continuing medical education course at Johns Hopkins University in Baltimore in 1976. President Khamenei nominated him for the post of prime minister, but he failed to get the approval of the Majlis on October 22, 1981. Velayati then resigned from the First Majlis to serve as foreign minister for sixteen years (1981–97). After leaving office, on August 21, 1997, Velayati became a foreign policy adviser to the supreme leader. He withdrew from the presidential contest in 2005 and ran unsuccessfully in the 2013 presidential election. In 2006, Ayatollah Khamenei appointed Velayati to the Strategic Council on Foreign Relations, and in January 2017, Khamenei appointed him as head of the founding committee of Islamic Azad University. A few weeks later he became the head of its board of trustees. Velayati is also the head of the Center for Strategic Research of the Expediency Discernment Assembly. Velayati's first wife, Shirin Khoshnevisan, died in medical surgery in 2005, and he then married Leila Enayat in 2008. Mrs. Enayat's sister is married to Sadeq Mahsuli, the interior minister under President Ahmadinejad.

Yahyavi, Seyyed Mohsen

Minister of housing and urban development in the Revolutionary Council cabinet (November 16,

1979–October 31, 1980); deputy of the Fourth (1992–96) and Fifth (1996–2000) Majlis, Tehran, Tehran; deputy of the Seventh Majlis, Borujerd, Lorestan (2004–8)

1942–, Borujerd, Lorestan

BS, civil engineering (USA); MA, political science, 1995

Civil servant

Seyyed Mohammad-Sadeq

No imprisonment

War veteran

Member of the Islamic Society of Engineers

Yahyavi became a POW on October 31, 1980, when Iraqi forces arrested him and minister of petroleum Mohammad-Javad Tondguyan during a visit to the front. He was released on September 15, 1990. He has held various positions, including member of the board of directors of the Housing Foundation and of the NIOC.

Yahyazadeh-Firozabad, Seyyed Jalal

Deputy of the Seventh (2004–8), Eighth (2008–12), and Ninth (2012–April 9, 2013) Majlis, Taft and Meybod, Yazd

1960–April 9, 2013, Meybod, Yazd

Clerical education, Qom Seminary

Clergyman

No imprisonment

War veteran

HI Yahyazadeh-Firozabad used to attend Ayatollah Khamenei's classes. He ran unsuccessfully for the Sixth Majlis. After he died of a heart attack, interim elections to replace him were not held in Taft.

Ya'qubi, Ali

Deputy of the Fourth (1992–96) and Fifth (1996–2000) Majlis, Bahar and Kabudarahang, Hamadan

1954–, Hamadan, Hamadan

BS, agricultural engineering, 1991; MA, political science, 1995

Shirzad

No imprisonment

Ya'qubi, Mehdi

Deputy of the Second Majlis, Torbat-e Heydariyyeh, Razavi Khorasan (1984–February 20, 1986)

1951–February 20, 1986, Torbat-e Heydariyyeh, Razavi Khorasan

Clerical education

Gholam-Nabi

Clergyman

No imprisonment

Not a war veteran

HI Ya'qubi was killed when Iraqi forces shot down his aircraft.

Ya'qubi-Bijarbaneh, Bahram

Deputy of the Fourth Majlis, Lahijan, Gilan (1992–96)

1957–, Lahijan, Gilan

BA, public administration; PhD

Ahmad

No imprisonment

In January 2015, Tehran Mayor Qalibaf appointed Ya'qubi-Bijarbaneh to the high council overseeing the development of Tehran. He had previously served as a manager in IRIB.

Yari, Ali

Deputy of the Sixth Majlis, Ilam, Eyvan, Mehran, Malekshahi, Shirvan, and Chardavol, Ilam (2000–2004)

1959–, Ilam, Ilam

MA, public administration

Kazem

Civil servant

No imprisonment

Yari ran unsuccessfully for the Seventh, Eighth, and Ninth Majlis.

Yar-Mohammadi, Alim

Deputy of the Tenth Majlis, Zahedan, Sistan and Baluchestan (2016–20)

1956–, Zahedan, Sistan and Baluchestan

BS, civil engineering, University of Sistan and Baluchestan, 1980; MA, public administration, Zahedan
   Center for Teaching Public Administration, 2004
Retired civil servant
No imprisonment
Yar-Mohammadi, a Sunni, worked in the roads and
   transportation department in Sistan and Baluchestan from 1982 until his retirement in 2012. He was
   director-general of the roads and transportation
   department in southern Sistan and Baluchestan
   from 2001 to 2006. He then continued his work as
   an official of the Engineering Council of Sistan and
   Baluchestan. His real name may be Alim Rigi.

Yar-Mohammadi, Ali-Reza

Deputy of the First Majlis, Bam, Kerman (1980–84)
1944–, Tehran, Tehran
High school diploma
Ebrahim, laborer
Laborer
No imprisonment
Not a war veteran

Yasrebi, Seyyed Ali-Mohammad

Deputy of the Sixth Majlis, Qom, Qom (2000–2004)
1951–, Qom, Qom
Clerical education; PhD, theology
Zeynol'abedin, clergyman
Clergyman (HI)
No imprisonment
In 2016, Yasrebi registered to run for the Tenth Majlis
   and the Fifth AE.

Yasrebi, Seyyed Mehdi

Member of the First Assembly of Experts, Isfahan
   (1983–90); member of the Second (1991–98) and
   Third (1999–2006) Assembly of Experts, Isfahan
1925–2006, Kashan, Isfahan
Clerical education, Qom Seminary
Seyyed Mohammad-Reza, clergyman (ayatollah)
Clergyman (HI)

No imprisonment
In 2016, Yasrebi registered to run for the Tenth Majlis
   and Fifth AE.
Not a war veteran
Ayatollah Yasrebi began to serve as the Friday prayer
   leader of Kashan in August 1979. On April 24,
   1983, he became Ayatollah Khomeini's representative in Kashan. His nephew is Hoseyn Mahlujchi,
   who was a member of the Majlis and minister of
   mining under President Hashemi-Rafsanjani.

Yavari, Mansur

Deputy of the Seventh Majlis, Golpayegan and Khan-
   sar, Isfahan (2004–8)
1951–, Golpayegan, Isfahan
BS, mechanical engineering
Mohammad
Civil servant, ministries
No imprisonment

Yazdi, Ebrahim

Member of the Revolutionary Council (1979–1980);
   ministerial adviser for revolutionary affairs (1979)
   and then minister of foreign affairs (April 24–No-
   vember 5, 1979) in PM Bazargan's cabinet; deputy
   of the First Majlis, Tehran, Tehran (1980–84)
1931–August 27, 2017, Qazvin, Qazvin
PhD, pharmacology, Tehran University, 1953
Mohammad-Sadeq, bazaar tradesman
Academia
No imprisonment
Not a war veteran
Secretary-general of the LMI (1995–2017)
Yazdi was active in the overseas Iranian opposition
   movement against the shah, and he served for nine
   years as Ayatollah Khomeini's representative in the
   United States. He was one of Khomeini's closest
   confidants, advisers, spokespersons, and translators
   during the ayatollah's stay in Paris (1978–79). In
   January and February 1979, Yazdi held a number
   of meetings with American diplomats in Paris
   and Tehran on behalf of Ayatollah Khomeini to

convince them not to oppose the revolution. Soon after the revolution, he performed the role of prosecutor in the kangaroo courts that sentenced high-level military commanders to death immediately. Because Yazdi carried an American green card, hardliners accused him of being an American agent. After serving briefly as PM Bazargan's ministerial adviser for revolutionary affairs, foreign minister and then one term as a member of the Majlis, Yazdi was shunned politically. The GC rejected his qualifications to run in the October 1981 and 1997 presidential elections and the 2000 parliamentary election. He remained active as an opposition politician, and the judiciary jailed him several times. Mohammad Tavassoli [-Hojjati], the first mayor of Tehran after the revolution, is his brother-in-law.

Yazdi, Mohammad

Member of the Assembly for the Final Examination of the Constitution, Kermanshah (1979); deputy of the First Majlis, Qom, Qom (1980–84); deputy of the Second Majlis, Tehran, Tehran (1984–88); chief justice (August 15, 1989–August 14, 1999); member of the Second (1988–89), Fourth (1999–2004), Fifth (2004–10), Sixth (2010–16), and Seventh (2016–19) Guardian Councils; member of the Second (1991–98), Third (1999–2006), and Fourth (2007–16) Assembly of Experts, Tehran; member of the Eighth Expediency Discernment Assembly (2017–22)
1931–, Isfahan, Isfahan
Clerical education, Qom Seminary
Ali, clergyman
Clergyman
Imprisoned and exiled before the revolution
Not a war veteran
Secretary of the SQSS; member of the central council of the SCC; and secretary of the HCRSQ
An archconservative ayatollah, Yazdi is one of the most prominent political personalities in postrevolutionary Iran. He was associated with the paramilitary group Devotees of Islam in his youth. In addition to the positions listed above, Yazdi has been head of Ayatollah Khomeini's office in

Qom, prosecutor and head of the revolutionary courts in Qom and Bakhtaran, deputy Speaker of the Majlis (1983–88), acting Friday prayer leader of Tehran (occasionally since June 1981), member of the IRGC's command council, and one of the two secretaries for the Council for Revision of the Constitution. In 2014, Yazdi defeated Akbar Hashemi-Rafsanjani to become the chairperson of the Fourth AE, but he was not elected to the Fifth AE in 2016. Ayatollah Yazdi's critics have accused him of financial wrongdoing.

Yeganli, Mir Mahmud

Deputy of the Sixth Majlis, Urmia, West Azerbaijan (2000–2004)
1954–, Urmia, West Azerbaijan
MS, mining
Mir Sami
Imprisoned before the revolution
He resigned from the Majlis on March 7, 2004, and worked in the mining field.

Yekta'i, Heybatollah

Member of the First Assembly of Experts, East Azerbaijan (1984–90)
1923–September 22, 2016, Karin, Ardabil
Clerical education, Qom Seminary
Abdolkhaleq, clergyman (ayatollah)
Clergyman
No imprisonment
Not a war veteran
Ayatollah Yekta'i was born in a village near Khalkhal. He was the first Friday prayer leader of Khalkhal after the revolution and held that post for seventeen years.

Yunesi, Ali

Public prosecutor-general of Tehran (1988–90); minister of intelligence in President Khatami's first (February 24, 1999–August 1, 2001), and second (August 22, 2001–August 2, 2005) cabinets

1955–, Nahavand, Hamadan

Clerical education, Haqqani Seminary; BA, judicial law, 1981; MA, political science

Father's name unknown, farmer

Clergyman and judiciary official

Imprisoned before the revolution

Not a war veteran

HI Yunesi received military training in Lebanon before the revolution. In 1984, then-president Khamenei put him in charge of the judicial affairs of the armed forces, and in 1989, he became the supreme leader's representative at the army's intelligence branch. Yunesi was a member of a three-person council appointed by President Khatami to look into the "chain murder" of intellectuals. On October 1, 2013, Yunesi became President Rouhani's adviser on the affairs of ethnic and religious minorities. His second wife, Fatemeh Amirani, was previously married to the revered martyred IRGC commander Mehdi Baqeri (1954–1985). Yunesi's son Hasan, who is a lawyer, was arrested after protesting the house arrest of presidential candidates Musavi and Karrubi in 2009.

Yusefi, Homayun

Deputy of the Tenth Majlis, Ahvaz, Khuzestan (2016–20)

1973–, Ahvaz, Khuzestan

MD, Shahid Beheshti University of Medical Sciences; specialization in cancer treatment, Ahvaz University of Medical Sciences

War veteran

Yusefi-Eshkevari, Hasan

Deputy of the First Majlis, Tonekabon, Mazandaran (1980–84)

1949–, Tonekabon, Mazandaran

Clerical education, Qom Seminary, 1979

Mohammad-Hashem, farmer

Clergyman (HI)

Imprisoned before the revolution

Not a war veteran

Yusefi-Eshkevari, who was sympathetic to the LMI and PMOI, became a dissident Islamic thinker. In 2000, he was sentenced to a seven-year prison term for having taken part in a conference in Berlin. He was imprisoned from 2000 to 2005, and then he settled in exile in Europe and abandoned his clerical robe.

Yusefiyan, Reza

Deputy of the Sixth Majlis, Shiraz, Fars (2000–2004)

1967–, Tehran, Tehran

MD, orthopedics, Shiraz University of Medical Sciences, 1991

Medical doctor

Mohammad

No imprisonment

Yusefiyan was a reformist activist.

Yusefiyan-Mola, Ezzatollah

Deputy of the Seventh (2004–8), Eighth (2008–12), Ninth (2012–16), and Tenth (2016–20) Majlis, Amol, Mazandaran

1951–, Amol, Mazandaran

BA, law, Shahid Beheshti University; PhD, private law

Asadollah

High-level judiciary official

No imprisonment

Yusefnezhad, Ali-Asghar

Deputy of the Fifth (1996–2000), Eighth (2008–12), and Tenth (2016–20) Majlis, Sari, Mazandaran

January 1, 1960–, Sari, Mazandaran

BS, industrial engineering, Iran University of Science and Technology, 1976; pursuing a PhD in planning

Mohammad

Dean of the Sari Agricultural Sciences and Natural Resources University (1991–96)

No imprisonment

War veteran

IRGC militiaman

Yusefnezhad was mayor of Sari in 1986 and worked as a research and planning deputy for Imam

Hoseyn University from 1990 to 1991. After his
unsuccessful run for the Ninth Majlis, he became
the parliamentary-legal deputy to the minister of
economic affairs (2013–15).

Yusefpur, Ali

Deputy of the Second (1984–88), Third (1988–92), and
Fourth (1992–96) Majlis, Ardal, Chahar Mahal
and Bakhtiari
1955–, Naghan, Chahar Mahal and Bakhtiari
BS, mechanical engineering, Iran University of
Science and Technology; MA, political science,
Shahid Beheshti University
Soltan-Ali
No imprisonment
IRGC militiaman
Martyr's family (brothers Zal and Najaf)
Founding member of the Alliance of Veterans of
the Islamic Revolution; founding member of
the ISFPD; member of the Islamic Society
of Bakhtiaris
Yusefpur, a conservative, was previously a member of the
IRGC command council in Hormozgan, Isfahan,
and Markazi, and he became deputy to the minister
of welfare during President Ahmadinejad's era. He
signed up to run in the election for the Tenth Majlis.

Zabeti-Tarqi, Mohammad

Deputy of the Eighth Majlis, Qamsar and Natanz,
Isfahan (2008–12)
1967–, Tehran, Tehran
MD, Isfahan University of Medical Sciences, 1993
Khosrow
Medical doctor and professor
No imprisonment
Zabeti-Tarqi was not elected to the Ninth Majlis.

Zadsar-Jirofti, Ali

Deputy of the Fourth (1992–96), Fifth (1996–2000),
and Seventh (2004–8) Majlis, Jiroft, Kerman
1958–, Jiroft, Kerman

Clerical education, Qom Seminary, 1989; studied
English literature at Shahid Bahonar University of
Kerman (1989–92)
Safar, farmer
Clergyman (HI)
Imprisoned before the revolution
War veteran (seven years; wounded)
Zadsar-Jirofti knew Ayatollah Khamenei before the
revolution, when the shah's regime exiled Khame-
nei to Jiroft. Besides fighting in the Iran–Iraq
War, he also fought in Lebanon in 1982.

Za'eri, Gholam-Abbas

Deputy of the First (1980–84), Second (1984–88),
Third (1988–92), and Fourth (1992–July 31, 1994)
Majlis, Bandar-e Abbas, Hormozgan
1946–, Bandar-e Abbas, Hormozgan
BA, Persian literature
Mohammad, academia
Civil servant
No imprisonment
Not a war veteran
Za'eri left the Fourth Majlis to become the governor of
Hormozgan Province under Hashemi-Rafsanjani.
He then joined the supreme leader's inspectorate.

Zafarzadeh, Ali

Deputy of the Sixth Majlis, Mashhad, Razavi Kho-
rasan (2000–2004)
1951–, Fariman, Razavi Khorasan
BS, laboratory sciences; MA, management
Mohammad-Heydar
Provincial civil servant
No imprisonment
Secretary-general of the Association of Producers
Zafarzadeh returned to civil service after finishing his
term in the Majlis.

Zahedi, Abdolqader

Member of the Third Assembly of Experts, Kurdistan
(1999–2005)

1907–December 19, 2005, Saqqez, Kurdistan
Clerical education
Abdollah, clergyman
Clergyman
No imprisonment
Not a war veteran
Mamosta Zahedi, a Sunni, was Friday prayer leader in
a number of cities in Kurdistan, including Saqqez.

Zahedi, Mohammad-Mehdi

Minister of science, research, and technology in
President Ahmadinejad's first cabinet (August
24, 2005–August 2, 2009); deputy of the Ninth
(2012–16) and Tenth (2016–20) Majlis, Kerman
and Ravar, Kerman
1954–, Kerman, Kerman
BS, mathematics, Isfahan University of Technology,
1979; MS, mathematics, Tarbiyat-e Modarres University, 1986; PhD, mathematics, Shahid Bahonar
University of Kerman, 1990
Masha'allah
Professor at Shahid Bahonar University of Kerman;
member of the Kerman City Council
No imprisonment
Not a war veteran
After he left the cabinet, Zahedi became ambassador
to Malaysia for a couple of years, and then he
was elected from Kerman to the Ninth Majlis.
He claimed the Cambridge International Center
chose him as "scientist of the year" in 1997. At
that time (1994–97), he was the research deputy at
Shahid Bahonar University of Kerman.

Zaheri, Ali-Asgar

Deputy of the Tenth Majlis, Masjed Soleyman, Khuz-
estan (2016–20)
1957–, Masjed Soleyman, Khuzestan
MA, public administration
Father's name unknown, oil worker
No imprisonment
Zaheri worked in the Construction Jihad and the
Public Health Organization.

Zahirnezhad, Qasemali

Commander of the Islamic Republic of Iran Ground
Forces (June 19, 1980–October 1, 1981); chief
of the joint staff of the Islamic Republic of Iran
Army (October 1, 1981–October 25, 1984)
1924–October 13, 1999, Ardabil, Ardabil
BS, military science, Ground Forces Officers'
Academy
Army officer (retired in 1973)
War veteran
Zahirnezhad retired from the army before the revolution with the rank of lieutenant colonel. He returned to active duty in March 1979 and became
the commander of Urmia brigade. On March
15, 1980, he was appointed as the commander of
the gendarmerie force, and a few months later
he became commander of the army's ground
forces. During the years of the Iran–Iraq War,
the plain-speaking Major General Zahirnezhad
fought forcefully with the IRGC command about
proper military tactics and strategies both in his
capacity as the commander of the army's ground
forces and as chief of JSIRIA. After Zahirnezhad
resigned from JSIRIA in October 1984, Ayatollah
Khomeini appointed him as one of his representatives in the Supreme Defense Council. In April
1987, Ayatollah Khomeini promoted him from
brigadier general to major general. On October
28, 1989, he became head of the military advisers
to the chief of the Armed Forces General Staff.
Zahirnezhad's sister was the wife of Ayatollah
Seyyed Abdolkarim Musavi-Ardabili.

Zahmatkesh, Hasan

Deputy of the Sixth Majlis, Astara, Gilan (2000–2004)
1947–, Astara, Gilan
Associate's degree
Asgar
Civil servant
No imprisonment
Zahmatkesh resigned from the Sixth Majlis along
with many other MPs to protest massive

disqualification of candidates for the Seventh
Majlis. He then returned to civil service.

Zajkaniha, Hoseyn

Deputy of the Fifth Majlis, Qazvin, Qazvin (1996–2000)
1950–, Qazvin, Qazvin
BA, economics
Ali-Akbar
No imprisonment
After Majlis, he was in charge of the Office to Enjoin the
    Good and Prohibit the Evil in Qazvin Province.

Zakani, Ali-Reza

Deputy of the Seventh (2004–8), Eighth (2008–12),
    and Ninth (2012–16) Majlis, Tehran, Tehran
1965–, Shahr-e Rey, Tehran
MD, nuclear medicine, Tehran University of Medical
    Sciences, 1997
Hoseyn, athlete and referee
Professor at Tehran University's medical school; nu-
    clear medicine doctor at Imam Khomeini Hospital
No imprisonment
War veteran (sixty-two months; wounded)
IRGC militiaman (nationwide director of student Basij)
Secretary-general of the Alliance of Wayfarers of the
    Islamic Revolution
Zakani, who is the proprietor of the conservative web-
    site Jahan News, was disqualified from running in
    the 2013 and 2017 presidential elections.

Zaker, Seyyed Salman

Deputy of the Eighth Majlis, Urmia, West Azerbaijan
    (2008–12)
1966–, Urmia, West Azerbaijan
Clerical education, Qom Seminary; MA, theology,
    Tarbiyat-e Modarres University
Mir Hamdollah
Clergyman (HI), judge, and university professor
No imprisonment
After running unsuccessfully for the Ninth Majlis,
    Zaker went back to the judiciary as a civil servant.

Zakeri, Mohammad-Baqer

Deputy of the Third (1988–92), Fifth (1996–2000), and
    Sixth (2000–2004) Majlis, Quchan, Razavi Khorasan
1952–, Quchan, Razavi Khorasan
Clerical education; BA, educational science
Abbas-Ali
Clergyman (HI)
No imprisonment
Member of the central council of NTP

Zali, Abbas-Ali

Minister of agriculture in PM Musavi's first (Decem-
    ber 7, 1983–85) and second (October 28, 1985–88)
    cabinets; deputy of the Third (1989–92) and
    Fourth (1992–96) Majlis, Karaj and Eshtehard,
    Tehran
March 20, 1938–, Golpayegan, Isfahan
BS, agronomy, Tehran University, 1964; MS, agricul-
    tural engineering, University of California, Davis
    (USA), 1968; PhD, agricultural engineering, Uni-
    versity of California, Davis (USA), 1970
Mohammad-Ali, farmer
Civil servant, ministries
No imprisonment
Not a war veteran
Zali, who was a professor at Tehran University before
    the revolution, did not receive a vote of confidence
    to continue serving in PM Musavi's second cabi-
    net. He was then elected to the Third Majlis from
    Karaj in interim elections, replacing Abdolmajid
    Shar'pasand, who had been dismissed. Later on,
    during the second term of President Khatami,
    Zali became the director of Iran Statistical Center.
    He was also the dean of Tehran University's Col-
    lege of Agriculture and Natural Resources.

Zali [Fazel-Golpayegani], Mohammad-Hasan

Member of the Fifth Assembly of Experts, Tehran
    (2016–22)
1948–, Golpayegan, Isfahan
Clerical education, Qom Seminary

Abdolali
Clergyman (ayatollah)
No imprisonment
Not a war veteran

Zamani, Hojjatollah

Deputy of the Second Majlis, Borujerd, Lorestan
(1984–88)
1947–, Arak, Markazi
Clerical education
Isa
Clergyman
No imprisonment
HI Zamani ran as an independent for the Second
Majlis and defeated ten other candidates with
strong factional backing. He was not in favor of
the notion of *velayat-e faqih*.

Zamani, Seyyed Javad

Deputy of the Eighth Majlis, Kangavar, Sahneh, and
Harsin, Kermanshah (2008–12)
1960–, Kangavar, Kermanshah
BA, Persian literature
Seyyed Torab, farmer
Academia
No imprisonment
Zamani was not elected to the Ninth Majlis.

Zamani, Valiyollah

Deputy of the Second Majlis, Babol, Mazandaran
(1984–88)
1937–2006, Shahmirzad, Mazandaran
MA, history, Tehran University
Farajollah
Imprisoned before the revolution
Zamani was a teacher before and after serving in the
Majlis.

Zamanifar, Hasan-Reza

Deputy of the Fifth (1997–2000) and Seventh (2004–8)
Majlis, Malayer, Hamadan

1958–, Malayer, Hamadan
MA, management
Reza
Civil servant
No imprisonment
Zamanifar, who also goes by the name Hasan
Zamani, became an adviser to Majlis Speaker Ali
Larijani in 2008.

Zamaniyan, Ahmad

Deputy of the First (1981–84), Second (1984–88), Third
(1988–92), and Fourth (1992–96) Majlis, Naha-
vand, Hamadan
1939–, Nahavand, Hamadan
Clerical education
Amir-Hoseyn
Clergyman
No imprisonment
Not a war veteran
Martyr's family
HI Zamaniyan was associated with military courts.

Zamaniyan-Dehkordi, Seyyed Sa'id

Deputy of the Ninth Majlis, Shahrekord, Chahar
Mahal and Bakhtiari (2012–16)
1960–, Shahrekord, Chahar Mahal and Bakhtiari
BA, public administration, Payam-e Nur University,
Shahrekord
Governor of Shahrekord
No imprisonment
Zamaniyan-Dehkordi, a martial arts master, has held
various positions in the MIIRI, and he has been a
deputy at FMVA.

Zangeneh, Hamid

Deputy of the Seventh Majlis, Ahvaz, Khuzestan
(2004–8)
1963–, Masjed Soleyman, Khuzestan
BA, management
Mozaffar
Civil servant
No imprisonment

Zangeneh, Seyyed Sabah

Deputy of the First Majlis, Shiraz, Fars (1980–84)
1951–, Karbala, Iraq
MS, biological sciences; clerical education
Seyyed Taqi, attorney
Academia
No imprisonment
Zangeneh became Iran's first ambassador to the Organization of Islamic Cooperation in October 1991. He has since left the post.

Zanjani-Hasanlu'i, Ali

Deputy of the Eighth Majlis, Naqadeh and Oshnaviyyeh, West Azerbaijan (2008–12)
1965–, Naqadeh, West Azerbaijan
BA, judicial law
Qanbar-Ali
Official in the intelligence unit of the Law Enforcement Forces
No imprisonment
Zanjani-Hasanlu'i was not elected to the Ninth Majlis.

Zarabadi, Mrs. Seyyedeh Hamideh

Deputy of the Tenth Majlis, Qazvin, Qazvin (2016–20)
1980–, Qazvin, Qazvin
BS, electrical engineering; MS, electrical engineering, Islamic Azad University–Science and Research Branch, 2011
Employee of the organization for radio communications and regulation in Qazvin Province
Zarabadi, whose grandfather was an ayatollah, has taught at a number of universities, including Iran University of Science and Technology.

Zarandi-Ma'sumi, Hoseyn [Mohammad]

Member of the First (1983–90), Third (1999–2006), and Fourth (2007–14) Assembly of Experts, Kermanshah
1932–2014, Zarand, Markazi

Clerical education, Qom Seminary
Ali-Akbar, farmer
Clergyman
Imprisoned before the revolution (1974–75)
Not a war veteran
HI Zarandi-Ma'sumi became the acting Friday prayer leader of Kermanshah in April 1984 and Ayatollah Khomeini's representative in the province in February 1986, where he served until 2007. During this time, he was considered the most powerful figure in Kermanshah Province.

Zare', Karim

Deputy of the Fourth Majlis, Shiraz, Fars (1992–96)
1950–, Bordaj, Fars
BS, chemistry, Tabriz University, 1974; MS, chemistry, Institut Pasteur (France), 1975; PhD, chemistry, Institut Pasteur (France), 1978; post-doctoral research in chemistry at Institut Pasteur
Hasan-Ali
University professor
No imprisonment
Not a war veteran

Zare', Rahim

Deputy of the Ninth (2012–16) and Tenth (2016–20) Majlis, Abadeh, Bavanat, and Khorrambid, Fars
1976–, Bavanat, Fars
BS, industrial management, Shiraz University; MA, business administration, Allameh Tabataba'i University; PhD, business administration, Allameh Tabataba'i University
Akbar
Tax controller
No imprisonment
Not a war veteran

Zare'i, Ali-Asghar

Deputy of the Eighth (2008–12) and Ninth (2012–16) Majlis, Tehran, Tehran
1956–, Tehran, Tehran

BS, electrical engineering; MA, public administration, Institute for Management and Planning Studies; PhD, electrical systems management, Tehran University

Donyam-Ali

No imprisonment

War veteran (wounded)

IRGC militiaman

Martyr's family (brother)

Founding member of the SFIR

Zare'i, one of the founders of Basiji faculty, was a faculty member and head of the college of engineering at Imam Hoseyn University when he ran for the Eighth Majlis. As an important official in the IRGC, he has headed Khatam al-Anbia's electronic warfare headquarters. He has also been the secretary of IRIB's High Council for Internet Policy. Zare'i, who reportedly is close to Ayatollah Mesbah-Yazdi, did not register to run for the Tenth Majlis election; instead, he returned to the IRGC and teaching at Imam Hoseyn University.

Zare'i, Gholam-Mohammad

Deputy of the Ninth (2012–16) and Tenth (2016–20) Majlis, Buyer Ahmad, Kohgiluyeh and Buyer Ahmad

1967–, Buyer Ahmad, Kohgiluyeh and Buyer Ahmad

MA, public administration

Gholam-Reza

Provincial civil servant (twenty years)

No imprisonment

IRGC militiaman

In 2016, Zare'i moved from the Ministry of Interior to the Ministry of Petroleum while serving as a MP.

Zare'i, Mostafa

Deputy of the Fifth Majlis, Sarvestan, Kavar, and Karbal, Fars (1996–2000)

1959–, Sarvestan, Fars

BA, theology

Ahmad-Qoli

Provincial civil servant

No imprisonment

Zare'i-Qanavati, Lotfollah

Deputy of the Fourth (1992–96) and Fifth (1996–2000) Majlis, Behbahan, Khuzestan

1943–2008, Behbahan, Khuzestan

MA, management

Nasir

No imprisonment

Zare'zadeh-Mehrizi, Dakhil-Abbas

Deputy of the Ninth Majlis, Mehriz, Bafq, Abarkuh, Khatam, and Bahabad, Yazd (2012–16)

1959–, Mehriz, Yazd

Clerical education, Qom Seminary

Clergyman (HI)

No imprisonment

IRGC militiaman

Zargar, Musa

Minister of health in the Revolutionary Council cabinet (November 19, 1979–July 22, 1980); deputy of the First Majlis, Shahriyar, Tehran (1980–84); deputy of the Second (1984–88) and Fifth (1996–2000) Majlis, Tehran, Tehran

1935–, Shahriyar, Tehran

MD, surgery, Tehran University, 1961

Azizollah

Surgeon and university professor

No imprisonment

Not a war veteran

Zargar became the caretaker of the Ministry of Health on November 4, 1979; the next day, Bazargan's cabinet resigned.

Zarghami, Seyyed Ezzatollah

Director-general of IRIB (May 23, 2004–November 8, 2014)

1959–, Tehran, Tehran

BS, civil engineering, Amirkabir University of Technology; MA, management, Islamic Azad University, 1997; thesis title: "The Role of Mid-level

Managers in Strategic Decision Making (Ministry of Culture and Islamic Guidance)"
Father's name unknown, laborer (National Iranian Oil Company)
IRIB official
No imprisonment
War veteran
IRGC militiaman
Zarghami and his sister were involved in the takeover of the American embassy in Tehran. For a while, he was in charge of Shahid Baqeri Industrial Group, which is heavily involved in Iran's missile development program. During his tenure as director of IRIB, the important 2009 presidential debates and the "confessions" of those arrested after the protests were aired. Zarghami is a member of the Supreme Council of Cyberspace. His brother was wounded in the Iran–Iraq War.

Zarhani, Seyyed Ahmad

Deputy of the First Majlis, Dezful, Khuzestan (1980–84)
1953–, Dezful, Khuzestan
BA, Persian literature, Tehran University; MA, cultural affairs management, Islamic Azad University; PhD, business administration, Islamic Azad University
Seyyed Mohammad-Baqer, bazaar tradesman
No imprisonment
Not a war veteran
After leaving the Majlis, Zarhani mainly worked in the educational field, including as educational deputy of the Islamic Schools of Thought Educational and Research Institute (2006–14) and as a member of the board of directors of the Headquarters for Prayer Adduction (1990–2014).

Zaribafan, Mas'ud

VP and head of FMVA in President Ahmadinejad's second cabinet (2009–13)
1957–, Tehran, Tehran
BS, civil engineering

Civil servant
No imprisonment
Not a war veteran
Member of the central council of the Alliance of Veterans of the Islamic Revolution
Massive embezzlement of funds allegedly took place during Zaribafan's tenure at FMVA. The GC disqualified him from running in the 2017 presidential election.

Zarif [-Khonsori], Mohammad-Javad

Permanent representative of Iran to the UN (2002–7); minister of foreign affairs in President Rouhani's first (August 15, 2013–August 13, 2017) and second (August 20, 2017–2021) cabinets
January 8, 1960–, Tehran, Tehran
BA, international relations, San Francisco State University (USA), 1981; MA, international relations, San Francisco State University (USA), 1982; MA, international relations, University of Denver (USA), 1984; PhD, international relations, University of Denver (USA), 1988; dissertation title: "Self-Defense in International Law and Policy"
Father's name unknown, bazaar merchant
Professor and Ministry of Foreign Affairs official
No imprisonment
Not a war veteran
Zarif attended the religiously inspired Alavi School and left Iran in 1976 to complete his high school in the United States. He was Iran's deputy permanent representative to the UN (1989–92), and deputy foreign minister for legal and international affairs (1992–2002). As foreign minister, he was Iran's chief nuclear negotiator with foreign powers from August 17, 2013, to October 18, 2015, bringing the negotiations to a successful resolution.

Zarringol, Morteza

Deputy of the Third Majlis, Sanandaj, Kurdistan (1988–92); deputy of the Fifth Majlis, Bijar, Kurdistan (1996–2000)
1950–, Bijar, Kurdistan

BS, civil engineering
Gholam-Hoseyn
No imprisonment
Zarringol is currently an official of Pars Oil and Gas
   Company.

Zavareh'i, Seyyed Reza

Revolutionary prosecutor-general of Tehran (1979);
   mayor of Tehran (1980); deputy of the First
   (1981–84) and Second (1984–88) Majlis, Tehran,
   Tehran; member of the Third (1995–96) and
   Fourth (1998–2004) Guardian Councils
1939–2005, Varamin, Tehran
BA, law
Seyyed Asghar, farmer
Revolutionary prosecutor of Tehran
No imprisonment
Not a war veteran
Member of the central council of the IRP and CIC/
   PCIC
Zavareh'i became the mayor of Tehran for less
   than a month in 1980. In the third presidential
   election held on October 2, 1981, he received less
   than 1 percent of the vote. Zavareh'i then held
   other posts, such as head of the State Organization for Registration of Deeds and Properties
   and deputy interior minister. He was a member
   of the editorial board of the conservative Resalat.
   In the summer of 1996, he resigned from the
   Third GC to run in the 1997 presidential election
   but received less than 3 percent of the vote. After
   he lost the race, he came back to the Fourth GC
   in 1998.

Zeynali, Seyyed Mohammad-Hoseyn

Deputy of the Fourth Majlis, Birjand, South Khorasan
   (1992–96)
1951–, Birjand, South Khorasan
High school diploma
Seyyed Mohammad-Baqer
Governor of Birjand and Qaenat, South Khorasan
No imprisonment

After serving in the Majlis, Zeynali became active as
   an entrepreneur in the private sector and was in
   charge of the Kavir Tire Company for many years.

Zeynali, Seyyed Shokrollah

Deputy of the First Majlis, Behbahan, Khuzestan
   (1980–84)
1940–, Behbahan, Khuzestan
BA, philosophy
Seyyed Hoseyn, farmer
Academia
No imprisonment

Ziyafat, Aflatun

Deputy of the Third Majlis, representing the Zoroastrian community (as a religious minority)
   (1988–92)
1947–, Yazd, Yazd
BS, agricultural engineering, Karaj Agricultural University; MS, public administration
Mehaban
No imprisonment
Ziyafat was head of the Zoroastrian Society of Tehran.

Ziya'i, Hoseyn-Ali

Deputy of the Third Majlis, Miyandoab and Takab,
   West Azerbaijan (1988–92)
1956–, Miyandoab, West Azerbaijan
BS, electrical engineering
Ali
No imprisonment
After leaving the Majlis, Ziya'i became a director-gen-
   eral in the Central Bank, and after some ten years,
   he became director of the social services adminis-
   tration under President Ahmadinejad.

Ziya'iniya, Seyyed Abdollah

Member of the Assembly for the Final Examination of
   the Constitution, Gilan (1979)
1923–1989, Daryakenar, Gilan

Clerical education; BA, education; PhD, theology,
Tehran University
Seyyed Hoseyn, farmer
Clergyman
Not a war veteran
After finishing his term in the AFEC, Ayatollah
Ziya'iniya returned to Qom and became the
secretary of the management council of Qom
Seminary.

Ziyapur-Razliqqi, Khosrow

Deputy of the Third Majlis, Gonbad-e Kavus, Goles-
tan (1988–92)
1946–, Gonbad-e Kavus, Golestan
MD, general surgery
Surgeon
Yusef
No imprisonment

Zolanvar, Seyyed Hoseyn

Deputy of the Seventh (2004–8), Eighth (2008–12),
and Ninth (2012–16) Majlis, Shiraz, Fars
1948–, Shiraz, Fars
BS, water engineering, Shiraz University, 1979
Seyyed Mohammad, clergyman (ayatollah)
Civil servant, ministries
No imprisonment
Not a war veteran
IRGC militiaman
Zolanvar was previously head of Qom Institute of
Technology, governor of Qom, and deputy direc-
tor of Iran's literacy campaign.

Zolanvar[i], Mojtaba

Deputy of the Tenth Majlis, Qom, Qom (2016–20)
1963–, Malayer, Hamadan
Clerical education, Qom Seminary; BA, English language, Tehran University; MS, defense sciences,
Imam Hoseyn University; pursuing a PhD in
strategic management at the Supreme National
Defense University

Clergyman
No imprisonment
Way veteran (eighty-four months)
IRGC militiaman
HI Zolanvar[i] is a cleric with a solid military back-
ground. He was a founder of the IRGC's Imam
Sadeq's 83 Brigade, comprised of clerics, and
commanded the brigade for twenty-three years.
Zolanvar[i] was also the deputy and chair of the
headquarters representing the supreme leader in
the IRGC (2008–11).

Zolqadr, Mohammad-Baqer

Deputy commander in chief of the IRGC (September
13, 1997–November 23, 2005); deputy chief of the
General Staff of Armed Forces in Basij Affairs
(December 11, 2007–May 23, 2010)
1954–, Shiraz, Fars
BA, economics, Tehran University
War veteran (commander of Ramazan base)
IRGC militiaman
Zolqadr was a member of the paramilitary Mansurron group before the revolution and after the
revolution parted ways with OMIRI over political
differences. Ayatollah Khamenei appointed him
to the post of deputy coordinator of the IRGC
(September 22, 1989–1997). In 1999, while serving
as IRGC's deputy commander in chief, Zolqadr
joined twenty-three other IRGC commanders who sent a threatening letter to President
Khatami urging a crackdown against protesting students. He was deputy interior minister
for security affairs from November 23, 2005 to
December 8, 2007 when he resigned. In 2010,
chief justice Larijani-Amoli appointed Zolqadr as
his deputy for preventing crimes. Zolqadr is on
the United States government list of sanctioned
individuals.

Zolqadr, Seyyed Mostafa

Deputy of the Second (1984–88), Third (1988–92),
and Tenth (2016–20) Majlis, Minab, Hormozgan;

deputy of the Sixth (2001–4) and Eighth (2008–12)
    Majlis, Bandar-e Abbas, Hormozgan
1946–, Minab, Hormozgan
Clerical education
Seyyed Ali, clergyman
Clergyman
No imprisonment
HI Zolqadr went to Najaf, Iraq, in the early 1960s and
    then moved to Kuwait in 1971. He was a deputy
    in the Ministry of Labor and Social Affairs as well
    as Iran's cultural attaché in Libya. He was not
    elected to the Ninth Majlis but served in the Tenth
    Majlis alongside his daughter, Fatemeh, who was
    an MP elected from Tehran.

Zolqadr, Mrs. Seyyedeh Fatemeh

Deputy of the Tenth Majlis, Tehran, Tehran (2016–20)
1970–
Seyyed Mostafa, clergyman (HI)
PhD, Arabic language and literature
Professor at Imam Sadeq and Alzahra universities
No imprisonment
Zolqadr is the daughter of Seyyed Mostafa Zolqadr,
    an MP from Hormozgan.

16

Family Ties of the Iranian Political Elite

To gain a more holistic view of the Iranian political elite, it helps to know something about their family ties. Over half a century ago, a perceptive American scholar wrote: "Nepotism is a strict family obligation in Iran" (Binder 1962, 159). In this section, we have provided a list of such ties for ten prominent clerical families that show how interwoven they are. We then provide a listing of the important family ties between other elites that are listed in the Who is Who section. The kinship ties among cousins, brothers-in-law, nephews, and the like demonstrates how nepotism is rife in the political system of the Islamic Republic of Iran.

Khomeini Family

Khomeini, Seyyed Ruhollah: husband of Khadijeh Saqafi, father of Seyyed Ahmad Khomeini, Seyyed Mostafa Khomeini, Sadiqeh Mostafavi, Farideh Mostafavi, and Zahra Mostafavi, grandfather of Seyyed Hasan Khomeini, Seyyed Yaser Khomeini, Lili Borujerdi, Masih Borujerdi, Na'imeh Eshraqi, Nafiseh Eshraqi, Zahra Eshraqi, Ali Eshraqi, Atefeh Eshraqi, Mohammad-Taqi Eshraqi, and Morteza Eshraqi, great-grandfather of Zahra-Sadat Rouhani, father-in-law of Mahmud Borujerdi, Mohammad-Hasan A'rabi and Shahabeddin Eshraqi

Khomeini, Seyyed Ahmad: son of Seyyed Ruhollah Khomeini, husband of Seyyedeh Fatemeh Tabataba'i, father of Seyyed Hasan Khomeini and Seyyed Yaser Khomeini, son-in-law of Seyyed Mohammad-Baqer Tabataba'i, and brother-in-law of Seyyed Sadeq Tabataba'i and Seyyed Morteza Tabataba'i

Khomeini, Seyyed Hasan: grandson of Seyyed Ruhollah Khomeini, son of Seyyed Ahmad Khomeini, brother of Seyyed Yaser Khomeini, and son-in-law of Seyyed Mohammad Musavi-Bojnurdi

Khomeini, Seyyed Mostafa: son of Ayatollah Ruhollah Khomeini and son-in-law of Morteza Ha'eri-Yazdi

Khomeini, Seyyed Yaser: grandson of Seyyed Ruhollah Khomeini, son of Seyyed Ahmad Khomeini, brother of Seyyed Hasan Khomeini, and son-in-law of Seyyed Mohammad Sadr

A'rabi, Fereshteh: granddaughter of Seyyed Ruhollah Khomeini, daughter of Farideh Mostafavi and Mohammad-Hasan A'rabi, wife of Seyyed Morteza Tabataba'i, mother of Seyyed Emadeddin and Seyyed Hoseyn Tabataba'i

Borujerdi, Lili: granddaughter of Seyyed Ruhollah Khomeini, daughter of Mahmud Borujerdi and Zahra Mostafavi, sister of Masih Borujerdi, wife of Seyyed Abdolhoseyn Tabataba'i, and mother of Seyyedeh Hoda Tabataba'i

Borujerdi, Mahmud: son-in-law of Seyyed Ruhollah Khomeini, husband of Zahra Mostafavi, and father of Masih Borujerdi and Lili Borujerdi, grandfather of Seyyedeh Hoda Tabataba'i

Borujerdi, Masih: grandson of Seyyed Ruhollah Khomeini, son of Mahmud Borujerdi and Zahra Mostafavi, brother of Lili Borujerdi, and son-in-law of Seyyed Abolfazl Mir Mohammadi [-Zarandi]

Eshraqi, Na'imeh: granddaughter of Seyyed Ruhollah Khomeini, daughter of Shahabeddin Eshraqi and Sadiqeh Mostafavi, and daughter-in-law of Seyyed Jalal Taheri-Isfahani

Eshraqi, Shahabeddin: son-in-law of Seyyed Ruhollah Khomeini, husband of Sadiqeh Mostafavi, and father of Na'imeh, Nafiseh, Zahra, Ali, Atefeh, Morteza and Mohammad-Taqi Eshraghi

Hashemi-Rafsanjani, Akbar: grandfather of Emad Hashemi-Bahremani who is the husband of Zahra-Sadat Rouhani

Musavi-Bojnurdi, Seyyed Mohammad: father-in-law of Seyyed Hasan Khomeini

Reza'i, Mohsen: father-in-law of Seyyedeh Hoda Tabataba'i

Rouhani, Zahra-Sadat: great-granddaughter of Seyyed Ruhollah Khomeini, daughter of Nafiseh Eshraqi and Seyyed Kazem Ruhani and wife of Emad Hashemi-Bahremani

Sadr, Seyyed Mohammad: father-in-law of Seyyed Yaser Khomeini

Tabataba'i, Seyyed Abdolhoseyn: son-in-law of Mahmud Borujerdi and Zahra Mostafavi, husband of Lili Borujerdi, brother-in-law of Masih Borujerdi, and father of Seyyedeh Hoda Tabataba'i

Tabataba'i, Seyyed Mohammad-Baqer: father-in-law of Seyyed Ahmad Khomeini, father of Seyyed Abdolhoseyn, Seyyed Sadeq Tabataba'i, Seyyed Morteza Tabataba'i, and Seyyedeh Fatemeh Tabataba'i

Tabataba'i, Seyyed Morteza: brother-in-law of Seyyed Ahmad Khomeini, son of Seyyed Mohammad-Baqer Tabataba'i, brother of Seyyed Sadeq, Seyyed Abdolhoseyn, and Seyyedeh Fatemeh Tabataba'i, and husband of Fereshteh A'rabi

Tabataba'i, Seyyed Sadeq: brother-in-law of Seyyed Ahmad Khomeini, son of Seyyed Mohammad-Baqer Tabataba'i, and brother of Seyyed Morteza, Seyyed Abdolhoseyn, and Seyyedeh Fatemeh Tabataba'i

Tabataba'i, Seyyedeh Fatemeh: daughter of Seyyed Mohammad-Baqer Tabataba'i, sister of Seyyed Abdolhoseyn Tabataba'i, Seyyed Sadeq Tabataba'i, and Seyyed Morteza Tabataba'i, wife of Seyyed Ahmad Khomeini, and cousin of Zohreh Sadeqi (wife of Seyyed Mohammad Khatami)

Tabataba'i, Seyyedeh Hoda: great-granddaughter of Seyyed Ruhollah Khomeini, daughter of Lili Borujerdi and Seyyed Abdolhoseyn Tabataba'i, wife of Ali Reza'i [-Mir Qaed], daughter-in-law of Mohsen Reza'i

Khamenei Family

Khamenei, Seyyed Ali: brother of Seyyed Hadi Khamenei and Seyyed Mohammad Khamenei, father of Seyyed Mojtaba Khamenei and Seyyed Mas'ud

Khamenei, and brother-in-law of Ali-Morad Tehrani (Shaikh Ali Tehrani)

Haddad-Adel, Gholam-Ali: father-in-law of Seyyed Mojtaba Khamenei

Khamenei, Seyyed Hadi: brother of Seyyed Ali Khamenei and Seyyed Mohammad Khamenei

Khamenei, Seyyed Mas'ud: son of Ali Khamenei and son-in-law of Seyyed Mohsen Kharrazi

Khamenei, Seyyed Mohammad: brother of Seyyed Ali Khamenei and Seyyed Hadi Khamenei

Khamenei, Seyyed Mojtaba: son of Ali Khamenei and son-in-law of Gholam-Ali Haddad-Adel

Kharrazi, Seyyed Mohsen: father-in-law of Seyyed Mas'ud Khamenei.

Tehrani, Ali-Morad: brother-in-law of Seyyed Ali Khamenei

Hashemi-Rafsanjani Family

Hashemi-Rafsanjani, Akbar: brother of Mohammad Hashemi-Bahremani, father of Fa'ezeh, Fatemeh, Mohsen, Yaser and Mehdi Hashemi-Bahremani, brother-in-law and cousin of Mohammad Hashemiyan, brother-in-law of Seyyed Hoseyn Mar'ashi, grandfather of Emad Hashemi-Bahremani, uncle of Marjan Hashemi-Bahremani, and cousin of Hoseyn Hashemiyan

Hashemi-Bahremani, Emad: grandson of Akbar Hashemi-Rafsanjani, son of Mohsen Hashemi-Bahremani, and husband of Zahra-Sadat Rouhani

Hashemi-Bahremani, Fa'ezeh: daughter of Akbar Hashemi-Rafsanjani, wife of Hamid Lahuti-Eshkevari, daughter-in-law of Hasan Lahuti-Eshkevari, and niece of Mohammad Hashemi-Bahremani

Hashemi-Bahremani, Marjan: niece of Akbar Hashemi-Rafsanjani and wife of Abolfazl Khansari's nephew

Hashemi-Bahremani, Mohammad: brother of Akbar Hashemi-Rafsanjani, and uncle of Fa'ezeh, Fatemeh, Mohsen, Yaser and Mehdi Hashemi-Bahremani. His daughter-in-law is a granddaughter of both Ayatollah Musavi-Ardabili and Ayatollah Javadi-Amoli.

Hashemiyan, Hoseyn: cousin of Akbar Hashemi-Rafsanjani and brother of Mohammad Hashemiyan

Hashemiyan, Mohammad: cousin and brother-in-law of Akbar Hashemi-Rafsanjani and Mohammad Hashemi-Bahremani, brother of Hoseyn Hashemiyan, and son-in-law of Mohammad-Ali Saduqi

Mar'ashi, Seyyed Hoseyn: brother-in-law of Akbar Hashemi-Rafsanjani

Saduqi, Mohammad-Ali: father-in-law of Mohammad Hashemiyan, and brother-in-law of Seyyed Mohammad Khatami and Seyyed Mohammad-Reza Khatami

Khatami Family

Khatami, Seyyed Ruhollah: father of Seyyed Mohammad Khatami and Seyyed Mohammad-Reza Khatami

Khatami, Seyyed Mohammad: son of Seyyed Ruhollah Khatami, brother of Seyyed Mohammad-Reza Khatami, husband of Zohreh Sadeqi, uncle of Seyyed Mohammad-Reza Tabesh, and brother-in-law of Mohammad-Ali Saduqi

Khatami, Seyyed Mohammad-Reza: son of Seyyed Ruhollah Khatami, brother of Seyyed Mohammad Khatami, brother-in-law of Mohammad-Ali Saduqi, and husband of Zahra Eshraqi. His son married the granddaughter of Seyyed Mohsen Kharrazi, and his daughter married Seyyed Mohammad-Sadeq Kharrazi. Hence, Seyyed Mohammad-Reza Khatami is also related to Seyyed Kamal Kharrazi, the uncle of Seyyed Sadeq.

Sadeqi, Zohreh: wife of Seyyed Mohammad Khatami and cousin of Seyyedeh Fatemeh Tabataba'i

Saduqi, Mohammad-Ali: brother-in-law of Seyyed Mohammad Khatami and Seyyed Mohammad-Reza Khatami, father-in-law of Mohammad Hashemiyan

Tabesh, Mohammad-Reza: nephew of Seyyed Mohammad Khatami and Seyyed Mohammad-Reza Khatami

Larijani Family

Larijani, Ali: son of Hashem Amoli, brother of Sadeq Larijani-Amoli and Mohammad-Javad Larijani, husband of Farideh Motahhari, and son-in-law of Morteza Motahhari.

Larijani, Mohammad-Javad: son of Hashem Amoli and brother of Ali Larijani and Sadeq Larijani-Amoli

Larijani-Amoli, Sadeq: son of Hashem Amoli, brother of Ali Larijani and Mohammad-Javad Larijani

Motahhari, Ali: son of Morteza Motahhari, and brother-in-law of Ali Larijani

Motahhari, Farideh: daughter of Morteza Motahhari, sister of Ali Motahhari, wife of Ali Larijani, and sister-in-law of Sadeq Larijani-Amoli and Mohammad-Javad Larijani

Motahhari, Morteza: father of Ali Motahhari and Farideh Motahhari, and father-in-law of Ali Larijani

Tavakkoli, Ahmad: cousin of Ali Larijani, Mohammad-Javad Larijani, and Sadeq Larijani-Amoli

Montazeri Family

Montazeri, Hoseyn-Ali: father of Mohammad-Ali Montazeri. His son Ahmad is married to Zahra, the daughter of Mohammad-Mehdi Rabbani-Amlashi.

Montazeri, Mohammad-Ali: son of Hoseyn-Ali Montazeri

Hashemi, Seyyed Mehdi: brother of Ayatollah Montazeri's son-in-law

Rabbani-Amlashi, Mohammad-Mehdi: father-in-law of Ahmad Montazeri

Motahhari Family

Motahhari, Morteza: father of Ali Motahhari and Farideh Motahhari, brother of Mohammad-Taqi Motahhari-Farimani, and father-in-law of Ali Larijani

Motahhari, Ali: son of Morteza Motahhari, brother of Farideh Motahhari, nephew of Mohammad-Taqi Motahhari, and brother-in-law of Ali Larijani

Motahhari, Farideh: daughter of Morteza Motahhari, sister of Ali Motahhari, and wife of Ali Larijani

Motahhari, Mohammad-Taqi: brother of Morteza Motahhari and uncle of Ali Motahhari and Farideh Motahhari

Larijani, Ali: son-in-law of Morteza Motahhari, husband of Farideh Motahhari, and brother-in-law of Ali Motahhari

Nateq-Nuri Family

Nateq-Nuri, Abbas-Ali: brother of Ahmad Nateq-Nuri and Ali-Akbar Nateq-Nuri

Nateq-Nuri, Ahmad: brother of Abbas-Ali Nateq-Nuri and Ali-Akbar Nateq-Nuri

Nateq-Nuri, Ali-Akbar: brother of Abbas-Ali Nateq-Nuri and Ahmad Nateq-Nuri, son-in-law of Seyyed Hashem Rasuli-Mahallati, and brother-in-law of Abbas-Ahmad Akhundi and Seyyed Mohammad-Ali Shahidi-Mahallati

Akhundi, Abbas-Ahmad: husband of Seyyed Hashem Rasuli-Mahallati's daughter

Shahidi-Mahallati, Seyyed Mohammad-Ali: husband of Seyyed Hashem Rasuli-Mahallati's daughter and father-in-law of Mohammad-Sa'id, Mohammad-Reza Mahdavi-Kani's son

Dastgheyb Family

Dastgheyb, Seyyed Abdolhoseyn: uncle of Seyyed Ali-Mohammad Dastgheyb, Seyyed Ali-Asghar Dastgheyb, and Gowharoshshari'eh Dastgheyb

Dastgheyb, Gowharoshshari'eh: niece of Seyyed Abdolhoseyn Dastgheyb and mother-in-law of Mostafa Mo'in

Dastgheyb, Seyyed Ahmad-Reza: son of Seyyed Ali-Asghar Dastgheyb and nephew of Seyyed Ali-Mohammad Dastgheyb

Dastgheyb, Seyyed Ali-Asghar: nephew of Seyyed Abdolhoseyn Dastgheyb, brother of Seyyed Ali-Mohammad Dastgheyb, and father of Seyyed Ahmad-Reza Dastgheyb

Dastgheyb, Seyyed Ali-Mohammad: nephew of Seyyed Abdolhoseyn Dastgheyb, brother of Seyyed Ali-Asghar Dastgheyb, and uncle of Seyyed Ahmad-Reza Dastgheyb

Mo'in, Mostafa: son-in-law of Gowharoshshari'eh Dastgheyb

Kharrazi Family

Kharrazi, Seyyed Mohsen: father of Seyyed Mohammad-Sadeq Kharrazi and Seyyed Mohammad-Baqer Kharrazi, brother of Seyyed Kamal Kharrazi, father-in-law of Seyyed Mas'ud Khamenei, and grandfather of Mohammad-Reza Khatami's son-in-law

Kharrazi, Seyyed Kamal: brother of Seyyed Mohsen Kharrazi, husband of Mansureh Ra'is-Qasem, and uncle of Seyyed Mohammad-Sadeq Kharrazi and Mohammad-Baqer Kharrazi

Kharrazi, Seyyed Mohammad-Baqer: son of Seyyed Mohsen Kharrazi, nephew of Seyyed Kamal Kharrazi, brother of Mohammad-Sadeq Kharrazi, and brother-in-law of Seyyed Mas'ud Khamenei

Kharrazi, Seyyed Mohammad-Sadeq: son of Seyyed Mohsen Kharrazi, nephew of Seyyed Kamal Kharrazi and Seyyed Mohammad-Baqer Kharrazi, and father of Mohammad-Reza Khatami's son-in-law; brother-in-law of Seyyed Mas'ud Khamenei

Khamenei, Seyyed Mas'ud: son-in-law of Seyyed Mohsen Kharrazi, brother-in-law of Seyyed Mohammad-Sadeq Kharrazi and Seyyed Mohammad-Baqer Kharrazi

Khatami, Seyyed Mohammad-Reza: father-in-law of Seyyed Mohsen Kharrazi's grandson

Family Ties of Other Elites

Abbaspur-Tehranifard, Ali: brother of Hasan Abbaspur-Tehranifard and brother-in-law of Abdollah Jasbi

Abbaspur-Tehranifard, Hasan: brother of Ali Abbaspur-Tehranifard

Abtahi, Seyyed Mohammad-Ali: nephew of Seyyed Habib Hasheminezhad

Abutorabifard, Seyyed Abbas: father of Seyyed Ali-Akbar Abutorabifard and Seyyed Mohammad-Hasan Abutorabifard

Abutorabifard, Seyyed Ali-Akbar: son of Seyyed Abbas Abutorabifard and brother of Seyyed Mohammad-Hasan Abutorabifard

Abutorabifard, Seyyed Mohammad-Hasan: son of Seyyed Abbas Abutorabifard and brother of Seyyed Ali-Akbar Abutorabifard

Ahadi, Ebrahim: nephew of Ja'far Shojuni

Ahmadi-Danesh-Ashtiyani, Mohammad-Hoseyn: father of Fakhreddin Ahmadi-Danesh-Ashtiyani

Ahmadinejad, Mahmoud: father-in-law of Esfandiyar Rahimmasha'i's daughter

Akhavan-Bitaraf, Nayyereh: wife of Hasan Kamran-Dastjerdi

Akhundi, Abbas-Ahmad: husband of Seyyed Hashem Rasuli-Mahallati's daughter

Alamolhoda, Seyyed Ahmad: father-in-law of Seyyed Ebrahim Ra`isi

Alavi, Seyyed Mahmud: father of Seyyed Mohsen Alavi

Alavi, Seyyed Mohsen: son of Seyyed Mahmud Alavi

Alavi-Hoseyni, Seyyed Mohammad-Hasan: uncle of Seyyed Ali Taheri-Gorgani and brother-in-law of Seyyed Habibollah Taheri-Gorgani

Aliahmadi, Ali-Reza: father-in-law of Mehrdad Bazrpash

Alikhani, Mohammad: son of Qodratollah Alikhani

Alikhani, Qodratollah: father of Mohammad Alikhani

Alizadeh, Ahmad: brother of Mohammad-Reza Alizadeh

Alizadeh, Mohammad-Reza: brother of Ahmad Alizadeh

Amani, Sa'id: father-in-law of Asadollah Badamchiyan, related by brother's marriage to Asadollah Ladjvardi

Angaji, Seyyed Javad: son of Seyyed Mohammad-Ali Angaji

Angaji, Seyyed Mohammad-Ali: father of Seyyed Javad

Aqa Hoseyni-Tabataba'i, Seyyed Hasan: brother of Seyyed Mohammad-Taqi Hoseyni-Tabataba'i

Ardalan, Ali: brother-in-law of Karim Sanjabi

Asgarowladi-Mosalman, Habibollah: brother-in-law of Abolfazl Haji-Heydari

Ava'i, Seyyed Ahmad: brother of Seyyed Ali-Reza Ava'i

Ava'i, Seyyed Ali-Reza: brother of Seyyed Ahmad Ava'i

Badamchiyan, Asadollah: son-in-law of Sa'id Amani-Hamadani

Bahonar, Mohammad-Javad: brother of Mohammad-Reza Bahonar

Bahonar, Mohammad-Reza: brother of Mohammad-Javad Bahonar and father-in-law of Ali-Akbar Mohtashamipur's granddaughter

Baniasadi, Mohammad-Hoseyn: son-in-law of Mehdi Bazargan

Banisadr, Seyyed Abolhasan: brother of Seyyed Fathollah Bani-Sadr and father-in-law of Ali-Reza Nowbari

Banisadr, Seyyed Fathollah: brother of Seyyed Abolhasan Banisadr

Bazargan, Mehdi: father-in-law of Mohammad-Hoseyn Baniasadi and maternal uncle of Ezzatollah Sahabi's wife

Bazrpash, Mehrdad: son-in-law of Ali-Reza Aliahmadi

Beheshti, Seyyed Mohammad: father-in-law of Mohammad-Javad Ezheh'i and husband of Zahra Pishgahifard's maternal aunt.

Dadvar, Khalil: brother-in-law of Seyyed Abufazel Razavi-Ardakani

Damadi, Ezzatollah: father of Mohammad Damadi

Damadi, Mohammad: son of Ezzatollah Damadi

Danesh-Ashtiyani, Gholam-Reza: brother of Ali Danesh-Monfared

Danesh-Ja'fari, Davud: His wife is the cousin of Seyyed Morteza Nabavi.

Daneshju, Farhad: brother of Kamran Daneshju

Daneshju, Kamran: brother of Farhad Daneshju

Danesh-Monfared, Ali: brother of Gholam-Reza Danesh-Ashtiyani

Ebadi, Seyyed Ali-Reza: brother of Seyyed Mehdi Ebadi and father of Seyyed Mohammad-Baqer Ebadi

Ebadi, Seyyed Mehdi: brother of Seyyed Ali-Reza Ebadi and uncle of Seyyed Mohammad-Baqer Ebadi

Ebadi, Seyyed Mohammad-Baqer: son of Seyyed Ali-Reza Ebadi and nephew of Seyyed Mehdi Ebadi

Ebtekar, Ma'sume: daughter-in-law of Seyyed Esma'il Hashemi-Isfahani

Eftekhari, Mohammad-Hoseyn: father of Mohammad-Mehdi Eftekhari

Eftekhari, Mohammad-Mehdi: son of Mohammad-Hoseyn Eftekhari

Ehsanbakhsh, Sadeq: grandfather of Mohammad-Mehdi Mofatteh

Erfani, Seyyed Mojtaba: son of Seyyed Yunes Erfani

Erfani, Seyed Yunes: father of Seyyed Mojtaba Erfani

Estaki, Fereydun: brother of Mojtaba Estaki and Rahman Estaki

Estaki, Mojtaba: brother of Fereydun Estaki and Rahman Estaki

Estaki, Rahman: brother of Mojtaba Estaki and Fereydun Estaki

Ezheh'i, Mohammad-Javad: son-in-law of Mohammad Beheshti

Fayyazbakhsh, Mohammad-Ali: father of Nafiseh Fayyazbakhsh

Fayyazbakhsh, Nafiseh: daughter of Mohammad-Ali Fayyazbakhsh

Fazel-Harandi, Mohyeddin: uncle of Mohammad-Hoseyn Saffar-Harandi

Fazel-Lankarani, Mohammad: father-in-law of Seyyed Kazem Nurmofidi

Haddad-Adel, Gholam-Ali: His daughter is married to Seyyed Mojtaba, the son of Ali Khamanei.

Ha'eri-Yazdi, Morteza: father-in-law of Mostafa, Ayatollah Khomeini's son

Haji-Heydari, Abolfazl: brother-in-law of Habibollah Asgarowladi

Hashemi-Isfahani, Seyyed Esma'il: father-in-law of Ma'sume Ebtekar

Hashemi-Shahrudi, Seyyed Mahmud: His daughter is married to the son of Seyyed Abdolkarim Musavi-Ardabil.

Hasheminezhad, Seyyed Habib: maternal uncle of Seyyed Mohammad-Ali Abtahi

Hezarjaribi, Gholam-Ali: father of Nabi Hezarjaribi

Hezarjaribi, Nabi: son of Gholam-Ali Hezarjaribi

Hoseyni, Seyyedeh Fatemeh: daughter of Seyyed Safdar Hoseyni

Hoseyni, Seyyed Emad: cousin of Seyyed Mas'ud Hoseyni

Hoseyni, Seyyed Mansur: brother of Seyyed Najib Hoseyni

Hoseyni, Seyyed Mas'ud: cousin of Seyyed Emad Hoseyni

Hoseyni, Seyyed Mohammad: related by brothers' marriage to Mohammad Hashemiyan, Akbar Hashemi-Rafsanjani, and Mohammad-Sadeq Khalkhali

Hoseyni, Seyyed Najib: brother of Seyyed Mansur Hoseyni

Hoseyni, Seyyed Safdar: father of Seyyedeh Fatemeh Hoseyni

Hoseyninezhad, Seyyed Akbar: brother of Seyyed Mohammad Hoseyninezhad

Hoseyninezhad, Seyyed Mohammad: brother of Seyyed Akbar Hoseyninezhad

Hoseyni-Shahrudi, Seyyed Abdolhadi: son of Seyyed Mohammad Hoseyni-Shahrudi

Hoseyni-Shahrudi, Seyyed Hasan: brother of Seyyed Hoseyn Hoseyni-Shahrudi

Hoseyni-Shahrudi, Seyyed Hoseyn: brother of Seyyed Hasan Hoseyni-Shahrudi

Hoseyni-Shahrudi, Seyyed Mohammad: father of Seyyed Abdolhadi Hoseyni-Shahrudi

Hoseyni-Tabataba'i, Seyyed Mohammad-Taqi: brother of Seyyed Hasan Aqa Hoseyni-Tabataba'i

Hoseyni-Vae'z, Seyyed Mahmud: son of Seyyed Hoseyn Hoseyni-Vae'z

Hoseyni-Vae'z, Seyyed Hoseyn: father of Seyyed Mahmud Hoseyni-Vae'z

Jabbari, Ahmad: uncle of Naser Sharifi

Jahromi, Seyyed Mohammad: son-in-law of Ali-Akbar Nateq-Nuri

Jannati, Ahmad: father of Ali Jannati

Jannati, Ali: son of Ahmad Jannati

Jasbi, Abdollah: brother-in-law of Ali Abbaspur-Tehranifard

Javadi-Amoli, Abdollah: His daughter is married to the son of Seyyed Abdolkarim Musavi-Ardabili. His granddaughter (daughter of the above marriage) is married to the son of Mohammad Hashemi-Bahremani. Another niece is Fatemeh Va'ez-Javadi.

Kadivar, Jamileh: wife of Seyyed Ataollah Mohajerani

Kalantari, Isa: brother of Musa Kalantari

Kalantari, Musa: brother of Isa Kalantari

Kamran-Dastjerdi, Hasan: husband of Nayyereh Akhavan-Bitaraf

Karami, Mohammad: brother of Mohammad-Mehdi Karami

Karami, Mohammad-Mehdi: brother of Mohammad Karami

Karimi [Kerman], Mohammad-Ali: His wife is the sister of Seyyed Hasan Khoshro.

Karrubi, Fatemeh: wife of Mehdi Karrubi

Karrubi, Mehdi: husband of Fatemeh Karrubi

Katira'i, Morteza: brother of Mostafa Katira'i

Katira'i, Mostafa: brother of Morteza Katira'i

Khalkhali, Mohammad-Sadeq: brother of Ghafur Sadeqi-Givi, brother-in-law of Seyyed Hashem Rasuli-Mahallati, and father-in-law of Asadollah Kiyan-Ersi

Khansari, Abolfazl: His nephew is married to Marjan Hashemi-Bahremani, the niece of Akbar Hashemi-Rafsanjani.

Khaz'ali, Seyyed Abolqasem: father-in-law of Mohammad-Hadi Marvi

Khoshro, Gholam-Ali: father-in-law of Maryam Fereydun (Hassan Rouhani's niece)

Khoshro, Seyyed Hasan: brother-in-law of Mohammad-Ali Karimi [Kerman]

Kiyan-Ersi, Asadollah: son-in-law of Mohammad-Sadeq Khalkhali

Kuchakzadeh, Mehdi: father-in-law of Hoseyn Mozaffar's son

Kuhsari, Gholam-Ali: brother of Ali Kuhsari

Kuhsari, Ali: brother of Gholam-Ali Kuhsari

Ladjvardi, Asadollah: related by sister's marriage to the brother of Sa'id Amani-Hamadani

Lahuti-Eshkevari, Hamid: son of Hasan Lahuti-Eshkevari, husband of Fa'ezeh Hashemi-Bahremani

Lahuti-Eshkevari, Hasan: father of Hamid Lahuti-Eshkevari, father-in-law of Fa'ezeh Hashemi-Bahremani

Mahdavi-Kani, Mohammad-Reza: brother of Mohammad-Baqer Mahdavi-Kani, father of Mohammad-Sa'id Mahdavi-Kani, and father-in-law of Seyyed Mohammad-Ali Shahidi-Mahallati's daughter

Mahdavi-Kani, Mohammad-Baqer: brother of Mohammad-Reza Mahdavi-Kani

Mahluji, Hoseyn: nephew of Seyyed Mehdi Yasrebi

Mahsuli, Sadeq: brother-in-law of Ali-Akbar Velayati

Malakuti, Ali: son of Moslem Malakuti

Malakuti, Moslem: father of Ali Malakuti

Malekhoseyni, Seyyed Keramatollah: father of Seyyed Sharafeddin Malekhoseyni

Malekhoseyni, Seyyed Sharafeddin: son of Seyyed Keramatollah Malekhoseyni

Mar'ashi, Salim: brother of Samad Mar'ashi

Mar'ashi, Samad: brother of Salim Mar'ashi

Marvi, Mohammad-Hadi: son-in-law of Seyyed Abolqasem Khaz'ali

Mesbah-Yazdi, Mohammad-Taqi: father-in-law of Mahmud Mohammadi-Araqi

Meshkini, Ali-Akbar: father-in-law of Mohammad Reyshahri

Milani-Hoseyni, Seyyed Mohammad: brother of Seyyed Mohammad-Reza Milani-Hoseyni

Milani-Hoseyni, Seyyed Mohammad-Reza: brother of Seyyed Mohammad Milani-Hoseyni

Mir Mohammadi [-Zarandi], Seyyed Abolfazl: father of Seyyed Mohammad Mir Mohammadi and father-in-law of Masih Borujerdi

Mir Mohammadi [-Zarandi], Seyyed Mohammad: son of Seyyed Abolfazl Mir Mohammadi

Mofatteh, Mohammad: father of Mohammad-Mehdi Mofatteh

Mofatteh, Mohammad-Mehdi: son of Mohammad Mofatteh and grandson of Sadeq Ehsanbakhsh

Mohajerani, Seyyed Ataollah: husband of Jamileh Kadivar

Mohammadi-Araqi, Mahmud: son-in-law of Mohammad-Taqi Mesbah-Yazdi

Mohseni-Sani, Mohammad-Reza: father-in-law of Abbas Va'ez-Tabasi's son

Mohtashamipur, Seyyed Ali-Akbar: His granddaughter is married to Mohammad-Reza Bahonar's son.

Mo'in, Mostafa: son-in-law of Gowharoshshari'eh Dastgheyb

Mojtahed-Shabestari, Javad: son of Mohsen Mojtahed-Shabestari and nephew of Mohammad Mojtahed-Shabestari

Mojtahed-Shabestari, Mohammad: brother of Mohsen Mojtahed-Shabestari and uncle of Javad Mojtahed-Shabestari

Mojtahed-Shabestari, Mohsen: brother of Mohammad Mojtahed-Shabestari and father of Javad Mojtahed-Shabestari

Mozaffar, Hoseyn: His son is married to the daughter of Mehdi Kuchakzadeh.

Musavi, Mir Hoseyn: His grandmother is Ali Khamenei's paternal aunt. He is also the brother-in-law of Mohammad-Hoseyn Sharifzadegan.

Musavi-Ardabili, Seyyed Abdolkarim: His wife was the sister of General Qasemali Zahirnezhad. One of his sons is married to Seyyed Mahmud Hashemi-Shahrudi's daughter, and another son is married to Abdollah Javadi-Amoli's daughter.

Musavi-Bojnurdi, Seyyed Mohammad: brother of Seyyed Mohammad-Kazem Musavi-Bojnurdi and father-in-law of Seyyed Hasan Khomeini

Musavi-Bojnurdi, Seyyed Mohammad-Kazem: brother of Seyyed Mohammad Musavi-Bojnurdi

Musavi-Ojaq, Seyyed Ayatollah: brother of Seyyed Mojtaba Musavi-Ojaq

Musavi-Ojaq, Seyyed Mojtaba: brother of Seyyed Ayatollah Musavi-Ojaq

Musavi-Tabrizi, Seyyed Hasan: brother of Seyyed Hoseyn Musavi-Tabrizi and Seyyed Mohsen Musavi-Tabrizi

Musavi-Tabrizi, Seyyed Hoseyn: brother of Seyyed Hasan Musavi-Tabrizi and Seyyed Mohsen Musavi-Tabrizi and son-in-law of Hoseyn Nuri-Hamadani.

Musavi-Tabrizi, Seyyed Mohsen: brother of Seyyed Hasan Musavi-Tabrizi and Seyyed Hoseyn Musavi-Tabrizi

Nabavi, Seyyed Morteza: His cousin is the wife of Davud Danesh-Ja'fari.

Namazi, Abdolnnabi: father of Hasan Namazi

Namazi, Hasan: son of Abdolnnabi Namaz

Nejabat, Ahmad: brother of Hoseyn Nejabat

Nejabat, Hoseyn: brother of Ahmad Nejabat

Nowbakht-Haqiqi, Ali: brother of Mohammad-Baqer Nowbakht-Haqiqi

Nowbakht-Haqiqi, Mohammad-Baqer: brother of Ali Nowbakht-Haqiqi

Nowbari, Ali-Reza: son-in-law of Seyyed Abolhasan Banisadr

Nuri, Abdollah: brother of Ali-Reza Nuri

Nuri, Ali-Reza: brother of Abdollah Nuri

Nuri-Hamadani, Hoseyn: father-in-law of Seyyed Hoseyn Musavi-Tabrizi

Nurmofidi, Seyyed Kazem: son-in-law of Mohammad Fazel-Lankarani

Paknezhad, Seyyed Reza: related to Mohammad Saduqi on his father's side

Pirmo'azzen, Kamaleddin: brother of Nureddin Pirmo'azzen

Pirmo'azzen, Nureddin: brother of Kamaleddin Pirmo'azzen

Pishgahifard, Zahra: related to Seyyed Mohammad Beheshti

Qazipur, Nader: son-in-law of Seyyed Hasan Va'ez-Musavi-Anzabi

Qazizadeh-Hashemi, Seyyed Amir-Hoseyn: brother of Seyyed Ehsan Qazizadeh-Hashemi and cousin of Seyyed Hasan Qazizadeh-Hashemi and Seyyed Hoseyn Qazizadeh-Hashemi

Qazizadeh-Hashemi, Seyyed Ehsan: brother of Seyyed Amir-Hoseyn Qazizadeh-Hashemi and cousin of Seyyed Hasan Qazizadeh-Hashemi and Seyyed Hoseyn Qazizadeh-Hashemi

Qazizadeh-Hashemi, Seyyed Hasan: brother of Seyyed Hoseyn Qazizadeh-Hashemi and cousin of Seyyed Ehsan Qazizadeh-Hashemi and Seyyed Amir-Hoseyn Qazizadeh-Hashemi

Qazizadeh-Hashemi, Seyyed Hoseyn: brother of Seyyed Hasan Qazizadeh-Hashemi and cousin of Seyyed Ehsan Qazizadeh-Hashemi and Seyyed Amir-Hoseyn Qazizadeh-Hashemi

Qomi, Mohammad: brother of Mohsen Qomi

Qomi, Mohsen: brother of Mohammad Qomi

Rabbani-Amlashi, Mohammad-Mehdi: father-in-law of Ahmad, Hoseyn-Ali Montazeri's son

Rahimi, Seyyed Fakhreddin: brother of Seyyed Nureddin Rahimi

Rahimi, Seyyed Nureddin: brother of Seyyed Fakhreddin Rahimi

Rahimi-Haji Abadi, Abbas: brother of Gholam-Reza Rahimi-Haji Abadi

Rahimi-Haji Abadi, Gholam-Reza: brother of Abbas Rahimi-Haji Abadi

Rahimmasha'i, Esfandiyar: father-in-law of Mahmoud Ahmadinejad's oldest son

Ra'isi, Seyyed Ebrahim: son-in-law of Seyyed Ahmad Alamolhoda

Raja'i, Mohammad-Ali: husband of Ateqeh Sadiqi

Ramezanpur-Nargesi, Ahmad: brother of Qasem Ramezanpur-Nargesi

Ramezanpur-Nargesi, Qasem: brother of Ahmad Ramezanpur-Nargesi

Rashidi-Kuchi, Habibollah: brother of Jalil Rashidi-Kuchi

Rashidi-Kuchi, Jalil: brother of Habibollah Rashidi-Kuchi

Rasuli-Mahallati, Seyyed Hashem: father-in-law of Ali-Akbar Nateq-Nuri, Seyyed Mohammad-Ali Shahi-di-Mahallati, and Abbas-Ahmad Akhundi. His sister was married to Mohammad-Sadeq Khalkhali.

Razavi-Ardakani, Seyyed Abufazel: brother-in-law of Khalil Dadvar

Reza'i, Mohsen: brother of Omidvar Reza'i and father-in-law of Seyyedeh Hoda Tabataba'i

Reza'i, Omidvar: brother of Mohsen Reza'i

Reyshahri, Mohammad: son-in-law of Ali-Akbar Meshkini

Rouhani, Hassan: uncle of Gholam-Ali Khoshro's daughter-in-law

Sadeqi, Mohammad-Hoseyn: father of Mahmud Sadeqi

Sadeqi, Mahmud: son of Mohammad-Hoseyn Sadeqi

Sadeqi-Givi, Ghafur: brother of Mohammad-Sadeq Khalkhali

Sadiqi, Ateqeh: wife of Mohammad-Ali Raja`i

Saduqi, Mohammad: father of Mohammad-Ali Saduqi. He is also related to Seyyed Reza Paknezhad and Seyyed Mohammad Khatami, and the family of Akbar Hashemi-Rafsanjani.

Saduqi, Mohammad-Ali: father-in-law of Mohammad Hashemiyan and brother-in-law of Seyyed Mohammad Khatami

Saffar-Harandi, Mohammad-Hoseyn: nephew of Mohyeddin Fazel-Harandi

Sahabi, Ezzatollah: son of Yadollah Sahabi. His wife was the niece of Mehdi Bazargan.

Sahabi, Yadollah: father of Ezzatollah Sahabi

Salehi, Ataollah: brother-in-law of Mohammad Shari'atmadari

Sane`i, Hasan: brother of Yusef Sane`i

Sane`i, Yusef: brother of Hasan Sane`i

Sanjabi, Karim: brother-in-law of Ali Ardalan

Sattari, Mansur: father of Sourena Sattari

Sattari, Sourena: son of Mansur Sattari

Sazegarnezhad, Jalil: brother of Mohammad-Amin Sazegarnezhad

Sazegarnezhad, Mohammad-Amin: brother of Jalil Sazegarnezhad

Seyyed Khamushi, Seyyed Ali-Naqi: brother of Seyyed Taqi Seyyed Khamushi

Seyyed Khamushi, Seyyed Taqi: brother of Seyyed Ali-Naqi Seyyed Khamushi

Shahcheraqi, Seyyed Mohammad: uncle of Seyyed Hasan Shahcheraghi

Shahcheraqi, Seyyed Hasan: nephew of Seyyed Mohammad Shahcheraghi

Shahidi-Mahallati, Seyyed Mohammad-Ali: husband of Seyyed Hashem Rasuli-Mahallati's daughter and father-in-law of Mohammad-Sa'id, Mohammad-Reza Mahdavi-Kani's son

Shar'i, Mohammad-Ali: brother of Abdolkarim Shar'i

Shar'i, Abdolkarim: brother of Mohammad-Ali Shar'i

Shari'atmadari, Mohammad: brother-in-law of Seyyed Ataollah Salehi

Sharifi, Naser: nephew of Ahmad Jabbari

Sharifzadegan, Mohammad-Hoseyn: brother-in-law of Mir Hoseyn Musavi

Shoja'ei-Kiyasari, Seyyed Hasan: uncle of Seyyed Ramezan Shoja'ei-Kiyasari

Shoja'ei-Kiyasari, Seyyed Ramezan: nephew of Seyyed Hasan Shoja'ei-Kiyasari

Shojuni, Ja'far: maternal uncle of Ebrahim Ahadi

Tabataba'i, Seyyed Mohammad-Baqer: father of Seyyed Sadeq Tabataba'i and Seyyed Morteza Tabataba'i and father-in-law of Seyyed Ahmad Khomeini

Tabataba'i, Seyyed Morteza: son of Seyyed Mohammad-Baqer Tabataba'i, brother of Seyyed Sadeq Tabataba'i, and brother-in-law of Seyyed Ahmad Khomeini

Tabataba'i, Seyyed Sadeq: son of Seyyed Mohammad-Baqer Tabataba'i, brother of Seyyed Morteza Tabataba'i, brother-in-law of Seyyed Ahmad Khomeini, and cousin of Seyyed Mohammad Khatami's wife

Tabataba'inezhad, Seyyed Abbas: brother of Seyyed Nureddin Tabataba'inezhad and Seyyed Yusef

Tabataba'inezhad and uncle of Seyyed Sadeq Tabataba'inezhad

Tabataba'inezhad, Seyyed Nureddin: brother of Seyyed Abbas Tabataba'inezhad and Seyyed Yusef Tabataba'inezhad and uncle of Seyyed Sadeq Tabataba'inezhad

Tabataba'inezhad, Seyyed Sadeq: son of Seyyed Yusef Tabataba'inezhad and nephew of Seyyed Abbas Tabataba'inezhad and Seyyed Nureddin Tabataba'inezhad

Tabataba'inezhad, Seyyed Yusef: father of Seyyed Sadeq Tabataba'inezhad and brother of Seyyed Nureddin Tabataba'inezhad and Seyyed Abbas Tabataba'inezhad

Tabesh, Mohammad-Reza: nephew of Seyyed Mohammad Khatami and Seyyed Mohammad-Reza Khatami

Taheri, Habibollah: brother-in-law of Seyyed Mohammad-Hasan Alavi-Hoseyni

Taheri-Gorgani, Seyyed Ali: son of Seyyed Habibollah Taheri-Gorgani and nephew of Seyyed Mohammad-Hasan Alavi-Hoseyni

Taheri-Gorgani, Seyyed Habibollah: father of Seyyed Ali Taheri-Gorgani and brother-in-law of Seyyed Mohammad-Hasan Alavi-Hoseyni

Taheri-Isfahani, Seyyed Jalal: father-in-law of Na'imeh Eshraqi

Taheri-Khorramabadi, Seyyed Hasan: father of Seyyed Mojtaba Taheri-Khorramabadi

Taheri-Khorramabadi, Seyyed Mojtaba: son of Seyyed Hasan Taheri-Khorramabadi

Tajgardun, Bahram: cousin of Gholam-Reza Tajgardun

Tajgardun, Gholam-Reza: cousin of Bahram Tajgardun

Taleqani, A'zam: daughter of Seyyed Mahmud Taleqani and sister of Vahideh Taleqani

Taleqani, Seyyed Mahmud: father of A'zam Taleqani and Vahideh Taleqani

Taleqani, Vahideh: daughter of Seyyed Mahmud Taleqani and sister of A'zam Taleqani

Tavassoli, Mohammad: brother-in-law of Ebrahim Yazdi

Tavassoli-Mahallati, Mohammad-Reza: father-in-law of Isa Vela'i

Tayyar, Atrak: father of Qarjeh Teyyar

Tayyar, Qarjeh: son of Atrak Teyyar

Yazdi, Ebrahim: brother-in-law of Mohammad Tavassoli

Va'ezi, Farajollah: father of Mohammad-Taqi Va'ezi

Va'ezi, Mohammad-Taqi: son of Farajollah Va'ezi

Va'ez-Javadi, Fatemeh: niece of Abdollah Javadi-Amoli

Va'ez-Musavi-Anzabi, Seyyed Hasan: father-in-law of Nader Qazipur

Va'ez-Tabasi, Abbas: father-in-law of Mohammad-Reza Mohseni-Sani's daughter

Vela'i, Isa: son-in-law of Ayatollah Mohammad-Reza Tavassoli-Mahallati

Velayati, Ali-Akbar: He and Sadeq Mahsuli married two sisters.

Yasrebi, Seyyed Mehdi: maternal uncle of Hoseyn Mahlujchi

Zahirnezhad, Qasemali: brother-in-law of Ayatollah Seyyed Abdolkarim Musavi-Ardabili

Zolqadr, Seyyed Mostafa: father of Seyyedeh Fatemeh Zolqadr

Zolqadr, Seyyedeh Fatemeh: daughter of Seyyed Mostafa Zolqadr

Glossary

References

Index

Glossary

Allameh: Honorific title given to a great scholar of Islamic sciences.

Astan-e Qods-e Razavi: Located in the city of Mashhad, this shrine, whose title translates as "The Holy Belongings of Imam Reza" or Imam Reza Shrine Foundation, is Iran's holiest shrine. It is visited by millions of Shia people every year. The charity arm of the shrine is a conglomerate that is involved in a wide range of economic activities.

ayatollah: "Sign of God," a title conferred upon a leading Shiite *mojtahed.*

ayatollahelozma: Grand ayatollah.

Baha'is: Adherents of a splinter movement from Shiism led by Baha'ullah (1817–92), who advocated the spiritual unity of mankind and was viewed by his followers as the manifestation of God on earth, considered by many Muslims as apostates.

bonyad: Foundation.

ejtehad: Exercise of independent reasoning in the (re)interpretation of Islamic sources (the Qur'an and the words of the Prophet and imams).

enqelab-e farhangi: Cultural revolution, a campaign which started in 1980 to purge leftist forces from university campuses. It led to the closure of Iranian universities for a couple of years.

faqih **(pl.** *foqaha*)**:** Jurist, an expert in Islamic jurisprudence.

Farmandar: Deputy governor-general.

fatwa: A binding religious edict issued by a qualified *mojtahed.*

Feda'iyan-e Islam (Devotees of Islam): A militant Islamic organization known for carrying out political assassinations in the 1940s and 1950s.

Hojjat al-Islam: "Proof of Islam," a clerical rank immediately below ayatollah.

Hoseyniyyeh-ye Ershad: An important mosque/teaching complex in Tehran.

howzeh: A center of theological learning, seminary.

imam: Spiritual leader, for Ja'fari Shiites one of the twelve infallible heirs to the Prophet descended from Ali.

Khatam al-Anbia: "Seal of the Prophets," name of the IRGC's main engineering firm.

komiteh: A revolutionary committee set up in the early days of the 1979 revolution in each neighborhood and city to provide law and order.

maddah: Panegyrist.

Majlis: The Iranian Parliament.

Majlis-e Khebregan-e Rahbari **(Assembly of Experts):** An assembly of religious experts charged with evaluating the performance of the supreme leader.

Majma'-e Tashkhis-e Maslahat-e Nezam **(Expediency Discernment Assembly):** A council with the mandate to resolve differences between the Majlis and the Guardian Council.

mamosta (Kurdish): A Sunni cleric.

Mansurron: A paramilitary group of Islamic militants that carried out several assassinations before the revolution and whose members came to occupy leadings posts in the IRGC, military, and security apparatuses.

marja'-e taqlid: "Source of emulation," the highest ranking *faqih.*

Marja'iyyat: The Shia principle of emulating a living *mojtahed.*

mojtahed: One who exercises *ejtehad.*

Qasr: Castle; an infamous prison in Iran.

Ruhaniyyat: The religious establishment.

SAVAK (Sazman-e Ettela'at va Amniyat-e Keshvar): The shah's notorious secret police.

Sepah-e Qods **(Qods Force):** A branch of IRGC responsible for foreign operations.

seyyed: A descendant of the Prophet.

Shari'a: The canonical law of Islam.

Showra-ye Enqelab **(Revolutionary Council):** A clandestine revolutionary council appointed by Ayatollah

Khomeini in 1978 to oversee the victory and consolidation of the revolution.

Showra-ye Negahban (Guardian Council): A clerically dominated council that determines who can run in elections and decides whether laws passed by the Majlis are compatible with Islam.

ulema: The collective term for religious leaders.

vali-ye faqih: Postrevolutionary Iran's most powerful political-religious figure who has the authority to overrule or dismiss the president, to appoint members of the Guardian Council and head of the judiciary, and to retain personal representatives in various institutions.

vazir-e sayar: A minister without portfolio.

velayat-e faqih (mandate of the jurist): The doctrine of guardianship of the jurist; popularized by Ayatollah Khomeini.

velayat-e motlaqeh-ye faqih: The absolute mandate of the jurist.

waqf: A religious endowment.

zendan-e Evin: An infamous prison in Tehran.

References

Abazari, Abdorrahim. 1378/1999. *Khaterat-e Haj Shaikh Reza Ostadi* [Memoirs of Haj Shaikh Reza Ostadi]. Tehran: Markaz-e Asnad-e Enqelab-e Islami.

———. 1386/2007. *Khaterat-e Ayatollah Shaikh Morteza Banifazl* [Memoirs of Ayatollah Shaikh Morteza Bani-fazl]. Tehran: Markaz-e Asnad-e Enqelab-e Islami.

Afshar, Haleh. 1985. "The Iranian Theocracy." In *Iran: A Revolution in Turmoil*, edited by Haleh Afshar, 220–43. Houndmills, UK: Macmillan Press.

Ahmadi, Ali. 1383/2004. *Majma'-e Tashkhis-e Maslahat-e Nezam* [Expediency Discernment Assembly of the State]. Tehran: Markaz-e Asnad-e Enqelab-e Islami.

Ahmadi [Miyanji], Ali. 1380/2001. *Khaterat-e Ayatollah Miyanji* [Memoirs of Ayatollah Miyanji]. Tehran: Markaz-e Asnad-e Enqelab-e Islami.

Ahmadipur, Zahra. 1378/1999. "Moruri Bar Tarikhcheh va Seyr-e Tahavvolat-e Taqsimat-e Keshvari dar Iran" [Review of the History and Evolution of Provincial Divisions in Iran]. *Roshd-e Amouzesh Jographia* 50: 27–35.

Akhavi, Shahrough. 1987. "Elite Factionalism in the Islamic Republic of Iran." *Middle East Journal* 41, no. 2 (spring): 181–201.

Akrami, Seyyed Kazem. 1389/2010. *Khaterat-e Seyyed Kazem Akrami* [Memoirs of Seyyed Kazem Akrami]. Tehran: Sureh-e Mehr.

Alamdari, Kazem. 2005. "The Power Structure of the Islamic Republic of Iran: Transition from Populism to Clientelism, and Militarization of the Government." *Third World Quarterly* 26: 407–42.

Alamiyan, Sa'id. 1392/2013. *Baraye Tarikh Miguyim: Khaterat-e Mohsen Rafiqdust 1357–1368* [I Tell This for History's Sake: Memoirs of Mohsen Rafiqdust 1978–1989]. Tehran: Sureh-e Mehr.

Alamuti, Mostafa. 1995. *Bazigaran-e Siyasi Az Mashruti-yyat Ta Sal-e 1357: Sharh-e Hal-e Nayebossaltaneh-ha va Ruzshomar-e Zendegi-ye Nokhost Vaziran-e Iran* [Political Players from the Constitutional Era to 1979: Biographies of Vicegerents and Chronology of the Lives of Iranian Prime Ministers]. London: Paka.

———. 1998. *Namdaran-e Mo'aser-e Iran: Zendegi-nameh-ye Yek Hezar Tan Az Shakhsiyat-haye Irani* [The Contemporary Elite of Iran: Biographies of 1,000 Iranian Figures]. Los Angeles, CA: Nashr-e Ketab.

Ale-'Eshaq, Ali. 1385/2006. *Khaterat-e Ayatollah Ali Ale-'Eshaq* [Memoirs of Ayatollah Ali Ale-'Eshaq]. Tehran: Markaz-e Asnad-e Enqelab-e Islami.

Alviri, Mohsen. 1387/2008. *Khaterat-e Ayatollah Seyyed Ahmad Alamolhoda* [Memoirs of Ayatollah Seyyed Ahmad Alamolhoda]. Tehran: Markaz-e Asnad-e Enqelab-e Islami.

Amir-Entezam, Abbas. 1381/2002. *An Sou-ye Etteham: Khaterat-e Abbas Amir-Entezam* [The Other Side of Accusation: Memoirs of Abbas Amir-Entezam]. Tehran: Ney.

Amiri, Hakimeh. 1386/2007. *Tarikh-e Shafahi-ye Hey'at-haye Mo'talefeh-ye Islami* [Oral History of Confederated Islamic Congregations]. Tehran: Markaz-e Asnad-e Enqelab-e Islami.

Amid-Zanjani, Abbas-Ali. 1379/2000. *Ravayati Az Enqelab-e Islami-ye Iran: Khaterat-e Hojjat al-Islam Valmoslemin Abbas-Ali Amid-Zanjani* [An Account of Iran's Islamic Revolution: Memoirs of Hojjat al-Islam Abbas-Ali Amid-Zanjani]. Tehran: Markaz-e Asnad-e Enqelab-e Islami.

Amjadi, Jalil. 1383/2004. *Tarikh-e Shafahi-ye Goruh-haye Haftganeh-ye Mosalman* [Oral History of Seven Militant Muslim Groups]. Tehran: Markaz-e Asnad-e Enqelab-e Islami.

Ansari, Ali M. 2006. *Confronting Iran: The Failure of American Foreign Policy and the Next Great Crisis in the Middle East*. New York: Basic Books.

———, ed. 2009. *Preliminary Analysis of the Voting Figures in Iran's 2009 Presidential Election*. London: Chatham

House and the Institute of Iranian Studies, Univ. of St. Andrews.

Aqa'i-Jireband, Abbas. 1387/2008. *Majlis-e Showra-ye Islami Dowreh-ye Dovvom* [Second Session of the Islamic Consultative Assembly]. Tehran: Markaz-e Asnad-e Enqelab-e Islami.

Aqa Shaikh Mohammad, Maryam. 1377/1998. *Golzar-e Mashahir: Zendeginameh-ye Dargozashtegan-e Mashahir Iran 1358–1376* [The Rose-Garden of Notables: Biographies of Deceased Notables 1979–1997]. Tehran: Anjoman-e Asar va Mafakher-e Farhangi-ye Iran and Nashr-e Barg-e Zeitun.

Aqeli, Baqer. 1372/1993. *Ruzshomar-e Tarikh-e Iran: Az Mashruteh Ta Enqelab-e Islami* [Chronology of Iran's History: From the Constitutional Revolution to the Islamic Revolution]. 2nd ed. 2 vols. Tehran: Goftar.

Asghari, Yunes. 1378/1999. *Barrasi-ye Tarkib-e Namayandegan-e Majlis-e Showra-ye Islami* [An Analysis of the Composition of MPs in the Islamic Consultative Assembly]. Tehran: Moshtaqan-e Falah.

Assembly for the Final Examination of the Constitution of the Islamic Republic of Iran. 1364–68/1985–89. *Surat-e Mashruh-e Mozakerat-e Majlis-e Barrasi-ye Naha'i-ye Qanun-e Asasi-ye Jomhuri-ye Islami-ye Iran* [Proceedings of the Assembly for the Final Examination of the Constitution of the Islamic Republic of Iran]. 4 vols. Tehran: Idareh-ye kol-e Omur-e Farhangi va Ravabet-e Omumi-ye Majlis-e Showra-ye Islami.

Assembly of Experts for the Leadership. 1379–80/2000–2001. *Khebregan-e Mellat: Sharh-e Hal-e Namayandegan-e Majlis-e Khebregan-e Rahbari* [People's Experts: Biographies of Representatives of the Assembly of Experts]. 3 vols. Tehran: Majlis-e Khebregan-e Rahbari.

Baktiari, Bahman. 1996. *Parliamentary Politics in Revolutionary Iran: The Institutionalization of Factional Politics*. Gainesville, FL: Univ. Press of Florida.

Bamdad, Mehdi. 1978. *Sharh-e Hal-e Rejal-e Iran dar Qarn-e 12, 13, 14 Hejri* [Bibliography of The Iranian Nobilities in 18th, 19th and 20th Centuries]. 6 vols. Tehran: Zavvar.

Bastami, Reza. 1385/2006. *Zendegi va Mobarezat-e Ayatollah Shahid Seyyed Asadollah Madani* [Life and Struggles of Martyr Ayatollah Seyyed Asadollah Madani]. Tehran: Markaz-e Asnad-e Enqelab-e Islami.

Behrooz, Karan. 1999. *Iran Who's Who*. Tehran: Iran Who's Who.

Besharati, Ali-Mohammad. 1383/2004. *Obur Az Shatt-e Shab* [Crossing the River of Night]. Tehran: Markaz-e Asnad-e Enqelab-e Islami.

Best, Heinrich and John Higley. 2010. "Introduction: Democratic Elitism Reappraised." In *Democratic Elitism: New Theoretical and Comparative Perspectives*, edited by Heinrich Best and John Higley, 1–22. Leiden: Brill.

Binder, Leonard. 1962. *Iran: Political Development in a Changing Society*. Los Angeles, CA: Univ. of California Press.

Blaydes, Lisa. 2011. *Elections and Distributive Politics in Mubarak's Egypt*. Cambridge, UK: Cambridge Univ. Press.

Boroujerdi, Mehrzad. 1997. "Khatami's Election: Implications for Iranian Politics," *Middle East Economic Survey* 40, no. 31 (August): D3-D5.

———. 2004. "The Reformist Movement in Iran." In *Oil in the Gulf: Obstacles to Democracy and Development*, edited by Daniel Heradstveit and Helge Hveem, 63–71. London: Ashgate.

Boroujerdi, Mehrzad, and Kourosh Rahimkhani. 2016. "The Office of the Supreme Leader: Epicenter of a Theocracy." In *Power and Change in Iran: Politics of Contention and Conciliation*, edited by Daniel Brumberg and Farideh Farhi, 135–65. Bloomington: Indiana Univ. Press.

Brownlee, Jason. 2007. *Authoritarianism in an Age of Democratization*. Cambridge, UK: Cambridge Univ. Press.

Buchta, Wilfried, 2001. *Who Rules Iran? The Structure of Power in the Islamic Republic*. Washington, DC: Washington Institute for Near East Policy.

Bureau for the Islamic Revolution Literature. 2005. *Farhang-e Namavaran-e Mo'aser Iran* [Encyclopedia of Contemporary Iranian Prominent Figures]. 2 vols. Tehran: Sureh-e Mehr.

Central Intelligence Agency. 1976. *Elites and the Distribution of Power in Iran*. Washington, DC: Directorate of Intelligence.

———. 1985. *Directory of Iranian Officials: A Reference Guide*. Washington, DC: Directorate of Intelligence. Declassified in August 2002.

———. 1987. *Directory of Iranian Clerics: A Reference Aid*. Washington, DC: Directorate of Intelligence. Declassified in part—sanitized copy approved for release on December 15, 2011.

Danesh-Monfared, Ali. 1384/2005. *Khatereat-e Ali Danesh-Monfared* [Memoirs of Ali Danesh-Monfared]. Tehran: Markaz-e Asnad-e Enqelab-e Islami.

Darabi, Ali. 1388/2009. *Jariyanshenasi-ye Siyasi dar Iran* [Political Currents in Contemporary Iran]. 4th ed. Tehran: Sazman-e Entesharat va Pazhuheshgah-e Farhang va Andisheh-ye Islami.

Dastgheyb, Seyyed Ali-Asghar. 1378/1999. *Khaterat-e Ayatollah Seyyed Ali-Asghar Dastgheyb* [Memoirs of Ayatollah Seyyed Ali-Asghar Dastgheyb]. Tehran: Markaz-e Asnad-e Enqelab-e Islami.

———. 1390/2011. *Khaterat-e Ayatollah Seyyed Ali-Asghar Dastgheyb Qabl Az Enqelab* [Memoirs of Ayatollah Seyyed Ali-Asghar Dastgheyb before the Revolution]. Tehran: Markaz-e Asnad-e Enqelab-e Islami.

Do'agu, Mohsen. 1382/2003. *Khaterat-e Hojjat al-Islam Do'agu* [Memoirs of Hojjat al-Islam Do'agu]. Tehran: Markaz-e Asnad-e Enqelab-e Islami.

Esma'ili, Kheyrollah. 1380/2001. *Dowlat-e Movaqqat* [Provisional Government]. Tehran: Markaz-e Asnad-e Enqelab-e Islami.

Fars News Agency, 2008. "Tablighat-e 4476 Namzad-e Vorood be Majlis-e Hashtom Aghaz Shod" [4,476 Candidates for the Parliament Begin Their Campaigns], Mar. 6.

Farzinfar, Laleh. 1390/2011. *Khaterat-e Marhum Seyyed Reza Zavareh'i* [Memoirs of the Late Seyyed Reza Zavareh'i]. Tehran: Markaz-e Asnad-e Enqelab-e Islami.

Fazel-Astarabadi, Mohammad. 1387/2008. *Khaterat-e Hojjat al-Islam Valmoslemin Haj Shaikh Mohammad Fazel-Astarabadi* [Memoirs of Hojjat al-Islam Shaikh Mohammad Fazel-Astarabadi]. Tehran: Markaz-e Asnad-e Enqelab-e Islami.

Fazeli-Birjandi, Mahmud. 1393/2014. *Az Mehdi Bazargan Ta Hasan Rouhani: Kabineh-ha Dar Jomhuri-ye Islami-ye Iran* [From Mehdi Bazargan to Hasan Rouhani: Cabinets in the Islamic Republic of Iran]. Tehran: Payan.

Fuller, Graham E. 1991. *The Center of the Universe: The Geopolitics of Iran*. Boulder, CO: Westview Press.

Gandhi, Jennifer. 2008. *Political Institutions under Dictatorship*. Cambridge, UK: Cambridge Univ. Press.

Geddes, Barbara. 1999. "What Do We Know About Democratization After Twenty Years?" *Annual Review of Political Science* 2, no. 1: 115–44.

Ghafurifard, Hasan. 1387/2008. *Khaterat-e Doktor Hasan Ghafurifard* [Memoirs of Dr. Hasan Ghafurifard]. Tehran: Markaz-e Asnad-e Enqelab-e Islami.

Ghayuri, Seyyed Ali. 1386/2007. *Ayenehdar-e Mehr: Khaterat-e Ayatollah Ghayuri* [Memoirs of Ayatollah Ghayuri]. Tehran: Markaz-e Asnad-e Enqelab-e Islami.

Guardian Council Research Center. 2002. *Majmu'eh-ye Nazariyyat-e Showra-ye Negahban, 1359–1380* [Collection of Guardian Council Opinions]. Tehran: Markaz-e Tahghighat-e Showra-ye Negahban.

———. 1385–91/2006–12. *Majmu'eh-ye Nazariyyat-e Showra-ye Negahban dar Mored-e Mosavvabat-e Majlis-e Showra-ye Islami: Doreh-ye Yek Ta Haftom* [Collection of Guardian Council Opinions on Legislations Passed by the Islamic Consultative Assembly: First to Seventh Terms]. 7 vols. Tehran: Markaz-e Tahghighat-e Showra-ye Negahban and Dadgostar.

Hasani [-Bozorgabad], Gholam-Reza. 1384/2003. *Khaterat-e Hojjat al-Islam Hasani Imam Jom'eh-ye Urmia* [Memoirs of Hojjat al-Islam Hasani the Friday Prayer Leader of Urmia]. Tehran: Markaz-e Asnad-e Enqelab-e Islami.

Hashemi-Rafsanjani, Akbar. 1376/1997. *Dowran-e Mobarezeh* [The Era of Struggle]. 2 vols. Tehran: Daftar-e Nashr-e Ma'aref-e Enqelab.

———. 1378/1999. *Obour Az Bohran: Karnameh va Khaterat-e 1360 Hashemi-Rafsanjani* [Passing through Crisis: Transcript and Memoirs of Hashemi-Rafsanjani in 1981]. Edited by Yaser Hashemi. Tehran: Daftar-e Nashr-e Ma'aref-e Enqelab.

———. 1386/2007. *Beh Sou-ye Sarnevesht: Karnameh va Khaterat-e 1363 Hashemi-Rafsanjani* [Toward Destiny: Transcript and Memoirs of Hashemi-Rafsanjani in 1984]. Edited by Mohsen Hashemi. 4th ed. Tehran: Daftar-e Nashr-e Ma'aref-e Enqelab.

———. 1389/2010. *Defa' va Siyasat: Karnameh va Khaterat-e 1366 Hashemi-Rafsanjani* [Defense and Politics: Transcript and Memoirs of Hashemi-Rafsanjani in 1987]. Edited by Ali-Reza Hashemi. Tehran: Daftar-e Nashr-e Ma'aref-e Enqelab.

———. 1391/2012. *Bazsazi va Sazandegi: Khaterat-e Sal-e 1368 (Hashemi-Rafsanjani)* [Reconstruction and Development: Memoirs of (Hashemi-Rafsanjani) in 1989]. Edited by Ali Lahuti. Tehran: Daftar-e Nashr-e Ma'aref-e Enqelab.

————. 1393/2014. *Sazandegi va Shokufa'i; Karnameh va Khaterat-e 1370 Hashemi-Rafsanjani* [Development and Flourishing: Transcript and Memoirs of Hashemi-Rafsanjani in 1991]. Edited by Emad Hashemi. Tehran: Daftar-e Nashr-e Ma'aref-e Enqelab.

————. 1394/2015. *Ronaq-e Sazandegi: Karnameh va Khaterat-e Hashemi-Rafsanjani Sal-e 1371* [The Momentum of Development: Transcript and Memoirs of Hashemi-Rafsanjani in 1992]. Edited by Hasan Lahuti. Tehran: Daftar-e Nashr-e Ma'aref-e Enqelab.

Hen-Tov, Elliot and Nathan Gonzalez. 2011. "The Militarization of Post-Khomeini Iran: Praetorianism 2.0." *The Washington Quarterly* 34, no. 1: 45–59.

Hojaji, Seyyed Sajjad. 1382/2003. *Khaterat-e Hojjat al-Islam Valmoslemin Haj Seyyed Sajjad Hojaji* [Memoirs of Hojjat al-Islam Seyyed Sajjad Hojaji]. Tehran: Markaz-e Asnad-e Enqelab-e Islami.

Hoseynia, Ahmad. 1384/2005. *Amir-e Khastegi Napazir: Zendeginameh-ye Sarlashgar Shahid Valiyollah Fallahi* [The Indefatigable Commander: Biography of Martyr Major General Valiyollah Fallahi]. 2nd ed. Tehran: Markaz-e Asnad-e Enqelab-e Islami.

Iran Publishing House. 2003. *Who's Who of Iran: An Insider Guide to the Islamic Republic*. London: Iran Publishing House.

Islamic Consultative Assembly. Various years. *Mashruh-e Mozakerat-e Majlis-e Showra-ye Islami* [Proceedings of the Islamic Consultative Assembly]. Tehran: Majlis-e Showra-ye Islami.

————. 1360/1981. *Ashna'i ba Namayandegan-e Majlis-e Showra-ye Islami* [Introducing the MPs of the Islamic Consultative Assembly]. Tehran: Dayerh-ye Tabliqat va Entesharat-e Majlis.

————. 1364/1985. *Negareshi beh Avvalin Dowreh-ye Majlis-e Showra-ye Islami* [A Glance at the First Islamic Consultative Assembly]. Tehran: Dayerh-ye Tablighat va Entesharat-e Majlis.

————. 1392/2013. *Mo'arrefi-ye Namayandegan-e Noh Dowreh-ye Majlis-e Showra-ye Islami* [Introducing the MPs in First through Ninth Islamic Consultative Assembly]. 2nd ed. Tehran: Edareh-ye Kol-e Farhangi va Ravabet-e Omumi-ye Majlis-e Showra-ye Islami.

Jahan-Mohammadi, Reza. 1389/2010. *Majlis-e Showra-ye Islami Doreye Sevvom* [Third Session of the Islamic Consultative Assembly]. Tehran: Markaz-e Asnad-e Enqelab-e Islami.

Jalali-Aziziyan, Hasan. 1382/2003. *Zendeginameh-ye Siyasi-ye Shahid Hasheminezhad* [Biography of Martyr Hasheminezhad]. Tehran: Markaz-e Asnad-e Enqelab-e Islami.

Jami, Gholam-Hoseyn. 1384/2005. *Khaterat-e Hojjat al-Islam Valmoslemin Gholam-Hoseyn Jami* [Memoirs of Hojjat al-Islam Ghomal-Hoseyn Jami]. Tehran: Markaz-e Asnad-e Enqelab-e Islami.

Jannati, Ali. 1381/2002. *Khaterat-e Ali Jannati* [Memoirs of Ali Jannati]. Tehran: Markaz-e Asnad-e Enqelab-e Islami.

Jasbi, Abdollah. 1382/2003. *Az Ghobar Ta Baran: Khaterat-e Doktor Abdollah Jasbi Salha-ye 1323–1342* [From Dust to Rain: Memoirs of Dr. Abdollah Jasbi in Years 1944–1963]. Tehran: Markaz-e Asnad-e Enqelab-e Islami.

Katouzian, Homa. 2010. "The Iranian Revolution at 30: The Dialectic of State and Society." *Middle East Critique* 19, no. 1: 35–53.

Kazemi, Mohsen. 1388/2009. *Khaterat-e Marziyeh Hadidchi-Dabbagh* [Memoirs of Marziyeh Hadidchi-Dabbagh]. 10th ed. Tehran: Soureh-ye Mehr.

Khajehnuri, Ibrahim. 1952. *Bazigaran-e Asr-e Tala'i* [The Players of the Golden Age]. 4 vols. Tehran: Javidan.

Khamenei, Seyyed Mohammad. 1392/2013. *Khaterat-e Ayatollah Seyyed Mohammad Khamenei* [Memoirs of Ayatollah Seyyed Mohammad Khamenei]. Edited by Javad Kamvar-Bakhshayesh and Javad Arabani. Tehran: Markaz-e Asnad-e Enqelab-e Islami.

Khatam-Yazdi, Abbas. 1381/2002. *Khaterat-e Abbas Khatam-Yazdi* [Memoirs of Abbas Khatam-Yazdi]. Tehran: Markaz-e Asnad-e Enqelab-e Islami.

Khaz'ali, Abolqasem. 1382/2003. *Khaterat-e Ayatollah Khaz'ali* [Memoirs of Ayatollah Khaz'ali]. Tehran: Markaz-e Asnad-e Enqelab-e Islami.

Khoda'i, Seyyed Ali-Akbar. 1385/2006. *Resaleh-ye Natamam: Zendeginameh-ye Shahid Doktor Seyyed Reza Paknezhad* [The Unfinished Manuscript: Biography of Martyr Dr. Seyyed Reza Paknezhad]. Tehran: Markaz-e Asnad-e Enqelab-e Islami.

Khomeini, Ruhollah. *Sahifeh-ye Imam Khomeini* [Treatise of Ayatollah Khomeini]. 21 vols. Available at www.imam-khomeini.ir/

Khoshzad, Akbar. 1386/2007. *Majlis-e Showra-ye Islami Dowreh-ye Avval* [First Session of the Islamic Consultative Assembly]. Tehran: Markaz-e Asnad-e Enqelab-e Islami.

Knoke, David. 1993. "Networks of Elite Structure and Decision Making." *Sociological Methods & Research* 22, no. 1: 23–45.

Künkler, Mirjam. 2012. "The Special Court of the Clergy [Dadgah-e Vizheh-ye Ruhaniyat] and the Repression of Dissident Clergy in Iran." In *The Rule of Law, Islam, and Constitutional Politics in Egypt and Iran*, edited by Said Arjomand and Nathan Brown, 57–100. Albany, NY: SUNY Press.

Kurzman, Charles. 2004. *The Unthinkable Revolution in Iran*. Cambridge, MA: Harvard Univ. Press.

Latifi-Pakdeh, Lotfali. 1390/2011. *Jariyanshenasi-ye Hezb-e Mo'talefeh-ye Islami* [Understanding (the History of the) Party of Confederated Islamic Congregations]. Qom: Pazhuheshkadeh-ye Tahqiqat-e Islami.

Limbert, John W. 2008. *Negotiating with the Islamic Republic of Iran*. United States Institute of Peace Special Report, no. 199 (January). Washington: USIP.

Lust-Okar, Ellen. 2006. "Elections under Authoritarianism: Preliminary Lessons from Jordan." *Democratization* 13, no. 3: 456–71.

———. 2009. "Competitive Clientelism in the Middle East." *Journal of Democracy* 20, no. 3: 122–35.

Mahdavi, Paasha. 2015. "Explaining the Oil Advantage: Effects of Natural Resource Wealth on Incumbent Reelection in Iran." *World Politics* 67, no. 2: 226–67.

Mahdavi-Kani, Mohammad-Reza. 1385/2006. *Khaterat-e Ayatollah Mahdavi-Kani* [Memoirs of Ayatollah Mahdavi-Kani]. Tehran: Markaz-e Asnad-e Enqelab-e Islami.

Malakuti, Moslem. 1385/2006. *Khaterat-e Ayatollah Moslem Malakuti* [Memoirs of Ayatollah Moslem Malakuti]. Tehran: Markaz-e Asnad-e Enqelab-e Islami.

Markaz-e Asnad-e Enqelab-e Islami. 1387/2008. *Farhangnameh-ye Nahadha-ye Enqelab-e Islami* [Dictionary of Institutions of the Islamic Revolution]. Tehran: Markaz-e Asnad-e Enqelab-e Islami.

———. 1387/2008. *Khaterat-e Shahid Amir Sepahbod Sayyad-Shirazi* [Memoirs of Martyr Lieutenant General Sayyad-Shirazi]. 4th ed. Tehran: Markaz-e Asnad-e Enqelab-e Islami.

———. 1387–89/2008–10. *Farhangnameh-ye Rejal-e Ruhani-ye Asr-e Imam Khomeini* [Dictionary of Clerical Elites in Imam Khomeini's Era]. 2 vols. Tehran: Markaz-e Asnad-e Enqelab-e Islami.

Marshall, Monty G., Ted Robert Gurr, and Keith Jaggers. 2016. *POLITY™ IV PROJECT, Political Regime Characteristics and Transitions, 1800–2015, Dataset Users' Manual*. Center for Systematic Peace. http://www.systemicpeace.org/.

Ministry of Culture and Islamic Guidance. 1997. *Majmu'eh-ye Mosavvabat-e Majma'-e Tashkhis-e Maslahat-e Nezam, 1367–1376* [Collected Legislation Approved by the Expediency Discernment Assembly of the System, 1988–1997]. Tehran: Moshiri.

Ministry of Interior. *Moshakhkhasat-e Tashakkol-haye Siyasi* [List of Registered Political Groupings]. Tehran: Edareh-ye Kol-e Siyasi-ye Vezarat-e Keshvar.

Mo'adikhah, Abdolmajid. 1382–85/2003–5. *Jam-e Shekasteh: Khaterat-e Hojjat al-Islam Abdolmajid Mo'adikhah* [Broken Chalice: Memoirs of Hojjat al-Islam Abdolmajid Mo'adikhah]. 2 vols. Tehran: Markaz-e Asnad-e Enqelab-e Islami.

Mo'men, Mohammad. 1387/2008. *Khaterat-e Ayatollah Mohammad Mo'men* [Memoirs of Ayatollah Mohammad Mo'men]. Tehran: Markaz-e Asnad-e Enqelab-e Islami.

Montajabniya, Rasul. 1383/2004. *Khaterat-e Hojjat al-Islam Valmoslemin Rasul Montajabniya* [Memoirs of Hojjat al-Islam Rasul Montajabniya]. Tehran: Markaz-e Asnad-e Enqelab-e Islami.

Montazeri, Hoseyn-Ali. 1379/2001. *Matn-e Kamel-e Khaterat-e Ayatollah Hoseyn-Ali Montazeri* [Full Version of Memoirs of Ayatollah Montazeri]. 2nd ed. Sweden, France, and Germany: Ettehad-e Nasherin-e Irani dar Urupa [Baran, Khavaran, Nima].

Moqaddam-Maragheh'i, Rahmatollah. 1386/2007. *Salha-ye Bohrani-ye Nasl-e Ma: Khaterat-e Mohandes Rahmatollah Moqaddam-Maragheh'i* [The Crisis Years of Our Generation: Memoirs of Engineer Rahmatollah Moqaddam-Maragheh'i]. Tehran: Nashr-e Elm.

Moslem, Mehdi. 2002. *Factional Politics in Post-Khomeini Iran*. Syracuse, NY: Syracuse Univ. Press.

Movahhedi-Savoji, Ali. 1381/2002. *Khaterat-e Marhum Hojjat al-Islam Movahhedi-Savoji* [Memoirs of the Late Hojjat al-Islam Movahhedi-Savoji]. 2nd ed. Tehran: Markaz-e Asnad-e Enqelab-e Islami.

Mozaffar, Mohammad-Javad. 1378/1999. *Avvalin Ra'is-e Jomhur* [The First President]. 3rd ed. Tehran: Kavir.

Musavi-Ashan, Mas'ud. 1384/2005. *Zendeginameh-ye Shahid Ayatollah Ali Qoddusi* [The Biography of Martyr Ayatollah Ali Qoddusi]. Tehran: Markaz-e Asnad-e Enqelab-e Islami.

Musavi-Ebadi, Ali-Asghar. 1378/1999. *Shahrdaran-e Tehran Az Asr-e Naseri Ta Dowlat-e Khatami* [Tehran's Mayors from the Mid-Qajar Era to Khatami's Government]. Qom: Khorram.

Musavi-Jazayeri, Seyyed Mohammad-Ali. 1377/1998. *Zendeginameh va Khaterati Az Dowran-e Enqelab-e Islami va Defa'-e Moqaddas* [Biography and Memories of the Eras of Islamic Revolution and Holy Defense]. Ahvaz: Darottahqiq-e Howzeh-ye Elmiyyeh-ye Ahvaz.

Nateq-Nuri, Ali-Akbar. 1384/2005. *Khaterat-e Hojjat al-Islam Valmoslemin Nateq-Nuri* [Memoirs of Hojjat al-Islam Nateq-Nuri]. 2nd ed. 2 vols. Tehran: Markaz-e Asnad-e Enqelab-e Islami.

Nazari, Heydar. 1384/2005. *Khaterat va Mobarezat-e Hojjat al-Islam Valmoslemin Dorri-Najafabadi* [Memoirs and Struggles of Hojjat al-Islam Dorri-Najafabadi]. Tehran: Markaz-e Asnad-e Enqelab-e Islami.

Nejati, Gholam-Reza. 1377/1998. *Shast Sal Khedmat va Moqavemat: Khaterat-e Mohandes Mehdi Bazargan dar Goftogu ba Sarhang Gholam-Reza Nejati* [60 Years of Service and Resistance: Memoirs of Engineer Mehdi Bazargan in Dialogue with Colonel Gholam-Reza Nejati]. 2 vols. Tehran: Mo'asseseh-ye Khadamat-e Farhangi-ye Rasa.

Nikbakht, Rahim. 1384/2005. *Zendegi va Mobarezat-e Ayatollah Shahid Doktor Mohammad Mofatteh* [Life and Struggles of the Martyr Ayatollah Dr. Mohammad Mofatteh]. Tehran: Markaz-e Asnad-e Enqelab-e Islami.

Nowzari, Ezzatollah. 1387/2008. *Tarikh-e Ahzab-e Siyasi dar Iran* [History of Political Parties in Iran]. 2nd ed. Shiraz: Navid-e Shiraz.

Nurmofidi, Seyyed [Mohammad] Kazem. 1385/2006. *Khaterat-e Ayatollah Nurmofidi: Az Tavallod Ta Piruzi-ye Enqelab* [Memoirs of Ayatollah Nurmofidi: From Birth until the Victory of the Revolution]. Tehran: Markaz-e Asnad-e Enqelab-e Islami.

Parsa, Misagh. 1989. *Social Origins of the Iranian Revolution*. New Brunswick: Rutgers Univ. Press.

Perthes, Volker. 2004. "Politics and Elite Change in the Arab World." In *Arab Elites: Negotiating the Politics of Change*, edited by Volker Perthes, 1–32. Boulder, CO: Lynne Rienner.

Peyqambari, Seyyed Mohammad-Hoseyn. 1394/2015. *Negahi Beh Amalkard-e Showra-ye Negahban* [A Look at the Performance of the Guardian Council]. Tehran: Pazhuheshgah-e Showra-ye Negahban.

Purardeshir, Tahereh. 1387/2008. "Gozaresh-e Khaneh-e Mellat Az Naqsh-e Zanan-e Qanungozar dar Keshvar" [Parliament's Report on the Role of Women Lawmakers in Iran]. April 6.

Purhadi, Yadollah. 1382/2003. *Khaterat-e Hojjat al-Islam Purhadi* [Memoirs of Hojjat al-Islam Purhadi]. Tehran: Markaz-e Asnad-e Enqelab-e Islami.

Purqasemi, Puneh. 1384/2005. *Majlis-e Haftom Az Negah-e Amar* [The Seventh Parliament: A Statistical Report]. Tehran: Sazman-e Khabargozari-ye Jomhuri-ye Islami.

Qasempur, Davud. 1388/2009. *Zendegi va Mobarezat-e Ayatollahelozma Seyyed Mahmud Hoseyni-Shahrudi* [Life and Struggles of Grand Ayatollah Seyyed Mahmud Hoseyni-Shahrudi]. Tehran: Markaz-e Asnad-e Enqelab-e Islami.

Qolizadeh-Olyar, Mostafa. 1388/2009. *Khaterat-e Hojjat al-Islam Valmoslemin Shaikh Abdolhamid Bonabi* [Memoirs of Hojjat al-Islam Shaikh Abdolhamid Bonabi]. Tehran: Markaz-e Asnad-e Enqelab-e Islami.

Qoreyshi, Mir Ali-Akbar. 1388/2009. *Khaterat-e Ayatollah Seyyed Ali-Akbar Qoreyshi* [Memoirs of Ayatollah Seyyed Ali-Akbar Qoreyshi]. Tehran: *Markaz-e Asnad-e Enqelab-e Islami*.

Rahnema, Saeed. 2004. "The Left and the Struggle for Democracy in Iran." In *Reformers and Revolutionaries in Modern Iran: New Perspectives on the Iranian Left*, edited by Stephanie Cronin, 250–67. London: Routledge.

Ra'i-Golloudje, Sajjad. 1382/2004. *Zendeginameh-ye Siyasi-e Shahid Raja'i* [The Political Biography of Martyr Raja'i]. Tehran: Markaz-e Asnad-e Enqelab-e Islami.

———. 1387/2008. *Dowlat-haye Shahid Raja'i va Shahid Bahonar va Ayatollah Mahdavi-Kani* [The Governments of Martyr Raja'i, Martyr Bahonar and Ayatollah Mahdavi-Kani]. Tehran: Markaz-e Asnad-e Enqelab-e Islami.

Raji, Mohammad-Mehdi. 1392/2013. *Aqay-e Safir: Goftogu ba Mohammad-Javad Zarif Safir-e Pishin-e Iran dar Sazman-e Melal-e Mottahed* [Mr. Ambassador: Dialogue with Iran's Former Ambassador to the United Nation Mohammad-Javad Zarif]. Tehran: Ney.

Randjbar-Daemi, Siavush. 2013. "Building the Islamic State: The Draft Constitution of 1979 Reconsidered." *Iranian Studies* 46, no. 4: 641–63.

Rasuli-Mahallati, Hashem. 1383/2004. *Khaterat-e Ayatollah Seyyed Hashem Rasuli-Mahallati* [Memoirs of Ayatollah Seyyed Hashem Rasuli-Mahallati]. Tehran: Markaz-e Asnad-e Enqelab-e Islami.

Razavi-Ardakani, Seyyed Abufazel. 1385/2006. *Khaterat-e Seyyed Abufazel Razavi-Ardakani* [Memoirs of

Seyyed Abufazel Razavi-Ardakani]. Tehran: Markaz-e Asnad-e Enqelab-e Islami.

Reyshahri [Mohammadinik], Mohammad. 1383/2004. *Khaterat-e Siyasi-ye Mohammadi Reyshahri* [Political Memoirs of Mohammad Mohammadi Reyshahri]. 3 vols. Tehran: Markaz-e Asnad-e Enqelab-e Islami.

Rouhani, Hassan. 1387/2008. *Khaterat-e Doktor Hassan Rouhani* [Memoirs of Dr. Hassan Rouhani]. Vol. 1. Tehran: Markaz-e Asnad-e Enqelab-e Islami.

Roy, Oliver. 1999. "The Crisis of Religious Legitimacy in Iran." *Middle East Journal* 53, no. 2: 201–16.

Saberi, Kiyumars. 1380/2001. *Mokatebat-e Raja'i ba Banisadr* [The Raja'i-Banisadr Correspondences]. Tehran: Vezarat-e Farhang va Ershad-e Islami.

Saberi-Hamadani, Ahmad. 1383/2004. *Khaterat-e Ayatollah Ahmad Saberi-Hamadani* [Memoirs of Ayatollah Ahmad Saberi-Hamadani]. Tehran: Markaz-e Asnad-e Enqelab-e Islami.

Sadeghi-Boroujerdi, Eskandar. 2017. "The Origins of Communist Unity: Anti-Colonialism and Revolution in Iran's Tri-Continental Moment." *British Journal of Middle Eastern Studies*. DOI: 10.1080/13530194.2017.1354967.

Sahabi, Ezzatollah. 1383/2004. *Nagofteha-ye Enqelab va Mabahes-e Bonyadi-ye Melli* [The Unspoken Facts of the Revolution and Fundamental National Discussions]. Tehran: Gam-e Now.

Sa'eli-Kordehdeh, Majid. 1384/2005. *Showra-ye Enqelab-e Islami-ye Iran* [The Islamic Revolutionary Council of Iran]. Tehran: Markaz-e Asnad-e Enqelab-e Islami.

Sa'idi, Mehdi. 1385/2006. *Sazman-e Mojahedin-e Enqelab-e Islami Az Ta'sis Ta Enhelal, 1356–1358* [Organization of Mojahedin of the Islamic Revolution of Iran from Formation until Dissolution, 1977–1979]. Tehran: Markaz-e Asnad-e Enqelab-e Islami.

Salek [-Kashani], Ahmad. 1385/2006. *Khaterat-e Hojjat al-Islam Shaikh Ahmad Salek* [Memoirs of Hojjat al-Islam Shaikh Ahmad Salek]. Tehran: Markaz-e Asnad-e Enqelab-e Islami.

Sanandaji, Kaveh-Cyrus. 2009. "The Eighth Majlis Elections in the Islamic Republic of Iran: A Division in Conservative Ranks and the Politics of Moderation." *Iranian Studies* 42, no. 4: 621–48.

Sanjabi, Karim. 1381/2002. *Khaterat-e Siyasi-ye Doktor Karim Sanjabi* [Political Memoirs of Dr. Karim Sanjabi]. Tehran: Seda-ye Mo'aser.

San'ati, Reza. 1387/2008. *Gofteman-e Mesbah: Gozareshi Az Zendegani-ye Elmi va Siyasi-ye Ayatollah Mesbah-Yazdi* [Mesbah's Discourse: A Report on the Scientific and Political Life of Ayatollah Mesbah-Yazdi]. Tehran: Markaz-e Asnad-e Enqelab-e Islami.

———. 1393/2014. *Hashemi dar Sal 88: Gozaresh-e Mavaze' Ayatollah Hashemi-Rafsanjani* [Hashemi-Rafsanjani in the Year 2009: A Report on Ayatollah Hashemi-Rafsanjani's Positions]. 3rd ed. Qom: Salman-e Farsi.

Schattsneider, Elmer E. 1960. *The Semisovereign People: A Realist's View of Democracy in America*. New York: Holt, Rinehart and Winston.

Schirazi, Asghar. 1997. *The Constitution of Iran: Politics and the State in the Islamic Republic*. London: I. B. Tauris.

Setad-e Entekhabat-e Keshvar. 1378/1999. *Showra-ha: Ancheh Gozasht: Majmu'eh-ye Mokatebat-e Setad-e Entekhabat-e Keshvar va Hey'at-e Markazi-ye Nezarat bar Entekhabat-e Showra-haye Islami* [What Happened in the Municipal Councils: Compilation of Correspondences Between the (Interior Ministry's) Election Headquarters and the Central Council Overseeing Islamic Municipal Council Elections]. Tehran: Hamshahri.

Shadlu, Abbas. 1388/2009. *Enqelab-e Islami Az Piruzi Ta Tahkim: Nagofteha-ye Tarikhi Az Dowlat-e Movaqqat Ta Soqut-e Banisadr, 1357–1360* [The Islamic Revolution from Victory to Consolidation: Unspoken Historical Facts from the Provisional Government to the Downfall of Banisadr, 1978–1981]. Tehran: Vozara.

———. 1392/2013. *Ettela'at Dar Bareh-ye Ahzab va Jenah-haye Siyasi-ye Iran-e Emruz* [Information on Political Parties and Factions in Today's Iran]. 2nd ed. Tehran: Vozara.

Shaji'i, Zahra. 1375/1996. *Naqsh-e Namayandegan dar Majalis-e Qanun-gozari-ye Asr-e Mashrutiyyat* [Role of MPs in the Parliaments of the Constitutional Era]. 3 vols. Tehran: Sokhan.

———. 1383/2004. *Nokhbegan-e Siyasi-ye Iran: Az Enqelab-e Mashrutiyyat Ta Enqelab-e Islami* [Iran's Political Elite: From the Constitutional Revolution to the Islamic Revolution]. 4 vols. Tehran: Sokhan.

Shojuni, Ja'far. 1381/2002. *Khaterat-e Hojjat al-Islam Ja'far Shojuni* [Memoirs of Hojjat al-Islam Ja'far Shojuni]. Tehran: Markaz-e Asnad-e Enqelab-e Islami.

Statistical Center of Iran. 1392/2013–14. *Salnameh-ye Amari-ye Keshvar 1392* [Statistical Yearbook of Iran 2013]. Tehran: Sazman-e Amar-e Iran.

————. 1393/2014–15. *Salnameh-ye Amari-ye Keshvar 1393* [Statistical Yearbook of Iran 2014]. Tehran: Sazman-e Amar-e Iran.

————. 1394/2015–16. *Salnameh-ye Amari-ye Keshvar 1394* [Statistical Yearbook of Iran 2015]. Tehran: Sazman-e Amar-e Iran.

Svolik, Milan W. 2012. *The Politics of Authoritarian Rule.* Cambridge, UK: Cambridge Univ. Press.

Taheri-Khorramabadi, Hasan. 1377–84/1998–2005. *Khaterat-e Ayatollah Taheri-Khorramabadi: Az Tab'id-e Imam Ta Piruzi-ye Enqelab-e Islami* [Memoirs of Ayatollah Taheri-Khorramabadi: From Imam (Khomeini's) Exile until the Victory of the Islamic Revolution]. 2 vols. Tehran: Markaz-e Asnad-e Enqelab-e Islami.

Takeyh, Ray. 2006. *Hidden Iran: Paradox and Power in the Islamic Republic.* New York: Times Books.

Tavakkoli, Ahmad. 1384/2005. *Khaterat-e Ahmad Tavakkoli: 1330–1360* [Memoirs of Ahmad Tavakkoli: 1951–1981]. Tehran: Markaz-e Asnad-e Enqelab-e Islami.

Tehranizadeh, Mohsen. 1373/1994a. *Fehrest-e Asami va Moshakhkhasat-e Ostadan va Daneshyaran-e Keshvar* [List of Names and Information of Iranian University Professors]. Tehran: Daftar-e Showra-ye Jazb-e Nokhbegan.

————. 1373/1994b. *Sharh-e Hal-e Takhassosi-ye Ostadan va Daneshyaran-e Keshvar* [Technical Biographies of Iranian Professors]. 3 vols. Tehran: Daftar-e Showra-ye Jazb-e Nokhbegan.

Teiri-qazi, Fatemeh and Rooznegar Publishing Research Bureau. 1380/2001. *Estizah dar Nezam-e Siyasi-e Iran* [Impeachment in Iran's Political System]. 2 vols. Tehran: Rooznegar.

Vahid-Qolfi, Mohammad. 1384/2005. *Majlis-e Khebregan va Hokumat-e Dini dar Iran* [Assembly of Experts and Islamic Government in Iran]. Tehran: Mo'asseseh-ye Chap va Nashr-e Orouj.

Vaziri, Nasrin. 1394/2015. *Bazigaran va Bazigardanan-e Majlis: Namayandegan-e Paytakht dar Parlemen-e Iran* [Parliament Players and Play Masters: Tehran's Representatives in the Iranian Parliament]. Tehran: Samadiyyeh.

Yazdi, Mohammad. 1380/2001. *Khaterat-e Ayatollah Mohammad Yazdi* [Memoirs of Ayatollah Mohammad Yazdi]. Tehran: Markaz-e Asnad-e Enqelab-e Islami.

Zakariya'i-Azizi, Hoseyn. 1386/2007. *Shagerd-e Avval: Zendegi va Mobarezat-e Shahid Doktor Mahmud Qandi* [The Top Student: Life and Struggles of Martyr Dr. Mahmud Qandi]. Tehran: Markaz-e Asnad-e Enqelab-e Islami.

Zonis, Marvin. 1971. *The Political Elite of Iran.* Princeton, NJ: Princeton Univ. Press.

Encyclopedias

Daneshnameh-ye Daneshgostar [Daneshgostar Encylopedia]. 1389/2010. 18 vols. Tehran: Daneshgostar Foundation.

Encyclopædia Iranica. Various volumes and website (http://www.iranicaonline.org/). New York: Columbia Univ.

Newspapers and Magazines

Andisheh-ye Puya

Arman-e Mellat

Ayandegan

Enqelab-e Islami

E'temad

Ettela'at

Haft-e-Sobh

Hayat-e Now

Hamshahri

Iran

Jame'eh

Jame'eh-ye Farda

Jomhuri-ye Islami

Keyhan

Mehrnameh

Mizan

Resalat

Ruznameh-ye Rasmi-ye Mozakerat-e Majlis

Salam

Shahrvand-Emruz

Tejarat-e Farda

Websites Consulted

The following websites were consulted while gathering research for the book.

http://81.91.157.27

http://www.aftabir.com

http://www.akhbar-rooz.com

http://alef.ir

http://www.asriran.com

http://www.bbc.com

http://www.bbc.com/persian
http://www.behdasht.gov.ir
http://www.cbi.ir/simplelist/1600.aspx
http://chehreha.iribtv.ir
http://www.dadsetani.ir/
http://www.darsahn.org/
http://www.digarban.com/
http://donya-e-eqtesad.com/
http://ethos.bl.uk
http://www.ettelaat.com/
http://eur-lex.europa.eu/legal-content/EN/TXT
    /?uri=CELEX%3A32011D0670
http://eur-lex.europa.eu/eli/reg/2011/359/2014-04-12
http://fararu.com
http://farsi.khamenei.ir
http://farsi.rouhollah.ir
http://www.farhang.gov.ir
http://www.farsnews.com
http://www.hamshahrionline.ir
http://hashemirafsanjani.ir
http://www.hawzah.net
www.historydocuments.ir
http://hamshahrionline.ir
http://ical.ir
http://www.ilna.ir/
http://www.imam-khomeini.ir
http://irandataportal.syr.edu
http://iran-newspaper.com
http://www.iran-resist.org
http://www.irc.ir
http://www.irdc.ir
http://www.irinn.ir/
http://www.irna.ir
http://www.isna.ir
https://isetad.ir/
http://www.jahannews.com
http://jameehmodarresin.org
http://kadivar.com
http://www.khabaronline.ir
http://www.khamenei.ir
http://www.leader.ir/fa
http://www.majlis.ir
http://www.majlesekhobregan.ir
https://www.mashreghnews.ir/
http://mehrkhane.com/
http://www.mehrnews.com

http://www.mizanonline.ir
http://www.moi.ir
http://www.mojehozoor.com
http://navideshahed.com/fa
http://nbo.ir
https://www.radiofarda.com
http://rc.majlis.ir/fa
http://www.parliran.ir
http://www.parsine.com/
http://www.payvand.com/calendar
http://www.president.ir
https://www.radiozamaneh.com
http://rasekhoon.net
http://rch.ac.ir
http://rc.majlis.ir
http://revolution.pchi.ir
http://www.rijaldb.com
http://www.rohaniatmobarez.ir
http://www.shahrara.com
http://sharghdaily.ir
http://www.shora-gc.ir
http://shora-tehran.ir
http://www.sociran.net
http://www.sunnidaily.net
http://tabnak.ir
http://talar.dadparvar.ir
http://tarikhirani.ir
https://www.tasnimnews.com
http://www.tebyan.net
http://www.theses.fr
http://thinker.irc.ir
https://www.treasury.gov

Other Sources

Reports produced by the Islamic Majlis Research Center.
Personal webpages, blogs, Facebook pages, email exchanges, and interviews.

Index

Italic page number denotes illustration or table.

Kuchaki-Borujeni, Mansur-Mirza, 562

Kuchakinezhad-Eramsadati, Jabar, 562

Kuchakzadeh, Mehdi, 562, 802

Kuhi-Baghanari, Nasrollah, 562

Kuhkan-Rizi, Mohsen, 562–63

Kuhsari, Ali, 563, 802

Kuhsari, Gholam-Ali, 563, 802

Kula'i, Elaheh, 563

Kurd, Ali, 563

Kurd, Baqer, 563

Kurdistan, 8, 15; Association for Defense of the People of Kurdistan, 331; Coordinating Council of the Societies of Kurdistan, 333; Kurdistan Autonomy Council, 334; Kurdistan Democratic Party-Followers of the Fourth Congress, 334; Kurdistan National Union, 343; Moftizadeh and, 342; Organization of National-Islamic Struggle of Kurdistan Province, 344; Toilers Revolutionary Party of Iranian Kurdistan, 339

Kurdistan Democratic Party of Iran (KDPI), 8, 9, 22, 24, 334

Kurdmandani, Khodabakhsh, 563

Kuwait, 23

Kuzehgar, Mohammad-Ali, 563–64

labor, 108, 127, 135, 137; Center for Coordination of Workers' Syndicates of Iran, 331; Freedom of Labor Group, 333; House of the Worker, 308; Islamic Assembly of Bank Employees, 309; Islamic Assembly of [Public Sector] Employees Following Imam's Line, 310; Islamic Association of Workers in Khorasan, 313; Islamic Labor Party, 313–14; Islamic Party of Workers' Welfare, 314; Islamic Society of Employees, 315; Islamic Society of Workers, 317; Labor Group, 334; Labor's Role Group, 334; Organization Struggling to Establish an Independent Labor Movement, 337

Ladjvardi, Asadollah, 26, 564, 802

Lahuti-Eshkevari, Hamid, 797

Lahuti-Eshkevari, Hasan, 564, 797, 802

Laingen, Bruce, 10

land ownership, 13

Larijani, Ali, 60, 564–65, 798

Larijani, Mohammad-Javad, 565, 798

Larijani-Amoli, Sadeq, 565, 798

Larijani family, 798

Latifiyan, Hedayat, 565–66

law: Association of Advocates of Law and Order, 303; Islamic Bar Association, 313; Islamic Society of Alumni of Legal Studies, 314; Legal Affairs, 142; Legal Jurist Guardian Council members, 56–57; on press, 28; Shari'a, 809

Law Enforcement Forces (LEF), 34n6; Chief of, 75; Deputy Chief of, 75; officials appointed to, 47

Lebanon, 17, 19, 25

LEF. See Law Enforcement Forces

Left Unity Organization, 334

Legal Affairs, 142

Legal Jurist Guardian Council members, 56–57

legislation, 58

Liberal Union, 343

Liberation Movement of Iran (LMI), 4, 25, 343

Liberation Party, 318

Libya, 25

Life Association, 318

Limbert, John, xvii

LMI. See Liberation Movement of Iran

Loqmaniyan, Hoseyn, 566

Lorestan Free Thinkers Association, 318

Lorestan Province, 310, 312

Lotfi, Hasan, 566

Lotfi, Mohammad-Taqi, 566

Lotfi-Ashtiyani, Seyyed Ahmad, 566

Madadi, Mohammad-Ali, 566

Madani, Seyyed Ahmad, 566–67

Madani-Bajestani, Seyyed Mahmud, 567

Madani-Dehkharqani, Mir Asadollah, 567

Madani-Kermani, Seyyed Jalaleddin, 567

maddah, 809

Maddahi, Mohammad-Ebrahim, 567

Mafi, Parvaneh, 567–68

Mahabad region, 333

Mahallati, Fazlollah, 568

Mahallati, Mohammad-Ja'far (Amir), 568

Mahbudi, Borzu, 568

Mahdavi, Seyyed Abolhasan, 568

Mahdavi-Abhari, Ahmad, 568–69

Mahdavi Haji, Mehdi, 568

Mahdavi-Kani, Mohammad-Reza, 9, 16–17, 31, 802; cabinet of, 106, 114–15, 146; overview of, 569

Mahdavi-Kani [Baqeri-Kani], Mohammad-Baqer, 569–70, 802

Mahdavi-Khanaki, Seyyed Mohammad-Baqer, 570

Mahdi (Vali-ye Asr) Society, 328

Mahestan Society, 318

Mahfuzi, Abbas, 570

Mahjub, Ali-Reza, 570

Mahlujchi [Mahluji], Hoseyn, 570, 802

Mahmudi, Morteza, 570–71

Mahmudi, Somayeh, 571

Mahmudi-Golpayegani, Seyyed Abutaleb, 571

Mahmudi-Sartangi, Seyyed Shahab, 571

Mahmudi-Shahneshin, Mohammad, 571

Mahmudiyan, Seyyed Nurmohammad, 571

Mahmud-Robati, Ahmad, 571

Mahmudzadeh, Jalal, 571–72

Mahsuli, Sadeq, 572, 802

Main Center of Councils of Turkoman Sahra, 334

Majdara, Mohammad, 572

Majidi, Mohammad-Reza, 572

Majlis (Iranian Parliament), xix, 18, 20–31, 809; age profile of deputies, 44; cabinet ministers impeached by, 158–59; deputies, in First Majlis (1980–84), 186–94; deputies, in Second Majlis (1984–88), 194–200; deputies, in Third Majlis (1988–92), 200–7; deputies, in Fourth Majlis (1992–96), 207–13; deputies, in Fifth Majlis (1996–2000), 213–20; deputies, in Sixth Majlis (2000–2004), 220–27; deputies, in Seventh Majlis (2004–8), 227–34; deputies, in Eighth Majlis (2008–12), 234–41; deputies, in Ninth Majlis (2012–16), 242–49; deputies, in Tenth Majlis (2016–20), 249–56; deputies representing religious minorities, 262; electoral districts, 168–73; fathers' professions of, 257; imprisoned deputies, before 1979, 42; incumbency rates for, 186; number of legislations

Experts seat distribution by, 272–73; Azerbaijan Province, 76; Bakhtaran Province, 76; Bushehr Province, 303, 320; explanatory note on, 76; Fars Province, 309; Gilan Province, 76, 302, 309, 323–24, 325; Golestan Province, 76, 302; gross income for urban households in, 78; Hormozgan Province, 300; Ilam Province, 327; Isfahan Province, 310, 312; Kerman Province, 306, 309, 321; Kermanshah Province, 307, 326; Khorasan Province, 76, 305, 315, 326; Khuzestan Province, 320, 327–28; Lorestan Province, 310, 312; Markazi Province, 76, 305, 317; Mazandaran Province, 76; North Khorasan Province, 76; number of female candidates in municipal council elections, by province, 292; number of male candidates in municipal council elections, by province, 291; number of rural and urban municipal councils in each province, in 2003 and 2013, 288–89; number of seats allocated to each, in Majlis 1980–2020, 167–68; number of total candidates elected in municipal councils, by province, 289–90; Qazvin Province, 76, 302, 326; Qom Province, 76, 301–2, 306, 311; Razavi Khorasan Province, 76, 303; South Khorasan Province, 76; Tehran Province, 68, 69, 298, 303, 310, 317, 319, 320, 325, 326; by territorial size and population percentage, 2016, 77; votes based on, in Assembly of Experts election of 1982, 265; votes based on, in Assembly of Experts election of 1990, 266; votes based on, in Assembly of Experts election of 1998, 267; votes based on, in Assembly of Experts election of 2006, 268; votes based on, in Assembly of Experts election of 2016, 269; votes based on, in presidential election of 1980, 85–86; votes based on, in presidential election of 1985, 88–89; votes based on, in presidential election of 1997, 91–92; votes based on, in presidential election of 2001, 93–95; votes based on, in presidential election of 2005,

96, 97–98; votes based on, in presidential election of 2009, 99; votes based on, in presidential election of 2013, 101; votes based on, in presidential election of 2017, 102–3; Zanjan Province, 76, 300, 326

Public Health Organization, 109, 139

public prosecutor-general, of Tehran, 68

Pudineh, Mohammad-Hoseyn, 664

Puladi, Shapur, 664–65

Purbafrani, Abbas-Ali, 665

Purdastan, Ahmad-Reza, 665

Purebrahimi-Davarani, Mohammad-Reza, 665

Purfatemi, Seyyed Mohammad-Mehdi, 665

Purgol, Mohammad-Mehdi, 665

Purhoseyn-Shaqlan, Shakur, 665–66

Purjazayeri, Samir, 666

Purmohammadi, Mohammad-Taqi, 666

Purmohammadi, Mostafa, 666

Purmohammadi-Fallah, Ali, 666

Purmokhtar, Mohammad-Ali, 666–67

Purnejati, Ahmad, 667

Purostad, Ali-Akbar, 667

Purqorban, Khan Ali, 667

Pursalari, Hoseyn, 667

Purshasb, Abdolali, 667

Purzaman, Rasul, 667

Puyandeh, Mohammad-Ja'far, 26

Qaderi, Ja'far, 667–68

Qaderi, Mohammad-Rauf, 668

Qaderi, Mostafa, 668

Qadermarzi, Hamed, 668

Qadiri, Mohammad-Hasan, 668

al-Qaeda, 28

Qa'edrahmat, Abbas, 668

Qaemi-Amiri, Ali, 668

Qaemifar [Mollay-e Semnani], Mehdi, 669

Qahremani, Mohammad-Mehdi, 669

Qalibaf, Mohammad-Baqer, 309, 669

Qamari, Daryush, 669

Qanbari-Adivi, Ali, 669

Qanbari-Maman, Jamshid, 669–70

Qanbari-Qazikolahi, Abdolali, 670

Qandehari, Qorbanali, 670

Qandi, Mahmud, 670

Qarani, Valiyollah, 7, 8–9, 670

Qarayi-Ashtiyani, Mohammad-Reza, 671

Qarhekhani-Alustani, Asadollah, 671

Qasemi, Abdolvahhab, 671

Qasemi, Fereydun, 671

Qasemi, Khodanazar, 671

Qasemi, Majid, 671

Qasemi, Rostam, 671–72

Qasemi[pur], Abdollah, 672

Qasemi-Golak, Yusef, 672

Qasemlu, Abdorrahman, 22, 334

Qasempur, Samad, 672

Qasemzadeh, Hoseyn-Ali, 672

Qashqavi, Hasan, 672

Qasr, 809

Qatmiri, Seyyed Hoseyn, 672

Qavami, Hadi, 672–73

Qavami, Karim, 673

Qavami, Seyyed Naser, 673

Qaza'i-Niyyari, Ahad, 673

Qazi-Dezfuli, Seyyed Majdeddin, 673

Qazipur, Mir Naqi, 673

Qazipur, Nader, 673–74, 803

Qazi-Tabatabai, Seyyed Mohammad, 11

Qazizadeh-Hashemi, Seyyed Amir-Hoseyn, 674, 803

Qazizadeh-Hashemi, Seyyed Ehsan, 674, 803

Qazizadeh-Hashemi, Seyyed Hasan, 674, 803

Qazizadeh-Hashemi, Seyyed Hoseyn, 674–75, 803

Qazvin Province, 76, 302; Society of Independent University Students and Alumni of Qazvin, 326

Qermezi, Shahriyar, 675

Qobadi, Khodadad, 675

Qobadi-Hamzehkhani, Ali-Akbar, 675

Qoddusi, Ali, 675

Qods Force (Sepah-e Qods), 74, 809

Qoli, Mohammad-Hasan, 675

Qolizadeh, Rahman-Qoli, 675

Qolizadeh, Yaghmor, 675–76

Qomi, Mohammad, 676, 803

Qomi, Mohsen, 676, 803

Qom Islamic Society of Admonishers, 324

Qom Province, 76, 301–2; Coordinating Assembly of Followers of Imam and the Leader in Qom Province, 306; Islamic Association of Educators of Qom Province, 311

MEHRZAD BOROUJERDI
is professor of political science and O'Hanley faculty
scholar at Syracuse University's Maxwell School of
Citizenship and Public Affairs.

KOUROSH RAHIMKHANI
is a doctoral candidate in the Department
of Political Science at State University
of New York at Binghamton.